GET YOUR CAPTAIN'S

FOURTH EDITION

Charlie Wing

with Jim Austin

Software by PEARSoft Corporation

International Marine / McGraw-Hill

Camden, Maine • New York • Chicago • San Francisco • Lisbon • London • Madrid
Mexico City • Milan • New Delhi • San Juan • Seoul • Singapore • Sydney • Toronto

The McGraw·Hill Companies

1 2 3 4 5 6 7 8 9 0 QPD QPD 0 9 8

© 2008 by Charlie Wing

All rights reserved. The name "International Marine" and the International Marine logo are trademarks of The McGraw-Hill Companies. Printed in the USA.

P/N
ISBN 978-0-07-160371-3
MHID 0-07-160371-9

Part of Set
ISBN 978-0-07-160369-0
MHID 0-07-160369-7

Library of Congress Cataloging-in-Publication Data is on file at the Library of Congress.

Questions regarding the content of this book should be addressed to
www.internationalmarine.com

Questions regarding the ordering of this book should be addressed to
The McGraw-Hill Companies
Customer Service Department
P.O. Box 547
Blacklick OH 43004
Retail customers: 1-800-262-4729
Bookstores: 1-800-722-4726

For questions regarding the operation of the CD please visit:
http://www.mhprofessional.com/techsupport/

CONTENTS

WHAT THIS BOOK IS ABOUT

Get your captain's license! What boater hasn't envied the title—because of the knowledge and experience it implies and because of the opportunities it offers. The reality is that most small-boat captain jobs pay mediocre wages. On the other hand, operating a boat is more fun than almost any other thing I can think of. To actually make money operating someone else's vessel, instead of endlessly pouring money into your own, is a proposition that is hard to beat. In addition, boating regulations get tougher every year. It is, in fact, illegal to accept as much as a beer from a guest on your boat unless you hold the proper Coast Guard-issued operator's license.

This book and its accompanying CD are designed to make the assimilation of knowledge as simple as possible. Some printed and classroom courses drill the student with just the answers required to pass the exam. Their educational philosophy is that passing the exam is all that counts; whether the student comprehends and later retains the material is irrelevant. Our approach is to explain the principles so that the student can not only answer the questions at the examination, but also come up with the answers in real-life situations years down the waterway.

Coast Guard examinations are divided into six subject areas: Rules of the Road, Deck General, Navigation General, Safety, Navigation Problems and Auxiliary Sail Endorsement. Each subject area covers numerous specific topics. As you will see in the Table of Contents, this book is organized in the same way. Each subject area is a chapter unto itself. Each chapter contains information-packed summaries of the topics, followed by the entire set of questions in that subject area from the Coast Guard database. Answers to the questions appear at the end of each chapter.

The instructional text and illustrations provide the answers to 95% of the questions. No reasonable amount of text—not even reading all 31 of the books the Coast Guard recommends (page 8)—could answer the more esoteric questions in the database, however. Some information can thus be gotten only from reading the questions and answers.

Once you have read an entire chapter, including questions and answers, start taking practice exams, either by selecting random questions from the back of the chapter or letting AutoExam do it for you. If you consistently pass the practice exams, move on to the next chapter. If not, read the chapter and questions again. And again. Find a boating friend—or better three—who also want licenses. Make up a game of "Trivial Pursuit" using the questions and answers. Learning the material can actually be fun!

Some students find it helpful to place marks next to the correct answers in the Question and Answer sections. For example:

3. A stopper used in securing the ground tackle for sea that consists of a grab attached to a turnbuckle is a

_____ .

    A. riding pawl
    B. buckler
    C. devil's claw
    D. locking ring

This way the question can be read as a statement:

"A stopper used in securing the ground tackle for sea that consists of a grab attached to a turnbuckle is a devil's claw."

What is NOT Included

The only thing we haven't included are the full-size, roll-up charts the Coast Guard uses in the navigation problems section of the exam:

12221 TR *Chesapeake Bay Entrance*
12354 TR *Long Island Sound—Eastern Part*
13205 TR *Block Island Sound and Approaches*
18531 *Columbia River*

The training (TR) charts are available through the mail for $3 each at many websites, including Blue Water Books (*www.bluewaterweb.com*) and Landfall Navigation (*www.landfallnavigation.com*). Chart 18531 can be purchased from any NOAA chart seller. Questions involving the Mississippi River require the publication *Flood Control and Navigation Maps Mississippi River Below Hannibal, Missouri to the Gulf of Mexico, 1998*. The maps are available for purchase in hardcopy ($20) and on CD-ROM ($5) from Vicksburg District Map Sales, (601) 631-5042. They are also available for free in PDF format for viewing, printing and downloading at: *http://www.mvd.usace.army.mil/Gis/navbook/html/instruct.htm*.

A Note on This Fourth Edition

We are pleased (and complimented) that many instructors of captain's license courses are using *Get Your Captain's License* as their textbook, primarily because of its illustrations and complete question-and-answer sets. In the third edition (2004) we incorporated the detailed, supplemental course materials developed by Dr./Capt. Jim Austin for use in his own courses. With the goal of presenting as much useful material as possible in a single volume, we invite suggestions for additional material from course instructors and students alike.

If You Question an Answer

The questions and answers in this book are those supplied by the Coast Guard. If you question an answer, you can download all current questions and answers in both Adobe Acrobat (PDF) and Microsoft Excel formats at the Coast Guard site:

http://www.uscg.mil/STCW/index.htm

USING PEARSOFT'S AUTOEXAM SOFTWARE

Main Menu

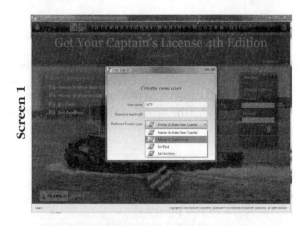

Screen 1

Drawing upon the complete database of over 14,500 Coast Guard questions, *AutoExam* automatically generates and grades examinations for four types of Coast Guard license:

1. OUPV (Six-Pack) License
2. Master and Mate Inland License
3. Master and Mate Near Coastal License
   Part 1: Rules of the Road (90% pass) 30 questions
   Part 2: Navigation General (70% pass) 20 questions
   Part 3: Navigation Problems (70% pass) 10 questions
   Part 4: Deck General and Safety (70% pass)
       60 questions (combined) for Licenses 1 and 2
       70 questions (combined) for License 3
4. Sail/Auxiliary Sail Endorsement (70% pass) 20 questions

The software consists of two main sections accessed through tab buttons:

Take Exams and **Review Past Exams**

Let's walk through a typical session:

1. From the Main Menu, if you're a new user, click the New User "**Click here**" link. In the Create New User window (Screen 1), enter a user name; password protection is optional. Finally, select your preferred product type. Creating this account enables a tracking mechanism which logs your performance for later review. Note that this account is local and exclusive to your computer.

If you've already created an account, use the Sign In window instead.

2. When you click **OK**, the Take Exams section appears (Screen 2). At this point you may be interested in configuring an exam just to see how you would do. Click the ⚙ (gear icon) and you'll see the Configure Exam window/Settings tab (Screen 3).

Screen 1

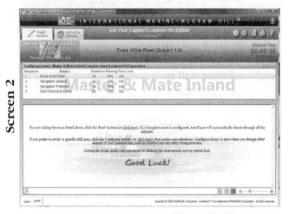
Screen 2

Screen 3

Screen 4

3. Let's try a Master and Mate Inland License. Notice that *AutoExam* has itemized the necessary subjects and appropriate question counts. If you wish a different exam, you can select from the Exam Types drop-down. Select a specific subject to drill in a singular subject. Check the **Use 100-ton filter** to limit the questions to only those appearing on exams of 100-ton vessels or less.

Within the Configure Exam window/Options tab (Screen 4), you can elect either to get your final score at the completion of a subject or to receive continuous feedback as you progress.

Would you like a second chance on questions you answer incorrectly? If so, select **Retry incorrect responses**. *AutoExam* will record incorrectly answered questions, allowing you to try again.

When an exam question references a diagram, *AutoExam* will precede the question with a thumbnail image. Click the thumbnail to bring up the image in an independent window, which can be adjusted to any size, as seen in Screen 5.

Now that we've set the options, let's take an exam.

4. Click the 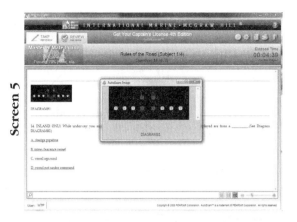 (start icon) when you're ready to go! You'll see numbered questions appear followed by potential answers represented as links; each potential answer is preceded by either A, B, C or D. Click the lettered link that you consider to be the correct response, as seen in Screen 5

If you would rather print an exam to take with you, click the ▤ (show all icon) and you'll get a full randomly generated exam ready to go (Screen 6).

The Review Exams section (Screen 7) allows you to review all aspects of previous exams. As you move through the list of questions, the correct answers appear side-by-side with your responses. Selecting an entry from the Past Exams list offers direct access to any past exam, including information on your performance, the date and time the exam started, as well as the elapsed time. Right click an entry and select **Chart** to display a chart of your performance, as seen in Screen 8.

Select **Show your incorrect responses** only from the Review Options window, which is accessed by clicking ⚙ (gear icon), to review only those questions you answered incorrectly.

If you ever need guidance, click ❓ (help icon).

Now get comfortable and start practicing. *AutoExam* never runs out of questions and never tires of randomly generating fresh exams. When you reach the point of consistently passing all subjects, call your local Regional Exam Center and tell them you are ready for the real thing. Good luck!

Screen 5

Screen 6

Screen 7

Screen 8

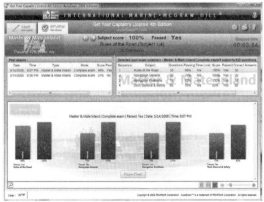

RECOMMENDED REFERENCES

The references listed below are those recommended by the Coast Guard in preparation for exams. The books in bold type are available during the exam. Supposedly, answers to all of the more than 6,000 questions can be found in the books listed.

Whether it is worth your time to read all of the books is doubtful. Better to read "Bowditch" (reference 2) two or three times than all books once.

Our recommendation is:
1. Become familiar with the books in bold so that you can quickly find answers during the exam.
2. Read Chapman (18) entirely at least twice.
3. Read the chapters in this book at least twice.
4. Read all of the questions and answers.
5. Take AutoExams until you consistently make grades well above passing.

REFERENCES
(Bold items are provided at exam)

1. *American Merchant Seaman's Manual*, Cornell and Hoffman
2. ***American Practical Navigator*** (Bowditch), Defense Mapping Agency Pub. #9
3. ***Code of Federal Regulations (CFR)***, Titles 33, 46 and 50, Government Printing Office
4. *Encyclopedia of Nautical Knowledge*, MacEwen and Lewis
5. ***International Code of Signals***, H.O. Pub. 102, National Geospatial Intelligence Agency
6. *Introduction to Steel Shipbuilding*, Baker
7. *Knight's Modern Seamanship*, Noel
8. ***List of Lights***, Pubs. 110, 111, National Geospatial Intelligence Agency
9. *Marine Fire Prevention, Firefighting and Fire Safety*, U.S. Maritime Administration
10. *Marine Radio User's Handbook*, Radio Technical Commission for Maritime Services
11. *Merchant Marine Officer's Handbook*, Turpin and MacEwen
12. *Meteorology*, Donn
13. *Modern Ships*, LaDage
14. ***Nautical Almanac***, U.S. Naval Observatory
15. *Dutton's Navigation and Piloting*, Cutler
16. *Navigation Rules*, U.S. Coast Guard
17. *Manual on Oil Pollution*, International Maritime Organization
18. *Chapman Piloting, Seamanship and Small Boat Handling*, Maloney
19. *Radar Navigation Manual*, NAVPUB 1310, National Geospatial Intelligence Agency
20. ***Radio Navigational Aids***, Pub. 117, National Geospatial Intelligence Agency
21. ***Sight Reduction Tables for Marine Navigation***, Pub. 229, National Geospatial Intelligence Agency
22. *Ship's Medicine Chest & Medical Aid at Sea*, U.S. Public Health Service
23. *Stability & Trim for the Ship's Officer*, LaDage and VanGemert
24. *This Is Sailing*, Creagh-Osborne
25. ***Tidal Current Tables***, National Ocean Service
26. ***Tide Tables***, National Ocean Service
27. *Tugs, Towboats and Towing*, Brady
28. ***U.S. Coast Pilots***, National Ocean Service
29. *Water Survival Guide*, Seafarers Harry Ludenberg School of Seamanship
30. *Weather for the Mariner*, Kotsch

QUALIFYING
FOR A LICENSE

DO YOU QUALIFY?

The Licensing Process

To obtain a license for either Operator of Uninspected Passenger Vessels or Master/Mate of Inspected Vessels to 100 gross tons, you must clear two hurdles:

- Prove to the Coast Guard that you *qualify* (meet all of the regulatory requirements for the license).

- Pass a written *exam* which includes multiple-choice questions on rules of the road, general navigation, safety and seamanship, and 10 hands-on chart navigation problems.

You cannot schedule an examination (hurdle 2) until the Coast Guard has evaluated your application and its supporting documentation.

A Changing Process

In line with the streamlining of government, the Coast Guard is working toward privatization of the examination process. The goal is to have the Coast Guard get out of the examination business entirely.

Instead, private schools are accredited by the Coast Guard to conduct courses, administer exams, and grant certificates qualifying an applicant for the knowledge portion of the license. The quality of the courses are periodically monitored. The list of schools offering the courses are available from the Coast Guard Regional Examination Centers (RECs) as well as online at: *http://www.uscg.mil/hq/ g-m/marpers/examques/oupv.pdf*. Many such schools exist. The courses are excellent, but considerably more expensive ($700–$1,200) than the price of a book. In order not to price applicants out of the process, applicants will still be able to study at home, then take the exam at a school for a lesser fee.

Further down the road the Coast Guard anticipates the use of computer simulation to examine the applicant's vessel-handling abilities and knowledge of the Rules of the Road.

Where to Apply

All phases of the licensing process are handled presently by RECs at each of the 17 Coast Guard Districts (addresses and telephone numbers listed on the facing page). This chapter supplies all of the information and forms you will require, but we suggest that you call the REC in your district for their *Small Vessel Licensing Information Package* to ensure that requirements haven't changed.

You will find that REC personnel are professional, courteous, and eager to assist, but will interpret the regulatory requirements strictly.

A Coast Guard document is a professional license—difficult to acquire and worthy of respect. We suggest you grant REC personnel and the licensing process the same respect. Lest you need further motivation, be aware that falsification of any information—such as sea service experience—is punishable by up to a $10,000 fine, five years in jail, or both!

Which License to Apply For

Operating licenses for vessels up to 100 gross tons (GT) fall into six categories, as shown on page 12. As you go through the requirements and the content of the exams for each, you should be struck by the fact that—except for the limited licenses (numbers 1 and 4)—the only significant differences are in experience (what the Coast Guard terms *sea service*). Our recommendation is to compute the sea service you can document and apply for the highest level license for which you are qualified. There is little sense settling for an OUPV ("Six-Pack" —a term the Coast Guard detests) if the exam is the same as that for a 100-ton Master!

Tonnage Limits

Licenses are issued in increments of 50 GT, except when the service was gained on vessels of less than 5 GT, in which case the limit will be 25 GT. Otherwise, the tonnage limit is calculated as the greater of:

1. the tonnage on which at least 25% of the required service was gained, or

2. 150% of the tonnage on which at least 50% of the required service was gained

Route (Waters)

The waters in which the license is valid depends on where the required sea service was gained:

Inland—inland of the Boundary Line, as specified in 46 CFR part 7. The Boundary Line is NOT THE SAME as the COLREGS Demarcation Line which separates International and Inland Rules of the Road waters. Contact the Coast Guard office in your area of operation for a definition.

Near Coastal—waters to seaward of the Boundary Line to 200 miles offshore. A Near Coastal license may be restricted to a smaller distance offshore, such as 100 miles. A Near Coastal license is also valid in Inland and Great Lakes waters.

Great Lakes—obviously valid in the Great Lakes. An Inland license is not valid in the Great Lakes unless it specifies Inland and Great Lakes.

Coast Guard Regional Examination Centers

ANCHORAGE, AK
USCG Regional Exam Center
800 E. Diamond Blvd., Suite 3-227
Anchorage, AK 99515
907-271-6736

JUNEAU, AK
USCG Regional Exam Center
2760 Sherwood Lane, Suite 2A
Juneau, AK 99801
907-463-2458

LONG BEACH, CA
USCG Regional Exam Center
501 W. Ocean Blvd., Suite 6200
Long Beach, CA 90802
562-495-1480

OAKLAND, CA
USCG Regional Exam Center
Oakland Federal Bldg., North Tower
1301 Clay Street, Room 180N
Oakland, CA 94612-5200
510-637-1124

MIAMI, FL
USCG Regional Exam Center
Claude Pepper Federal Building
51 S.W. 1st Ave., 6th Floor
Miami, FL 33130-1608
305-536-6548/6874

HONOLULU, HI
USCG Regional Exam Center
433 Ala Moana Boulevard (Pier 4)
Honolulu, HI 96813-4909
808-522-8264

NEW ORLEANS, LA
USCG Regional Exam Center
4250 Highway 22, Suite F
Mandeville, LA 70471
985-624-5700

BALTIMORE, MD
USCG Regional Exam Center
Customhouse, 40 South Gay Street
Baltimore, MD 21202-4022
410-962-5132

BOSTON, MA
USCG Regional Exam Center
455 Commercial Street
Boston, MA 02109-1045
617-223-3040

ST. LOUIS, MO
USCG Regional Exam Center
1222 Spruce Street, Suite 8.104E
St. Louis, MO 63103-2835
314-539-3091

NEW YORK, NY
USCG Regional Exam Center
Battery Park Building
1 South Street
New York, NY 10004-1466
212-668-7492

TOLEDO, OH
USCG Regional Exam Center
420 Madison Ave., Suite 700
Toledo, OH 43604
419-418-6010

PORTLAND, OR
USCG Regional Exam Center
6767 North Basin Avenue
Portland, OR 97217-3992
503-240-9346

CHARLESTON, SC
USCG Regional Exam Center
196 Tradd Street
Charleston, SC 29401-1899
843-720-3250

MEMPHIS, TN
USCG Regional Exam Center
200 Jefferson Avenue, Suite 1302
Memphis, TN 38103
901-544-3297

HOUSTON, TX
USCG Regional Exam Center
8876 Gulf Freeway, Suite 200
Houston, TX 77017-6595
713-948-3350

SEATTLE, WA
USCG Regional Exam Center
915 Second Ave., Room 194
Seattle, WA 98174-1067
206-220-7327

EXPERIENCE REQUIREMENTS

UNINSPECTED VESSELS

1. **License for Operating Uninspected Passenger Vessels at Yacht Clubs, Marinas, Formal Camps or Educational Institutions**—*AKA "Launchtender" or "Fishing Guide"*

   a. Minimum age: 17

   b. Satisfactory completion within the past five years of a safe boating course approved by the National Association of State Boating Law Administrators or conducted by the USPS, Red Cross, or CG Auxiliary

   c. 90 days in the last 3 years operating same type of vessel

   d. Letter from prospective employer stating type of vessel and area of operation

2. **License for Operating Uninspected Passenger Vessel Upon Inland Waters**—*AKA "Six-Pack"*

   a. Minimum age: 18

   b. 360 days operating a small vessel

   c. 90 of the 360 days must have been within the past three years

3. **License for Operating Uninspected Passenger Vessel Upon Near Coastal Waters**—*AKA "Six-Pack"*

   a. Minimum age: 18

   b. 360 days operating a small vessel, of which 90 days must have been on ocean or near coastal waters

   c. 90 of the 360 days must have been within the past three years

INSPECTED VESSELS

4. **License for Operating Inspected Inland Passenger Vessels at Yacht Clubs, Marinas, Formal Camps or Educational Institutions**

   a. Minimum age: 17

   b. Satisfactory completion within the past 5 years of a safe boating course approved by the National Association of State Boating Law Administrators or conducted by the USPS, Red Cross, or CG Auxiliary

   c. 120 days operating same type of vessel, of which 90 days must be within the preceding three years

   d. Letter from prospective employer stating type of vessel and area of operation

5. **Master of Inland Steam or Motor Vessels of Not More Than 100 Gross Tons**

   a. Minimum age: 19

   b. 360 days operating a small vessel, of which 90 days must have been within the preceding three years

   c. For Auxiliary Sail Endorsement, 180 days service on a sail or auxiliary sail vessel

6. **Master of Near Coastal Steam or Motor Vessels of Not More Than 100 Gross Tons**

   a. Minimum age: 19

   b. 720 days operating a small vessel, of which 90 days must have been within the preceding three years

   c. Of the 720 total days, 360 must have been on ocean or near coastal waters

   d. For Auxiliary Sail Endorsement, 360 days service on a sail or auxiliary sail vessel

ENDORSEMENTS

Auxiliary Sail Endorsement

   a. On an Inland Master License, a minimum of 180 days of service on a sail or auxiliary sail vessel

   b. On a Near Coastal Master License, a minimum of 360 days of service on a sail or auxiliary sail vessel

COMPLETING THE FORMS

1. Application Form (Pages 15–17)

Applicants for an original license, complete Sections I, II, III, IV, V, and VI. Applicants for an original license submit two sets of fingerprints. You can have fingerprints made at your police station or at the Coast Guard REC. The prints will be forwarded to the FBI for verification of the arrest and conviction information on your application.

All applicants for an original license are required to supply three recommendations attesting to the applicant's suitability for a Coast Guard License.

Applications are valid for one year from receipt. After one year you must submit a new application. Original supporting documentation submitted with the application will be returned to the applicant.

2. Physical Exam Form (Pages 18–20)

The Coast Guard Physical Exam Form (CG-719K) must be completed in full by a licensed physician, a licensed physician's assistant, or a licensed nurse practitioner. The examination must be completed before submission of the application and no more than 12 months before issuance of the license.

An incomplete examination form will delay your application. Make sure the physician completes the entire form. If medication side effects are experienced, they must be listed. If no side effects are experienced, a statement to that effect must be entered.

Blood pressure may not be higher than 150/90, regardless of treatment or medication. Uncorrected vision should be at least 20/200, correctable to 20/40, in each eye. A waiver for simple myopia over 20/200 may be granted.

Not meeting a vision, hearing, or general physical condition requirement does not automatically disqualify the applicant. The examining physician may attach a request for waiver based on the opinion that the condition does not endanger the vessel or her passengers. Conditions the Coast Guard probably would not accept include major psychological disorder, unstable diabetes, heart condition, and epilepsy.

The Coast Guard has access to your records through the FBI, so be sure to list all convictions for drugs and OUI. Prior conviction does not automatically disqualify you. Severity and age at convictions are considered. If the state won't give you a license, however, you can be sure the Coast Guard won't either.

3. Drug Test Form (Pages 21–23)

All applicants must be certified "Drug Free." An individual can be documented "Drug Free" by:

- The examining physician or program vendor collects a urine sample and sends it to a Substance Abuse and Mental Health Services Administration (SAMHSA) approved lab. Upon receipt of the results, the physician or vendor completes the form on page 21 and returns it to the REC. *Do not submit copies of the custody control forms or laboratory forms to the REC.* Tests performed by non-approved labs will not be accepted. The lab test must be performed within six months of the application.

- A letter on company letterhead from a marine employer signed by a company official indicating that the applicant has **a)** passed a test for dangerous drugs required by the Coast Guard within the previous six months with no subsequent positive chemical tests during the remainder of the six-month period; or **b)** during the previous 185 days, has been subject to a Coast Guard-required random testing program for at least 60 days and did not fail or refuse to participate in a Coast Guard-required chemical test for dangerous drugs.

- A letter from an active-duty military command or a federal employee supervisor indicating that the applicant has **a)** passed a test for dangerous drugs within the previous six months with no subsequent positive chemical tests during the remainder of the six-month period; or **b)** during the previous 185 days been subject to a random testing program for at least 60 days and did not fail or refuse to participate in a chemical test for dangerous drugs.

4. Sea Service Form (Pages 24–25)

You must tabulate your experience in operating vessels on the Sea Service Form. Use a separate copy of the form for each vessel. Service on other vessels may be provided by a letter (page 25) from the owner, operator or master of the vessel.

One day of service consists of eight hours underway—not at the dock. The CG *may* reduce the requirement to four hours on vessels less than 100 gross tons if the operating schedule limits the service. Do not claim additional days on any one day even if you served more than eight hours.

Service listed on the Sea Service Form must be supported by proof of vessel ownership. State registration, documentation certificate, bill of sale, and insurance policy may be acceptable proofs.

5. Proof of Age and Citizenship

Age and citizenship must be verified by one of the following:

- Birth Certificate (original or certified copy)

- Passport (original or certified copy)

- Baptismal Certificate (issued within a year of birth)

- Certificate of Naturalization (original only)

If your current name is different from what appears on your proof of citizenship, supply documentation of the name change. A married woman must present marriage licenses and divorce decrees.

6. Character References

The applicant must supply written recommendations from three persons who have knowledge of the applicant's suitability for duty.

7. Proof of Social Security Number

A photocopy of your Social Security Card may be submitted for evaluation, but you must supply an original or duplicate card before the license will be issued. If you do not have your original card, apply for a duplicate from the Social Security Administration.

8. First Aid Card

Applicants for all licenses, except Launchtender, must present a certificate for a first aid course, dated within 12 months of the application date. Acceptable courses include:

- American Red Cross Standard First Aid and Emergency Care

- American Red Cross Multi-Media Standard First Aid

- Any other Coast Guard-approved first aid course

9. CPR Certificate

Applicants for all licenses, except Launchtender, must present a certificate for a cardiopulmonary resuscitation (CPR) course. The certificate must be valid at the time of the application. Acceptable courses include:

- American Red Cross CPR

- American Heart Association CPR

- Any other Coast Guard-approved CPR course

10. Boating Course Certificate

Applicants for limited licenses (Launchtender, etc.) must present evidence of satisfactory completion within the past five years of a safe boating course approved by the National Association of State Boating Law Administrators or one of the public education courses conducted by the U.S. Power Squadrons, the Coast Guard Auxiliary, or the American Red Cross.

11. Fees

The fees depend on the category of license and are assessed in three phases:

Evaluation—processing the application, including review of documents and records submitted with the application

Examination—scheduling, proctoring, and grading examination sections, as well as notifying applicants of results

Issuance—preparing, reviewing, and signing documents by appropriate REC personnel

You pay only for the phases you use. Fees may be paid in person or mailed to the REC. Check, money order, or cash in the exact amount are accepted in person. For mail-ins, fees must be paid by check or money order. Checks and money orders are to be made out to the U.S. Coast Guard and must include the applicant's social security number so that the payment is credited to the correct applicant.

Fee Schedule

	Evaluation	Exam	Issuance
Original License	$100	$110	$45
Launchtender License	$100	$95	$45
Raise of Grade	$100	$45	$45
Renewal License	$50	$45	$45
Endorsement Only	$50	$45	$45
Continuity Endorsement[1]	0	0	$45
Duplicate/Replacement	0	0	$45

[1] *A Continuity Endorsement is an endorsement on an expired license which preserves the license in an inactive state until a requirement such as sea service is fulfilled.*

Application Forms

DEPARTMENT OF HOMELAND SECURITY U.S. COAST GUARD CG-719B (Rev 03/04)	Application for License as an Officer, Staff Officer, or Operator and for Merchant Mariner's Document	O.M.B 1625-0040 Expires 07/31/2009 Page 1

Section I - Personal Data

	(For CG Use Only) Date Application Received

Name (Last, First, Middle) (Maiden Name if applicable)	Social Security Number

Date of Birth (Month, Day, Year) ____ / ____ / ____	Place of Birth (City, State, Country)	Country of Citizenship

Color of Eyes	Color of Hair	Height ____ft ____in	Weight ____lbs

Mailing Address, City, State, Zip Code (PO Boxes are acceptable)	Phone Number ( ) -
	FAX Number ( ) -
	E-mail Address

Next of Kin's Name and Mailing Address, City, State, Zip Code	Relationship
	Next of Kin's Phone Number ( ) -
	Next of Kin's E-mail Address

Parental or Guardian's Consent

☐ I am under 18 years old and a notarized statement of parental/guardian consent is attached.

Section II - Type of Transaction

Transaction	Original	Renewal	Raise in Grade	Endorsement	Duplicate*
☐ License	☐	☐	☐	☐	☐
☐ Merchant Mariner's Document (MMD)	☐	☐	☐	☐	☐
☐ STCW Certificate	☐	☐	☐	☐	☐
☐ Certificates of Registry	☐	☐	☐	☐	☐
☐ Certificate of Discharge Sea Service					

*If requesting a duplicate for a lost or stolen License/MMD attach a signed statement explaining how, when and where your credentials were lost or stolen and your efforts to recover them.

Applying for:

Grade of License (include tonnage, waters, propulsion mode, horsepower, etc.); or MMD rating (Able Seaman, QMED-Oiler, etc.)

State Current or Previous License/Merchant Mariner's Document

Description of License/Merchant Mariner's Document	Place of Issue	Date of Issue

Previous Edition Obsolete

Section III - Narcotics, DWI/DUI, and Conviction Record

Conviction means found guilty by judgment or by plea and includes cases of deferred adjudication (no contest, adjudication withheld, etc.) or where the court required you to attend classes, make contribution of time or money, receive treatment, submit to any manner of probation or supervision, or forgo appeal of a trial court finding. Expunged convictions must be reported unless the expungement was based upon a showing that the court's earlier conviction was in error.

Yes (X)	No (X)	Indicate your answers to the following questions; sign and date at the bottom of this section.
		Have you ever been convicted of violating a dangerous drug law of the United States, District of Columbia, or any state, or territory of the United States? (This includes marijuana.) *(If yes, attach statement)*
		Have you ever been a user of/or addicted to a dangerous drug, including marijuana? *(If yes, attach statement)*
		Have you ever been convicted by any court – including military court – for an offense other than a minor traffic violation? *(If yes, attach statement)*
		Have you ever been convicted of a traffic violation arising in connection with a fatal traffic accident, reckless driving or racing on the highway or operating a motor vehicle while under the influence of, or impaired by, alcohol or a controlled substance? *(If yes, attach statement)*
		Have you ever had your driver's license revoked or suspended for refusing to submit to an alcohol or drug test? *(If yes, attach statement)*
		Have you ever been given a Coast Guard Letter of Warning or been assessed a civil penalty for violation of maritime or environmental regulations? *(If yes, attach statement)*
		Have you ever had any Coast Guard license or document held by you revoked, suspended or voluntarily surrendered? *(If yes, attach statement)*

I have attached a statement of explanation for all areas marked "yes" above. I signed this section with full understanding that a false statement is grounds for denial of the application as well as criminal prosecution and financial penalty. I understand that failure to answer *every* question will delay my application.

X Signature of Applicant agreeing to the above statement	Date

Section IV – Character References (For Original License Applicants Only)

☐ I am an Original License Applicant and have attached three letters of written recommendation.

Section V - Mariner's Consent

National Driver Registry (NDR) (Mandatory): I authorize the National Driver Registry to furnish the U.S. Coast Guard (USCG) information pertaining to my driving record. This consent constitutes authorization for a single access to the information contained in the NDR to verify information provided in this application. I understand the USCG will make the information received from the NDR available to me for review and written comment prior to taking any action against my License or Merchant Mariner's Document. Authority: 46 U. S. C. 7101(g) and 46 U. S. C. 7302(c).

X Signature of Applicant	Date

Mariner's Tracking System (Optional): I consent to voluntary participation in the Mariner's Tracking System to be used by the Maritime Administration (MARAD) in the event of a national emergency or sealift crisis. In such an emergency, MARAD would disseminate my contact information to an appropriate maritime employment office to determine my availability for possible employment on a sealift vessel. Once consent is given, it remains effective until revoked in writing. Send signed notice of revocation to the USCG National Maritime Center (NMC-4A), 4200 Wilson Blvd., Suite 630, Arlington, VA 22203-1804

X Signature of Applicant	Date

Section VI - Certification and Oath

Certification (Mandatory)

Whoever, in any manner within the jurisdiction of any department or agency of the United States, knowingly and willfully falsifies, conceals or covers up by any trick, scheme, or device a material fact, or makes any false, fictitious or fraudulent statements or representations, or makes or uses any false writing or document knowing the same to contain any false, fictitious or fraudulent statement or entry, violates the U. S. Criminal Code at Title 18 U. S. C. 1001 which subjects the violator to Federal prosecution and possible incarceration, fine or both.

I certify that the information on this application is true and correct and that I have not submitted any application of any type to the Officer-in-Charge, Marine Inspection in any port and been rejected or denied within 12 months of this application.

X Signature of Applicant agreeing to the above statement	Date

Oath (For originals only. Coast Guard official must witness applicant signature.)

I do solemnly swear or affirm that I will faithfully and honestly, according to my best skill and judgment, and without concealment and reservation, perform all the duties required of me by the laws of the United States. I will faithfully and honestly carry out the lawful orders of my superior officers aboard a vessel.

X Signature of Applicant	Date	Signature of Coast Guard Official	Date

U.S. Coast Guard Use Only

Section VII – REC Application Approval

Signature of Approving Official		REC	(Application has been approved on this date) Date

Section VIII – REC Citizenship Verification & Credential Issuance

Indicate Proof of Citizenship below (For non U.S. also include I.N.S. Alien Registration #)

License Endorsement(s) Issued	Document Rating(s) Issued
Issue Number	License Serial Number	MMD Serial Number
Expiration Date	Expiration Date

☐ Check box if corresponding STCW certificate was issued.

Signature of Issuing Official	REC	Date

Section IX – NMC Verification of Duplicate Transactions

Ratings/Endorsements Authorized

Signature of Approving NMC Official: _____ Date: _____

Department of Homeland Security U.S. Coast Guard CG-719K (Rev 03/04)	**Merchant Mariner Physical Examination Report**	OMB 1625-0040 Expires 07/31/2009 **Page 1**

Instructions

If you are applying for:

1. **ORIGINAL LICENSE AND/OR QUALIFIED RATING DOCUMENT** (i.e., *First Rating* of Able Seaman, Qualified Member of the Engine Department, and Tankerman) – Submit this report, completed by your physician.

2. **RENEWAL OF LICENSE AND/OR QUALIFIED RATING DOCUMENT** – You may:
   - Submit this report, completed by your physician; **or**
   - Submit a certification by a physician in accordance with Title 46, CFR, 10.209(d) or 12.02-27(d).

3. **RAISE-IN-GRADE (LICENSES)** – You may:
   - Submit this report, completed by your physician; **or**
   - Submit a certification by a physician in accordance with Title 46, CFR, 10.207(e).

Instructions for Licensed Physician / Physician Assistant / Nurse Practitioner

The U. S. Coast Guard requires a physical examination / certification be completed to ensure that all holders of Licenses and Merchant Mariner Documents are physically fit and free of debilitating illness and injury. Physicians completing the examination should ensure that mariners:

- Are of sound health.
- Have no physical limitations that would hinder or prevent performance of duties.
- Are physically and mentally able to stay alert for 4 to 6-hour shifts.
- Are free from any medical conditions that pose a risk of sudden incapacitation, which would affect operating, or working on vessels.

Below is a partial list of physical demands for performing the duties of a merchant mariner in most segments of the maritime industry:

- Working in cramped spaces on rolling vessels.
- Maintaining balance on a moving deck.
- Rapidly donning an exposure suit.
- Stepping over doorsills of 24 inches in height.
- Opening and closing watertight doors that may weigh up to 56 pounds.
- Pulling heavy objects, up to 50 lbs. in weight, distances of up to 400 feet.
- Climbing steep stairs or vertical ladders without assistance.
- Participating in firefighting and lifesaving efforts, including wearing a self-contained breathing apparatus (SCBA), and lifting/controlling fully charged fire hoses.

1. Detailed guidelines on potentially disqualifying medical conditions are contained in Navigation and Vessel Inspection Circular (NVIC) 02-98. Physicians should be familiar with the guidelines contained within this document. NVIC 02-98 may be obtained from www.uscg.mil/hq/g-m/index or by calling the nearest USCG Regional Examination Center.

2. Examples of physical impairment or medical conditions that could lead to disqualification include impaired vision, color vision or hearing; poorly controlled diabetes; multiple or recent myocardial infarctions; psychiatric disorders; and convulsive disorders. In short, any condition that poses an inordinate risk of sudden incapacitation or debilitating complication, and any condition requiring medication that impairs judgment or reaction time are potentially disqualifying and will require a detailed evaluation.

3. Engineer Officer, Radio Officer, Offshore Installation Manager, Barge Supervisor, Ballast Control Operator, QMED and Tankerman applicants need only to have the ability to distinguish the colors **red**, **green**, **blue** and **yellow**. The physician should indicate in Section IV the method used to determine the applicant's ability to distinguish these colors.

4. This applicant should present photo identification before the physical examination/certification.

Previous Editions Obsolete

Section I – Applicant Information

Name (Last, First, Middle) of Applicant

Date of Birth (Month, Day, Year) | Social Security Number

Section II - Physical Information

Eye Color | Hair Color | Weight _____ lbs | Distinguishing Marks

Height _____ ft _____ in | Blood Pressure Systolic _____ / Diastolic _____ | Pulse Resting _____ ☐ Regular ☐ Irregular

Section III - Vision (if you have corrected vision, BOTH uncorrected & corrected MUST be shown)

UNCORRECTED	CORRECTABLE TO	FIELD OF VISION
Right 20 / _____	Right 20 / _____	☐ Normal
Left 20 / _____	Left 20 / _____	☐ Abnormal

The applicant must have **100** degrees horizontal field of vision

Section IV – Color Vision

☐ PASS ☐ FAIL

Deck Officers/Ratings (masters, mates, pilots, operators, able-seaman) must be tested using one of the following tests. For all other licenses/ratings, see page 1, note 3.

Pseudoisochromatic Plates

☐ Divorine - 2nd Edition
☐ AOC
☐ AOC Revised Edition
☐ AOC - HRR
☐ Ishihara 16, 24, 38 Plate Edition

☐ Eldridge - Green Perception Lantern
☐ Farnsworth Lantern (FALANT)
☐ Keystone Orthoscope
☐ Keystone Telebinocular
☐ SAMCTT- School of Aviation Medicine
☐ Titmus Optical Vision Test
☐ Williams Lantern

Section V - Hearing

☐ NORMAL ☐ IMPAIRED (If impaired, complete Audiometer and Functional Speech Discrimination Test)

Audiometer (Threshold Value)	500 Hz	1000 Hz	2000 Hz	3000 Hz
Right Ear (Unaided)				
Left Ear (Unaided)				
Right Ear (Aided)				
Left Ear (Aided)				

Functional Speech Discrimination Test at 55 dB

Right Ear (Unaided) _____ % | Left Ear (Unaided) _____ %
Right Ear (Aided) _____ % | Left Ear (Aided) _____ %

Section VI - Medications

List all current medications, including dosage and possible side effects. State the condition(s) for which the medication(s) are taken.

☐ NO PRESCRIPTION MEDICATIONS

Section VII – Certification of Physical Impairment or Medical Conditions

Does the applicant have or ever suffered from any of the following?
If YES, PROVIDE TEST RESULTS, AS INDICATED.

If YES:
- Identify the condition
- Any limitations
- Is condition controlled
- Date of diagnosis
- Prognosis

Remarks (Please Print)

Yes	No	
		1. Circulatory System
		a. Heart disease **(Stress Test within the past year)**
		b. Hypertension **(Recent BP reading)**
		c. Chronic renal failure
		d. Cardiac surgery **(Stress Test within the past year)**
		e. Blood disorder/vascular disease
		2. Digestive System
		a. Severe digestive disorder
		3. Endocrine System
		a. Thyroid dysfunction **(TSH level within the past year)**
		b. Diabetes **(State effects on vision & HgbAlc w/in 30 days)**
		4. Infectious
		a. Communicable disease
		b. Hepatitis A, B or C
		c. HIV
		d. Tuberculosis
		5. Mental System
		a. Psychiatric disorder
		b. Depression
		c. Attempted suicide
		d. Alcohol abuse
		e. Drug abuse
		f. Loss of memory
		6. Musculoskeletal System
		a. Amputations
		b. Impaired range of motion
		c. Impaired balance/coordination
		7. Nervous System
		a. Epilepsy/seizure
		b. Dizziness/unconsciousness
		c. Paralysis
		8. Respiratory System
		a. Asthma **(PFT results within the past year)**
		b. Lung disease **(PFT results within the past year)**
		9. Other
		a. Debilitating allergies
		b. Other eye disease **(Corrected/Uncorrected Visual acuity)**
		c. Glaucoma **(Pressure test results within the past year)**
		d. Recent or repetitive surgery
		e. Sleepwalking
		f. Severe speech impediment
		g. Other illness or disability not listed

Considering the findings in this examination, and noting the physical demands that may be placed upon the applicant, I consider the applicant **(please check one)**

☐ **Competent**   ☐ **Not competent**   ☐ **Needing further review**

Name of Physician/Physician Assistant/Nurse Practitioner	License Number	Telephone Number	Office Address, City, State, Zip

Signature of Physician/Physician Assistant/Nurse Practitioner	Date

I certify that all information provided by me is complete and true to the best of my knowledge

X **Signature of Applicant** | **Date**

Drug Test

DEPARTMENT OF HOMELAND SECURITY U.S. COAST GUARD CG-719P (Rev 03/04)	DOT/USCG Periodic Drug Testing Form	OMB 1625-0040 Expires 07/31/2009 Page 1

INSTRUCTIONS: This form MAY be used to satisfy the requirements for "Periodic Drug Testing" in accordance with Title 46 CFR 16.220. If you participate in a USCG "random or pre-employment drug test program," this form may not be necessary. (See page 2 for details).
NOTE: The cost of the drug test is the **sole** responsibility of the applicant, not the Coast Guard.

Section I – Applicant Consent

I certify that I am the described applicant and that I have provided the specimen(s) described below in accordance with Department of Transportation procedures given in 49 CFR 40. I also understand that making in any way, a false or fraudulent statement, entry, or evidence is a violation of the U.S Criminal Code at Title 18 U.S.C. 1001 which subjects the violator to federal prosecution and possible incarceration, fine, or both.

Name: (Last, First, Middle) of Applicant (Print or Type)	Social Security Number
X Signature of Applicant	Date

Section II – Name of SAMHSA Accredited Laboratory (Type or Print)

Name	Address

Section III – Medical Review Officer

DATE SPECIMEN COLLECTED: _____ **Specimen Analyzed For (DOT 5 Panel):** • **Marijuana metabolite** • **Cocaine metabolites** • **Opiates metabolites** • **Phencyclidine** • **Amphetamines**	The laboratory report has been reviewed in accordance with procedures given in **49 CFR Part 40, Subpart G,** and the verified test results are: (CIRCLE ONE) **NEGATIVE** **POSITIVE/SUBSTITUTED/ADULTERATED or INVALID TEST (Test Cancelled)** (Please complete the next block for all non-negative results)

FOR POSITIVE/ADULTERATED/CANCELLED DRUG TESTS ONLY: (To be reported to the nearest USCG Marine Safety Office).
This specimen is verified **POSITIVE** for _____.
The specimen was identified as being **SUBSTITUTED** or containing the **ADULTERANT**:

_____

The test was **CANCELLED** because (insert reason): _____

I certify that I meet the qualifications for a Medical Review Officer as outlined in Title 49 CFR 40.121. I have reviewed the results and determined that the applicant's verified test result is in accordance with Title 49 CFR 40 Subpart G.

MEDICAL REVIEW OFFICER CONTACT INFORMATION: Name: _____ Address: _____ _____ _____ Phone: _____	MEDICAL REVIEW OFFICER AUTHORITY: Name: *(Printed)* _____ Signature: _____ *(MRO signature stamp is authorized for negative results only)* Name of MRO Qualifying Organization: _____ Registration Number Issued by Qualifying Organization: _____

"An agency may not conduct or sponsor, and a person is not required to respond to a collection of information unless it displays a valid OMB control number." "The Coast Guard estimates that the average burden for this report is 5 minutes. You may submit any comments concerning the accuracy of this burden estimate or any suggestions for reducing the burden to: Commanding Officer, U. S. Coast Guard National Maritime Center, 4200 Wilson Boulevard, Suite 630, Arlington, VA 22203-1804 or Office of Management and Budget, Paperwork Reduction Project (1625-0040), Washington, DC 20503."

REQUIREMENTS	• A drug test is required for all transactions EXCEPT endorsements, duplicates and STCW certificates. • ONLY a DOT 5 Panel (SAMHSA 5 Panel, formerly NIDA 5), testing for Marijuana, Cocaine, Opiates, Phencyclidine, and Amphetamines will be accepted.
OPTION I **PERIODIC TESTING PROGRAM**	• A USCG drug test conducted within the past 185 days by a laboratory accredited by Substance Abuse and Mental Health Services Administration (SAMHSA), Department of Health and Human Services. • **COLLECTION** of a urine sample may be conducted by an independent medical facility, private physician or at an employer-designated site as long as the collection agent meets the qualification requirements to be a collection agent given Title 49 CFR Part 40.31. It is CRITICAL that the sample is sent to an accredited SAMHSA laboratory for ANALYSIS or the drug test is <u>invalid</u>. A list of service agents that can assist in meeting these requirements is included or a list of service agents can be obtained at *www.uscg.mil/hq/g-m/moa/dapip.htm.* • The ORIGINAL results are required. A FACSIMILE is acceptable, if it is originated from the Medical Review Officer (MRO) or the Service Agent assisting the mariner, and sent directly to our office. The drug test result must be signed and dated by the MRO or by a representative of the service agent who assisted you in meeting this requirement.
OPTION II **RANDOM TESTING**	• An ORIGINAL DATED letter on marine employer stationary or, for ACTIVE DUTY MILITARY MEMBERS, an ORIGINAL DATED letter from your command on command letterhead attesting to participation in random drug testing programs. **EXAMPLE (From Marine Employers)**: *APPLICANT'S NAME / SSN* has been subject to a random testing program meeting the criteria of Title 46 CFR 16.230 for at least 60 days during the previous 185 days and has not failed nor refused to participate in a chemical test for dangerous drugs. **EXAMPLE (Active Duty Military/Military Sealift Command/N.O.A.A./ Army Corps of Engineers)**: *APPLICANT'S NAME / SSN* has been subject to a random testing program and has never refused to participate in or failed a chemical drug test for dangerous drugs.
OPTION III **PRE-EMPLOYMENT TESTING**	• An ORIGINAL DATED letter on marine employer stationary signed by a company official, stating that you have passed a pre-employment chemical test for dangerous drugs within the past 185 days. **EXAMPLE**: *APPLICANT'S NAME / SSN* passed a chemical test for dangerous drugs, required under Title 46 CFR 16.210 within the previous six months of the date of this letter with no subsequent positive drug test results during the remainder of the six month period.

PRIVACY ACT STATEMENT

IN ACCORDANCE WITH 5 U. S. C. 552a(e)(3), THE FOLLOWING INFORMATION IS PROVIDED TO YOU WHEN SUPPLYING PERSONAL INFORMATION TO THE U.S. COAST GUARD.

1. AUTHORITY WHICH AUTHORIZED THE SOLICITATION OF INFORMATION 46 U. S. C. 7302, 7305, 7314, 7316, 7319, AND 7502 (SEE 46 CFR PARTS 10, 12, 13, AND 16).
2. PRINCIPLE PURPOSES FOR WHICH INFORMATION IS INTENDED TO BE USED:
   A. TO ESTABLISH ELIGIBILITY FOR A MERCHANT MARINER'S LICENSE AND DOCUMENT ISSUED BY THE COAST GUARD.
   B. TO ESTABLISH AND MAINTAIN A CONTINUOUS RECORD OF THE PERSON'S DOCUMENTATION TRANSACTIONS.
   C. PART OF THE INFORMATION IS TRANSFERRED TO A FILE MANAGEMENT COMPUTER SYSTEM FOR A PERMANENT RECORD.
3. THE ROUTINE USES WHICH MAY BE MADE OF THE INFORMATION:
   A. TO MAINTAIN RECORDS REQUIRED BY 46 U. S. C. 7319 AND 7502.
   B. TO ENABLE ELIGIBLE PARTIES (*i.e. the mariner's heirs or properly designated representative*) TO OBTAIN INFORMATION.
   C. TO PROVIDE INFORMATION TO THE U.S. MARITIME ADMINISTRATION FOR USE IN DEVELOPING MANPOWER STUDIES AND TRAINING BUDGET NEEDS.
   D. TO DEVELOP INFORMATION AT THE REQUEST OF COMMITTEES OF CONGRESS.
   E. TO PROJECT BILLET ASSIGNMENTS AT COAST GUARD MARINE INSPECTION/SAFETY OFFICES.
   F. TO PROVIDE INFORMATION TO LAW ENFORCEMENT AGENCIES FOR CRIMINAL OR CIVIL LAW ENFORCEMENT PURPOSES.
   G. TO ASSIST U.S. COAST GUARD INVESTIGATING OFFICERS AND ADMINISTRATIVE LAW JUDGES IN DETERMINING MISCONDUCT, CAUSES OF CASUALTIES, AND APPROPRIATE SUSPENSION AND REVOCATION ACTIONS.
4. WHETHER OR NOT DISCLOSURE OF SUCH INFORMATION IS MANDATORY OR VOLUNTARY (*Required by law or optional*) AND THE EFFECTS ON THE INDIVIDUAL, IF ANY, OF NOT PROVIDING ALL OR PART OF THE REQUESTED INFORMATION IS VOLUNTARY, DISCLOSURE OF THIS INFORMATION IS VOLUNTARY, BUT FAILURE TO PROVIDE MAY RESULT IN NON-ISSUANCE OF THE REQUESTED DOCUMENT(S).

Drug Test Assistance

THE FOLLOWING INSTRUCTION WILL ASSIST YOU IN MEETING THE DRUG TEST REQUIREMENTS FOR LICENSE AND/OR MERCHANT MARINER DOCUMENT ISSUANCE:

1. Look in the local phone book in the Yellow Pages.
2. Go to the category **"DRUG TESTING DETECTION SERVICES OR DRUG DETECTION SERVICES."**
3. In that category, look for a business entity that can assist in providing a **DOT (Department of Transportation)** drug test.
4. Contact that business and explain that you need a DOT drug test to complete your USCG license/MMD transaction.
5. The business entity should be able to provide a one-stop service to include arranging for the collection of the specimen, laboratory analysis of the specimen at a SAMHSA-accredited laboratory, and Medical Review Officer (MRO) services for review of the specimen results.

THINGS TO LOOK FOR:

1. The chain-of-custody form should have the words on the top line **"Federal Drug Testing Custody and Control Form."** If those words are not present on the form in the top space, it is not a DOT (Federal) drug test and will not be accepted by the USCG Regional Examination Center (REC).
2. Make sure that the name of the MRO appears in Section 1 on the right-hand side.

AFTER TAKING THE TEST OR HAVING THE SPECIMEN COLLECTED:

1. You should be given **Copy 5 (Donor's copy)** to take with you. That is your copy and receipt that you have taken the drug test. **THIS DOES NOT HAVE THE TEST RESULTS ON IT.**
2. The test results should be available approximately 24 to 48 hours after the time that you had your specimen collected.
3. When arranging for the drug test services, ensure that you will be able to get the results back.
4. Drug test results need to be submitted with your complete application package to the REC that is handling your transaction.
5. Acceptable proof of a drug test result can be any one of the following:
   a. Copy 2 of the Federal Drug Testing Custody and Control Form signed by the MRO. Make sure that the test result can be seen clearly; or
   b. Completion of the DOT/USCG PERIODIC DRUG TESTING FORM (CG-719P) that was issued to you by the REC. The MRO needs to complete this form; or
   c. A letter issued by the business entity that made the arrangements for you to take a drug test. The letter should contain the following:
      i. Your name and Social Security Number.
      ii. The date that the specimen was collected.
      iii. The name and address of the SAMHSA-accredited laboratory that did the analysis of your specimen.
      iv. The MRO's name, address, and registration number showing that the MRO meets DOT requirements for performing MRO services for DOT-regulated individuals.
      v. The final verified test results as reported by the MRO.

IF YOU HAVE ANY QUESTIONS REGARDING THE DRUG TESTING PROCESS, PLEASE CONTACT YOUR LOCAL USCG REGIONAL EXAMINATION CENTER.

Sea Service Form

<table>
<tr>
<td>DEPARTMENT OF
HOMELAND SECURITY
U.S. COAST GUARD

CG - 719S (REV 03/04)</td>
<td>Small Vessel Sea Service Form</td>
<td>OMB 1625-0040
Expires 07/31/2009

PAGE 1</td>
</tr>
</table>

Section I – Applicant Information (Note: Complete One Form per Vessel)

Name (Last, First, Middle)	Social Security Number

Vessel Name	Official Number or State Registration Number

Vessel Gross Tons	Length	Width (if known)	Depth (if known)

Propulsion (Motor/Steam/Gas Turbine/Sail/Aux Sail)	Served As: (Master/Mate/Operator/Deckhand/etc.)

Name of body or bodies of water upon which vessel was underway (Geographic Locations)

Section II – Record of Underway Service

In the block under the appropriate month, write in the number of days you served for that year (you can show more than one year)

January (year / days)	February (year / days)	March (year / days)	April (year / days)	May (year / days)	June (year / days)
___/___	___/___	___/___	___/___	___/___	___/___
___/___	___/___	___/___	___/___	___/___	___/___
___/___	___/___	___/___	___/___	___/___	___/___
___/___	___/___	___/___	___/___	___/___	___/___

July (year / days)	August (year / days)	September (year / days)	October (year / days)	November (year / days)	December (year / days)
___/___	___/___	___/___	___/___	___/___	___/___
___/___	___/___	___/___	___/___	___/___	___/___
___/___	___/___	___/___	___/___	___/___	___/___
___/___	___/___	___/___	___/___	___/___	___/___

Total number of days served on this vessel: [ ]

Average hours underway (per day): [ ]

Average distance offshore: [ ]

Number of days served on Great Lakes: [ ]

Number of days served on waters shoreward of the boundary line as defined in 46 CFR Part 7:

Number of days served on waters seaward of the boundary line as defined in 46 CFR Part 7: [ ]

Section III – Signature and Verification   Applicant Read Before Signing!

I certify that I have served on the above vessel as stated. I am making this statement in order that I, the applicant, may obtain a license/document to operate a vessel under the provisions of Title 46 CFR, as applicable. I understand that if I make any false or fraudulent statement in this certification of service, I may be subject to a fine or imprisonment of up to five (5) years or both (18 U. S. C. 1001).

X **Signature of Applicant**	Date

NOTE:
- If you were not the owner, the Owner, Operator, or Master must complete the remainder of this form.
- If you were the owner of the above vessel, proof of ownership must be provided with this form.

Owner, Operator or Master Read Before Signing!

I certify that the above individual has served on the above vessel as stated. I am making this statement in order that the applicant may obtain a license to operate a vessel under the provisions of Title 46 CFR, as applicable. I understand that if I make any false or fraudulent statement in this certification of service, I may be subject to a fine or imprisonment of up to five (5) years or both (18 U. S. C. 1001).

X **Signature and title of person attesting to experience**	Date

Owner's, Operator's, or Master's Name (Last, First Middle):	Owner's, Operator's, or Master's address and phone number:

SEA SERVICE LETTER

<COMPANY LETTERHEAD>

<DATE>

U.S. Coast Guard
Regional Examination Center
<ADDRESS>
<CITY>, <STATE> <ZIP>

Dear Sir,

Please be advised that <EMPLOYEE NAME> <SOCIAL SECURITY NUMBER> is employed by our company as a <POSITION>. The following is an accumulation of <EMPLOYEE NAME>'s seatime.

Vessel Name	Official Number	Type	Tons	HP	Position	From	To	Days Underway
			** *SAMPLE FORMAT* **					
							Total Days Underway: <u>NUMBER OF DAYS</u>	

The listed seatime consists of <8 OR 12> hour days underway on <WATERS (WESTERN RIVERS/INLAND/NEAR COASTAL/OCEANS>.

Whoever, in any matter within the jurisdiction of any department or agency of the United States knowingly and willfully falsifies, conceals, or covers up by any trick, scheme, or device a material fact, or makes any false, fictitious, or fraudulent statement or entry, shall be fined not more than $10,000 or imprisoned for not more than 5 years or both (18 U.S.C. 1001).

I certify that this statement is true and correct to the best of my knowledge and is in accordance with the warning notice listed above (18 U.S.C. 1001).

<SIGNATURE BY AUTHORIZED COMPANY REPRESENTATIVE>

Denied Applications

Top Reasons Coast Guard Licensing and MMD Applications Are Delayed/Denied (Source: MLD-SP-REC-08 (04))

1. Applications

If the application is not complete, it will be returned for correction. Three signatures are mandatory: Section III ("Have you ever . . . ?" questions), Section V (consent of National Driver Registry check), and Section VI (application certification). When the "Applying for:" block is left blank or is incomplete, the REC is left to guess what you want.

2. Drug Screen

A drug screen is often rejected because it does not contain either the Medical Review Officer's (MRO) signature, the MRO Certification Number, it is a photocopy, or a company compliance letter is not written to meet the requirements of the Code of Federal Regulations, Title 46, Part 16, Section 220.

3. Photographs

Merchant Mariner's Documents (MMDs) and STCW certificates cannot be printed without a photograph. Two passport-size photos are needed when applying for an MMD or STCW.

4. Physical Exam

If the Merchant Marine Personnel Physical Examination/Certification Report is not complete, it will be returned for correction. Particular attention is paid to the "competent," "not competent," and "needs further review" boxes, which are frequently blank. Often the type of color vision exam given in Section IV is not indicated, or mariners who wear glasses and/or contacts submit exams without their uncorrected vision listed in Section III.

5. Original Certificates

Photocopies of essential documents, even if notarized, are not accepted. Certified copies from the issuing authority are authorized. Only original signatures, those documents signed by the issuing authority (e.g., course completion certificates) or official custodian (e.g., birth certificates) are acceptable. Original certificates will be returned when the evaluation is completed and the REC mails the newly issued credentials to the applicant.

6. User Fees

No or incorrect fees are included with the application. Licensing user fees changed as of October 4, 1999. Current fees are published in the most recent Code of Federal Regulations, Title 46, Part 10, Section 109 and on the web at: *http://www.uscg.mil/STCW/l-userfees.htm.*

7. Current or Past License, Document, and/or STCW

A mariner who is holding, or has held, a license, MMD, and/or STCW certificate does not indicate it in the history (Section II of the application) or does not include a copy of their credentials (front and back) with the application package. This especially applies for renewals and mariners with past transactions at other RECs.

8. Sea Service

Missing or conflicting information on the sea service letter (e.g., not including tonnage or horsepower, the position listed does not agree with other documents in the application package, or conflicting waters). Service should be documented with discharges, letters from marine employers, or small boat sea service forms. If a small boat service form is used, it must be certified and signed by the owner or proof of individual ownership is required.

9. Disclosure

If an applicant marks "Yes" in any block of Section III, a written statement is required. Note that all questions beginning with "Have you ever . . ." include all past convictions, even ones that may have already been disclosed. Simply stating "on file" will not suffice, statements should include the what, when, where, and penalties assessed for each incident, if it has already been disclosed to the REC, and whether there have been any new incidents. The applicant must sign and date the statement. *You are strongly advised to be truthful, upfront, and complete when listing all convictions. Failure to do so may result in legal action, including denial of the application.*

10. Medical Condition

Additional medical information is required whenever a medical condition is identified on the Merchant Marine Personnel Physical Examination Report.

RULES OF THE ROAD

Two sets of rules exist: **a)** The International Regulations for the Prevention of Collision at Sea (COLREGS), and **b)** The United States Inland Rules (Inland Rules). The latter consolidated the previous: Inland Rules, Western Rivers Rules, Great Lakes Rules and parts of the Motorboat Act of 1940. *Navigation Rules: International-Inland* is a Coast Guard publication containing both sets of rules. Rules covering the same situation carry the same rule numbers in both sets. In most cases the rules are identical, but there are a few exceptions of which you must be aware.

The following chapter explains the COLREGS in less formal language than that of the official text, which appears in full in the Appendix, page 813. It is meant to serve as an easy introduction to, rather than a replacement for, the Rules. In the full version (Appendix), differences between the COLREGS and Inland Rules are highlighted in italics.

PART A—GENERAL

RULE 1. Application

(a) The International Rules ("Colregs") apply on all oceans and connected navigable waters, except inside the dashed magenta Colregs Demarcation lines shown on charts, where Inland Rules apply.

(b) In spite of (a), special rules may apply to harbors, rivers, and canals.

(c) Vessels fishing in a fleet and warships may use special lights, shapes, and sound signals, as long as they cannot be confused with those in the Rules.

(d) Vessels of unusual construction or use may deviate in the characteristics of light and sound-signaling devices, as long as they comply as closely as possible.

RULE 2. Responsibility

(a) The owner, master, and crew are all charged with obeying the Rules.

(b) (General Prudential Rule) All dangers of navigation and collision, as well as *special circumstances* which may require departure from the Rules to avoid *immediate danger*, must be taken into account.

RULE 3. General Definitions

Vessel: any watercraft usable for transport on water.

Power-driven vessel: vessel propelled in whole or in part by machinery. A sailboat under both sail and power is a power-driven vessel under the Rules.

Sailing vessel: vessel being propelled by sail alone.

Vessel engaged in fishing: vessel *fishing with equipment that restricts maneuverability (nets, trawls, etc.).* Does not include fishing boats when not fishing, nor angling or trolling recreational boats.

Seaplane: aircraft which can maneuver on water.

Vessel not under command: vessel unable to maneuver *due to some exceptional circumstance* such as equipment failure.

Vessel restricted in her ability to maneuver: vessel which, *due to the nature of her work,* cannot maneuver easily (*examples*—buoy tending, laying cable, dredging, surveying, diving, transferring materials, launching or recovering aircraft, minesweeping, towing).

Vessel constrained by her draft: a power-driven vessel which, because of her draft in relation to the depth and width of navigable water, is severely restricted in ability to deviate from the course she is following (COLREGS only).

Underway: vessel not anchored, grounded, or otherwise attached to shore. Includes vessel dead in water and not making way.

Length and breadth: length overall (LOA) and beam.

In sight: seen with the eyes.

Restricted visibility: any atmospheric condition reducing visibility.

PART B—STEERING AND SAILING
Section I—Conduct of Vessels in Any Condition of Visibility

RULE 4. Application
The rules in this section apply generally, regardless of whether or not the vessels can see each other.

RULE 5. Look-Out
Every vessel must maintain a lookout by sight and hearing, as well as all available means, in order to be able to appraise the situation and risk of collision.

RULE 6. Safe Speed
A vessel is required to limit her speed so that she can avoid collision and be stopped within a distance appropriate to the prevailing circumstances and conditions. Factors include visibility, traffic, maneuverability, background lights, wind and sea, currents, navigational hazards, depth, draft, and the limitations of radar.

RULE 7. Risk of Collision
A vessel must use all available means to determine if collision with another boat is possible. Collision is possible if the compass bearing (or relative bearing, if on a steady course) to another vessel remains constant while the distance is decreasing. If in doubt, assume collision is possible.

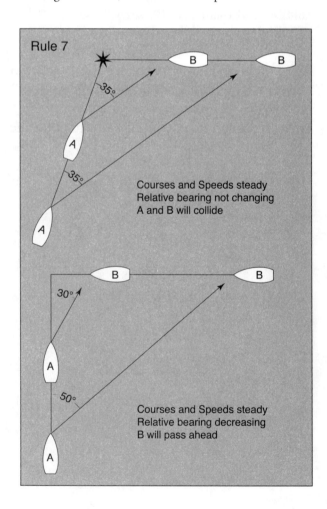

Rule 7

35°
35°
A
A
B
B

Courses and Speeds steady
Relative bearing not changing
A and B will collide

30°
50°
A
A
B
B

Courses and Speeds steady
Relative bearing decreasing
B will pass ahead

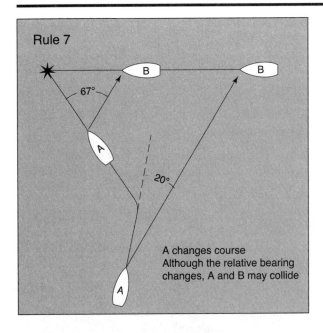

Rule 7

67°

20°

B

B

A

A

A changes course
Although the relative bearing
changes, A and B may collide

RULE 8. Action to Avoid Collision

(a) If you must take action to avoid collision, the action must be substantial and early enough to indicate clearly to the other vessel you are taking action.

(b) Changes of course and/or speed should be large enough to be obvious to the other vessel. At night, for example, the change should be large enough to show a shift in aspect of sidelights and/or masthead(s).

(c) Change of course is often preferable to change of speed (because it is more obvious), unless it will result in another bad situation.

(d) The action must result in passing at safe distance.

(e) If necessary, a vessel shall (must) slow or stop in order to avoid collision.

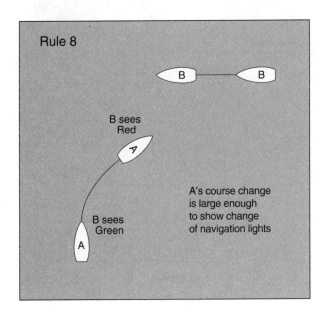

Rule 8

B

B

B sees
Red

A

A's course change
is large enough
to show change
of navigation lights

B sees
Green

A

RULE 9. Narrow Channels

(a) Stay on the starboard side of a narrow channel. Note: a power-driven vessel operating in narrow channels or fairways on the Great Lakes, Western Rivers, or waters specified by the Secretary, and proceeding downbound with a following current has the right-of-way over an upbound vessel.

(b) Sailing vessels and vessels <20 m are not to impede any vessel confined to the channel.

(c) Fishing vessels are not to impede any vessel confined to the channel.

(d) Don't cross a channel if it will impede the progress of a vessel confined to the channel.

(e) If an overtaken vessel must take action to be safely passed, the vessels must use the signals in Rule 34(c). The overtaking vessel is also subject to Rule 13.

(f) Vessels approaching a bend obscuring visibility must sound one prolonged (4–6 second) blast. Vessels approaching in opposite direction must respond in like manner.

(g) Don't anchor in a narrow channel.

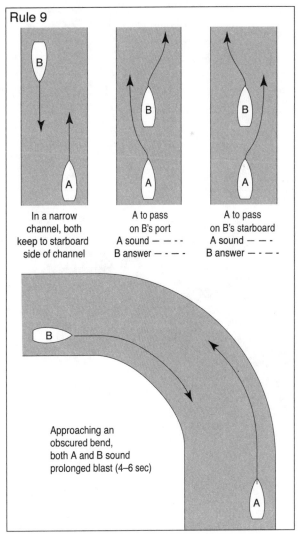

Rule 9

B

A

In a narrow channel, both keep to starboard side of channel

B

A

A to pass on B's port
A sound — — - - -
B answer — — - — -

B

A

A to pass on B's starboard
A sound — — - —
B answer — - - — -

B

A

Approaching an obscured bend, both A and B sound prolonged blast (4–6 sec)

RULE 10. Traffic Separation Schemes (TSS)

(a) This applies to official Traffic Separation Schemes.

(b) When using a TSS, use the correct lane, keep clear of separation lines and zones, and try to enter and leave at the termination points. If you must enter or exit elsewhere, do so at a small angle.

(c) If you must cross a TSS, do so at a right angle.

(d) In general, use the TSS, but vessels sailing and fishing and vessels under 20 meters may use the inshore zones.

(e) Other than when entering, leaving, or crossing a TSS, do not cross a separation line or enter a separation zone except to avoid immediate danger or to engage in fishing in the separation zone.

(f) Be especially careful near terminations because vessels will be heading in all directions.

(g) Do not anchor in a TSS or near terminations.

(h) Unless using a TSS, stay as far away as possible from it.

(i) Vessels engaged in fishing should not impede the passage of any vessel in a traffic lane.

(j) Vessels sailing and vessels under 20 meters should not impede the passage of power-driven vessels in traffic lanes.

(k, l) Vessels involved in maintenance of navigation aids and vessels working on underwater cables are exempt from Rule 10.

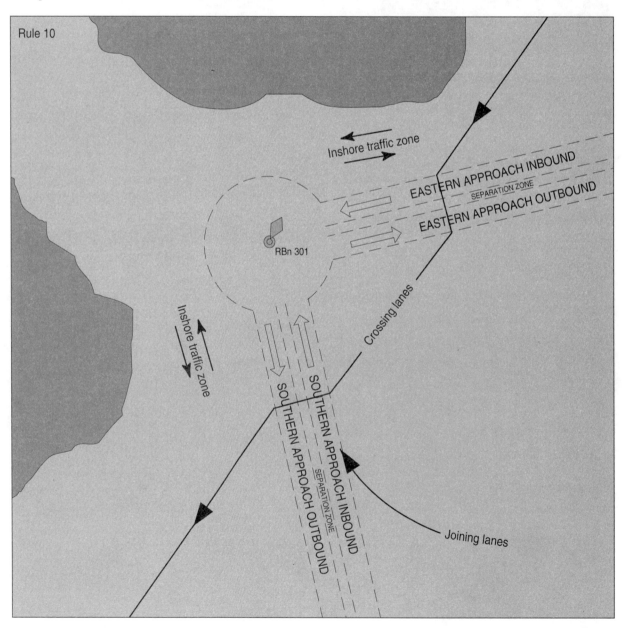

Rule 10

Section II—Conduct of Vessels in Sight

RULE 11. Application
Section II applies to vessels that can see each other.

RULE 12. Sailing Vessels
(1) If two sailboats are on different tacks (side opposite the main boom), the boat on port tack shall stay clear.

(2) If two sailboats are on the same tack (any point of sail), the windward boat shall stay clear.

(3) If in doubt as to the other boat's tack, a vessel on a port tack seeing a vessel to windward on an unknown tack shall stay clear.

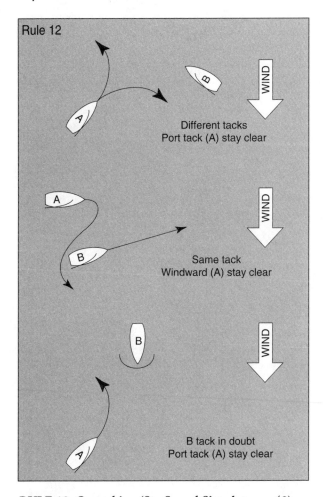

RULE 13. Overtaking (See Sound Signals, page 42)
(a) Regardless of any other rule, an overtaking vessel must keep out of the way.

(b) A vessel is overtaking when approaching another vessel from within the arc of its sternlight (more than 22.5 degrees abaft her beam).

(c) If in doubt, assume you are overtaking.

(d) After passing forward of the arc of the sternlight arc, you remain the give-way vessel until past and clear.

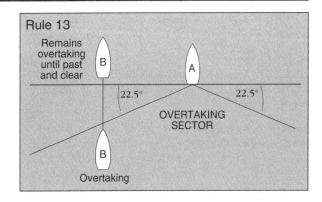

RULE 14. Head-on (See Sound Signals, page 42)
Power-driven vessels meeting head-on should both alter course to starboard and pass port-to-port. If there is any doubt as to whether the meeting is head-on or crossing, assume head-on. See Note under Rule 9(a) for Great Lakes and Western Rivers (Inland Rules) exception.

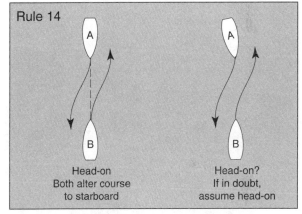

RULE 15. Crossing (See Sound Signals, page 42)
When two power-driven vessels cross paths, one on your starboard should stand on, i.e., not change course or speed; one on your port must give way. The give-way vessel should not pass ahead of the stand-on vessel. Remember, the vessel on your starboard sees your green (go) light, while the vessel on your port sees your red (stop) light.

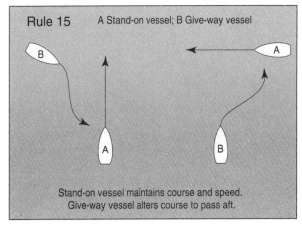

RULE 16. Action by Give-way Vessel

The give-way vessel should make her give-way action early and obvious.

RULE 17. Action by Stand-on Vessel

The stand-on vessel is required to maintain course and speed.

If the give-way vessel does not take early and obvious action, then the stand-on vessel *may* take action to avoid collision, except for altering course to port for a give-way vessel on her port. If the situation deteriorates to the point where collision cannot be avoided by action of the give-way vessel alone, the stand-on vessel *must* take action, including altering course to port if that is judged safest.

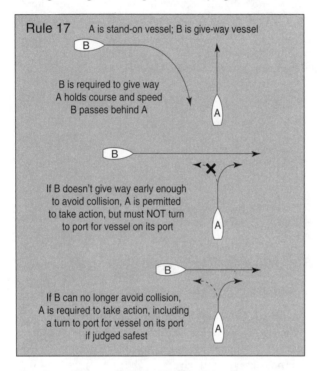

Rule 17   A is stand-on vessel; B is give-way vessel

B is required to give way
A holds course and speed
B passes behind A

If B doesn't give way early enough
to avoid collision, A is permitted
to take action, but must NOT turn
to port for vessel on its port

If B can no longer avoid collision,
A is required to take action, including
a turn to port for vessel on its port
if judged safest

RULE 18. Responsibilities Between Vessels

Rule 18 establishes a "pecking order" between vessel types. Vessels above you have the right-of-way; you have right-of-way over vessels below you. The list:

> Vessel not under command
> Vessel restricted in ability to maneuver
> Vessel constrained by draft
> Vessel engaged in fishing
> Sailing vessel
> Power-driven vessel
> Seaplane

The status a vessel claims is indicated by the lights or shapes she displays. Note that a fishing vessel not displaying either fishing or trawling lights or shapes, a sailing vessel using its engine, and a tug not displaying the lights or shapes for a vessel restricted in ability to maneuver—are all simply power-driven vessels.

Section III—Conduct of Vessels in Restricted Visibility

RULE 19. Conduct of Vessels in Restricted Visibility

Vessels must proceed at safe speed (allowing avoidance upon sighting), determined by conditions.

If you see another vessel only on radar, you must evaluate risk of collision. If risk exists (constant bearing, decreasing range), you must take avoiding action without: 1) altering course to port for vessels forward of your beam (unless overtaking); 2) altering course toward vessels abeam or abaft your beam.

Unless you know there is no risk of collision, when you hear the fog signal of another vessel forward of your beam, you must reduce your speed to bare steerageway or, if necessary, stop.

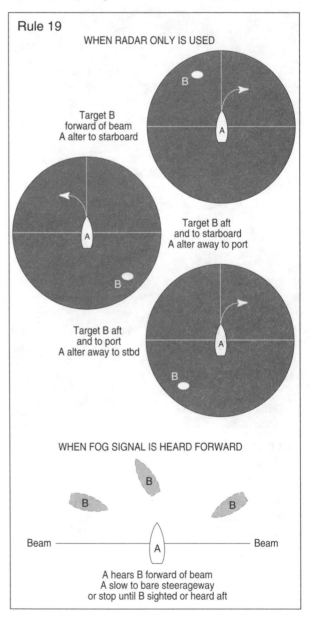

Rule 19

WHEN RADAR ONLY IS USED

Target B
forward of beam
A alter to starboard

Target B aft
and to starboard
A alter away to port

Target B aft
and to port
A alter away to stbd

WHEN FOG SIGNAL IS HEARD FORWARD

Beam ——————— Beam

A hears B forward of beam
A slow to bare steerageway
or stop until B sighted or heard aft

PART C—LIGHTS AND SHAPES

RULE 20. Application

Lights must be displayed at night (sunset to sunrise) and during the day in restricted visibility. Shapes must be displayed by day, regardless of visibility. Lights that could be confused with the official required lights or impair your lookout are prohibited.

RULE 21. Definitions

Masthead light (also known as *steaming light*): white light on centerline showing from forward to 22.5° abaft the beam on either side (225° arc).

Sidelights: green on starboard and red on port, each visible from dead ahead to 22.5° abaft the beam. On vessels less than 20 meters (65 feet), the sidelights may be combined in one unit on the centerline.

Sternlight: white light at the stern showing aft from 22.5° abaft the beam on either side (135° arc).

Towing light: same as a sternlight, except yellow.

All-around light: light of any color that shows 360°.

Flashing light: light flashing 120 per min. minimum.

Special flashing light (Inland only): yellow light flashing 50–70 per minute, centered ahead, showing on an arc of 180° to 225° centered on forward tow.

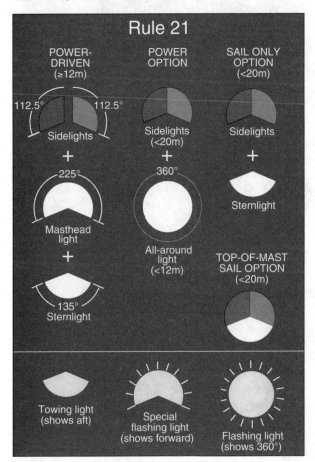

RULE 22. Visibility of Lights

Type of Light	Vessel Length, in meters	Visibility, in miles
Masthead	under 12	2
	12 up to 20	3
	20 up to 50	5
	50 or more	6
Side	under 12	1
	12 up to 50	2
	50 or more	3
Stern, Towing, and All-around	under 50	2
	50 or more	3

RULES 23–31. Lights for Vessel Types

To simplify the presentation of Rules 23 through 31, which describe the required lights for different vessels, we will first group the lights and shapes by activity. By considering what the vessel is doing, we can then specify the lights or shapes she must display.

Light/Shape Groupings

Group	Lights	Shapes
Masthead		Motor-sailing
Anchored		
Trawling		
Fishing	Gear side	+ Gear side
Not Under Command		
Restricted in Ability to Maneuver		
Mineclearing		
Constrained by Draft (COLREGS only)		Cylinder
Pilot		Flag "H"

POWER-DRIVEN VESSELS UNDERWAY (Rule 23)

VESSEL/RULE	GROUPS	SHAPES	VIEW FROM STARBOARD SIDE	BOW	STERN
INLAND—GREAT LAKES ONLY Rule 23(a) Power-driven ≥50 m	Masthead Sidelights All-around for 2nd 　masthead + stern	None			
BOTH COLREGS AND INLAND Rule 23(a) Power-driven ≥50 m	2 Mastheads Sidelights Sternlight	None			
Rule 23(a) Power-driven <50 m	Masthead Sidelights Sternlight	None			
Rule 23(c) Power-driven optional <12 m	Sidelights All-around in lieu of masthead and stern	None			
COLREGS ONLY Rule 23(c)(ii) Power-driven <7 m & <7 kn max.	Sidelights 　if practical All-around	None			
BOTH COLREGS AND INLAND Rule 23(a) Submarine	2 Mastheads Sidelights Sternlight Flashing Y, 1/sec. for 3 sec., followed by 3 sec. off	None			
Rule 23(b) Hovercraft in displacement mode <50 m	Masthead Sidelights Sternlight	None			
Rule 23(b) Hovercraft in non- displacement mode <50 m	Masthead Sidelights Sternlight Flashing Y	None			
INLAND Rule 23(a) Law Enforcement <50 m	Masthead Sidelights Sternlight Flashing Blue	None			

TOWING & PUSHING (Rule 24)

RULE/VESSEL	GROUPS	SHAPES	VIEW FROM STARBOARD SIDE	BOW	STERN
BOTH COLREGS AND INLAND					
24(a)/Towing astern (Tow ≤ 200 m) — If vessel ≥50m, add	2 vert. Mastheads / Sidelights / Sternlight / Towlight / Masthead aft ●	None			
24(a)/Towing astern (Tow > 200 m) — If vessel ≥50m, add	3 vert. Mastheads / Sidelights / Sternlight / Towlight / Masthead aft ●	◆			
24(b)/Composite (treated as single power vessel) — If composite ≥50m, add	Masthead / Sidelights / Sternlight / Masthead aft ●	None			
24(e)/Vessel/object being towed astern (other than 24(g)) (Tow ≤ 200 m)	Sidelights fwd / Sternlight	None			
24(e)/Vessel/object being towed astern (other than 24(g)) (Tow > 200 m)	Sidelights fwd / Sternlight	◆			
24(g)/Partly submerged 100 m long (<25 m wide)	All-round fore & aft	◆			
(≥25 m wide)	Add all-round on beam ●				
Partly submerged >100 m long) (<25 m wide)	All-round fore & aft and every 100 m	◆ aft ◆ fwd			
(≥25 m wide)	All-round fore & aft / Add beam every 100 m ●	If tow >200 m			
COLREGS ONLY					
24(c)/Pushing ahead or towing alongside (not composite) — If vessel ≥50m, add	2 vert. Mastheads / Sidelights / Sternlight / Masthead aft ●	None			
24(f)/Multiple vessels/objects pushed ahead	Sidelights fwd	None			
24(f)/Multiple objects towed alongside	Sidelights / Sternlight	None			
INLAND ONLY					
24(c)/Pushing ahead or towing alongside (not composite) — If vessel ≥50m, add	2 vert. Mastheads / Sidelights / 2 towing lights / Masthead aft ●	None			
24(f)/Multiple vessels/objects pushed ahead	Sidelights fwd / Special flashing	None			
24(f)/Multiple vessels/objects towed alongside	Sidelights / Sternlight / Special flashing	None			
24(f)/Multiple vessels/objects towed alongside BOTH sides	Sidelights / 2 Sternlights / Special flashing	None			
INLAND Western Rivers except below Huey Long Bridge					
24(i)/Pushing ahead or towing alongside (not composite)	Sidelights / 2 Towing lights / NO mastheads	None			

SAILING VESSELS UNDERWAY & VESSELS UNDER OARS (Rule 25)

VESSEL/RULE	GROUPS	SHAPES	VIEW FROM STARBOARD SIDE	BOW	STERN
BOTH COLREGS AND INLAND					
25(a) Sailing any length	Sidelights Sternlight	None			
25(b) Sailing <20 m option	Tri-color	None			
25(c) Sailing only optional any length	Sidelights Sternlight R/G all-around	None			
25(d)(i) Sailing or Rowing <7 m	Sidelights Sternlight	None			
25(d)(ii) Sailing or Rowing <7 m option	All-round or show only to prevent collision	None			
25(e) Motorsailing ≥50 m	2 Mastheads Sidelights Sternlight	▼			
25(e) Motorsailing <50 m	Masthead Sidelights Sternlight	▼			
25(e) Motorsailing <12 m	Masthead Sidelights Sternlight	▼ Optional under Inland Rules			

FISHING VESSELS ENGAGED IN FISHING (Rule 26)

VESSEL/RULE	GROUPS	SHAPES	VIEW FROM STARBOARD SIDE	BOW	STERN

BOTH COLREGS AND INLAND

VESSEL/RULE	GROUPS
26(b) Trawling Making way ≥50 m	2 Mastheads Sidelights Sternlight G/W All-around
26(b) Trawling Making way <50 m	Sidelights Sternlight G/W All-around
26(b) Trawling Not making way If ≥50 m	G/W All-around Masthead
26(c) Fishing other than trawling Making way Any length	Sidelights Sternlight R/W All-around
26(c) Fishing other than trawling Not making way Any length	R/W All-around
26(c) Fishing other than trawling Making way Gear out >150 m	Sidelights Sternlight R/W All-around All-around gear side
26(c) Fishing other than trawling Not making way Gear out >150 m	R/W All-around All-around gear side

NOT UNDER COMMAND or RESTRICTED IN ABILITY TO MANEUVER (Rule 27)

VESSEL/RULE	GROUPS	SHAPES	VIEW FROM STARBOARD SIDE	BOW	STERN
COLREGS AND INLAND					
27(a) Not Under Command Making way	Sidelights Sternlight R/R All-around				
27(a) Not Under Command Not making way	R/R All-around				
27(b) Restricted in Ability to Maneuver Making way <50 m	Masthead Sidelights Sternlight R/W/R All-around				
27(b) Restricted in Ability to Maneuver Making way ≥50 m	2 Mastheads Sidelights Sternlight R/W/R All-around				
27(b) Restricted in Ability to Maneuver Not making way	R/W/R All-around				
27(b) Restricted in Ability to Maneuver Anchored <50 m	R/W/R All-around W All-around				
27(b) Restricted in Ability to Maneuver Anchored ≥50 m	R/W/R All-around 2 W All-around				
27(d) Dredging or Underwater Operations Not making way	R/W/R All-around R/R All-rnd obstr. side G/G All-rnd clear side	obstr. clear side side			
27(e) Diving, but unable to display Underwater Operations lights	R/W/R All-around	Int'l Code Flag "A"			
27(f) Mine clearing Making way ≥50 m	2 Mastheads Sidelights Sternlight 3 G (Δ) All-around				
27(f) Mine clearing Making way <50 m	Masthead Sidelights Sternlight 3 G (Δ) All-around				

VESSELS CONSTRAINED BY THEIR DRAFT (Rule 28) International Only

VESSEL/RULE	GROUPS	SHAPES	VIEW FROM STARBOARD SIDE	BOW	STERN
COLREGS ONLY					
28/Constrained by Draft Making way <50 m	Masthead Sidelights Sternlight R/R/R All-around	cylinder			
28/Constrained by Draft Making way ≥50 m	2 Mastheads Sidelights Sternlight R/R/R All-around	cylinder			

PILOT VESSELS (Rule 29)

VESSEL/RULE	GROUPS	SHAPES	VIEW FROM STARBOARD SIDE	BOW	STERN
BOTH COLREGS AND INLAND					
29(a) Pilot Vessel on Duty Underway	Sidelights Sternlight W/R All-around	Int'l Code Flag "H"			
29(a) Pilot Vessel on Duty Anchored	W/R All-around Anchor light(s)	Int'l Code Flag "H"			
29(b) Pilot Vessel off Duty Making way <50 m	Masthead Sidelights Sternlight	None			

ANCHORED VESSELS & VESSELS AGROUND (Rule 30)

VESSEL/RULE	GROUPS	SHAPES	VIEW FROM STARBOARD SIDE	BOW	STERN
BOTH COLREGS AND INLAND					
30(a) Anchored 50–100 m	W All-around fwd Lower W All-around aft	●			
30(b) Anchored ≥7 m and <50 m	W All-around	●			
30(c) Anchored ≥100 m	2 W All-around All deck lights	●			
30(d) Aground ≥50 m	W All-around fwd Lower W All-around aft (if practicable INLAND)	● ● ●			
30(d) Aground <50 m and ≥12 m	W All-around R/R All-around (if practicable INLAND)	● ● ●			
30(f) Aground <12 m	W All-around	●			

SEAPLANE (Rule 31)

VESSEL/RULE	GROUPS	SHAPES	VIEW FROM STARBOARD SIDE	BOW	STERN
BOTH COLREGS AND INLAND					
31 Seaplane Underway	Masthead Sidelights Sternlight	None			

LIGHTING MEMORY AIDS

Why Memory Aids?

The materials on this page are not part of the Rules, but are included to help you remember the complexities of lighting rules. In the Rules section of the examination, you must score at least 90 percent to pass. In piloting a vessel, ANY mistake may lead to misunderstanding and collision. So memorize these aids!

Identification Lights

The following all-around, vertically arranged lights signify a particular function or limitation of the vessel displaying them. The colors are Red (R), Green (G), and White (W).

Lights	Vessel	Memory Rhyme
R/R	Not Under Command (NUC) (If aground combined with anchor lights)	"Red over red; the captain is dead."
R/R/R	Maneuvering Constrained by Draft	"Red—red—red; constrained by red."
R/W/R	Restricted in Ability to Maneuver (RAM)	"Red—white—red; RAM ahead."
R/G	Sailing Underway (optional at top of mast)	"Red over green; a sailing machine."
R/W	Fishing (lines or nets)	"Red over white; fishing tonight."
G/W	Fishing (trawling)	"Green over white; trawling tonight."
W/R	Pilot on Duty	"White over red; pilot ahead."
G/G/G	Mine clearing (mineclearing)	"Green—green—green; danger extreme."

The following lights are NOT all-around. White (W) is a masthead light showing ahead through 225 degrees; Yellow (Y) is a towing light showing astern through 135 degrees.

W/W	Towing	"White over white; there's a tow in sight."
W/W/W	Towing—length of tow exceeds 200 m	"White—white—white; a LONG tow in sight."
Y/W	Towing Astern	"Yellow over white; the tow's behind."
Y/Y	Towing Alongside or Pushing Ahead	"Yellow over white; the tow's ahead or alongside."

Remembered Best by Exception

Vessels NOT showing mastheads:

- Pilot vessel ON duty
- Fishing vessels fishing (except ≥50 m trawler)
- Not Under Command (NUC)
- Restricted in Ability to Maneuver, not making way
- Towing (pushing or alongside) above H. Long Br.
- Sailing vessels under sail only.

Vessels showing ID only, underway but not making way:

- Fishing vessels fishing (except ≥50 m trawler)
- Restricted in Ability to Maneuver
- Not Under Command

When the above begin making way they must show sidelights, sternlight (plus masthead light(s) on RAM).

Vessels showing yellow lights:

- Tug towing
- Tow pushed or alongside (Inland Rules)
- Submarine
- Air-cushion vessel
- Purse seiner in close proximity
- Public service (yellow alternates with red).

Towing Generalities

1. Tugs towing (whether astern, pushing ahead or alongside) show two vertical mastheads (exception: three vertical mastheads when tow exceeds 200 m).

2. All ≥50 m power-driven vessels, including tugs, require second (after) masthead.

3. When a tug's vertical mastheads are aft, she shows another masthead forward, regardless of length.

4. Yellow towing light over white stern light (Y/W) shown ONLY when towing astern.

5. Two vertical towing lights (Y/Y) are shown ONLY when pushing ahead or towing alongside.

6. Western Rivers (above H. Long Bridge) when pushing ahead or alongside—tug mastheads off.

7. COLREGS—pushing ahead or alongside—special flashing light (tow) and towing lights (tug) off.

8. Composite Units (tug and tow functioning as a single vessel) are lit as a power-driven vessel.

9a. Barges towed astern are lit individually.

9b. Barges pushed ahead are lit as a single unit.

9c. Barges along one side are lit as a single unit.

9d. Barges along both sides are lit as a single unit (Inland) or as separate units (COLREGS).

PART D—SOUND AND LIGHT SIGNALS

RULE 32. Definitions

Short blast: 1 second (●)

Prolonged blast: 4–6 seconds (—)

Whistle: any sound device meeting the specifications:

Length	Hertz	Decibels	Range
12 ≤ 20 m	280–700 (*250–525*)	120	0.5 nm
20 ≤ 75 m	280–700 (*250–525*)	130	1.0 nm

RULE 33. Equipment for Sound Signals

The type of required sound apparatus depends on the length of the vessel.

Length	Any Means	Whistle	Bell	Gong
<12 m	✔			
12 to <20 m		✔		
20 to <100 m		✔	✔	
≥100 m		✔	✔	✔

RULE 34. Maneuvering and Warning Signals

Under the International Rules, the signals below announce action to be taken. No delay for agreement is required before action.		*Under the Inland Rules, the signals below announce proposed action. Proposed maneuver should be delayed until the other vessel agrees.*	
When a maneuver is required in open water and within sight of each other:		*When meeting or crossing within ¹/₂ mile of each other and within sight:*	
I am altering course to starboard	●	*I will leave you on my port*	●
I am altering course to port	● ●	*I will leave you on my starboard*	● ●
I am operating astern propulsion	● ● ●	*I am operating astern propulsion*	● ● ●
In sight in a narrow channel or fairway:		*In sight in a narrow channel or fairway:*	
I intend to overtake on your starboard	— — ●	*I intend to overtake on your starboard*	●
I intend to overtake on your port	— — ● ●	*I intend to overtake on your port*	● ●
I agree to be overtaken	— ● — ●	*I agree to be overtaken—answer*	● *or* ● ●
I don't understand your intentions	● ● ● ● ●	*I don't understand your intentions*	● ● ● ● ●
Approaching a bend in a channel	—	*Approaching a bend in a channel*	—
		Leaving berth or dock	—

RULE 35. Sound Signals in Restricted Visibility

Power making way	— @ 2 min.	Being towed, if manned	— ● ● ● @ 2 min.
Power stopped	— — @ 2 min.	At anchor <100 m	rapid 5-sec. bell @ 1 min.
Not under command	— ● ● @ 2 min.	≥100 m	5 sec. fore, then 5 sec. gong aft
Restricted	— ● ● @ 2 min.	added option	● — ●
Constrained by draft	— ● ● @ 2 min.	Aground <100 m	3 claps of bell + rapid 5-sec. bell + 3 claps, all @ 1 min.
Sailing	— ● ● @ 2 min.		
Fishing	— ● ● @ 2 min.	≥100 m	same as above + 5 sec. gong aft
Towing or pushing	— ● ● @ 2 min.	Vessel <12 m option	any sound @ 2 min.
Fishing, at anchor	— ● ● @ 2 min.	Pilot vessel on duty	● ● ● ● after her fog signal
Restricted, at anchor	— ● ● @ 2 min.		

@ means that the signal must be sounded at an interval less than or equal to the value indicated.

RULE 36. Signals to Attract Attention

In attracting the attention of another vessel, you may use any light or sound signal that cannot be mistaken for any of the signals given in the Rules. The only exception is a prohibition of high-intensity flashing or revolving lights—such as strobes—in the International Rules.

RULE 37. Distress Signals

Vessels in distress and requiring assistance shall use one or more of the distress signals listed in Annex IV of the Rules (see below). The only exception is permission to use strobes in Inland waters.

ANNEX IV. Distress Signals

- A gun fired once per minute

- Continuous sounding of fog horn

- Red star rockets or shells

- Morse Code SOS (●●● — — — ●●●) by radio, light, sound, or any other method

- Spoken word "Mayday" on radio

- International Flags "N" + "C"

- Square flag and a ball

- Flames on deck, such as burning oil in a barrel

- Rocket parachute flare

- Red hand flare

- Orange-colored smoke

- Slow, repeated raising and lowering of arms at sides

- Radiotelegraph alarm signal

- Radiotelephone alarm signal

- EPIRB

- Dye marker

- Orange canvas with black square and circle

- *High-intensity flashing white light (strobe), at 50–70/minute*

Sound Memory Aids
Bells, Gongs and Whistles

Why THREE different sound makers?

- Bells and gongs indicate a vessel either anchored or aground.

- Whistles (horns) are for vessels under way.

- Gongs indicate a *large* vessel, 100 m or over.

- Three claps of a bell indicate a vessel *aground.*

COLREGS vs. Inland Comparisons

Though there are few differences between the COLREGS and Inland Rules, they are concentrated in two areas: lights and sounds. Here is a summary of the differences in sound requirements:

Situation	COLREGS	Inland
Power-driven vessel leaving dock	No mention	Must sound
In a narrow channel and doubt intentions	May sound	Must sound
Radio agreement; are maneuvering sound signals still required?	Yes	No
Approaching a bend restricting visibility	Must sound	Must sound
Whistle/light signals Color Synchronized?	White Not required	White or Yellow Required

RULES OF THE ROAD QUESTIONS

The illustrations cited in the questions are shown on pages 796–801.

1. INLAND ONLY
You are navigating in a narrow channel and must remain in the channel for safe operation. Another vessel is crossing the channel ahead of you from your starboard and you doubt whether your vessel will pass safely. Which statement is TRUE?

A. You must stop your vessel, since the other vessel is the stand-on.
B. You must sound one short blast of the whistle and turn to starboard.
C. You must sound the danger signal.
D. You must stop your engines and you may sound the danger signal.

2. INLAND ONLY
What is the required whistle signal for a power-driven vessel leaving a dock or berth?

A. One short blast
B. One prolonged blast
C. Two short blasts
D. Two prolonged blasts

3. INLAND ONLY
In a narrow channel, you are underway on vessel A and desire to overtake vessel B. After you sound two short blasts on your whistle, vessel B sounds five short and rapid blasts on the whistle. You should:

A. pass with caution on the port side of vessel B
B. hold your relative position, and then sound another signal after the situation has stabilized
C. answer the five short blast signal then stop your vessel until the other vessel initiates a signal
D. slow or stop and expect radical maneuvers from B

4. INLAND ONLY
A vessel proceeding downstream in a narrow channel on the Western Rivers sights another vessel moving upstream. Which vessel has the right of way?

A. The vessel moving upstream against the current
B. The vessel moving downstream with a following current
C. The vessel located more toward the channel centerline
D. The vessel sounding the first whistle signal

5. INLAND ONLY
You are overtaking a power-driven vessel in a narrow channel and wish to leave her on your starboard side. You may _____.

A. attempt to contact her on the radiotelephone to arrange for the passage
B. proceed to overtake her without sounding whistle signals
C. sound five short blasts
D. All of the above

6. INLAND ONLY
A vessel displaying a flashing blue light is _____.

A. transferring dangerous cargo
B. a law enforcement vessel
C. a work boat
D. engaged in a race

7. INLAND ONLY
When power-driven vessels are crossing, a signal of one short blast by either vessel means _____.

A. I intend to leave you on my port side
B. I intend to hold course and speed
C. I intend to change course to starboard
D. I request a departure from the Rules

8. INLAND ONLY
If you were coming up on another power-driven vessel from dead astern and desired to overtake on the other vessel's starboard side, which whistle signal would you sound?

A. One short blast
B. One prolonged blast
C. Two short blasts
D. Two prolonged blasts

9. INLAND ONLY
Which statement is TRUE concerning narrow channels?

A. You should keep to that side of the channel which is on your port side.
B. You should avoid anchoring in a narrow channel.
C. A vessel having a following current will propose the manner of passage in any case where two vessels are meeting.
D. All of the above

10. INLAND ONLY
Which term is NOT defined in the Inland Navigation Rules?

A. Seaplane
B. Restricted visibility
C. Underway
D. Vessel constrained by her draft

11. INLAND ONLY
When you are overtaking another vessel and desire to pass on her left or port hand, you should sound _____.

A. one short blast
B. one long blast
C. two short blasts
D. two prolonged blasts

12. INLAND ONLY
Your vessel is meeting another vessel head-on. To comply with the steering and sailing rules, you should _____.

A. sound the danger signal
B. sound one prolonged and two short blasts
C. exchange two short blasts
D. exchange one short blast

13. INLAND ONLY
Yellow lights are NOT used to identify:

A. U.S. submarines
B. vessels pushing ahead
C. law enforcement vessels
D. dredge pipelines on trestles

14. INLAND ONLY
You have made your vessel up to a tow and are moving from a pier out into the main channel. Your engines are turning ahead. What whistle signal should you sound?

A. One prolonged and two short blasts
B. Three long blasts
C. One prolonged blast
D. Five or more short rapid blasts

15. INLAND ONLY
Under the Inland Navigation Rules, what is the meaning of the two short blasts signal used when meeting another vessel?

A. I am turning to starboard.
B. I am turning to port.
C. I intend to leave you on my starboard side.
D. I intend to leave you on my port side.

16. INLAND ONLY
For the purpose of the Inland Navigation Rules, the term Inland Waters includes _____.

A. the Western Rivers
B. the Great Lakes on the United States side of the International Boundary

C. harbors and rivers shoreward of the COLREGS demarcation lines
D. All of the above

17. INLAND ONLY
A power-driven vessel crossing a river on the Western Rivers has the right of way over ____.

A. vessels ascending the river
B. vessels descending the river
C. all vessels ascending and descending the river
D. None of the above

18. INLAND ONLY
Which lights are required for a barge, not part of a composite unit, being pushed ahead?

A. Sidelights and a sternlight
B. Sidelights, a special flashing light, and a sternlight
C. Sidelights and a special flashing light
D. Sidelights, a towing light, and a sternlight

19. INLAND ONLY
A power-driven vessel operating in a narrow channel with a following current on the Great Lakes or Western Rivers is meeting an upbound vessel. Which statement is TRUE?

A. The downbound vessel has the right-of-way.
B. The downbound vessel must initiate the required maneuvering signals.
C. The downbound vessel must propose the manner and place of passage.
D. All of the above

20. INLAND ONLY
Your vessel is proceeding down a channel, and can safely navigate only within the channel. Another vessel is crossing your bow from port to starboard, and you are in doubt as to her intentions. Which statement is TRUE?

A. The sounding of the danger signal is optional.
B. The sounding of the danger signal is mandatory.
C. You should sound two short blasts.
D. You should sound one prolonged and two short blasts.

21. INLAND ONLY
The stand-on vessel in a crossing situation sounds one short blast of the whistle. This means that the vessel:

A. intends to hold course and speed
B. is changing course to starboard
C. is changing course to port
D. intends to leave the other on her port side

22. INLAND ONLY
You are crossing the course of another vessel which is to your starboard. You have reached an agreement by radiotelephone to pass astern of the other vessel. You MUST:

A. sound one short blast
B. sound two short blasts
C. change course to starboard
D. None of the above

23. INLAND ONLY
Passing signals shall be sounded on inland waters by ____.

A. all vessels upon sighting another vessel rounding a bend in the channel
B. towing vessel when meeting another towing vessel on a clear day with a 0.6 mile CPA (Closest Point of Approach)
C. a power-driven vessel when crossing less than half a mile ahead of another power-driven vessel
D. All of the above

24. DIAGRAM 16. INT & INLAND
Which of the dayshapes shown would you show on the after end of an inconspicuous partially submerged vessel or object being towed less than 200 meters in length?

A. A
B. B
C. C
D. No dayshape would be shown.

25. INLAND ONLY
In a narrow channel, a power-driven vessel desiring to overtake another power-driven vessel on the other vessel's starboard side will sound a whistle signal of ____.

A. one short blast
B. two short blasts
C. two prolonged blasts followed by one short blast
D. two prolonged blasts followed by two short blasts

26. INLAND ONLY
A law enforcement boat may display a ____.

A. blue flag

B. flashing blue light
C. flashing red light
D. flashing amber light

27. INLAND ONLY
Your vessel is meeting another vessel head-on. To comply with the rules, you should exchange ____.

A. one short blast, alter course to port, and pass starboard to starboard
B. one short blast, alter course to starboard, and pass port to port
C. two short blasts, alter course to port, and pass starboard to starboard
D. two short blasts, alter course to starboard, and pass port to port

28. INLAND ONLY
A vessel overtaking another in a narrow channel, and wishing to pass on the other vessel's port side, would sound a whistle signal of ____.

A. one short blast
B. two short blasts
C. two prolonged blasts followed by one short blast
D. two prolonged blasts followed by two short blasts

29. INLAND ONLY
A fleet of moored barges extends into a navigable channel. What is the color of the lights on the barges?

A. Red
B. Amber
C. White
D. None of the above

30. INLAND ONLY
Which signal must a power-driven vessel give, in addition to one prolonged blast, when backing out of a berth with another vessel in sight?

A. 2 short blasts
B. 1 blast
C. 3 short blasts
D. 4 blasts

31. INLAND ONLY
At night, a light signal consisting of two flashes by a vessel indicates ____.

A. an intention to communicate over radiotelephone
B. that the vessel is in distress
C. an intention to leave another vessel to port
D. an intention to leave another vessel to starboard

32. INLAND ONLY
You are overtaking a power-driven vessel in a narrow channel and wish to leave her on your starboard side. You may ____.

A. proceed to overtake her without sounding whistle signals
B. attempt to contact her on the radiotelephone to arrange for the passage
C. sound four short blasts
D. Any of the above

33. INLAND ONLY
For the purpose of the Inland Navigation Rules, the term *inland waters* includes ____.

A. the Great Lakes on the United States side of the International Boundary
B. the water surrounding any islands of the United States
C. the coastline of the United States, out to one mile offshore
D. any lakes within state boundaries

34. INLAND ONLY
A barge more than 50 meters long is required to show how many white anchor lights when anchored in a Secretary of Transportation approved special anchorage area?

A. 2
B. 1
C. 3
D. 4

35. DIAGRAM 9. INLAND ONLY
You are on vessel B and vessel A desires to overtake you on your starboard side as shown. After the vessels have exchanged one blast signal, you should ____.

A. alter course to the left
B. slow your vessel until vessel A has passed
C. hold course and speed
D. alter course to the left or right to give vessel A more sea room

36. INLAND ONLY
Which type of vessel is NOT mentioned in the Inland Navigation Rules?

A. An inconspicuous, partly submerged vessel
B. A seaplane
C. An air-cushion vessel
D. A vessel constrained by her draft

37. INLAND ONLY
You are operating a vessel through a narrow channel and your vessel must stay within the channel to be navigated safely. Another vessel is crossing your course from starboard to port, and you are in doubt as to her intentions. You ____.

A. must sound the danger signal
B. are required to back down
C. may sound the danger signal
D. should sound one short blast to show that you are holding course and speed

38. INLAND ONLY
Your vessel is meeting another vessel head-on. To comply with the rules, you should exchange ____.

A. one short blast, alter course to the left, and pass starboard to starboard
B. two short blasts, alter course to the left, and pass starboard to starboard
C. one short blast, alter course to the right, and pass port to port
D. two short blasts, alter course to the right, and pass port to port

39. INLAND ONLY
Which indicates the presence of a partly submerged object being towed?

A. A diamond shape on the towed object
B. An all-around light at each end of the towed object
C. A searchlight beamed from the towing vessel in the direction of the tow
D. All of the above

40. INLAND ONLY
The light used to signal passing intentions is a(n) ____.

A. all-around white light ONLY
B. all-around yellow light ONLY
C. all-around white or yellow light
D. light of any color

41. INLAND ONLY
Two vessels in a crossing situation have reached agreement by radiotelephone as to the intentions of the other. In this situation, whistle signals are ____.

A. required
B. not required, but may be sounded
C. required if crossing within half a mile
D. required when crossing within one mile

42. INLAND ONLY
You are underway in a narrow channel, and are being overtaken by another power-driven vessel. The overtaking vessel sounds the signal indicating his intention to pass you on your starboard side. You signal your agreement by sounding ____.

A. one short blast
B. two prolonged blasts
C. two prolonged followed by two short blasts
D. one prolonged, one short, one prolonged, and one short blast in that order

43. INLAND ONLY
You are meeting another vessel head-on and sound one short blast as a passing signal. The other vessel answers with two short blasts. What should be your next action?

A. Pass on the other vessel's starboard side.
B. Sound the danger signal.
C. Pass astern of the other vessel.
D. Hold your course and speed.

44. INLAND ONLY
What lights are required for a barge being pushed ahead, not being part of a composite unit?

A. Sidelights and a sternlight
B. Sidelights and a special flashing light
C. Sidelights, a towing light, and a sternlight
D. Sidelights, a special flashing light, and a sternlight

45. INLAND ONLY
You are overtaking another power-driven vessel in a narrow channel, and you wish to overtake on the other vessel's port side. You will sound a whistle signal of ____.

A. one short blast
B. two short blasts
C. two prolonged blasts followed by one short blast
D. two prolonged blasts followed by two short blasts

46. INLAND ONLY
At night, a barge moored in a slip used primarily for mooring purposes shall ____.

A. not be required to be lighted
B. show a white light at each corner
C. show a red light at the bow and stern
D. show a flashing yellow light at each corner

47. INLAND ONLY
A flashing blue light is used to identify ____.

A. law enforcement vessels
B. U.S. submarines
C. air-cushion vessels in the nondisplacement mode
D. dredge pipelines on trestles

48. INLAND ONLY

Which statement is TRUE concerning the fog signal of a vessel 15 meters in length anchored in a special anchorage area approved by the Secretary of Transportation?

A. The vessel is not required to sound a fog signal.
B. The vessel shall ring a bell for 5 seconds every minute.
C. The vessel shall sound one blast of the foghorn every 2 minutes.
D. The vessel shall sound three blasts on the whistle every 2 minutes.

49. INLAND ONLY

A power-driven vessel, when leaving a dock or berth, is required to sound:

A. four short blasts
B. one long blast
C. one prolonged blast
D. No signal is required.

50. DIAGRAM 29. INLAND ONLY

Vessels A and B are meeting on a river as shown and will pass about 1/4 mile apart. Which statement is TRUE?

A. Both vessels should continue on course and pass without sounding any whistle signals.
B. The vessels should exchange two blast whistle signals and pass port to port.
C. The vessels should exchange two blast whistle signals and pass starboard to starboard.
D. The vessels should pass port to port and must sound whistle signals only if either vessel changes course.

51. INLAND ONLY

Which statement is TRUE concerning the Inland Navigation Rules?

A. They list requirements for Traffic Separation Schemes.
B. They define moderate speed.
C. They require communication by radiotelephone to reach a passing agreement.
D. All of the above

52. INLAND ONLY

Whistle signals shall be exchanged by vessels in sight of one another when:

A. they are passing within half a mile of each other
B. passing agreements have been made by radio
C. course changes are necessary to pass
D. doubt exists as to which side the vessels will pass on

53. DIAGRAM 38. INLAND ONLY

You are on vessel A and vessel B desires to overtake you on the starboard side as shown. After the vessels have exchanged one blast signals you should _____.

A. alter course to the left
B. slow your vessel until vessel B has passed
C. hold course and speed
D. alter course to the left or right to give vessel B more sea room

54. INLAND ONLY

A barge over 50 m long would be required to show how many white anchor lights when anchored in a Secretary of Transportation approved special anchorage area?

A. 1
B. 2
C. 3
D. 4

55. DIAGRAM 75. INLAND ONLY

The lights shown are those of a _____.

A. pipeline
B. vessel towing by pushing ahead
C. vessel being towed astern
D. vessel underway and dredging

56. INLAND ONLY

Your vessel must remain in a narrow channel for safe operation. Another vessel is crossing the channel from your starboard. You do not think she will pass safely. You MUST _____.

A. stop your vessel, since the other vessel has the right of way
B. sound one short blast of the whistle, and turn to starboard
C. sound the danger signal
D. stop your engines, and you may sound the danger signal

57. INLAND ONLY

While underway during the day you sight a small motorboat showing a flashing blue light. The blue light indicates a _____.

A. law enforcement boat
B. boat involved in a race
C. Coast Guard Auxiliary Vessel on regatta patrol
D. rescue boat

58. DIAGRAM 81. INLAND ONLY

While underway, you sight the lights as shown, with the yellow lights flashing. You should _____.

A. wait until vessel ahead crosses your bow
B. stop until the red lights turn green
C. proceed leaving all the lights on your starboard side
D. pass between the two sets of vertical red lights

59. INLAND ONLY

When power-driven vessels are in a crossing situation, one short blast by either vessel would mean _____.

A. I intend to leave you on my port side
B. I intend to hold course and speed
C. I intend to change course to starboard
D. I request a departure from the rules

60. INLAND ONLY

Two vessels are meeting on a clear day and will pass less than half a mile apart. In this situation whistle signals:

A. must be exchanged
B. may be exchanged
C. must be exchanged if passing agreements have not been made by radio
D. must be exchanged only if course changes are necessary by either vessel

61. INLAND ONLY

Your power-driven vessel is overtaking another power-driven vessel in a narrow channel. You wish to overtake her on her starboard side. You should sound a whistle signal of _____.

A. one short blast
B. two prolonged blasts followed by one short blast
C. one prolonged and one short blast
D. at least five short blasts

62. INLAND ONLY

Which is TRUE of a vessel downbound with a following current when meeting an upbound vessel on the Western Rivers?

A. She has the right-of-way only if she is a power-driven vessel.
B. She has the right-of-way only if she has a tow.

C. She does not have the right-of-way, since the other vessel is not crossing the river.
D. She must wait for a whistle signal from the upbound vessel.

63. INLAND ONLY
A vessel of less than 20 meters in length at anchor at night in a special anchorage area designated by the Secretary ____.

A. must show one white light
B. need not show any lights
C. must show two white lights
D. need show a light only on the approach of another vessel

64. INLAND ONLY
At night, which lights are required on barges moored in group formation at a bank of a river?

A. A white light placed at the corners farthest from the bank on each of the upstream and downstream ends of the group.
B. A white light placed at the corners farthest from the bank of each barge in the group.
C. A flashing yellow light placed at each of the upstream and downstream ends of the group.
D. Two red lights in a vertical line placed at the corners farthest from the bank on each of the upstream and downstream ends of the group.

65. INLAND ONLY
A power-driven vessel intends to overtake another power-driven vessel on the overtaken vessel's port side. Which whistle signal should be sounded in order to state this intention?

A. 1 short blast
B. 2 short blasts
C. 2 prolonged and 1 short blast
D. 2 prolonged and 2 short blasts

66. INLAND ONLY
A towing vessel pushing ahead on the Western Rivers above the Huey P. Long bridge must show ____.

A. sidelights only
B. sidelights and towing lights
C. sidelights, towing lights, and two masthead lights
D. sidelights, towing lights, and three masthead lights

67. INLAND ONLY
A power-driven vessel, when leaving a dock or berth, is required to sound ____.

A. two short blasts
B. one long blast
C. one prolonged blast
D. the danger signal

68. INLAND ONLY
Which is CORRECT regarding a special flashing light?

A. It must be yellow in color.
B. It must be placed as far forward as possible.
C. It must not show through an arc of more than 225°.
D. All of the above

69. INLAND ONLY
For the purpose of the Inland Navigation Rules, the term Inland Waters includes ____.

A. the Western Rivers, extending to the COLREGS demarcation line
B. harbors and rivers to the outermost aids to navigation
C. waters along the coast of the United States to a distance of two miles offshore
D. None of the above

70. DIAGRAM 29. INLAND ONLY
Vessels A and B are meeting in a narrow channel as shown. Which statement is TRUE concerning whistle signals between the vessels?

A. Both vessels should sound two short blasts.
B. Both vessels should sound one short blast.
C. Vessel A should sound one short blast and vessel B should sound two short blasts.
D. Neither vessel should sound any signal as no course change is necessary.

71. INLAND ONLY
Which is TRUE of a power-driven vessel, bound downstream, when meeting an upbound vessel on the Western Rivers?

A. She has the right-of-way.
B. She shall propose the manner of passage.
C. She shall initiate maneuvering signals.
D. All of the above

72. DIAGRAM 75. INLAND ONLY
You are approaching a vessel displaying the lights as shown. This is a(n):

A. meeting head-on situation
B. crossing situation

C. overtaking situation
D. special circumstance situation

73. INLAND ONLY
You are overtaking a power-driven vessel in a narrow channel and wish to leave her on your starboard side. You may ____.

A. sound one short blast
B. sound four short blasts
C. overtake her without sounding whistle signals
D. attempt to contact her on the radiotelephone to arrange for the passage

74. INLAND ONLY
Which term is NOT used in the Inland Navigation Rules?

A. A vessel engaged in mineclearing operations
B. A vessel constrained by her draft
C. A vessel towing
D. A vessel engaged in fishing

75. DIAGRAM 31. INLAND ONLY
You are on vessel A, and vessel B desires to overtake you on your starboard side as shown. After the vessels have exchanged one blast signals, you should ____.

A. alter course to the left
B. slow your vessel until vessel B has passed
C. hold course and speed
D. alter course to the left to give vessel B more sea room

76. INLAND ONLY
A special flashing light is used on a vessel(s) ____.

A. being pushed ahead
B. at anchor in a fairway
C. towed astern
D. All of the above

77. DIAGRAM 41. INLAND ONLY
Vessels A and B are meeting on a river as shown and will pass about 1/4 mile apart. What action should the vessels take?

A. Both vessels should continue on course and pass without sounding any whistle signals.
B. The vessels should exchange two blast whistle signals and pass starboard to starboard.

C. The vessels should exchange one blast whistle signals and pass starboard to starboard.
D. The vessels should pass starboard to starboard and must sound whistle signals only if either vessel changes course.

78. INLAND ONLY
Under the Inland Navigation Rules, what is the meaning of a one short blast signal used when meeting another vessel?

A. I am turning to starboard.
B. I am turning to port.
C. I intend to leave you on my starboard side.
D. I intend to leave you on my port side.

79. INLAND ONLY
On the Western Rivers, a power-driven vessel crossing a river must _____.

A. maintain course and speed as you have the right of way over all vessels
B. keep out of the way of any vessel descending the river
C. keep out of the way of a power-driven vessel ascending or descending the river
D. None of the above

80. INLAND ONLY
While underway at night, you see two yellow lights displayed in a vertical line. This should indicate to you a(n):

A. opening in a pipeline
B. vessel broken down
C. vessel pushing ahead
D. vessel fishing

81. INLAND ONLY
When two power-driven vessels are meeting on the Great Lakes, Western Rivers, or waters specified by the Secretary, where there is a current, which vessel shall sound the first passing signal?

A. The vessel going upstream stemming the current
B. The vessel downbound with a following current
C. The vessel that is towing regardless of the current
D. Either vessel

82. INLAND ONLY
A vessel leaving a dock or berth must sound a prolonged blast of the whistle only if _____.

A. other vessels can be seen approaching

B. she is a power-driven vessel
C. visibility is restricted
D. her engines are going astern

83. INLAND ONLY
If your tug is pushing a barge ahead at night and it is not a composite unit, which light(s) should show aft on your vessel?

A. A white sternlight
B. Two red lights
C. Two towing lights
D. A towing light over the sternlight

84. INLAND ONLY
You are in charge of a power-driven vessel crossing a river on the Western Rivers. You must keep out of the way of a _____.

A. sail vessel descending the river
B. power-driven vessel ascending the river
C. sail vessel ascending the river
D. All of the above

85. INLAND ONLY
A power-driven vessel crossing a river on the Great Lakes or Western Rivers must keep out of the way of a power-driven vessel _____.

A. descending the river with a tow
B. ascending the river with a tow
C. ascending the river without a tow
D. All of the above

86. INLAND ONLY
What is the whistle signal used to indicate a power-driven vessel leaving a dock?

A. One short blast
B. Three short blasts
C. One prolonged blast
D. Three prolonged blasts

87. INLAND ONLY
Which statement is TRUE concerning the light used for maneuvering signals?

A. It must be synchronized with the whistle.
B. It may be white or yellow.
C. It must be an all-around light.
D. All of the above

88. DIAGRAM 37. INLAND ONLY
Two power-driven vessels are meeting in the situation as shown. One short blast by vessel A means_____.

A. I am altering my course to starboard
B. I intend to leave you on my port side
C. My intention is to hold course and speed
D. I intend to pass on your starboard side

89. INLAND ONLY
Your vessel must stay within a narrow channel to be navigated safely. Another vessel is crossing your course from starboard to port. You do NOT think she will pass safely. You:

A. may sound the danger signal
B. must sound the danger signal
C. should sound one short blast to indicate that you are holding course and speed
D. are required to back down

90. INLAND ONLY
Two vessels are in a starboard to starboard meeting situation and will pass well clear approximately 1/4 mile apart. Which action should each vessel take?

A. Sound a one blast whistle signal and turn to starboard.
B. Maintain course and sound no signal.
C. Sound a two blast whistle signal and maintain course.
D. Sound a three blast whistle signal and turn to port.

91. DIAGRAM 16. INT & INLAND
Which of the dayshapes shown would you show on the after end of an inconspicuous partially submerged vessel or object being towed over 200 meters in length?

A. A
B. B
C. C
D. No dayshape would be shown.

92. INLAND ONLY
A power-driven vessel pushing ahead or towing alongside on the Mississippi River, below the Huey P. Long Bridge, shall carry:

A. two masthead lights, sidelights and sternlight
B. two masthead lights, sidelights and two towing lights
C. sidelights and two towing lights
D. one masthead light, sidelights and sternlight

93. INLAND ONLY
While underway in a harbor you hear a vessel sound a prolonged blast. This signal indicates that this vessel _____.

A. desires to overtake your vessel
B. is at anchor
C. is backing her engines
D. is moving from a dock

94. INLAND ONLY

You are overtaking another power-driven vessel and sound a whistle signal indicating that you intend to pass the vessel along her starboard side. If the other vessel answers your signal with five short and rapid blasts, you should ____.

A. not overtake the other vessel until both vessels exchange the same passing signal
B. not overtake the other vessel until she sounds another five short and rapid blast signal
C. pass the other vessel along her starboard side
D. sound five short and rapid blasts and pass along her starboard side

95. INLAND ONLY

You are meeting another vessel in inland waters, and she sounds one short blast on the whistle. This means that she ____.

A. is changing course to starboard
B. is changing course to port
C. intends to leave you on her port side
D. desires to depart from the Rules

96. INLAND ONLY

You are approaching a sharp bend in a river. You have sounded a prolonged blast and it has been answered by a vessel on the other side of the bend. Which statement is TRUE?

A. Both vessels must exchange passing signals when in sight and passing within one-half mile of each other.
B. No further whistle signals are necessary.
C. The vessel downriver must stop her engines and navigate with caution.
D. Both vessels must immediately sound passing signals whether or not they are in sight of each other.

97. INLAND ONLY

Which statement is TRUE concerning a passing agreement made by radiotelephone?

A. Such an agreement is prohibited.
B. A vessel which has made such an agreement must also sound whistle signals.
C. Whistle signals must still be exchanged when passing within half a mile of each other.
D. If agreement is reached by radiotelephone, whistle signals are optional.

98. INLAND ONLY

You are aboard the stand-on vessel in a crossing situation. You sound a one blast whistle signal. The give-way vessel answers with a two blast whistle signal. You should sound the danger signal and ____.

A. maintain course and speed as you are the stand-on vessel
B. come around sharply to port
C. take precautionary action until a safe passing agreement is made
D. maneuver around the stern of the other vessel

99. INLAND ONLY

A power-driven vessel when pushing ahead or towing alongside on the Western Rivers (above the Huey P. Long Bridge on the Mississippi River) shall exhibit ____.

A. two masthead lights, sidelights, and sternlight
B. two masthead lights, sidelights, and two towing lights
C. sidelights and two towing lights
D. one masthead light, sidelights, and sternlight

100. INLAND ONLY

Only law enforcement vessels are permitted to show ____.

A. two red lights in a vertical line
B. a flashing yellow light
C. an alternately flashing red and yellow light
D. a flashing blue light

101. INLAND ONLY

You are overtaking another power-driven vessel in a narrow channel. The other vessel will have to move to allow you to pass. You wish to overtake the other vessel on her starboard side. Your first whistle signal should be ____.

A. one short blast
B. two short blasts
C. two prolonged blasts followed by one short blast
D. two prolonged blasts followed by two short blasts

102. DIAGRAM 16. INT & INLAND

Which of the dayshapes shown must you show when at anchor?

A. A
B. B
C. C
D. D

103. INLAND ONLY

Which light display would mark the open ing in a pipeline where vessels could pass through?

A. Three red lights in a vertical line on each side of the opening
B. Two red lights in a vertical line on each side of the opening
C. Three white lights in a vertical line on each side of the opening
D. Two white lights in a vertical line on each side of the opening

104. INLAND ONLY

Which light(s) shall be shown at night on a moored barge which reduces the navigable width of any channel to less than 80m?

A. A white light placed on the two corners farthest from the bank
B. Two yellow lights in a vertical line at the stern
C. A red light placed on all four corners
D. A red light placed on the two corners farthest from the bank

105. INLAND ONLY

You are overtaking another power-driven vessel in a narrow channel. The other vessel will have to move to allow you to pass. You wish to overtake the other vessel and leave her on your starboard side. Your FIRST whistle signal should be ____.

A. one short blast
B. two short blasts
C. two prolonged blasts followed by one short blast
D. two prolonged blasts followed by two short blasts

106. INLAND ONLY

You are overtaking another power-driven vessel and sound a whistle signal indicating that you intend to pass the vessel along her starboard side. If the other vessel answers your signal with five short and rapid blasts, you should ____.

A. pass the other vessel along her starboard side
B. sound five short and rapid blasts and pass along her starboard side
C. not overtake the other vessel until both vessels exchange the same passing signal
D. not overtake the other vessel until she sounds another five short and rapid blast signal

107. INLAND ONLY

A power-driven vessel intends to overtake another power-driven vessel on the overtaken vessel's port side. What whistle signal should be sounded in order to state this intention?

A. 1 prolonged and 1 short blast
B. 1 short blast
C. 2 prolonged and 2 short blasts
D. 2 short blasts

108. INLAND ONLY
You are overtaking another power-driven vessel in a narrow channel. The other vessel will have to move to allow you to pass. You wish to overtake the other vessel and leave her on your starboard side. Your first whistle signal should be ____.

A. two prolonged blasts followed by one short blast
B. two prolonged blasts followed by two short blasts
C. one short blast
D. two short blasts

109. DIAGRAM 17. INT & INLAND
Vessel A is overtaking vessel B as shown. Vessel B is an air-cushion vessel operating in the nondisplacement mode. In addition to a steady white light, which other light will vessel A observe on vessel B?

A. Steady green light
B. Flashing red light
C. Flashing yellow light
D. Flashing white light

110. INLAND ONLY
Which statement is TRUE concerning the fog signal of a sailing vessel 25 m in length anchored in a special anchorage area approved by the Secretary of Transportation?

A. The vessel is not required to sound a fog signal.
B. The vessel shall ring a bell for 5 seconds every minute.
C. The vessel shall sound one blast of the whistle every 2 minutes.
D. The vessel shall sound three blasts on the whistle every 2 minutes.

111. INLAND ONLY
Which light display marks the opening in a pipeline where vessels could pass through?

A. Two red lights in a vertical line on each side of the opening
B. Three red lights in a vertical line on each side of the opening
C. Two yellow lights in a vertical line on each side of the opening
D. Three white lights in a vertical line on each side of the opening

112. DIAGRAM 81. INLAND ONLY
While underway, you sight the lights shown, with the yellow lights flashing. You should ____.

A. wait until the vessel ahead crosses your bow
B. stop until the red lights turn green
C. pass between the two sets of vertical red lights
D. proceed, leaving all the lights on your starboard side

114. INLAND ONLY
At night, what lights are required on barges moored in a group formation at a river bank?

A. A flashing yellow light placed at the upstream and downstream ends of the group
B. A white light placed at the corners farthest from the bank of each barge in the group
C. A white light placed at the corners farthest from the bank on each of the upstream and downstream ends of the group
D. Two red lights in a vertical line placed at the corners farthest from the bank on each of the upstream and downstream ends of the group

115. INLAND ONLY
What is true of a special flashing light?

A. It may show through an arc of 180°.
B. It flashes at the rate of 120 flashes per minute.
C. It is optional below the Baton Rouge Highway Bridge.
D. All of the above

116. DIAGRAM 16. INT & INLAND
You are on a 30-meter fishing vessel. Which day shape must you show while engaged in fishing?

A. A
B. B
C. C
D. D

117. INLAND ONLY
Which is a characteristic of a special flashing light?

A. It is required for all vessels being pushed ahead as part of a composite unit.
B. It must show through an arc of not less than 180° nor more than 225°.

C. It must be of the same character and construction as the masthead light.
D. All of the above

118. DIAGRAM 16. INT & INLAND
You are on a vessel engaged in fishing, other than trawling, and have gear extending more than 150 meters horizontally from the vessel. Which dayshape must you show in the direction of the outlying gear?

A. A
B. B
C. C
D. D

119. INLAND ONLY
What MAY be used to indicate the presence of a partly submerged object being towed?

A. A black cone, apex upward
B. Two all-around yellow lights at each end of the tow
C. The beam of a search light from the towing vessel shown in the direction of the tow
D. All of the above

120. INLAND ONLY
What shall be used to indicate the presence of a partly submerged object being towed?

A. A black cone, apex downward
B. An all-around white light at each end of the tow
C. A flare-up light
D. All of the above

122. INLAND ONLY
A barge more than 50 meters long is required to show how many white anchor lights when anchored in a Secretary of Transportation approved special anchorage area?

A. None
B. One
C. Two
D. One, on the near approach of another vessel

123. INLAND ONLY
What is not contained in the Inland Navigation Rules?

A. An inconspicuous, partly submerged object
B. Lights on pipelines
C. A vessel constrained by her draft
D. An air-cushion vessel

124. INLAND ONLY
Which term is NOT defined in the Inland Navigation Rules?

A. Towing light
B. Vessel constrained by her draft
C. In sight
D. Restricted visibility

125. INLAND ONLY
Under the Inland Navigation Rules, the term Inland Waters includes _____.

A. any waters marked by U.S. aids to navigation
B. harbors and rivers to the outermost aids to navigation
C. waters along the coast of the United States to a distance of two miles offshore
D. the Western Rivers, extending to the COLREGS demarcation line

126. INLAND ONLY
For the purpose of the Inland Rules, the term Inland Waters includes _____.

A. the waters surrounding any islands of the U.S.
B. the Great Lakes on the United States side of the boundary
C. the coastline of the United States, out to one mile offshore
D. any lakes within state boundaries

127. INLAND ONLY
You are on board the stand-on vessel in a crossing situation. You sound a one blast whistle signal, and the give-way vessel answers with a two-blast signal. You should then sound the danger signal and _____.

A. maintain course and speed
B. come around sharply to port
C. maneuver around the stern of the other vessel
D. stop and back your vessel if necessary until signals are agreed upon

128. DIAGRAM 16. INT & INLAND
You are on a sailing vessel. While under sail you decide to use your engine to assist in propulsion. Which day signal would you show?

A. D
B. C
C. B
D. None of these day signals are correct.

129. INLAND ONLY
You are proceeding in a channel in inland waters and are meeting an outbound vessel. Your responsibilities include _____.

A. keeping to that side of the channel which is on your vessel's port side
B. exchanging whistle signals if passing within half a mile
C. stopping your vessel and letting the outbound vessel initiate signals for passing
D. giving the outbound vessel the right of way

130. INLAND ONLY
Your vessel must stay within a narrow channel to be navigated safely. Another vessel is crossing your course from starboard to port. You do NOT think she will pass safely. You are required to _____.

A. slow to bare steerageway
B. back down
C. sound one short blast to indicate that you are holding course and speed
D. sound the danger signal

131. INLAND ONLY
You are navigating in a narrow channel and must remain in the channel for safe operation. Another vessel is crossing the channel ahead of you from your starboard. You are doubtful of intention of the crossing vessel. You MUST _____.

A. stop your vessel, since the other vessel has the right of way
B. sound the danger signal
C. contact him on the radiotelephone to make a passing agreement
D. stop your engines until you have slowed to bare steerageway

132. INLAND ONLY
Which statement is TRUE of a power-driven vessel proceeding downbound with the current, when meeting an upbound vessel on the Western Rivers?

A. She shall not impede the upbound vessel.
B. She shall pass on the port side of the other.
C. She shall propose the manner of passage.
D. All of the above

133. INLAND ONLY
A power-driven vessel operating in a narrow channel with a following current on the Great Lakes or Western Rivers is meeting an upbound vessel. Which statement is TRUE?

A. The downbound vessel has right of way.
B. The upbound vessel must initiate the required maneuvering signals.
C. The upbound vessel must propose the manner of passing.
D. All of the above

134. INLAND ONLY
Which is TRUE of a vessel downbound with a following current when meeting an upbound vessel on the Western Rivers?

A. Neither vessel has the right-of-way.
B. She has the right-of-way only if she is power-driven.
C. She does not have the right-of-way, since the other vessel is not crossing the river.
D. She must wait for a whistle signal from the upbound vessel.

135. DIAGRAM 16. INT & INLAND
You are on a 30-meter trawler. Which day signal must you show while trawling?

A. A
B. B
C. C
D. None of these day signals are correct.

136. INLAND ONLY
Yellow lights are NOT used to identify:

A. a dredge pipeline on a trestle
B. the heads of tows being pushed ahead by tugboats
C. purse seiners
D. a seaplane on the water

137. INLAND ONLY
A vessel displaying an alternating red and yellow light is _____.

A. in distress
B. enforcing the law
C. engaged in public safety activities
D. restricted in its ability to maneuver

138. INLAND ONLY
A law enforcement vessel patrolling a marine regatta may show either a flashing blue light or _____.

A. two amber lights in a horizontal line
B. an alternately flashing red and yellow light
C. a high intensity flashing white light (strobe)
D. a fixed green light over a red flashing light

139. DIAGRAM 16. INT ONLY
Which dayshape must you show on the forward end of an inconspicuous partially submerged vessel or object being towed more than 200 meters in length?

A. A
B. B
C. D
D. No dayshape must be shown.

140. INLAND ONLY
You are the stand-on vessel in a crossing situation. The other vessel is showing an alternating red and yellow light. Which action should you take?

A. Stand on.
B. Heave to.
C. Alter course to assist.
D. Yield the right-of-way.

141. INLAND ONLY
You are the stand-on vessel in an overtaking situation. The other vessel is showing an alternately flashing red-and-yellow light. What action should you take?

A. Alter course to assist
B. Give-way
C. Stand on
D. Heave to

142. INLAND ONLY
The special light for a vessel engaged in public safety activities must ____.

A. be on top of the mast or highest structure of the vessel
B. not interfere with the visibility of the navigation lights
C. be as far forward as possible
D. not be visible more than 22-1/2 degrees abaft the beam

143. INLAND ONLY
A light used to signal passing intentions must be an ____.

A. alternating red and yellow light
B. alternating white and yellow light
C. all-around white or yellow light
D. all-around white light only

144. INLAND ONLY
A light used to signal passing intentions must be an ____.

A. all-around yellow light only
B. all-around white light only
C. alternating red and yellow light
D. all-around white or yellow light

145. INLAND ONLY
A light used to signal passing intentions must be a(n) ____.

A. all-around white or yellow light
B. all-around yellow light only
C. all-around white light only
D. 225° white light only

146. INLAND ONLY
What characteristic must a light have if used to signal passing intentions?

A. an all-around white light.
B. an alternating blue and white light.
C. either an all-around white or an all-around yellow light.
D. an alternating red and yellow light.

147. INLAND ONLY
What characteristic must a light used to indicate passing intentions have?

A. an alternating red and yellow light.
B. an all-around white light.
C. an all-around yellow light.
D. either an all-around white or an all-around yellow light.

148. INLAND ONLY
In a narrow channel, you are underway on vessel A and desire to overtake vessel B. After you sound two short blasts on your whistle, vessel B sounds five short and rapid blasts on the whistle. You should ____.

A. pass with caution on the port side of vessel B
B. wait for the other vessel to initiate a signal
C. initiate another signal after the situation has stabilized
D. immediately answer with the danger signal, and then sound one short blast

149. INLAND ONLY
A power-driven vessel pushing ahead or towing alongside on the Mississippi River, above the Huey P. Long Bridge, shall carry ____.

A. two masthead lights, sidelights, and sternlight
B. two masthead lights, sidelights, and two towing lights
C. sidelights and two towing lights
D. one masthead light, sidelights, and sternlight

150. INLAND ONLY
A power-driven vessel, when leaving a dock or berth, must sound what signal?

A. Three short blasts
B. A long blast
C. A prolonged blast
D. No signal is required.

151. DIAGRAM 22. INT & INLAND
Which vessel is indicated by the day signal shown?

A. A dredge indicating the side with the obstruction
B. A fishing vessel with gear extending more than 150 meters horizontally
C. A tug with a tow exceeding 200 meters which limits her ability to maneuver
D. A vessel engaged in underwater operations with a diver down

152. DIAGRAM 22. INT & INLAND
The vessel showing the day signal is:

A. engaged in mine clearance operations
B. a fishing vessel with gear extending more than 150 meters horizontally
C. a trawler shooting nets in the direction indicated
D. a tug with a tow exceeding 200 meters unable to deviate from course

153. DIAGRAM 47. INT & INLAND
You are underway at night and you sight the lights shown. You know these lights indicate a ____.

A. fishing vessel engaged in fishing
B. trawler dragging nets
C. sailing vessel
D. dredge at work

154. DIAGRAM 47. INT & INLAND
You are underway at night and you sight the lights shown. You know these lights indicate a ____.

A. sailing vessel
B. trawler dragging nets
C. vessel engaged in mine clearance
D. dredge at work

155. DIAGRAM 47. INT & INLAND
You are underway at night and you sight the lights shown. You know these lights indicate a(n) ____.

A. sailing vessel
B. air-cushion vessel operating in the non-displacement mode
C. submarine operating on the surface

D. vessel pushing a barge ahead

156. DIAGRAM 47. INT & INLAND
You are underway at night and you sight the lights shown. You know these lights indicate a _____.

A. vessel towing astern
B. sailing vessel
C. submarine operating on the surface
D. vessel pushing a barge ahead

157. DIAGRAM 49. INT & INLAND
The lights shown are exhibited by a vessel _____.

A. restricted in her ability to maneuver
B. engaged in fishing
C. not under command
D. on pilotage duty

158. DIAGRAM 49. INT & INLAND
The lights shown are exhibited by a vessel _____.

A. dredging while underway
B. not under command
C. engaged in trawling
D. engaged in mineclearance

159. DIAGRAM 49. INT & INLAND
The lights shown are exhibited by a(n) _____.

A. submarine on the surface
B. air-cushion vessel in the non-displacement mode
C. vessel engaged in trawling
D. vessel not under command

160. DIAGRAM 49. INT & INLAND
The lights shown are exhibited by a(n) _____.

A. vessel not under command
B. air-cushion vessel in the non-displacement mode
C. vessel engaged in fishing
D. vessel engaged in underwater operations

161. DIAGRAM 51. INT & INLAND
You are on a vessel heading due south and see the lights shown one point on the port bow. This vessel could be heading _____.

A. NW
B. SW
C. NE
D. SE

162. DIAGRAM 51. INT & INLAND
You are on a vessel heading due south and see the lights shown one point on the port bow. This vessel could be heading _____ .

A. SSW
B. NW
C. NE
D. SE

163. INLAND ONLY
A commercial vessel engaged in public safety activities may display a(n):

A. flashing yellow light
B. flashing blue light
C. alternately flashing blue and red light
D. alternately flashing red and yellow light

164. DIAGRAM 51. INT & INLAND
You are on a vessel heading due south and see the lights shown one point on your port bow. This vessel could be heading _____.

A. SE
B. NE
C. NW
D. SW

165. DIAGRAM 51. INT & INLAND
You are on a vessel heading due south and see the lights shown one point on your port bow. This vessel could be heading _____.

A. SE
B. NE
C. SW
D. NW

166. DIAGRAM 51. INT & INLAND
You are on a vessel heading due north and see the lights shown one point on your port bow. This vessel could be heading _____.

A. SE
B. NE
C. SW
D. NW

168. DIAGRAM 51. INT & INLAND
You are on a vessel heading due north and see the lights shown one point on your port bow. This vessel could be heading _____.

A. NW
B. SW
C. NE
D. SE

169. DIAGRAM 51. INT & INLAND
You are on a vessel heading due north and see the lights shown one point on your port bow. This vessel could be heading _____.

A. NW
B. SW
C. SE
D. NE

170. DIAGRAM 59. INT & INLAND
You are on a vessel and see ahead the lights shown. They indicate a _____.

A. vessel crossing from your starboard
B. vessel crossing from your port
C. vessel being overtaken
D. vessel meeting head-on

171. DIAGRAM 59. INT & INLAND
You are on a vessel and see ahead the lights shown. They indicate a _____.

A. vessel being overtaken
B. vessel meeting head-on
C. vessel crossing from your starboard
D. vessel crossing from your port

172. DIAGRAM 59. INT & INLAND
You are on watch and sight a vessel showing only these lights. They indicate a _____.

A. sailing vessel
B. vessel engaged in trawling
C. power-driven vessel
D. mineclearance vessel

173. DIAGRAM 59. INT & INLAND
You are on watch and sight a vessel showing only these lights. They indicate a _____.

A. submarine on the surface
B. power-driven vessel
C. sailing vessel
D. vessel engaged in trawling

175. DIAGRAM 71. INT & INLAND
You see the display of lights shown. They indicate a vessel _____.

A. trawling
B. approaching head-on
C. fishing with nets extending more than 150 meters
D. dredging

176. DIAGRAM 64. INT & INLAND
You see the display of lights shown. This could indicate a _____.

A. 40m tug with tow exceeding 200m

B. tug unable to maneuver as required by the Rules
C. range marking a channel beneath a drawbridge
D. 60-meter tug pushing a barge ahead

177. DIAGRAM 64. INT & INLAND
You see the display of lights shown. This could indicate a ____.

A. 35-meter tug towing more than one barge astern
B. dredge restricted in its ability to maneuver
C. 55-meter tug towing astern, length of tow exceeds 200 meters
D. 65-meter tug towing astern, length of tow 150 meters

178. DIAGRAM 72. INT & INLAND
Which display of lights shown indicates a 65-meter tug towing a barge astern, length of tow 120 meters?

A. A
B. B
C. C
D. D

179. DIAGRAM 72. INT & INLAND
Which display of lights shown indicates a dredge underway and not dredging?

A. A
B. B
C. C
D. D

181. DIAGRAM 74. INT & INLAND
At night, you see the display of lights shown. They indicate a(n) ____.

A. sailing vessel
B. 8-meter power-driven vessel
C. vessel not under command
D. 12-meter fishing vessel

182. DIAGRAM 74. INT & INLAND
At night, you see the display of lights shown. They indicate a(n) ____.

A. vessel under oars
B. sailing vessel
C. law enforcement vessel
D. air-cushion vessel

183. INT & INLAND
Which vessel must show an after masthead light, if over 50 meters in length?

A. A vessel engaged in fishing
B. A vessel at anchor

C. A vessel not under command
D. A vessel trawling

185. DIAGRAM 54. INT & INLAND
You see the display of lights shown. It could be a ____.

A. pilot vessel with a motor launch alongside
B. fishing vessel adrift and fishing with hand– lines
C. fishing vessel at anchor
D. fishing vessel with outlying gear more than 150 meters

186. DIAGRAM 54. INT & INLAND
You see the display of lights shown. It could be a ____.

A. pilot vessel with a motor launch alongside
B. fishing vessel adrift and fishing with handlines
C. fishing vessel making way
D. dredge making way

187. INT & INLAND
You are in charge of a power-driven vessel making way in dense fog. You observe what appears to be another vessel on radar half a mile distant on your port bow and closing. You must:

A. sound the danger signal
B. exchange passing signals
C. sound one prolonged blast
D. sound one short, one prolonged, and one short blast

188. INT ONLY
Yellow lights are NOT shown by ____.

A. towing vessels pushing ahead
B. air cushion vessels in a nondisplacement mode
C. purse seiners
D. U.S. submarines

189. DIAGRAM 39. INT & INLAND
You are on vessel A towing a barge alongside and meeting vessel B as shown. Which action should you take?

A. Alter course to port
B. Alter course to starboard
C. Back down to reduce the strain on the lines
D. Maintain course and speed

190. DIAGRAM 75. INLAND ONLY
At night, you see the lights shown. They are shown on a ____.

A. barge being pushed ahead
B. barge being towed astern
C. tug pushing a barge ahead
D. tug towing a barge astern

191. DIAGRAM 75. INLAND ONLY
At night, you see the lights shown. They are shown on a ____.

A. bow of a barge being pushed ahead
B. stern of a barge being towed astern
C. masthead of a tug towing astern
D. stern of a tug pushing ahead

193. DIAGRAM 40. INT & INLAND
You are on vessel B and crossing a narrow channel. Vessel A , who can only navigate within the channel, is on your port bow and crossing as shown. Which action should you take?

A. Maintain course and speed as the ship is on your port bow.
B. Give way to the other vessel.
C. Increase speed and cross his bow.
D. Sound the danger signal.

194. DIAGRAM 40. INT & INLAND
You are on vessel A and proceeding down a narrow channel as shown. You can only navigate within the channel and vessel B is crossing so as to involve risk of collision. Which action would be most prudent?

A. Back down and allow vessel B to cross ahead.
B. Alter course to starboard to give him more room.
C. Maintain course and speed.
D. Sound the danger signal and take evasive action.

195. DIAGRAM 78. INT & INLAND
At night, you see a vessel with only the lights shown. This would indicate a ____.

A. vessel restricted in her ability to maneuver
B. fishing vessel underway
C. pilot vessel underway
D. vessel not under command

197. INT ONLY
A partially submerged object towed by a vessel must show during the day one ____.

A. diamond shape when the length of the tow is 200 meters or less
B. diamond shape when the length of the tow exceeds 200 meters in length

C. black ball
D. black ball only when the length of the tow exceeds 200 meters in length

198. INT ONLY
You are on a vessel that cannot comply with the spacing requirement for masthead lights. What is required in this situation?

A. The vessel must carry only the lights that comply with the rules; the others may be omitted.
B. The vessel's lights must comply as closely as possible, as determined by her government.
C. The vessel must be altered to permit full compliance with the rules.
D. An all-around light should be substituted for the after masthead light and the sternlight.

199. INLAND ONLY
You are on a vessel that the Secretary has determined cannot comply with the spacing requirement for masthead lights. What is required in this situation?

A. The vessel must carry only the lights that comply with the rules; the others may be omitted.
B. The vessel's lights must comply as closely as possible.
C. The vessel must be altered to permit full compliance with the rules.
D. An all-around light should be substituted for the after masthead light and the sternlight.

200. INLAND ONLY
A partially submerged object towed by a vessel must show during the day one ____.

A. diamond shape regardless of length of the tow
B. diamond shape only when the length of the tow exceeds 200 meters in length
C. black ball
D. black ball only when the length of the tow exceeds 200 meters in length

204. DIAGRAM 14. INT ONLY
Vessels A and B are in a crossing situation on the high seas as shown in DIAGRAM 14. Vessel B sounds one short blast. What is the proper action for vessel A to take?

A. Answer with one blast and hold course and speed
B. Hold course and speed
C. Answer with one blast and keep clear of

vessel B
D. Sound danger signal

205. INT ONLY
Which whistle signal may be sounded by one of two vessels in sight of each other?

A. Four short blasts
B. One prolonged blast
C. One short blast
D. One short, one prolonged, and one short blast

206. INT ONLY
What lights are required for a single barge being towed alongside?

A. Sidelights and a stern light
B. Sidelights, a special flashing light, and a stern light
C. Sidelights and a special flashing light
D. Sidelights, a towing light, and a stern light

207. INLAND ONLY
What lights are required for a single barge being towed alongside?

A. Sidelights and a stern light
B. Sidelights, a special flashing light, and a stern light
C. Sidelights and a special flashing light
D. Sidelights, a towing light, and a sternlight

208. INT ONLY
A single vessel being towed alongside shall show ____.

A. one all-around white light
B. sidelights and a stern light
C. only the outboard sidelight and a stern-light
D. a masthead light, sidelights, and a stern-light

209. INLAND ONLY
A single vessel being towed alongside shall show ____.

A. one all-around white light
B. sidelights and a stern light
C. only the outboard sidelight and a stern light
D. a special flashing light, sidelights, and a stern light

210. INLAND ONLY
A single vessel being towed alongside shall exhibit ____.

A. one all-around white light

B. sidelights, stern light and a special flashing light
C. only the outboard sidelight and a stern light
D. a masthead light, sidelights, and stern light

211. INT ONLY
A single vessel being towed alongside shall exhibit ____.

A. one all-around white light
B. sidelights, stern light and a special flashing light
C. only the outboard sidelight and a stern light
D. sidelights and a stern light

212. DIAGRAM 54. INT & INLAND
You see the display of lights shown. This indicates a vessel engaged ____.

A. in fishing at anchor
B. in fishing underway but not making way
C. in trawling making way
D. on pilotage duty making way

213. DIAGRAM 66. INT ONLY
You see the lights shown. This is a ____.

A. pilot vessel with a launch alongside
B. vessel towing astern and her tow
C. vessel towing a barge alongside
D. vessel pushing a barge ahead

214. DIAGRAM 55. INT ONLY
At night, you sight the lights shown. What do the lights indicate?

A. A tug with a tow astern
B. A tug with a tow alongside
C. A tug not under command
D. A pipeline

215. DIAGRAM 66. INT ONLY
At night you sight the lights shown. What do the lights indicate?

A. A tug with a tow astern
B. A tug with a tow alongside
C. A ship being assisted by a tug
D. A vessel engaged in fishing

216. INLAND ONLY
Signals shall be sounded by a power-driven vessel intending to overtake:

A. any vessel when within half a mile of that vessel
B. another power-driven vessel when both power-driven vessels are in sight of one another

C. any vessel when both are in sight of one another
D. another power-driven vessel only when within half a mile of that power-driven vessel

217. DIAGRAM 17. INT & INLAND
Vessel A is overtaking vessel B as shown. Vessel A is the _____.

A. give-way vessel
B. stand-on vessel
C. overtaken vessel
D. None of the above

218. INLAND ONLY
Your tug is pushing a barge ahead at night. What light(s) should show aft on your vessel?

A. The light(s) in Diagram 60.
B. The light(s) in Diagram 75.
C. The light(s) in Diagram 46.
D. The light(s) in Diagram 70.

219. INLAND ONLY
You are proceeding up a channel in Chesapeake Bay and are meeting an outbound vessel. There is no current. You MUST _____.

A. keep to that side of the channel which is on your vessel's port side
B. stop your vessel, letting the outbound vessel sound the signals for meeting and passing
C. propose or answer one- or two-blast whistle signals given by the other vessel if passing within 1/2 mile
D. give the outbound vessel the right-of-way

221. INLAND ONLY
A barge more than 50 meters long would be required to show how many white anchor lights when anchored in a Secretary of Transportation approved special anchorage area?

A. 4
B. 3
C. 2
D. 1

222. INLAND ONLY
A barge more than 50 meters long, at anchor in a special anchorage area designated by the Secretary , is required to show how many white anchor lights?

A. 1
B. 3

C. 4
D. 2

223. INLAND ONLY
A barge more than 50 meters long, at anchor in a special anchorage area designated by the Secretary, is required to show how many white anchor lights?

A. Two
B. One
C. One, on the near approach of another vessel
D. None

224. INLAND ONLY
A barge more than 50 meters long, at anchor in a special anchorage area designated by the Secretary, is required to show how many white anchor lights?

A. None
B. Two
C. One
D. One, on the near approach of another vessel

225. INLAND ONLY
A barge more than 50 meters long, at anchor in a special anchorage area designated by the Secretary, is required to show how many white anchor lights?

A. One
B. None
C. One, on the near approach of another vessel
D. Two

226. INLAND ONLY
While underway and in sight of another vessel a mile ahead you put your engines on astern propulsion. Which statement concerning whistle signals is TRUE?

A. You must sound three short blasts on the whistle.
B. You must sound one blast if backing to starboard.
C. You must sound whistle signals only if the vessels are meeting.
D. You need not sound any whistle signals.

227. INLAND ONLY
A commercial vessel engaged in public safety activities may display a(n):

A. alternately flashing red and yellow light
B. flashing blue light
C. flashing yellow light
D. alternately flashing blue and red light

228. INLAND ONLY
A vessel engaged in public safety activities may display an alternately flashing red and yellow light. This special light may be used by a vessel engaged in _____.

A. law enforcement
B. patrolling a regatta
C. hauling in pairs
D. river bank protection

229. DIAGRAM 17. INT & INLAND
Vessel A is overtaking vessel B as shown. Vessel A is the _____.

A. overtaken vessel
B. give-way vessel
C. stand-on vessel
D. None of the above

230. DIAGRAM 17. INT & INLAND
Vessel A is overtaking vessel B as shown. Vessel B is the _____.

A. stand-on vessel
B. give-way vessel
C. burdened vessel
D. None of the above

231. DIAGRAM 17. INT & INLAND
Vessel A is overtaking vessel B as shown. Vessel B is the _____.

A. give-way vessel
B. overtaken vessel
C. passing vessel
D. None of the above

232. DIAGRAM 17. INT & INLAND
Vessel A is overtaking vessel B as shown. Vessel B _____.

A. should change course to the right
B. should slow down until vessel A has passed
C. should hold her course and speed
D. may steer various courses and vessel A must keep clear

233. DIAGRAM 17. INT & INLAND
Vessel "A" is overtaking vessel "B" as shown. and will pass without changing course. Vessel "B" is an air-cushion vessel operating in the nondisplacement mode. Which light will vessel "A" observe from vessel "B"?

A. green light
B. flashing red light
C. flashing yellow light
D. flashing white light

234. DIAGRAM 17. INT & INLAND
Vessel A is overtaking vessel B as shown. Which color light will vessel A observe on vessel B ?

A. Green
B. White
C. Flashing red
D. Yellow over yellow

235. DIAGRAM 17. INLAND ONLY
Vessel A is overtaking vessel B as shown and will pass without changing course. Vessel A should sound _____.

A. one short blast
B. two short blasts
C. one prolonged blast
D. no signal

236. DIAGRAM 17. INT ONLY
Vessel "A" is overtaking vessel "B" on open waters as shown and will pass without changing course. Vessel "A" should sound _____.

A. one short blast
B. two short blasts
C. one prolonged blast
D. no whistle signal

237. DIAGRAM 17. INT ONLY
Vessel "A" is overtaking vessel "B" on open waters as shown and will pass without changing course. Vessel "A" should sound _____.

A. no whistle signal
B. two short blasts
C. two prolonged blasts followed by two short blasts
D. at least five short and rapid blasts

238. DIAGRAM 29. INT & INLAND
Vessels A and B are meeting in a narrow channel as shown but are not in sight of one another due to restricted visibility. Which statement is TRUE concerning whistle signals between the vessels?

A. Both vessels should sound two short blasts.
B. Both vessels should sound one short blast.
C. Vessel A should sound one short blast and vessel B should sound two short blasts.
D. None of the above statements is TRUE.

239. DIAGRAM 29. INLAND ONLY
Vessels A and B are meeting on a river as shown and will pass 1/4 mile apart. Which statement is TRUE?

A. Both vessels should continue on course and pass without sounding any whistle signals.
B. The vessels must exchange two blast whistle signals and pass port to port.
C. The vessels must exchange one blast whistle signals and pass starboard to starboard.
D. The vessels may reach agreement by radiotelephone and sound no whistle signal.

240. DIAGRAM 17. INT & INLAND
Vessel A is overtaking vessel B as shown and will pass without changing course. Which light will vessel A observe on vessel B ?

A. yellow towing light
B. white sternlight
C. green sidelight
D. None of the above

241. DIAGRAM 29. INLAND ONLY
Vessels A and B are meeting on a river as shown and will pass 1/4 mile apart. Which statement is TRUE?

A. Whistle signals must be exchanged in all cases when passing within one half mile of each other.
B. The vessels should exchange two blast signals and pass port to port.
C. If a passing agreement is reached by radiotelephone, whistle signals are optional, and the vessels should pass starboard to starboard as agreed.
D. The vessels should pass port to port and must sound whistle signals only if either vessel changes course.

242. DIAGRAM 32. INT & INLAND
You are on Vessel A engaged in fishing as shown in a narrow channel. Vessel B is a tanker proceeding in the channel. Vessel B sounds five short and rapid blasts. You feel it is not safe for vessel B to overtake you at the present time. You should _____.

A. not answer the whistle signals from vessel B
B. maintain course and speed
C. not impede the passage of vessel B
D. sound one prolonged followed by two short blasts

243. DIAGRAM 32. INT ONLY
You are on vessel A as shown. Vessel B sounds two short blasts. You should:

A. sound two prolonged blasts followed by two short blasts

B. not answer the whistle signal from vessel B
C. sound two short blasts and maintain course and speed
D. sound one prolonged, one short, one prolonged and one short blast

244. DIAGRAM 32. INT & INLAND
You are on a 15-meter vessel A in a narrow channel as shown. Vessel B , a large tanker which can safely navigate only within the channel, sounds five short and rapid blasts. You should:

A. sound one prolonged followed by two short blasts
B. not answer the whistle signal from vessel B
C. maintain course and speed
D. not impede the passage of vessel B

245. DIAGRAM 32. INT ONLY
You are on vessel A as shown. Vessel B sounds two short blasts. You should:

A. sound two prolonged blasts followed by two short blasts
B. sound two short blasts
C. maintain course and speed
D. None of the above

246. DIAGRAM 32. INLAND ONLY
You are on vessel A as shown in a narrow channel. Vessel B sounds two short blasts. If you are in agreement you should _____.

A. sound two short blasts
B. sound two prolonged followed by two short blasts
C. not answer the whistle signals from vessel B
D. None of the above

247. DIAGRAM 36. INLAND ONLY
You are on vessel I and in sight of vessel II as shown. Vessel II sounds one short blast. If you agree, you should _____.

A. sound one short blast and hold course and speed
B. hold course and speed and sound no signal
C. sound one short blast and slow down or turn to starboard
D. sound the danger signal and slow to moderate speed

248. DIAGRAM 36. INT & INLAND
Vessels I and II are power-driven vessels. You are on vessel I as shown. You are the _____.

A. give-way vessel
B. stand-on vessel
C. overtaking vessel
D. None of the above

249. DIAGRAM 36. INLAND ONLY
You are on a power-driven vessel I as shown. Vessel II is a power-driven vessel engaged in fishing within 1/2 mile of your vessel. Which action should you take?

A. Hold course and speed without giving a signal.
B. Sound the danger signal and slow to moderate speed.
C. Sound one short blast, slow down and turn to starboard.
D. Sound one short blast and await response from the fishing vessel.

250. DIAGRAM 36. INLAND ONLY
You are on a power-driven vessel I as shown. Vessel II is a power-driven vessel engaged in fishing within 1/2 mile of your vessel. You sound one short blast on the whistle. Vessel II does not sound any signal. Which action should you take?

A. Hold course and speed without giving a signal.
B. Sound the danger signal and slow to moderate speed.
C. Sound one short blast, slow down and turn to starboard.
D. Sound two short blasts and change course to port.

251. DIAGRAM 41. INLAND ONLY
Vessels "A" and "B" are meeting on a river as shown and will pass about 1/4 mile apart. Which action should the vessels take?

A. The vessels should continue on course and pass without sounding any whistle signals.
B. The vessels should exchange two blast whistle signals and pass starboard to starboard.
C. The vessels should exchange one blast whistle signals and pass starboard to starboard.
D. The vessels should pass starboard to starboard and must sound whistle signals only if either vessel changes course.

252. DIAGRAM 41. INT ONLY
Vessels A and B are meeting on a river as shown and will pass 1/4 mile apart. Which action should the vessels take?

A. The vessels should continue on course

and pass without sounding any whistle signals.
B. The vessels should exchange two blast whistle signals and pass starboard to starboard.
C. The vessels should exchange one blast whistle signals and pass starboard to starboard
D. The vessel with the tow should initiate the whistle signals.

253. DIAGRAM 41. INLAND ONLY
Vessels A and B are meeting on a river as shown and will pass 1/4 mile apart. Which light(s) on vessel B will you see if you are on vessel A?

A. special flashing light
B. two white masthead lights in a vertical line
C. green sidelight
D. All of the above

254. DIAGRAM 41. INLAND ONLY
Vessels A and B are meeting on a river as shown and will pass 1/4 mile apart. Which is one of the lights on vessel B that you will see if you are on vessel A?

A. red sidelight
B. yellow towing light
C. special flashing light
D. All of the above

255. DIAGRAM 41. INT ONLY
Vessels A and B are meeting on a river as shown and will pass 1/4 mile apart. Which light on vessel B will you see if you are on vessel A?

A. special flashing yellow light
B. flashing blue light
C. two yellow towing lights
D. None of the above

256. DIAGRAM 41. INT ONLY
Vessels A and B are meeting on a river as shown and will pass 1/4 mile apart. Which light(s) on vessel B will you see if you are on vessel A?

A. special flashing yellow light
B. two white masthead lights in a vertical line
C. two yellow towing lights
D. None of the above

257. DIAGRAM 37. INLAND ONLY
Two power-driven vessels are meeting in the situation as shown. One short blast from either vessel means ____.

A. "I am altering my course to starboard."
B. "I intend to leave you on my port side."
C. "I intend to hold course and speed."
D. "I intend to pass on your starboard side."

258. DIAGRAM 41. INLAND ONLY
Vessels A and B are meeting on a river as shown and will pass 1/4 mile apart. Which statement is TRUE?

A. Whistle signals must be exchanged in all situations when passing within one half mile.
B. If a passing agreement is reached by radiotelephone, whistle signals are optional.
C. If a passing agreement is reached by radio-telephone whistle signals are still required.
D. None of the above

259. INT & INLAND
Barges being towed at night must exhibit navigation lights ____.

A. at all times
B. only if manned
C. only if towed astern
D. Need not be lighted

260. INLAND ONLY
A vessel engaged in public safety activities may display an alternately flashing red and yellow light. This special light may be used by a vessel engaged in ____.

A. search and rescue
B. restricted in ability to maneuver
C. not under command
D. river bank protection

261. INLAND ONLY
While underway and in sight of another vessel more than 0.5 mile away, you put your engines full speed astern. Which statement concerning whistle signals is TRUE?

A. You must sound three short blasts on the whistle.
B. You must sound one blast if backing to starboard.
C. You must sound whistle signals only if the vessels are meeting.
D. You need not sound any whistle signals.

262. INLAND ONLY
When power-driven vessels are in sight of one another, passing signals shall be sounded when ____.

A. meeting or crossing within half a mile of each other

B. meeting within one mile of each other
C. meeting or crossing at any distance
D. crossing within one mile of each other

264. DIAGRAM 37. INT ONLY
Two power-driven vessels are meeting in the situation as shown. One short blast from either vessel means:

A. I am altering my course to starboard.
B. I intend to leave you on my port side.
C. I intend to hold course and speed.
D. I am altering my course to port.

265. DIAGRAM 36. INT ONLY
You are on a power-driven vessel I as shown. Vessel II is a vessel engaged in fishing. Which action should you take?

A. Hold course and speed without giving a signal.
B. Sound the danger signal and slow to moderate speed.
C. Sound one short blast, turn to starboard and reduce speed.
D. Sound one short blast and hold course and speed.

266. DIAGRAM 37. INLAND ONLY
Two power-driven vessels are meeting in a narrow channel on the Great Lakes as shown. Vessel A is downbound with a following current. Vessel B shall ____.

A. propose the manner of passage
B. have the right of way
C. initiate the maneuvering signals
D. None of the above

267. DIAGRAM 37. INT ONLY
Two power-driven vessels are meeting in the situation as shown. Two short blasts from either vessel means ____.

A. I am altering my course to starboard.
B. I intend to leave you on my port side.
C. I am altering my course to port.
D. I am operating astern propulsion.

268. DIAGRAM 37. INLAND ONLY
Two power-driven vessels are meeting in the situation as shown and will pass within 1/2 mile of each other. Two short blasts from either vessel means ____.

A. I intend to leave you on my starboard side.
B. I intend to leave you on my port side.
C. I am altering my course to port.
D. I am altering my course to starboard.

269. DIAGRAM 37. INLAND ONLY
Two power-driven vessels are meeting in a narrow channel on the Great Lakes as shown. Vessel A is downbound with a following current. Vessel A shall ____.

A. propose the manner of passage
B. have the right of way
C. initiate the maneuvering signals
D. All of the above

270. DIAGRAM 37. INLAND ONLY
Two power-driven vessels are meeting in a narrow channel as shown. Which statement is TRUE?

A. Whistle signals must be exchanged in all situations when passing within one half mile of each other.
B. If agreement is reached by radio-telephone whistle signals are optional.
C. If agreement is reached by radiotelephone whistle signals must still be exchanged.
D. None of the above

272. DIAGRAM 37. INT & INLAND
Two vessels are meeting as shown in a narrow channel. Vessel A is a sailing vessel. Vessel B is a power-driven vessel which can safely navigate only within the channel. Vessel B sounds the danger signal. Vessel A shall ____.

A. maintain course and speed
B. not impede the passage of vessel B
C. sound one prolonged followed by two short blasts
D. have the right of way

273. DIAGRAM 81. INLAND ONLY
While underway you sight the lights shown with the yellow lights flashing, you should ____.

A. wait until the vessel ahead crosses your bow
B. stop until the red lights turn green
C. proceed leaving all the lights on your starboard side
D. pass between the two sets of vertical red lights

274. DIAGRAM 81. INLAND ONLY
While underway you sight the lights shown with the yellow lights flashing, you should ____.

A. wait until the vessel ahead crosses your bow
B. stop until the red lights turn green
C. pass between the two sets of vertical red lights

D. proceed leaving all the lights on your starboard side

275. DIAGRAM 81. INLAND ONLY
While underway you sight the lights shown with the yellow lights flashing, you should ____.

A. wait until the vessel ahead crosses your bow
B. pass between the two sets of vertical red lights
C. stop until the red lights turn green
D. proceed leaving all the lights on your starboard side

276. DIAGRAM 81. INLAND ONLY
While underway you sight the lights shown with the yellow lights flashing, you should ____.

A. pass between the two sets of vertical red lights
B. wait until the vessel ahead crosses your bow
C. stop until the red lights turn green
D. proceed leaving all the lights on your starboard side

277. DIAGRAM 81. INLAND ONLY
While underway you sight the lights shown with the yellow lights flashing. The lights displayed should be ____.

A. visible at night and during periods of restricted visibility
B. visible for at least one mile
C. more than 50 meters apart
D. flashing at 120 flashes per minute

278. DIAGRAM 81. INLAND ONLY
While underway you sight the lights shown with the yellow lights flashing. The lights displayed should be ____.

A. visible for at least one mile
B. more than 50 meters apart
C. visible at night and during periods of restricted visibility
D. flashing at 120 flashes per minute

279. DIAGRAM 81. INLAND ONLY
While underway you sight the lights shown with the yellow lights flashing. The lights displayed should be ____.

A. visible for at least one mile
B. visible at night and during periods of restricted visibility
C. more than 50 meters apart
D. flashing at 120 flashes per minute

280. DIAGRAM 81. INLAND ONLY
While underway you sight the lights shown

with the yellow lights flashing. The lights displayed should be _____.

A. visible for at least one mile
B. flashing at 120 flashes per minute
C. more than 50 meters apart
D. visible at night and during periods of restricted visibility

282. DIAGRAM 81. INLAND ONLY
While underway you sight the lights shown with the yellow lights flashing. The lights displayed are from a _____.

A. vessel not under command
B. dredge pipeline
C. vessel aground
D. vessel not under command

283. DIAGRAM 81. INLAND ONLY
While underway you sight the lights shown with the yellow lights flashing. The lights displayed are from a _____.

A. seaplane
B. minesweeper
C. dredge pipeline
D. vessel not under command

284. DIAGRAM 81. INLAND ONLY
While underway you sight the lights shown with the yellow lights flashing. The lights displayed are from a _____.

A. vessel aground
B. mine clearance vessel
C. vessel not under command
D. dredge pipeline

288. DIAGRAM 24. INT & INLAND
The tow shown is less than 200 meters in length and severely restricted in her ability to deviate from her course. Which day-shape(s) would be displayed by day from the vessel(s)?

A. ball-diamond-ball on the towing vessel
B. diamond on the towing vessel
C. diamond on the last barge
D. All of the above

289. DIAGRAM 24. INT & INLAND
The tow shown is less than 200m in length and severely restricted in her ability to deviate from her course. Which dayshape(s) would be displayed by day from the vessel?

A. ball-diamond-ball on the towing vessel
B. diamond on the towing vessel
C. diamond on the last barge
D. None of the above

290. DIAGRAM 24. INT & INLAND
The tow shown is greater than 200 meters in length and severely restricted in her ability to deviate from her course. Which day-shape(s) would be displayed by day from the vessel(s)?

A. ball-diamond-ball on the towing vessel
B. diamond on the towing vessel
C. diamond on the barges
D. All of the above

292. DIAGRAM 24. INT & INLAND
The tug shown is greater than 50 meters and severely restricted in her ability to deviate from her course. Which lights would be displayed from the towing vessel?

A. Two white masthead lights, red-white-red all-around lights, sidelights, stern light and a towing light
B. Three white masthead lights, red-white-red all round lights, sidelights and two towing lights
C. Three white masthead lights, two all-around red lights, sidelights, stern light and a towing light
D. None of the above

293. DIAGRAM 48. INT & INLAND
A vessel displaying the lights below is a _____.

A. a vessel towing astern
B. sailing vessel
C. a vessel not under command
D. a submarine on the surface

294. DIAGRAM 48. INT & INLAND
A vessel displaying the lights below is a _____.

A. a submarine on the surface
B. sailing vessel
C. a vessel not under command
D. None of the above

295. DIAGRAM 48. INT & INLAND
A vessel displaying the lights below is a _____.

A. submarine on the surface
B. vessel towing astern
C. vessel restricted in her ability to maneuver
D. vessel not under command

296. DIAGRAM 48. INT & INLAND
A vessel displaying the lights below is a _____.

A. submarine on the surface
B. vessel constrained by her draft
C. vessel towing astern
D. vessel not under command

297. DIAGRAM 48. INT & INLAND
A vessel displaying the lights below is a _____.

A. vessel towing astern
B. vessel constrained by her draft
C. vessel in the nondisplacement mode
D. vessel not under command

298. DIAGRAM 79. INT & INLAND
A vessel displaying the lights shown is a _____.

A. vessel constrained by her draft
B. law enforcement vessel
C. vessel not under command
D. vessel towing astern

299. DIAGRAM 79. INT & INLAND
A vessel displaying the lights shown is a _____.

A. vessel towing astern
B. vessel restricted in ability to maneuver
C. vessel not under command
D. vessel aground

300. DIAGRAM 79. INT & INLAND
A vessel displaying the lights shown is a _____.

A. sailing vessel
B. vessel towing astern
C. vessel engaged in fishing
D. vessel dredging

301. DIAGRAM 79. INT & INLAND
A vessel displaying the lights shown is a vessel _____.

A. engaged in submarine operations
B. dredging
C. engaged in fishing
D. towing astern

302. DIAGRAM 79. INT & INLAND
A vessel displaying the lights shown is a vessel _____.

A. engaged in fishing
B. dredging
C. engaged in launching or recovery of aircraft
D. towing astern

311. DIAGRAM 85. INLAND ONLY
Identify the operation indicated by the lights exhibited as shown.

A. Aircraft carrier engaged in the launching and recovery of aircraft
B. A submarine engaged in underway replenishment
C. A vessel aground assisted by tugs
D. None of the above

312. DIAGRAM 85. INLAND ONLY
You see the lights shown while proceeding in a channel. What should you do?

A. Proceed at full speed through the two sets of double red lights.
B. Stop the vessel and await the red lights to change to green.
C. Slow down and pass between the two sets of double red lights.
D. None of the above

313. DIAGRAM 85. INLAND ONLY
You see the lights shown while proceeding in a channel. Where should you pass?

A. A
B. B
C. C
D. D

314. DIAGRAM 85. INLAND ONLY
Identify the operation indicated by the lights shown.

A. An aircraft carrier engaged in the launching and recovery of aircraft
B. A submarine engaged in underway replenishment at sea
C. A dredge engaged in dredging
D. A vessel aground assisted by tugs

315. DIAGRAM 82. INT & INLAND
At night a vessel displaying the lights as shown is _____.

A. fishing
B. sailing
C. a pilot boat
D. anchored

316. DIAGRAM 82. INT & INLAND
At night a vessel displaying the lights as shown is _____.

A. a pilot boat
B. sailing
C. fishing
D. anchored

317. DIAGRAM 82. INT & INLAND
At night a vessel displaying the lights as shown is _____.

A. a pilot boat
B. sailing
C. anchored
D. fishing

318. DIAGRAM 82. INT & INLAND
Which dayshape(s) would be displayed by the vessel engaged in the operation indicated by the lights shown.

A. two cones with apexes together
B. a ball, a diamond and another ball
C. a cylinder
D. a diamond

319. DIAGRAM 82. INT & INLAND
Which dayshape(s) would be displayed by the vessel engaged in the operation indicated by the lights shown.

A. a cylinder
B. two cones with apexes together
C. a ball, a diamond and another ball
D. a diamond

320. DIAGRAM 82. INT & INLAND
Which dayshape(s) would be displayed by the vessel engaged in the operation indicated by the lights shown.

A. a cylinder
B. a ball, a diamond and another ball
C. two cones with apexes together
D. a diamond

321. DIAGRAM 82. INT & INLAND
Which dayshape(s) would be displayed by the vessel engaged in the operation indicated by the lights shown.

A. a cylinder
B. a diamond
C. a ball, a diamond and another ball
D. two cones with apexes together

322. DIAGRAM 82. INT & INLAND
The vessel whose lights are shown is navigating in a narrow channel. Which statement about this vessel is TRUE?

A. It shall not impede the passage of any other vessel navigating within the channel or fairway
B. It is the stand-on vessel
C. It may anchor in the channel or fairway
D. It shows two balls

323. DIAGRAM 23. INT & INLAND
Which diagram shows the arc of visibility of a red sidelight?

A. A
B. B
C. C
D. D

324. DIAGRAM 23. INT & INLAND
Which diagram shows the arc of visibility of a green sidelight?

A. A
B. B
C. C
D. D

325. DIAGRAM 23. INT & INLAND
Diagram B shows the arc of visibility of a _____.

A. white masthead light
B. red sidelight
C. green sidelight
D. stern light

326. DIAGRAM 23. INT & INLAND
Diagram A shows the arc of visibility of a _____.

A. white masthead light
B. red sidelight
C. green sidelight
D. stern light

327. DIAGRAM 23. INT & INLAND
Diagram A shows the arc of visibility of a _____.

A. white masthead light
B. green sidelight
C. red sidelight
D. stern light

328. DIAGRAM 23. INT & INLAND
Diagram D shows the arc of visibility of a _____.

A. white masthead light
B. green sidelight
C. stern light
D. None of the above

329. DIAGRAM 23. INT & INLAND
Diagram C shows the arc of visibility of a _____.

A. white masthead light
B. red sidelight
C. stern light
D. None of the above

330. DIAGRAM 23. INT & INLAND
Diagram B shows the arc of visibility of a ____.

A. white masthead light
B. green sidelight
C. red sidelight
D. stern light

331. DIAGRAM 23. INT & INLAND
Diagram A shows the arc of visibility of a ____.

A. yellow flashing light
B. green sidelight
C. masthead light
D. None of the above

332. DIAGRAM 23. INT & INLAND
Diagram A shows the arc of visibility of a ____.

A. red sidelight
B. green sidelight
C. masthead light
D. stern light

333. DIAGRAM 23. INT & INLAND
Diagram B shows the arc of visibility of a ____.

A. yellow flashing light
B. red sidelight
C. green sidelight
D. stern light

334. DIAGRAM 23. INT & INLAND
Diagram A shows the arc of visibility of a ____.

A. yellow flashing light
B. red sidelight
C. green sidelight
D. stern light

335. DIAGRAM 23. INT & INLAND
Diagram C shows the arc of visibility of a ____.

A. yellow flashing light
B. red sidelight
C. green sidelight
D. None of the above

336. DIAGRAM 42. INLAND ONLY
Two power-driven vessels are crossing within a half a mile of each other as shown. Vessel A sounds one short blast on the whistle. Vessel B should ____.

A. maintain course and speed without sounding any signals

B. alter course to the right or slowdown
C. sound one short blast and maintain course and speed
D. sound the danger signal and slow to moderate speed

337. DIAGRAM 42. INLAND ONLY
Two power-driven vessels are crossing within a half a mile of each other as shown. Vessel A sounds one short blast on the whistle. Vessel B should sound ____.

A. one short blast
B. two short blasts
C. two prolonged blasts followed by two short blasts
D. three short blasts

338. DIAGRAM 42. INLAND ONLY
Two power-driven vessels are crossing within a half a mile of each other as shown. Vessel A sounds one short blast on the whistle. Vessel B should sound ____.

A. one prolonged, one short, one prolonged and one short blast
B. one short blast
C. two prolonged blasts followed by one short blast
D. two short blasts

339. DIAGRAM 42. INLAND ONLY
Two power-driven vessels are crossing within a half a mile of each other as shown. Vessel A sounds one short blast on the whistle. Vessel B should sound ____.

A. one prolonged, one short, one prolonged and one short blast
B. two short blasts
C. one short blast
D. None of the above

340. DIAGRAM 42. INLAND ONLY
Two power-driven vessels are crossing within a half a mile of each other as shown. Vessel A sounds one short blast on the whistle. Vessel B should sound ____.

A. one prolonged, one short, one prolonged and one short blast
B. one prolonged blast
C. two short blasts
D. None of the above

341. DIAGRAM 42. INLAND ONLY
Two power-driven vessels are crossing within a half a mile of each other as shown. Vessel A sounds one short blast on the whistle. This signal means ____.

A. I intend to leave you on my port side
B. I intend to overtake you on your port side
C. I am altering my course to starboard
D. None of the above

342. DIAGRAM 42. INLAND ONLY
Two power-driven vessels are crossing within a half a mile of each other as shown. Vessel A sounds one short blast on the whistle. This signal means ____.

A. I intend to leave you on my starboard side
B. I am operating astern propulsion port side
C. I am altering my course to starboard
D. None of the above

343. DIAGRAM 42. INLAND ONLY
Two power-driven vessels are crossing within a half a mile of each other as shown. Vessel A sounds one short blast on the whistle. This signal means ____.

A. I intend to leave you on my starboard side
B. I intend to leave you on my port side
C. I am altering my course to starboard
D. None of the above

345. DIAGRAM 42. INLAND ONLY
Two power-driven vessels are crossing within a half a mile of each other as shown. Vessel A sounds one short blast on the whistle. This signal means ____.

A. I intend to overtake you on my starboard side
B. I am operating astern propulsion
C. I intend to leave you on my port side
D. None of the above

346. DIAGRAM 42. INLAND ONLY
Two power-driven vessels are crossing within a half a mile of each other as shown. Vessel A sounds one short blast on the whistle. This signal means ____.

A. I intend to overtake you on my port side
B. I am operating astern propulsion
C. I intend to leave you on my starboard side D. None of the above

347. DIAGRAM 42. INT ONLY
Two power-driven vessels are crossing within one half mile of each other as shown. Vessel A sounds one short blast of the whistle. Vessel B should ____.

A. sound the danger signal and slow to moderate speed

B. alter course to the right or slow down
C. sound one short blast and maintain course and speed
D. None of the above

348. DIAGRAM 42. INT ONLY
Two power-driven vessels are crossing within one half mile of each other as shown. Vessel A sounds one short blast of the whistle. Vessel B should ____.

A. maintain course and speed
B. alter course to the right or slow down
C. sound one short blast and maintain course and speed
D. sound the danger signal and slow to moderate speed

349. DIAGRAM 42. INT ONLY
Two power-driven vessels are crossing within one half mile of each other as shown. Vessel A sounds one short blast of the whistle. Vessel B should sound ____.

A. one prolonged, one short, one prolonged and one short blast
B. one short blast
C. two short blasts
D. None of the above

350. DIAGRAM 42. INT ONLY
Two power-driven vessels are crossing within one half mile of each other as shown. Vessel A sounds one short blast of the whistle. Vessel B should sound ____.

A. one prolonged, one short, one prolonged and one short blast
B. one prolonged blast
C. two short blasts
D. None of the above

351. DIAGRAM 42. INT ONLY
Two power-driven vessels are crossing within one half mile of each other as shown. Vessel A sounds one short blast of the whistle. This signal means ____.

A. I am altering my course to starboard
B. I am operating astern propulsion
C. I am altering my course to port
D. None of the above

352. INLAND ONLY
A commercial vessel engaged in public safety activities may display a(n) ____.

A. flashing blue light
B. alternately flashing red and yellow light
C. flashing yellow light
D. alternately flashing blue and red light

353. DIAGRAM 42. INT ONLY
Two power-driven vessels are crossing within one half mile of each other as shown. Vessel A sounds one short blast of the whistle. This signal means ____.

A. "I intend to overtake you on your starboard side."
B. "I am operating astern propulsion."
C. "I intend to leave you on my port side."
D. none of the above

354. DIAGRAM 42. INT ONLY
Two power-driven vessels are crossing within one half mile of each other as shown. Vessel A sounds one short blast of the whistle. This signal means ____.

A. I intend to leave you on your starboard side
B. I am altering my course to starboard
C. I am altering my course to port
D. None of the above

355. DIAGRAM 42. INT ONLY
Two power-driven vessels are crossing within one half mile of each other as shown. Vessel A sounds one short blast of the whistle. This signal means ____.

A. I am altering my course to starboard
B. I intend to leave you on my port side
C. I am altering my course to port
D. None of the above

356. DIAGRAM 42. INT ONLY
Two power-driven vessels are crossing within one half mile of each other as shown. Vessel A sounds one short blast of the whistle. This signal means ____.

A. I intend to leave you on my port side
B. I intend to overtake you on your port side
C. I am altering my course to starboard
D. None of the above

357. DIAGRAM 42. INT ONLY
Two power-driven vessels are crossing within one half mile of each other as shown. Vessel A sounds one short blast of the whistle. This signal means ____.

A. I intend to leave you on my starboard side
B. I intend to overtake you on your port side
C. I am altering my course to port
D. None of the above

358. DIAGRAM 42. INT ONLY
Two power-driven vessels are crossing

within one half mile of each other as shown. Vessel A sounds one short blast of the whistle. Vessel B is the ____.

A. burdened vessel
B. give-way vessel
C. overtaking vessel
D. none of the above

359. DIAGRAM 42. INT & INLAND
Two power-driven vessels are crossing as shown. Vessel A sounds one short blast on the whistle. You are on vessel B and doubt that sufficient action is being taken by vessel A to avoid collision. You should ____.

A. maintain course and speed
B. alter course to the left and increase speed
C. sound one short blast and maintain course and speed
D. None of the above

360. DIAGRAM 42. INT & INLAND
Two power-driven vessels are crossing as shown. Vessel A sounds one short blast on the whistle. You are on vessel B and doubt that sufficient action is being taken by vessel A to avoid collision. You should ____.

A. maintain course and speed
B. alter course to the right or slow down
C. sound one short blast and maintain course and speed
D. sound at least five short and rapid blasts

361. DIAGRAM 42. INT & INLAND
Two power-driven vessels are crossing as shown. Vessel A sounds two short blasts on the whistle. You are on vessel B and are in doubt that sufficient action is being taken by vessel A to avoid collision. You should:

A. maintain course and speed
B. alter course to the left and increase speed
C. sound five or more short and rapid blasts
D. None of the above

362. DIAGRAM 42. INT & INLAND
Two power-driven vessels are crossing as shown. Vessel A sounds two short blasts on the whistle. You are on vessel B and are in doubt that sufficient action is being taken by vessel A to avoid collision. You should:

A. maintain course and speed
B. alter course to the right or slow down
C. sound one short blast and maintain course and speed
D. sound 5 or more short and rapid blasts

363. DIAGRAM 42. INT & INLAND
Two power-driven vessels are crossing as shown. Vessel A sounds one short blast on the whistle. Vessel B is the ____.

A. burdened vessel
B. give-way vessel
C. overtaking vessel
D. None of the above

364. DIAGRAM 42. INT & INLAND
Two power-driven vessels are crossing as shown. Vessel A sounds one short blast on the whistle. Vessel B is the ____.

A. burdened vessel
B. give-way vessel
C. stand-on vessel
D. overtaking vessel

365. DIAGRAM 42. INT & INLAND
Two power-driven vessels are crossing as shown. Vessel A sounds one short blast on the whistle. Vessel B is the ____.

A. stand-on
B. give-way vessel
C. overtaking vessel
D. None of the above

366. DIAGRAM 42. INT & INLAND
Two power-driven vessels are crossing as shown. Vessel A sounds one short blast on the whistle. Vessel B is the ____.

A. give-way vessel
B. stand-on vessel
C. overtaking vessel
D. burdened vessel

367. DIAGRAM 42. INT & INLAND
Two power-driven vessels are crossing as shown. Vessel A sounds one short blast on the whistle. Vessel A is the ____.

A. give-way vessel
B. stand-on vessel
C. overtaking vessel
D. None of the above

368. DIAGRAM 42. INT & INLAND
Two power-driven vessels are crossing as shown. Vessel A sounds one short blast on the whistle. Vessel A is the ____.

A. stand-on vessel
B. give-way vessel
C. overtaking vessel
D. None of the above

369. DIAGRAM 42. INT & INLAND
Two power-driven vessels are crossing as shown. Vessel A sounds one short blast on the whistle. Vessel A is the ____.

A. stand-on vessel
B. overtaking vessel
C. give-way vessel
D. None of the above

370. INLAND ONLY
If a towing vessel and her tow are severely restricted in their ability to deviate from their course, they may show lights in addition to their towing identification lights. These additional lights shall be shown if the tow is____.

A. pushed ahead
B. towed alongside
C. towed astern
D. Any of the above

371. INT ONLY
If a towing vessel and her tow are severely restricted in their ability to deviate from their course, the towing vessel shall show lights in addition to her towing identification lights. These additional lights shall be shown if the tow is ____.

A. pushed ahead
B. towed alongside
C. towed astern
D. Any of the above

372. DIAGRAM 32. INLAND ONLY
You are on vessel A as shown and hear vessel B sound a signal indicating his intentions to overtake you. You feel it is not safe for vessel B to overtake you at the present time. You should ____.

A. sound two short blasts
B. sound one prolonged followed by three short blasts
C. not answer the whistle signal from vessel B
D. None of the above

374. DIAGRAM 29. INLAND ONLY
Vessels A and B are meeting on a river as shown and will pass 1/4 mile apart. Which statement is TRUE?

A. Whistle signals must be exchanged in all situations when passing within one half mile.
B. The vessels should exchange two blast whistle signals and pass port to port.
C. If a passing agreement is reached by radiotelephone whistle signals are optional.
D. The vessels should pass port to port and must sound whistle signals only if either vessel changes course.

375. DIAGRAM 24. INT & INLAND
The tug shown is made up of inconspicuous, partly submerged vessels and is 150m in length. The towed vessels are less than 25m in breadth and less than 100m in length. Which lights would be displayed from the towed vessels?

A. Sidelights and stern light on each vessel towed
B. One all-around white light at the after end of each vessel towed
C. One all-around white light at or near each end of each vessel towed
D. One all-around white light at each end and one all-around white light at the extremities of its breadth of each vessel towed

376. INT & INLAND
Which vessel must show forward and after masthead lights when making way?

A. A 75-meter vessel restricted in her ability to maneuver
B. A 100-meter sailing vessel
C. A 150-meter vessel engaged in fishing
D. A 45-meter vessel engaged in towing

377. DIAGRAM 51. INT & INLAND
You are on a vessel heading due north and see the lights shown one point on your port bow. This vessel could be heading____.

A. NW
B. SE
C. SW
D. NW

378. DIAGRAM 42. INLAND ONLY
Two power-driven vessels are crossing within a half a mile of each other as shown. Vessel A sounds one short blast on the whistle. This signal means ____.

A. I am altering my course to starboard
B. I intend to leave you on my port side
C. I intend to overtake you on your port side
D. I am operating astern propulsion

379. DIAGRAM 24. INT & INLAND
A seagoing tug has a tow greater than 200 meters as shown and is severely restricted in her ability to deviate from her course. Which lights would be displayed from the towing vessel?

A. Three white masthead lights, red-white-red all-around lights, sidelights, stern light and a towing light
B. Three white masthead lights, red-white-red all-around lights, sidelights and two towing lights
C. Three white masthead lights, two all-around red lights, sidelights, stern light and a towing light
D. None of the above

380. DIAGRAM 81. INLAND ONLY
While underway you sight the lights shown with the yellow lights flashing. The lights displayed are from a _____.

A. dredge pipeline
B. mine clearance vessel
C. vessel aground
D. vessel not under command

383. INLAND ONLY
You are meeting "head on" a tug towing a barge alongside about a mile away. In addition to the white masthead lights which other lights do you see on the tug and tow combined?

A. one green and one red sidelight on the outside of the unit
B. one green and one red sidelight and a special flashing light
C. only the green and red sidelights marking each vessel
D. the green and red sidelights marking each vessel and a special flashing light

384. DIAGRAM 78. INT & INLAND
At night, you see the lights shown. This would indicate a _____.

A. vessel restricted in her ability to maneuver
B. fishing vessel underway
C. pilot vessel underway
D. vessel not under command

385. INLAND ONLY
Which statement is TRUE concerning the fog signal of a canal boat 25 meters in length, anchored in a "special anchorage area" approved by the Secretary?

A. The vessel is not required to sound a fog signal.
B. The vessel shall ring a bell for 5 seconds every minute.
C. The vessel shall sound one blast of the whistle every 2 minutes.

D. The vessel shall sound three blasts on the whistle every 2 minutes.

386. INLAND ONLY
Which statement is TRUE concerning the fog signal of a barge 35 meters in length, anchored in a "special anchorage" area approved by the Secretary?

A. The vessel shall ring a bell for 5 seconds every minute.
B. The vessel is not required to sound a fog signal.
C. The vessel shall sound one blast of the whistle every 2 minutes.
D. The vessel shall sound three blasts on the whistle every 2 minutes.

388. INT & INLAND
Lighting requirements in inland waters are different from those in international waters for _____.

A. barges being pushed ahead
B. vessels being towed alongside
C. vessels pushing ahead
D. all of the above

389. DIAGRAM 80. INT & INLAND
You see ONLY the light shown. This could be a vessel _____.

A. not under command
B. engaged in fishing
C. under oars
D. towing

390. DIAGRAM 80. INT & INLAND
You see ONLY the light shown. This could be a vessel _____.

A. not under command
B. under oars
C. engaged in fishing
D. towing

391. DIAGRAM 80. INT & INLAND
You see ONLY the light shown. This could be a vessel _____.

A. under oars
B. on pilotage duty
C. engaged in fishing
D. towing

392. DIAGRAM 80. INT & INLAND
You see ONLY the light shown. This could be a _____.

A. law enforcement vessel
B. vessel on pilotage duty

C. vessel engaged in fishing
D. sailing vessel

393. DIAGRAM 80. INT & INLAND
You see ONLY the light shown. This could be a _____.

A. sailing vessel
B. vessel on pilotage duty
C. vessel engaged in fishing
D. power-driven vessel

394. DIAGRAM 80. INT & INLAND
You see ONLY the light shown. This could be a _____.

A. law enforcement vessel
B. vessel on pilotage duty
C. sailing vessel
D. power-driven vessel

395. DIAGRAM 80. INT & INLAND
You see ONLY the light shown. This could be a _____.

A. law enforcement vessel
B. sailing vessel
C. vessel engaged in trawling
D. power-driven vessel

396. DIAGRAM 80. INT & INLAND
You see ONLY the light shown. This could be a _____.

A. vessel aground
B. submarine on the surface
C. vessel engaged in trawling
D. vessel under oars

401. DIAGRAM 37. INLAND ONLY
Two power-driven vessels are meeting in the situation as shown in a narrow channel on the Great Lakes. Vessel "A" is down-bound with a following current. Vessel "B" should _____.

A. take action to permit safe passage
B. have the right of way
C. initiate the maneuvering signals
D. none of the above

402. INT & INLAND
While underway in fog, you hear a prolonged blast from another vessel. This signal indicates a _____.

A. sailboat making way
B. power-driven vessel making way, towing
C. power-driven vessel making way
D. vessel being towed

727. INLAND ONLY

Maneuvering signals shall be sounded on inland waters by _____.

A. all vessels when meeting, crossing, or overtaking and in sight of one another
B. all vessels meeting or crossing at a distance within half a mile of each other and not in sight of one another
C. power-driven vessels overtaking and in sight of one another
D. power-driven vessels crossing at a distance within half a mile of each other and NOT in sight of one another

728. INLAND ONLY

A vessel engaged in public safety activities may display an alternately flashing red and yellow light. This special light may be used by a vessel engaged in _____.

A. river bank protection
B. conducting submarine operations
C. firefighting
D. law enforcement

821. INLAND ONLY

One and two short blast signals must be sounded on inland waters when _____.

A. two sailing vessels are in sight of one another and meeting at a distance of 1/4 mile
B. two power-driven vessels are in sight of one another and will cross at a distance of 1 mile
C. two power-driven vessels are crossing within 1/2 mile of each other and NOT in sight of each other
D. two power-driven vessel are in sight of one another and are meeting at a distance of 1/2 mile

1000. INT & INLAND

You hear the fog signal of another vessel forward of your beam. Risk of collision may exist. You MUST _____.

A. begin a radar plot
B. stop your engines
C. take all way off, if necessary
D. All of the above

3683. INT & INLAND

The rules require that a stand-on vessel SHALL take action to avoid collision when she determines that _____.

A. risk of collision exists
B. the other vessel will cross ahead of her
C. the other vessel is not taking appropriate action

D. collision cannot be avoided by the give-way vessel's maneuver alone

4000. INT & INLAND

Your vessel is 75 meters in length and restricted in her ability to maneuver. Visibility is restricted. What signal do you sound if you are carrying out your work at anchor?

A. Five seconds ringing of a bell at intervals of not more than one minute
B. One prolonged blast followed by two short blasts on the whistle at intervals of not more than two minutes
C. Five seconds ringing of a bell and five second sounding of a gong at intervals of not more than one minute
D. Four short blasts on the whistle at intervals of not more than two minutes

4001. INT & INLAND

The maximum length of a power-driven vessel which may show an all-around white light and sidelights instead of a masthead light, sidelights and a stern light is _____.

A. 6.9 meters
B. 9.9 meters
C. 11.9 meters
D. 19.9 meters

4002. INT & INLAND

While underway in fog, you hear a prolonged blast from another vessel. This signal indicates a _____.

A. sailboat underway
B. vessel underway, towing
C. power-driven vessel underway, making way
D. vessel being towed

4003. INT & INLAND

What is used to show the presence of a partly submerged object being towed?

A. A diamond shape on the towed object
B. An all-around light at each end of the towed object
C. A searchlight from the towing vessel in the direction of the tow
D. All of the above

4004. INT & INLAND

At night, a barge being towed astern must display _____.

A. red and green sidelights only
B. a white sternlight only
C. sidelights and a sternlight
D. one all-around white light

4005. INT & INLAND

Which is recognized as a distress signal?

A. Directing the beam of a searchlight at another vessel
B. A smoke signal giving off orange colored smoke
C. A whistle signal of one prolonged and three short blasts
D. International Code Signal PAN spoken over the radiotelephone

4006. INT & INLAND

Your vessel is approaching a bend. You hear a prolonged blast from around the bend. You should _____.

A. back your engines
B. stop your engines and drift
C. answer with one prolonged blast
D. sound the danger signal

4007. INT & INLAND

If you do NOT understand the course or intention of an approaching vessel you should sound _____.

A. one short blast
B. one prolonged blast
C. not less than five short blasts
D. not less than five prolonged blasts

4008. INT & INLAND

If you are the stand-on vessel in a crossing situation, you may take action to avoid collision by your maneuver alone. When may this action be taken?

A. At any time you feel it is appropriate
B. Only when you have reached extremis
C. When you determine that your present course will cross ahead of the other vessel
D. When it becomes apparent to you that the give-way vessel is not taking appropriate action

4009. INT & INLAND

Your 15-meter tug is underway and crossing a deep and narrow channel. A large container vessel is off your port bow on a steady bearing. Which statement is TRUE concerning this situation?

A. You should maintain course and speed.
B. The container vessel is the stand-on as it is the larger vessel.
C. You are not to impede the safe passage of the container vessel in the channel.
D. None of the above

4010. INT & INLAND
If your vessel is underway in fog and you hear one prolonged and three short blasts, this is a ____.

A. vessel not under command
B. sailing vessel
C. vessel being towed (manned)
D. vessel being towed (unmanned)

4011. INT & INLAND
A pilot vessel on pilotage duty at night will show sidelights and a sternlight ____.

A. when at anchor
B. only when making way
C. at any time when underway
D. only when the identifying lights are not being shown

4012. DIAGRAM 6. INT & INLAND
A vessel which displays the day signal shown may be engaged in ____.

A. submarine cable laying
B. pilotage duty
C. fishing
D. mineclearance

4013. DIAGRAM 11. INT & INLAND
A vessel displaying the dayshapes shown is ____.

A. towing
B. conducting underwater operations
C. drifting
D. aground

4014. INT & INLAND
A power-driven vessel underway in fog making NO way must sound what signal?

A. One long blast
B. Two prolonged blasts
C. One prolonged blast
D. One prolonged and two short blasts

4015. INT & INLAND
A 95-meter vessel aground sounds which fog signal?

A. A rapid ringing of a bell for 5 seconds every two minutes
B. A whistle signal of one short, one prolonged, and one short blast
C. A prolonged blast of the whistle at intervals not to exceed one minute
D. A rapid ringing of a bell for 5 seconds, preceded and followed by three separate and distinct strokes on the bell

4016. INT & INLAND
Which statement is TRUE concerning a vessel equipped with operational radar?

A. She must use this equipment to obtain early warning of risk of collision.
B. The radar equipment is only required to be used in restricted visibility.
C. The use of a radar excuses a vessel from the need of a look-out.
D. The safe speed of such a vessel will likely be greater than that of vessels without radar.

4017. INT & INLAND
A 200-meter vessel is aground in fog. Which signal is optional?

A. A bell signal
B. A gong signal
C. A whistle signal
D. All of the above

4018. INT & INLAND
Which is a distress signal?

A. A triangular flag above or below a ball
B. The International Code Signal of distress indicated by "JV"
C. A green smoke signal
D. Flames on the vessel as from a burning tar barrel

4020. INT & INLAND
A vessel must proceed at a safe speed ____.

A. in restricted visibility
B. in congested waters
C. during darkness
D. at all times

4021. INT & INLAND
A light signal of three flashes means:

A. I am in doubt as to your actions
B. My engines are full speed astern
C. I desire to overtake you
D. I am operating astern propulsion

4022. INT & INLAND
A sailing vessel underway may exhibit ____.

A. a red light over a green light at the masthead
B. a green light over a red light at the masthead
C. two white lights in a vertical line at the stern
D. an all-around white light at the bow

4023. DIAGRAM 43. INT & INLAND
A sailing vessel is overtaking a tug and tow as shown. Which statement is CORRECT?

A. The sailing vessel is the stand-on vessel because it is overtaking.
B. The sailing vessel is the stand-on vessel because it is under sail.
C. The tug is the stand-on vessel because it is being overtaken.
D. The tug is the stand-on vessel because it is towing.

4024. INT & INLAND
The word *vessel*, in the Rules, includes ____.

A. sailing ships
B. nondisplacement craft
C. seaplanes
D. All of the above

4025. INT & INLAND
A sailing vessel with the wind abaft the beam is navigating in fog. She should sound ____.

A. three short blasts
B. one prolonged blast
C. one prolonged and two short blasts
D. two prolonged blasts

4026. INT & INLAND
Which is a distress signal?

A. Firing of green star shells
B. Sounding 5 short blasts on the whistle
C. Answering a one blast whistle signal with two blasts
D. A flaming barrel of oil on deck

4028. INT & INLAND
If two sailing vessels are running free with the wind on the same side, which one must keep clear of the other?

A. The one with the wind closest abeam
B. The one with the wind closest astern
C. The one to leeward
D. The one to windward

4029. INT & INLAND
The masthead light may be located at other than the fore and aft centerline on a power-driven vessel ____.

A. less than 20 meters in length
B. less than 12 meters in length

C. which has separate sidelights carried on the outboard extremes of the vessel's breadth
D. engaged in fishing

4030. INT & INLAND
The NAVIGATION RULES define a *vessel not under command* as a vessel which ____.

A. from the nature of her work is unable to keep out of the way of another vessel
B. through some exceptional circumstance is unable to maneuver as required by the rules
C. by taking action contrary to the rules has created a special circumstance situation
D. is moored, aground or anchored in a fairway

4031. INT & INLAND
Additional light signals are provided in the Annexes to the Rules for vessels ____.

A. engaged in fishing
B. not under command
C. engaged in towing
D. under sail

4032. INT & INLAND
Which vessel may combine her sidelights and sternlight in one lantern on the fore and aft centerline of the vessel?

A. A 16-meter sailing vessel
B. A 25-meter power-driven vessel
C. A 28-meter sailing vessel
D. Any non-self-propelled vessel

4033. INT & INLAND
The duration of a prolonged blast of the whistle is ____.

A. 2 to 4 seconds
B. 4 to 6 seconds
C. 6 to 8 seconds
D. 8 to 10 seconds

4034. INT & INLAND
A vessel restricted in her ability to maneuver is one which ____.

A. from the nature of her work is unable to maneuver as required by the rules
B. through some exceptional circumstance is unable to maneuver as required by the rules
C. due to adverse weather conditions is unable to maneuver as required by the rules
D. has lost steering and is unable to maneuver

4035. INT & INLAND
When underway in restricted visibility, you might hear, at intervals of two minutes, any of the following fog signals EXCEPT ____.

A. one prolonged blast
B. two prolonged blasts
C. one prolonged and two short blasts
D. ringing of a bell for five seconds

4036. INT & INLAND
You are preparing to cross a narrow channel. You see a vessel that can only be navigated safely within the channel. You should ____.

A. not cross the channel if you might impede the other vessel
B. initiate an exchange of passing signals
C. sound the danger signal
D. hold your course and speed

4038. INT & INLAND
A bell is used to sound a fog signal for a ____.

A. power-driven vessel underway
B. sailing vessel at anchor
C. vessel engaged in fishing
D. vessel not under command

4039. INT & INLAND
You see another vessel approaching, and its compass bearing does not significantly change. This would indicate that ____.

A. you are the stand-on vessel
B. risk of collision exists
C. a special circumstances situation exists
D. the other vessel is dead in the water

4040. DIAGRAM 16. INT & INLAND
Which of the dayshapes shown indicates a vessel with a tow exceeding 200 meters in length?

A. A
B. B
C. C
D. D

4042. INT & INLAND
A towing vessel pushing a barge ahead and rigidly connected in a composite unit shall show the lights of ____.

A. a vessel towing by pushing ahead
B. a power-driven vessel, not towing
C. a barge being pushed ahead
D. either answer A or answer B

4043. INT & INLAND
You are the watch officer on a power-driven vessel and notice a large sailing vessel approaching from astern. You should ____.

A. slow down
B. sound one short blast and change course to starboard
C. sound two short blasts and change course to port
D. hold your course and speed

4044. INT & INLAND
You see a vessel's green sidelight bearing due east from you. The vessel might be heading ____.

A. east (090°)
B. northeast (045°)
C. northwest (315°)
D. southwest (225°)

4045. INT & INLAND
A vessel shall be deemed to be overtaking when she can see at night ____.

A. only the sternlight of the vessel
B. a sidelight and one masthead light of the vessel
C. only a sidelight of the vessel
D. any lights except the masthead lights of the vessel

4046. DIAGRAM 14. INT & INLAND
You are underway on vessel A and sight vessel B which is a vessel underway and fishing as shown. Which statement is true?

A. Vessel A must keep out of the way of vessel B because B is to port.
B. Vessel A must keep out of the way of vessel B because B is fishing.
C. Vessel B must keep out of the way of vessel A because A is to starboard.
D. In this case, both vessels are required by the Rules to keep clear of each other.

4047. INT & INLAND
A vessel trawling will display a ____.

A. red light over a white light
B. green light over a white light
C. yellow light over a red light
D. white light over a green light

4048. INT & INLAND
If it becomes necessary for a stand-on vessel to take action to avoid collision, she shall NOT, if possible, ____.

A. decrease speed
B. increase speed
C. turn to port for a vessel on her own port side
D. turn to starboard for a vessel on her own port side

4049. INT & INLAND
Your vessel is NOT making way, but is not in any way disabled. Another vessel is approaching you on your starboard beam. Which statement is TRUE?

A. The other vessel must give way since your vessel is stopped.
B. Your vessel is the give-way vessel in a crossing situation.
C. You should be showing the lights or shapes for a vessel not under command.
D. You should be showing the lights or shapes for a vessel restricted in her ability to maneuver.

4050. INT & INLAND
A 22-meter sailing vessel when also being propelled by machinery shall show during daylight hours a ____.

A. black diamond
B. black cone
C. black ball
D. basket

4051. INT & INLAND
The rules concerning lights shall be complied with in all weathers from sunset to sunrise. The lights ____.

A. shall be displayed in restricted visibility during daylight hours
B. need not be displayed when no other vessels are in the area
C. shall be set at low power when used during daylight hours
D. need not be displayed by unmanned vessels

4052. DIAGRAM 44. INT & INLAND
The lights displayed would be shown by a vessel which is ____.

A. aground
B. not under command and is dead in the water
C. not under command and is making way
D. laying or picking up navigation marks

4053. INT & INLAND
Two vessels meeting in a head-on situation are directed by the Rules to ____.

A. alter course to starboard and pass port to port
B. alter course to port and pass starboard to starboard
C. decide on which side the passage will occur by matching whistle signals
D. slow to bare steerageway

4054. INT & INLAND
A vessel is engaged in fishing when ____.

A. her gear extends more than 100 meters from the vessel
B. she is using any type of gear, other than lines
C. she is using fishing apparatus which restricts her maneuverability
D. she has any fishing gear on board

4055. INT & INLAND
When shall the stand-on vessel change course and speed?

A. The stand-on vessel may change course and speed at any time as it has the right-of-way
B. After the give-way vessel sounds one blast in a crossing situation
C. When action by the give-way vessel alone cannot prevent collision
D. When the two vessels become less than half a mile apart

4056. INT & INLAND
A sailing vessel with the wind abaft the beam is navigating in restricted visibility. She should sound ____.

A. three short blasts
B. one prolonged blast
C. one prolonged and two short blasts
D. two prolonged blasts

4057. INT & INLAND
You see a vessel displaying the code flag LIMA below which is a red ball. The vessel is ____.

A. trolling
B. getting ready to receive aircraft
C. aground
D. in distress

4058. INT & INLAND
Which factor is listed in the Rules as one which must be taken into account when determining safe speed?

A. The construction of the vessel
B. The maneuverability of the vessel
C. The experience of vessel personnel

D. All of the above must be taken into account.

4059. INT & INLAND
Which statement is TRUE concerning seaplanes on the water?

A. A seaplane must show appropriate lights but need not exhibit shapes.
B. A seaplane should exhibit the lights for a vessel constrained by her draft.
C. In situations where a risk of collision exists, a seaplane should always give way.
D. A seaplane on the water shall, in general, keep well clear of all vessels.

4060. INT & INLAND
A vessel approaching your vessel from 235° relative is in what type of situation?

A. Meeting
B. Overtaking
C. Crossing
D. Passing

4061. DIAGRAM 26. INT & INLAND
Vessels A and B are crossing as shown. Which statement is TRUE?

A. The vessels should pass starboard to starboard.
B. Vessel B should pass under the stern of vessel A.
C. Vessel B should alter course to the right.
D. Vessel A must keep clear of vessel B.

4062. INT & INLAND
You are in charge of a power-driven vessel navigating at night. You sight the red sidelight of another vessel on your port bow. The other vessel's after masthead light is to the right of her forward masthead light. You should ____.

A. hold course and speed
B. alter course to port
C. stop engines
D. sound the danger signal

4063. INT & INLAND
There are two classes of vessels which, to the extent necessary to carry out their work, do not have to comply with the rule regarding traffic separation schemes. One of these is a vessel ____.

A. engaged in fishing in a traffic lane
B. servicing a submarine cable
C. towing another
D. engaged on pilotage duty

4065. INT & INLAND
You are underway in fog when you hear the rapid ringing of a bell for five seconds followed by the sounding of a gong for five seconds. This signal indicates a vessel____.

A. aground
B. more than 100m in length, at anchor
C. fishing while making no way through the water
D. fishing in company with another vessel

4066. INT & INLAND
The wind is ESE, and a sailing vessel is steering NW. Which fog signal should she sound?

A. One blast at one-minute intervals
B. One blast at two-minute intervals
C. Two blasts at one-minute intervals
D. One prolonged and two short blasts at two-minute intervals

4067. INT & INLAND
At night, which lights are required to be shown by a dredge on the side of the dredge which another vessel may pass?

A. One red light
B. Two red lights
C. One white light
D. Two green lights

4068. DIAGRAM 2. INT & INLAND
In the situation illustrated, vessel I is a power-driven vessel. Vessel II is a sailing vessel with the wind dead aft. Which statement about this situation is correct?

A. Vessel I should keep out of the way of Vessel II.
B. Vessel II should keep out of the way of Vessel I.
C. Vessel II would normally be the stand-on vessel, but should stay out of the way in this particular situation.
D. The Rules of Special Circumstances applies, and neither vessel is the stand-on vessel.

4069. INT & INLAND
Which lights are shown by a vessel restricted in her ability to maneuver to indicate that the vessel is making way?

A. Masthead lights, sidelights and sternlight
B. Masthead lights and sidelights only
C. Sidelights and sternlight only
D. Sidelights only

4070. INT & INLAND
You are underway and hear a vessel continuously sounding her fog whistle. This indicates the other vessel ____.

A. desires to communicate by radio
B. desires a pilot
C. is in distress
D. is aground

4072. INT & INLAND
A 30-meter tug is underway and NOT towing. At night, this vessel must show sidelights and ____.

A. one masthead light and a sternlight
B. two masthead lights and a sternlight
C. three masthead lights and a sternlight
D. a sternlight ONLY

4073. INT & INLAND
While underway in fog, you hear a signal of one prolonged blast followed by three short blasts. This is the fog signal for a vessel ____.

A. towing
B. manned being towed
C. unmanned being towed
D. at anchor

4074. INT & INLAND
Which statement is TRUE concerning a vessel of 75 meters in length, at anchor?

A. She must show an all-around white light forward.
B. She must show a second all-around white light aft.
C. She may use her working lights to illuminate her decks.
D. All of the above

4075. INT & INLAND
You are approaching another vessel. She is about one mile distant and is on your starboard bow. You believe she will cross ahead of you. She then sounds a whistle signal of five short blasts. You should ____.

A. answer the signal and hold course and speed
B. reduce speed slightly to make sure she will have room to pass
C. make a large course change, and slow down if necessary
D. wait for another whistle signal from the other vessel

4076. INT & INLAND
If a rowboat underway does NOT show the lights specified for a sailing vessel underway, it shall show a ____.

A. white light from sunset to sunrise
B. combined lantern showing green to starboard and red to port and shown from sunset to sunrise
C. combined lantern showing green to starboard and red to port and shown in sufficient time to prevent collision
D. white light shown in sufficient time to prevent collision

4077. INT & INLAND
A vessel at anchor shall display, between sunrise and sunset, on the forward part of the vessel where it can best be seen ____.

A. one black ball
B. two black balls
C. one red ball
D. two orange and white balls

4078. INT & INLAND
You are making headway in fog and hear a fog signal of two prolonged blasts on your starboard quarter. You should ____.

A. stop your vessel
B. change course to the left
C. change course to the right
D. hold your course and speed

4080. INT & INLAND
You are underway, in fog, when you hear a whistle signal of one prolonged blast followed by two short blasts. This signal could indicate a vessel ____.

A. not under command
B. being towed
C. aground
D. All of the above

4081. DIAGRAM 27. INT & INLAND
You are aboard vessel A, a power-driven vessel, on open waters and vessel B, a sailing vessel, is sighted off your port bow as shown. Which vessel is the stand-on vessel?

A. Vessel A because it is towing
B. Vessel A because it is to starboard of vessel B
C. Vessel B because it is sailing
D. Vessel B because it is to port of vessel A

4082. INT & INLAND
Which vessel must exhibit three white masthead lights in a vertical line?

A. Any vessel towing astern
B. A vessel whose tow exceeds 200 meters astern
C. A vessel not under command, at anchor
D. A vessel being towed

4083. INT & INLAND
All of the following are distress signals EXCEPT ____.

A. the continuous sounding of any fog signal apparatus
B. giving five or more short and rapid blasts of the whistle
C. firing a gun at intervals of about a minute
D. a barrel with burning oil in it, on deck

4084. INT & INLAND
If you are approaching a bend, and hear a whistle signal of one prolonged blast from around the bend, you should answer with a signal of ____.

A. a short blast
B. a prolonged blast
C. one short, one prolonged, and one short blast
D. a long blast

4086. DIAGRAM 15. INT & INLAND
You are on vessel A and approaching vessel B as shown. You are not sure whether your vessel is crossing or overtaking vessel B. You should ____.

A. change course to make the situation definitely either crossing or overtaking
B. consider it to be a crossing situation
C. consider it to be an overtaking situation
D. consider it a crossing situation if you can cross ahead safely

4087. INT & INLAND
A flashing light , by the definition given in the rules, is a light that____.

A. is red in color
B. is visible over an arc of the horizon of 360°
C. flashes at regular intervals at a frequency of 120 flashes or more per minute
D. All of the above

4088. INT & INLAND
The term restricted visibility as used in the Rules refers ____.

A. only to fog
B. only to visibility of less than one-half of a mile
C. to visibility where you cannot see shore
D. to any condition where visibility is restricted

4089. INT & INLAND
A vessel engaged in mineclearing shows special identity lights ____.

A. in addition to the lights required for a power-driven vessel
B. which mean that other vessels should not approach within 1000 meters of the mineclearing vessel
C. which are green and show all-around
D. All of the above

4090. INT & INLAND
According to the Navigation Rules, you may depart from the Rules when:

A. no vessels are in sight visually
B. no vessels are visible on radar
C. you are in immediate danger
D. out of sight of land

4091. INT & INLAND
An authorized light to assist in the identification of submarines operating on the surface is a(n) ____.

A. blue rotating light
B. intermittent flashing amber/yellow light
C. flashing white light
D. flashing sidelight

4093. INT & INLAND
Which statement is TRUE concerning two sailing vessels?

A. A sailing vessel with the wind forward of the beam on her port side shall keep out of the way of a sailing vessel with the wind forward of the beam on the starboard side.
B. When both vessels have the wind on the same side, the vessel to leeward shall keep out of the way.
C. A sail vessel with the wind abaft of the beam must keep out of the way of a vessel sailing into the wind.
D. None of the above

4094. DIAGRAM 20. INT & INLAND
You are aboard vessel A which is towing on open waters when vessel B, a sailing vessel, is sighted off your port bow as shown. Which vessel is the stand-on?

A. Vessel A is the stand-on vessel because it is towing.
B. Vessel A is the stand-on vessel because it is to starboard of vessel B.
C. Vessel B is the stand-on vessel because it is sailing.
D. Vessel B is the stand-on vessel because it is to port of vessel A.

4095. INT & INLAND
When underway in a channel, you should keep to the ____.

A. middle of the channel
B. starboard side of the channel
C. port side of the channel
D. side of the channel that has the widest turns

4096. INT & INLAND
While underway, in fog, you hear a whistle signal of one prolonged blast followed by two short blasts. This signal is sounded by a vessel ____.

A. not under command
B. being towed
C. on pilotage duty
D. aground

4097. INT & INLAND
When navigating in restricted visibility, a power-driven vessel shall ____.

A. stop her engines when hearing a fog signal forward of her beam, even if risk of collision does not exist
B. have her engines ready for immediate maneuver
C. when making way, sound one prolonged blast at intervals of not more than one minute
D. operate at a speed to be able to stop in the distance of her visibility

4098. INT & INLAND
You can indicate that your vessel is in distress by ____.

A. displaying a large red flag
B. displaying three black balls in a vertical line
C. sounding four or more short rapid blasts on the whistle
D. continuously sounding the fog whistle

4099. INT & INLAND
During the day, a dredge will indicate the side on which it is safe to pass by displaying ____.

A. two balls in a vertical line
B. two diamonds in a vertical line
C. a single black ball
D. no shape is shown during the day

4100. INT & INLAND
A 45-meter vessel is pulling a 210-meter tow. She may exhibit ____.

A. a masthead light forward, and two masthead lights in a vertical line aft
B. three masthead lights forward and one aft
C. two masthead lights forward and no after masthead light
D. three masthead lights aft and none forward

4101. INT & INLAND
Which statement is TRUE concerning the danger signal?

A. When any vessel fails to understand the intentions of an approaching vessel she must sound the danger signal.
B. Only the stand-on vessel can sound the danger signal.
C. Distress signals may be used in place of the danger signal.
D. The danger signal consists of 4 or more short blasts of the whistle.

4102. INT & INLAND
A distress signal ____.

A. consists of 5 or more short blasts of the fog signal apparatus
B. may be used separately or with other distress signals
C. consists of the raising and lowering of a large white flag
D. is used to indicate doubt about another vessel's intentions

4103. INT & INLAND
Which is the danger signal?

A. A continuous sounding of the fog signal
B. Firing a gun every minute
C. Five or more short rapid blasts on the whistle
D. One prolonged blast on the whistle

4104. INT & INLAND
A vessel is in sight of another vessel when ____.

A. she can be observed by radar
B. she can be observed visually from the other vessel

C. she can be plotted on radar well enough to determine her heading
D. her fog signal can be heard

4105. INT & INLAND
Which statement is TRUE concerning two sailing vessels approaching each other?

A. A sailing vessel overtaking another is the give-way vessel.
B. When each is on a different tack, the vessel on the starboard tack shall keep out of the way.
C. A sailing vessel seeing another to leeward on an undetermined tack shall hold her course.
D. All of the above

4106. INT & INLAND
What type of vessel or operation is indicated by a vessel showing two cones with the apexes together?

A. Sailing vessel
B. Vessel trawling
C. Mineclearing
D. Dredge

4107. INT & INLAND
A power-driven vessel has on her port side a sailing vessel which is on a collision course. The power-driven vessel is to ____.

A. maintain course and speed
B. keep clear, passing at a safe distance
C. sound one blast and turn to starboard
D. stop her engines

4108. INT & INLAND
At specified intervals, a vessel towing in fog shall sound ____.

A. one prolonged blast
B. two prolonged blasts
C. one prolonged and two short blasts in succession
D. one prolonged and three short blasts in succession

4109. INT & INLAND
A vessel towing in fog shall sound a fog signal of ____.

A. one prolonged blast every one minute
B. two prolonged blasts every two minutes
C. one prolonged and two short blasts every two minutes
D. one prolonged blast every two minutes

4110. INT & INLAND
Continuous sounding of a fog whistle by a vessel is a signal ____.

A. that the vessel is anchored
B. to request the draw span of a bridge to be opened
C. of distress
D. that the vessel is broken down and drifting

4111. INT & INLAND
A 50-meter vessel is towing astern and the length of the tow is 100 meters. In addition to sidelights, which lights may she show to fully comply with the Rules?

A. Two masthead lights forward, a sternlight, and a towing light above the sternlight
B. A masthead light forward, two masthead lights aft, a sternlight, and a towing light above the sternlight
C. No masthead light forward, two masthead lights aft, a sternlight, and a towing light above the sternlight
D. Three masthead lights forward, one masthead light aft, and two towing lights in a vertical line at the stern

4112. INT & INLAND
A vessel, which is unable to maneuver due to some exceptional circumstance, shall exhibit ____.

A. during the day, three balls in a vertical line
B. during the day, three shapes, the highest and lowest being balls and the middle being a diamond
C. when making way at night, two all-around red lights, sidelights, and a sternlight
D. when making way at night, masthead lights, sidelights, and a sternlight

4113. INT & INLAND
Which signal, other than a distress signal, can be used by a vessel to attract attention?

A. Searchlight beam
B. Continuous sounding of a fog signal apparatus
C. Burning barrel
D. Orange smoke signal

4114. INT & INLAND
Which statement is TRUE concerning the light used with whistle signals?

A. Use of such a light is required.
B. The light shall have the same characteristics as a masthead light.
C. It is only used to supplement short blasts of the whistle.
D. All of the above

4115. INT & INLAND
What is the minimum sound signaling equipment required aboard a vessel 14 meters in length?

A. A bell only
B. A whistle only
C. A bell and a whistle
D. Any means of making an efficient sound signal

4116. INT & INLAND
The towing light is a(n) _____.

A. flashing amber light
B. yellow light with the same characteristics as the sternlight
C. all-around yellow light
D. yellow light with the same characteristics as the masthead light

4117. INT & INLAND
An all-around flashing yellow light may be exhibited by a(n) _____.

A. vessel not under command
B. air-cushion vessel in the nondisplacement mode
C. vessel towing a submerged object
D. vessel engaged in diving operations

4118. INT & INLAND
When should the fog signal of a manned vessel under tow be sounded?

A. After the towing vessel's fog signal
B. Before the towing vessel's fog signal
C. Approximately one minute after the towing vessel's fog signal
D. If the towing vessel is sounding a fog signal, the manned vessel being towed is not required to sound any fog signal.

4119. INT & INLAND
A lantern combining a vessel's navigation lights may be shown on a _____.

A. 15-meter sailing vessel
B. 20-meter vessel engaged in fishing and making way

C. 25-meter power-driven vessel trolling
D. 25-meter pilot vessel

4120. INT & INLAND
A vessel engaged in fishing during the day would show _____.

A. one black ball
B. two cones with bases together
C. a cone, apex downward
D. two cones, apexes together

4121. INT & INLAND
A sailing vessel is NOT required to keep out of the way of a _____.

A. power-driven vessel
B. vessel not under command
C. vessel restricted in her ability to maneuver
D. vessel engaged in fishing

4122. INT & INLAND
Which vessel may sound the danger signal?

A. The stand-on vessel in a crossing situation
B. The give-way vessel in a crossing situation
C. A vessel at anchor
D. All of the above

4123. INT & INLAND
While underway in fog, you hear a vessel sound one prolonged blast followed by two short blasts on the whistle. What does this signal indicate?

A. A vessel towing
B. A vessel engaged in pilotage duty
C. A vessel being towed
D. A vessel aground

4124. DIAGRAM 28. INT & INLAND
Vessel A is underway and pushing ahead when vessel B is sighted off the starboard bow as shown. Which vessel is the stand-on vessel?

A. Vessel A is the stand-on vessel because it is to port.
B. Vessel A is the stand-on vessel because it is pushing ahead.
C. Vessel B is the stand-on vessel because it is to starboard of vessel A.
D. Neither vessel is the stand-on vessel.

4125. INT & INLAND
If you saw flames aboard a vessel but could see the vessel was not on fire, you would know that the _____.

A. crew was trying to get warm
B. vessel required immediate assistance
C. vessel was attempting to attract the attention of a pilot boat
D. vessel was being illuminated for identification by aircraft

4126. INT & INLAND
By day, when it is impracticable for a small vessel engaged in diving operations to display the shapes for a vessel engaged in underwater operations, she shall display _____.

A. three black balls in a vertical line
B. two red balls in a vertical line
C. a black cylinder
D. a rigid replica of the International Code flag A

4127. INT & INLAND
A vessel will NOT show sidelights when _____.

A. underway but not making way
B. making way, not under command
C. not under command, not making way
D. trolling underway

4128. INT & INLAND
Which display indicates a vessel conducting mineclearance operations?

A. Three balls in a vertical line
B. Two balls in a vertical line
C. One ball near the foremast and one ball at each yardarm
D. One diamond near the foremast and one ball at each yardarm

4129. INT & INLAND
Which vessel MUST show two masthead lights in a vertical line?

A. A power-driven vessel less than 50 meters in length with a 20-meter tow
B. A sailing vessel towing a small vessel astern
C. A vessel not under command
D. A vessel engaged in dredging

4130. INT & INLAND
The duration of each blast of the whistle signals used in meeting and crossing situations is _____.

A. about 1 second
B. 2 or 4 seconds
C. 4 to 6 seconds
D. 8 to 10 seconds

4131. INT & INLAND
What dayshape should a vessel being towed exhibit if the tow EXCEEDS 200 meters?

A. Two balls
B. Two diamonds
C. One ball
D. One diamond

4133. INT & INLAND
Which statement is TRUE when you are towing more than one barge astern at night?

A. Only the last barge in the tow must be lighted.
B. Only the first and last barges in the tow must be lighted.
C. All barges in the tow must be lighted.
D. All barges, except unmanned barges, must be lighted.

4134. DIAGRAM 9. INT & INLAND
Vessel A is overtaking vessel B as shown. Which vessel is the stand-on vessel?

A. Vessel A
B. Vessel B
C. Neither vessel
D. Both vessels must keep clear of the other.

4135. INT & INLAND
A vessel is being propelled both by sail and by engines. Under the Rules, the vessel is ____.

A. a special circumstance vessel
B. not covered under any category
C. a sail vessel
D. a power-driven vessel

4136. INT & INLAND
The white masthead light required for a power-driven vessel under the Rules is visible over how many degrees of the horizon?

A. 022.5°
B. 112.5°
C. 225.0°
D. 360.0°

4137. INT & INLAND
Which statement is TRUE concerning lights and shapes for towing vessels?

A. If a tow exceeds 200 meters in length, the towing vessel will display a black ball during daylight.

B. When towing astern, a vessel will carry her identification lights at the masthead in addition to her regular masthead light.
C. When towing astern, the towing vessel may show either a sternlight or a towing light, but not both.
D. If the towing vessel is over 50 meters in length, she must carry forward and after masthead lights.

4138. INT & INLAND
A vessel may use any sound or light signals to attract the attention of another vessel as long as ____.

A. white lights are not used
B. red and green lights are not used
C. the vessel signals such intentions over the radiotelephone
D. the signal cannot be mistaken for a signal authorized by the Rules

4139. INT & INLAND
What type of vessel or operation is indicated by a vessel displaying two cones with the apexes together?

A. Sailing
B. Trawling
C. Minesweeping
D. Dredging

4140. INT & INLAND
The rule regarding look-outs applies:

A. in restricted visibility
B. between dusk and dawn
C. in heavy traffic
D. All of the above

4141. INT & INLAND
While underway and towing, your vessel enters fog. Which fog signal should you sound?

A. One prolonged blast
B. Two prolonged blasts
C. One prolonged blast and two short blasts
D. Three distinct blasts

4142. INT & INLAND
A vessel engaged in fishing must display a light in the direction of any gear that extends outward more than 150 meters. The color of this light is:

A. white
B. green
C. red
D. yellow

4143. INT & INLAND
Which statement is true concerning a towing light when a towing vessel is towing astern?

A. When a towing light is shown, no sternlight is necessary.
B. When a sternlight is shown, no towing light is necessary.
C. The towing light is shown below the sternlight.
D. The towing light is shown above the sternlight.

4144. INT & INLAND
At night, a vessel which is less than 7 meters in length and anchored in an area where other vessels do not normally navigate is ____.

A. not required to show any anchor lights
B. required to show a flare-up light
C. required to show one white light
D. required to show sidelights and a sternlight

4145. INT & INLAND
You are in charge of a 120-meter power-driven vessel at anchor in fog, sounding the required anchor signals. You hear the fog signal of a vessel underway off your port bow. You may sound ____.

A. at least five short and rapid blasts
B. two short blasts
C. one short, one prolonged, and one short blast
D. three short blasts

4146. INT & INLAND
When taking action to avoid collision, you should ____.

A. make sure the action is taken in enough time
B. not make any large course changes
C. not make any large speed changes
D. All of the above

4147. INT & INLAND
Which vessel would have no white lights visible when meeting her head-on?

A. A vessel trawling
B. A vessel restricted in her ability to maneuver
C. A vessel mineclearing
D. A vessel not under command

4148. INT & INLAND
You are in restricted visibility and hear a fog signal forward of the beam. Nothing appears on your radar screen. You must ____.

A. stop your engines
B. sound two prolonged blasts of the whistle
C. sound the danger signal
D. slow to bare steerageway

4149. DIAGRAM 84. INT & INLAND
A vessel displaying the lights shown is ____.

A. not under command
B. showing improper lights
C. towing
D. dredging

4150. INT & INLAND
A towing vessel 30 meters in length is pushing barges ahead. How many white masthead lights is the vessel REQUIRED to show at night?

A. One
B. Two
C. Three
D. Four

4151. INT & INLAND
While underway in fog you hear a vessel sound one prolonged blast followed by two short blasts. What does this signal indicate?

A. A vessel towing
B. A vessel being towed
C. A pilot vessel engaged on pilotage duty
D. A vessel aground

4152. INT & INLAND
A power-driven vessel with a 150-meter stern tow shall display ____.

A. three masthead lights in a vertical line
B. a towing light above the sternlight
C. two towing lights in a vertical line
D. a red light over a white light at the masthead

4153. INT & INLAND
A vessel transferring cargo while underway is classified by the Rules as a vessel ____.

A. not under command
B. in special circumstances
C. restricted in her ability to maneuver
D. constrained by her draft

4154. INT & INLAND
Which vessel, when anchored at night, is NOT required to show anchor lights?

A. A power-driven vessel
B. A vessel engaged on pilotage duty
C. A vessel dredging
D. A vessel restricted in her ability to maneuver

4155. INT & INLAND
A vessel towing is showing three forward white masthead lights in a vertical line. This means that the length of the ____.

A. towing vessel is less than 50 meters
B. towing vessel is greater than 50 meters
C. tow is less than 200 meters
D. tow is greater than 200 meters

4156. INT & INLAND
Which vessel is underway under the Rules of the Road?

A. A vessel at anchor with the engine running
B. A vessel with a line led to a tree onshore
C. A vessel drifting with the engine off
D. A vessel aground

4157. INT & INLAND
Which vessel may exhibit identifying lights when not actually engaged in her occupation?

A. A trawler
B. A fishing vessel
C. A tug
D. None of the above

4158. INT & INLAND
A 25-meter vessel trawling will show the dayshape(s) consisting of ____.

A. a basket
B. two balls
C. two cones, apexes together
D. a cone, apex downward

4159. INT & INLAND
A power-driven vessel underway shall keep out of the way of a ____.

A. vessel not under command
B. vessel engaged in fishing
C. sailing vessel
D. All of the above

4160. INT & INLAND
A fog signal of one short, one prolonged, and one short blast may be sounded by a ____.

A. vessel at anchor
B. vessel not under command
C. vessel towing
D. All of the above

4161. INT & INLAND
A continuous sounding of a fog-signal apparatus indicates ____.

A. the vessel is in distress
B. the vessel has completed loading dangerous cargo
C. it is safe to pass
D. the vessel is anchored

4162. DIAGRAM 83. INT & INLAND
A vessel at night, displaying the lights shown is ____.

A. fishing
B. not under command
C. towing
D. being towed

4163. INT & INLAND
You are underway in restricted visibility. You hear the fog signal of another vessel about 22° on your starboard bow. If danger of collision exists you must ____.

A. reduce your speed to bare steerageway
B. slow your engines and let the other vessel pass ahead of you
C. alter the course to starboard to pass around the other vessel's stern
D. alter course to port to pass the other vessle on its port side

4164. INT & INLAND
While underway in fog you hear a whistle signal consisting of one prolonged blast followed immediately by two short blasts. This signal is sounded in fog by ____.

A. vessels at anchor, not engaged in fishing
B. vessels underway and towing
C. vessels in danger
D. pilot vessels

4165. INT & INLAND
Which statement is TRUE of a 30-meter sailing vessel underway?

A. She must show sidelights and a sternlight in restricted visibility.
B. She may show an all-around white light at the top of the mast.
C. She need not show a sternlight if she is showing all-around lights on the mast.

D. If she is using propelling machinery, she shall show forward a shape consisting of two cones, apexes together.

4166. INT & INLAND
A power-driven vessel towing another vessel astern (tow less than 200 meters) shall show ____.

A. three masthead lights in a vertical line instead of either the forward or after masthead light
B. two masthead lights in a vertical line instead of either the forward or after masthead lights
C. two towing lights in a vertical line at the stern
D. a small white light aft of the funnel

4167. INT & INLAND
A vessel which is restricted in her ability to maneuver under the Rules, is a vessel which is ____.

A. mineclearing
B. engaged in fishing
C. at anchor
D. not under command

4168. INT & INLAND
When a vessel signals her distress by means of a gun or other explosive signal, the firing should be at intervals of approximately ____.

A. 10 minutes
B. 1 minute
C. 1 hour
D. 3 minutes

4169. INT & INLAND
A head-on situation shall be deemed to exist at night when a power-driven vessel sees another power-driven vessel ahead and ____.

A. one sidelight and the masthead light are visible
B. the vessels will pass closer than half a mile
C. both vessels sound one prolonged blast
D. both sidelights and masthead light(s) are visible

4170. INT & INLAND
A 20-meter vessel is towing another vessel astern. The length of the tow from the stern of the towing vessel to the stern of the tow is 75 meters. How many white towing masthead lights shall the towing vessel show at night?

A. 1
B. 2
C. 3
D. 4

4171. INT & INLAND
A vessel enagaged in fishing, and at anchor, shall show ____.

A. an anchor light
B. sidelights and a sternlight
C. three lights in a vertical line, the highest and lowest being red, and the middle being white
D. None of the above

4173. INT & INLAND
A power-driven vessel underway shall keep out of the way of a vessel:

A. not under command
B. restricted in her ability to maneuver
C. engaged in fishing
D. All of the above

4174. INT & INLAND
A vessel sounding a fog signal of one short, one prolonged, and one short blast is indicating that the vessel is:

A. fishing
B. in distress
C. at anchor
D. not under command

4175. DIAGRAM 57. INT & INLAND
A vessel displaying the lights shown is ____.

A. restricted in her ability to maneuver and not making way
B. engaged in fishing and not making way
C. a pilot vessel underway and making way on pilotage duty
D. towing and making way

4176. INT & INLAND
Two all-around red lights displayed in a vertical line are shown by a vessel:

A. being towed
B. pushing a barge ahead
C. at anchor
D. not under command

4177. INT & INLAND
Your vessel is underway in reduced visibility. You hear the fog signal of another vessel about 30° on your starboard bow. If danger of collision exists, you must ____.

A. alter course to starboard to pass around the other vessel's stern
B. slow your engines and let the other vessel pass ahead of you
C. reduce your speed to bare steerageway
D. alter course to port and pass the other vessel on its port side

4178. INT & INLAND
You are underway in fog and you hear one prolonged blast followed by two short blasts. This is a vessel ____.

A. towing
B. engaged on pilotage duty
C. aground in a fairway
D. stopped and making no way through the water

4179. INT & INLAND
A sailing vessel is NOT allowed to show the all-around red over green lights on the mast if ____.

A. she is showing sidelights
B. her sidelights are combined and shown on the fore and aft centerline of the vessel
C. she is showing a sternlight
D. her sidelights and sternlight are combined in one lantern and shown on the mast

4180. INT & INLAND
A power-driven vessel, when towing astern, shall show ____.

A. two towing lights in a vertical line
B. a towing light in a vertical line above the sternlight
C. two towing lights in addition to the sternlight
D. a small white light in lieu of the sternlight

4181. INT & INLAND
According to the Rules, which vessel is NOT restricted in her ability to maneuver?

A. A vessel servicing a navigation marker
B. A sailing vessel
C. A vessel mineclearing
D. A vessel dredging

4182. INT & INLAND
Distress signals may be ____.

A. red flares
B. smoke signals
C. sound signals
D. Any of the above

4183. INT & INLAND
When anchoring a 25-meter vessel at night, you must show _____.

A. one all-around white light
B. two all-around white lights
C. one all-around white light and the sidelights
D. the sidelights and a sternlight

4184. INT & INLAND
You are approaching another vessel at night. You can see both red and green sidelights and, above the level of the sidelights, three white lights in a vertical line. The vessel may be _____.

A. not under command
B. towing a tow more than 200 m astern
C. trawling
D. underway and dredging

4185. INT & INLAND
A vessel engaged in fishing, and at anchor, should exhibit _____.

A. an anchor light
B. sidelights and sternlight
C. three lights in a vertical line, the highest and lowest being red, and the middle being white
D. None of the above

4186. DIAGRAM 1. INT & INLAND
A vessel fishing should display which of the day signals shown.

A. A
B. B
C. C
D. D

4187. INT & INLAND
In a crossing situation on open waters, a sailing vessel shall keep out of the way of all the following vessels EXCEPT a _____.

A. vessel not under command
B. vessel restricted in her ability to maneuver
C. power-driven vessel approaching on her starboard side
D. vessel fishing

4188. INT & INLAND
You are at anchor in fog on a 120-meter power-driven vessel. You hear the fog signal of a vessel approaching off your port bow. You may sound _____.

A. one prolonged, one short and one prolonged
B. two short blasts
C. one short, one prolonged, and one short blast
D. one prolonged blast

4189. DIAGRAM 6. INT & INLAND
You see a vessel displaying the day signal shown. The vessel may be _____.

A. not under command
B. fishing with trawls
C. laying cable
D. aground

4190. INT & INLAND
A power-driven vessel making way through water sounds a fog signal of:

A. one prolonged blast at intervals of not more than two minutes
B. two prolonged blasts at intervals of not more than two minutes
C. one prolonged blast at intervals of not more than one minute
D. two prolonged blasts at intervals of not more than one minute

4191. INT & INLAND
You are on watch in the fog. Your vessel is proceeding at a safe speed when you hear a fog signal ahead of you. The Rules require you to navigate with caution and, if danger of collision exists, _____.

A. slow to less than 2 knots
B. stop your engines
C. reduce to bare steerageway
D. begin a radar plot

4192. INT & INLAND
In restricted visibility, a vessel fishing with nets shall sound at intervals of two minutes _____.

A. one prolonged blast
B. one prolonged followed by two short blasts
C. one prolonged followed by three short blasts
D. two prolonged blasts in succession

4193. INT & INLAND
A 20-meter sailing vessel underway must exhibit a _____.

A. sternlight
B. combined lantern
C. red light over a green light at the masthead

D. All of the above

4194. INT & INLAND
At night, you are towing a partly submerged vessel, 20 meters in length and 4 meters in breadth. What lights must you display on the towed vessel?

A. A white light at the stern
B. Two white lights side by side at the stern
C. A white light at the forward end and a white light at the after end
D. Two red lights in a vertical line at the after end

4195. INT & INLAND
All of the following vessels are restricted in their ability to maneuver EXCEPT a vessel _____.

A. laying a pipeline
B. dredging
C. mineclearing
D. not under command

4196. INT & INLAND
What lights must be shown on a barge being towed astern at night?

A. A white light at each corner
B. A white light fore and aft
C. Sidelights and a sternlight
D. A sternlight only

4197. INT & INLAND
A vessel which is unable to maneuver due to some exceptional circumstance shall show two red lights in a vertical line and _____.

A. during the day, three balls in a vertical line
B. during the day, three shapes, the highest and lowest being balls and the middle being a diamond
C. when making way at night, sidelights and a sternlight
D. when making way at night, masthead lights, sidelights, and a sternlight

4198. INT & INLAND
You are underway and approaching a bend in the channel where vessels approaching from the opposite direction cannot be seen. You should sound _____.

A. one blast, 4 to 6 seconds in duration
B. three blasts, 4 to 6 seconds in duration
C. one continuous blast until you are able to see around the bend
D. one blast, 8 to 10 seconds in duration

4199. INT & INLAND
A vessel which is fishing must show sidelights and a sternlight only when:

A. anchored
B. underway
C. dead in the water
D. underway and making way

4201. INT & INLAND
A power-driven vessel towing astern shall show ____.

A. two towing lights in a vertical line
B. a towing light in a vertical line above the sternlight
C. two towing lights in addition to the sternlight
D. a small white light in lieu of the sternlight

4202. INT & INLAND
You are underway in fog when you hear the following signal: one short blast, one prolonged blast and one short blast in succession. Which of the following would it be?

A. A sailing vessel underway with the wind abaft the beam
B. A power-driven vessel underway and making way through the water
C. A vessel at anchor
D. A vessel towing

4203. INT & INLAND
If you hear the firing of a gun at one minute intervals from another vessel, this indicates that ____.

A. the gun is being used to sound passing signals
B. the vessel is in distress
C. all vessels are to clear the area
D. all is clear and it is safe to pass

4204. INT & INLAND
Fog signals, required under the Rules for vessels underway, shall be sounded ____.

A. only on the approach of another vessel
B. only when vessels are in sight of each other
C. at intervals of not more than one minute
D. at intervals of not more than two minutes

4205. INT & INLAND
A towing vessel is towing two barges astern. The length of the tow from the stern of the tug to the stern of the last barge is 250 meters. The towing vessel is 45 meters in length. How many white masthead lights should be displayed on the tugboat at night?

A. 1
B. 2
C. 3
D. 4

4206. INT & INLAND
At night, a vessel shall indicate that she is restricted in her ability to maneuver by showing in a vertical line two ____.

A. red lights
B. red lights and two white lights
C. red lights with a white light in between
D. white lights with a red light in between

4207. INT & INLAND
Your power-driven vessel is underway when you sight a sailing vessel on your port bow. Which vessel is the stand-on vessel?

A. The sailboat, because it is to port of your vessel
B. The sailboat, because it is under sail
C. Your vessel, because it is a power-driven vessel
D. Your vessel, because it is to starboard of the sailboat

4208. INT & INLAND
Five or more short blasts on a vessel's whistle indicates that she is:

A. in doubt that another vessel is taking sufficient action to avoid a collision
B. altering course to starboard
C. altering course to port
D. the stand-on vessel and will maintain course and speed

4209. INT & INLAND
Which statement concerning maneuvering in restricted visibility is FALSE?

A. A vessel which cannot avoid a close-quarters situation with a vessel forward of her beam shall reduce her speed to bare steerageway.
B. A vessel which hears a fog signal forward of her beam shall stop her engines.
C. A vessel which hears a fog signal forward of the beam shall navigate with caution.
D. If a vessel determines by radar that a close-quarters situation is developing, she shall take avoiding action in ample time.

4210. INT & INLAND
A vessel being towed astern shall show at night ____.

A. the lights required for a power-driven vessel underway
B. only the required masthead lights
C. a sternlight only
D. sidelights and a sternlight

4211. INT & INLAND
In order for a stand-on vessel to take action in a situation, she must determine that the other vessel ____.

A. is restricted in her ability to maneuver
B. has sounded the danger signal
C. is not taking appropriate action
D. has not changed course since risk of collision was determined

4212. INT & INLAND
While underway your vessel approaches a bend in a river where, due to the bank, you cannot see around the bend. You should ____.

A. keep to the starboard side of the channel and sound one short blast
B. sound the danger signal
C. sound one prolonged blast
D. slow your vessel to bare steerageway

4213. INT & INLAND
Which statement concerning whistle signals is FALSE?

A. When a pushing vessel and a vessel pushed are connected in a composite unit, the unit sounds the fog signal of a power-driven vessel.
B. A vessel at anchor may sound one short, one prolonged, and one short blast.
C. A pilot vessel may sound an identity signal on the whistle.
D. A vessel engaged in towing in fog shall sound a fog signal at intervals of one minute.

4214. INT & INLAND
A sailing vessel of over 20 meters in length underway must show a ____.

A. red light over a green light at the masthead
B. white masthead light

C. combined lantern
D. sternlight

4215. INT & INLAND
An inconspicuous, partly submerged vessel or object being towed, where the length of tow is 100 meters, shall show _____.

A. yellow lights at each end
B. two red lights in a vertical line
C. a black ball
D. a diamond shape

4216. INT & INLAND
You are approaching a narrow channel. You see a vessel that can only be navigated safely within the channel. You should _____.

A. initiate an exchange of passing signals
B. not cross the channel if you might impede the other vessel
C. sound the danger signal
D. hold your course and speed

4217. INT & INLAND
A man aboard a vessel, signaling by raising and lowering his outstretched arms to each side, is indicating _____.

A. danger, stay away
B. all is clear, it is safe to pass
C. the vessel is anchored
D. a distress signal

4218. DIAGRAM 7. INT & INLAND
A vessel displaying the day signal shown is _____.

A. not under command
B. a dredge underway and dredging
C. fishing
D. a hydrographic survey vessel underway

4219. INT & INLAND
Your 15-meter vessel is crossing a narrow channel and a large cargo vessel to port is within the channel and crossing your course. You must:

A. hold course and speed
B. sound the danger signal
C. initiate an exchange of passing signals
D. do not cross the channel if you might impede the other vessel.

4220. INT & INLAND
A vessel towed astern shall show:

A. masthead lights
B. sidelights
C. a special flashing light
D. All of the above

4221. INT & INLAND
A power-driven vessel making way through the water sounds which fog signal?

A. Two short blasts every one minute
B. One short blast every one minute
C. Two prolonged blasts every two minutes
D. One prolonged blast every two minutes

4222. INT & INLAND
You are towing two barges astern. The length of the tow from the stern of the tug to the stern of the last barge is 150 meters. How many white towing identification lights should be displayed on the tugboat at night?

A. 1
B. 2
C. 3
D. 4

4223. INT & INLAND
Which vessel may show three lights in a vertical line, the top and bottom being red and the middle being white?

A. A vessel engaged in diving operations
B. A pilot vessel
C. A vessel trawling
D. All of the above

4224. INT & INLAND
A power-driven vessel has on her port side a sailing vessel which is on a collision course. The power-driven vessel is required to _____.

A. maintain course and speed
B. keep clear
C. sound one blast and turn to starboard
D. stop her engines

4225. INT & INLAND
A single towing light will be carried above a vessel's sternlight _____.

A. only if she is towing astern
B. only if the tow exceeds 200 meters
C. at any time when towing
D. if the towing vessel is part of a composite unit

4226. INT & INLAND
Which dayshape must be shown by a vessel 25 meters in length aground during daylight hours?

A. One black ball
B. Two black balls
C. Three black balls
D. Four black balls

4227. INT & INLAND
An orange flag showing a black circle and square is a _____.

A. signal indicating a course change
B. distress signal
C. signal of asking to communicate with another vessel
D. signal indicating danger

4228. INT & INLAND
When is a stand-on vessel FIRST allowed by the Rules to take action in order to avoid collision?

A. When the two vessels are less than half a mile from each other.
B. When the give-way vessel is not taking appropriate action to avoid collision.
C. When collision is imminent.
D. The stand-on vessel is never allowed to take action.

4229. INT & INLAND
You are crossing a narrow channel in a 15-meter vessel when you sight a tankship off your port bow coming up the channel. Which statement is TRUE?

A. Yours is the give-way vessel because it is less than 30 meters long.
B. You shall not impede the safe passage of the tankship.
C. The tankship is the stand-on vessel because it is to port of your vessel.
D. The tankship is the stand-on vessel because it is the larger of the two vessels.

4230. INT & INLAND
In restricted visibility, a vessel restricted in her ability to maneuver, at anchor, would sound a fog signal of:

A. the rapid ringing of a bell for five seconds every minute
B. two prolonged and two short blasts every two minutes
C. one prolonged and two short blasts every two minutes

D. two prolonged and one short blast every two minutes

4231. INT & INLAND
A 15-meter sailing vessel would be required to show _____.

A. sidelights, sternlight, and a red light over a green light on the mast
B. sidelights, and sternlight, but they may be in a combined lantern on the mast
C. separate sidelights and sternlight
D. sidelights only

4232. INT & INLAND
The use of the signal consisting of five or more short blasts on the ship's whistle _____.

A. replaces directional signals
B. makes the other vessel the give-way vessel
C. indicates doubt as to the other vessel's action
D. makes it necessary to slow or stop

4233. INT & INLAND
While underway in fog, you hear the fog signal of another vessel ahead. If a risk of collision exists, you must:

A. slow to bare steerageway and navigate with caution
B. sound three short blasts and back your engines
C. stop your engines and navigate with caution
D. continue on your course and speed until the other vessel is sighted

4234. INT & INLAND
What lights, if any, would you exhibit at night if your vessel were broken down and being towed by another vessel?

A. None
B. Same lights as for a power-driven vessel underway
C. A white light forward and a white light aft
D. The colored sidelights and a white sternlight

4235. DIAGRAM 7. INT & INLAND
A vessel displaying the dayshapes shown is _____.

A. broken down
B. fishing
C. a minesweeper
D. transferring dangerous cargo

4236. INT & INLAND
If your vessel is underway in fog and you hear one prolonged and three short blasts, this indicates a _____.

A. vessel not under command
B. sailing vessel
C. vessel in distress
D. vessel being towed

4237. INT & INLAND
At night, which lights would you see on a vessel engaged in fishing, other than trawling?

A. Two red lights, one over the other
B. A green light over a red light
C. A red light over a white light
D. A white light over a red light

4239. INT & INLAND
You are on a vessel nearing a bend in the channel where, because of the height of the bank, you cannot see a vessel approaching from the opposite direction. You should sound _____.

A. one short blast
B. one prolonged blast
C. one long blast
D. five or more short blasts

4240. INT & INLAND
Systems of inbound and outbound lanes to promote the safe flow of vessel traffic in certain areas around the world are known as _____.

A. merchant vessel reporting systems
B. traffic separation schemes
C. collision avoidance fairways
D. restricted maneuverability channels

4241. INT & INLAND
A tug is towing three manned barges in line in fog. The first vessel of the tow should sound _____.

A. no fog signal
B. one short blast
C. one prolonged and three short blasts
D. one prolonged, one short, and one prolonged blast

4242. INT & INLAND
All fog signals shall be sounded every two minutes with the exception of a vessel _____.

A. underway or making way
B. under sail or under tow

C. anchored or aground
D. not under command or restricted in her ability to maneuver

4243. INT & INLAND
In reduced visibility, you hear two prolonged blasts of a whistle. This signal is sounded by a _____.

A. power-driven vessel dead in the water
B. sailing vessel on the port tack
C. vessel not under command
D. vessel fishing with nets

4244. INT & INLAND
A 200-meter vessel restricted in her ability to maneuver, at anchor, will sound a fog signal of _____.

A. a 5 second ringing of a bell forward and a 5 second sounding of a gong aft at intervals of 1 minute
B. one prolonged followed by two short blasts every 2 minutes
C. one prolonged followed by three short blasts every minute
D. one prolonged followed by three short blasts every 2 minutes

4245. DIAGRAM 62. INT & INLAND
Underway at night, a vessel displaying the lights shown is _____.

A. engaged in fishing
B. mine sweeping
C. a pilot boat
D. under sail

4247. INT & INLAND
What dayshape is to be shown by a vessel aground?

A. A cylinder
B. Two cones with their apexes together
C. Two black balls in a vertical line
D. Three black balls in a vertical line

4248. INT & INLAND
What is NOT a distress signal?

A. Red flares or red rockets
B. Continuous sounding of fog signaling apparatus
C. International Code Flags November and Charlie
D. Basket hanging in the rigging

4249. INT & INLAND
Which statement is TRUE concerning a vessel equipped with operational radar?

A. She must use this equipment to obtain early warning of risk of collision.
B. The use of a radar excuses a vessel from the need of a look-out.
C. The radar equipment is only required to be used in restricted visibility.
D. The safe speed of such a vessel will likely be greater than that of vessels without radar.

4250. DIAGRAM 60. INT & INLAND
A vessel displaying the lights shown is _____.

A. towing
B. being towed
C. broken down
D. fishing

4251. DIAGRAM 70. INT & INLAND
At night, if you see a vessel ahead displaying the lights shown you should:

A. provide assistance as the vessel is in distress
B. stay clear as the vessel is transferring dangerous cargo
C. stay clear as the vessel is fishing
D. change course to the right as the vessel is crossing your bow

4253. INT & INLAND
A pilot vessel on pilotage duty shall show identity lights _____.

A. at any time while underway
B. while at anchor
C. while alongside a vessel
D. All of the above

4254. INT & INLAND
You are underway in restricted visibility and hear a fog signal forward of the beam. Nothing appears on your radar screen. You must _____.

A. stop your engines
B. sound two prolonged blasts of the whistle
C. sound the danger signal
D. slow to bare steerageway

4255. INT & INLAND
A stand-on vessel in a crossing situation is allowed to take action when:

A. on a collision course
B. the vessels will pass within one mile
C. it becomes apparent to her that the give-way vessel is not taking appropriate action
D. the relative speed of the vessels indicates collision in less than six minutes

4256. INT & INLAND
Traffic separation schemes established by the International Maritime Organization _____.

A. provide inbound and outbound lanes to promote the safe flow of vessel traffic
B. provide vessel reporting systems to assist in search and rescue in the event of a vessel casualty
C. provide routing and vessel scheduling procedures to reduce shipping delays
D. prohibit vessels carrying hazardous cargoes from entering waters that are environmentally sensitive

4257. INT & INLAND
Which vessel is required to sound a fog signal of one prolonged followed by two short blasts?

A. A vessel not under command
B. A sailing vessel, underway
C. A vessel restricted in its ability to maneuver, at anchor
D. All of the above

4258. INT & INLAND
At night, a broken-down vessel being towed would show the same lights as:

A. a power-driven vessel underway
B. the towing vessel
C. a barge
D. a vessel at anchor

4259. INT & INLAND
What is the optional whistle signal which may be sounded by a vessel at anchor?

A. Two prolonged followed by one short blast
B. One short followed by two prolonged blasts
C. One short, one prolonged, followed by one short blast
D. Four short blasts

4260. INT & INLAND
The minimum length of a power-driven vessel that must show forward and after masthead lights is _____.

A. 30 meters
B. 50 meters
C. 75 meters
D. 100 meters

4261. INT & INLAND
What light(s), if any, would you show at night if your vessel was broken down and being towed astern by another vessel?

A. None
B. Same lights as for a power-driven vessel underway
C. A white light forward and a white light aft
D. The colored sidelights and a white sternlight

4262. INT & INLAND
A vessel not under command making way at night would show _____.

A. two all-around red lights in a vertical line
B. anchor lights and sidelights
C. two all-around white lights in a vertical line, sidelights and a sternlight
D. two all-around red lights in a vertical line, sidelights, and a sternlight

4263. INT & INLAND
In a dense fog, you hear a whistle signal of one prolonged blast followed by three short blasts. This signal is sounded by a _____.

A. manned vessel being towed
B. fishing vessel underway trawling
C. pilot vessel underway making a special signal
D. vessel not under command

4265. INT & INLAND
While underway and pushing a barge ahead, your vessel enters a heavy rain storm. You should sound _____.

A. a prolonged blast every two minutes
B. two prolonged blasts every two minutes
C. one prolonged and two short blasts every two minutes
D. one prolonged and three short blasts every two minutes

4266. INT & INLAND
On open waters, a power-driven vessel shall keep out of the way of a _____.

A. vessel on her port side that is crossing her course
B. vessel that is overtaking her
C. seaplane on the water
D. sailing vessel

4267. INT & INLAND
You are overtaking a vessel at night and you see a yellow light showing above the sternlight of the overtaken vessel. The overtaken vessel is _____.

A. underway and dredging
B. pushing ahead or towing alongside
C. towing astern
D. a pilot vessel

4268. INT & INLAND
Your vessel is at anchor in fog. The fog signal of another vessel, apparently underway, has been growing louder and the danger of collision appears to exist. In addition to your fog signal, what signal may be used to indicate your presence?

A. No signal other than your fog signal may be used.
B. One prolonged, one short, and one prolonged whistle blast
C. One prolonged followed by two short whistle blasts
D. One short, one prolonged, and one short whistle blast

4269. INT & INLAND
All of the following are distress signals under the Rules EXCEPT _____.

A. International Code Signal AA
B. orange-colored smoke
C. red flares
D. the repeated raising and lowering of outstretched arms

4270. DIAGRAM 70. INT & INLAND
A vessel displaying the lights shown is a _____.

A. pilot boat
B. sailboat
C. fishing vessel
D. motorboat

4271. INT & INLAND
A tug is towing three manned barges in line in fog. The third vessel of the tow should sound _____.

A. no fog signal
B. one prolonged and two short blasts
C. one prolonged and three short blasts
D. one prolonged, one short and one prolonged blast

4272. INT & INLAND
A power-driven vessel, when towing an-
other vessel astern shall show the light(s) in Diagram _____.

A. 75
B. 60
C. 54
D. 46

4273. INT & INLAND
Which vessel is NOT classified as restricted in her ability to maneuver?

A. A vessel picking up a navigation mark
B. A vessel transferring cargo while underway
C. A vessel whose anchor is fouled
D. A vessel in a towing operation that restricts the ability of the vessel and her tow to change their course

4274. INT & INLAND
During the day, a vessel picking up a submarine cable shall carry _____.

A. three shapes; the highest and lowest shall be red balls, and the middle shall be a white diamond
B. two black balls
C. three shapes; the highest and lowest shall be black balls, and the middle shall be a red diamond
D. three shapes; the highest and lowest shall be black balls and the middle shall be a black diamond

4276. INT & INLAND
While underway your vessel enters fog. You stop your engines and the vessel is dead in the water. Which fog signal should you sound?

A. One prolonged blast every two minutes
B. Two prolonged blasts every two minutes
C. Three short blasts every two minutes
D. One prolonged and three short blasts every two minutes

4277. INT & INLAND
You are underway in a fog when you hear a whistle signal of one prolonged blast followed by two short blasts. This signal could indicate all of the following EXCEPT a vessel _____.

A. being towed
B. not under command
C. fishing with trawls
D. towing astern

4278. INT & INLAND
A light signal consisting of three flashes means _____.

A. I am in doubt as to your actions
B. My engines are full speed astern
C. I desire to overtake you
D. I am operating astern propulsion

4279. INT & INLAND
You are watching another vessel approach and her compass bearing is not changing. This means that _____.

A. you are the stand-on vessel
B. a risk of collision exists
C. a special circumstances situation exists
D. the other vessel is dead in the water

4280. DIAGRAM 33. INT & INLAND
Vessels I and II are underway as shown. Vessel I is a sailing vessel with the wind dead aft. Vessel II is a power-driven vessel trawling. Which statement is TRUE?

A. Vessel I is to keep clear because the other vessel is fishing.
B. Vessel II is to keep clear because she is a power-driven vessel.
C. Vessel II is to keep clear because the other vessel is to its starboard.
D. Both vessels are to take action to stay clear of each other.

4281. INT & INLAND
A vessel 30 meters in length and aground would display a dayshape consisting of _____.

A. a cylinder
B. one black ball
C. two black balls in a vertical line
D. three black balls in a vertical line

4282. DIAGRAM 63. INT & INLAND
A vessel displaying the lights shown is _____.

A. towing astern
B. underway and more than 50 meters in length
C. broken down
D. fishing

4283. INT & INLAND
What is NOT a distress signal?

A. A continuous sounding of the fog horn
B. Firing a gun every minute
C. Five or more short rapid blasts on the whistle

D. A square flag and ball flown from the mast

4284. INT & INLAND
Which statement is true concerning a vessel equipped with operational radar?

A. The Master of the vessel must be on the bridge when the radar is in use.
B. The radar equipment is only required to be used in restricted visibility.
C. The use of a radar excuses a vessel from the need of a look-out.
D. This equipment must be used to obtain early warning of risk of collision.

4285. INT & INLAND
While underway in fog you hear another vessel sounding two prolonged blasts every two minutes. This signal indicates a vessel ____.

A. making way through the water
B. towing
C. drifting
D. anchored

4286. DIAGRAM 69. INT & INLAND
A vessel which is underway at night and displaying the lights shown is____.

A. engaged in trawling
B. minesweeping
C. under sail
D. a pilot boat

4287. INT & INLAND
Fog signals for vessels at anchor or aground shall be sounded at intervals of not more than ____.

A. 15 minutes
B. 5 minutes
C. 2 minutes
D. 1 minutes

4288. INT & INLAND
A vessel is carrying three lights in a vertical line. The highest and lowest of these are red and the middle light is white. Which statement is always TRUE?

A. During the day, she would display three balls in a vertical line.
B. If making way, she would show masthead lights at night.
C. If at anchor, she need not show anchor lights while displaying identifying lights.
D. Her fog signal would consist of a rapid ringing of a bell for five seconds every minute.

4289. INT & INLAND
You are on a power-driven vessel in fog. Your vessel is proceeding at a safe speed when you hear a fog signal ahead of you. The Rules require you to navigate with caution and, if danger of collision exists ____.

A. slow to less than 2 knots
B. reduce to bare steerageway
C. stop your engines
D. initiate a radar plot

4290. INT & INLAND
While underway in a fog you hear a signal of three strokes of a bell, a rapid ringing of the bell, and three more strokes of the bell. This signal is made by a vessel ____.

A. at anchor and giving warning
B. aground
C. at anchor and greater than 100 meters in length
D. not under command and at anchor

4292. INT & INLAND
While underway in fog, you hear a signal of one prolonged blast followed by three short blasts. This is the fog signal for a vessel ____.

A. towing
B. being towed (manned)
C. under sail
D. at anchor

4293. INT & INLAND
Which vessel is to sound a fog signal of one prolonged followed by two short blasts?

A. A vessel not under command
B. A sailing vessel underway
C. A vessel restricted in its ability to maneuver, at anchor
D. All of the above

4294. INT & INLAND
At night you observe a vessel ahead show three flashes of a white light. This signal indicates that the vessel ahead is ____.

A. in distress
B. approaching a bend in the channel
C. operating astern propulsion
D. intending to overtake another vessel

4295. INT & INLAND
The use of the danger signal ____.

A. replaces directional signals
B. makes the other vessel the stand-on vessel

C. indicates doubt as to another vessels actions
D. is the same as a MAYDAY signal

4296. INT & INLAND
Which power-driven vessel is NOT required to carry a light in the position of the after masthead light?

A. A pushing vessel and a vessel being pushed, in a composite unit and 100 meters in length
B. A vessel of 60 meters in length towing astern
C. A vessel of 45 meters in length trolling
D. Any vessel constrained by her draft

4297. INT & INLAND
Which requirement must be met in order for a stand-on vessel to take action to avoid collision?

A. Risk of collision must exist.
B. The give-way vessel must have taken action first.
C. The vessels must be within half a mile of each other.
D. There are no requirements to be met. The stand-on vessel may take action anytime.

4298. INT & INLAND
A single vessel being towed alongside shall exhibit ____.

A. one all-around white light
B. sidelights and a sternlight
C. only the outboard sidelight and a sternlight
D. a masthead light, sidelights, and a sternlight

4299. DIAGRAM 40. INT & INLAND
You are crossing a narrow channel on your 15-meter vessel. A deeply loaded cargo vessel is proceeding down the channel as shown. In this situation, which statement is correct?

A. You are the stand-on vessel because you are less than 65 feet in length.
B. You cannot impede the passage of the cargo vessel.
C. The cargo vessel is the stand-on vessel because she is running with the current.
D. The Rule of Special Circumstances applies in this case.

4300. DIAGRAM 46. INT & INLAND
At night, a vessel displaying the light shown is ____.

A. sailing
B. fishing and making way
C. a pilot boat making way
D. fishing and anchored

4301. INT & INLAND
In which situation would risk of collision definitely exist?

A. A vessel is 22 degrees on your port bow, range increasing, bearing changing slightly to the right.
B. A vessel is broad on your starboard beam, range decreasing, bearing changing rapidly to the right.
C. A vessel is 22 degrees abaft your port beam, range increasing, bearing is constant.
D. A vessel is on your starboard quarter, range decreasing, bearing is constant.

4302. INT & INLAND
A vessel nearing a bend or an area of a channel or fairway where other vessels may be obscured by an intervening obstruction shall sound ____.

A. one long blast
B. one prolonged blast
C. the danger signal
D. two short blasts

4303. INT & INLAND
In fog, you hear apparently forward of your beam a fog signal of 2 prolonged blasts in succession every two minutes. This signal indicates a:

A. power-driven vessel making way through the water
B. vessel being pushed ahead
C. vessel restricted in her ability to maneuver
D. power-driven vessel underway but stopped and making no way through the water

4304. INT & INLAND
A vessel being towed will show ____.

A. a forward masthead light
B. sidelights and a sternlight
C. a towing light
D. All of the above

4305. INT & INLAND
In fog, a vessel being towed, if manned, shall sound a fog signal of:

A. two short blasts
b. three short blasts

C. one prolonged and two short blasts
D. one prolonged and three short blasts

4306. INT & INLAND
Which vessel is directed not to impede the passage of a vessel which can only navigate inside a narrow channel?

A. A vessel of less than 20 meters in length
B. A vessel not under command
C. A vessel engaged in surveying
D. All of the above

4309. INT & INLAND
What dayshape must be shown on a partly submerged vessel which is being towed?

A. A diamond
B. A cone
C. One black ball
D. Two black balls in a vertical line

4310. INT & INLAND
Which vessel is to be regarded as a vessel restricted in her ability to maneuver?

A. A vessel fishing with trawls
B. A vessel which has lost the use of her steering gear
C. A vessel with a draft of such depth that she cannot change her course
D. A vessel engaged in mineclearing

4311. INT & INLAND
Which vessel would show 3 dayshapes in a vertical line, the highest and lowest being balls and the middle shape being a diamond?

A. Vessel not under command
B. Vessel constrained by her draft
C. Vessel minesweeping
D. Vessel restricted in her ability to maneuver

4312. INT & INLAND
A power-driven vessel not under command at night must show which lights in a vertical line?

A. Three red
B. Two red
C. Two white
D. Three white

4313. DIAGRAM 71. INT & INLAND
While underway at night, you sight a vessel ahead displaying the lights shown. How should the vessels pass?

A. Both vessels should alter course to star-

board and pass port to port.
B. Both vessels should alter course to port and pass starboard to starboard.
C. Your vessel should hold course and speed and the other vessel should keep clear.
D. You should sound an appropriate overtaking signal.

4314. INT & INLAND
In order for a vessel to be engaged in fishing she must be ____.

A. underway
B. using gear which extends more than 50 meters outboard
C. using a seine of some type
D. using gear which restricts her maneuverability

4315. INT ONLY
While underway and in sight of another vessel you put your engines on astern propulsion. Which statement concerning whistle signals is TRUE?

A. You must sound three short blasts on the whistle.
B. You must sound one blast if backing to starboard.
C. You must sound whistle signals only if the vessels are meeting.
D. You need not sound any whistle signals.

4316. INT & INLAND
When shall the stand-on vessel in a crossing situation take action to avoid the other vessel?

A. When a risk of collision exists
B. When action by the give-way vessel alone will not prevent a collision
C. When the bearing to give-way vessel becomes steady
D. When the vessels become less than 1/2 mile apart

4317. INT & INLAND
What signal would a vessel aground show during daylight?

A. One black ball
B. Two black balls
C. Three black balls
D. Four black balls

4318. INT & INLAND
Which is NOT a distress signal?

A. Flames on a vessel

B. Vertical motion of a white lantern at night
C. Code flags November and Charlie
D. Dye marker on the water

4319. INT & INLAND
Which statement about a 25-meter auxiliary sailboat is TRUE?

A. The sidelights and sternlight may be combined in one lantern.
B. When operating under sail, her fog signal would consist of one prolonged blast.
C. She may show a green light over a red light at the masthead.
D. She must show fixed sidelights.

4320. INT & INLAND
Which vessel shall NOT impede the passage of a vessel which can safely navigate only within a narrow channel or fairway?

A. A vessel of less than 20 meters
B. A vessel sailing
C. A vessel fishing
D. All of the above

4321. INT & INLAND
While underway in a fog, you hear a whistle signal of one prolonged blast followed by two short blasts. This signal could mean all of the following EXCEPT a vessel ____.

A. not under command
B. towing astern
C. fishing with trawls
D. being towed

4322. INT & INLAND
In which situation do you think a risk of collision exists?

A. A vessel is 22° on your port bow, range increasing, bearing changing slightly to the right.
B. A vessel is broad on your starboard beam, range decreasing, bearing changing rapidly to the right.
C. A vessel is 22° abaft your port beam, range increasing, bearing is constant.
D. A vessel is on your starboard quarter, range decreasing, bearing is constant.

4323. DIAGRAM 53. INT & INLAND
A vessel displaying ONLY the lights shown is a ____.

A. vessel engaged on pilotage duty underway
B. vessel engaged in fishing
C. vessel under sail
D. power-driven vessel underway

4325. INT & INLAND
A vessel aground in fog shall sound, in addition to the proper anchor signal, which of the following?

A. Three strokes on the gong before and after sounding the anchor signal
B. Three strokes on the bell before and after the anchor signal
C. Four short blasts on the whistle
D. One prolonged and one short blast on the whistle

4327. INT & INLAND
Two vessels are approaching each other near head on. What action should be taken to avoid collision?

A. The first vessel to sight the other should give way.
B. The vessel making the slower speed should give way.
C. Both vessels should alter course to starboard.
D. Both vessels should alter course to port.

4328. DIAGRAM 10. INT & INLAND
A vessel displaying the dayshape shown____.

A. is at anchor
B. is not under command
C. has a tow that exceeds 200 meters
D. has a tow that is carrying dangerous cargo

4329. INT & INLAND
Your vessel is 25 meters long and anchored in restricted visibility. You are required to sound the proper fog signal at intervals of not more than:

A. 30 seconds
B. one minute
C. two minutes
D. three minutes

4330. INT & INLAND
While underway in fog, you hear a short blast, a prolonged blast, and a short blast of a whistle. This signal indicates a ____.

A. vessel towing in fog
B. sailboat underway in fog
C. vessel being towed in fog
D. vessel anchored in fog

4331. DIAGRAM 77. INT & INLAND
You see the lights shown. What would it be?

A. A vessel pushing barges ahead
B. A vessel towing barges astern
C. A pipeline
D. A stationary dredge

4332. INT & INLAND
You are the stand-on vessel in a crossing situation. You may hold your course and speed until ____.

A. the other vessel takes necessary action
B. the other vessel gets to within half a mile of your vessel
C. action by the give-way vessel alone will not prevent collision
D. the other vessel gets to within a quarter mile of your vessel

4334. INT & INLAND
In narrow channels, vessels of less than what length shall not impede the safe passage of vessels which can navigate only inside that channel?

A. 20 meters
B. 50 meters
C. 65 meters
D. 100 meters

4335. DIAGRAM 82. INT & INLAND
At night a vessel displaying the lights shown is ____.

A. sailing
B. fishing
C. a pilot boat
D. anchored

4336. INT & INLAND
While underway and in sight of another vessel crossing less than 0.5 mile away, you put your engines full speed astern. Which statement concerning whistle signals is TRUE?

A. You must sound three short blasts on the whistle.
B. You must sound one blast if backing to starboard.
C. You must sound whistle signals only if the vessels are meeting.

D. You need not sound any whistle signals.

4337. INT & INLAND
A vessel showing a yellow light over a white light at night is a vessel ____.

A. engaged in piloting
B. towing astern
C. engaged in fishing
D. in distress

4338. INT & INLAND
A vessel hearing a fog signal forward of her beam has not determined if risk of collision exists. She shall reduce speed to ____.

A. moderate speed
B. safe speed
C. half speed
D. bare steerageway

4339. INT & INLAND
Two vessels are in an overtaking situation. Which of the lights on the overtaken vessel will the overtaking vessel see?

A. Two masthead lights
B. One masthead light and a sidelight
C. Both sidelights
D. Sternlight only

4340. INT & INLAND
While underway and making way your vessel enters fog. Which fog signal should you sound every two minutes?

A. One prolonged blast
B. Two prolonged blasts
C. Three short blasts
D. A prolonged blast and three short blasts

4341. INT & INLAND
On open water, a vessel fishing is in a crossing situation with a vessel sailing located on the fishing vessel's starboard side. Which vessel is the stand-on vessel?

A. The fishing vessel because it is to port of the sailing vessel.
B. The fishing vessel because it is fishing.
C. The sailing vessel because it is to starboard of the fishing vessel.
D. The sailing vessel because it is sailing.

4342. INT & INLAND
The lights prescribed by the Rules shall be exhibited ____.

A. from sunrise to sunset in restricted visibility
B. at all times

C. from sunset to sunrise, and at no other time
D. whenever a look-out is posted

4343. INT & INLAND
Risk of collision may exist ____.

A. if the compass bearing of an approaching vessel does NOT appreciably change
B. even when an appreciable bearing change is evident, particularly when approaching a vessel at close range
C. if you observe both sidelights of a vessel ahead for an extended period of time
D. All of the above

4344. INT & INLAND
Safe speed is defined as that speed where ____.

A. you can stop within your visibility range
B. you can take proper and effective action to avoid collision
C. you are traveling slower than surrounding vessels
D. no wake comes from your vessel

4345. INT & INLAND
A vessel showing a green light over a white light in a vertical line above the level of the sidelights is ____.

A. engaged in underwater construction
B. under sail and power
C. a pilot vessel
D. trawling

4346. INT & INLAND
A vessel being towed at night must show ____.

A. a white all-around light
B. sidelights and a sternlight
C. a flashing yellow light
D. forward and after masthead lights

4347. INT & INLAND
To determine if risk of collision exists, a vessel which is fitted with radar must use ____.

A. radar scanning
B. radar plotting
C. compass bearings
D. All of the above

4348. DIAGRAM 12. INT & INLAND
You are on vessel A pushing a barge ahead and meeting vessel B as shown. How should the vessels pass?

A. Both vessels must alter course to starboard and pass port to port.
B. Both vessels must alter course to port and pass starboard to starboard.
C. Vessel A should maintain course and vessel B alter course.
D. The vessels should determine which will alter course by sounding whistle signals.

4349. INT & INLAND
If a vessel is engaged in fishing according to the definitions in the Rules, it will have ____.

A. gear extending from the side or stern
B. gear that restricts maneuverability
C. less than 50 percent trolling lines
D. None of the above

4350. INT & INLAND
While underway in fog you hear the rapid ringing of a bell. What does this signal indicate?

A. A vessel backing down
B. A sailboat underway
C. A vessel at anchor
D. A vessel drifting

4351. INT & INLAND
Two power-driven vessels are crossing so as to involve risk of collision. Which statement is TRUE, according to the Rules?

A. The vessel which has the other on her own port side shall keep out of the way.
B. If the stand-on vessel takes action, she shall avoid changing course to port.
C. If the give-way vessel takes action, she shall avoid changing course to starboard.
D. The give-way vessel should keep the other vessel to her starboard.

4352. INT & INLAND
What is the minimum vessel length which must show two white masthead lights, one forward and one aft, when underway at night?

A. 7 meters
B. 20 meters
C. 50 meters
D. 100 meters

4353. INT & INLAND
Every vessel that is to keep out of the way of another vessel must take positive early action to comply with this obligation and must ____.

A. avoid crossing ahead of the other vessel
B. avoid passing astern of the other vessel
C. sound one prolonged blast to indicate compliance
D. alter course to port for a vessel on her port side

4354. INT & INLAND

At night, a power-driven vessel less than 12 meters in length may, instead of the normal navigation lights, show sidelights and one ____.

A. white light
B. yellow light
C. flashing white light
D. flashing yellow light

4355. INT & INLAND

You are crossing a narrow channel in an 18-meter tug when you sight a loaded tankship off your port bow coming up the channel. Which statement is correct?

A. Neither vessel is the stand-on vessel because the tankship is crossing.
B. You cannot impede the safe passage of the tankship.
C. The tankship is the stand-on vessel because it is in the channel.
D. The tankship is the stand-on vessel because it is the larger of the two vessels.

4356. INT & INLAND

A vessel engaged in fishing underway sounds the same fog signal as a ____.

A. power-driven vessel stopped and making no way through the water
B. vessel being towed
C. vessel restricted in her ability to maneuver at anchor
D. sailing vessel at anchor

4357. INT & INLAND

A vessel 15 meters in length which is proceeding under sail as well as being propelled by machinery shall exhibit during the daytime ____.

A. one black ball
B. a basket
C. a cone with its apex downward
D. two cones with their apexes together

4358. INT & INLAND

Which vessel should not impede the navigation of a power-driven vessel?

A. A vessel not under command
B. A vessel engaged in fishing

C. A sailing vessel
D. A seaplane

4359. INT & INLAND

Your vessel is underway but stopped and making no way through the water when fog sets in. Which fog signal should you sound?

A. One prolonged blast on the whistle
B. One prolonged blast and two short blasts on the whistle
C. Two prolonged blasts on the whistle
D. One short, one prolonged, and one short blast on the whistle

4360. DIAGRAM 6. INT & INLAND

While underway, you see a vessel displaying the dayshapes shown. Which action should you take?

A. Maintain course and speed
B. Provide assistance, the other vessel is in distress
C. Stay clear, the other vessel is maneuvering with difficulty
D. Stop your vessel and sound passing signals

4362. INT & INLAND

A vessel underway and fishing shall keep out of the way of a ____.

A. power-driven vessel underway
B. vessel not under command
C. vessel sailing
D. vessel engaged on pilotage duty

4363. DIAGRAM 10. INT & INLAND

A vessel displaying the day shape shown is ____.

A. broken down
B. anchored
C. towing
D. fishing

4364. INT & INLAND

The whistle signal for a vessel operating astern propulsion is ____.

A. one long blast
B. one prolonged blast
C. three short blasts
D. four or more short blasts

4365. INT & INLAND

An anchored vessel is servicing an aid to navigation and is restricted in her ability to maneuver. Which lights will she show?

A. Three lights in a vertical line, the highest and lowest red and the midddle white, and anchor lights
B. Three lights in a vertical line, the highest and lowest red and the middle white, ONLY
C. Anchor lights ONLY
D. Anchor lights and sidelights ONLY

4366. INT & INLAND

Which vessel is a vessel restricted in her ability to maneuver under the Rules?

A. A vessel mineclearing
B. A vessel engaged in fishing
C. A vessel at anchor
D. A vessel not under command

4367. INT & INLAND

What would NOT be a distress signal?

A. MAYDAY sent by radiotelephone
B. Continuous sounding of fog horn
C. Green star shells fired from a launcher
D. Square flag and ball in a vertical line

4368. INT & INLAND

In a dense fog you hear a whistle signal ahead of one prolonged blast followed by three short blasts. This signal indicates a ____.

A. fishing vessel underway trawling
B. manned vessel being towed
C. pilot vessel underway making a special signal
D. vessel not under command

4369. INT & INLAND

If a towing vessel and her tow are severely restricted in their ability to deviate from their course, they may show lights in addition to their towing identification lights. These additional lights may be shown if the tow is ____.

A. pushed ahead
B. towed alongside
C. towed astern
D. any of the above

4371. INT & INLAND

A head-on situation at night is one in which you see ____.

A. one sidelight of a vessel ahead of you
B. one sidelight and a masthead light of a vessel ahead of you
C. one sidelight, a masthead light, and a range light of a vessel ahead of you

D. both sidelights of a vessel dead ahead of you

4372. INT & INLAND
You are the stand-on vessel in a crossing situation. If you think the give-way vessel is NOT taking sufficient action to avoid collision, you should sound ____.

A. one short blast and maintain course
B. two short blasts, alter to port, and pass astern
C. no signal and maneuver at will
D. the danger signal

4373. INT & INLAND
A lantern combining the two sidelights and sternlight may be shown on a ____.

A. 10-meter sailing vessel
B. 20-meter vessel engaged in fishing and making way
C. 25-meter power-driven vessel engaged in trolling
D. 25-meter pilot vessel

4374. INT & INLAND
A vessel aground would show the same dayshape as a ____.

A. vessel towing a submerged object
B. dredge underway and dredging
C. hydrographic survey vessel at anchor and surveying
D. None of the above

4375. INT & INLAND
You are underway in fog when you hear a signal of three strokes of a bell, a rapid ringing of the bell, and three more strokes of the bell. This signal indicates a vessel ____.

A. at anchor, giving warning
B. aground
C. at anchor, greater than 100 meters
D. not under command at anchor

4376. INT & INLAND
A power-driven vessel not under command at night must show her sidelights when ____.

A. making headway
B. making no headway
C. moored to a buoy
D. at anchor

4377. INT & INLAND
The term prolonged blast means a blast of ____.

A. two to four seconds duration
B. four to six seconds duration
C. six to eight seconds duration
D. eight to ten seconds duration

4378. INT & INLAND
While you are underway, navigation lights must be displayed on your vessel ____.

A. during all periods of restricted visibility
B. at all times
C. at night only when other vessels may be in the area
D. at night only when vessels are detected on radar

4379. INT & INLAND
Which statement is TRUE concerning risk of collision?

A. The stand-on vessel must keep out of the way of the other vessel when risk of collision exists.
B. Risk of collision always exists when two vessels pass within one mile of each other.
C. Risk of collision always exists when the compass bearing of an approaching vessel changes appreciably.
D. Risk of collision may exist when the compass bearing of an approaching vessel is changing appreciably.

4380. INT & INLAND
A vessel nearing a bend where other vessels may be obscured shall sound:

A. one short blast
B. one long blast
C. two short blasts
D. one prolonged blast

4381. INT & INLAND
A vessel that is defined as restricted in her ability to maneuver is unable to keep out of the way of another vessel due to ____.

A. her draft
B. the nature of her work
C. some exceptional circumstances
D. a danger of navigation

4382. INT & INLAND
While underway in fog, you hear a vessel sound four short blasts in succession. What does this signal indicate?

A. A pilot vessel
B. A vessel being towed
C. A vessel fishing
D. A sailboat

4383. INT & INLAND
You are in charge of a stand-on vessel in a crossing situation. The other vessel is 1.5 miles to port. You believe that risk of collision exists. You should ____.

A. take avoiding action immediately upon determining that risk of collision exists
B. immediately sound the danger signal
C. take avoiding action only after providing the give-way vessel time to take action, and determining that her action is not appropriate
D. hold course and speed until the point of extremis, and then sound the danger signal, taking whatever action will best avert collision

4384. DIAGRAM 8. INT & INLAND
In DIAGRAM 8, vessel A and vessel B (which is pushing ahead) are meeting head-on as shown. How must the vessels pass?

A. Vessel A must alter course while vessel B continues on its present course.
B. The vessels should determine which will alter course by exchanging whistle signals.
C. Both vessels should alter course to port and pass starboard to starboard.
D. Both vessels should alter course to starboard and pass port to port.

4385. INT & INLAND
To be considered engaged in fishing according to the Rules of the Road, a vessel must be ____.

A. using fishing apparatus which restricts maneuverability
B. using trolling lines
C. power-driven
D. showing lights or shapes for a vessel restricted in her ability to maneuver

4386. INT & INLAND
While underway in fog you hear a rapid ringing of a bell ahead. This bell indicates a ____.

A. vessel at anchor
B. vessel in distress
C. sailboat underway
D. vessel backing out of a berth

4387. INT & INLAND
An overtaking situation would be one in which one vessel is approaching another from more than how many degrees abaft the beam?

A. 0°
B. 10°
C. 22.5°
D. None of the above

4388. INT & INLAND
A stand-on vessel is ____.

A. required to give way in a crossing situation
B. required to sound the first passing signal in a meeting situation
C. free to maneuver in any crossing or meeting situation as it has the right-of-way
D. required to maintain course and speed in a crossing situation but may take action to avoid collision

4389. INT & INLAND
An overtaking situation at night would be one in which one vessel sees which light(s) of a vessel ahead?

A. Masthead lights and sidelights
B. One sidelight, the masthead lights and sternlight
C. Both sidelights
D. Sternlight

4390. INT & INLAND
What lights must sailboats show when underway at night?

A. One all-around white light
B. A sternlight
C. Red and green sidelights
D. Red and green sidelights and a sternlight

4391. INT & INLAND
You are crossing a narrow channel in a small motorboat. You sight a tankship off your port bow coming up the channel. Which statement is TRUE?

A. You are the stand-on vessel because the tankship is to port.
B. You cannot impede the safe passage of the tankship.
C. The tankship is the stand-on vessel because it is to port of your vessel.
D. The tankship is the stand-on vessel because it is the larger of the two.

4392. INT & INLAND
Which vessel does NOT sound a fog signal of one prolonged followed by two short blasts?

A. A vessel dredging
B. A vessel being towed

C. A vessel engaged in fishing
D. A sailing vessel

4393. INT & INLAND
Which light(s) is(are) AMONG those shown by a 200-m vessel at anchor?

A. In the forepart of the vessel, a 225° white light
B. In the after part of the vessel, a 135° white light
C. Any available working lights to illuminate the decks
D. In the fore part of the vessel, a 135° white light

4394. INT & INLAND
A partly submerged vessel or object being towed, which is not readily noticeable, shall show ____.

A. yellow lights at each end
B. two red lights in a vertical line
C. a black ball
D. a diamond shape

4395. DIAGRAM 73. INT & INLAND
The lights displayed indicate a ____.

A. fishing vessel trolling
B. vessel laying submarine cable
C. vessel towing astern
D. vessel dredging

4396. INT & INLAND
Concerning the identification signal for a pilot vessel, in fog, which statement is TRUE?

A. When at anchor, the pilot vessel is only required to sound anchor signals.
B. The identification signal must be sounded any time the pilot vessel is underway.
C. The pilot vessel may only sound the identity signal when making way.
D. All of the above

4397. INT & INLAND
In a crossing situation, a vessel fishing must keep out of the way of a vessel which is ____.

A. under sail
B. towing
C. restricted in her ability to maneuver
D. engaged in pilotage duty

4398. DIAGRAM 10. INT & INLAND
A tugboat displaying the dayshape shown ____.

A. is at anchor
B. is not under command
C. has a tow that exceeds 200 meters in length
D. has a tow that is carrying dangerous cargo

4399. INT & INLAND
Which vessel would display a cone, apex downward?

A. A fishing vessel with outlying gear
B. A vessel proceeding under sail and machinery
C. A vessel engaged in diving operations
D. A vessel being towed

4400. INT & INLAND
When action to avoid a close quarters situation is taken, a course change alone may be the most effective action provided that ____.

A. it is done in a succession of small course changes
B. it is NOT done too early
C. it is a large course change
D. the course change is to starboard

4401. INT & INLAND
You are underway in heavy fog. You hear the fog signal of a vessel which is somewhere ahead of your vessel. You must ____.

A. slow to moderate speed and navigate with caution
B. maintain speed and sound the danger signal
C. stop engines and navigate with caution
D. slow to bare steerageway and navigate with caution

4402. INT & INLAND
A vessel at anchor will show a ____.

A. ball
B. cone
C. cylinder
D. double cone, apexes together

4403. INT & INLAND
What dayshape must be shown by a vessel over 20 meters fishing which has gear extending more than 150 meters horizontally outward from it?

A. One black ball
B. One diamond shape
C. One cone with its apex upwards
D. One basket

4404. INT & INLAND
A vessel towing astern in an operation which severely restricts the towing vessel and her tow in their ability to change course shall, when making way, exhibit ____.

A. the masthead lights for a towing vessel
B. the lights for a vessel restricted in its ability to maneuver
C. sidelights, sternlight and towing light
D. All of the above

4405. INT & INLAND
A vessel underway but not making way and fishing other than trawling will show which lights?

A. A white light over a red light
B. A red light over a white light
C. A white light over a red light, sidelights, and a sternlight
D. A red light over a white light, sidelights, and a sternlight

4406. DIAGRAM 42. INT & INLAND
Two power-driven vessels are crossing as shown. Vessel A sounds three short blasts on the whistle. This signal means that vessel A ____.

A. intends to hold course and speed
B. is sounding the danger signal
C. is backing engines
D. proposes to cross ahead of the other vessel

4407. INT & INLAND
A 200-meter vessel is aground in restricted visibility. Which signal is optional?

A. A bell signal
B. A gong signal
C. A whistle signal
D. All of the above

4408. DIAGRAM 67. INT & INLAND
A fishing vessel displaying the lights shown is ____.

A. anchored
B. underway but not fishing
C. tending a small fishing boat
D. fishing by trawling

4409. INT & INLAND
A vessel or object being towed astern shall display a(n) ____.

A. forward masthead light
B. after masthead light
C. sternlight
D. All of the above

4410. INT & INLAND
The rules state that vessels may depart from the requirements of the Rules when ____.

A. there are no other vessels around
B. operating in a narrow channel
C. the Master enters it in the ship's log
D. necessary to avoid immediate danger

4411. INT & INLAND
For the purpose of the Rules, except where otherwise required, the term ____.

A. vessel includes seaplanes
B. seaplane includes nondisplacement craft
C. vessel engaged in fishing includes a vessel fishing with trolling lines
D. vessel restricted in her ability to maneuver includes fishing vessels

4412. DIAGRAM 44. INT & INLAND
A vessel displaying the lights shown is ____.

A. towing
B. conducting underwater survey operations
C. drifting
D. aground

4413. INT & INLAND
Which statement is TRUE concerning a 75-meter power-driven vessel underway at night?

A. She must exhibit an all-around white light at the stern.
B. She must exhibit forward and after masthead lights.
C. She must exhibit only a forward masthead light.
D. She may exhibit a red light over a green light forward.

4414. INT & INLAND
Every vessel which is directed by these Rules to keep out of the way of another vessel shall, if the circumstances of the case admit, avoid ____.

A. crossing ahead of the other
B. crossing astern of the other
C. passing port to port
D. passing starboard to starboard

4415. INT & INLAND
Which signal may be used by a vessel that is in doubt as to whether sufficient action is being taken by another vessel to avoid collision?

A. A continuous sounding of the fog horn
B. Firing a gun every minute
C. Five or more short rapid blasts on the whistle
D. One prolonged blast on the whistle

4416. INT & INLAND
Navigation lights must be displayed in all weathers from sunset to sunrise. They also ____.

A. must be displayed when day signals are being used
B. must be displayed when moored to a pier
C. may be extinguished at night on open waters when no other vessels are in the area
D. may be displayed during daylight

4417. INT & INLAND
What describes a head-on situation?

A. Seeing a vessel displaying both sidelights ONLY dead ahead
B. Seeing two forward white towing identification lights in a vertical line on a towing vessel directly ahead
C. Seeing both sidelights of a vessel directly off your starboard beam
D. Seeing both sidelights and masthead light(s) of a vessel dead ahead

4418. INT & INLAND
When two vessels are in immediate danger of collision, the stand-on vessel must ____.

A. abandon ship
B. assist in taking whatever action is necessary to avoid collision
C. hold course and speed
D. sound a distress signal

4419. INT & INLAND
A vessel 25 meters in length must have which sound signaling appliance onboard?

A. None is required
B. Whistle only
C. Whistle and bell only
D. Whistle, bell, and gong

4420. INT & INLAND

A vessel transferring provisions or cargo at sea shall display during the day ____.

A. two black balls in a vertical line
B. three black balls in a vertical line
C. three shapes in a vertical line; the highest and lowest shall be red balls and the middle a white diamond
D. three black shapes in a vertical line; the highest and lowest shall be balls and the middle one a diamond

4421. INT & INLAND

You see a red sidelight bearing NW (315°). That vessel may be heading:

A. south (180°)
B. east (090°)
C. northeast (045°)
D. west (270°)

4422. INT & INLAND

Each prolonged blast on whistle signals used by a power-driven vessel in fog, whether making way or underway but not making way, is ____.

A. about one second
B. two to four seconds
C. four to six seconds
D. eight to ten seconds

4423. INT & INLAND

Which statement is TRUE concerning a vessel engaged in fishing?

A. The vessel may be using nets, lines, or trawls.
B. The vessel may be trolling.
C. The vessel shows 2 lights in a vertical line, white over red.
D. The vessel sounds the same fog signal as a vessel underway, making no way.

4424. INT & INLAND

The Rules state that risk of collision shall be deemed to exist ____.

A. whenever two vessels approach from opposite directions
B. if the bearing of an approaching vessel does not appreciably change
C. whenever a vessel crosses ahead of the intended track of another vessel
D. if one vessel approaches another so as to be overtaking

4425. INT & INLAND

A power-driven vessel exhibits the same lights as a ____.

A. vessel towing, when not underway
B. vessel towing astern
C. sailing vessel
D. pushing vessel and a vessel being pushed, when they are in a composite unit

4426. INT & INLAND

A power-driven vessel is underway in fog but stopped and making no way through the water. What is the required fog signal?

A. One prolonged blast at not more than one-minute intervals
B. Two prolonged blasts at not more than one-minute intervals
C. One prolonged blast at not more than two-minute intervals
D. Two prolonged blasts at not more than two-minute intervals

4427. INT & INLAND

A towing light, according to the Rules, is a ____.

A. white light
B. red light
C. yellow light
D. blue light

4428. INT & INLAND

Which signal shall a power-driven vessel sound when making way in fog?

A. One short blast every two minutes
B. One prolonged blast every two minutes
C. One prolonged and two short blasts every two minutes
D. Three short blasts every two minutes

4429. INT & INLAND

Two vessels are meeting head-on. How must the vessels pass?

A. One vessel must alter course while the other must continue on its course.
B. The vessels should determine which will alter course by sounding whistle signals.
C. Both vessels should alter course to port and pass starboard to starboard.
D. Both vessels should alter course to starboard and pass port to port.

4430. INT & INLAND

Which vessel does NOT sound a fog signal of one prolonged followed by two short blasts?

A. A vessel engaged in dredging

B. A sailing vessel
C. A vessel being towed
D. A vessel engaged in fishing

4431. INT & INLAND

A vessel 50 meters in length at anchor must sound which fog signal?

A. 5-second ringing of a bell every minute
B. 5-second ringing of a bell every two minutes
C. 5-second sounding of a gong every minute
D. 5-second sounding of both a bell and gong every two minutes

4432. DIAGRAM 61. INT & INLAND

A vessel displaying ONLY the lights shown is ____.

A. fishing
B. a pilot vessel at anchor
C. a fishing vessel aground
D. fishing and hauling her nets

4433. INT & INLAND

Which vessel is NOT to be regarded as restricted in her ability to maneuver?

A. A vessel transferring provisions while underway
B. A pushing vessel and a vessel being pushed when connected in a composite unit
C. A vessel servicing a navigation mark
D. A vessel launching aircraft

4434. INT & INLAND

Which statement correctly applies to a situation where a sailing vessel is overtaking a power-driven vessel?

A. The power-driven vessel must keep out of the way of the sailing vessel.
B. A special circumstance situation exists.
C. The sailing vessel must keep out of the way of the power-driven vessel.
D. The vessel which has the other vessel to the right must keep out of the way.

4435. INT & INLAND

Which procedure(s) shall be used to determine risk of collision?

A. Watching the compass bearing of an approaching vessel
B. Systematic observation of objects detected by radar

C. Long-range radar scanning
D. All of the above

4436. INT & INLAND
A white masthead light shows through an arc of how many degrees?

A. 90°
B. 112.5°
C. 225°
D. 360°

4437. INT & INLAND
What is the minimum length of an anchored vessel which is required to show a white light both forward and aft?

A. 50 meters
B. 100 meters
C. 150 meters
D. 200 meters

4438. INT & INLAND
You are at anchor in fog. The fog signal of a vessel underway has been steadily growing louder and the danger of collision appears to exist. In addition to your fog signal, what signal may be used to indicate the presence of your vessel?

A. Three blasts on the whistle; one prolonged, one short, and one prolonged.
B. Three blasts on the whistle; one short, one prolonged, and one short.
C. Three blasts on the whistle; one prolonged followed by two short.
D. No signal other than your fog signal may be used.

4439. INT & INLAND
Signals required for vessels aground include ____.

A. by night, the anchor lights for a vessel of her length, and three red lights in a vertical line
B. a short, a prolonged, and a short blast
C. by day, three black balls in a vertical line
D. All of the above

4440. INT & INLAND
Which craft would be considered a power-driven vessel under the Rules of the Road?

A. An auxiliary sail vessel, using her engine
B. A canoe being propelled by a small outboard motor
C. A tug powered by a diesel engine
D. All of the above

4441. INT & INLAND
At night, power-driven vessels less than 12 meters in length may, instead of the underway lights for vessels under 50 meters, show which lights?

A. Sidelights and sternlight
B. One all-around white light and sidelights
C. Masthead light only
D. Sternlight only

4442. INT & INLAND
Which vessel shall not impede the passage of a vessel which can only navigate inside a narrow channel?

A. A vessel of less than 20 meters in length
B. A vessel not under command
C. A vessel engaged in surveying
D. All of the above

4443. INT & INLAND
Which statement is TRUE in an overtaking situation?

A. One vessel is approaching another vessel from more than 20° abaft the beam.
B. It is the duty of the vessel being overtaken to get out of the way.
C. Any later change of bearing between the two vessels shall not make the overtaking vessel a crossing vessel.
D. All of the above

4444. INT & INLAND
Which vessel must exhibit a conical shape, apex downwards?

A. A 10-meter vessel engaged in fishing
B. A 15-meter vessel proceeding under sail when also being propelled by machinery
C. A 20-meter vessel restricted in her ability to maneuver
D. All of the above

4445. INT & INLAND
Which vessel must show a towing light above the sternlight?

A. A vessel pushing three barges ahead
B. A vessel towing alongside
C. A vessel with a 150-meter tow astern
D. None of the above

4446. INT & INLAND
Which is NOT a distress signal?

A. A continuous sounding with any fog signal apparatus
B. A signal sent by radiotelephone consisting of the spoken word "Mayday"

C. An International Code Signal of N.C.
D. The firing of green star rockets or shells

4447. INT & INLAND
A rigid replica of the International Code flag A may be shown by a vessel:

A. pulling a submarine cable
B. engaged in diving operations
C. engaged in underway replenishment
D. transferring explosives

4448. DIAGRAM 5. INT & INLAND
Vessel A is underway and pushing ahead when vessel B is sighted off the starboard bow as shown. Which statement is TRUE?

A. Vessel A is the stand-on vessel because it is to the port side of vessel B.
B. Vessel A is the stand-on vessel because it is pushing ahead.
C. Vessel B is the stand-on vessel because it is to starboard of vessel A.
D. Neither vessel is the stand-on vessel.

4449. INT & INLAND
In a crossing situation, which vessel may sound the danger signal?

A. Give-way vessel
B. Stand-on vessel
C. Either vessel
D. Neither vessel

4451. INT & INLAND
Every vessel should at all times proceed at a safe speed. *Safe speed* is defined as that speed where ____.

A. you can stop within your visibility range
B. you can take proper and effective action to avoid collision
C. you are traveling slower than surrounding vessels
D. no wake comes from your vessel

4452. INT & INLAND
You are underway in fog and you hear three distinct bell strokes followed by five seconds of rapid bell ringing followed by three distinct bell strokes. This signal indicates a vessel:

A. aground
B. engaged in underwater construction
C. at anchor
D. in distress

4453. DIAGRAM 30. INT & INLAND
Vessels A and B are crossing as shown.

Which statement is TRUE?

A. The vessels should pass starboard to starboard.
B. Vessel B should pass astern of vessel A.
C. Vessel B should alter course to the right.
D. Vessel A must keep clear of vessel B.

4454. INT & INLAND

In a crossing situation, a stand-on vessel which is forced to take action in order to avoid collision with a vessel on her own port side shall, if possible, avoid ____.

A. turning to port
B. turning to starboard
C. decreasing speed
D. increasing speed

4455. INT & INLAND

Which vessel is underway within the meaning of the Rules?

A. A vessel at anchor with the engine turning
B. A vessel tied to an offshore mooring buoy
C. A vessel aground with the engine turning
D. A vessel drifting with the engine stopped

4456. INT & INLAND

What is the required fog signal for a manned vessel being towed at night?

A. One prolonged followed by one short blast
B. One prolonged followed by three short blasts
C. One prolonged followed by two short blasts
D. Two prolonged blasts

4457. INT & INLAND

If you anchor your 25-meter vessel in a harbor, what light(s) must you show?

A. One all-around white light
B. Two all-around white lights
C. One all-around red light
D. All the deck house lights

4458. DIAGRAM 50. INT & INLAND

You see the lights shown on your port bow. You should ____.

A. hold course and speed
B. alter course to port

C. stop engines
D. sound the danger signal

4459. INT & INLAND

Three short blasts of the whistle means ____.

A. danger
B. I am in distress
C. the vessel is not under command (broken down)
D. I am operating astern propulsion

4460. INT & INLAND

Of the vessels listed, which must keep out of the way of all the others?

A. A sailing vessel
B. A vessel restricted in her ability to maneuver
C. A vessel not under command
D. A vessel engaged in fishing

4461. INT & INLAND

During the day, a vessel with a tow over 200 meters in length will show:

A. a black ball
B. a diamond shape
C. two cones, apexes together
D. one cone, apex upward

4462. INT & INLAND

A fog signal of one prolonged blast followed by four short blasts would mean the presence of a ____.

A. vessel being towed
B. fishing vessel trawling
C. vessel at anchor warning of her location
D. power-driven pilot vessel on station underway

4463. DIAGRAM 38. INT & INLAND

You are underway on vessel B approaching vessel A, as shown. You are unable to see any sidelights on vessel A. This is a(n) ____.

A. meeting situation
B. crossing situation
C. overtaking situation
D. special circumstances situation

4464. INT & INLAND

A vessel not under command, underway but not making way, would show:

A. two all-around red lights in a vertical line
B. sidelights

C. a sternlight
D. All of the above

4465. INT & INLAND

Traffic separation schemes ____.

A. provide routing and scheduling procedures to reduce shipping delays
B. provide traffic patterns in congested areas, so that vessels can operate without having a separate lookout
C. provide inbound and outbound lanes to promote the safe flow of vessel traffic
D. prohibit vessels carrying hazardous cargoes from entering waters that are environmentally sensitive

4466. INT & INLAND

Which lights shall a 200-meter vessel exhibit when at anchor?

A. In the forepart of the vessel, a 225-degree white light
B. In the after part of the vessel, a 112.5-degree white light
C. Working lights to illuminate the decks
D. In the forepart of the vessel, a 112.5-degree white light

4467. INT & INLAND

Under the Rules, the term vessel includes ____.

A. non-self-propelled raft
B. seaplanes
C. hovercrafts
D. All of the above

4468. INT & INLAND

You see a vessel displaying three lights in a vertical line. The highest and lowest lights are red and the middle light is white. She is also showing a white light at the stern, which is lower than the forward light. It could be a ____.

A. survey vessel
B. vessel not under command
C. vessel aground
D. pilot vessel with port side to you

4469. INT & INLAND

A pilot vessel may continue to sound an identity signal in fog if she is ____.

A. aground
B. at anchor
C. not under command
D. no longer on pilotage duty

4470. INT & INLAND
You are in charge of a stand-on vessel in a crossing situation. The other vessel is 1.5 miles to port. You believe that risk of collision exists. You should ____.

A. take avoiding action immediately upon determining that risk of collision exists
B. immediately sound the danger signal, and change course
C. take avoiding action only after giving the give-way vessel time to take action, and determining that her action is not appropriate
D. hold course and speed until the point of extremis, and then sound the danger signal, taking whatever action will best avoid collision

4471. INT & INLAND
A vessel towing astern in an operation which severely restricts the towing vessel and her tow in their ability to deviate from their course shall, when making way, show ____.

A. the masthead lights for a towing vessel
B. the lights for a vessel restricted in its ability to maneuver
C. sidelights, sternlight and towing light
D. All of the above

4472. INT & INLAND
Which statement is TRUE concerning seaplanes on the water?

A. A seaplane must exhibit appropriate lights but need not exhibit shapes.
B. A seaplane should show the lights for a vessel constrained by her draft.
C. In situations where a risk of collision exists, a seaplane should always give way.
D. A seaplane on the water shall, in general, keep well clear of all vessels.

4473. INT & INLAND
A head-on situation at night is one in which you see dead ahead a vessel showing ____.

A. one sidelight
B. one sidelight and a masthead light
C. one sidelight and two masthead lights
D. both sidelights of a vessel and her masthead light(s)

4474. INT & INLAND
In a crossing situation, the stand-on vessel should normally ____.

A. take action to cross ahead of the other vessel
B. take action to pass astern of the other vessel
C. maintain course and speed
D. change course and increase speed

4475. INT & INLAND
A self-propelled dredge not engaged in dredging but proceeding to a dredging location at night would ____.

A. not be required to show any lights
B. be required to show the lights characteristic of a dredge
C. be required to show the lights of a stationary dredge
D. be required to show the lights of a power-driven vessel underway

4476. INT & INLAND
At night you sight a vessel displaying one green light. This light could indicate a ____.

A. vessel drifting
B. vessel at anchor
C. small motorboat underway
D. sailboat underway

4477. INT & INLAND
There is a provision to depart from the Rules, if necessary, to avoid ____.

A. a close-quarters situation
B. an overtaking situation
C. immediate danger
D. Any of the above

4478. INT & INLAND
Risk of collision exists when an approaching vessel has a(n) ____.

A. generally steady bearing and decreasing range
B. generally steady range and increasing bearing
C. increasing range and bearing
D. decreasing bearing only

4479. INT & INLAND
What signal indicates doubt that sufficient action is being taken by another vessel to avoid collision?

A. Five short and rapid blasts of the whistle
B. Three long blasts of the whistle
C. Three short rapid blasts of the whistle
D. One prolonged blast followed by three short blasts of the whistle

4480. INT & INLAND
A power-driven vessel towing another vessel astern (tow less than 200 meters) shall show ____.

A. a small white light abaft the funnel
B. three masthead lights in a vertical line instead of either the forward or after masthead lights
C. two masthead lights in a vertical line instead of either the forward or after masthead lights
D. two towing lights in a vertical line at the stern

4481. INT & INLAND
While underway in fog, you hear the rapid ringing of a bell for about five seconds followed by the sounding of a gong for about five seconds. This signal came from a ____.

A. vessel engaged in fishing at anchor
B. sailing vessel at anchor
C. vessel 150 meters in length at anchor
D. vessel aground

4482. INT & INLAND
You are underway in a narrow channel and you are being overtaken by a vessel astern. The overtaking vessel sounds a signal indicating his intention to pass your vessel on your starboard side. If such an action appears dangerous you should sound ____.

A. five short and rapid blasts
B. three short and rapid blasts
C. one prolonged followed by one short blast
D. one prolonged, one short, one prolonged, and one short blast in that order

4483. INT & INLAND
A vessel restricted in her ability to maneuver shall ____.

A. turn off her sidelights when not making way
B. when operating in restricted visibility, sound a whistle signal of two prolonged and one short blast
C. show a dayshape of two diamonds in a vertical line
D. keep out of the way of a vessel engaged in fishing

4484. INT & INLAND
A power-driven vessel at anchor, not fishing or otherwise restricted in its ability to maneuver, sounds her fog signal at

intervals of not _____.

A. more than one minute
B. more than two minutes
C. more than three minutes
D. less than two minutes

4485. INT & INLAND
You are underway in reduced visibility. You hear the fog signal of another vessel about 20° on your starboard bow. Risk of collision may exist. You should _____.

A. alter course to starboard to pass around the other vessel
B. reduce your speed to bare steerageway
C. slow your engines and let the other vessel pass ahead of you
D. alter course to port to pass the other vessel on its port side

4486. INT & INLAND
What dayshape would a vessel at anchor show during daylight?

A. One black ball
B. Two black balls
C. Three black balls
D. No signal

4487. DIAGRAM 34. INT & INLAND
A vessel displaying the dayshape shown is _____.

A. towing
B. fishing
C. anchored
D. being towed

4488. INT & INLAND
You are approaching a bend in a channel. You cannot see around the bend because of the height of the bank. You should _____.

A. stop engines and navigate with caution
B. stay in the middle of the channel
C. sound passing signals to any other vessel that may be on the other side of the bend
D. sound a whistle blast of 4 to 6 seconds duration

4489. INT & INLAND
Which statement is TRUE concerning a vessel of 150 meters in length, at anchor?

A. She may show an all-around white light where it can best be seen.
B. She must show an all-around white light forward and a second such light aft.
C. The showing of working lights is optional.

D. None of the above

4490. INT & INLAND
Which vessel would be required to show a white light from a lantern exhibited in sufficient time to prevent collision?

A. A 9-meter sailing vessel
B. A rowboat
C. A 6-meter motorboat
D. A small vessel fishing

4491. INT & INLAND
Barges being towed at night _____.

A. must be lighted at all times
B. must be lighted only if manned
C. must be lighted only if towed astern
D. need not be lighted

4492. INT & INLAND
You sight another power-driven vessel dead-ahead showing both the red and green sidelights. The required action to take would be to _____.

A. carefully watch his compass bearing
B. start a radar plot in order to ascertain his course
C. alter your course to port
D. alter your course to starboard

4493. INT & INLAND
You are underway in fog and hear one short, one prolonged, and one short blast in succession. What is the meaning of this signal?

A. A vessel is in distress and needs assistance.
B. A vessel is fishing, hauling nets.
C. A vessel is at anchor, warning of her position.
D. A vessel is towing.

4494. INT & INLAND
An anchored vessel on pilotage duty must show which light(s) at night?

A. A sternlight only
B. Anchor lights only
C. A white light over a red light only
D. A white light over a red light and anchor lights

4496. INT & INLAND
A vessel which is fishing is required to show sidelights and a sternlight only when _____.

A. anchored
B. underway

C. dead in the water
D. underway and making way

4497. INT & INLAND
What is a requirement for any action taken to avoid collision?

A. When in sight of another vessel, any action taken must be accompanied by sound signals.
B. The action taken must include changing the speed of the vessel.
C. The action must be positive and made in ample time.
D. All of the above

4498. INT & INLAND
In the daytime, you see a large sailing vessel on the beam. You know that she is also propelled by machinery if she shows _____.

A. a basket
B. a black ball
C. a black cone
D. two black cones

4499. DIAGRAM 76. INT & INLAND
At night, the lights shown would indicate a vessel _____.

A. trawling
B. laying submarine cable
C. towing astern
D. dredging

4500. INT & INLAND
Your vessel is stopped and making no way, but is not in any way disabled. Another vessel is approaching you on your starboard beam. Which statement is TRUE?

A. The other vessel must give way since your vessel is stopped.
B. Your vessel is the give-way vessel in a crossing situation.
C. You should be showing the lights or shapes for a vessel not under command.
D. You should be showing the lights or shapes for a vessel restricted in her ability to maneuver.

4501. INT & INLAND
For identification purposes at night, U.S. Navy submarines on the surface may display an intermittent flashing light of which color?

A. Amber (yellow)
B. White
C. Blue
D. Red

4502. INLAND ONLY
Vessels engaged in fishing may show the additional signals described in Annex II to the Rules when they are:

A. trolling
B. fishing in a traffic separation zone
C. in a narrow channel
D. in close proximity to other vessels engaged in fishing

4503. INT & INLAND
Which vessel must show a masthead light abaft of and higher than her identifying lights?

A. A 55-m vessel fishing
B. A 55-m vessel trawling
C. A 100-m vessel not under command
D. A 20-m vessel engaged on pilotage duty

4504. INT & INLAND
While underway in a narrow channel, a vessel should stay _____.

A. in the middle of the channel
B. to the starboard side of the channel
C. to the port side of the channel
D. to the side of the channel that has the widest bends

4505. INT & INLAND
Vessels of less than what length may not impede the passage of other vessels which can safely navigate only within a narrow channel or fairway?

A. 10 meters
B. 20 meters
C. 30 meters
D. 40 meters

4506. INT & INLAND
A lantern combining the sidelights and sternlight MAY be shown on a _____.

A. sailing vessel of 25 meters in length
B. 20-meter vessel engaged in fishing and making way
C. 25-meter power-driven vessel engaged in trolling
D. 6-meter vessel under oars

4507. INT & INLAND
The lights required by the Rules must be shown _____.

A. from sunrise to sunset in restricted visibility
B. at all times

C. ONLY from sunset to sunrise
D. whenever a look-out is posted

4508. INT & INLAND
Which vessel may carry her sidelights and sternlight in a combined lantern on the mast?

A. An 18-meter sailing vessel
B. A 10-meter sailing vessel also being propelled by machinery
C. A 25-meter sailing vessel
D. All of the above

4509. INT & INLAND
A vessel nearing a bend or an area of a channel or fairway where other vessels may be hidden by an obstruction shall _____.

A. sound the danger signal
B. sound a prolonged blast
C. take all way off
D. post a look-out

4510. INT & INLAND
You are approaching a vessel dredging during the day and see two balls in a vertical line on the port side of the dredge. These shapes mean that _____.

A. you should pass on the port side of the dredge
B. there is an obstruction on the port side of the dredge
C. the dredge is not under command
D. the dredge is moored

4511. INT & INLAND
Which statement is TRUE concerning the light used to accompany whistle signals?

A. It is mandatory to use such a light.
B. The light shall have the same characteristics as a masthead light.
C. It is used to supplement short blasts of the whistle.
D. All of the above

4512. INT & INLAND
Which vessel must sound her fog signal at intervals not to exceed one minute?

A. A power-driven vessel underway, not making way
B. A vessel constrained by her draft
C. A vessel engaged in fishing, at anchor
D. A vessel aground

4513. INT & INLAND
By day, you sight a vessel displaying three shapes in a vertical line. The top and bottom shapes are balls, and the middle shape is a diamond. It could be a _____.

A. vessel trolling
B. mineclearing vessel
C. trawler
D. vessel engaged in replenishment at sea

4514. INT & INLAND
You are heading due east (090°) and observe a vessel's red sidelight on your port beam. The vessel may be heading _____.

A. northwest (315°)
B. north (000°)
C. southeast (135°)
D. southwest (225°)

4516. INT & INLAND
Which vessel is, by definition, unable to keep out of the way of another vessel?

A. Vessel engaged in fishing
B. Vessel restricted in her ability to maneuver
C. Sailing vessel
D. Vessel towing

4517. INT & INLAND
Which vessel must exhibit forward and after masthead lights when underway?

A. A 200-meter sailing vessel
B. A 50-meter power-driven vessel
C. A 100-meter vessel engaged in fishing
D. All of the above

4518. INT & INLAND
As defined in the Rules, a towing light is a yellow light having the same characteristics as a(n) _____.

A. masthead light
B. all-around light
C. sidelight
D. sternlight

4519. INT & INLAND
A vessel underway and making way in fog shall sound every two minutes _____.

A. one prolonged blast
B. two prolonged blasts
C. one prolonged blast and three short blasts
D. three distinct blasts

4520. INT & INLAND
When anchoring a 20-meter vessel at night, you must show _____.

A. one all-around white light
B. two all-around white lights
C. one all-around white light and the sternlight
D. one all-around white light and a flare up light

4521. INT & INLAND
According to the Navigation Rules, all of the following are engaged in fishing EXCEPT a vessel _____.

A. setting nets
B. trawling
C. using a dredge net
D. trolling

4522. INT & INLAND
When a vessel sounds three short blasts on the whistle, this indicates that _____.

A. danger is ahead
B. her engines are going astern
C. the vessel is not under command (broken down)
D. all other vessels should stand clear

4523. INT & INLAND
A vessel is overtaking when she approaches another from more than how many degrees abaft the beam?

A. 0.0°
B. 11.25°
C. 22.5°
D. 45.0°

4524. INT & INLAND
What equipment for fog signals is required for a vessel 20 meters in length?

A. Whistle only
B. Bell only
C. Whistle and bell only
D. Whistle, bell, and gong

4525. INT & INLAND
Sailing vessels are stand-on over power-driven vessels except _____.

A. in a crossing situation
B. in a meeting situation
C. when they are the overtaking vessel
D. on the inland waters of the U.S.

4526. INT & INLAND
Which statement is TRUE concerning risk of collision?

A. Risk of collision never exists if the compass bearing of the other vessel is changing.
B. Proper use shall be made of radar equipment to determine risk of collision.
C. Risk of collision must be determined before any action can be taken by a vessel.
D. Risk of collision exists if the vessels will pass within half a mile of each other.

4527. INT & INLAND
You are fishing at night, and you sight a vessel showing three lights in a vertical line. The upper and lower lights are red and the middle light is white. Which statement is TRUE?

A. You must keep out of the way of the other vessel.
B. The other vessel is responsible to keep out of your way.
C. The other vessel is at anchor.
D. The rule of special circumstances applies.

4528. INT & INLAND
Which vessel is to sound a fog signal of one prolonged followed by two short blasts?

A. A vessel not under command
B. A sailing vessel, underway
C. A vessel restricted in her ability to maneuver when carrying out her work at anchor
D. All of the above

4529. INT & INLAND
A vessel may exhibit lights other than those prescribed by the Rules as long as the additional lights _____.

A. do not interfere with the keeping of a proper look-out
B. are not the color of either sidelight
C. have a lesser range than the prescribed lights
D. All of the above

4530. INT & INLAND
Which statement is TRUE concerning a partly submerged vessel being towed?

A. It must show a yellow light at each end.
B. It will show red lights along its length.
C. A diamond shape will be carried at the

aftermost extremity of the tow.
D. All of the above

4531. INT & INLAND
Your vessel enters fog. You stop your engines, and the vessel is dead in the water. Which fog signal should you sound?

A. One prolonged blast every two minutes
B. Two prolonged blasts every two minutes
C. Three short blasts every two minutes
D. One prolonged and two short blasts every two minutes

4532. INT & INLAND
The term power-driven vessel refers to any vessel _____.

A. with propelling machinery onboard whether in use or not
B. making way against the current
C. with propelling machinery in use
D. travelling at a speed greater than that of the current

4533. INT ONLY
In which situation do the Rules require both vessels to change course?

A. Two power-driven vessels meeting head-on
B. Two power-driven vessels crossing when it is apparent to the stand-on vessel that the give-way vessel is not taking appropriate action
C. Two sailing vessels crossing with the wind on the same side
D. All of the above

4534. INT & INLAND
A vessel towing where the tow prevents her from changing course shall carry _____.

A. only the lights for a vessel towing
B. only the lights for a vessel restricted in her ability to maneuver
C. the lights for a towing vessel and the lights for a vessel restricted in her ability to maneuver
D. the lights for a towing vessel and the lights for a vessel not under command

4535. INT & INLAND
Which statement is TRUE concerning the danger signal?

A. May be sounded by the stand-on vessel only
B. Indicates that the vessel is in distress

C. Is used to indicate a course change

D. May be supplemented by an appropriate light signal

4536. INT & INLAND

If a sailing vessel with the wind on the port side sees a sailing vessel to windward and cannot tell whether the other vessel has the wind on the port or starboard side, she shall ____.

A. hold course and speed

B. sound the danger signal

C. keep out of the way of the other vessel

D. turn to port and come into the wind

4537. INT & INLAND

Vessel A is on course 000°T. Vessel B is on a course such that she is involved in a head-on situation and is bearing 355°T, 2 miles away from vessel A. To ensure a safe passing, vessel A should ____.

A. maintain course

B. alter course to port

C. alter course to ensure a starboard to starboard passing

D. maneuver to ensure a port to port passing

4538. INT & INLAND

What is a vessel restricted in her ability to maneuver?

A. A vessel not under command

B. A vessel constrained by her draft

C. A vessel underway in fog

D. A vessel towing unable to deviate from her course

4539. INT & INLAND

All of the following are distress signals under the Rules EXCEPT ____.

A. a green star signal

B. orange-colored smoke

C. red flares

D. the repeated raising and lowering of outstretched arms

4540. DIAGRAM 58. INT & INLAND

The lights shown are those of a ____.

A. vessel being towed

B. power-driven vessel of less than 50 meters in length

C. fishing vessel at anchor

D. sailboat

4541. INT & INLAND

The Rules state that vessels may depart from the Rules when ____.

A. there are no other vessels around

B. operating in a narrow channel

C. the Master enters it in the ship's log

D. necessary to avoid immediate danger

4542. INT & INLAND

A vessel is towing and carrying the required lights on the masthead. What is the visibility arc of these lights?

A. 112.5°

B. 135.0°

C. 225.0°

D. 360.0°

4543. INT & INLAND

Which situation would be a special circumstance under the Rules?

A. Vessel at anchor

B. More than two vessels meeting

C. Speed in fog

D. Two vessels crossing

4544. INT & INLAND

You are approaching another vessel on crossing courses. She is approximately half a mile distant and is presently on your starboard bow. You believe she will cross ahead of you. She then sounds a whistle signal of five short blasts. You should ____.

A. answer the signal and hold course and speed

B. reduce speed slightly to make sure she will have room to pass

C. make a large course change, accompanied by the appropriate whistle signal, and slow down if necessary

D. wait for another whistle signal from the other vessel

4545. INT & INLAND

You are approaching another vessel and are not sure whether danger of collision exists. You must assume ____.

A. there is risk of collision

B. you are the give way vessel

C. the other vessel is also in doubt

D. All of the above are correct.

4546. INT & INLAND

Which vessel may use the danger signal?

A. The vessel to starboard when two power-driven vessels are crossing

B. A vessel engaged in fishing, crossing the course of a sailing vessel

C. Either of two power-driven vessels meeting head-on

D. All of the above

4547. INT & INLAND

What is the minimum sound signaling equipment required aboard a vessel 10 meters in length?

A. A bell only

B. A whistle only

C. A bell and a whistle

D. Any means of making an efficient sound signal

4548. INT & INLAND

Which statement is TRUE regarding equipment for sound signals?

A. A vessel of less than 12 meters in length need not have any sound signaling equipment.

B. Any vessel over 12 meters in length must be provided with a gong.

C. Manual sounding of the signals must always be possible.

D. Automatic sounding of the signals is not permitted.

4549. DIAGRAM 3. INT & INLAND

Two sailing vessels are approaching each other as shown. Which statement is correct?

A. Vessel I should stand on because she has the wind on her port side.

B. Vessel II should stand on because she has the wind on her starboard side.

C. Neither vessel is the stand-on vessel because they are meeting head-on.

D. Vessel I should stand on because she is close-hauled.

4550. INT & INLAND

Which statement concerning an overtaking situation is correct?

A. The overtaking vessel is the stand-on vessel.

B. Neither vessel is the stand-on vessel.

C. The overtaking vessel must maintain course and speed.

D. The overtaking vessel must keep out of the way of the other.

4551. INT & INLAND

The Rules state that a vessel overtaking another vessel is relieved of her duty to keep clear when ____.

A. she is forward of the other vessel's beam

B. the overtaking situation becomes a crossing situation

C. she is past and clear of the other vessel
D. the other vessel is no longer in sight

4552. INT & INLAND
Which statement is TRUE concerning fog signals?

A. All fog signals for sailing vessels are to be given at intervals of not more than one minute.
B. A vessel not under command sounds the same fog signal as a vessel towed.
C. A pilot vessel underway and making way sounds the pilot identity signal and no other signal.
D. A vessel aground may sound a whistle signal.

4553. INT & INLAND
Which dayshape would a vessel aground show during daylight?

A. One black ball
B. Two black balls
C. Three black balls
D. Four black balls

4554. INT & INLAND
Which vessel must have a gong, or other equipment which will make the sound of a gong?

A. A sailing vessel
B. Any vessel over 50 meters
C. Any vessel over 100 meters
D. A power-driven vessel over 75 meters

4555. INT & INLAND
A sailing vessel is proceeding along a narrow channel and can safely navigate ONLY inside the channel. The sailing vessel approaches a vessel engaged in fishing. Which statement is TRUE?

A. The fishing vessel is directed not to impede the passage of the sailing vessel.
B. The sailing vessel must keep out of the way of the fishing vessel.
C. Each vessel should move to the edge of the channel on her port side.
D. Each vessel should be displaying signals for a vessel constrained by her draft.

4556. INT & INLAND
Dayshapes MUST be shown _____.

A. during daylight hours
B. during daylight hours except in restricted visibility
C. ONLY between 8 AM and 4 PM daily
D. between sunset and sunrise

4557. INT & INLAND
Rule 14 describes the action to be taken by vessels meeting head-on. Which of the following conditions must exist in order for this rule to apply?

A. Both vessels must be power-driven.
B. They must be meeting on reciprocal or nearly reciprocal courses.
C. The situation must involve risk of collision.
D. All of the above

4558. INT & INLAND
The sternlight shall be positioned such that it will show from dead astern to how many degrees on each side of the stern of the vessel?

A. 22.5°
B. 67.5°
C. 112.5°
D. 135.0°

4559. INT & INLAND
A vessel aground at night is required to show two red lights in a vertical line as well as _____.

A. not under command lights
B. restricted in her ability to maneuver lights
C. anchor lights
D. sidelights and a sternlight

4560. INT & INLAND
When towing more than one barge astern at night _____.

A. only the last barge on the tow must be lighted
B. only the first and the last barges in the tow must be lighted
C. each barge in the tow must be lighted
D. only manned barges must be lighted

4561. INT & INLAND
Your vessel is aground in fog. In addition to the regular anchor signals, you will be sounding _____.

A. three strokes of the gong before and after the rapid ringing of the gong
B. a blast on the whistle
C. three strokes of the bell before and after the rapid ringing of the bell
D. no additional signals

4562. INT & INLAND
In a crossing situation, the vessel which has the other on her own starboard side shall _____.

A. if the circumstances of the case admit, avoid crossing ahead of the other
B. change course to port to keep out of the way
C. reduce her speed
D. All of the above

4563. DIAGRAM 32. INT & INLAND
You are on vessel A in DIAGRAM 32, and hear vessel B sound a signal indicating her intention to overtake you. You feel it is not safe for vessel B to overtake you at the present time. You should _____.

A. sound five or more short rapid blasts
B. sound two short blasts
C. not answer the whistle signal from vessel B
D. sound three blasts of the whistle

4564. INT & INLAND
Which vessel sounds the same fog signal when underway or at anchor?

A. A sailing vessel
B. A vessel restricted in her ability to maneuver
C. A vessel constrained by her draft
D. A vessel not under command

4565. INT & INLAND
You are approaching a bend in a river where, due to the bank, you cannot see around the other side. A vessel on the other side of the bend sounds one prolonged blast. You should _____.

A. sound passing signals
B. not sound any signal until you sight the other vessel
C. sound a prolonged blast
D. sound the danger signal

4567. DIAGRAM 5. INT & INLAND
In DIAGRAM 5, vessel A, which is pushing ahead, and vessel B are crossing. Which is the stand-on vessel?

A. Vessel A is the stand-on vessel because she is to port of vessel B.
B. Vessel A is the stand-on vessel because she is pushing ahead.
C. Vessel B is the stand-on vessel because she is to starboard of vessel A.
D. Neither vessel is the stand-on vessel in this situation.

4568. INT & INLAND
Which vessel is underway according to the Rules?

A. A vessel made fast to a single point mooring buoy
B. A purse seiner hauling her nets
C. A pilot vessel at anchor
D. A vessel which has run aground

4569. INT & INLAND
When two power-driven vessels are crossing, the vessel which has the other to starboard must keep out of the way if _____.

A. she is the faster vessel
B. the situation involves risk of collision
C. the vessels will pass within half a mile of each other
D. whistle signals have been sounded

4570. INT & INLAND
Which signal may at some time be exhibited by a vessel trawling?

A. Two white lights in a vertical line
B. A white light over a red light in a vertical line
C. Two red lights in a vertical line
D. All of the above

4571. INT & INLAND
Risk of collision is considered to exist if _____.

A. four vessels are nearby
B. a vessel has a steady bearing at a constant range
C. there is any doubt that a risk of collision exists
D. a special circumstance situation is apparent

4572. INT & INLAND
You are underway in low visibility and sounding fog signals. What changes would you make in the fog signal immediately upon losing propulsion?

A. Begin sounding two prolonged blasts at two-minute intervals.
B. Begin sounding one prolonged blast followed by three short blasts at two-minute intervals.
C. Begin sounding one prolonged blast followed by two short blasts at two-minute intervals.
D. No change should be made in the fog signal.

4573. INT & INLAND
A power-driven vessel shows the same lights as a _____.

A. vessel engaged in towing, when not underway
B. vessel towing astern
C. sailing vessel
D. pushing vessel and a vessel being pushed, when they are rigidly connected in a composite unit

4574. INT & INLAND
Which vessel shall NOT show her sidelights?

A. A fishing vessel that is not making way
B. A sailing vessel which is becalmed
C. A vessel engaged in underwater operations
D. A vessel that is not under command making way

4575. INT & INLAND
A vessel is overtaking when she can see which light(s) of a vessel ahead?

A. Only the sternlight of the vessel
B. One sidelight and a masthead light of the vessel
C. Only a sidelight of the vessel
D. The masthead lights of the vessel

4577. INT & INLAND
Which statement about the Navigation Rules is TRUE?

A. The rules require vessels to comply with Traffic Separation Scheme regulations.
B. The rules use the term safe speed.
C. The Rules permit a stand-on vessel to take action prior to being in extremis.
D. All of the above are correct.

4578. INT & INLAND
A short blast on the whistle has a duration of _____.

A. 1 second
B. 4 to 6 seconds
C. 8 to 12 seconds
D. 12 to 15 seconds

4579. INT & INLAND
As defined in the Rules, the term *vessel* includes _____.

A. seaplanes
B. nondisplacement craft
C. barges
D. All of the above

4580. DIAGRAM 45. INT & INLAND
You see a vessel displaying ONLY the lights shown. This could be a _____.

A. pilot vessel less than 50 meters, underway and NOT engaged on pilotage duty
B. vessel engaged in fishing
C. vessel aground less than 50 meters
D. vessel engaged in dredging at anchor with an obstruction on one side

4581. INT & INLAND
A vessel shall slacken her speed, stop, or reverse her engines, if necessary, to _____.

A. avoid collision
B. allow more time to assess the situation
C. be stopped in an appropriate distance
D. All of the above

4582. DIAGRAM 52. INT & INLAND
At night, a vessel displaying the lights shown is _____.

A. towing by pushing ahead
B. underway
C. towing a submerged object
D. engaged in dredging

4583. INT & INLAND
An anchor ball need NOT be exhibited by an anchored vessel if she is _____.

A. under 50 meters in length, and anchored in an anchorage
B. over 150 meters in length
C. rigged for sail
D. less than 7 meters in length, and not in or near an area where other vessels normally navigate

4584. INT AND INLAND
A vessel that is not equipped with towing lights should show that it has a vessel in tow by _____.

A. continuously sounding its horn
B. sounding one prolonged followed by two short blasts at intervals of not more than two minutes
C. shining a searchlight on the towline of the towed vessel
D. None of the above; a vessel shall not engage in towing at night without proper navigation lights

4585. INT & INLAND

While underway at night you are coming up on a vessel from astern. What lights would you expect to see?

A. Red and green sidelights
B. Two white lights
C. One white light and red and green sidelights
D. One white light

4586. INT & INLAND

What describes a head-on situation?

A. Seeing one red light of a vessel directly ahead
B. Seeing two forward white towing lights in a vertical line on a towing vessel directly ahead
C. Seeing both sidelights of a vessel directly off your starboard beam
D. Seeing both sidelights of a vessel directly ahead

4587. INT & INLAND

A vessel anchored in fog may warn an approaching vessel by sounding ____.

A. the whistle continuously
B. one short, one prolonged, and one short blast of the whistle
C. five or more short and rapid blasts of the whistle
D. three distinct strokes on the bell before and after sounding the anchor signal

4588. INT & INLAND

While underway in fog, you hear a vessel ahead sound two prolonged blasts on the whistle. You should ____.

A. sound two blasts and change course to the left
B. sound whistle signals only if you change course
C. sound only fog signals until the other vessel is sighted
D. not sound any whistle signals until the other vessel is sighted

4589. INT & INLAND

You are operating in restricted visibility and hear a signal of a rapidly ringing bell followed by the rapid sounding of a gong. It could be a ____.

A. 30-meter sail vessel at anchor
B. 150-meter power-driven vessel aground
C. vessel in distress
D. 300-meter power-driven vessel at anchor

4590. INT & INLAND

A vessel being towed, if manned, shall sound a fog signal of ____.

A. two short blasts
B. three short blasts
C. one prolonged and two short blasts
D. one prolonged and three short blasts

4591. INT & INLAND

A vessel using a traffic separation scheme shall ____.

A. only anchor in the separation zone
B. cross a traffic lane at as small an angle as possible
C. avoid anchoring in areas near the termination of the scheme
D. utilize the separation zone for navigating through the scheme if she is impeding other traffic due to her slower speed

4592. INT & INLAND

A proper look-out shall be maintained:

A. only at night
B. only during restricted visibility
C. at night and during restricted visibility
D. at all times

4593. INT & INLAND

Risk of collision may be deemed to exist ____.

A. if the compass bearing of an approaching vessel does NOT appreciably change
B. even when an appreciable bearing change is evident, particularly when approaching a vessel at close range
C. if you observe both sidelights of a vessel ahead for an extended period of time
D. All of the above

4594. INT & INLAND

The Rules state that certain factors are to be taken into account when determining safe speed. Those factors include ____.

A. state of wind, sea, and current, and the proximity of navigational hazards
B. maximum attainable speed of your vessel
C. temperature
D. aids to navigation that are available

4595. INT & INLAND

Which vessel, when anchored at night, would NOT be required to show anchor lights?

A. A power-driven vessel

B. A vessel on pilotage duty
C. A vessel dredging
D. A vessel restricted in her ability to maneuver

4596. DIAGRAM 13. INT & INLAND

A vessel displaying the dayshape is:

A. fishing
B. towing
C. being towed
D. anchored

4597. INT & INLAND

A vessel not under command shall display ____.

A. two red lights at night and two black balls during daylight
B. two red lights at night and three black balls during daylight
C. three red lights at night and two black balls during daylight
D. three red lights at night and three black balls during daylight

4598. INT & INLAND

A vessel engaged in fishing while at anchor shall sound a fog signal of ____.

A. one prolonged and two short blasts at two-minute intervals
B. one prolonged and three short blasts at two-minute intervals
C. a rapid ringing of the bell for five seconds at one-minute intervals
D. a sounding of the bell and gong at one-minute intervals

4599. INT & INLAND

Underway at night you see the red sidelight of a vessel well off your port bow. Which statement is TRUE?

A. You are required to alter course to the right.
B. You must stop engines.
C. You are on a collision course with the other vessel.
D. You may maintain course and speed.

4600. INT & INLAND

Which vessel would sound a fog signal consisting of the ringing of a bell for 5 seconds?

A. A vessel engaged in fishing, at anchor
B. A vessel restricted in its ability to maneuver, at anchor
C. A sailing vessel, at anchor
D. A sailing vessel becalmed

4601. INT & INLAND

A vessel towing a barge astern would show, at the stern ____.

A. only a sternlight
B. a towing light above the sternlight
C. two towing lights in a vertical line
D. two white lights in a vertical line

4602. INT & INLAND

A fog signal consisting of one prolonged blast followed by four short blasts would indicate the presence of a ____.

A. vessel being towed
B. fishing vessel engaged in trawling
C. vessel at anchor warning of her location
D. power-driven pilot vessel on station underway

4603. INT & INLAND

In addition to sidelights what light should a vessel being towed astern show?

A. A sternlight
B. A masthead light
C. Not under command lights
D. Range lights

4604. INT & INLAND

A pilot vessel may continue to sound an identity signal if she is ____.

A. aground
B. at anchor
C. not under command
D. being towed

4605. INT & INLAND

When two power-driven vessels are meeting head-on and there is a risk of collision, each shall ____.

A. stop her engines
B. alter course to starboard
C. sound the danger signal
D. back down

4606. INT & INLAND

A power-driven vessel when towing and the length of the tow exceeds 200 meters shall exhibit during daylight hours where they can best be seen which of the following shapes?

A. a diamond shape
B. two cones, apexes together
C. a black ball
D. one cone, apex upward

4607. INT & INLAND

What is the minimum length of vessels required to show two anchor lights?

A. 40 meters
B. 50 meters
C. 60 meters
D. 70 meters

4608. INT & INLAND

A vessel showing a rigid replica of the International Code flag A is engaged in ____.

A. diving operations
B. dredging
C. fishing
D. mineclearance operations

4609. INT & INLAND

In determining safe speed, all of the following must be taken into account EXCEPT the ____.

A. maximum horsepower of your vessel
B. presence of background lights at night
C. draft of your vessel
D. maneuverability of your vessel

4610. INT & INLAND

You are aboard the give-way vessel in a crossing situation. What should you NOT do in obeying the Rules?

A. Cross ahead of the stand-on vessel
B. Make a large course change to starboard
C. Slow your vessel
D. Back your vessel

4611. INT & INLAND

A vessel, which does not normally engage in towing operations, is towing a vessel in distress. She ____.

A. need not show the lights for a vessel engaged in towing, if it is impractical to do so
B. may show the lights for a vessel not under command
C. must show a yellow light above the sternlight
D. must show the lights for a vessel towing

4612. INT & INLAND

An all-around flashing yellow light may be exhibited by a(n) ____.

A. vessel laying cable
B. vessel towing a submerged object
C. vessel not under command
D. air-cushion vessel

4613. INT & INLAND

Working lights shall be used to illuminate the decks of a vessel ____.

A. over 100 meters at anchor
B. not under command
C. constrained by her draft
D. Any of the above

4614. INT & INLAND

Which vessel may show identifying lights when not actually engaged in her occupation?

A. A fishing vessel
B. A pilot vessel
C. A mineclearance vessel
D. None of the above

4615. INT & INLAND

A pilot vessel may continue to sound an identity signal if she is ____.

A. underway, but not making way
B. aground
C. being towed
D. not engaged in pilotage duty

4616. INT & INLAND

If your vessel is the stand-on vessel in a crossing situation ____.

A. you must keep your course and speed
B. you may change course and speed as the other vessel must keep clear
C. the other vessel must keep her course and speed
D. both vessels must keep their course and speed

4617. INT & INLAND

A vessel proceeding along a narrow channel shall ____.

A. avoid crossing the channel at right angles
B. not overtake any vessels within the channel
C. keep as near as safe and practicable to the limit of the channel on her starboard side
D. when nearing a bend in the channel, sound a long blast of the whistle

4618. INT & INLAND

Which vessel would exhibit sidelights when underway and not making way?

A. A vessel towing astern
B. A vessel trawling
C. A vessel not under command

D. A vessel engaged in dredging operations

4619. INT & INLAND
Which vessel is NOT to impede the passage of a vessel which can only navigate safely within a narrow channel?

A. Any vessel less than 20 m in length
B. Any sailing vessel
C. A vessel engaged in fishing
D. All of the above

4620. INT & INLAND
A tug is towing three manned barges in line in fog. The second vessel of the tow should sound ____.

A. no fog signal
B. one short blast
C. one prolonged and three short blasts
D. one prolonged and two short blasts

4621. INT & INLAND
The steering and sailing rules for vessels in restricted visibility apply to vessels ____.

A. in sight of one another in fog
B. navigating in or near an area of restricted visibility
C. only if they are showing special purpose lights
D. only if they have operational radar

4622. INT & INLAND
The Navigation Rules state that a vessel shall be operated at a safe speed at all times so that she can be stopped within ____.

A. the distance of visibility
B. 1/2 the distance of visibility
C. a distance appropriate to the existing circumstances and conditions
D. the distance that it would require for the propeller to go from full ahead to full astern

4623. INT & INLAND
A towing vessel 35 meters in length, with a tow 100 meters astern, must show a minimum of how many masthead lights?

A. 1
B. 2
C. 3
D. 4

4624. DIAGRAM 56. INT & INLAND
A vessel displaying the lights shown could be a vessel ____.

A. towing a barge alongside
B. underway and laying cable
C. at anchor and dredging
D. underway and carrying dangerous cargo

4625. INT & INLAND
What must be TRUE in order for a stand-on vessel to take action to avoid collision by her maneuver alone?

A. She must be in sight of the give-way vessel.
B. There must be risk of collision.
C. She must determine that the give-way vessel is not taking appropriate action.
D. All of the above

4626. INT & INLAND
A vessel being towed astern, where the length of the tow exceeds 200 meters, will exhibit ____.

A. two balls in a vertical line
B. a diamond shape where it can best be seen
C. a ball on each end of the tow
D. no dayshape

4627. DIAGRAM 6. INT & INLAND
While underway you sight a vessel displaying the dayshapes shown. You should ____.

A. contact the vessel on VHF radio-telephone
B. provide assistance, the other vessel is in distress
C. stay clear, the other vessel cannot get out of the way
D. stop your vessel and sound passing signals

4628. DIAGRAM 35. INT & INLAND
A sailing vessel displaying the dayshape shown is indicating that she is ____.

A. being propelled by power as well as sail
B. on a starboard tack
C. close-hauled and has difficulty maneuvering
D. fishing as well as sailing

4629. INT & INLAND
For a stand-on vessel to take action to avoid collision she shall, if possible, NOT ____.

A. decrease speed
B. increase speed
C. turn to port for a vessel on her port side
D. turn to starboard for a vessel on her port side

4630. INT & INLAND
You hear the fog signal of another vessel forward of your beam. Risk of collision may exist. You MUST ____.

A. reduce speed to bare steerageway
B. stop your engines
C. begin a radar plot
D. All of the above

4631. INT & INLAND
Two barges are being pushed ahead by a tugboat. Which statement is TRUE concerning lights on the barges?

A. Each vessel should show sidelights.
B. Each vessel should show at least one white light.
C. The barges should be lighted as separate units.
D. The barges should be lighted as one vessel.

4632. INT & INLAND
The Rules state that a seaplane shall:

A. not be regarded as a vessel
B. in general, keep well clear of all vessels
C. proceed at a slower speed than surrounding vessels
D. when making way, show the lights for a vessel not under command

4633. INT & INLAND
If practical, when shall a manned vessel being towed sound her fog signal?

A. Immediately before the towing vessel sounds hers
B. Immediately after the towing vessel sounds hers
C. As close to the mid-cycle of the towing vessel's signals as possible
D. At any time as long as the interval is correct

4634. INT & INLAND
Your tug is underway at night and NOT towing. What light(s) should your vessel show aft to other vessels coming up from astern?

A. One white light
B. Two white lights
C. One white light and one yellow light
D. One white light and two yellow lights

4635. INT & INLAND
A vessel conducting mineclearing operations will show ____.

A. three balls in a vertical line
B. two balls in a vertical line
C. one ball near the foremast and one ball at each fore yard
D. one diamond near the foremast head and one ball at each fore yard

4636. INT & INLAND
A vessel sailing shall keep out of the way of all of the following vessels except a vessel ____.

A. not under command
B. engaged on pilotage duty
C. restricted in her ability to maneuver
D. engaged in fishing

4637. INT & INLAND
Which statement is TRUE concerning a vessel under oars?

A. She must show a sternlight.
B. She is allowed to show the same lights as a sailing vessel.
C. She must show a fixed all-around white light.
D. She must show a dayshape of a black cone.

4638. INT & INLAND
A power-driven vessel is underway and fishing with trolling lines. This vessel ____.

A. must keep out of the way of sailing vessels
B. must sound a one prolonged, two short blasts signal in restricted visibility
C. is the stand-on vessel when overtaking power-driven vessels
D. All of the above

4639. INT & INLAND
At night you sight a vessel displaying a single green light. This is a ____.

A. vessel at anchor
B. small motorboat underway
C. vessel drifting
D. sailing vessel

4640. INT & INLAND
When two power-driven vessels are crossing, which vessel is the stand-on vessel?

A. The vessel which is to starboard of the other vessel
B. The vessel which is to port of the other vessel
C. The larger vessel
D. The vessel that sounds the first whistle signal

4641. INT & INLAND
Which vessel must exhibit forward and after white masthead lights when making way?

A. A 75-meter vessel restricted in her ability to maneuver
B. A 100-meter sailing vessel
C. A 150-meter vessel engaged in fishing
D. A 45-meter vessel engaged in towing

4642. INT & INLAND
By radar alone, you detect a vessel ahead on a collision course, about 3 miles distant. Your radar plot shows this to be a meeting situation. You should ____.

A. turn to port
B. turn to starboard
C. maintain course and speed and sound the danger signal
D. maintain course and speed and sound no signal

4643. INT & INLAND
A sailing vessel underway at night may show ____.

A. a red light over a green light at the masthead
B. a green light over a red light at the masthead
C. two white lights in a vertical line at the stern
D. an all-around white light at the bow

4644. INT & INLAND
A vessel engaged in trawling will show identification lights of ____.

A. a red light over a white light
B. a white light over a red light
C. a green light over a white light
D. two red lights in a vertical line

4645. INT & INLAND
What is required of a vessel navigating near an area of restricted visibility?

A. A power-driven vessel shall have her engines ready for immediate maneuver
B. She must sound appropriate sound signals
C. If she detects another vessel by radar, she shall determine if risk of collision exists
D. All of the above

4646. INT & INLAND
By night, you sight the lights of a vessel engaged in underwater operations. If an obstruction exists on the port side of the vessel, it will be marked by ____.

A. a floodlight
B. two red lights in a vertical line
C. a single red light
D. any visible lights

4647. DIAGRAM 65. INT & INLAND
At night a vessel displaying the lights shown is ____.

A. fishing
B. anchored
C. being towed
D. drifting

4649. INT & INLAND
Which vessel may carry her sidelights and sternlight in one combined lantern?

A. A 10-meter power-driven vessel
B. A 15-meter vessel propelled by sail and machinery
C. A 10-meter sailing vessel
D. All of the above

4650. INT & INLAND
Which lights would be shown at night by a vessel which is restricted in her ability to deviate from her course?

A. Three red lights in a vertical line
B. Three white lights in a vertical line
C. Three lights in a vertical line, the highest and lowest white and the middle red
D. Three lights in a vertical line, the highest and lowest red and the middle white

4651. INT & INLAND
Which vessel is the stand-on vessel when two vessels crossing in fog are NOT in sight of one another?

A. The vessel which has the other on her own starboard side
B. The vessel which has the other on her own port side
C. The one which hears the other's fog signal first

D. Neither vessel is the stand-on vessel.

4652. DIAGRAM 18. INT & INLAND
A vessel displaying the dayshapes shown is
____.

A. towing astern with a tow greater than
200 meters in length
B. not under command
C. dredging
D. carrying dangerous cargo

4653. DIAGRAM 34. INT & INLAND
A vessel showing this dayshape ____.

A. has a tow which exceeds 200 meters in
length
B. is engaged in surveying or underwater
work
C. is not under command
D. is fishing

4654. INT & INLAND
A vessel engaged in fishing shall keep out
of the way of a vessel ____.

A. under sail
B. restricted in her ability to maneuver
C. crossing a channel
D. All of the above

4655. INT & INLAND
Which vessels shall turn off their sidelights?

A. All vessels that are not under command
B. All fishing vessels that are not making
way
C. All sailing vessels which are becalmed
D. All vessels engaged in underwater oper-
ations

4656. INT & INLAND
A vessel fishing at night, with gear extending more than 150 meters horizontally outward, will show in the direction of the gear
____.

A. one white light
B. two vertical white lights
C. one yellow light
D. two vertical yellow lights

4657. INT & INLAND
In restricted visibility, a vessel which detects by radar alone the presence of another vessel shall determine if a close-quarters
situation is developing or risk of collision
exists. If so, she shall ____.

A. sound the danger signal

B. when taking action, make only course
changes
C. avoid altering course toward a vessel
abaft the beam
D. All of the above

4658. INT & INLAND
A 60-meter vessel which is trawling is
required to show how many white
masthead lights at night?

A. 1
B. 2
C. 3
D. 4

4659. INT & INLAND
A vessel servicing a pipeline during the day
shall display ____.

A. three black shapes in a vertical line; the
highest and lowest are balls, and the middle one is a diamond
B. three shapes in a vertical line; the highest and lowest are red balls, and the middle
one is a white diamond
C. three black balls in a vertical line
D. two black balls in a vertical line

4660. INT & INLAND
In fog you observe your radar and
determine that risk of collision exists with a
vessel which is 2 miles off your port bow.
You should ____.

A. stop your engines
B. sound the danger signal at two-minute
intervals
C. hold course and speed until the other
vessel is sighted
D. take avoiding action as soon as possible

4661. INT & INLAND
Which statement is TRUE concerning a
towing vessel which, due to the nature of
her work, is unable to keep out of the way
of another vessel?

A. By day, she shall carry a black
cylinder shape.
B. By day, she shall carry two black balls in a
vertical line.
C. By night, she would show the same
lights as a vessel not under command.
D. By day, she would show the same
shapes as a vessel restricted in her ability to
maneuver.

4662. DIAGRAM 12. INT & INLAND
Vessel A (towing) and vessel B are meeting
as shown. In this situation, which
statement is TRUE?

A. Both vessels should alter course to star-
board and pass port to port.
B. Both vessels should alter course to port
and pass starboard to starboard.
C. Vessel A should hold course while vessel
B alters course to starboard.
D. Vessel A is the stand-on in this situation.

4663. INT & INLAND
Which statement is TRUE regarding equipment for bell and gong signals?

A. A vessel of less than 12 meters in length
need not have any sound signaling equipment.
B. Manual sounding of the signals must always be possible.
C. Any vessel over 12 meters in length
must be provided with a gong.
D. Signals must be able to be sounded
manually and automatically.

4664. INT & INLAND
You are approaching a narrow channel.
You see a vessel that can only be navigated
safely within the channel. You MUST ____.

A. hold your course and speed
B. sound the danger signal
C. not cross the channel if you might
impede the other vessel
D. initiate an exchange of passing signals

4665. INT & INLAND
What is the minimum sound-signaling
equipment required aboard a vessel 10
meters in length?

A. Any means of making an efficient sound
signal
B. A bell only
C. A whistle only
D. A bell and a whistle

4666. INT & INLAND
Which vessel must have a gong, or other
equipment which will make the sound of a
gong?

A. A sailing vessel
B. Any vessel over 50 meters
C. A power-driven vessel over 75 m
D. Any vessel over 100 meters

4667. INT & INLAND
While underway and in sight of another vessel, less than one half mile away, you put your engines on astern propulsion. Which statement concerning whistle signals is TRUE?

A. You need not sound any whistle signals.
B. You must sound one blast if backing to starboard.
C. You must sound whistle signals only if the vessels are meeting.
D. You must sound three short blasts on the whistle.

4668. DIAGRAM 42. INT & INLAND
Two power-driven vessels are crossing as shown. Vessel A sounds three short blasts on the whistle. This signal means that vessel A ____.

A. intends to hold course and speed
B. is uncertain about the actions of B
C. proposes to cross ahead of the other vessel
D. is backing engines

4669. INT & INLAND
Which statement is TRUE concerning the light used with whistle signals?

A. Use of such a light is required.
B. Its purpose is to supplement short blasts of the whistle.
C. The light shall have the same characteristics as a masthead light.
D. All of the above

4670. INT & INLAND
What determines if a vessel is restricted in her ability to maneuver?

A. Whether or not all of the vessel's control equipment is in working order
B. The vessel's draft in relation to the available depth of water
C. Whether the nature of the vessel's work limits maneuverability required by the Rules
D. Whether or not the vessel is the give-way vessel in a meeting situation

4671. INT & INLAND
Which statement is true concerning the light used to accompany whistle signals?

A. It is only used to supplement short blasts of the whistle.
B. It is mandatory to use such a light.
C. The light shall have the same characteristics as a masthead light.

D. All of the above

4672. INT & INLAND
Which statement is TRUE concerning the danger signal?

A. Only the stand-on vessel can sound the danger signal.
B. Radio transmissions may be used in place of the danger signal.
C. A vessel in doubt as to the other vessel's intentions must sound the danger signal.
D. The danger signal consists of 5 or more prolonged blasts of the whistle.

4673. INT & INLAND
Which vessel may sound the danger signal?

A. Either vessel in a meeting situation
B. The give-way vessel in a crossing situation
C. A vessel at anchor
D. All of the above

4674. INT & INLAND
You are on watch in fog. Which vessel is in sight?

A. A vessel that you can see from the bridge
B. A radar target of which you have determined the course and speed
C. A vessel from which you can hear the fog signal
D. All of the above

4675. INT & INLAND
In a meeting situation, which vessel may sound the danger signal?

A. Stand-on vessel
B. Give-way vessel
C. Either vessel
D. Neither vessel

4676. INT & INLAND
You are underway in a narrow channel and are being overtaken by a vessel astern. The overtaking vessel sounds a signal indicating her intention to pass you on your starboard side. If such an action appears dangerous, you should sound ____.

A. one prolonged followed by one short blast
B. one prolonged, one short, one prolonged, and one short blast in that order
C. five short and rapid blasts
D. three short and rapid blasts

4677. DIAGRAM 32. INT & INLAND
You are on vessel A, as shown and hear vessel B sound a signal indicating his intention to overtake you. You feel it is not safe for vessel B to overtake you at the present time. You should ____.

A. sound two short blasts
B. sound five or more short and rapid blasts
C. not answer the whistle signal from vessel B
D. sound three blasts of the whistle

4678. INT & INLAND
Which is a light signal authorized by the Secretary of the Navy as an additional navigational light for a ship of war?

A. Intermittent flashing amber (yellow) beacon for submarines
B. Green masthead and yardarm lights indicating mine clearance operations
C. Red-white-red lights in a vertical line for a carrier, launching aircraft
D. Yellow flares indicating torpedo firing exercises

4680. INT & INLAND
Dayshapes must be displayed ____.

A. between sunset and sunrise
B. only between 8 AM and 4 PM
C. during daylight hours in any visibility
D. during daylight hours in unrestricted visibility only

4681. INT & INLAND
A vessel may exhibit lights other than those prescribed by the Rules as long as the additional lights ____.

A. are not the same color as either side light
B. have a lesser range of visibility than the prescribed lights
C. do not impair the visibility or distinctive character of the prescribed lights
D. All of the above

4682. INT & INLAND
A vessel may exhibit lights other than those prescribed by the Rules as long as the additional lights ____.

A. do not interfere with the keeping of a proper look-out
B. do not impair the visibility or distinctive character of the prescribed lights
C. cannot be mistaken for the lights specified elsewhere in the Rules
D. All of the above

4683. INT & INLAND

The sternlight shall be positioned such that it will show from dead astern to how many degrees on each side of the stern of the vessel?

A. 135.0°
B. 112.5°
C. 67.5°
D. 22.5°

4684. INT & INLAND

You see a red sidelight bearing 315°. The vessel may be heading ____.

A. northwest (315°)
B. east (090°)
C. southwest (225°)
D. west (270°)

4685. INT & INLAND

What does the word *breadth* mean?

A. Greatest breadth
B. Molded breadth
C. Breadth on the main deck
D. Breadth at the load waterline

4686. INT & INLAND

If underway in low visibility and sounding fog signals, what changes would you make in the fog signal IMMEDIATELY upon losing the power plant and propulsion?

A. Begin sounding one prolonged blast followed by two short blasts at two-minute intervals.
B. Begin sounding one prolonged blast followed by three short blasts at two-minute intervals.
C. Begin sounding two prolonged blasts at two-minute intervals.
D. No change should be made in the fog signal.

4687. INT & INLAND

A vessel engaged in fishing while at anchor shall sound a fog signal of ____.

A. one prolonged and three short blasts at one minute intervals
B. a rapid ringing of the bell for five seconds at one minute intervals
C. one prolonged and two short blasts at two minute intervals
D. a sounding of the bell and gong at one minute intervals

4688. INT & INLAND

What is the fog signal for a vessel 75 meters in length, restricted in her ability to maneuver, at anchor?

A. One prolonged blast followed by two short blasts at intervals of not more than two minutes
B. Five second ringing of a bell at intervals of not more than one minute
C. Four short blasts at intervals of not more than two minutes
D. Five second ringing of a bell and five second sounding of a gong at intervals of not more than one minute

4689. INT & INLAND

Which vessel sounds the same fog signal when underway or at anchor?

A. A sailing vessel
B. A vessel constrained by her draft
C. A vessel restricted in her ability to maneuver
D. A vessel not under command

4690. INT & INLAND

Which vessel would sound a fog signal consisting of the ringing of a bell for 5 seconds?

A. A vessel engaged in fishing, at anchor
B. A vessel restricted in its ability to maneuver, at anchor
C. A sailing vessel, at anchor
D. All of the above

4691. INT & INLAND

A 200-meter vessel is aground in fog. Which signal is optional?

A. A bell signal
B. A whistle signal
C. A gong signal
D. All of the above are mandatory.

4692. INT & INLAND

What is NOT a vessel restricted in her ability to maneuver?

A. A vessel engaged in laying submarine cable
B. A vessel towing with limited maneuverability due to a large unwieldy tow
C. A deep-draft vessel that can only navigate in a dredged channel
D. A towing vessel underway with a fuel barge alongside and taking on fuel

4693. INT & INLAND

A 200-meter vessel is aground in restricted visibility. Which signal is optional?

A. A whistle signal
B. A gong signal
C. A bell signal
D. All of the above are optional.

4694. INT & INLAND

Which statement is TRUE concerning fog signals?

A. All fog signals for sailing vessels are to be given at intervals of not more than one minute.
B. A vessel aground may sound a whistle signal.
C. A vessel not under command sounds the same fog signal as a vessel towed.
D. The identity signal of a pilot vessel is the only fog signal sounded by such a vessel.

4695. INT & INLAND

While underway in fog, you hear a vessel ahead sound two short blasts on the whistle. You should ____.

A. not sound any whistle signals until the other vessel is sighted
B. sound only fog signals until the other vessel is sighted
C. sound whistle signals only if you change course
D. sound two short blasts and change course to the left

4696. INT & INLAND

You are underway in fog when you hear the rapid ringing of a bell for five seconds followed by the sounding of a gong for five seconds. This signal indicates a vessel ____.

A. engaged in pair trawling
B. fishing while making no way through the water
C. more than 100 meters in length, at anchor
D. engaged on pilotage duty

4697. INT & INLAND

A tug is towing three barges astern in restricted visibility. The second vessel of the tow should sound ____.

A. one prolonged and two short blasts
B. one prolonged and three short blasts
C. one short blast
D. no fog signal

4699. INT & INLAND
What is the identity signal which may be sounded by a vessel engaged on pilotage duty in fog?

A. 2 short blasts
B. 3 short blasts
C. 4 short blasts
D. 5 short blasts

4700. INT & INLAND
What does the word length refer to?

A. Length between the perpendiculars
B. Length overall
C. Waterline length
D. Register length

4701. INT & INLAND
A fog signal of one prolonged blast followed by four short blasts would mean the presence of a _____.

A. vessel being towed
B. power-driven pilot vessel on station underway
C. fishing vessel trawling
D. vessel at anchor warning of her location

4702. INT & INLAND
You are heading due east (090°) and observe a vessel's red sidelight on your port beam. The vessel may be heading _____.

A. northwest (315°)
B. southeast (135°)
C. northeast (045°)
D. southwest (225°)

4703. INT & INLAND
A towing light is a yellow light having the same characteristics as a(n) _____.

A. special flashing light
B. anchor light
C. sternlight
D. masthead light

4704. INT & INLAND
The masthead light may be located at other than the fore and aft centerline on a vessel _____.

A. less than 50 meters in length
B. less than 20 meters in length
C. of special construction
D. engaged in trolling

4705. INT & INLAND
In complying with the Rules, of what must the mariner take due regard?

A. Limited backing power of his vessel
B. Radar information about nearby vessels
C. The occupation of the other vessel, if known
D. All of the above

4706. INT & INLAND
A flashing light is a light that _____.

A. flashes at regular intervals at a frequency of 120 flashes or more per minute
B. is yellow in color
C. is visible over an arc of the horizon of not less than 180° nor more than 225°
D. All of the above

4707. INT & INLAND
While underway at night you are coming up on a vessel from astern. Which light(s) would you expect to see?

A. A sternlight only
B. Two masthead lights
C. Both sidelights and the sternlight
D. Sidelights only

4708. DIAGRAM 52. INT & INLAND
At night, a vessel displaying the lights shown is _____.

A. at anchor
B. aground
C. underway
D. dredging

4709. DIAGRAM 52. INT & INLAND
At night, a vessel displaying the lights shown is _____.

A. aground
B. underway
C. at anchor
D. transferring dangerous cargo

4710. INT & INLAND
Which vessel would exhibit sidelights when underway and not making way?

A. A vessel engaged in fishing
B. A vessel not under command
C. A vessel engaged in dredging
D. A power-driven vessel

4711. INT & INLAND
Which vessel would exhibit sidelights when underway and not making way?

A. A vessel trawling
B. A vessel not under command
C. A pilot vessel
D. A vessel engaged in dredging

4713. INT & INLAND
What equipment for fog signals is required for a vessel 20 m in length?

A. Whistle and bell only
B. Whistle only
C. Bell only
D. Whistle, bell, and gong

4714. INT & INLAND
Which vessel would exhibit sidelights when underway and not making way?

A. A vessel not under command
B. A vessel towing by pushing ahead
C. A vessel engaged in dredging
D. A vessel trawling

4715. INT & INLAND
What is a vessel restricted in her ability to maneuver?

A. A deep-draft vessel that can only navigate in a dredged channel
B. A vessel fishing with a bottom trawl that must remain on course
C. A large tanker that is being towed as a dead ship to dry dock
D. A vessel laying revetment mats to provide bank protection along a channel

4716. INT & INLAND
Which dayshape should a vessel being towed exhibit if the tow EXCEEDS 200 meters?

A. A cone, apex downward
B. A cone, apex upward
C. A diamond
D. A ball

4717. INT & INLAND
A sailing vessel underway at night MAY show _____.

A. a green light over a red light
B. a red light over a white light
C. two white lights at the stern
D. None of the above

4718. DIAGRAM 56. INT & INLAND
A vessel displaying the lights shown could be a vessel _____.

A. fishing at anchor
B. dredging while underway
C. transferring dangerous cargo at a berth
D. restricted in her ability to maneuver, underway but not making way

4719. DIAGRAM 68. INT & INLAND
The lights shown mean that another vessel should pass no closer than ____.

A. 500 meters
B. 1000 meters
C. 1500 meters
D. 2000 meters

4721. INT & INLAND
Which vessel when anchored at night, would not be required to show anchor lights?

A. A vessel engaged in underwater operations
B. A vessel engaged in mine clearance
C. A vessel engaged on pilotage duty
D. A vessel engaged in survey operations

4722. INT & INLAND
Which vessel, when anchored at night, is not required to show anchor lights?

A. A power-driven vessel
B. A vessel engaged in survey operations
C. A vessel engaged on pilotage duty
D. A vessel engaged in fishing

4723. DIAGRAM 45. INT & INLAND
You see a vessel displaying ONLY the lights shown. This could be a ____.

A. vessel engaged in fishing at anchor
B. pilot vessel on pilotage duty
C. vessel engaged in launching or recovering aircraft
D. power-driven vessel underway

4724. DIAGRAM 65. INT & INLAND
At night, a vessel displaying the lights shown is ____.

A. trawling
B. not under command
C. anchored
D. drifting

4725. INT & INLAND
What is the minimum sound signaling equipment required aboard a vessel 14 meters in length?

A. Any means of making an efficient sound signal
B. A bell only
C. A whistle only
D. A bell and a whistle

4726. INT & INLAND
A tug is towing three unmanned barges astern in fog. The third vessel of the tow should sound ____.

A. no fog signal
B. one short blast
C. one prolonged and three short blasts
D. one prolonged, one short, and one prolonged blast

4728. INT & INLAND
Which statement is TRUE, according to the Rules?

A. A vessel engaged in fishing shall keep out of the way of a sailing vessel.
B. A vessel not under command shall keep out of the way of a vessel engaged in fishing.
C. A vessel engaged in fishing while underway shall, so far as possible, keep out of the way of a vessel restricted in her ability to maneuver.
D. A vessel not under command shall keep out of the way of a vessel restricted in her ability to maneuver.

4729. INT & INLAND
Which statement is TRUE, according to the Rules?

A. A vessel engaged in fishing shall keep out of the way of a sailing vessel.
B. A vessel engaged in fishing while underway shall, so far as possible, keep out of the way of a vessel restricted in her ability to maneuver.
C. A vessel not under command shall keep out of the way of a vessel restricted in her ability to maneuver.
D. A vessel not under command shall keep out of the way of a vessel engaged in fishing.

4730. INLAND ONLY
Which of the following signals may be exhibited by a vessel trawling in close proximity to other fishing vessels?

A. Two white lights in a vertical line
B. A red light over a white light in a vertical line
C. Two fixed yellow lights in a vertical line
D. All of the above

4731. INT & INLAND
Additional light signals are provided in the Annexes to the Rules for vessels ____.

A. not under command
B. engaged in fishing
C. engaged in towing
D. under sail

4732. INLAND ONLY
Vessels engaged in fishing may show the additional signals described in Annex II to the Rules when they are ____.

A. trolling
B. fishing in a traffic separation zone
C. in close proximity to other vessels engaged in fishing
D. in a narrow channel

4733. INT & INLAND
A distress signal ____.

A. consists of 5 or more short blasts of the fog signal apparatus
B. consists of the raising and lowering of a large white flag
C. may be used separately or with other distress signals
D. is used to indicate doubt about another vessel's intentions

4734. INT & INLAND
A vessel may use any sound or light signals to attract the attention of another vessel as long as ____.

A. white lights are not used
B. red and green lights are not used
C. the signal cannot be mistaken for a signal authorized by the Rules
D. the vessel signals such intentions over the radiotelephone

4735. INT & INLAND
One of the signals, other than a distress signal, that can be used by a vessel to attract attention is a(n) ____.

A. red star shell
B. searchlight
C. burning barrel
D. orange smoke signal

4736. INT & INLAND
In restricted visibility a towed vessel must sound a fog signal when it is ____.

A. the last vessel in the tow
B. the last vessel in the tow and it is carrying a crew
C. manned, regardless of its position in the tow

D. None of the above are correct

4737. INT & INLAND
You are approaching a narrow channel. Another vessel in the channel can only be navigated safely in that channel. You should ____.

A. not cross the channel if you might impede the other vessel
B. hold your course and speed if she is on your port bow
C. sound three short blasts, and take all way off your vessel
D. sound two prolonged blasts followed by one short blast

4738. INT & INLAND
You are the stand-on vessel in a crossing situation. If you think the give-way vessel is NOT taking sufficient action to avoid collision, you should sound ____.

A. one short blast and maintain course
B. five short and rapid blasts
C. no signal and maneuver at will
D. two short blasts, alter to port, and pass astern

4739. INT & INLAND
Which statement is TRUE?

A. A vessel not under command shall keep out of the way of a vessel restricted in her ability to maneuver.
B. A vessel not under command shall keep out of the way of a vessel engaged in fishing.
C. A vessel engaged in fishing while underway shall, so far as possible, keep out of the way of a vessel restricted in her ability to maneuver.
D. A vessel engaged in fishing shall keep out of the way of a sailing vessel.

4745. INT & INLAND
You are approaching a narrow channel. Another vessel in the channel can only be navigated safely in that channel. You should ____.

A. hold your course and speed if he is on your port bow
B. sound three short blasts, and take all way off your vessel
C. not cross the channel if you might impede the other vessel
D. sound two prolonged blasts followed by one short blast

4770. INT & INLAND
While underway in fog, you hear a vessel ahead sound two prolonged blasts on the whistle. You should ____.

A. sound two blasts and change course to the left
B. sound whistle signals only if you change course
C. not sound any whistle signals until the other vessel is sighted
D. sound only fog signals until the other vessel is sighted

4780. INT & INLAND
You are the stand-on vessel in a crossing situation. If you think the give-way vessel is NOT taking sufficient action to avoid collision, you should sound ____.

A. the danger signal
B. two short blasts, alter to port, and pass astern
C. no signal and maneuver at will
D. one short blast and maintain course

4818. INT & INLAND
A vessel engaged in mineclearance operations shows special identity lights ____.

A. instead of the masthead lights
B. which mean that other vessels should not approach within 1000 meters
C. that are 225° green lights
D. All of the above

4819. DIAGRAM 87. INT & INLAND
Which breadth shown represents the breadth as defined in the Rules?

A. A
B. B
C. C
D. D

4820. INT & INLAND
You are about to cross a narrow channel when you see an approaching vessel that can only be navigated safely within the channel. You should:

A. cross the channel as you are the stand-on vessel
B. cross only if the vessel in the channel is approaching on your port side
C. not cross the channel if you might impede the other vessel
D. sound the danger signal

4825. INT & INLAND
What is a light signal authorized by the Secretary of the Navy as an additional navigational light for a ship of war?

A. Two yellow lights in a vertical line for a carrier launching aircraft
B. Green masthead and yardarm lights for a vessel engaged in mineclearing operations
C. Flashing amber beacon for submarines
D. Yellow flares indicating torpedo firing exercises

4826. INT & INLAND
According to the Navigation Rules, you may depart from the Rules when:

A. you do so to avoid immediate danger
B. no vessels are visible on radar
C. you are in a close-quarters situation
D. out of sight of land

4827. INT & INLAND
The Rules state that vessels may depart from the requirements of the Rules when ____.

A. operating in restricted visibility
B. operating in a narrow channel
C. necessary to avoid immediate danger
D. the Master enters it in the ship's log

4828. INT & INLAND
The Rules state that vessels may depart from the Rules when ____.

A. there are other vessels in the vicinity
B. operating in a traffic separation scheme
C. engaged in a situation involving more than two vessels
D. necessary to avoid immediate danger

4829. INT & INLAND
The term restricted visibility, when used in the Rules, refers to ____.

A. situations when you can see vessels on radar that you cannot see visually
B. visibility of less than half a mile
C. any condition where visibility is restricted
D. visibility where you cannot see shore

4830. INT & INLAND
The Navigation Rules define a vessel not under command as a vessel which:

A. from the nature of her work is unable to keep out of the way of another vessel

B. does not have a proper look-out
C. by taking action contrary to the Rules has created a special circumstance situation
D. through some exceptional circumstance is unable to maneuver as required by the Rules

4831. INT & INLAND
Which craft is a power-driven vessel under the Rules of the Road?

A. An auxiliary sailing vessel, using her engine
B. A canoe propelled by a small outboard motor
C. A trawler on her way to the fishing grounds
D. All of the above

4832. INT & INLAND
A vessel is in sight of another vessel when she ____.

A. can be observed by radar
B. has determined that risk of collision exists
C. is sounding a fog signal which can be heard on the other vessel
D. can be observed visually from the other vessel

4833. INT & INLAND
Which statement is TRUE concerning a vessel engaged in fishing?

A. The vessel is classified as restricted in her ability to maneuver
B. Her gear will not affect the vessel's maneuverability.
C. The vessel may be using nets, lines, or trawls.
D. She sounds the same fog signal as a vessel underway but stopped and making no way.

4834. INT & INLAND
To be considered engaged in fishing under the Rules, a vessel must be ____.

A. power-driven
B. showing lights or shapes for a vessel restricted in its ability to maneuver
C. using nets
D. using fishing apparatus which restricts maneuverability

4835. INT & INLAND
The word vessel, in the Rules, includes ____.

A. a barge permanently affixed to the shore
B. nondisplacement craft
C. a drilling unit attached to the Outer Continental Shelf
D. All of the above

4836. INT & INLAND
Which vessel is, by definition, unable to keep out of the way of another vessel?

A. Vessel engaged in fishing
B. Vessel not making way
C. Vessel sailing
D. Vessel restricted in her ability to maneuver

4837. INT & INLAND
A vessel restricted in her ability to maneuver is one which ____.

A. through some exceptional circumstance is unable to maneuver as required by the Rules
B. from the nature of her work is unable to maneuver as required by the Rules
C. due to adverse weather conditions is unable to maneuver as required by the Rules
D. has lost steering and is unable to maneuver

4838. INT & INLAND
What determines if a vessel is restricted in her ability to maneuver?

A. Whether or not all of the vessel's control equipment is in working order
B. The vessel's draft in relation to the available depth of water
C. Whether the vessel is operating in a narrow channel
D. The nature of the vessel's work, limiting maneuverability required by the Rules

4839. INT & INLAND
A vessel is considered to be restricted in her ability to maneuver under the Rules if she is ____.

A. at anchor
B. mineclearing
C. engaged in fishing
D. engaged in towing

4841. INT & INLAND
A vessel transferring cargo while underway is classified by the Rules as a vessel ____.

A. restricted in her ability to maneuver
B. in special circumstances
C. not under command
D. constrained by her draft

4842. INT & INLAND
Which vessel is underway according to the Rules?

A. A vessel made fast to a single point mooring buoy
B. A vessel engaged in towing, not making way
C. A pilot vessel at anchor
D. A vessel which has run aground

4843. INT & INLAND
According to the Rules, a vessel's length is her ____.

A. length between the perpendiculars
B. length along the waterline
C. length overall
D. registered length

4844. INT & INLAND
What does the word breadth mean in the Rules?

A. Breadth on the uppermost continuous deck
B. Molded breadth
C. Greatest breadth
D. Breadth at the load waterline

4845. DIAGRAM 86. INT & INLAND
What represents the length of a vessel as defined by the Rules?

A. A
B. B
C. C
D. D

4846. INT & INLAND
In determining safe speed, the Rules list all of the following as factors which must be taken into account EXCEPT the ____.

A. limitations of radar equipment
B. presence of background lights at night
C. maximum horsepower of your vessel
D. maneuverability of your vessel

4847. INT & INLAND
The rules require which factor to be taken into account when determining safe speed?

A. The construction of the vessel
B. The experience of the vessel's crew
C. The location of vessels detected by radar
D. All of the above

4848. INT & INLAND

The Rules state that certain factors are to be taken into account when determining safe speed. One of the factors is the _____.

A. radio communications that are available
B. maximum speed of your vessel
C. temperature
D. current

4849. INT & INLAND

Safe speed is defined as that speed where _____.

A. you can stop within your visibility range
B. the vessel is not subject to vibrations
C. you are traveling slower than surrounding vessels
D. you can take proper and effective action to avoid collision

4850. INT & INLAND

The Rules state that risk of collision shall be deemed to exist _____.

A. whenever two vessels are on opposite courses
B. whenever a vessel crosses ahead of the intended track of another vessel
C. if the bearing of an approaching vessel does not appreciably change
D. if one vessel approaches another so as to be overtaking

4851. INT & INLAND

In which situation would you consider a risk of collision to exist?

A. A vessel is one point on your starboard bow, range increasing, bearing changing slightly to the right.
B. A vessel is broad on your starboard beam, range decreasing, bearing changing rapidly to the right.
C. A vessel is two points abaft your port beam, range decreasing, bearing constant.
D. A vessel is on your starboard quarter, range increasing, bearing is constant.

4852. INT & INLAND

What is TRUE when operating in fog and other vessels are detected by radar?

A. You should make an ample change to port for a vessel crossing on the starboard bow.
B. You should maneuver in ample time if a close-quarters situation is developing.
C. You should determine the course and speed of all radar contacts at six minute intervals.

D. Long-range scanning will provide early warning of ALL other vessels within the radar's range.

4853. INT & INLAND

You are approaching another vessel on crossing courses. She is about one mile distant and is on your starboard bow. You believe she will cross ahead of you but she sounds a whistle signal of five short blasts. You should _____.

A. answer the signal and hold course and speed
B. reduce speed slightly
C. initiate a passing signal that will allow for a half mile clearance
D. make a large course change, and slow down if necessary

4854. INT & INLAND

You are approaching another vessel on crossing courses. She is approximately half a mile distant on your starboard bow. You believe she will cross ahead of you but she sounds a whistle signal of five short blasts. You should _____.

A. sound a signal of one prolonged blast
B. make a large course change
C. reduce speed slightly to make sure she will have room to pass
D. wait for another whistle signal from the other vessel

4855. INT & INLAND

Under the Rules, any vessel may slacken her speed, stop, or reverse her engines to _____.

A. create a crossing situation
B. allow more time to assess the situation
C. attract the attention of another vessel
D. All of the above

4856. INT & INLAND

When in sight of another vessel, any action taken to avoid collision must:

A. be accompanied by sound signals
B. not result in another close-quarters situation
C. include a speed change
D. All of the above

4857. INT & INLAND

A vessel approaching a narrow channel shall _____.

A. avoid crossing the channel if it impedes another vessel navigating in the channel

B. not overtake any vessels within the channel
C. keep as close as possible to the edge of the channel on her port side
D. anchor only in the middle of the channel

4858. INT & INLAND

When underway in a channel, you should if safe and practicable _____.

A. stay near the middle of the channel
B. keep to the starboard side of any vessels you meet
C. exchange whistle signals with any other vessels in the channel
D. keep to the side of the channel which lies to your starboard

4859. INT & INLAND

A sailing vessel is proceeding along a narrow channel and can safely navigate ONLY inside the channel. The sailing vessel approaches a vessel engaged in fishing in the narrow channel. Which statement is TRUE?

A. Each vessel should move to the edge of the channel on her port side.
B. The vessels are required to exchange signals.
C. The fishing vessel is directed not to impede the passage of the sailing vessel.
D. Each vessel should be displaying signals for a vessel constrained by her draft.

4860. INT & INLAND

A vessel engaged in mineclearance operations shows special identity lights _____.

A. in addition to the lights required for a power-driven vessel
B. which means that other vessels should not approach closer than 500 meters on either side of the vessel
C. that are green and show through an arc of the horizon of 225°
D. All of the above

4861. INT & INLAND

When navigating in thick fog with the radar on, you should _____.

A. station the look-out in the wheelhouse to keep a continuous watch on the radar
B. secure the sounding of fog signals until a vessel closes within five miles
C. station a look-out as low down and far forward as possible
D. keep the radar on the shortest available range for early detection of approaching vessels

4862. INT & INLAND

You are underway in thick fog. You have not determined if risk of collision exists. Which statement is TRUE?

A. Your speed must be reduced to bare steerageway.
B. A look-out is not required if the radar is on.
C. Fog signals are only required when a vessel is detected by radar.
D. The radar should always be kept on a short-range scale.

4863. INT & INLAND

A sailing vessel is proceeding along a narrow channel and can safely navigate ONLY inside the channel. The sailing vessel approaches a vessel engaged in fishing. Which statement is TRUE?

A. The fishing vessel must sound the danger signal.
B. The fishing vessel shall not impede the passage of the sailing vessel.
C. Each vessel should move to the edge of the channel on her port side.
D. Both vessels should be displaying the signal for a vessel restricted in her ability to maneuver.

4864. INT & INLAND

Which vessel shall NOT impede the passage of a vessel which can safely navigate only within a narrow channel or fairway?

A. A vessel dredging
B. A sailing vessel
C. A vessel servicing an aid to navigation
D. All of the above

4865. INT & INLAND

Your 15-meter vessel is crossing a narrow channel and a large cargo vessel to starboard is within the channel and crossing your course. You should _____.

A. hold your course and speed
B. sound the danger signal
C. keep out of the way of the cargo vessel
D. do not cross the channel

4866. INT & INLAND

If two sailing vessels are running free with the wind on the same side, which one must keep clear of the other?

A. The one with the wind closest abeam
B. The one to windward
C. The one to leeward

D. The one that sounds the first whistle signal

4868. INT & INLAND

Which statement is TRUE concerning two sailing vessels approaching each other?

A. The vessel making the most speed is the give-way vessel.
B. A sailing vessel overtaking another is the give-way vessel.
C. A sailing vessel seeing another to leeward on an undetermined tack shall hold her course.
D. All of the above

4869. INT & INLAND

Power-driven vessels must keep out of the way of sailing vessels except:

A. in a crossing situation
B. when they are making more speed than the power-driven vessel
C. when the sailing vessel is overtaking
D. on the Inland Waters of the United States

4870. INT & INLAND

When do the Rules require both vessels to change course?

A. Any time the danger signal is sounded
B. When two power-driven vessels are crossing and it is apparent to the stand-on vessel that the give-way vessel is not taking appropriate action
C. When two power-driven vessels are meeting head-on
D. All of the above

4871. INT & INLAND

Your vessel is NOT making way, but is not in any way disabled. Another vessel is approaching you on your starboard beam. Which statement is TRUE?

A. Your vessel is obligated to stay out of the way.
B. The other vessel must give way, since your vessel is stopped.
C. You should be showing the lights or shapes for a vessel not under command.
D. You should be showing the lights or shapes for a vessel restricted in her ability to maneuver.

4872. INT & INLAND

If you are the stand-on vessel in a crossing situation, you may take action to avoid collision by your maneuver alone. When may this action be taken?

A. As soon as you determine that risk of collision exists
B. Only when you have reached extremis
C. When it becomes apparent to you that the give-way vessel is not taking appropriate action
D. When you determine that your present course will cross ahead of the other vessel

4873. INT & INLAND

In a crossing situation on open waters, a sailing vessel shall keep out of the way of all the following vessels EXCEPT a vessel _____.

A. not under command
B. restricted in her ability to maneuver
C. engaged in towing
D. fishing

4874. INT & INLAND

What would be a special circumstance under the Rules?

A. Vessel at anchor
B. Two vessels meeting
C. Speed in fog
D. More than two vessels crossing

4875. INT & INLAND

In restricted visibility, a vessel being towed, if manned, shall sound a signal of _____.

A. one prolonged and three short blasts
B. one prolonged and two short blasts
C. three short blasts
D. two short blasts

4876. INT & INLAND

You are approaching a narrow channel. Another vessel in the channel can only be navigated safely in that channel. You should _____.

A. sound two prolonged blasts followed by one short blast
B. not cross the channel if you might impede the other vessel
C. sound three short blasts, and take all way off your vessel
D. hold your course and speed if he is on your port bow

4877. INT & INLAND

You are the stand-on vessel in a crossing situation. If you think the give-way vessel is NOT taking sufficient action to avoid collision, you should sound _____.

A. one short blast and maintain course

B. two short blasts, alter to port, and pass astern
C. the danger signal
D. no signal and maneuver at will

5000. INT & INLAND
While underway in fog, you hear a vessel ahead sound two prolonged blasts on the whistle. You should ____.

A. sound only fog signals until the other vessel is sighted
B. not sound any whistle signals until the other vessel is sighted
C. sound two blasts and change course to the left
D. sound whistle signals only if you change course

5100. INT & INLAND
Lighting requirements in inland waters are different from those for international waters for ____.

A. barges being towed astern
B. vessels not under command
C. vessels pushing ahead
D. All of the above

5150. INT & INLAND
There are two classes of vessels which do not have to comply with the rule regarding traffic separation schemes, to the extent necessary to carry out their work. One of those is a vessel ____.

A. engaged in fishing
B. towing another
C. servicing a navigational aid
D. on pilotage duty

5200. INT & INLAND
In a traffic separation scheme, when joining a traffic lane from the side, a vessel shall do so ____.

A. only in case of an emergency or to engage in fishing within the zone
B. as nearly as practical at right angles to the general direction of traffic flow
C. at as small an angle as possible
D. only to anchor within the zone

5300. INT & INLAND
A traffic separation zone is that part of a traffic separation scheme which:

A. is located between the scheme and the nearest land
B. separates traffic proceeding in one direc-

tion from traffic proceeding in the opposite direction
C. is designated as an anchorage area
D. contains all the traffic moving in the same direction

5350. INT & INLAND
A vessel using a traffic separation scheme shall ____.

A. avoid anchoring in areas near the termination of the scheme
B. avoid crossing traffic lanes, but if obliged to do so, shall cross on as small an angle as is practical
C. only anchor in the separation zone
D. use the separation zone for navigating through the scheme if she is hindering other traffic due to her slower speed

5400. INT & INLAND
A vessel using a traffic separation scheme shall NOT ____.

A. cross a traffic lane
B. engage in fishing the separation zone
C. proceed in an inappropriate traffic lane
D. enter the separation zone

5500. INT & INLAND
A vessel using a traffic separation scheme shall ____.

A. only anchor in the separation zone
B. avoid crossing traffic lanes, but if obliged to do so, shall cross on a heading at as small an angle as is practical
C. avoid anchoring in areas near the termination of the scheme
D. use the separation zone for navigation through the scheme if she is hindering other traffic due to her slower speed

6000. INT & INLAND
While underway in fog, you hear a vessel ahead sound two prolonged blasts on the whistle. You should ____.

A. sound two blasts and change course to the left
B. sound only fog signals until the other vessel is sighted
C. sound whistle signals only if you change course
D. not sound any whistle signals until the other vessel is sighted

6500. INT & INLAND
A towing vessel and her tow are severely restricted in their ability to change course.

When making way, the towing vessel will show ONLY ____.

A. the masthead lights for a towing vessel
B. the lights for a vessel restricted in her ability to maneuver
C. sidelights, stern light, and towing light
D. All of the above.

6510. INT & INLAND
You hear the fog signal of another vessel forward of your beam. Risk of collision may exist. You MUST ____.

A. take all way off, if necessary
B. stop your engines
C. begin a radar plot
D. All of the above

6520. INT & INLAND
A fog signal of one short, one prolonged, and one short blast may be sounded by a ____.

A. vessel not under command
B. vessel at anchor
C. vessel towing
D. All of the above

6530. INT & INLAND
You hear the fog signal of another vessel forward of your beam. Risk of collision may exist. You MUST ____.

A. stop your engines
B. take all way off, if necessary
C. begin a radar plot
D. All of the above

6540. INT & INLAND
A vessel may enter a traffic separation zone ____.

A. in an emergency
B. to engage in fishing within the zone
C. to cross the traffic separation scheme
D. All of the above

6550. INT & INLAND
In a traffic separation scheme, when joining a traffic lane from the side, a vessel shall do so ____.

A. at as small an angle as possible
B. as nearly as practical at right angles to the general direction of traffic flow
C. only in case of an emergency or to engage in fishing within the zone
D. never

6560. INT & INLAND

A vessel using a traffic separation scheme is forbidden to ____.

A. proceed through an inappropriate traffic lane
B. engage in fishing in the separation zone
C. cross a traffic lane
D. enter the separation zone, even in a emergency

6570. INT & INLAND

A traffic separation zone is that part of a traffic separation scheme which:

A. is between the scheme and the nearest land
B. contains all the traffic moving in one direction
C. is designated as an anchorage area
D. separates traffic proceeding in one direction from traffic proceeding in the opposite direction

8000. INT ONLY

To indicate that a vessel is constrained by her draft, a vessel may display, in a vertical line, ____.

A. three 360° red lights
B. two 225° red lights
C. three 360° blue lights
D. two 225° blue lights

8001. INT ONLY

A power-driven vessel pushing ahead or towing alongside displays navigation lights and ____.

A. two all-around red lights in a vertical line
B. two yellow towing lights in a vertical line
C. two white masthead lights in a vertical line
D. two lights on the stern, one yellow and one white

8002. INT ONLY

Which statement is true concerning a vessel constrained by her draft?

A. She must be a power-driven vessel.
B. She is not under command.
C. She may be a vessel being towed.
D. She is hampered because of her work.

8004. INT ONLY

When moving from a berth alongside a quay (wharf), a vessel must sound:

A. three short blasts
B. a long blast
C. a prolonged blast
D. No signal is required.

8005. INT ONLY

You are in charge of a 250-meter freight vessel constrained by her draft proceeding down a narrow channel. There is a vessel engaged in fishing on your starboard bow half a mile away. According to Rule 9, which statement is TRUE?

A. You are not to impede the fishing vessel.
B. If you are in doubt as to the fishing vessel's intentions you may sound at least five short and rapid blasts on the whistle.
C. You are to slow to bare steerageway until clear of the fishing vessel.
D. You must sound one prolonged blast to alert the fishing vessel.

8006. INT ONLY

The International Rules of the Road apply ____.

A. to all waters which are not inland waters
B. only to waters outside the territorial waters of the United States
C. only to waters where foreign vessels travel
D. upon the high seas and connecting waters navigable by seagoing vessels

8007. INT ONLY

A towing light is ____.

A. shown at the bow
B. white in color
C. shown in addition to the sternlight
D. an all-around light

8008. INT ONLY

In a narrow channel, an overtaking vessel which intends to pass on the other vessel's port side would sound:

A. one prolonged followed by two short blasts
B. one short blast
C. two short blasts
D. two prolonged followed by two short blasts

8009. INT ONLY

You are underway on the high seas in restricted visibility. You hear a fog signal of one prolonged and two short blasts. It

could be any of the following EXCEPT a vessel ____.

A. minesweeping
B. engaged in fishing
C. constrained by her draft
D. being towed

8010. INT ONLY

A vessel displaying three red lights in a vertical line is ____.

A. not under command
B. aground
C. dredging
D. constrained by her draft

8011. INT ONLY

At night, a power-driven vessel underway of less than 7 meters in length where its maximum speed does not exceed 7 knots may show, as a minimum, ____.

A. sidelights and a sternlight
B. the lights required for a vessel more than 7 meters in length
C. sidelights only
D. one all-around white light

8012. INT ONLY

In a narrow channel, a signal of intent which must be answered by the other vessel, is sounded by a vessel ____.

A. meeting another head-on
B. crossing the course of another
C. overtaking another
D. Any of the above

8013. INT ONLY

When two vessels are in sight of one another, all of the following signals may be given EXCEPT ____.

A. a light signal of at least five short and rapid flashes
B. four short whistle blasts
C. one prolonged, one short, one prolonged and one short whistle blast
D. two short whistle blasts

8014. INT ONLY

A power-driven vessel leaving a quay or wharf must sound what signal?

A. Three short blasts
B. A long blast
C. A prolonged blast
D. No signal is required.

8015. INT & INLAND

Lighting requirements in inland waters are different from those in international waters for ____.

A. barges being pushed ahead
B. vessels constrained by their draft
C. vessels towing by pushing ahead
D. All of the above

8016. INT ONLY

What whistle signal, if any, would be sounded when two vessels are meeting, but will pass clear starboard to starboard?

A. One short blast
B. Two short blasts
C. Five or more short blasts
D. No signal is required.

8017. INT ONLY

In a narrow channel, a vessel trying to overtake another on the other vessel's port side would sound a whistle signal of ____.

A. one short blast
B. two short blasts
C. two prolonged blasts followed by one short blast
D. two prolonged blasts followed by two short blasts

8018. INT ONLY

On open water, a power-driven vessel coming up dead astern of another vessel and altering her course to starboard so as to pass on the starboard side of the vessel ahead would sound ____.

A. two short blasts
B. one short blast
C. two prolonged blasts followed by one short blast
D. one long and one short blast

8019. INT ONLY

If a vessel displays three all-around red lights in a vertical line at night, during the day she may show ____.

A. three balls in a vertical line
B. a cylinder
C. two diamonds in a vertical line
D. two cones, apexes together

8020. INT ONLY

A vessel not under command sounds the same fog signal as a vessel ____.

A. towing
B. constrained by her draft
C. under sail
D. All of the above

8021. INT ONLY

Your vessel is crossing a narrow channel. A vessel to port is within the channel and crossing your course. She is showing a black cylinder. What is your responsibility?

A. Hold your course and speed.
B. Sound the danger signal.
C. Begin an exchange of passing signals.
D. Do not cross the channel if you might impede the other vessel.

8022. INT ONLY

You are approaching another vessel and will pass starboard to starboard without danger if no course changes are made. You should ____.

A. hold course and sound a two blast whistle signal
B. hold course and sound no whistle signal
C. change course to the right and sound one blast
D. hold course and sound two prolonged and two short blasts

8023. INT & INLAND

A fishing vessel is approaching a vessel not under command. Which statement is TRUE?

A. The fishing vessel must keep clear of the vessel not under command.
B. If the vessel not under command is a power-driven vessel, she must keep clear of the fishing vessel.
C. They must exchange whistle signals.
D. Both vessels are required to take action to stay clear of each other.

8024. INT ONLY

Which signal is required to be sounded by a power-driven vessel ONLY?

A. A signal meaning, I am altering my course to starboard.
B. A signal meaning, I intend to overtake you on your starboard side.
C. A signal meaning that the vessel sounding it is in doubt as to the other vessel's actions.
D. A signal sounded when approaching a bend.

8025. INT ONLY

The light which may be used with a vessel's whistle is to be ____.

A. used when the whistle is broken
B. used prior to sounding the whistle
C. used only at night
D. a white light

8026. INT ONLY

You are in sight of another vessel in a crossing situation, and the other vessel sounds one short blast. You are going to hold course and speed. You should ____.

A. answer with one short blast
B. answer with two short blasts
C. sound the danger signal
D. sound no whistle signal

8027. INT ONLY

Two prolonged blasts followed by one short blast on the whistle is a signal which could be sounded by a ____.

A. fishing vessel
B. vessel anchored
C. mineclearing vessel
D. vessel overtaking another in a narrow channel

8028. INT ONLY

In a crossing situation on international waters, a short blast by the give-way vessel indicates that the vessel ____.

A. is holding course and speed
B. is turning to starboard
C. intends to pass port to port
D. will keep out of the way of the stand-on vessel

8029. INT ONLY

What dayshape is prescribed for a vessel constrained by her draft?

A. A black cone, apex upward
B. A black cone, apex downward
C. Two vertical black balls
D. A cylinder

8030. INT ONLY

A vessel not under command sounds the same fog signal as a vessel ____.

A. engaged in towing
B. constrained by her draft
C. under sail
D. All of the above

8031. INT ONLY

Which statement(s) is(are) TRUE concerning light signals?

A. The time between flashes shall be about five seconds.
B. The time between successive signals shall be not less than ten seconds.
C. The light signals are to be used when not using sound signals.
D. All of the above

8032. INT ONLY

Under what circumstances would an overtaking vessel sound a whistle signal of two prolonged followed by one short blast?

A. When overtaking in restricted visibility
B. When overtaking in a narrow channel
C. When overtaking on open waters
D. When no other vessels are in the immediate area

8038. INT ONLY

In which case would an overtaking vessel sound a whistle signal of two prolonged followed by one short blast?

A. When overtaking in restricted visibility
B. When overtaking in a narrow channel
C. When overtaking on open waters
D. When no other vessels are in the immediate area

8039. INT ONLY

When vessels are in sight of one another, two short blasts from one of the vessels means _____.

A. I am altering my course to starboard
B. I am altering my course to port
C. I intend to change course to starboard
D. I intend to change course to port

8040. INT ONLY

Which vessel may NOT exhibit two red lights in a vertical line?

A. A vessel constrained by her draft
B. A trawler fishing in close proximity to other trawlers
C. A vessel aground
D. A dredge

8041. INT ONLY

Vessel A is overtaking vessel B on open waters and will pass without changing course. Vessel A _____.

A. should sound two short blasts
B. should sound the danger signal

C. should sound one long blast
D. will not sound any whistle signals

8042. INT ONLY

Of the vessels listed, which must keep out of the way of all the others?

A. A vessel constrained by her draft
B. A vessel restricted in her ability to maneuver
C. A vessel on pilotage duty
D. A vessel engaged in fishing

8043. INT ONLY

Which vessel would NOT sound a fog signal of one prolonged and two short blasts?

A. A vessel not under command
B. A vessel constrained by her draft
C. A vessel being towed
D. A vessel sailing

8044. DIAGRAM 36. INT ONLY

In international waters, you are on Vessel I in the situation as shown. Vessel II sounds one short blast. Which action should you take?

A. Sound one short blast and hold course and speed
B. Hold course and speed
C. Sound one short blast and slow down or turn to starboard
D. Sound two short blasts, slow down and turn to port

8045. INT ONLY

You intend to overtake a vessel in a narrow channel, and you intend to pass along the vessel's port side. How should you signal your intention?

A. No signal is necessary.
B. Two prolonged blasts
C. Two short blasts
D. Two prolonged followed by two short blasts

8046. INT ONLY

A vessel sounds two short blasts. This signal indicates the vessel _____.

A. intends to alter course to port
B. intends to pass starboard to starboard
C. is altering course to port
D. will alter course to port

8047. INT ONLY

A vessel sounds one short blast. This signal indicates the vessel _____.

A. intends to alter course to starboard
B. intends to pass starboard to starboard
C. is altering course to starboard
D. intends to pass port to port

8048. INT ONLY

You are underway in a narrow channel, and you are being overtaken by a vessel astern. After the overtaking vessel sounds the proper signal indicating his intention to pass your vessel on your starboard side, you signal your agreement by sounding _____.

A. one short blast
B. two prolonged blasts
C. two prolonged followed by two short blasts
D. one prolonged, one short, one prolonged, and one short blast in that order

8049. INT ONLY

Which signal is sounded ONLY when vessels are NOT in sight of each other?

A. A signal of at least five short and rapid blasts
B. Four short blasts on the whistle
C. One prolonged, one short, one prolonged, and one short blast on the whistle, in that order
D. Two short blasts on the whistle

8050. INT ONLY

A sailing vessel is overtaking a power-driven vessel in a narrow channel, so as to pass on the power-driven vessel's port side. The overtaken vessel will have to move to facilitate passage. The sailing vessel is the _____.

A. stand-on vessel and would sound two short blasts
B. give-way vessel and would sound no whistle signal
C. stand-on vessel and would sound no whistle signal
D. give-way vessel and would sound two prolonged blasts followed by two short blasts

8051. INT ONLY

A vessel constrained by her draft may display _____.

A. three all-around red lights
B. two 225° red lights
C. three all-around blue lights
D. two 225° blue lights

8052. INT ONLY

Two power-driven vessels are meeting. A two blast whistle signal by either vessel means ____.

A. I intend to alter course to port
B. I desire to pass starboard to starboard
C. I desire to pass port to port
D. I am altering course to port

8053. INT ONLY

A 20-meter power-driven vessel pushing ahead or towing alongside will display ____.

A. a single white light forward
B. two masthead lights in a vertical line
C. two towing lights in a vertical line
D. two all-around red lights where they can best be seen

8054. INT ONLY

Which statement applies to a vessel constrained by her draft?

A. She is severely restricted in her ability to change her course because of her draft in relation to the available depth of water.
B. The term applies only to vessels in marked channels.
C. She is designated as a vessel restricted in her ability to maneuver.
D. The vessel must be over 100 meters in length.

8056. INT ONLY

A whistle signal of one prolonged, one short, one prolonged and one short blast is sounded by a vessel ____.

A. at anchor
B. towing a submerged object
C. being overtaken in a narrow channel
D. in distress

8057. INT ONLY

Your vessel is backing out of a slip in a harbor and you can see that other vessels are approaching. You should sound ____.

A. three short blasts when leaving the slip
B. one prolonged blast followed by three short blasts when the last line is taken aboard
C. one prolonged blast only
D. the danger signal

8058. INT ONLY

Which vessel is to keep out of the way of the others?

A. A vessel constrained by her draft
B. A vessel engaged in underwater operations
C. A vessel engaged in trawling
D. A vessel not under command

8059. INT ONLY

You are in sight of a power-driven vessel that sounds two short blasts of the whistle. This signal means that the vessel ____.

A. is altering course to port
B. is altering course to starboard
C. intends to leave you on her port side
D. intends to leave you on her starboard side

8060. INT ONLY

You are operating a vessel in a narrow channel. Your vessel must stay within the channel to be navigated safely. Another vessel is crossing your course from starboard to port, and you are in doubt as to his intentions. According to Rule 9, you:

A. may sound the danger signal
B. must sound one prolonged and two short blasts
C. should sound one short blast to indicate that you are holding course and speed
D. are required to back down

8061. DIAGRAM 17. INT ONLY

Vessel A is overtaking vessel B on open waters as shown and will pass without changing course. Vessel A ____.

A. should sound two short blasts
B. should sound the danger signal
C. should sound one long blast
D. need not sound any whistle signals

8062. INT ONLY

If you sighted three red lights in a vertical line on another vessel at night, it would be a vessel ____.

A. aground
B. constrained by her draft
C. dredging
D. moored over a wreck

8063. INT ONLY

On open water two vessels are in an overtaking situation. The overtaking vessel has just sounded one short blast on the whistle. What is the meaning of this whistle signal?

A. I request permission to pass you on my port side.

B. I will maintain course and speed and pass you on your starboard side.
C. On which side should I pass?
D. I am changing course to starboard.

8064. INT ONLY

You are underway in fog and hear a fog signal consisting of one prolonged and two short blasts. It could be any of the following EXCEPT a vessel ____.

A. engaged in mineclearance
B. engaged in fishing
C. constrained by her draft
D. being towed

8067. INT ONLY

Which vessel shall avoid impeding the safe passage of a vessel constrained by her draft?

A. A vessel not under command
B. A fishing vessel
C. A vessel restricted in her ability to maneuver
D. All of the above

8068. INT ONLY

A signal of one prolonged, one short, one prolonged, and one short blast, in that order is given by a vessel ____.

A. engaged on pilotage duty
B. in distress
C. at anchor
D. being overtaken in a narrow channel

8069. INT ONLY

Which signal is sounded ONLY by a vessel in sight of another and NOT in or near an area of restricted visibility?

A. Four short blasts on the whistle
B. One prolonged blast on the whistle
C. One short blast on the whistle
D. One short, one prolonged, and one short blast on the whistle

8070. INT ONLY

In addition to her running lights, an underway vessel constrained by her draft may carry in a vertical line:

A. a red light, a white light, and a red light
B. two red lights
C. two white lights
D. three red lights

8071. INT ONLY

Which vessel is NOT regarded as being restricted in her ability to maneuver?

A. A vessel servicing an aid to navigation
B. A vessel engaged in dredging
C. A towing vessel with tow unable to deviate from its course
D. A vessel constrained by her draft

8072. INT ONLY
When two vessels are in sight of one another and NOT in or near an area of restricted visibility, any of the following signals may be given EXCEPT:

A. a light signal of at least five short and rapid flashes
B. one prolonged, one short, one prolonged, and one short whistle blast
C. four short whistle blasts
D. two short whistle blasts

8073. INT ONLY
In a narrow channel, an overtaking vessel which intends to PASS on the other vessel's port side would sound:

A. one prolonged followed by two short blasts
B. one short blast
C. two prolonged followed by two short blasts
D. two short blasts

8074. INT ONLY
Two prolonged blasts followed by one short blast on the whistle is a signal which would be sounded by a vessel:

A. overtaking another in a narrow channel
B. anchored
C. engaged in mineclearance
D. engaged in fishing

8075. INT ONLY
You intend to overtake a vessel in a narrow channel, and you intend to pass along the vessel's port side. How should you signal your intention?

A. Two short blasts followed by two prolonged blasts
B. Two prolonged followed by two short blasts
C. Two prolonged blasts only
D. Two short blasts only

8076. INT ONLY
You are underway in a narrow channel, and you are being overtaken by a vessel astern. After the overtaking vessel sounds the proper signal indicating his intention to

pass your vessel on your starboard side, you signal your agreement by sounding _____.

A. two prolonged followed by two short blasts
B. one prolonged, one short, one prolonged, and one short blast
C. one short blast
D. two prolonged blasts

8077. INT ONLY
Vessel A is overtaking vessel B on open waters and will pass without changing course. Vessel A should _____.

A. sound two prolonged blasts followed by two short blasts
B. sound the danger signal
C. not sound any whistle signals
D. sound one long blast

8078. DIAGRAM 17. INT ONLY
Vessel A is overtaking vessel B on open waters as shown and will pass without changing course. Vessel A _____.

A. need not sound any whistle signals
B. should sound two short blasts
C. should sound the danger signal
D. should sound one long blast

8080. INT ONLY
Which signal is sounded ONLY by a vessel in sight of another?

A. One short blast on the whistle
B. Four short blasts on the whistle
C. One prolonged blast on the whistle
D. One short, one prolonged, and one short blast on the whistle

8081. INT ONLY
The light which may be used with a vessel's whistle must be _____.

A. used when the whistle is broken
B. a white light
C. used only at night
D. used prior to sounding the whistle

8082. INT ONLY
Which statement is TRUE concerning light signals?

A. The time between flashes shall be about five seconds.
B. The light signals are to be used when not using sound signals.
C. The time between successive signals

shall be not less than ten seconds.
D. All of the above

8083. INT ONLY
While underway and in sight of another vessel, you put your engines full speed astern. Which statement concerning whistle signals is TRUE?

A. You must sound three short blasts on the whistle.
B. You must sound one blast if backing to starboard.
C. You must sound whistle signals only if the vessels are meeting.
D. You need not sound any whistle signals.

8084. INT ONLY
While underway at night, a power-driven vessel of less than 7 meters in length, whose maximum speed which does not exceed 7 knots, may show:

A. sidelights combined in a single lantern, only
B. an all-around flashing yellow light, only
C. one all-around white light, only
D. a lantern showing a white light exhibited in sufficient time to prevent collision, only

8085. INT ONLY
At night, a power-driven vessel less than 7 meters in length, with a maximum speed which does not exceed 7 knots, MUST show when underway at least _____.

A. one white 360° light
B. a white light on the near approach of another vessel
C. sidelights and a sternlight
D. the lights required of a vessel less than 12 meters in length

8087. INT ONLY
Lighting requirements in inland waters are different from those for international waters for _____.

A. barges being towed by pushing ahead
B. vessels restricted in their ability to maneuver
C. vessels towing astern
D. barges being towed astern

8088. INT ONLY
A 20-meter power-driven vessel pushing ahead or towing alongside will display _____.

A. two towing lights in a vertical line
B. a towing light above the sternlight
C. two all-around red lights at the masthead
D. two masthead lights in a vertical line

8089. INT ONLY
A towing light _____.

A. flashes at regular intervals of 50-70 flashes per minute
B. is yellow in color
C. shows an unbroken light over an arc of the horizon of not less than 180° nor more than 225°
D. All of the above

8090. INT & INLAND
A towing light is _____.

A. shown below the sternlight
B. white in color
C. displayed at the masthead
D. a yellow light having the same characteristics as the stern light

8092. INT ONLY
A light used to signal passing intentions must be an _____.

A. alternating red and yellow light
B. alternating white and yellow light
C. all-around white or yellow light
D. all-around white light only

8096. INT ONLY
A vessel constrained by her draft may display _____.

A. three all-around red lights instead of the lights required for a power-driven vessel of her class
B. the same lights as a vessel restricted in her ability to maneuver
C. three all-around red lights in addition to the lights required for a power-driven vessel of her class
D. the lights for a power-driven vessel which is not under command

8097. INT ONLY
Which dayshape is prescribed for a vessel constrained by her draft?

A. A black diamond
B. A cylinder
C. A black ball
D. A black cone, apex upward

8098. INT ONLY
If at night a vessel displays three all-around red lights in a vertical line, during the day she may show _____.

A. two cones, base to base
B. three black balls in a vertical line
C. a cylinder
D. a cone, apex downward

8099. INT ONLY
A vessel displaying three red lights in a vertical line is _____.

A. restricted in her ability to maneuver
B. not under command
C. engaged in mineclearing operations
D. constrained by her draft

8100. INT ONLY
The International Rules of the Road apply _____.

A. to all waters
B. to any waters inside the territorial waters of the U.S.
C. only to waters where foreign vessels travel
D. upon the high seas and connecting waters navigable by seagoing vessels

8101. INT ONLY
Which statement applies to a vessel constrained by her draft?

A. The term only applies to vessels in narrow channels.
B. She is severely restricted in her ability to change her course because of her draft in relation to the available depth and width of navigable water.
C. She is designated as a vessel restricted in her ability to maneuver.
D. The vessel must be over 100 meters in length.

8102. INT ONLY
Which statement is TRUE concerning a vessel constrained by her draft?

A. She is hampered because of her work.
B. She is unable to maneuver due to some exceptional circumstance.
C. She may be a vessel being towed.
D. She must be a power-driven vessel.

8103. INT ONLY
Which vessel is NOT restricted in her ability to maneuver?

A. A vessel servicing an aid to navigation
B. A vessel constrained by her draft
C. A towing vessel with tow, unable to deviate from its course
D. A vessel engaged in dredging

8104. INT ONLY
Your vessel is constrained by her draft and operating in a narrow channel. Another vessel is crossing your course from starboard to port. You are in doubt as to her intentions. According to Rule 9, you _____.

A. should sound one short blast to indicate that you are holding course and speed
B. must sound one prolonged blast
C. may sound the danger signal
D. are required to back down

8105. INT ONLY
Your vessel is crossing a narrow channel. A vessel to port is within the channel and crossing your course. She is showing a black cylinder. You should _____.

A. hold your course and speed
B. not impede the other vessel
C. exchange passing signals
D. sound the danger signal

8111. INT ONLY
Your vessel is backing out of a slip in a harbor. Visibility is restricted. You should sound _____.

A. one prolonged blast only
B. one prolonged blast followed by three short blasts when the last line is taken aboard
C. one prolonged blast followed by three short blasts when leaving the slip
D. the danger signal

8113. INT ONLY
You are approaching another vessel and will pass safely starboard to starboard without changing course. You should _____.

A. hold course and sound no whistle signal
B. hold course and sound a two blast whistle signal
C. change course to starboard and sound one blast
D. hold course and sound one blast

8114. INT & INLAND
Which statement is TRUE concerning a situation involving a fishing vessel and a vessel not under command?

A. They are required to communicate by radiotelephone.
B. If the vessel not under command is a power-driven vessel, she must keep clear of the fishing vessel.
C. The fishing vessel must keep out of the way of the vessel not under command.
D. Both vessels are required to take action to stay clear of each other.

8115. INT ONLY
Of the vessels listed, which must keep out of the way of all the others?

A. A vessel constrained by her draft
B. A vessel restricted in her ability to maneuver
C. A vessel pushing a barge
D. A vessel engaged in fishing

8116. INT ONLY
Which vessel shall avoid impeding the safe passage of a vessel constrained by her draft?

A. A vessel not under command
B. A sailing vessel
C. A vessel restricted in her ability to maneuver
D. All of the above

8118. INT ONLY
A signal of intent must be sounded in international waters by ____.

A. a vessel meeting another head-on
B. a vessel overtaking another in a narrow channel
C. a vessel crossing the course of another
D. the give-way vessel in a crossing situation

8120. INT ONLY
A light used to signal passing intentions must be an ____.

A. all-around yellow light only
B. all-around white light only
C. all-around blue light only
D. alternating red and yellow light

8121. INT ONLY
Which statement is TRUE, according to the Rules?

A. A vessel engaged in fishing while underway shall, so far as possible, keep out of the

way of a vessel restricted in her ability to maneuver.
B. A vessel not under command shall keep out of the way of a vessel restricted in her ability to maneuver.
C. A fishing vessel while underway has the right-of-way over a vessel constrained by her draft.
D. A vessel not under command shall avoid impeding the safe passage of a vessel constrained by her draft.

8126. INT ONLY
A light used to signal passing intentions must be an ____.

A. all-around white or yellow light
B. all-around yellow light only
C. all-around white light only
D. Any colored light is acceptable.

8127. INT ONLY
Which statement is TRUE, according to the Rules?

A. A vessel constrained by her draft shall keep out of the way of a vessel engaged in fishing.
B. A vessel engaged in fishing while underway shall, so far as possible, keep out of the way of a vessel restricted in her ability to maneuver.
C. A vessel not under command shall avoid impeding the safe passage of a vessel constrained by her draft.
D. A vessel not under command shall keep out of the way of a vessel restricted in her ability to maneuver.

8128. INT ONLY
Which statement is TRUE, according to the Rules?

A. A vessel engaged in fishing while underway shall, so far as possible, keep out of the way of a vessel restricted in her ability to maneuver.
B. A vessel not under command shall keep out of the way of a vessel restricted in her ability to maneuver.
C. A vessel engaged in fishing shall keep out of the way of a sailing vessel.
D. A vessel not under command shall keep out of the way of a vessel engaged in fishing.

8129. INT ONLY
Which statement is TRUE, according to the Rules?

A. A vessel not under command shall keep out of the way of a vessel restricted in her ability to maneuver.
B. A vessel not under command shall avoid impeding the safe passage of a vessel constrained by her draft.
C. A vessel constrained by her draft shall keep out of the way of a vessel engaged in fishing.
D. A vessel engaged in fishing while underway shall, so far as possible, keep out of the way of a vessel restricted in her ability to maneuver.

8131. INT ONLY
What characteristic must a light have if used to signal passing intentions?

A. It must be an all-around white light.
B. It must be an alternating blue and white light.
C. It must be an all-around white or yellow light.
D. It must be an alternating red and yellow light.

8135. INT ONLY
What characteristic must a light used to indicate passing intentions have?

A. It must be an alternating red and yellow light.
B. It must be an all-around white light.
C. It must be an all-around yellow light.
D. It must be an all-around blue light.

8136. INT ONLY
A power-driven vessel pushing ahead or towing alongside will show sidelights, a sternlight, and ____.

A. an all-around red light where it can best be seen
B. two yellow masthead lights in a vertical line
C. two masthead lights in a vertical line
D. a single white light forward

RULES OF THE ROAD
ANSWERS

NBR	ANS	NBR	ANS	NBR	ANS	NBR	ANS	NBR	ANS	NBR	ANS	NBR	ANS	NBR	ANS
1	C	59	A	119	C	182	B	248	B	321	D	384	C	4044	D
2	B	60	C	120	B	183	D	249	D	322	A	385	A	4045	A
3	B	61	A	122	C	185	D	250	B	323	A	386	B	4046	B
4	B	62	A	123	C	186	C	251	B	324	B	388	D	4047	B
5	A	63	B	124	B	187	C	252	A	325	C	389	C	4048	C
6	B	64	A	125	D	188	A	253	D	326	B	390	B	4049	B
7	A	65	B	126	B	189	B	254	C	327	C	391	A	4050	B
8	A	66	B	127	D	190	C	255	D	328	D	392	D	4051	A
9	B	67	C	128	D	191	D	256	B	329	D	393	A	4052	A
10	D	68	D	129	B	193	B	257	B	330	B	394	C	4053	A
11	C	69	A	130	D	194	D	258	B	331	D	395	B	4054	C
12	D	70	A	131	B	195	C	259	A	332	A	396	D	4055	B
13	C	71	D	132	C	197	A	260	A	333	C	401	A	4056	C
14	C	72	C	133	A	198	B	261	D	334	B	402	B	4057	D
15	C	73	D	134	B	199	B	262	A	335	D	727	C	4058	B
16	D	74	B	135	C	200	A	263	C	336	C	728	C	4059	B
17	D	75	C	136	D	204	B	264	A	337	A	821	D	4060	B
18	C	76	A	137	C	205	C	265	C	338	B	1000	C	4061	D
19	D	77	B	138	B	206	A	266	D	339	C	3683	D	4062	A
20	B	78	D	139	B	207	B	267	C	340	D	4000	B	4063	B
21	D	79	C	140	A	208	B	268	A	341	A	4001	B	4065	B
22	D	80	C	141	C	209	D	269	D	342	D	4002	C	4066	D
23	C	81	B	142	B	210	B	270	B	343	B	4003	D	4067	D
24	B	82	B	143	C	211	D	272	B	345	C	4004	C	4068	A
25	A	83	C	144	D	212	A	273	D	346	D	4005	B	4069	A
26	B	84	D	145	A	213	C	274	C	347	D	4006	C	4070	C
27	B	85	D	146	C	214	B	275	B	348	A	4007	C	4072	A
28	B	86	C	147	D	215	B	276	A	349	D	4008	D	4073	B
29	C	87	D	148	C	216	B	277	A	350	D	4009	C	4074	D
30	C	88	B	149	C	217	A	278	C	351	A	4010	C	4075	C
31	D	89	B	150	C	218	B	279	B	352	B	4011	C	4076	D
32	B	90	C	151	C	219	C	280	D	353	D	4012	A	4077	A
33	A	91	B	152	D	221	C	282	B	354	B	4013	D	4078	D
34	A	92	B	153	C	222	D	283	C	355	A	4014	B	4080	A
35	C	93	D	154	A	223	A	284	D	356	C	4015	D	4081	C
36	D	94	A	155	A	224	B	288	A	357	D	4016	A	4082	B
37	A	95	C	156	B	225	D	289	A	358	D	4017	C	4083	B
38	C	96	A	157	C	226	D	290	D	359	D	4018	D	4084	B
39	D	97	D	158	B	227	A	292	D	360	D	4020	D	4086	C
40	C	98	C	159	D	228	B	293	A	361	C	4021	D	4087	C
41	B	99	C	160	A	229	B	294	D	362	D	4022	A	4088	D
42	A	100	D	161	A	230	A	295	B	363	D	4023	C	4089	D
43	B	101	A	162	B	231	B	296	C	364	C	4024	D	4090	C
44	B	102	A	163	D	232	C	297	A	365	A	4025	C	4091	B
45	B	103	B	164	C	233	C	298	D	366	B	4026	D	4093	A
46	A	104	A	165	D	234	B	299	A	367	A	4028	D	4094	C
47	A	105	B	166	A	235	B	300	B	368	B	4029	B	4095	B
48	A	106	C	168	D	236	D	301	D	369	C	4030	B	4096	A
49	C	107	D	169	C	237	A	302	D	370	D	4031	A	4097	B
50	C	108	D	170	B	238	D	311	D	371	C	4032	A	4098	D
51	A	109	C	171	D	239	D	312	C	372	D	4033	B	4099	B
52	A	110	B	172	C	240	B	313	A	374	C	4034	A	4100	B
53	C	111	A	173	B	241	C	314	C	375	C	4035	D	4101	A
54	B	112	C	175	B	242	C	315	A	376	A	4036	A	4102	B
55	B	114	C	176	A	243	B	316	C	377	B	4038	B	4103	C
56	C	115	A	177	D	244	D	317	D	378	B	4039	B	4104	B
57	A	116	C	178	C	245	C	318	A	379	A	4040	B	4105	A
58	D	117	B	179	B	246	A	319	B	380	A	4042	B	4106	B
		118	D	181	A	247	A	320	C	383	D	4043	D	4107	B

4108 C	4168 B	4229 B	4294 C	4358 D	4419 C	4479 A	4540 B
4109 C	4169 D	4230 C	4295 C	4359 C	4420 D	4480 C	4541 D
4110 C	4170 B	4231 B	4296 C	4360 C	4421 A	4481 C	4542 C
4111 B	4171 D	4232 C	4297 A	4362 B	4422 C	4482 A	4543 B
4112 C	4173 D	4233 A	4298 B	4363 C	4423 A	4483 A	4544 C
4113 A	4174 C	4234 D	4299 B	4364 C	4424 B	4484 A	4545 A
4114 C	4175 A	4235 A	4300 A	4365 A	4425 D	4485 B	4546 D
4115 C	4176 D	4236 D	4301 D	4366 A	4426 D	4486 A	4547 D
4116 B	4177 C	4237 C	4302 B	4367 C	4427 C	4487 B	4548 C
4117 B	4178 A	4239 B	4303 D	4368 B	4428 B	4488 D	4549 B
4118 A	4179 D	4240 B	4304 B	4369 C	4429 D	4489 B	4550 D
4119 A	4180 B	4241 A	4305 D	4371 D	4430 C	4490 B	4551 C
4120 D	4181 B	4242 C	4306 A	4372 D	4431 A	4491 A	4552 D
4121 A	4182 D	4243 A	4309 A	4373 A	4432 B	4492 D	4553 C
4122 D	4183 A	4244 B	4310 D	4374 D	4433 B	4493 C	4554 C
4123 A	4184 B	4245 D	4311 D	4375 B	4434 C	4494 D	4555 A
4124 C	4185 D	4247 D	4312 B	4376 A	4435 D	4496 D	4556 A
4125 B	4186 B	4248 D	4313 A	4377 B	4436 C	4497 C	4557 D
4126 D	4187 C	4249 A	4314 D	4378 A	4437 A	4498 C	4558 B
4127 C	4188 C	4250 A	4315 A	4379 D	4438 B	4499 A	4559 C
4128 C	4189 C	4251 C	4316 B	4380 D	4439 C	4500 B	4560 C
4129 A	4190 A	4253 D	4317 C	4381 B	4440 D	4501 A	4561 C
4130 A	4191 C	4254 D	4318 B	4382 A	4441 B	4502 D	4562 A
4131 D	4192 B	4255 C	4319 D	4383 C	4442 A	4503 B	4563 A
4133 C	4193 A	4256 A	4320 D	4384 D	4443 C	4504 B	4564 B
4134 B	4194 C	4257 D	4321 D	4385 A	4444 B	4505 B	4565 C
4135 D	4195 D	4258 C	4322 D	4386 A	4445 C	4506 D	4567 C
4136 C	4196 C	4259 C	4323 A	4387 C	4446 D	4507 A	4568 B
4137 D	4197 C	4260 B	4325 B	4388 D	4447 B	4508 A	4569 B
4138 D	4198 A	4261 D	4327 C	4389 D	4448 C	4509 B	4570 D
4139 B	4199 D	4262 D	4328 C	4390 D	4449 C	4510 B	4571 C
4140 D	4201 B	4263 A	4329 B	4391 B	4451 B	4511 C	4572 C
4141 C	4202 C	4265 C	4330 D	4392 B	4452 A	4512 D	4573 D
4142 A	4203 B	4266 D	4331 B	4393 C	4453 D	4513 D	4574 A
4143 D	4204 D	4267 C	4332 C	4394 D	4454 A	4514 D	4575 A
4144 A	4205 C	4268 D	4334 A	4395 C	4455 D	4516 B	4577 D
4145 C	4206 C	4269 A	4335 B	4396 A	4456 B	4517 B	4578 A
4146 A	4207 B	4270 C	4336 A	4397 C	4457 A	4518 D	4579 D
4147 D	4208 A	4271 C	4337 B	4398 C	4458 A	4519 A	4580 A
4148 D	4209 B	4272 B	4338 D	4399 B	4459 D	4520 A	4581 D
4149 A	4210 D	4273 C	4339 D	4400 C	4460 A	4521 D	4582 B
4150 B	4211 C	4274 D	4340 A	4401 D	4461 B	4522 B	4583 D
4151 A	4212 C	4276 B	4341 B	4402 A	4462 D	4523 C	4584 C
4152 B	4213 D	4277 A	4342 A	4403 C	4463 C	4524 C	4585 D
4153 C	4214 D	4278 D	4343 D	4404 D	4464 A	4525 C	4586 D
4154 C	4215 D	4279 B	4344 B	4405 B	4465 C	4526 B	4587 B
4155 D	4216 B	4280 A	4345 D	4406 C	4466 C	4527 A	4588 C
4156 C	4217 D	4281 D	4346 B	4407 C	4467 D	4528 D	4589 D
4157 D	4218 A	4282 A	4347 D	4408 D	4468 A	4529 A	4590 D
4158 C	4219 D	4283 C	4348 A	4409 C	4469 B	4530 C	4591 C
4159 D	4220 B	4284 D	4349 B	4410 D	4470 C	4531 B	4592 D
4160 A	4221 D	4285 C	4350 C	4411 A	4471 D	4532 C	4593 D
4161 A	4222 B	4286 A	4351 B	4412 D	4472 D	4533 A	4594 A
4162 B	4223 A	4287 D	4352 C	4413 B	4473 D	4534 C	4595 C
4163 A	4224 B	4288 B	4353 A	4414 A	4474 C	4535 D	4596 D
4164 B	4225 A	4289 B	4354 A	4415 C	4475 D	4536 C	4597 A
4165 A	4226 C	4290 B	4355 B	4416 D	4476 D	4537 D	4598 A
4166 B	4227 B	4292 B	4356 C	4417 D	4477 C	4538 D	4599 D
4167 A	4228 B	4293 D	4357 C	4418 B	4478 A	4539 A	4600 C

4601 B	4661 D	4724 C	4864 B	8030 D	8103 B
4602 D	4662 A	4725 D	4865 C	8031 B	8104 C
4603 A	4663 B	4726 A	4866 B	8032 B	8105 B
4604 B	4664 C	4728 C	4868 B	8038 B	8111 A
4605 B	4665 A	4729 B	4869 C	8039 B	8113 A
4606 A	4666 D	4730 A	4870 C	8040 A	8114 C
4607 B	4667 D	4731 B	4871 A	8041 D	8115 C
4608 A	4668 D	4732 C	4872 C	8042 C	8116 B
4609 A	4669 B	4733 C	4873 C	8043 C	8118 B
4610 A	4670 C	4734 C	4874 D	8044 B	8120 B
4611 A	4671 A	4735 B	4875 A	8045 D	8121 A
4612 D	4672 C	4736 B	4876 B	8046 C	8126 C
4613 A	4673 D	4737 A	4877 C	8047 C	8127 B
4614 D	4674 A	4738 B	5000 A	8048 D	8128 A
4615 A	4675 C	4739 C	5100 C	8049 B	8129 D
4616 A	4676 C	4745 C	5150 C	8050 D	8131 A
4617 C	4677 B	4770 D	5200 C	8051 A	8135 B
4618 A	4678 A	4780 A	5300 B	8052 D	8136 C
4619 D	4680 C	4818 B	5350 A	8053 B	
4620 A	4681 C	4819 A	5400 C	8054 A	
4621 B	4682 D	4820 C	5500 C	8056 C	
4622 C	4683 C	4825 C	6000 B	8057 A	
4623 B	4684 C	4826 A	6500 D	8058 C	
4624 B	4685 A	4827 C	6510 A	8059 A	
4625 D	4686 A	4828 D	6520 B	8060 A	
4626 B	4687 C	4829 C	6530 B	8061 D	
4627 C	4688 A	4830 D	6540 D	8062 B	
4628 A	4689 C	4831 D	6550 A	8063 D	
4629 C	4690 C	4832 D	6560 A	8064 D	
4630 A	4691 B	4833 C	6570 D	8067 B	
4631 D	4692 C	4834 D	8000 A	8068 D	
4632 B	4693 A	4835 B	8001 C	8069 C	
4633 B	4694 B	4836 D	8002 A	8070 D	
4634 A	4695 B	4837 B	8004 D	8071 D	
4635 C	4696 C	4838 D	8005 B	8072 C	
4636 B	4697 D	4839 B	8006 D	8073 C	
4637 B	4699 C	4841 A	8007 C	8074 A	
4638 A	4700 B	4842 B	8008 D	8075 B	
4639 D	4701 B	4843 C	8009 D	8076 B	
4640 A	4702 D	4844 C	8010 D	8077 C	
4641 A	4703 C	4845 C	8011 D	8078 A	
4642 B	4704 C	4846 C	8012 C	8080 A	
4643 A	4705 D	4847 C	8013 B	8081 B	
4644 C	4706 A	4848 D	8014 D	8082 C	
4645 D	4707 A	4849 D	8015 D	8083 A	
4646 B	4708 C	4850 C	8016 D	8084 C	
4647 B	4709 B	4851 C	8017 D	8085 A	
4649 C	4710 D	4852 B	8018 B	8087 A	
4650 D	4711 C	4853 D	8019 B	8088 D	
4651 D	4713 A	4854 B	8020 D	8089 B	
4652 C	4714 B	4855 B	8021 D	8090 D	
4653 D	4715 D	4856 B	8022 B	8092 D	
4654 B	4716 C	4857 A	8023 A	8096 C	
4655 B	4717 D	4858 D	8024 A	8097 B	
4656 A	4718 B	4859 C	8025 D	8098 C	
4657 C	4719 B	4860 A	8026 D	8099 D	
4658 A	4721 A	4861 C	8027 D	8100 D	
4659 A	4722 D	4862 A	8028 B	8101 B	
4660 D	4723 D	4863 B	8029 D	8102 D	

DECK GENERAL

SHIP HANDLING

Propeller Forces

Propellers can be single or twin, and described as right- or left-handed depending upon their direction of rotation when viewed from astern (clockwise = right-handed, etc.). When the prop rotates, it draws water via a suction screw current and expels water via a discharge screw current. The terminology applies whether going ahead or astern.

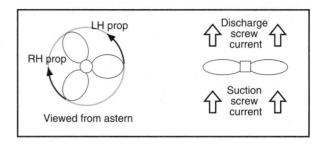

A propeller produces three forces. Much the same as an aircraft wing, the intake face of the blade corresponds to an upper wing surface, thus experiencing a lower pressure than the blade discharge face (lower wing surface). This pressure differential results in a force ("lift") acting perpendicular to the blade face. Since the blade is angled to the horizontal, that lift is resolved into two components: a horizontal thrust acting in the direction of motion, and a vertical thrust lifting the vessel's stern. The vertical thrust is not apparent, however, unless the prop is angled strongly downward, because the prop's depth acts also to rotate the vessel's bow upward. Because the rotating propeller imparts rotation to the discharge current, an equal and opposite torque is imparted to the prop shaft. This is most noticeable when getting underway, an RH prop causing the vessel to roll to port.

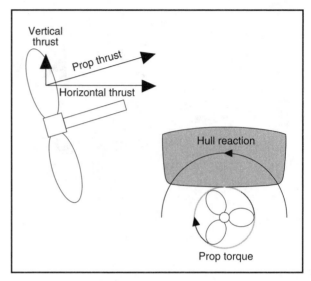

Prop-walk. Because the shaft is at an angle to the underwater hull, and the blade is perpendicular to the shaft, the blade strikes the suction screw current at an angle. As the figure shows, the descending blade thus has greater pitch than the ascending blade, resulting in a torque on the vessel termed "prop-walk." When going ahead with a right-handed prop, the torque "walks" the stern to starboard, with the effects being reversed when going astern. In twin-screw vessels, contra-rotating props cancel the effect.

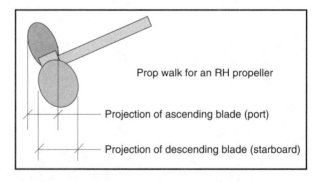

Three common variations on propeller geometry are:
- *Kort nozzle*, a cylindrical shroud surrounding the propeller. It increases efficiency at lower speeds when going ahead, but is less efficient when going astern.
- *Inboard-outboard ("I/O") and outboard engines*, achieving directional control by changing the direction of prop thrust, there being no rudder as such.
- *Bow thrusters*, providing lateral control of the bow at slow speeds. The effectiveness drops off at higher speeds.

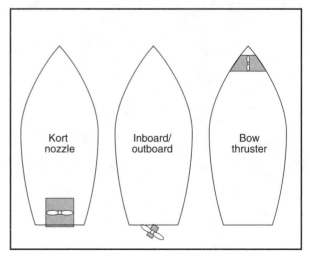

Rudder Forces

Although directional control is achieved in I/O and outboard units without a rudder, and twin-screw vessels can maneuver with engine control only, "steerageway" implies speed through the water sufficient to allow rudder forces to take effect. A vessel making 4 knots over the ground in a 4-knot following current has zero speed relative to the water, thus no steerageway since there is no relative flow over the rudder blade. Rudder force is generated perpendicular to the rudder blade face, and this force can be resolved into two components, one acting to turn the vessel on the direction of the rudder and the other causing a heel—usually inboard and toward the direction of turn.

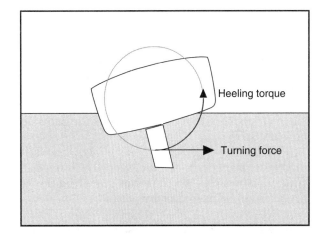

In larger vessels the rudder is fabricated around a stock supported by the rudderpost. In smaller vessels, pintles (pins) on the rudder fit into and are supported by gudgeons on the stern or rudderpost.

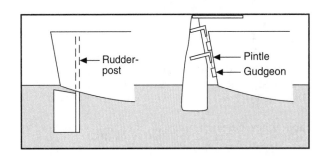

Three types of rudders are: (a) balanced, (b) semi-balanced and (c) unbalanced. The balanced rudder has a short section of blade forward of the rudder stock running the height of the blade. When the rudder is put over, water striking that portion of the blade forward of the vertical axis of rotation partially balances the force pushing on the main part of the blade. This results in less force being required to put the rudder over than in the unbalanced type, which hangs completely astern of the stock. The semi-balanced rudder has a shorter vertical section forward of the stock, thus less counterbalance than the "balanced" but more than the unbalanced.

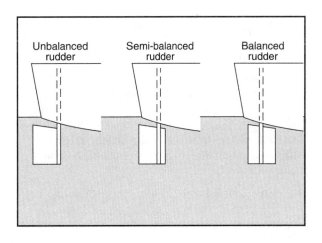

Propeller vs. Rudder Forces

Since the rudder is exposed to a weak suction current when backing, its steering control is initially overcome by prop-walk effect of the screw. Only after considerable sternway is achieved does rudder effect predominate. As an example, a LEFT-handed screw backing will initially swing the stern to starboard, and only after good sternway is reached will the rudder take effect.

Turning Characteristics

When the rudder is put over, the circle in the water is inscribed by the vessel's pivot point, that point, for a power boat, being approximately 1/3 aft of the bow when going ahead and 1/3 forward of the stern when backing. For a sailboat with a fin keel, the pivot point is roughly centered on the keel. The pivot point should be kept in mind when maneuvering in close quarters in order to predict the paths of bow and stern.

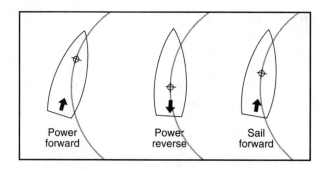

In plotting maneuvers—required for large ships in constrained waters—several terms describing the geometry of the maneuver are used:

- *Head Reach*—distance traveled from the time of full astern to dead in the water.
- *Turning Circle*—path followed by the pivot point of a vessel.
- *Advance*—distance gained in the original direction after turning 90 degrees.
- *Transfer*—distance gained at right angles to a vessel's original course after turning through 90 degrees.

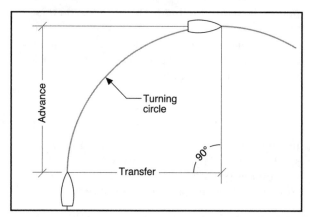

Maneuvering in Shallow Water

In shallow water, rudder control can be sluggish and sometimes unpredictable. *Squat* is the pulling of the stern of a vessel toward the bottom of a shallow channel by the lowering of pressure due to increased water velocity (the Bernoulli effect), as well as by the suction of the propellers.

The obvious problem with squat is that it affects draft, reducing available under-keel clearance.

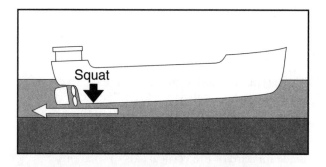

Interactions with Banks and Ships

Narrow-channel effects include bank cushion and bank suction:

- *Bank cushion* is the pushing of the bow of a vessel away from the bank of a narrow channel by water piled up between the bow and the bank by the vessel's bow wave.
- *Bank suction* is the pulling of the stern of a vessel toward the bank of a narrow channel by the lowering of pressure due to increased water velocity (the Bernoulli effect), as well as by the suction of the propellers.

The same two effects occur when two large vessels pass close aboard. In an overtaking situation, the overtaking vessel assumes the burden of compensating for the effects.

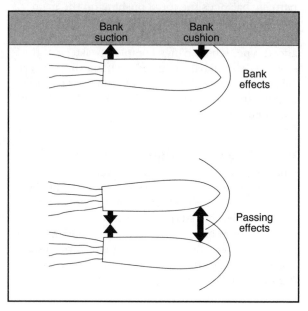

HEAVY WEATHER OPERATIONS

Ship Handling in Heavy Weather

Heavy weather maneuvering provokes endless controversy. As William Van Dorn observes in his *Oceanography and Seamanship*, ". . . no one approach to a given condition is universally successful." The vessel, crew, available sea room, etc., collectively present unique situations preventing a cookie-cutter approach.

The first object, of course, is to avoid it altogether. This requires attention to radio, weatherfax and local observation. If in port and the weather is questionable, it very well may worsen. "If in doubt, don't" is a good maxim to follow, but if caught out:

- Rig inboard lifelines.
- Don life jackets and harnesses.
- If under sail and questioning whether it's time to shorten sail, it is . . . or was!
- Clear the bilges and fill tanks to eliminate free surfaces (see, Stability, beginning page 151).
- Maintain a plot and be able to quickly transmit your position in an emergency. Know where you are relative to a lee shore.
- If involved with a tropical cyclone (hurricane) determine the low's center and your position relative to the dangerous/navigable semicircles. The Weather chapter discusses these as well as recommended evasive maneuvers.
- For less strain on vessel and crew, given ample sea room, run downwind with the wind on your quarter. If accelerating too much and in danger of overrunning a crest (and thus plunging into the trough, tripping and pitchpoling), bear off and let the crest get ahead a little. Trailing a drogue helps control heading and speed.
- Heaving-to is an option for sailing vessels. With storm jib sheeted to windward and trysail amidships and rudder to windward most vessels will jog slowly to windward with no attention to the helm.

Vessel Motions

Rotation:

- *Roll* is motion about the length axis. It can be most uncomfortable for people who are prone to motion sickness due to its rhythmic, unceasing nature. It can be lessened by tacking—taking the waves on the bow or stern quarter in a zigzag course.

- *Pitch* is motion about the width axis. It is made worse by speed and is punishing to the vessel. It can be lessened by slowing and tacking.

- *Yaw* is turning about the vertical axis. Following waves can make a vessel yaw by throwing the stern to the side. It can be lessened by increasing speed, by shifting weight to the stern, and by taking seas on the quarter rather than dead astern. When running a narrow inlet with following seas, it is best to keep the seas dead astern, though this requires quick reactions—even anticipation.

Translation:

- *Sway* is side-to-side motion caused by the horizontal component of wave motion.

- *Surge* is fore-and-aft motion caused by the horizontal component of wave motion.

- *Heave* is up-and-down motion caused by the vertical component of wave motion.

Broaching:

Broaching is yawing out of control until the vessel lies parallel to the waves. Combined with the centrifugal force of the turn, it can capsize a marginally stable vessel.

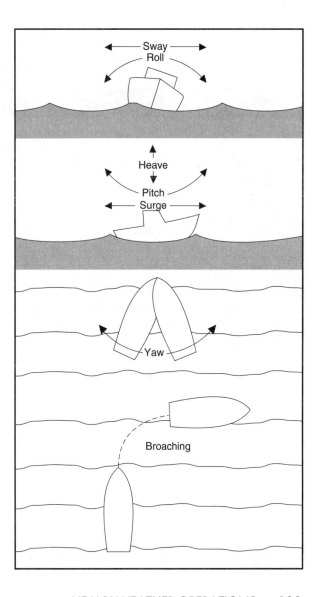

DOCKING AND UNDOCKING

Dock Lines

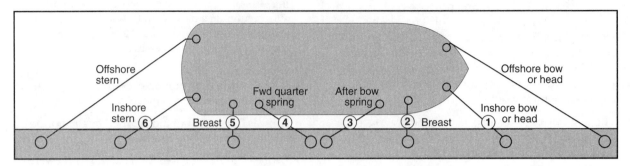

Docking Procedures for a Single RH Prop

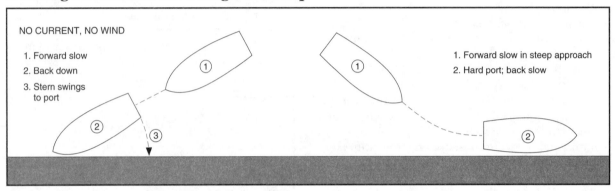

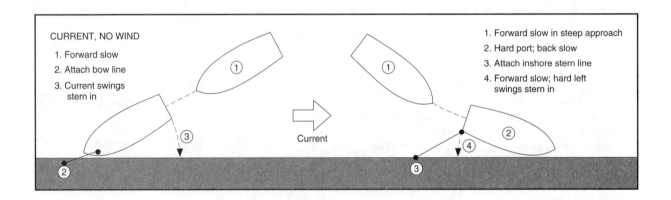

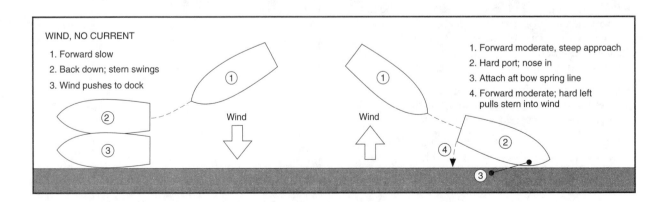

Dockline Handling Terminology

Hold the line—don't let the line slip

Check the line—hold, but ease if necessary to prevent parting

Slack the line—remove all tension; form a bight

Take a strain—put line under tension

Take in number "x"—take in line "x" after it is cast off (see line numbering at left)

Single up—take in all lines but leaving one standing part at all stations.

Getting Underway with a Single RH Prop

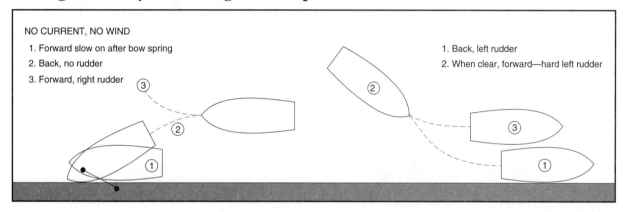

NO CURRENT, NO WIND

1. Forward slow on after bow spring
2. Back, no rudder
3. Forward, right rudder

1. Back, left rudder
2. When clear, forward—hard left rudder

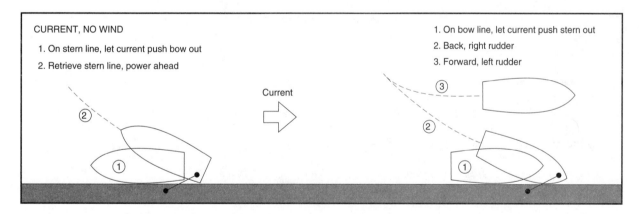

CURRENT, NO WIND

1. On stern line, let current push bow out
2. Retrieve stern line, power ahead

1. On bow line, let current push stern out
2. Back, right rudder
3. Forward, left rudder

Current

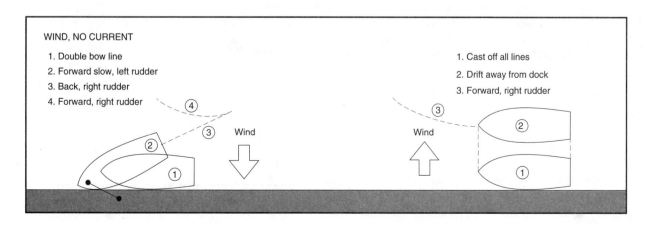

WIND, NO CURRENT

1. Double bow line
2. Forward slow, left rudder
3. Back, right rudder
4. Forward, right rudder

1. Cast off all lines
2. Drift away from dock
3. Forward, right rudder

Wind

Wind

MOORING AND ANCHORING

Moorings

A mooring system is ground tackle designed for long-term tethering of a vessel. A typical mooring consists of—starting at the bottom:

- *Mushroom anchor* or *large concrete or granite block*. A mushroom should weigh 10 lb. per foot of boat length.

- *Heavy chain*. Chain length should equal that of the vessel. Typical chain link diameter is 1 inch.

- *Swivel shackle*. Shackle size should match that of the heavy chain.

- *Light chain*. Chain length should equal the maximum depth of water.

- *Mooring ball*. Ball or buoy should easily support the light chain; material should be non-marring.

- *Nylon pendant*. The pendant(s) should be of length 12–20 feet and be secured directly to the chain with a thimble and shackle.

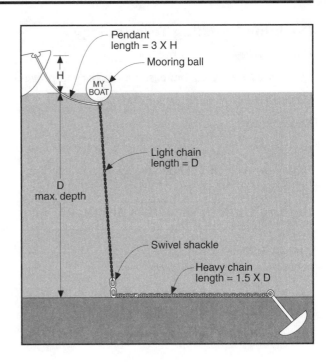

Anchoring and Ground Tackle

The term "ground tackle" refers to all of the equipment used in anchoring: windlass, rode (wire, rope or chain) and anchor.

Windlass

Windlasses may be horizontal (axle horizontal) or vertical. A typical horizontal anchor windlass is shown at right. The smooth gypsy is used to haul on rope; the socketed wildcat engages and hauls in chain. A riding pawl locks the wildcat, preventing chain from running out. A chain stripper disengages the chain links from the wildcat and feeds them down the hawsepipe to the chain locker below. A devil's claw (not shown) takes the strain of the deployed chain and acts as a preventer and/or snubber.

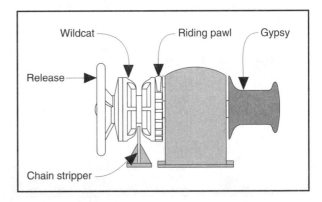

Chain

Small boat chain comes in three types (in order of increasing strength): Proof coil, BBB, and High test. Chain "size" is the nominal diameter of the material of the link. When new, the diameter of U.S. chain is actually about 1/32″ greater than the nominal.

Chain links are either open or studded. Studding prevents the chain from kinking and increases the chain's strength by about 15%.

Chain is purchased and measured in 15-fathom (90′) "shots" (smaller lengths can be purchased at boating stores). An all-chain rode is often marked with paint and/or wire wrapped around the detachable links found between the shots as shown in the table.

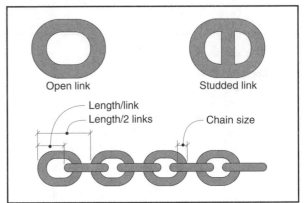

Marking Anchor Chain

	Colored Detachable Link (DL)	Number of Links Either Side of DL Painted White	Turns of Wire Around Stud Links Adjacent to DL
1 shot (15 fathoms/90 feet)	red	one either side	one wire 1st stud
2 shots (30 fathoms/180 feet)	white	two either side	two wires 2nd stud
3 shots (45 fathoms/270 feet)	blue	three either side	three wires 3rd stud
4 shots (60 fathoms/360 feet)	red	four either side	four wires 4th stud
5 shots (75 fathoms/450 feet)	white	five either side	five wires 5th stud
6 shots (90 fathoms/540 feet)	blue	six either side	six wires 6th stud

Example: Three Shots

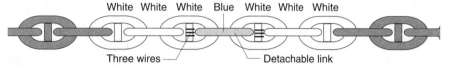

White White White Blue White White White

Three wires — Detachable link

The Stockless or Navy Anchor

The modern stockless anchor is used by large vessels. The absence of a stock allows the shank to be housed in the hawsepipe.

- *Arm*: arm that supports the flukes.
- *Bill:* point of the fluke.
- *Crown:* reinforced point at which arm and shank are joined by a ball joint.
- *Fluke:* part that resists pulling out of the bottom.
- *Head:* top of the shank which engages the stock.
- *Palm:* flat face of the fluke.
- *Shank:* long member connecting arm to stock.
- *Tripping palm:* inclined surface which causes flukes to dig in when anchor drags across bottom.

TYPICAL STOCKLESS ANCHOR — Ring — Head — Shank — Bill — Fluke — Crown — Arm — Tripping palm

Small Vessel Anchor Types

- *Fisherman:* also known as a Yachtsman and as a kedge. These anchors are not intended primarily to bury themselves in mud, but to catch on a rocky bottom.
- *Danforth:* the classic lightweight anchor, designed to dig into a soft bottom. It thus depends more on fluke area than on weight. A disadvantage is that when the wind shifts, the Danforth sometimes flips out instead of pivoting to follow the rode. The Fortress is an ultra-low-weight aluminum version of the Danforth. It is so light that it is sometimes difficult to lower in a strong current.
- *Plow:* This anchor literally plows itself into a soft bottom. An advantage is that, once set, it will turn to follow the rode without flipping out.
- *Bruce:* similar to the plow, but rigid and easier to handle. A disadvantage is that it can become fouled with a lump of clay and may not reset.

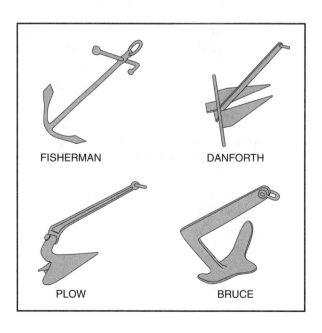

FISHERMAN DANFORTH PLOW BRUCE

Anchoring Large Vessels

Large vessels are often required to anchor in special anchorages, shown on harbor charts as lettered or numbered circles. The center of the circles indicates where the anchor is to be dropped, and the radius of the circle is the radius through which the ship is permitted to swing at anchor.

Dropping the Anchor

1. Plot an *approach course* from a prominent landmark through the center of the selected *anchor circle* and extending outward toward your position.

2. Mark a *letting-go point* on the approach course indicating the position of the vessel's bridge when the bow is at the *drop point* (center of circle).

3. From that point draw a *letting-go bearing* to another prominent landmark approximately 90° from the approach course.

3. Approach the drop point along the approach course (by maintaining constant bearing to the landmark) and stop when you reach the letting-go bearing. Pass the word to "let go the anchor."

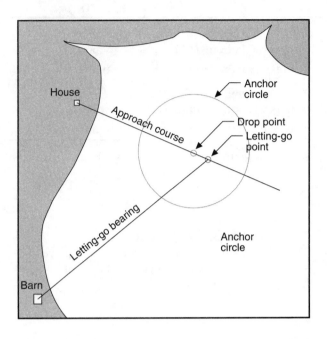

After Dropping the Anchor

1. While backing, veer (let out) length of chain equal to 5 to 7 (the scope) times the depth of water.

2. Continue backing the engines slowly, as needed, until the anchor sets and the vessel stops moving.

3. Plot your position (*bridge position*) and *anchor-set position* (forward of the bridge position by the length of chain plus distance from bridge to bow).

4. From the anchor-set position, draw two circles:

a) the *swing circle* (radius = chain out + vessel length)

b) the *drag circle* (radius = chain out + bridge-to-bow distance)

5. Maintain an anchor watch. Using radar and visual bearings, plot the bridge position at least hourly. All positions should fall within the drag circle. If not, the anchor is dragging.

6. If the anchor is dragging, veer out more chain. If this doesn't stop dragging, reset the anchor.

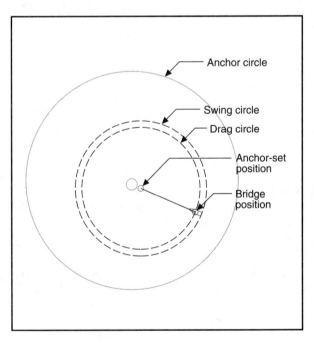

Anchoring Small Vessels

Single anchor. Pick your spot and calculate the length of rode, L. Approach into the wind (or current, if stronger) and stop upwind the distance, L, from where you want your boat to ride. Put the engine into reverse, lower the anchor, and pay out rode for a 4:1 scope. Snub the rode on a cleat (if chain, tighten windlass brake). If the anchor digs in (indicated by the rode going taut), pay out more rode for a 6:1 scope. Power back until the rode goes taut again. When the anchor sets the bow will dip suddenly and the boat will spring forward. Finally, pay out rode to match the conditions: calm—6:1; average—7:1; heavy wind—up to 10:1.

Two anchors off the bow. Set the first anchor, as above, to port of the position you would place a single anchor. After setting the first anchor, power to starboard to a point equidistant on the other side and drop the second anchor. Carefully drop back, paying out a scope of 6:1, then set the anchor. Finally, pay out rode until the two rodes are of equal length.

Bahamian moor. Prepare two anchors on the bow and calculate final lengths of rode, L. Power upwind or up current. Drop the first anchor the distance, L, downwind of your desired spot. Feed out rode until you have let out 2L. Drop the second anchor and set as with a single anchor. Retrieve L of the first rode.

Mediterranean moor. Calculate the length of rode, L. Drop the anchor a distance of L plus one boat length out from fastening point on shore. Back down toward the shore, setting the anchor, as in the single anchor. Adjust dock lines and rode for final position. If your boat backs poorly, run the anchor out in a dinghy.

Breaking Out

Power the boat slowly forward in the direction of the anchor while the foredeck crew takes in the rode. Since the helmsman cannot see the rode, the crew should occasionally point in its direction for guidance.

As soon as the rode is vertical, the crew quickly snubs the rode around a cleat. The inertia and buoyancy of the boat will exert a great force straight up or slightly forward, breaking the anchor out of the bottom. You will know when the anchor is free because the bow will dip, then spring back as the anchor releases its grip. The anchor is then retrieved with the boat in neutral or slow ahead.

With a chain rode, have a snubber line with a chain hook already cleated. As the rode goes vertical, snub the chain with the hook. This will prevent the chain from jumping out of the wildcat.

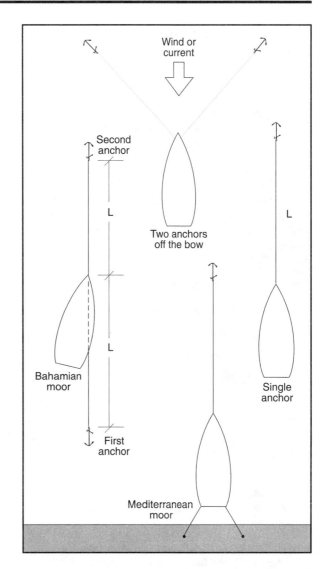

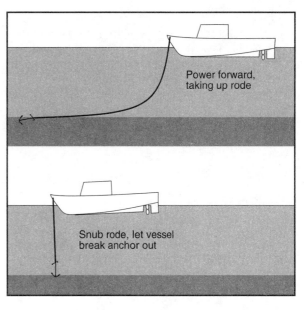

MEASURING DEPTH

Measuring Depth of Water

Fathometer

A fathometer is an electronic instrument for measuring water depth. The transducer (the part that emits and receives the sound signals) is usually mounted near the bottom of the vessel. The display can often be adjusted to indicate depth under the keel, depth under the transducer, or depth of water (from the surface).

The principle of the transducer utilizes the fact that sound travels through water at a nearly constant 4,800 feet per second. By measuring the time for an emitted sound pulse to return as an echo, the approximate depth can be determined.

For example, if an echo returns in 0.08 seconds, the sound has traveled down and up a total distance of:

$$0.08 \text{ sec.} \times 4{,}800 \text{ ft./sec.} = 384 \text{ feet}$$

The depth is half of the total distance traveled:

$$1/2 \times 384 \text{ ft.} = 192 \text{ ft.}$$

Fathometers can be subject to several errors:

- Due to variations in salinity, pressure and temperature, sound transmission is often faster, thus actual depth can be somewhat greater than indicated, providing a safety factor.

- A soft mud bottom may return a double echo, one for the mud and the other for the hard layer beneath.

- A very hard bottom may result in a multiple bottom return, or "double bounce," one twice the (actual) other.

- A "deep scattering layer" due to masses of microscopic life can show between the surface and the bottom, often around 200 fathoms (less at night).

The Lead Line

While it may seem archaic in this age of electronics, electrical systems fail. The prudent mariner thus carries (and the Coast Guard examines on) the lead line—a line with lead weight attached, and the following sequence of leather and cloth markings:

2 fathoms	2 strips leather
3 fathoms	3 strips leather
5 fathoms	white rag
7 fathoms	red rag
10 fathoms	leather with hole
13 fathoms	3 strips leather
15 fathoms	white rag
17 fathoms	red rag
20 fathoms	line with 2 knots
25 fathoms	line with 1 knot
30 fathoms	line with 3 knots
35 fathoms	line with 1 knot
40 fathoms	line with 4 knots

Note the repetitions at:

3 fathoms and 13 fathoms

5 fathoms and 15 fathoms

7 fathoms and 17 fathoms

TOWING OPERATIONS

Towing Terms

Ocean towing has its own language. In order to discuss towing operations, it helps to understand the terminology:

Backing Wire: wire from a tow string barge led forward and across to an adjacent drag string which transmits its pull when backing.

Back-Up Wires: wires on barge that carry the load in case bitts or padeyes give away. Are never left slack. Add safety, distribute the load and provide additional strength.

Bollard Pull: pull, normally measured in tons, that the tug can exert against a static object; measurement of a tug's towing power.

Brake Horsepower: HP available at the shaft.

Breasted Tow: see On the Hip.

Breasted Tug Towing: two tugs pulling tow on separate hawsers. If staggered in length, stronger tug ahead.

Bridle: two equal length chains forming legs of a triangle when rigged for towing. The ends connected to the fishplate form the apex and the other ends at the tow form the base. The SWL of each leg should be equal to the SWL of the main hawser. The legs should make a small angle at the fishplate for maximum strength and yaw control.

Button: a round deck fitting to receive an eye or serve as a fairlead.

Cable: wire rope (see Hawser).

Catenary: curve described by a bight of line supported at both ends.

Capstan Line: line from tug's capstan, around a timberhead on the tow to the new barge in order to pull it into position.

Check Line: function is to slow barge headway; use at least three round turns at timberhead.

Chocks: fairleads that provide chafe protection.

Christmas Tree (Honolulu): a method of tandem towing in which all tows ride to a single hawser with each being connected to the hawser via a short wire and its own fishplate. In the *Modified Christmas Tree* the last tow rides on its own wire connected to the master fishplate.

Drag String: row (string) of barges outboard of, and parallel to, the tow string (on either or both sides).

Face Up: to bring the bow of the tug firmly against the barge ahead using appropriate wires, etc.

Face Wire: wire(s) connecting tug to barge directly ahead. Parting of face wires one of the greatest hazards when pushing ahead.

Fairlead: used to redirect a line/wire. Can be chocks, roller chocks, double bitts. Also can be fabricated shape used to change direction of a flexible member of the tow hook-up.

Fishplate: triangular plate connecting two bridle legs from the tow to tug's towing hawser; prevents twisting of the tow bridle.

Flanking Rudders: installed in pairs on either side and slightly ahead of propellers. Their function is to affect propeller discharge current when going astern where they have max effect; effect negligible when going ahead.

Flounder Plate: see Fishplate.

Gird: see Trip.

Gob Rope (Gogeye): chain or wire running transversely across tug's stern and secured at either end at padeyes. A shackle attached to the rope at the tug's centerline with the hawser led through, thereby limiting its athwartship movement protecting crew and gear.

Hanging a Barge Off: mooring a barge to a bank.

Hawser: manila or synthetic, usually nylon (see Cable).

Hawser Towing: towing astern.

Headlog: reinforced end of a barge enabling it to withstand pushing pressure.

Heart-Shaped Shackle: can substitute for fishplate on lighter tows.

Indicated Horsepower: HP theoretically available.

In Irons: tug unable to make way since she is, in effect, anchored to the bottom by her hawser with danger of overrunning by her tow. To get it off the bottom, reduce catenary by speeding up or taking in.

Integrated Tow: multiple barges connected together, acting as a unit under tow.

Intermediate Spring Hawser (Surge Pendant): heavy chain or nylon run between fishplate and main hawser acting as shock absorber.

Jewelry: portable barge rigging including lines, shackles, steamboat ratchets, etc.

Jockey Lines (Wires): led from centerline of tug's bow to each quarter of barge ahead. Function is to prevent tug's knees from shifting in a turn. Wires run in an X pattern connecting two adjacent barges are jockey lines but used in this fashion are referred to as *Scissor Wires*.

Kevel: a cleat.

Kort Nozzle: shroud or cylinder within which the propeller rotates providing increased thrust up to about 15 kts.

Lashings: couplings; short wires used to secure adjacent barges together.

Lizzard: short line with an eye at one end used as a stopper. Typical use in hawser towing is while transferring hawser from capstan to towing bitts.

Norman Pins: two vertical heavy steel rods or bars mounted on tug's stern either side of centerline. They fairlead the hawser to the centerline. Can be retracted automatically on some installations.

Notch: opening between barge headlogs that don't meet.

On the Hip (Breasted Tow): towing alongside.

Pelican Hook: quick release mechanism used both in towing and anchor gear.

Pike Pole: pole with hook and spike at ends used to retrieve lines.

Preventers: prevents tow line whip in case of emergency hawser let-go.

Push Knees: strength members on the bow of a tug used for pushing ahead accomplishing two functions: (a) distribution of the load over a wider area of the barge being pushed and (b) preventing the barge headlog from riding up over the bow of the tug.

Scissor Wire: see Jockey Lines.

Steamboat Ratchet: device for tightening remaining slack in wire rope; essentially a turnbuckle with a ratchet in the center of the barrel. The ratchet handle operates the turnbuckle using a "cheater bar" for leverage. The turnbuckle is connected to a pelican hook which is prevented from turning while the turnbuckle is rotating by the "toothpick."

Stern Wire: led from each quarter of the tug outboard to the outboard quarters of the face barge if there are no drag strings, or, to the same points on the drag string if there are. Function is to prevent barges from spreading when backing.

Swing Line: line to a stationary barge off the beam to pull it into position.

Tandem Tow: one or more tows in line behind the tug; includes Christmas Tree, Modified Christmas Tree, Tandem.

Tandem Tug Towing: two tugs, one astern (the stronger) the other.

Timberhead: bollard-appearing structure used to secure lines to and/or as a fairlead.

Toothpick: spike passed through a shackle in the steamboat ratchet assembly to prevent its rotation when turnbuckle taken up.

Tow: generic term including astern hawser towing, pushing ahead and alongside (on the hip).

Tow Hook: the tug connection for the towing strap which in turn is connected to the main hawser providing for hawser quick release.

Towing Arch: horizontal span across tug stern preventing hawser from fouling deck gear (see Tow Span).

Towing Engine: heavy duty winch on tug to which hawser is run. Can automatically take in and pay out hawser to dampen any surging with the goal of maintaining a steady strain. Not all are automatic.

Towing Strap: length of fiber line joined to a length of chain. The line is secured to a tow hook on the tug. The chain end shackled to the main towing hawser assumes chafing duty as it is the section of the strap that rides over the stern.

Towing Winch: see Towing Engine.

Tow Span (Bar): on stern of tug to prevent fouling of deck gear by the hawser. Also called a Dutch tow bar.

Tow String: barges directly ahead of the tug. Drag strings are alongside.

Tow Wire: transmits thrust when going ahead from either (or both) tug to barge, or tow string to drag string.

Trip: to be pulled sidewise due to a lateral pull on the tug. The higher the line is secured at the tug, and the closer amidships, the greater the possibility of a trip and capsize.

Tripping Rope: used to retrieve outboard legs of the bridle where they are connected to the fishplate. This allows the fishplate to be brought aboard for a disconnect without having to retrieve the whole bridle to get to the fishplate and hawser.

Tug Boat/Tow Boat: generally speaking a "tug" boat is used for hawser (astern) towing, but in some cases can also push ahead or alongside (on the hip). Tow boats are primarily push boats.

Towing Equipment

Ocean towing is done mostly with one or more *hawsers*. The main hawser may be of wire (usually) or rope. A *bridle*, consisting of equal lengths of wire cable or chain connected by a triangular *fishplate*, distributes the load on the tow and helps to prevent yawing.

The hawser is made as long as practicable in order to form a large, deep *catenary*, which reduces the shock load. A *spring hawser* may be added between the bridle and main hawser to reduce shock even more.

The length of the hawser is adjusted to keep tug and tow in phase with the waves, further reducing both shock load and tendency for the tow to yaw.

At the tug end a wire hawser is taken in and out with a *towing machine*—a winch which continually adjusts the tension. Rope hawsers are secured to a pair of H-bitts, generally located a little forward of the rudder in order to increase maneuverability.

Rope hawsers are fixed, so chafe is a serious consideration where the heavily strained rope passes over the tug's gunwale. Chafe protection consists of layers of canvas wrapped around the hawser at the point of contact, as well as grease applied to the gunwale.

A *gob rope*—a chain or wire running across the tug's stern, with a shackle through which the hawser is led—is sometimes used to hold the hawser on the tug's centerline. A pair of pins or rollers in the stern can serve the same purpose.

If a towing engine is being used, don't use chafing gear on the hawser—it could jam.

Ensure bridle legs of adequate length. If too short, the resulting wide angle at the fishplate results in excessive strain and yaw of the tow.

The safe working load (SWL) of each bridle leg should be equal to that of the hawser.

On the towed vessel, the line is secured to the forward-most bitts.

If necessary to release the tow, the towing vessel should release first to avoid fouling the screws.

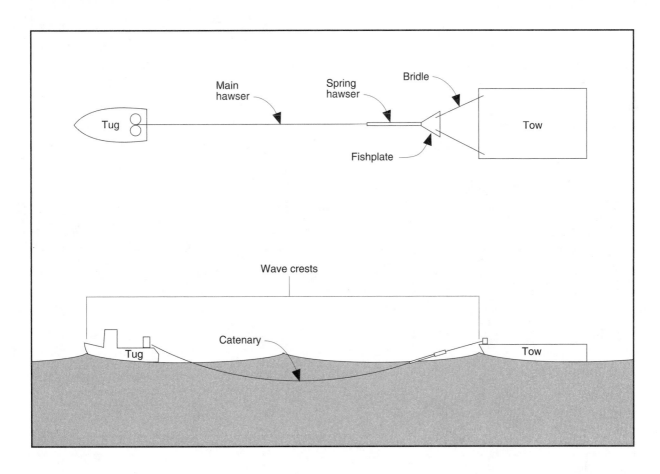

Towing Dangers

An obvious danger when towing a large, heavily loaded barge is being overrun by the barge. This can happen when a tug loses power, if the catenary is allowed to drag on the bottom, or if the tug slows too much in shortening the hawser.

Another danger, particularly when the barge is shipping water, is sinking of the tow. In deep water the tow must be released immediately. In shallow water, where the hawser length is greater than the depth of water, the hawser is cut and used to tether a marker buoy.

With extremely long hawsers, the connection between tug and tow is sometimes not apparent. Thus there is the danger of another vessel running over the hawser. If this happens the hawser should be paid out quickly, allowing the catenary to sink. The offending vessel may be alerted by the use of VHF CH 13 or 16, or a searchlight directed at the

tow or at the vessel itself, if necessary. If the offending vessel is large, the tug should be prepared to release or cut the hawser immediately.

The most common danger to a tug, however, is tripping from a lateral hawser pull. Extreme yawing, by pulling the tug sideways, can lead to tripping, as shown. Yaw can be minimized by:

- trimming the tow down by the stern

- deploying a stern drogue

- lengthening the bridle legs

- shortening one of the bridle legs (keeping in mind that uneven legs could place all of the load on one leg, causing it to fail).

Tripping situations can also be induced when the tow overruns the tug or when the tug attempts to slow the tow with S-turns.

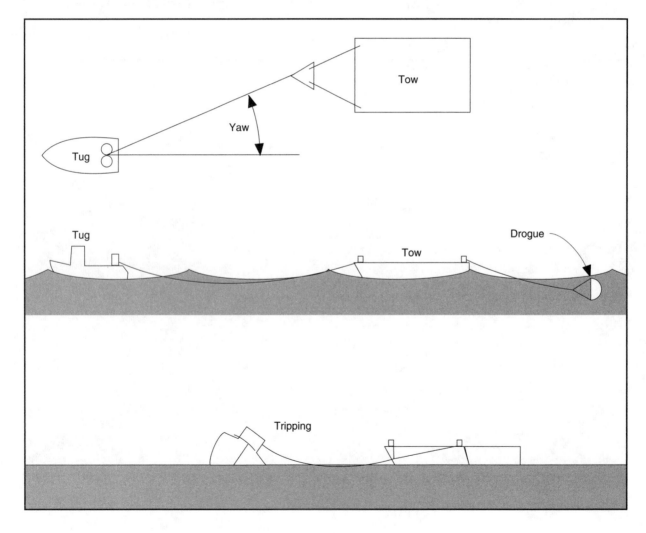

Ocean and Coastal Towing Options

The *single tow* is self-explanatory.

The *breasted tow* offers the greatest control over the tow. The most powerful tug provides a steady pull, while the smaller tug varies its output to control speed and tow orientation.

In the *tandem tow*, each tow is attached by its own hawser to the tow ahead.

Tandem tug towing uses two tugs in a line to pull the tow (which may be a single or multiple tow). The smaller tug usually tows the larger tug, using the latter's hull to transmit the pull.

The *Honolulu (Christmas-tree) tow* is a tandem (in a line) arrangement of tows. The hawser passes under the tows, each tow being connected to the hawser with its own bridle.

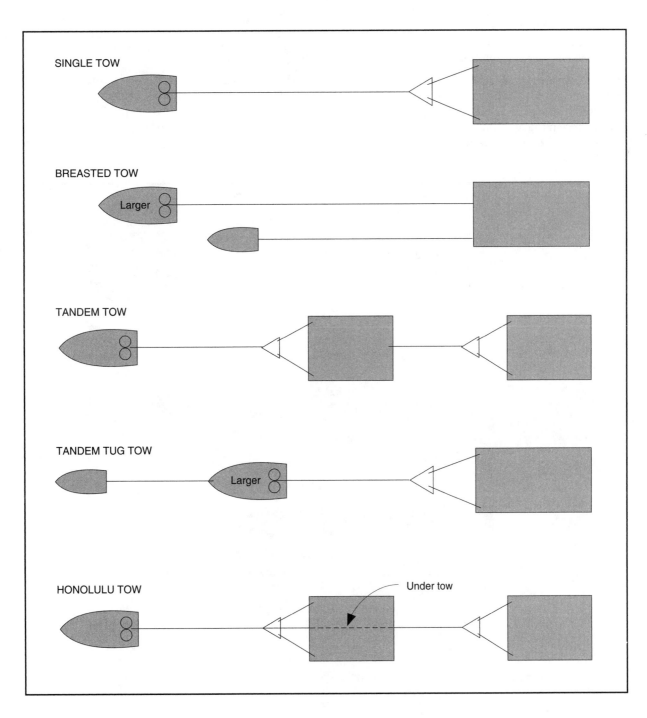

SINGLE TOW

BREASTED TOW — Larger

TANDEM TOW

TANDEM TUG TOW — Larger

HONOLULU TOW — Under tow

Pushing Ahead

In rivers and other inland waters, control of the tow is more important, and large waves are less of a problem. Here the most common options are pushing and towing alongside.

A tow boat pushing ahead is fitted with "knees" as part of the bow structure—two heavy vertical supports which act to distribute the forces over a wider area of the barge's headlog. They also prevent the barge from riding up and over the tug's bow. The tug can be linked to the tow string by facing one barge directly ("facing square") or by lining up with the tug's centerline in line with the space between two adjacent barges ("splitting-on-heads").

In "notch towing" a notch in the stern of the face barge is designed to receive the bow of a specially designed tow boat. Some designs are integrated units wherein tug and tow are rigidly connected, riding as one unit in a seaway.

When the tow is pushed ahead of the tug, it is imperative that the two be rigidly connected so that they act as a single vessel. Two principle types of lashings are used to assure immobility:

- *Face lines (face wires)* are wire(s) connecting the tug to the barge directly ahead. The parting of face wires poses one of the greatest hazards to tug personnel when pushing ahead. The same term is applied to the short lines connecting the quarters of two barges in line.

- *Jockey lines (jockey wires)* are led from the centerline of the tug's bow to each quarter of the barge ahead. Their function is to prevent tug's knees from shifting in a turn. Wires run in an X pattern connecting two adjacent barges are jockey lines but used in this fashion are referred to as "scissor wires."

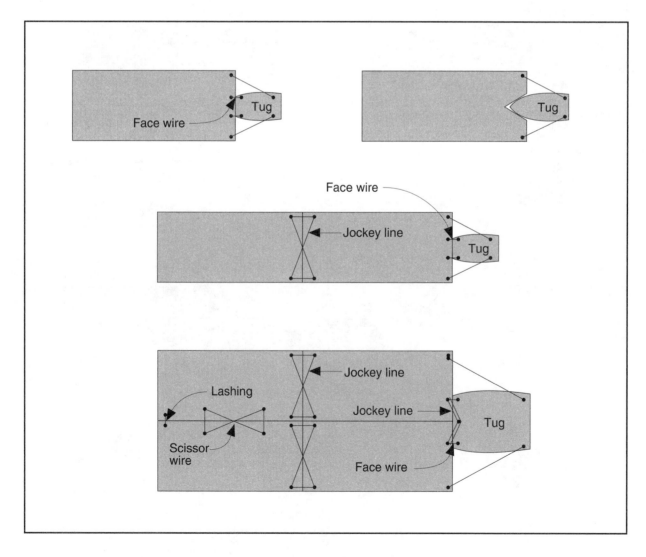

Towing Alongside

Towing alongside—also known as hip towing—requires a rigid connection between tug and tow. The tug is lashed to an aft quarter of the tow so that its propeller and rudder are well clear aft of the tow. Placing propulsion and steering aft also maximizes turning ability. It is essential that tug and tow be as rigidly connected as possible. For this reason, and for safety, non-stretch lines are used. While nylon's elasticity makes it desirable for astern towing, it makes it unsuitable for towing alongside.

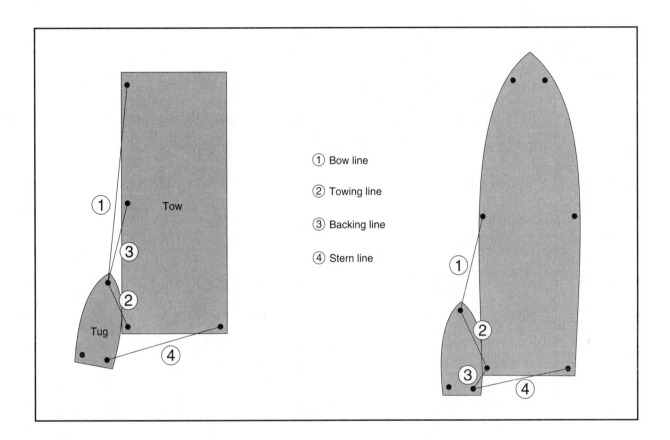

1 Bow line

2 Towing line

3 Backing line

4 Stern line

Additional Towing Tips

The safety factor provided by back-up wires is due to added strength and load distribution—therefore never leave slack.

If a towing engine is being used, don't use chafing gear on the hawser—it could jam.

Ensure bridle legs of adequate length. If too short, the resulting wide angle at the fishplate results in excessive strain and yaw of the tow.

The safe working load (SWL) of each bridle leg should be equal to that of the hawser.

Connect towing bridle on the tow with figure 8s.

Tripping becomes a greater threat when the towline is secured amidships on the tug.

If a tow line fails, attempt to retrieve the bridle.

In making up a tow, the heaviest barges should be adjacent to the tug and centered (in the tow string). Not doing so would have the same effect as a heavy weight on the end of a string—inertia could cause the tow to swing out of control.

Two hawsers are joined using the double carrick bend.

On the towed vessel, the line is secured to the forward-most bitts.

If necessary to release the tow, the towing vessel should release first to avoid fouling the screws.

Barge sizes 175′ × 26′ (standard) and 195′ × 35′ (jumbo).

SHIP CONSTRUCTION

Construction

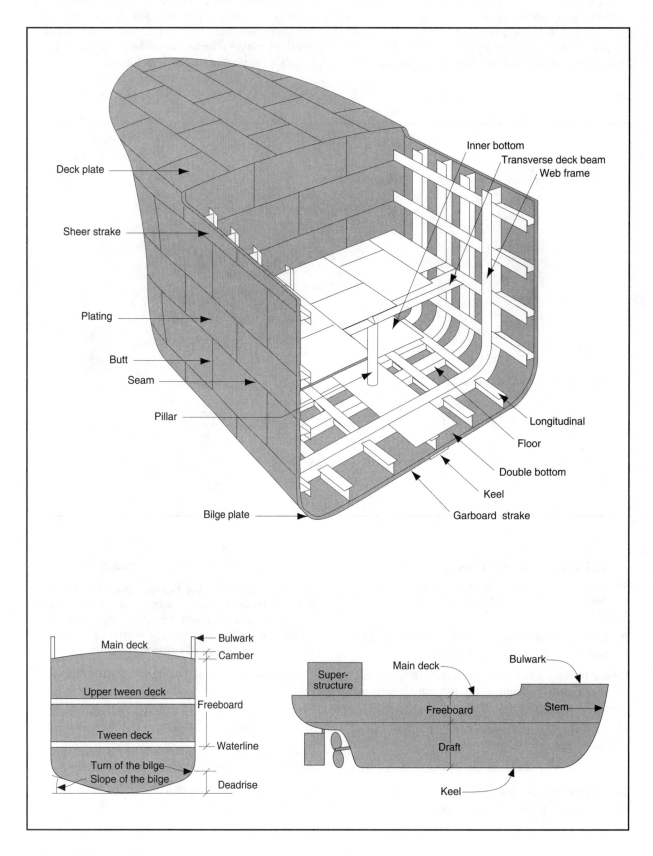

Deck plate

Sheer strake

Plating

Butt

Seam

Pillar

Bilge plate

Inner bottom

Transverse deck beam

Web frame

Longitudinal

Floor

Double bottom

Keel

Garboard strake

Bulwark

Main deck

Camber

Upper tween deck

Freeboard

Tween deck

Waterline

Turn of the bilge

Slope of the bilge

Deadrise

Super-structure

Main deck

Bulwark

Freeboard

Stem

Draft

Keel

Ship Construction

Terminology

1. Structural hull members include the *framing* (including stem and sternpost), *shell* and *inner bottom plating*, *bulkheads*, and *decks*. A ship is constructed essentially as a "box girder."

2. The watertight boundary (the skin of the vessel) is established by:

    a) *shell plating*—rows (*strakes*) of sheet metal plates whose vertical edges join adjacent plates at *butts* and horizontal edges at *seams*.

    b) *deck plating*—the "roof." The outboard strakes (the *stringer plates*) on either side strengthen the joints between *frames* and *beams*.

3. The *keel* acts as the vessel's spine or backbone. The *keelson* is a strength member atop the keel.

4. *Transverse frames*, joined to the keel, run laterally up each side of the vessel. These are the "ribs" and provide the vessel its contour.

5. Forward, shell plating is attached to the *stem*; aft, to the *sternpost*.

6. *Cant frames* are tipped frames at bow and stern which, because of the hull shape at those locations, are not perpendicular to the keel as are other frames.

7. *Beams* are horizontal members running athwartship and attached to the frames, providing vessel strength and underside deck support.

8. *Girders (stringers)* are longitudinal members serving the same function as the beams.

9. *Stanchions (pillars)* are interior vertical deck supports.

10. Below-deck, watertight integrity is provided by:

    a) Watertight transverse *bulkheads*. Passage is gained through gasketed watertight doors, secured tightly with dogs, closed individually or multiply with a bar or wheel.

    b) The *collision bulkhead*, the first bulkhead aft of the vessel's stem through which no penetrations (doors, piping, wiring, etc.) are allowed.

    c) The *double bottom* (usually in commercial vessels), a separate layer of horizontal plating located above the outer bottom, allowing for accidental penetration of the outer shell. The space between is subdivided into tanks which can carry fuel, fresh water or ballast.

    d) The *floors* are vertical members running transversely, separating inner and outer bottom platings.

11. The propeller *shaft* is supported by the *stern bearing*. Misalignment or wear results in a wobbly shaft and vibration. When the shaft becomes misaligned, the engine should be shut down or the revolutions reduced. The shaft passes through the hull via a watertight gland or *stuffing box*, sealing the hull. Damage to the packing could result in flooding.

Framing Methods

Depending on the function of the vessel, one of two framing methods is employed:

    a) *Transverse*—many athwartship frames, rib-like, closely spaced running from keel to main deck. Fewer longitudinal frames, supplemented by intercostals running longitudinally.

    b) *Longitudinal*—many closely spaced longitudinal frames, augmented by widely spaced deep transverse web frames. The latter are supplemented by intercostals running transversely. Deep web frames interfere with break-bulk cargo stowage, therefore these vessels generally use transverse framing.

An unbroken frame is *continuous*, a broken or interrupted frame is an *intercostal*.

Hull Shape

1. Hull shape is generally determined by a compromise between speed, comfort, space, etc.

2. The shape of the underbody is described by:

    a) *Deadrise*—the vertical distance from the keel to the turn of the bilge.

    b) *Slope of the bilge*—the angle between the bottom of the hull and the horizontal.

    c) *Entrance*—the tapered section of the hull forward of the midsection.

    d) *Run*—the tapered section of the hull from the midsection to the stern.

3. Above the waterline the vessel sides may slope outward or inward to the main deck as they rise from the waterline:

    a) *Flare*—the horizontal distance the hull shapes outboard.

    b) *Tumblehome*—the horizontal distance the hull shapes inward.

4. The shape of the deck is described by:

    a) *Camber*—the slope from amidships to deck edge for rapid water clearance.

    b) *Sheer*—the curvature of the deckline up or down from the horizontal from the midship section to the bow and stern. Upward is positive; downward is negative. The former allows for drier decks.

Hull Definitions

Bilge keel—longitudinal members running alongside the bilge on either side to reduce rolling.

Breast hook—triangular horizontal plates fitted across the forepeak at regular intervals to which are joined peak frames, stem and shell plating.

Bulwark—framing and plating extending above the weather deck providing crew protection and water deflection.

Camber—the transverse slope of the main deck downward from midship to deck edge in order to facilitate drainage.

Cant frame—frames at bow and stern tipped relative to the keel providing the contour and strength to the shell plating.

Carling—longitudinal discontinuous strength members running between transverse deck beams.

Ceiling—wooden planking inside a ship; deck installed over tank tops.

Chock—opening in solid bulwark for mooring lines.

Cofferdam—void space between bulkheads to protect adjacent bulkhead from fire, collision, etc.

Double-skin construction—structural framing is outside the cargo space.

Fidley—raised framework over engine/boiler room.

Floor—continuation of transverse framing across ship's bottom, intersecting longitudinals.

Freeboard—distance from waterline to deck edge.

Freeing ports—openings in bulwarks for drainage.

Furnace plate—shell plating that has curvature in two directions and must be hammered into shape over special forms.

Girders—longitudinal deck supporting strength members.

Hawsepipe—tube lining a hole in the bow for anchor chain.

Hogged—center section of vessel curving upward due to uneven loading of cargo.

Inner bottom—top of shell plating of a double bottomed vessel.

Limber holes—holes in floor bottoms allowing water access to bilge for pumping overboard.

Manger—perforated elevated chain locker bottom.

Margin plate—outboard strake on each side of an inner bottom where it joins shell plating at the bilge.

Molded breadth—greatest breadth of a vessel.

Orlop deck—partial deck in a hold.

Outer bottom—bottom shell plating of a double bottom vessel.

Permissible length—maximum allowable length between main transverse bulkheads.

Pillar (stanchion)—vertical column supporting deck.

Plating—steel plates forming vessel's skin, arranged in rows, or "strakes."

Rise of bottom—vertical distance between the bottom at centerline and the bottom at any given point.

Sagged—center section of vessel curves downward; opposite of *hogged*. Due to uneven cargo loading.

Scantlings—dimensions of frames, plating, girders, etc., making up the vessel's structure. Standards established by ABS and Lloyds.

Scupper—any opening through vessel's side to allow drainage.

Single-skin construction—structural framing inside cargo space.

Slope of the bilge—angle between hull bottom and the horizontal.

Spar deck—upper or weather deck.

Spill pipe—tube leading from windlass to chain locker.

Stiffener—angle or T-bar reinforcers attached to a bulkhead to stiffen plating.

Strake—row of plates running longitudinally on hull and deck joining each other longitudinally at a butt and vertically at a seam. Three named strakes: 1) *sheer strake*—top row of side plating meeting the deck; the lower seam of the sheer strake is riveted (instead of welded) as a crack arrestor; 2) *bilge strake*—strakes of curved plating at turn of the bilge; 3) *garboard strakes*—strakes adjacent to the keel.

Stringer plates—outboard strake of deck plating fastened to the frames.

Stringers—lighter longitudinal strength members used to reinforce bilge, deck, etc.

Tonnage opening—opening in uppermost deck bulkhead which has only a temporary means of closure; an attempt to obtain exception in tonnage requirement.

Tween deck—space between two continuous decks.

Web frame—deep transverse frame used in longitudinal framing.

STABILITY

Stability

Stability is the tendency of a vessel to return to its original position if inclined by an external force. In order to understand stability, we need to understand three key concepts: Archimedes' Principle, center of buoyancy, and center of gravity.

The Weight of Water

Volume conversion 7.48 gal/ft³

Water	Density	Specific Gravity
Fresh	62.4 lbs/ft³	1.000
Salt	64.0 lbs/ft³	1.025

Archimedes' Principle

Archimedes' Principle states that a floating object is buoyed up by a force equal to the weight of the fluid displaced. The obvious corollary is that if the body hasn't displaced its weight by the time it sinks to deck level—it's all over.

Center of Buoyancy (figure below)

Since buoyancy is the weight of the water displaced by a floating (or submerged) object, the center of buoyancy, B, is the geometric center of the submerged portion of the object.

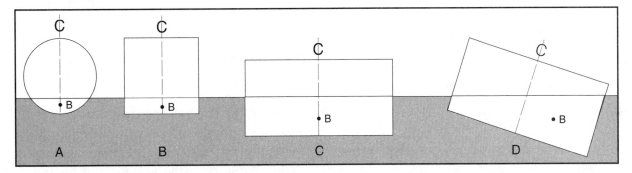

Center of Gravity (figure below)

Center of gravity, G, is defined as the point in a body around which its weight is evenly distributed and through which the force of gravity acts.

A. Homogeneous empty cylinder. Since the cylinder is uniform and empty, its center of gravity is in the exact center. If set in motion, the cylinder will not stop because it is neither stable nor unstable.

B. Same cylinder with weight in bottom. The weight shifts the center of gravity downward. Being stable, the cylinder will return to its original position.

C. Same cylinder with weight concentrated at top. The weight shifts the center of gravity upward. The unstable cylinder will flip 180° to look like the stable cylinder B.

D. Homogeneous cube. Since the cube is empty, its center of gravity, G, is in the exact center. If

tipped less than 45°, it will return to level. If tipped more than 45°, it will flip on its side.

E. Cube with weight in bottom. The weight shifts the center of gravity downward. The cube is more stable than either cylinder B or cube D and will nearly always return to its original position.

F. Cube with weight at top. The weight shifts the center of gravity, G, upward. Has stability like D for small tilts, but flips like C for large tilts.

Note that if the weight in B had been a fluid, the fluid would always flow to the lowest point, therefore *contributing nothing to stability*.

The stability of a floating object is a function of:

- Shape—flatter is more stable
- Location of G—lower is more stable
- Weight—if location is low, more is more stable

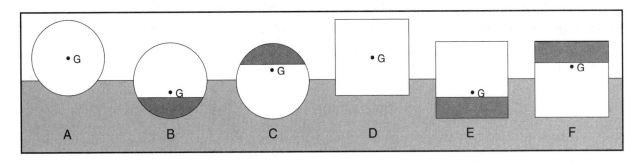

Stability Definitions

Angle of Loll—angle of list caused by a negative GM. The vessel may "flop" from one side to the other.

Buoyancy—upward vertical force supplied by the liquid displaced by a floating object.

Center of Buoyancy (B)—the point at which all the buoyant forces are considered to act; the center of volume of the immersed portion of the hull.

Center of Gravity (G)—point at which all the vertical downward forces of weight are considered to act; the vessel's center of mass. Note that when a vessel heels (barring a weight shift), G does not move relative to the hull.

Compartment Standard—number of compartments that can be flooded up to the margin line and the vessel not sink. This assumes 65% permeability for cargo spaces and 80% for machinery spaces.

Couple—two equal forces acting in parallel but opposite directions.

Density—weight per unit volume of a material.

Displacement—the weight of water displaced by a floating object.

Draft—distance from keel to waterline.

Freeboard—distance from waterline to highest enclosed deck. This determines the angle of deck-edge immersion which itself is an indicator of maximum (overall) stability—and thus the angle of maximum list. Freeboard has no effect on *initial stability.*

Free Surface—condition existing when a liquid is free to move in a compartment or tank resulting in a *virtual rise* in the vessel's center of gravity.

Heel—transverse inclination due to external forces.

Initial Stability—stability of a vessel at small angles of inclination (up to about 10 degrees); determined by GM.

Intact Buoyancy—intact space below the surface of a flooded area.

List—transverse inclination due to internal forces.

Mean Draft—average of the fore and aft drafts.

Metacenter (M)—intersection of the line of force through B when the vessel is erect with the line of force through B when the vessel is inclined through a small angle—usually about 10 degrees.

Metacentric Height (GM)—length in feet from G to M; GM is the indicator of *initial stability* only since at angles greater than about 10 degrees, M is no longer in a fixed position.

Metacentric Radius (BM)—length in feet from the arc's center at M to B. This applies to angles less than about 10 degrees.

Moment—the distance between the forces of the couple multiplied by the force.

Overall (Maximum) Stability—stability at large angles of inclination; a function of GZ.

Permeability—percentage of volume of a compartment which can be occupied by water if flooded.

Range of Stability—angle to which a vessel inclines before the righting arm (GZ) becomes zero; occurs when B moves vertically below G.

Reserve Buoyancy—volume of the watertight portion of the vessel above the waterline.

Righting Arm (GZ)—the horizontal distance from G to Z (Z is the point where that horizontal intersects BM). GZ is the indicator of *overall stability.*

Righting Moment (GZ × W)—force tending to right the vessel. The product of righting arm and displacement.

Slack Tank—partially filled tank, 10–90%.

Stiff—large GM; fast snapping roll; uncomfortable and structurally stressing.

Synchronous Rolling—undesirable situation existing when the vessel's natural rolling period, T, is the same as the period of the sea. Severe rolling and capsize could occur. Solution is to change course and/or speed.

Tender (cranky)—small GM; top-heavy with slow roll.

Tipping Center—center of gravity of the waterline plane; the point about which a vessel trims or lists.

TPI—tons per inch immersion.

Virtual Rise in G—an effective rise in the center of gravity due to surging (swashing) of liquid in a slack tank.

Stability Calculations

Transverse vs. Longitudinal Stability

While the focus of this section is on transverse stability, it must be pointed out that longitudinal stability is also of concern to a ship's officers. Trim (rotation about a transverse axis) is to longitudinal stability as list (rotation about a longitudinal axis) is to transverse stability. The examples and computations below are all related to transverse stability.

Righting Arm (GZ) and Overall Stability

The *couple* (equal forces acting in parallel but opposite directions) and the *moment* they induce (the product of one of the equal forces and the distance between them) are responsible for the twisting effect tending to provide stability. Those parallel but opposite acting forces are buoyancy (B) acting vertically upward and gravity (G) acting vertically downward.

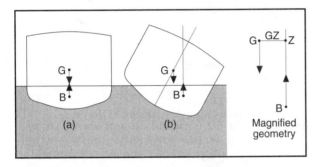

When a vessel is heeled by an external force, B moves to the side of the inclination since more of the hull on that side is immersed. As B moves outboard, it lengthens the lever arm GZ, thus increasing the moment (GZ × W) where W is the vessel's displacement.

It is apparent from the diagram that anything that lengthens GZ increases overall stability. These can be a lower G or a hull shape allowing B to move outboard.

The Metacenter (M)

Imagine a vertical line (KB) projected from K through B in the upright vessel. When the vessel heels, the center of buoyancy (B) moves out on the immersed side and a vertical drawn from B will intersect KB at a point referred to as the *metacenter* (M). As the inclination progresses through approximately 10 degrees and verticals from B are drawn, they will continue to pass through the original posi-

tion of M. For this reason, BM is referred to as the *metacentric radius* since as the vessel inclines B moves along an arc with M as its center. GM is the indicator of stability at small angles. Beyond that angle, the position of M is no longer fixed and it moves downward; thus at larger angles the indicator of overall stability is GZ as noted above.

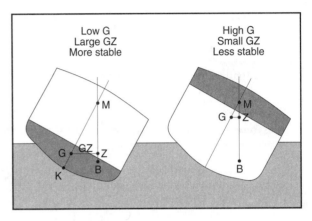

To summarize the terms:

KG	height of vessel's G above the keel
KM	height if the metacenter above the keel
GM	metacentric height
BM	metacentric radius
GZ	the lever arm
GZ (W)	righting moment

Note that GM = KM − KG

Initial Stability vs. Overall Stability

Initial stability (up to about 10 degrees) indicated by GM (metacentric height). Overall stability (over 10 degrees) is indicated by GZ (righting arm).

Classification of initial stability:

Stable	(GM positive)	G below M
Neutral	(GM zero)	G at M
Unstable	(GM negative)	G above M

Correcting List

- A list to either side to the angle of loll results from a negative GM (high weight)
- A list to one side results from off-center weight

It is critical to determine the cause of a list before attempting to correct it. Flopping side to side to an angle of loll is due to a negative GM, and the solution is to lower the G. Moving weight to the high side could just aggravate the situation and result in a capsize.

Effects on the Position of G

1. Raising G (thus reducing GM)
   a) adding weight above the G (stores, cargo, ice accumulation, etc.)
   b) loss of weight below the G (fuel, water, stores consumption, pumping bilges)
   c) virtual rise in the G due to free surface effect of fluids in a slack tank

2. Lowering G (thus increasing GM)
   a) adding weight below the G
   b) discharging weight from above the G
   c) eliminating free surface—emptying or pressing up slack tanks

3. Off-center G
   a) asymmetric cargo loading
   b) asymmetric cargo discharging
   c) shifting cargo

Note that accumulation of ice combines (1) and (3)—the worst of both worlds.

Period of Roll, T

A roll is one cycle—the time to go from maximum starboard to port and back to starboard. A very stable, "stiff," vessel has a short rolling period; a marginally stable, "tender," vessel has a long period. The period, in seconds, can be calculated from the metacentric height, GM, and the beam, W, where both measurements are in feet:

$$T = 0.44W/(GM)^{1/2}$$

Example: a vessel has a beam of 15′3″ and a metacentric height of 2′6″:

$$T = 0.44 \times 15.25/(2.5)^{1/2}$$
$$= 6.71/1.58$$
$$= 4.24 \text{ seconds}$$

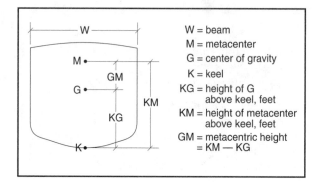

W = beam
M = metacenter
G = center of gravity
K = keel
KG = height of G above keel, feet
KM = height of metacenter above keel, feet
GM = metacentric height = KM — KG

Determining the G of a Deck Load

1. Tabulate each weight and its center of gravity above the deck. Multiply each weight by its G to find the *moment* for that particular unit. Weight will generally be in long tons (2,200 lb) and G in feet. If the height of the G for the unit isn't given, use one-half of the height of the unit.

2. Total the weights and the moments, then divide the sum of the moments by the sum of the weights. to determine the G of the entire deck load. Note that the G of the deck load is not simply the sum of the individual Gs.

Example 1:
   a) 5 containers, 8 tons each, 4 feet high
   b) 8 trucks, G 3 ft., 1 ton each
   c) 10 steel beams, G 1 ft., 0.5 ton each

Items	Tons	G	Moment
5 × 8	40	2	80
8 × 1	8	3	24
10 × 0.5	5	1	5
TOTALS	53		109

G of this deck load = 109/53 = 2.06 ft.

A variation on the problem is the situation wherein a deck load with specific weight and G exists and the question becomes what additional weight with what G can be added without exceeding given limits as to either weight or G of the load.

Example 2:

The existing deck cargo is 18 tons with a G of 3 ft. If the Stability Letter limits the deck load to 34 tons with a G of 2.5 feet, what additional weight with what G can be added?

Simply use what you already know to solve it. It amounts to simply filling in the blanks!

	T	G	M	T	G	M
Existing	18	3	?	18	3	54
Added	?	?	?	16	1.9	31
Allowed	34	2.5	?	34	2.5	85

Subtracting the existing 18 tons from the allowed 34 tons yields 16 added tons. Multiplying the allowed 34 tons by the allowed 2.5 ft. yields the total allowed moment of 85 ft. tons. Since the existing moment is 18 tons × 3 ft. = 54 ft. tons, the allowed increase in moment is 85 – 54 = 31 ft. tons. The allowed G for the added 16 tons is thus 31/16 = 1.9 ft.

Vertical Shift in G Due to Moving Cargo

Moving a cargo of weight, w, on a vessel of weight, W, moves G proportionally

$$w(d) = W(\Delta G)$$

Example:

A cargo of 800 tons is shifted upward 4 ft. on 8,000-ton vessel whose KG is 14 ft.

$$w(d) = W(\Delta G)$$

$$\Delta G = w(d)/W$$

$$= 800(4)/8,000$$

$$= 0.4 \text{ ft.}$$

Therefore, the new KG is 14 + 0.4 = 14.4 ft. Had the weight been moved down, the new KG would be 14 – 0.4 = 13.6 ft.

Vertical Shift in G Due to Loading or Discharging Cargo

This is similar to determing the G of a deck load, except here we are determining the G of the ship and previous load plus the new load.

Example:

What is the shift in KG if 600 tons is loaded 8 ft. above the keel of a 6,000-ton vessel with KG of 15 ft.?

	Tons	KG	Moment
Existing	6,000	15	90,000
Added	+600	8	+4,800
TOTALS	6,600		94,800

New KG = 94,800/6,600 = 14.36 ft.

So the KG is shifted by 15 – 14.36 = –0.64 ft.

Remember to either add or subtract both the weight and the moment, depending on whether weight is loaded or discharged.

Determining the Virtual Shift in G Due to the Free-Surface Effect

This calculates the *free-surface effect* of an incompletely filled (*slack*) tank on the vessel's G. The result, the *virtual rise in G*, reduces GM as well as GZ with resultant reduction in stability. The effect is a function of the specific gravity of the liquid in the tank and the water floating the vessel, the length and breadth of the tank and the vessel's displacement. Note that, though the volume of liquid in the tank has no effect, the breadth of the tank is a huge factor.

$$\Delta G = R(L)(B^3)/420(W)$$

ΔG = virtual rise of G (ft.)
  R = sp. gr. of: liquid in tank/outside hull
  L = tank length (ft.)
  B = tank breadth (ft.)
  W = vessel displacement
420 = a constant

Example:

Determine the free-surface effect of a slack tank 90 ft. long, 30 ft. wide, carrying liquid with specific gravity of 0.7. The 13,000-ton vessel is in salt water.

$$R = 0.7/1.025 = 0.68$$

$$\Delta G = R(L)(B^3)/420(W)$$
$$= 0.68(90)(30^3)/420(13,000)$$
$$= 0.3 \text{ ft.}$$

Now notice the effect if the tank had one centerline baffle.

$$\Delta G = 2(0.68)(90)(15^3)/420(13,000)$$
$$= 0.075 \text{ ft. } (1/4 \text{ of the original effect})$$

And if the tank had two equispaced baffles.

$$\Delta G = 3(0.68)(90)(10^3)/420(13,000)$$
$$= 0.033 \text{ ft. } (1/9 \text{ of the original effect})$$

The Stability Letter

Based on the results of stability tests and calculations, the U.S. Coast Guard issues a Stability Letter for the vessel. The purpose of the document is to detail certain parameters of loading in order to ensure maintenance of adequate stability. The Stability Letter specifies:

a) allowed deck cargo tonnage, with variations on that limit depending upon whether or not below-deck cargo or ballast is aboard.

b) the maximum allowed height of the center of gravity of the deck load.

c) ballast requirements.

d) draft limits.

e) whether towing is allowed.

f) whether or not drilling fluids may be carried (service vessels) and if so, their maximum specific gravity.

Example:

A vessel's Stability Letter states that its maximum allowable deck load is 50 tons and the limit on drafts is 6′3″ forward and 7′1″ aft. The vessel is carrying no below-deck cargo or ballast. It has 25 T of deck cargo aboard. Draft forward 5′9″ and aft 6′6″. Tests document a TPI (tons/inch-immersion) of 5 T/inch. What additional deck load is allowable?

Since the maximum allowed deck load is 50 tons, no more than 25 T can be added (from a purely weight point of view).

The difference between the allowed (per Stability Letter) and current drafts are 6″ forward and 7″ aft, therefore a draft increase of 6″ forward is limiting the additional tonnage (at 5 T/in.) to 30 tons.

In this case, the maximum deck load (25 tons) is the controlling limit

DISPLACEMENT AND LOAD LINES

Displacement and Tonnage

According to Archimedes' Principle, a vessel displaces a weight of water equal to its own weight. Therefore, *displacement* is a measure of a vessel's weight.

Displacement is expressed in either:

- *short tons* (2,000 lb.), or
- *long tons* (2,240 lb.)

Tonnage is a measure of the load-carrying capacity of cargo vessels, where one ton equals 100 cubic feet of interior volume:

- *gross tons* = volume inside watertight bulkheads
- *net tons* = volume inside watertight bulkheads less the volume of operational spaces

Draft Marks

Draft marks at both bow and stern indicate the depth of the keel below the waterline. A vessel that is neither trimmed down by the bow nor trimmed down by the stern can have different drafts fore and aft.

Draft marks are 6″ high and spaced 12″ from base to base. The base of a number indicates the number of feet exactly. If the waterline is at the top of a number, the draft is the number of feet, plus six inches.

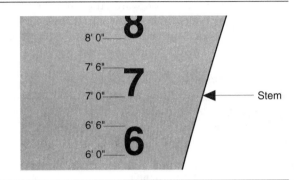

Load Lines and the Plimsoll Mark

A set of load lines, painted at the midpoints on both sides of a vessel, is collectively called the *Plimsoll Mark*. The horizontal bars indicate the maximum depth to which the vessel may be loaded, depending on the season and whether the water is salt or fresh.

To one side is a circle with a horizontal bisecting bar, at the level of the summer seawater line. There may be letters at the ends of the bisecting bar which indicate the vessel's registration society or agency. In the United States, the certifying agency is the American Bureau of Shipping (ABS).

The "freshwater allowance" allows a vessel, loading for an ocean voyage in a freshwater river or lake, to be trimmed below the fresh water line if it will later rise to the appropriate salt water line.

A = Deck line
B = Tropical fresh water
C = Fresh water
D = Tropical seawater
E = Summer seawater
F = Winter seawater
G = Winter North Atlantic

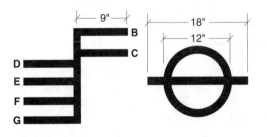

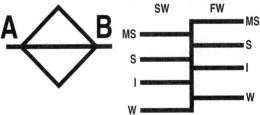

Great Lakes Load Lines

Great Lakes load lines—for vessels registered in the Great Lakes—are similar to the Plimsoll Mark, but with more freshwater gradations.

SW = Salt water
FW = Fresh water
MS = Midsummer
S = Summer
I = Intermediate
W = Winter

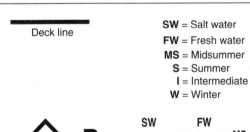

Fiber Rope

Rope is what you buy on spools at the chandlery. Rope becomes line as soon as it has a designated purpose, i.e., "dockline" or "halyard." Until recently, rope was made from natural fibers, usually hemp (sisal) or manila (wild banana plant). While less expensive and more "nautical," all of the natural fibers are inferior to synthetic rope in several important regards. Natural fibers are subject to rot, so must be dried before stowing. If used in salt water, they must first be rinsed in fresh water because salt attracts moisture. Last, natural fiber rope has about half the strength of the same size of nylon rope when new.

Natural Materials
Manila
- strongest of the natural fiber ropes
- easy to work
- subject to rot

Sisal
- strength 80% that of manila
- less expensive than manila
- fibers are brittle and easily break
- stiff, difficult to work

Hemp
- used only for small stuff (<1 inch circumference)
- tarred marline used for whipping, seizing, worming and serving

Synthetic Materials
Nylon
- easy to handle
- 5x stronger than manila
- SWL = 20% of breaking strength
- unique ability to stretch up to 40% and recover
- 3-strand parts at 50% stretch; double-braid parts at 30% stretch
- well suited for use as docklines and anchor rodes
- must be careful when towing because, when it parts, it snaps back like a lethal elastic band

Dacron
- easy to handle
- nearly as strong as nylon
- stretches little
- well suited for use as sailboat running rigging
- manufactured in a variety of finishes, from hard and slick to soft and fuzzy, and a variety of colors
- UV resistant

Polypropylene
- difficult to handle; subject to kinking
- floats (USCG specifies for thrown lifelines)
- doesn't hold knots well
- inexpensive

Braids

- *Three-strand* is the classic "rope," made up of material twisted into fibers, yarns, and strands. When holding a piece of right-hand laid (most common) rope vertically, the strands run up and to the *right*. The twists of fibers, yarns and strands are alternated to reduce the tendency of the rope to twist under tension and to build in a tension that holds the rope tightly together. The twists are not perfectly balanced, however, so that right-hand laid rope "wants to be" coiled clockwise (CW) to avoid kinking.

- *Single-braid* is a modern developement, made possible by braiding machines. Its chief advantage is that it has little tendency to twist and therefore kink. Coil braided halyards, sheets and docklines CW, just to develop the habit so you won't coil three-strand the wrong way. Braided anchor rode and tow lines can be faked down in a figure-eight pattern without kinking. Single-braid, being hollow, is reasonably simple to splice.

- *Double-braid* consists of a braided core inside a braided shell. The core and shell are often of different materials, giving the rope a range of characteristics. It is extremely flexible and easy on the hands, making it ideal for running rigging and docklines.

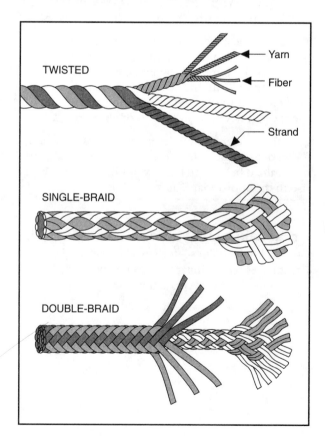

Caring for Fiber Rope
Unspooling
A new coil of manila is placed on deck, the tagged end pulled up through the coil. Synthetic line and wire rope are pulled directly from the reel.

Coiling
Rope should be coiled in the same direction as the lay, or twist, as seen looking along the rope with the bitter end held away. Nearly all three-strand rope has a clockwise lay. It is considered standard practice to coil braided rope clockwise, as well.

Flemish is to make a Flemish coil—the end of a line laid in a tight spiral flat on the deck. It looks good, but serves no useful purpose.

Faking—or faking down—is to lay a rope on deck in a series of figure-eights, so that the rope will run free without tangling.

Flaking—often confused with "faking"—consists of laying out on deck in parallel rows.

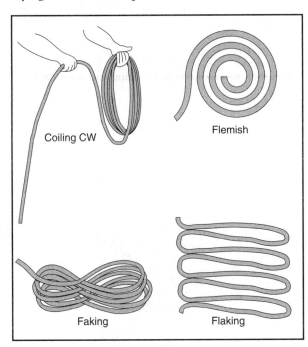

Coiling CW

Flemish

Faking

Flaking

Cleaning and Stowing
Natural fibers are vulnerable to salt water and dampness and are thus subject to rot. Before putting a natural fiber rope away, rinse it with fresh water and allow it to dry completely; store dry.

Synthetic materials are vulnerable to sunlight, oils and greases. Before storing a synthetic rope, wash with detergent, rinse with fresh water, and dry. Store out of direct sunlight.

How Fiber Rope is Measured
Rope (and line) are measured by circumference. (If you have forgotten your math, circumference (C) equals pi (π) $\times$ diameter (D):

$$C = \pi \times D$$
$$= 3.14 \times D$$

Rope is manufactured, starting at 1/4 inch, in 1/4-inch circumference increments (although you may have a hard time finding all sizes).

• *Small stuff* is line <1 inch in circumference
• *Large lines* are those >1-3/4 inch in circumference
• *Hawsers* are lines >5 inches in circumference

Safe Working Loads for Fiber Ropes
The table below lists the minimum breaking strength in pounds of twisted ropes of different materials and sizes (circumferences).

Size (in.)	Material			
	Manila	Nylon	Dacron	Poly
3/4	600	1,500	1,500	1,100
1	1,000	2,500	2,500	1,700
1-1/4	1,750	4,500	4,500	2,500
1-1/2	2,650	5,500	5,000	3,700
2	4,400	8,400	8,000	6,000
3	9,000	22,000	18,500	13,000
4	15,000	37,500	31,000	21,500
5	22,500	57,000	48,000	32,000
6	31,000	81,000	68,000	44,000

Of course one can't use a rope at its breaking strength without great risk. The rope's minimum breaking strength (from the table above) must be divided by a safety factor—usually taken to be 5 for less critical applications and 10 for more.

The definition of safety factor (SF) is minimum breaking strength (BS)/maximum allowed load (L).

Example:
What size nylon rope is required to lift a load of 6,000 lb. with a safety factor of 5?

$$SF = BS/L$$
$$BS = SF \times L$$
$$= 5 \times 6,000 \text{ lb}$$
$$= 30,000 \text{ lb.}$$

From the table, we see that a 4-inch (circumference) rope is required.

Wire Rope

Wire rope might also be called wire-reinforced rope, as it is mostly wires twisted into strands, which are then twisted around a fiber rope core. Sometimes the strands have fiber cores, as well. The fiber cores are not for strength, but to give the wire rope greater flexibility.

A wire rope's *size* is its *maximum diameter*, as shown in the figure.

Wire rope is specified by four descriptors:
- diameter, in inches
- the lay—# strands × wires per strand, i.e., 6 × 12
- wire material: improved plow steel (IPS), galvanized improved plow steel (GIPS)
- the core: fiber (FC), wire strand core (WSC)

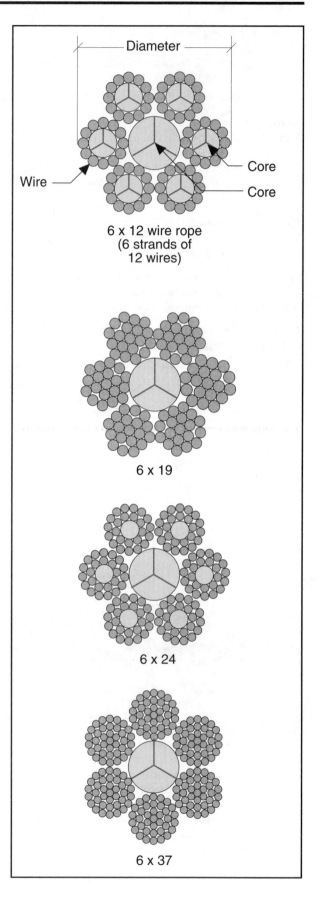

6 x 12 wire rope
(6 strands of
12 wires)

6 x 19

6 x 24

6 x 37

Safe Working Loads for Wire Ropes

The table below lists the minimum breaking strength, in pounds, of common wire ropes of different sizes (maximum diameter).

Size (in.)	Material 6x12*	6x19**	6x24*	6x37**
1/4	3,020	5,480	—	5,180
3/8	6,720	12,200	9,540	11,540
1/2	11,820	21,400	16,800	20,400
5/8	18,320	33,400	26,000	31,600
3/4	26,200	47,600	37,200	45,200
1	46,000	83,600	65,600	79,600
1-1/4	71,200	129,200	101,400	123,000

* Galvanized Improved Plow Steel (GIPS) with fiber core
** Improved Plow Steel (IPS) with fiber core

Calculating a safe working load for wire rope is the same, in principle, to that for fiber ropes (see previous page). Use a table, such as that above, if available. If no table is available, however, the breaking strength (BS) of IPS/FC rope may be approximated by the formula:

$$BS = 5,000 \times (\pi \times D)^2$$

where π is 3.14

D is size (maximum diameter of rope)

Example:
What is the breaking strength of 3/4″ IPS/FC rope?

$$
\begin{aligned}
BS &= 5,000 \times (\pi \times D)^2 \\
&= 5,000 \times (3.14 \times 0.75)^2 \\
&= 27,730 \text{ lb.}
\end{aligned}
$$

Splices

Eye splice

Stronger than any knot in forming a loop, the eye splice is common on one end of dock lines, as well as at the anchor end of a rode. For the anchor rode, a metal or plastic thimble inserted in the eye eliminates chafe. Unless the eye is very tight around the thimble, the eye should be whipped tight.

Short splice

The strongest way to connect two ropes. Because there are six strands in the cross section, the short splice is thick and may not run through a properly sized block.

Long splice

The long splice—where each strand of one rope replaces a strand of the second—is uniform in diameter, so can run through blocks. It is weaker than the short splice, however.

Back (or end) splice

The back splice is an impressive way to prevent unravelling of the end of a line. As with the short splice, the cross-sectional area of the back splice is twice that of its rope, so it cannot be used where the rope has to be pulled through a block or fairlead.

Wire rope eye

Not really a splice, the wire rope eye is formed around a thimble and seized with three wire rope clips. Note that the U-sides of the clips lie against the short (dead) end of the wire. A memory aid is the old nautical saying, "Don't saddle a dead horse."

Knots

The knots on the following page are those you will see in the exam. Don't bother looking for knots A through D; they don't exist. We have simply labeled the knots as you will see them in the exam.

Pay attention to the uses of the knots. Most of the examination questions have to do with the uses, not simply identifying the knots.

- *Timber hitch and half hitch (E)*: used for hauling timbers and starting lashings.

- *Round turn and double half hitch (F):* used to tie up when the length of line needs to be adjusted; faster but less secure than the bowline. If you want the adjustment to hold, add a third half hitch.

- *Fisherman's bend (G):* also known as an *anchor bend*, its primary use is in tying a rode to an anchor; more secure and less chafing than the bowline. The seizing shown is not part of the knot.

- *Becket* or *sheet bend (H):* used instead of square knot for tying lines of different diameter together.

- *Bowline on a bight (I):* used for rescue; a conscious victim puts one leg through each loop; if unconscious, put both legs through one loop and the chest and arms through the other.

- *Plain whipping (J):* a fast way to whip the end of a line, but more likely to slip off than the sailmaker's whip.

- *Sailmaker's whip (K):* requires a sailmaker's needle, but will not slip off, even with severe use.

- *Double blackwall hitch (L):* same as the single blackwall hitch—for attaching a line to a cargo hook—but more secure.

- *Carrick bend (M):* for connecting two hawsers (rope >5 inches in circumference); more secure than the square knot. The seizing shown is not part of the knot.

- *Stopper (N):* used to hold (stop) another line, such as an anchor rode, while the hauling part is moved or secured. Don't confuse the stopper with knots, such as the figure-eight, tied at the ends of lines to prevent their running out of a block.

- *Barrel hitch (O):* used for lifting barrels upright.

- *Rolling hitch (P):* used for fastening a line under tension to a spar. It can also fasten to another, larger line. The rolling hitch is often confused with the *stopper* (N) because it can be used as a stopper, and because it actually forms the first part of the stopper. Make sure you are clear on what the USCG considers the *stopper* and the *rolling hitch*.

- *Bowline (Q):* the most useful knot aboard a boat; will not slip, but can always be untied.

- *Double sheet bend (R):* used to secure two lines of different diameter; more secure than the single sheet bend.

- *Blackwall hitch (S):* a quick way to temporarily attach a line to a cargo hook.

- *French bowline (T):* also sometimes known as the "Portuguese bowline" and the "caulker's bowline"; used to support a victim. If the victim is conscious, one leg goes through each of the loops, while the victim holds on the standing part. If the victim is unconscious, both legs go through one loop and the trunk through the second loop.

- *Half hitch (U):* generally a turn of a line around an object with the bitter end being led back through the bight; the basis of many other knots. Unfortunately, the USCG has chosen a poor example for the illustration. The knot shown is identical to the marling hitch (V). Make sure you remember which is which. As a memory aid, perhaps, "Illustration U is Unfortunate."

- *Marling hitch (V):* used to lash canvas to a spar. Watch out because the USCG calls it a *marline hitch*.

- *Square knot or reef knot (W):* used to connect two lines of equal diameter; easy to untie except when under strain.

- *Clove hitch (X):* used to attach line to a piling; more secure if followed with a single half hitch.

Marlinspike Definitions

Becket—metal or fiber eye for receiving a hook.

Bend—knot used to join two lines together.

Bight—a loop formed by crossing the bitter end over itself.

Bitter end—the free end of a line.

Block—shell of wood or steel mounting sheaves.

Dipping the eye—to bring a mooring line's eye up from below and through the eye of a line already on a bollard, allowing either's removal without disturbing the other.

End-for-end—reversing a line's attachments in order to distribute the wear.

Fid—pointed wood device used in splicing.

Hauling part—that portion of a line (fall) to which the force is applied.

Heaving line—a lightweight line with a weight at the end, used to haul on heavy hawser.

Hitch—knot used to join a line to a post, spar, etc.

Knot—used to form an eye or to secure a line.

Lanyard—small stuff secured to an object to prevent it from going adrift.

Lay—how the components of a rope are twisted together.

Line—name for rope once aboard. The few *ropes* aboard a vessel are *man, head, hand, ship, bell*, and *buoy*. An exception is wire rope.

Marlinespike—pointed metal device used in working wire rope.

Messenger—line attached to a heaving line on one end and a heavier line on the other (hawser, etc.).

Parceling—winding strips of canvas over, and in the same direction as, worming. See *worming*.

Running rigging—rigging which moves in performing its function, usually in sail control as in sheets, halyards, etc.

Seizing—wrapping twine or tape around rope to bind two ropes together or a rope to another object.

Serving—winding small line against the lay and over worming and parceling to protect rope from chafe and water damage.

Sheave—rotating grooved wheel within a block for wire or fiber line.

Small stuff—line less than 1 inch in circumference.

Splice—weaving strands of a rope to itself or to a second piece of rope.

Standing part—the longer part of a line which is fixed during the tying of a knot.

Standing rigging—does not move, as in shroud, stays on sail craft.

Tackle—an assembly of blocks and falls used to achieve mechanical advantage in applying a force, as in lifting.

Thoroughfoot a line—to clear it if twists by coiling against the lay and bringing end up through the center.

Turn—a loop formed around a post, rail, or the rope itself.

Whipping—wrapping twine or tape around a rope end to prevent unraveling.

Worming—laying smaller line in the spiral grooves (with the lay) between rope strands. Worming, parceling, and serving are anachronisms from the days of natural-fiber rope. The purpose of the process is to prevent water from penetrating between the strands of a rope and causing it to rot. Regardless, you should learn the terminology because you will probably see it in a question!

The difference between worming, parceling and serving can be remembered from the ditty,

> "Worm and parcel with the lay,
> Turn and serve the other way."

BLOCK AND TACKLE

Construction and Terminology

The figure at right shows the parts of a basic block. When a line is passed through a block (or blocks), the line is said to be *rove*. When rove, the block(s) and line are known as a *tackle*.

The block which remains fixed is the *standing block*. The *moving block* is attached to the load. The end of the line you pull on is the *hauling part*. The other end of the line is the *standing part*.

To separate the blocks is to *overhaul*. To bring the blocks closer together is to *round in* or to *round up*. When the two blocks come together, they are *two-blocked* or *chock-a-block*.

To properly size a block and its line, use the following rules, where circumference = 3.14 × diameter:

- fiber: block diameter = 3 × rope circumference
    sheave diameter = 2 × rope circumference

- wire: sheave diameter = 20 × rope diameter

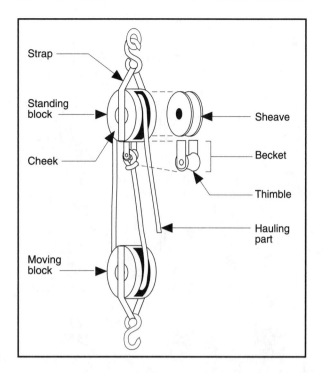

Mechanical Advantage

The figure on the following page shows the names of the tackles on which you will be examined.

The theoretical (no friction) mechanical advantage (MA) of a tackle depends on two factors:

- the number of sheaves or pulleys

- whether the hauling part comes from the standing block or the moving block

Imagine the tackle to be lifting a weight against gravity. *The theoretical mechanical advantage equals the number of lines pulling in the direction of the motion of the load.* Obviously, a greater advantage obtains when the hauling line is pulling on the load; in this case, the tackle is said to be *rove to advantage*. If not, the tackle is said to be *rove to disadvantage*.

In the real world, however, there is friction—both in the turning sheave and within the rope itself. To account for friction in calculating MA, add 10% of the load for each sheave.

Example 1:
What pull is required to lift a 1,000 lb. weight using a twofold purchase rove to advantage?

> As seen at right, there are 4 sheaves and the theoretical MA is 5. Add 4 × 10% of the weight, so the load becomes 140% of 1,000 lb., or 1,400 lb.
>
> Pull = 1,400 lb./5 = 280 lb.

Name of Tackle	Rove to Advantage	Theoretical Advantage	Advantage w/Friction
Whip	No	1	0.91
Runner	Yes	2	1.82
Gun tackle	No	2	1.67
Gun tackle	Yes	3	2.50
Single luff tackle	No	3	2.31
Luff tackle	Yes	4	3.07
Twofold purchase	No	4	2.86
Twofold purchase	Yes	5	3.57
Double luff tackle	No	5	3.33
Double luff tackle	Yes	6	4.00
Threefold purchase	No	6	3.75
Threefold purchase	Yes	7	4.38

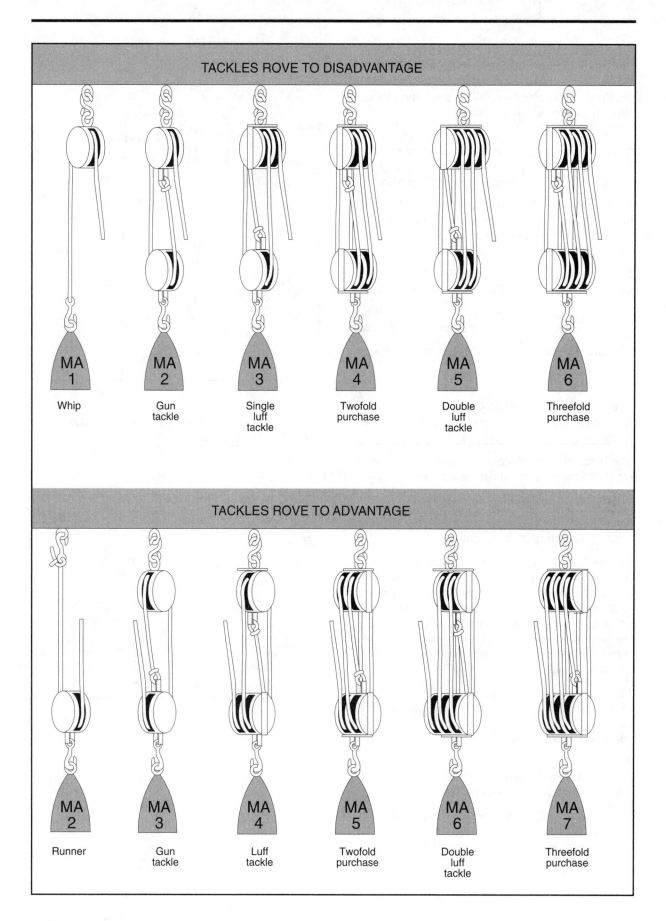

TACKLES ROVE TO DISADVANTAGE

MA 1 — Whip

MA 2 — Gun tackle

MA 3 — Single luff tackle

MA 4 — Twofold purchase

MA 5 — Double luff tackle

MA 6 — Threefold purchase

TACKLES ROVE TO ADVANTAGE

MA 2 — Runner

MA 3 — Gun tackle

MA 4 — Luff tackle

MA 5 — Twofold purchase

MA 6 — Double luff tackle

MA 7 — Threefold purchase

SHIP'S BUSINESS

Documents

Certificate of Documentation (USCG)

Any U.S. vessel of at least 5 net tons *can be* documented, but documentation is *required* of all merchant vessels regardless of flag. The certificate must be aboard and current. It is issued by the USCG at the port of registry and its intent is to identify and describe the vessel, identify the owner(s), its financial status (liens, mortgages, etc.), and to specify by endorsements the trades in which the vessel is entitled to engage. It is effective for one year with the date specified by a sticker attached to the Document. Renewal must be effected by the end of the month during which it expires and is done by submitting an application.

Home Port is defined as the port with a documentation office closest to the owner's home. *Hailing Port* is any port designated by the owner. The *Official Number* is that assigned by the Coast Guard, is on the Document, and must be marked on some clearly visible interior structural part of the hull by any method that cannot be obliterated or obscured. The numerals are to be block Arabic, at least 3″ high.

Certificate of Inspection (USCG)

This document attests (by inspection) that the vessel conforms with the laws and regulations that apply to her, and defines the conditions under which she can legally operate. It is to be posted under glass and if on a passenger vessel >100 GT it shall be posted in the dining room or lounge (if there is no dining room). Vessels requiring such a Certificate include:
- vessels carrying passengers for hire (except uninspected passenger vessels <100 GT).
- vessels >15 GT carrying freight for hire.
- vessels carrying flammable or combustible liquid cargo in bulk containers >100 gallons.
- vessels carrying dangerous cargo, when required by the USCG.

Stability Letter (USCG)

Required of every U.S. vessel, the Letter states that the vessel can be maintained in a satisfactory stability state as a result of calculations which have been made. Any operating restrictions which exist (referring to their effect on stability) are stated in the letter and must be complied with. It must be posted under glass in the wheelhouse.

Load Line Certificate (ABS)

A Load Line Certificate is required of merchant vessels of ≥150 GT engaged in international, intercoastal and coastwise voyages. The purpose is to certify the correctness of the load lines for that vessel, and that they have been correctly marked on the hull. It specifies the maximum draft in terms of minimum freeboard according to the area she is to operate and the season involved. Load Line Regulations (46 CFR Parts 41-47) are to be carried aboard each American flagged vessel.

Station License (FCC)

Any installed equipment emitting electromagnetic radiation (VHF, SSB, RADAR, EPIRB) must be listed on the vessel's FCC Station License. The license is good for 5 years, must be renewed before it expires, and must be posted near the equipment.

Radio Operator's License (FCC)

Required of the radio operator (could be Master) of:
- SSB equipment transmitting >100 W
- vessel >65 ft. operating on the Great Lakes
- vessel carrying >6 passengers for hire
- vessel >300 GT
- tug >26 ft. towing
- vessel >100 GT carrying 1 or more passengers
- dredge
- floating power plant

Official Log

An official logbook is to be maintained by the Master of the vessel. Entries are to be free of erasures, with corrections to be made by drawing a light line through the entry and initialing the correction. The Log is required on:
- U.S. merchant vessels from a U.S. to a foreign port
- A vessel of ≥100T on an intercoastal voyage

Oil Record Book

Required of tankers of more than 150 GT and other ships over 400 GT, the Oil Record Book is a legally required book containing a record of discharges from machinery spaces, cargo and ballast operations, etc. It must be current and available for examination when entering port. Note that since it is required only on larger ships, you are unlikely to be asked a question about it.

Radiotelephone (RT) Log

This daily log of the ship's radio status and distress calls heard is to be maintained in the pilothouse near the radio equipment. The record of radio condition is to be kept for one year, but the log of emergency or disaster messages (either sent or received) must be kept for three years.

POLLUTION REGULATIONS

Definitions

Cargo Record Book—a log required by any vessel carrying bulk "noxious liquid substances."

33 CFR Part 156—the title and part of the *Code of Federal Regulations* that concerns oil transfer operations and procedures.

Clean ballast—ballast water producing no "sheen" on the water and containing less than 15 ppm oil.

COW—"Crude Oil Washing," using crude oil as the washdown medium instead of water as is used in the Butterworth system.

Declaration of Inspection—a form required by the applicable CFR, which must be completed prior to transferring oil to or from a vessel. The person in charge at both the transferring and receiving facilities must sign it. This form functions to ensure that appropriate steps, personnel, communications, etc., are in such condition as to make oil transfer a safe and non-polluting event. Copies must be retained for a minimum of one month.

Discharge—intentional or unintentional emission; includes spilling, leaking, pumping, pouring, emptying or dumping.

Garbage—includes food wastes, glass, metal, crockery, rags, paper. Note that "garbage" does *not* include plastics.

Inert gas system—a system by which inert gas whose oxygen content is <5% is introduced into a tank in order to maintain the oxygen present below 8%. The inert gasses are obtained from (a) the vessel's flue gasses (after passing through a scrubber to remove impurities), or (b) an inert gas generator.

IOPP Certificate—the International Oil Pollution Prevention Certificate, issued by the flag country certifying that the vessel has been surveyed and will not pollute. It must be carried by:

- any oil tanker 150 GT or greater
- any other vessel of 400 GT or greater if on foreign voyages or to offshore terminals

The certificate is good for 5 years (4 years for an Inspected U.S. vessel).

In addition, an intermediate survey is required within 6 months of the halfway point of the certificate's life. U.S. inspected vessels require an intermediate survey every year.

Load on top—allowing an oil-water mixture to separate naturally, discharging the clean water overboard, then loading the next cargo on top of the separated oil.

MARPOL 73/78—International Convention for the Prevention of Pollution from Ships, 1973 (amended in 1978). Annexes thereto cover pollution by:

I   Oil
II Noxious liquid substances
III Chemicals in package form
IV Sewage
V   Plastic and Garbage

The regulations apply to the navigable waters adjoining the shorelines and contiguous waters of the U.S. Note that Annex V does not apply to U.S. Government vessels. A port in which medical or hazardous waste is to be discharged requires 24 hours advance notice.

MSD—Marine Sanitation Device.

Noxious Liquid Substances—hazardous liquid cargoes which are transported in bulk and covered under 46 CFR Subchapter O.

Oil—oil of any kind, in any form, including petroleum, fuel oil, sludge, oil refuse, and oil mixed with wastes (but not dredged spoil).

Oily mixture—a mixture with an oil content of at least 100 ppm.

OPA 90—The Oil Pollution Act of 1990.

Pollution—oil, garbage, hazardous substances and plastics.

Special areas—areas of the world where, because of the absence of tidal action, *any* oil discharge is prohibited. These include the Persian Gulf, the Mediterranean, and the Black, Red and North Seas.

Tank vessel—a vessel constructed or adapted to carry oil or hazardous material in bulk as cargo or cargo residue.

Discharge Regulations—Permitted

Within 3 miles—dishwater or gray water. This includes dishwasher, shower, bath, washbasin and laundry drainage. Does not include drainage from toilets, urinals, hospital or cargo spaces.

> *Between 3 and 12 miles*—the above plus glass, metal, crockery, bottles, food waste, paper, rags, dunnage (all ground to less than one inch); toilets.

> *Between 12 and 25 miles*—the above even if not ground but not including garbage that floats or dunnage.

> *25 miles or more*—the above plus floating garbage and dunnage.

Note that plastics are prohibited from discharge anywhere or anytime.

Penalties

Any oil discharge *must* be reported to the USCG.

- Penalty for discharge: $5,000
- Failing to report: $10,000, 1 year in jail, or both.

Pollution Regulations (MARPOL) apply on:

- navigable waters
- adjoining shorelines
- contiguous zones of the U.S.

Violation may result in a civil penalty of up to $25,000 per violation, plus a criminal penalty of up to $50,000 and/or imprisonment up to 5 years.

When a vessel violates the pollution law, *any person* connected with the vessel involved in the operation is liable for prosecution.

Pollution Placard

Vessels greater than or equal to 26 feet in length must display a durable and conspicuously placed placard in machinery spaces and/or bilge pump control spaces stating the following:

> "The Federal Water Pollution Control Act prohibits the discharge of oil or oily waste into or upon the navigable waters of the United States or the waters of the contiguous zone if such discharge causes a film or sheen upon, or discoloration of, the surface of the water, or causes a sludge or emulsion beneath the surface of the water. Violators are subject to a penalty of $5,000."

Oil Transfer Operations

A waiver of requirements of the regulations for oil transfer is submitted to the Captain of the Port at least 30 days prior to the scheduled transfer.

A certified tankerman must be familiar with all pollution laws and regulations.

If an order to suspend oil transfer operations is issued, it will include a statement of each condition requiring immediate action to prevent oil discharge.

In the case of a facility and a vessel transferring oil, the decision to start lies with the person in charge at both facilities.

For a single person to act as "person in charge" of both transferring and receiving facilities, the Captain of the Port must approve.

Action in Case of a Spill

In case of a spill:

- stop the discharge;
- notify the USCG;
- prevent spreading and remove as much as possible.

Types of control:

- containment (booms)
- mechanical (skimmers)
- absorbents (straw or reclaimed fibers)
- chemical (detergents)
- sinking agents (carbon, sand, chalk)

Note that use of dispersants (detergents) or sinking agents is generally *prohibited* in the U.S. as they are harmful to marine life.

Marine Sanitation Devices (MSD)

The regulations (33 CFR, Subchapter O, Part 159) state that no boat with an *installed* toilet may be operated on the navigable waters of the U.S. without a USCG-certified MSD.

The regulations further prohibit discharge of untreated sewage (human body wastes from toilets or other receptacles intended to receive or retain body wastes) into U.S. waters out to the margin of the Territorial Seas. The extent of the latter is marked on most charts, but, in general, it extends 3 miles beyond the low water mark. In the Great Lakes, sewage is expanded to include graywater (bath and galley waste water).

The current certified MSD classes are:

- Type I—discharge contains a fecal coliform bacteria count of ≤1,000 per 100 milliliters and no visible floating solids.

- Type II—discharge contains a fecal coliform bacteria count of ≤200 per 100 milliliters and suspended solids of ≤150 milligrams per liter.

- Type III—essentially a holding tank.

Vessels ≤65 feet and under may use types I, II or III. Vessels >65 feet must have an installed type II or III.

Note that a portable toilet (Porta-Potti) is an acceptable head solution for vessels ≤ 65 feet even though it is not *certifiable* (since it is not an *installed* unit). Portable toilets utilizing throwaway bags are not acceptable, however, because the bags are easily thrown overboard.

REGULATIONS (CFRs)

Code of Federal Regulations (CFRs)

Congress passes *laws*. By necessity, Congress cannot deal with the vast amount of detail required to administer the spirit of a law. For this reason, a regulatory agency, specified by the law, is charged with developing and enforcing the details as *regulations*. These are incorporated into a body of work known as the *Code of Federal Regulations* (the CFRs). Those of maritime interest fall within the purview of the U.S. Coast Guard. Titles 33 (Navigation and Navigable Waters) and 46 (Shipping) are those of specific concern.

Title 33 comprises three volumes and Title 46 nine, two of the former and seven of the latter being of interest. Within each *Title*, specific topics are assigned to *Subchapters*. For example, within Title 46 is Subchapter C devoted to Uninspected Vessels. Each Subchapter is further divided into *Parts*, each Part covering a specific aspect of the main topic. Continuing the example above, Subchapter C has four Parts covering General Provisions, Requirements, Operations, and Requirements (Fishing Vessels)—all applicable to Uninspected Vessels.

When attempting to locate a specific regulation, first determine the applicable Title (33 or 46). After finding the appropriate Subchapter (in the front of the book—a sort of Table of Contents), it is then necessary to locate the Part covering that particular topic. This is done by using the index at the end of the Subchapter (if there is one!). Most, but not all, Subchapters have an index. Where one isn't provided, it is necessary to go to the List of Contents at the beginning of each Part.

The CFRs are provided in the exam room, so you can fumble your way through them, trying to find the Part(s) that apply to a specific question. It would speed things up, however, if you had a rough idea of where to look before taking the exam. Here is the breakdown:

33 CFR: NAVIGATION & NAVIGABLE WATERS

Sub	Parts	Subject
A	1–27	General
B	40–55	Personnel
C	60–76	Aids to Navigation
D	80–82	International Navigation Rules
E	84–90	Inland Navigation Rules
F	95–96	Vessel Operating Regulations
G	100	Regattas, Marine Parades
I	109–110	Anchorages
J	114–118	Bridges
K	120–124	Security of Vessels
L	125–128	Waterfront Facilities
M	133–138	Marine Pollution—Financial Responsibility and Compensation
N	140–147	Outer Continental Shelf Activities
NN	148–150	Deepwater Ports
O	151–159	Pollution
P	160–169	Ports and Waterways Safety
S	173–199	Boating Safety

46 CFR: SHIPPING

Sub	Parts	Subject
A	1–9	Procedures Applicable to the Public
B	10–16	Merchant Marine Officers and Seamen
C	24–28	Uninspected Vessels
D	30–38	Tank Vessels
E	41–47	Load Lines
F	50–64	Marine Engineering
G	66–69	Vessel Documentation & Measurement
H	70–89	Passenger Vessels
I	90–105	Cargo and Miscellaneous Vessels
J	107–109	Mobile Offshore Drilling Units
K	114–124	Small Passenger Vessels carrying >150 passengers or with overnight accommodations for >49 passengers
L	125–139	Offshore Supply Vessels
N	140–149	Dangerous Cargoes
O	150–155	Certain Bulk Dangerous Cargoes
P	156–158	Manning of Vessels (Reserved)
Q	159–165	Equipment; Construction; Material
R	166–169	Nautical Schools
S	170–174	Subdivision and Stability
T	175–187	Small Passenger Vessels Under 100 GT
U	188–196	Oceanographic Research Vessels
V	197–198	Marine Occupations; Safety; Health Stds.
W	199	Lifesaving Appliances & Arrangements

Looking Up an Answer

Since most 100-ton and under Master and Mate licenses are used to operate inspected small passenger vessels ("T-boats"), most of your questions will come from Title 46, Subchapter T. So that you can familiarize yourself with the contents of Subchapter T, we reprint its full index here.

A simple example should suffice to demonstrate the process of finding an answer from the CFRs supplied at the exam.

Example:
How many paddles must accompany life floats on inspected passenger vessels of under 100 tons?

1. The vessel is an inspected small passenger vessel under 100 GT. It falls under Title 46, Subchapter T; thus the term "T-boat."

2. Look for key words in the index at the end of Subchapter T. Key words for this question might be *paddles*, *life floats*, and *lifesaving equipment*.

3. Looking in the index, we score all three times.

Under "paddles":
Paddles **180.15**

Under "life floats":
Life floats, equipment for **180.15**

Under "lifesaving equipment":
Lifesaving equipment:
Application 180.01-1
Approved 180.05-1
Buoyant apparatus 180.10, 180.15
For vessels in Great Lakes service 180.10-15
For vessels in lakes, bays, and sounds service 180.10-20
For vessels in ocean or coastwise service 180.10-5
For vessels in river service .180.10-25
Inspection of 176.25-22
Installed but not required 180.10-5, 181.05-5
Intent 180.01-5
Life floats 180.10-1, **180.15-1**

4. It appears that Part 180, Section 15 is where we will most likely find the answer. Going there we find:

Subpart 180.15—Equipment for Life Floats and Buoyant Apparatus

§ 180.15-1 Equipment required.

(a) Each life float shall be fitted with a life line and shall be equipped with two paddles, a water light and a painter.

Answer: two paddles

DECK GENERAL
QUESTIONS

The illustrations cited in the questions are shown on pages 802–805.

2. You are standing the wheelwatch when you hear the cry, "Man overboard starboard side." You should _____.

A. give full right rudder
B. give full left rudder
C. put the rudder amidships
D. throw a life ring to mark the spot

3. A stopper used in securing the ground tackle for sea that consists of a grab attached to a turnbuckle is a _____.

A. riding pawl
B. buckler
C. devil's claw
D. locking ring

5. You are standing the wheelwatch when you hear the cry, "Man overboard starboard side." You should be ready to _____.

A. give full left rudder
B. give full right rudder
C. put the rudder amidships
D. throw a life ring to mark the spot

6. Which statement about a tunnel bow thruster is TRUE?

A. It provides lateral control without affecting headway.
B. It is fully effective at speeds up to about six knots.
C. It can be used to slow the ship in addition to backing down.
D. It will allow you to hold a position when the current is from astern.

7. Illustration D044DG. The mooring line labeled "F" is called a _____.

A. breast line
B. bow line
C. forward spring line
D. None of the above

9. Defense plans may cause the operation of electronic aids to navigation to be suspended with _____.

A. no notice
B. one day's notice
C. a week's notice
D. thirty (30) days notice

11. A person is found operating a vessel while intoxicated. He is liable for _____.

A. imprisonment for up to one year

B. a civil penalty of not more than $5,000
C. seizure of his/her vessel and forfeiture of the title
D. a fine of not more than $1,000

12. The maximum length allowed between main, transverse bulkheads on a vessel is referred to as the _____.

A. floodable length
B. factor of subdivision
C. compartment standard
D. permissible length

13. In illustration D044DG, the mooring line labeled "G" is called a(n) _____.

A. inshore bow line
B. offshore bow line
C. forward breast line
D. forward spring line

15. Floors aboard ship are _____.

A. frames to which the tank top and bottom shell are fastened on a double bottomed ship
B. transverse members of the ships frame which support the decks
C. longitudinal beams in the extreme bottom of a ship from which the ship's ribs start
D. longitudinal angle bars fastened to a surface for strength

16. When underway and proceeding ahead, as the speed increases, the pivot point tends to _____.

A. move aft
B. move forward
C. move lower
D. remain stationary

17. Illustration D044DG. The mooring line labeled "E" is called a(n) _____.

A. bow spring line
B. aft spring line
C. forward breast line
D. bow line

19. The vessel's "quarter" is located _____.

A. abeam
B. dead astern
C. just forward of the beam on either side
D. on either side of the stern

22. A wildcat is a _____.

A. deeply grooved drum on the windlass with sprockets which engage the links of the anchor chain
B. winch that is running out of control due to a failure of the overspeed trips
C. line that has jumped off the gypsy head while under strain
D. nylon line that parts under strain and whips back in a hazardous manner

24. A crack in the deck plating of a vessel may be temporarily prevented from increasing in length by _____.

A. cutting a square notch at each end of the crack
B. drilling a hole at each end of the crack
C. slot-welding the crack
D. welding a doubler over the crack

25. The turning circle of a vessel making a turn over 360 degrees is the path followed by the _____.

A. center of gravity
B. bow
C. bridge
D. centerline

26. The pivoting point of a fully loaded vessel with normal trim proceeding ahead at sea speed is _____.

A. right at the bow
B. one-third the length of the vessel from the bow
C. one-half the length of the vessel from the bow
D. two-thirds the length of the vessel from the bow

27. Under title 46 of the United States Code, the person in charge of a documented vessel who fails to report a complaint of a sexual offense may be _____.

A. fined up to $5,000
B. imprisoned for up to one year
C. charged with accessory to sexual assault
D. All of the above

29. You are in charge of a U.S. documented vessel. Under title 46 of the United States Code, if you fail to report a complaint of a sexual offense, you may be _____.

A. criminally charged and jailed
B. civilly charged and fined

C. held personally liable by the victim and sued
D. All of the above are correct

31. An embarked Pilot _____.

A. is a specialist hired for his local navigational knowledge
B. is solely responsible for the safe navigation of the vessel
C. relieves the Master of his duties
D. relieves the officer of the watch

36. The distance that a vessel travels from the time that the order to put engines full astern until the vessel is dead in the water is known as _____.

A. advance
B. head reach
C. surge
D. transfer

37. Your enrolled vessel is bound from Baltimore, MD, to Norfolk, VA, via Chesapeake Bay. Which statement about the required Pilot is TRUE?

A. The Pilot must be licensed by either Virginia or Maryland.
B. The Pilot need only be licensed by the Coast Guard.
C. The Pilot must be licensed by Virginia and Maryland.
D. The Pilot must be licensed by Virginia, Maryland and the Coast Guard.

43. In illustration D044DG, the mooring line labeled "D" is called a(n) _____.

A. after spring line
B. forward spring line
C. waist breast line
D. stern line

45. Which shallow water effect will increase dramatically if you increase your ship's speed past its "critical speed"?

A. Squatting
B. Smelling the bottom
C. Sinkage
D. Bank cushion

46. Which statement concerning the handling characteristics of a fully loaded vessel as compared with those of a light vessel is FALSE?

A. A fully loaded vessel will be slower to respond to the engines.
B. A fully loaded vessel will maintain her headway further.
C. A light vessel will be more affected by the wind.
D. A light vessel loses more rudder effect in shallow water.

49. Flammable liquid means any liquid which gives off flammable vapors at or below _____.

A. 40°F (4.4°C)
B. 80°F (26.7°C)
C. 110°F (43.3°C)
D. 150°F (65.6°C)

50. A vessel is entering port and has a Pilot conning the vessel. The Master is unsure that the Pilot is taking sufficient action to prevent a collision. What should the Master do?

A. Nothing; the Pilot is required by law and is solely responsible for the safety of the vessel.
B. State his concerns to the Pilot but do not interfere with the handling of the vessel.
C. Recommend an alternative action and if not followed relieve the Pilot.
D. Direct the Pilot to stop the vessel and anchor if necessary until the situation clears.

51. You are the licensed Master of a 100 GT towing vessel sailing coastwise. What percentage of the deck crew must be able to understand any order spoken by the officers?

A. 50%
B. 65%
C. 75%
D. 100%

53. The objective of shoring a damaged bulkhead is to _____.

A. force the warped, bulged, or deformed sections back into place
B. support and hold the area in the damaged position
C. withstand subsequent additional damage
D. make a watertight seal at the damaged area

54. Your vessel has grounded on a bar. What should you do?

A. If you cannot get clear immediately, lighten the ship by pumping all ballast overboard.
B. Run the engine full astern to keep from being set further onto the bar.
C. Switch to the high suction for condenser circulating water, if it is submerged.
D. All of the above

55. You are in charge of a U.S. documented vessel. Under title 46 of the United States Code, if you fail to report a complaint of a sexual offense, you may be _____.

A. held personally liable by the victim and sued
B. criminally charged and jailed
C. civilly charged and fined
D. All of the above are correct.

56. The effect of wind on exposed areas of the vessel is most noticeable when _____.

A. backing
B. going slow ahead
C. going full ahead
D. turning

61. Deckhands onboard towing vessels shall be divided into 3 watches when on a trip exceeding _____.

A. 600 miles
B. 700 miles
C. 800 miles
D. 1000 miles

63. Which space(s) is(are) deducted from gross tonnage to derive net tonnage?

A. Boatswain's stores
B. Chart room
C. Spaces for the exclusive use of the officers or crew
D. All of the above

64. Which statement about damage control is TRUE?

A. A hole in the hull at the waterline is more dangerous than a hole below the inner bottom.
B. The amount of water entering a ship through a hole varies inversely to the area of the hole.
C. Water flowing into a lower compartment on a ship is more dangerous than water on deck or flowing into an upper compartment.
D. Water flowing over the fo'c'sle bulwark is more dangerous than a hole in the hull at the waterline.

65. Under title 46 of the United States Code, the person in charge of a documented vessel who fails to report a complaint of a sexual offense may be _____.

A. charged with accessory to sexual assault
B. imprisoned for up to one year
C. fined up to $5,000
D. All of the above

66. Most of your vessel's superstructure is forward. How will the vessel lie when drifting with no way on?

A. With the wind from ahead
B. With the wind off the port beam
C. With the wind off the starboard beam
D. With the wind from abaft the beam

67. You are in charge of a U.S. documented vessel. Under title 46 of the United States Code, if you fail to report a complaint of a sexual offense, you may be _____.

A. civilly charged and fined
B. criminally charged and jailed
C. held personally liable by the victim and sued
D. All of the above are correct.

73. Aboard ship, vertical flat plates running transversely and connecting the vertical keel to the margin plates are called _____.

A. floors
B. intercostals
C. girders
D. stringers

75. Frames to which the tank top and bottom shell are fastened are called _____.

A. floors
B. intercostals
C. stringers
D. tank top supports

76. Leeway is the _____.

A. difference between the true course and the compass course
B. momentum of a vessel after her engines have been stopped
C. lateral movement of a vessel downwind of her intended course
D. displacement of a vessel multiplied by her speed

77. When steering a vessel, a good helmsman will _____.

A. use as much rudder as possible to keep the vessel on course
B. apply rudder to move the compass card toward the lubbers line when off course
C. repeat back to the watch officer any rudder commands before executing them
D. keep the rudder amidships except when changing course

82. Floors aboard ship are _____.

A. also called decks
B. vertical transverse plates connecting the vertical keel with the margin plates
C. large beams fitted in various parts of the vessel for additional strength
D. found in passenger and berthing spaces only

83. In illustration D044DG, the mooring line labeled "A" is called a(n) _____.

A. offshore stern line
B. onshore stern line
C. after spring line
D. after breast line

84. The ceiling is _____.

A. the overhead in berthing compartments
B. a wooden protection placed over the tank top
C. material driven into seams or cracks to prevent leaking
D. None of the above are correct

85. The wooden planking that protects the tank top from cargo loading is called _____.

A. ceiling
B. shores
C. frames
D. toms

86. The turning circle of a vessel making a turn of over 360 degrees is the path followed by the _____.

A. bow
B. bridge
C. centerline
D. center of gravity

87. A set of interior steps on a ship leading up to a deck from below is known as _____.

A. a companionway
B. tween-decks
C. stairs
D. Any of the above are acceptable

93. A lookout can leave his station _____.

A. only when properly relieved
B. at the end of the watch
C. 15 minutes before the end of the watch
D. at any time

94. All of the following records are usually maintained by the watch-standing officers aboard a vessel EXCEPT the _____.

A. deck logbook
B. official logbook
C. compass record book
D. chronometer error book

95. You should keep clear of _____.

A. any line under a strain
B. lines that are paying out
C. lines that are coiled down only
D. None of the above are correct

96. The distance a vessel moves at right angles to the original course, when a turn of 180° has been completed, is called the _____.

A. advance
B. pivoting point
C. tactical diameter
D. kick

97. Chafing gear should be placed _____.

A. at all wearing points of mooring lines
B. at the bitter ends of all standing rigging
C. around running rigging
D. on wire rope only

100. Which statement is ALWAYS true?

A. Keep clear of any line that is under a strain.
B. A line will creak, make snapping sounds, and smoke before it parts.
C. Only synthetic lines will snap back after parting.
D. Stepping on the bight of a line is safer than stepping in the bight of a line.

101. You can safely step in the bight of a line _____.

A. when it is not under strain
B. if both ends are made fast
C. in an emergency
D. at no time

103. Your ship is in shallow water and the

bow rides up on its bow wave while the stern sinks into a depression of its transverse wave system. What is this called?

A. Broaching
B. Fish tailing
C. Squatting
D. Parallel sinkage

106. In relation to the turning circle of a ship, the term "kick" means the distance _____.

A. around the circumference of the turning circle
B. gained at right angles to the original course
C. gained in the direction of the original course
D. or throw of a vessel's stern from her line of advance upon putting the helm hard over

111. You are the licensed Master of a towing vessels operating between New York and Tampa, Florida. If you carry four (4) deckhands onboard, how many must be able seamen?

A. 1
B. 2
C. 3
D. 4

113. During the course of a voyage, a seaman falls on the main deck and injures his ankle. The Master should submit a Report of Marine Accident, Injury or Death if the _____.

A. injury results in loss of life only
B. injury is the result of misconduct
C. injured is incapacitated
D. injured needs first aid

114. You are on watch at sea on course 090°T. A man falls overboard on your starboard side. You immediately start a Williamson Turn. Which step is NOT a part of a Williamson Turn?

A. Step 1: Come right full rudder until the vessel heads 150°T.
B. Step 2: Stop the engines until clear of the man.
C. Step 3: Shift the helm to left full rudder.
D. Step 4: Continue with left rudder until on course 270°T.

115. During the course of a voyage, a seaman falls on the main deck and injures his ankle. The Master should submit a Report of Marine Accident, Injury or Death if the _____.

A. injury is the result of misconduct
B. injury results in loss of life only
C. injured need first aid
D. injured is incapacitated

116. In relation to the turning circle of a ship, the term "transfer" means the distance _____.

A. gained in the direction of the original course
B. gained at right angles to the original course
C. the ship moves sidewise from the original course away from the direction of the turn after the rudder is first put over
D. around the circumference of the turning circle

117. If two mooring lines are to be placed on the same bollard, which method is BEST?

A. Place the eye from the forward line on the bollard and then place the eye from the second line directly over the first.
B. It makes no difference how the lines are placed.
C. Place the eye from either line on the bollard, and then bring the eye of the other line up through the eye of the first, and place it on the bollard.
D. Place both eyes on the bollard, in any manner, but lead both lines to the same winch head on the vessel and secure them on the winch.

123. When patching holes in the hull, pillows, bedding, and other soft materials can be used as _____.

A. shores
B. gaskets
C. strongbacks
D. wedges

124. Bilge soundings indicate _____.

A. the amount of condensation in the hold
B. whether the cargo is leaking or not
C. whether the vessel is taking on water
D. All of the above

125. Chafing gear is normally used _____.

A. for portable fenders
B. for ground tackle
C. on the inside of the hawsepipe
D. on mooring lines

126. The distance a vessel moves parallel to the original course from the point where the rudder is put over to any point on the turning circle is called the _____.

A. advance
B. drift angle
C. pivoting point
D. transfer

127. In illustration D044DG, the mooring line labeled "C" is called a _____.

A. breast line
B. shore line
C. spring line
D. stern line

129. Which knot is suitable for hoisting an unconscious person?

A. Bowline on a bight
B. Fisherman's loop
C. French bowline
D. Spider hitch

136. Under the federal regulations, what minimum level of Blood Alcohol Content (BAC) constitutes a violation of the laws prohibiting Boating Under the Influence of Alcohol (BUI) on commercial vessels?

A. 0.18% BAC
B. 0.10% BAC
C. 0.06% BAC
D. 0.04% BAC

144. The lookout sights a vessel dead ahead. This should be reported on the bell with _____.

A. one bell
B. two bells
C. three bells
D. four bells

146. When turning a ship in restricted space with a strong wind, it is normally best to _____.

A. go ahead on both engines with the rudder hard to one side, if on a twin-screw vessel

B. back down with the rudder hard to one side, if on a single-screw vessel
C. take advantage of the tendency to back to port, if on a twin-screw vessel
D. turn so that the tendency to back into the wind can be used, if on a single-screw vessel

147. In illustration D044DG, the mooring line labeled "B" is called a(n) _____.

A. inshore stern line
B. offshore stern line
C. after spring line
D. after breast line

153. The proper way to correct a mistake in the logbook is to _____.

A. erase the entry and rewrite
B. draw several lines through the entry, rewrite, and initial the correction
C. completely black out the entry, rewrite, and initial the correction
D. draw one line through the entry, rewrite, and initial the correction

154. A look-out at the bow sights an object on your port side. How many bell strokes should he sound?

A. One
B. Two
C. Three
D. Four

156. When heading on a course, you put your rudder hard over. The distance traveled parallel to the direction of the original course from where you put your rudder over to any point on the turning circle is known as _____.

A. advance
B. head reach
C. tactical diameter
D. transfer

157. The proper way to correct a mistake in the logbook is to _____.

A. draw a line through the entry, rewrite, and initial the correction
B. draw several lines through the entry, rewrite, and initial the correction
C. erase the entry and rewrite
D. completely black out the entry, rewrite, and initial the correction

164. A look-out should report objects

sighted using _____.

A. true bearings
B. magnetic bearings
C. gyro bearings
D. relative bearings

166. The distance gained in the direction of the original course when you are making a turn is known as _____.

A. advance
B. drift
C. tactical diameter
D. transfer

167. You are on a large merchant vessel entering a U.S. port. There is a Pilot on board and he has the conn. Which statement is TRUE?

A. The Pilot is solely responsible for the safe maneuvering of the ship only if he is required to be on board by law.
B. The Master is responsible for the safe navigation of the ship and the Pilot is employed for his local knowledge.
C. The Pilot is soley responsible for the internal working of the ship.
D. The Pilot becomes soley responsible for the safe navigation of the vessel only if the Master relinquishes the conn.

171. Illustration DO35DG. You have determined the maneuvering characteristics of your vessel by taking the radar ranges and bearings of an isolated light while making a turn. The results are as listed. Based on this data what is the transfer for a turn of 30°?

A. 40 yards
B. 140 yards
C. 190 yards
D. 230 yards

174. A proper look-out must be kept _____.

A. only in fog
B. only between the hours of sunset and sunrise
C. only when entering and leaving port
D. at all times

175. While the Pilot is maneuvering the vessel to a dock, what is the primary responsibility of the watch officer?

A. Judge the appropriateness of the Pilot's orders and countermand them if necessary

B. Insure that helm and throttle orders given by the Pilot are correctly executed
C. Record the bells and their times in the bell book
D. Supervise the signaling and flag etiquette

176. The turning circle of a vessel is the path followed by the _____.

A. tipping center
B. bow
C. outermost part of the ship while making the circle
D. center of gravity

177. The measurement of the amount of force a towing vessel is capable of applying to a motionless tow is called _____.

A. shaft horsepower
B. delivered horsepower
C. bollard pull
D. towrope pull

184. You are standing look-out duty at night. A dim light on the horizon will be seen quickest by looking _____.

A. at an area just a little below the horizon
B. at the horizon, where the sky and water appear to meet
C. a little above the horizon
D. well below the horizon

185. Before a Master relieves a Pilot of the conn, the _____.

A. Master should foresee any danger to the vessel on the present course
B. vessel must be in extremis
C. Master should agree to sign a release of liability form
D. Master must first request the Pilot to take corrective action

186. The pivoting point of a vessel going ahead is _____.

A. at the hawsepipe
B. about one-third of the vessel's length from the bow
C. about two-thirds of the vessel's length from the bow
D. near the stern

187. You are standing the wheel watch on entering port and the Master gives you a rudder command which conflicts with a

rudder command from the Pilot. What should you do?

A. Ask the Pilot if he relinquishes control.
B. Obey the Pilot.
C. Obey the Master.
D. Bring the rudder to a position midway between the two conflicting positions.

192. Illustration D044DG. The mooring line labeled "H" is called a(n) _____.

A. offshore bow line
B. onshore bow line
C. offshore spring line
D. forward breast line

194. A vessel spotted at 45° relative can be reported as _____.

A. on the starboard beam
B. broad on the starboard bow
C. 4 points forward of starboard bow
D. 4 points abaft the starboard beam

197. Serving is _____.

A. marline or ratline wound along the grooves of a rope
B. narrow strips of light canvas or cotton cloth spiral-wrapped along the rope
C. marline tightly wound on the rope by means of a board or mallet
D. a splice made by laying the strand of one rope into the vacated grooves of another rope

203. How does the effect known as "bank suction" act on a single-screw vessel proceeding along a narrow channel?

A. It pulls the bow toward the bank.
B. It pushes the entire vessel away from the bank.
C. It pulls the stern toward the bank.
D. It heels the vessel toward the bank.

204. What does the helm command "shift the rudder" mean?

A. Put the rudder over to the opposite side, the same number of degrees it is now.
B. Put the rudder amidships and hold the heading steady as she goes.
C. Shift the rudder control to the alternate steering method.
D. Stop the swing of the ship.

206. In stopping distances of vessels, "head reach" can best be described as the _____.

A. difference between the vessel's speed through the water at any instant and the new speed ordered on the telegraph
B. distance the vessel has actually run through the water since a change of speed was ordered
C. distance the vessel will run between taking action to stop her and being stationary in the water
D. speed at which a vessel should proceed to ensure that she will run a predetermined distance, once her engines have been stopped

207. A towing vessel's capability is BEST measured by horsepower, maneuverability, displacement, and _____.

A. stability
B. propeller design
C. bollard pull
D. towing winch horsepower

208. Your vessel has been damaged and you must shore a bulkhead. You should cut the shore _____.

A. approximately 1/2 inch longer than the measured length to allow for trimming
B. approximately 1/2 inch shorter than the measured length to allow for wedges
C. approximately 1/2 inch shorter per foot of shoring to allow for wet expansion
D. to the same length as the measured length

212. Your vessel is port side to a pier with a spring line led aft from the bow. In calm weather, putting the engines ahead with the rudder hard left should bring _____.

A. the bow in and the stern out
B. both the bow and stern in
C. the bow out and the stern in
D. both the bow and stern out

213. You are the Master of a single-screw vessel. You are docking at a port which has no tugs available. You decide to drop the offshore anchor to help in docking. The amount of chain you should pay out is _____.

A. 5 to 7 times the depth of the water
B. 1-1/2 to 2 times the depth of the water
C. equal to the depth of the water
D. you should NEVER use the anchor to help in docking

214. The helm command "meet her" means _____.

A. use rudder to check the swing
B. decrease the rudder angle which is on
C. steer more carefully
D. note the course and steady on that heading

215. How does the effect known as "bank suction" act on a single-screw vessel proceeding along a narrow channel?

A. It pulls the bow toward the bank.
B. It heels the vessel toward the bank.
C. It pushes the entire vessel away from the bank.
D. It pulls the stern toward the bank.

216. As a ship moves through the water, it drags with it a body of water called the wake. The ratio of the wake speed to the ship's speed is called _____.

A. propeller velocity
B. speed of advance
C. wake distribution
D. wake fraction

217. The holding capability of an anchor is primarily determined by the _____.

A. shape of the anchor
B. stowage of the anchor on board
C. anchor's ability to dig in
D. size of the vessel and its draft

220. The best method to secure a towline to bitts is to _____.

A. take a round turn on the bitt farthest from the pull and use figure-eights
B. take a round turn on the bitt closest to the pull and use figure-eights
C. use figure-eights and take a round turn at the top of the bitts
D. use only figure-eights

224. The term "shift the rudder" means _____.

A. put the rudder amidships
B. use right or left rudder
C. check, but do not stop the vessel from swinging
D. change from right to left or left or right

225. For safety reasons, when assistance towing _____.

A. the disabled vessel should be towed to the nearest port

B. the disabled vessel should be inspected for flammable gases
C. passengers should always be removed from the disabled vessel
D. personnel on the disabled vessel should don PFDs

226. Which statement is TRUE concerning the vessel's slipstream?

A. It has no effect on steering of the vessel.
B. It has no effect on the rudder when the helm is amidships.
C. Its velocity is the same as that of the wake.
D. The propeller gives it a helical motion.

227. An ocean towing bridle should _____.

A. have equal legs of sufficient length
B. have a large angle between the legs
C. be formed on a bight of cable through a ring
D. never be made up of chain

232. The angle at which the fluke penetrates the soil is called the _____.

A. fluke angle
B. tripping angle
C. penetration angle
D. holding angle

233. A vessel brought alongside should be fended off the towing vessel by _____.

A. crew members using their arms
B. crew members using the strong muscles of their legs
C. fenders
D. No fending is necessary due to the rugged construction of most towing vessels.

234. The helm command "shift your rudder" means _____.

A. double your rudder angle or go to full rudder
B. bring your rudder amidships
C. change from right rudder to left rudder, or vice versa, an equal number of degrees
D. check the swing of the vessel

236. As the propeller turns, voids are formed on the trailing and leading edges of the propeller blades causing a loss of propulsive efficiency, pitting of the blades, and vibration. These voids are known as _____.

A. advance
B. cavitation
C. edging
D. slip

237. The latch of a safety hook _____.

A. increases the strength of the hook
B. prevents the sling ring from coming out of the hook if the strain is abruptly eased
C. prevents the sling ring from coming out of the hook if there is a strain on the sling ring
D. All of the above

239. Flame screens are used to _____.

A. contain flammable fumes
B. protect firefighters from flames
C. prevent flames from entering tanks
D. keep flames and sparks from getting out of an engine's exhaust system

243. A towing vessel becomes tripped while towing on a hawser astern. What factor is MOST important when assessing the risk of capsizing?

A. Length of the towline
B. Height of the towline connection
C. Longitudinal position of the towline connection
D. Direction of opposing force

244. "Hard right rudder" means _____.

A. put the rudder over to the right all the way
B. jam the rudder against the stops
C. meet a swing to the right, then return to amidships
D. put the rudder over quickly to 15° right rudder

245. The fitting that allows a boom to move freely both vertically and laterally is called the _____.

A. swivel
B. lizard
C. spider band
D. gooseneck

246. The force exerted by a propeller which tends to throw the stern right or left is called _____.

A. slip
B. sidewise force
C. rotational force
D. thrust

253. The forward movement of a vessel in one revolution of its propeller is measured by _____.

A. advance
B. head reach
C. the pitch
D. transfer

254. "Ease the rudder" means to _____.

A. move the rudder slowly in the direction of the most recent rudder command
B. bring the rudder amidships
C. decrease the rudder angle
D. steer the course which is your present heading

263. Which type of hull damage should be repaired FIRST?

A. Damage below the waterline
B. Damage to interior watertight boundaries
C. Damage in way of machinery rooms
D. Damage at or just above the waterline

264. The total weight of cargo, fuel, water, stores, passengers and crew, and their effects that a ship can carry is the _____.

A. bale cubic
B. deadweight
C. gross tonnage
D. loaded displacement

265. Which statement is TRUE about hooks and shackles?

A. Hooks are stronger than shackles of the same diameter.
B. Shackles are stronger than hooks of the same diameter.
C. Hooks and shackles of the same diameter are of equal strength.
D. All the above may be true, depending on the hook's or shackle's overall length.

266. The distance that a ship moves forward with each revolution of its propeller, if there is no slip, is called _____.

A. advance
B. head reach
C. pitch
D. transfer

270. The disadvantage of using a heaving line to pass a towline is that _____.

A. it increases the likelihood of collision between the towing vessel and the disabled vessel
B. recreational boaters tend to make the heaving line fast to the towed vessel as if it were the towline
C. the monkey fist may injure someone
D. it may reduce the catenary and increase yawing

271. Total responsibility for shipping and discharging the seamen is that of the _____.

A. Master of the vessel
B. steamship company
C. U.S. Customs Service
D. U.S. Coast Guard

274. What is the difference between net tonnage and gross tonnage?

A. Net tonnage is the gross tonnage less certain deductible spaces.
B. Net tonnage is tonnage of cargo compared to tonnage of whole ship.
C. Net tonnage is gross tonnage minus engine and bunker spaces.
D. Net tonnage is the net weight of the ship.

275. You have taken another vessel in tow. You can tell that the towing speed is too fast when the _____.

A. vessels are not in step
B. tow line feels like it is "jumping" when touched
C. catenary comes clear of the water
D. towed vessel goes "in irons"

276. As a ship moves through the water, it causes a wake, which is also moving forward relative to the sea. In addition to a fore and aft motion, this wake also has a(n) _____.

A. downward and inward flow
B. downward and outward flow
C. upward and inward flow
D. upward and outward flow

282. The owner, agent, Master or person-in-charge of a "T-Boat" involved in a marine casualty causing injury that requires professional medical treatment must _____.

A. immediately notify the nearest USCG MSO, MIO, or Group Office

B. keep all voyage records and make them available to Coast Guard investigators
C. file a written report (CG2692) of the casualty within five days
D. All of the above

284. The beam of a vessel refers to the _____.

A. depth between decks
B. internal cubic capacity
C. molded depth of the vessel
D. width of the vessel

285. Which form of navigation may be suspended without notice under defense planning?

A. celestial
B. electronic
C. piloting
D. None of the above

286. Sidewise force of the propeller tends to throw a vessel's stern to the right or left, depending on rotation. This force is caused by _____.

A. back current from the rudder
B. greater pressure on the right or left side of the propeller, depending on rotation
C. lower pressure on the right or left side of the propeller, depending on rotation
D. torque from the velocity and angle at which the surrounding water impinges upon the propeller blades

291. You are the licensed operator of a 100 GT towing vessel making coastwise runs. Whenever a crew member is discharged from your vessel you must _____.

A. issue a Certificate of Discharge and make an entry in his Continuous Discharge Book
B. issue a Certificate of Discharge or make an entry in his Continuous Discharge Book
C. retain the crew member's Continuous Discharge Book onboard
D. retain the crew member's Certificate of Discharge onboard

293. Which space(s) is(are) NOT exempt when measuring gross tonnage?

A. Auxiliary machinery spaces above the deck
B. Steering gear room

C. Cargo holds
D. Galley in a deckhouse

294. Displacement refers to the _____.

A. cubic capacity of a vessel
B. deadweight carrying capacity of a vessel
C. gross tonnage of a vessel
D. number of long tons of water displaced by a vessel afloat

300. On which form do you provide a written report of Marine Casualty to the nearest Coast Guard Marine Safety Office?

A. DD 214
B. CG 2692
C. DOT 211
D. CG 5511

303. What requires a Report of Marine Accident, Injury or Death?

A. Collision with a bridge
B. Injury beyond first aid
C. loss of life
D. All of the above

304. To warp a vessel means to _____.

A. anchor the vessel
B. bring the head into the wind
C. clean the decks
D. move the vessel by hauling on lines

306. You are aboard a single-screw vessel with a right-handed propeller. The vessel is dead in the water and the rudder is amidships. If you reverse your engine you would expect your vessel to _____.

A. kick its stern to port
B. kick its stern to starboard
C. move astern without swinging
D. swing its stern to starboard, then to port

310. Operators of Uninspected Passenger Vessels are required to keep their Coast Guard License aboard _____.

A. only when operating more than one mile from shore
B. only when operating at night
C. only when carrying passengers for hire
D. At all times

313. With the exception of a Coast Guard approved commercial hybrid Personal

Flotation Device (PFD), which type of life preserver must be carried for each person on board an uninspected passenger vessel?

A. Type I
B. Type II
C. Type III
D. None of the above

314. "Avast" means _____.

A. let go
B. pull
C. slack off
D. stop

315. A vessel must have one approved ring life buoy on board if its length is over how many feet?

A. 6 feet
B. 16 feet
C. 26 feet
D. 36 feet

324. A "chock" is a _____.

A. deck fitting used to secure mooring lines
B. casting fitted at the side of a weather-deck, used as a fairlead
C. sharp block of wood used to support hygroscopic cargo
D. smoke pipe for the galley stove

325. A deck fitting, used to secure line or wire rope, consisting of a single body with two protruding horns is called a _____.

A. bitt
B. bollard
C. capstan
D. cleat

326. In order to back a right-handed, single-screw vessel in a straight line, you will probably need to use _____.

A. very little rudder
B. some left rudder
C. some right rudder
D. full left rudder

332. The helm command "Meet her" means _____.

A. steer more carefully
B. use rudder to check the swing
C. decrease the existing rudder angle
D. note the course and steady on that heading

334. The space above the engine room is called the _____.

A. fidley
B. gold locker
C. middle hatch
D. noble

335. You are steaming in a heavy gale and find it necessary to heave to. Under most circumstances, this is best done by _____.

A. stopping the engines and drifting beam to the seas
B. going slow astern and taking the seas on the quarter
C. taking the sea fine on the bow and reducing the speed to the minimum to hold that position
D. maintaining speed and taking the sea broad on the bow

336. When a vessel with a single right-hand propeller backs to port the _____.

A. bow falls off to starboard
B. vessel moves to port without changing heading
C. bow swings to port
D. vessel moves to starboard without changing heading

340. Argon is classified as a _____.

A. corrosive
B. flammable gas
C. flammable liquid
D. nonflammable gas

341. The Certificate of Freeboard is the _____.

A. Load Line Certificate
B. Certificate of Inspection
C. Admeasurer's Certificate
D. Forecastle Card

344. The purpose of a bilge well is to_____.

A. afford access to the shell through the double bottoms
B. collect water to be pumped out
C. provide access for the pneumercator
D. provide a base line for sounding measurements

345. What does the helm command "shift the rudder" mean?

A. Put the rudder amidships and hold the heading steady as she goes.
B. Put the rudder over to the opposite side, the same number of degrees it is now.
C. Shift the rudder control to the alternate steering method.
D. Stop the swing of the ship.

346. A vessel is equipped with a single right-handed screw. With rudder amidships and calm wind, the vessel will most likely back _____.

A. straight astern
B. to port
C. to starboard
D. in no particular direction

351. Which certificate is issued by the American Bureau of Shipping?

A. Certificate of Inspection
B. Load Line Certificate
C. Safety Equipment Certificate
D. Permit to Proceed for repairs

354. A "stopper" is _____.

A. a short length of line used for temporarily holding another line
B. a snatch block for handling a topping lift
C. an engine order telegraph
D. the brake on a cargo winch

355. Generally, you can best keep a vessel under steering control when the vessel has _____.

A. headway
B. sternway
C. no way on, with engines stopped
D. no way on, with engines full ahead

357. What does the proof test load of an anchor chain demonstrate?

A. Breaking strength of the chain
B. Strength of the chain to a specified limit
C. Adequate holding power for new bottom conditions
D. Safe working load of the chain

361. The strictest load line regulations apply to _____.

A. gas carriers
B. freighters (break-bulk)
C. passenger ships
D. tankers

362. A towing vessel is tripped when _____.

A. it is overtaken by the tow
B. it is pulled sideways by the tow
C. the weight of the towing hawser causes loss of maneuverability
D. the propeller is fouled by the towing hawser

363. Which space(s) is(are) deducted from gross tonnage to derive net tonnage?

A. Companions and booby hatches
B. Chart room
C. Open structures
D. All of the above

364. A long ton is _____.

A. 1,000 pounds
B. 2,000 pounds
C. 2,240 pounds
D. 2,400 pounds

366. When backing down with sternway, the pivot point of a vessel is _____.

A. at the bow
B. about one-third of the vessel's length from the bow
C. about one-quarter of the vessel's length from the stern
D. aft of the propellors

370. Cottonseed oil is classed as a _____.

A. combustible liquid
B. flammable liquid
C. flammable solid
D. poison B

371. In the United States, the load line markings are set by the _____.

A. American Bureau of Shipping
B. Coast Guard
C. Federal Maritime Board
D. IMO

372. Keeping the draft at or below the load line mark will insure that the vessel has adequate _____.

A. ballast
B. reserve buoyancy
C. displacement
D. rolling periods

374. Holes in the bulwark, which allow deck water to drain into the sea, are _____.

A. doggers
B. fidleys
C. freeing ports
D. swash ports

375. The best line for towing small vessels is _____.

A. three-strand nylon
B. double-braided nylon
C. polypropylene
D. manila

376. You are aboard a right-handed single-screw vessel with headway on. The engine is put full astern and the rudder hard left. What will the bow do?

A. It will swing to the left, and will swing left faster as the vessel loses way.
B. It will swing to the left, straighten out and then swing to the right as the vessel loses way.
C. It will swing to the left without increasing or decreasing its swing.
D. The bow will swing to the right.

384. A "strongback" refers to a _____.

A. bar securing a cargo port
B. centerline vertical bulkhead
C. deep beam
D. spanner stay

386. You are maneuvering a vessel with a right-hand propeller. The rudder is amidships. The vessel will generally back _____.

A. to port
B. to starboard
C. in a straight line directly astern
D. downstream, the stern going in the direction of the current

394. The rope which is rove from the truck to be used with a bos'n's chair is called a _____.

A. gantline
B. life line
C. strop
D. whip

395. The vertical motion of a floating vessel in which the entire hull is lifted by the force of the sea is known as _____.

A. surge
B. sway
C. heave
D. pitch

396. A vessel is equipped with twin propellers, both turning outboard with the engines half ahead. If there is no wind or current and the rudders are amidships, what will happen?

A. The bow will swing to starboard.
B. The bow will swing to port.
C. The vessel will steer a zigzag course.
D. The vessel will steer a fairly straight course.

404. A vessel's "quarter" is that section which is _____.

A. abeam
B. dead astern
C. just aft of the bow
D. on either side of the stern

406. A twin-screw vessel with a single rudder is making headway. The engines are full speed ahead. There is no wind or current. Which statement is FALSE?

A. If one screw is stopped, the ship will turn toward the side of the stopped screw.
B. The principal force which turns the ship is set up by the wake against the forward side of the rudder.
C. Turning response by use of the rudder only is greater than on a single-screw vessel.
D. With the rudder amidships, the ship will steer a fairly steady course.

413. A person is found operating a vessel while intoxicated. He is liable for _____.

A. imprisonment for up to three years
B. a civil penalty of not more than $5,000
C. a fine of not more than $3,000
D. a fine of not more than $10,000

414. To "ease" a line means to _____.

A. cast off
B. double up so that one line does not take all the strain
C. pay out line to remove most of the tension
D. slack it off quickly

416. While moving ahead, a twin-screw ship has an advantage over a single-screw ship because _____.

A. correct trim will be obtained more easily
B. drag effect will be cancelled out
C. side forces will be eliminated
D. speed will be increased

417. When inspecting wire rope that has been in use for some time, one must look for _____.

A. fishhooks
B. kinks
C. worn spots
D. All of the above

422. Which method should be used to secure a synthetic fiber line to two bitts?

A. Two round turns on the bitt closest to the strain and then figure eights
B. Two round turns on the bitt farthest from the strain and then figure eights
C. Figure eights and then a round turn at the top of both bitts
D. Only figure eights are necessary on both bitts

423. When securing a synthetic line to a bitt what is the minimum number of round turns you should take before figure-eighting the line?

A. None
B. 1
C. 2
D. 3

424. Faking a line means to _____.

A. arrange it on deck in long bights
B. coil it down on deck
C. put a whipping on it
D. stow it below

426. You are stopped with no way upon your vessel at the pilot station. Your vessel is a large twin-screw ship. You must come around 180° to board your Pilot. How should you use the engines and rudder to turn the ship fastest in the least amount of space?

A. Full ahead on the engines and hard over rudder
B. Full ahead on one engine, full astern on the other
C. Half ahead with hard over rudder, then full astern on inboard engine
D. Slow ahead with hard over rudder

427. What is the greatest danger of an overriding tow?

A. Fouling of the towing hawser
B. Loss of steering
C. Tripping
D. Collision between the tow and the stern of the towing vessel

431. Official proof of an American vessel's nationality is contained in the _____.

A. Certificate of Inspection
B. Official Log
C. Certificate of Documentation
D. Shipping Articles

433. When a tow is trimmed by the stern it is said to _____.

A. hog
B. sag
C. drag
D. list

434. To "belay" a line means to _____.

A. coil it down
B. heave it taut
C. stow it below
D. secure it to a cleat

435. The amount of force a tug can exert on a stationary pull is called its _____.

A. brake horsepower
B. indicated horsepower
C. shaft horsepower
D. bollard pull

436. The rudders are amidships and both screws are going ahead. What will happen if the starboard screw is stopped?

A. The bow will go to port.
B. The bow will go to starboard.
C. The bow will remain steady.
D. The stern will go to starboard.

437. Prior to getting underway in fresh or brackish water, the Master must _____.

A. log the density of the water
B. secure all overboard discharges
C. take on fresh water ballast
D. clean the sides with fresh water

441. The document which shows a vessel's nationality, ownership, and tonnage is the _____.

A. Manifest Certificate
B. Bill of Lading Certificate
C. Certificate of Documentation
D. Official Logbook

442. "Ease the rudder" means to _____.

A. move the rudder slowly in the direction of the most recent rudder command
B. decrease the rudder angle
C. bring the rudder amidships
D. steer the course which is your present heading

444. A metal object on the pier resembling a tree stump and made to receive mooring lines is a _____.

A. bight
B. bollard
C. chock
D. camel

445. Where are the towing bitts best placed for towing purposes?

A. Near the centerline and over the rudders
B. On each side of the vessel near the stern
C. Forward of the rudder post and close to the tug's center of pivot
D. As far aft as possible

446. A twin-screw vessel can clear the inboard propeller and maneuver off a pier best by holding a(n) _____.

A. forward spring line and going slow ahead on the inboard engine
B. after spring line and going slow astern on the outboard engine
C. forward spring line and going slow ahead on both engines
D. forward spring line and going slow ahead on the outboard engine

447. One reason a tug's towing bitts are located forward of the rudders is because _____.

A. it makes it easier to hook up the towing hawser
B. this is where the towhook is located
C. this allows more responsive steering
D. it is traditional

451. What is official proof of a vessel's ownership?

A. Certificate of Documentation
B. Bill of Lading

C. Transfer Certificate
D. Logbook

452. Where should the foundation supports for towing bitts terminate?

A. Forward of the towing winch
B. In the frames or other substantial structural members below decks
C. On the deck plates in the engine room
D. On deck, aft of the towing winch

454. A rope ladder with wooden rungs is a _____.

A. drop ladder
B. life ladder
C. Jacob's ladder
D. jury ladder

455. A vessel having continuous closely spaced transverse strength members is _____.

A. longitudinally framed
B. transversely framed
C. cellular framed
D. web framed

456. You are conning a twin-screw vessel going ahead with rudders amidships. If the port screw stops turning the bow will _____.

A. go to port
B. go to starboard
C. not veer to either side
D. go first to port and then to starboard

462. The safe working load (SWL) of wire rope with a safety factor of 6 is what percent of its strength?

A. 10%
B. 17%
C. 50%
D. 80%

465. Which structural members improve a towing vessel's chance of surviving punctured shell plating?

A. Stringers
B. Longitudinals
C. Transverse watertight bulkheads
D. The rake

466. A twin-screw vessel, making headway with both engines turning ahead, will turn more readily to starboard if you _____.

A. reverse port engine, apply right rudder
B. reverse port engine, rudder amidships
C. reverse starboard engine, apply right rudder
D. reverse starboard engine, rudder amidships

467. Of which type of material may a towing hawser be constructed?

A. Wire rope
B. Nylon, Dacron, polypropylene or a blend of other synthetic fibers
C. Manila
D. All of the above

470. A fiber towing hawser should be stowed _____.

A. in an enclosed rope locker with adequate air circulation
B. by spooling it on the winch
C. by coiling it on deck
D. by hanging it in the engine room

471. The official identification of a vessel is found in the _____.

A. Certificate of Inspection
B. Classification Certificate
C. Load Line Certificate
D. Certificate of Documentation

472. On a long ocean tow, the bridle should be made up of two equal lengths of _____.

A. chain
B. wire
C. nylon
D. manila

474. On an anchor windlass, the wheel over which the anchor chain passes is called a _____.

A. brake compressor wheel
B. devil's claw
C. wildcat
D. winchhead

475. In illustration D044DG, the mooring line labeled "F" is called a _____.

A. bow line
B. breast line
C. forward spring line
D. None of the above

476. You are backing on twin engines with rudders amidships, when your port engine stalls. To continue backing on course, you should _____.

A. apply left rudder
B. apply right rudder
C. increase engine speed
D. keep your rudder amidships

477. When underway with a tow, you are required to notify the Coast Guard in which casualty situation?

A. An injury requiring first aid treatment
B. Damage of bridge-to-bridge radio capability
C. Accidental stranding or grounding
D. Damage to property amounting to $12,500

481. Which U.S. agency assigns an official number to a vessel?

A. American Bureau of Shipping
B. Collector of Customs
C. Treasury Department
D. Coast Guard

4484. On stud-link anchor chain the addition of the stud increases the strength of the link by about _____.

A. 10%
B. 15%
C. 20%
D. 50%

485. To clean a dirty fiber towing hawser used in ocean towing, you should _____.

A. use lye or other mild detergent
B. wash it with fresh water, dry and store it
C. wash it with salt water
D. use cleaning fluid on nylon, Dacron and other synthetic lines

486. You are backing on twin engines with rudders amidships. Your starboard engine stalls. To continue backing on course, you should _____.

A. apply left rudder
B. apply right rudder
C. increase your engine speed
D. keep your rudder amidships

487. One method of removing kinks from fiber rope is to _____.

A. coil the line against the lay
B. tow the line astern until it straightens
C. stretch the line until it reaches its elastic limit
D. cut out each kink and splice

491. A change of a documented vessel's name can only be made by the _____.

A. American Bureau of Shipping
B. Commissioner of Customs
C. Treasury Department
D. Coast Guard

493. What does "end for end" mean in regard to a towing hawser?

A. To take the kinks out of the hawser
B. To fake it down in figure eights
C. To increase the catenary
D. To swap ends of the hawser to minimize wear

494. What best describes an anchor buoy?

A. A black ball that is hoisted when the ship anchors
B. A buoy attached to the anchor
C. A buoy attached to the scope of an anchor chain
D. A mark of the number of fathoms in an anchor chain

495. Which space(s) is (are) deducted from gross tonnage to derive net tonnage?

A. Boatswain's stores
B. Companions and booby hatches
C. Passenger spaces
D. All of the above

496. Your twin-screw vessel is moving ASTERN with rudders amidships. The starboard screw suddenly stops turning. Your vessel's head will _____.

A. go to port
B. go to starboard
C. remain stationary
D. suddenly drop down

497. Which type of fiber towing hawser is preferred for towing astern?

A. Manila
B. Polypropylene
C. Nylon
D. Dacron

503. Which statement is FALSE?

A. Nylon can stretch approximately 40% and still recover.
B. Only nylon stoppers should be used on nylon hawsers.
C. Nylon is most practical for use on hip towing.
D. With proper care nylon hawsers will greatly outlast manila and other natural fibers.

504. Anchors are prevented from running out when secured by the _____.

A. brake
B. devil's claw
C. pawls
D. All of the above

505. Which form of navigation may be suspended without notice under defense planning?

A. celestial
B. piloting
C. electronic
D. None of the above

506. With rudders amidships and negligible wind, a twin-screw vessel moving astern with both engines backing will back _____.

A. to port
B. to starboard
C. in a fairly straight line
D. in a circular motion

512. When paying out nylon line from around the bitts _____.

A. stand clear of the bitts and use two or more round turns under your figure eights
B. you can surge the line even with a single turn
C. no extra turns are necessary since nylon has a high coefficient of friction
D. stand in the bight of the line

513. Wire rope is used in the towing industry _____.

A. for backup wires and main towing hawsers
B. for face wires or jockeys when pushing ahead
C. as stern wires when pushing ahead
D. All of the above

514. The part of an anchor which takes hold on the bottom is the _____.

A. arm
B. base
C. fluke
D. stock

515. When compared to a fiber towing hawser, what is NOT an advantage of a wire towing hawser?

A. Wire is easy to handle when properly spooled on the drum of a towing winch.
B. Wire has more spring and shock resistance than fiber.
C. Wire can be used to tow heavier loads because of its smaller diameter and more manageable size.
D. Wire is subject to less deterioration if properly maintained.

516. You are going ahead on twin engines with rudder amidships. Your starboard engine stalls. To continue on course, you should _____.

A. apply left rudder
B. apply right rudder
C. increase engine speed
D. keep your rudder amidships

517. What is the purpose of the intermediate spring?

A. Serves as a backup for the main tow hawser in case of failure.
B. Provides weight and flexibility to the total tow makeup.
C. Lengthens the main tow hawser to keep the tow in step.
D. Distributes the towing load.

524. The purpose of the stripping bar on an anchor windlass is to _____.

A. clean off any mud that may have accumulated on the chain
B. engage or disengage the wildcat
C. fairlead the chain from the hawsepipe to the wildcat
D. prevent the chain from fouling the wildcat

525. To lay out a towing hawser in a fore-and-aft direction so each bight is clear and can run out freely without snagging describes _____.

A. flemishing
B. faking
C. spooling
D. worming, parceling and serving

526. You are going ahead on twin engines with rudders amidships. Your port engine stalls. To continue your course you should _____.

A. apply right rudder
B. apply left rudder
C. keep your rudder amidships
D. increase engine speed

534. Which is part of the ground tackle?

A. Charlie noble
B. Devil's claw
C. Gooseneck
D. Rat's tail

535. In illustration D044DG, the mooring line labeled "G" is called a(n) _____.

A. offshore bow line
B. inshore bow line
C. forward breast line
D. forward spring line

536. Your vessel is backing on the starboard screw, and going ahead on the port screw. The bow will _____.

A. back on a straight line
B. move ahead on a straight line
C. swing to port
D. swing to starboard

539. Which type of shackle is used for most towing connections?

A. Safety shackles
B. Round pin anchor shackles
C. Screw pin schackles
D. Heart shaped schackles

540. As seen from the tow, what should connect the leading ends of both towing bridle legs to the main towing hawser?

A. A cable clamp
B. A fishplate, flounder, or towing plate
C. A padeye
D. The towing bitts

541. The official number of a documented vessel is _____.

A. not required to be marked anywhere on the vessel
B. required to be permanently marked on the vessel's structure
C. required to be painted on the vessel's stern
D. required to be painted on the vessel's bow

542. Which best describes a "fishplate" used in towing?

A. A triangular-shaped heavy steel plate with a round hole inset from each corner
B. A steel plate in the shape of a flat fish
C. A rectangular-shaped piece of heavy steel plate with four holes
D. A circular piece of heavy steel with three holes forming an equilateral triangle

543. You would be most likely to use a fishplate _____.

A. when towing alongside
B. on a hawser tow
C. when pushing ahead or in the notch
D. when running "light boat"

544. If the winch should fail while you are hauling in the anchor, what prevents the anchor cable from running out?

A. Chain stopper
B. Devil's claw
C. Hawse ratchet
D. Riding pawl

545. Repairing damage to the hull at or above the waterline reduces the threat of _____.

A. free surface effects
B. capsizing
C. continued progressive flooding
D. wind heel

546. A twin-screw ship going ahead on the starboard screw only tends to move _____.

A. in a straight line
B. to port
C. from side to side
D. to starboard

550. If the towing bridle legs are not of equal length _____.

A. excessive strain is placed on the shorter leg
B. the shorter leg may fail
C. the longer leg is slack
D. All of the above

551. The name and hailing port of a documented commercial vessel is _____.

A. not required to be marked anywhere on the vessel
B. required to be marked on both bows and on the keel
C. required to be marked on the stern with the name of the vessel marked on both bows
D. required to be marked on the keel, stern, and both bows

552. Which type of bridle is the most effective for a heavy ocean tow?

A. Nylon because of its strength
B. Polypropylene because it floats and is easier to handle
C. Stud link anchor chain for chafe resistance and strength
D. Wire rope for flexibility and strength

553. A bridle for an ocean tow consists of _____.

A. two chains of equal length
B. a single nylon pendant rove through a heavy ring free to move on the pendant
C. two long legs of wire rope shackled to a fishplate
D. a single length of heavy chain with both ends secured on deck to welded padeyes

554. Which part of the patent anchor performs the same function as the stock of an old fashioned anchor; that is, forces the flukes to dig in?

A. Bill or pea
B. Arm
C. Shank
D. Tripping palm

555. A chain bridle is used when towing astern because it _____.

A. is easy to connect
B. provides an effective catenary and absorbs shock due to its weight
C. makes rigging a swivel unnecessary

D. prevents the tow from yawing by the drag of the chains in a seaway

556. You may BEST turn a twin-screw vessel about, to the right, in a narrow channel by using _____.

A. both engines ahead and helm
B. one engine only
C. port engine ahead and the starboard engine astern
D. both engines astern and use helm

561. Which space cannot be deducted from gross tonnage when calculating net tonnage?

A. Crew messroom
B. Forepeak ballast tank
C. Master's cabin
D. Chain locker

563. While the Pilot is maneuvering the vessel to a dock, what is the PRIMARY responsibility of the watch officer?

A. Supervise the signaling and flag etiquette.
B. Record the bells and their times in the bell book.
C. Insure that helm and throttle orders given by the Pilot are correctly executed.
D. Judge the appropriateness of the Pilot's orders and countermand them if necessary.

564. The anchors on the bow are known as _____.

A. bower anchors
B. kedge anchors
C. spare anchors
D. stream anchors

565. When the Pilot is embarked he or she _____.

A. relieves the officer of the watch
B. relieves the Master of his duties
C. is solely responsible for the safe navigation of the vessel
D. is a specialist hired for his or her local navigational knowledge

566. The BEST way to steer a twin-screw vessel if you lose your rudder is by using _____.

A. one engine and a steering oar
B. both engines at the same speed

C. one engine at a time
D. one engine running at reduced speed and controlling the vessel with the other

567. Your enrolled vessel is bound from Baltimore, MD, to Norfolk, VA, via Chesapeake Bay. Which statement about the required Pilot is TRUE?

A. The Pilot must be licensed by Virginia and Maryland.
B. The Pilot must be licensed by either Virginia or Maryland.
C. The Pilot need only be licensed by the Coast Guard.
D. The Pilot must be licensed by Virginia, Maryland and the Coast Guard.

570. A chain bridle is preferable to a wire rope towing bridle on a long ocean tow because chain _____.

A. is more flexible and has the ability to absorb shock because of its weight
B. is less subject to wear and damage from abrasion
C. requires little maintenance
D. All of the above

571. You are in port A in the United States, and your Certificate of Inspection has expired. You wish to go to port B in the United States for repairs and to complete the inspection. If the Officer-in-Charge, Marine Inspection deems it safe, he may issue a _____.

A. Certificate of Seaworthiness
B. Limited Certificate of Inspection
C. Temporary Certificate of Inspection
D. Permit to Proceed

572. A vessel is entering port "A" for the first time and has a Pilot conning the vessel. The Master is unsure that the Pilot is taking sufficient action to prevent a collision. What should the Master do?

A. Nothing; the Pilot is required by law and is solely responsible for the safety of the vessel.
B. State his concerns to the Pilot but do not interfere with the handling of the vessel.
C. Direct the Pilot to stop the vessel and anchor if necessary until the situation clears.
D. Recommend an alternative action and if not followed relieve the Pilot.

573. An ocean towing bridle whose legs are of equal length, but too short, may _____.

A. fail to provide spring in the hawser
B. cause unequal distribution of the load to one leg
C. cause the bridle legs to jump clear of the chocks or fairleads
D. None of the above

574. Which type of link is generally used to connect shots of anchor chain?

A. Detachable
B. Open
C. Pear shaped
D. Stud link

575. What is a correct reply to a Pilot's request, "How's your head"?

A. "Steady"
B. "Checked"
C. "Passing 200°"
D. "Eased to 10° rudder"

576. In twin-screw engine installations while going ahead, maneuvering qualities are most effective when the tops of the propeller blades both turn _____.

A. to starboard
B. outboard from the center
C. to port
D. inboard toward the center

577. You are signing on a crew. A man presents a Merchant Mariner's Document that you suspect has been tampered with. Which action should you take?

A. Confiscate the document and deliver it to the Coast Guard.
B. Sign the man on and notify the Coast Guard at the first U.S. port of call.
C. Refuse to sign the man on articles until authorized by the Coast Guard.
D. Refuse to sign the man on and notify the FBI of unauthorized use of a federal document.

580. Which statement is FALSE about using a wire bridle on an ocean tow?

A. The inboard end of each bridle leg should have a large eyesplice to fit over the bitts.
B. The strength of each leg should be at least one-half that of the main towing hawser.
C. Each leg should be at least 60 to 90 feet long.
D. None of the above

582. In illustration D044DG, the mooring line labeled "E" is called a(n) _____.

A. after spring line
B. bow spring line
C. forward breast line
D. bow line

583. Which factor(s) must you consider when making up a towing bridle?

A. The horsepower of the tug
B. The desired amount of swing in the tow hook up
C. The weight of the tow
D. All of the above

592. When a helmsman receives the command "Right 15 degrees rudder," the helmsman's immediate reply should be _____.

A. "Right 15 degrees rudder"
B. "Aye Aye Sir"
C. "Rudder is right 15 degrees"
D. No reply is necessary, just carry out the order.

593. To lead the towing hawser over the center of the stern when not under a strain you could _____.

A. fairlead it through a stern roller chock
B. lead it through the Norman pins
C. hold it in the median position by a gob rope or lizard stopper
D. All of the above when so equipped

594. A bollard is found on the _____.

A. beach
B. deck
C. pier
D. towed vessel

595. The turning circle of a vessel is the path followed by the _____.

A. outermost part of the ship while making the circle
B. center of gravity
C. bow
D. tipping center

597. Wages due a seaman may be attached by the court for the _____.

A. payment of monthly bills
B. payment of creditors
C. support of a minor child
D. All of the above

601. Your vessel has completed an inspection for certification and is issued a temporary certificate. This _____.

A. expires six months after it is issued
B. must be exchanged for a regular Certificate of Inspection before going foreign or out of state
C. has the full force of a regular Certificate of Inspection
D. must be posted in the vicinity of the officers' licenses

602. Which emergency equipment should you keep near the towing bitts?

A. A self-contained breathing apparatus (SCBA)
B. A boat hook and a spanner wrench
C. A fire ax and/or cutting torch
D. A Stokes litter basket

603. To reduce the amount of catenary you may _____.

A. shorten the hawser or increase the tug's speed
B. lengthen the hawser or reduce the tug's speed
C. place your tug in irons
D. make a sharp turn

604. The term "lee side" refers to the _____.

A. side of the vessel exposed to the wind
B. side of the vessel sheltered from the wind
C. port side
D. starboard side

605. You would properly secure a bos'n's chair to a gantline with a _____.

A. fisherman's bend
B. bowline
C. double sheetbend
D. double blackwall hitch

607. A lashing used to secure two barges side by side, lashed in an "X" fashion, is called a _____.

A. scissor wire
B. towing wire
C. breast wire
D. cross wire

612. When backing down with sternway, the pivot point of a vessel is _____.

A. at the bow

B. about one-third of the vessel's length from the bow
C. aft of the propellers
D. about one-quarter of the vessel's length from the stern

613. A lookout can leave his station _____.

A. at the end of the watch
B. only when properly relieved
C. at any time
D. 15 minutes before the end of the watch

614. A fid is a _____.

A. mallet used when splicing wire rope
B. sharp pointed crow bar used to unlay wire rope
C. tapered steel pin used to separate wire rope
D. tapered wooden pin used when splicing heavy rope

615. When a wedge of water builds up between the head of the barge and the bank it is referred to as _____.

A. bank cushion
B. bank suction
C. bow wave
D. veering cushion

616. "Ice blink" is _____.

A. the dark appearance of the underside of a cloud layer due to reflection of a surface of open water
B. the soft light appearance on the underside of a cloud layer due to reflection from a surface of open water
C. the yellowish-white glare on the underside of a cloud layer
D. "water sky"

617. In illustration D044DG, the mooring line labeled "A" is called a(n) _____.

A. onshore stern line
B. offshore stern line
C. after breast line
D. after spring line

622. A predictable result of a vessel nearing a bank or edge of a channel is that the _____.

A. stern is drawn to the bank as the bow sheers off
B. bow sheers toward the bank

C. vessel continues in a straight line, but with greatly reduced maneuverability
D. vessel will be drawn bodily into the bank unless the engines are stopped

623. When hugging a bank in a narrow channel, you should take precautions against _____.

A. bank suction, squat and the effects of vessels passing close aboard
B. clogged sea chests, plugged sea strainers and overheated machinery
C. striking underwater obstructions close to the bank
D. All of the above

624. A serving mallet is used in _____.

A. covering wire or fiber rope
B. forcing fids into a line
C. dogging hatches
D. splicing lines

625. Which statement is FALSE?

A. Your stern is sucked down and your draft increases when going from deep to shallow water.
B. Excessive speed while passing moored vessels may cause them to surge and break their moorings.
C. Excessive speed while passing a tow being pushed ahead or pushing a tow into an eddy too fast may break up the tow.
D. None of the above

627. Your ship is steaming at night with the gyropilot engaged when you notice that the vessel's course is slowly changing to the right. What action should you take FIRST?

A. switch to hand steering
B. shift steering to the emergency steering station
C. call the Master
D. notify the engine room

630. You are doing a Williamson turn. Your vessel has swung about 60° from the original course heading. You should _____.

A. put the rudder amidships and check the swing
B. stop the engines and prepare to maneuver to pick up the man in the water
C. shift your rudder
D. increase to maximum speed

631. At least one reinspection shall be made on each vessel holding a Certificate of Inspection valid for two years. This inspection shall be held between the tenth and fourteenth months of the duration period of the certificate and shall be _____.

A. at the discretion of the inspector, but in no greater detail than required for original certification
B. at the discretion of the inspector, but in no lesser detail than required for original certification
C. generally similar in scope to the inspection required for certification, but in less detail
D. equivalent to the inspection required for certification

632. What does the helm command "shift the rudder" mean?

A. Stop the swing of the ship.
B. Shift the rudder control to the alternate steering method.
C. Put the rudder over to the opposite side, the same number of degrees that it is now.
D. Put the rudder amidships and hold the heading steady as she goes.

633. A tug is best positioned for towing and maneuvering on rivers and other restricted waters where wave action is limited when _____.

A. directly astern and pushing the tow
B. towing on a hawser
C. towing alongside and parallel to the vessel it is towing
D. towing on the hip

634. The "iron mike" is a(n) _____.

A. pilot
B. speaker
C. standby wheel
D. automatic pilot

636. The use of an anchor to assist in turning in restricted waters is _____.

A. a last resort
B. good seamanship
C. the sign of a novice shiphandler
D. to be used only with a single-screw vessel

637. A tow bridle is attached to the main tow hawser at the _____.

A. bight ring
B. tow hook
C. fishplate
D. swivel

640. Which factor(s) can affect the performance of a river towboat?

A. The draft of the towboat and the draft of the barges under tow
B. The placement of the barges within the tow
C. The presence of flanking rudders and Kort nozzles
D. All of the above

641. Which document shows the minimum required crew a vessel must have to navigate from one port in the United States to another?

A. Articles
B. Certificate of Inspection
C. Crew List
D. Register

642. In illustration D044DG, the mooring line labeled "B" is called a(n) _____.

A. offshore stern line
B. inshore stern line
C. after spring line
D. after breast line

644. The "lay" of a line refers to _____.

A. its normal location of stowage
B. the direction of twist in the strands
C. the manner in which it is coiled
D. the manner in which it is rigged

645. A vessel's Certificate of Documentation _____.

A. may be retained by the owner at the home port OR kept on the vessel
B. must be posted under transparent material in the pilothouse
C. must be carried on board
D. must be kept on file at the corporate offices of the owner or operator

647. Synchronous towing means that the _____.

A. tug is on the crest of a wave while the tow is in the trough
B. tug is in the trough while the tow is riding on the crest of a wave

C. tug and tow are both in the same relative position on different waves at the same time
D. port and starboard engines on the tug are turning at the same RPM

650. A crew member has just fallen overboard off your port side. Which action should you take?

A. Immediately put the rudder over hard right.
B. Immediately put the rudder over hard left.
C. Immediately put the engines astern.
D. Wait until the stern is well clear of the man and then put the rudder over hard right.

651. Fire fighting equipment requirements for a particular vessel may be found on the _____.

A. Certificate of Inspection
B. Certificate of Seaworthiness
C. Classification Certificate
D. Certificate of Registry

652. When plugging holes below the waterline you should _____.

A. eliminate all water entering the hole
B. only plug holes in machinery or other vital spaces
C. reduce the entry of water as much as possible
D. plug the largest holes first

654. A rope made of a combination of wire and fiber is known as _____.

A. independent
B. lang lay
C. preformed
D. spring lay

655. Good seamanship while towing in heavy weather requires all of the following EXCEPT _____.

A. reducing speed to reduce surging on the towline
B. lashing down or stowing all loose gear
C. dogging all hatches and watertight doors
D. streaming all of your towing hawser

657. Which space(s) is(are) deducted from gross tonnage to derive net tonnage?

A. Companions and booby hatches
B. Open structures

C. Spaces for the exclusive use of the officers or crew
D. Water ballast spaces

660. You receive word that a person has fallen overboard from the starboard side. You should FIRST _____.

A. notify the Master
B. put the wheel hard right
C. put the engines full astern
D. sound the man overboard alarm

661. The number of certificated lifeboatmen required for a vessel is found on the _____.

A. Certificate of Inspection
B. Station Bill
C. lifeboats
D. Register or Enrollment

663. While towing astern, if your towing hawser becomes taut it results in _____.

A. more catenary in the towing hawser
B. less catenary in the towing hawser
C. more yaw
D. less yaw

664. Coiling new rope against the lay, bringing the lower end up through the center of the coil, then coiling with the lay, in order to remove the kinks, is known as

_____.

A. coiling
B. faking
C. flemishing
D. thoroughfooting

665. The catenary _____.

A. acts as a reserve length of towing hawser when the tug applies more power, and it dampens the surge effect of the tow
B. gives an approximation of the amount of strain on the towing hawser
C. is the dip in the towing hawser between the tug and the tow
D. All of the above

666. You are proceeding at a slow speed with your starboard side near the right bank of a channel. If your vessel suddenly sheers toward the opposite bank, the best maneuver would be _____.

A. full ahead, hard left rudder
B. full ahead, hard right rudder

C. full astern, hard left rudder
D. full astern, hard right rudder

667. While towing in shallow water you should consider _____.

A. using a short towing hawser
B. using a floating hawser
C. the catenary and the effect it may have on the tow
D. All of the above

669. Which statement describes the motion of a yawing tow?

A. The tow twists, sometimes violently, astern of the tug
B. The tow sheers to one side behind the tug and maintains a position in a line diagonal to the tug's forward movement
C. The tow snakes behind the tug
D. All of the above

670. You must evacuate a seaman by helicopter lift. Which statement is TRUE?

A. The ship should be stopped with the wind off the beam while the helicopter is hovering overhead.
B. The basket or stretcher must not be allowed to touch the deck.
C. The tending line of the litter basket should be secured to the ship beyond the radius of the helicopter blades.
D. The hoist line should be slack before the basket or stretcher is hooked on.

672. When towing alongside (breasted tow), more forward movement will be imparted to the tow by _____.

A. increasing the angle of line pull to the keel axis of the tow
B. reducing the angle of line pull to the keel axis of the tow
C. positioning the towing vessel on the forward end of the tow
D. shortening the length of the tow line

673. In illustration D044DG, the mooring line labeled "C" is called a _____.

A. shore line
B. breast line
C. spring line
D. stern line

674. Stuffer-braid rope has _____.

A. a yarn core
B. no core

C. three strands
D. 12 threads

675. An advantage of the Christmas Tree towing method is to _____.

A. increase the towing hawser's catenary and provide more spring
B. reduce catenary, allow operation in shallower water, and to release one barge without breaking up the entire tow
C. enable one tug and its crew without any outside assistance to make up or break down the tow
D. provide rapid delivery of logs from the northwestern United States to Hawaiian sawmills

676. Conditions for crossing a rough bar are usually best at _____.

A. low water slack
B. high water slack
C. high water ebb
D. high water flood

677. In illustration D044DG, the mooring line labeled "D" is called a(n) _____.

A. forward spring line
B. after spring line
C. waist breast line
D. stern line

680. You must medevac a critically injured seaman by helicopter hoist. Which statement is TRUE?

A. The ship's relative wind should be from dead ahead at 10 to 30 knots.
B. The deck crew at the hoist point should not wear baseball hats.
C. The helicopter's drop line should be secured to the ship not more than 15 feet from the hoist position.
D. When using a "horsecollar," the bight of the loop should be around the chest of the injured seaman.

681. A Cargo Ship Safety Radiotelegraphy Certificate and a Cargo Ship Safety Radiotelephony Certificate shall be issued for a period of not more than _____.

A. 6 months
B. 12 months
C. 18 months
D. 24 months

682. Illustration D044DG. The mooring line labeled "H" is called a(n) _____.

A. forward breast line
B. offshore bow line
C. offshore spring line
D. onshore bow line

683. Barges and vessels are ballasted before departure to _____.

A. improve their stability
B. avoid polluting waters where liquid ballast may not be discharged
C. prevent free surface effects
D. allow movement of liquids within the barge for tank cleaning

684. Right-laid line should be coiled _____.

A. clockwise
B. counterclockwise
C. either clockwise or counterclockwise
D. on a reel

685. Which type of ballast is most commonly used in barges and ships?

A. Water
B. Oil
C. Concrete and barite
D. Sand, rock and gravel

686. The effect known as "bank cushion" acts in which of the following ways on a single-screw vessel proceeding along a narrow channel?

A. It forces the bow away from the bank.
B. It forces the stern away from the bank.
C. It forces the entire vessel away from the bank.
D. It heels the vessel toward the bank.

689. When your tug reduces speed to shorten tow, the _____.

A. length of the tow gets shorter as the strain is reduced
B. tow may continue its momentum and overtake the tug
C. towing hawser may drag the bottom and put the tug in irons
D. All of the above

690. A rescue helicopter's hoist area should have a radius of at least _____.

A. 6 feet of clear deck
B. 10 feet of clear deck
C. 25 feet of clear deck
D. 50 feet of clear deck

691. On U.S. flag vessels, which certificate is always issued by the Coast Guard?

A. Load Line Certificate
B. Safety Equipment Certificate
C. Safety Construction Certificate
D. Register of cargo gear

692. The tow makeup that is designed to keep the catenary of the tow hawser to a minimum is called the _____.

A. Christmas tree tow
B. tandem tow
C. British tow
D. tandem tug tow

693. The effect of excessive catenary in shallow water may be _____.

A. dragging the towing hawser along the bottom and chafing it
B. snagging sunken or submerged objects
C. slowing, stopping or endangering the towing operation by placing the tug in irons
D. All of the above

694. An advantage of nylon rope over manila rope is that nylon rope _____.

A. can be used in conjunction with wire or spring-lay rope
B. can be stored on decks exposed to sunlight
C. can hold a load even when a considerable amount of the yarns have been abraded
D. gives audible warning of overstress whereas manila does not

695. A tug is "in irons" when held in a fixed position by _____.

A. the weight of its tow, its being anchored, or grounded
B. the weight of its towing hawser on the bottom
C. an adverse current
D. lack of power or an engine breakdown

696. A vessel traveling down a narrow channel, especially if the draft is nearly equal to the depth of the water, may set off the nearer side. This effect is known as _____.

A. smelling the bottom
B. squatting
C. bank suction
D. bank cushion

697. What imminent danger results from tripping?

A. A crew member being knocked over the side
B. Capsizing your tug
C. Your tug being pulled backwards by your tow
D. The tow being thrown off course

699. Under which condition is a tug likely to be tripped?

A. when the tow "jumps" on the line
B. while making up to tow a large oil rig
C. when the towing hawser leads forward of the quarter
D. when the tug exerts maximum bollard pull with the tow close astern

704. Laying out a line in successive circles flat on deck with the bitter end in the center is known as _____.

A. coiling
B. faking
C. flemishing
D. lining

705. A tug may be in danger of tripping when _____.

A. towed sideways by an overwhelming force on the towline
B. her tow moves parallel to and forward on either side of the tug
C. the tow is no longer directly astern but moves up on her quarter
D. All of the above

706. How does the effect known as "bank suction" act on a single-screw vessel proceeding along a narrow channel?

A. It pulls the bow toward the bank.
B. It pulls the stern toward the bank.
C. It pushes the entire vessel away from the bank.
D. It heels the vessel toward the bank.

707. Is tripping limited to harbor and coastal towing?

A. No! Forces tending to capsize a tug are as dangerous on the high seas as they are in harbor and coastal work.
B. Yes! The long towing hawser used in ocean towing eliminates the danger of tripping.

C. No! Tripping is common in ocean towing because of more frequent maneuvering
D. Yes! Because of increased water depths, forces required to capsize a tug are not usually found in ocean towing

710. Which statement is FALSE, concerning the Williamson turn?

A. In a large vessel (VLCC) much of the headway will be lost thereby requiring little astern maneuvering.
B. When the turn is completed, the vessel will be on a reciprocal course and nearly on the original track line.
C. The initial actions are taken at well-defined points and reduce the need for individual judgement.
D. The turn will return the vessel to the man's location in the shortest possible time.

712. What is the effect of releasing the towline in a tripping situation?

A. It disconnects the capsizing force and allows the tug to recover from its list.
B. It frees the tug from its towing responsibilities.
C. There is no effect other than relief.
D. Yawing

713. How do the height and location of a tug's towing bitts relate to the danger of tripping?

A. The further forward and closer to amidships the more readily the tug will trip.
B. Placement further aft permits more effective pulling, better steering and eliminates the danger of tripping.
C. Installing the bitts down low lowers the center of gravity.
D. The height and position of towing bitts has no significance.

714. Using a safety factor of 6, determine the safe working load of manila line with a breaking stress of 8 tons.

A. 0.75 tons
B. 1.25 tons
C. 1.33 tons
D. 8.00 tons

715. The term "overriding" or "over-running" when applied to towing, implies that _____.

A. there is more crew on board than required
B. the tow has overtaken its tug
C. the towing hawser comes out of the water
D. the Norman pins are not effective

716. Your vessel is proceeding along a narrow channel. The effect called bank cushion has which effect on the vessel?

A. Forces the bow away from the bank
B. Forces the stern away from the bank
C. Forces the entire vessel bodily away from the bank
D. Decreases the draft at the bow

717. It is the responsibility of the Master to ensure that _____.

A. the muster list is posted in each compartment
B. temporary personnel and visitors are advised of emergency stations
C. names of crew members are listed on the muster list
D. no changes are made to the muster list

720. You suspect that a crewmember has fallen overboard during the night and immediately execute a Williamson turn. What is the primary advantage of this maneuver under these circumstances?

A. You will be on a reciprocal course and nearly on the trackline run during the night.
B. The turn provides the maximum coverage of the area to be searched.
C. The turn enables you to reverse course in the shortest possible time.
D. You have extra time to maneuver in attempting to close in on the man for rescue.

721. Illustration D044DG. The mooring line labeled "F" is called a _____.

A. bow line
B. forward spring line
C. breast line
D. None of the above

722. A tow can override its tug as a result of _____.

A. a mechanical breakdown on the tug
B. adverse tidal current conditions
C. the tug reducing its speed
D. All of the above

724. Using a safety factor of five, determine what is the safe working load for 3-1/2 inch manila line with a breaking stress of 4.9 tons.

A. 0.82 ton
B. 0.98 ton
C. 2.45 tons
D. 12.25 tons

725. By law, a user of marijuana shall be subject to _____.

A. loss of pay during the period of such use
B. reprimand by the U.S. Coast Guard
C. revocation of license or certificate
D. termination of employment

726. A common occurrence when a vessel is running into shallow water is that _____.

A. the wake is less pronounced
B. the vessel is more responsive to the rudder
C. "squat" will cause a decrease in bottom clearance and an increase in draft
D. All of the above

727. Which space(s) is(are) deducted from gross tonnage to derive net tonnage?

A. Galley fitted with range or oven
B. Open structures
C. Passenger spaces
D. Boatswain's stores

730. In a Williamson turn, the rudder is put over full until the _____.

A. vessel has turned 90° from her original course
B. vessel has turned 60° from her original course
C. vessel is on a reciprocal course
D. emergency turn signal sounds

732. Which action should be taken FIRST if your tow is sinking in shallow water?

A. Pay out the towline until the sunken tow reaches bottom.
B. Sever the towline.
C. Immediately head for the nearest shoreline.
D. Contact the Coast Guard.

733. Before leaving port on an ocean tow, a tug captain should assure himself of all the following EXCEPT _____.

A. the towing hawser can be released quickly in an emergency
B. the correct navigation lights are rigged and operable on the tug and tow
C. an insurance underwriter has prepared a pre-sailing survey
D. a pick-up wire has been rigged on the tow in case of a breakaway.

734. What is the computed breaking strength of a 4-inch manila line?

A. 5,280 lbs.
B. 7,700 lbs.
C. 12,200 lbs.
D. 14,400 lbs.

736. You notice that your speed has decreased, the stern of your vessel has settled into the water, and your rudder is sluggish in responding. The MOST likely cause is _____.

A. mechanical problems with the steering gear
B. shallow water
C. loss of lubricating oil in the engine
D. current

740. The extension of the after part of the keel in a single-screw vessel upon which the stern post rests is called the _____.

A. boss
B. knuckle
C. skeg
D. strut

741. A vessel has sustained damage in a collision with another vessel. It is necessary to have a Seaworthy Certificate before the vessel sails. Who will issue this certificate?

A. American Consul
B. Classification Society
C. Captain of the Port
D. Officer in Charge, Marine Inspection

742. Lighter longitudinal stiffening frames on the vessel's side plating are called _____.

A. stringers
B. side frames
C. side stiffeners
D. intercostals

744. When using natural-fiber rope, you should NEVER _____.

A. dry the line before stowing it
B. reverse turns on winches periodically to keep out kinks
C. try to lubricate the line
D. use chafing gear

746. Which effect does speed through the water have on a vessel which is underway in shallow water?

A. A decrease in the speed results in a decrease in steering response and maneuverability.
B. An increase in speed results in the stern sucking down lower than the bow.
C. An increase in speed results in the vessel rising on an even plane.
D. A decrease in speed results in the vessel sucking down on an even plane.

750. On a single-screw vessel the stern frame _____.

A. furnishes support to the rudder, propeller shaft, and transom frame
B. provides foundations for after mooring winches
C. provides foundations for the main propulsion engines
D. transfers the driving force of the propeller to the hull

751. A document which has a list of names, birthplaces, and residences of persons employed on a merchant vessel bound from a U.S. port on a foreign voyage and is required at every port is called the _____.

A. Certified Crew List
B. Crew Manifest
C. Shipping Articles
D. Station Bill

754. Which method is used to detect rot in manila lines?

A. Feeling the surface of the line for broken fibers
B. Measuring the reduction in circumference of the line
C. Observing for the appearance of mildew on the outer surface
D. Opening the strands and examining the inner fibers

759. The equipment used to control, protect and connect a towline is called _____.

A. cat head
B. terminal gear

C. level wind
D. poured socket

760. The connection to the towline must be secured with a _____.

A. galvanized screw-pin shackle
B. hardened steel thimble
C. shackle secured with a nut and cotter pin
D. shackle fitted with a swivel piece

763. A vessel that tows astern must have a/an _____.

A. towing winch
B. method to easily release the towline
C. oxyacetylene cutting torch
D. ax or knife mounted near the towing bitts

764. Roundline is a _____.

A. four-stranded, left- or right-handed line
B. three-stranded, right-handed line
C. three-stranded, left-handed line
D. small tarred hempline of three strands laid left-handed

765. The owner or Master of a vessel pushing ahead or towing alongside must ensure that each of the following is appropriate for the vessel's horsepower and tow arrangement EXCEPT _____.

A. hydraulic couplings
B. face wires
C. push gear
D. spring lines

766. Insufficient space between the hull and bottom in shallow water will prevent normal screw currents resulting in _____.

A. waste of power
B. sudden sheering to either side
C. sluggish rudder response
D. All of the above

769. The owner or Master of a towing vessel must ensure that each person that directs and controls the movement of the vessel knows all of the following EXCEPT _____.

A. the effects of maneuvering on the vessel and its tow
B. the speed and direction of any current for the area being transited
C. how to apply variation and deviation to readings from a magnetic compass

D. the ownership of the vessel(s) being towed

770. The ratio of the height of a vessel's rudder to its width is referred to as the _____.

A. aspect ratio
B. constriction ratio
C. rudder ratio
D. steering ratio

772. To reduce stress on the towing hawser when towing astern (ocean tow), the hawser should be _____.

A. secured to the aftermost fitting on the towing vessel
B. just touching the water
C. underwater
D. as short as possible

774. The strongest of the natural fibers is _____.

A. cotton
B. hemp
C. manila
D. sisal

775. You are on a large merchant vessel entering a U.S. port. There is a Pilot onboard and he has the conn. Which statement is TRUE?

A. The Pilot becomes solely responsible for the safe navigation of the vessel only if the Master relinquishes the conn.
B. The Pilot is solely responsible for the internal working of the ship.
C. The Pilot is solely responsible for the safe maneuvering of the ship only if he is required to be on board by law.
D. The Master is responsible for the safe navigation of the ship and the Pilot is employed for his local knowledge.

776. In most cases, when a large merchant vessel enters shallow water at high speed the _____.

A. maneuverability will increase
B. speed will increase
C. bow will squat farther than the stern
D. vessel will rise slightly, on a level plane

777. Before a Master relieves a Pilot of the conn, the _____.

A. Master must always request the Pilot to take corrective action

B. Master should foresee any danger to the vessel on the present course
C. Master should agree to sign a release of liability form
D. vessel must be in extremis

780. Bilge keels are more effective at dampening rolls as the _____.

A. pitching increases
B. list increases
C. rolling increases
D. draft decreases

781. The trim and stability booklet must be approved by the _____.

A. International Maritime Organization
B. National Cargo Bureau
C. Society of Naval Architects and Marine Engineers
D. United States Coast Guard

782. The owner or Master of a towing vessel shall ensure that each person that directs and controls the movement of the vessel can accurately fix the vessel's position using all of the following EXCEPT _____.

A. installed navigational equipment
B. buoys alone
C. all available aids to navigation
D. depths soundings and hydrographic contour lines

783. The owner or Master of a towing vessel shall ensure that each person that directs and controls the movement of the vessel can accomplish all of the following EXCEPT _____.

A. evaluate the danger of each closing visual or radar contact
B. adjust speed with due regard for the weather and visibility
C. reduce speed only where local speed limits are posted
D. enter all required test and inspection results in the vessel's log or other record carried on board

784. Marline is _____.

A. four-stranded sisal line
B. three-stranded cotton line
C. sail twine
D. two-stranded hemp cord

785. With rudders amidships and negligible wind, a twin-screw vessel moving

ahead on the port screw and backing on the starboard screw will _____.

A. move in a straight line
B. pivot to starboard
C. pivot to port
D. walk sideways to starboard

786. You are on a single-screw vessel with a right-handed propeller, and you are making headway. When you enter shallow water, _____.

A. you will have better rudder response
B. your speed will increase without a change in your throttle
C. your rudder response will become sluggish
D. your vessel will tend to ride higher

794. "White Line" is made from _____.

A. cotton
B. hemp
C. manila
D. sisal

796. When you enter shallow water, you would expect your rudder response to _____.

A. be sluggish and your speed to decrease
B. be sluggish and your speed to increase
C. improve and your speed to decrease
D. improve and your speed to increase

799. Temporary Certificates of Inspection are effective until the _____.

A. Solas Certificate is issued
B. Load Line Certificate is renewed
C. classification society approval is issued
D. permanent Certificate of Inspection is issued

800. A Kort nozzle is a(n) _____.

A. hollow tube surrounding the propeller used to improve thrust
B. nozzle attached to a firefighting hose
C. intake valve on a diesel engine
D. piston cylinder on a diesel engine

802. You are on watch at sea on course 090°T. A man falls overboard on your starboard side. You immediately start a Williamson Turn. Which action is NOT a part of a Williamson Turn?

A. Stop the engines until clear of the man.
B. Come right full rudder until the vessel heads 150°T.
C. Shift the helm to left full rudder.
D. Continue with left rudder until on course 270°T.

804. Line is called "small stuff" if its circumference is less than _____.

A. 1/2"
B. 3/4"
C. 1"
D. 1-3/4"

806. Which will most likely occur when entering shallow water?

A. Rudder action will become more effective.
B. The vessel's list will change.
C. The vessel's trim will change.
D. An increase in speed will occur.

810. In nautical terminology a "dog" is a _____.

A. crow bar
B. device to force a water tight door against the frame
C. heavy steel beam
D. wedge

814. In the manufacture of line, plant fibers are twisted together to form _____.

A. cable
B. line
C. strands
D. yarns

816. Water may boil up around the stern of a vessel in a channel due to _____.

A. slack water when upbound
B. shallow water
C. a cross current
D. a head current

817. In illustration D044DG, the mooring line labeled "G" is called a(n) _____.

A. forward spring line
B. forward breast line
C. inshore bow line
D. offshore bow line

820. A partial deck in a hold is called a(n) _____.

A. weather deck
B. orlop deck
C. shelter deck
D. main deck

824. The larger sizes of manila line are measured by their _____.

A. radius
B. diameter
C. circumference
D. weight per foot

825. Who is responsible for establishing watches aboard a U.S. vessel?

A. The owner of the vessel
B. The company that operates the vessel
C. The company that charters the vessel
D. The Master of the vessel

826. In order to reduce your wake in a narrow channel you should _____.

A. apply enough rudder to counter the effect of the current
B. change your course to a zigzag course
C. reduce your speed
D. shift the weight to the stern

827. The pitch of a propeller is a measure of the _____.

A. angle that the propeller makes with a free stream of water
B. angle that the propeller makes with the surface of the water
C. number of feet per revolution the propeller is designed to advance in still water without slip
D. positive pressure resulting from the difference of the forces on both sides of the moving propeller in still water without slip

829. In terms of vessel manning, a watch is the _____.

A. direct performance of deck or engine operations in a scheduled and fixed rotation
B. performance of maintenance work necessary for the vessel's safe operation, on a daily basis
C. performance of lookout duties
D. direct performance of cargo loading and discharge operations only

833. The Master may require part of the crew to work when needed for _____.

A. maneuvering, shifting berth, mooring and unmooring
B. performing work necessary for the safety of the vessel, its passengers, crew or cargo
C. performing fire, lifeboat or other drills in port or at sea
D. All of the above

834. A whipping on a fiber line _____.

A. keeps the ends from fraying
B. strengthens it
C. protects your hands
D. becomes part of a splice

836. River currents tend to _____.

A. pick up speed where the channel widens
B. run slower in the center of the channel
C. hug the inside of a bend
D. cause the greatest depth of water to be along the outside of a bend

840. The terms "cant frame" and "counter" are associated with the vessel's _____.

A. cargo hatch
B. forecastle
C. steering engine
D. stern

844. Using a safety factor of five, determine the safe working load of a line with a breaking strain of 20,000 pounds.

A. 4,000
B. 5,000
C. 20,000
D. 100,000

845. The terminology "able to understand any order spoken by the officers" refers to all of the following situations EXCEPT _____.

A. in response to a fire
B. directing the use of lifesaving equipment
C. for deck department crew members to understand the terminology used in the engine room
D. in response to a man overboard

846. A vessel proceeding along the bank of a river or channel has the tendency to _____.

A. continue in line with the bank
B. hug the bank

C. sheer away from the bank
D. increase speed

847. When towing astern what equipment should be stowed ready for use near the towline?

A. First aid kit
B. Ax or cutting torch
C. Fire extinguisher
D. Chafing gear

850. Panting frames are located in the _____.

A. after double bottoms
B. centerline tanks on tankships
C. fore and after peaks
D. forward double bottoms

852. How can the Coast Guard determine that a crew member is "able to understand any order spoken by the officers"?

A. Require a demonstration by the officer and the crew member
B. Require a written test
C. Require that an interpreter be provided
D. All of the above

853. Who is responsible for properly manning a vessel in accordance with all applicable laws, regulations and international conventions?

A. The (USCG) Officer in Charge of Marine Inspection
B. The (USCG) Captain of the Port
C. The owner or operator of the vessel
D. The Master of the vessel

854. A piece of small stuff (small line) secured to an object to prevent it from going adrift is a _____.

A. lanyard
B. keeper
C. noose
D. stopper

855. Which party must ensure that legal work hour limitations (for both officers and crew members), rest periods and regulations governing work on Sundays and holidays are followed when the vessel is in a safe harbor?

A. The owner of the vessel
B. The company operating the vessel

C. The Master of the vessel
D. The company chartering the vessel

856. A wedge of water building up between the bow and nearer bank which forces the bow out and away describes _____.

A. bank cushion
B. bank suction
C. combined effect
D. bend effect

861. Every entry required to be made in the Official Logbook shall be signed by the _____.

A. Mate on watch
B. Master and Chief Mate or other member of the crew
C. Master only
D. Purser, one of the Mates, and some other member of the crew

862. The term "pintle" and "gudgeon" are associated with the _____.

A. anchor windlass
B. jumbo boom
C. rudder
D. steering engine

864. During the manufacture of line, yarns are twisted together in the _____.

A. opposite direction from which the fibers are twisted together to form strands
B. same direction the fibers are twisted to form strands
C. opposite direction from which the fibers are twisted together to form the line
D. opposite direction from which the fibers are twisted together forming cables

865. A nylon line is rated at 15,000 lbs. breaking strain. Using a safety factor of 5, what is the safe working load (SWL)?

A. 3,000 lbs
B. 5,000 lbs
C. 15,000 lbs
D. 65,000 lbs

866. For the deepest water when rounding a bend in a river, you should navigate your vessel _____.

A. toward the inside of the bend
B. toward the outside of the bend

C. toward the center of the river just before the bend, then change course for the river's center after the bend
D. in the river's center

867. Who may perform as a lookout?

A. A member of the engineering watch
B. A member of the navigational watch
C. A member of the Stewards Department
D. All of the above

870. The terms "ceiling" and "margin plate" are associated with the _____.

A. crew's quarters
B. engine room
C. main deck
D. tank top

871. In writing up the logbook at the end of your watch, you make an error in writing an entry. What is the proper means of correcting this error?

A. Cross out the error with a single line, and write the correct entry, then initial it.
B. Carefully and neatly erase the entry and rewrite it correctly.
C. Remove this page of the log book, and rewrite all entries on a clean page.
D. Blot out the error completely and rewrite the entry correctly.

873. At the required fire drill, all persons must report to their stations and demonstrate their ability to perform the duties assigned to them _____.

A. by the Coast Guard regulations
B. in the station bill
C. by the person conducting the drill
D. at the previous safety meeting

874. Which type of line would have the LEAST resistance to mildew and rot?

A. Manila
B. Nylon
C. Dacron
D. Polypropylene

876. You intend to overtake a vessel in a narrow channel. As you approach the other vessel's stern _____.

A. you will gain speed
B. both vessels will gain speed
C. the vessels will drift together

D. the vessels will drift apart

880. The projecting lugs of the rudderpost which furnish support to the rudder are called _____.

A. bases
B. gudgeons
C. pintles
D. rudder lugs

881. The proper way to correct a mistake in the logbook is to _____.

A. erase the entry and rewrite
B. completely black out the entry and rewrite
C. draw a line through the entry, rewrite, and initial
D. draw several lines through the entry and rewrite

882. The owner or Master of a towing vessel that tows astern must keep records of the towline(s) that include all of the following information EXCEPT _____.

A. the towline's initial minimum breaking strength as determined by the manufacturer
B. an invoice showing the cost of the towline
C. the towline's nautical miles of use or time in service
D. the history of loading of the towline

883. The size and material used for towline(s) must meet all of the following requirements, EXCEPT _____.

A. be appropriate to the vessel's horsepower or bollard pull
B. be strong enough to handle any static or dynamic loads expected during its service life
C. fit any spare wire clips carried on board the vessel for repair purposes
D. be suitable for exposure to the marine environment

884. When towing astern, each towline must meet all of these requirements, EXCEPT _____.

A. being suitable for use as soon as it is removed from its normal stowage location
B. having wire clips for other than a temporary repair

C. having the end either spliced with a thimble or fitted with a poured socket
D. being free of knots

885. How many wire clips must be used to make a temporary repair to a tow wire?

A. 3
B. 4
C. 5
D. Wire clips are never, under any circumstances, permitted

886. Two vessels are abreast of each other and passing port to port in a confined waterway. What should you expect as your bow approaches the screws of the other vessel?

A. Your speed will significantly increase.
B. Your draft will significantly decrease.
C. Your bow will sheer toward the other vessel.
D. Your bow will sheer away from the other vessel.

887. The condition of a towline must be monitored by _____.

A. keeping record of the towline's initial minimum breaking strength
B. keeping record of each retest of the towline's minimum breaking strength
C. conducting routine visual inspections of the towline
D. All of the above

889. The owner or Master of a towing vessel must evaluate whether the entire towline, or a part of it, is no longer serviceable. The towline should be removed from service in all cases EXCEPT _____.

A. when recommended by the manufacturer or an authorized classification society
B. in accordance with a replacement schedule
C. when the vessel is underway
D. depending on the mileage or time that the towline has been in service

890. A term applied to the bottom shell plating in a double-bottom ship is _____.

A. bottom floor
B. outer bottom
C. shear plating
D. tank top

892. On a shallow water tow, the catenary of the towline should be _____.

A. large
B. small
C. eliminated
D. adjusted frequently

894. When taking a length of new manila rope from the coil, you should _____.

A. mount the coil so it will turn like a spool and unreel from the outside
B. roll the coil along the deck and allow the rope to fall off the coil
C. lay the coil on end with the inside end down, then pull the inside end up through the middle of the coil
D. lay the coil on end with the inside end up then unwind the rope from the outside of the coil

895. Which factor would NOT lead to removing a towline from service?

A. An excessive number of miles of towing service.
B. Failing a tensile strength test that proved the towline was no longer appropriate for expected sea conditions.
C. When heavy grease on the towline saturates the core of the wire rope.
D. Its surface condition is noted, including its corrosion and discoloration.

896. A V-shaped ripple with the point of the V pointing upstream in a river may indicate a _____.

A. submerged rock, not dangerous to navigation
B. sunken wreck, not dangerous to navigation
C. towed-under buoy
D. All of the above

897. Which factor(s) might indicate that a towline should be removed from service?

A. Visible damage to the towline, including fishhooks.
B. Measurements showing a decrease in diameter.
C. A surface condition of corrosion and discoloration.
D. All of the above

899. When must the owner or Master of a towing vessel retest a towline or remove it from service?

A. When the record of its material condition lapses for 3 months or more.
B. After it jams on the towing winch.
C. After it drags on the bottom.
D. When it has not been used for over 60 days.

900. Camber, in a ship, is usually measured in _____.

A. feet per feet of breadth
B. feet per feet of length
C. inches per feet of breadth
D. inches per feet of length

902. The number of able seamen required on board is stated in the _____.

A. American Bureau of Shipping code
B. Solas Certificate
C. Classification Certificate
D. Certificate of Inspection

904. In order to help protect a natural fiber rope from rotting, the line must be _____.

A. dried, and stowed in a place with adequate ventilation
B. stowed in a hot, moist compartment
C. stowed on deck at all times
D. stowed in any compartment

905. When should you conduct a visual inspection of your towline?

A. Whenever its serviceability is in doubt.
B. In accordance with the manufacturer's recommendation.
C. At least once a month.
D. All of the above

906. A snag or other underwater obstruction may form a _____.

A. V-shaped ripple with the point of the V pointing upstream
B. V-shaped ripple with the point of the V pointing downstream
C. small patch of smooth water on a windy day
D. smoothing out of the vessel's wake

912. You are aboard vessel "A" in a narrow channel and the pilot is approaching vessel "B" as shown in DIAGRAM 25. The reason he has not previously changed course to the starboard side of the channel is _____.

A. to avoid vessel squat in the shallower water near the bank

B. to avoid the effects of bank cushion and bank suction
C. because there is less chance of striking submerged objects in mid-channel
D. because the current has less eddies in mid-channel

914. When natural fiber rope gets wet, the _____.

A. overall strength of the line will decrease
B. line shrinks in length
C. line will become more elastic
D. line will be easier to handle

916. A condition where two currents meet at the downstream end of a middle bar can be determined by a _____.

A. small whirlpool
B. smooth patch of water
C. V-shaped ripple with the point of the V pointing downstream
D. V-shaped ripple with the point of the V pointing upstream

925. In illustration D044DG, the mooring line labeled "E" is called a(n) _____.

A. bow line
B. after spring line
C. bow spring line
D. forward breast line

926. Usually the most gentle way of riding out a severe storm on a larger vessel is _____.

A. head on at slow speeds
B. hove to
C. running before the seas
D. to rig a sea anchor

934. Which method is used to detect rot in manila lines?

A. Opening the strands and examining the inner fibers
B. Measuring the reduction in circumference of the line
C. Observing for the appearance of mildew on the outer surface
D. Feeling the surface of the line for broken fibers

937. When towing astern, you notice that another vessel is about to pass between the towing vessel and the tow. You should immediately _____.

A. turn away from the approaching vessel
B. shine a spotlight in the direction of the approaching vessel
C. sever the towline
D. slow down and pay out the main tow hawser

944. When caring for natural-fiber line, you should NEVER _____.

A. dry the line before stowing it
B. lubricate the line
C. protect the line from weather
D. slack off taut lines when it rains

950. The upward slope of a ship's bottom from the keel to the bilge is known as _____.

A. camber
B. slope
C. deadrise
D. keel height

954. In order to correctly open a new coil of manila line, you should _____.

A. pull the tagged end from the top of the coil
B. pull the tagged end through the eye of the coil
C. secure the outside end and unroll the coil
D. unreel the coil from a spool

956. When a vessel is swinging from side to side off course due to quartering seas, the vessel is _____.

A. broaching
B. pitchpoling
C. rolling
D. yawing

957. Your vessel has completed an inspection for certification and is issued a Temporary Certificate of Inspection. The Temporary Certificate _____.

A. has the full force of the regular Certificate of Inspection
B. expires six months after it is issued
C. must be exchanged for a regular Certificate of Inspection within 3 months
D. is retained in the custody of the Master

960. Gross tonnage indicates the vessel's _____.

A. displacement in metric tons

B. total weight including cargo
C. volume in cubic feet
D. draft in feet

964. To coil a left-hand laid rope, you should coil the line in _____.

A. a clockwise direction only
B. a counterclockwise direction only
C. an alternating clockwise and counterclockwise direction
D. either a clockwise or a counterclockwise direction

966. When a boat turns broadside to heavy seas and winds, thus exposing the boat to the danger of capsizing, the boat has _____.

A. broached
B. pitchpoled
C. trimmed
D. yawed

968. The Master may have his/her license suspended or revoked for _____.

A. carrying stowaways
B. sailing shorthanded
C. being negligent
D. All of the above

970. What is the difference between net tonnage and gross tonnage?

A. Net tonnage is the gross tonnage less certain deductions for machinery and other areas.
B. Net tonnage is tonnage of cargo compared to tonnage of whole ship.
C. Net tonnage is the net weight of the ship.
D. There is no difference.

976. When the period of beam seas equals the natural rolling period of a vessel, what will most likely occur?

A. Excessive pitching
B. Excessive yawing
C. Excessive rolling
D. No change should be evident

977. An ocean tow is sinking in deep water. Attempts to sever the towing hawser are unsuccessful. Which action should now be taken?

A. Abandon the towing vessel.
B. Radio for emergency assistance.

C. Slip the towline and allow it to run off the drum.
D. Secure all watertight openings on the towing vessel.

978. Anyone voluntarily surrendering their license to a U.S. Coast Guard investigating officer signs a statement indicating that _____.

A. all title to the license is given up for 5 years
B. their rights to a hearing are waived
C. they may be issued a new license in 5 years after passing another written examination
D. All of the above

980. The perforated, elevated bottom of the chain locker, which prevents the chains from touching the main locker bottom and allows seepage water to flow to the drains, is called a _____.

A. cradle
B. draft
C. harping
D. manger

984. To coil a right-laid rope, you should coil the line in _____.

A. a clockwise direction
B. a counterclockwise direction
C. alternating clockwise and counterclockwise directions
D. either a clockwise or counterclockwise directions

986. When running before a heavy sea, moving weights aft will affect the handling of a vessel by _____.

A. reducing rolling
B. increasing rolling
C. reducing yawing
D. increasing yawing

987. What does the helm command "shift the rudder" mean?

A. Stop the swing of the ship.
B. Shift the rudder control to the alternate steering method.
C. Put the rudder amidships and hold the heading steady as she goes.
D. Put the rudder over to the opposite side, the same number of degrees it is now.

990. Freeboard is measured from the upper edge of the _____.

A. bulkwark
B. deck line
C. gunwale bar
D. sheer strake

993. Your vessel is docking, but not yet alongside. Which line will be the most useful when maneuvering the vessel alongside the pier?

A. Bow breast line
B. Bow spring line
C. Inshore head line
D. Offshore head line

994. Manila lines in which the strands are right-hand laid _____.

A. should be coiled in a clockwise direction
B. should be coiled in a counterclockwise direction
C. may be coiled either clockwise or counterclockwise
D. should never be coiled

995. The maneuver which will return your vessel in the shortest time to a person who has fallen overboard is _____.

A. a single turn with hard rudder
B. engine(s) crash astern, no turn
C. a Williamson Turn
D. two 180° turns

996. With a following sea, a vessel will tend to _____.

A. heave to
B. pound
C. reduce speed
D. yaw

1004. Uncoiling manila line improperly can result in a(n) _____.

A. number of fishhooks
B. kink in the line
C. 50% loss of efficiency of the line
D. increase in deterioration of the line

1005. Which device is designed to automatically hold the load if power should fail to an electric winch?

A. Pneumatic brake
B. Electromagnetic brake
C. Hand brake
D. Motor controller

1006. Which action reduces the yawing of a vessel in a following sea?

A. Increasing GM
B. Pumping out tanks aft
C. Shifting weights to the bow
D. Shifting weights to the stern

1007. When using the term "limber system" one is referring to a _____.

A. cleaning system
B. drainage system
C. strengthening system
D. weight reduction system

1008. When anyone voluntarily deposits their license or document with a Coast Guard investigating officer _____.

A. they permanently give up their rights to the license or document
B. it may be for reasons of mental or physical incompetence
C. it must be for reason of addiction to narcotics
D. All of the above

1010. When the longitudinal strength members of a vessel are continuous and closely spaced, the vessel is _____.

A. transversely framed
B. longitudinally framed
C. intermittently framed
D. web framed

1011. After your vessel has been involved in a casualty, you are required to make your logbooks, bell books, etc., available to _____.

A. attorneys for opposition parties
B. marine surveyors
C. U.S. Coast Guard officials
D. All of the above

1012. In illustration D044DG, the mooring line labeled "A" is called a(n) _____.

A. after breast line
B. after spring line
C. offshore stern line
D. inshore stern line

1014. In order to detect rot in manila lines, you should _____.

A. feel the surface of the line for broken fibers
B. measure the reduction in circumference of the line
C. observe any mildew on the surface

D. open the strands and examine the inner fibers

1016. Your vessel is off a lee shore in heavy weather and laboring. Which action should you take?

A. Put the sea and wind about two points on either bow and reduce speed.
B. Heave to in the trough of the sea.
C. Put the sea and wind on either quarter and proceed at increased speed.
D. Put the bow directly into the sea and proceed at full speed.

1018. Which U.S. Government agency can suspend or revoke a Merchant Mariner's license for violating the load line act?

A. American Bureau of Shipping
B. U.S. Coast Guard
C. U.S. Customs Service
D. U.S. Maritime Administration

1020. The Plimsoll Mark on a vessel is used to _____.

A. align the vessel's tailshaft
B. determine the vessel's trim
C. determine the vessel's freeboard
D. locate the vessel's centerline

1021. A vessel's Classification Certificate is issued by the _____.

A. American Bureau of Shipping
B. National Cargo Bureau
C. United States Coast Guard
D. United States Customs

1024. A natural fiber rope can be ruined by dampness because it may _____.

A. rot
B. shrink
C. stretch
D. unlay

1026. When making way in heavy seas you notice that your vessel's screw is being lifted clear of the water and racing. One way to correct this would be to _____.

A. increase speed
B. decrease speed
C. move more weight forward
D. shift the rudder back and forth several times

1030. If an attempt is made to hoist a load

that exceeds the capacity of an electric winch, an overload safety device causes a circuit breaker to cut off the current to the winch motor _____.

A. when the line pull reaches the rated winch capacity
B. after the line pull exceeds the rated winch capacity
C. after a short build-up of torque
D. immediately

1041. The document on a vessel, annually endorsed by an American Bureau of Shipping surveyor, is called the _____.

A. Certificate of Inspection
B. Classification Certificate
C. Load Line Certificate
D. Seaworthy Certificate

1044. Using a safety factor of 6, determine the safe working load of a line with a breaking strain of 30,000 pounds.

A. 4,000 lbs.
B. 5,000 lbs.
C. 20,000 lbs.
D. 100,000 lbs.

1045. If a hydraulic pump on a winch accidentally stops while hoisting, the load will stay suspended because _____.

A. a check valve will close and prevent reverse circulation
B. a centrifugal counterweight counteracts the force of gravity.
C. the electric pump motor will cut out
D. the control lever will move to the stop position

1046. In a following sea, a wave has overtaken your vessel and thrown the stern to starboard. To continue along your original course, you should _____.

A. use more right rudder
B. use more left rudder
C. increase speed
D. decrease speed

1048. You are the person in charge of a vessel involved in a marine casualty. You must notify the nearest Coast Guard Marine Inspection Office if the property damage is over _____.

A. $1,500
B. $10,000

C. $25,000
D. $50,000

1050. The "margin plate" is the_____.

A. outboard strake of plating on each side of an inner bottom
B. outer strake of plating on each side of the main deck of a vessel
C. plate which sits atop the center vertical keel
D. uppermost continuous strake of plating on the shell of a vessel

1051. A vessel arrives in San Francisco from a foreign voyage. When MUST the Master make formal entry at the custom house?

A. Within 24 hours after arrival, Sundays and holidays excepted
B. Within 48 hours after arrival, Sundays and holidays excepted
C. Within 48 hours and before all foreign cargo is discharged for that port
D. Within 24 hours after arrival

1052. A term used to describe the dip in a towline that acts as a shock absorber is _____.

A. catenary
B. step
C. shock dip
D. bight

1054. Which mooring line has the least elasticity?

A. Dacron
B. Nylon
C. Esterlene
D. Polypropylene

1056. In which situation could a vessel most easily capsize?

A. Running into head seas
B. Running in the trough
C. Running with following seas
D. Anchored with your bow into the seas

1058. The damage to a vessel is over $25,000. Who must notify the nearest Coast Guard Marine Safety or Marine Inspection Office as soon as possible?

A. The owner of the vessel
B. The Master of the vessel
C. The person in charge of the vessel at the time of casualty

D. Any one of the above

1064. Which factor is most likely to impair the strength and durability of synthetic line?

A. Dry rot
B. Mildew
C. Sunlight
D. Washing with mild soap

1066. If your propeller is racing in rough weather, you should _____.

A. decrease your engine speed
B. ignore it
C. increase your engine speed
D. stop your engine until the rough weather passes

1074. A new coil of nylon line should be opened by _____.

A. pulling the end up through the eye of the coil
B. taking a strain on both ends
C. uncoiling from the outside with the coil standing on end
D. unreeling from a spool

1075. You are standing wheelwatch on entering port, and the Master gives you a rudder command that conflicts with a rudder command from the Pilot. What should you do?

A. Obey the Pilot
B. Obey the Master
C. Ask the Pilot for guidance
D. Bring the rudder to midships

1076. You are underway in heavy weather and your bow is into the seas. To prevent pounding, you should _____.

A. change course, in order to take the seas at an 85 degree angle from the bow
B. decrease speed
C. increase speed
D. secure all loose gear

1078. By law, the maximum penalty for failing (without reasonable cause) to give aid in the case of collision is _____.

A. one year imprisonment or $500
B. two years imprisonment or $1000
C. two years imprisonment or $1500
D. two years imprisonment or $2000

1080. The "inner bottom" is the _____.

A. tank top
B. compartment between the tank top and shell of the vessel
C. inner side of the vessel's shell
D. space between two transverse bottom frames

1082. A lashing used to secure two barges side by side, lashed in an "X" fashion, is called a _____.

A. backing wire
B. scissor wire
C. face wire
D. breast wire

1087. The turning circle of a vessel is the path followed by the _____.

A. center of gravity
B. outermost part of the ship while making the circle
C. bow
D. tipping center

1088. As Master or person in charge, you must notify the U.S. Coast Guard if an injury leaves a crewman unfit to perform routine duties for more than _____.

A. 24 hours
B. 48 hours
C. 72 hours
D. Any amount of time

1089. The system of valves and cargo lines in the bottom piping network of a tank vessel that connects one section of cargo tanks to another section is called a _____.

A. crossover
B. runaround
C. come-along
D. manifold

1090. A chock _____.

A. is a deck fitting used to shackle gear to the deck
B. permits easy jettisoning of deck cargo in an emergency
C. prevents stress concentration in the bulwark
D. provides openings through the bulwark for mooring lines

1092. When a helmsman receives the command "Right 15 degrees rudder," the

helmsman's immediate reply should be _____.

A. "Rudder is right 15 degrees"
B. "Aye Aye Sir"
C. "Right 15 degrees rudder"
D. No reply is necessary, just carry out the order.

1094. Which statement is TRUE with respect to the elasticity of nylon mooring lines?

A. Nylon can stretch over forty percent without being in danger of parting.
B. Nylon can be elongated by one-hundred percent before it will part.
C. Nylon will part if it is stretched any more than twenty percent.
D. Under load, nylon will stretch and thin out but will return to normal size when free of tension.

1100. What is the purpose of the freeing ports on a vessel with solid bulwarks?

A. Allow water which may be shipped on deck to flow off rapidly
B. Permit easy jettisoning of deck cargo in an emergency
C. Prevent the formation of any unusual stress concentration points
D. Lighten the above deck weight caused by a solid bulwark

1102. In illustration D044DG, the mooring line labeled "B" is called a(n) _____.

A. after breast line
B. after spring line
C. inshore stern line
D. offshore stern line

1104. Nylon line can be dangerous because it _____.

A. breaks down when wet
B. kinks when wet
C. is not elastic
D. stretches

1110. One function of a bulwark is to _____.

A. help keep the deck dry
B. prevent stress concentrations on the stringer plate
C. protect against twisting forces exerted on the frame of the vessel
D. reinforce the side stringers

1112. What is an advantage of the 6 X 37 class of wire rope over the 6X19 class of wire rope of the same diameter?

A. Greater flexibility
B. More resistance to corrosion
C. More resistance to elongation
D. Lower weight per foot

1114. What type of stopper would you use on a nylon mooring line?

A. Chain
B. Nylon
C. Manila
D. Wire

1115. The proper way to correct a mistake in the logbook is to _____.

A. draw several lines through the entry, rewrite, and initial the correction
B. draw a line through the entry, rewrite, and initial the correction
C. completely black out the entry, rewrite, and initial the correction
D. erase the entry and rewrite

1116. On a single-screw vessel, when coming port side to a pier and being set off the pier, you should _____.

A. swing wide and approach the pier so as to land starboard side to
B. approach the pier on a parallel course at reduced speed
C. make your approach at a greater angle than in calm weather
D. point the vessel's head well up into the slip and decrease your speed

1122. Freeing ports on a vessel with solid bulwarks _____.

A. prevent stress concentration in the bulwark
B. permit easy jettison of deck cargo in an emergency
C. provide openings through the bulwarks for mooring lines
D. allow water shipped on deck to flow off rapidly

1124. Which material makes the strongest mooring line?

A. Dacron
B. Manila
C. Nylon
D. Polyethylene

1125. The pivoting point of a vessel going ahead is _____.

A. about one-third of the vessel's length from the bow
B. about two-thirds of the vessel's length from the bow
C. at the hawsepipe
D. near the stern

1126. You are approaching a pier and intend to use the port anchor to assist in docking port side to. You would NOT use the anchor if _____.

A. the current was setting you on the pier
B. another vessel is berthed ahead of your position
C. the wind was blowing from the starboard side
D. there is shallow water enroute to the berth

1130. The fittings used to secure a watertight door are known as _____.

A. clamps
B. clasps
C. dogs
D. latches

1132. A lookout can leave his station _____.

A. at the end of the watch
B. at any time
C. ONLY when properly relieved
D. 15 minutes before the end of the watch

1134. The critical point in nylon line elongation is about _____.

A. 20%
B. 30%
C. 40%
D. 50%

1136. Your vessel is to dock bow first at a pier without the assistance of tugboats. Which line will be the most useful when maneuvering the vessel alongside the pier?

A. Bow breast line
B. Bow spring line
C. Inshore head line
D. Stern breast line

1139. The pivoting point of a vessel going ahead is _____.

A. near the stern
B. at the hawsepipe

C. about one-third of the vessel's length from the bow
D. about two-thirds of the vessel's length from the bow

1140. In a transversely framed ship, the transverse frames are supported by all of the following EXCEPT _____.

A. girders
B. longitudinals
C. side stringers
D. web plates

1141. A vessel has arrived in a U.S. port from a foreign voyage. Preliminary entry has been made. Formal entry at the U.S. Customs House must be made within how many hours after arrival (Sundays and holidays excepted)?

A. 12
B. 24
C. 48
D. 72 without exception

1144. Which rope has the greatest breaking strength?

A. Manila
B. Nylon
C. Polyethelene
D. Polypropylene

1148. The document which acknowledges that the cargo has been received and is in the carrier's custody is called the _____.

A. Dock Receipt
B. Hatch Report and Recapitulation
C. Cargo Manifest
D. Stowage Plan

1150. In ship construction, frame spacing is _____.

A. greater at the bow and stern
B. reduced at the bow and stern
C. uniform over the length of the vessel
D. uniform over the length of the vessel, with the exception of the machinery spaces, where it is reduced due to increased stresses

1154. Which line would be least likely to kink?

A. Braided
B. Left-handed laid

C. Right-handed laid
D. Straight laid

1156. The best time to work a boat into a slip is _____.

A. when the wind is against you
B. with the current setting against you
C. at slack water
D. with a cross current

1157. What is a correct reply to a pilot's request, "How's your head"?

A. "Steady"
B. "Passing 150°"
C. "Checked"
D. "Eased to 5° rudder"

1160. In a longitudinally framed ship, the longitudinal frames are held in place and supported by athwartship members called _____.

A. floors
B. margin plates
C. stringers
D. web frames

1164. Which type of line floats?

A. Dacron
B. Nylon
C. Old manila
D. Polypropylene

1165. The station bill shows each person's lifeboat station, duties during abandonment, basic instructions, and _____.

A. all emergency signals
B. instructions for lowering the lifeboats
C. the time each weekly drill will be held
D. work schedule

1166. You are 15 feet off a pier and docking a vessel using only a bow and stern breast line. Once the slack is out of both lines you begin to haul in on the bow breast line. What is the effect on the vessel?

A. The bow will come in and the stern will go out.
B. The whole ship moves toward the pier.
C. The bow will come in and the stern will remain the same distance off the pier.
D. The stern will come in and the bow will remain the same distance off the pier.

1170. Transverse frames are more widely spaced on a ship that is designed with the _____.

A. centerline system of framing
B. isometric system of framing
C. longitudinal system of framing
D. transverse system of framing

1174. Compared to manila line, size for size, nylon line _____.

A. has less strength than manila line
B. has more strength than manila line
C. is equivalent to manila line
D. will rot quicker than manila line

1181. Uncleared crew curios remaining on board during a domestic coastwise voyage after returning from foreign should be _____.

A. listed in the Official Logbook
B. cleared prior to the next foreign voyage
C. noted in the Traveling Curio Manifest
D. retained under locked security by the owner

1184. A new coil of nylon line should be opened by _____.

A. pulling the end up through the eye of the coil
B. uncoiling from the outside with the coil standing on end
C. taking a strain on both ends
D. unreeling from a spool

1185. Illustration D044DG. As shown, the mooring line labeled "C" is called a _____.

A. stern line
B. spring line
C. breast line
D. shore line

1192. A person has fallen overboard and is being picked up with a lifeboat. If the person appears in danger of drowning, the lifeboat should make _____.

A. an approach from leeward
B. an approach from windward
C. the most direct approach
D. an approach across the wind

1193. The main advantage of a Chinese stopper over the one line stopper is that it _____.

A. will not jam on the mooring line
B. is stronger
C. is easier to use when under heavy tension
D. is safer to use when under heavy tension

1194. What type of line melts easiest?

A. Wire
B. Dacron
C. Nylon
D. Polypropylene

1196. You are landing a single-screw vessel, with a right-hand propeller, starboard side to the dock. When you have approached the berth and back the engine, you would expect the vessel to _____.

A. lose headway without swinging
B. turn her bow toward the dock
C. turn her bow away from the dock
D. head into the wind, regardless of the side the wind is on

1206. You are landing a single-screw vessel with a left-handed propeller, starboard side to the dock. As you approach the dock you back your engine with your rudder amidships. You would expect the vessel to _____.

A. lose headway without swinging
B. turn its bow toward the dock
C. turn its stern toward the dock
D. drift away from the dock

1210. To rigidly fasten together the peak frames, the stem, and the outside framing, a horizontal plate is fitted across the forepeak of a vessel. This plate is known as a(n) _____.

A. apron plate
B. breasthook
C. intercostal plate
D. joiner

1214. Which statement is TRUE about nylon line?

A. Manila line will usually last longer than nylon line.
B. Nylon line is excellent for use in alongside towing.
C. A normal safe working load will stretch nylon line 50%.
D. Nylon stoppers should be used with nylon line.

1216. It is easier to dock a right-hand, single-screw vessel _____.

A. starboard side to the wharf
B. either side to the wharf
C. port side to the wharf
D. stern to the wharf

1217. The proper way to correct a mistake in the logbook is to _____.

A. erase the entry and rewrite
B. draw a line through the entry, rewrite, and initial the correction
C. draw several lines through the entry, rewrite, and initial the correction
D. completely black out the entry, rewrite, and initial the correction

1224. Which is NOT a recommended practice when handling nylon line?

A. Nylon lines which become slippery because of oil or grease should be scrubbed down.
B. Manila line stoppers should be used for holding nylon hawsers.
C. When easing out nylon line, keep an extra turn on the bitt to prevent slipping.
D. Iced-over nylon lines should be thawed and drained before stowing.

1230. Which statement concerning solid floors is TRUE?

A. They must be watertight.
B. They may have lightening, limber, or air holes cut into them.
C. They are built of structural frames connected by angle struts and stiffeners, with flanged plate brackets at each end.
D. They are lighter than open floors.

1234. Which type of line will stretch the most when under strain?

A. Polypropylene
B. Dacron
C. Nylon
D. Manila

1236. You are docking a ship with a single-screw tug assisting on your starboard bow. How should the tug be tied up if you are anticipating that she will have to hold your bow off while you stem the current?

A. One head line would be sufficient.
B. The tug would need at least two head lines.

207

C. The tug should put a spring line up, leading astern on the ship.
D. The tug should put a stern line up, leading ahead on the ship.

1240. Bilge keels are fitted on ships to _____.

A. assist in drydock alignment
B. improve the vessel's stability
C. protect the vessel from slamming against piers
D. reduce the rolling of the vessel

1244. Nylon line is NOT suitable for _____.

A. towing
B. lashings
C. stoppers
D. mooring lines

1250. The floors in a vessel's hull structure are kept from tripping, or folding over, by _____.

A. face plates
B. bottom longitudinals
C. longitudinal deck beams
D. transverse deck beams

1252. Control of flooding should be addressed _____.

A. first
B. following control of fire
C. following restoration of vital services
D. only if a threat exists

1254. Under identical load conditions, nylon, when compared with natural fiber line, will stretch _____.

A. less and have less strength
B. more and have less strength
C. more and have greater strength
D. less and have greater strength

1260. The function of the bilge keel is to _____.

A. reduce the rolling of the vessel
B. serve as the vessel's main strength member
C. add strength to the bilge
D. protect the vessel's hull when alongside a dock

1264. Which type of line is best able to withstand sudden shock loads?

A. Polypropylene
B. Nylon
C. Dacron
D. Manila

1265. You are picking up an unconscious person that has fallen overboard in a fresh breeze. For safety reasons a small craft should approach with the _____.

A. victim to leeward
B. victim to windward
C. wind on your port side
D. wind on your starboard side

1269. What is meant by the term "topping the boom"?

A. Lowering the boom
B. Raising the boom
C. Spotting the boom over the deck
D. Swinging the boom athwartships

1270. When a man who is conscious and has fallen overboard is being picked up by a lifeboat, the boat should approach with the wind _____.

A. astern and the victim just off the bow
B. ahead and the victim just off the bow
C. just off the bow and the victim to windward
D. just off the bow and the victim to leeward

1271. The citizenship of a crew member of a vessel in a U.S. port is determined solely by the _____.

A. Customs Officer
B. Immigration Officer
C. Coast Guard
D. Union Official

1274. If given equal care, nylon line should last how many times longer than manila line?

A. Three
B. Four
C. Five
D. Six

1275. The tension on an anchor cable increases so that the angle of the catenary to the seabed at the anchor reaches 10°. How will this affect the anchor in sandy soil?

A. It will have no effect.

B. It will increase the holding power.
C. It will reduce the holding power.
D. It will cause the anchor to snag.

1276. When moored with a Mediterranean moor, the ship should be secured to the pier by having _____.

A. a stern line and two quarter lines crossing under the stern
B. a stern line, 2 bow lines, and 2 quarter lines leading aft to the pier
C. all regular lines leading to the pier in opposition to the anchor
D. two bow lines and two midship lines leading aft to the pier

1280. Vertical structural members attached to the floors that add strength to the floors are called _____.

A. boss plates
B. buckler plates
C. stiffeners
D. breast hooks

1282. When evacuating a seaman by helicopter lift, the vessel should be _____.

A. stopped with the wind dead ahead
B. stopped with the wind on the beam
C. underway with the wind 30° on the bow
D. underway on a course to provide no apparent wind

1286. The anchors should be dropped well out from the pier while at a Mediterranean moor to _____.

A. eliminate navigational hazards by allowing the chain to lie along the harbor bottom
B. increase the anchor's reliability by providing a large catenary in the chain
C. permit the ship to maneuver in the stream while weighing anchors
D. prevent damage to the stern caused by swinging against the pier in the approach

1287. The term "shift the rudder" means _____.

A. change from right (left) to left (right) rudder an equal amount
B. use right or left rudder
C. check, but do not stop the vessel from swinging
D. put the rudder amidships

1289. What would you use to adjust the height of a cargo boom?

A. Lizard
B. Spanner guy
C. Topping lift
D. Working guy

1290. What is NOT an advantage of double bottom ships?

A. The tanktop forms a second skin for the vessel.
B. The center of gravity of a loaded bulk cargo ship may be raised to produce a more comfortable roll.
C. The floors and longitudinals distribute the upward push of the water on the ship's bottom.
D. They are less expensive to construct because of increased access space.

1296. To ensure the best results during the Mediterranean moor, the chains should _____.

A. be crossed around the bow
B. tend out at right angles to the bow
C. tend aft 60° from each bow
D. tend forward 30° on either bow

1299. Which part of a conventional cargo gear rig provides for vertical control and positioning of a boom?

A. Cargo whip
B. Gooseneck fitting
C. Spider band
D. Topping lift

1302. Reinforcing frames attached to a bulkhead on a vessel are called _____.

A. side longitudinals
B. intercostals
C. stiffeners
D. brackets

1304. A nylon line is rated at 12,000 lbs. breaking strain. Using a safety factor of 5, what is the safe working load (SWL)?

A. 2,000 lbs.
B. 2,400 lbs.
C. 12,000 lbs.
D. 60,000 lbs.

1305. What is an advantage of the 6X19 class of wire rope over the 6X37 class of wire rope of the same diameter?

A. Greater holding power
B. Better for towing
C. More resistance to elongation
D. More resistance to corrosion

1306. You are making mooring lines fast to bitts, stern to, as in some Mediterranean ports. A swell is liable to make the vessel surge. How should you tie up?

A. Use manila or synthetic fiber hawsers only.
B. Use wires only from the stern and each quarter.
C. Use synthetic fiber and/or manila hawsers as required.
D. Use wires from each quarter and manila hawsers from the stern.

1307. Which type of ice is a hazard to navigation?

A. Ice rind
B. Pancake ice
C. Frazil ice
D. Growlers

1312. In illustration D044DG, the mooring line labeled "D" is called a(n) _____.

A. stern line
B. forward spring line
C. after spring line
D. waist breast line

1313. Where should a vessel being towed alongside be positioned for increased maneuverability?

A. Stern of the towed vessel aft of the stern of the towing vessel
B. Stern of the towed vessel even with the stern of the towing vessel
C. Stern of the towed vessel forward of the stern of the towing vessel
D. Bow of the towed vessel even with the bow of the towing vessel

1314. A wire rope rove through two single blocks with two parts at the moving block is used for a boat fall. The weight of the 100-person boat is 5 tons. Compute the required breaking strain. Safety Factor—6, weight per person—165 lbs., 10% friction per sheave (2 sheaves).

A. 18.30 tons B.S.
B. 20.29 tons B.S.
C. 22.27 tons B.S.
D. 24.31 tons B.S.

1316. The anchor chain should be kept moderately taut during a Mediterranean moor to _____.

A. facilitate speed of recovery during the weighing process
B. indicate the anchor's location to passing or mooring ships
C. prevent damage to the stern in the event of a headwind
D. provide a steady platform for the gangway between the fantail and pier

1319. In relation to cargo gear, what does "SWL" mean?

A. Safe working load
B. Ship's working lift
C. Starboard wing lift
D. Stress, weight, load

1320. A cofferdam is _____.

A. any deck below the main deck and above the lowest deck
B. a member that gives fore-and-aft strength
C. made by placing two bulkheads a few feet apart
D. a heavy fore-and-aft beam under the deck

1323. "Ease the rudder" means to _____.

A. decrease the rudder angle
B. move the rudder slowly in the direction of the most recent rudder command
C. bring the rudder amidships
D. steer the course which is your present heading

1324. The forecastle card is a(n) _____.

A. copy of the shipping agreement
B. quarters allocation
C. station bill
D. unlicensed shipping card from the union

1325. You are signing on crew members. The minimum number of people required aboard, and the qualifications of each, is listed on the _____.

A. Crew list
B. Certificate of Inspection
C. Articles of Agreement
D. fo'c'sle card

1326. After casting off moorings at a mooring buoy in calm weather, you should _____.

A. go full ahead on the engine(s)
B. back away a few lengths to clear the buoy and then go ahead on the engines
C. go half ahead on the engines and put the rudder hard right
D. go half ahead on the engines and pass upstream of the buoy

1329. A pelican hook _____.

A. can be released while under strain
B. is used for boat falls
C. is used for extra heavy loads
D. is used for light loads only

1330. Beams are cambered to _____.

A. increase their strength
B. provide drainage from the decks
C. relieve deck stress
D. All of the above

1336. When picking up your mooring at the buoy, the correct method is to _____.

A. approach the buoy with the wind and current astern
B. approach the buoy with the wind and current ahead
C. approach the buoy with wind and sea abeam
D. stop upwind and up current and drift down on the buoy

1344. When working with wire rope, which must be considered?

A. Metal sheaves should be lined with wood or leather.
B. It needs better care than hemp or manila.
C. It should be lubricated annually.
D. The diameter of a sheave over which a rope is worked should be ten times that of the rope.

1346. The best method of determining if a vessel is dragging anchor is to note _____.

A. the amount of line paid out
B. how much the vessel sheers while at anchor
C. any change in the tautness of the anchor chain
D. changes in bearings of fixed objects onshore

1350. A deck beam does NOT_____.

A. act as a beam to support vertical deck loads
B. lessen the longitudinal stiffness of the vessel
C. act as a tie to keep the sides of the ship in place
D. act as a web to prevent plate wrinkling due to twisting action on the vessel

1354. A 6x19 wire rope would be _____.

A. 6 inches in diameter and 19 fathoms long
B. 6 inches in circumference with 19 strands
C. 6 strands with 19 wires in each strand
D. 19 strands with 6 wires in each strand

1356. If your vessel is dragging her anchor in a strong wind, you should _____.

A. shorten the scope of anchor cable
B. increase the scope of anchor cable
C. put over the sea anchor
D. put over a stern anchor

1357. Illustration D033DG. The area indicated by the letter G is known as the _____.

A. entrance
B. stringer plate
C. turn of the bilge
D. garboard

1360. What are reef points used for?

A. Reduce the area of a sail
B. Keep the sail taut in light airs
C. Reduce the draft if the boat runs aground
D. Increase the strength of the mast

1364. Which molten substance is poured into the basket of a wire rope socket being fitted to the end of a wire rope?

A. Babbitt
B. Bronze
C. Lead
D. Zinc

1365. A person who sees someone fall overboard should _____.

A. call for help and keep the individual in sight
B. run to the radio room to send an emergency message

C. immediately jump in the water to assist the individual
D. go to the bridge for the distress flares

1366. The best method to stop a vessel from dragging anchor in a sand bottom is to _____.

A. reduce the length of the cable
B. pay out more anchor cable
C. back the engines
D. swing the rudder several times to work the anchor into the bottom

1368. Fire and abandon ship stations and duties may be found on the _____.

A. crewman's duty list
B. Certificate of Inspection
C. shipping articles
D. muster list

1369. What is meant by "spotting the boom"?

A. Lowering it into a cradle
B. Placing it in a desired position
C. Spotting it with wash primer and red lead
D. Two-blocking it

1370. The strength of a deck will be increased by adding _____.

A. camber
B. deck beam brackets
C. hatch beams
D. sheer

1374. Which type of stopper should be used to stop off wire rope?

A. Chain
B. Manila
C. Polypropylene
D. Wire

1375. A chain stripper is used to _____.

A. prevent chain from clinging to the wildcat
B. clean the marine debris from the chain
C. flake chain from a boat's chain locker
D. clean chain prior to an x-ray inspection

1376. Generally speaking, the most favorable bottom for anchoring is _____.

A. very soft mud

B. rocky
C. a mixture of mud and clay
D. loose sand

1380. The deck beam brackets of a transversely framed vessel resist _____.

A. hogging stresses
B. sagging stresses
C. racking stresses
D. shearing stresses

1384. The wire rope used for cargo handling on board your vessel has a safe working load of eight tons. It shall be able to withstand a breaking test load of _____.

A. 32 tons
B. 40 tons
C. 48 tons
D. 64 tons

1389. A band or collar on the top end of a boom to which the topping lift, midships guy, and outboard guys are secured is called the _____.

A. collar band
B. guy band
C. padeye collar
D. spider band

1392. In illustration D044DG, the mooring line labeled "H" is called a(n) _____.

A. forward breast line
B. offshore spring line
C. offshore bow line
D. onshore bow line

1394. Galvanizing would be suitable for protecting wire rope which is used for _____.

A. cargo runners
B. stays
C. topping lifts
D. All of the above

1396. Lifting the anchor from the bottom is called _____.

A. broaching the anchor
B. shifting the anchor
C. walking the anchor
D. weighing the anchor

1399. Which part of a cargo boom has the greatest diameter?

A. Head
B. Middle
C. Heel
D. It has the same diameter along its complete length.

1402. What form of ice is of land origin?

A. Shuga
B. Floe
C. Spicule
D. Bergy bit

1404. Galvanizing would not be suitable for protecting wire rope which is used for _____.

A. cargo runners
B. mooring wires
C. shrouds
D. stays

1406. How many fathoms are in a shot of anchor cable?

A. 6
B. 15
C. 20
D. 30

1410. The result of two forces acting in opposite directions and along parallel lines is an example of what type of stress?

A. Tensile
B. Compression
C. Shear
D. Strain

1414. A wire rope that has been overstrained will show _____.

A. a bulge in the wire where the strain occurred
B. a decrease in diameter where the strain occurred
C. a kink in the wire where the strain occurred
D. no visible effects of an overstrain

1416. What is meant by veering the anchor chain?

A. Bringing the anchor to short stay
B. Heaving in all the chain
C. Locking the windlass to prevent more chain from running out
D. Paying out more chain

1420. Tensile stress is a result of two forces acting in _____.

A. opposite directions on the same line, tending to pull the material apart
B. opposite directions on the same line, tending to compress the object
C. opposite directions along parallel lines
D. the same direction along parallel lines

1424. A wire rope for a 10-ton boom on a vessel shows signs of excessive wear and must be replaced. What safety factor should be used when ordering a new wire?

A. 4
B. 5
C. 6
D. 7

1426. Forty-five fathoms is marked on the anchor chain by _____.

A. one turn of wire on the first stud from each side of the detachable link
B. two turns of wire on the second stud from each side of the detachable link
C. three turns of wire on the third stud from each side of the detachable link
D. four turns of wire on the fourth stud from each side of the detachable link

1427. Which letter in illustration D030DG represents a plain whipping?

A. E
B. F
C. J
D. V

1430. A vessel's bottom will be subjected to tension when weight is concentrated _____.

A. amidships
B. aft
C. at both ends of the vessel
D. forward

1434. In the manufacture of wire rope, if the wires are shaped to conform to the curvature of the finished rope before they are laid up, the rope is called _____.

A. composite
B. left-lay
C. improved
D. preformed

1435. Illustration D030DG. Which letter shown represents a clove hitch?

A. X
B. U
C. T
D. R

1436. How many feet are there in 2 shots of anchor chain?

A. 50
B. 60
C. 180
D. 360

1443. The Safety of Life at Sea Convention was developed by the _____.

A. U.S. Coast Guard
B. American Bureau of Shipping
C. International Maritime Organization
D. American Institute of Maritime Shipping

1444. If kinking results while wire rope is being coiled clockwise, you should _____.

A. coil it counterclockwise
B. not coil it
C. take a turn under
D. twist out the kinks under a strain

1446. The marking on an anchor chain for 30 fathoms is _____.

A. two links on each side of the 30 fathom detachable link painted white
B. one link on each side of the 30 fathom detachable link painted white
C. three links on each side of the 30 fathom detachable link painted white
D. only the detachable link painted red

1448. Nylon line is better suited than manila for _____.

A. towing alongside
B. towing astern
C. holding knots and splices
D. resisting damage from chemicals

1452. The helm command "Check her" means _____.

A. test the steering control
B. read the compass heading
C. stop the swing using hard over rudder
D. slow the swing using moderate rudder

1455. Illustration D030DG. Which letter represents a bowline on a bight?

A. H
B. I
C. M
D. W

1458. The catenary in a towline is _____.

A. a short bridle
B. the downward curvature of the hawser
C. another name for a pelican hook
D. used to hold it amidships

1459. When handling cargo, the majority of cargo gear breakdowns is due to _____.

A. compression bending of the boom
B. extension failure of the boom
C. guy failures
D. topping lift failures

1460. Weight concentration in which area will cause a vessel's bottom to be subjected to tension stresses?

A. Aft
B. Amidships
C. At both ends
D. Forward

1462. Two mooring lines may be placed on the same bollard and either one cast off first if _____.

A. the eye of the second line is dipped
B. the mooring lines are doubled
C. the bollard has two horns
D. one of the lines is a breast line

1463. On a small boat, which knot is best suited for attaching a line to the ring of an anchor?

A. Clove hitch
B. Figure-eight knot
C. Fisherman's bend
D. Overhand knot

1464. When talking about wire rope, the lay of the wire is the _____.

A. direction wires and strands are twisted together
B. number of strands in the wire
C. direction the core is twisted
D. material used in the core

1465. The maneuver which will return your vessel in the shortest time to a person who has fallen overboard is _____.

A. engine(s) crash astern, no turn
B. a single turn with hard rudder
C. a Williamson Turn
D. two 180° turns

1466. When dropping anchor, you are stationed at the windlass brake. The most important piece(s) of gear is(are) _____.

A. a hard hat
B. a long sleeve shirt
C. gloves
D. goggles

1468. What will NOT reduce yawing of a tow?

A. Increasing the length of the towing hawser
B. Trimming the tow by the stern
C. Stowing deck loads forward
D. Drogues put over the stern

1470. Signs of racking stresses generally appear at the _____.

A. bow and stern shell frames and plating
B. junction of the frames with the beams and floors
C. garboard strake, at each side of the keel
D. thrust bearing of the main shaft

1472. Illustration D030DG. Which knot represents a single becket bend?

A. E
B. F
C. G
D. H

1473. The carrick bend is used to _____.

A. add strength to a weak spot in a line
B. join two hawsers
C. be a stopper to transfer a line under strain
D. join lines of different sizes

1474. To find the distance the strands should be unlaid for an eyesplice, multiply the diameter of the wire in inches by _____.

A. 12
B. 24
C. 36
D. 48

1475. In illustration D044DG, the mooring line labeled "G" is called a(n) _____.

A. forward spring line
B. offshore bow line
C. forward breast line
D. inshore bow line

1476. How is the size of chain determined?

A. Length of link in inches
B. Diameter of metal in link in inches
C. Links per fathom
D. Weight of stud cable in pounds

1478. What does "in step" refer to in regards to towing?

A. The towed vessel follows exactly in the wake of the towing vessel.
B. There is no catenary in the towing hawser.
C. When turning, both the towed and towing vessels turn at the same time.
D. Both the towed and towing vessels reach a wave crest or trough at the same time.

1482. The two courses of action if the underwater hull is severely damaged are to plug the openings or to _____.

A. establish and maintain flooding boundaries
B. dewater the compartment
C. secure power to the compartment
D. ballast to maintain even keel

1483. The knot used to join two lines or two large hawsers for towing is called a _____.

A. square knot
B. carrick bend
C. sheet bend
D. bowline

1486. Which is NOT a part of an anchor?

A. Bill
B. Devil's claw
C. Palm
D. Crown

1487. You are approaching a disabled vessel in order to remove survivors from it. If your vessel drifts faster than the disabled vessel, how should you make your approach?

A. To windward of the disabled vessel
B. To leeward of the disabled vessel
C. Directly astern of the disabled vessel
D. At three times the drifting speed of the disabled vessel

1488. What does the term "end-for-end" refer to in regard to a wire towing hawser?

A. Cutting off the bitter and towing ends of the wire rope
B. Splicing two wire ropes together
C. Removing the wire rope from the drum and reversing it so that the towing end becomes the bitter end
D. Removing the wire rope from the drum and turning it over so that the wire bends in the opposite direction when rolled on a drum

1493. The knot used to join two lines of different diameter is a _____.

A. square knot
B. carrick bend
C. becket bend
D. sheepshank

1494. After splicing an eye in a piece of wire rope, the splice should be parceled and served to _____.

A. strengthen the line
B. increase its efficiency
C. prevent hand injury by covering loose ends
D. make the line more flexible

1495. A common class of wire rope is the 6X37 class. What does the 37 represent?

A. Number of wires in the inner core
B. Number of strands per wire rope
C. Tensile strength of the wire
D. Number of wires per strand

1496. The purpose of a devil's claw is to _____.

A. act as a chain stopper
B. prevent the windlass from engaging
C. prevent the chain from fouling on deck
D. control the wildcat

1498. The biggest problem you generally encounter while towing a single tow astern is _____.

A. the catenary dragging on the bottom
B. swamping of the tow

C. the tow tending to dive
D. yaw

1499. In illustration D044DG, the mooring line labeled "E" is called a(n) _____.

A. bow line
B. forward breast line
C. after spring line
D. bow spring line

1503. Which knot should be used to send a man over the side when he may have to use both hands?

A. Bowline
B. French bowline
C. Bowline on a bight
D. Running bowline

1506. The sprocket wheel in a windlass, used for heaving in the anchor, is called a _____.

A. capstan
B. dog wheel
C. fairlead
D. wildcat

1508. While towing, sudden shock-loading caused during heavy weather can be reduced by _____.

A. using a short tow hawser
B. using a nonelastic type hawser
C. using a heavier hawser
D. decreasing the catenary in the hawser

1513. Which knot is suitable for hoisting an unconscious person?

A. Bowline in a bight
B. French bowline
C. Fisherman's loop
D. Spider hitch

1514. A 6X12, two-inch wire rope has _____.

A. 12 strands and a two-inch diameter
B. 12 strands and a two-inch circumference
C. 6 strands and a two-inch diameter
D. 6 strands and a two-inch circumference

1516. The length of a standard "shot" of chain is _____.

A. 12 fathoms
B. 15 fathoms
C. 18 fathoms
D. 20 fathoms

1517. Which picture in illustration D030DG represents a timber hitch?

A. E
B. F
C. N
D. U

1518. Your vessel is being towed and back-up wires have been installed. Back-up wires carry the towing load in the event that the _____.

A. bridle legs part
B. towing bitt or padeye fails
C. bight ring fails
D. main towing hawser parts

1520. A welded joint's effectiveness is considered _____.

A. 48%
B. 90%
C. 100%
D. 121%

1523. When making a short splice in wire rope _____.

A. all tucks go against the lay
B. all tucks go with the lay
C. the first three wires are tucked against the lay and the last three go with the lay
D. the first three wires are tucked with the lay and the last three go against the lay

1524. A mooring line is described as being 6X24, 1-3/4 inch wire rope. What do the above numbers refer to?

A. Strands, yarns, circumference
B. Strands, wires, diameter
C. Wires, yarns, diameter
D. Strands, circumference, wires

1525. The term "shift the rudder" means _____.

A. use right or left rudder
B. change from right (left) to left (right) rudder an equal amount
C. check, but do not stop the vessel from swinging
D. put the rudder amidship

1526. One shot of anchor chain is equal to how many feet (meters)?

A. 6 (1.8 meters)
B. 15 (4.6 meters)
C. 45 (13.7 meters)
D. 90 (27.4 meters)

1528. You are being towed by one tug. As you lengthen the bridle legs you _____.

A. increase your chances of breaking the towing hawser
B. reduce the yawing of your vessel
C. reduce the spring effect of the tow connection
D. increase your chances of breaking the bridle legs

1530. Shell plating is _____.

A. the galvanizing on steel
B. a hatch cover
C. the outer plating of a vessel
D. synonymous with decking

1532. To determine the number of portable fire extinguishers required on an inspected vessel, you should check the _____.

A. hot work permit
B. Certificate of Inspection
C. Safety of Life at Sea Certificate
D. station bill

1533. What is the best splice for repairing a parted synthetic fiber mooring line?

A. Liverpool splice
B. Locking long splice
C. Long splice
D. Short splice

1534. Which statement(s) is(are) TRUE concerning wire rope?

A. Wire rope should be condemned if the outside wires are worn to one-half their original diameter.
B. Wire rope should be condemned if the fiber core appears moist.
C. Wire rope which is right-hand laid should be coiled counterclockwise to prevent kinking.
D. All of the above

1536. When anchoring, it is a common rule of thumb to use a length of chain _____.

A. five to seven times the depth of water
B. seven to ten times the depth of water
C. twice the depth of water
D. twice the depth of water plus the range of tide

1537. Which is NOT a potential hazard of approaching close to an iceberg?

A. The brash ice in the vicinity may clog sea intakes.

B. The berg may calve with the bergy bit hitting the vessel.
C. There may be underwater rams extending out from the berg.
D. The berg may suddenly tilt or capsize due to uneven melting and hit the vessel.

1540. In ship construction, keel scantlings should be the greatest _____.

A. at each frame
B. amidships
C. one-third the distance from the bow
D. one-third the distance from the stern

1543. Which is normally used to hold wire rope for splicing?

A. Come-along
B. Jigger
C. Rigger's screw
D. Sealing clamp

1544. The main function of the core of a wire rope is to _____.

A. give flexibility
B. support the strands laid around it
C. allow some circulation around the strands
D. allow lubrication inside the rope

1546. What is the best guide for determining the proper scope of anchor chain to use for anchoring in normal conditions?

A. One shot of chain for every ten feet of water
B. One shot of chain for every fifteen feet of water
C. One shot of chain for every thirty feet of water
D. One shot of chain for every ninety feet of water

1548. What could be used as fairleads on a towed vessel?

A. Chocks
B. Double bitts
C. Roller chocks
D. All of the above

1549. On your vessel, a wire rope for the cargo gear shows signs of excessive wear and must be replaced. In ordering a new wire for this 10-ton boom, what safety factor should you use?

A. Three

B. Five
C. Six
D. Seven

1550. Keel scantlings of any vessel are greatest amidships because _____.

A. connections between forebody and afterbody are most crucial
B. of maximum longitudinal bending moments
C. of severest racking stresses
D. resistance to grounding is at a maximum amidships

1552. Illustration D030DG. Which picture represents a stopper hitch?

A. M
B. N
C. R
D. L

1553. The correct way to make an eye in a wire rope with clips is to place the clips with the _____.

A. first and third U-bolts on the bitter end and the second U-bolt on the standing part
B. first and third U-bolts on the standing part and the second U-bolt on the bitter end
C. U-bolts of all clips on the bitter end
D. U-bolts of all clips on the standing part

1556. When anchoring, good practice requires 5 to 7 fathoms of chain for each fathom of depth. In deep water you should use _____.

A. the same ratio
B. more chain for each fathom of depth
C. less chain for each fathom of depth
D. two anchors with the same ratio of chain

1557. When relieving the helm, the new helmsman should find it handy to know the _____.

A. amount of helm carried for a steady course
B. variation in the area
C. leeway
D. deviation on that heading

1558. When making up a tow connection, you should use _____.

A. safety hooks
B. plain eye hooks

C. round pin shackles
D. screw pin shackles

1560. Which arrangement of shell plating is used most in modern shipbuilding?

A. Clinker
B. Flush
C. In-and-Out
D. Joggled

1563. Which statement about two lines spliced together is TRUE?

A. Splicing is used to increase the circumference of each line.
B. Splicing two lines together is stronger than knotting two lines together.
C. Splicing is used to increase the overall strength of the line.
D. Splicing is used to prevent rotting of the lines bitter end.

1564. What is the main reason to slush a wire rope?

A. Keep the wire soft and manageable
B. Lubricate the inner wires and prevent wear
C. Prevent kinking
D. Prevent rotting

1566. In bad weather, what length of chain should be used with a single anchor?

A. 3 times the depth of water
B. 6 times the depth of water
C. 10 times the depth of water
D. 15 times the depth of water

1567. Illustration D044DG. The mooring line shown as "A" is called a(n) _____.

A. after breast line
B. after spring line
C. onshore stern line
D. offshore stern line

1568. A tackle is "two blocked" when the blocks are _____.

A. equally sharing the load
B. jammed together
C. as far apart as possible
D. rove to the highest mechanical advantage

1570. What is NOT an advantage of ship construction methods using welded butt joints in the shell plating?

A. Keeps practically 100% of tensile strength at the joints
B. Reduces frictional resistance
C. Reduces plate stress
D. Reduces weight

1573. Which statement about splices is TRUE?

A. A back splice is used to permanently connect two lines together.
B. A long splice is used to connect two lines that will pass through narrow openings.
C. A short splice is used to temporarily connect two lines.
D. In splicing fiber rope, you would splice with the lay of the line.

1574. Wire rope is galvanized to _____.

A. protect it from corrosion due to contact with saltwater
B. make it bend more easily
C. increase its strength
D. increase its circumference

1575. The key to rescuing a man overboard is _____.

A. good communication
B. a dedicated crew
C. good equipment
D. well-conducted drills

1576. Using a scope of five, determine how many shots of chain you should put out to anchor in 5 fathoms of water?

A. 1
B. 2
C. 3
D. 5

1578. A stream of water immediately surrounding a moving vessel's hull, flowing in the same direction as the vessel is known as _____.

A. directional current
B. forward current
C. propeller current
D. wake current

1580. Shell plating that has curvature in two directions and must be heated and hammered to shape over specially prepared forms is called _____.

A. compound plate
B. furnaced plate

C. flat plate
D. rolled plate

1582. Which is an example of failure to exercise due diligence?

A. Overloading
B. Sailing short of union manning requirements
C. Sailing with less than 30% reserve fuel oil supply
D. Sailing short of being full and down

1583. Which statement concerning a short splice is TRUE?

A. It is used to temporarily join two lines together.
B. A short splice is stronger than two lines joined by a knot.
C. A short splice decreases the diameter of the line.
D. None of the above

1584. The size of wire rope is determined by the _____.

A. number of strands
B. number of wires in each strand
C. circumference
D. diameter

1586. By paying out more anchor cable, you _____.

A. decrease the holding power of your anchor
B. decrease the swing of your vessel while at anchor
C. increase the holding power of your anchor
D. increase the possibility that your vessel will drag anchor

1588. You are aboard a single-screw vessel (right-hand propeller) going full ahead with good headway. The engine is put astern and the rudder is placed hard left. The stern of the vessel will swing to _____.

A. starboard until headway is lost and then to port
B. port
C. port until headway is lost and then may possibly swing to starboard
D. port slowly at first and then quickly to port

1589. Why is 6X19 class wire rope more commonly used for cargo runners than the more flexible 6X37 wire rope?

A. It resists abrasion better.
B. It is longer.
C. It hugs the winch drum better.
D. It is less expensive.

1593. A long splice in a line _____.

A. is used in running rigging
B. doubles the size of the line
C. is only used on fiber rope
D. is very weak

1594. What is the breaking strain of steel wire rope with a 5/8" diameter?

A. 1.0 ton
B. 6.6 tons
C. 9.6 tons
D. 15.6 tons

1595. Which picture in illustration D030DG represents a barrel hitch?

A. O
B. U
C. E
D. P

1596. Using a scope of five, determine how many feet of chain you should put out to anchor in 12 fathoms of water.

A. 60 feet (18 meters)
B. 72 feet (22 meters)
C. 360 feet (110 meters)
D. 450 feet (137 meters)

1598. On a vessel with a single propeller, transverse force has the most effect on the vessel when the engine is put _____.

A. full ahead
B. full astern
C. half ahead
D. slow astern

1600. A person who sees someone fall overboard should _____.

A. call for help and keep the individual in sight
B. immediately jump in the water to assist the individual
C. run to the radio room to send an emergency message
D. go to the bridge for the distress flares

1603. Which weakens a line the LEAST?

A. Clove hitch

B. Long splice
C. Short splice
D. Square knot

1604. Which knot would serve best as a safety sling for a person working over the side?

A. Bowline on a bight
B. French bowline
C. Jug sling
D. Lifting hitch

1605. The pivoting point of a vessel going ahead is _____.

A. near the stern
B. about two-thirds of the vessel's length from the bow
C. at the hawsepipe
D. about one-third of the vessel's length from the bow

1606. To safely anchor a vessel there must be sufficient "scope" in the anchor cable. Scope is the ratio of _____.

A. weight of cable to weight of vessel
B. weight of cable to weight of anchor
C. length of anchor to depth of water
D. length of cable to depth of water

1607. Using a scope of 6, how much cable would have to be used in order to anchor in 24 feet of water?

A. 4 feet
B. 18 feet
C. 30 feet
D. 144 feet

1608. Your ship is dead in the water with the rudder amidships. As the right-handed screw starts to turn ahead, the bow will tend to go _____.

A. to starbaord
B. to port
C. straight ahead
D. as influenced by the tide and sea

1613. Which splice should you use in order to make a permanent loop in a line?

A. Back splice
B. Eye splice
C. Long splice
D. Short splice

1614. Which bend or knot is used to tie a small line to a larger one?

A. Becket bend
B. Bowline
C. Clove hitch
D. Lark's head

1615. A towing vessel should be on the crest of a wave at the same time as its tow and in the trough at the same time. The term used to describe this is _____.

A. tow strain
B. catenary length
C. being in step
D. Williamson's Tow

1616. In moderate wind and current what should be the length of chain with a single anchor?

A. 5 times the depth of the water in good holding ground
B. 10 times the depth of the water in shallow water
C. 2 times the depth of the water in poor holding ground
D. 8 times the depth of the water in deep water

1618. A twin-screw vessel is easier to maneuver than a single-screw vessel because the twin-screw vessel _____.

A. permits the rudder to move faster
B. generates more power
C. can turn without using her rudder
D. can suck the water away from the rudder

1622. What is NOT an indication that pack ice may be nearby?

A. The presence of icebergs
B. Ice blink
C. Absence of wave motion
D. Sighting a walrus in the Arctic

1623. A short splice in a line _____.

A. decreases the size of the line
B. should be used if the line is going through a block
C. should only be used in wire rope
D. doubles the size of the line

1624. Which kind of hitch should you use to secure a spar?

A. Blackwall hitch
B. Stage hitch
C. Timber hitch
D. Two half hitches

1625. All inspected vessels on unrestricted ocean routes must have equipment on board for testing an individual's _____.

A. blood
B. breath
C. urine
D. All of the above

1626. Using a scope of 6, determine how many feet of anchor cable you should put out to anchor in 12 feet (3.7 meters) of water.

A. 2 feet (0.6 meters)
B. 18 feet (5.5 meters)
C. 48 feet (14.6 meters)
D. 72 feet (21.9 meters)

1628. You are going ahead on twin engines when you want to make a quick turn to port. Which actions will turn your boat the fastest?

A. Reverse port engine; apply left rudder
B. Reverse port engine; rudder amidship
C. Reverse starboard engine; apply left rudder
D. Reverse starboard engine; rudder amidship

1630. The fore and aft run of deck plating which strengthens the connection between the beams and the frames and keeps the beams square to the shell is called the _____.

A. garboard strake
B. limber strake
C. sheer strake
D. stringer strake

1632. In which casualty case is it UNNECESSARY to notify the local Coast Guard Marine Safety Office?

A. Your vessel strikes a pier and does $1,500 damage to the pier but none to the vessel.
B. A nylon mooring line parts while the vessel is tied up and kills a harbor worker who was on the pier.
C. A seaman is injured and in the hospital for four days.

D. Your vessel is backing from a dock and runs aground, but is pulled off by tugs in 30 minutes.

1633. The strongest way to join the ends of two ropes is with a _____.

A. back splice
B. short splice
C. square knot
D. carrick bend

1634. A monkey fist is found on a _____.

A. heaving line
B. leadline
C. manrope
D. mooring line

1635. In illustration D044DG, the mooring line labeled "B" is called a(n) _____.

A. after breast line
B. after spring line
C. offshore stern line
D. inshore stern line

1636. When anchoring a vessel under normal conditions, which scope of chain is recommended?

A. Four times the depth of water
B. Two and one-half times the depth of water
C. Five to seven times the depth of water
D. Fifteen times the depth of water

1638. On a twin-screw, twin-rudder vessel, the most effective way to turn in your own water, with no way on, is to put _____.

A. one engine ahead and one engine astern, with full rudder
B. one engine ahead and one engine astern, with rudders amidships
C. both engines ahead, with full rudder
D. both engines astern, with full rudder

1640. The garboard strake is the _____.

A. raised flange at the main deck edge
B. riveted crack arrester strap on all-welded ships
C. riveting pattern most commonly used in ship construction
D. row of plating nearest the keel

1641. The helm command "Steady as you go" means _____.

A. steer the course you are on now
B. steer the course when the swing stops
C. maintain the rate of swing
D. don't allow the vessel to swing off course so much

1642. Illustration D030DG. Which illustration represents a carrick bend?

A. H
B. J
C. L
D. M

1643. The splice designed to pass easily through a block is called a(n) _____.

A. eye splice
B. short splice
C. long splice
D. block splice

1644. A rolling hitch can be used to _____.

A. make a temporary eye
B. mouse a hook
C. secure a line around a spar
D. shorten a line

1646. What is the normal length of anchor cable used to anchor a vessel?

A. An amount equal to the depth of the water
B. Two times the depth of water
C. Three to four times the depth of water
D. Five to seven times the depth of water

1648. When steaming through an anchorage, a shipmaster should _____.

A. avoid crossing close astern of the anchored ships
B. avoid crossing close ahead of the anchored ships
C. keep the ship moving at a good speed to reduce set
D. transit only on a flood tide

1651. Which document is NOT required by law to be posted aboard a vessel?

A. Official Crew List
B. Certificate of Inspection
C. Officer's licenses
D. Muster List

1653. Which tool is used to open the strands of fiber lines when making an eye splice?

A. Belaying spike
B. Fid
C. Heaver
D. Pricker

1654. Which knot should be used to bend two hawsers together for towing?

A. Double carrick bend
B. Fisherman's bend
C. Heaving line bend
D. Rolling hitch

1655. Illustration D030DG. Which knot represents a double blackwall hitch?

A. F
B. G
C. L
D. R

1657. What is the perimeter of a circle with a radius of 5.1 feet?

A. 81.71 ft.
B. 64.08 ft.
C. 40.85 ft.
D. 32.04 ft.

1660. The strake on each side of the keel is called a _____.

A. sheer strake
B. gatewood strake
C. insulation strake
D. garboard strake

1661. Which document is NOT required by law to be posted aboard a vessel?

A. Certificate of Inspection
B. Official Crew List
C. Officers' licenses
D. Muster list

1662. Under defense plans, operation of electronic aids to navigation may be temporarily suspended with _____.

A. one day's notice
B. thirty (30) days notice
C. no notice
D. a week's notice

1664. A method used to make an eye in a bight of line where it cannot be spliced is known as _____.

A. braiding
B. plaiting

C. seizing
D. serving

1666. While anchoring your vessel, the best time to let go the anchor is when the vessel is _____.

A. dead in the water
B. moving slowly astern over the ground
C. moving fast ahead over the ground
D. moving fast astern over the ground

1668. Your ship is steaming at night with the gyropilot engaged. You notice that the vessel's course is slowly changing to the right. Which action should you take FIRST?

A. Notify the engine room of the steering malfunction.
B. Change to hand steering.
C. Call the Master.
D. Send the Quartermaster to the emergency steering station.

1670. The term "strake" is used in reference to _____.

A. rudder mountings
B. anchor gear
C. hull plating
D. vessel framing

1671. The number of certificated able seamen and lifeboatmen required on a vessel is determined by the _____.

A. International Maritime Organization
B. Corps of Engineers
C. Coast Guard
D. American Bureau of Shipping

1673. A sail hook is used for _____.

A. hoisting a windsail
B. parceling
C. sewing canvas
D. testing canvas

1674. Which is NOT a type of seizing?

A. Flat seizing
B. Racking seizing
C. Throat seizing
D. Tube seizing

1675. Illustration D003DG. What is the name of the mark indicated by the letter D?

A. Tropical load line

B. Summer load line
C. Fresh load line
D. Winter load line

1676. When preparing to hoist the anchor, you should FIRST _____.

A. engage the wildcat
B. put the brake in the off position
C. take off the chain stopper
D. take the riding pawl off the chain

1677. A vessel is entering port and has a Pilot conning the vessel. The Master is unsure that the Pilot is taking sufficient action to prevent a collision. What should the Master do?

A. Recommend an alternative action and if not followed relieve the Pilot.
B. Nothing; the Pilot is required by law and is solely responsible for the safety of the vessel.
C. Direct the Pilot to stop the vessel and anchor if necessary until the situation clears.
D. State his concerns to the Pilot but do not interfere with the handling of the vessel.

1680. In vessel construction, the garboard strake is _____.

A. located next to and parallel to the keel
B. located next to and parallel to the gunwale
C. another term for the bilge keel
D. another term for the rub rail

1683. "Herringbone" is a term associated with _____.

A. anchoring
B. mooring
C. sewing
D. splicing

1684. Temporary seizings on wire rope are made with _____.

A. marline
B. sail twine
C. tape
D. wire

1686. When weighing anchor in a rough sea, how would you avoid risk of damaging the bow plating?

A. Heave it home as fast as you can.
B. Heave it home intermittently, between swells.

C. Leave the anchor under foot, until the vessel may be brought before the sea.
D. Wait for a calm spot between seas, then house it.

1687. What is the perimeter of a circle with a radius of 4.2 feet?

A. 26.39 ft.
B. 21.19 ft.
C. 17.81 ft.
D. 13.20 ft.

1689. Illustration D044DG. The mooring line shown as "C" is called a _____.

A. stern line
B. spring line
C. shore line
D. breast line

1693. What is the stress on the hauling part when lifting a 4900 lbs. weight using a twofold purchase rove to least advantage? (Allow 10 percent of the weight per sheave for friction.)

A. 980 lbs.
B. 1225 lbs.
C. 1715 lbs.
D. 1837 lbs.

1694. A "whipping" is _____.

A. a messenger
B. a stopper for nylon line
C. a U-bolt for securing a cargo whip to the winch drum
D. turns of twine around a rope end

1695. What is the perimeter of a circle with a radius of 3.7 feet?

A. 11.62 ft.
B. 17.49 ft.
C. 23.25 ft.
D. 25.72 ft.

1696. Mooring with two bow anchors has which major advantage over anchoring with one bow anchor?

A. The vessel will not reverse direction in a tidal current.
B. The radius of the vessel's swing will be shortened.
C. A mooring approach may be made from any direction.
D. The vessel will not swing with a change in wind.

1700. Illustration D001DG. Which letter designates the bilge strake of the vessel?

A. A
B. B
C. C
D. D

1703. What is the stress on the hauling part when lifting a 4,200 lbs. weight using a threefold purchase rove to advantage? (Allow 10 percent of the weight per sheave for friction.)

A. 571.4
B. 715.2
C. 960
D. 1066.7

1704. Whipping the bitter end of a fiber rope _____.

A. increases circumference of the rope
B. makes for easier handling
C. prevents fraying of the bitter end
D. prevents moisture from entering the bitter end

1706. Your vessel is anchored in an open roadstead with three shots of chain out on the port anchor. The wind freshens considerably and the anchor begins to drag. Which action should you take FIRST?

A. Drop the starboard anchor short with about one shot of chain.
B. Sheer out to starboard using the rudder, then drop the starboard anchor with about four shots of chain.
C. Put the engines slow ahead to help the anchor.
D. Veer out more chain on the port anchor.

1709. The force acting on a single cargo runner which is vertically lifting or lowering a load is greatest when _____.

A. decelerating when lowering the load
B. decelerating when raising the load
C. lowering the load at constant speed
D. raising the load at constant speed

1713. The cheek length of a block in inches should be about _____.

A. three times the circumference of a manila line
B. five times the diameter of a manila line
C. twice the diameter of its sheaves for manila line

D. twenty times the diameter of a manila line

1714. A sheepshank is used to _____.

A. keep a line from fraying
B. join lines of unequal size
C. stop off a line
D. shorten a line

1716. Which is the correct procedure for anchoring a small to medium size vessel in deep water?

A. Let the anchor fall free from the hawsepipe, but apply the brake at intervals to check the rate of fall.
B. Back the anchor slowly out of the hawsepipe a few feet, and then let it fall in the normal fashion.
C. Let the anchor fall off the brake right from the hawsepipe, but keep a slight strain on the brake.
D. Under power, back the anchor out until it is near, but clear, of the bottom before letting it fall.

1717. With a large tow astern, there is immediate danger to the tug in the event of the _____.

A. tug losing power
B. tow line parting
C. bridle twisting
D. tow broaching

1719. What is a CORRECT reply to a pilot's request, "How's your head"?

A. "Steady"
B. "Eased to 10° rudder"
C. "Checked"
D. "Passing 50°"

1720. Your vessel is to dock bow first at a pier. Which line will be the most useful when maneuvering the vessel alongside the pier?

A. Bow spring line
B. Bow breast line
C. Stern breast line
D. Inshore head line

1723. What is meant by the term "two-blocked"?

A. The bottom block touches the top block.
B. The line has jumped the sheaves.
C. There are turns in the fall.

D. You have two blocks.

1724. A bowline is used to _____.

A. join lines of equal size
B. form a temporary eye (loop) at the end of a line
C. be a stopper
D. keep a line from fraying

1725. The term "shift the rudder" means _____.

A. use right or left rudder
B. check, but do not stop the vessel from swinging
C. change from right (left) to left (right) rudder an equal amount
D. put the rudder amidships

1726. When attempting to free an anchor jammed in the hawsepipe, the simplest method of freeing it may be _____.

A. starting the disengaged windlass at high speed
B. rigging a bull rope to pull it out
C. to grease the hawsepipe
D. to pry it loose with a short piece of pipe

1728. You are trying to rescue survivors from a wrecked vessel on fire. You should approach _____.

A. to leeward of the wrecked vessel
B. at a speed of at most one-half that of the wrecked vessel
C. at a speed of at least that of the wrecked vessel
D. to windward of the wrecked vessel

1730. A disk with a horizontal line through its center, equivalent to the summer load line, is called the _____.

A. deadrise mark
B. maximum allowable draft mark
C. Plimsoll Mark
D. tonnage mark

1732. Which picture in illustration D030DG represents a half hitch?

A. U
B. S
C. K
D. H

1733. Separating both blocks of a tackle to prepare it for reuse is called _____.

A. chockablocking
B. out-hauling
C. over-hauling
D. two-blocking

1734. Which knot reduces the strength of a line by the LEAST amount?

A. Bowline
B. Clove hitch
C. Sheet bend
D. Two half hitches

1736. Before letting the anchor go, you should check that the _____.

A. chain is clear
B. anchor is clear of obstructions
C. wildcat is disengaged
D. All of the above

1737. When evacuating a seaman by helicopter lift, which course should the ship take?

A. Downwind so that the apparent wind is close to nil.
B. A course that will keep a free flow of air, clear of smoke, over the hoist area.
C. A course that will have the hoist area in the lee of the superstructure.
D. With the wind dead ahead because the helicopter is more maneuverable when going into the wind.

1739. If two falls are attached to lift a one-ton load, what angle between the falls will result in the stress on each fall being equal to the load being lifted?

A. 60°
B. 75°
C. 120°
D. 150°

1740. Illustration D003DG. The group of markings shown is called a _____.

A. loft mark
B. load line mark
C. test mark
D. water mark

1741. The load line regulations are administered by the _____.

A. U.S. Coast Guard
B. Maritime Administration
C. Lloyd's Register of Shipping
D. National Cargo Bureau

1743. A mooring line leading at nearly right angles to the keel is a _____.

A. bow line
B. breast line
C. spring line
D. stern line

1746. Which would you NOT use to report the amount of anchor chain out? "Three shots _____."

A. at the water's edge
B. on deck
C. on the bottom
D. well in the water

1750. A grapnel is a _____.

A. device for securing a chain topping lift
B. hook to prevent the anchor cable from slipping
C. device used to drag for a submerged cable or line
D. type of clam bucket used for discharging bulk cargo

1751. The load line certificate is issued by _____.

A. the American Bureau of Shipping
B. the National Cargo Bureau
C. the United States Coast Guard
D. United States Customs

1755. Illustration D030DG. Which knot shown is a French bowline?

A. L
B. T
C. Q
D. W

1756. When anchoring a vessel, it is best to release the anchor when _____.

A. going full astern
B. going full ahead
C. going slow astern
D. dead in the water

1760. A hook that will release quickly is a _____.

A. longshore hook
B. margin hook
C. marginal hook
D. pelican hook

1761. Load lines for U.S. vessels are assigned by _____.

A. the U.S. Coast Guard
B. the American Bureau of Shipping
C. Lloyd's Register of Shipping
D. the National Cargo Bureau

1762. What is the perimeter of a circle with a radius of 2.5 feet?

A. 7.86 ft.
B. 15.71 ft.
C. 19.63 ft.
D. 22.71 ft.

1763. You are in charge while handling a synthetic hawser on a capstan. The hawser has a heavy strain and you wish to avoid the hawser's slipping on the capstan drum. Which action should you take?

A. Back off on the capstan a bit and have the seaman take several more turns on the drum.
B. Have the seaman take a strain on the hawser and carefully have several turns added on the drum.
C. Have more than one seaman hold a good strain on the hawser and continue to heave easy.
D. While continuing to heave slowly on the capstan, have the seaman take several more turns on the drum.

1764. The "square knot" is used for_____.

A. forming temporary eyes in lines
B. joining two lines of equal size
C. keeping line from unlaying or fraying
D. joining two lines of different size

1766. When anchoring in a current, you should _____.

A. drop the anchor with the bow headed downstream
B. back your vessel into the current
C. anchor while stemming the current
D. All of the above

1767. Illustration D003DG. What is the name of the mark indicated by the letter E?

A. Fresh water line
B. Winter water line
C. Tropical water line
D. Summer water line

1768. As a rule, ships of most configurations, when drifting in calm water with neglible current, will lie _____.

A. bow to the wind
B. beam to the wind
C. stern to the wind
D. with the wind on the quarter

1771. The agency which assigns load lines and issues Load Line Certificates is the _____.

A. American Bureau of Shipping
B. Secretary of Commerce
C. U.S. Customs
D. U.S. Coast Guard

1773. What size block shell should be used with a 4-inch manila line?

A. 8"
B. 12"
C. 16"
D. 24"

1774. Which knot is used to attach two different sized lines together?

A. Granny knot
B. Sheet bend
C. Square knot
D. Thief knot

1776. When anchoring in calm water, it is best to _____.

A. maintain slight headway when letting go the anchor
B. wait until the vessel is dead in the water before letting go the anchor
C. have slight sternway on the vessel while letting go the anchor
D. let the anchor go from the stern with the anchor cable leading from the bow

1778. You are landing a single-screw vessel with a right-handed propeller port side to a dock. As you approach the dock, you back down on your engine with rudder amidships. You would expect the vessel to _____.

A. drift away from the dock
B. lose headway without swinging
C. swing its stern toward the dock
D. swing its stern away from the dock

1781. Which organization usually assigns load lines to U.S. vessels?

A. National Load-Line Agency
B. National Shipping Bureau
C. American Bureau of Shipping
D. American Regulations Council

1782. When evacuating a seaman by helicopter lift, which statement is TRUE?

A. The vessel should be stopped with the wind dead ahead during the hoisting operation.
B. Flags should be flown to provide a visual reference as to the direction of the apparent wind.
C. The drop line should be grounded first then secured as close to the hoist point as possible.
D. The hoist area should be located as far aft as possible so the pilot will have a visual reference while approaching.

1783. Which mooring line is likely to undergo the most strain when docking a ship under normal conditions?

A. Bow line
B. Breast line
C. Spring line
D. Stern line

1784. The rolling hitch could be used to _____.

A. join two lines of different sizes
B. join two lines of equal sizes
C. add strength to a weak spot in a line
D. act as a stopper to transfer a line under strain

1786. You are anchoring in a river where the current is from one direction only. The best way to lay out two anchors is to have them _____.

A. directly in line with the bow
B. side by side, with their lines on the port and starboard side
C. so that their lines form an angle
D. on top of one another

1787. Illustration D030DG. Which picture represents a blackwall hitch?

A. F
B. H
C. P
D. S

1788. Illustration D019DG. Which position shown is the most dangerous when tying up?

A. I
B. II
C. III
D. IV

1790. Which space(s) is(are) exempt when measuring gross tonnage?

A. Auxiliary machinery spaces above the uppermost continuous deck
B. Steering gear room
C. Part of the wheelhouse used to control vessel
D. All of the above

1791. Which factor does NOT affect the required freeboard of a cargo vessel?

A. Season of the year
B. Geographic zone of operation
C. Density of the water
D. Condition of trim in normal operation

1792. Illustration D003DG. What is the name of the mark indicated by the letter F?

A. Fresh water load line
B. Summer load line
C. Winter load line
D. Tropical load line

1793. The lines led forward from the bow and aft from the stern when a vessel is moored to the dock are _____.

A. bow and stern lines
B. breast lines
C. halyards
D. warps

1794. A figure eight knot is used to _____.

A. be a stopper
B. shorten a line
C. join lines of equal size
D. keep a line from passing through a sheave

1795. Illustration D030DG. Which knot represents a double sheet bend?

A. F
B. L
C. R
D. T

1796. Which safety check(s) should be made before letting go the anchor?

A. See that the anchor is clear of obstructions.
B. See that the chain is all clear.
C. See that the wildcat is disengaged.
D. All of the above

1798. You are on a single-screw vessel with a left-handed propeller making no way in the water. How will your vessel react when you apply right rudder?

A. Bow will kick to starboard
B. Bow will kick to port
C. Rudder alone has no effect on the vessel
D. Stern will kick to port, then slowly swing to starboard

1800. The figure obtained by dividing the total volume of the ship in cubic feet (after omission of exempted spaces) by 100 is the _____.

A. bale cubic
B. gross tonnage
C. light displacement
D. net tonnage

1802. Illustration D030DG. Which picture represents a bowline?

A. G
B. H
C. L
D. Q

1803. A snatch block is a _____.

A. block used only with manila rope
B. chock roller
C. hinged block
D. strong block used for short, sharp pulls

1804. Instead of whipping an end of a line, a temporary means of preventing the line from unraveling is to tie a _____.

A. becket bend
B. blackwall hitch
C. figure-eight knot
D. square knot

1805. In towing it is desirable for the tug and the tow to ride wave crests simultaneously because _____.

A. shock loading on the tow line is reduced
B. towing speed is improved

C. the tow is more visible from the tug
D. the catenary of the towline is reduced

1806. If the situation arose where it became necessary to tow a disabled vessel, which statement is TRUE concerning the towing line?

A. The towing line between the two vessels should be clear of the water.
B. The towing line should be taut at all times between the vessels.
C. There should be a catenary so the line dips into the water.
D. None of the above

1807. When evacuating a seaman by helicopter lift, which statement is TRUE?

A. Evacuation should be from an area forward of the bridge.
B. The vessel should be slowed to bare steerageway.
C. If the hoist is at the stern, booms extending aft at the stern should be cradled with the topping lifts hove taut.
D. The litter should not be touched until it has been grounded.

1811. You are towing a large barge on a hawser. Your main engine suddenly fails. What is the greatest danger?

A. The tug and the tow will go aground.
B. The tow will endanger other traffic.
C. The tow will overrun tug.
D. The tow will block the channel.

1813. A snatch block would most likely be used as a _____.

A. boat fall
B. fairlead
C. riding pawl
D. topping lift

1814. In illustration D044DG, the mooring line labeled "D" is called a(n) _____.

A. stern line
B. forward spring line
C. waist breast line
D. after spring line

1815. "Ease the rudder" means to _____.

A. steer the course which is your present heading
B. move the rudder slowly in the direction of the most recent rudder command

C. bring the rudder amidships
D. decrease the rudder angle

1816. Illustration D030DG. Which picture shown represents a square knot?

A. W
B. R
C. P
D. H

1818. When comparing twin-screw tug to single-screw tugs, which statement about a twin-screw tug is FALSE?

A. If one engine fails, you do not lose control of the tow.
B. It is more maneuverable.
C. It develops more bollard pull for the same horsepower.
D. It is generally subject to more propeller damage from debris in the water.

1819. Illustration D033DG. The stringer plate is represented by which letter?

A. A
B. C
C. I
D. N

1820. If a drill required by regulations is not completed, the Master or person in charge must _____.

A. report this immediately to the Commandant of the Coast Guard
B. log the reason for not completing the drill
C. conduct two of the required drills at the next opportunity
D. All of the above

1821. While towing, what is the principal danger in attempting to swing a barge on a short hawser in order to slow the barge's speed?

A. The barge may capsize from the sharp turn.
B. The barge may swing too quickly and run over the tug.
C. Free-surface effect of liquid inside the barge may rupture the barge bulkheads when turning too quickly.
D. Dangerous wakes may result from the swinging barge and capsize the tug.

1822. What is the principal danger in attempting to swing a barge on a hawser in order to slow the barge's speed?

A. Dangerous wakes may result from the swinging barge and capsize the tug.
B. The barge may swing too quickly and run over the tug.
C. Free-surface effect of liquid inside the barge may rupture the barge bulkheads if the turn is too quick.
D. The barge may pass under the hawser and capsize the tug.

1823. Chafing gear _____.

A. reduces and prevents corrosion of standing rigging
B. prevents corrosion of running rigging
C. reduces and prevents wear caused by the rubbing of one object against another
D. protects the body against extreme cold

1828. Your vessel is broken down and rolling in heavy seas. You can reduce the danger of capsizing by _____.

A. constantly shifting the rudder
B. moving all passengers to one side of the boat
C. rigging a sea anchor
D. moving all passengers to the stern

1829. The term "shift your rudder" means _____.

A. change from right rudder to left rudder an equal number of degrees
B. double your rudder angle or go to full rudder
C. bring your rudder amidships
D. check the swing of the vessel

1831. A loose tow may cause all of the following EXCEPT _____.

A. loss of maneuverability
B. lines to part
C. damage to the towing vessel and tow
D. a saving in the transit time

1832. Illustration D033DG. The run of plating labeled A is known as the _____.

A. sheer strake
B. stringer plate
C. deck strake
D. deck longitudinal

1833. The standing part of a tackle is _____.

A. all the fall except the hauling part
B. the hook that engages the weight to be moved

C. that part to which power is applied
D. that part of the falls made fast to one of the blocks

1836. While towing, what is the principal danger in attempting to swing a barge on a hawser in order to slow the barge's speed?

A. The barge may swing too quickly and run over the tug.
B. The barge may pass under the hawser and capsize the tug.
C. Free-surface effect of liquid inside the barge may rupture the barge bulkheads when turning too quickly.
D. Dangerous wakes may result from the swinging barge and capsize the tug.

1838. You are docking a vessel. If possible, you should _____.

A. go in with the current
B. go in against the current
C. approach the dock at a 90° angle and swing to
D. pass a mooring line to the dock with a heaving line and let the crew pull the vessel in

1839. When relieving the helm, the new helmsman should find it handy to know the _____.

A. leeway
B. variation in the area
C. amount of helm carried for a steady course
D. deviation on that heading

1840. You are approaching a steamer that is broken down and are preparing to take her in tow. BEFORE positioning your vessel to pass the towline, you must _____.

A. compare the rate of drift between the ships
B. install chafing gear on the towline
C. secure the bitter end of the towing hawser to prevent loss if the tow is slipped
D. have traveling lizards rigged to guide the towline while it is paid out

1841. If a tow sinks in shallow water, you should _____.

A. release it immediately
B. attempt to beach it before it goes under
C. pay out cable until it's on the bottom and place a buoy on the upper end

D. shorten cable to keep it off the bottom

1842. Illustration D030DG. The knot shown lettered W is a _____.

A. clove hitch
B. square knot
C. barrel hitch
D. stopper knot

1843. The sheave diameter to be used with a 3-inch manila rope is _____.

A. 3 inches
B. 6 inches
C. 9 inches
D. 12 inches

1844. A wooden float placed between a ship and a dock to prevent damage to both is called a _____.

A. camel
B. dolphin
C. rat guard
D. wedge

1848. You are docking a vessel. Wind and current are most favorable when they are

_____.

A. crossing your course in the same direction
B. crossing your course in opposite directions
C. parallel to the pier from ahead
D. setting you on the pier

1849. Illustration D030DG. The knot lettered U is a _____.

A. half hitch
B. round knot
C. becket bend
D. plain whipping

1852. What is normally used to pass a mooring line to a dock?

A. Distance line
B. Gantline
C. Heaving line
D. Tag line

1854. Illustration DO33DG. The structural member indicated by the letter F is known as a(n) _____.

A. erection
B. pillar

C. girder
D. deck support

1855. Which problem is virtually impossible to detect during an in-service inspection of used anchor chain?

A. Cracks
B. Elongation
C. Loose studs
D. Fatigue

1856. When passing a hawser to the dock you would first use what line?

A. Gantline
B. Heaving line
C. Preventer
D. Warp

1858. The easiest way to anchor a vessel in a current is to _____.

A. stem the current and make very slow headway when the anchor is dropped
B. stem the current and be falling aft very slowly when the anchor is dropped
C. stem the current and endeavor to make neither headway nor sternway when the anchor is dropped
D. stop all headway through the water and keep the current astern when the anchor is dropped

1859. You are attempting to take a dead ship in tow. All lines have been passed and secured. How should you get underway?

A. Order minimum turns until the towing hawser is just clear of the water, then reduce speed to that necessary to keep the line clear of the water.
B. If the towline is properly adjusted and weighted you can order slow or dead slow and the towline will act as a spring to absorb the initial shock.
C. Order minimum turns until the towing hawser is taut and then continue at that speed until towing speed is attained.
D. Order minimum turns until the catenary almost breaks the water, then stop. Order more turns as the hawser slackens but keep the catenary in the water.

1860. A towline should be fastened to _____.

A. the chocks at the bow of a towed vessel
B. the most forward, centermost point of a towed vessel such as a sturdy bow rail

C. the mast of a towed sailboat
D. a secure fitting near the bow of the towed vessel

1862. How much force would be required to lift a weight of 200 lbs. using a gun tackle rigged to disadvantage (do not consider friction)?

A. 50 lbs.
B. 100 lbs.
C. 150 lbs.
D. 200 lbs.

1863. If a mooring line should part while you are tying up at a dock, you should make a temporary eye by tying a _____.

A. becket bend
B. clove hitch
C. bowline
D. square knot

1868. When being towed by one tug, the towing bridle should be connected to towing _____.

A. bitts with figure eights
B. padeyes with pelican hooks
C. padeyes with safety hooks
D. All of the above

1870. Illustration D030DG. The knot lettered S is a _____.

A. bowline
B. blackwall hitch
C. half hitch
D. hook hitch

1873. How much weight can you lift by applying 100 lbs. of force to a twofold purchase rigged to disadvantage (do not consider friction)?

A. 200 lbs.
B. 300 lbs.
C. 400 lbs.
D. 500 lbs.

1875. A seam is indicated by which letter in illustration D033DG?

A. E
B. H
C. L
D. M

1878. When being towed, a fairlead is a _____.

A. fabricated shape used to change the direction of a flexible member of the tow hookup
B. fabricated shape used to secure the tow hookup to the towed vessel
C. line connecting the fishplate to the bridle legs
D. line connecting the tow bridle to the towed vessel

1879. What is the mechanical advantage of a threefold purchase when rove to disadvantage and neglecting friction?

A. 3
B. 4
C. 5
D. 6

1883. The most common method of securing a line to a cleat is a _____.

A. half hitch, then round turns
B. round turn, then figure eights
C. figure eight, then round turns
D. figure eight, then half hitches

1886. Illustration DO30DG. The knot lettered R is a _____.

A. double becket bend
B. bowline
C. fisherman's bend
D. round turn and two half hitches

1887. A small light tackle with blocks of steel or wood that is used for miscellaneous small jobs is called a _____.

A. snatch block
B. threefold purchase
C. handy-billy
D. chockablock

1888. How many legs does the bridle for an ocean tow have?

A. One
B. Two
C. Three
D. Four

1889. The helm command "Nothing to the left" means do NOT _____.

A. use left rudder
B. steer left of the ordered course
C. steer right of the ordered course
D. leave any bouys on the port side

1893. A block and tackle is "rove to advantage." This means that the _____.

A. blocks have been overhauled
B. hauling parts of two tackles are attached
C. hauling part leads through the movable block
D. hauling part leads through the standing block

1894. A load line is assigned by _____.

A. the U.S. Customs
B. the U.S. Department of Energy
C. the U.S. Army Corps of Engineers
D. a recognized classification society approved by the U.S. Coast Guard

1895. The knot lettered Q in illustration D030DG is a _____.

A. square knot
B. clove hitch
C. bowline
D. round knot

1896. You are on a large merchant vessel entering a U.S. port. There is a Pilot on board and he has the conn. Which statement is TRUE?

A. The Master is responsible for the safe navigation of the ship and the Pilot is employed for his local knowledge.
B. The Pilot is solely responsible for the safe maneuvering of the ship only if he is required to be on board by law.
C. The Pilot is solely responsible for the internal working of the ship.
D. The Pilot becomes solely responsible for the safe navigation of the vessel only if the Master relinquishes the conn.

1902. Illustration D033DG. The joint indicated by letter D is a _____.

A. seam
B. butt
C. span
D. sheet line

1903. When securing a manila line to a bitt what is the minimum number of round turns you should take before figure-eighting the line?

A. None
B. 1
C. 2
D. 3

1905. You have a large, broken-down vessel in tow with a wire rope and anchor cable towline. Both vessels have made provision for slipping the tow in an emergency; however, unless there are special circumstances _____.

A. the towing vessel should slip first
B. the vessel towed should slip first
C. they should slip simultaneously
D. either vessel may slip first

1908. When towing astern, increased catenary will _____.

A. increase control of the tow
B. prevent the towing vessel from going in irons
C. make the towing vessel less maneuverable
D. reduce shock stress on the towing hawser

1910. Illustration D030DG. The knot lettered J is a _____.

A. plain whipping
B. bowline
C. marline hitch
D. becket bend

1913. An example of a messenger is a _____.

A. fairlead
B. heaving line
C. stay
D. warp

1914. You need to make a fixed loop at the end of a line in order to use the line as a mooring line. You have insufficient time to make a splice. Which knot should you use?

A. Clove hitch
B. Fisherman's bend
C. Bowline
D. Round turn and two half hitches

1915. Illustration D033DG. A butt is indicated by which letter?

A. J
B. F
C. E
D. D

1918. Which statement is TRUE concerning hawser towing?

A. The catenary in a hawser should be sufficient so that the hawser just touches the bottom.
B. The hawser is of sufficient length for towing when taut between tug and tow.
C. Increasing speed usually increases the catenary in the hawser.
D. Shortening the tow hawser generally decreases the maneuverability of the tug.

1919. The disadvantage of using three strand nylon line for towing is its _____.

A. inherent weakness
B. tendency to rot if left damp
C. danger to crew if it parts
D. strength and shock absorbing abilities

1920. Which form of navigation may be suspended without notice under defense planning?

A. electronic
B. celestial
C. piloting
D. None of the above

1923. Disregarding friction, a twofold purchase when rove to disadvantage has a mechanical advantage of _____.

A. 2
B. 3
C. 4
D. 5

1924. The knot lettered I in illustration D030DG is a _____.

A. square knot
B. round knot
C. bowline on a bight
D. timber hitch

1928. Which towing method maintains the most control over the tow?

A. Tandem towing
B. Honolulu towing
C. Tandem tug towing
D. Breasted tug towing

1930. The holding capabilities of an anchor are determined PRIMARILY by the _____.

A. design of the anchor
B. weight of the anchor
C. scope of the anchor chain
D. size of the vessel

1931. Illustration D029DG. You are using tackle number 12 to lift a weight of 300 lbs. If you include 10 percent of the weight for each sheave for friction, what is the pull on the hauling part required to lift the weight?

A. 80 lbs.
B. 69 lbs.
C. 55 lbs.
D. 50 lbs.

1933. When checking a mooring line, you should _____.

A. ensure the bight is not fouled between the ship and the dock by taking up slack
B. pay out slack smartly and keep free for running
C. secure more turns to hold the line against any strain, then clear the area
D. surge the line so that it maintains a strain without parting

1935. The knot lettered H in illustration D030DG is a _____.

A. becket bend
B. bowline
C. plain whipping
D. crown knot

1936. A gypsy or gypsyhead is a _____.

A. punt used for painting over the side
B. small, reciprocating steam engine
C. spool-shaped drum fitted on a winch
D. swinging derrick

1938. Towing a structure using two tugs approximately side by side, each using one hawser, is referred to as a _____.

A. tandem tow
B. Honolulu tow
C. breasted tug tow
D. tandem tug tow

1939. You are on a vessel that has broken down and are preparing to be taken in tow. You will use your anchor cable as part of the towline. Which statement is TRUE?

A. The anchor cable should be veered enough to allow the towline connection to be just forward of your bow.
B. The anchor cable should be veered enough to allow the towline connection to be immediately astern of the towing vessel.

C. The strain of the tow is taken by the riding pawl, chain stopper, and anchor windlass brake.

D. The anchor cable should be led out through a chock, if possible, to avoid a sharp nip at the hawsepipe lip.

1941. The helm command "Left twenty" means _____.

A. change course twenty degrees to the left

B. put the rudder left twenty degrees

C. put the rudder hard left for the first twenty degrees of swing

D. put the rudder left twenty degrees and then ease back as the vessel starts swinging

1943. In order to pay out or slack a mooring line which is under strain, you should _____.

A. sluice the line

B. surge the line

C. stopper the line

D. slip the line

1944. Illustration D033DG. The garboard strake is indicated by which letter?

A. A

B. B

C. G

D. H

1945. One of your crew members falls overboard from the starboard side. You should IMMEDIATELY _____.

A. apply left rudder

B. throw the crew member a life preserver

C. begin backing your engines

D. position your vessel to windward and begin recovery

1948. The Honolulu (Christmas tree) tow was devised to _____.

A. keep the catenary to a minimum

B. allow easy removal of a center tow

C. reduce hawser length

D. increase the catenary

1949. Using a scope of 5, determine how many feet of cable you should put out to anchor in 5 fathoms of water.

A. 100 feet

B. 150 feet

C. 200 feet

D. 250 feet

1950. You are proceeding to a distress site and expect large numbers of people in the water. Which statement is TRUE?

A. You should stop to windward of the survivors in the water and only use the ship's boats to recover the survivors.

B. If the survivors are in inflatable rafts you should approach from windward to create a lee for the survivors.

C. An inflatable life raft secured alongside can be an effective boarding station for transfer of survivors from the boats.

D. Survivors in the water should never be permitted alongside due to the possibility of injury from the vessel.

1953. What is likely to occur when you are surging synthetic mooring lines on the gypsyhead during mooring operations?

A. The lines may jam and then jump off the gypsyhead.

B. If there is sudden strain on the line, the man tending the line may be pulled into the gypsyhead.

C. The lines' surging may cause the vessel to surge.

D. The heat generated may cause the lines to temporarily fuse to the gypsyhead.

1957. Illustration D033DG. The strake of shell plating indicated by letter H is known as the _____.

A. sheer strake

B. outboard keel plate

C. garboard strake

D. bilge strake

1958. When tandem tug towing, the more powerful of the two tugs should be _____.

A. the lead tug

B. behind the lead tug

C. towing at a right angle to the smaller tug

D. towing at a faster speed than the smaller tug

1960. The knot lettered G in illustration D030DG is a _____.

A. round turn and two half hitches

B. fisherman's bend

C. timber hitch

D. barrel hitch

1961. A sufficient amount of chain must be veered when anchoring a vessel to ensure _____.

A. the vessel has enough room to swing while at anchor

B. the anchor flukes bite into the ocean bottom

C. there is a sufficient scope of chain to keep the anchor on the bottom

D. there is more chain out than there is in the chain locker

1962. The maximum draft to which a vessel can legally be submerged is indicated by the _____.

A. load line mark

B. Certificate of Inspection

C. station bill

D. tonnage mark

1963. What should you do to a line to prevent fraying where it passes over the side of the vessel?

A. Worm that part of the line.

B. Splice that part of the line.

C. Cover it with chafing gear.

D. Install a cleat.

1966. The turning circle of a vessel making a turn of over 360 degrees is the path followed by the _____.

A. bow

B. bridge

C. center of gravity

D. centerline

1969. If you shorten the scope of anchor cable, your anchor's holding power _____.

A. decreases

B. increases

C. remains the same

D. has no relation to the scope

1970. Illustration D033DG. The structural member indicated by the letter L is a _____.

A. web frame

B. bilge keel

C. side keel
D. longitudinal

1973. Which statement is TRUE about placing the eyes of two mooring lines on the same bollard?

A. Put one line at the low point and one at the high point of the bollard so they don't touch.
B. Take the eye of the second line up through the eye of the first line before putting the second line on the bollard.
C. Never put two mooring lines on the same bollard.
D. The mooring line forward should be put on the bollard first.

1976. Illustration D033DG. Which letter indicates a longitudinal?

A. C
B. E
C. L
D. M

1977. On a crane, the boom indicator tells the operator what angle the boom angle is compared to the _____.

A. vertical position
B. horizontal position
C. boom stop angle
D. minimum radius angle

1978. When towing, the least amount of tension will be on each bridle leg when the two legs _____.

A. form a large angle with each other
B. form a small angle with each other
C. are of unequal length
D. are joined by a fishplate

1979. What is a proper size block to use with a 3-inch circumference Manila line?

A. At least a 12-inch sheave
B. 9-inch cheek, 6-inch sheave
C. 8-inch cheek, any size sheave
D. 6-inch cheek, 4-inch sheave

1980. Illustration D003DG. What is the name of the mark indicated by the letter C?

A. Fresh water line
B. Tropical water line
C. Summer water line
D. Winter North Atlantic water line

1982. Illustration D029DG. You are using tackle number 8 to lift a weight of 100 lbs. If you include 10 percent of the weight for each sheave for friction, what is the pull on the hauling part required to lift the weight?

A. 120 lbs.
B. 55 lbs.
C. 40 lbs.
D. 37 lbs.

1983. When a line is subject to wear where it passes through a mooring chock, it should be _____.

A. wormed, parceled, and served
B. wrapped with heavy tape
C. wrapped with chafing gear
D. wrapped in leather

1988. When towing, what is the main reason for using a chain bridle on a wire hawser?

A. It makes for an easy connection.
B. It gives a spring effect to cushion the shock.
C. It eliminates the necessity of a swivel.
D. It does not chafe.

1989. If you were to pass a stopper on a wire rope, what should the stopper be made of?

A. Wire
B. Manila
C. Nylon
D. Chain

1992. While the Pilot is embarked he or she _____.

A. is solely responsible for the safe navigation of the vessel
B. is a specialist hired for his or her local navigational knowledge
C. relieves the officer of the watch
D. relieves the Master of his duties

1993. The usual method of arranging a line on deck so that it will run out easily without kinking or fouling is _____.

A. coiling the line
B. faking down the line
C. flemishing the line
D. racking the line

1994. Illustration D033DG. The space indicated by the letter J is known as the _____.

A. double bottom
B. flooding barrier
C. floor space
D. bilge tank

1995. The single turn method of returning to a man overboard should be used ONLY if _____.

A. the man is reported missing rather than immediately seen as he falls overboard
B. the vessel is very maneuverable
C. the conning officer is inexperienced
D. a boat will be used to recover the man

1996. Which method should be used to secure a manila line to bitts?

A. A round turn on the bitt farthest from the strain and then figure eights
B. A round turn on the bitt closest to the strain and then figure eights
C. Figure eights and then a round turn at the top of both bitts
D. Only figure eights are necessary on both bitts

1997. Illustration D029DG. What is the name of tackle number 12?

A. Threefold purchase
B. Davit tackle
C. Deck tackle
D. Gin tackle

1998. When towing in an open seaway, it is important to use a towing line _____.

A. made only of wire rope, due to possible weather conditions
B. that will have the tow on a crest while your vessel is in a trough
C. that will have the tow on a crest while your vessel is on a crest
D. with little dip to gain maximum control of the tow

1999. When shoring a damaged bulkhead, effort should be taken to spread the pressure over the _____.

A. maximum possible area
B. minimum possible area
C. nearest watertight door
D. nearest longitudinal girder

2000. Illustration D025DG. The vessel has broken down and you are going to take her in tow. The wind is on her starboard beam. Both vessels are making the same amount of leeway. Where should you position your vessel when you start running lines?

A. A
B. B
C. C
D. D

2002. Illustration D033DG. The structural member indicated by the letter K was fitted in segments between continuous longitudinals. It is known as which type of floor?

A. Intercostal
B. Open
C. Lightened
D. Nonwatertight

2003. Chafing gear is used to _____.

A. anchor the boat
B. pick up heavy loads
C. protect fiber rope from abrasion
D. strengthen mooring lines

2005. A block that can be opened at the hook or shackle end to receive a bight of the line is a _____.

A. bight block
B. gin block
C. heel block
D. snatch block

2007. The helm command "shift your rudder" means _____.

A. double your rudder angle or go to full rudder
B. change from right rudder to left rudder an equal number of degrees
C. bring your rudder amidships
D. check the swing of the vessel

2008. When towing another vessel, the length of the towing line should be _____.

A. as long as possible
B. as short as possible under the circumstances and not over two wave lengths
C. such that one vessel will be on a crest while the other is in a trough
D. such that the vessels will be in step

2011. Illustration D033DG. The structural member indicated by the letter K is a _____.

A. longitudinal frame
B. stringer
C. girder
D. floor

2013. A mooring line that checks forward motion of a vessel at a pier is a _____.

A. bow line
B. forward bow line
C. stern line
D. stern breast line

2014. Illustration D029DG. You are using tackle number 12, as shown, to lift a weight. The hauling part of this tackle is bent to the weight hook (w) of tackle number 2. What is the mechanical advantage of this rig?

A. 9
B. 10
C. 14
D. 21

2015. During a period of "whiteout," you should expect which of the following?

A. Snowfall or blowing snow
B. Lack of ability to estimate distance
C. Harsh contrast between sun-illuminated snow cover and the background
D. Hazy horizons with extensive mirage effects

2018. When towing astern, one way to reduce yawing of the tow is to _____.

A. trim the tow by the stern
B. trim the tow by the head
C. have the tow on an even keel
D. list the tow on the side it is yawing

2019. A man was sighted as he fell overboard. After completing a Williamson turn, the man is not sighted. What type of search should be conducted?

A. Expanding circle
B. Sector search
C. Parallel track pattern
D. Datum-drift search

2020. To facilitate passing the end of a large rope through a block, you could use a _____.

A. gantline
B. head line
C. reeving line
D. sail line

2022. In determining the scope of cable to be used when anchoring, what would NOT be considered?

A. Depth of the water
B. Character of the holding ground
C. Maintenance cost for the chain
D. Type of anchor cable

2023. A mooring line leading at nearly right angles to the keel is a _____.

A. spring line
B. bow line
C. stern line
D. breast line

2025. What is the chief hazard encountered when surging synthetic mooring lines on the gypsyhead during operations?

A. If there is sudden strain, the man tending the line may be pulled into the gypsyhead.
B. The lines may jam and then jump off the gypsyhead.
C. The lines' surging may cause the vessel to surge.
D. The heat generated may cause the lines to temporarily fuse to the gypsyhead.

2028. When making up a long, large coastwise tow, which of the following procedures is INCORRECT?

A. A chain towing bridle is generally preferred
B. Safety shackles should be used when connecting to the fishplate
C. Rig tripping ropes (retrieving lines)
D. Back-up wires are left slack

2029. When anchored, increasing the scope of the anchor chain normally serves to _____.

A. prevent fouling of the anchor
B. decrease swing of the vessel
C. prevent dragging of the anchor
D. reduce strain on the windlass

2030. Safety equipment on board vessels must be approved by the _____.

A. U.S. Coast Guard
B. Safety Standards Bureau

C. Occupational Health and Safety Agency (OSHA)
D. National Safety Council

2031. Multi-year ice is the hardest sea ice and should be avoided if possible. It is recognizable because of what tone to its surface color?

A. Greenish
B. Bluish
C. Grey
D. Grey-white

2033. A spring line leads _____.

A. fore and aft from the ship's side
B. to the dock at a right angle to the vessel
C. through the bull nose or chock at the bow
D. through the chock at the stern

2034. You are ordering a new block to use with a 3-inch circumference manila line. Which represents a proper size block for this line?

A. 6-inch cheek, 4-inch sheave
B. 8-inch cheek, any size sheave
C. 9-inch cheek, 6-inch sheave
D. At least a 12-inch sheave

2037. You are riding to a single anchor. The vessel is yawing excessively. Which action should be taken to reduce the yawing?

A. Veer chain to the riding anchor
B. Heave to a shorter scope of chain on the riding anchor
C. Drop the second anchor at the extreme end of the yaw and veer the riding anchor
D. Drop the second anchor at the extreme end of the yaw, then adjust the cables until the scope is equal

2038. With a large ocean tow in heavy weather, you should NOT _____.

A. keep the stern of the tug well down in the water
B. adjust the towline so the tug is on the crest when the tow is in the trough
C. keep the low point of the catenary in the water
D. use a long towing hawser

2040. Illustration D033DG. The plating indicated by the letter N is known as the _____.

A. inner bottom

B. floor riders
C. tank-top rider plating
D. ceiling

2041. Which tackle arrangement has the LEAST mechanical advantage?

A. Single whip
B. Gun tackle
C. Luff tackle
D. Twofold purchase

2042. Which statement about the deck line is TRUE?

A. The top of the deck line is marked at the highest point of the freeboard deck, including camber, at the midships point.
B. A vessel with wooden planks on a steel deck will have the deck line marked at the intersection of the upper line of the wood sheathing with the side shell.
C. The deck edge is marked at the intersection of the freeboard deck with the side shell, at the lowest point of sheer, with the vessel at even trim.
D. On a vessel with a rounded stringer-sheer plate, the deck line is marked where the stringer plate turns down from the plane of the deck line.

2043. A mooring line that prevents a vessel from moving sideways away from the dock is a _____.

A. bow line
B. breast line
C. stern line
D. spring line

2045. When relieving the helm, the new helmsman will find it helpful to know the _____.

A. deviation on that heading
B. variation in the area
C. leeway
D. amount of helm carried for a steady course

2046. The structural member indicated by the letter I in illustration D033DG is the _____.

A. garboard strake
B. center pillar
C. keel
D. girder

2047. Progressive flooding is controlled by securing watertight boundaries and _____.

A. transferring water ballast
B. jettisoning cargo
C. pumping out flooded compartments
D. abandoning ship

2048. The MINIMUM acceptable size for a towing bridle would be that size in which the safe working load (SWL) of each leg of the bridle is equal to _____.

A. one-half the SWL of the main towing hawser
B. three-fourths the SWL of the main towing hawser
C. that of the main towing hawser
D. twice that of the main towing hawser

2049. While the Pilot is maneuvering the vessel to a dock, what is the PRIMARY responsibility of the watch officer?

A. Supervise the signaling and flag etiquette.
B. Record the bells and their times in the bell book.
C. Judge the appropriateness of the Pilot's orders and countermand them if necessary.
D. Insure that helm and throttle orders given by the Pilot are correctly executed.

2050. In illustration D044DG, the mooring line labeled "H" is called a(n) _____.

A. forward breast line
B. offshore spring line
C. onshore bow line
D. offshore bow line

2053. A mooring line leading 45° to the keel, used to check forward or astern movement of a vessel, is called a _____.

A. spring line
B. warp line
C. bow line
D. breast line

2054. Illustration D003DG. What is the name of the mark indicated by the letter B in the diagram?

A. Timber summer load line
B. Tropical fresh water load line
C. Tropical load line
D. Summer load line

2058. What is NOT suitable for use in making up the towing rig for a heavy, long ocean tow?

A. Chain
B. Ring
C. Solid thimble
D. A fishplate

2059. You are handling a mooring line and are instructed to "Check the line." What should you do?

A. Ensure the bight is not fouled by taking up slack.
B. Pay out the line smartly and keep it free for running.
C. Secure the line by adding more turns.
D. Surge the line so it maintains a strain without parting.

2060. In polar regions you should NOT expect to see _____.

A. mirage effects
B. sea smoke
C. extensive snowfall
D. false horizons

2061. A sheave is a _____.

A. grooved wheel in a block
B. line to hold a lifeboat next to the embarkation deck
C. partial load of grain
D. seaman's knife

2062. Illustration D025DG. The vessel shown has broken down and you are going to take her in tow. The wind is on her starboard beam. She is making more leeway than you. Where should you position your vessel when you start running lines?

A. A
B. B
C. C
D. D

2063. A spring line is _____.

A. any wire rope used for mooring
B. a fire-warp
C. a mooring line running diagonally to the keel
D. a mooring line perpendicular to the keel

2064. While underway in thick fog you are on watch and hear the cry "man overboard." Which type of maneuver should you make?

A. Figure eight turn
B. Round turn
C. Racetrack turn
D. Williamson turn

2065. A continual worsening of the list or trim indicates _____.

A. negative GM
B. progressive flooding
C. structural failure
D. an immediate need to ballast

2067. Illustration D029DG. What is the mechanical advantage, neglecting friction, of tackle number 12?

A. 3
B. 5.5
C. 6
D. 7

2068. You intend to tow a barge with one tug and expect continuous high winds from the north. To reduce the yaw of your tow, you should _____.

A. reduce the draft of the barge
B. shorten one leg of the bridle
C. place bulky deck loads as far aft as possible
D. trim the barge down by the bow

2069. A spring line is a _____.

A. mooring line made of spring lay wire rope
B. mooring line running diagonally to the keel
C. mooring line parallel to the keel
D. wire rope used for securing an anchor buoy

2070. Which statement about the Williamson turn is FALSE?

A. It requires the highest degree of shiphandling skills to accomplish.
B. It is the slowest of the methods used in turning the vessel.
C. It is the best turn to use when the victim is not in sight due to reduced visibility.

D. It returns the vessel to the original trackline on a reciprocal course.

2073. When rigging a bos'n's chair on a stay with a shackle, _____.

A. mouse the shackle to the chair
B. never allow the shackle pin to ride on the stay
C. secure it with small stuff
D. seize the end of the shackle

2075. The knot lettered E in illustration D030DG is a _____.

A. stopper hitch
B. blackwall hitch
C. timber and half hitch
D. bowline on a bight

2076. A person who sees someone fall overboard should _____.

A. immediately jump in the water to assist the individual
B. go to the bridge for the distress flares
C. run to the radio room to send an emergency message
D. call for help and keep the individual in sight

2078. While towing, bridle legs of unequal lengths may cause _____.

A. the bridle to foul
B. the shorter leg to fail
C. chafing on the fairlead or bitts
D. a bent swivel

2081. A seaman is reported missing in the morning and was last seen after coming off the mid-watch. Which type of turn would you use to return to the trackline steamed during the night?

A. Williamson
B. Racetrack
C. 180°
D. Anderson

2086. Illustration D029DG. What is the mechanical advantage of tackle number 11?

A. 7
B. 6
C. 5.5
D. 5

2088. You have been towing astern and have just let go the tow. Your deckhands are pulling in and faking the towline by hand on the stern. The most dangerous action to take is to _____.

A. continue ahead at slow speed
B. continue ahead at half speed
C. stop your engines
D. back down on your engines

2091. When operating in an area where sea ice and icebergs are present, which statement is TRUE?

A. Icebergs may travel in a direction many degrees different from the sea ice.
B. Both icebergs and sea ice will move in approximately the same direction and at the same speed.
C. Icebergs and sea ice will move in the same direction, but at different speeds due to the sail effect of the berg.
D. Icebergs and sea ice will move in the same direction, but the iceberg will move slower because of its underwater bulk.

2093. Illustration D029DG. What is the mechanical advantage of tackle number 10?

A. 4
B. 4.5
C. 5
D. 5.5

2095. You are using a racetrack turn to recover a man overboard. The vessel is first steadied when how many degrees away from the original heading?

A. 60° to 70°
B. 90°
C. 135°
D. 180°

2097. Illustration D029DG. What is the name of tackle number 11?

A. Three-two purchase
B. Double luff tackle
C. Gun tackle
D. Topping lift

2098. Snow has obliterated surface features and the sky is covered with uniform, altostratus clouds. There are no shadows and the horizon has disappeared. What is this condition called?

A. Ice blink
B. Whiteout
C. Water sky
D. Aurora reflection

2100. The primary purpose of a load line is to establish required _____.

A. minimum freeboard
B. GM
C. transverse stability
D. fresh water allowances

2104. You are proceeding to a distress site where the survivors are in life rafts. Which action will assist in making your vessel more visible to the survivors?

A. Steering a zigzag course with 5 to 10 minutes on each leg
B. Steering a sinuous course
C. Dumping debris over the side to make a trail to your vessel
D. Making smoke in daylight

2106. A racetrack turn would be better than a Williamson turn in recovering a man overboard if _____.

A. the man has been missing for a period of time
B. the sea water is very cold and the man is visible
C. there is thick fog
D. the wind was from astern on the original course

2107. Illustration D003DG. What is the name of the mark indicated by the letter A?

A. Winter North Atlantic load line
B. Fresh water load line
C. Deck line
D. Plimsoll line

2111. You are anchoring in 16 fathoms of water. On a small to medium size vessel, the _____.

A. anchor may be dropped from the hawsepipe
B. anchor should be lowered to within 2 fathoms of the bottom before being dropped
C. scope should always be at least ten times the depth of the water
D. scope should always be less than 5 times the depth of the water

2113. One major advantage of the round turn maneuver in a man overboard situation is that it _____.

A. is the fastest method
B. is easy for a single-screw vessel to perform
C. requires the least shiphandling skills to perform
D. can be used in reduced visibility

2116. What is the name of tackle number 10 in illustration D029DG?

A. Two-two purchase
B. Deck purchase
C. Twofold purchase
D. Double runner

2117. When a vessel is involved in a casualty, the cost of property damage includes the _____.

A. cost of labor and material to restore the vessel to the service condition which existed before the casualty
B. loss of revenue while the vessel is being repaired, up to a maximum of $50,000
C. damage claims awarded to individuals or companies involved in the casualty
D. All of the above

2119. You are coming to anchor in 8 fathoms of water. In this case, the _____.

A. anchor may be dropped from the hawsepipe
B. anchor should be lowered to within 2 fathoms of the bottom before being dropped
C. anchor should be lowered to the bottom then the ship backed and the remainder of the cable veered
D. scope should be less than 3 times the depth of the water

2122. Illustration D029DG. What is the name of tackle number 9?

A. Single purchase
B. One-two tackle
C. Double whip
D. Luff tackle

2124. You are on watch aboard a vessel heading NW, with the wind from dead ahead, in heavy seas. You notice a man fall overboard from the starboard bow. Which action would NOT be appropriate?

A. Hard right rudder
B. Throw a lifebuoy to the man, if possible
C. Send a man aloft
D. Get the port boat ready

2126. You have anchored in a mud and clay bottom. The anchor appears to be dragging in a storm. What action should you take?

A. Shorten the scope of the cable.
B. Veer cable to the anchor.
C. Drop the other anchor underfoot.
D. Drop the second anchor, veer to a good scope, then weigh the first anchor.

2127. The maneuver which will return your vessel to a person who has fallen overboard in the shortest time is _____.

A. a Williamson Turn
B. engine(s) crash astern, no turn
C. a single turn with hard rudder
D. two 180° turns

2130. In a racetrack turn, to recover a man overboard, the vessel is steadied for the SECOND time after a turn of how many degrees from the original heading?

A. 60°
B. 135°
C. 180°
D. 360°

2135. A load line certificate is valid for how many years?

A. 1
B. 2
C. 3
D. 5

2136. Your enrolled vessel is bound from Baltimore, MD, to Norfolk, VA, via Chesapeake Bay. Which statement about the required Pilot is TRUE?

A. The Pilot need only be licensed by the Coast Guard.
B. The Pilot must be licensed by either Virginia or Maryland.
C. Tlhe Pilot must be licensed by Virginia and Maryland.
D. The Pilot must be licensed by Virginia, Maryland and the Coast Guard.

2143. Your vessel was damaged and initially assumed a significant list and trim; however, further increase has been slow. Based on this data, what should you expect?

A. The slowing is only temporary and the vessel will probably suddenly capsize or plunge from loss of stability due to change in the waterplane area.
B. The vessel can probably be saved if further flooding can be stopped.
C. The vessel will continue to slowly list and/or trim due to the free-surface effect and free-communication effect.
D. The vessel will suddenly flop to the same or greater angle of list on the other side and may capsize.

2144. "Hard right rudder" means _____.

A. jam the rudder against the stops
B. put the rudder over quickly to 15 degrees right rudder
C. meet a swing to the right, then return to amidships
D. put the rudder over to the right all the way

2146. You are on a single-screw vessel with a right-handed propeller. The vessel is going full speed astern with full right rudder. The bow will swing _____.

A. quickly to port, then more slowly to port
B. probably to port
C. slowly to port, then quickly to starboard
D. probably to starboard

2147. Illustration D029DG. What is the name of tackle number 8?

A. Parbuckle
B. Gun tackle
C. Single purchase
D. Single luff tackle

2149. When anchoring in a clay bottom, what is one hazard that may cause the anchor to drag?

A. The flukes may dig in unevenly and capsize the anchor when under stress.
B. The flukes may not dig in.
C. The anchor may get shod with clay and not develop full holding power.
D. The anchor will tend to dig in and come to rest near the vertical.

2150. Illustration D025DG. The vessel shown has broken down and you are going to take her in tow. The wind is coming from her starboard beam. You are making more leeway than she. Where should you position your vessel when you start running lines?

A. A
B. B
C. C
D. D

2156. You are standing watch on entering port and the Master gives a rudder command which conflicts with a rudder command from the Pilot. You should ensure the helmsman _____.

A. obeys the Master
B. obeys the Pilot
C. brings the rudder to a position midway between the two conflicting positions
D. asks the Pilot if he has relinquished control

2157. You are in a fresh water port loading logs with gear rated at 5 tons, and suspect the weight of the logs exceeds the SWL of the gear. The logs are floating in the water alongside the vessel and have 95% of their volume submerged. The average length of the logs is 15 feet and the average diameter is 4.4 feet. What is the nearest average weight of the logs, based on these average measurements?

A. 5.5 tons
B. 6.0 tons
C. 7.7 tons
D. 24.1 tons

2159. Illustration D029DG. What is the mechanical advantage of tackle number 9?

A. 1
B. 2
C. 3
D. 4

2163. Illustration D029DG. What is the name of tackle number 7?

A. Runner
B. Inverted whip
C. Whip
D. Single purchase

2168. Illustration D029DG. What is the name of tackle number 6?

A. Triple purchase

B. Clew garnet tackle
C. Boat falls
D. Threefold purchase

2169. Illustration D029DG. What is the mechanical advantage of tackle number 8?

A. 3
B. 1.5
C. 1
D. 0.5

2171. The order of importance in addressing damage control is _____.

A. control flooding, control fire, repair structural damage
B. restore vital services, control fire, control flooding
C. control fire, restore vital services, control flooding
D. control fire, control flooding, repair structural damage

2173. Illustration D029DG. What is the name of tackle number 5?

A. 3-2 purchase
B. Double luff tackle
C. Twofold purchase
D. Fourfold whip

2179. A design modification of an anchor chain which prevents kinking is the _____.

A. detachable link
B. stud link
C. Kenter link
D. connecting link

2181. When relieving the helm, the new helmsman should know the _____.

A. course per magnetic steering compass
B. gyro error
C. variation
D. maximum rudder angle previously used

2182. Illustration D029DG. What is the name of tackle number 4?

A. Double whip
B. Luff tackle
C. Twofold purchase
D. 2-2 tackle

2185. Illustration D029DG. You are using tackle number 7 to lift a weight of 100 lbs. If you include 10 percent of the weight for each sheave for friction, what is the pull on the hauling part required to lift the weight?

A. 200 lbs.
B. 150 lbs.
C. 110 lbs.
D. 55 lbs.

2186. Illustration D029DG. What is the mechanical advantage of tackle number 7?

A. 0
B. 0.5
C. 1
D. 2

2189. Illustration D034DG. You are conducting trials to determine the maneuvering characteristics of your vessel. While making a turn you take the ranges and bearings of an isolated light with the results shown. Based on this information, what is the transfer for a turn of 75°?

A. 340 yards (306 meters)
B. 280 yards (252 meters)
C. 230 yards (207 meters)
D. 190 yards (171 meters)

2190. Illustration D029DG. What is the name of tackle number 3?

A. 1-2 purchase
B. Gun tackle
C. Single luff tackle
D. Double whip

2191. Illustration D033DG. A wooden deck installed on top of the plating lettered N is known as _____.

A. spar decking
B. furring
C. ceiling
D. flooring

2192. The part of a windlass which physically engages the chain during hauling or paying out is the _____.

A. devil's claw
B. bull gear
C. wildcat
D. cat head

2193. Illustration D035DG. You have determined the maneuvering characteristics of your vessel by taking the radar ranges and bearings of an isolated light while making a turn. The results are listed in illustration D035DG. Based on this data what is the tactical diameter of the turning circle?

A. 755 yards
B. 780 yards
C. 820 yards
D. 880 yards

2194. Illustration D029DG. What is the mechanical advantage of tackle number 6?

A. 6
B. 5.5
C. 5
D. 3

2195. Illustration D035DG. You have determined the maneuvering characteristics of your vessel by taking the radar ranges and bearings of an isolated light while making a turn. The results are as listed. Based on this data what is the transfer for a turn of 180°?

A. 745 yards
B. 770 yards
C. 840 yards
D. 890 yards

2196. Illustration D029DG. You are using tackle number 10 to lift a weight. The hauling part of this tackle is bent to the weight hook (w) of tackle number 4. What is the mechanical advantage of this rig?

A. 24
B. 20
C. 13
D. 9

2197. You are signing on crew members. The minimum number of people required aboard, and the qualifications of each, is listed on the _____.

A. Crew list
B. fo'c'sle card
C. Certificate of Inspection
D. Articles of Agreement

2198. Illustration D034DG. You are conducting trials to determine the maneuvering characteristics of your vessel. While making a turn, you take ranges and bearings of an isolated light with the results as shown. Based on this information, what is the transfer for a turn of 90°?

A. 355 yards
B. 380 yards
C. 410 yards
D. 455 yards

2199. Illustration D029DG. What is the name of tackle number 2?

A. Whip
B. Onefold purchase
C. Single purchase
D. Gun tackle

2203. A Chinese stopper (two lines) will hold best when you _____.

A. fasten the bitter ends to the mooring line with half hitches
B. twist the ends together and hold them in the direction of the pull
C. twist the ends together and hold them in the direction opposite to the pull
D. twist the ends together and hold them at right angles to the mooring line

2204. While writing in the logbook at the end of your watch, you make an error in writing an entry. What is the proper way of correcting this error?

A. Blot out the error completely and rewrite the entry correctly.
B. Carefully and neatly erase the entry and rewrite it correctly.
C. Cross out the error with a single line, write the correct entry, and initial it.
D. Remove this page of the log book and rewrite all entries on a clean page.

2207. Repair of vital machinery and services should start _____.

A. after control of fire, flooding, and structural repairs
B. immediately
C. after control of fire, but before control of flooding
D. after stability is restored

2211. Illustration D029DG. What is the mechanical advantage, neglecting friction, of tackle number 5?

A. 2
B. 4
C. 5
D. 5.5

2212. Illustration D035DG. You have determined the maneuvering characteristics of your vessel by taking the radar ranges and bearings of an isolated light while making a turn. The results are listed in illustration D035DG. Based on this data what is the advance for a turn of 30°?

A. 380 yards
B. 420 yards
C. 470 yards
D. 525 yards

2213. Illustration D029DG. You are using tackle number 6 to lift a weight. The hauling part of this tackle is bent to the weight hook (w) of tackle number 8. Disregarding friction, what is the mechanical advantage of this rig?

A. 11
B. 16
C. 18
D. 24

2214. Illustration D034DG. You are conducting trials to determine the maneuvering characteristics of your vessel. While making a turn, you take ranges and bearings of an isolated light with the results as shown. Based on this information, what is the advance for a turn of 90°?

A. 820 yards
B. 870 yards
C. 930 yards
D. 975 yards

2216. Illustration D029DG. What is the mechanical advantage, neglecting friction, of tackle number 4?

A. 1
B. 2
C. 3
D. 4

2217. Illustration D030DG. The knot lettered P is a _____.

A. rolling hitch
B. clove hitch
C. round turn and two half hitches
D. marline hitch

2219. Illustration D029DG. You are using tackle number 5 to lift a weight of 300 lbs. If you include 10 percent of the weight for each sheave for friction, what is the pull on the hauling part required to lift the weight?

A. 50 lbs.
B. 75 lbs.
C. 90 lbs.
D. 112 lbs.

2221. Illustration D029DG. You are using tackle number 5 to lift a weight. The hauling part of this tackle is bent to the weight

hook (w) of tackle number 8. What is the mechanical advantage of this rig?

A. 20
B. 15
C. 10
D. 5

2222. Illustration D033DG. The lower seam of the strake indicated by the letter B is sometimes riveted. This is done to _____.

A. increase the strength in a highly stressed area
B. provide the flexibility inherent in a riveted seam
C. serve as a crack arrestor and prevent hull girder failure
D. reduce construction costs

2223. Illustration D029DG. What is the mechanical advantage of tackle number 3?

A. 1
B. 2
C. 3
D. 4

2224. Illustration D030DG. When improperly tied, which knot shown is called a granny or thief's knot?

A. F
B. M
C. R
D. W

2225. Illustration D030DG. Which knot should be used to secure a line to a spar when the pull is perpendicular to the spar?

A. E
B. F
C. N
D. P

2226. Illustration D030DG. The knot lettered O is a _____.

A. timber hitch
B. barrel hitch
C. carrick bend
D. blackwall hitch

2228. You have determined the maneuvering characteristics of your vessel by taking the radar ranges and bearings of an isolated light while making a turn. The results are listed. Based on this data what is the transfer for a turn of 60°?

A. 140 yards (126 meters)
B. 180 yards (162 meters)
C. 225 yards (203 meters)
D. 270 yards (243 meters)

2229. Illustration D029DG. You are using tackle number 5 to lift a weight. The hauling part of this tackle is bent to the weight hook of tackle number 9. What is the mechanical advantage of this rig?

A. 20
B. 9
C. 5
D. 4

2230. Illustration D029DG. What is the name of tackle number 1?

A. Whip
B. Onefold purchase
C. Gun tackle
D. Runner

2231. Illustration D029DG. What is the mechanical advantage of tackle number 2?

A. 0.5
B. 1
C. 2
D. 3

2232. The MAIN use of the knot lettered M is to _____.

A. marry two hawsers
B. form a temporary eye in the end of a line
C. secure a heaving line to a hawser
D. provide a seat for a man to work over the side

2233. The knot lettered N in illustration D030DG is a _____.

A. timber hitch
B. rolling bowline
C. stopper
D. heaving line hitch

2235. Illustration D034DG. You are conducting trials to determine the maneuvering characteristics of your vessel. While making a turn, you take ranges and bearings of an isolated light with the results as shown. Based on this information, what is the advance for a turn of 75°?

A. 800 yards (720 meters)
B. 860 yards (774 meters)
C. 910 yards (819 meters)

D. 955 yards (860 meters)

2236. Another name for the garboard strake is the _____.

A. A strake
B. Z strake
C. side keel plate
D. stringer plate

2238. What is the area of a circle with a radius of 12 feet after a sector of 60° has been removed?

A. 18.85 square feet
B. 75.40 square feet
C. 94.25 square feet
D. 376.99 square feet

2239. Illustration D029DG. You are using tackle number 3 to lift a weight of 120 lbs. If you include 10 percent of the weight for each sheave for friction, what is the pull on the hauling part required to lift the weight?

A. 52 lbs.
B. 49 lbs.
C. 40 lbs.
D. 27 lbs.

2240. Illustration D029DG. What is the mechanical advantage of tackle number 1?

A. 0.5
B. 1
C. 1.5
D. 2

2241. Illustration D033DG. The letter M indicates a(n) _____.

A. web frame
B. intercostal
C. stringer
D. cant frame

2242. What is the area of a circle with a radius of 21 feet after a sector of 120° has been removed?

A. 115.45 ft.
B. 230.91 ft.
C. 461.81 ft.
D. 923.63 ft.

2243. Illustration D029DG. You are using tackle number 4, as shown, to lift a weight. The hauling part of this tackle is bent to the weight hook of tackle number 11. What is the mechanical advantage of this rig?

A. 4
B. 6
C. 10
D. 24

2245. To determine the number of certificated lifeboatmen required on a vessel, you should check the _____.

A. Load Line Certificate
B. Certificate of Inspection
C. Safety of Life at Sea Certificate
D. operations manual

2249. Illustration D030DG. Which knot should be used to secure a line to a spar when the pull is parallel to the spar?

A. G
B. F
C. P
D. Q

2250. Illustration D035DG. You have determined the maneuvering characteristics of your vessel by taking radar ranges and bearings of an isolated light while making a turn. The results are as shown. Based on this data what is the transfer for a turn of 90°?

A. 380 yards
B. 430 yards
C. 485 yards
D. 525 yards

2251. Illustration D033DG. The letter I indicates the keel. Which of the following plates is NOT part of the keel?

A. Center vertical keel
B. Rider plate
C. Longitudinal girder
D. Flat plate keel

2253. What is the area of a circle with a radius of 17 feet after a sector of 57° has been removed?

A. 764.17 ft.
B. 190.66 ft.
C. 145.27 ft.
D. 36.85 ft.

2254. Illustration D029DG. You are using tackle number 4 to lift a weight. The hauling part of this tackle is bent to the weight hook (w) of tackle number 10. What is the mechanical advantage of this rig?

A. 4
B. 5
C. 9
D. 20

2255. Illustration D029DG. You are using tackle number 2 to lift a weight of 100 lbs. If you include 10 percent of the weight for each sheave for friction, what is the pull on the hauling part required to lift the weight?

A. 50 lbs.
B. 55 lbs.
C. 60 lbs.
D. 110 lbs.

2256. You are conducting trials to determine the maneuvering characteristics of your vessel. While making a turn, you take ranges and bearings of an isolated light with the results shown in illustration D034DG. Based on this information, what is the transfer for a turn of 180°?

A. 875 yards
B. 910 yards
C. 975 yards
D. 1015 yards

2259. Illustration D035DG. You have determined the maneuvering characteristics of your vessel by taking radar ranges and bearings of an isolated light while making a turn. The results are as shown. Based on this data what is the advance for a turn of 90°?

A. 490 yards
B. 350 yards
C. 800 yards
D. 885 yards

2261. The machinery associated with heaving in and running out anchor chain is the _____.

A. winch
B. windlass
C. draw works
D. dynamic pay out system

2264. When you "end for end" a wire rope, you _____.

A. cut off the free end and bitter end of the rope
B. splice two wire ropes together
C. remove the wire rope from the drum and reverse it so that the free end becomes the bitter end

D. remove the wire rope from the drum and turn it over, so the wire bends in the opposite direction

2265. You are conducting trials to determine the maneuvering characteristics of your vessel. While making a turn, you take ranges and bearings of an isolated light with the results shown in illustration D034DG. Based on this information, what is the transfer for a turn of 45°?

A. 130 yards
B. 165 yards
C. 195 yards
D. 230 yards

2266. Your vessel has been damaged and is partially flooded. The first step to be taken in attempting to save the vessel is to _____.

A. establish flooding boundaries and prevent further spread of flood water
B. plug the hole(s) in the outer shell
C. pump out the water inside the vessel
D. calculate the free-surface effect and lost buoyancy to determine the vessel's stability

2268. The helm command "shift your rudder" means _____.

A. check the swing of the vessel
B. double your rudder angle or go to full rudder
C. bring your rudder amidships
D. change from right rudder to left rudder, or vice versa, an equal number of degrees

2271. You are signing on a crew. You can determine the minimum number and qualifications of the crew that you are required to carry by consulting which document?

A. Crew list
B. Certificate of Inspection
C. Articles of Agreement
D. fo'c'sle card

2272. Illustration D030DG. Which knot is secure only when there is a strain on the line?

A. H
B. I
C. L
D. P

2273. What is the area of a circle with a ra-

dius of 4 feet after a sector of 111° has been removed?

A. 3.90 ft.
B. 8.67 ft.
C. 34.77 ft.
D. 50.27 ft.

2275. When inspecting wire rope before a hoisting operation, one must look for _____.

A. fishhooks
B. kinks
C. worn spots
D. All of the above

2276. Illustration D035DG. You have determined the maneuvering characteristics of your vessel by taking radar ranges and bearings of an isolated light while making a turn. The results are as shown. Based on this data what is the advance for a turn of 60°?

A. 665 yards
B. 710 yards
C. 745 yards
D. 780 yards

2279. In plugging submerged holes, rags, wedges, and other materials should be used in conjunction with plugs to _____.

A. reduce the water pressure on the hull
B. reduce the possibility of stress fractures
C. prevent progressive flooding
D. reduce the water leaking around the plugs

2280. You are conducting trials to determine the maneuvering characteristics of your vessel. While making a turn, you take ranges and bearings of an isolated light with the results shown in illustration D034DG. Based on this information, what is the advance for a turn of 45°?

A. 590 yards
B. 635 yards
C. 690 yards
D. 740 yards

2281. Your vessel has run hard aground in an area subject to heavy wave action. Backing full astern failed to free her. Which action should be taken next?

A. Continue backing to scour out the bottom.

B. Wait for high tide and then try backing.
C. Flood empty tanks to increase bottom pressure and prevent inshore creep.
D. Shift weight aft to reduce the forward draft.

2283. What is the area of a circle with a radius of 2 feet after a sector of 86° has been removed?

A. 2.39 ft.
B. 3.02 ft.
C. 9.55 ft.
D. 12.57 ft.

2284. In determining the scope of anchor line to pay out when anchoring a small boat, one must consider the _____.

A. charted depth of water only
B. depth of water, including tidal differences
C. type of line being used for the anchor rope
D. type of anchor being used

2285. While writing in the logbook at the end of your watch, you make an error in writing an entry. What is the proper way of correcting this error?

A. Remove this page of the log book and rewrite all entries on a clean page.
B. Carefully and neatly erase the entry and rewrite it correctly.
C. Blot out the error completely and rewrite the entry correctly.
D. Cross out the error with a single line, write the correct entry, and initial it.

2288. What will cause wire rope to fail?

A. Operating the winch too fast
B. Using a sheave 9 times the wire's diameter
C. Kinking
D. All of the above

2290. The sprocket teeth on a wildcat are known as the _____.

A. pawls
B. devil's claws
C. whelps
D. pockets

2291. Before a Master relieves a Pilot of the conn, the _____.

A. Master must first request the Pilot to take corrective action

B. Master should agree to sign a release of liability form
C. Master should foresee any danger to the vessel on the present course
D. vessel must be in extremis

2292. The biggest problem encountered when towing bridle legs are too short is _____.

A. retrieval
B. adjusting tension
C. excessive strain
D. hookup to main towline

2293. As defined in the regulations governing marine casualties a "marine employer" may be the _____.

A. owner
B. agent
C. Master
D. All of the above

2301. In towing, chocks are used to _____.

A. protect the towline from chafing
B. secure the end of the towline on the tug
C. stop off the towline while retrieving it
D. absorb shock loading on the towline

2302. What is NOT required to be approved or certified by the U.S. Coast Guard before being used on inspected vessels?

A. Lifesaving equipment that is in excess of the regulatory minimum
B. Ship's stores that are Class A poisons or Class A explosives
C. Steel plate used in hull construction
D. EPIRBs

2305. Which will cause a wire rope to fail?

A. Using a medium graphite grease as a lubricant
B. Operating a winch too slow
C. Using a sheave with an undersized throat
D. A sheave diameter of 24 times the wire's diameter

2315. Which splice is used to connect two separate lines together?

A. Back splice
B. Chain splice
C. Eye splice
D. Long splice

2316. A lookout can leave his/her station _____.

A. at any time
B. at the end of the watch
C. 15 minutes before the end of the watch
D. only when properly relieved

2321. Your vessel has run aground and is touching bottom for the first one-quarter of its length. What is the LEAST desirable method from the standpoint of stability to decrease the bottom pressure?

A. Discharge forward deck cargo.
B. Pump out the forepeak tank.
C. Shift deck cargo aft.
D. Flood an after double-bottom tank.

2322. Fittings used for towing must be _____.

A. Coast Guard approved
B. stamped with maximum working loads
C. securely fastened
D. positioned exactly at the bow of the towed vessel

2325. Which line cannot be spliced?

A. Braided line with a hollow core
B. Double-braided line
C. Braided line with a solid core
D. Any line can be spliced

2335. When two lines are spliced together, _____.

A. the size of the lines at the splice decreases
B. they are stronger than if knotted together
C. the overall strength of each line is increased
D. the bitter ends will resist rotting

2336. The maneuver which will return your vessel in the shortest time to a person who has fallen overboard is _____.

A. engine(s) crash astern, no turn
B. two 180° turns
C. a Williamson Turn
D. a single turn with hard rudder

2341. The grooved wheel inside a block is called a _____.

A. cheek
B. gypsy

C. sheave
D. drum

2342. How many tons of salt water can be loaded into a flat ended cylindrical tank with a diameter of 3 feet and a length of 8 feet?

A. 1.62
B. 1.98
C. 3.23
D. 6.46

2343. When securing a hook to the end of a wire rope you should use _____.

A. a bowline knot
B. a long splice
C. an overhand knot with a wire rope clip
D. wire rope clips with a thimble eye

2344. An example of an anchor which has a stock is a _____.

A. Bruce anchor
B. Dunn anchor
C. Hook anchor
D. Danforth anchor

2345. A splice that can be used in running rigging, where the line will pass through blocks, is a _____.

A. short splice
B. long splice
C. back splice
D. spindle splice

2346. What is the volume of a sphere with a radius of 11 feet?

A. 506.75 cubic ft.
B. 696.78 cubic ft.
C. 5,575.28 cubic ft.
D. 44,593.82 cubic ft.

2347. What is an advantage of having wire rope with a fiber core over that of a wire rope of the same size with a wire core?

A. Fiber core rope offers greater strength.
B. Fiber core rope offers greater flexibility.
C. Fiber core rope can be used at higher operating temperatures.
D. Fiber core rope is the only type authorized for cargo runners.

2349. What is the volume of a sphere with a radius of 7 feet?

A. 11,491.87 cubic ft.
B. 1,436.76 cubic ft.
C. 963.72 cubic ft.

D. 205.21 cubic ft.

2350. A temporary wire eye splice made with three wire rope clamps will hold approximately what percentage of the total rope strength?

A. 20%
B. 50%
C. 80%
D. 99%

2351. What is the area of a circle with a diameter of 12 feet after a sector of 86° has been removed?

A. 108.57 square ft.
B. 86.08 square ft.
C. 28.65 square ft.
D. 27.14 square ft.

2352. The recessed areas on a wildcat are called _____.

A. pawls
B. sockets
C. pockets
D. devil's claws

2353. Which mooring line prevents sideways motion of a vessel moored to a pier?

A. A line led forward from the bow
B. A line led aft from the bow
C. A line led in the same direction as the keel
D. A line led at a right angle to the keel

2354. What is the area of a circle with a diameter of 21 feet after a sector of 72° has been removed?

A. 277.09 square ft.
B. 149.43 square ft.
C. 69.27 square ft.
D. 52.78 square ft.

2355. The metal, teardrop-shaped object sometimes used within an eyesplice is a _____.

A. grommet
B. reinforcement
C. splice form
D. thimble

2356. "Hard right rudder" means _____.

A. jam the rudder against the stops
B. meet a swing to the right, then return to amidships

C. put the rudder over to the right all the way
D. put the rudder over quickly to 15 degrees right rudder

2360. Splices made in nylon should _____.

A. be long splices only
B. have extra tucks taken
C. be short splices only
D. be around a thimble

2361. The BEST information on the nature and extent of damage to the vessel is obtained from _____.

A. alarms and monitoring devices
B. the engine room watch
C. personnel at the scene of the damage
D. the bridge watch

2365. A six-strand composite rope made up of alternate fiber and wire strands around a fiber core is called _____.

A. spring lay
B. lang lay
C. cable lay
D. alternate lay

2367. What is the volume of a sphere with a radius of 5 feet?

A. 4,188.00 cubic ft.
B. 523.60 cubic ft.
C. 129.62 cubic ft.
D. 65.44 cubic ft.

2384. What is the volume of a sphere with a radius of 3 feet?

A. 113.08 cubic ft.
B. 96.57 cubic ft.
C. 37.69 cubic ft.
D. 28.23 cubic ft.

2387. What is the area of a circle with a diameter of 2 feet after a sector of 60° has been removed?

A. 0.25 square ft.
B. 0.52 square ft.
C. 2.09 square ft.
D. 2.62 square ft.

2388. What is the area of a circle with a diameter of 4 feet after a sector of 120° has been removed?

A. 2.67 square ft.

B. 4.19 square ft.
C. 8.38 square ft.
D. 10.67 square ft.

2389. What is the area of a circle with a diameter of 17 feet after a sector of 111° has been removed?

A. 36.94 square ft.
B. 156.99 square ft.
C. 226.98 square ft.
D. 627.47 square ft.

2394. Determine the area of a triangle with a base of 3.5 feet and a height of 4.0 feet.

A. 7.0 square ft.
B. 7.5 square ft.
C. 11.5 square ft.
D. 14.0 square ft.

2395. Determine the area of a triangle with a base of 4.7 feet and a height of 6.3 feet.

A. 29.6 square ft.
B. 26.2 square ft.
C. 18.5 square ft.
D. 14.8 square ft.

2396. Determine the area of a triangle with a base of 5.8 feet and a height of 2.1 feet.

A. 12.2 square ft.
B. 7.9 square ft.
C. 6.1 square ft.
D. 3.0 square ft.

2397. Determine the area of a triangle with a base of 6.7 feet and a height of 9.1 feet.

A. 61.0 square ft.
B. 30.5 square ft.
C. 22.9 square ft.
D. 15.8 square ft.

2398. How many tons of salt water can be loaded into a flat-ended cylindrical tank with a diameter of 4.5 feet and a length of 8 feet?

A. 1.82
B. 3.64
C. 7.27
D. 14.54

2399. You are standing wheel watch on entering port and the Master gives you a rudder command which conflicts with a

rudder command from the Pilot. What should you do?

A. Obey the Pilot.
B. Bring the rudder to a position midway between the two conflicting positions.
C. Ask the Pilot if he relinquishes control.
D. Obey the Master.

2400. The turning circle of a vessel is the path followed by the _____.

A. bow
B. outermost part of the ship while making the circle
C. center of gravity
D. tipping center

2450. Which statement is NOT true concerning precautions during fueling operations?

A. All engines, motors, fans, etc. should be shut down when fueling.
B. All windows, doors, hatches, etc., should be closed.
C. A fire extinguisher should be kept nearby.
D. Fuel tanks should be topped off with no room for expansion.

2451. A safety shackle is identified by its _____.

A. shape
B. pin
C. certification stamp
D. color code

2452. Which is an advantage of using watertight longitudinal divisions in double bottom tanks?

A. Cuts down free surface effect
B. Increases the rolling period
C. Decreases weight because extra stiffeners are unneeded
D. Lowers the center of buoyancy without decreasing GM

2454. You are going astern (single-screw, right-handed propeller) with the anchor down at a scope of twice the depth of the water. As the anchor dredges, you should expect the _____.

A. stern to walk to the same side as the anchor being used
B. vessel to back in a straight line
C. stern to walk to port but at a reduced rate

D. stern to walk to port at a faster rate than normal

2456. Which term describes a part of a natural fiber line?

A. Lacings
B. Lays
C. Strands
D. Twines

2459. Tripping defects in anchors frequently occur in _____.

A. deep water
B. shallow water
C. stiff soils
D. soft soils

2460. You are operating a twin-screw vessel and lose your port engine. You continue to operate on your starboard engine only. Which action would you take to move your vessel ahead in a straight line?

A. Compensate with right rudder.
B. Compensate with left rudder.
C. Surge the starboard engine.
D. Rudder amidships—no compensation is necessary on a twin-screw vessel.

2461. In writing up the logbook at the end of your watch, you make an error in writing an entry. What is the proper way of correcting this error?

A. Carefully and neatly erase the entry and rewrite it correctly.
B. Cross out the error with a single line, write the correct entry, and initial it.
C. Blot out the error completely and rewrite the entry correctly.
D. Remove this page of the log book and rewrite all entries on a clean page.

2462. Which term describes a part of a natural fiber line?

A. Twines
B. Fibers
C. Lays
D. Lacings

2464. Which term describes a part of a natural fiber line?

A. Yarns
B. Twines
C. Lacings
D. Lays

2470. Which type of bottom provides most anchors with the best holding ability?

A. Clay and rocks
B. Soft mud
C. Sandy mud
D. Soft sand

2471. To determine the number of able seamen required on an inspected vessel, you should check the _____.

A. Load Line Certificate
B. operations manual
C. Safety of Life at Sea Certificate
D. Certificate of Inspection

2474. Generally speaking, the more destructive storms occurring on the Great Lakes usually come from the _____.

A. northeast or east
B. southwest or west
C. northwest or north
D. southeast or south

2480. A Danforth lightweight anchor does NOT hold well in which type of bottom?

A. Mud
B. Grass
C. Sand
D. Clay

2489. A post on a dock or wharf used to secure mooring lines or hawsers is called a _____.

A. bitt
B. bollard
C. cleat
D. capstan

2490. The best method of protecting that portion of a fiber anchor line nearest the anchor from chafing on the bottom is by _____.

A. using a small scope ratio
B. replacing that portion with a short length of chain
C. using a hockle to keep that portion of the anchor line off the bottom
D. using a synthetic line

2492. When a tug makes up to a large vessel, the spring line should lead from the forwardmost part of the tug so that _____.

A. friction on the spring line is minimized

B. the length of the spring line is minimized
C. the head line and spring line can be worked simultaneously
D. the tug can pivot freely

2494. The major components which determine the length of a catenary in a deployed anchor cable are water depth, cable weight, and _____.

A. cable tension
B. water temperature
C. bottom conditions
D. water density

2500. Which part of an anchor actually digs into the bottom?

A. Stock
B. Fluke
C. Shank
D. Crown

2510. Mooring lines should be turned end-for-end occasionally. This is because _____.

A. a line is weakened by constantly pulling on it in one direction
B. normal wear on the line is thus distributed to different areas
C. it prevents the line from kinking or un-laying
D. it prevents permanent misalignment of the line's internal strands

2520. When a line is spirally coiled about its end and lying flat on deck, it is said to be _____.

A. coiled
B. faked
C. flemished
D. seized

2521. The period of roll is the time difference between _____.

A. zero inclination to full inclination on one side
B. full inclination on one side to full inclination on the other side
C. full inclination on one side to the next full inclination on the same side
D. zero inclination to the next zero inclination

2530. Your vessel has gone aground in waters where the tide is falling. The BEST action you can take is to _____.

A. set out a kedge anchor
B. shift the vessel's load aft and repeatedly surge the engine(s) astern
C. shift the vessel's load forward and wait until the next high tide
D. slowly bring the engine(s) to full speed astern

2533. You should attach a towline to a trailer eye bolt using a(n) _____.

A. eye splice
B. bowline
C. towing hitch
D. square knot

2534. Great Lakes vessels, using life rafts, must have sufficient life raft capacity on each side of the vessel to accommodate at least _____.

A. 50% of the persons on board
B. 100% of the persons on board
C. 100% of the persons normally assigned to those spaces
D. 150% of the crew

2536. Wages due a seaman may be attached by the court for the _____.

A. payment of any fines imposed by the court
B. payment of back taxes to the IRS
C. support of a spouse
D. All of the above

2540. In small craft terminology, all of the anchor gear between a boat and her anchor is called the _____.

A. stock
B. chock
C. scope
D. rode

2549. An example of a modern anchor which has a stock is a(n) _____.

A. articulated anchor
B. Flipper Delta anchor
C. Baldt anchor
D. Danforth anchor

2550. When a small craft's anchor fouls in a rocky bottom, the first attempt to clear it should be made by _____.

A. hauling vertically on the line
B. making the line fast to the bitt and bringing the vessel further forward

C. reversing the angle and direction of pull, with moderate scope
D. increasing the scope and running slowly in a wide circle with the anchor line taut

2552. When using a Mediterranean moor, the vessel is moored with her _____.

A. bow to the pier
B. anchors crossed
C. anchor chains forward, side to the pier
D. stern to the pier

2553. The key to rescuing a man overboard is _____.

A. good equipment
B. a dedicated crew
C. well-conducted drills
D. good communication

2558. A sling is a device used in _____.

A. hoisting cargo aboard a vessel
B. hoisting personnel aboard a vessel
C. securing a small boat to a large vessel
D. hoisting the anchor

2559. A vessel in Great Lakes service shall carry anchors in accordance with standards established by the _____.

A. American Bureau of Shipping
B. Canadian Coast Guard
C. U.S. Coast Guard
D. underwriter of the vessel

2562. As you hold a piece of manila line vertically in front of you, the strands run from the lower left to the upper right. Which type of line is this?

A. Right-hand laid
B. Cable-laid
C. Sennet-laid
D. Water-laid

2564. The major components which determine the length of catenary in a deployed anchor cable are water depth, cable tension, and _____.

A. environmental forces
B. bottom conditions
C. cable weight
D. water density

2567. When relieving the helm, the new helmsman should know the _____.

A. variation
B. gyro error
C. course per magnetic steering compass
D. maximum rudder angle previously used

2568. You are proceeding along the right bank of a narrow channel aboard a right-handed single-screw vessel. The vessel starts to sheer due to bank suction/cushion effect. You should _____.

A. stop engines and put the rudder left full
B. back full with rudder amidships
C. decrease speed and put the rudder right full
D. increase speed and put the rudder right full

2570. When a line is laid down in loose, looping figure-eights, it is said to be _____.

A. faked
B. flemished
C. coiled
D. chined

2572. A tug would NOT assist a ship to steer if the tug is made up to the large vessel _____.

A. by a tow line ahead of the vessel
B. forward on either bow of the vessel
C. approximately amidships of the vessel
D. on the vessel's quarter

2574. You are proceeding down a channel and lose the engine(s). You must use the anchors to stop the ship. Which statement is true?

A. Pay out all of the cable before setting up on the brake to insure the anchors dig in and hold.
B. For a mud, mud and clay, or sandy bottom pay out a scope of 5 to 7 times the depth before setting up on the brake.
C. Use one or both anchors with a scope of twice the depth before setting the brake.
D. Drop the anchor to short stay and hold that scope.

2580. You want to double the strength of a mooring line by using two lines. To accomplish this, the second line must _____.

A. be 1-1/2 times the diameter of the first
B. be married to the first
C. not cross the first
D. be of the same length

2581. How does the effect known as "bank suction" act on a single-screw vessel proceeding along a narrow channel?

A. It pulls the stern toward the bank.
B. It heels the vessel toward the bank.
C. It pushes the entire vessel away from the bank.
D. It pulls the bow toward the bank.

2589. The angle at which the anchor flukes penetrate the soil is the _____.

A. burial angle
B. penetration angle
C. fluke angle
D. holding angle

2590. Which method of adjusting mooring lines is MOST useful for leaving a boat free to rise and fall with the tide?

A. Crossing the spring lines
B. Slacking all forward running lines while keeping all after running lines taut
C. Doubling up on spring or breast lines
D. Slacking bow and stern lines

2591. A tow astern is veering from side to side on its towline. The best way of controlling the action is to _____.

A. trim the tow by the bow
B. trim the tow by the stern
C. list the tow to windward
D. adjust the length of the towing bridle

2595. Yawing can be described as _____.

A. jumping on the towline as the tow pitches
B. jumping on the towline as the tow slams into waves
C. veering from side to side on the end of the towline
D. corkscrew motion of the tow due to wave action

2596. A person who sees someone fall overboard should _____.

A. immediately jump into the water to assist the individual
B. call for help and keep the individual in sight
C. run to the radio room to send an emergency message
D. go to the bridge for the distress flares

2597. On a small boat, if someone fell overboard and you did not know over which side the person fell, you should _____.

A. immediately reverse the engines
B. stop the propellers from turning and throw a ring buoy over the side
C. increase speed to full to get the vessel away from the person
D. first put the rudder hard over in either direction

2598. Where, due to the arrangement of the vessel, lifejackets may become inaccessible, additional lifejackets shall be carried _____.

A. for the people on bridge watch
B. for the forward lifeboats
C. as determined by the OCMI
D. for 50% of the crew of the vessel, not including those assigned to engineering duties

2600. A smooth, tapered pin, usually of wood, used to open up the strands of a rope for splicing is called a(n)_____.

A. batten
B. bench hook
C. awl
D. fid

2601. To determine the number of inflatable life rafts required on a vessel, you should check the _____.

A. Load Line Certificate
B. SOLAS Certificate
C. Stability Letter
D. Certificate of Inspection

2602. As you hold a piece of manila line vertically in front of you, the strands run from the lower right to the upper left. Which type of line is this?

A. Plain-laid
B. Shroud-laid
C. Left-hand laid
D. Water-laid

2608. Most very large oceangoing vessels, such as bulk carriers and large tankers, tend to squat _____.

A. by the bow
B. by the stern
C. at the end nearest the bottom
D. evenly fore and aft

2612. When using the anchor to steady the bow while approaching a dock you must be aware of the fact that _____.

A. the vessel will tend to take a large sheer toward the side where the anchor is down
B. steering control is ineffective in trying to turn to the side opposite to that of the anchor being used
C. the anchor cable must never lead under the hull
D. using an offshore anchor decreases the chances of the anchor holding

2619. On the Great Lakes, the term "controlling depth" means the _____.

A. designed dredging depth of a channel constructed by the Corps of Engineers
B. minimum amount of tail water available behind a dam
C. distance in units of the chart (feet, meters or fathoms) from the reference datum to the bottom
D. least depth within the limits of the channel which restricts the navigation

2622. You must shore up the collision bulkhead due to solid flooding forward. The bulkhead approximates a triangle. The center of pressure of the shores on the bulkhead should be located _____.

A. evenly over the surface of the bulkhead
B. approximately one-half the height of the bulkhead
C. approximately one-third the height of the bulkhead
D. at the bottom of the bulkhead

2632. The horizontal flat surfaces where the upper stock joins the rudder are the _____.

A. rudder keys
B. rudder palms
C. lifting flanges
D. shoes of the rudder

2642. Which line is two-stranded, left-handed small stuff?

A. Houseline
B. Marline
C. Ratline
D. Lagline

2652. You are using the anchor to steady the bow while maneuvering. You have the proper scope of anchor cable when the _____.

A. bow is held in position with the engines coming slowly ahead
B. anchor is just touching the bottom
C. scope is not more than 5 times the depth of the water
D. cable enters the water at an angle between 60° and 85° from the horizontal

2658. A Kip is equal to _____.

A. 1000 lbs.
B. 1000 kgs.
C. 2000 lbs.
D. 2240 lbs.

2659. The shearing stresses on a ship's structure are usually greatest at _____.

A. the bow
B. the stern
C. midships
D. the ship's quarter-length points

2664. You must shore up a bulkhead due to solid flooding forward. The bulkhead approximates a rectangle. The center of pressure of the shores on the bulkhead should be located _____.

A. evenly over the surface of the bulkhead
B. approximately one-half the height of the bulkhead
C. approximately one-third the height of the bulkhead
D. at the bottom of the bulkhead

2666. On the Great Lakes, short-term fluctuations in water levels may be a result of any of the following EXCEPT _____.

A. strong winds
B. sudden changes in barometric pressure
C. seiches
D. below normal rain fall

2672. The term "scantlings" refers to the _____.

A. draft of a vessel
B. measurements of structural members
C. requirements for ship's gear
D. placement of a vessel's loadline

2674. You operate a harbor craft on inland waters exclusively. If you regularly service or contact foreign flag vessels in the course of business, which statement is TRUE?

A. Your vessel must be inspected.

B. Your crew must have identification credentials.
C. A customs official must be on board when contacting a foreign flag vessel.
D. All contacts with a foreign flag vessel must be reported to the U.S. Coast Guard.

2684. Which statement about bilge keels is CORRECT?

A. They are critical strength members and require careful design consideration.
B. They increase resistance to rolling.
C. They attach to a low stress area.
D. They provide support when the vessel is drydocked.

2688. What would have the greatest affect on a vessel's longitudinal strength?

A. Collision damage to the bow, forward of the collision bulkhead
B. Grounding damage to the bilge strake, just aft of midships
C. Extensive corrosion to the centerline deck plating
D. Damage to the side shell, midway between the bilge and the stringer plate

2692. Illustration D031DG. Your vessel is on a voyage from Ogdensburg, NY, to Chicago, IL, via the Great Lakes. The date is October 3 of the current year. If your vessel is subject to the load line requirements, to which of her marks should she be loaded?

A. Fresh water—Winter
B. Salt water—Intermediate
C. Fresh water—Intermediate
D. Salt water—Winter

2694. When relieving the helm, the new helmsman should know the _____.

A. gyro error
B. course per magnetic steering compass
C. variation
D. maximum rudder angle previously used

2696. You are on a power-driven vessel proceeding down a channel, with the current, on a river on the Great Lakes System. If you meet another power-driven vessel who is upbound, your responsibilities include _____.

A. backing down to get out of the way of the other vessel
B. waiting for the other vessel to signal her intentions, and then answering promptly

C. proposing a safe way to pass
D. All of the above

2704. The legs of a tow bridle are joined together with a _____.

A. bridle plate
B. shackle
C. fishplate
D. tri-link

2708. Illustration D031DG. Which statement is TRUE with respect to the load line markings shown?

A. A vessel displaying these marks may load in the salt waters of the St. Lawrence River.
B. Vessels engaged solely on Great Lakes voyages are not required to show these marks.
C. U.S. flag vessels less than 100 feet in length and less than 200 gross tons are not required to show these marks.
D. U.S. flag vessels of 100 gross tons and upward must show these marks.

2712. Which two Great Lakes are considered hydraulically as one?

A. Lakes Superior–Huron
B. Lakes Michigan–Huron
C. Lakes Erie–St. Clair
D. Lakes Erie–Ontario

2714. The major components which determine the length of catenary in a deployed anchor cable are cable tension, cable weight, and _____.

A. water density
B. bottom conditions
C. environmental forces
D. water depth

2716. A channel is stated as having a controlling depth of 38 feet. Which statement is TRUE?

A. At least 80% of the channel is cleared to the charted depth.
B. At least 50% of the channel is cleared to the charted depth.
C. 100% of the channel width is clear to 38 feet.
D. The sides of the channel conform to at least 50% of the controlling depth.

2718. On Great Lakes vessels, midsummer load lines apply _____.

A. April 16 through April 30 and September 16 through September 30
B. May 1 through September 15
C. July 16 through August 30
D. June 16 through September 16

2719. Which publication would give detailed information on the commercial vessel traffic reporting system for connecting waters from Lake Erie to Lake Huron?

A. United States Coast Pilot—Great Lakes #6
B. U.S. Coast Guard Light List—Vol. VII
C. Code of Federal Regulation—Title 33
D. The appropriate Great Lakes Navigation Chart

2722. "Limber" is a term associated with _____.

A. emergency gear
B. drainage
C. deck cargo storage
D. securing gear

2729. Illustration D031DG. The load line markings shown are inscribed on the vessel's _____.

A. port side
B. starboard side
C. port and starboard sides
D. stern

2732. Flanking rudders effect a vessel's heading because of the _____.

A. effect of the propeller flow on the rudders
B. water flow due to the vessel's movement through the water
C. tunnel affect of the water flow past opposing rudders
D. discharge current being channeled to impinge on the vessel's deadwood

2735. Periodic surveys to renew the load line assignment must be made at intervals NOT exceeding _____.

A. 18 months
B. two years
C. three years
D. five years

2736. Distances on the Great Lakes System are generally expressed in _____.

A. miles above the entrance to the St. Lawrence Seaway (MASLW)

B. miles above the head of the passes (AHP)
C. nautical miles
D. statute miles

2738. Assume that your vessel has just entered Lake Michigan via the Straits of Mackinac and is proceeding south to Chicago. Which statement is TRUE with respect to the aids to navigation you will encounter along this route?

A. Aids to navigation are serviced jointly by the U.S. and Canadian Coast Guards.
B. Red buoys should be passed down your starboard side.
C. Green buoys mark the location of wrecks or obstructions which must be passed by keeping the buoy on the right hand.
D. All solid colored buoys are numbered, the red buoys bearing odd numbers and green buoys bearing even numbers.

2745. While standing look-out at night, a dim light on the horizon will be seen quickest by looking _____.

A. a little above the horizon
B. directly toward the light
C. a little below the horizon
D. quickly above then quickly below the horizon

2746. Which of the Great Lakes experiences the least amount of water level fluctuation between seasonal high and low water marks?

A. Lake Huron
B. Lake Erie
C. Lake Superior
D. Lake Michigan

2752. Which is a correct reply to a Pilot's request, "How's your head"?

A. "Passing 040°"
B. "Steady"
C. "Checked"
D. "Eased to 15° rudder"

2759. Which of the Great Lakes is most affected by short-term lake level fluctuations?

A. Lake Superior
B. Lake Michigan
C. Lake Huron
D. Lake Erie

2760. When the wave period and the apparent rolling period are the same _____.

A. synchronous rolling occurs
B. roll period decreases
C. roll period increases
D. roll amplitude is dampened

2761. A short ton is a unit of weight consisting of _____.

A. 1,000 pounds
B. 2,000 pounds
C. 2,205 pounds
D. 2,240 pounds

2768. Which of the Great Lakes lies entirely within the United States?

A. Lake Ontario
B. Lake St. Clair
C. Lake Michigan
D. Lake Superior

2774. There are basically three categories of water level fluctuations on the Great Lakes. What is NOT included as one of these?

A. Long range fluctuations
B. Controlled outflow fluctuations
C. Seasonal fluctuations
D. Short period fluctuations

2776. How are aids to navigation on the Great Lakes arranged geographically?

A. In a westerly and northerly direction, except on Lake St. Clair
B. In an easterly and southerly direction, except on Lake Erie
C. In a westerly and northerly direction, except on Lake Michigan
D. In an easterly and southerly direction, except on the New York State Barge Canal

2778. Assume that your vessel has just entered Lake Erie by way of the Welland Canal and is proceeding in a southwesterly direction. Which statement about the aids to navigation you can expect to encounter along the route is TRUE?

A. The characteristics of buoys and other aids are as if "returning from seaward" when proceeding in this direction.
B. All aids are maintained by the U.S. Coast Guard, 9th Coast Guard District, Cleveland, Ohio.
C. All red even-numbered buoys should be

kept on your port side when proceeding in this direction.
D. Lighted aids, fog signals, and radiobeacons maintained by Canada are not included in the Great Lakes Light List.

2783. The effect of ocean current is usually more evident on a tug and tow than on a tug navigating independently because the _____.

A. speed of the tug and tow is less
B. towline catches the current
C. current causes yawing
D. current will offset the tow

2784. Which of the Great Lakes generally has the shortest navigation season?

A. Lake Erie
B. Lake Huron
C. Lake Michigan
D. Lake Superior

2792. When relieving the helm, the new helmsman should find it handy to know the _____.

A. variation in the area
B. amount of helm carried for a steady course
C. leeway
D. deviation on that heading

2794. The Great Lakes Edition of the Notice to Mariners is published _____.

A. weekly by the 9th Coast Guard District
B. monthly by the Army Corps of Engineers
C. monthly by the Naval Oceanographic office
D. biweekly by the Commandant, U.S. Coast Guard

2798. The primary purpose of the stud is to prevent the anchor chain from _____.

A. kinking
B. distorting
C. elongating
D. breaking

2799. Who publishes the "Canadian List of Lights, Buoys and Fog Signals"?

A. The U.S. Coast Guard
B. The Canadian Coast Guard
C. The U.S. Hydrographic Service
D. The Canadian Hydrographic Service

2802. Illustration D031DG. The single line located directly above the diamond is the _____.

A. load line
B. water line
C. freeboard line
D. deck line

2805. "Hard right rudder" means _____.

A. jam the rudder against the stops
B. put the rudder over to the right all the way
C. meet a swing to the right, then return to amidships
D. put the rudder over quickly to 15 degrees right rudder

2808. Under the forces of its own weight, the suspended length of line will fall into a shape known as a _____.

A. polygon
B. holding arc
C. catenary curve
D. parabolic curve

2810. Which document lists all the lifesaving equipment required for a vessel?

A. Certificate of Inspection
B. American Bureau of Shipping Classification Certificate
C. International Convention for the Safety of Life at Sea Certificate
D. Certificate of Registry

2812. If a tug equipped with flanking rudders is to be turned in a confined circle, when going astern, the stern will move to port the quickest if _____.

A. the rudder is hard to port and the flanking rudders are hard to port
B. the rudder is amidships and the flanking rudders are hard to port
C. the rudder is hard to port and the flanking rudders are hard to starboard
D. all rudders are hard to starboard

2814. Your vessel is crossing a river on the Great Lakes System. A power-driven vessel is ascending the river, crossing your course from port to starboard. Which statement is TRUE?

A. The vessel ascending the river has the right of way.

B. Your vessel has the right of way, but you are directed not to impede the other vessel.
C. The other vessel must hold as necessary to allow you to pass.
D. You are required to propose the manner of passage.

2816. Which statement is TRUE concerning lighting requirements for Great Lakes vessels?

A. The showing of a forward masthead light is optional for vessels under 150 meters.
B. An all-round white light may be carried in lieu of the second masthead light and sternlight.
C. Sidelights for vessels over 50 meters are required to have only a two-mile range of visibility.
D. Great Lakes vessels are exempted from the requirement to show yellow towing lights.

2817. The command "meet her" means the helmsman should _____.

A. decrease the rudder angle
B. steer more carefully
C. use rudder to slow the vessel's swing
D. note the course and steady on that heading

2819. On which of the Great Lakes would shore ice be the most pronounced?

A. Lake Michigan
B. Lake Superior
C. Lake Huron
D. Lake Erie

2822. Which statement about stopping a vessel is TRUE?

A. A lightly laden vessel requires as much stopping distance as a fully laden vessel when the current is from astern.
B. A vessel is dead in the water when the back wash from astern operation reaches the bow.
C. A tunnel bow thruster can be used in an emergency to reduce the stopping distance.
D. When a vessel is dead in the water any speed displayed by doppler log reflects the current.

2832. You are transiting the Straits of Mack-

inac by way of an improved channel. You have information which indicates that the channel's Federal project depth is 28 ft. Which of the following statements is true with regards to this channel?

A. The least depth within the limits of the channel is 28 ft.
B. The design dredging depth of the channel is 28 ft.
C. The channel has 28 ft. in the center but lesser depths may exist in the remainder of the channel.
D. The maximum depth which may be expected within the limits of the channel is 28 ft.

2836. Which of the Great Lakes is generally the last to reach its seasonal low and seasonal high water marks?

A. Lake Superior
B. Lake Michigan
C. Lake Huron
D. Lake Ontario

2848. Nautical charts published by the Canadian Hydrographic Service which are referenced in the United States Coast Pilot are identified by _____.

A. the abbreviation "can" preceding the chart number
B. the letter "C" in parentheses following the chart number
C. an asterisk preceding the chart number
D. a footnote number

2852. On a small passenger vessel the collision bulkhead is _____.

A. amidships forward of the engine room
B. just forward of the steering compartment
C. in the engine room
D. A distance of 5% to 15% of the waterline length abaft the stem measured at the load waterline

2854. The term "Great Lakes," as defined by the Inland Rules of the Road, does NOT include _____.

A. portions of the Chicago River
B. portions of the Calumet River
C. the St. Lawrence River to Trois Rivieres
D. Saginaw Bay

2855. A 150-meter vessel is proceeding

down the course of a narrow channel in the Great Lakes System. A 60-meter vessel is starting to cross the channel. Which statement is TRUE?

A. If the smaller vessel is engaged in fishing, he shall not impede the passage of the other vessel.
B. The crossing vessel has the right of way.
C. The vessel in the channel must slow to her steerageway.
D. The larger vessel is considered to be a vessel restricted in her ability to maneuver.

2858. Which characteristic is a disadvantage of a controllable-pitch propeller as compared to a fixed-pitch propeller?

A. Slightly higher fuel consumption
B. Lack of directional control when backing
C. Inefficient at high shaft RPM
D. Some unusual handling characteristics

2861. A vessel is entering port and has a Pilot conning the vessel. The Master is unsure that the Pilot is taking sufficient action to prevent a collision. What should the Master do?

A. Direct the Pilot to stop the vessel and anchor if necessary until the situation clears.
B. Recommend an alternative action and if not followed relieve the Pilot.
C. State his concerns to the Pilot but do not interfere with the handling of the vessel.
D. Nothing; the Pilot is required by law and is solely responsible for the safety of the vessel.

2870. A single-screw vessel going ahead tends to turn more rapidly to port because of propeller _____.

A. discharge current
B. suction current
C. sidewise force
D. thrust

2872. The Sheer Plan _____.

A. shows a longitudinal side elevation
B. is an endwise view of the ship's molded form
C. is usually drawn for the port side only
D. has the forebody to the right of centerline and afterbody to the left of centerline

2879. The vertical reference for all water levels and bench marks on the Great

Lakes–St. Lawrence River System is known as _____.

A. Mean Sea Level Datum
B. International Great Lakes Datum
C. Great Lakes Low Water Datum
D. North Central Reference Datum

2882. Illustration D031DG. What does the line labeled "MS" denote on the Great Lakes load line model shown?

A. Mean sea level
B. Midseason
C. Maximum submergence
D. Midsummer

2883. While you are on watch entering port, the Master gives the helmsman a rudder command which conflicts with a rudder command from the Pilot. You should make sure the helmsman _____.

A. brings the rudder to a point midway between the two conflicting positions
B. obeys the Pilot
C. asks you for instructions
D. obeys the Master

2889. What is the minimum size required before a vessel can be documented?

A. 5 net tons
B. 100 gross tons
C. 26 feet length
D. 65 feet length

2894. The term "Great Lakes," as defined by the Inland Rules of the Road, includes part of the _____.

A. Calumet River
B. Chicago River
C. St. Lawrence River
D. All of the above

2896. You are proceeding against the current on a river in the Great Lakes System. You are meeting a downbound vessel. Both vessels are power-driven. The other vessel sounds one short blast. You must _____.

A. change course to port
B. hold course and speed
C. sound three short blasts
D. sound one short blast

2902. Which basic category of water level fluctuations on the Great Lakes is the most

regular?

A. Seasonal fluctuations
B. Outflow fluctuations
C. Short-term fluctuations
D. Long-term fluctuations

2906. You are planning to anchor in an area where several anchors have been lost due to fouling. As a precaution, you should _____.

A. anchor using both anchors
B. anchor with scope of 8 or more to 1
C. use a stern anchor
D. fit a crown strap and work wire to the anchor

2910. Your vessel is a single-screw ship with a right-hand propeller. There is no current. The easiest way to make a landing is _____.

A. port side to
B. starboard side to
C. dropping anchor and swinging the ship in to the pier
D. either port or starboard side to, with no difference in degree of difficulty

2914. Your vessel has been ordered to proceed to the United Grain Growers Wharf at Thunder Bay, Lake Superior, for the purpose of taking on a load of wheat. Which publication(s) would you consult for such information as the length of the wharf, the depth of the water alongside, and the loading capacity at the facility?

A. The Navigational Chart and Light List Vol. VII
B. The International Guide to Canadian Ports and Facilities
C. The Lake Carriers Association Facilities Directory
D. The United States Coast Pilot #6

2920. You are on a large vessel fitted with a right-handed controllable-pitch propeller. When making large speed changes while decreasing pitch, which statement is TRUE?

A. You will probably have full directional control throughout the speed change.
B. You may lose rudder control until the ship's speed has dropped to correspond to propeller speed.
C. The stern will immediately slew to starboard due to unbalanced forces acting on the propeller.

D. The stern will immediately slew to port due to unbalanced forces acting on the propeller.

2922. A long pole with a hook at one end, used to reach for lines, is known as a _____.

A. pike pole
B. jack staff
C. line rod
D. hooker

2924. You are on a large vessel fitted with a right-handed controllable-pitch propeller set at maximum forward pitch. Which statement about reversing is TRUE?

A. When the pitch is reversed, the stern will slew to port even with headway.
B. The vessel will respond to the rudder until sternway is developed, then the stern will slew to starboard.
C. There will probably be a loss of steering control.
D. The vessel will have full rudder control throughout the speed change from ahead to astern.

2930. A large vessel is equipped with a controllable pitch propeller. Which statement is TRUE?

A. When dead in the water, it is often difficult to find the neutral position and slight headway or sternway may result.
B. When going directly from full ahead to full astern, there is complete steering control.
C. When the vessel has headway and the propeller is in neutral, there is no effect on rudder control.
D. When maneuvering in port, full ahead or astern power can usually be obtained without changing shaft RPM.

2932. Which type of rudder may lose its effectiveness at angles of 10 or more degrees?

A. Contra-guide
B. Balanced spade
C. Unbalanced
D. Flat plate

2933. Your vessel is to dock bow first at a pier. Which line will be the most useful when maneuvering the vessel alongside the pier?

A. Stern breast line
B. Bow spring line
C. Bow breast line
D. Inshore head line

2936. Storms that enter the Great Lakes Basin from the west and northwest at a peak in October are the products of pressure systems known as _____.

A. Northwesters
B. Alberta lows
C. Fata morgana
D. Polar highs

2938. Which statement concerning storm surges on the Great Lakes is FALSE?

A. They are common along the deeper areas of the lakes.
B. They cause rapid differences in levels between one end of the lake and the other.
C. The greatest water level difference occurs when the wind is blowing along the axis of the lake.
D. If the wind subsides rapidly, a seiche effect will most likely occur.

2939. A vessel operating on the Great Lakes, and whose position is south of an approaching eastward-moving storm center, would NOT experience _____.

A. a falling barometer
B. lowering clouds and drizzle
C. a southwest to west wind
D. rain or snow

2940. A vessel reduces speed without backing. The rate that her speed through the water decreases depends primarily on the _____.

A. vessel's horsepower
B. sea state
C. number of propellers
D. vessel's displacement

2950. In relation to the turning circle of a ship, the term "advance" means the distance _____.

A. gained at right angles to the original course
B. gained in the direction of the original course
C. moved sidewise from the original course when the rudder is first put over

D. around the circumference of the turning circle

2951. The helm command "meet her" means _____.

A. decrease the rudder angle
B. note the course and steady on that heading
C. steer more carefully
D. use rudder to check the swing

2954. An intermediate spring is _____.

A. fitted in each leg of the towing bridle
B. generally located between the "fish-plate" and the main towing hawser
C. secured at the "H" bitts
D. usually made of manila hawser

2957. Your vessel is to dock bow in at a pier without the assistance of tugboats. Which line will be the most useful when maneuvering the vessel alongside the pier?

A. Bow breast line
B. Inshore head line
C. Stern breast line
D. Bow spring line

2958. The bow thruster generally is ineffective at _____.

A. over 3 knots headway
B. at any speed astern
C. at any speed ahead
D. over 1 knot sternway

2959. A metal ring on the bottom of a block, to which the standing part of a tackle is spliced, is known as a(n) _____.

A. becket
B. loop
C. swivel
D. eye

2960. When cutting wire rope, seizings are put on each side of the cut. The seizings prevent the wire from unlaying and also _____.

A. maintain the original balance of the tension in the wires and strands
B. prevent moisture from entering between the wires at the cut end
C. forces lubricant from the core to protect the raw, cut end
D. All of the above

2964. "Seiche" is defined as a(n) _____.

A. unusually strong storm system which approaches the Great Lakes System generally from the Northeast
B. lake current which is predominant during the spring and fall navigation season on the Great Lakes
C. oscillation caused by the diminishing of forces which cause lake level fluctuations
D. higher than normal high water or lower than normal low water

2968. On the Great Lakes, winter storms compound the ice threat by bringing a variety of wind, wave, and weather problems on an average of every _____.

A. two days
B. three days
C. four days
D. five days

2969. Fog can form in any season on the Great Lakes, but it is most likely to occur over open waters in _____.

A. summer and early autumn
B. autumn and early winter
C. winter and early spring
D. spring and early summer

2970. What material may be substituted for zinc when making a poured metal socket ending to a wire rope?

A. Lead
B. Babbitt
C. Solder
D. Nothing

2981. When the anchor is brought to and holding, the horizontal component of anchor cable tensions should equal the _____.

A. displacement tonnage
B. weight forces
C. buoyancy forces
D. environmental forces

2988. You are mooring to a buoy. You should approach the buoy with the current from _____.

A. ahead
B. broad on the bow
C. abeam
D. astern

2990. When cutting regular-lay wire rope, what is the minimum number of seizings to be placed on each side of the cut?

A. One
B. Two, and three on rope diameters over 1 inch
C. Three, and more on larger diameter wire ropes
D. Four

2994. Nearly half of all storms that enter the Great Lakes Basin during the period from October through May come from _____.

A. highs which originate in the east and east-central USA
B. lows which originate in north-central and western Canada
C. highs which originate in northeastern and eastern Canada
D. lows which originate in the central and western USA

2996. Advection fog, a common occurrence on the Great Lakes, forms when _____.

A. air comes in contact with a rapidly cooling land surface
B. frigid arctic air moves across the lakes and becomes saturated
C. relatively warm air flows over cooler water
D. cool air contacts warm river currents

3013. Which will NOT reduce yawing of a tow?

A. Increasing the length of the towing hawser
B. Trimming the tow by the bow
C. Trimming the tow by the stern
D. Drogues put over the stern

3016. To obtain better steering control when you are towing alongside, your vessel should be positioned with its _____.

A. bow extending forward of the tow
B. stern amidships of the tow
C. stern extending aft of the tow
D. bow even with the bow of the tow

3018. When turning a vessel in shallow water, which statement is TRUE?

A. The rate of turn is increased.
B. The rate of turn is decreased.
C. The turning diameter increases.
D. The turning diameter remains the same.

3026. Which type of fog is the most dense and widely spread of those that occur on the Great Lakes?

A. Steam fog
B. Advection fog
C. Radiation fog
D. Lake effect fog

3028. The term "inland waters," as defined in the Rules of the Road, includes _____.

A. the Great Lakes in their entirety
B. the Mississippi River System
C. U.S. waters out to three miles offshore
D. the St. Lawrence River to Anticosti Island

3031. Before a Master relieves a Pilot of the conn, the _____.

A. vessel must be in extremis
B. Master must request the Pilot to take corrective action
C. Master should release the Pilot from all liability
D. Master should foresee any danger to the vessel on the present course

3032. Ice is often strong enough to halt navigation through the St. Lawrence Seaway by mid- _____.

A. October
B. November
C. December
D. January

3044. When you have a tow alongside, your stern should extend aft of the tow in order to _____.

A. avoid obscuring your stern light
B. provide a better lead for your lines
C. obtain better steering control
D. let the barge deflect floating objects from your propeller

3047. When backing down with sternway, the pivot point of a vessel is _____.

A. about one-quarter of the vessel's length from the stern
B. at the bow
C. about one-third of the vessel's length from the bow
D. aft of the propellors

3048. The proximity of pack ice may be indicated by _____.

A. changes in seawater salinity
B. glare on clouds on the horizon
C. changes in air temperature
D. icebergs

3054. The phenomenon known as a "seiche" is most likely to occur on Lake Erie _____.

A. during the passage of a rapidly moving warm front
B. when strong winds from the Northeast suddenly diminish
C. during the months of May through August
D. when the Moon and Sun are in alignment

3056. Advection fog holds longest over which portions of the lakes?

A. Northwest
B. Southeast
C. Northeast
D. Southwest

3067. A lashing used to secure two barges side by side, lashed in an "X" fashion, is called a _____.

A. face wire
B. cross wire
C. scissor wire
D. breast wire

3073. You are on a large merchant vessel entering a U.S. port. There is a Pilot on board and he has the conn. Which statement is TRUE?

A. The Pilot becomes solely responsible for the safe navigation of the vessel only if the Master relinquishes the conn.
B. The Pilot is solely responsible for the safe maneuvering of the ship only if he is required to be on board by law.
C. The Master is responsible for the safe navigation of the ship and the Pilot is employed for his local knowledge.
D. The Pilot is solely responsible for the internal working of the ship.

3074. In securing a towing cable, consideration must be given to letting go in an emergency. The possible whip of towlines when released can be overcome by _____.

A. increasing the shaft RPM prior to release
B. using a pelican hook for quick release
C. using preventers

D. using a short chain for the lead through the stern chock

3076. Illustration D038DG. The part of the anchor indicated by the letter K is the _____.

A. crown
B. ring
C. shank
D. bending shot

3082. Which statement is FALSE with regards to the Great Lakes Light List?

A. The Light List does not contain information on any of the navigational aids maintained by Canada.
B. Volume VII does not include information on Class III private aids to navigation.
C. The Light List does not include Coast Guard mooring buoys, special purpose buoys, or buoys marking fish net areas.
D. The Light List should be corrected each week from the appropriate Notice to Mariners.

3083. You are signing on crew members. The minimum number of people required aboard, and the qualifications of each, is listed on the _____.

A. fo'c'sle card
B. Crew list
C. Articles of Agreement
D. Certificate of Inspection

3088. A "check" line is _____.

A. a safety line attached to a man working over the side
B. used to measure water depth
C. used to slow the headway of a barge
D. used to measure the overhead height of a bridge

3091. Towlines should be inspected for chafing where the towline _____.

A. passes over the stern of the towing vessel
B. passes through chocks
C. is attached to the disabled vessel
D. All of the above

3092. Illustration D024DG. Item A is the _____.

A. lashing
B. drag wire

C. scissor wire
D. tandem wire

3094. Your vessel is underway and approaching an overhead obstruction on Lake Superior. Given the following information, determine the clearance between your vessel and the obstruction. Highest point on vessel: 74 ft. Lowest point of obstruction: 126 (LWD) Monthly lake level: +2 (LWD) International Great Lakes Datum: 600.0 (182.88 meters)

A. 474 feet
B. 400 feet
C. 175 feet
D. 50 feet

3095. You are standing the wheelwatch when you hear the cry, "Man overboard starboard side." You should be ready to _____.

A. give full left rudder
B. put the rudder amidships
C. give full right rudder
D. throw a life ring to mark the spot

3098. A weight of 1,000 short tons is equivalent to _____.

A. 1,500 foot-pounds
B. 2,240 long tons
C. 2,000 pounds
D. 2,000 kips

3099. A lashing used to secure two barges side by side, lashed in an "X" fashion, is called a _____.

A. quarter line
B. back line
C. peg line
D. jockey line

3100. A holder of a license as Master of towing vessels may work each 24 hours for a period not to exceed _____.

A. 6 hours
B. 12 hours
C. 18 hours
D. 24 hours

3102. When hip towing, a line led from the stern of the towboat forward to the barge provides the towing pull when _____.

A. going ahead
B. dead in the water

C. in a following current
D. backing

3104. When maneuvering a heavy barge up a wide channel with a tug, the tow may be most closely controlled by making up to the barge _____.

A. with a short tow astern
B. nearly bow to bow, at a small angle
C. amidships, parallel to the barge
D. nearly stern to stern, at a small angle to the barge

3109. When hip towing, a line led from the bow of the towing vessel aft to the vessel being towed would be a _____.

A. backing line
B. towing line
C. stern line
D. breast line

3111. While the Pilot is maneuvering the vessel to a dock, what is the PRIMARY responsibility of the watch officer?

A. Insure that helm and throttle orders given by the Pilot are correctly executed.
B. Judge the appropriateness of the Pilot's orders and countermand them if necessary.
C. Supervise the signaling and flag etiquette.
D. Record the bells and their times in the bell book.

3114. Illustration D024DG. Which item is rigged to transmit the thrust from one barge to another barge when going ahead?

A. I
B. H
C. E
D. B

3122. When a tug is "in irons," she _____.

A. is made fast to the dock with engines secured
B. is in dry dock
C. may be in danger of being overrun by her tow
D. should pay out more towline

3130. What is NOT required on an uninspected towing vessel?

A. Certificate of Documentation
B. Certificate of Inspection
C. Operators Merchant Marine license
D. FCC Station License

3132. What may prevent a tug from tripping or capsizing when towing a large vessel?

A. Surge lines
B. Norman pins
C. Under riders
D. Safety shackles

3138. When pushing ahead, wires leading from the quarters of the after outboard barges to the bow of a towboat _____.

A. prevent the towboat from sliding when the rudder is moved
B. prevent the barges from spreading out when backing down
C. hold the towboat securely to the barges
D. prevent the sidewise movement of the face barges

3142. Why are stern towing bitts placed well forward of the rudder when hawser towing?

A. To keep the hawser from fouling the rudder
B. To keep the towing bitts as far away as possible from the tugs pivoting point
C. To allow the stern to swing more freely when using rudder
D. To have as much of the towing hawser in use as possible

3148. Illustration D038DG. The part of the anchor indicated by the letter H is the _____.

A. fluke
B. shank
C. tripping palm
D. crown

3152. The danger of a towing vessel tripping is increased the closer the towline is secured to _____.

A. the stern
B. amidships
C. the bow
D. the quarter

3162. When maneuvering from pull towing to breasted (alongside) towing, a twin-

screw vessel is more likely than a single-screw vessel of equal horsepower to _____.

A. trip or capsize
B. foul the towline
C. go into irons
D. part the towing strap

3165. When steering a vessel, a good helmsman does NOT _____.

A. consider steering a vessel a highly responsible job
B. use as much rudder as possible to keep the vessel on course
C. use as little rudder as possible to keep the vessel on course
D. advise his relief of the course being steered

3168. Illustration D024DG. Which item is rigged to transmit the thrust from one barge to another when backing down?

A. I
B. H
C. C
D. B

3176. Illustration D038DG. The part of the anchor indicated by the letter G is the

_____.

A. fluke
B. shank
C. tripping palm
D. crown

3180. A license issued by the U.S. Coast Guard for Master of Towing Vessels is valid for _____.

A. 2 years and must be renewed
B. 3 years and must be renewed
C. 5 years and must be renewed
D. life and need not be renewed

3200. A license issued by the U.S. Coast Guard for apprentice mate (steersman) of Uninspected Towing Vessels is valid for

_____.

A. 2 years and must be renewed
B. 3 years and must be renewed
C. 5 years and must be renewed
D. None of the above

3201. You are on watch entering port, and the Master gives the helmsman a rudder command which conflicts with a rudder command from the Pilot. You should make sure the helmsman _____.

A. obeys the Pilot
B. asks you for instructions
C. obeys the Master
D. brings the rudder to a point midway between the two conflicting positions

3204. What term indicates the immersed body of the vessel forward of the parallel mid-body?

A. Run
B. Flare
C. Entrance
D. Sheer

3218. The term "bollard pull" refers to a towing vessel's _____.

A. propulsion horsepower available
B. pulling ability at cruise power
C. towing winch capability
D. pulling ability under static conditions

3220. If you are guilty of failure to properly perform your duties as Master of Unin-spected Towing Vessels, which of the following actions may NOT be taken?

A. Issuance of a letter of warning
B. Suspension of your license
C. Revocation of your license
D. A fine placed against your license

3234. Rolling is angular motion of the vessel about what axis?

A. Longitudinal
B. Transverse
C. Vertical
D. Centerline

3239. Which term indicates the rise in height of the bottom plating from the plane of the base line?

A. Deadrise
B. Camber
C. Molded height
D. Sheer

3242. What term indicates the line drawn at the top of the flat plate keel?

A. Base line
B. Molded line
C. Designer's waterline
D. Keel line

3244. Illustration D038DG. The shank is indicated by which letter?

A. K
B. J
C. H
D. F

3248. The rope which is the lightest is _____.

A. manila
B. nylon
C. polypropylene
D. Dacron

3250. You are operator of a towing vessel which collides with a buoy and drags it off station. What should you do if the damage to your vessel is not serious?

A. If the buoy is afloat, no action is necessary.
B. Wait one week and submit form CG-2692 to the nearest Coast Guard Marine Safety or Inspection Office.
C. Immediately notify the nearest Coast

Guard Marine Safety or Inspection Office and no further action is necessary.

D. Immediately notify the nearest Coast Guard Marine Safety or Inspection Office and then submit form CG-2692.

3260. When underway with a tow, you must notify the Coast Guard of which casualty?

A. Damage to property amounting to $1,500
B. Loss of bridge-to-bridge radio capability
C. An injury requiring first aid
D. Loss of main propulsion

3262. Fracture damage to the end links of the anchor cable, or to the Jews' harp may be eliminated by _____.

A. using a small diameter connecting shackle
B. ensuring the swivel is well lubricated and free to turn
C. installing the connecting shackle with the bow toward the anchor
D. securing a piece of wood to the Jews' harp

3269. What provides little or no indication that a vessel is dragging?

A. Changing range to an object abeam
B. Drift lead with the line tending forward
C. The cable alternately slackening and then tightening
D. Changing bearing to a fixed distant object abeam

3270. A vessel is tide rode when it is _____.

A. carrying extra rudder to compensate for the current
B. necessary to adjust the course steered to allow for the current
C. at anchor and stemming the current
D. being forced off of a pier by the hydraulic effect of the current

3282. What term indicates the immersed body of the vessel aft of the parallel mid-body?

A. Run
B. Stern
C. Counter
D. Flow

3288. The angular movement of a vessel about a horizontal line drawn from its bow to its stern is _____.

A. pitching
B. rolling
C. heaving
D. swaying

3291. The riding pawl is _____.

A. a safety interlock in a cargo winch that prevents the runner from overspeeding
B. a stopper that prevents the anchor cable from running free if the cable jumps the wildcat
C. the device that locks the deck lashings of the Peck and Hale system
D. the lug that rides on the eccentric rib and engages the locking ring on the windlass

3292. The forecastle card is a(n) _____.

A. unlicensed shipping card from the union
B. quarters allocation
C. copy of the shipping agreement
D. station bill

3294. Your vessel is to dock bow in at a pier without the assistance of tugboats. Which line will be the most useful when maneuvering the vessel alongside the pier?

A. Bow breast line
B. Stern breast line
C. Bow spring line
D. Inshore head line

3300. You are heading into the sea during rough weather. Having too much weight forward can cause your small boat to _____.

A. broach
B. plunge into the wave
C. rise rapidly over the wave
D. list

3308. What term indicates a curvature of the decks in a longitudinal direction?

A. Deadrise
B. Camber
C. Sheer
D. Flare

3309. Catenary as applied to tow lines denotes the _____.

A. dip of the line
B. stretch of the line
C. strain on the line
D. length of the line

3320. Which type of bottom is best suited for holding an anchor of a small boat?

A. Mud and clay
B. Rocky
C. Sandy
D. Gravel

3321. By law, the maximum penalty for failing (without reasonable cause) to give aid in the case of collision is _____.

A. one year imprisonment or $500
B. two years imprisonment or $500
C. two years imprisonment or $1000
D. two years imprisonment or $2000

3322. Illustration D038DG. The fluke is indicated by which letter?

A. F
B. G
C. H
D. I

3324. What descriptive term indicates that the dimension is measured from the inner face of the shell or deck plating?

A. Molded
B. Register
C. Tonnage
D. Effective

3325. Flammable liquids should have what kind of label?

A. Skull and crossbones
B. Yellow
C. Red
D. White

3327. The upward slope of a vessels bottom from the keel to the bilge is called _____.

A. camber
B. sheer
C. rake
D. rise of bottom

3328. The vertical motion of a floating vessel is known as _____.

A. surge
B. sway
C. heave
D. yaw

3330. When towing astern, chafing gear should NOT be used on a hawser which is _____.

A. attached to an "H" bitt
B. attached to an automatic towing engine
C. held amidships by a gob rope
D. connected to a swivel

3338. What is used to prevent wear on towlines that bear on hard surfaces?

A. Chafing gear
B. Chocks
C. Grease
D. Boots

3339. Pitching is angular motion of the vessel about what axis?

A. Longitudinal
B. Transverse
C. Vertical
D. Centerline

3340. It is NOT advisable to use nylon for alongside towing because it _____.

A. stretches too much
B. is too difficult to make fast

C. parts too readily
D. is too susceptible to mildew

3342. Which term refers to a transverse curvature of the deck?

A. Deadrise
B. Camber
C. Freeboard
D. Flare

3346. When connecting the tow bridle to a tug, the end of the bridle is passed with a _____.

A. heaving line
B. shot line
C. high line
D. messenger line

3347. The opening in the deck beneath the anchor windlass that leads to the chain locker is the _____.

A. hawsepipe
B. fallpipe
C. drop-pipe
D. spill pipe

3350. It is not advisable to use nylon for alongside towing because it _____.

A. stretches too much
B. is too expensive for everyday towing usage
C. binds on the cleats
D. parts too readily

3360. On a light tow, what could you substitute for a fishplate?

A. heart-shaped shackle
B. pelican hook
C. swivel
D. ring

3370. In astern towing, a tow span, also called the "tow bar" or "towing arch," is used to _____.

A. insure that the hawser leads directly aft as it passes over the stern of the towing vessel
B. increase the stability of the towing vessel by raising the hawser off the deck
C. reduce chafing of the towing hawser
D. prevent fouling of the hawser on deck gear located on the stern of the towing vessel

3372. The lead of a tow bridle is usually redirected with a _____.

A. bollard
B. chock
C. padeye
D. devil's claw

3374. Angular motion about the longitudinal axis of a vessel is known as _____.

A. pitch
B. surge
C. sway
D. roll

3378. Illustration D038DG. The part of the anchor indicated by the letter F is the _____.

A. shank
B. bar
C. stock
D. shot

3390. When towing, a tow hook is used to _____.

A. provide quick release of the hawser
B. pull a tow alongside
C. attach a hawser to a tow which has no bitts or padeyes
D. join two hawsers for lengthening a tow

3392. What term indicates the midships portion of a vessel that has a constant cross section?

A. Half length
B. Amidships
C. Middle body
D. Molded length

3394. Illustration D038DG. The crown is indicated by which letter?

A. K
B. J
C. H
D. G

3395. The holding power of an anchor at a given scope of cable increases when the _____.

A. amount of chain lying along the bottom increases
B. length of the catenary is reduced
C. mooring line tension is increased
D. amount of chain lying along the bottom decreases

3396. A tow that veers to the side on the end of the towline is said to _____.

A. yaw
B. surge
C. sway
D. swing

3400. In a tow made up astern, the fishplate _____.

A. connects the hawser to the bridle
B. connects the bridle to the tow
C. keeps the hawser amidships on the tug
D. is the capping piece on the "H" bitt

3411. When steering a vessel, a good helmsman does NOT _____.

A. consider steering a vessel a highly responsible job
B. use as little rudder as possible to maintain course
C. use as much rudder as possible to keep the vessel on course
D. advise his relief of the course being steered

3420. A face line is used to _____.

A. prevent barge movement in a lock
B. secure two barges end-to-end
C. secure barges to the towboat
D. secure barges side-by-side

3432. A vessel is wind rode when it is _____.

A. at anchor and heading into the wind
B. backing into the wind
C. carrying lee rudder
D. necessary to apply a leeway correction to the course

3434. The Scharnow turn should be used in a man overboard situation only when _____.

A. the man can be kept in sight from the bridge while maneuvering
B. the turn is started immediately when the man goes over
C. there has been sufficient time elapsed since the man went over to complete the maneuver

D. the vessel has twin screws to assist in making the turn

3438. One advantage of chain over wire rope for a tow bridle is that chain _____.

A. is better suited for inland towing
B. resists damage from chafing
C. handles more easily
D. equalizes towing forces better

3439. Horizontal fore or aft motion of a vessel is known as _____.

A. pitch
B. surge
C. sway
D. roll

3440. The circular steel structure installed around the propeller of a towboat is the _____.

A. nozzle
B. shroud
C. strut
D. hood

3442. Illustration D038DG. The part of the anchor indicated by the letter J is the _____.

A. crown
B. shank
C. bill
D. tip

3447. The best method to secure a tow line to a cleat is to _____.

A. take a turn around the cleat, then figure-eights, and a half-hitch
B. make figure-eights, followed by a half-hitch, then a figure-eight knot
C. take a turn, a half turn, and a figure-eight
D. take several turns around the cleat only

3448. When inspecting ground tackle, fractures are most frequently found in the _____.

A. anchor shank
B. end links
C. swivel
D. fluke

3449. What term indicates an inward curvature of the ship's hull above the waterline?

A. Camber
B. Tumble home
C. Deadrise
D. Flare

3450. Kort nozzles are installed around the propellers of some vessels to _____.

A. increase the thrust of the propeller
B. protect the propeller from striking sawyers
C. prevent the propeller from striking barges towed on the hip
D. prevent the propeller from touching bottom in low water

3452. A drift lead indicates that the vessel is dragging anchor when the line is _____.

A. taut and leading forward
B. slack
C. leading out perpendicular to the centerline
D. leading under the hull

3456. The vertical movement of a vessel in the water is called _____.

A. pitch
B. sway
C. heave
D. roll

3459. Illustration D038DG. The pea is indicated by which letter?

A. J
B. H
C. G
D. F

3460. You would NOT secure a line to a _____.

A. kevel
B. stand pipe
C. button
D. timber head

3462. Under U.S. law, what is the penalty for assaulting the Master?

A. Fine of not more than $1000
B. Fine of not more than $500 and/or imprisonment for not more than 1 year
C. Imprisonment for not more than 2 years
D. Revocation of the Merchant Mariner's Document (and license if applicable)

3463. Deckhands onboard towing vessels shall be divided into 3 watches when the trip exceeds _____.

A. 1000 miles
B. 800 miles
C. 700 miles
D. 600 miles

3464. The ultimate or maximum strength of a wire rope is referred to as the _____.

A. operating strength
B. working load
C. breaking strength
D. lifting load

3465. Illustration D038DG. Which type of anchor is illustrated?

A. Stockless
B. Danforth
C. Old-fashioned
D. Kedge

3466. What is a spill pipe?

A. A drainage pipe that carries rain or spray from an upper deck to a lower deck
B. A pipe under the anchor windlass leading to the chain locker
C. A chute, usually over the stern, to lead dumped garbage clear of the hull
D. An opening in the deck leading outside the hull

3476. The strongest method of forming an eye in wire rope is using _____.

A. three wire rope clamps
B. an eye splice with four or five tucks
C. a thimble fastened with four or five tucks
D. a wire rope socket attached with zinc

3484. You are on watch and see a man fall overboard. Which man-overboard turn should NOT be used in this situation?

A. Scharnow
B. Single
C. Racetrack
D. Williamson

3487. The opening in the deck that leads the anchor cable outside the hull is the _____.

A. hawsepipe
B. fall pipe

C. drop-pipe
D. spill pipe

3488. Angular motion about the vertical axis of a vessel is called _____.

A. yaw
B. surge
C. sway
D. roll

3490. A device used to tighten up remaining slack in wire rope when you are making up to a tow in inland waters is a _____.

A. tripping line
B. tripping bracket
C. norman pin
D. steamboat ratchet

3492. The Master of a passenger vessel which is not required to maintain an Official Logbook must keep a record of the number of passengers received and delivered from day to day. This record must be available for a period of _____.

A. 6 months
B. 12 months
C. 24 months
D. 36 months

3494. Nylon rope is often used in the make-up of a towline because it _____.

A. floats
B. stretches
C. handles easily
D. resists rot

3500. Small hull leaks can be temporarily repaired by _____.

A. parceling
B. parbuckling
C. caulking
D. seizing

3501. What must be accurately determined to assess the potential for progressive flooding after a vessel has been damaged?

A. The integrity of the water tight boundaries
B. The capacity of the water sprinkler systems
C. The operation of the machinery space bilge level alarms
D. All of the above

3502. The point that is halfway between the forward and after perpendicular and is a reference point for vessel construction is the _____.

A. half length
B. mid-body
C. center line
D. amidships

3504. Metal plates that cover the top of the hawsepipe are called _____.

A. footings
B. plugs
C. buckler plates
D. stop waters

3508. A situation has occurred in which your vessel must be towed. When the towing vessel passes the towing line to you, you should secure the line _____.

A. to the base of the foremast
B. to the forward-most bitts
C. to the forward part of the deckhouse
D. at the stern

3511. The wheel on the windlass with indentations for the anchor chain is the _____.

A. grabber
B. wildcat
C. locking ring
D. pawl

3514. Illustration D038DG. Which type of anchor is depicted?

A. Stock
B. Danforth
C. Patent
D. Old-fashioned

3518. A tug's horsepower available at the shaft is _____.

A. indicated horsepower
B. brake horsepower
C. dynamic horsepower
D. net horsepower

3519. Strengthening damaged bulkheads by using wood or steel is called _____.

A. bracing
B. battening
C. blocking
D. shoring

3520. A situation has occurred where it becomes necessary for you to be towed. What action should be taken to prevent your vessel from yawing?

A. Shift weight to the bow
B. Shift weight to the center of the boat
C. Shift weight to the stern
D. Throw excess weight overboard

3521. Once a towline is connected between the towing vessel and the disabled vessel, the towing vessel should _____.

A. not exceed bare steerageway during the transit
B. take a strain as soon as you can to control the tow
C. come up to speed very slowly and maintain a "safe speed"
D. come up to speed quickly, then cut back power considerably to ease the strain

3530. Which is NOT a duty of a look-out?

A. Refuse to talk to others, except as required by duty.
B. Remain standing during your watch.
C. Report every sighting.
D. Supervise any deck work going on in the area.

3540. While on duty as a look-out, which other duty may you perform?

A. Sweep down the fo'c'sle
B. Paint any area near your station
C. Overhaul a block, as long as it is at your look-out station
D. None of the above

3544. Wire rope should be renewed when the _____.

A. outer wires are rusted
B. outer wires are worn to half their original diameter
C. inner core appears dry
D. certification period expires

3550. When can a look-out leave his duty station?

A. 15 minutes before the end of the watch
B. At the end of the watch
C. When properly relieved
D. At any time

3556. The choice of length of tow bridle legs is governed by the _____.

A. expected towing forces
B. capability of retrieving gear
C. freeboard of the unit being towed
D. need to reduce yaw

3560. What should look-outs report?

A. Discolored water
B. Shoals
C. Floating objects
D. All of the above

3561. A holder of a license as Operator of Uninspected Towing Vessels may work each 24 hours for a period not to exceed _____.

A. 24 hours
B. 18 hours
C. 12 hours
D. 6 hours

3564. The angle at which the fluke penetrates the soil is called the _____.

A. tripping angle
B. fluke angle
C. penetration angle
D. holding angle

3565. The safety stopper that prevents the anchor cable from running free if the cable jumps the wildcat is the _____.

A. riding pawl
B. devil's claw
C. buckler plate
D. spill pipe

3570. As look-out, you spot an object 45° off your port bow. You should report the object as _____.

A. broad on the port bow
B. 3 points on the port bow
C. 3 points forward of the port beam
D. on the port beam

3576. Heave is motion along the _____.

A. longitudinal axis
B. transverse axis
C. vertical axis
D. centerline axis

3580. You are standing the wheelwatch on entering port and the Master gives you a rudder command which conflicts with a rudder command from the Pilot. What should you do?

A. Obey the Master.
B. Obey the Pilot.
C. Bring the rudder to a position midway between the two conflicting orders.
D. Ask the Pilot if he relinquishes control.

3584. Illustration D038DG. The tripping palm is indicated by which letter?

A. F
B. G
C. H
D. J

3586. The last shot of an anchor cable is usually painted _____.

A. white
B. international orange
C. yellow
D. red

3587. Following a serious marine incident, a device to test an individual's breath can be used by _____.

A. any individual trained to conduct such tests
B. the marine employer
C. qualified medical personnel only
D. any USCG licensed deck officer

3588. Conventional anchors are least likely to hold in a bottom consisting of _____.

A. soft clay
B. hard mud
C. sand
D. rock

3590. When steering a vessel, a good helmsman does NOT _____.

A. use as much rudder as possible to maintain course
B. consider steering a vessel a highly responsible job
C. use as little rudder as possible to maintain course
D. advise his relief of the course being steered

3599. What term indicates the outward curvature of the hull above the waterline?

A. sheer
B. tumble home
C. deadrise
D. flare

3600. A helmsman receives the command "Right 15 degrees rudder." The helmsman's IMMEDIATE reply should be _____.

A. "Aye Aye Sir"
B. "Right 15 degrees rudder"
C. "Rudder is right 15 degrees"
D. No reply is necessary, just carry out the order

3602. What is the penalty for desertion?

A. Fine of not more than 2000 dollars and forfeiture of wages
B. Imprisonment for not more than 2 years and/or a fine of not more than 2000 dollars
C. Revocation of Merchant Mariner's Document (and license if applicable) and forfeiture of wages due
D. Forfeiture of money and property left on the vessel, and wages due

3604. Illustration D038DG. The Jews' harp is indicated by which letter?

A. K
B. J
C. H
D. F

3606. A spreader bar is used to _____.

A. increase the lifting capacity
B. increase the lifting radius
C. protect the slings
D. protect the upper part of a load

3608. The horizontal port or starboard movement of a vessel is called _____.

A. yaw
B. sway
C. surge
D. heave

3614. While you are on watch, you learn that a crewman has not been seen on board for the past three hours. Which type of turn is best in this man-overboard situation?

A. Round
B. Scharnow
C. Racetrack
D. Single turn of 180°

3616. A tug in irons is _____.

A. rudder bound
B. being tripped by the towline
C. unable to maneuver
D. broached

3631. The number of certificated able seamen and lifeboatmen required on board is listed in the _____.

A. Certificate of Inspection
B. American Bureau of Shipping code
C. station bill
D. Safety of Life at Sea Convention

3644. You are drifting in calm water, there is no current. As a rule, your vessel will lie _____.

A. bow to the wind
B. beam to the wind
C. stern to the wind
D. with the wind on the quarter

3645. Conventional anchors are least likely to hold in a bottom consisting of _____.

A. soft clay
B. hard mud
C. very soft mud
D. sand

3654. Horizontal transverse motion of a vessel is known as _____.

A. pitch
B. surge
C. sway
D. heave

3662. Unless extremely flexible wire rope is used, the sheave diameter should always be as large as possible, but should never be less than _____.

A. 20 times the rope diameter
B. 10 times the rope diameter
C. 2 times the rope diameter
D. the rope diameter

3681. While you are on watch entering port, the Master gives the helmsman a rudder command which conflicts with a rudder command from the Pilot. You should make sure the helmsman _____.

A. obeys the Pilot
B. obeys the Master
C. asks you for instructions

D. brings the rudder to a point midway between the two conflicting positions

3684. In towing, heaving lines are used for _____.

A. passing a tow bridle to the tug
B. passing a messenger line
C. heaving in the tow bridle
D. service lines with rocket line throwers

3686. If the towline parts, you should_____.

A. start towing by pushing ahead
B. abandon the towing vessel
C. retrieve the tow bridle
D. relieve strain on the retrieving line

3689. The wildcat is linked to the central drive shaft on most windlasses by _____.

A. an electromagnetic brake
B. a hydraulic coupling
C. aligning the keyways on both and inserting a key
D. a mechanical coupling where lugs engage detents

3690. Illustration D038DG. The part of the anchor indicated by the letter I is the _____.

A. tripping palm
B. fluke
C. bill
D. stock

3692. What provides little or no indication that a vessel is dragging anchor?

A. Increasing radar range to a fixed object ahead
B. Drift lead with the line leading perpendicular to the centerline
C. Vibrations felt by placing a hand on the cable
D. Changing bearings to distant fixed objects abeam

3693. When the Pilot is embarked he or she _____.

A. relieves the Master of his duties
B. is solely responsible for the safe navigation of the vessel
C. is a specialist hired for his or her local navigational knowledge
D. relieves the officer of the watch

3694. Your enrolled vessel is bound from Baltimore, MD, to Norfolk, VA, via Chesapeake Bay. Which statement about the required pilot is TRUE?

A. The pilot must be licensed by Virginia or Maryland.
B. The Pilot must be licensed by either Virginia or Maryland.
C. The Pilot must be licensed by Virginia, Maryland and the Coast Guard.
D. The Pilot need only by licensed by the Coast Guard.

3710. A new crewman reports on board. He must be trained in the use of the ship's lifesaving appliances within what time period?

A. 2 months
B. 1 month
C. 2 weeks
D. Before sailing

3719. Besides saving distance along the track line, another advantage of the Scharnow Turn over the Williamson Turn in a man overboard situation is because _____.

A. it is faster
B. it can be used in both the immediate action and the delayed action situations
C. in fog, if the turn is started as soon as the man goes over, the vessel will be at the point where he went over when the turn is completed
D. it returns the vessel to the original track line on a reciprocal course

3722. The next-to-last shot of an anchor cable is usually painted _____.

A. white
B. international orange
C. yellow
D. red

3724. What part of the ground tackle is the most likely to develop fractures due to extensive anchor use?

A. Anchor shank
B. Swivel
C. Jews' harp
D. Fluke

3728. The main reason a long towline is used during an ocean tow is that _____.

A. a margin of safety is provided should the line part

B. the towline will wear more evenly
C. there will be less stress on the towline
D. a slight increase in speed will be realized

3740. Instructions to the crew in the use of all the ship's lifesaving equipment shall be completed _____.

A. before sailing
B. within one week of sailing
C. in one month and repeated quarterly
D. within any two-month period

3742. It is good practice to use long towlines for ocean tows because the _____.

A. wear on the towline is equalized
B. weight of the towline increases the towing force
C. dip in the towline absorbs shock loads
D. danger of overriding is reduced

3790. The locking pin that joins the parts of a detachable link is held in position by _____.

A. a tack weld
B. the self-locking characteristics of its taper
C. a cotter pin
D. a lead plug

3820. When making a Scharnow turn, the _____.

A. rudder must be put over toward the side the man went over
B. initial turn direction is away from the side the man went over
C. rudder is put hard over and the initial turn is maintained until about 240° from the original course
D. man overboard must be not more than 300 feet astern when starting the turn

3960. The line with the most stretch is _____.

A. manila
B. nylon
C. polypropylene
D. Dacron

3982. Fairleads perform the same function as _____.

A. deadeyes
B. bollards
C. bitts
D. chocks

4009. What is used to prevent twisting of a towing bridle?

A. A bitt
B. A bulkhead
C. A V-spring
D. A fishplate

4011. Under defense plans, operation of electronic aids may be temporarily suspended with _____.

A. thirty (30) day's notice
B. a week's notice
C. one day's notice
D. no notice

4012. Illustration D024DG. The purpose of item G is to _____.

A. distribute the vessel's thrust over a wider area
B. prevent the towboat from capsizing if item I should part
C. prevent the knee from shifting when the rudder is put hard over
D. keep the barges from shifting fore and aft

4013. What is the minimum size required before a vessel can be documented?

A. 26 feet, end-to-end over the deck excluding sheer
B. 100 gross tons
C. 5 net tons
D. 26 feet between perpendiculars

4014. Illustration D024DG. The facewire refers to item _____.

A. I
B. H
C. B
D. A

4016. Which statement is TRUE concerning weather conditions on the Great Lakes?

A. When a vessel is south of an eastward-moving storm center, the approach of the low is evidenced by winds from the north to northeast.
B. When a vessel is north of an eastward-moving storm center, changes in the weather are less distinctive than when sailing south of the center.
C. The most destructive storms usually come from the northwest or north.

D. Thunderstorms are most likely to develop from November through April.

4018. The BEST holding ground for conventional anchors is _____.

A. sand
B. very soft mud
C. shale
D. rock

4026. Illustration D024DG. One of the greatest hazards of towing by pushing ahead is parting which item shown?

A. A
B. B
C. F
D. I

4040. When towing another vessel astern, the length of the towline should be _____.

A. as long as possible
B. such that one vessel will be on a crest while the other is in a trough
C. such that the vessels will be "in step"
D. not over two wave lengths in seas up to 10 feet

4043. When backing down with sternway, the pivot point of a vessel is _____.

A. aft of the propellers
B. about one-quarter of the vessel's length from the stern
C. about one-third of the vessel's length from the bow
D. at the bow

4046. Which statement about tunnel bow thrusters fitted to large vessels is TRUE?

A. They are effective on most vessels at speeds up to 10 knots.
B. Because of their location, most modern installations have as much power as a tug.
C. They are fully effective at all drafts.
D. When going astern at slow speed, they provide effective steering control.

4047. Your vessel is to dock bow in at a pier. Which line will be the most useful when maneuvering the vessel alongside the pier?

A. Inshore head line
B. Bow spring line
C. Stern breast line
D. Bow breast line

4048. You are arriving in port and are assigned to anchor in anchorage circle B-4. It has a diameter of 600 yards and your vessel's LOA is 525 feet. If you anchor in 10 fathoms at the center of the circle, what is the maximum number of shots of chain you can use and still remain in the circle?

A. 4 shots
B. 5 shots
C. 6 shots
D. 7 shots

4049. Tugs sometimes shackle a length of chain in the towline in order to _____.

A. take the wear should the towline drag bottom
B. assure that if the towline is overstressed it will part close to the bridle
C. prevent the towline from whipping should it part
D. put spring in the towline

4051. You are the operator of an uninspected vessel which is involved in an accident. You are not required to assist people affected by the accident if _____.

A. the other vessel did not appear to be sinking
B. it would unduly delay your voyage
C. the other vessel was at fault
D. it would cause serious danger to your vessel

4052. You are arriving in port and are assigned to anchor in anchorage circle B-4. It has a diameter of 700 yards and your vessel's LOA is 600 feet. If you anchor in 11 fathoms at the center of the circle, what is the maximum number of shots of chain can use and still remain in the circle?

A. 4 shots
B. 5 shots
C. 6 shots
D. 7 shots

4054. "Hanging a barge off" means to _____.

A. moor a damaged barge to the bank and leave
B. remove and deliver a loaded barge from a multiple tow
C. remove a barge while locking through
D. tow an empty barge astern

4057. Your vessel is to dock bow in at a pier without the assistance of tugboats. Which line will be the most useful when maneuvering the vessel alongside the pier?

A. Bow spring line
B. Inshore head line
C. Stern breast line
D. Bow breast line

4060. You are arriving in port and are assigned to anchor in anchorage circle B-4. It has a diameter of 550 yards and your vessel's LOA is 449 feet. If you anchor in 9 fathoms at the center of the circle, what is the maximum number of shots of chain you can use and still remain in the circle?

A. 6 shots
B. 5 shots
C. 4 shots
D. 3 shots

4061. The two factors which make underwater hull repair difficult are accessibility and the _____.

A. availability of tools
B. shape of the hull
C. pressure exerted by the water
D. threat of progressive flooding

4063. The knot at the end of the heaving line used to pass the towing hawser is called a _____.

A. monkey's fist
B. ball or baseball knot
C. heaving knot
D. three strand Turk's head

4067. When steering a vessel, a good helmsman does NOT _____.

A. use as little rudder as possible to maintain course

B. advise his relief of the course being steered
C. consider steering a vessel a highly responsible job
D. use as much rudder as possible to maintain course

4069. The horizontal fore-and-aft movement of a vessel is called _____.

A. yaw
B. sway
C. heave
D. surge

4070. Small floes of rough, hummocky sea ice capable of damaging a vessel _____.

A. can usually be detected by radar in a smooth sea at a range of 4 to 6 kilometers
B. are indistinguishable from sea return on the PPI
C. are invisible to radar when covered with a thick layer of snow
D. are usually seen at night before they are close enough to provide a radar echo

4090. The BEST holding ground for conventional anchors is _____.

A. very soft mud
B. hard mud
C. shale
D. rock

4091. The turning circle of a vessel making a turn of over 360 degrees is the path followed by the _____.

A. bow
B. center of gravity
C. centerline
D. bridge

4092. To reconnect a broken tow line, it is better to use a polypropylene messenger line because it _____.

A. has great strength
B. is very supple
C. floats
D. absorbs shock by stretching

4096. Yawing is angular motion of the vessel about what axis?

A. Longitudinal
B. Transverse
C. Vertical
D. Centerline

4379. When relieving the helm, the new helmsman should know the _____.

A. maximum rudder angle previously used
B. gyro error
C. variation
D. course per magnetic steering compass

4390. When a helmsman receives the command "Right 15 degrees rudder," the helmsman's immediate reply should be _____.

A. "Rudder is right 15 degrees"
B. "Aye Aye Sir"
C. No reply is necessary, just carry out the order
D. "Right 15 degrees rudder"

4440. You are standing the wheelwatch when you hear the cry, "Man overboard, starboard side." You should be ready to _____.

A. give full left rudder
B. throw a life ring to mark the spot
C. put the rudder amidships
D. give full right rudder

DECK GENERAL
ANSWERS

DECK GENERAL ANSWERS

1	B	113	C	245	D	396	D	515	B	623	D	710	D	820	B
2	A	114	B	246	B	404	D	516	A	624	A	712	A	824	C
3	C	115	D	253	C	406	C	517	B	625	D	713	A	825	D
5	B	116	B	254	C	413	B	524	D	627	A	714	C	826	C
6	A	117	C	263	D	414	C	525	B	630	C	715	B	827	C
7	A	123	B	264	B	416	C	526	A	631	C	716	A	829	A
9	A	124	D	265	B	417	D	534	B	632	C	717	B	833	D
11	B	125	D	266	C	422	A	535	B	633	A	720	A	834	A
12	D	126	A	270	B	423	C	536	D	634	D	721	C	836	D
13	A	127	A	271	A	424	A	539	A	636	B	722	D	840	D
15	A	129	C	274	A	426	C	540	B	637	C	724	B	844	A
16	B	136	D	275	C	427	D	541	B	640	D	725	C	845	C
17	A	144	C	276	C	431	C	542	A	641	B	726	C	846	C
19	D	146	D	282	D	433	C	543	B	642	B	727	D	847	B
22	A	147	A	284	D	434	D	544	D	644	B	730	B	850	C
24	B	153	D	285	B	435	D	545	C	645	C	732	A	852	A
25	A	154	B	286	D	436	B	546	B	647	C	733	C	853	D
26	B	156	A	291	B	437	A	550	D	650	B	734	D	854	A
27	A	157	A	293	C	441	C	551	C	651	A	736	B	855	C
29	B	164	D	294	D	442	B	552	C	652	C	740	C	856	A
31	A	166	A	300	B	444	B	553	A	654	D	741	B	861	B
36	B	167	B	303	D	445	C	554	D	655	D	742	A	862	C
37	B	171	A	304	D	446	D	555	B	657	C	744	C	864	A
43	A	174	D	306	A	447	C	556	C	660	B	746	B	865	A
45	A	175	B	310	C	451	A	561	B	661	A	750	A	866	B
46	D	176	D	313	A	452	B	563	C	663	B	751	A	867	B
49	B	177	C	314	D	454	C	564	A	664	D	752	C	870	D
50	C	184	C	315	C	455	B	565	D	665	D	754	D	871	A
51	C	185	A	324	B	456	A	566	D	666	B	759	B	873	B
53	B	186	B	325	D	462	B	567	C	667	B	760	C	874	A
54	C	187	C	326	C	465	C	570	D	669	D	763	B	876	C
55	C	192	A	332	B	466	C	571	D	670	D	764	B	880	B
56	A	194	B	334	A	467	D	572	D	672	B	765	A	881	C
61	A	197	C	335	C	470	A	573	A	673	B	766	D	882	B
63	D	203	C	336	A	471	D	574	A	674	A	769	D	883	C
64	A	204	A	340	D	472	A	575	C	675	B	770	A	884	A
65	C	206	C	341	A	474	C	576	B	676	B	772	C	885	C
66	D	207	C	344	B	475	B	577	C	677	B	774	C	886	C
67	A	208	B	345	B	476	B	580	B	680	B	775	D	887	D
73	A	212	A	346	B	477	C	582	B	681	B	776	C	889	C
75	A	213	B	351	B	481	D	583	D	682	B	777	B	890	B
76	C	214	A	354	A	482	B	592	A	683	A	780	C	892	B
77	C	215	D	355	A	484	B	593	D	684	A	781	D	894	C
82	B	216	D	357	B	485	B	594	C	685	A	782	B	895	C
83	A	217	C	361	C	486	A	595	B	686	A	783	C	896	C
84	B	220	B	362	B	487	B	597	C	689	D	784	D	897	D
85	A	222	D	363	B	491	D	601	C	690	D	785	B	899	A
86	D	224	D	364	C	493	D	602	C	691	B	786	C	900	C
87	A	225	D	366	C	494	B	603	A	692	A	794	A	902	D
93	A	226	D	370	A	495	A	604	B	693	D	796	A	904	A
94	B	227	A	371	A	496	A	605	C	694	C	799	D	905	D
95	A	232	B	372	B	497	C	607	A	695	B	800	A	906	A
96	C	233	C	374	C	503	C	612	D	696	D	802	A	912	B
97	A	234	C	375	B	504	D	613	B	697	B	804	D	914	B
100	A	236	B	376	B	505	C	614	D	699	C	806	C	916	C
101	D	237	B	384	A	506	C	615	A	704	C	810	B	925	C
103	C	239	C	386	A	512	A	616	C	705	D	814	D	926	C
106	D	243	B	394	A	513	D	617	B	706	B	816	B	934	A
111	C	244	A	395	C	514	C	622	A	707	A	817	C	937	D

944	B	1088	D	1265	B	1410	C	1532	B	1630	D	1732	A	1823	C
950	C	1089	A	1269	B	1414	B	1533	D	1632	A	1733	C	1828	C
954	B	1090	D	1270	D	1416	D	1534	A	1633	B	1734	D	1829	A
956	D	1092	C	1271	B	1420	A	1536	A	1634	A	1736	D	1831	D
957	A	1094	D	1274	C	1424	B	1537	A	1635	D	1737	B	1832	B
960	C	1100	A	1275	C	1426	C	1540	B	1636	C	1739	C	1833	D
964	B	1102	C	1276	A	1427	C	1543	C	1638	A	1740	B	1836	B
966	A	1104	D	1280	C	1430	A	1544	B	1640	D	1741	A	1838	B
968	C	1110	A	1282	C	1434	D	1546	B	1641	A	1743	B	1839	C
970	A	1112	A	1286	C	1435	A	1548	D	1642	D	1746	C	1840	A
976	C	1114	B	1287	A	1436	C	1549	B	1643	C	1750	C	1841	C
977	C	1115	B	1289	C	1443	C	1550	B	1644	C	1751	A	1842	B
978	B	1116	C	1290	D	1444	C	1552	B	1646	D	1755	B	1843	B
980	D	1122	D	1296	D	1446	A	1553	C	1648	B	1756	C	1844	A
984	A	1124	C	1299	D	1448	B	1556	C	1651	A	1760	D	1848	C
986	C	1125	A	1302	C	1452	D	1557	A	1653	B	1761	B	1849	A
987	D	1126	D	1304	B	1455	B	1558	D	1654	A	1762	B	1852	C
990	B	1130	C	1305	D	1458	B	1560	B	1655	C	1763	A	1854	B
993	B	1132	C	1306	A	1459	C	1563	B	1657	D	1764	B	1855	D
994	A	1134	C	1307	D	1460	B	1564	B	1660	D	1766	C	1856	B
995	A	1136	B	1312	C	1462	A	1566	C	1661	B	1767	D	1858	B
996	D	1139	C	1313	C	1463	C	1567	D	1662	C	1768	B	1859	D
1004	B	1140	D	1314	C	1464	A	1568	B	1664	C	1771	A	1860	D
1005	B	1141	C	1316	C	1465	B	1570	C	1666	B	1773	B	1862	B
1006	D	1144	B	1319	A	1466	D	1573	B	1668	B	1774	B	1863	C
1007	B	1148	A	1320	C	1468	C	1574	A	1670	C	1776	C	1868	A
1008	B	1150	B	1323	A	1470	B	1575	D	1671	C	1778	C	1870	B
1010	B	1154	A	1324	A	1472	D	1576	B	1673	C	1781	C	1873	C
1011	C	1156	C	1325	B	1473	B	1578	D	1674	D	1782	B	1875	A
1012	C	1157	B	1326	B	1474	C	1580	B	1675	A	1783	C	1878	A
1014	D	1160	D	1329	A	1475	D	1582	A	1676	A	1784	D	1879	D
1016	A	1164	D	1330	B	1476	B	1583	B	1677	A	1786	C	1883	B
1018	B	1165	A	1336	B	1478	D	1584	D	1680	A	1787	D	1886	A
1020	C	1166	C	1344	B	1482	A	1586	C	1683	C	1788	A	1887	C
1021	A	1170	C	1346	D	1483	B	1588	A	1684	D	1790	D	1888	B
1024	A	1174	B	1350	B	1486	B	1589	A	1686	C	1791	D	1889	B
1026	B	1181	C	1354	C	1487	A	1593	A	1687	A	1792	C	1893	C
1030	B	1184	D	1356	B	1488	C	1594	C	1689	D	1793	A	1894	D
1041	C	1185	C	1357	C	1493	C	1595	A	1693	C	1794	D	1895	C
1042	B	1192	C	1360	A	1494	C	1596	C	1694	D	1795	C	1898	D
1044	B	1193	A	1364	D	1495	D	1598	B	1695	C	1796	D	1902	B
1045	A	1194	D	1365	A	1496	A	1600	A	1696	B	1798	C	1903	B
1046	A	1196	B	1366	B	1498	D	1603	C	1700	D	1800	B	1905	A
1048	C	1206	C	1368	D	1499	D	1604	B	1703	C	1802	D	1908	D
1050	A	1210	B	1369	B	1503	B	1605	D	1704	C	1803	C	1910	A
1051	B	1214	D	1370	B	1506	D	1606	D	1706	D	1804	C	1913	B
1052	A	1216	C	1374	A	1508	C	1607	D	1709	A	1805	A	1914	C
1054	A	1217	B	1375	A	1513	B	1608	B	1713	A	1806	C	1915	D
1056	B	1224	B	1376	C	1514	C	1613	B	1714	D	1807	D	1918	D
1058	D	1230	B	1380	C	1516	B	1614	A	1716	D	1811	C	1919	C
1064	C	1234	C	1384	B	1517	A	1615	C	1717	A	1813	B	1920	A
1066	A	1236	D	1389	D	1518	B	1616	A	1719	D	1814	D	1923	C
1074	D	1240	D	1392	C	1520	C	1618	C	1720	A	1815	D	1924	C
1075	B	1244	B	1394	B	1523	A	1622	A	1723	A	1816	A	1928	D
1076	B	1250	B	1396	D	1524	B	1623	D	1724	B	1818	C	1930	C
1078	B	1252	B	1399	B	1525	B	1624	C	1725	C	1819	A	1931	B
1080	A	1254	C	1402	D	1526	D	1625	B	1726	A	1820	B	1933	D
1082	B	1260	A	1404	A	1528	B	1626	D	1728	D	1821	B	1935	A
1087	A	1264	B	1406	B	1530	C	1628	A	1730	C	1822	D	1936	C

No.	Ans	No.	Ans	No.	Ans	No.	Ans	No.	Ans	No.	Ans	No.	Ans	No.	Ans
1938	C	2033	A	2150	A	2250	A	2388	C	2601	D	2832	B	3073	C
1939	C	2034	C	2152	D	2251	C	2389	B	2602	C	2836	A	3074	C
1941	B	2037	D	2155	B	2253	A	2394	A	2608	A	2848	C	3076	B
1943	B	2038	B	2156	A	2254	D	2395	D	2612	D	2852	D	3082	A
1944	D	2040	A	2157	B	2255	C	2396	C	2619	D	2854	C	3083	D
1945	B	2041	A	2159	D	2256	B	2397	B	2622	B	2855	A	3088	C
1948	A	2042	B	2163	A	2259	C	2398	B	2632	B	2858	D	3091	D
1949	B	2043	B	2168	D	2261	B	2399	D	2642	B	2861	B	3092	A
1950	C	2045	D	2169	A	2264	C	2400	C	2652	A	2870	C	3094	D
1951	A	2046	C	2171	D	2265	A	2450	D	2658	A	2872	A	3095	C
1953	D	2047	C	2173	B	2266	A	2451	B	2659	D	2879	B	3098	D
1957	C	2048	C	2179	B	2268	D	2452	A	2664	C	2882	D	3099	D
1958	B	2049	D	2181	A	2271	B	2454	C	2666	D	2883	D	3100	B
1960	B	2050	D	2182	C	2272	C	2456	C	2672	B	2889	A	3102	D
1961	B	2053	A	2185	D	2273	C	2459	D	2674	B	2894	D	3103	A
1962	A	2054	B	2186	D	2275	D	2460	A	2684	B	2896	D	3104	D
1963	C	2058	B	2189	B	2276	A	2461	B	2688	B	2902	A	3109	B
1966	C	2059	D	2190	C	2279	D	2462	B	2692	C	2906	D	3111	A
1969	A	2060	C	2191	C	2280	C	2464	A	2694	B	2910	A	3114	C
1970	D	2061	A	2192	C	2281	C	2470	C	2696	C	2914	D	3122	C
1973	B	2062	D	2193	D	2283	C	2471	D	2704	C	2920	B	3130	B
1976	C	2063	C	2194	A	2284	B	2474	B	2708	A	2922	A	3132	B
1977	B	2064	D	2195	C	2285	D	2480	B	2712	B	2924	C	3138	B
1978	B	2065	B	2196	B	2288	D	2489	B	2714	D	2930	A	3142	C
1979	B	2067	D	2197	C	2290	C	2490	B	2716	C	2932	B	3148	D
1980	A	2068	B	2198	B	2291	C	2492	D	2718	B	2933	B	3152	B
1982	C	2069	B	2199	D	2292	C	2494	A	2719	C	2936	B	3162	B
1983	C	2070	A	2203	B	2293	D	2500	B	2722	B	2938	A	3165	B
1988	B	2073	B	2204	C	2301	A	2510	B	2729	C	2939	C	3168	C
1989	D	2075	C	2207	A	2302	C	2520	C	2732	A	2940	D	3176	C
1992	B	2076	D	2211	C	2305	C	2521	C	2735	D	2950	B	3180	C
1993	B	2078	B	2212	C	2315	D	2530	A	2736	D	2951	D	3200	C
1994	A	2081	A	2213	C	2316	D	2533	B	2738	B	2954	B	3201	C
1995	B	2086	B	2214	B	2321	B	2534	B	2745	A	2957	D	3204	C
1996	B	2088	D	2216	D	2322	C	2536	C	2746	C	2958	A	3218	D
1997	A	2091	A	2217	A	2325	C	2540	D	2752	A	2959	A	3220	D
1998	C	2093	C	2219	C	2335	B	2549	D	2759	D	2960	A	3234	A
1999	A	2095	D	2221	B	2336	D	2550	C	2760	A	2964	C	3239	A
2000	C	2097	B	2222	C	2341	C	2552	D	2761	B	2968	C	3242	A
2002	A	2098	B	2223	C	2342	A	2553	C	2768	C	2969	D	3244	D
2003	C	2100	A	2224	D	2343	D	2558	A	2774	B	2970	D	3248	C
2005	D	2104	D	2225	B	2344	D	2559	A	2776	C	2981	D	3250	C
2007	B	2106	B	2226	B	2345	B	2562	A	2778	A	2988	A	3260	D
2008	D	2107	C	2228	A	2346	C	2564	C	2783	A	2990	C	3262	D
2011	D	2111	B	2229	A	2347	B	2567	C	2784	D	2994	D	3269	A
2013	C	2113	A	2230	A	2349	B	2568	D	2792	B	2996	C	3270	C
2014	C	2119	A	2231	C	2350	C	2570	A	2794	A	3013	B	3282	A
2015	B	2122	D	2232	A	2351	B	2572	C	2798	A	3016	C	3288	B
2016	B	2124	D	2233	C	2352	C	2574	C	2799	B	3018	C	3291	B
2018	A	2126	D	2235	A	2353	D	2580	D	2802	D	3026	B	3292	C
2019	B	2127	C	2236	A	2354	A	2581	A	2805	B	3028	B	3294	C
2020	C	2130	D	2238	D	2355	D	2589	C	2808	C	3031	D	3300	B
2022	C	2135	D	2239	A	2356	C	2590	A	2810	A	3032	C	3308	C
2023	D	2136	A	2240	B	2360	B	2591	B	2812	A	3044	C	3309	A
2025	D	2143	B	2241	A	2361	C	2595	C	2814	A	3047	A	3320	A
2028	D	2144	D	2242	D	2365	A	2596	B	2816	B	3048	B	3321	C
2029	C	2146	B	2243	D	2367	B	2597	B	2817	C	3054	B	3322	D
2030	A	2147	B	2245	B	2384	A	2598	C	2819	B	3056	A	3324	A
2031	B	2149	C	2249	C	2387	D	2600	D	2822	D	3067	C	3325	C

3327	D	3521	C	4043	B
3328	C	3530	D	4046	D
3330	B	3540	D	4047	B
3338	A	3544	B	4048	A
3339	B	3550	C	4049	D
3340	A	3556	D	4051	D
3342	B	3560	D	4052	B
3346	D	3561	C	4054	A
3347	D	3564	A	4057	A
3350	A	3565	A	4060	C
3360	A	3570	A	4061	C
3370	D	3576	C	4063	A
3372	B	3580	A	4067	D
3374	D	3584	B	4069	D
3378	A	3586	D	4070	A
3390	A	3587	A	4090	B
3392	C	3588	D	4091	B
3394	C	3590	A	4092	C
3395	A	3599	D	4096	C
3396	A	3600	B	4379	D
3400	A	3602	D	4390	D
3411	C	3604	A	4440	D
3420	C	3606	D		
3432	A	3608	B		
3434	C	3614	B		
3438	B	3616	C		
3439	B	3631	A		
3440	A	3644	B		
3442	C	3645	C		
3447	A	3654	C		
3448	B	3662	A		
3449	B	3681	B		
3450	A	3684	B		
3452	A	3686	C		
3456	C	3689	D		
3459	A	3690	B		
3460	B	3692	B		
3462	C	3693	C		
3463	D	3694	D		
3464	C	3710	C		
3465	A	3719	A		
3466	B	3722	C		
3476	D	3724	C		
3484	A	3728	C		
3487	A	3740	D		
3488	A	3742	C		
3490	D	3790	D		
3492	B	3820	C		
3494	B	3960	B		
3500	C	3982	D		
3501	A	4009	D		
3502	D	4011	D		
3504	C	4012	C		
3508	B	4013	C		
3511	B	4014	A		
3514	C	4016	B		
3518	B	4018	A		
3519	D	4026	D		
3520	C	4040	C		

NAVIGATION GENERAL

The Elements of Weather

The Greeks believed everything in the world to consist of four basic elements: earth, air, fire and water. Although this has turned out not to be the case, they are the four elements of the weather machine.

Earth. Even though 70% of its surface is covered by water, "earth" is the name we give our little sphere in space. The earth acts as a heat sump, absorbing heat energy from the sun and re-radiating heat energy back to outer space in a delicate balancing act. Different areas of the earth absorb, retain and re-radiate heat to differing degrees, resulting in the large-scale movement of air we call the weather.

Air. The fluid set into motion by the earth's heat imbalances is air. The earth's atmosphere contains the gas vital for human life (21% oxygen, 78% nitrogen, and traces of other gases). Another vital component of the atmosphere is water vapor, the gaseous form of water. The amount of water vapor air can hold is extremely dependent on the temperature of the air. This temperature dependence has implications for cloud and fog formation, precipitation, and dew point temperature. Air is the primary medium distributing the earth's heat energy, as the planet strives to even things out.

Fire. Energy from the sun passes through an ultraviolet (UV) filtering ozone layer, then through the earth's atmosphere. The roughly 50% of the energy finally reaching the surface consists of residual UV, visible, and infrared radiation. Due to the differences in reflectivity (albedo) of water, vegetation, snow, etc., the percentage of energy reflected back into space varies widely over the earth's surface. This uneven heating of different areas of the earth is the underlying cause of weather. Further, because of a difference in specific heats (the specific heat of a substance is defined as the number of calories required to raise one gram of the substance one centigrade degree) land and water do not warm or cool at the same rates. It takes more energy (thus more time) to raise the temperature of the ocean than it does that of the land. Conversely, it takes the ocean longer than the land to cool as winter approaches.

Water. Essential for life and covering 70% of the earth's surface, water acts as a massive energy sink and transport medium, both as ocean currents and as water vapor in the air. If air is the transport vehicle, then water is the fuel. Water in vapor form holds prodigious amounts of stored, or latent, heat (540 cal./gm). The millions of tons of water vapor contained in the vortex of air sweeping into the wall of a hurricane condense and release this heat, driving the engine of the tropical cyclone.

Water Vapor and Humidity

Water exists in three states: solid (ice), liquid (water), and gas (water vapor), temperature determining which. The capacity of air to hold water vapor is also determined by its temperature—warm air being able to hold more vapor than cold. Cooling air down effectively wrings the moisture out of it. As the cooling air loses capacity, the excess vapor is forced out (condenses) as liquid droplets or solid crystals, forming clouds, fog, dew, rain, snow, etc.

Relative humidity (RH) is the ratio of water vapor in air at a certain temperature to its capacity, expressed as a percentage. When air is holding its maximum amount, it is saturated, and its RH is 100%.

Dew point is the temperature to which a parcel of air must be cooled to become saturated. The dew point is a function of the air's present temperature and relative humidity. The dew point of more humid air is higher than that of drier air at the same temperature.

The figure below (the psychrometric chart) shows the relationships between humidity, temperature and relative humidity. A parcel of air can be represented by a single point on the chart. The air's temperature is shown by the horizontal scale, while its humidity is shown on the vertical scale. The top curve is the line of saturation, where the air is holding as much moisture as it can. The similarly shaped curves below are lines of equal relative humidity.

The arrows on the chart show what happens when air at 40% RH and 70°F (Point A) is cooled to its dew point (Point B) at 45°F. At the dew point the air is saturated; cooling the air below 45°F will force (condense) water out of the air.

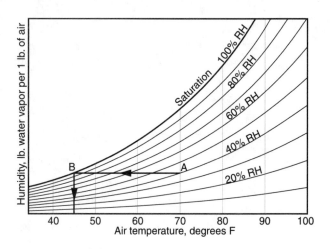

Condensation

Condensation takes many forms: dew, frost, clouds, fog, rain, snow and sleet.

Dew usually occurs overnight when a clear sky allows the escape of IR radiation and cooling of the earth's surface. As we saw above, the temperature at which dew forms (the dew point) is determined by the amount of water vapor in the air. If the air has a high relative humidity it doesn't require much cooling to bring the air to saturation. If the DP is above freezing, dew forms. If the DP is below freezing, frost forms by sublimation (going directly from vapor to solid, skipping the liquid phase). Frost is not frozen dew.

Clouds are similarly condensation of excess water vapor from the air. As air rises, pressure drops and the air expands and cools. The natural rate of temperature drop with altitude is termed the adiabatic lapse rate. Air heated during the day through contact with the sun-warmed ground expands and rises. As it rises it expands even further and cools. If cooled below its DP, the excess water vapor condenses into minute droplets—clouds.

The rising air may be a convective current rising from warmed land as just described, air wedged aloft by an advancing front, or a parcel of air forced upward over a mountain chain (orographic lifting). In the severest of all mechanisms, it is moist air hurtling inwards in an ever tightening spiral toward a zone of very low pressure, at which point it rushes upward and outward forming the dense clouds and precipitation in the eyewall of a hurricane.

If the condensation proceeds long enough, the density of water droplets causes the small droplets to coalesce into larger drops, eventually heavy enough to fall through the rising current of air. Temperature conditions dictate whether that precipitation occurs as rain, freezing rain, snow, sleet or hail.

Air Masses

An *air mass* is a continent-sized parcel of air (see the illustration above) with fairly uniform temperature and moisture characteristics. Like a fingerprint, an air mass will carry the imprint of where it was formed, whether Continental or Maritime (dry or moist) and Polar or Tropical (cold or warm). It is also may be labeled as to its temperature relative to the surface over which it travels.

Air mass types and their meteorological labels are:

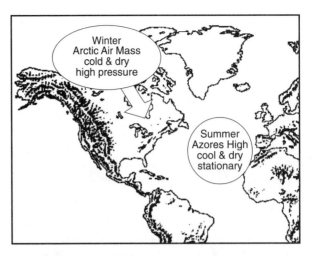

cP Continental Polar
mP Maritime Polar
cT Continental Tropical
mT Maritime Tropical
E Equatorial

In addition, a *w* (warm) or *k* (cold) can be appended to indicate the temperature of the mass relative to the surface over which it is passing (i.e., *mTw*).

As an air mass moves out of its source region, it eventually collides with a mass of different temperature and moisture content. The boundary between the two masses is referred to as a *front* and is a source of "weather." It is important to understand that while air masses are three-dimensional, fronts on a weather chart show where the two masses meet at the earth's *surface*. The actual frontal surface extends upward into the atmosphere at an angle, the degree of the angle varying with the type of front and speed of advance. It is the magnitude of the differences in air mass characteristics (temperature, moisture and density) which dictates the violence of the weather at the front. Keep in mind that cold, dry air is more dense than warm, moist air.

Fronts

Although air characteristics are fairly uniform within an air mass, where two dissimilar masses come together is generally an area of conflict, or "weather." A cold air mass advancing into an area occupied by warm air is a cold front. A warm front is the reverse. The type of weather experienced by the passage of one is very different from that of the other. An advancing warm front incites relatively prolonged, gray, drizzly days until the front passes. On the other hand, the advancing cold front is quicker, more intense with gusty winds, thunderstorms, occasional hail and temperature drop.

Stationary Fronts

These are stand-offs in that neither air mass moves, one waiting for the other to "blink"! Weather in the vicinity of a stationary front is that of a mild warm front. If and when a low pressure center develops along the front, arriving upper air support (a jet stream trough) can spur development of a mid-latitude cyclone. On either side of a stationary front, winds blow parallel to the front but in opposite directions. An upper level low (jet stream trough) can cause a surface low center to develop along the front.

The Cold Front

Air density is greatest in cold and dry air. As a cold front advances into warmer and more moist air, it wins the density contest. The greater the differences, the faster its advance and the steeper the frontal surface. As it advances, it burrows under and lifts the warm air, with the frontal surface tipping backward at an angle of up to 1:50. Because of this steep slope, the weather disturbance associated with a cold front is relatively short and intense compared to that of a warm front. It occurs in a narrow band along, or just ahead of, the cold front.

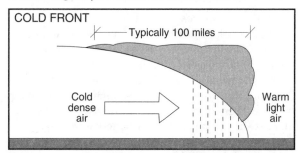

COLD FRONT — Typically 100 miles — Cold dense air → Warm light air

Warm air is unstable air and will rise like a hot air balloon. This warm, moist rising air cools rapidly to its dew point, forming clouds and precipitation. The relatively steep and rapid uplift of a cold front generates more active (sometimes violent) weather than that of a warm front. Line Squalls can occur in the warm air sector 50–150 miles ahead of the advancing cold front. They move quickly and may be spotted on the horizon as a very dark cloud band. The cold front cloud pattern includes building cumulus and cumulonimbus, characteristic of the "cumuliform" pattern of vertical development. With frontal passage, the temperature drops rapidly and the winds shift clockwise to the west and northwest. Skies clear, the barometer rises, and it remains cool with gusty winds.

The Warm Front

A warm front is preceded by several days of increasing cloud cover—cirrus to cirrostratus to altostratus to nimbostratus. The cloud deck (the bottom of the cloud cover) gradually lowers with a

succession of clouds having the horizontal (stratiform) characteristic of the warm front. This lengthy process is due to the more shallow slope (1:150) of the frontal surface as the warm air rides

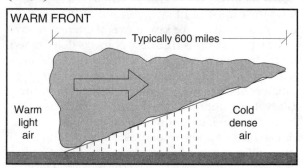

WARM FRONT — Typically 600 miles — Warm light air → Cold dense air

up and over the cooler air, gradually displacing it. The actual frontal passage is much less intense, usually accompanied by heavier rain and a slowly rising temperature. As the front passes, the falling barometer levels off and sees little change thereafter. Winds shift clockwise to the southeast and south, often diminishing. Most cloudiness and precipitation occur over a broad band to the north and east of the surface front.

Frontal Waves

Cold fronts tend to move more rapidly than warm fronts. This leads to the development of frontal waves that sweep across the U.S. from west to east. The wind shifts clockwise as the warm front passes and shifts clockwise again when the cold front passes.

As the cold front closes in on the warm front, the wave becomes steeper, pressure at the crest decreases (the low "deepens") and wind and rain become more intense. Ultimately, the two fronts merge as an occluded front. After occlusion, the cold air lifts the entire warm air mass, the fronts disappear and weather settles down.

The Occluded Front

An occluded front exists when a faster-moving cold front catches up with a warm front and pushes it off the ground. If the advancing cold air is colder than the cool air ahead of the warm front, then a "cold front occlusion" occurs, and the warm air followed by the cool air is forced aloft. If the advancing cool air is not as cold as the cold air ahead of the warm front, then the warm air is again pushed aloft and the oncoming cool air also rides up over the cold air slope ahead of it. This constitutes a *warm front occlusion*. The weather associated with a cold front occlusion is similar to that of a cold front, while the weather for the warm front occlusion resembles that of a warm front.

The Coriolis Effect

The so-called "Coriolis Force" has bedeviled students for years, mainly because of the word "force." Not a force at all, it is simply an observed effect—a result of the earth's rotation. While a fixed spot on the equator travels eastward at almost 900 knots, the speed of similar fixed spots north or south of the equator diminish to zero at the poles.

Were you able to hover in space at the north pole while the earth spun below, and you observed a baseball being thrown toward the equator, you would think, "That guy has an arm!" Relative to space, the ball is traveling in a straight line, but during its flight, the aiming point at the equator is moving east. To an observer, the ball seemingly veers to the right toward a point to the west, as that point moves under the landing point of the ball.

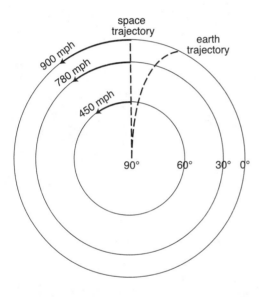

Another way to look at the situation is that a point to the west (to the pitcher's right as he faces south) has now moved under the point of his original aim—and that is where the ball lands.

Remember that this is the perspective of the space-walker, not that of an earthbound observer. To the observer traveling with the earth, the ball appears to curve to the right. In the reverse situation, the passer is on the equator, traveling east with it at 900 knots. When the ball is thrown toward the pole, it has the earth's initial eastward velocity component, and thus travels in a northeast direction relative to earth—again to the right of its initial trajectory.

Due to this Coriolis Effect, winds do not blow directly from high pressure to low pressure. They deviate to the right in the Northern Hemisphere and left in the Southern.

Atmospheric Circulation

If the earth's axis wasn't tilted, if there were no land masses to provide friction, if there were no Coriolis Effect, if land and water had the same specific heats . . . then the equator would receive maximum solar radiation, with symmetrically reduced amounts at higher latitudes and minimum amounts at the poles. Heated air would rise at the equator, flow northward and southward to the poles (losing heat as it went), sink at the poles and return along the surface to the equator to begin the cycle again.

In reality heating of the earth's surface is uneven. However, there is still an overall prevailing wind pattern over which the frontal system weather is superimposed. The discussion here is for the Northern Hemisphere. The Southern Hemisphere is the mirror image.

From the high pressure zone centered at about 30 degrees, surface winds move south toward the equator as the northeast trades and north as the prevailing westerlies. Why they do not flow due south and north, respectively, was discussed above.

The prevailing westerlies flow northeast, warm through contact with the earth as they go, and rise at about 60°N (creating a low pressure zone). At altitude the flow splits into a branch heading north and another branch heading south. These flows feed the high at the pole and at 30°N, respectively.

Study the action of the rising and falling air masses and the generation of winds in the illustration below. Memorize the names of the zones and their locations.

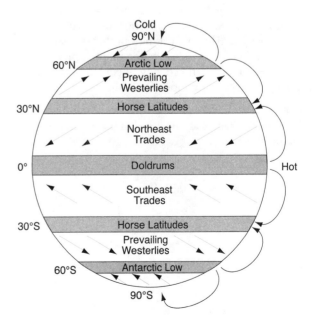

High and Low Pressure Areas

Barometric pressure refers to the weight of the air column over a particular place at a specific time. The reference air column is called the standard atmosphere, at sea level, at 15°C (59°F). The pressure of this standard atmosphere, in three different measurement units, is:

29.92 inches of Hg (mercury)

1013.25 millibars (mb)

14.7 lbs./sq. in.

On a weather map points of equal pressure are connected by continuous curves (isobars), drawn at 4 mb intervals. Adjacent high and low pressure areas create a pressure differential, causing air to move "downhill" (in a pressure sense) as wind. The closer the spacing of the isobars, the steeper the pressure gradient, and the greater the air movement (wind). It helps to think of geographic maps on which steep terrain is indicated by closely spaced iso-heights (curves of equal heights). The closer the iso-heights, the steeper the hill, and the faster a ball would roll down the hill.

The Cyclone

A cyclone, or low pressure area, often forms along fronts where warm air is rising and clouds and precipitation occur. Winds circulate counterclockwise around a low and at an angle of about 15 degrees in from the isobar toward the center. Note that *cyclone* is a generic term applying to a low pressure area with counterclockwise winds, not a specific type of storm system (with the exception of the name for a hurricane in the Indian Ocean).

The Anticyclone

An anticyclone, or high pressure area, exists where cool air is descending from upper levels. As it does so, it compresses and warms, resulting in generally lower relative humidity and clear weather. Winds circulate around a high in a clockwise direction and at an angle of about 15 degrees out from the isobar and away from the center.

The significance of highs and lows lies in their effect on weather. The high can be considered a mountain of subsiding and clearing air which brings clear and calm weather. The low features air that is rushing in at the surface, then rising (generating the pressure drop), expanding, and cooling. If cooled to the dew point, clouds and precipitation result.

Note that the above circulations about both high and low pressure areas are reversed in the Southern Hemisphere.

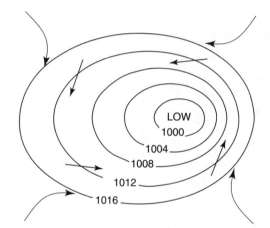

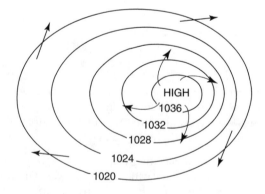

Buys Ballot's Law

Buys Ballot's Law provides a simple way to determine the location of a low pressure system relative to your position. Facing the wind, the low pressure area will be to the right and slightly behind your right shoulder (approximately 110 degrees relative). The law applies to the Northern Hemisphere; reverse it for the Southern. (If facing the wind it will be behind your left shoulder.)

Wind Shifts

Because winds flow around low and high pressure centers, as these centers move we can expect local winds to change in direction. As with Buys Ballot's law, understanding the direction of flow around lows and highs will allow you to picture the movement of the centers as they pass by.

Passage of a Northern Hemisphere Low

The illustration at right depicts a low pressure system (cyclone) moving from west to east. As the center moves, an observer to the north of the track will find himself sequentially in positions 1, 2, and 3. The wind directions change from SE to NE to N. This counterclockwise shifting of the wind is called *backing*. (Remember, *counter*clockwise = *backing*.)

An observer to the south of the track will experience the wind shift sequence 4, 5, and 6. The wind will shift clockwise from S to SW to W. A clockwise shift of the wind is called *veering*.

Passage of a Northern Hemisphere High

The illustration at right depicts a high pressure system (anticyclone) moving from west to east. As the center moves, an observer to the north of the track is in relative positions 1, 2, and 3. The wind directions change from NW to W to SW. The shift is counterclockwise and so is *backing*.

An observer to the south of the track will experience the wind shift sequence 4, 5, and 6. The wind will shift clockwise from N to NE to E. The shift is clockwise, so the wind is *veering*.

The same rule thus applies to both lows and highs: if the wind backs, a pressure center will pass to your south.

Note that both a high and a low passing north of the observer results in a veering wind, while on passing south a backing wind.

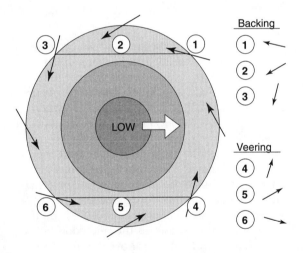

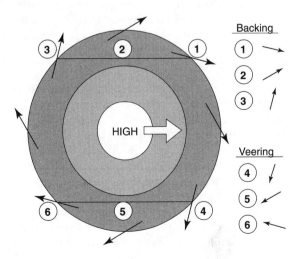

Local Winds

In addition to the winds of the general circulation and those associated with cyclones and anticyclones, there are numerous local winds which influence the weather in various places.

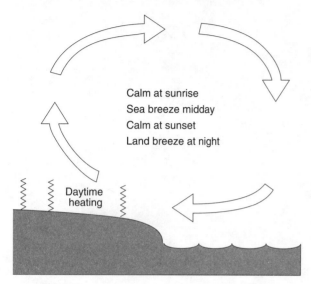

Calm at sunrise
Sea breeze midday
Calm at sunset
Land breeze at night

Daytime heating

The most common are the land and sea breeze*s*, caused by alternate heating and cooling of land adjacent to water. By day the land is warmer than the water, and by night it is cooler. This effect occurs along many coasts during the summer. Between about 0900 and 1100 local time the temperature of the land becomes greater than that of the adjacent water. The lower levels of air over the land are warmed, and the air rises, drawing in cooler air from the sea. This is the *sea breeze*. Late in the afternoon, when the sun is low in the sky, the temperature of the two surfaces equalizes and the breeze stops. After sunset, as the land cools below the sea temperature, the air above it is also cooled. The contracting cool air becomes more dense, increasing the pressure near the surface. This results in an outflow of winds to the sea. This is the *land breeze*, which blows during the night and dies away near sunrise.

Since the atmospheric pressure changes associated with this cycle are not great, the accompanying winds generally do not exceed gentle to moderate breezes. The circulation is usually of limited extent, reaching a distance of perhaps 20 miles inland, and not more than 5 or 6 miles offshore, and to a height of a few hundred feet. In the doldrums and subtropics, this process is repeated with great regularity throughout most of the year. As the latitude increases, it becomes less prominent, being masked by winds of migratory cyclones and anticyclones.

Varying conditions of topography produce a large variety of local winds throughout the world. Winds tend to follow valleys, and to be deflected from high banks and shores. In mountain areas wind flows in response to temperature distribution and gravity. An *anabatic wind* is one that blows up an incline, usually as a result of surface heating. A *katabatic wind* is one which blows down an incline. There are two types, foehn and fall wind.

The *foehn* (fan) is a warm dry wind which initiates from horizontally moving air encountering a mountain barrier. As it blows upward to clear the mountains, it is cooled below the dew point, resulting in clouds and rain on the windward side. As the air continues to rise, its rate of cooling is reduced because the condensing water vapor gives off heat to the surrounding atmosphere. After crossing the mountain barrier, the air flows downward along the leeward slope, being warmed by compression as it descends to lower levels. Since it loses less heat on the ascent than it gains during descent, and since it has lost its moisture during ascent, it arrives at the bottom of the mountains as very warm, dry air. This accounts for the warm, arid regions along the eastern side of the Rocky Mountains and in similar areas. In the Rocky Mountain region this wind is known by the name *chinook*. It may occur at any season of the year, at any hour of the day or night, and have any speed from a gentle breeze to a gale. It may last for several days, or for a very short period. Its effect is most marked in winter, when it may cause the temperature to rise as much as 20°F to 30°F within 15 minutes, and cause snow and ice to melt within a few hours. On the west coast of the United States, a foehn wind, given the name *Santa Ana*, blows through a pass and down a valley of that name in Southern California. This wind is frequently very strong and may endanger small craft immediately off the coast.

A cold wind blowing down an incline is called a *fall wind*. Although it is warmed somewhat during descent, as is the foehn, it remains cold relative to the surrounding air. It occurs when cold air is dammed up in great quantity on the windward side of a mountain and then spills over suddenly, usually as an overwhelming surge down the other side. It is usually quite violent, sometimes reaching hurricane force. A different name for this type of wind is given at each place where it is common. The *tehuantepecer* of the Mexican and Central American coast, the *pampero* of the Argentine coast, the *mistral* of the western Mediterranean, and the *bora* of the eastern Mediterranean are examples of this wind.

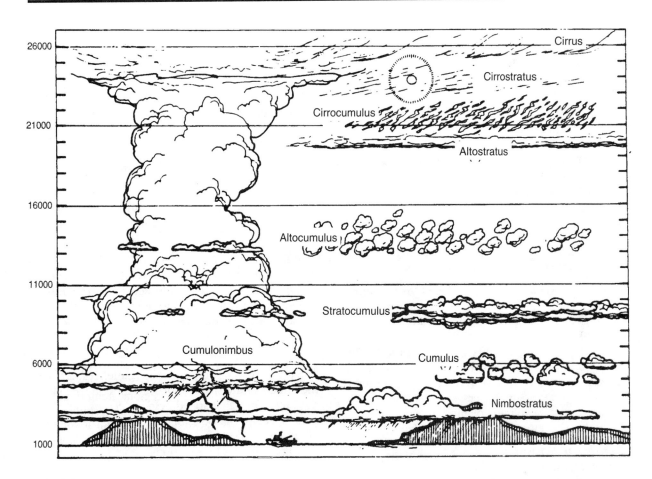

Clouds
Development Descriptors

- *Stratiform* (horizontal development): stable air gently lifted spreads out in layers, forming flat sheets covering large areas
- *Cumuliform* (vertical development): unstable air, warmer than the surrounding air, rises rapidly and involves smaller areas

Appearance Descriptors

- *Cirrus:* gauze-like, thin, wispy, delicate
- *Stratus:* flat, continuous cover, stratified, layered
- *Cumulus:* cotton-ball like, cauliflower, separate

Principal Cloud Types (see Illustration)

Cirrus (Ci)—detached, delicate and fibrous high clouds. Also, "mare's tails." Generally associated with fair weather. If followed by lower clouds, however, they foretell rain within 24–48 hours.

Cirrostratus (Cs)—thin, whitish veil producing halos around sun and moon. Foretells rain.

Cirrocumulus (Cc)—white scales, arranged in rows, known as "mackerel sky." Associated with fair weather. Followed by lower clouds, they foretell rain.

Altostratus (As)—gray veil. The sun appears out of focus with corona. When nimbostratus appear below them, expect continuous rain within a few hours.

Altocumulus (Ac)—cottony masses, usually uniformly distributed with blue sky between. May lead to thunderstorms, but of short duration.

Stratocumulus (Sc)—low, soft, grayish, roll-shaped masses. Usually form after altocumulus and are followed by a clear night.

Cumulus (Cu)—dense with flat base and much vertical development. They never cover the entire sky. Usually associated with fair weather.

Nimbostratus (Ns)—low, dark, shapeless layer. The "rain cloud." Rain is steady or intermittent, but not showery.

Cumulonimbus (Cb)—tremendous vertical development. Top may spread out horizontally in form of an anvil. Typically results in lightning and rain.

Stratus (St)—uniform low cloud with base often below 1,000 feet. If thick, makes the sky dark. Often produces steady mist.

The Hurricane

The *tropical cyclone* is referred to as a "typhoon" in the East Indies and Japan, as a "cyclone" in the Indian Ocean, a "willy-willy" off Australia, a "baguio" near the Philippines, and as a "hurricane" in the Atlantic, Caribbean and Gulf of Mexico.

As noted, *cyclone* is a generic term applied to a counterclockwise-rotating low pressure system often associated with stormy conditions. The weather discussed previously applies to the extra-tropical (mid-latitude) cyclone—one that develops in the middle latitudes, supported and steered east by the jet stream and the prevailing westerlies. That storm system is born of the meeting of cold-dry and warm-moist air masses. A low forms along a stationary front and, with upper air support, the rest is history.

The tropical cyclone is a different beast. As the term implies, its birth is in the tropics—generally off the West African coast. Somewhere at sea an *easterly wave* of low pressure forms, generating a tropical disturbance featuring a band of thunderstorms to the east of the wave. Imbedded in the northeast trades, this easterly wave moves west. If conditions are right the barometric pressure lowers, isobars close, winds increase, and the evolution begins. The conditions required for development are discussed later.

tropical depression	winds to 34 knots
tropical storm	winds 35 to 64 knots
hurricane	winds 65+ knots

As in any cyclone, winds circulate counter-clockwise (clockwise in the Southern Hemisphere) and inward. Development of the storm requires heat and moisture. Thus, passing over land or cooler water deprives the gigantic heat engine of its fuel, and the engine sputters.

Advance Warning

As a hurricane approaches, there are several warning signs:

Several days away: long low swells (15-second period), cirrus bands radiating toward the storm center, slow steady fall of the barometer. It is important to note that the direction of swells indicates the direction of the eye at the time they were generated, not the present location of the center. At some point during this interval the skies may clear and the barometer actually rise a little. This is due to subsiding air from the outflow of the storm. Subsidence results in compression, heating, reduced RH, and increased barometric pressure.

24-48 hours: drop in barometric pressure in excess of the usual diurnal fluctuation, increasing winds and steady rain, cirrus and cirrostratus clouds.

Storm center at 15 miles: torrential rains and wall clouds, mountainous seas; rapid fall of the barometer.

At the eye: confused mountainous seas, very low pressure, wind roar subsides, may see blue sky overhead.

After the eye passes: wind shifts to opposite direction and the pattern repeats in reverse order.

The Dangerous Semicircle

If a line is drawn through the eye of the storm and in the direction of travel, it bisects the storm into a dangerous semicircle (DS) to the right of the line and a navigable semicircle (NS) to the left. The semicircles are reversed in the Southern Hemisphere.

The terms "dangerous" and "navigable" result from the effects of the storm's forward motion (see illustration below), that speed being added to the wind speed in the DS (since they are in the same direction) and subtracted from it in the NS, since they are in opposite directions.

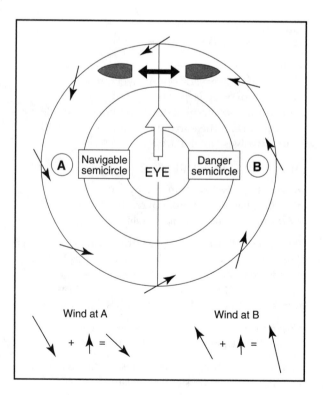

A vessel caught out with a hurricane approaching must first determine the position of the storm center relative to his vessel and its probable direction of movement. Usually some information is available from onboard radio and weatherfax, but there are things the navigator can do for himself. First, use Buys Ballot's law to determine the direction to the center of the low. Then, while holding a steady course, determine whether the wind seems to be veering or backing, and increasing or decreasing in velocity.

- A veering wind indicates you are in the dangerous semicircle.

- A backing wind indicates you are in the navigable semicircle.

- A steady wind direction, increasing speed, and falling barometer indicates you are directly in the path of the storm.

- A steady wind direction, decreasing speed, and rising barometer indicates the storm is past and moving away from you.

Avoidance Maneuvers
- If on the storm track, put the wind two points on your starboard quarter (a bearing of 158° relative).

- If in the dangerous semicircle, put the wind on your starboard bow (bearing of 45° relative).

- If in the navigable semicircle, put the wind on your starboard quarter (bearing of 135° relative).

- If on the track but behind the storm, take the best riding course that increases your distance from the eye.

The Thermodynamics of the Hurricane
There are significant differences between the mid-latitude (extra-tropical) cyclone and the tropical cyclone (hurricane). The hurricane (a.k.a. typhoon, willy-willy, baguio) encompasses an air mass which is comparatively uniform in temperature and moisture, as opposed to the mid-latitude storm and its conflicting cold and warm air sectors. It has no front. It is a rather circular storm system whose pressures (as indicated by closed isobars) are symmetric about the storm's center. In vertical cross-section, pressure gradients are steep, with the rate of gradient change increasing as the eye approaches.

This warm-core system is a self-sustaining one, given the appropriate conditions. These conditions include:

- a sea-surface temperature of at least 80°F to a depth of 200 feet;

- a thermal trough of low pressure often arising in the eastern Atlantic;

- a cyclonic rotation generated by the Coriolis effect; and

- the absence of any significant vertical wind shear which could interrupt the necessary vertical stacking (think of a chimney) necessary for convection.

Hurricanes generally originate in the eastern North Atlantic off the West Coast of Africa where the Northeast Trades predominate. If induced by a weak trough of low pressure, an easterly wave develops along that flow and the stage is set for convection, lowered surface pressure, and surface convergence. As this warm, humid air rises, it cools and its vapor condenses, surrendering the latent heat of vaporization (540 cal/gm). This heat increases the already existing instability, even as increasing volumes of rising air stimulate steadily increasing cyclonic convergence at the surface. With increasing volumes of air converging and rising, increasing quantities of heat are released, accelerating further the convection. Divergence aloft deepens the surface low, inducing increased surface convergence, causing more warm, moist air to ascend and release its heat, etc. The hurricane is a true self-sustaining heat engine—or, as the Caribs labeled it, a "God of Evil."

As the mass of surface air approaches the hurricane's center, it is rotating counterclockwise and starts a slowly ascending spiral—the wall cloud or eye wall. This is essentially a tube of violent air rotating about the eye. The tube ranges from 10 to 50 miles in diameter and is marked by dense cumulonimbus development, high winds, updrafts, heavy rains, and thunderstorms. In the center of this nearly circular tube of violence is the eye—a zone of clear sky, warmer air, minimum pressure (average 950 mb) and confused seas. Air descends within the eye with the usual compression-related effects, i.e., heating, lowered relative humidity, and clearing. As the eye passes, the opposite side of the storm greets the unfortunate observer. The size of the eye (the diameter of the wall cloud) decreases with intensification of the storm. (The spinning figure skater increases her rate of rotation by pulling her arms in.) At about the 200 mb level the cyclonic rotation reverses to clockwise to provide accelerated outflow of the huge volumes or rising air. The average diameter of a tropical cyclone is 400 nm.

Destructive Effects

The hurricane, for all its concentrated power, is actually a relatively small storm, averaging about 1/3 the diameter of the typical mid-latitude cyclone. Its destructive effects are the result of high winds, spawned tornadoes, heavy rains, and the one that takes the most lives, the storm surge.

Winds: The force exerted by wind increases as the square of the wind speed. If the wind increases from 30 kts to 60 kts (factor of 2), the force exerted on a structure is 4 times that at 30 kts. If it goes from 30 to 90 kts (factor of 3), the force is 9 times that at 30 kts. Since winds of 100+ kts are typical, the destructive effects are not difficult to picture.

Tornadoes: These violent offshoots are not unusual after the storm makes landfall and starts its curve to the N/NE. They form most often in the northeast quadrant of the storm and beyond the areas suffering hurricane force winds.

Heavy Rains: Heavy rainfall is a given. All that condensing water vapor has to come down, and does so in torrents. Satellite pictures of hurricanes showing thick clouds spiraling in toward the center are rain bands. The rainfall adds to flooding problems generated by the most life-threatening complication of such a storm, the storm surge.

Storm Surge: Three factors combine to produce abnormally high water levels along exposed coastlines. The extreme low pressures associated with the tropical storm allow a rise in water level—essentially a mound of water beneath the low pressure zone. This mound moves ashore along with wind-driven wave action. If timed to coincide with a high tide, a destructive surge of water descends upon an already rain-drenched shoreline. The majority of storm-related fatalities are a direct result of the effects of the storm surge. With the direction of forward movement taken as the axis, the surge will be maximum on the right side of the storm where the wind direction and forward motion coincide (the dangerous semicircle).

The factors that favor development of the tropical storm cause its demise by their absence. The driving force is vapor-laden warm air; its fuel is the latent heat of evaporation. Movement over cooler waters, as the storm moves north, gradually robs the storm of its energy source. Moving over land not only removes the source of heat and vapor sources, but blunts wind velocities with surface friction. As cooler and less humid air moves into the center, it literally runs out of gas, the engine sputters and dies.

While the storm's tropical characteristics may weaken, it usually continues on as a more widespread weather system, as an awaiting polar front supplies cold air, allowing for the evolution of a typical extra-tropical cyclone.

Some comparisons between mid-latitude (sub-tropical) and tropical (hurricane) systems.

	Sub-Tropical	Tropical
Core	cold	warm
Structure	frontal	circular
Made of	opposing cold/ warm air masses	homogeneous warm air
Energy source	temperature gradients	latent heat
Center	Rising cool air	Descending warm air
Pressure gradient	gradual	steep
Area	large	small

Not having respect for this serious weather phenomenon has cost many lives. Anyone who has been at sea in one never wants to repeat the experience. A review of the loss of 4 destroyers to the Pacific typhoon of 1944 is testament to the incredible power of the tropical cyclone. Caught with low fuel, they were fearful of salt water ballasting lest the remaining fuel be contaminated with the salt water, resulting in instant loss of their boilers and propulsion. Inability to ballast the empty tanks resulted in a raised center of gravity, loss of adequate stability, and subsequent capsize.

The Saffir-Simpson Hurricane Scale grades tropical cyclones by sustained winds and relates those to predicted damage.

Category	Wind, mph	Damage
1	74–95	Minimal
2	96–110	Moderate
3	111–130	Extensive
4	131–155	Extreme
5	>155	Catastrophic

Wind Scales and Warnings

Beaufort Wind Scale

Beaufort Force	Knots	Miles per Hr	WMO Description	Observed Effects
0	0-1	0-1	Calm	Sea like a mirror
1	1-3	1-3	Light air	Ripples with the appearance of scales
2	4-6	4-7	Light breeze	Small wavelets; crests of glassy appearance, not breaking
3	7-10	8-12	Gentle breeze	Large wavelets; crests begin to break, scattered whitecaps
4	11-16	13-18	Moderate	Small waves, becoming longer; numerous whitecaps
5	17-21	19-24	Fresh	Moderate waves of longer form; many whitecaps; some spray
6	22-27	25-31	Strong	Larger waves forming; whitecaps everywhere; more spray
7	28-33	32-38	Near gale	Sea heaps up; white foam from breaking waves begins to blow in streaks
8	34-40	39-46	Gale	Moderately high waves of greater length; edges of crests begin to break into spindrift; foam blown in well-marked streaks
9	41-47	47-54	Strong gale	High waves; sea begins to roll; dense streaks of foam; spray may reduce visibility
10	48-55	55-63	Storm	Very high waves with overhanging crests; sea takes white appearances; foam is blown in very dense streaks; rolling is heavy and visibility reduced
11	56-63	64-73	Violent storm	Exceptionally high waves; sea covered with white foam patches; visibility still more reduced
12	64+	74+	Hurricane	Air filled with foam; sea completely white with driving spray; visibility greatly reduced

Storm Warnings

SMALL CRAFT ADVISORY Wind to 33 kt (38 mph)	GALE WARNING Wind 34–47 kt (39–54 mph)	STORM WARNING Wind 48–63 kt (55–73 mph)	HURRICANE WARNING Wind over 63 kt (over 73 mph)
DAYTIME SIGNALS (FLAGS)			
RED	RED RED	RED/ BLACK	RED/ BLACK
NIGHT SIGNALS (LIGHTS)			
RED WHITE	WHITE RED	RED RED	RED WHITE RED

Synoptic Map Symbols

Weather maps received by facsimile recorders are synoptic maps, meaning that they show simultaneous weather conditions at many weather stations. To avoid the necessity of words, conditions at each weather station are shown by symbols.

You will probably not be asked to interpret a full station report, but you may be asked to identify one or more weather symbols. The illustration at right shows the most likely symbols.

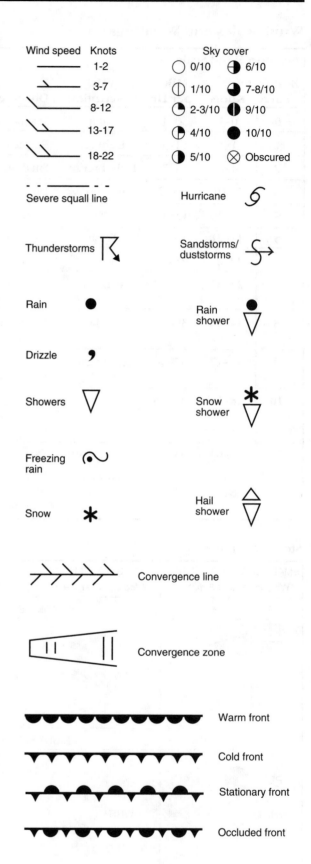

Fog

Fog is a condensation of tiny water droplets close to the surface, over land or water. It requires the presence of moist air and a cooling medium.

Radiation Fog

Sometimes called ground fog, this type of fog occurs on a clear night over land when the absence of significant cloud cover allows the earth to radiate infrared energy. Warm moist air overlying the cooling earth is gradually cooled, and if cooled to its dew point, condensation and fog occur. A version of this is *valley fog,* formed when colder, heavier air drains downhill and collects in valley bottoms. A very slight breeze adds to the mixing needed to bring new parcels of humid air into contact with the cooling mechanism, the ground. As the sun warms the earth again, the fog appears to "lift" as it thins and evaporates from the bottom up.

Advection Fog

The word advection implies horizontal flow and therefore applies to the movement of moist warm air over a cold surface. Contact of this air with the cooling surface lowers its temperature to the dew point and condenses the vapor to water droplets forming fog. This can occur over water or land. An over-water example is warm moist air (mT) moving north over the Labrador Current producing the dense fog banks over the Grand Banks. An overland example is in the early spring when fog may be caused by warm moist air flowing over a snow layer. Unlike radiation fog, advection fog can form day or night, over land or water, and be extremely persistent as over the Grand Banks.

Sea Smoke

Also known as *arctic smoke* and *steam fog*, sea smoke develops when very cold air moves over cold water. The water vapor just above the surface is cooled to its dew point with the usual result—condensation (fog) which looks like steam rising from the water's surface. Notice the difference between sea smoke, in which the cooling medium is the air above the water surface, and advection fog, in which the cooling medium is the water surface—a case of meteorologic role reversal.

Frontal Fog

Rarely, fog forms ahead of a warm front or behind a cold front. At a cold front there is warm air aloft and behind the frontal surface, while at a warm front there is warm air above and ahead of the frontal surface. In both cases evaporation from raindrops can raise the humidity and dew point of the cold air to saturation, resulting in the formation of fog.

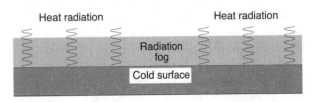

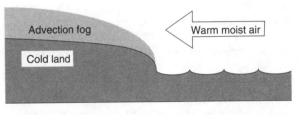

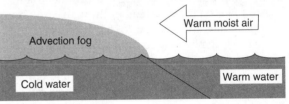

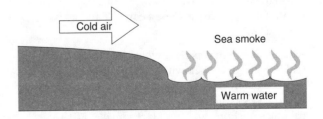

NORTH ATLANTIC RIGHT WHALES

North Atlantic right whales are the world's most endangered large whale, there remaining only an estimated 300 individuals. Right whales migrate annually along the east coast of the United States between the feeding grounds off New England and the southern calving grounds of Florida, Georgia and South Carolina. Because right whales mate, rest, feed and nurse their young at the surface, and often do not move out of the way of oncoming ships, they are highly vulnerable to being struck. Calves traveling north with their mothers from the southern calving grounds appear to be particularly vulnerable to collisions with ships. Ship strikes are one of two known sources of human-related mortality.

Description

The species reaches lengths of 45 to 55 feet and is black in color. The best field identification marks (see illustrations on the next page) are a broad back with no dorsal fin, irregular bumpy white patches (callosities) on the head, and a distinctive two-column V-shaped blow when viewed from directly behind or in front of the whale. They have broad, paddle-shaped flippers and a broad, deeply notched tail.

Seasonal Occurrence

Right whales may occur south of Cape Henry, VA within 30 miles of the Atlantic coast to the Atlantic coast of Florida from November through April; however peak migratory periods occur September through December, when right whales migrate toward the calving grounds from critical habitat feeding areas off New England and Canada, and January through April, when right whales and their calves migrate northward from the critical habitat calving grounds off Florida, Georgia and South Carolina. Occasionally in the calving season, November 15 through April 15, calving right whales have been sighted as far north as Cape Fear, NC and as far south as Miami, FL.

An area designated as right whale *critical habitat* (calving ground) is shown at right. This area extends approximately from the mouth of the Altamaha River, GA to Jacksonville, FL from the shoreline to 15 nautical miles offshore; and from Jacksonville, FL to Sabastian Inlet, FL from the shoreline to 5 nautical miles offshore. Seasonal advisories and sighting reports are broadcast periodically for these areas by Coast Guard Broadcast Notice to Mariners, NAVTEX, NOAA Weather Radio, and in the return message from the Right Whale Mandatory Ship Reporting (MSR) system, which applies to all vessels over 300GT.

Detailed local requirements pertaining to right whales can be found in each of the Coast Pilots.

Precautions

It is illegal to approach a whale closer than 500 yards. (See 50 CFR 224.103(c), chapter 2 for limits, regulations and exceptions.) If a whale is sighted underway, a vessel must steer a course away from the right whale and immediately leave the area at slow safe speed.

Any whale struck, any dead whale carcass, and any whale observed entangled should be reported immediately to the Coast Guard noting the precise location, date, and time of the accident or sighting. In the event of a strike or sighting, the following information should be provided to the Coast Guard:

- location, date, and time of the accident or sighting or of a carcass or an entangled whale,
- speed of the vessel,
- size of the vessel,
- water depth,
- wind speed and direction,
- description of the impact,
- fate of the animal, and
- species and size, if known.

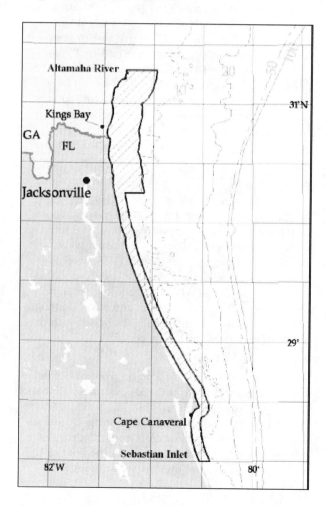

Northern Right Whale Identifiers (from Coast Pilot No. 4)

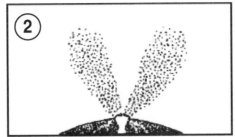

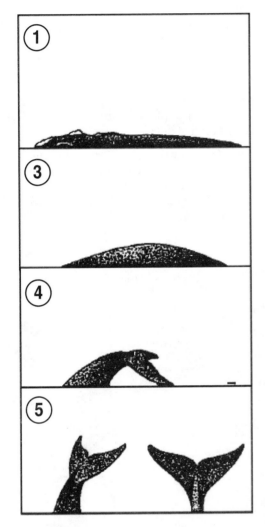

1. Whitish patches of raised and roughened skin (called callosities) on top of the head

2. V-shaped blow easily visible from in front or behind whale

3. No dorsal fin on the back

4. Tall flukes often lifted vertically when the whale dives

5. All black tail on the top and underside

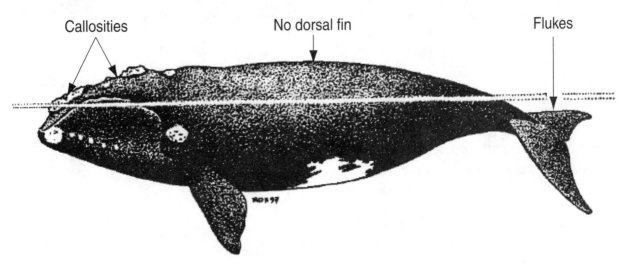

Callosities   No dorsal fin   Flukes

TIDES

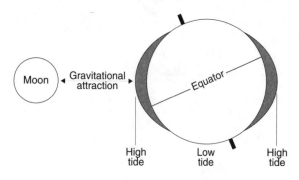

Causes

The periodic rise and fall of ocean waters is due to a combination of factors:

- *Gravitational attraction* between the water and the moon and sun. Due to its proximity, the moon exerts the greater force.
- *Declination (angular distance above or below the equator)* of the moon and sun.
- *Centrifugal force* on the water opposite the moon or sun as the earth spins.
- *Barometric pressure* on the ocean surface, a difference of one inch of mercury causing a sea level change of about one foot.
- *Geometry* of water bodies, resulting in resonant oscillations and in piling up at the ends of funnel-shaped bodies.

The earth rotates once per 24 hours. The moon, however, revolves about the earth once per month and rises 52 minutes later each day. High tides, therefore, occur about 52 minutes later each day.

Heights

The *range of the tide* is the difference in heights between successive high and low waters.

Spring Tides occur at new and full moon. The moon and sun are directly in line, so their pulls work together. Tidal heights are higher than normal and lows lower than normal; thus a larger than normal range. Note that in this context, *spring* has nothing to do with the season.

Neap Tides occur with the moon at quadrature (1st and 3rd quarters). With the moon and sun 90° out of phase, their attractions subtract. Tidal highs are lower than normal, and lows are higher than normal; thus a smaller than normal range.

Perigean Tides occur when the moon is closest to the earth in its elliptical orbit, increasing its pull.

Apogean Tides occur when the moon is farthest from the earth in its orbit, decreasing its pull.

Tropic Tides occur when the moon is at maximum declination, increasing the diurnal range.

Types

All coasts are affected by tides. For various reasons, some experience two highs and lows per day, others but one.

- *Semi-diurnal tides* have two highs and two lows per day. They occur along the U.S. East Coast and have small differences between the two highs and two lows than do mixed tides.
- *Diurnal tides* occur just once per day and are usually of small amplitude. Much of the U.S. Gulf Coast has diurnal tides.
- *Mixed tides* occur twice daily, with the amplitude of one tide being markedly different from that of the other. Galveston, TX, has diurnal tides, followed by mixed tides, depending on the declination of the moon.

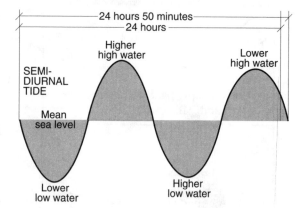

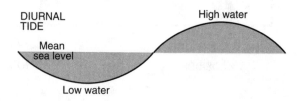

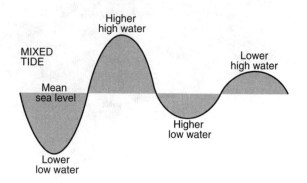

Tide Tables

Tide tables were published by National Ocean Service (NOS) until 1995. Since then NOS has made the information available to private publishers who offer the data to the public in book form. Four annual volumes are available:

- *Tide Tables: Europe & West Coast of Africa*
- *Tide Tables: East Coast of North & South America*
- *Tide Tables: West Coast of North & South America*
- *Tide Tables: Central & Western Pacific Ocean and Indian Ocean*

Each volume contains eight tables, the first three being of direct concern. The following two pages are taken from Tables 1 and 2, *Tide Tables 1995: East Coast of North and South America.*

Table 1 contains the times and heights of high and low waters for the entire year for 50 primary stations. The one shown is a sample for April, May, and June of 1995.

Table 2 contains tidal differences to be applied to the data in Table 1 for approximately 2,500 subordinate stations. The example page contains stations subordinate to Portland, ME.

Table 3 allows determination of height of tide at any intermediate time.

Table 1—Primary Stations

Table 1 is in geographic order of primary station. Once you have found the port of interest, find the page containing the month and day. The data for 8 and 9 May, 1995, is shaded on the sample page.

After the month and day, the first column lists the times of high and low water in Standard Time. To convert to Daylight Savings Time, add one hour. The next column shows the height in feet above datum, which for Portland, ME, is mean lower low water. Obviously, the higher numbers refer to high tides. The third column lists the same tide heights in centimeters.

On 8 May, 1995, the first high water is 8.7 feet above datum at 0439 (4:39 AM). The low water that follows is 1.1 feet above datum at 1058.

Tidal data for May 9 is shown because there are only three tides shown for the date. Three-tide days occur about once every seven days because the four-tide semidiurnal cycle takes 24 hr 50 min.

Table 2—Subordinate Station Differences

Table 2 is listed in the geographic order from north to south of subordinate stations. You can find subordinate stations either by paging through Table 2 or by looking up the name of the station location in the index at the back of the book. Let's look up Station 861, Peaks Island, ME.

Following the number and name of the station, the next two columns list the latitude and longitude of the station. The next two columns show time corrections for high and low waters to be applied to the corresponding times for the primary station in Table 1. The next pair of columns list height corrections for high and low waters. Height corrections indicated by an asterisk (*) are multipliers. If there is no asterisk, the correction is in feet to be added or subtracted. The last three columns show the mean range (mean high water–mean low water), mean spring range (average range at the times of spring tides), and mean tide (the average of mean high and mean low). The mean tide isn't halfway between datum and mean high water because datum is NOT mean low water, but mean *lower* low water.

For Peaks Island, ME, we find differences to be applied to Portland, ME, of:

- time of high water (–0 04)
- time of low water (–0 08)
- height of high water (*0.99)
- height of low water (*0.99)

Using Table 1 and Table 2 Together

Using both Table 1 and Table 2, we can find the heights and times of tides at any subordinate stations for any day.

Example: Find the height and time of the second high tide on 8 May, 1995, at Peaks Island, ME.

Solution: Find Peaks Island, ME, either in the index or directly in Table 2. In Table 2 we find that Peaks Island is Station 861 and is based on Portland, ME.

In Table 1, find Portland, ME, and the date 8 May, 1995. The second high tide for that date is 8.5 feet at 1719.

In Table 2 find Station 861, Peaks Island. The height correction is *0.99 and the time of high water correction is –0 04 minutes. The answer is, therefore:

$$(8.5 \times 0.99) = 8.4 \text{ feet}$$

$$\text{at } (1719 - 0\ 04) = 1715.$$

Table 1—Tides

Portland, Maine, 1995

Times and Heights of High and Low Waters

April

Day	Time (h m)	Height (ft)	Height (cm)	Day	Time (h m)	Height (ft)	Height (cm)
1 Sa	0547	-0.5	-15	16 Su	0509	-1.5	-46
	1159	9.8	299		1123	10.5	320
	1800	0.1	3		1724	-0.8	-24
					2337	11.4	347
2 Su	0011	10.1	308	17 M	0558	-1.7	-52
	0625	-0.4	-12		1213	10.5	320
	1238	9.5	290		1813	-0.8	-24
	1837	0.4	12				
3 M	0046	9.9	302	18 Tu	0026	11.5	351
	0704	-0.1	-3		0649	-1.6	-49
	1316	9.1	277		1305	10.3	314
	1913	0.7	21		1904	-0.6	-18
4 Tu	0123	9.6	293	19 W	0119	11.3	344
	0743	0.2	6		0743	-1.4	-43
	1356	8.8	268		1401	10.0	305
	1952	1.1	34		1959	-0.2	-6
5 W	0203	9.3	283	20 Th	0215	10.9	332
	0824	0.6	18		0841	-1.0	-30
	1438	8.4	256		1501	9.7	296
	2034	1.4	43		2100	0.2	6
6 Th	0246	9.0	274	21 F ○	0316	10.5	320
	0909	0.9	27		0944	-0.5	-15
	1525	8.1	247		1605	9.4	287
	2120	1.7	52		2206	0.5	15
7 F	0334	8.7	265	22 Sa	0423	10.0	305
	0958	1.2	37		1050	-0.1	-3
	1616	7.9	241		1713	9.3	283
	2212	1.9	58		2316	0.7	21
8 Sa ◑	0427	8.5	259	23 Su	0534	9.7	296
	1052	1.4	43		1157	0.1	3
	1711	7.6	238		1820	9.3	283
	2308	1.9	58				
9 Su	0524	8.5	259	24 M	0027	0.7	21
	1149	1.4	43		0643	9.5	290
	1808	8.0	244		1301	0.2	6
					1923	9.5	290
10 M	0008	1.8	55	25 Tu	0132	0.5	15
	0623	8.6	262		0747	9.5	290
	1244	1.2	37		1400	0.2	6
	1902	8.3	253		2018	9.7	296
11 Tu	0105	1.4	43	26 W	0230	0.2	6
	0719	8.8	268		0844	9.5	290
	1335	0.9	27		1451	0.2	6
	1952	8.8	268		2108	9.9	302
12 W	0158	0.8	24	27 Th	0321	0.0	0
	0812	9.2	280		0934	9.6	293
	1423	0.5	15		1538	0.3	9
	2038	9.4	287		2152	10.1	308
13 Th	0248	0.2	6	28 F	0406	-0.2	-6
	0901	9.7	296		1019	9.6	293
	1509	0.0	0		1619	0.3	9
	2122	10.1	308		2231	10.1	308
14 F	0335	-0.5	-15	29 Sa ●	0448	-0.3	-9
	0948	10.1	308		1100	9.5	290
	1553	-0.4	-12		1657	0.5	15
	2206	10.7	326		2308	10.1	308
15 Sa ○	0422	-1.1	-34	30 Su	0526	-0.2	-6
	1035	10.4	317		1138	9.3	283
	1638	-0.7	-21		1733	0.7	21
	2251	11.2	341		2343	10.0	305

May

Day	Time (h m)	Height (ft)	Height (cm)	Day	Time (h m)	Height (ft)	Height (cm)
1 M	0602	-0.1	-3	16 Tu	0542	-1.9	-58
	1215	9.2	280		1158	10.5	320
	1808	0.9	27		1755	-0.7	-21
2 Tu	0017	9.9	302	17 W	0009	11.8	360
	0638	0.0	0		0635	-1.8	-55
	1251	9.0	274		1252	10.4	317
	1843	1.1	34		1849	-0.5	-15
3 W	0053	9.7	296	18 Th	0104	11.6	354
	0715	0.3	9		0730	-1.6	-49
	1329	8.8	268		1349	10.2	311
	1921	1.3	40		1947	-0.2	-6
4 Th	0131	9.5	290	19 F	0202	11.1	338
	0753	0.5	15		0828	-1.1	-34
	1409	8.6	262		1449	10.0	305
	2001	1.5	46		2048	0.1	3
5 F	0212	9.3	283	20 Sa	0303	10.6	323
	0834	0.7	21		0928	-0.7	-21
	1452	8.4	256		1551	9.8	299
	2045	1.6	49		2153	0.4	12
6 Sa	0256	9.0	274	21 Su ○	0408	10.1	308
	0919	0.9	27		1030	-0.2	-6
	1538	8.3	253		1654	9.7	296
	2134	1.8	55		2300	0.7	21
7 Su ◐	0345	8.8	268	22 M	0515	9.6	293
	1007	1.1	34		1133	0.2	6
	1627	8.3	253		1756	9.6	293
	2227	1.7	52				
8 M	0439	8.7	265	23 Tu	0008	0.7	21
	1058	1.1	34		0621	9.3	283
	1719	8.5	259		1234	0.5	15
	2324	1.6	49		1856	9.7	296
9 Tu	0535	8.7	265	24 W	0111	0.6	18
	1152	1.0	30		0723	9.1	277
	1812	8.9	271		1331	0.7	21
					1951	9.8	299
10 W	0022	1.2	37	25 Th	0208	0.4	12
	0634	8.9	271		0820	9.0	274
	1246	0.8	24		1423	0.8	24
	1905	9.4	287		2040	9.8	299
11 Th	0119	0.7	21	26 F	0259	0.3	9
	0731	9.2	280		0911	9.0	274
	1339	0.5	15		1510	0.9	27
	1956	10.0	305		2125	9.9	302
12 F	0214	0.0	0	27 Sa	0345	0.1	3
	0827	9.6	293		0957	9.0	274
	1430	0.1	3		1552	0.9	27
	2046	10.6	323		2205	10.0	305
13 Sa	0307	-0.7	-21	28 Su	0426	0.1	3
	0920	10.0	305		1038	9.0	274
	1521	-0.3	-9		1630	1.0	30
	2136	11.2	341		2242	10.0	305
14 Su	0358	-1.3	-40	29 M ●	0504	0.0	0
	1012	10.3	314		1116	9.0	274
	1611	-0.6	-18		1707	1.1	34
	2226	11.6	354		2317	9.9	302
15 M	0450	-1.7	-52	30 Tu	0540	0.1	3
	1105	10.5	320		1153	8.9	271
	1702	-0.7	-21		1742	1.2	37
	2317	11.9	363		2352	9.9	302
				31 W	0615	0.2	6
					1229	8.8	268
					1817	1.2	37

June

Day	Time (h m)	Height (ft)	Height (cm)	Day	Time (h m)	Height (ft)	Height (cm)
1 Th	0027	9.8	299	16 F	0050	11.6	354
	0650	0.3	9		0715	-1.6	-49
	1305	8.8	268		1334	10.4	317
	1854	1.3	40		1933	-0.3	-9
2 F	0104	9.6	293	17 Sa	0147	11.2	341
	0726	0.4	12		0810	-1.2	-37
	1342	8.7	265		1430	10.3	314
	1933	1.4	43		2032	0.0	0
3 Sa	0143	9.5	290	18 Su	0246	10.6	323
	0804	0.5	15		0906	-0.7	-21
	1422	8.7	265		1528	10.1	308
	2015	1.4	43		2133	0.3	9
4 Su	0225	9.3	283	19 M ○	0346	10.0	305
	0845	0.6	18		1003	-0.2	-6
	1504	8.7	265		1626	9.9	302
	2101	1.4	43		2237	0.6	18
5 M	0311	9.1	277	20 Tu	0448	9.4	287
	0929	0.7	21		1102	0.3	9
	1549	8.9	271		1725	9.7	296
	2152	1.4	43		2340	0.7	21
6 Tu	0401	9.0	274	21 W ◐	0551	9.0	274
	1017	0.7	21		1200	0.8	24
	1638	9.1	277		1822	9.6	293
	2247	1.2	37				
7 W	0456	8.9	271	22 Th	0042	0.8	24
	1109	0.7	21		0653	8.7	265
	1730	9.4	287		1256	1.0	30
	2345	0.9	27		1917	9.6	293
8 Th	0555	9.0	274	23 F	0140	0.7	21
	1204	0.6	18		0750	8.6	262
	1824	9.8	299		1349	1.2	37
					2008	9.6	293
9 F	0045	0.4	12	24 Sa	0232	0.6	18
	0656	9.1	277		0843	8.5	259
	1301	0.4	12		1438	1.3	40
	1920	10.4	317		2054	9.6	293
10 Sa	0145	-0.2	-6	25 Su	0319	0.5	15
	0757	9.4	287		0930	8.6	262
	1358	0.1	3		1523	1.3	40
	2016	10.9	332		2137	9.7	296
11 Su	0243	-0.8	-24	26 M	0402	0.4	12
	0855	9.7	296		1013	8.6	262
	1454	-0.2	-6		1603	1.3	40
	2111	11.4	347		2216	9.8	299
12 M ○	0338	-1.3	-40	27 Tu ●	0441	0.3	9
	0952	10.1	308		1052	8.7	265
	1549	-0.4	-12		1641	1.2	37
	2206	11.8	360		2252	9.8	299
13 Tu	0433	-1.7	-52	28 W	0517	0.2	6
	1048	10.3	314		1129	8.8	268
	1644	-0.6	-18		1717	1.2	37
	2300	11.9	363		2328	9.9	302
14 W	0527	-1.9	-58	29 Th	0551	0.2	6
	1143	10.5	320		1204	8.8	268
	1739	-0.7	-21		1752	1.2	37
	2355	11.9	363				
15 Th	0621	-1.8	-55	30 F	0003	9.8	299
	1238	10.5	320		0624	0.2	6
	1835	-0.6	-18		1239	8.9	271
					1829	1.1	34

TABLE 2 – TIDAL DIFFERENCES AND OTHER CONSTANTS

No.	PLACE	POSITION Latitude	POSITION Longitude	DIFFERENCES Time High Water	DIFFERENCES Time Low Water	DIFFERENCES Height High Water	DIFFERENCES Height Low Water	RANGES Mean	RANGES Spring	Mean Tide Level
		North	West	h m	h m	ft	ft	ft	ft	ft
	MAINE, Casco Bay–cont. Time meridian, 75° W				on Portland, p.32					
833	Little Flying Point, Maquoit Bay	43° 50'	70° 03'	−0 01	−0 01	*0.99	*0.99	9.0	10.3	4.8
835	South Freeport	43° 49'	70° 06'	+0 12	+0 10	*0.99	*0.99	9.0	10.3	4.8
837	Chebeague Point, Great Chebeague Island	43° 46'	70° 06'	−0 04	−0 09	*0.99	*0.99	9.0	10.4	4.8
839	Prince Point	43° 46'	70° 10'	0 00	0 00	*1.01	*1.00	9.2	10.6	4.9
841	Doyle Point	43° 45'	70° 08'	−0 02	−0 03	*1.00	*0.88	9.2	10.5	4.9
843	Falmouth Foreside	43° 44'	70° 12'	+0 01	0 00	*1.00	*1.03	9.1	10.5	4.9
845	Great Chebeague Island	43° 43'	70° 08'	+0 03	+0 03	*1.00	*1.00	9.1	10.5	4.9
847	Cliff Island, Luckse Sound	43° 42'	70° 07'	−0 02	−0 02	*1.00	*1.00	9.1	10.4	4.9
849	Vaill Island	43° 41'	70° 09'	+0 05	+0 01	*0.98	*1.03	9.0	10.3	4.8
851	Long Island	43° 41'	70° 10'	−0 01	0 00	*1.00	*1.00	9.1	10.4	4.9
853	Cow Island	43° 41'	70° 11'	−0 01	0 00	*1.00	*1.00	9.1	10.5	4.9
855	Presumpscot River Bridge	43° 41'	70° 15'	+0 01	+0 04	*1.01	*1.06	9.2	10.6	5.0
857	Back Cove	43° 41'	70° 15'	+0 02	+0 06	*0.97	*0.97	9.1	10.5	4.9
859	Great Diamond Island	43° 40'	70° 12'	−0 01	0 00	*0.99	*1.00	9.0	10.4	4.9
861	Peaks Island	43° 39'	70° 12'	−0 04	−0 08	*0.99	*0.99	9.0	10.4	4.8
863	Cushing Island	43° 39'	70° 12'	+0 01	0 00	*0.99	*1.00	9.0	10.4	4.9
865	PORTLAND	43° 40'	70° 15'		Daily predictions			9.1	10.4	4.9
867	Fore River	43° 38'	70° 17'	+0 02	+0 02	*1.00	*1.00	9.1	10.5	4.9
869	Portland Head Light	43° 37'	70° 12'	−0 02	−0 02	*0.97	*0.97	8.9	10.2	4.8
	MAINE, outer coast–cont.									
871	Richmond Island	43° 33'	70° 14'	−0 03	−0 03	*0.98	*0.98	8.9	10.1	4.8
873	Old Orchard Beach	43° 31'	70° 22'	0 00	−0 06	*0.97	*0.97	8.8	10.1	4.7
875	Wood Island Harbor	43° 27'	70° 21'	+0 02	−0 04	*0.96	*0.96	8.7	9.9	4.7
877	Cape Porpoise	43° 22'	70° 26'	+0 12	+0 14	*0.95	*0.95	8.7	9.9	4.7
879	Kennebunkport	43° 21'	70° 28'	+0 16	+0 16	*0.94	*0.94	8.6	9.9	4.6
881	York Harbor	43° 08'	70° 38'	+0 03	+0 13	*0.95	*0.95	8.6	9.9	4.6
883	Seapoint, Cutts Island	43° 05'	70° 40'	+0 01	−0 04	*0.96	*0.96	8.8	10.1	4.7
	MAINE and NEW HAMPSHIRE									
	Portsmouth Harbor									
885	Jaffrey Point	43° 03'	70° 43'	−0 03	−0 05	*0.95	*0.95	8.7	10.0	4.7
887	Gerrish Island	43° 04'	70° 42'	−0 02	−0 03	*0.95	*0.95	8.7	10.0	4.7
889	Fort Point	43° 04'	70° 43'	+0 03	+0 07	*0.94	*0.94	8.6	9.9	4.6
891	Kittery Point	43° 05'	70° 42'	−0 07	+0 01	*0.96	*0.96	8.7	10.0	4.7
893	Seavey Island	43° 05'	70° 45'	+0 20	+0 18	*0.89	*0.89	8.1	9.4	4.4
895	Portsmouth	43° 05'	70° 45'	+0 22	+0 17	*0.86	*0.86	7.8	9.0	4.2
	Piscataqua River									
897	Atlantic Heights	43° 05'	70° 46'	+0 37	+0 28	*0.82	*0.82	7.5	8.6	4.0
899	Dover Point	43° 07'	70° 50'	+1 33	+1 27	*0.70	*0.70	6.4	7.4	3.4
901	Salmon Falls River entrance	43° 11'	70° 50'	+1 35	+1 52	*0.75	*0.75	6.8	7.8	3.6
903	Squamscott River RR. Bridge	43° 03'	70° 55'	+2 19	+2 41	*0.75	*0.75	6.8	7.8	3.6
905	Gosport Harbor, Isles of Shoals	42° 59'	70° 37'	+0 02	−0 02	*0.93	*0.93	8.5	9.8	4.5
907	Hampton Harbor	42° 54'	70° 49'	+0 14	+0 32	*0.91	*0.91	8.3	9.5	4.5
	MASSACHUSETTS, outer coast									
909	Merrimack River entrance	42° 49'	70° 49'	+0 20	+0 24	*0.91	*0.91	8.3	9.5	4.4
911	Newburyport, Merrimack River	42° 49'	70° 52'	+0 31	+1 11	*0.86	*0.86	7.8	9.0	4.2
913	Plum Island Sound (south end)	42° 43'	70° 47'	+0 12	+0 37	*0.94	*0.94	8.6	9.9	4.6
915	Annisquam	42° 39'	70° 41'	0 00	−0 07	*0.96	*0.96	8.7	10.1	4.7
917	Rockport	42° 40'	70° 37'	+0 04	+0 02	*0.94	*0.94	8.6	10.0	4.6
					on Boston, p.36					
919	Gloucester Harbor	42° 36'	70° 40'	−0 01	−0 04	*0.91	*0.91	8.7	10.1	4.6
921	Manchester Harbor	42° 34'	70° 47'	0 00	−0 04	*0.92	*0.92	8.8	10.2	4.7
923	Beverly	42° 32'	70° 53'	+0 02	−0 03	*0.94	*0.94	9.0	10.4	4.8
925	Salem	42° 31'	70° 53'	+0 04	+0 03	*0.92	*0.92	8.8	10.2	4.7
927	Marblehead	42° 30'	70° 51'	0 00	−0 04	*0.95	*0.95	9.1	10.6	4.8
	Broad Sound									
929	Nahant	42° 25'	70° 55'	+0 01	0 00	*0.94	*0.94	9.0	10.4	4.8
931	Lynn Harbor	42° 27'	70° 58'	+0 10	+0 06	*0.96	*0.96	9.2	10.7	4.9
	Boston Harbor									
933	Boston Light	42° 20'	70° 53'	+0 02	+0 03	*0.94	*0.94	9.0	10.4	4.8
935	Lovell Island, The Narrows	42° 20'	70° 56'	+0 04	+0 03	*0.95	*0.95	9.1	10.6	4.8
937	Deer Island (south end)	42° 21'	70° 58'	+0 01	0 00	*0.97	*0.97	9.3	10.8	4.9
939	Belle Isle Inlet entrance	42° 23'	71° 00'	+0 20	+0 17	*1.00	*1.00	9.5	11.0	5.0
941	Castle Island	42° 20'	71° 01'	0 00	+0 02	*0.99	*0.99	9.4	10.9	5.0
943	BOSTON	42° 21'	71° 03'		Daily predictions			9.5	11.0	5.1
945	Dover St. Bridge, Fort Point Channel	42° 21'	71° 04'	+0 06	+0 08	*1.01	*1.01	9.6	11.0	5.1
	Charles River									
947	Charlestown Bridge	42° 22'	71° 04'	+0 04	+0 04	*1.00	*1.00	9.5	11.0	5.0
949	Charles River Dam	42° 22'	71° 04'	+0 07	+0 06	*1.00	*1.00	9.5	11.0	5.0
951	Charlestown	42° 22'	71° 03'	0 00	+0 01	*1.00	*1.00	9.5	11.0	5.0
953	Chelsea St. Bridge, Chelsea River	42° 23'	71° 01'	+0 01	+0 06	*1.01	*1.01	9.6	11.1	5.1
955	Neponset, Neponset River	42° 17'	71° 02'	−0 02	+0 03	*1.00	*1.00	9.5	11.0	5.0
957	Moon Head	42° 19'	70° 59'	+0 01	+0 04	*0.99	*0.99	9.4	10.9	5.0
959	Rainsford Island, Nantasket Roads	42° 19'	70° 57'	0 00	+0 02	*0.95	*0.95	9.1	10.6	4.8

TIDAL CURRENTS

Types of Tidal Current

Tidal currents in the open ocean are *rotary*, i.e., the direction of the water flow rotates 360° during a full tidal period, 12 hours 25 minutes. Rotary currents tend to be small and have little effect on navigation. You may be asked a rotary-current question, however, so we will explain them at the end of this section.

The type of tidal current you definitely will be examined on is the *periodic ebb and flood* in constricted water bodies, such as estuaries. This type of flow is nearly linear because the shape of the water body constrains it to be so.

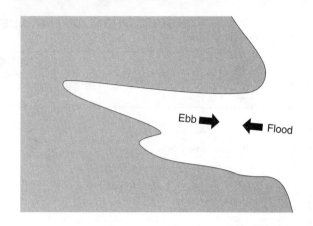

Tidal Current Terminology

- *Flood* is the movement of tidal current into or up a tidal river or estuary.

- *Ebb* is the movement of tidal current out of or down a tidal river or estuary.

- *Slack water* is the state of the tide when its current is zero, or as close to zero as it gets.

Tidal Current Tables

Tidal current tables are published in three annual volumes:

- *Tidal Current Tables: Atlantic Coast of North America*

- *Tidal Current Tables: Pacific Coast of North America and Asia*

- *Regional Tide and Tidal Current Tables: New York Harbor to Chesapeake Bay*

Each volume contains five tables, with the first three of main concern. Sample pages from Tables 1 and 2 follow. Table 3 allows determination of current at any intermediate time.

Table 1 contains the times of slack water and the times and magnitudes of maximum flood and maximum ebb for the entire year for 25 primary stations, including the sample, Chesapeake Bay Entrance.

Table 2 contains current differences to be applied to the currents in Table 1 for approximately 1,200 subordinate stations. The example page contains stations subordinate to Chesapeake Bay Entrance.

Table 1—Primary Stations

Find the primary station nearest your location and the page covering the month and day. The data for Chesapeake Bay Entrance, 3 June, 1995, is shaded on the sample page.

After the month and day, the first column lists the times of slack water in Standard Time. To convert to Daylight Savings Time add one hour. The next column shows the times of maximum current. The third column shows the magnitude of the maximum current in knots and whether it is an ebb or a flood.

On 3 June, 1995, the first slack water is at 0216 (2:16 AM). The next maximum current is an ebb of 1.0 knots occurring at 0553. Following the ebb the current goes slack again at 0934.

Table 2—Subordinate Station Differences

You can find subordinate stations by paging through Table 2 or by looking up the station name in the index. Let's look up Station 4556, York Spit Channel, N of Buoy "26."

Following the number and name of the station, the next three columns list the water depth, latitude and longitude of the station. The next four columns show time corrections for minimum (slack) before flood, maximum flood, slack before ebb, and maximum ebb. The next pair of columns list speed ratios (multipliers) to apply to maximum flood and ebb currents.

Using Table 1 and Table 2 Together

Using Table 1 and Table 2, we can find the maximum currents and slack waters at any subordinate stations for any day.

Example: Find the time and maximum speed of the first ebb on 3 June, 1995, at York Spit Channel.

Solution: Find the time and speed of first maximum ebb at the primary station, Chesapeake Bay Entrance (found above as 1.0 knots at 0553). Next find the time difference and speed multiplier for maximum ebb at York Spit Channel (+ 1 26 and 0.9). Finally, apply the difference factors to find the answers:

time of maximum ebb 05 53 + 1 26 = 07 19

speed of maximum ebb 1.0 kt × 0.9 = 0.9 kt

Current Diagrams

The time of maximum flood increases as you proceed further into an estuary. You can take advantage of this phenomenon to "go with the flow" and minimize transit time between locations in the diagram. The example diagram below is one of five in the Atlantic Coast tidal current volume.

Select a sloped line from the two sets below, according to your vessel's speed through the water and whether northbound or southbound. Using a parallel rule, transfer the chosen line to the flood (shaded) or ebb (unshaded) zone, keeping the line as close to the center of the zone as possible between your departure and destination points.

Example: You wish to go from York Spit Light to Thomas Point Light on the flood tide. Your vessel's cruising speed is 10 knots. At what time should you leave to derive maximum benefit from the flood current?

Solution: Transfer the 10 knot northbound slope to the flood (shaded) zone between York Spit (nm 20 on the left scale) to Thomas Point Light (nm 120). Move the slope line until it is centered in the zone. From the intersection of the slope line to the horizontal line at 20 nm, draw a vertical line down to read the optimum departure time. The answer is 2.5 hours after slack before flood at Chesapeake Bay Entrance. To get the actual time, find the time of slack before flood from Table 1, as shown on the previous page, and add two hours and 30 minutes.

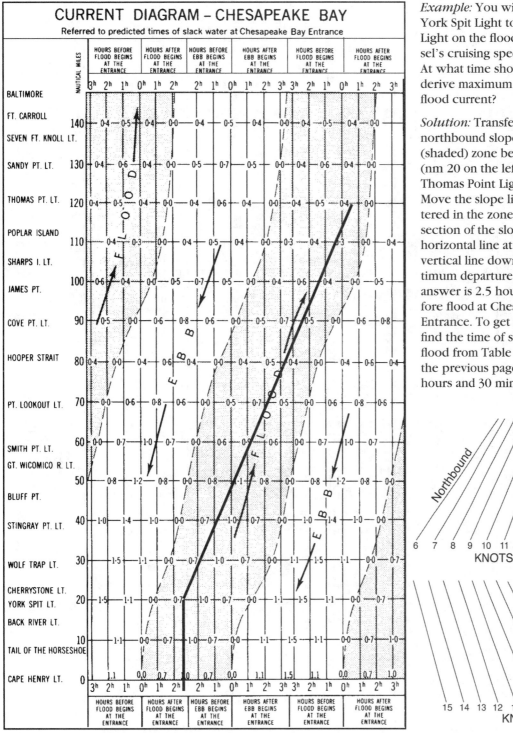

Table 1—Daily Current Predictions

Chesapeake Bay Entrance, Virginia, 1995

F—Flood, Dir. 300° True   E—Ebb, Dir. 129° True

April

Day	Slack h m	Max h m	knots	Day	Slack h m	Max h m	knots
1 Sa		0323	1.4E	**16** Su		0249	1.7E
	0632	0852	0.8F		0557	0821	1.0F
	1141	1514	1.4E		1115	1454	1.8E
	1820	2105	1.1F		1754	2044	1.6F
2 Su	0032	0400	1.3E	**17** M	0017	0336	1.8E
	0719	0932	0.8F		0649	0909	1.0F
	1215	1544	1.3E		1203	1541	1.7E
	1900	2142	1.0F		1843	2131	1.5F
3 M	0110	0439	1.2E	**18** Tu	0107	0428	1.7E
	0805	1013	0.6F		0743	1000	1.0F
	1249	1617	1.2E		1256	1633	1.6E
	1940	2222	0.9F		1938	2222	1.4F
4 Tu	0148	0523	1.1E	**19** W	0158	0527	1.6E
	0852	1058	0.5F		0840	1055	0.9F
	1324	1657	1.0E		1350	1734	1.5E
	2023	2305	0.8F		2035	2318	1.3F
5 W	0227	0612	0.9E	**20** Th	0252	0629	1.5E
	0944	1148	0.4F		0942	1157	0.8F
	1401	1746	0.9E		1453	1840	1.3E
	2109	2353	0.7F		2138		
6 Th	0310	0700	0.8E	**21** F		0018	1.1F
	1042	1239	0.3F		0354	0732	1.4E
	1442	1839	0.9E		1049	1301	0.7F
	2202			○	1610	1947	1.2E
					2249		
7 F		0041	0.6F	**22** Sa		0121	0.9F
	0404	0748	0.8E		0502	0836	1.3E
	1146	1333	0.3F		1156	1411	0.6F
	1539	1931	0.8E		1735	2100	1.1E
	2303						
8 Sa ◗		0134	0.5F	**23** Su	0001	0231	0.7F
	0505	0843	0.8E		0607	0944	1.3E
	1242	1442	0.3F		1259	1547	0.7F
	1703	2030	0.8E		1848	2215	1.2E
9 Su	0005	0238	0.5F	**24** M	0115	0356	0.7F
	0600	0943	0.7E		0705	1045	1.3E
	1329	1557	0.4F		1356	1653	0.8F
	1816	2138	0.8E		1954	2317	1.2E
10 M	0102	0347	0.5F	**25** Tu	0221	0457	0.7F
	0649	1033	1.0E		0758	1136	1.3E
	1407	1641	0.5F		1445	1735	0.9F
	1919	2240	1.0E		2052		
11 Tu	0158	0437	0.6F	**26** W		0012	1.3E
	0735	1115	1.2E		0319	0541	0.7F
	1440	1716	0.7F		0844	1222	1.3E
	2016	2332	1.1E		1528	1811	1.0F
					2140		
12 W	0248	0517	0.8F	**27** Th		0104	1.4E
	0819	1156	1.3E		0408	0622	0.7F
	1513	1751	1.0F		0924	1305	1.3E
	2107				1604	1847	1.0F
					2222		
13 Th		0022	1.3E	**28** F		0150	1.4E
	0334	0558	0.9F		0451	0703	0.7F
	0903	1239	1.5E		0959	1342	1.3E
	1549	1830	1.2F		1639	1925	1.1F
	2155				2300		
14 F		0113	1.5E	**29** Sa ●		0231	1.4E
	0420	0643	1.0F		0534	0748	0.7F
	0946	1324	1.6E		1033	1416	1.3E
	1628	1913	1.4F		1714	2003	1.1F
	2241				2337		
15 Sa ○		0202	1.6E	**30** Su		0308	1.3E
	0508	0731	1.0F		0618	0829	0.7F
	1029	1410	1.7E		1106	1445	1.3E
	1709	1958	1.5F		1751	2041	1.1F
	2328						

May

Day	Slack h m	Max h m	knots	Day	Slack h m	Max h m	knots
1 M	0013	0341	1.3E	**16** Tu	0000	0321	1.8E
	0701	0909	0.6F		0631	0851	1.0F
	1141	1515	1.2E		1144	1524	1.8E
	1829	2118	1.0F		1824	2114	1.6F
2 Tu	0050	0415	1.2E	**17** W	0051	0412	1.8E
	0745	0950	0.6F		0727	0944	1.0F
	1219	1548	1.2E		1241	1617	1.7E
	1909	2156	0.9F		1920	2206	1.5F
3 W	0126	0452	1.1E	**18** Th	0142	0509	1.7E
	0830	1032	0.5F		0823	1040	0.9F
	1257	1627	1.1E		1342	1719	1.5E
	1951	2236	0.8F		2019	2302	1.3F
4 Th	0203	0538	1.0E	**19** F	0236	0611	1.6E
	0918	1120	0.4F		0923	1142	0.8F
	1337	1714	0.9E		1447	1826	1.4E
	2034	2320	0.7F		2122		
5 F	0240	0625	0.9E	**20** Sa		0002	1.1F
	1009	1210	0.3F		0332	0711	1.5E
	1419	1809	0.9E		1027	1246	0.8F
	2121				1601	1932	1.2E
					2230		
6 Sa		0006	0.6F	**21** Su ○		0103	0.9F
	0322	0710	0.9E		0433	0810	1.4E
	1102	1301	0.3F		1130	1352	0.7F
	1513	1902	0.8E		1720	2041	1.1E
	2215				2342		
7 Su ◖		0055	0.6F	**22** M		0207	0.7F
	0409	0755	0.9E		0533	0913	1.3E
	1151	1354	0.3F		1230	1517	0.7F
	1632	1957	0.8E		1832	2154	1.1E
	2316						
8 M		0144	0.5F	**23** Tu	0055	0323	0.6F
	0501	0845	1.0E		0628	1015	1.3E
	1233	1457	0.4F		1327	1633	0.8F
	1748	2059	0.8E		1937	2259	1.1E
9 Tu	0018	0244	0.5F	**24** W	0204	0431	0.6F
	0550	0939	1.1E		0717	1107	1.2E
	1312	1554	0.6F		1417	1718	0.9F
	1850	2206	1.0E		2035	2355	1.2E
10 W	0118	0348	0.6F	**25** Th	0304	0517	0.6F
	0637	1029	1.2E		0802	1152	1.2E
	1350	1637	0.8F		1500	1751	0.9F
	1948	2303	1.1E		2124		
11 Th	0215	0440	0.7F	**26** F		0046	1.2E
	0725	1116	1.4E		0354	0557	0.6F
	1430	1716	1.1F		0843	1232	1.2E
	2041	2356	1.3E		1539	1825	0.9F
					2206		
12 F	0308	0525	0.8F	**27** Sa		0133	1.2E
	0815	1203	1.5E		0438	0638	0.5F
	1512	1757	1.3F		0920	1311	1.2E
	2132				1615	1901	1.0F
					2243		
13 Sa		0049	1.5E	**28** Su		0214	1.2E
	0358	0613	0.9F		0518	0721	0.5F
	0906	1252	1.7E		0957	1346	1.2E
	1557	1843	1.5F		1650	1940	1.0F
	2220				2319		
14 Su ○		0142	1.7E	**29** M ●		0249	1.2E
	0447	0704	1.0F		0559	0805	0.5F
	0958	1344	1.8E		1033	1418	1.2E
	1641	1932	1.6F		1727	2019	1.0F
	2309				2355		
15 M		0232	1.8E	**30** Tu		0321	1.2E
	0538	0758	1.0F		0640	0847	0.5F
	1049	1434	1.8E		1112	1451	1.2E
	1731	2023	1.6F		1804	2057	1.0F
				31 W	0031	0352	1.1E
					0723	0928	0.5F
					1153	1526	1.2E
					1843	2134	0.9F

June

Day	Slack h m	Max h m	knots	Day	Slack h m	Max h m	knots
1 Th	0107	0427	1.1E	**16** F	0126	0449	1.7E
	0808	1009	0.5F		0803	1023	1.0F
	1236	1604	1.1E		1330	1702	1.6E
	1924	2211	0.9F		2004	2245	1.3F
2 F	0142	0507	1.1E	**17** Sa	0216	0548	1.6E
	0850	1053	0.4F		0900	1123	0.9F
	1319	1650	1.0E		1433	1808	1.4E
	2005	2251	0.8F		2105	2343	1.1F
3 Sa	0216	0553	1.0E	**18** Su	0306	0645	1.5E
	0934	1141	0.4F		0959	1225	0.8F
	1403	1742	0.9E		1541	1912	1.3E
	2049	2335	0.7F		2210		
4 Su	0250	0637	1.1E	**19** M ○		0041	0.9F
	1019	1229	0.4F		0359	0740	1.6E
	1455	1837	0.9E		1059	1324	0.8F
	2139				1655	2017	1.1E
					2320		
5 M		0019	0.7F	**20** Tu		0139	0.7F
	0326	0720	1.1E		0453	0837	1.3E
	1101	1314	0.5F		1157	1432	0.7F
	1605	1930	0.9E		1805	2127	1.1E
	2238						
6 Tu ◐		0107	0.6F	**21** W ◐	0030	0243	0.6F
	0408	0804	1.1E		0545	0936	1.2E
	1142	1404	0.5F		1251	1555	0.7F
	1719	2028	0.9E		1908	2234	1.0E
	2340						
7 W		0200	0.6F	**22** Th	0139	0355	0.5F
	0457	0855	1.2E		0631	1031	1.1E
	1223	1501	0.7F		1343	1650	0.8F
	1822	2133	1.0E		2007	2331	1.0E
8 Th	0042	0302	0.6F	**23** F	0242	0448	0.4F
	0548	0949	1.3E		0715	1117	1.1E
	1308	1556	0.9F		1430	1728	0.8F
	1920	2237	1.1E		2059		
9 F	0145	0404	0.7F	**24** Sa		0022	1.1E
	0641	1042	1.4E		0333	0529	0.4F
	1354	1644	1.2F		0758	1158	1.1E
	2016	2332	1.3E		1513	1801	0.9F
					2143		
10 Sa	0242	0458	0.8F	**25** Su		0109	1.1E
	0736	1134	1.6E		0416	0609	0.5F
	1442	1730	1.4F		0840	1237	1.1E
	2110				1551	1837	0.9F
					2221		
11 Su		0027	1.5E	**26** M		0151	1.1E
	0337	0548	0.9F		0455	0652	0.5F
	0834	1227	1.7E		0923	1314	1.2E
	1531	1818	1.5F		1628	1917	0.9F
	2201				2257		
12 M ○		0122	1.6E	**27** Tu ●		0226	1.1E
	0428	0640	1.0F		0534	0738	0.5F
	0932	1322	1.8E		1006	1352	1.2E
	1621	1910	1.6F		1704	1958	0.9F
	2252				2332		
13 Tu		0215	1.7E	**28** W		0258	1.1E
	0519	0736	1.0F		0614	0823	0.5F
	1030	1417	1.8E		1048	1429	1.2E
	1714	2004	1.6F		1741	2036	1.0F
	2343						
14 W		0305	1.8E	**29** Th	0008	0327	1.2E
	0611	0833	1.0F		0657	0905	0.5F
	1129	1509	1.8E		1132	1506	1.2E
	1809	2058	1.6F		1819	2112	1.0F
15 Th	0035	0355	1.8E	**30** F	0044	0400	1.2E
	0708	0927	1.0F		0737	0945	0.5F
	1229	1603	1.7E		1218	1545	1.2E
	1906	2150	1.5F		1859	2148	0.9F

Table 2—Current Differences

No.	PLACE	Meter Depth (ft)	POSITION Latitude North	POSITION Longitude West	TIME DIFF. Min. before Flood (h m)	TIME DIFF. Flood (h m)	TIME DIFF. Min. before Ebb (h m)	TIME DIFF. Ebb (h m)	SPEED RATIOS Flood	SPEED RATIOS Ebb	AVG Min. before Flood (knots)	AVG Min. before Flood (Dir.)	AVG Maximum Flood (knots)	AVG Maximum Flood (Dir.)	AVG Min. before Ebb (knots)	AVG Min. before Ebb (Dir.)	AVG Maximum Ebb (knots)	AVG Maximum Ebb (Dir.)
	CHESAPEAKE BAY Time meridian, 75° W																	
4441	Cape Henry Light, 1.1 n.mi. NNE of	15d	36°56.33'	75°59.98'	+0 26	+0 03	−0 04	+0 10	1.3	1.3	—	—	1.0	298°	—	—	1.7	113°
4446	Cape Henry Light, 2.0 n.mi. north of	38d	36°56.33'	75°59.98'	−1 42	−1 41	−1 36	−1 52	1.4	1.0	0.2	003°	1.1	275°	0.2	189°	1.2	106°
	do.	15d	36°57.53'	76°00.63'	+0 12	+0 25	+1 00	+0 20	1.5	0.9	0.1	210°	1.2	289°	—	—	1.1	110°
	do.	39d	36°57.53'	76°00.63'	−0 23	+0 10	+0 55	−0 17	1.5	0.5	0.1	012°	1.2	277°	0.1	190°	0.7	110°
	do.	54d	36°57.53'	76°00.63'	−1 03	+0 07	+0 34	−1 05	1.1	0.4	0.0	002°	0.9	263°	0.2	177°	0.5	111°
4451	CHESAPEAKE BAY ENTRANCE	15d	36°58.80'	75°59.88'		Daily predictions on Chesapeake Bay Entrance, p.44					—	—	0.8	300°	0.0	—	1.2	129°
4456	Cape Henry Light, 4.6 miles north of		37°00.1'	75°59.3'	−0 27	−0 09	+0 19	+0 23	1.6	1.0	0.1	228°	1.3	294°	—	—	1.3	104°
4461	Cape Henry Light, 5.9 n.mi. north of	14d	37°01.40'	75°59.55'	−0 59	−0 09	−0 26	−0 36	0.8	0.5	—	—	0.6	307°	—	—	0.7	140°
4466	Lynnhaven Roads		36°55.1'	76°04.9'	−0 20	+0 18	+0 15	−0 10	1.0	0.7	—	—	0.8	280°	—	—	0.9	070°
4471	Lynnhaven Inlet bridge		36°54.4'	76°05.6'	−1 18	−1 10	−1 43	−2 30	0.7	1.1	—	—	0.6	180°	—	—	1.4	000°
	Chesapeake Bay Bridge Tunnel																	
4476	Chesapeake Beach, 1.5 miles north of	15d	36°56.69'	76°07.33'	+0 29	−0 48	+0 06	+0 00	1.0	0.7	0.1	228°	0.8	305°	—	—	0.9	100°
4481	Thimble Shoal Channel (Buoy "10")	45d	36°58.73'	76°07.57'	−0 04	+0 30	+0 45	+0 16	1.4	0.6	0.1	—	1.1	302°	—	—	0.7	122°
	do.		36°58.73'	76°07.57'	−0 55	+0 15	+1 25	−0 17	0.8	0.2	—	—	0.7	285°	—	—	0.3	105°
4486	Tail of the Horseshoe	12	36°59.57'	76°06.20'	+0 05	+0 30	+0 16	+0 28	1.1	0.8	—	—	0.9	300°	—	—	1.0	110°
4491	Cape Henry Light, 8.3 mi. NW of		37°02.20'	76°06.60'	+0 16	+0 43	+0 45	+0 26	1.2	0.9	—	—	1.0	329°	—	—	1.1	133°
4496	Chesapeake Channel (bridge tunnel)	13d	37°02.50'	76°04.33'	−0 30	+0 38	+0 32	+0 29	2.2	1.2	0.2	037°	1.8	335°	—	—	1.5	145°
4501	Chesapeake Channel (Buoy "15")	34d	37°03.40'	76°05.58'	−0 21	+0 33	+0 50	+0 38	0.8	0.4	0.2	032°	0.6	311°	0.1	229°	0.4	125°
	do.		37°03.40'	76°05.58'	−0 22	−0 27	+0 57	−0 07	0.7	0.3	0.2	—	0.6	309°	0.1	232°	1.6	139°
4506	Fishermans Island, 3.2 miles WSW of		37°04.00'	76°02.25'	−0 22	−0 12	−0 17	−0 36	1.5	1.3	—	—	1.2	330°	—	—	1.1	135°
4511	Fishermans Island, 1.4 miles WSW of		37°04.78'	76°00.25'	−1 09	−0 09	−0 12	−1 02	2.2	0.9	—	—	1.8	330°	—	—	1.1	140°
4516	Fishermans I.Bridge 1.4 n.mi. S of	16d	37°03.37'	75°58.33'	−0 19	−0 29	−0 15	−0 26	1.0	1.1	0.2	218°	1.0	297°	—	—	1.4	126°
	do.	26d	37°03.37'	75°58.33'	−0 37	−0 19	−0 16	−0 34	1.0	0.8	—	—	0.8	290°	—	—	1.0	120°
4521	Fishermans I. Bridge, 0.7 n.mi. S of	15d	37°04.85'	75°58.83'	−0 57	−0 15	−0 24	−0 35	1.9	1.5	0.2	223°	1.5	306°	0.1	218°	1.9	140°
4526	Fishermans I., 0.4 mile west of		37°05.57'	75°59.33'	−0 21	−0 08	−0 06	−0 42	2.5	1.6	—	—	2.0	005°	—	—	2.0	175°
4531	Fishermans I., 1.4 n.mi. WNW of	16d	37°06.10'	76°00.33'	−0 28	−0 14	−0 12	−0 27	1.4	1.0	0.1	060°	1.2	333°	0.1	247°	1.2	155°
4536	Fishermans I., 1.1 miles northwest of		37°06.88'	75°58.30'	−0 39	+0 20	+0 23	−0 19	2.2	1.3	—	—	1.8	355°	—	—	1.6	165°
4541	Cape Charles, off Wise Point	5	37°06.05'	76°00.78'	+0 09	+0 37	+0 56	+1 20	0.9	0.2	—	—	0.7	305°	—	—	0.2	075°
4546	Little Creek, 0.2 n.mi. N of east jetty	15d	36°56.05'	76°01.60'	−1 01	−1 18	−0 39	+1 02	0.4	0.3	—	—	0.3	278°	—	—	0.3	092°
4551	Butler Bluff, 2.1 n.mi. WSW of	14d	37°09.37'	76°00.50'	+0 02	+0 14	+0 57	+1 02	0.9	0.7	—	—	0.8	348°	—	—	0.8	164°
4556	York Spit Channel. N of Buoy "26"	7	37°12.90'	76°04.10'	+1 33	+1 50	+1 24	+1 26	1.0	0.9	0.8	010°	0.8	010°	—	—	1.1	195°
4561	Old Plantation Flats Lt. 0.5 mi. W of	15d	37°14.10'	76°05.62'	+1 31	+2 01	+1 55	+1 06	1.5	1.0	0.2	280°	1.2	005°	0.1	094°	1.3	175°
4566	Cape Charles City, 3.3 n.mi. west of	40d	37°15.87'	76°05.62'	+0 38	+1 18	+1 03	+1 01	1.2	0.8	—	—	1.0	355°	0.1	284°	1.0	187°
	do.	95d	37°15.87'	76°11.45'	+0 16	+0 43	+1 10	+0 30	1.1	0.7	—	—	0.9	356°	—	—	0.8	182°
	do.	15d	37°17.40'	76°11.9'	+0 29	+1 00	+1 37	+1 24	1.2	0.8	0.1	223°	1.0	322°	0.3	098°	0.8	138°
4571	New Point Comfort, 4.1 n.mi. ESE of	15d	37°23.1'	76°04.3'	+1 07	+1 22	+0 46	+0 46	1.1	1.0	0.3	296°	0.8	018°	—	—	1.0	202°
4576	Wolf Trap Light, 0.5 mile west of		37°23.4'	76°00.78'	+1 43	+2 00	+1 34	+1 36	0.6	0.9	—	—	1.0	015°	—	—	1.2	190°
4581	Wolf Trap Light, 5.8 miles east of		37°24.20'	76°03.83'	+2 23	+2 40	+2 14	+2 16	1.6	0.9	0.2	275°	1.2	015°	0.2	098°	1.3	175°
4586	Church Neck Point, 1.9 n.mi. W of	14d	37°24.50'	76°03.83'	+1 40	+1 58	+1 36	+0 50	1.6	0.9	0.4	006°	0.4	003°	0.2	279°	0.4	177°
4591	Wolf Trap Light, 6.1 n.mi. ENE of	29d	37°24.50'	76°05.00'	+0 26	+0 55	+2 28	+2 11	1.3	0.9	0.7	012°	0.7	006°	0.2	098°	1.1	191°
4596	Wolf Trap Light, 5.2 n.mi. ENE of	40d	37°24.50'	76°05.00'	+1 43	+2 34	+1 27	+2 09	1.0	0.5	1.3	010°	1.3	012°	0.2	098°	1.1	173°
	do.	63d	37°24.50'	76°05.00'	+1 07	+2 24	+2 43	+1 19	1.4	0.7	1.3	010°	1.0	352°	0.2	266°	0.7	187°
	do.	15d	37°24.50'	76°05.00'	+0 24	+1 22	+2 05	+1 11	0.7	0.4	1.0	352°	0.8	343°	—	—	0.6	183°
	do.		37°24.67'	76°10.57'	+1 38	+2 16	+1 52	+1 19	0.8	0.5	—	—	1.1	005°	—	—	0.6	158°
4601	Wolf Trap Light, 1.4 n.mi. NNE of	14d	37°25.00'	76°05.00'	+0 33	+0 33	+1 05	+0 08	1.2	0.4	0.2	088°	0.6	345°	0.2	088°	1.2	175°
4606	Wolf Trap Light, 2.0 n.mi. NW of	13d	37°29.97'	75°59.37'	+1 16	+1 43	+1 56	+1 36	0.7	0.7	—	—	0.6	352°	—	—	0.6	166°
4611	Nassawadox Point, 1.9 n.mi. NW of	14d	37°29.70'	76°06.50'	+2 03	+3 03	+2 48	+2 33	1.2	0.6	0.2	270°	1.0	357°	0.1	270°	0.6	178°
4616	Gwynn Island, 8.0 n.mi. east of	28d	37°30.03'	76°14.70'	+0 33	+1 07	+1 46	+0 23	0.6	0.7	0.2	267°	0.6	013°	0.3	090°	1.0	175°
	do.	16d	37°33.8'	76°10.4'	+0 59	+0 54	+0 54	+0 22	1.2	0.6	0.2	102°	0.6	331°	0.1	281°	0.6	209°
4621	Gwynn Island, 1.5 n.mi. east of		37°35.45'	76°02.3'	+2 28	+3 36	+3 21	+2 32	0.8	0.5	—	—	0.5	343°	0.1	227°	0.5	159°
4626	Stingray Point, 5.5 miles east of		37°34.60'	75°58.10'	+2 18	+3 00	+2 09	+2 36	1.2	0.6	—	—	1.0	030°	—	—	0.9	179°
4631	Stingray Point, 12.5 miles east of		37°34.60'	76°03.80'	+1 21	+1 29	+1 54	+1 23	0.8	0.5	0.1	101°	0.6	030°	0.1	284°	0.8	175°
4636	Powells Bluff, 2.2 n.mi. NW of	17d		76°03.80'	+2 18	+2 57	+3 04	+2 46	1.1	0.7	0.1	270°	0.9	359°	0.1	095°	0.6	201°
4641	Windmill Point Light, 8.3 n.mi. ESE of	14d			+1 06	+1 22	+3 07	+2 14	0.8	0.5	0.1	101°	0.6	015°	0.1	284°	0.6	182°
	do.	33d							0.6	0.3	0.2	099°	0.5	017°	0.2	255°	0.4	172°

TIDAL CURRENTS 291

Rotary Currents

Most open ocean tidal currents rotate clockwise (CCW south of equator) in direction through the tidal period of 12 hours 26 minutes. The tidal current volumes contain information on rotary currents for a few dozen offshore locations (former lightship stations). The illustration at right was drawn from the data listed for Frying Pan Shoals, off Cape Hatteras. The arrows show the direction the current is flowing at the number of hours after the time of maximum flood at Charleston (listed in Table 1). The speeds are monthly averages. Speeds increase by 15–20% at times of full and new moons, and decrease by the same amount at quadrature.

Note that there is no slack water in a rotary current. Instead, there is a minimum current and a maximum current, separated by three hours, thus corresponding to low and high tides.

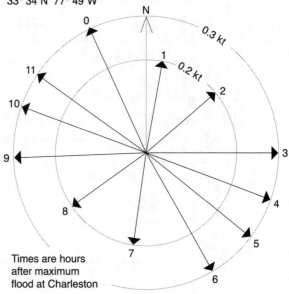

Rotary Currents at Frying Pan Shoals
33° 34′N 77° 49′W

Times are hours after maximum flood at Charleston

Wind-Driven Current

Wind will cause a surface current due to friction. Just as in the atmosphere, the wind-driven current will be deflected to the right in the Northern Hemisphere. Observed current vs. wind speed at most light ships averaged:

Wind, mph	10	20	30	40	50
Current, kt	0.2	0.3	0.4	0.5	0.6

While the Coriolis force causes an average current deflection of 30° to the right of the wind, the configuration of the coast can alter the direction. The Atlantic Coast tidal current volume lists data for 20 lightship stations. Here are the deflections for Frying Pan Shoals, where + means to the right and – means to the left of the wind direction. Wind from:

N (34°)	NE (18°)	E (2°)	SE (48°)
S (48°)	SW (26°)	W (–7°)	NW (–27°)

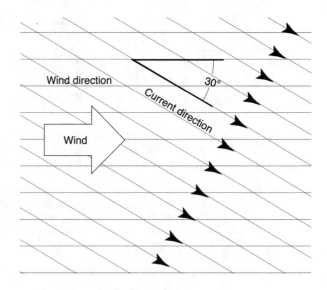

Combined Effects

Rotary and wind-driven currents combine the same way as vessel speed through the water and current. *Example:* the wind at Frying Pan Shoals has been northwesterly at an average velocity of 22 knots. The predicted set and drift of the rotary current are 125° at 0.6 knot. What current should you expect?

Solution: plot the rotary current vector of 0.6 kt @ 125°T. The 22-knot wind should produce a 0.3 kt wind-driven current. With the wind from the NW, the deflection is –27°, so the wind-driven vector is 0.3 kn @ (135° – 27°) = 108°, which we add to the rotary vector. The resultant current is 0.9 kt @ 119°.

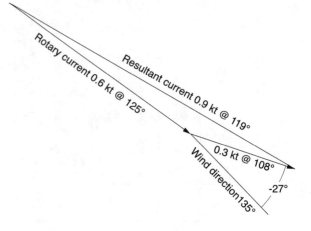

CHARTS AND PUBLICATIONS

Chart Projections

Several projection methods exist, the chart's use dictating which is employed. They are:

- Mercator (Cylindrical Projection)
- Gnomonic (Plane Projection)
- Lambert Conformal (Conic Projection)

The Mercator Projection

At the equator, the distance on the earth's surface represented by one degree of latitude is approximately that of one degree of longitude, 60 nautical miles.

Moving to higher latitudes (north or south) on the globe, the linear distances covered by one degree of latitude and longitude are not the same. The former remains 60 nautical miles while the latter gradually shortens as the meridians converge toward zero at the poles.

In order to stretch this curved/wedge shape into a plane, the converging meridians of longitude are made parallel, resulting in a distortion which increases with increasing latitude. In order to maintain accurate angular relationships, the east-west distortion is matched by a factor of north-south lengthening, thus ensuring that the parallels of latitude and meridians of longitude are expanded proportionally. As the meridians converge toward each pole, a greater compensatory expansion of latitude occurs on this projection, until finally at the pole, that expansion approaches infinity, making the practical useful limit of this projection about 80 degrees of latitude. For the interested, the increase in length of the meridian (the factor noted above) is equal to the secant of the latitude, at that latitude.

The advantage of the Mercator projection is the fact that a course line plots as a straight (rhumb) line, making the same angle with all meridians that it crosses. This means that one course holds from departure to destination, and also that measurement of bearings and distances are simple. The disadvantage is that for longer distances (unless due north-south, or east-west at the equator), the rhumb-line distance is not the shortest, the shortest being a great circle route. The ability to plot a great circle track as a straight line is the advantage of the gnomonic projection (see next page).

MERCATOR PROJECTION

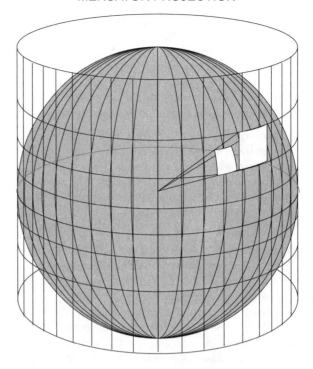

With the high degree of magnification occurring in the latitude scale when moving from equator to poles, it is apparent why it is important when using the latitude scale for distance measurement, to use the scale nearest to the latitude of the distance involved. Large-scale charts provide a distance scale at the margin. Small-scale charts covering areas with large latitudinal changes do not provide such a scale since no one scale could be accurate over the entire chart.

Longitude scales are never to be used as distance scales, no matter what the projection.

To summarize, the Mercator projection is used for two very good reasons:

1) rhumb lines plot as straight lines

2) the vertical scale is 1′ of latitude = 1 nautical mile.

The Gnomonic Projection

The *gnomonic projection* is produced by placing a plane tangent to the equator, and from the center of the sphere, projecting through its surface and onto the plane. The *oblique gnomonic projection* places the tangent point at a latitude other than the equator. Any two projected points form one edge of a plane—that plane passing through the earth's center. The latter is the definition of a great circle.

The importance of a great circle lies in its property of being the shortest distance between two points on a sphere. The utility of a gnomonic projection, therefore, lies in the fact that a great circle plots as a straight line. A chart using that projection allows for the plot of a great circle route by simply drawing a straight line.

The limitation of this projection lies in the fact that a straight line does not cross all meridians at the same angle, and (since a great circle is a curve on the globe) direction is constantly changing, requiring a slow but continuous course change. The route (long distance sailing) is plotted on a "great circle chart" (a gnomonic projection). Then, at convenient intervals of longitude (often five degrees), Lat/Long points are transferred to a Mercator chart, and rhumb-line courses are steered between those points. This results in a sequence of straight-line courses whose cumulative length is very little longer than the great circle track.

The Lambert Conformal Projection

A *conic projection* is produced by transferring points from the surface of the earth to a cone or series of cones. The cone is then cut along a meridian and spread flat. If the axis of the cone coincides with the earth's axis, parallels appear as circular arcs, and meridians appear as straight lines converging toward the pole.

A single tangent cone results in a *simple conic projection*. In this projection only the parallel of latitude to which the cone is tangent is correct in scale. All other parallels are magnified.

If the cone is shrunk so that cone and earth intersect along two parallels, then the scale is correct at the two "standard" latitudes, too small in between, and too large beyond. This is the *secant conic projection*.

If the spacing of the parallels is adjusted so the distortion is the same along both parallels and meridians, the result is the *Lambert conformal projection*. The utility of this projection is that, between the two standard latitudes, straight lines are very close to great circles.

OBLIQUE GNOMONIC PROJECTION

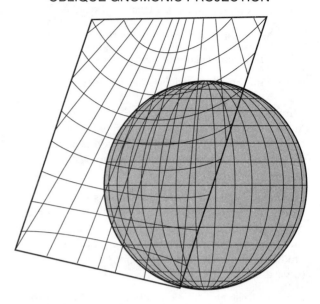

SIMPLE CONIC PROJECTION

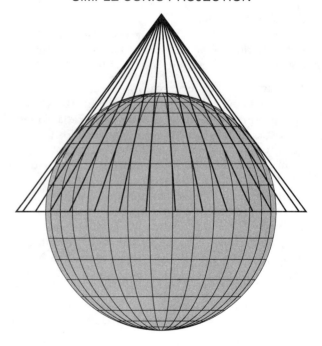

Chart Scales

Chart scale is the ratio of a unit of distance on the chart to the distance represented on the earth in the same units. Scale is represented in two ways:

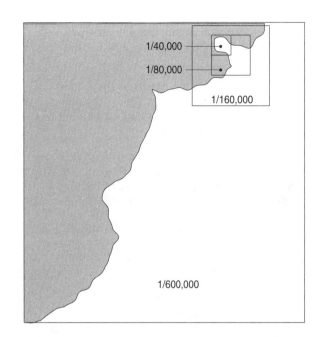

- a fraction, such as 1/80,000, meaning that 1 inch on the chart represents 80,000 inches on the earth. Note that a *larger denominator* indicates a *smaller scale*.

- a subdivided bar indicating nautical miles, statute miles and sometimes yards.

Four common NOS classifications by scale are:

Sailing charts—>600,000 for sailing between distant ports and for making landfalls.

General charts—150,000–600,000 for cruising outside the major buoys and shoals.

Coastal charts—50,000–150,000 for coastal navigation inside the furthest out buoys.

Harbor charts—<50,000 for inside harbors.

Chart Numbering System

NOS and DMAHTC share a common numbering system, where North America is designated as Region 1. South and Central America fall in Region 2.

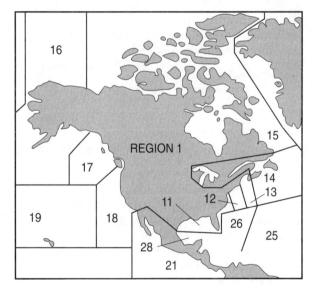

Most charts employ a five-digit system. The first indicates the region, the sub-region by the second, with the last three digits being assigned by geographical sequence within that sub-region. An example is the chart for Lake Champlain (14782). The numeral (1) represents the Atlantic Region; (4) for the Gulf of St. Lawrence–Richeleau River–Lake Champlain Sub-Region. (782) is the sequence of that chart within the sub-region.

The Atlantic and Gulf Coasts are covered by:

11xxx—Gulf Coast, Florida, thence north to NC

12xxx—North Carolina to New York

13xxx—New York through Maine

The illustration at right shows the subdivisions of Region 1. Learn these subdivisions. You may see them on the exam.

NOS offers chart catalogs (free through chart dealers) which show the numbering system in detail. Get the catalog for your area.

What Is on a Chart?

A *chart* presents primarily water areas with adjacent land margins, whereas a *map* is the reverse.

Printed on the lower left margin is the edition and publication date of the chart. That date also reflects the latest *Notice to Mariners* date to which it has been corrected.

Corrections are published weekly by the U.S. Coast Guard in its *Notice to Mariners* (DMA) and *Local Notice to Mariners* (each Coast Guard District). Revised chart printings are issued either for low stock situations or for minor corrections. New editions are printed when required by extensive corrections.

The *Catalog* is a quarterly listing of the most recent issue of each chart.

Chart No. 1 is not a chart at all, but a booklet displaying and explaining the symbols, abbreviations and terms seen on charts.

River charts are published by the U.S. Army Corps of Engineers, usually in fanfold form.

Categories of Data

Information available from the nautical chart falls into four categories:

1. Basic Data
- who published the chart
- date of publication
- chart scale
- depth scale (ft. vs. fathoms)
- datum for height above water (generally MHW)

2. Margin and Overlaid Information (not all charts)
- latitude and longitude scales
- distance scales (larger scale charts only)
- logarithmic time/speed/distance scale
- Loran linear interpolator
- Loran chain and station identifiers
- special notices regarding restricted areas, traffic separation schemes
- compass rose

3. Land Features
- shoreline features (bluffs, etc.)
- high water mark (solid line)
- contiguous areas that uncover at chart datum (MLLW)
- landmarks useful in piloting:
    radio towers
    spires
    cupolas
    tanks
    standpipes
    movie screens

4. Navigation Aids
- lighthouses
- beacons
- ranges

5. Water Features
- depth contours
- soundings in feet/fathoms
- aids to navigation

6. Chart Title Block
- area covered by the chart
- survey datum (usually MLLW)
- scale
- soundings (in feet or fathoms)
- projection

7. Magnetic variation—located at the center of the compass rose, including annual change. Local anomalies noted as margin notes.

8. Lettering
- vertical—dry at high water
- slanted—underwater or floating

9. Shoreline
- solid line indicates land/water boundary at Mean High Water
- dotted line may indicate the Low Water mark with some charts showing a tint in the zone between high and low water marks
- hatching indicates adjacent areas which may uncover at chart datum
- Sides of dredged channels marked by broken lines

10. Soundings
- chart datum is reference depth for soundings on that chart
- old charts of the West, Gulf and East Coast referenced to a Mean Low Water (MLW) datum
- datum now Mean Lower Low Water (MLLW)

11. Aids to Navigation
- primary seacoast aids: lighthouses and large navigational buoys (LNB)
- secondary lights (beacons)
- lighted and unlighted buoys
- unlighted fixed aids (daybeacons or daymarks)
- radar transponder beacons (RACONS)
- fixed charted objects ashore ("landmarks")
    radio towers
    movie screens
    standpipes
    cupolas
    tanks
    spires

Chart No. 1

Chart No. 1 is not a chart. No longer in print, it was a collaboration between NOS and DMAHTC, listing all of the symbols (in color), abbreviations and terms used on NOS and DMAHTC charts. It is now available for download at *http://pollux.nss.nima.mil/pubs/*. Below and on the next page are the more common symbols. Navigation aids are covered later in this chapter. (Full text of Chart 1 is also available in *How to Read a Nautical Chart*, by Nigel Calder.)

Relief

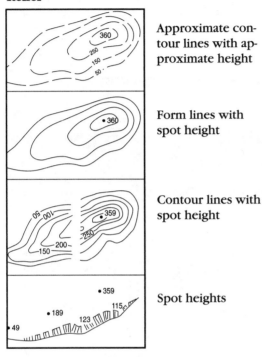

Approximate contour lines with approximate height

Form lines with spot height

Contour lines with spot height

Spot heights

Water Features

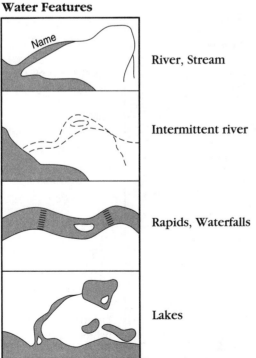

River, Stream

Intermittent river

Rapids, Waterfalls

Lakes

Bridges

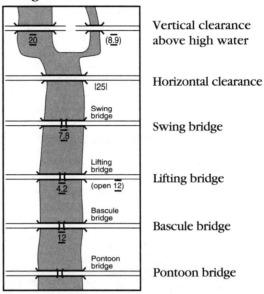

Vertical clearance above high water

Horizontal clearance

Swing bridge

Lifting bridge

Bascule bridge

Pontoon bridge

Ports

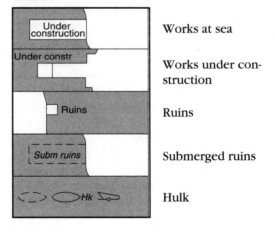

Works at sea

Works under construction

Ruins

Submerged ruins

Hulk

Canals

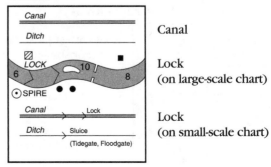

Canal

Lock
(on large-scale chart)

Lock
(on small-scale chart)

Tidal Levels and Charted Data

Planes of reference are not exactly as shown below, for all charts. They are usually defined in notes under chart titles.

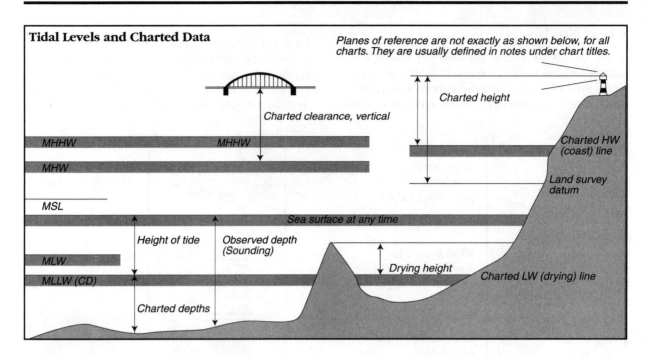

Depth Contours

Feet	Fm/m	Green / Blue
0	0	
6	1	
12	2	
18	3	
24	4	
30	5	
36	6	
60	10	
120	20	
180	30	
240	40	
300	50	
600	100	
1200	200	
1800	300	
2400	400	
3000	500	
6000	1000	

Types of Seabed, Intertidal Areas

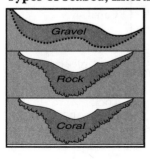

Area with stones, gravel or shingle

Rocky area, which covers and uncovers

Coral reef, which covers and uncovers

Obstructions

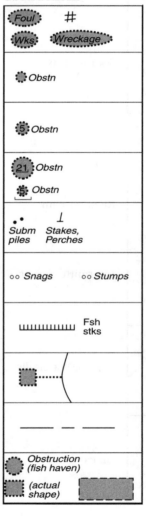

Remains, not dangerous to navigation

Obstruction, depth unknown

Obstruction, least depth known

Obstruction, swept by wire or diver

Stumps of posts or piles, submerged

Submerged pile, stump or snag (with exact position)

Fishing stakes

Fish trap, fish weirs, tunny nets

Fish trap area, tunny nets area

Fish haven (artificial fishing reef)

Publications Other Than Charts

Agency	Pub.	Title	Contents
DMAHTC	9	*American Practical Navigator (Bowditch)*	Piloting, electronic navigation, celestial navigation, navigational mathematics, navigational safety, oceanography and meteorology.
	151	*Distances Between Ports*	Distances between major ports, considering currents and climatic conditions. Used with *Sailing Directions (Planning Guide)*.
	102	*International Code of Signals*	Safety, distress, medical, and operational information to be transmitted by Morse light and sound, flag, radio, and semaphore flag.
		List of Lights, Radio Aids, and Fog Signals	Foreign lighted navigation aids, sound signals, storm signals, signal stations, racons, and radiobeacons, but NOT lighted harbor buoys.
		Notice to Mariners	Weekly updates affecting navigational safety, including changes in charted depths, channels, and aids to navigation.
	117	*Radio Navigational Aids*	Worldwide stations broadcasting RDF, radar, time signals, navigation warnings, distress and safety, medical advice, long-range navigation aids, AMVER, and wartime procedures for U.S. vessels.
		Sailing Directions (Enroute)	Essentially "Coast Pilots" for foreign coasts, in 37 volumes.
		Sailing Directions (Planning Guide)	Ten guides cover eight ocean basins, including pilotage, signals, and shipping regs for bordering countries, meteorological and oceanographic info, danger areas, recommended routes, traffic separation schemes, and lights, beacons, buoys, and radio aids.
		Summary of Corrections	Six-month summary of regional Notice to Mariners corrections.
NOS		*Chart Catalog*	1. Atlantic and Gulf Coasts, PR, and VI, 2. Pacific Coast and HI, 3. Alaska and Aleutians, 4. Great Lakes and Rivers, 5. Bathymetry.
		Chart No. 1	DMA, DMAHTC, NOS, and IHO-recommended chart symbols (available only at: *http://pollux.nss.nima.mil/pubs/*).
		Tidal Current Charts	Hourly currents in Boston, Charleston, LI Sound, Narragansett Bay, Puget Sound, Upper Chesapeake Bay, and Tampa Bay.
		Tidal Current Diagrams	Graphs of current vs. time and location for Vineyard Sound, East River, NY Harbor, Delaware Bay and Chesapeake Bay.
		Tidal Current Tables	Hourly current tables for: 1. East Coast, 2. West Coast and Asia.
		Tide Tables	Hourly tidal heights for: 1. East Coast of N & S America, 2. West Coast of N & S America, 3. Asia, 4. Europe.
		United States Coast Pilots	Channels, harbors, anchorages, supplies, repairs, canals, bridges, and the ICW, covering U.S. coastline and Great Lakes in 9 volumes.
USCG		*Light Lists (U.S. Waters)*	Complete descriptions of all navigation aids clockwise around the U.S. Coast, plus luminous and geographic range tables. In 7 vol.
		Local Notice to Mariners	Weekly updates affecting navigational safety within each of 11 local Coast Guard Districts. Free by request to District Commander.
		Navigation Rules, Int.-Inland	COLREGS plus U.S. Inland Rules in one illustrated volume.
USNO		*Nautical Almanac*	Annual data for celestial navigation, plus sun and moon rise and set.
	229	*Sight Reduction Tables*	Tabular solutions of the celestial triangle to be used with *Nautical Almanac*, in 6 vol., each covering 15° of latitude.

Key: DMAHTC (Defense Mapping Agency Hydrographic/Topographic Center), NOS (National Ocean Service), USCG (United States Coast Guard), USNO (United States Naval Observatory)

AIDS TO NAVIGATION

Lights

Lights, being the only visual reference at night for many vessels, comprise a huge part of the general category, *aids to navigation*. There are three principal sources of information on lighted aids to navigation. The first is the chart where the light is shown accompanied by an abbreviated descriptor. The second—and primary—is the USCG *Light List* (see below). Third is the DMAHTC *List of Lights* (see also below).

Before discussing the lights in detail it helps to become familiar with the terminology.

Aeronautical lights—not a marine aid to navigation and, therefore, not listed in the *Light List*.

Alternating light—a flashing light where the colors of the light alternate.

Beacon—a fixed aid on shore or in shallow water. An unlighted beacon is a *daybeacon* mounting *dayboards*. If lit, is a *minor light*. "Bn" on a chart indicates a beacon whether or not lighted. Color(s) and number conform to the Lateral System.

Bridge lights—lights marking piers, abutments and channel margins. Multi-span bridges may have green lights marking mid-channel with red lights marking channel margins (unless the piers are the margins). In the case of a multi-span, the main channel is indicated by three vertical white lights above the green.

Characteristics—the color/shape of a mark; the color/phase of a light (i.e., flashing, group flash, etc.).

Daybeacon—an unlighted beacon.

Dayboard—small geometric boards having lateral significance.

Daymark—the characteristics which allow daytime recognition of a beacon.

Eclipse—an interval of dark in a flashing light.

Geographic range—the distance an object (light) can be seen, given its height and that of the observer.

Isophase—a flashing light where the periods of light and dark are equal.

Large navigational buoy (LNB)—a 40-foot diameter buoy replacing a lightship.

Light—a beacon emitting light.

Light List—USCG publication in 7 volumes, listing all U.S. lighted navigation aids, unlighted buoys, radiobeacons, radio direction finder calibration stations, daybeacons, racons, and Loran stations.

Light sector—the arc covered by a distinguishing color (red) indicating an area of danger (shoals, etc). The sector limits are shown on the chart and in the *Light List* as the number of *degrees true from the vessel to the light*.

List of Lights—DMAHTC publication (full title: *List of Lights, Radio Aids, and Fog Signals*) listing lighted aids to navigation and fog signals in foreign water, as well as storm signals, signal stations, racons, radio beacons, radio direction finder calibration stations, and aeronautical lights on the U.S. coast. Not to be confused with the USCG *Light List*.

Major light—a high-intensity light exhibited from a fixed structure or a marine site.

Minor light—a low- to moderate-intensity light in harbors and marking channels and rivers, usually distinguished by number, color, light, and sound having lateral significance.

NAVAID—a short range aid to navigation; includes lighted and unlighted beacons, buoys and ranges.

Period—the time for a light to complete one cycle. Whereas a light's *characteristic* is what it's doing, its *period* is how often it's doing it.

Range—a set of two lights or dayboards placed in line with the rear higher than the front, placed so when seen in-line they mark mid-channel to an observer.

Light Patterns and Their Chart Abbreviations

Fixed (F)—a continuous light.

Flashing (Fl)—dark period > light period; a light flashing a maximum of 30/second.

Fixed and Flashing (F Fl)—flashing light against a background of a fixed light.

Group Flashing (Fl2)—repetition of fixed number of flashes each period.

Composite Group Flashing (Fl 2+1)—repetition of two specific numbers of flashes.

Long Flashing (LFl)—flash of 2 seconds or longer.

Quick Flashing (Q)—flashes not fewer than 60/min.

Very Quick Flashing (VQ)—80–160 flashes/min.

Morse A (MoA)—a light flashing the Morse A code (dot-dash).

Isophase (Iso)—equal periods of light and dark.

Occulting (Oc)—light period > dark period.

Alternating (Alt)—light showing different colors alternating.

Light Phase Characteristics

F — FIXED A light showing continuously and steadily

Oc — SINGLE-OCCULTING A light in which the duration of light in a period is longer than the duration of darkness and the eclipse is regularly repeated

Oc (2) — GROUP-OCCULTING A light in which the duration of light in a period is longer than the duration of darkness and the eclipses repeat in groups

Oc (2+1) — COMPOSITE GROUP-OCCULTING A light similar to a group-occulting light, except that successive groups in a period have different numbers of eclipses

Iso — ISOPHASE A light in which all durations of light and darkness are equal

Fl — SINGLE-FLASHING A flashing light in which a flash is repeated regularly (frequency not exceeding 30 flashes per minute)

Fl (2) — GROUP-FLASHING A flashing light in which a group of flashes, specified in number, is regularly repeated

Fl (2+1) — COMPOSITE GROUP-FLASHING A light similar to a group-flashing light except that successive groups in the period have different numbers of flashes

Q — CONTINUOUS QUICK A light in which flashes are produced at a rate of 60 flashes per minute

IQ — INTERRUPTED QUICK A quick light in which the sequence of flashes is interrupted by regularly repeated eclipses of constant and long duration

Mo (A) — MORSE CODE A light in which appearances of light of two clearly different durations (dots and dashes) are grouped to represent a character or characters in the Morse code

FFl — FIXED AND FLASHING A light in which a fixed light is combined with a flashing light of higher luminous intensity

Al RW — ALTERNATING A light showing different colors alternately

The USCG *Light List*

(1) No.	(2) Name and location	(3) Position	(4) Characteristic	(5) Height	(6) Range	(7) Structure	(8) Remarks
		N/W					
	CASCO BAY (Chart 13290)						
	PORTLAND HARBOR (Chart 13292)						
	Portland Harbor						
7565	**Portland Head Light**	43 37.4 70 12.5	**Fl W 4ˢ**	101 80	24	White conical tower, _connected dwelling.	HORN: 1 blast ev 15ˢ (2ˢ bl). Lighted throughout 24 hours.
7570	**Portland Head Directional Light**	43 37.4 70 12.5	**F W (R+G sector)**	23	W 15 R 11 G 11	At base of Portland Head Light.	Shows red from 271.3° to 274.3°; white from 274.3° to 275.8°, green from 275.8° to 279.3°.
7575	**Ram Island Ledge Light**	43 37.9 70 11.3	**Fl (2) W 6ˢ** 1ˢ fl 1.0ˢ ec. 1ˢ fl 3.0ˢ ec.	77	12	Light-gray, conical, granite tower.	Emergency light of reduced intensity when main light is extinguished. HORN: 1 blast ev 10ˢ (1ˢ bl).
7580	– *Main Approach Lighted Bell Buoy 12*	43 38.0 70 12.5	**Fl R 4ˢ**		4	Red.	
7590	– *Midchannel Lighted Gong Buoy PH*	43 38.4 70 13.0	**Mo (A) W**		6	Red and white stripes with red spherical topmark.	
7595	Portland Main Approach Buoy 14					Red nun.	

Description of Columns

1. *Light List* number.

2. Name of the aid. When preceded by a dash (–) the bold heading is part of the name of the aid.

3. Geographic position in latitude and longitude. Note: position is approximate and is listed only to facilitate locating the aid on the chart.

4. Light characteristic for a lighted aid. Morse characteristic for a radiobeacon.

5. Height above water from mean high water to the focal plane of a fixed light.

6. Nominal range of lighted aids, in nm, listed by color for alternating lights. Effective range for radiobeacons in nautical miles. Not listed for ranges, directional lights or private aids to navigation.

7. Structural characteristic of the aid, including dayboard, description of fixed structure, color, and type of buoy and height above ground.

8. General remarks, including fog signal and Racon characteristics, light sector arc of visibility, radar reflector if installed on fixed structure, emergency lights, seasonal remarks, and private aid identification.

Abbreviations

Al	Alternating	LNB	Lrg Nav Buoy
bl	blast	MHz	Megahertz
C	Canadian	Mo	Morse Code
ec	eclipse	Oc	Occulting
ev	every	ODAS	Anch. Ocean. Data Buoy
F	Fixed		
fl	flash	Q	Quick Flashing
Fl	Flashing	Ra ref	Radar reflector
FS	Fog Signal	RBN	Radiobeacon
Fl(2)	Group flashing	R	Red
G	Green	s	seconds
I	Interrupted	si	silent
Iso	Isophase	SPM	Single Point Mooring Buoy
kHz	kiloHertz		
LFl	Long Flash	W	White
lt	Lighted	Y	Yellow

Determining the Range of a Light

The range of a light is the distance at which it can be seen as determined by: (a) intensity (*nominal range*), (b) meteorologic visibility which, when combined with the nominal range, yields the *luminous range,* and (c) the heights of the light and the observer which yield the *geographic range.*

Geographic Range

The illustration at top right shows how the earth's curvature limits geographic (line-of-sight) range. The distance, D_E, from the height of the eye, H_E, to the tangent to the earth's surface is called the distance to the horizon.

D_E (and D_L—distance to horizon of light) can be found from the Geographic Range Table at right (found in the *Light Lists*). It can also be calculated using a simple 4-function calculator as:

$$D_E = 1.17\sqrt{H_E}$$

Example: $H_E = 20$ feet. $D_E = 1.17\sqrt{20} = 5.2$ nm.

Don't forget, the total geographic range is the sum of $D_E + D_L$!

Nominal Range

The range listed in the *Light Lists* (column 6) and on the chart is the nominal range of the light, simple as that.

Luminous Range

The nominal range of a light (on a chart or in the *Light List*) assumes a meteorological visibility of 10 nm. The Luminous Range Diagram at right (found in the front of the *Light List*) allows you to find luminous range, given nominal range and the actual meteorological visibility. To use the diagram, enter at the bottom with nominal range, follow the vertical line to where it intersects the meteorological visibility curve, then run horizontally to find luminous range.

Example: The *Light List* shows that a navigational light has a nominal range of 10 miles and a height above water of 38 feet. Your height of eye is 25 feet and the visibility is 5 miles. At what approximate range will you first sight the light?

Solution:

Geographic range = D_E (5.9 nm) + D_L (7.2 nm) = 13.1 nm

Nominal range = 10 nm

Luminous range = 6 nm

Answer: 6 nm

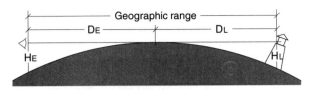

Geographic Range Table

Height Feet	Distance nm	Height Feet	Distance nm	Height Feet	Distance nm
5	2.6	70	9.8	250	18.5
10	3.7	75	10.1	300	20.3
15	4.5	80	10.5	350	21.9
20	5.2	85	10.8	400	23.4
25	5.9	90	11.1	450	24.8
30	6.4	95	11.4	500	26.2
35	6.9	100	11.7	550	27.4
40	7.4	110	12.3	600	28.7
45	7.8	120	12.8	650	29.8
50	8.3	130	13.3	700	31.0
55	8.7	140	13.8	800	33.1
60	9.1	150	14.3	900	35.1
65	9.4	200	16.5	1000	37.0

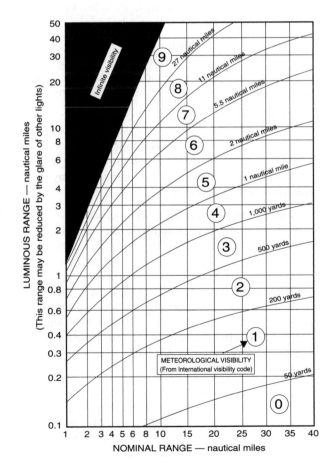

Aids to Navigation Systems

Under the IALA (International Association of Lighthouse Authorities) there are two buoyage systems: Lateral and Cardinal. The former is the one you are undoubtedly most familiar with, the latter (page 306, top) is more suited for offshore isolated dangers.

Two divisions within the Lateral System are A and B. The IALA-A System applies to Europe. The IALA-B System applies to North, Central and South America, Philippines, Korea and Japan.

The primary difference between the A and B systems is which shape carries which color. Where the A system uses red, the B system uses green. Thus:

IALA-A   "Green right returning" (green nun to stbd.)

IALA-B   "Red right returning" (red nun to stbd.)

IALA-B Lateral System Buoyage (pages 305–307)

The general rule incorporates shape, color and number with even-numbered red nuns to starboard and odd-numbered green cans to port on entering, returning from sea or up-channel ("Red–Right–Returning"). Marks carrying sound and/or light apparatus are identified by number and light/buoy color. Only solid red or green marks will be numbered.

For buoyage located offshore, "returning" is considered to be clockwise, i.e., south on the Atlantic coast, west across the Gulf and north on the Pacific Coast. Going south on the ICW is also returning.

Fairway (midchannel)—indicates good water on both sides. This mark is vertically striped red and white, carries one spherical red topmark, shows a white light flashing the MoA code and may be lettered, indicating its position. An unlighted buoy is spherical and striped as above.

Preferred Channel (bifurcation or junction)—indicates a preferred channel, and often applies to the entering direction only. Be sure to check the chart. This is a horizontally banded red and green mark with the top color indicating the side to take the mark for the channel preferred. If unlit, the buoy will be a can or nun, with the shape corresponding to the top band color. If lit, the light will correspond to the top band color and show a composite group flash (Gp Fl 2+1). The buoy may also be lettered.

Isolated Danger—horizontally banded black and red, with two spherical black topmarks and showing a group flashing white light (Fl 2). This buoy is moored over a shoal, sunken wreck, etc., and has good water all around. It may be lettered.

Wreck Buoy—is a numbered buoy placed on the channel or seaward side of a wreck and carries the color and shape appropriate to its position, i.e., red nun or green can. If there is a light, it will be a quick flash (red or green).

Special Purpose Marks—used to mark pipelines, jetties, anchorages, spoil areas, traffic separation schemes, and military exercise zones. The marks are yellow and may be lettered. If lit, the light is yellow with a fixed or flashing light.

Information/Regulatory/Warning Marks—used to indicate warning and exclusion areas, speed control, etc. These buoys are white with orange markings. If there is a light, it will be a white light flashing any rhythm *except* quick flash or flashing (2).

Circle—certain operating restrictions (speed)

Open Diamond—danger

Diamond surrounding a cross—exclusion area

Rectangle or Square—will contain directions

Other Systems Based on IALA-B Lateral System

Intracoastal Waterway. The ICW employs a system of beacons (fixed on shore or in shallow water, lighted or unlighted boards) marking the edges of the channel.

Running south in the ICW is "returning" in the lateral system. A mark serving the ICW exclusively will have a yellow horizontal stripe. Yellow squares or triangles are used on dual-purpose marks, those serving two intersecting waterways.

A mark at the intersection of the ICW with another waterway will have either a yellow triangle, indicating that it is to be treated as a nun (TY) or a yellow square (SY) if treated as a can—keeping in mind that "returning" is running south in the waterway.

Example: a daybeacon shown on the chart as TR-TY, indicates that it's to be taken as a nun if in either waterway. TR-SY would indicate that it's to be taken as a can by vessels in the ICW and as a nun if in the other.

Western Rivers (page 308). The Mississippi River above Baton Rouge, LA, and other major rivers draining to the Gulf of Mexico are marked with a system of beacons also similar to those of IALA-B, except the port side (green, proceeding upriver) and starboard side (red, proceeding upriver) boards have neither numbers nor yellow shapes.

U.S. AIDS TO NAVIGATION SYSTEM
on navigable waters except Western Rivers

LATERAL SYSTEM AS SEEN ENTERING FROM SEAWARD

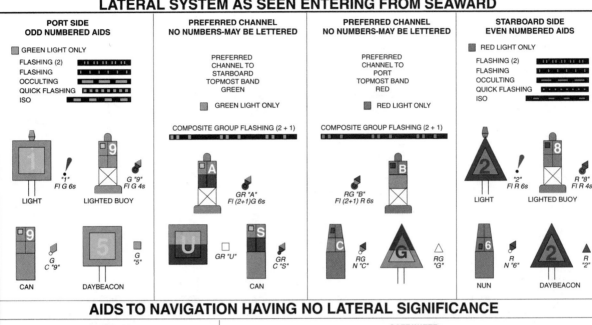

AIDS TO NAVIGATION HAVING NO LATERAL SIGNIFICANCE

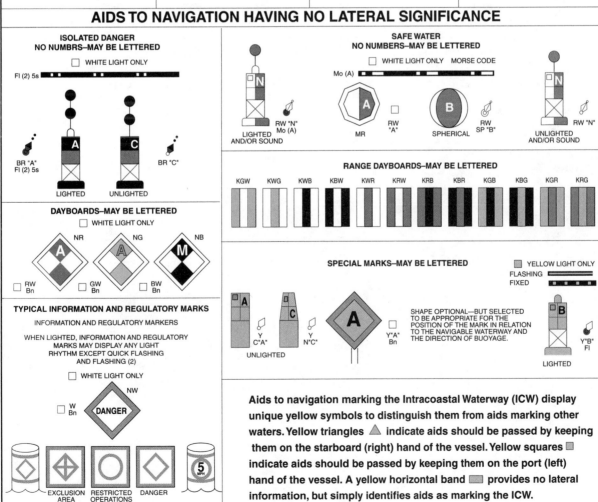

Aids to navigation marking the Intracoastal Waterway (ICW) display unique yellow symbols to distinguish them from aids marking other waters. Yellow triangles △ indicate aids should be passed by keeping them on the starboard (right) hand of the vessel. Yellow squares ▢ indicate aids should be passed by keeping them on the port (left) hand of the vessel. A yellow horizontal band ▭ provides no lateral information, but simply identifies aids as marking the ICW.

Cardinal System Buoyage

This system is used mostly along coasts to mark isolated danger spots where the Lateral System is not appropriate. It employs distinguishing double-cone topmarks to indicate one of the four Cardinal compass directions to safe water. A North mark indicates good water to the north of the mark (thus danger is to its south). The mark itself is a pillar or spar supporting topmarks. The danger direction is indicated by horizontal stripes on the pillar, the topmark pattern, and if lit, a flashing sequence.

IALA Cardinal Marks

	Topmarks	Color Bands	Qk Flash Pattern
N	Two cones both points up	B over Y	Uninterrupted quick
E	Two cones bases together	B, Y, B	3 quick in a group
S	Two cones both down	Y over B	6 quick + 1 long
W	Two cones points together	Y, B, Y	9 flashes in a group

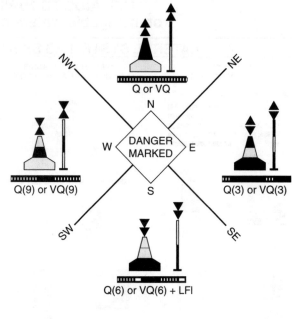

Memory aid: the number of quick flashes corresponds to the numbers on a clock: North—0, East—3, South—6, West—9

A Fictitious Nautical Chart Demonstrating the IALA-B Lateral System

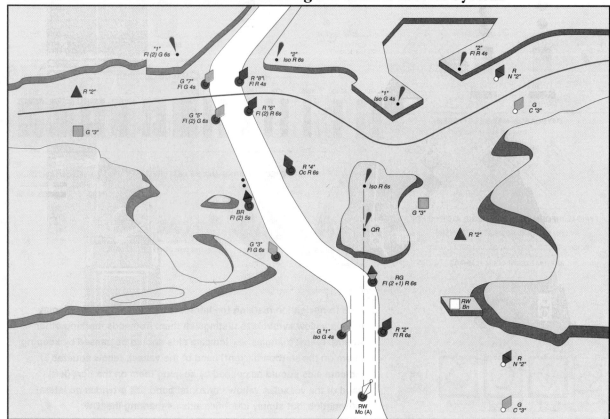

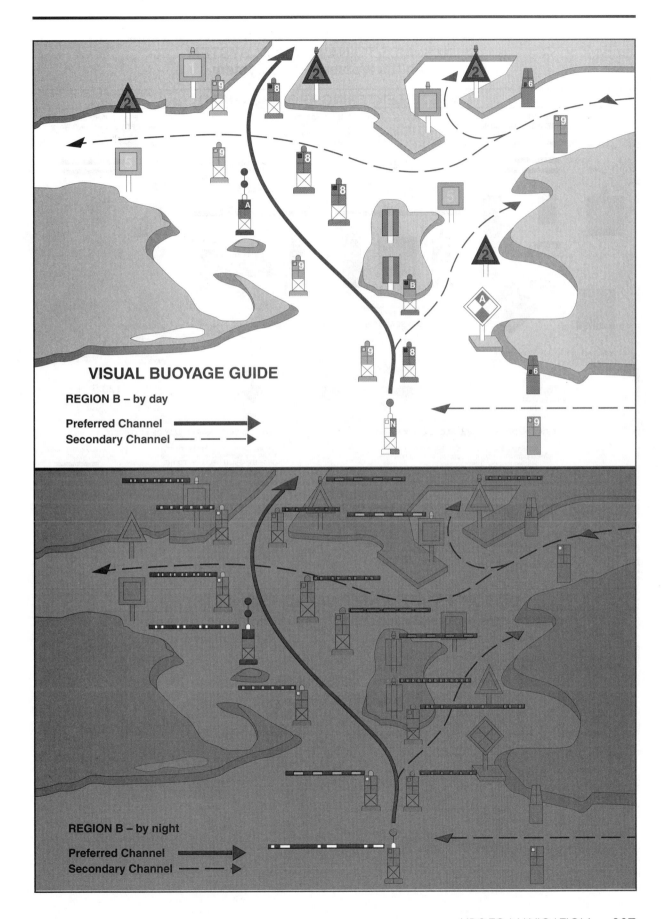

VISUAL BUOYAGE GUIDE

REGION B – by day

Preferred Channel →
Secondary Channel - - →

REGION B – by night

Preferred Channel →
Secondary Channel - - →

U.S. AIDS TO NAVIGATION SYSTEM
on the Western River System

AS SEEN ENTERING FROM SEAWARD

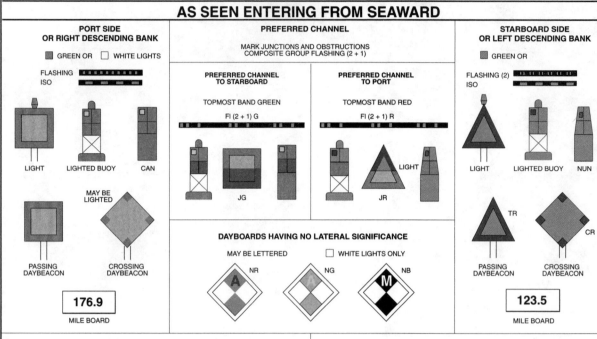

PORT SIDE OR RIGHT DESCENDING BANK

■ GREEN OR □ WHITE LIGHTS

FLASHING
ISO

LIGHT LIGHTED BUOY CAN

MAY BE LIGHTED

PASSING DAYBEACON CROSSING DAYBEACON

176.9
MILE BOARD

PREFERRED CHANNEL

MARK JUNCTIONS AND OBSTRUCTIONS
COMPOSITE GROUP FLASHING (2 + 1)

PREFERRED CHANNEL TO STARBOARD

TOPMOST BAND GREEN

Fl (2 + 1) G

JG

PREFERRED CHANNEL TO PORT

TOPMOST BAND RED

Fl (2 + 1) R

LIGHT

JR

DAYBOARDS HAVING NO LATERAL SIGNIFICANCE

MAY BE LETTERED   □ WHITE LIGHTS ONLY

NR   NG   NB

STARBOARD SIDE OR LEFT DESCENDING BANK

■ GREEN OR

FLASHING (2)
ISO

LIGHT LIGHTED BUOY NUN

TR

CR

PASSING DAYBEACON CROSSING DAYBEACON

123.5
MILE BOARD

TYPICAL INFORMATION AND REGULATORY MARKS

INFORMATION AND REGULATORY MARKERS
WHEN LIGHTED, INFORMATION AND REGULATORY
MARKS MAY DISPLAY ANY LIGHT
RHYTHM EXCEPT QUICK FLASHING
AND FLASHING (2)

NW □ WHITE LIGHTS ONLY

DANGER

EXCLUSION AREA   RESTRICTED OPERATIONS   DANGER

SPECIAL MARKS–MAY BE LETTERED

SHAPE: OPTIONAL—BUT SELECTED
TO BE APPROPRIATE FOR THE POSITION
OF THE MARK IN RELATION TO THE
NAVIGABLE WATERWAY AND THE
DIRECTION OF BUOYAGE

■ YELLOW LIGHT ONLY

FIXED
FLASHING

A   C   A   B

UNLIGHTED   LIGHTED

UNIFORM STATE WATERWAY MARKING SYSTEM

STATE WATERS AND DESIGNATED STATE WATERS FOR PRIVATE AIDS TO NAVIGATION

REGULATORY MARKERS

BOAT EXCLUSION AREA

SWIM   AREA

EXPLANATION MAY BE PLACED
OUTSIDE THE CROSSED DIAMOND
SHAPE, SUCH AS DAM, RAPIDS,
SWIM AREA, ETC.

DANGER

ROCK

THE NATURE OF DANGER MAY BE
INDICATED INSIDE THE DIAMOND
SHAPE, SUCH AS ROCK, WRECK,
SHOAL, DAM, ETC.

CONTROLLED AREA

SLOW

NO   WAKE

TYPE OF CONTROL IS INDICATED
IN THE CIRCLE, SUCH AS SLOW,
NO WAKE, ANCHORING, ETC.

INFORMATION

MULLET LAKE
BLACK RIVER

FOR DISPLAYING INFORMATION
SUCH AS DIRECTIONS, DISTANCES,
LOCATIONS, ETC.

BUOY USED TO DISPLAY
REGULATORY MARKERS

MAY SHOW WHITE LIGHT
MAY BE LETTERED

5 MPH

LATERAL SYSTEM

MAY SHOW GREEN
REFLECTOR OR LIGHT

3

USUALLY FOUND IN PAIRS
PASS BETWEEN THESE BUOYS

PORT SIDE   STARBOARD SIDE

— LOOKING UPSTREAM —

SOLID BLACK BUOY

MAY SHOW RED
REFLECTOR OR LIGHT

4

SOLID RED BUOY

CARDINAL SYSTEM

MAY SHOW WHITE REFLECTOR OR LIGHT

RED-STRIPED
WHITE BUOY

MAY BE LETTERED
DO NOT PASS BETWEEN
BUOY AND NEAREST SHORE

7

BLACK-TOPPED
WHITE BUOY

MAY BE NUMBERED
PASS TO NORTH
OR EAST OF BUOY

RED-TOPPED
WHITE BUOY

PASS TO SOUTH
OR WEST OF BUOY

MOORING BUOY

WHITE WITH
BLUE BAND

MAY SHOW WHITE
REFLECTOR OR LIGHT

LOCKS AND DAMS

Locks and Dams

Most locks and dams are controlled by the Army Corps of Engineers (C of E). Information on lock regulations, sound and light signals, and radio communications is provided in the *Coast Pilot* for the area. The pecking order for lockage, as established by the Corps, is:

- U.S. military vessels
- Mail boats
- Commercial passenger vessels
- Commercial tows
- Commercial fishing boats
- Pleasure craft

Lights

The illustration at right, borrowed from the exam illustrations, shows lock terminology and the lights displayed to identify the lock geometry.

In addition, lights are used to communicate with vessels desiring to lock through. These are:

- Flashing Red   Stand clear; do not enter
- Flashing Amber   Approach under full control
- Flashing Green   Single lock ready to enter

Sound Signals

Sound signals are generally exchanged when the approaching vessel is within one mile. These are:

— -	I desire a single lockage
— - -	I desire a double lockage
—	Enter the landward lock
— —	Enter the riverward lock
-	Leave the landward lock
- -	Leave the riverward lock

Locks with Movable Dams

Some dams have movable "wickets" that are raised or lowered to control the height of the dam. When the wickets are lowered, the water level is the same on both sides of the dam, eliminating the need for lockage. In such a case, vessels are to pass through the clear channel of a "bear trap"—a deeper section —somewhere along the dam.

When the wickets are down and the lock not in use, the lights displayed at the lock are as shown at right. In addition, signals indicating that the bear trap is open include:

- a white circular disk near the bear trap
- a red light over an amber light
- depth of the bear trap in red numbers on a white background

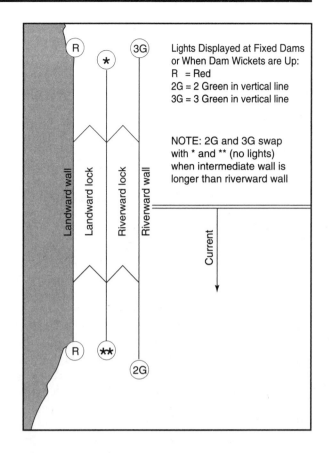

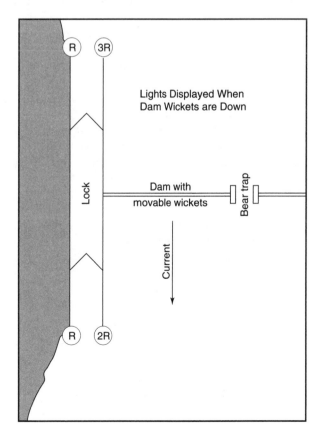

COMPASS

The Compass—Magnetic and Gyro

In any measurement, a number or value is meaningless without a reference. In the case of direction, two references are employed—true north and magnetic north. True north can be determined by either the gyrocompass directly, or with a **magnetic compass** after applying corrections for **variation** and **deviation**. This chapter is about correcting the magnetic compass.

The Compass Rose

On any chart will be found a *compass rose*, essentially two concentric circles with markings at either one or five degree increments, depending upon the size of the rose. The outer circle has its true-north orientation parallel to the meridians (on a Mercator projection) with a star just above the north (000) point. The inner circle is labeled magnetic, and the position of its north point will depend upon the area covered by that particular chart. It will be rotated to the left (west) or to the right (east), the amount depending upon the magnitude of the magnetic variation in the area covered by that particular chart. If there is no variation in that area, the north points of both circles will be in line, indicating no variation. The amount of the variation and the amount of annual change in variation are given in a note at the center of the rose.

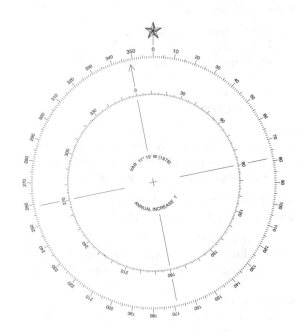

The Magnetic Compass and Its Errors

The modern compass has evolved over centuries, starting with a piece of naturally occurring magnetic "lodestone" floating on a chip of wood in a container of water. The modern compass (except for the solid-state fluxgate compass) is basically several magnets mounted beneath a *card*, imprinted with one- to five-degree markings, depending upon the size of the card. Cardinal and intercardinal points are often labeled. The magnets cause the card to align itself along the earth's magnetic lines of force existing at that location. As the vessel changes course, the card remains aligned to the local magnetic meridian while the vessel rotates about the card. A fixed reference on the compass casing (the *lubber's line*) rotates with the vessel, while the card remains fixed in space, the lubber's line indicating the compass heading.

A common cause of error in chart work is that related to compass correction when plotting bearings and courses. It is critical to remember that while *variation* is a function of geographic location, *deviation* is a function of heading. Keep this in mind while studying the material that follows.

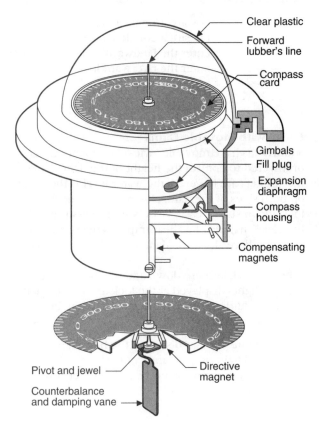

Clear plastic
Forward lubber's line
Compass card
Gimbals
Fill plug
Expansion diaphragm
Compass housing
Compensating magnets

Pivot and jewel
Directive magnet
Counterbalance and damping vane

Magnetic Variation

Soon after mariners began using the magnetic compass it was realized that the north it indicated wasn't the geographic north pole, but somewhere to the east or west of it, depending on the location of the compass. The amount that the magnetic direction varied from the true at any one location was called variation, and charts appeared with lines of equal variation (*isogonic lines*). The compass rose with its two concentric circles indicates the variation applicable to the area of the chart by the amount the inner (magnetic) rose is offset from the outer (true) rose. Thus, the variation for an area can be found by examining the concentric circles of the rose, the center of the rose, or the isogonic lines.

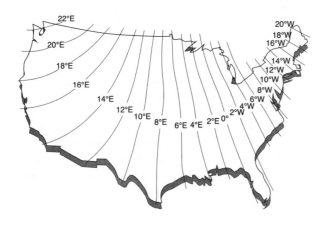

Although variation is considered one of the two compass errors, it is really only an error when attempting to determine true north from magnetic north. It is simply the difference between the two directions at that location.

Whereas variation is the result of the earth's magnetic field causing the compass needle to indicate a direction which varies from true north (an external effect), an internal (shipboard) cause exists for the second compass error, the deviation. The latter is the result of iron and electromagnetic fields aboard the vessel affecting the magnetic compass. As with variation, the effect (error) can be east, west, or zero, depending on the magnetic heading.

Compass Error Corrections

Compass Error (CE) is the algebraic sum of deviation and variation:

Deviation 4E / Variation 14W . . . CE = 10W
Deviation 3E / Variation 12E . . . CE = 15E

Aboard small vessels, the magnetic compass is the directional aid. It allows bearings to be taken for a fix and courses to be steered, but before doing so corrections must be made. A bearing must be corrected to magnetic (referenced to the magnetic pole) or true (referenced to the geographic pole) before plotting. An intended course taken from the chart must be corrected before a helm order given.

A mnemonic traditionally used is:

Can	**Dead**	**Men**	**Vote**	**Twice**
Compass (psc) ±	Deviation =	Magnetic ±	Variation =	True

Psc stands for "Per steering compass" or "per standard compass," and it's what a specific magnetic compass on a specific boat under specific conditions reads. It can be affected by nearby metal, electrical currents, etc.

Deviation errors can be either east or west. Instead of memorizing four rules, learn one, and that is when going from left to right as in the mnemonic above, ADD EAST; from that all else follows:

• if east is added left to right, it is subtracted right to left

• if east is added left to right, west is subtracted left to right, but added right to left.

A convenient way of checking your work is to do the problem as above, then compute the CE and apply it to the psc or true (depending on which is needed).

When plotting, which compass rose should be used, magnetic or true? While many texts advocate always plotting in true, it is important to understand that it makes no difference—as long as the reference used is indicated on the plot as either magnetic (M) or true (T). If magnetic bearings are corrected for deviation and plotted, use the magnetic rose. If they are corrected for both deviation and variation, use the true rose.

The reverse also applies. A course read from the true rose needs both variation and deviation applied to obtain psc—the course to steer. That same line read from the magnetic rose needs only its deviation applied to obtain psc. All that is done is to let the rose do the correction for variation. On a large gyro-equipped vessel, where courses are steered using a true reference and bearings are taken with gyro repeaters, "plotting in true" is obviously preferred.

One caveat. If the plot is "in magnetic" be aware that when doing current problems, currents are tabulated in true. Be sure you use the correct rose.

Compensating a Compass for Deviation (Swinging the Compass)

While variation changes with geographic position, deviation changes with vessel heading. Small vessel compasses usually contain internal compensators. Larger vessels usually have external compensators.

While it is best to utilize the services of a compass adjustor, the small boat operator can often make his own adjustments. The first step is to swing the vessel, that is to turn the vessel through a circle in 15-degree increments while taking bearings on a charted object, preferably a range. The chart provides the true bearing of the object or range. After correction for local variation, the resulting magnetic bearing is compared with the compass bearing to yield the deviation for that heading.

When heading directly at or away from the range, it is a simple matter to read the bearing directly from the steering compass, but a pelorus is needed when crossing the range at an angle. The pelorus is a gimbal-mounted compass card with two sighting vanes. The card is set to the compass course being steered at the time, so the bearing read on the pelorus card will be a compass bearing. For example, if a range has a charted true bearing of 330° in an area of 15°W variation, the magnetic bearing is 345°. If the compass course being steered directly up the range is 342°, then the deviation on that heading is 3°E.

Continuing to swing the vessel, the range is crossed on a compass course of 000°. The pelorus card is set to 000° so that when the bearing of the range is taken with the pelorus it will be, in effect, a compass bearing. If that bearing is 344°, then the deviation is 1°E. This sequence is continued at 15-degree increments, and from this data, a deviation card is constructed.

Compass Compensation on Steel Vessels

The compass of a steel vessel is subject to two types of magnetism:

> *Permanent (hard-iron)*—resulting from the magnetic orientation of the shipbuilding ways and the stresses on the steel during shipbuilding.

> *Induced (soft-iron)*—due to the earth's magnetic field, having both horizontal and vertical components which vary with position relative to the magnetic equator.

Since soft iron is subject to magnetism induced by the earth's magnetic field, and since that field has a maximum horizontal component at the earth's mag-

netic equator and minimal component at the magnetic pole, two correctors are employed to compensate for both horizontal and vertical components:

> *Quadrantial spheres*—the balls seen on either side of the compass binnacle. These compensate for the horizontal component of induced magnetism.

> *Flinders bar*—several lengths of soft iron in a tube vertically mounted in the compass binnacle, which compensate for the vertical component of induced magnetism.

It is important that both the spheres and the Flinder's bar be free of any permanent magnetism before any adjustment is undertaken. Unlike the heeling magnet, these are simple masses of iron, not magnets.

The actual adjustments of these components are beyond the scope of this text. *Bowditch* and *Dutton* are the standard references for the procedures.

The Gyrocompass

The gyroscope is a gimbal-mounted heavy spinning rotor, free to rotate about three mutually perpendicular axes. The unique property of the gyroscope—that of maintaining the orientation of its spin axis in space, is utilized in the gyroscopic compass by orienting the spin axis to the local geographic meridian. Sensors then detect differences in the direction of the spin axis (true north) and the ship's heading to yield direction relative to true north.

The gyrocompass is subject to errors in the range of one to two degrees. How the error is applied is simple to remember. Recall that when correcting magnetic compass errors for deviation and variation, easterly errors are added when going from compass to magnetic to true. The same rule applies here. When correcting from gyro to true, add easterly and subtract westerly error ("CAE").

Advantages of the gyrocompass:
- no magnetic effects (no deviation)
- indicates true instead of magnetic north (no variation)
- functions near the magnetic poles where the magnetic compass would be useless
- errors tend to be small (nevertheless important to compensate for).

Disadvantages of the gyrocompass:
- loss of accuracy at very high latitudes
- dependence on electrical power
- need for technical attention for maintenance.

Sample Compass Correction Problems

Use the mnemonic, "Can Dead Men Vote Twice?" and the rule, "Correct Add East" to solve the problems.

<u>C</u>an	<u>D</u>ead	<u>M</u>en	<u>V</u>ote	<u>T</u>wice
Compass ±	Deviation =	Magnetic ±	Variation =	True

Abbreviations:

C = compass reading	M = magnetic heading
D = deviation	T = true heading
V = variation	G = gyro reading
CE = compass error	GE = gyro error

Example 1: D = 4°E, V =10°W, C = 150°, Find T

Compass	±	Deviation	=	Magnetic	±	Variation	=	True
150	+	4E	=	?	–	10W	=	?
150	+	4	=	154	–	10	=	144

Example 2: C = 270°, V =14°W, T = 259°, Find D and M

Compass	±	Deviation	=	Magnetic	±	Variation	=	True
270	±	?	=	?	–	14W	=	259
270	+	3E	=	273	–	14	=	259

Example 3: D = 4°E, T =169°, C = 155°, Find V and M

Compass	±	Deviation	=	Magnetic	±	Variation	=	True
155	+	4E	=	?	±	?	=	169
155	+	4E	=	159	+	10E	=	169

Example 4: D = 4°E, V =10°W, M = 270°, Find C and T

Compass	±	Deviation	=	Magnetic	±	Variation	=	True
?	+	4E	=	270	–	10W	=	?
266	+	4E	=	270	–	10W	=	260

Now let's throw in gyro heading (G) and gyro error (GE). Observing the same "correct add east" rule, east gyro errors are added to gyro headings to find true headings. We append GE and G to the equation, but we must now work backward (from G to GE to T) to keep the signs right.

Example 5: G = 211°, T =210°, M = 208°, C = 210°, Find D, V, and GE

Compass	±	Deviation	=	Magnetic	±	Variation	=	True	=	GE	±	G
210	±	?	=	208	±	?	=	210	=	?	±	211
210	–	2W	=	208	+	2E	=	210	=	1W	–	211

Example 6: G = 085°, GE =2°E, V = 2°E, D = 4°E, Find C, M, and T

Compass	±	Deviation	=	Magnetic	±	Variation	=	True	=	GE	±	G
?	+	4E	=	?	+	2E	=	?	=	2E	+	085
081	+	4E	=	085	+	2E	=	087	=	2E	+	085

Example 7: D = 3°E, V =3°W, C = 187°, GE = 1°E, Find M, T, and G

Compass	±	Deviation	=	Magnetic	±	Variation	=	True	=	GE	±	G
187	+	3E	=	?	–	3W	=	?	=	1E	±	?
187	+	3E	=	190	–	3W	=	187	=	1E	+	186

LORAN

Loran

The Loran-C system consists of chains of radio stations, operating on a carrier frequency of 100 kHz, and separated by hundreds of miles. Within a chain, one station is designated as the master and the others as secondaries. There are a minimum of two and a maximum of four secondaries for each master.

Masters and secondaries transmit pulses at precise time intervals. A shipboard Loran receiver measures the time differences (TDs) between arrival of the master and secondary pulse pairs. The receiver displays either the TDs in microseconds, or latitude and longitude, which it computes from the TDs.

The time difference between arrival of master and secondary pulses is a measure of the difference in distances between the receiver and the two transmitters. Locations with constant time differences (TDs) fall along hyperbolic curves, as shown in the chart at right. That is why Loran is known as a hyperbolic radio navigation system.

By comparing the overall pulse envelopes, Loran receivers can measure TDs to about 0.01 microseconds—equivalent to 10 feet. Using the radio waves that travel along the ground (the ground wave), Loran is very *repeatable* to about 1,200 miles. Reception of sky waves, which bounce off the earth's ionosphere, allows degraded reception to about 3,000 miles.

Unfortunately, topography and variations in the earth's conductivity affect travel times and so distort the hyperbolas. Uncorrected *accuracy* is more like ±0.25 mile. Sophisticated Loran receivers store correction factors (ASFs), which they use to improve the latitude/longitude conversion. *Absolute accuracy* is the difference between the Loran position vs. the geographic position; *repeatable accuracy* is the difference in Loran positions at the same location.

At turn-on, Loran receivers acquire signals and match cycles automatically. Most receivers will be "tracking" (producing reliable positions) within five minutes. When a secondary station becomes unreliable, it transmits a coded signal that causes the receiver to "blink" and alert the operator.

All of North America is blanketed by a series of overlapping Loran chains, each having its own Group Repetition Interval (GRI). It is up to the operator to select the best GRI for his area. "Best" involves distance from the chain—which controls signal strength and spacing of hyperbola—and crossing angle of the LOPs. The figure at right shows that, for a given TD uncertainty, the area of position uncertainty is much less for steep crossing angles than for shallow angles. As a rule of thumb any angle >30° is acceptable.

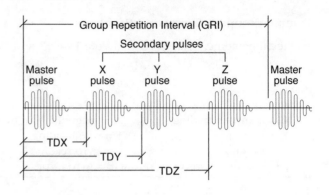

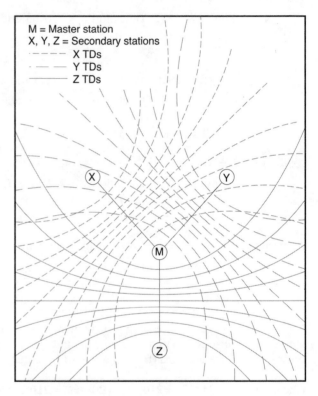

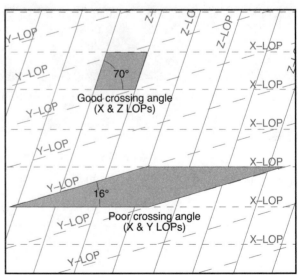

GPS

How GPS Works

The principle of GPS is solving a time-speed-distance problem. The speed of the signal (186,000 miles/sec.) combined with the time for the signal to travel from satellite to receiver yields the distance. (The GPS receiver is programmed so as to be able to measure signal travel time between it and a specific satellite.) The distance from one satellite describes a circle of position on the earth's surface. Range data from a second inscribes a circle that intersects the first at two points, one of which is discarded as impossible. To compensate for clock error, position data from a third satellite provides 2-D accuracy, and a three-dimensional fix requires inputs from four satellites.

Accuracy

The basic accuracy of the system is limited by:

- satellite and receiver clock timing errors
- ephemeris (positions of satellites) errors
- atmospheric propagation variations
- signal reflections (multipath error)

As an indicator of accuracy, the satellites continually broadcast a Horizontal Dilution of Position (HDOP) number that may be displayed by the receiver. A low HDOP, such as 2, indicates a good fix.

Selective Availability (SA)

To render GPS less useful to foreign enemies, the U.S. military: 1) has the option of shutting the system down at any time, and 2) introduces a purposeful error (Selective Availability, SA) into the system. Degraded SA fixes fall within a circle of radius 100 meters 95% of the time. In the early years SA was in effect a high percentage of time. One never knew whether it was on or off, so the useful accuracy of the system was about 100 m. Since nearly every vessel now uses GPS as its primary navigation system, the military has been keeping the SA feature off.

Differential GPS

Since two GPS units within a few hundred miles suffer nearly identical errors, comparing fixes between roving units and a receiver fixed in a known position allows removal of most error. "Differential GPS" units contain a separate 300 kHz receiver to pick up the errors broadcast by a chain of coastal differential transmitters and are accurate to within about 10 meters.

Wide Area Augmentation System (WAAS)

In a brilliant stroke, the GPS operators put several WAAS satellites into orbit. These receive and retransmit differential signals, so any WAAS-enabled receiver in the line of sight of a WAAS satellite now enjoys an accuracy of 3–5 meters.

1 SATELLITE

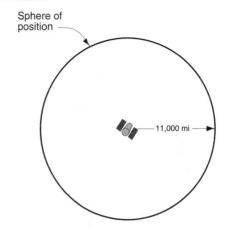

Sphere of position

11,000 mi

2 SATELLITES

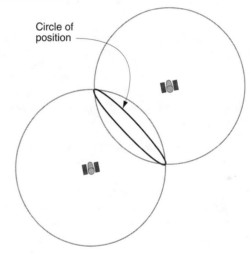

Circle of position

3 SATELLITES

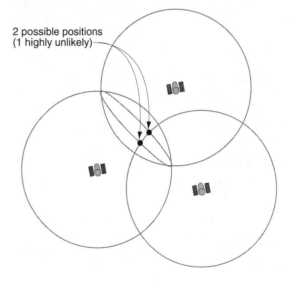

2 possible positions (1 highly unlikely)

RADAR

How Radar Works

Radar is the only navigation system in which the signals originate at the vessel (unless you consider a depth sounder a navigation system). A radar system sends out extremely high frequency pulses from a rotating antenna, the direction of which is indicated by a rotating line on the screen called the sweep. When a pulse strikes an object, a portion of the energy is reflected back to the antenna where it is received, amplified and displayed in the direction of the sweep as a "pip." The distance of the pip from the center of the screen indicates its range; the direction of the sweep when the pip occurs is its bearing.

Pulse length is the duration of the pulse in microseconds. It limits range discrimination of a target, as well as the minimum range at which a target can be detected. The strength of the reflected pulse depends not only on target size, but material and orientation:

- Reflectivity is proportional to electrical conductivity, so metals reflect best, followed by water, rock, wood, and plastics. Wood and plastic vessels require metal radar reflectors.

- Assuming the same material and size, targets with flat surfaces perpendicular to the bearing reflect better.

Horizontal beam width is the arc width of the transmitted pulse, measured in degrees. It is inversely proportional to the width of the antenna. The radar set cannot resolve (present as separate) targets that are closer together than its horizontal beam width. Beam width for a 30″ antenna is 3.8°, for a 48″ antenna 1.9°. When taking tangent bearings, one-half of the beam width is added to left-tangent bearings and subtracted from right-tangent bearings.

Range is a function of transmitted power, height of the antenna, and height of the target. Although radar transmission is theoretically line-of-sight (cannot see over the horizon), there is some bending (refraction) of the energy around the earth's contour due to the change of atmospheric density with height. The maximum theoretical range of a radar system is calculated in the same way as the visible range of a light (see page 303).

False Echoes

Practice is required to separate the real returns from "false returns."

Indirect returns are false echoes produced when portions of the returning pulse reflect from the ship's superstructure into the antenna. The echoes appear at the same range as the target but at the angles of the surfaces from which they were reflected. They can be identified by displaying constant bearing despite a change in true bearing to the target.

Second traces are echoes that result when pulses return to the antenna after the following pulse has been transmitted.

Side lobes of smaller intensity are transmitted along with the main pulse. These often result in one or more echoes on both sides of the main echo and at the same range. If the target is close, they may blend into an apparent arc.

Multiple echoes are due to the pulse being reflected back and forth between the vessel and the target, causing multiple pips at ranges that are multiples of the true range.

Controls

Practice is required to separate the real returns from false echoes.

Fast Time Constant (Differentiator)—eliminates echoes with little depth (snow, rain, etc.).

Gain—used to increase or decrease the strength of the incoming signals. It is usually adjusted to give a lightly speckled appearance to the display when set at a long range scale.

Range—controls the range, or farthest distance from the vessel, of echoes that will be displayed. The display will usually display fixed range rings subdividing the maximum range for better estimation of distance to a target.

Sensitivity Time Control—selectively reduces the gain for close returns in order to eliminate the clutter of reflections from waves (sea return).

Variable Range Ring—may be adjusted to any distance, so is useful to quickly determine whether range to a target is increasing or decreasing.

Variable Bearing Line—may be adjusted to any bearing and is used to determine whether the bearing of a target is increasing or decreasing.

Tune—adjusts the frequency of the set's receiver to match the frequency of its transmitter. As with a radio, signals at a frequency too different from that of the receiver will not be detected. This control needs adjustment infrequently.

Brightness—controls the intensity of the display, allowing optimum viewing under different ambient light conditions. Newer sets with LCD displays also have a contrast control.

Displays and Tracking Targets

Figure A at top right shows the components of a typical display. The fixed vertical line is the ship's heading for a "relative display" or north for a "stabilized display" connected to a gyrocompass. Range and bearing of the target is indicated by variable range and bearing markers that the operator controls.

Figure B shows a sequence of reflections with decreasing range but constant bearing. The radar plot shows that the vessel and the target are on collision courses and must take avoiding action.

Figure C shows a sequence of reflections where both range and bearing are changing. By drawing a line between successive reflections, you can tell that risk of collision does not exist. In fact, you can measure the projected distance of closest approach.

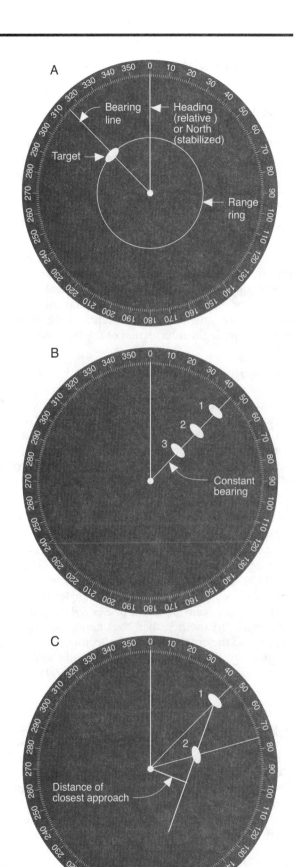

Navigating with Radar

LOP from Range Only

Due to beam width, range determined by radar is generally more accurate than bearing. A single range reading establishes a circle of position centered on the nearest point of the target. Figure D shows a series of such circles of position centered on the edge of a coastline. The vessel must be on the line of position (LOP) tangent to all of the circles of position.

Fix from a Single Range and Bearing

Figure E shows a target of known position on a chart. The vessel is known to be somewhere along the circle of position centered on the target and of radius equal to the range. At the same time, the vessel must be somewhere along the bearing line drawn through the target. The location of the vessel is, therefore, at the intersection of the two lines of position.

Fix from Two or Three Ranges

Figure F shows three separate charted targets along a shoreline. The range of each is drawn as a circle of position centered on the respective targets. Only two circles of position are required to fix the location of the vessel, but three circles are better. The best estimate of the vessel's position is at the center of the "cocked hat" formed by the three circles.

Reflectors and Racons

Several devices are used to enhance the return of radar pulses. *Radar reflectors* are passive metal objects designed to maximize the return regardless of the direction to the target. The most common reflector is similar to the three-cornered mirror, i.e., three flat metal or foil plates at right angles to each other. Theoretically, a radar pulse is reflected from one surface to another, then back along the original path to the antenna. These reflectors are lightweight, sturdy and inexpensive, and should be hung from the mast of every wood or fiberglass vessel.

Racons are active transponders (RACON = RAdar transponder beaCON) placed on some large navigational buoys. When the Racon detects a radar pulse, it sends out a coded pulse of its own, such as a Morse Code letter. On a radar screen a buoy having a Racon will appear as the normal buoy pip, accompanied by a pattern on the same bearing, at slightly greater range. The greater range is due to a slight delay in sending out the code. If searching for a Racon, make sure the radar's sea clutter control is turned off.

D. LOP from Range Only

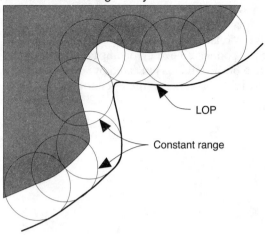

LOP

Constant range

E. Fix from Single Range and Bearing

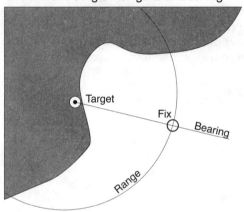

Target

Fix

Bearing

Range

F. Fix from Three Ranges

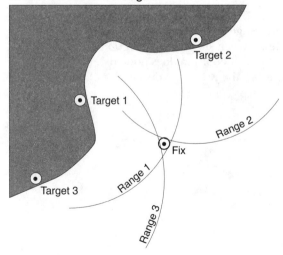

Target 2

Target 1

Range 2

Fix

Target 3

Range 1

Range 3

NAVIGATION GENERAL QUESTIONS

The illustrations cited in the questions are shown on pages 806–811.

1. Unlighted, red and green, horizontally banded buoys with the topmost band red _____.

A. are cylindrical in shape and called can buoys
B. are conical in shape and called nun buoys
C. may either be cylindrical or conical since the shape has no significance
D. are triangular in shape to indicate that it may not be possible to pass on either side of the buoy

2. On an isomagnetic chart, the line of zero variation is the _____.

A. zero variation line
B. isogonic line
C. variation line
D. agonic line

3. Blinking of a Loran-C signal indicates _____.

A. the signal is in proper sequence
B. there will be no increase or decrease in kHz
C. there is an error in the transmission of that signal
D. that it has the proper GRI

4. Gyrocompass repeaters reproduce the indications of the master gyrocompass. They are _____.

A. accurate only in the polar regions
B. accurate electronic servomechanisms
C. hand operated
D. accurate only if the vessel is underway

5. A vessel is steaming in east longitude on January 25 and crosses the International Date Line on an eastbound course at 0900 zone time. What is the date and time at Greenwich when the vessel crosses the line?

A. 0900, 24 January
B. 2100, 24 January
C. 2100, 25 January
D. 0900, 26 January

6. Wind velocity varies _____.

A. directly with the temperature of the air mass
B. directly with the pressure gradient
C. inversely with the barometric pressure
D. inversely with the absolute humidity

7. The period at high or low tide during which there is no change in the height of the water is called the _____.

A. range of the tide
B. plane of the tide
C. stand of the tide
D. reversing of the tide

8. When you are steering on a pair of range lights and find the upper light is above the lower light you should _____.

A. come left
B. come right
C. continue on the present course
D. wait until the lights are no longer in a vertical line

9. When displayed under a single-span fixed bridge, red lights indicate _____.

A. the channel boundaries
B. that vessels must stop
C. the bridge is about to open
D. that traffic is approaching from the other side

10. The wind at Frying Pan Shoals has been northwesterly at an average velocity of 22 knots. The predicted set and drift of the rotary current are 125° at 0.6 knot. What current should you expect?

A. 119° at 0.9 knot
B. 172° at 1.1 knots
C. 225° at 0.6 knot
D. 340° at 0.4 knot

11. A buoy having red and green horizontal bands would have a light characteristic of _____.

A. interrupted quick flashing
B. composite group flashing
C. Morse (A)
D. quick flashing

12. Lines on a chart which connect points of equal magnetic variation are called _____.

A. magnetic latitudes
B. magnetic declinations
C. dip
D. isogonic lines

13. Most modern Loran-C receivers, when not tracking properly, have a(n) _____.

A. bell alarm to warn the user
B. lighted alarm signal to warn the user
C. alternate signal keying system
D. view finder for each station

14. You have replaced the chart paper in the course recorder. What is NOT required to ensure that a correct trace is recorded?

A. Test the electrical gain to the thermograph pens
B. Set the zone pen on the correct quadrant
C. Line the course pen up on the exact heading of the ship
D. Adjust the chart paper to indicate the correct time

15. What is the length of a nautical mile?

A. 1,800 meters
B. 2,000 yards
C. 6,076 feet
D. 5,280 feet

16. The direction of the surface wind is _____.

A. directly from high pressure toward low pressure
B. directly from low pressure toward high pressure
C. from high pressure toward low pressure deflected by the earth's rotation
D. from low pressure toward high pressure deflected by the earth's rotation

17. Stand of the tide is that time when _____.

A. the vertical rise or fall of the tide has stopped
B. slack water occurs
C. tidal current is at a maximum
D. the actual depth of the water equals the charted depth

18. A vessel's position should be plotted using bearings of _____.

A. buoys close at hand
B. fixed known objects on shore
C. buoys at a distance
D. All of the above

19. You are approaching a swing bridge at night. You will know that the bridge is open for river traffic when _____.

A. the fixed, green light starts to flash
B. the amber light changes to green

C. the red light is extinguished
D. the red light changes to green

20. You are underway on course 050°T and your maximum speed is 12 knots. The eye of a hurricane bears 120°T, 110 miles from your position. The hurricane is moving toward 285°T at 25 knots. If you maneuver at 12 knots to avoid the hurricane, what could be the maximum CPA?

A. 77 miles
B. 82 miles
C. 87 miles
D. 93 miles

21. Which buoy is NOT numbered?

A. Green can buoy
B. Preferred-channel buoy
C. Red lighted buoy
D. Green gong buoy

22. Charts showing the coast of Mexico are produced by the United States _____.

A. National Imagery and Mapping Agency
B. Coast Guard
C. Naval Observatory
D. National Ocean Service

23. If Loran-C signals become unsynchronized, the receiver operator is warned because _____.

A. signals begin to blink
B. signals begin to shift
C. stations discontinue transmission
D. stations transmit grass

24. When the gyropilot is used for steering, what control is adjusted to compensate for varying sea conditions?

A. Rudder control
B. Sea control
C. Lost motion adjustment
D. Weather adjustment

25. You are in LONG 144°E. The date is 6 February, and the zone time is 0800. The Greenwich date and time are _____.

A. 2200, 5 February
B. 2300, 5 February
C. 1700, 6 February
D. 1800, 6 February

26. Wind direction may be determined by observing all of the following EXCEPT _____.

A. low clouds
B. waves
C. whitecaps
D. swells

27. Spring tides are tides that _____.

A. have lows lower than normal and highs higher than normal
B. have lows higher than normal and highs lower than normal
C. are unpredictable
D. occur in the spring of the year

28. When using a buoy as an aid to navigation which of the following should be considered?

A. The buoy should be considered to always be in the charted location.
B. If the light is flashing, the buoy should be considered to be in the charted location.
C. The buoy may not be in the charted position.
D. The buoy should be considered to be in the charted position if it has been freshly painted.

29. You are approaching a multiple-span bridge at night. The main navigational channel span will be indicated by _____.

A. a quick-flashing red or green aid to navigation
B. a steady blue light in the center of the span
C. 3 white lights in a vertical line in the center of the span
D. a flashing green light in the center of the span

31. When approaching a preferred-channel buoy, the best channel is NOT indicated by the _____.

A. light characteristic
B. color of the uppermost band
C. shape of an unlighted buoy
D. color of the light

32. The datum used for soundings on charts of the Atlantic Coast of the United States is mean _____.

A. low water
B. lower low water
C. high water springs
D. high water

34. The Local Notice to Mariners is usually published _____.

A. daily
B. weekly
C. monthly
D. semiannually

35. You are on a vessel at 0400 ZT on 3 July, and the ZD for your position is −8. What is the GMT?

A. 1200, 3 July
B. 2000, 3 July
C. 1200, 2 July
D. 2000, 2 July

36. A strong, often violent, northerly wind occurring on the Pacific coast of Mexico, particularly during the colder months, is a _____.

A. Papagayo
B. fall wind
C. foehn
D. williwaw

37. What does the term "tide" refer to?

A. Horizontal movement of the water
B. Vertical movement of the water
C. Mixing tendency of the water
D. Salinity content of the water

38. When navigating a vessel, you _____.

A. can always rely on a buoy to be on station
B. can always rely on a buoy to show proper light characteristics
C. should assume a wreck buoy is directly over the wreck
D. should never rely on a floating aid to maintain its exact position

40. The predicted time that the flood begins at the entrance to Delaware Bay is 1526. You are anchored off Chestnut St. in Philadelphia. If you get underway bound for sea at 1600 and turn for 8 knots, at what point will you lose the ebb current?

A. Billingsport
B. Marcus Hook
C. Mile 63
D. Mile 52

41. Mean high water is the reference plane used for _____.

A. all vertical measurements
B. heights above water of land features such as lights
C. soundings on the East and West Coasts
D. water depths on the East Coast only

42. The datum used for soundings on charts of the the East Coast of the United States is _____.

A. mean low water springs
B. mean low water
C. mean lower low water
D. half tide level

43. A buoy with a composite group-flashing light indicates a(n) _____.

A. anchorage area
B. fish net area
C. bifurcation
D. dredging area

44. The speed of sound through ocean water is nearly always _____.

A. faster than the speed of calibration for the fathometer
B. the same speed as the speed of calibration for the fathometer
C. slower than the speed of calibration for the fathometer
D. faster than the speed of calibration for the fathometer, unless the water is very warm

46. What wind reverses directions seasonally?

A. Monsoon winds
B. Hooked trades
C. Jet stream
D. Secondary winds

47. The range of tide is the _____.

A. distance the tide moves out from the shore
B. duration of time between high and low tide
C. difference between the heights of high and low tide
D. maximum depth of the water at high tide

48. When should a navigator rely on the position of floating aids to navigation?

A. During calm weather only
B. During daylight only

C. Only when inside a harbor
D. Only when fixed aids are not available

49. While steering a course of 150°T, you wish to observe a body for a latitude check. What would the azimuth have to be?

A. 000°T
B. 090°T
C. 150°T
D. 240°T

50. The difference between the heights of low and high tide is the _____.

A. period
B. range
C. distance
D. depth

51. In the U.S. Aids to Navigation System, red and green horizontally banded buoys mark _____.

A. channels for shallow draft vessels
B. general anchorage areas
C. fishing grounds
D. junctions or bifurcations

52. The reference datum used in determining the heights of land features on most charts is _____.

A. mean sea level
B. mean high water
C. mean low water
D. half-tide level

56. A strong, often violent, northerly wind occurring on the Pacific coast of Mexico, particularly during the colder months, is called _____.

A. Tehuantepecer
B. Papagayo
C. Norther
D. Pampero

57. The height of tide is the _____.

A. depth of water at a specific time due to tidal effect
B. difference between the depth of the water and the area's tidal datum
C. difference between the depth of the water and the high water tidal level
D. difference between the depth of the water at high tide and the depth of the water at low tide

58. You should plot your dead-reckoning position _____.

A. at every course change
B. hourly
C. at every speed change
D. All of the above are correct.

59. For navigational purposes, each great circle on the Earth has a length of _____.

A. 3,600 miles
B. 5,400 miles
C. 12,500 miles
D. 21,600 miles

60. The predicted time that the ebb begins at the entrance to Delaware Bay is 1526. You are anchored off Chestnut St. in Philadelphia. If you get underway bound for sea at 1630 and turn for 12 knots, at what point will you lose the flood current?

A. New Castle
B. Reedy Island
C. Mile 44
D. Ship John Shoal Lt.

61. Red lights may appear on _____.

A. horizontally banded buoys
B. vertically striped buoys
C. yellow buoys
D. spherical buoys

62. Charted depth is the _____.

A. vertical distance from the chart sounding datum to the ocean bottom, plus the height of tide
B. vertical distance from the chart sounding datum to the ocean bottom
C. average height of water over a specified period of time
D. average height of all low waters at a place

63. A full service Loran-C receiver will provide _____.

A. matching pulse rates of at least 20 stations
B. an automatic on-and-off switch
C. a horizontal matching of all delayed hyperbolic signals
D. automatic signal acquisition and cycle matching

64. Mean lower low water is the reference plane used for _____.

A. all vertical measurements
B. heights above water for lights, mountains, etc.
C. soundings on the U.S. east and west coasts
D. water depths on the U.S. east coast only

66. What will a veering wind do?

A. Change direction in a clockwise manner in the Northern Hemisphere
B. Circulate about a low pressure center in a counterclockwise manner in the Northern Hemisphere
C. Vary in strength constantly and unpredictably
D. Circulate about a high pressure center in a clockwise manner in the Southern Hemisphere

67. What is the definition of height of tide?

A. The vertical distance from the tidal datum to the level of the water at any time
B. The vertical difference between the heights of low and high water
C. The vertical difference between a datum plane and the ocean bottom
D. The vertical distance from the surface of the water to the ocean floor

68. A position obtained by taking lines of position from one object at different times and advancing them to a common time is a(n) _____.

A. dead-reckoning position
B. estimated position
C. fix
D. running fix

70. D001NG. The station located at A is the _____.

A. on station
B. off station
C. master station
D. secondary station

71. A preferred-channel buoy may be _____.

A. lettered
B. spherical
C. showing a white light
D. All of the above

72. The datum from which the predicted heights of tides are reckoned in the tide tables is _____.

A. mean low water
B. the same as that used for the charts of the locality
C. the highest possible level
D. given in table three of the tide tables

74. When operated over a muddy bottom, a fathometer may indicate _____.

A. a shallow depth reading
B. a zero depth reading
C. no depth reading
D. two depth readings

76. In the Northern Hemisphere, a wind that shifts counterclockwise is a _____.

A. veering wind
B. backing wind
C. reverse wind
D. chinook wind

77. When there are small differences between the heights of two successive high tides or two low tides, in a tidal day, the tides are called _____.

A. diurnal
B. semidiurnal
C. solar
D. mixed

78. A single line of position combined with a dead-reckoning position results in a(n) _____.

A. assumed position
B. estimated position
C. fix
D. running fix

80. When the moon is at first quarter or third quarter phase, what type of tides will occur?

A. Apogean
B. Perigean
C. Neap
D. Spring

81. A buoy with a composite group-flashing light indicates a(n) _____.

A. bifurcation
B. fish net area
C. anchorage area
D. dredging area

82. On the west coast of North America, charted depths are taken from _____.

A. high water
B. mean tide level
C. mean low water
D. mean lower low water

83. All Loran-C transmitting stations are equipped with cesium frequency standards which permit _____.

A. every station in one chain to transmit at the same time
B. each station to transmit without reference to another station
C. on-line transmission of single-line transmitters at the same time
D. each station to only depend on the master for synchronization and signal ratio

84. When using an echo sounder in deep water, it is NOT unusual to _____.

A. receive a strong return at about 200 fathoms (366 meters) during the day, and one nearer the surface at night
B. receive a first return near the surface during the day, and a strong return at about 200 fathoms (366 meters) at night
C. receive false echoes at a constant depth day and night
D. have to recalibrate every couple of days due to inaccurate readings

86. A weather forecast states that the wind will commence backing. In the Northern Hemisphere, this would indicate that it will _____.

A. shift in a clockwise manner
B. shift in a counterclockwise manner
C. continue blowing from the same direction
D. decrease in velocity

87. A tide is called diurnal when _____.

A. only one high and one low water occur during a lunar day
B. the high tide is higher and the low tide is lower than usual
C. the high tide and low tide are exactly six hours apart
D. two high tides occur during a lunar day

88. Which position includes the effects of wind and current?

A. Dead-reckoning position
B. Leeway position
C. Estimated position
D. Set position

90. When the moon is new or full, which type of tides occur?

A. Neap
B. Spring
C. Diurnal
D. Apogean

91. A preferred-channel buoy will show a _____.

A. white light whose characteristic is Morse (A)
B. group-occulting white light
C. composite group-flashing (2 + 1) white light
D. composite group-flashing (2 + 1) red or green light

92. When utilizing a Pacific Coast chart, the reference plane of soundings is _____.

A. mean low water springs
B. mean low water
C. mean lower low water
D. lowest normal low water

93. The time interval between the transmission of signals from a pair of Loran-C stations is very closely controlled and operates with _____.

A. an atomic time standard
B. Daylight Savings Time
C. Eastern Standard Time
D. Greenwich Mean Time

94. When using a recording depth finder in the open ocean, what phenomena is most likely to produce a continuous trace that may not be from the actual ocean bottom?

A. Echoes from a deep scattering layer
B. Echoes from schools of fish
C. Multiple returns reflected from the bottom to the surface and to the bottom again
D. Poor placement of the transducer on the hull

95. The difference in local time between an observer on 114°W and one on 119°W is _____.

A. 1.25 minutes
B. 5 minutes
C. 20 minutes
D. 75 minutes

96. A weather forecast states that the wind will commence veering. In the Northern Hemisphere this indicates that the wind will _____.

A. shift in a clockwise manner
B. shift in a counterclockwise manner
C. continue blowing from the same direction
D. increase in velocity

97. The lunar or tidal day is _____.

A. about 50 minutes shorter than the solar day
B. about 50 minutes longer than the solar day
C. about 10 minutes longer than the solar day
D. the same length as the solar day

98. A position that is obtained by applying estimated current and wind to your vessel's course and speed is a(n) _____.

A. dead-reckoning position
B. estimated position
C. fix
D. None of the above

99. You are enroute to Jacksonville, FL, from San Juan, P.R. There is a fresh N'ly wind blowing. As you cross the axis of the Gulf Stream you would expect to encounter _____.

A. smoother seas and warmer water
B. steeper waves, closer together
C. long swells
D. cirrus clouds

100. You are underway on course 050°T and your maximum speed is 12 knots. The eye of a hurricane bears 080°T, 100 miles from your position. The hurricane is moving towards 265°T at 22 knots. What course should you steer at 12 knots to have the maximum CPA?

A. 219°
B. 208°
C. 199°
D. 190°

101. A lighted preferred-channel buoy may show a _____.

A. fixed red light
B. Morse (A) white light

C. composite group-flashing light
D. yellow light

102. Which statement about a NIMA chart with stock no. 23BHA23433 is TRUE?

A. This is a non-navigational or special purpose chart.
B. It is not included in the portfolio.
C. It is a chart of an area in subregion 23.
D. It depicts a major portion of an ocean.

103. In Loran-C the high accuracy of atomic time and frequency controls allows each station to operate _____.

A. at higher frequencies
B. on schedule, independently
C. at 1,975 kHz
D. in a multiplex phase

104. What should you apply to a fathometer reading to determine the depth of water?

A. Subtract the draft of the vessel.
B. Add the draft of the vessel.
C. Subtract the sea water correction.
D. Add the sea water correction.

105. If the GMT is 1500, the time at 75°E longitude is _____.

A. 1000
B. 1500
C. 1700
D. 2000

106. A local wind which occurs during the daytime and is caused by the different rates of warming of land and water is a _____.

A. foehn
B. chinook
C. land breeze
D. sea breeze

107. The average height of the surface of the sea for all stages of the tide over a 19 year period is called _____.

A. mean high water
B. mean low water
C. half-tide level
D. mean sea level

108. A position that is obtained by using two or more intersecting lines of position taken at nearly the same time is a(n) _____.

A. dead-reckoning position
B. estimated position
C. fix
D. running fix

109. D021NG. While proceeding along the Norwegian coast on course 039°T, you sight the black-yellow-black banded buoy shown bearing 053°T. What action should you take?

A. Alter course to 053° and leave the buoy close aboard on either side
B. Maintain course
C. Alter course to 060° and ensure that the true bearings decrease
D. Alter course to port to rapidly open the bearing to the right

110. A millibar is a unit of _____.

A. humidity
B. precipitation
C. pressure
D. temperature

111. Green lights may appear on _____.

A. horizontally banded buoys
B. vertically striped buoys
C. yellow buoys
D. spherical buoys

112. Which chart number indicates a NIMA chart designed for inshore coastwise navigation?

A. LCORR5868
B. COMBT800564
C. 17XHA17365
D. 16ACO16595

113. The type of transmission used in Loran-C is a _____.

A. single pulse
B. wide pulse
C. multipulse
D. narrow pulse

114. All echo-sounders can measure the _____.

A. actual depth of water
B. actual depth of water below keel
C. average depth from waterline to hard bottom
D. average depth of water to soft bottom

116. Which wind results from a land mass cooling more quickly at night than an adjacent water area?

A. Coastal breeze
B. Sea breeze
C. Land breeze
D. Mistral

117. Mean high water is the average height of _____.

A. the higher high waters
B. the lower high waters
C. the lower of the two daily tides
D. all high waters

118. What describes an accurate position that is NOT based on any prior position?

A. Dead-reckoning position
B. Estimated position
C. Fix
D. Running fix

119. D020NG. While proceeding along the Mediterranean coast of Spain, you sight the black and yellow buoy shown. Your course is 039°T, and the buoy bears 053°T. What action should you take?

A. Alter course to 053°T and pass the buoy close aboard on either side
B. Alter course to 060° and ensure that the bearings decrease
C. Maintain course and ensure that the bearings increase
D. Alter course towards the buoy and leave the buoy well clear on either side

120. You are underway on course 050°T and your maximum speed is 13 knots. The eye of a hurricane bears 100°T, 120 miles from your position. The hurricane is moving toward 275°T at 25 knots. If you maneuver at 13 knots to avoid the hurricane, what could be the maximum CPA?

A. 72 miles
B. 78 miles
C. 83 miles
D. 89 miles

121. A safe water mark may be _____.

A. vertically striped
B. spherical
C. showing a white light
D. All of the above

122. The subregions of the United States Gulf and East Coasts are numbered 11, 12 and 13 within the chart numbering system. Which chart number indicates a chart for either the Gulf or East Coast?

A. 11250
B. 18411
C. 21228
D. 17136

123. If the radio signal ground wave extends out for less distance than the minimum skywave distance, there is an area in which no signal is received. This is called the _____.

A. skip zone
B. blackout zone
C. diffraction zone
D. shadow zone

124. An electronic depth finder operates on the principle that _____.

A. radio signals reflect from a solid surface
B. sound waves travel at a constant speed through water
C. radar signals travel at a constant speed through water
D. pressure increases with depth

125. The GMT is 0445 and your zone description is +1. Your zone time is _____.

A. 0445
B. 0345
C. 0545
D. 1545

126. A katabatic wind blows _____.

A. up an incline due to surface heating
B. in a circular pattern
C. down an incline due to cooling of the air
D. horizontally between a high and a low pressure area

127. Mean low water is the average height of _____.

A. the surface of the sea
B. high waters and low waters
C. all low waters
D. the lower of the two daily low tides

128. A position obtained by applying only your vessel's course and speed to a known position is a _____.

A. dead-reckoning position
B. fix
C. probable position
D. running fix

130. The distance between the surface of the water and the tidal datum is the _____.

A. range of tide
B. height of tide
C. charted depth
D. actual water depth

131. A vertically striped buoy may be _____.

A. striped black and green
B. striped black and yellow
C. lighted with a red light
D. lighted with a white light

132. The value of sixty nautical miles per degree of geodetic latitude is most correct at _____.

A. the equator
B. latitude 45°
C. the poles
D. all latitudes

133. The line connecting the Loran-C master station with a secondary station is called the _____.

A. focus line
B. base line
C. side line
D. center line

134. The recording fathometer produces a graphic record of the _____.

A. bottom contour only up to depths of 100 fathoms
B. depth underneath the keel against a time base
C. contour of the bottom against a distance base
D. depth of water against a distance base

135. The standard meridian for the time zone +1 is _____.

A. 0°
B. 7-1/2°W
C. 15°W
D. 7-1/2°E

136. Which Beaufort force indicates a wind speed of 65 knots?

A. Beaufort force 0
B. Beaufort force 6.5
C. Beaufort force 12
D. Beaufort force 15

137. Priming of the tides occurs _____.

A. at times of new and full Moon
B. when the Earth, Moon, and Sun are lying approximately on the same line
C. when the Moon is between first quarter and full and between third quarter and new
D. when the Moon is between new and first quarter and between full and third quarter

138. The path that a vessel is expected to follow, represented on a chart by a line drawn from the point of departure to the point of arrival, is the _____.

A. DR plot
B. track line
C. heading
D. estimated course

140. You are underway on course 050°T and your maximum speed is 12 knots. The eye of a hurricane bears 080°T, 100 miles from your position. The hurricane is moving toward 265°T at 22 knots. If you maneuver at 12 knots to avoid the hurricane, what could be the maximum CPA?

A. 76 miles
B. 69 miles
C. 63 miles
D. 56 miles

141. You are enroute to assist vessel A. Vessel A is underway at 6 knots on course 133°T, and bears 042°T, 105 miles from you. What is the time to intercept if you make 10 knots?

A. 12h 30m
B. 12h 44m
C. 12h 58m
D. 13h 22m

142. Which nautical charts are intended for coastwise navigation outside of outlying reefs and shoals?

A. Approach charts
B. General charts
C. Sailing charts
D. Coast charts

143. Under the IALA-A Buoyage System, a buoy used as a port hand mark would not show which light characteristic?

A. Isophase
B. Quick flashing
C. Long flashing
D. Group Flashing (2 + 1)

144. In modern fathometers the sonic or ultrasonic sound waves are produced electrically by means of a(n) _____.

A. transmitter
B. transducer
C. transceiver
D. amplifier

145. The standard time meridian for zone description −1 is _____.

A. 0°
B. 7-1/2°W
C. 7-1/2°E
D. 15°E

146. D049NG. What change in the wind could be expected at position D if the low was moving northeasterly?

A. Decreasing and veering to the west
B. Decreasing and backing to the north
C. Increasing and veering to the southwest
D. Increasing and backing to the east

147. Which statement is TRUE concerning equatorial tides?

A. They occur when the Sun is at minimum declination north or south.
B. They occur when the Moon is at maximum declination north or south.
C. The difference in height between consecutive high or low tides is at a minimum.
D. They are used as the basis for the vulgar establishment of the port.

148. When possible, a DR plot should always be started from where?

A. Any position
B. A known position
C. An assumed position
D. None of the above

149. You are underway on course 050°T and your maximum speed is 13 knots. The eye of a hurricane bears 100°T, 120 miles from your position. The hurricane is moving towards 275°T at 25 knots. What course

should you steer at 13 knots to have the maximum CPA?

A. 339°
B. 333°
C. 326°
D. 320°

150. An alternating light _____.

A. shows a light with varying lengths of the lighted period
B. shows a light that changes color
C. marks an alternate lesser-used channel
D. is used as a replacement for another light

151. Under the U.S. Aids to Navigation System, spherical buoys may be _____.

A. numbered
B. lettered
C. lighted
D. All of the above

152. A chart with a natural scale of 1:160,000 is classified as a _____.

A. sailing chart
B. general chart
C. coast chart
D. harbor chart

153. D004NG. The line extending beyond the stations at A and B is referred to as the _____.

A. slave line
B. zero line
C. baseline extension
D. centerline

154. Which factor has the greatest effect on the amount of gain required to obtain a fathometer reading?

A. Salinity of water
B. Temperature of water
C. Atmospheric pressure
D. Type of bottom

155. The velocity of the current in large coastal harbors is _____.

A. predicted in Tidal Current Tables
B. unpredictable
C. generally constant
D. generally too weak to be of concern

156. In reading a weather map, closely spaced pressure gradient lines would indicate _____.

A. high winds
B. high overcast clouds
C. calm or light winds
D. fog or steady rain

157. Tropic tides are caused by the _____.

A. Moon being at its maximum declination
B. Moon crossing the equator
C. Sun and Moon both being near 0° declination
D. Moon being at perigee

158. Discounting slip, if your vessel is turning RPM for 10 knots and making good a speed of 10 knots, the current could be _____.

A. with you at 10 knots
B. against you at 10 knots
C. slack
D. with you at 2 knots

159. The apparent wind can be zero when the true wind is from _____.

A. ahead and equal to the ship's speed
B. astern and equal to the ship's speed
C. ahead and twice the ship's speed
D. astern and equal to twice the ship's speed

161. How is a safe water mark, that can be passed close aboard on either side, painted and lighted?

A. Black and white stripes with an interrupted quick flashing light
B. Black and red stripes with a Morse (A) light
C. Black and red stripes with an interrupted quick flashing light
D. Red and white stripes with a Morse (A) light

162. A chart with a scale of 1:80,000 would fall into the category of a _____.

A. sailing chart
B. general chart
C. coastal chart
D. harbor chart

163. How many fixed objects are needed to plot a running fix?

A. None
B. One
C. Two
D. Three

166. On the pole side of the high pressure belt in each hemisphere, the pressure diminishes. The winds along these gradients are diverted by the Earth's rotation toward the east and are known as the _____.

A. geostrophic winds
B. doldrums
C. horse latitudes
D. prevailing westerlies

167. When the Moon's declination is maximum north, which of the following will occur?

A. Mixed-type tides
B. Higher high tides and lower low tides
C. Tropic tides
D. Equatorial tides

168. Your vessel is making way through the water at a speed of 12 knots. Your vessel traveled 30 nautical miles in 2 hours 20 minutes. What current are you experiencing?

A. A following current at 2.0 knots
B. A head current of 2.0 knots
C. A following current of 0.9 knot
D. A head current of 0.9 knot

169. You want to transit Hell Gate on 23 July 1983. What is the period of time around the AM (ZD +4) slack before ebb when the current will be less than 0.5 knot?

A. 0939 to 0957
B. 0943 to 0953
C. 0844 to 0852
D. 0348 to 0356

170. Which of the buoy symbols in illustration D032NG indicates a safe water mark?

A. D
B. C
C. B
D. A

171. Under the U.S. Aids to Navigation System, a lighted buoy with a spherical topmark marks _____.

A. safe water
B. a fish trap area

C. a hazard to navigation
D. a bifurcation in the channel

172. A chart with a scale of 1:45,000 is a
_____.

A. harbor chart
B. coast chart
C. general chart
D. sailing chart

176. Which wind pattern has the most influence over the movement of frontal weather systems over the North American continent?

A. Subpolar easterlies
B. Northeast trades
C. Prevailing westerlies
D. Dominant southwesterly flow

177. How many high waters usually occur each day on the East Coast of the United States?

A. One
B. Two
C. Three
D. Four

178. You are steering a southerly course, and you note that the chart predicts an easterly current. Without considering wind, how may you allow for the set?

A. Head your vessel slightly to the right
B. Head your vessel slightly to the left
C. Decrease your speed
D. Increase your speed

179. You are proceeding up a channel at night. It is marked by a range which bears 185°T. You steady up on a compass course of 180° with the range in line dead ahead. This indicates that you(r) _____.

A. must come right to get on the range
B. course is in error
C. compass has some easterly error
D. are being affected by a southerly current

180. What is a lighted safe water mark fitted with to aid in its identification?

A. A spherical topmark
B. Red and white retroreflective material
C. A sequential number
D. A red and white octagon

181. Which navigational mark may only be lettered?

A. An unlighted, green, can buoy
B. A spherical buoy
C. A red buoy
D. A port side dayshape

182. The scale on a chart is given as 1:5,000,000. This means that _____.

A. 1 inch is equal to 5,000 inches on the Earth's surface
B. 1 nautical mile on the chart is equal to 5,000 inches on the Earth's surface
C. 1 inch is equal to 5,000,000 inches on the Earth's surface
D. 1 nautical mile on the chart is equal to 5,000,000 inches on the Earth's surface

185. A ship is in longitude 54°00'W on a true course of 270°. The ship's clocks are on the proper time zone. At what longitude should the clocks be changed to maintain the proper zone time?

A. 45°00'W
B. 52°30'W
C. 60°00'W
D. 67°30'W

186. In the doldrums you will NOT have _____.

A. high relative humidity
B. frequent showers and thunderstorms
C. steep pressure gradients
D. frequent calms

187. Which statement is TRUE concerning apogean tides?

A. They occur only at quadrature.
B. They occur when the Moon is nearest the Earth.
C. They cause diurnal tides to become mixed.
D. They have a decreased range from normal.

188. Off Barnegat, NJ, with the wind coming out of the east, the wind-driven current will be flowing approximately _____.

A. 286°
B. 254°
C. 106°
D. 016°

190. You are enroute to Jacksonville, FL,

from San Juan, P.R. There is a fresh N'ly wind blowing. As you cross the axis of the Gulf Stream you would expect to encounter _____.

A. steeper waves, closer together
B. long swells
C. cirrus clouds
D. smoother seas and warmer water

191. Safe water buoys may show ONLY _____.

A. flashing red lights
B. flashing green lights
C. white lights
D. yellow lights

192. The description "Racon" beside an illustration on a chart would mean a _____.

A. radar conspicuous beacon
B. circular radiobeacon
C. radar transponder beacon
D. radar calibration beacon

193. In using Loran-C, skywave reception gives greater range but is _____.

A. only accurate during daylight hours
B. much less accurate
C. only accurate at twilight
D. more accurate than using ground waves

194. The horizon glass of a sextant is _____.

A. silvered on its half nearer the frame
B. mounted on the index arm
C. between the horizon and the shade glasses
D. All of the above

196. The area of strong westerly winds occurring between 40°S and 60°S latitude is called the _____.

A. polar easterlies
B. prevailing westerlies
C. roaring forties
D. jet streams

197. Chart legends printed in capital letters show that the associated landmark is _____.

A. conspicuous
B. inconspicuous
C. a government facility or station
D. a radio transmitter

198. You are enroute to assist vessel A. Vessel A is underway at 6 knots on course 133°T, and bears 343°T at 92 miles from you. What is the time to intercept if you make 9 knots?

A. 7h 44m
B. 7h 12m
C. 6h 43m
D. 6h 08m

200. When navigating using GPS, what is an indicator of the geometery of the satellites that your receiver is locked onto?

A. Horizontal Dilution of Precision
B. Selective Availability
C. Doppler Shifting
D. Precision Coding

201. What is a lighted safe water mark fitted with to aid in its identification?

A. Red and white retroreflective material
B. A spherical topmark
C. A sequential number
D. A red and white octagon

202. On charts of U.S. waters, a magenta marking is NOT used for marking a _____.

A. radiobeacon
B. lighted buoy
C. prohibited area
D. 5-fathom curve

203. In any Loran-C chain, there are three or more stations transmitting pulses which radiate in all directions. One of the stations is the master station, and the others in the chain are the _____.

A. radio stations
B. secondary stations
C. monitor stations
D. pulse stations

206. The winds you would expect to encounter in the North Atlantic between latitudes 5° and 30° are known as the

_____.

A. doldrums
B. westerlies
C. trades
D. easterlies

207. An important lunar cycle affecting the tidal cycle is called the nodal period. How long is this cycle?

A. 16 days
B. 18 days
C. 6 years
D. 19 years

208. The moon is full and at perigee on 20 January 1983. What is the maximum current you could expect at 2350 (ZD +5) at Nantucket Shoals?

A. 0.5 knot
B. 0.7 knot
C. 0.8 knot
D. 1.0 knot

209. The West Wind Drift is located _____.

A. near 60°S
B. on each side of the Equatorial Current
C. in the North Atlantic between Greenland and Europe
D. in the South Pacific near 5°S

210. D051NG. The position labeled C is a(n) _____.

A. fix
B. running fix
C. estimated position
D. dead reckoning position

211. The light rhythm of Morse (A) is shown on _____.

A. preferred-channel buoys
B. starboard- or port-side buoys
C. special marks
D. safe water buoys

212. Which aid is NOT marked on a chart with a magenta circle?

A. Radar station
B. Radar transponder beacon
C. Radiobeacon
D. Aero light

213. When using GPS, how many position lines are required for a 2D (dimensional) fix?

A. 1
B. 2
C. 3
D. 4

216. The prevailing winds in the band of latitude from approximately 5°N to 30°N are the _____.

A. prevailing westerlies
B. northeast trade winds
C. southeast trade winds
D. doldrums

217. In some parts of the world there is often a slight fall in tide during the middle of the high water period. The effect is to create a longer period of stand at higher water. This special feature is called a(n) _____.

A. apogean tide
B. double high water
C. perigean tide
D. bore

218. Lines of position may be _____.

A. hyperboles
B. straight lines
C. arcs
D. All of the above

219. The predicted time that the flood begins at the entrance to Delaware Bay is 1526. You are anchored off Chestnut St. in Philadelphia. If you get underway bound for sea at 1300 and turn for 13 knots, at what point will you lose the flood current?

A. Mile 52
B. New Castle
C. Marcus Hook
D. Billingsport

220. At 0000 you fix your position and plot a new DR track line. At 0200 you again fix your position and it is 0.5 mile east of your DR. Which statement is TRUE?

A. The current is westerly at 0.5 knot.
B. You must increase speed to compensate for the current.
C. The current cannot be determined.
D. The drift is 0.25 knot.

221. In United States waters, a buoy having red and white vertical stripes has a light characteristic of _____.

A. group occulting
B. Morse (A)
C. interrupted quick flashing
D. quick flashing

222. D010NG. Which statement concerning the illustration is correct? (Soundings and heights are in meters.)

A. Maury Lightship swings about her anchor on a circle with a 21 m diameter.
B. The position of the lightship is indicated by the center of the star on the symbol's mast.
C. There is a 12-meter deep hole inside the 5-meter curve just west of Beito Island.
D. The sunken wreck southwest of Beito Island shows the hull or superstructure above the sounding datum.

223. D003NG. In the Loran-C configuration shown, the stations located at X, Y, and Z are called _____.

A. repeater stations
B. secondary stations
C. composite stations
D. alternate stations

226. What winds blow towards the equator from the area about 30° north?

A. Prevailing westerlies
B. Roaring thirties
C. Equatorial flow
D. Northeast trades

227. The class of tide that prevails in the greatest number of important harbors on the Atlantic Coast is _____.

A. interval
B. mixed
C. diurnal
D. semidiurnal

228. D042NG. The Illustration shows the symbols used on radiofacsimile weather charts. Which of these symbols indicates a convergence line?

A. L
B. F
C. M
D. Q

229. The shoreline on charts generally represents the mean _____.

A. high water line
B. low water line
C. low water spring line
D. tide level

230. If the LORAN-C ground wave does NOT extend out as far as the skywave skip distance, there will be a skip zone in which _____.

A. no LORAN-C signal is received
B. only ground waves are received
C. only skywaves are received
D. both ground waves and skywaves are received

231. You are outbound in a buoyed channel on course 015°T. You sight a white light showing a Morse (A) characteristic bearing 359° relative. For safety, you should _____.

A. change course to 359°T to pass near to the buoy
B. stay in the channel and leave the buoy to port
C. alter course to 000°T and leave the buoy well clear to starboard
D. check the chart to see where the marked danger lies in relation to the buoy

232. D010NG. Which statement concerning the chartlet is TRUE? (Soundings and heights are in meters)

A. Maury lightship is visible for 17 miles.
B. The bottom to the south-southeast of the lightship is soft coral.
C. There is a 12-meter deep hole west of Beito Island and inside the 5-meter line.
D. There is a dangerous eddy southeast of Beito Island.

234. When the declination of the Moon is 0°12.5'S, you can expect some tidal currents in Gulf Coast ports to _____.

A. exceed the predicted velocities
B. become reversing currents
C. have either a double ebb or a double flood
D. become weak and variable

236. The winds with the greatest effect on the set, drift, and depth of the equatorial currents are the _____.

A. doldrums
B. horse latitudes
C. trade winds
D. prevailing westerlies

237. Neap tides occur when the _____.

A. Moon is in its first quarter and third quarter phases
B. Sun and Moon are on opposite sides of the Earth
C. Moon's declination is maximum and opposite to that of the Sun
D. Sun and Moon are in conjunction

238. The predicted time that the flood begins at the entrance to Delaware Bay is 1526. You are anchored off Chestnut St. in Philadelphia. If you get underway bound for sea at 1430 and turn for 11 knots, at what point will you lose the ebb current?

A. New Castle
B. Liston Pt.
C. Arnold Pt.
D. Ship John Shoal Lt.

239. As you enter a channel from seaward in a U.S. port, the numbers on the starboard side buoys _____.

A. decrease and the buoys are black
B. increase and the buoys are green
C. decrease and the buoys are red
D. increase and the buoys are red

240. In a river subject to tidal currents, the best time to dock a ship without the assistance of tugs is _____.

A. at high water
B. when there is a following current
C. at slack water
D. at flood

241. A spherical buoy may be_____.

A. numbered
B. lettered
C. green
D. red

242. The difference between the heights of low and high tide is the _____.

A. range
B. period
C. depth
D. distance

243. The loran lines drawn on navigation charts represent _____.

A. ground waves
B. skywaves
C. either ground waves or skywaves interchangeably
D. an average between ground wave and skywave positions

244. To make sure of getting the full advantage of a favorable current, you should reach an entrance or strait at what time in relation to the predicted time of the favorable current?

A. One hour after the predicted time
B. At the predicted time
C. 30 minutes before flood, one hour after an ebb
D. 30 minutes before the predicted time

246. The consistent winds blowing from the horse latitudes to the doldrums are called the _____.

A. prevailing westerlies
B. polar easterlies
C. trade winds
D. roaring forties

247. Neap tides occur _____.

A. at the start of spring, when the Sun is nearly over the equator
B. only when the Sun and Moon are on the same sides of the Earth and are nearly in line
C. when the Sun and Moon are at approximately 90° to each other, as seen from the Earth
D. when the Sun, Moon, and Earth are nearly in line, regardless of alignment order

249. When using GPS, how many position lines are required for a 3D (dimensional) fix that takes into account altitude?

A. 1
B. 2
C. 3
D. 4

250. Weather systems in the middle latitudes generally travel from _____.

A. west to east
B. east to west
C. north to south
D. None of the above

251. A mid-channel buoy, if lighted, will show a _____.

A. fixed red light
B. Morse (A) white light
C. green light
D. flashing red light

252. D015NG. A large automated navigational buoy, such as those that have replaced some lightships, would be shown on a chart by which symbol?

A. A

B. B
C. C
D. D

253. Loran-C is which type of system?

A. Reflected electron
B. Electrical radiation
C. Quarterpoint electrical navigation
D. Hyperbolic radio navigation

254. The range of tide is the _____.

A. difference between the heights of high and low tide
B. distance the tide moves out from the shore
C. duration of time between high and low tide
D. maximum depth of the water at high tide

255. On March 17, at 0500 zone time, you cross the 180th meridian steaming eastward to west longitude. What is your local time?

A. You are in –12 time zone.
B. It is 1700, March 18.
C. It is 0500, March 16.
D. It is 0500, March 18.

256. The belt of light and variable winds between the westerly wind belt and the northeast trade winds is called the _____.

A. subtropical high pressure belt
B. intertropical convergence zone
C. doldrum belt
D. polar frontal zone

257. Spring tides occur _____.

A. at the start of spring, when the Sun is nearly over the equator
B. only when the Sun and Moon are on the same side of the Earth and nearly in line
C. when the Sun and Moon are at approximately 90° to each other as seen from the Earth
D. when the Sun, Moon, and Earth are nearly in line, in any order

258. You are enroute to Savannah, GA, from Recife, Brazil. There is a strong N'ly wind blowing. As you cross the axis of the Gulf Stream you would expect to encounter _____.

A. cirrus clouds
B. long swells
C. smoother seas and warmer water
D. steeper waves, closer together

259. D042NG. The Illustration shows the symbols used on radiofacsimile weather charts. The symbol indicated at letter Q represents a _____.

A. convergence zone
B. squall line
C. convergence line
D. weather boundary

260. The National Ocean Service publishes the _____.

A. Light Lists
B. Coast Pilots
C. pilot charts
D. Sailing Directions

261. You are heading out to sea in a buoyed channel and see a quick-flashing green light on a buoy ahead of you. In U.S. waters, you should leave the buoy _____.

A. well clear on either side
B. about 50 yards off on either side
C. to port
D. to starboard

262. Which of the buoy symbols in illustration D032NG indicates a safe water mark?

A. A
B. B
C. C
D. D

263. Loran-C uses the multiple pulse system because _____.

A. less signal energy is necessary for receiver operation
B. more signal energy is available at the receiver
C. it significantly increases the peak power
D. it increases the signal capacity

265. It is 1200 local time for an observer at 54°E longitude. Which statement is TRUE?

A. It is afternoon at Greenwich.
B. It is midnight at 126°E longitude.
C. The observer is in time zone –4.
D. All of the above are true.

266. The horse latitudes are characterized by _____.

A. weak pressure gradients and light, variable winds
B. the formation of typhoons or hurricanes in certain seasons
C. steady winds in one direction for six months followed by wind reversal for the next six months
D. steady winds generally from the southeast in the Southern Hemisphere

267. D047NG. You are inbound in a channel marked by a range. The range line is 309°T. You are steering 306°T and have the range in sight as shown. The range continues to open. What action should you take?

A. Alter course to the right to 309°T or more to bring the range in line.
B. Alter course to the left until the range closes, then steer to the left of 306°T.
C. Alter course to the left to close the range, then alter course to 309°T.
D. Maintain course as it is normal for the range to open as you get close.

268. D042NG. The illustration shows the symbols used on radiofacsimile weather charts. The symbol indicated at letter L represents a _____.

A. convergence line
B. maritime air mass
C. warm front
D. convergence zone

269. The wind at Frying Pan Shoals has been south-southwesterly at an average velocity of 30 knots. The predicted set and drift of the rotary current are 232° at 0.8 knot. What current should you expect?

A. 065° at 1.2 knots
B. 092° at 1.3 knots
C. 139° at 0.6 knot
D. 224° at 0.4 knot

270. D047NG. You are entering port and have been instructed to anchor, as your berth is not yet available. You are on a SW'ly heading, preparing to drop anchor, when you observe the range lights as shown on your starboard beam. You should _____.

A. drop the anchor immediately as the range lights mark an area free of obstructions

B. drop the anchor immediately as a change in the position of the range lights will be an indication of dragging anchor
C. ensure your ship will NOT block the channel or obstruct the range while at anchor
D. NOT drop the anchor until the lights are in line

271. Your vessel is leaving New York harbor in dense fog. As the vessel slowly proceeds toward sea, you sight a green can buoy on the starboard bow. Which action should you take?

A. Turn hard right to get back into the channel.
B. Pass the buoy close to, leaving it to your port.
C. Stop and fix your position.
D. Stand on, leaving the buoy to your starboard.

272. D033NG. What does the symbol shown indicate on a chart?

A. A sunken vessel marked by a buoy
B. A safe water beacon
C. A red and white can buoy
D. A can buoy with a rotating white light

273. Loran-C is which type of navigation system?

A. Hyperbolic, long-range navigation system
B. Short-range electronic
C. Long-range, high frequency navigation system
D. Long-range, with a frequency of 1950 kHz

275. Which statement concerning illustration D010NG is correct? (Soundings and heights are in meters.)

A. The sunken wreck southwest of Beito Island shows the hull or superstructure above the sounding datum.
B. There is a 12-meter deep hole inside the 5-meter curve just west of Beito Island.
C. The position of the lightship is indicated by the center of the star on the symbol's mast.
D. Maury Lightship swings about her anchor on a circle with a 21-meter diameter.

276. The region of high pressure extending

around the Earth at about 35°N latitude is called the _____.

A. prevailing westerlies
B. horse latitudes
C. troposphere
D. doldrums

277. Your vessel goes aground in soft mud. You would have the best chance of refloating it on the next tide if it grounded at _____.

A. low water neap
B. low water spring
C. high water neap
D. high water spring

278. You are underway on course 050°T and your maximum speed is 11 knots. The eye of a hurricane bears 070°T, 80 miles from your position. The hurricane is moving towards 270°T at 19 knots. If you maneuver at 11 knots to avoid the hurricane, what could be the maximum CPA?

A. 84 miles
B. 79 miles
C. 74 miles
D. 66 miles

279. As a vessel changes course to starboard, the compass card in a magnetic compass _____.

A. remains aligned with compass north
B. also turns to starboard
C. first turns to starboard then counterclockwise to port
D. turns counterclockwise to port

280. Under the U.S. Aids to Navigation System, a lighted buoy with a spherical topmark marks _____.

A. the port side of the channel
B. safe water
C. a hazard to navigation
D. the position of underwater cables

281. A lighted buoy to be left to starboard, when entering a U.S. port from seaward, shall have a _____.

A. white light
B. red light
C. green light
D. light characteristic of Morse (A)

282. The symbol which appears beside a light on a chart reads Gp Fl R (2) 10 sec 160 ft 19M. Which characteristic describes the light?

A. It is visible 10 miles.
B. Its distinguishing number is 19M.
C. It has a radar reflector.
D. None of the above

283. Loran-C operates on a single frequency centered on _____.

A. 100 kHz
B. 500 kHz
C. 1,850 kHz
D. 1,950 kHz

285. The apparent wind is zero when the true wind is _____.

A. zero
B. from ahead and equal to the ship's speed
C. from astern and equal to the ship's speed
D. from astern and is twice the ship's speed

286. On the pole side of the trade wind belt, there is an area of high pressure with weak pressure gradients and light, variable winds. This area is called the _____.

A. prevailing westerlies
B. geostrophic winds
C. doldrums
D. horse latitudes

287. The datum from which the predicted heights of tides are reckoned in the tide tables is the same as that used for the charts of the locality. The depression of the datum below mean sea level for Hampton Roads, Virginia, is _____.

A. between –0.7 and +0.5 feet
B. between 1.9 and 3.2 feet
C. 4.1 feet
D. 1.2 feet

288. When using a radar in a unstabilized mode, fixes are determined most easily from _____.

A. center bearings
B. tangent bearings
C. ranges
D. objects that are close aboard

289. A position obtained by crossing lines

of position taken at different times and advanced to a common time is a(n) _____.

A. running fix
B. dead-reckoning position
C. fix
D. estimated position

290. The true wind is from 330°T, speed 6 knots. You want the apparent wind to be 30 knots from 10° on your port bow. To what course and speed must you change?

A. Cn 240°, 28.0 knots
B. Cn 270°, 28.0 knots
C. Cn 180°, 30.0 knots
D. Cn 090°, 32.5 knots

291. A buoy marking a wreck will show a(n) _____.

A. white light FL (2) and a topmark of 2 black spheres
B. occulting green light and may be lettered
C. yellow light and will be numbered
D. continuous quick white light and may be numbered

292. The symbol which appears beside a light on a chart reads "Gp Fl R (2) 10 sec 160 ft 19M." Which characteristic does the light possess?

A. It is visible two nautical miles.
B. Its distinguishing number is 19M.
C. It has a red light.
D. It flashes once every ten seconds.

293. The use of pulse groups and extremely precise timing at each Loran-C station makes possible the use of _____.

A. high frequency pulses
B. combinations of high and low frequency pulses
C. the same frequency for all stations in a chain
D. varied long and short pulses

296. The wind flow from the horse latitudes to the doldrums is deflected due to _____.

A. Coriolis force
B. the mid-latitude, semi-permanent high
C. differing atmospheric pressures
D. the prevailing westerlies

297. The tides in Boston Harbor generally _____.

A. are diurnal in nature
B. have their variations caused by the changing declination of the Moon
C. have a greater range than the tides in Gulf Coast ports
D. All of the above

298. A great circle crosses the equator at 173°E. It will also cross the equator at what other longitude?

A. 7°W
B. 73°E
C. 73°W
D. 173°W

299. Steady precipitation is typical of _____.

A. coming cold weather conditions
B. a warm front weather condition
C. high pressure conditions
D. scattered cumulus clouds

300. D018NG. Which of the symbols shown represents a warm front?

A. A
B. B
C. C
D. D

301. In the U.S. Aids to Navigation System, lateral aids as seen entering from seaward will display lights with which characteristic?

A. Flashing
B. Occulting
C. Quick Flashing
D. All of the above

302. Which symbol represents a 20-fathom curve?

A. —..—..—..—..—
B. — — — — — — — —
C. — —.— —.— —.— —.
D. — — — — — — — —

305. In Region A of the IALA Buoyage System, when entering from seaward, the port side of a channel would be marked by a _____.

A. red can buoy
B. black can buoy
C. red conical buoy
D. black conical buoy

306. Weather conditions in the middle latitudes generally move _____.

A. eastward
B. westward
C. northward
D. southward

307. The time meridian that is used when computing the currents for Pensacola Bay, Florida, is _____.

A. 60°W
B. 75°W
C. 90°W
D. 105°W

308. The wind at Frying Pan Shoals has been west-northwesterly at an average velocity of 40 knots. The predicted set and drift of the rotary current are 323° at 0.6 knot. What current should you expect?

A. 001° at 0.7 knot
B. 018° at 0.4 knot
C. 052° at 0.6 knot
D. 089° at 0.9 knot

309. You are underway on course 050°T and your maximum speed is 12 knots. The eye of a hurricane bears 120°T, 110 miles from your position. The hurricane is moving towards 285°T at 25 knots. What course should you steer at 12 knots to have the maximum CPA?

A. 332°
B. 339°
C. 346°
D. 357°

311. You are steaming southward along the west coast of the United States when you encounter a buoy showing a flashing red light. The buoy should be left on _____.

A. the vessel's starboard side
B. the vessel's port side
C. either side close aboard
D. either side well clear

312. The depth of water on a chart is indicated as 23 meters. This is equal to _____.

A. 11.5 fathoms
B. 12.6 fathoms
C. 69.0 feet
D. 78.6 feet

313. The Loran-C receiver _____.

A. is not affected by interference
B. can be used at any distance with accuracy
C. can be affected by interference
D. is reliable only from sunrise to sunset

316. According to Buys Ballot's law, when an observer in the Northern Hemisphere experiences a northwest wind, the center of low pressure is located to the _____.

A. northeast
B. west-southwest
C. northwest
D. south-southeast

317. The time meridian used for tide computations in New York Harbor is_____.

A. 52°30'W
B. 60°00'W
C. 75°00'W
D. 82°30'W

318. Vessels required to have an Automatic Radar Plotting Aid must have a device to indicate the _____.

A. distance to the next port
B. speed of the vessel over the ground or through the water
C. time of the next navigational satellite pass
D. None of the above

319. D042NG. The Illustration shows the symbols used by radiofacsimile weather charts. The symbol indicated at letter F represents a _____.

A. maritime air mass
B. weather boundary
C. convergence zone
D. squall line

320. Sometimes foreign charts are reproduced by NIMA. On such a chart, a wire-dragged, swept area may be shown in green or _____.

A. red
B. black
C. purple
D. yellow

321. Which buoy may be even numbered?

A. Mid-channel buoy
B. Unlighted nun buoy

C. Lighted green buoy
D. All of the above

323. The position accuracy of Loran-C degrades with increasing distance from the transmitting stations as_____.

A. gains are made over the signal path
B. a result of variation in propagation conditions
C. the frequency of the pulses increases
D. the stations shift pulses

326. You are steaming west in the North Atlantic in an extratropical cyclonic storm, and the wind is dead ahead. According to the law of Buys Ballot, the center of low pressure lies to the _____.

A. north
B. south
C. east
D. west

327. When daylight savings time is kept the times of tide and current calculations must be adjusted. One way of doing this is to _____.

A. subtract one hour from the times listed under the reference stations
B. add one hour to the times listed under the reference stations
C. apply no correction, as the times in the reference stations are adjusted for daylight savings time
D. add 15° to the standard meridian when calculating the time difference

328. The direction of prevailing winds in the Northern Hemisphere is caused by the _____.

A. magnetic field at the North Pole
B. Gulf Stream
C. Earth's rotation
D. Arctic cold fronts

329. D042NG. The symbols shown are used on radiofacsimile weather charts. Which symbol indicates a weather boundary?

A. I
B. H
C. G
D. F

330. You are taking bearings on two known objects ashore. The BEST fix is obtained

when the angle between the lines of position is _____.

A. 90°
B. 30°
C. 45°
D. 60°

331. What indicates a buoy that should be left to port when entering from seaward? (U.S. Aids to Navigation System)

A. White light
B. Group flashing characteristic
C. Nun shape
D. Odd number

333. Loran-C stations transmit groups of pulses at specific times. The time interval between transmissions from the master station is the _____.

A. coding delay
B. group repetition interval
C. pulse interval
D. phase code

336. You are steaming eastward in the North Atlantic in an extratropical cyclonic storm and the wind is dead ahead. According to the law of Buys Ballot, the center of the low pressure lies _____.

A. ahead of you
B. astern of you
C. to the north
D. to the south

337. To predict the actual depth of water using the Tide Tables, the number obtained from the Tide Tables is _____.

A. the actual depth
B. added to or subtracted from the charted depth
C. multiplied by the charted depth
D. divided by the charted depth

338. D042NG. The illustration shows the symbols used on radio facsimile weather charts. The symbol indicated at letter N represents _____.

A. hail
B. freezing rain
C. rain
D. snow

339. The wind at Frying Pan Shoals has been north-northeasterly at an average velocity of 30 knots. The predicted set and

drift of the rotary current are 355° at 0.8 knot. What current should you expect?

A. 010° at 1.1 knots
B. 047° at 0.3 knot
C. 325° at 0.7 knot
D. 279° at 1.0 knot

340. Information about the direction and velocity of rotary tidal currents is found in the _____.

A. Mariner's Guide
B. Nautical Almanac
C. Tide Tables
D. Tidal Current Tables

341. Buoys which only mark the left or right side of the channel will never exhibit a light with which characteristic?

A. Flashing
B. Quick flashing
C. Composite group flashing
D. Equal interval (isophase)

342. A polyconic projection is based on a _____.

A. plane tangent at one point
B. cylinder tangent at one parallel
C. cone tangent at one parallel
D. series of cones tangent at selected parallels

345. A navigator fixing a vessel's position by radar _____.

A. should never use radar bearings
B. should only use radar bearings when the range exceeds the distance to the horizon
C. can use radar information from one object to fix the position
D. must use information from targets forward of the beam

346. If your weather bulletin shows the center of a low pressure area to be 100 miles due east of your position, what winds can you expect in the Northern Hemisphere?

A. East to northeast
B. East to southeast
C. North to northwest
D. South to southeast

347. D042NG. The illustration shows the symbols used on radiofacsimile weather charts. Which of these symbols indicates rain?

A. N
B. M
C. I
D. G

348. When using a radar in an unstabilized mode, fixes are determined most easily from _____.

A. center bearings
B. tangent bearings
C. objects that are close aboard
D. ranges

349. The direction of the southeast trade winds is a result of the_____.

A. equatorial current
B. humidity
C. rotation of the earth
D. change of seasons

350. When making landfall at night, the light from a powerful lighthouse may sometimes be seen before the lantern breaks the horizon. This light is called the _____.

A. diffusion
B. backscatter
C. loom
D. elevation

351. Which buoy may be odd-numbered?

A. A spherical buoy
B. An unlighted can buoy
C. A red buoy
D. A yellow buoy

352. Which chart projection would be most suitable for marine surveying?

A. Gnomonic
B. Lambert conformal
C. Mercator
D. Polyconic

355. During the month of October the Sun's declination is _____.

A. north and increasing
B. north and decreasing
C. south and increasing
D. south and decreasing

356. When facing into the wind in the Northern Hemisphere the center of low pressure lies _____.

A. directly in front of you
B. directly behind you
C. to your left and behind you
D. to your right and behind you

357. On 10 August 1983 you will dock near Days Point, Weehawken, on the Hudson River, at 1800 DST (ZD +4). The charted depth alongside the pier is 24 feet (7.3 meters). What will be the depth of water when you dock?

A. 23.5 feet (7.1 m)
B. 23.9 feet (7.2 m)
C. 24.9 feet (7.5 m)
D. 26.3 feet (8.0 m)

358. What will be the set of the rotary current at Nantucket Shoals at 1245 (ZD +5) 14 January 1983?

A. 015°
B. 125°
C. 162°
D. 225°

359. You are enroute to assist vessel A. Vessel A is underway at 4.5 knots on course 233°T, and bears 264°T, 68 miles from you. What is the time to intercept if you make 13 knots?

A. 6h 31m
B. 6h 47m
C. 7h 03m
D. 7h 34m

360. D042NG. The Illustration shows the symbols used on radiofacsimile weather charts. The symbol indicated at letter M represents _____.

A. rain
B. snow
C. hail
D. ice

361. As your vessel is heading southward along the east coast of the United States, you encounter a buoy showing a red flashing light. How should you pass this buoy?

A. Pass it about 50 yards off on either side.
B. Leave it to your starboard.
C. Leave it to your port.
D. Pass it well clear on either side.

362. Which statement about a simple conic chart projection is TRUE?

A. It is an equal-area projection.
B. It is a conformal projection.
C. Meridians appear as curved lines.
D. The scale is correct along any meridian.

363. Your dead-reckoning position should be plotted _____.

A. whenever an estimated position is plotted
B. when it agrees with your loran position
C. when coming on or going off soundings
D. at least every hour on the hour in the open waters of the sea

365. The Sun at a maximum declination north would be approximately at _____.

A. aphelion
B. perihelion
C. autumnal equinox
D. first point of Aries

366. If an observer in the Northern Hemisphere faces the surface wind, the center of low pressure is to his_____.

A. left, slightly behind him
B. right, slightly behind him
C. left, slightly in front of him
D. right, slightly in front of him

367. What will be the time after 0800 EST (ZD +5) that the height of the tide at South Freeport, ME, will be 6.0 feet (1.8 meters) on 7 November 1983?

A. 0936
B. 0942
C. 0951
D. 1001

368. A great circle crosses the equator at 134°E. It will also cross the equator at what other longitude?

A. 46°W
B. 124°W
C. 134°W
D. 34°E

369. You are underway on course 050°T and your maximum speed is 11 knots. The eye of a hurricane bears 070°T, 80 miles from your position. The hurricane is moving towards 270°T at 19 knots. What course should you steer at 11 knots to have the maximum CPA?

A. 250°
B. 234°

C. 227°
D. 215°

370. Prevailing winds between 30°N and 60°N latitude are from the _____.

A. north
B. south
C. east
D. west

371. Which buoy may be odd-numbered?

A. Mid-channel buoy
B. Unlighted nun buoy
C. Lighted green buoy
D. All of the above

372. You would find the variation on a polyconic projection chart _____.

A. on the compass rose
B. on the mileage scale
C. written on the chart title
D. at each line of longitude

373. How is a navigation light on the Mississippi River identified on an Army Corps of Engineers navigation map?

A. Name and light characteristic
B. Name and miles from a reference point
C. Light characteristic and miles A.H.P.
D. None of the above

376. According to Buys Ballot's law, when an observer in the Northern Hemisphere experiences a northeast wind the center of low pressure is located to the _____.

A. northeast
B. west-southwest
C. northwest
D. south-southeast

377. Determine the height of the tide at 2045 EST (ZD +5) at Augusta, ME, on 8 March 1983.

A. 1.4 feet (0.5 meter)
B. 1.9 feet (0.6 meter)
C. 2.3 feet (0.7 meter)
D. 2.6 feet (0.8 meter)

378. A navigator fixing a vessel's position by radar _____.

A. should never use radar bearings
B. can use radar information from one object to fix the position

C. should only use radar bearings when the range exceeds the distance to the horizon
D. must use information from targets forward of the beam

379. The steady current circling the globe at about 60°S is the _____.

A. Prevailing Westerly
B. Sub-Polar Flow
C. West Wind Drift
D. Humboldt Current

380. Prevailing winds between 30°N and 60°N latitude are from the_____.

A. east
B. west
C. north
D. south

381. A nun buoy will _____.

A. be green in color
B. have an even number
C. be left to port when entering from seaward
D. be cylindrical in shape

382. Which would you consult for information about the general current circulation in the North Atlantic Ocean?

A. Pilot chart
B. Coast Pilot
C. Current Table
D. Climatological Atlas

386. Your vessel is on course 180°T speed 22 knots. The apparent wind is from 70° off the port bow, speed 20 knots. The true direction and speed of the wind are _____.

A. 45°T, 21.0 knots
B. 51°T, 24.0 knots
C. 58°T, 21.2 knots
D. 64°T, 26.0 knots

388. You are underway on course 120°T and your maximum speed is 12 knots. The eye of a hurricane bears 150°T, 120 miles from your position. The hurricane is moving towards 295°T at 20 knots. If you maneuver at 12 knots to avoid the hurricane, what could be the maximum CPA?

A. 89 miles
B. 96 miles
C. 105 miles
D. 117 miles

389. The edge of a hurricane has overtaken your vessel in the Gulf of Mexico, and the northwest wind of a few hours ago has shifted to the west. This is an indication that you are located in the _____.

A. navigable semicircle
B. dangerous semicircle
C. low pressure area
D. eye of the storm

390. During the winter months, the southeast trade winds are _____.

A. stronger than during the summer months
B. weaker than during the summer months
C. drier than during the summer months
D. wetter than during the summer months

391. When outbound from a U.S. port, a buoy displaying a flashing red light indicates _____.

A. a junction with the preferred channel to the left
B. a sharp turn in the channel to the right
C. the port side of the channel
D. a wreck to be left on the vessel's starboard side

392. A pilot chart does NOT contain information about _____.

A. average wind conditions
B. tidal currents
C. magnetic variation
D. average limits of field ice

393. If your position is LAT 25°N, LONG 35°W, what is the correction you would apply to an RDF bearing received from a transmitting station in LAT 30°N, LONG 40°W?

A. −1.3°
B. +1.3°
C. −2.1°
D. +2.1°

394. An instrument designed to maintain a continuous record of atmospheric pressure is a(n) _____.

A. mercurial barometer
B. aneroid barometer
C. barograph
D. thermograph

396. Your vessel is on course 150°T, speed 17 knots. The apparent wind is from 40° off the starboard bow, speed 15 knots. What is the speed of the true wind?

A. 9.0 knots
B. 10.2 knots
C. 11.0 knots
D. 12.0 knots

397. The mean tide level at Peaks Island, ME, is _____.

A. 1.8 feet (0.5 meter)
B. 2.5 feet (0.8 meter)
C. 3.2 feet (1.0 meter)
D. 4.5 feet (1.4 meters)

398. The velocity of the apparent wind can be less than the true wind and from the same direction, if certain conditions are present. One condition is that the _____.

A. ship's speed is more than the true wind velocity
B. true wind is from dead astern
C. true wind is on the beam
D. true wind is from dead ahead

399. Where will you find information about the duration of slack water?

A. American Practical Navigator
B. Sailing Directions
C. Tide Tables
D. Tidal Current Tables

400. Information about the currents for the Pacific Coast of the U. S. are found in the _____.

A. Ocean Current Tables
B. Nautical Almanac
C. Tide Tables
D. Tidal Current Tables

401. You are steaming in a westerly direction along the Gulf Coast. You see ahead of you a lighted buoy showing a red isophase light. Which action should you take?

A. Alter course to port and leave the buoy to starboard.
B. Alter course to starboard and leave the buoy to port.
C. Alter course and leave the buoy nearby on either side.
D. Alter course and pass the buoy well-off on either side.

402. All of the following can be found on a Pilot Chart EXCEPT information concerning the _____.

A. percentage of frequency of wave heights
B. percentage of poor visibility conditions
C. sea surface temperatures
D. amounts of precipitation

404. An aneroid barometer is an instrument _____.

A. used to measure the speed of wind
B. in which the pressure of the air is measured
C. that tells which direction a storm is coming from
D. used to measure the height of waves

406. Your vessel is on course 135°T, speed 18 knots. From the appearance of the sea you estimate the speed of the true wind as 24.5 knots. The apparent wind is 40° on the starboard bow. Determine the speed of the apparent wind.

A. 24.2 knots
B. 28.4 knots
C. 32.2 knots
D. 36.0 knots

407. What would be the height of the tide at Crisfield, MD, at 0310 DST (ZD +4) on 6 May 1983?

A. 0.1 foot
B. 0.5 foot
C. 1.1 feet
D. 1.6 feet

408. A buoy bears 176°T at 3000 yards. What is the course to make good to leave the buoy 100 yards to port?

A. 174°T
B. 176°T
C. 178°T
D. 180°T

409. On November 1st the zone time is 1700 EST (ZD +5) in LONG 75°W. What is the corresponding zone time and date in LONG 135°E?

A. 0700, November 2nd
B. 0700, November 1st
C. 2200, November 1st
D. 2200, October 31st

410. The height of the tide at low water is 0.0 feet. The range is 9.0 feet. The duration is 06h 00m. The height of the tide 02h 12m before high water will be _____.

A. 8.3 feet
B. 6.3 feet
C. 4.7 feet
D. 2.7 feet

411. When entering from seaward, a buoy displaying a single-flashing red light would indicate _____.

A. a junction with the preferred channel to the left
B. a sharp turn in the channel to the right
C. the starboard side of the channel
D. a wreck to be left on the vessel's port side

412. If you were sailing in the North Pacific and were interested in the ice and iceberg limits, you could find this information in the _____.

A. Pilot Chart
B. Coast Pilot
C. Notice to Mariners
D. None of the above

413. You would need to apply the conversion angle to an RDF bearing, prior to plotting the bearing on a chart, when the ship and the station are both on _____.

A. latitude 50°S, 200 miles apart
B. longitude 50°W, 150 miles apart
C. the equator, 175 miles apart
D. latitude 30°N, 50 miles apart

414. The barometer is an instrument for measuring the _____.

A. temperature
B. relative humidity
C. dew point
D. atmospheric pressure

416. A ship is on course 195° at a speed of 15 knots. The apparent wind is from 40° on the port bow, speed 30 knots. The direction and speed of the true wind are _____.

A. 068°T, 30 knots
B. 127°T, 21 knots
C. 263°T, 42 knots
D. 292°T, 42 knots

417. On 6 July 1983, at 1830 DST (ZD +4), what will be the predicted height of tide at Newburgh, NY?

A. 3.3 feet
B. 2.6 feet
C. 2.4 feet
D. 2.0 feet

418. In most cases, the direction of the apparent wind lies between the bow and _____.

A. the direction of the true wind
B. true north
C. the beam on the windward side
D. the beam on the lee side

419. The ocean bottom that extends from the shoreline out to an area where there is a marked change in slope to a greater depth is the _____.

A. abyssal plain
B. continental shelf
C. borderland
D. offshore terrace

420. D047NG. You are inbound in a channel marked by a range. The range line is 309°T. You are steering 306°T and have the range in sight as shown. The range continues to open. What action should you take?

A. Alter course to the left until the range closes then steer to the left of 306°T.
B. Maintain course as it is normal for the range to open as you get close.
C. Alter course to the left to close the range, then alter course to 309°T.
D. Alter course to the right to 309°T or more to bring the range in line.

421. Daylight savings time is a form of zone time that adopts the time _____.

A. one zone to the west
B. one zone to the east
C. two zones to the west
D. two zones to the east

422. If you are sailing from the East Coast of the United States to the Caribbean Sea, which publication would contain information on weather, currents, and storms?

A. Sailing Charts of the Caribbean Sea
B. Pilot Charts of the North Atlantic
C. Light Lists, Atlantic and Gulf Coast
D. Tidal Current Tables

423. You have calibrated your RDF. When compiling the calibration table, the correction to be applied to any future RDF bearings is listed against the _____.

A. true bearing of the transmitter
B. relative bearing of the transmitter
C. heading of the vessel
D. time of reception

424. For an accurate barometer check, you would _____.

A. check it with a barometer on another vessel
B. take readings from several barometers and average them
C. check it with the barometer at the ship chandlery
D. check it against radio or National Weather Service reports of the immediate vicinity

426. The wind speed and direction observed from a moving vessel is known as _____.

A. coordinate wind
B. true wind
C. apparent wind
D. anemometer wind

427. On 23 March 1983, at Kingston Point, NY, what is the earliest time after 1700 EST (ZD +5) that the predicted tide will be +2.0 feet?

A. 1730
B. 1800
C. 1854
D. 2030

428. A buoy bears 178°T at 3000 yards (2700 meters). What is the course to make good to leave the buoy 100 yards (90 meters) to starboard?

A. 174°T
B. 176°T
C. 178°T
D. 180°T

429. A great circle crosses the equator at 127°W. It will also cross the equator at what other longitude?

A. 127°E
B. 53°E
C. 27°E
D. 27°W

430. The southeast trade winds actually blow toward the _____.

A. southeast
B. south
C. east
D. northwest

431. When a buoy marks a channel bifurcation, the preferred channel is NOT indicated by _____.

A. the shape of an unlighted buoy
B. the light color of a lighted buoy
C. the color of the topmost band
D. whether the number is odd or even

432. When using a Lambert conformal chart in high latitudes, angles such as bearings are measured in reference to _____.

A. the meridian through the object of the bearing
B. the meridian through the ship's position
C. the meridian midway between the ship and the object
D. any meridian

433. You are swinging ship to calibrate the RDF. The gyro error is 2°W. The RDF gyro bearing of a station is 308° at the same time the visual bearing is 307°. At the time of the bearing, you are heading 270°T. When you prepare the calibration chart, you would indicate the _____.

A. correction is –1° when the relative bearing is 035°
B. error is –1° when the heading is 270°
C. correction is +1° when the relative bearing is 325°
D. error is –1° on all headings

434. The purpose of the set hand on an aneroid barometer is to _____.

A. adjust the barometer
B. indicate any change in the reading of the barometer
C. provide a correction for height above sea level
D. provide a correction for temperature changes

436. A wind vane on a moving vessel shows _____.

A. dead reckoning wind direction
B. true wind direction

C. apparent wind direction
D. estimated wind direction

437. Your vessel will be docking at Chester, PA, during the evening of 22 April 1983. The chart shows a depth of 20 feet (6.1 meters) at the pier. What will be the depth of water available at 1856 EST (ZD +5)?

A. 22.4 feet (6.8 meters)
B. 23.4 feet (7.2 meters)
C. 24.9 feet (7.6 meters)
D. 25.7 feet (7.8 meters)

438. Your longitude is 124°E, and your local mean time is 0520 on the 5th of the month. The mean time and date at Greenwich is _____.

A. 1336 on the 4th
B. 1336 on the 5th
C. 2104 on the 4th
D. 2104 on the 5th

439. If a weather bulletin shows the center of a low pressure system to be 100 miles due east of you, what winds can you expect in the Southern Hemisphere?

A. South-southwesterly
B. North-northwesterly
C. South-southeasterly
D. North-northeasterly

440. D047NG. You are inbound in a channel marked by a range. The range line is 309°T. You are steering 306°T. The range appears as shown and is closing. Which action should you take?

A. Continue on the present heading until the range is in line, then alter course to the left.
B. Immediately alter course to the right to bring the range in line.
C. Immediately alter course to 309°T.
D. Continue on course until the range is closed, then alter course to the right.

441. A yellow buoy may exhibit a(n) _____.

A. fixed red light
B. flashing light
C. white light
D. occulting light

442. In very high latitudes, the most practical chart projection is the _____.

A. Mercator
B. gnomonic
C. azimuthal
D. Lambert conformal

443. You are swinging ship to calibrate the RDF. The RDF gyro bearing is 054° at the same time the visual bearing is 053°pgc. Gyro error is 1°W. At the time of the bearings the heading was 339°pgc. Which statement about the calibrations is TRUE?

A. 1° must be subtracted from all RDF bearings.
B. 1° must be subtracted from all bearings when the ship is headed 339°T.
C. 1° must be subtracted from all RDF bearings of 053°T.
D. 1° must be subtracted from all RDF bearings of 075° relative.

444. A sylphon cell is a part of a _____.

A. maximum thermometer
B. barograph
C. thermograph
D. hygrometer

446. The usual sequence of directions in which a tropical cyclone moves in the Southern Hemisphere is _____.

A. northwest, west, and south
B. southwest, south, and southeast
C. north, northwest, and east
D. west, northwest, and north

447. On 27 April 1983, at 1105 DST (ZD +4), what will be the predicted height of tide at Falkner Island, CT?

A. 5.3 feet (1.6 m)
B. 5.6 feet (1.7 m)
C. 6.2 feet (1.9 m)
D. 6.8 feet (2.7 m)

448. Mean high water is the reference datum used to measure _____.

A. soundings on the east coast of the United States
B. soundings in European waters
C. heights of topographical features in the United States
D. both heights and soundings worldwide

449. You are enroute to assist vessel A. Vessel A is underway at 5 knots on course 063°T, and bears 136°T at 78 miles from

you. What is the course to steer at 13 knots to intercept vessel A?

A. 340°
B. 295°
C. 158°
D. 114°

450. You are enroute to Jacksonville, FL, from San Juan, P.R. There is a fresh N'ly wind blowing. As you cross the axis of the Gulf Stream you would expect to encounter _____.

A. cirrus clouds
B. smoother seas and warmer water
C. steeper waves, closer together
D. long swells

451. Which light characteristic may be used on a special purpose mark?

A. Fixed
B. Occulting
C. Equal interval
D. Quick flashing

452. When navigating in high latitudes and using a chart based on a Lambert conformal projection, _____.

A. a straight line drawn on the chart approximates a great circle
B. the chart should not be used outside of the standard parallels
C. the course angle is measured at the mid-longitude of the track line
D. distance cannot be measured directly from the chart

453. The quadrantal correction to be applied to an RDF bearing is determined _____.

A. from Bowditch Vol. II
B. from a table on board your ship
C. by requesting the calibration station to provide the information after the RDF is calibrated
D. by comparing the true and relative bearings of the transmitter

454. On what does the operation of an aneroid barometer depend?

A. Thin, metal, airtight cell
B. Curved tube containing alcohol
C. Column of mercury supported by atmospheric pressure
D. Expansion of mercury in a closed tube

456. Which condition exists in the eye of a hurricane?

A. Wind rapidly changing direction
B. A temperature much lower than that outside the eye
C. Towering cumulonimbus clouds
D. An extremely low barometric pressure

457. Find the height of the tide at Port Wentworth, GA, on 5 October 1983, at 1840 DST (ZD +4).

A. 3.0 feet
B. 3.5 feet
C. 4.0 feet
D. 4.4 feet

458. The prevailing westerlies of the Southern Hemisphere blow 18–30 knots_____.

A. all year long
B. during the summer months only
C. during the winter only
D. during spring only

459. A buoy bears 178°T at 3000 yards (2700 meters). What is the course to make good to leave the buoy 100 yards (90 meters) to port?

A. 174°T
B. 176°T
C. 178°T
D. 180°T

460. When using horizontal sextant angles of three objects to fix your position, an indeterminate position will result in which situation?

A. The objects lie in a straight line.
B. The vessel is inside of a triangle formed by the objects.
C. The vessel is outside of a triangle formed by the objects.
D. A circle will pass through your position and the three objects.

461. Under the U.S. Aids to Navigation System, a yellow buoy may _____.

A. mark a fish net area
B. be lighted with a white light
C. show a fixed red light
D. All of the above

462. For what purpose would using a Lambert conformal chart be more convenient than using a Mercator?

A. Plotting radio bearings over a long distance
B. Determining latitude and longitude of a fix
C. Measuring rhumb line distances
D. Measuring rhumb line directions

463. The signal transmitted by a radiobeacon station is called its _____.

A. group sequence
B. frequency
C. directional signal
D. characteristic signal

464. Prior to reading an aneroid barometer, you should tap the face lightly with your finger to _____.

A. expose any loose connections
B. demagnetize the metal elements
C. bring the pointer to its true position
D. contract and expand the glass face

466. In the relatively calm area near the hurricane center, the seas are _____.

A. moderate but easily navigated
B. calm
C. mountainous and confused
D. mountainous but fairly regular as far as direction is concerned

467. At what time after 1400 EST (ZD +5), on 4 January 1983, will the height of the tide at Port Wentworth, GA, be 3.0 feet?

A. 1612
B. 1630
C. 1653
D. 1718

468. Which of the symbols in illustration D018NG represents a cold front?

A. A
B. B
C. C
D. D

469. Where are the prevailing westerlies of the Southern Hemisphere located?

A. Between the Equator and 10° latitude
B. Between 10° and 20° latitude
C. Between 30° and 60° latitude
D. Between 60° and 90° latitude

470. You are underway on course 120°T and can make 12 knots. The eye of a hurricane bears 150°T at 120 miles. The hurricane is on course 295° at 20 knots. What course should you steer at 12 knots to have the maximum CPA?

A. 312°
B. 330°
C. 348°
D. 001°

471. Yellow lights may appear on _____.

A. special-purpose buoys
B. vertically striped buoys
C. horizontally banded buoys
D. spherical buoys

472. Which conic projection chart features straight lines which closely approximate a great circle?

A. Polyconic
B. Lambert conformal
C. Orthographic
D. Stereographic

473. The quadrantal error of a radio bearing is caused by _____.

A. polarization at sunrise and sunset
B. not taking the bearing from the transmitting antenna
C. the signal passing over land before it reaches sea
D. the metal in a ship's structure

474. Which indication on the barometer is most meaningful in forecasting weather?

A. The words Fair—Change—Rain
B. The direction and rate of change of barometric pressure
C. The actual barometric pressure
D. The relative humidity

476. Tropical cyclones normally form within which of the following belts of latitude?

A. 5° to 15°
B. 15° to 30°
C. 30° to 45°
D. 45° to 60°

477. Determine the height of the tide at 1430 EST (ZD +5) at New Bedford, MA, on 10 April 1983.

A. 1.1 feet
B. 1.2 feet

C. 1.4 feet
D. 1.7 feet

478. The velocity of the apparent wind can be more than the true wind, and come from the same direction, if certain conditions are present. One condition is that the _____.

A. ship's speed must be less than the true wind velocity
B. true wind must be from dead astern
C. true wind velocity must be faster than the ship's speed
D. true wind must be from dead ahead

479. You are enroute to assist vessel A. Vessel A is underway at 5 knots on course 063°T, and bears 136°T at 78 miles from you. What is the course to steer at 13 knots to intercept vessel A?

A. 114°
B. 158°
C. 295°
D. 340°

480. What kind of pressure systems travel in easterly waves?

A. High pressure
B. Low pressure
C. Subsurface pressure
D. Terrastatic pressure

481. A special mark (yellow buoy), if lighted, may exhibit which light rhythm?

A. Flashing
B. Morse A
C. Equal interval
D. Occulting

482. Which statement about a gnomonic chart is correct?

A. A rhumb line appears as a straight line.
B. Distance is measured at the midlatitude of the track line.
C. Meridians appear as curved lines converging toward the nearer pole.
D. Parallels, except the equator, appear as curved lines.

483. Coral atolls, or a chain of islands at right angles to the radar beam, may show as a long line rather than as individual targets due to _____.

A. the effects of beam width
B. limitations on range resolution
C. the pulse length of the radar
D. the multiple-target resolution factor

484. The needle of an aneroid barometer points to 30.05 on the dial. This indicates that the barometric pressure is _____.

A. 30.05 inches of mercury
B. 30.05 millimeters of mercury
C. 30.05 millibars
D. falling

486. Tropical cyclones do not form within 5° of the Equator because _____.

A. there are no fronts in that area
B. it is too hot
C. it is too humid
D. of negligible Coriolis force

487. What will be the time after 0600 (ZD +3), on 6 March 1983, that the height of the tide at Puerto Rosales, Argentina, will be 9.0 feet (2.7 meters)?

A. 0740
B. 0754
C. 0840
D. 0922

488. A great circle crosses the equator at 93°W. It will also cross the equator at what other longitude?

A. 13°E
B. 87°E
C. 177°E
D. 177°W

489. You are anchored in the Aleutian Island chain and receive word that a tsunami is expected to strike the islands in six hours. What is the safest action?

A. Get underway and be in deep, open-ocean water when the tsunami arrives.
B. Increase the scope of the anchor cable and drop the second anchor underfoot at short stay.
C. Get underway and be close inshore on the side of the island away from the tsunami.
D. Plant both anchors with about a 60° angle between them, and let out a long scope to each anchor.

490. You are underway on course 050°T and your maximum speed is 10 knots. The eye of a hurricane bears 100°T, 90 miles from your position. The hurricane is moving towards 285°T at 19 knots. Which course should you steer at 10 knots to have the maximum CPA?

A. 221°
B. 226°
C. 233°
D. 238°

491. A special-purpose buoy shall be _____.

A. lighted with a white light
B. striped black and red
C. lighted with a red light
D. yellow

492. Which type of projection is formed if a plane is tangent to the Earth, and points are projected geometrically from the center of the Earth?

A. Lambert conformal
B. Oblique gnomonic
C. Mercator
D. Transverse conic

493. D011NG. The picture shown represents the geographic location of a vessel and the radar presentation at the same time. Which statement is TRUE?

A. Ship No. 1 is not detected due to the shadow effect of the headland.
B. The small island is not detected due to the effect of beam width.
C. A tangent bearing of the headland to the south-southeast should be corrected by adding one-half of the beam width.
D. Ship No. 2 is not detected due to the reflective mass of the background mountain overpowering the ship's reflective signals.

494. Barometers are usually calibrated to indicate atmospheric pressure in _____.

A. inches of mercury and centimeters
B. feet of mercury and millibars
C. inches of mercury and millimeters
D. inches of mercury and millibars

496. Severe tropical cyclones (hurricanes, typhoons) occur in all warm-water oceans except the _____.

A. Indian Ocean
B. North Pacific Ocean
C. South Pacific Ocean
D. South Atlantic Ocean

497. What will be the time after 0300 (ZD +4), on 5 March 1983, when the height of the tide at Port of Spain, Trinidad, will be 2.5 feet (.76 meters) ?

A. 0548
B. 0602
C. 0618
D. 0634

498. What is an advantage of the magnetic compass aboard vessels?

A. Compass error is negligible at or near the earth's magnetic poles.
B. It does not have to be checked as often.
C. It is reliable due to its essential simplicity.
D. All points on the compass rose are readily visible.

499. D018NG. Which of the symbols shown represents an occluded front?

A. A
B. B
C. C
D. D

500. The National Imagery and Mapping Agency would produce a chart of the coast of _____.

A. Alaska
B. Canada
C. Puerto Rico
D. Hawaii

501. Which of the buoys listed below could be used to mark an anchorage?

A. White buoy numbered 3
B. White buoy with a green top
C. White buoy with orange bands
D. Yellow buoy lettered N

502. A gnomonic projection is based on a(n) _____.

A. plane tangent at one point
B. cylinder tangent at the equator
C. cone tangent at one parallel
D. infinite series of cones tangent at selected parallels

503. You are approaching a light fitted with a RACON. The light may be identified on the radar by _____.

A. a dashed line running from the center of the scope to the light

B. an audible signal when the sweep crosses the light
C. a circle appearing on the scope surrounding the light
D. a coded signal appearing on the same bearing at a greater range than the light

504. Barometer readings in weather reports are given in terms of pressure at _____.

A. sea level
B. Washington, D.C.
C. the weather station
D. the broadcasting station

506. You are to sail from Elizabethport, N.J., on 22 May 1983, with a maximum draft of 28 feet. You will pass over an obstruction in the channel near Sandy Hook that has a depth of 26.5 feet. The steaming time from Elizabethport to the obstruction is 1h 40m. What is the earliest time (ZD + 4) you can sail on the afternoon of 22 May and pass over the obstruction with 2 feet of clearance?

A. 1454
B. 1424
C. 1405
D. 1329

507. What will be the time after 1000 EST (ZD +5), on 4 March 1983, that the height of the tide at City Island, NY, will be 2.4 feet?

A. 1228
B. 1240
C. 1244
D. 1248

508. Which statement about the chartlet in illustration D010NG is TRUE? (Soundings and heights are in meters.)

A. There is a dangerous eddy southeast of Beito Island.
B. Maury lightship is visible for 17 miles.
C. The bottom to the south-southeast of the lightship is soft coral.
D. There is a 12-meter deep hole west of Beito Island and inside the 5-meter line.

509. A line of position derived by radar range from an identified point on a coast will be a(n) _____.

A. straight line
B. arc

C. parabola
D. line parallel to the coast

510. Which aid is NOT marked on a chart with a magenta circle?

A. Aero light
B. Radar station
C. Radar transponder beacon
D. Radiobeacon

511. A survey (special-purpose mark) buoy _____.

A. must be lighted
B. may have a flashing red light
C. may have a fixed white light
D. None of the above

512. On a gnomonic chart, a great circle track between Los Angeles and Brisbane will appear as a _____.

A. loxodromic curve
B. curved line concave to the equator
C. straight line
D. spiral approaching the poles as a limit

513. D017NG. You are radar scanning for a buoy fitted with a racon. Which radar screen represents the presentation you should expect on the PPI?

A. A
B. B
C. C
D. D

514. What instrument measures wind velocity?

A. Hydrometer
B. Barometer
C. Psychrometer
D. Anemometer

516. A hurricane moving northeast out of the Gulf passes west of your position. You could expect all of the following EXCEPT _____.

A. higher than normal swells
B. high winds
C. winds veering from south, through west, to northwest
D. light showers

517. On 5 March 1983, at 0630 EST (ZD +5), what will be the predicted height of tide at Ocracoke, Ocracoke Inlet, NC?

A. 0.1 foot
B. 1.2 feet
C. 1.9 feet
D. 2.3 feet

518. With regard to GPS, a civilian receiver will have the same accuracy as a military receiver if _____.

A. selective availability is set to zero
B. the satellites are all below 15° in elevation
C. your vessel is equipped with a Doppler receiver
D. horizontal dilution of precision is high

519. The chart of a beach area shows a very flat slope to the underwater beach bottom. What type of breakers can be expected when trying to land a boat on this beach?

A. Surging
B. Spilling
C. Plunging
D. Converging

520. On charts of U.S. waters, a magenta marking is NOT used for marking a _____.

A. 5-fathom curve
B. prohibited area
C. lighted buoy
D. radiobeacon

522. All straight lines represent great circle tracks on a chart based on a(n) _____.

A. Mercator projection
B. polyconic projection
C. orthographic projection
D. gnomonic projection

523. A radar display in which North is always at the top of the screen is a(n) _____.

A. unstabilized display
B. stabilized display
C. composition display
D. relative display

524. An anemometer on a moving vessel measures _____.

A. apparent wind speed only
B. true wind speed and true wind direction
C. true wind speed only
D. apparent wind speed and true wind direction

526. When a hurricane passes over colder water or land and loses its tropical characteristics, the storm becomes a(n) _____.

A. high pressure area
B. extratropical low-presure system
C. tropical storm
D. easterly wave

527. On 6 June 1983, at 1719 EST (ZD +5), what will be the predicted height of tide at Chester, PA?

A. 0.8 foot (0.2 meter)
B. 1.1 feet (0.3 meter)
C. 3.5 feet (1.1 meters)
D. 4.7 feet (1.4 meters)

528. What should you expect when you encounter a tsunami in the open ocean?

A. Violent seas from mixed directions
B. No noticeable change from the existing sea state
C. Winds increasing to gale force from the northwest in the Northern Hemisphere
D. A major wave of extreme height and length

529. In some river mouths and estuaries the incoming high-tide wave crest overtakes the preceding low-tide trough. This results in a wall of water proceeding upstream, and is called a _____.

A. seiche
B. bore
C. boundary wave
D. surge

530. Under the U.S. Aids to Navigation System, a lighted buoy with a spherical topmark marks_____.

A. the port side of the channel
B. the position of underwater cables
C. safe water
D. a hazard to navigation

531. You have been informed that dredging operations may be underway in your vicinity. Which buoy indicates the dredging area?

A. White buoy with a green top
B. White and international orange buoy
C. Yellow buoy
D. Yellow and black vertically striped buoy

532. In a river subject to tidal currents, the best time to dock a ship without the assistance of tugs is _____.

A. at high water
B. at slack water
C. at flood tide
D. when there is a following current

533. You are using a radar in which your own ship is shown at the center, and the heading flash always points to 0°. If bearings are measured in relation to the flash, what type of bearings are produced?

A. Relative
B. True
C. Compass
D. Magnetic

534. What is TRUE concerning an anemometer on a moving vessel?

A. It measures true wind speed.
B. It measures true wind speed and true wind direction.
C. It measures apparent wind speed.
D. It measures apparent wind speed and true wind direction.

536. You are enroute from Puerto Rico to New York. A hurricane makes up and is approaching. If the wind veers steadily, this indicates that your vessel is _____.

A. in the dangerous semicircle
B. in the navigable semicircle
C. directly in the path of the storm
D. in the storm center

537. What will be the height of tide at Gargathy Neck, VA, at 1800 DST (ZD +4), on 16 August 1983?

A. 2.3 feet
B. 2.9 feet
C. 3.3 feet
D. 3.6 feet

538. D018NG. Which symbol shown represents a stationary front?

A. A
B. B
C. C
D. D

539. You are underway on course 050°T and your maximum speed is 13 knots. The eye of a hurricane bears 120°T, 100 miles from your position. The hurricane is moving towards 265°T at 25 knots. What course should you steer at 13 knots to have the maximum CPA?

A. 324°T
B. 306°T
C. 299°T
D. 276°T

540. A white buoy with an orange rectangle on it is used to indicate_____.

A. danger
B. a controlled area
C. an exclusion area
D. general information

541. A yellow buoy may mark a(n)_____.

A. wreck
B. shoal area
C. anchorage area
D. middle ground

542. The only cylindrical chart projection widely used for navigation is the _____.

A. Lambert conformal
B. Mercator
C. azimuthal
D. gnomonic

543. A radar display which is oriented, so that north is always at the top of the screen is called a(n)_____.

A. relative display
B. composite display
C. stabilized display
D. unstabilized display

544. The instrument most commonly used to gather the data for determining the relative humidity is the _____.

A. hydrometer
B. psychrometer
C. barometer
D. anemometer

546. If it is impossible to avoid a hurricane in the Northern Hemisphere, the most favorable place to be when the storm passes is in _____.

A. the dangerous semicircle
B. the eye (center) of the storm
C. that half of the storm lying to the right of the storm's path

D. that half of the storm lying to the left of the storm's path

547. On 2 November 1983, at 1630 EST (ZD +5), what will be the predicted height of tide at Fulton, FL?

A. 2.8 feet (0.8 meters)
B. 3.4 feet (1.0 meters)
C. 4.2 feet (1.3 meters)
D. 5.6 feet (1.7 meters)

548. When the declination of the Moon is 0°12.5'S, you can expect some tidal currents in Gulf Coast ports to _____.

A. have either a double ebb or a double flood
B. become reversing currents
C. become weak and variable
D. exceed the predicted velocities

549. On a working copy of a weather map, an occluded front is represented by which color line?

A. Red
B. Blue
C. Alternating red and blue
D. Purple

550. The description "Racon" beside an illustration on a chart would mean a _____.

A. radar transponder beacon
B. radar conspicuous beacon
C. radar calibration beacon
D. circular radiobeacon

551. Spoil grounds, anchorage areas, cable areas, and military exercise areas are all marked by yellow buoys. Which special mark on the buoy will indicate the specific area you are in?

A. A topmark triangular in shape
B. A topmark spherical in shape
C. Lettering on the buoy
D. A topmark consisting of two cones with the points up

552. A Mercator chart is a _____.

A. cylindrical projection
B. simple conic projection
C. polyconic projection
D. rectangular projection

553. The beam width of your radar is 2°. The left tangent bearing of a small island,

as observed on the PPI scope, is 056°pgc. If the gyro error is 2°E, what bearing would you plot on the chart?

A. 052°
B. 056°
C. 059°
D. 060°

554. A sling psychrometer is a(n) _____.

A. type of cargo gear
B. instrument used in celestial navigation
C. instrument used to measure relative humidity
D. instrument used to measure specific gravity

556. In a tropical cyclone in the Northern Hemisphere, a vessel hove to with the wind shifting counterclockwise would be _____.

A. in the navigable semicircle
B. in the dangerous semicircle
C. directly in the path of the center
D. ahead of the storm

557. Your vessel has a draft of 23 feet. On 23 June 1983 you wish to pass over a temporary obstruction near Beaufort, SC, that has a charted depth of 22 feet. Allowing for a safety margin of 3 feet, what is the earliest time after 1600 DST (ZD +4) that this passage can be made?

A. 1751
B. 1815
C. 1855
D. 1944

558. A buoy bears 176°T at 3000 yards. What is the course to make good to leave the buoy 100 yards to starboard?

A. 174°T
B. 176°T
C. 178°T
D. 180°T

559. A great circle crosses the equator at 162°E. It will also cross the equator at what other longitude?

A. 62°E
B. 126°W
C. 162°W
D. 18°W

561. Buoys which mark dredging areas are painted _____.

A. black
B. yellow
C. green
D. red

562. You wish to measure the distance on a Mercator chart between a point in latitude 42°30'N and a point in latitude 40°30'N. To measure 30 miles at a time you should set the points of the dividers at _____.

A. 41°15' and 41°45'
B. 41°45' and 42°15'
C. 42°15' and 42°45'
D. 42°00' and 42°30'

563. Your radar has a beam width of 2°. The radar gyro bearing of the right tangent of an island is 316°. The gyro error is 1°E. Which true bearing should be plotted on the chart?

A. 313°
B. 314°
C. 316°
D. 317°

564. A hygrometer is a device used for determining _____.

A. the absolute temperature
B. atmospheric pressure
C. wind velocity
D. relative humidity

566. You are attempting to locate your position relative to a hurricane in the Northern Hemisphere. If the wind direction remains steady, but with diminishing velocity, you are most likely _____.

A. in the right semicircle
B. in the left semicircle
C. on the storm track ahead of the center
D. on the storm track behind the center

567. The charted channel depth at Eastport, ME, is 28 feet. You are drawing 31.5 feet and wish 2 feet clearance under the keel. What is the earliest time after 1700 DST (ZD +4), on 6 September 1983, that you can enter the channel?

A. 1803
B. 1815
C. 1921
D. 2208

568. The chart of a beach area shows a very steep slope to the underwater beach bottom. Which type of breakers can be expected when trying to land a boat on this beach?

A. Surging
B. Converging
C. Spilling
D. Plunging

569. A line of position formed by sighting two charted objects in line is called a(n) _____.

A. relative bearing
B. range line
C. track line
D. estimated position

570. Chart legends printed in capital letters show that the associated landmark is _____.

A. inconspicuous
B. conspicuous
C. a government facility or station
D. a radio transmitter

571. The Coast Guard Captain of the Port has excluded all traffic from a section of a port, while a regatta is taking place. The buoys marking this exclusion area will be _____.

A. nun- or can-shaped to conform to the overall direction of navigation
B. yellow
C. orange and white
D. marked with a spherical topmark

572. You wish to measure the distance on a Mercator chart between a point in latitude 43°30′N and a point in latitude 40°30′N. To measure 30 miles at a time, you should set the points of the dividers at _____.

A. 41°30′ and 42°00′
B. 41°45′ and 42°15′
C. 42°00′ and 42°30′
D. 42°15′ and 42°45′

573. What is the name of the movable, radial guide line used to measure direction on a radar?

A. Compass rose
B. Cursor
C. Plan position indicator
D. Variable range marker

574. If your mercurial barometer reads 30.50 inches (1033 millibars) and the temperature is 56°F (13°C), what is the correct reading at 55°N, 150°W?

A. 30.42 inches (1030 millibars)
B. 30.45 inches (1031 millibars)
C. 30.50 inches (1032 millibars)
D. 30.53 inches (1033 millibars)

576. In a tropical cyclone in the Southern Hemisphere, a vessel hove to with the wind shifting clockwise would be _____.

A. ahead of the storm center
B. in the dangerous semicircle
C. directly behind the storm center
D. in the navigable semicircle

577. Your vessel has a draft of 24 feet. On 7 April 1983 you wish to pass over a temporary obstruction near Lovell, MA, that has a charted depth of 22 feet. Allowing for a safety margin of 3.1 feet under your keel, what is the earliest time after 0100 EST (ZD +5) that this passage can be made?

A. 0248
B. 0304
C. 0334
D. 0356

579. Low pressure disturbances, which travel along the intertropical convergence zone, are called _____.

A. permanent waves
B. tidal waves
C. tropical waves
D. tropical storms

581. The Captain of the Port has closed to navigation, and buoyed, a section of a harbor. These buoys would be painted _____.

A. red or green to conform with the other lateral aids
B. red and green horizontally-striped
C. solid yellow
D. white with orange marks

582. Distance along a track line is measured on a Mercator chart by using the _____.

A. latitude scale near the middle of the track line
B. longitude scale near the middle of the track line
C. latitude scale at the midlatitude of the chart
D. latitude or longitude scale at the middle of the scale

583. The radar control used to reduce sea return at close ranges is the _____.

A. gain control
B. sensitivity time control
C. fast time constant
D. pulse length control

584. The correction(s) which must be applied to an aneroid barometer reading include(s) _____.

A. height error
B. gravity error
C. temperature error
D. All of the above

586. The approximate distance to a storm center can be determined by noting the hourly rate of fall of the barometer. If the rate of fall is 0.08–0.12 inches, what is the approximate distance to the storm center?

A. 50 to 80 miles
B. 80 to 100 miles
C. 100 to 150 miles
D. 150 to 250 miles

587. Your vessel has a draft of 34 feet. On 8 October 1983 you wish to pass over an obstruction near Jaffrey Point, NH, that has a charted depth of 31 feet. Allowing for a safety margin of 3 feet, what is the earliest time after 0900 DST (ZD +4) that this passage can be made?

A. 0920
B. 1028
C. 1120
D. 1159

588. You are underway on course 050°T and your maximum speed is 10 knots. The eye of a hurricane bears 100°T, 90 miles from your position. The hurricane is moving towards 285°T at 19 knots. If you maneuver at 10 knots to avoid the hurricane, what could be the maximum CPA?

A. 39 miles
B. 45 miles

C. 53 miles
D. 59 miles

591. White lights may be found on _____.

A. special-purpose buoys
B. preferred channel buoys
C. information and regulatory buoys
D. numbered buoys

592. To measure distance on a Mercator chart between the parallels of LAT 34°30′N and LAT 31°30′N, which 30 mile scale should be used?

A. 33°00′N to 33°30′N
B. 32°30′N to 33°00′N
C. 32°45′N to 33°15′N
D. 32°15′N to 32°45′N

593. Radar makes the most accurate determination of the _____.

A. direction of a target
B. distance to a target
C. size of a target
D. shape of a target

594. Barometers are calibrated at a standard temperature of _____.

A. 0°F
B. 32°F
C. 60°F
D. 70°F

596. Which condition would NOT indicate the approach of a tropical storm?

A. Long, high swells
B. Cirrus clouds
C. Halos about the Sun or Moon
D. Decrease in wind velocity

597. You will be loading in Boston Harbor to a maximum draft of 32′06. The charted depth of an obstruction in the channel near Boston Light is 30 feet and you wish to have 3 feet of keel clearance. The steaming time from the pier to the obstruction is 01h 05m. What is the latest time (ZD +4) you can sail on 17 May 1983 and meet these requirements?

A. 1610
B. 1726
C. 1821
D. 2350

598. A great circle crosses the equator at 141°E. It will also cross the equator at what other longitude?

A. 180°E
B. 41°E
C. 141°W
D. 39°W

599. Magnetic compass deviation _____.

A. varies depending upon the bearing used
B. is the angular difference between magnetic north and compass north
C. is published on the compass rose on most nautical charts
D. is the angular difference between geographic and magnetic meridians

600. The dangerous semicircle of a typhoon in the Southern Hemisphere is that area _____.

A. measured from due south clockwise 180°
B. measured from due south counterclockwise 180°
C. to the left of the storm's track
D. ahead of the typhoon measured from the storm's track to 90° on each side

601. White and orange buoys, if lighted, show which color light?

A. White
B. Orange
C. Red
D. Alternating yellow and white

602. Between the equator and the 46th parallel of latitude, there are 3099 meridional parts. How many degrees of equatorial longitude does 3099 meridional parts represent?

A. 35°52′45
B. 51°39′00
C. 74°21′11
D. 82°36′12

603. What is the approximate wave length of an X Band Radar operating on a frequency of approximately 9500 MHz?

A. 3 cm
B. 10 cm
C. 30 cm
D. 100 cm

606. Early indications of the approach of a hurricane may be all of the following EXCEPT _____.

A. short confused swells
B. gradually increasing white clouds (mare's tails)
C. pumping barometer
D. continuous fine mist-like rain

607. The charted depth alongside the south face of Mystic Pier, Charlestown, MA, is 35 feet. Your maximum draft is 38 feet. You wish to have 2 feet under the bottom, on a rising tide, when you go alongside to discharge a heavy lift. What is the earliest time after 0900 EST (ZD +5), on 2 February 1983, that you can dock?

A. 1020
B. 1050
C. 1120
D. 1150

608. In which voyage, between two points, is the rhumb line distance NOT approximately the same as the great circle distance?

A. The two points are in low latitudes in the same hemisphere.
B. The two points are in high latitudes in the same hemisphere.
C. The two points are near the equator, but in different hemispheres.
D. One point is near the equator, one point is in a high latitude, and both are near the 180th meridian.

609. A tropical wave is located 200 miles due west of your position, which is north of the equator. Where will the wave be in 24 hours?

A. Farther away to the west
B. Farther away to the east
C. In the same place
D. Closer and to the west

610. The apparent wind's speed can be zero, but only when two conditions are present. One condition is that the true wind _____.

A. must be from dead ahead
B. speed must be zero
C. must be from dead astern
D. must be on the beam

611. Information markers, when lighted, will display _____.

A. yellow lights
B. green lights
C. white lights
D. red lights

612. Which statement is TRUE concerning a Mercator projection?

A. Degrees of longitude decrease in length as latitude increases.
B. The length of the meridians is increased to provide for equal expansion in all directions.
C. The mileage between the meridians is increased as the latitude increases.
D. All of the above

613. Your radar indicates a target; however, there is no visible object at the point indicated. A large mountain, approximately 50 miles away on the same bearing as the target, is breaking the horizon. You should suspect the radar target is caused by _____.

A. a submerged submarine
B. ducting
C. sub-refraction
D. ionospheric skip waves

615. The spinning motion of a planet around its axis is called _____.

A. revolution
B. rotation
C. orbit
D. space motion

617. You are bound for the Chelsea docks in the Hudson River. The Captain wants to arrive at the docks at the first slack water on 28 July 1983. You are keeping daylight saving time. What time should you be at the docks?

A. 0215
B. 0530
C. 0811
D. 0911

619. According to Buys Ballot's Law, when an observer in the Southern Hemisphere experiences a northwest wind, the center of the low pressure is located to the _____.

A. east-northeast
B. south-southwest
C. east-southeast
D. west-southwest

620. Chart legends which indicate a conspicuous landmark are printed in _____.

A. capital letters
B. italics
C. boldface print
D. underlined letters

621. Navigational marks used for informational or regulatory purposes are _____.

A. solid yellow
B. white with orange geometric shapes
C. red and white vertically striped
D. green and red horizontally banded

622. The scale of a Mercator projection is 4 inches equals 1° LONG. What is the expansion in inches between the 60th and 61st parallels?

A. 8.11 inches
B. 7.70 inches
C. 7.48 inches
D. 6.98 inches

623. An indirect radar echo is caused by a reflection of the main lobe of the radar beam off the observer's vessel. Which of the following is NOT a characteristic of indirect echoes?

A. Their bearing is almost constant, even when the true bearing of the contact changes appreciably.
B. They always appear on a bearing of 90° from the true bearing of the contact.
C. The indirect echoes usually appear in shadow sectors.
D. When plotted, their movements are usually abnormal.

625. The center of a circle of equal altitude, plotted on the surface of the Earth, is the _____.

A. dead reckoning position of the observer
B. assumed position of the observer
C. geographical position of the body
D. assumed position of the body

626. What indicates the arrival of a hurricane within 24 to 36 hours?

A. The normal swell becoming lower and from a steady direction
B. Long bands of nimbostratus clouds radiating from a point over the horizon

C. The barometer drops 2 millibars between 1000 and 1600
D. Unusually good weather with above average pressures followed by a slow fall of 4 millibars in six hours

627. You are on a coastwise voyage bound for Marcus Hook, PA. Your speed is 15 knots. You wish to use the flood tide to facilitate docking starboard side to, heading seaward. To have the most favorable tide throughout, you should time your arrival at the entrance to Delaware Bay _____.

A. for 1 hour before flood begins
B. for 1 hour after flood begins
C. for 3 hours after flood begins
D. for 1 hour before ebb begins

629. The rise and fall of the ocean's surface due to a distant storm is known as _____.

A. sea
B. waves
C. fetch
D. swell

630. What kind of weather would you expect to accompany the passage of a tropical wave?

A. Heavy rain and cloudiness
B. Good weather
C. A tropical storm
D. Dense fog

631. A light characteristic of composite group flashing indicates that there is a(n) _____.

A. sharp turn in the channel
B. narrowing in the channel at that point
C. junction in the channel
D. obstruction that must be left to port

632. You must construct a Mercator projection for an area bounded by latitudes 40°–47°N and longitudes 176°E to 176°W on a paper 28 X 36 inches. Allow a neat line of one inch. What will be the separation between meridians?

A. 3.190 inches
B. 3.249 inches
C. 3.529 inches
D. 3.714 inches

633. You have another ship overtaking you close aboard to starboard. You have 3 radar targets bearing 090° relative at ranges of

0.5 mile, 1 mile, and 1.5 miles. In this case, the unwanted echoes are called _____.

A. multiple echoes
B. spoking
C. indirect echoes
D. side-lobe echoes

635. A low HDOP (Horizontal Dilution of Precision) number such as 2 indicates a _____.

A. poor fix
B. good fix
C. poor signal quality
D. good signal quality

636. Tropical cyclones are classified by form and intensity. Which system does not have closed isobars?

A. Hurricane
B. Tropical disturbance
C. Tropical depression
D. Cyclone

637. Your draft is 24 feet. You wish to pass over an obstruction near Lovell Island, MA, on 6 May 1983. The charted depth is 22 feet. Allowing a safety margin of 3.0 feet, what is the earliest time after 0200 DST (ZD +4) that this passage can be made?

A. 0215
B. 0245
C. 0310
D. 0350

638. Swell is the rise and fall of the ocean's surface due to _____.

A. fetch
B. distant winds
C. local storms
D. the pull of the moon

639. In the Northern Hemisphere, what type of cloud formations would you expect to see to the west of an approaching tropical wave?

A. Cumulus clouds lined up in rows extending in a northeast to southwest direction
B. High altostratus clouds in the morning hours
C. Cirrostratus clouds lined up in rows extending in a northeast to southwest direction
D. Cirrostratus clouds lined up in rows extending in a north to south direction

641. Buoys which mark isolated dangers are painted with alternating _____ .

A. red and black bands
B. green and black bands
C. red and white stripes
D. green and white bands

642. Which government agency publishes the U.S. Coast Pilot?

A. Army Corps of Engineers
B. National Imagery and Mapping Agency
C. National Ocean Service
D. U.S. Coast Guard

643. When using the radar for navigating _____.

A. the best fix is obtained by using a tangent bearing and a range
B. and using two radar ranges for a fix, the objects of the ranges should be close to reciprocal bearings
C. and using ranges, the most rapidly changing range should be measured last
D. and crossing a radar range of one object with the visual bearing of a second object, the two objects should be 80° to 110° apart

646. You have determined that you are in the right semicircle of a tropical cyclone in the Northern Hemisphere. What action should you take to avoid the storm?

A. Place the wind on the starboard quarter and hold that course.
B. Place the wind on the port quarter and hold that course.
C. Place the wind on the port bow and hold that course.
D. Place the wind on the starboard bow and hold that course.

647. You will enter Argentia, Newfoundland, at 1200 on 5 October 1983, while keeping zone description +3 on the ship's clocks. What will be the height of tide at this time (based on the Canadian chart datum)?

A. 0.5 foot
B. 1.2 feet
C. 2.1 feet
D. 3.4 feet

648. Weather systems in the middle latitudes generally travel from _____.

A. north to south
B. west to east

C. east to west
D. None of the above

650. What classification of tropical cyclone would have closed isobars, counterclockwise rotary circulation and sustained winds between 34 and 63 kt?

A. A tropical disturbance
B. A tropical depression
C. A tropical storm
D. A hurricane

651. Which topmark in illustration D023NG identifies an isolated danger?

A. A
B. B
C. C
D. D

652. What agency of the U.S. Government issues charts of U.S. waters and Coast Pilots?

A. National Ocean Service
B. National Imagery and Mapping Agency
C. U.S. Coast Guard
D. U.S. Naval Observatory

653. You have been observing your radar screen and notice that a contact on the screen has remained in the same position, relative to you, for several minutes. Your vessel is making 10 knots through the water. Which statement is TRUE?

A. The contact is dead in the water.
B. The contact is on the same course and speed as your vessel.
C. The contact is on a reciprocal course at the same speed as your vessel.
D. The radar is showing false echoes and is probably defective.

656. In the Northern Hemisphere you are caught in the dangerous semicircle with plenty of sea room available. The best course of action is to bring the wind on the _____.

A. starboard bow and make as much headway as possible
B. starboard quarter, and make as much headway as possible
C. port quarter, and make as much headway as possible
D. port bow, and make as much headway as possible

657. Current refers to the _____.

A. vertical movement of the water
B. horizontal movement of the water
C. density changes in the water
D. None of the above

658. Monsoons are characterized by _____.

A. light, variable winds with little or no humidity
B. strong, gusty winds that blow from the same general direction all year
C. steady winds that reverse direction semi-annually
D. strong, cyclonic winds that change direction to conform to the passage of an extreme low pressure system

660. What is the length of a nautical mile?

A. 1,850 meters
B. 5,280 feet
C. 1,760 yards
D. 6,076 feet

661. Under the IALA Buoyage Systems, safe water marks may show a _____.

A. composite group-flashing, Fl(2 + 1), red light
B. composite group-flashing, Fl(2 + 1), green light
C. quick-flashing, Q(9)15s, white light
D. white Morse (A) light

662. What publication contains descriptions of the coast line, buoyage systems, weather conditions, port facilities, and navigation instructions for the United States and its possessions?

A. Coast Pilots
B. Sailing Directions
C. Port Index
D. Light List

663. You are underway at 10 knots. At 1800 you note a radar contact dead ahead at a range of 10 miles. At 1812 the contact is dead ahead at a range of 8 miles. The estimated speed of the contact is _____.

A. dead in the water
B. 5 knots
C. 10 knots
D. 15 knots

665. 17 degrees of latitude is equal to _____.

A. 68 miles

B. 510 miles
C. 1020 miles
D. 4080 miles

666. In the Northern Hemisphere, your vessel is believed to be in the direct path of a hurricane, and plenty of sea room is available. The best course of action is to bring the wind on the _____.

A. starboard bow, note the course, and head in that direction
B. starboard quarter, note the course, and head in that direction
C. port quarter, note the course, and head in that direction
D. port bow, note the course, and head in that direction

667. The navigable semicircle of a typhoon in the Southern Hemisphere is the area

_____.

A. behind the typhoon, measured from 90° to 180° from each side of the storm's track
B. to the right of the storm's track
C. ahead of the typhoon, measured from the storm's track to 90° on each side
D. measured from due south, counterclockwise 180°

668. You are enroute to assist vessel A. Vessel A is underway at 6 knots on course 133°T, and bears 042° at 105 miles from you. What is the course to steer at 10 knots to intercept vessel A?

A. 063°
B. 068°
C. 073°
D. 079°

669. It is desirable that a vessel encountering hurricane or typhoon conditions sends weather reports to the closest meteorological service at least every _____.

A. hour
B. 3 hours
C. 6 hours
D. 8 hours

671. You sight a buoy fitted with a double-sphere topmark. If sighted at night, this buoy would show a _____.

A. quick-flashing red light
B. quick-flashing green light
C. flashing white light showing a group of two flashes

D. flashing red light showing a group of three flashes

672. You are planning to enter an unfamiliar U.S. port. Which publication provides information about channel depths, dangers, obstructions, anchorages, and marine facilities available in that port?

A. American Practical Navigator
B. Notice to Mariners
C. Coast Pilot
D. Sailing Directions

673. You are underway at 5 knots and see on your radar a contact 10 miles directly astern of you. 12 minutes later, the contact is 8 miles directly astern of you. What is the estimated speed of the contact?

A. Dead in the water
B. 1 knot
C. 10 knots
D. 15 knots

675. 15° of latitude is equal to _____.

A. 600 miles
B. 900 miles
C. 1200 miles
D. 1500 miles

676. If you are caught in the left semicircle of a tropical storm, in the Southern Hemisphere, you should bring the wind _____.

A. on the starboard quarter, hold course and make as much way as possible
B. 2 points on the port quarter, and make as much way as possible
C. on the port bow, and make as much way as possible
D. dead ahead and heave to

677. A swift current occurring in a narrow passage connecting two large bodies of water, which is produced by the continuously changing difference in height of tide at the two ends of the passage, is called a

_____.

A. hydraulic current
B. rectilinear current
C. rotary current
D. harmonic current

679. A tropical wave is usually preceded by _____.

A. tropical storms
B. good weather

C. heavy rain and cloudiness
D. heavy seas

680. The apparent wind's speed can be zero, but only when two conditions are present. One condition is that the true _____.

A. wind must be on the beam
B. wind's speed must be zero
C. wind must be from dead ahead
D. wind's speed equals the ship's speed

681. D027NG. You sight a spar buoy with the top mark shown in the illustration. You must _____ .

A. pass to the east of the buoy
B. pass to the south of the buoy
C. pass to the north of the buoy
D. keep well clear of the buoy and pass on either side

682. Which table is NOT found in the U.S. Coast Pilots?

A. Climatological table
B. Luminous range table
C. Meteorological table
D. Coastwise distance table

683. A radar contact will remain stationary on a relative motion radar display only when it is _____.

A. on the same course as your vessel
B. at the same speed as your vessel
C. on the same course and speed as your vessel
D. on a reciprocal course at the same speed as your vessel

685. Thirty-two meters equals_____.

A. 17.50 feet
B. 58.52 feet
C. 96.00 feet
D. 104.99 feet

686. The pressure gradient between the horse latitudes and doldrums runs _____.

A. east to west
B. north to south
C. northeast to southwest
D. northwest to southeast

687. The drift and set of tidal, river, and ocean currents refer to the _____.

A. position and area of the current
B. speed and direction toward which the current flows
C. type and characteristic of the current's flow
D. None of the above

688. In mid-ocean, the characteristics of a wave are determined by three factors. What is NOT one of these factors?

A. Effect of the moon's gravity
B. Fetch
C. Wind velocity
D. Length of time a wind has been blowing

690. What level of development of a tropical cyclone has a hundred mile radius of circulation, gale force winds, less than 990 millibars of pressure and vertically formed cumulonimbus clouds?

A. A tropical disturbance
B. A tropical depression
C. A tropical storm
D. A typhoon

691. D019NG. Of the four light characteristics shown which one does NOT represent a safe water mark of the IALA Buoyage System?

A. A
B. B
C. C
D. D

692. Which publication should you check for complete information on Puget Sound weather conditions?

A. Sailing Directions
B. Light List
C. Coast Pilot
D. Chart of the area

693. Which general statement concerning radar is FALSE?

A. Raising the antenna height increases the radar range.
B. The ability of radar to detect objects is unaffected by weather conditions.
C. Radar bearings are less accurate than radar ranges.
D. Radar should be checked regularly during clear weather to ensure that it is operating properly.

696. The diurnal pressure variation is most noticeable in the _____.

A. polar regions
B. horse latitudes
C. roaring forties
D. doldrums

697. The set of the current is the _____.

A. speed of the current at a particular time
B. maximum speed of the current
C. direction from which the current flows
D. direction in which the current flows

698. You are in LONG 165°E, zone time at 0400, 1 November 1981. What is the zone time and date in LONG 165°W?

A. 0600, 31 October
B. 1800, 31 October
C. 1800, 1 November
D. 0600, 1 November

700. You are enroute to Savannah, GA, from Recife, Brazil. There is a strong N'ly wind blowing. As you cross the axis of the Gulf Stream you would expect to encounter _____.

A. smoother seas and warmer water
B. long swells
C. steeper waves, closer together
D. cirrus clouds

701. In the IALA Buoyage System, buoys with alternating red and green horizontal bands are used to indicate _____.

A. fishing areas
B. spoil grounds
C. the preferred channel
D. isolated dangers

702. Which publication contains information on navigation regulations, landmarks, channels, anchorages, tides, currents, and clearances of bridges for Chesapeake Bay?

A. Coast Pilot
B. Light List
C. Sailing Directions
D. Pilot Charts

703. Which statement concerning the operation of radar in fog is TRUE?

A. Radar ranges are less accurate in fog.
B. Navigation buoys will always show up on radar.

C. A sandy beach will show up clearer on radar than a rocky cliff.
D. Small wooden boats may not show up on radar.

705. The precession of the equinoxes occurs in a(n) _____.

A. easterly direction
B. westerly direction
C. northerly direction
D. southerly direction

706. A steep barometric gradient indicates _____.

A. calms
B. light winds
C. strong winds
D. precipitation

707. Set of the current is _____.

A. its velocity in knots
B. direction from which it flows
C. estimated current
D. direction towards which it flows

709. A sea breeze is a wind _____.

A. that blows towards the sea at night
B. that blows towards an island during the day
C. caused by cold air descending a coastal incline
D. caused by the distant approach of a hurricane

710. What is the FIRST sign of the existence of a well-developed tropical cyclone?

A. Gale force winds from the north
B. An unusually long ocean swell
C. Steep, short-period waves and light wind
D. Thunderstorms and higher than usual humidity

711. In the IALA Maritime Buoyage System, a red and white vertically striped buoy is used as a(n)_____.

A. safe water mark
B. cardinal mark
C. isolated danger mark
D. special mark not primarily used for navigation

712. Information about the pilotage available at Miami harbor may best be obtained from which publication?

A. World Port Index
B. Sailing Directions
C. Pilot Chart
D. United States Coast Pilot

713. The closest point of approach (CPA) of a contact on a relative motion radar may be determined _____.

A. immediately when the contact is noted on radar
B. only if the radar scope is watched constantly
C. after the contact has been marked at least twice
D. by an occasional glance at the radar

716. Standard atmospheric pressure in inches of mercury is _____.

A. 30
B. 28.92
C. 29.92
D. 29

717. Which term refers to the direction a current is flowing?

A. Set
B. Drift
C. Vector direction
D. Stand

718. You are to sail from Elizabethport, NJ, on 22 May 1983 with a maximum draft of 28 feet. You will pass over an obstruction in the channel near Sandy Hook that has a charted depth of 27 feet. The steaming time from Elizabethport to the obstruction is 1h 40m. What is the earliest time (ZD +4) you can sail on the afternoon of 22 May and pass over the obstruction with 3 feet of clearance?

A. 1406
B. 1330
C. 1300
D. 1242

720. Which change in the condition of the seas could indicate the formation of a tropical storm or hurricane several hundred miles from your location?

A. A long swell from an unusual direction
B. A lengthy lull in the wind and seas
C. Large seas coming from different directions
D. A brisk chop from the southeast

721. Under the IALA Buoyage System, a red and white vertically striped buoy would NOT indicate _____.

A. a landfall
B. the extreme end of an islet
C. a mid-channel
D. a center line

722. Which publication would describe the explosive anchorages in the ports on the east coast of the United States?

A. Sailing Directions
B. Pilot Rules for Inland Waters
C. Coast Pilot
D. Notice to Mariners

723. If there is any doubt as to the proper operation of a radar, which statement is TRUE?

A. Only a radar expert can determine if the radar is operating.
B. All radars have indicator lights and alarms to signal improper operation.
C. A radar range compared to the actual range of a known object can be used to check the operation of the radar.
D. The radar resolution detector must be energized to check the radar.

724. Which statement concerning GPS is TRUE?

A. It cannot be used in all parts of the world.
B. There are 12 functioning GPS satellites at present.
C. It may be suspended without warning.
D. Two position lines are used to give a 2D fix.

726. Atmospheric pressure at sea level is equal to _____.

A. 14.7 pounds per square inch
B. 29.92 inches of mercury
C. 1013.25 millibars
D. All of the above

727. What is an ebb current?

A. A current at minimum flow
B. A current coming in
C. A current going out
D. A current at maximum flow

729. The doldrums are characterized by _____.

A. steady, light to moderate winds
B. frequent calms
C. clear skies
D. low humidity

730. In the Northern Hemisphere, the largest waves or swells created by a typhoon or hurricane will be located _____.

A. in the southeast quadrant of the storm
B. directly behind the storm center
C. forward and to the right of its course
D. behind and to the left of its course

731. Under the IALA Buoyage Systems, a vertically striped buoy may be striped red and _____.

A. green
B. black
C. white
D. yellow

732. What publication has information on the climate, distances, navigation regulations, outstanding landmarks, channels and anchorages of Long Island Sound?

A. Light List
B. Coast Pilot
C. Sailing Directions
D. Pilot Chart

733. What would give the best radar echo?

A. The beam of a three masted sailing vessel with all sails set.
B. A 110-foot fishing vessel with a radar reflector in its rigging.
C. A 300-foot tanker, bow on.
D. A 600-foot freighter, beam on.

734. You are approaching Chatham Strait from the south in foggy weather. You have Coronation Island and Hazy Islands on the radar. Suddenly the radar malfunctions. You then resort to using whistle echoes to determine your distance off Coronation Island. Your stopwatch reads 16.3 seconds for the echo to be heard. How far are you off Coronation Island?

A. 1.0 mile
B. 1.5 miles
C. 2.0 miles
D. 2.5 miles

736. A line on a weather chart connecting places which have the same barometric pressure is called an _____.

A. isotherm
B. isallobar
C. isobar
D. isotope

737. What describes an ebb current?

A. Horizontal movement of the water away from the land following low tide
B. Horizontal movement of the water toward the land following low tide
C. Horizontal movement of the water away from the land following high tide
D. Horizontal movement of the water toward the land following high tide

738. Most GPS receivers use the doppler shift of the carrier phase to compute _____.

A. Latitude
B. Longitude
C. Speed
D. Time

739. The upper vertex of a great circle track is in LONG 156°00'E. Sailing eastward, the great circle track will cross the equator in LONG _____.

A. 114°00'W
B. 110°00'W
C. 66°00'W
D. 66°00'E

740. A very light breeze that causes ripples on a small area of still water is a _____.

A. cat's paw
B. hog's breath
C. williwaw
D. chinook

741. What is the light phase characteristic of a lighted isolated-danger mark?

A. Interrupted quick flashing
B. Very quick flashing
C. Long flashing
D. Group flashing

742. You are preparing to take a tow from San Diego to Portland, OR. Good seamanship would require that you have on board, available for reference and use, all of the following EXCEPT the _____.

A. Coast Pilot
B. harbor and coastal charts for ports of refuge enroute
C. Sailing Directions (Enroute)
D. Light List

743. The Consol navigation system, used in Russian and Northern European waters, can be used _____.

A. for precise navigation in coastal waters
B. by measuring the phase difference of the dots and dashes
C. as an aid to ocean navigation
D. if the vessel is fitted with a special Consol receiver

744. A handheld instrument used to measure distances between objects and the ship is a _____.

A. vernier
B. psychrometer
C. hygrometer
D. stadimeter

746. Lines drawn through points on the Earth having the same atmospheric pressure are known as _____.

A. isothermal
B. millibars
C. isobars
D. seismics

747. The movement of water away from the shore or downstream is called a(n) _____.

A. reversing current
B. ebb current
C. flood current
D. slack current

748. You are steaming west in the South Atlantic in an extratropical cyclonic storm, and the wind is dead ahead. According to the law of Buys Ballot, the center of low pressure lies _____.

A. to the north of you
B. to the south of you
C. dead ahead of you
D. dead astern of you

749. You are enroute to assist vessel A. Vessel A is underway at 4.5 knots on course 233°T, and bears 264°T at 68 miles from you. What is the course to steer at 13 knots to intercept vessel A?

A. 249°
B. 256°
C. 262°
D. 268°

750. On a working copy of a weather map, a cold front is represented by what color line?

A. Red
B. Blue
C. Alternating red and blue
D. Purple

751. Under the IALA Buoyage Systems, a yellow buoy may mark _____.

A. fish net areas
B. spoil areas
C. military exercise zones
D. All of the above

752. Which publication would NOT be used on a voyage from Houston to New York?

A. Coast Pilot
B. Light List
C. Radio Navigational Aids
D. Sailing Directions (Enroute)

754. Deviation in a compass is caused by the _____.

A. vessel's geographic position
B. vessel's heading
C. earth's magnetic field
D. influence of the magnetic materials of the vessel

756. What is a common unit of measure for atmospheric pressure?

A. Centimeters
B. Inches
C. Degrees
D. Feet

757. The term flood current refers to that time when the water _____.

A. is flowing towards the land
B. is moving towards the ocean
C. level is not changing
D. level is rising because of heavy rains

758. A tropical cyclone has recurved and entered temperate latitudes. In the Northern Hemisphere when a large high pressure system lies north of the storm, what situation may occur?

A. The low may suddenly deepen, and the cyclone intensify and pick up speed.
B. The left semicircle may become the dangerous semicircle.

C. The low and the high may merge and cancel out the weather characteristics of each.
D. The high may force the cyclone to reverse its track.

759. At 0000 you fix your position and plot a new DR track line. At 0200 you again fix your position and it is 0.5 mile west of your DR. Which statement is TRUE?

A. The set is 090°, drift 0.5 knot.
B. The set is 270°, drift 0.25 knot.
C. The set is 270°, drift 0.5 knot.
D. The set is 270°, drift 1.0 knot.

760. As a vessel changes course to starboard, the compass card in a magnetic compass _____.

A. first turns to starboard then counterclockwise to port
B. also turns to starboard
C. remains aligned with compass north
D. turns counterclockwise to port

761. Under the IALA Buoyage Systems, a safe water mark may NOT _____.

A. be spherical
B. display a white light
C. be lettered
D. show a quick flashing light

762. Chart correction information is NOT disseminated through the _____.

A. Summary of Corrections
B. Local Notice to Mariners
C. Daily Memorandum
D. Chart Correction Card

763. Time signals broadcast by WWV and WWVH are transmitted _____.

A. every 15 minutes
B. every 30 minutes
C. every hour
D. continuously throughout day

764. Magnetic variation changes with a change in _____.

A. the vessel's heading
B. sea conditions
C. seasons
D. the vessel's position

765. Diurnal aberration is due to _____.

A. motion of the Earth in its orbit
B. rotation of the Earth on its axis
C. the body's orbital motion during the time required for its light to reach the Earth
D. a false horizon

766. Which position includes the effects of wind and current?

A. Dead reckoning position
B. Leeway position
C. Set position
D. Estimated position

767. What describes a flood current?

A. Horizontal movement of the water toward the land after high tide
B. Horizontal movement of the water toward the land after low tide
C. Horizontal movement of the water away from the land following high tide
D. Horizontal movement of the water away from the land following low tide

768. The wind velocity is higher in the dangerous semicircle of a tropical cyclone because of the _____.

A. wind circulation and forward motion of the storm
B. extension of the low pressure ridge
C. recurvature effect
D. direction of circulation and pressure gradient

769. What does not contribute to the commercial GPS receiver position error?

A. Satellite clock
B. Ship's speed
C. Atmospheric/ionospheric propagation
D. Receiver

770. You are plotting a running fix in an area where there is a determinable current. How should this current be treated in determining the position?

A. The course and speed made good should be determined and used to advance the LOP.
B. The drift should be added to the ship's speed.
C. The current should be ignored.
D. The set should be applied to the second bearing.

771. Under the IALA Buoyage Systems, a spherical buoy will mark _____.

A. safe water
B. the port side of the channel
C. a hazard to navigation
D. the position of an underwater cable

773. What is the basic principle of the magnetic compass?

A. Magnetic materials of the same polarity repel each other and those of opposite polarity attract.
B. The Earth's magnetic lines of force are parallel to the surface of the Earth.
C. Magnetic meridians connect points of equal magnetic variation.
D. The compass needle(s) will, when properly compensated, lie parallel to the isogonic lines of the Earth.

774. Variation is not constant; it is different with every change in _____.

A. speed
B. vessel heading
C. geographical location
D. cargo

776. You are navigating in pilotage waters using running fixes. The maximum time between fixes should be about _____.

A. 4 hours
B. 1 hour
C. 30 minutes
D. 5 minutes

777. With respect to a reversing current, slack water occurs when there is _____.

A. little or no horizontal motion of the water
B. little or no vertical motion of the water
C. a weak ebb or flood current
D. when winds cause water to back up in a river mouth

778. The navigable semicircle of a hurricane in the Northern Hemisphere is that area of the storm measured _____.

A. from true north clockwise to 180°T
B. from true north counterclockwise to 180°T
C. from the bow counterclockwise to 180° relative
D. from the direction of the storm's movement counterclockwise 180°

780. Apparent wind speed blowing across your vessel while underway can be measured by a(n) _____.

A. barometer
B. wind vane
C. anemometer
D. thermometer

781. The IALA Buoyage Systems do NOT apply to _____.

A. the sides and centerlines of navigable channels
B. natural dangers and other obstructions, such as wrecks
C. lighthouses and lightships
D. areas in which navigation may be subject to regulation

782. Mariners are FIRST warned of serious defects or important changes to aids to navigation by means of _____.

A. marine broadcast Notice to Mariners
B. Weekly Notices to Mariners
C. corrected editions of charts
D. Light Lists

783. Magnetism which is present only when the material is under the influence of an external field is called _____.

A. permanent magnetism
B. induced magnetism
C. residual magnetism
D. terrestrial magnetism

784. Variation is the angular measurement between _____.

A. compass north and magnetic north
B. compass north and true north
C. magnetic meridian and the geographic meridian
D. your vessel's heading and the magnetic meridian

786. The greater the pressure difference between a high and a low pressure center, the _____.

A. dryer the air mass will be
B. cooler the temperature will be
C. greater the force of the wind will be
D. warmer the temperature will be

787. You are on a voyage from New Orleans to Boston. When navigating off the Florida coast, you will get the greatest benefit from the Gulf Stream if you navigate _____

A. about 45 miles east of Cape Canaveral
B. about 25 miles east of Daytona Beach
C. along the 50-fathom curve
D. close inshore between Fowey Rocks and Jupiter Inlet

788. What is the minimum number of measurement(s) from satellites for GPS to give an exact position?

A. 4
B. 3
C. 2
D. 1

789. The dangerous semicircle of a hurricane in the Northern Hemisphere is that area of the storm _____.

A. to the right of the storm's track
B. measured from true north clockwise to 180°T
C. measured from true north counterclockwise to 180°T
D. between the ship's heading and the bearing to the eye

791. Under the IALA Buoyage Systems, the topmark of a red and white vertically striped buoy shall be _____.

A. X-shaped
B. two black spheres
C. a single red sphere
D. a single red cone

792. Information about temporary, short term changes affecting the safety of navigation in U.S. waters is distributed to navigational interests by the _____.

A. Daily Memorandum
B. HYDROLANT or HYDROPAC broadcasts
C. Local Notice to Mariners
D. Summary of Corrections

793. The permanent magnetism of a vessel may change in strength due to _____.

A. a collision with another vessel
B. being moored on a constant heading for a long period of time
C. being struck by lightning
D. All of the above

794. Your position is LAT 30°N, LONG 45°W. From this position you receive an RDF bearing from a transmitting vessel in LAT 32°N, LONG 40°W. The bearing corrected for calibration error is 63.7°. What is the direction of the rhumb line between these two positions?

A. 65.9°
B. 65.0°
C. 63.7°
D. 62.4°

796. Cyclones tend to move _____.

A. perpendicular to the isobars in their warm sectors
B. parallel to the isobars in their warm sectors
C. parallel to the line of the cold front
D. perpendicular to the line of the cold front

797. Which statement is TRUE concerning the current of the Gulf Stream?

A. It reaches its daily maximum speed a few hours before the transit of the Moon.
B. It is slower at the time of neap tides than at spring tides.
C. When the Moon is at its maximum declination the stream is narrower than when the Moon is on the equator.
D. Variations in the trade winds affect the current.

799. In Region A of the IALA Buoyage System, when entering from seaward, the starboard side of a channel would be marked by a _____.

A. green can buoy
B. red can buoy
C. green conical buoy
D. red conical buoy

800. You are to sail from Elizabethport, NJ, on 17 November 1983 with a maximum draft of 27 feet. You will pass over an obstruction in the channel near Sandy Hook that has a charted depth of 26 feet. The steaming time from Elizabethport to the obstruction is 1h 50m. What is the earliest time (ZD +5) you can sail on 17 November and pass over the obstruction with 2 feet of clearance?

A. 0100
B. 0124
C. 0154

D. 0218

801. You are entering an African port and see ahead of you a red can-shaped buoy. What action should you take?

A. Alter course to leave the buoy to port
B. Alter course to leave the buoy to starboard
C. Pass the buoy close aboard on either side
D. Pass the buoy well clear on either side

802. Which is a weekly publication advising mariners of important matters affecting navigational safety?

A. Light List
B. Notice to Mariners
C. Coast Pilot
D. Sailing Directions

803. Which buoy will NOT display white retroreflective material?

A. Safe water mark
B. Isolated danger mark
C. Preferred channel mark
D. Daymark of no lateral significance

804. A relative bearing is always measured from _____.

A. true north
B. magnetic north
C. the vessel's beam
D. the vessel's head

806. Temperature and moisture characteristics are modified in a warm or cold air mass due to _____.

A. pressure changes in the air mass
B. movement of the air mass
C. the heterogeneous nature of the air mass
D. upper level atmospheric changes

807. The approximate mean position of the axis of the Gulf Stream east of Palm Beach, FL, is _____.

A. 35 nautical miles
B. 25 nautical miles
C. 15 nautical miles
D. 5 nautical miles

808. On a working copy of a weather map, a stationary front is represented by which color line?

A. Red
B. Blue
C. Alternating red and blue
D. Purple

809. The compass rose on a nautical chart indicates both variation and _____.

A. deviation
B. annual rate of variation change
C. precession
D. compass error

810. D051NG. The position labeled B is a(n) _____.

A. fix
B. running fix
C. estimated position
D. dead reckoning position

811. Under the IALA-A Buoyage System, a green spar buoy with a triangular topmark would indicate that the buoy _____.

A. should be left to port when heading out to sea
B. may be left close aboard on either side
C. is on the north side of a point of interest
D. is marking the preferred channel

812. You are informed of defects or changes in aids to navigation by _____.

A. Local Notice to Mariners
B. Weekly Notice to Mariners
C. marine broadcasts
D. All of the above

813. At the magnetic equator there is no induced magnetism in the vertical soft iron because _____.

A. the lines of force cross the equator on a 0°–180° alignment
B. the quadrantal error is 0°
C. there is no vertical component of the Earth's magnetic field
D. the intercardinal headings have less than 1° error

814. Steam smoke will occur when _____.

A. extremely cold air from shore passes over warmer water
B. warm dry air from shore passes over cooler water
C. cold ocean water evaporates into warm air

D. cool rain passes through a warm air mass

815. When entering from seaward, a buoy displaying a composite group (2+1) flashing red light indicates _____.

A. a junction with the preferred channel to the left
B. a sharp turn in the preferred channel to the right
C. the starboard side of the secondary channel
D. a wreck to be left on the vessel's port side

816. Cyclones that have warm sectors usually move _____.

A. westerly
B. parallel to the isobars in the warm sector
C. toward the nearest high pressure area
D. faster than the accompanying cold front

817. Which current would you encounter on a direct passage from London, England, to Capetown, South Africa?

A. Falkland Current
B. Brazil Current
C. Norway Current
D. Benguela Current

818. Ocean swells originating from a typhoon can move ahead of it at speeds near _____.

A. 10 knots
B. 20 knots
C. 30 knots
D. 50 knots

820. A position obtained by crossing lines of position taken at different times and advanced to a common time is a(n) _____.

A. dead-reckoning position
B. running fix
C. estimated position
D. fix

821. In addition to monitoring channel 16, all Corps of Engineer locks may use as working channels _____.

A. 06, 12 and 22A
B. 01A, 05A and 07A
C. 12, 13 and 14
D. 14, 24 and 28

822. Charts should be corrected by using information published in the _____.

A. Light List
B. American Practical Navigator
C. Notice to Mariners
D. Coast Pilot

823. The greatest directive force is exerted on the magnetic compass when the _____.

A. needles are nearly in line with the meridian
B. vessel is near the magnetic poles
C. variation is near zero
D. vessel is near the magnetic equator

824. An atoll cloud forming over an island due to heating of the land during the daytime would be which type?

A. Cirrus
B. Cumulus
C. Stratus
D. Nimbus

826. In the U.S., in which direction do air masses usually move?

A. Easterly
B. Southerly
C. Northerly
D. Southwesterly

827. The Benguela Current flows in a _____.

A. SW'ly direction along the NW coast of Africa
B. S'ly direction off the East Coast of Australia
C. NW'ly direction along the SW coast of Africa
D. SW'ly direction along the SE coast of Greenland

828. The true wind has been determined to be from 210°T, speed 12 knots. You desire the apparent wind to be 30 knots from 10° on the port bow. What course must you steer, and what speed must you make for this to occur?

A. 235°T, 18.6 knots
B. 245°T, 20.0 knots
C. 325°T, 22.4 knots
D. 335°T, 23.6 knots

829. You are plotting a running fix in an area where there is a determinable current.

How should this current be treated in determining the position?

A. The drift should be added to the ship's speed.
B. The set should be applied to the second bearing.
C. The current should be ignored.
D. The course and speed made good should be determined and used to advance the LOP.

830. The highest frequency of tropical cyclones in the North Atlantic Ocean occurs during _____.

A. January, February and March
B. April, May and June
C. August, September and October
D. July, November and December

831. Under the IALA-A Buoyage system, a buoy marking the starboard side of the channel when approaching from seaward may have a _____.

A. triangular topmark
B. red light
C. can shape
D. isophase light

832. What is the most important source of information to be used in correcting charts and keeping them up to date?

A. Fleet Guides
B. Notice to Mariners
C. Sailing Directions
D. Pilot Charts

833. The magnetic compass magnets are acted on by the horizontal component of the Earth's total magnetic force. This magnetic force is GREATEST at the _____.

A. north magnetic pole
B. south magnetic pole
C. magnetic prime vertical meridian
D. magnetic equator

834. In many areas atoll clouds (clouds of vertical development) are produced over small islands. These are the result of _____.

A. rising air currents produced by the warm islands
B. warm air from the sea rising over higher land areas
C. cool land air mixing with warm sea air
D. descending air over the islands

836. In North America the majority of the weather systems move from _____.

A. north to south
B. south to north
C. east to west
D. west to east

837. The Brazil Current flows in which general direction?

A. Northwesterly
B. Southwesterly
C. Southerly
D. Northerly

838. A navigator fixing a vessel's position by radar _____.

A. must use information from targets forward of the beam
B. should never use radar bearings
C. should only use radar bearings when the range exceeds the distance to the horizon
D. can use radar information from one object to fix the position

839. When using a radar in an unstabilized mode, fixes are determined most easily from _____.

A. ranges
B. center bearings
C. tangent bearings
D. objects that are close aboard

840. Which position includes the effects of wind and current?

A. Estimated position
B. Set position
C. Leeway position
D. Dead-reckoning position

841. Under the IALA-A Buoyage system, a buoy marking the port hand of the channel when approaching from seaward may NOT have a _____.

A. red light
B. conical shape
C. group-flashing light
D. square topmark

842. Coast Pilots and navigational charts are kept corrected and up-to-date by using the _____.

A. pilot charts

B. Notices to Mariners
C. Tide Tables
D. Current Tables

843. The line which connects the points of zero magnetic dip is _____.

A. an agonic line
B. the magnetic equator
C. a magnetic meridian
D. All of the above

844. A cloud of marked vertical development (often anvil-shaped) would be classified as _____.

A. cirrus
B. cirrocumulus
C. altocumulus
D. cumulonimbus

846. Weather systems in the middle latitudes generally travel from _____.

A. east to west
B. north to south
C. west to east
D. None of the above

847. On a voyage from Halifax, N.S., to Dakar, West Africa, the Canary Current will _____.

A. set the vessel to the left
B. set the vessel to the right
C. offer resistance in the form of a head current
D. furnish additional thrust in the form of a fair or following current

848. It is unlawful to approach within how many yards of a northern right whale?

A. 200
B. 300
C. 400
D. 500

849. The Light List shows that a navigational light has a nominal range of 12 miles and a height above water of 25 feet (7.6 meters). Your height of eye is 30 feet (9.1 meters) and the visibility is 0.5 mile. At what approximate range will you first sight the light?

A. 0.5 mile
B. 1.4 miles
C. 5.2 miles

D. 12.0 miles

850. When is the peak of the hurricane season in the western North Pacific?

A. January through March
B. April through June
C. July through October
D. November through December

851. You would expect to find channels marked with the IALA-A Buoyage System in _____.

A. the Philippines
B. Australia
C. Republic of Korea
D. Chile

852. What is published by the U.S. Coast Guard?

A. Light List
B. Nautical Charts
C. Tide Tables
D. U.S. Coast Pilot

853. The standard magnetic compass heading differs from the true heading by _____.

A. compass error
B. latitude
C. variation
D. deviation

854. The appearance of nimbostratus clouds in the immediate vicinity of a ship at sea would be accompanied by which of the following conditions?

A. Rain and poor visibility
B. Dropping barometric pressure and backing wind in the Northern Hemisphere
C. High winds and rising sea
D. Severe thunderstorms

855. Which condition exists at the summer solstice in the Northern Hemisphere?

A. The north polar regions are in continual darkness.
B. The Northern Hemisphere is having short days and long nights.
C. The Southern Hemisphere is having winter.
D. The Sun shines equally on both hemispheres.

856. The flow of air around an anticyclone in the Southern Hemisphere is _____.

A. clockwise and outward
B. counterclockwise and outward
C. clockwise and inward
D. counterclockwise and inward

857. The current that, in many respects, is similar to the Gulf Stream is the _____.

A. Kuroshio
B. California Current
C. Oyashio
D. Benguela Current

858. Your ship is proceeding on course 320°T at a speed of 25 knots. The apparent wind is from 30° off the starboard bow, speed 32 knots. What is the relative direction, true direction and speed of the true wind?

A. Relative 80°true, 040°T, 16.2 knots
B. Relative 40°true, 080°T, 16.4 knots
C. Relative 80°true, 060°T, 15.2 knots
D. Relative 60°true, 040°T, 18.6 knots

860. The Light List shows that a navigational light has a nominal range of 10 miles and a height above water of 38 feet (11.6 meters). Your height of eye is 52 feet (15.8 meters) and the visibility is 11.0 miles. At which approximate range will you first sight the light?

A. 10.5 miles
B. 13.9 miles
C. 15.6 miles
D. 18.0 miles

861. You would expect to find channels marked with the IALA-A Buoyage System in _____.

A. Argentina
B. Japan
C. India
D. Canada

862. The U.S. Coast Guard publishes _____.

A. Light Lists
B. U.S. Coast Pilots
C. Radio Navigational Aids
D. All of the above

863. The compass heading of a vessel differs from the true heading by _____.

A. compass error
B. variation
C. magnetic dip
D. deviation

864. Uniform, grayish-white cloud sheets that cover large portions of the sky, and are responsible for a large percentage of the precipitation in the temperate latitudes, are called _____.

A. altostratus
B. altocumulus
C. cirrostratus
D. cirrocumulus

865. The radius of a circle of equal altitude of a body is equal to the _____.

A. coaltitude of the body
B. altitude of the body
C. codeclination of the body
D. polar distance

866. Anticyclones are usually characterized by _____.

A. dry, fair weather
B. high winds and cloudiness
C. gustiness and continuous precipitation
D. overcast skies

867. Which ocean current is warm based on the latitude in which it originates and on the effect it has on climate?

A. Kuroshio Current
B. Benguela Current
C. Peru Current
D. California Current

869. Tropical storms and hurricanes are most likely to form in the Southern hemisphere during _____.

A. January through March
B. April through May
C. June through August
D. September through November

870. Vessels should maintain a sharp lookout, especially during December through March, when navigating the right whale's only known calving grounds which lie off the coasts of _____.

A. Nova Scotia
B. Maine and Massachusetts
C. Georgia and NE Florida
D. California and Mexico

871. Under the IALA-A Buoyage System, a buoy marking the starboard side of the channel when approaching from seaward must have a(n) _____.

A. pillar shape
B. green color
C. square topmark
D. even number

872. Which agency publishes the Light Lists?

A. United States Coast Guard
B. National Ocean Service
C. Oceanographic Office
D. Army Corps of Engineers

873. Compass error is equal to the _____.

A. deviation minus variation
B. variation plus compass course
C. combined variation and deviation
D. difference between true and magnetic heading

874. Altocumulus clouds are defined as _____.

A. high clouds
B. middle clouds
C. low clouds
D. vertical development clouds

876. A generally circular low pressure area is called a(n) _____.

A. cyclone
B. anticyclone
C. cold front
D. occluded front

877. Cold water flowing southward through the western part of the Bering Strait between Alaska and Siberia is joined by water circulating counterclockwise in the Bering Sea to form the _____.

A. Alaska Current
B. Subarctic Current
C. Kuroshio Current
D. Oyashio Current

879. You are enroute to assist vessel A. Vessel A is underway at 4.5 knots on course 233°T, and bears 346°T at 68 miles from you. What is the course to steer at 13 knots to intercept vessel A?

A. 328°
B. 323°
C. 318°
D. 314°

880. You are taking bearings on two known objects ashore. The BEST fix is obtained when the angle between the lines of position is _____.

A. 60°
B. 90°
C. 45°
D. 30°

881. Under the IALA-A Buoyage System, when entering from seaward, a buoy indicating the preferred channel is to starboard may have a _____.

A. green light
B. long-flashing light characteristic
C. square topmark
D. conical shape

882. Some lights used as aids to marine navigation have a red sector to indicate a danger area. The limits of a colored sector of a light are listed in the Light List in which of the following manners?

A. Geographical positions outlining the area of the sector
B. True bearings as observed from the ship toward the light
C. An outline of the area of the sector
D. True bearings as observed from the light toward the ship

883. When changing from a compass course to a true course you should apply _____.

A. variation
B. deviation
C. variation and deviation
D. a correction for the direction of current set

884. Which cloud type is normally associated with thunderstorms?

A. Cirrus
B. Stratus
C. Cumulus
D. Cumulonimbus

886. The circulation around a low pressure center in the Northern Hemisphere is _____.

A. counterclockwise
B. variable
C. clockwise
D. anticyclonic

887. Which current would you encounter on a direct passage from southern Africa to Argentina, South America?

A. South Atlantic
B. South Equatorial
C. Agulhas
D. Guinea

888. Recurvature of a hurricane's track usually results in the forward speed _____.

A. increasing
B. decreasing
C. remaining the same
D. varying during the day

889. The Light List shows that a navigational light has a nominal range of 6 miles and a height above water of 18 feet (5.5 meters). Your height of eye is 47 feet (14.3 meters) and the visibility is 1.5 miles. At what approximate range will you first sight the light?

A. 1.5 miles
B. 2.0 miles
C. 6.0 miles
D. 12.7 miles

890. If several navigational lights are visible at the same time, each one may be positively identified by checking all of the following EXCEPT what against the Light List?

A. Rhythm
B. Period
C. Intensity
D. Color

891. Under the IALA-A Buoyage System, a buoy indicating the preferred channel is to port would have _____.

A. an even number
B. an odd number
C. a pillar shape
D. horizontal bands

892. When a buoy is in position only during a certain period of the year, where may the dates when the buoy is in position be found?

A. Light List

B. Notice to Mariners
C. On the chart
D. Coast Pilot

893. One point of a compass is equal to how many degrees?

A. 7.5
B. 11.25
C. 17.5
D. 22.5

894. On a clear, warm day, you notice the approach of a tall cumulus cloud. The cloud top has hard well-defined edges and rain is falling from the dark lower edge. Should this cloud pass directly overhead _____.

A. it will be preceded by a sudden increase in wind speed
B. it will be preceded by a sudden decrease in wind speed
C. the wind speed will not change as it passes
D. the wind will back rapidly to left in a counterclockwise direction as it passes

896. The wind direction around a low pressure area in the Northern Hemisphere is _____.

A. clockwise and inward
B. clockwise and outward
C. counterclockwise and inward
D. counterclockwise and outward

897. What current flows southward along the west coast of the United States and causes extensive fog in that area?

A. Davidson Current
B. North Pacific Current
C. Alaska Current
D. California Current

900. An orange and white buoy with a rectangle on it is a(n) _____.

A. informational buoy
B. junction buoy
C. safe water buoy
D. All of the above

901. Under the IALA-A Buoyage System, a buoy indicating that the preferred channel is to port when entering from seaward can have a _____.

A. can shape
B. group-flashing (2) light

C. red-and-green vertical stripes
D. green light

902. All of the following information concerning lighted aids to navigation may be read directly from the Light List EXCEPT the _____.

A. location
B. height of light above water
C. luminous range
D. light characteristics

903. Eight points of a compass are equal to how many degrees?

A. 45
B. 90
C. 180
D. 360

904. All of the following are associated with cumulonimbus clouds EXCEPT _____.

A. steady rainfall
B. hail storms
C. thunderstorms
D. tornadoes or waterspouts

906. In the Northern Hemisphere, an area of counterclockwise wind circulation surrounded by higher pressure is a _____.

A. low
B. high
C. warm front
D. cold front

907. In which month will the equatorial countercurrent be strongest?

A. January
B. April
C. August
D. October

908. From LAT 07°12′N, LONG 80°00′W, to LAT 47°12′S, LONG 169°18′E, the initial great circle course angle is 137.25°. How would you name this course?

A. N 137.25°E
B. S 137.25°E
C. N 137.25°W
D. S 137.25°W

909. What is the average speed of movement of a hurricane prior to recurvature?

A. 4 to 6 knots

B. 6 to 8 knots
C. 10 to 12 knots
D. 15 to 20 knots

910. The Light List shows that a navigational light has a nominal range of 12 miles and a height above water of 25 feet (7.6 meters). Your height of eye is 38 feet (11.6 meters) and the visibility is 5.5 miles. At what approximate range will you FIRST sight the light?

A. 5.5 miles
B. 6.3 miles
C. 8.0 miles
D. 12.0 miles

911. Under the IALA-B Buoyage System, a buoy displaying a red light will _____.

A. be left to starboard when entering from seaward
B. show a light characteristic of Morse Code A
C. be lettered
D. have a radar reflector

912. The Light List does NOT contain information on _____.

A. the Global Positioning System (GPS)
B. aeronautical lights useful for marine navigation
C. radiobeacon systems
D. radio direction finder calibration stations

913. How many points are there in a compass card?

A. 4
B. 8
C. 24
D. 32

914. If the sky was clear, with the exception of a few cumulus clouds, it would indicate _____.

A. rain
B. hurricane weather
C. fair weather
D. fog setting in

916. Stormy weather is usually associated with regions of _____.

A. low barometric pressure
B. high barometric pressure
C. steady barometric pressure
D. changing barometric pressure

917. As the South Equatorial Current approaches the east coast of Africa, it divides with the main part flowing south to form the warm _____.

A. Agulhas Current
B. Canary Current
C. Benguela Current
D. Madagascar Current

919. You are plotting a running fix in an area where there is a determinable current. How should this current be treated in determining the position?

A. The drift should be added to the ship's speed.
B. The course and speed made good should be determined and used to advance the LOP.
C. The current should be ignored.
D. The set should be applied to the second bearing.

920. What is the average speed of the movement of a hurricane following the recurvature of its track?

A. 5 to 10 knots
B. 20 to 30 knots
C. 40 to 50 knots
D. Over 60 knots

921. Under the IALA-B Buoyage System, a conical buoy will be_____.

A. red in color
B. numbered with an odd number
C. left to port when entering from seaward
D. All of the above

922. How is the intensity of a light expressed in the Light Lists?

A. Luminous range
B. Geographic range
C. Nominal range
D. Meteorological range

923. A magnetic compass card is marked in how many degrees?

A. 90
B. 180
C. 360
D. 400

924. The form of cloud often known as mackerel sky which is generally associated with fair weather is _____.

A. nimbostratus
B. stratus
C. cirrocumulus
D. cumulonimbus

926. When a low pressure area is approaching, the weather generally _____.

A. improves
B. worsens
C. remains the same
D. is unpredictable

927. The set of the equatorial countercurrent is generally to the_____.

A. north
B. east
C. southwest
D. northwest

928. D051NG. The position labeled D was plotted because _____.

A. a dead reckoning position is plotted for each course change
B. a dead reckoning position is plotted withen 30 minutes of a running fix
C. the vessel's speed changed at 1125
D. All of the above

929. Which error is NOT included in the term current when used in relation to a fix?

A. Poor steering
B. Leeway
C. Known compass error
D. Ocean currents

931. Under the IALA-B Buoyage System, when entering from seaward, a buoy that should be left to port will be _____.

A. black
B. red
C. green
D. yellow

932. To find the specific phase characteristic of a lighthouse on a sound of the United States you would use the _____.

A. American Practical Navigator
B. Light List
C. Nautical Chart Catalog
D. U.S. Coast Pilot

933. How many degrees are there on a compass card?

A. 360°
B. 380°
C. 390°
D. 420°

934. Clouds that form as small white flakes or scaly globular masses covering either small or large portions of the sky are _____.

A. cirrus
B. cirrostratus
C. altostratus
D. cirrocumulus

935. The Light List shows that a navigational light has a nominal range of 5 miles and a height above water of 21 feet (6.4 meters). Your height of eye is 32 feet (9.8 meters) and the visibility is 1.0 mile. At what approximate range will you first sight the light?

A. 1.0 mile
B. 1.5 miles
C. 5.0 miles
D. 11.7 miles

936. A cyclone in its final stage of development is called a(n) _____.

A. tornado
B. anticyclone
C. occluded cyclone or occluded front
D. polar cyclone

937. The north equatorial current flows to the _____.

A. east
B. northeast
C. southwest
D. west

938. If within 500 yards (460m) of a Northern Right Whale you are lawfully obligated to _____.

A. turn away from the whale and leave at full speed
B. turn away from the whale and leave at slow speed
C. slow to bare steerageway until the whale swims away
D. stop the vessel and sound repeated blasts on the ship's whistle to scare the whale away

939. That half of the hurricane to the right hand side of its track (as you face the same

direction that the storm is moving) in the Northern Hemisphere is called the _____.

A. windward side
B. leeward side
C. safe semicircle
D. dangerous semicircle

940. What is the length of a nautical mile?

A. 6,076 feet
B. 5,280 feet
C. 2,000 yards
D. 1,850 meters

941. While preparing to enter a Brazilian port, you see ahead a red and green horizontally striped buoy. The upper band is red. What action should you take?

A. Alter course to leave the buoy to port.
B. Alter course to leave the buoy to starboard.
C. Pass the buoy close aboard on either side.
D. Pass the buoy well clear on either side.

942. Light Lists for coastal waters are _____.

A. published every year and require no corrections
B. published every second year and must be corrected
C. published every five years and require no correction
D. accurate through NM number on title page and must be corrected

943. You should plot your dead reckoning position _____.

A. when you obtain an estimated position
B. ONLY in piloting waters
C. at every speed change
D. All of the above are correct.

944. High clouds, composed of small white flakes or scaly globular masses, and often banded together to form a mackerel sky, would be classified as _____.

A. cirrus
B. cirrocumulus
C. altostratus
D. cumulonimbus

946. The wind circulation around a high pressure center in the Northern Hemisphere is _____.

A. counterclockwise and moving towards the high
B. counterclockwise and moving outward from the high
C. clockwise and moving towards the high
D. clockwise and moving outward from the high

947. The cold ocean current which meets the warm Gulf Stream between latitudes 40° and 43°N to form the cold wall is called the _____.

A. North Cape Current
B. Labrador Current
C. Greenland Current
D. North Atlantic Current

949. In Region A of the IALA Buoyage System, when entering from seaward, the port side of a channel would be marked by a _____.

A. black can buoy
B. red can buoy
C. black conical buoy
D. red conical buoy

950. Where is the dangerous semicircle located on a hurricane in the Southern Hemisphere?

A. To the left of the storm's track
B. To the right of the storm's track
C. In the high pressure area
D. On the south side

951. In which country would you expect the channels to be marked with the IALA-B Buoyage System?

A. Poland
B. Morocco
C. Peru
D. Saudi Arabia

952. What is TRUE concerning new editions of Light Lists?

A. Supplements to new editions are issued monthly by the U.S. Coast Guard.
B. New editions are published by the National Ocean Service.
C. New editions are corrected through the date shown on the title page.
D. None of the above

953. The magnetic compass operates on the principle that _____.

A. like magnetic poles attract
B. unlike magnetic poles repel
C. unlike poles attract
D. the poles of the compass line up with the geographic poles of the earth

954. A thin, whitish, high cloud popularly known as mares' tails is _____.

A. altostratus
B. stratus
C. cumulus
D. cirrus

956. Good weather is usually associated with a region of _____.

A. low barometric pressure
B. high barometric pressure
C. falling barometric pressure
D. pumping barometric pressure

957. The Humboldt Current flows in which direction?

A. North
B. South
C. East
D. West

960. The Light List shows that a navigational light has a nominal range of 15 miles and a height above water of 29 feet (8.8 meters). Your height of eye is 52 feet (15.8 meters) and visibility is 6.0 miles. At which approximate range will you first sight the light?

A. 9.0 miles
B. 11.0 miles
C. 14.5 miles
D. 15.0 miles

961. In which country would you expect the channels to be marked with the IALA-B Buoyage System?

A. Brazil
B. Tanzania
C. New Zealand
D. Norway

962. Chart legends which indicate a conspicuous landmark are printed in _____.

A. underlined letters
B. boldfaced print
C. italics
D. capital letters

963. To center a compass bowl in its binnacle, you should have the ship on an even keel, heading north or south, and adjust the screws until _____.

A. the compass heading is in line with the lubber's line
B. there is no lost motion in the gimbal rings
C. no change of heading by compass is observed if you raise and lower the heeling magnet
D. the gimbal rings do not strike the compass frame when they are tilted

964. The thin, whitish, high clouds composed of ice crystals, popularly known as mares' tails, are _____

A. cirrus
B. cirrocumulus
C. altostratus
D. nimbostratus

966. Most high pressure areas in the United States are accompanied by _____.

A. precipitation
B. clear, cool weather
C. humid, sticky weather
D. cool fogs

967. On an Atlantic Ocean voyage from New York to Durban, South Africa, you should expect the Agulhas Current to present a strong _____.

A. offshore set
B. onshore set
C. head current
D. fair or following current

968. The world is divided into NAVAREAS by the National Imagery and Mapping Agency for the dissemination of important marine information. Which NAVAREAS include the U.S. coasts?

A. I and II
B. IV and XII
C. V and X
D. VI and VII

969. The population of northern right whales, an endangered species, numbers approximately _____.

A. 300
B. 5000
C. 100,000

D. 1,000,000

971. You are in British waters on course 090°T when you sight a flashing white light with a characteristic of VQ(9)10s. You immediately change course to 030°T. After one hour, you sight another flashing white light with the characteristic of VQ. You must pass well _____.

A. south of this buoy
B. west of this buoy
C. north of this buoy
D. east of this buoy

972. In which source could you find the number of a chart for a certain geographic area?

A. Chart No. 1
B. Catalog of Charts
C. American Practical Navigator
D. U.S. Coast Guard Light List

973. The heading of a vessel is indicated by what part of the compass?

A. Card
B. Needle
C. Lubber's line
D. Gimbals

974. Which cloud commonly produces a halo about the Sun or Moon?

A. Cirrostratus
B. Cirrocumulus
C. Altostratus
D. Altocumulus

976. The atmosphere in the vicinity of a high pressure area is called a(n) _____.

A. anticyclone
B. cold front
C. occluded front
D. cyclone

977. In the Sargasso Sea there are large quantities of seaweed and no well-defined currents. This area is located in the _____.

A. Central North Atlantic Ocean
B. Caribbean Sea
C. Western North Pacific Ocean
D. area off the west coast of South America

978. The wind velocity is higher in the dangerous semicircle of a tropical cyclone because of the _____.

A. recurvature effect
B. extension of the low pressure ridge
C. wind circulation and forward motion of the storm
D. direction of circulation and pressure gradient

979. Which kind of conditions would you observe as the eye of a storm passes over your vessel's position?

A. Huge waves approaching from all directions, clearing skies, light winds, and an extremely low barometer
B. Flat calm seas, heavy rain, light winds, and an extremely low barometer
C. Flat calm seas, heavy rain, light winds, and high pressure
D. Huge waves approaching from all directions, clearing skies, light winds, and high pressure

980. When the declination of the Moon is 0°12.5'S, you can expect some tidal currents in Gulf Coast ports to _____.

A. have either a double ebb or a double flood
B. become weak and variable
C. become reversing currents
D. exceed the predicted velocities

981. The characteristic of a lighted cardinal mark may be _____.

A. very quick flashing
B. flashing
C. fixed
D. occulting

982. The National Imagery and Mapping Agency's (NIMA) List of Lights for coasts other than the United States and its possessions does NOT provide information on _____.

A. lighted buoys in harbors
B. storm signal stations
C. radio direction finder stations at or near lights
D. radiobeacons located at or near lights

983. Error may be introduced into a magnetic compass by _____.

A. making a structural change to the vessel
B. a short circuit near the compass
C. belt buckles
D. All of the above

984. The bases of middle clouds are located at altitudes of between _____.

A. 3,000 to 6,500 feet (914 to 1981 meters)
B. 6,500 to 20,000 feet (1981 to 6096 meters)
C. 10,000 to 35,000 feet (3048 to 10,668 meters)
D. 20,000 to 60,000 feet (6096 to 18,288 meters)

986. A warm air mass is characterized by _____.

A. stability
B. instability
C. gusty winds
D. good visibility

987. Which current is responsible for the movement of icebergs into the North Atlantic shipping lanes?

A. Iceland Current
B. Baltic Current
C. Labrador Current
D. Baffin Current

989. The Light List shows that a navigational light has a nominal range of 18 miles and a height above water of 22 feet (6.7 meters). Your height of eye is 16 feet (4.9 meters) and the visibility is 2.0 miles. At which approximate range will you first sight the light?

A. 2.0 miles
B. 2.7 miles
C. 4.2 miles
D. 5.8 miles

990. You plot a fix using three lines of position and find they intersect in a triangle. You should plot the position of the vessel _____.

A. outside of the triangle
B. anywhere in the triangle
C. on the line of position from the nearest object, between the other two lines of position
D. in the geometric center of the triangle

991. You are underway in the North Sea on course 328°T when you sight a buoy broad on your port bow. You are in the best navigable water if the buoy _____.

A. has a topmark of two cones with points down

B. is a western quadrant buoy
C. is painted yellow on the top half and black on the bottom
D. exhibits a light with the characteristic of VQ(3)5s

992. Which publication contains information on Naval Control of Shipping (NCS) in time of emergency or war?

A. Pub. 117, Radio Navigational Aids
B. Appropriate volume of the Sailing Directions
C. Pub. 102, International Code of Signals
D. Light List

993. When crossing the magnetic equator the _____.

A. Flinders bar should be inverted
B. heeling magnet should be inverted
C. the quadrantal spheres should be rotated 180°
D. Flinders bar should be moved to the opposite side of the binnacle

994. Which list of clouds is in sequence, from highest to lowest in the sky?

A. Altostratus, cirrostratus, stratus
B. Cirrostratus, altostratus, stratus
C. Stratus, cirrostratus, altostratus
D. Altostratus, stratus, cirrostratus

996. Warm air masses will generally have _____.

A. turbulence within the mass
B. stratiform clouds
C. heavy precipitation
D. good visibility

997. A coastal current _____.

A. is generated by waves striking the beach
B. flows outside the surf zone
C. flows in a circular pattern
D. is also known as a longshore current

998. The navigable semicircle of a tropical storm in the South Indian Ocean is located on which side of the storm's track?

A. Rear
B. Front
C. Left
D. Right

1000. D047NG. You are inbound in a channel marked by a range. The range line is

309°T. You are steering 306°T. The range appears as shown and is closing. Which action should you take?

A. Continue on course until the range is closed, then alter course to the right.
B. Continue on the present heading until the range is in line, then alter course to the left.
C. Immediately alter course to the right to bring the range in line.
D. Immediately alter course to 309°T to bring the range in line.

1001. While steaming in English waters on course 280°T, you sight a buoy showing a very quick-flashing (VQ) white light well to port. Maintaining course, you sight another buoy showing a quick-flashing (Q) white light. You should pass _____.

A. north of the buoy
B. west of the buoy
C. east of the buoy
D. south of the buoy

1002. What publication contains information about the port facilities in Cadiz, Spain?

A. World Port Index
B. United States Coast Pilot
C. Nautical Index
D. Sailing Directions

1003. The quadrantal spheres are used to _____.

A. remove deviation on the intercardinal headings
B. remove deviation on the cardinal compass headings
C. remove heeling error
D. compensate for induced magnetism in vertical soft iron

1004. A low, uniform layer of cloud resembling fog, but not resting on the ground, is called _____.

A. cumulus
B. nimbus
C. stratus
D. cirrus

1005. The refraction correction table given in the Nautical Almanac is based on a standard or average atmospheric density with a temperature of 50°F (10°C) and atmospheric pressure of _____.

A. 29.72 inches (1006 millibars)
B. 29.83 inches (1010 millibars)
C. 29.89 inches (1012 millibars)
D. 29.93 inches (1014 millibars)

1006. An air mass is termed warm if _____.

A. it is above 70°F
B. the ground over which it moves is cooler than the air
C. it originated in a high pressure area
D. it originated in a low pressure area

1007. When a current flows in the opposite direction to the waves, the wave _____.

A. length is increased
B. height is increased
C. velocity increases
D. length is unchanged

1008. The Light List indicates that a light has a nominal range of 18 miles and is 38 feet high. If the visibility is 6 miles and your height of eye is 15 feet, at which distance will you sight the light?

A. 18.0 nm
B. 14.8 nm
C. 11.7 nm
D. 6.0 nm

1010. What is a characteristic of a rhumb line?

A. It is the shortest distance between two points on the Earth.
B. It plots as a straight line on a Lambert conformal chart.
C. It cuts each meridian at the same angle.
D. The course angle constantly changes to form the loxodromic curve.

1011. D025NG. You are underway in the North Sea on course 127°T. You sight a buoy with the topmarks shown bearing two points on the starboard bow. Which action must be taken?

A. Alter course to starboard until the buoy is at least two points on the port bow, then hold course.
B. Alter course to port until the buoy is broad on the starboard quarter, then hold course.
C. Change course to have the buoy close aboard either side.
D. Ensure the bearings change to the right.

1012. General information about the location, characteristics, facilities, and services for U.S. and foreign ports may be obtained from which publication?

A. World Port Index
B. Sailing Directions
C. Distances Between Ports
D. Coast Pilot

1013. The purpose of the soft iron spheres mounted on arms on the binnacle is to compensate for _____.

A. the vertical component of the permanent magnetism of the vessel
B. the residual deviation
C. magnetic fields caused by electrical currents in the vicinity
D. induced magnetism in the horizontal soft iron

1014. Relative humidity is the percentage of water vapor that is in the air as compared to the maximum amount it can hold at _____.

A. a specific barometric pressure
B. a specific temperature
C. a specific wind speed
D. any time

1016. A source of an air mass labeled mTw is _____.

A. the equator
B. the Gulf of Mexico
C. Alaska
D. Canada

1017. Which statement(s) concerning the effect of Coriolis force on ocean currents is(are) correct?

A. The deflection of the current is to the left in the Northern Hemisphere.
B. The Coriolis force is greater in the lower latitudes.
C. The Coriolis force is more effective in deep water.
D. All of the above

1018. An aneroid barometer reading should be corrected for differences in _____.

A. elevation
B. temperature
C. wind speed
D. latitude

1020. The Light List shows that a navigational light has a nominal range of 6 miles and a height above water of 18 feet (5.5 meters). Your height of eye is 40 feet (12.2 meters) and the visibility is 27.0 miles. At which approximate range will you first sight the light?

A. 5.6 miles
B. 6.4 miles
C. 9.8 miles
D. 12.1 miles

1021. You are underway in the North Sea on course 142°T when you sight a buoy bearing 105°T. The buoy's white light has a characteristic of continuous very quick-flashing. To ensure that your vessel remains in the best navigable water you would _____.

A. continue on course and ensure that the bearings change to the left
B. pass between the buoy and another buoy showing a fixed white light
C. alter course to port and pass the buoy close aboard to either side
D. alter course to port and pass north of the buoy

1022. What is the approximate geographic range of Fenwick Island Light, Delaware, if your height of eye is 37 feet (11.6 meters)? Refer to Reprints from the Light Lists and Coast Pilots.

A. 24.8 nm
B. 17.8 nm
C. 15.9 nm
D. 10.3 nm

1023. Which compensates for induced magnetism in the horizontal soft iron of a vessel?

A. Iron spheres mounted on the binnacle
B. A single vertical magnet under the compass
C. The Flinders bar
D. Magnets in trays inside the binnacle

1024. The dew point is reached when the _____.

A. temperature of the air equals the temperature of the seawater
B. atmospheric pressure is 14.7 lbs. per square inch
C. relative humidity reaches 50%
D. air becomes saturated with water vapor

1026. An air mass that has moved down from Canada would most likely have the symbols _____.

A. mPk
B. cPk
C. cTk
D. cTw

1027. In the Northern Hemisphere the major ocean currents tend to flow _____.

A. clockwise around the North Atlantic and North Pacific Oceans
B. clockwise or counterclockwise depending on whether it is warm or cold current
C. counterclockwise except in the Gulf Stream
D. counterclockwise around the North Atlantic and North Pacific Oceans

1028. At what angle to the isobars do surface winds blow over the open sea?

A. About 90°
B. About 50°
C. About 25°
D. About 15°

1031. While steaming north of the Irish coast, you sight a buoy which shows the light rhythm shown in illustration D028NG. How would you pass this buoy?

A. North of the buoy
B. East of the buoy
C. South of the buoy
D. West of the buoy

1032. What is the approximate geographic range of Point Judith Light, Rhode Island, if your height of eye is 62 feet (18.9 meters)? Refer to Reprints from the Light Lists and Coast Pilots.

A. 9.6 nm
B. 16.5 nm
C. 18.6 nm
D. 20.7 nm

1033. Deviation which is maximum on intercardinal compass headings may be removed by the _____.

A. Flinders bar
B. transverse magnets
C. fore-and-aft magnets
D. soft iron spheres on the sides of the compass

1034. The expression the air is saturated means _____.

A. the relative humidity is 100%
B. the vapor pressure is at its minimum for the prevailing temperature
C. precipitation has commenced
D. cloud cover is 100%

1036. A frontal thunderstorm is caused by _____.

A. pronounced local heating
B. wind being pushed up a mountain
C. a warm air mass rising over a cold air mass
D. an increased lapse rate caused by advection of warm surface air

1037. Generally speaking, a ship steaming across the North Pacific from Japan to Seattle is likely to experience _____.

A. adverse currents for practically the entire crossing
B. favorable currents for practically the entire crossing
C. favorable currents in the summer months and adverse currents in the winter months
D. variable currents having no significant effect on the total steaming time

1039. While taking weather observations, you determine that the wind is coming from the west. In the weather log, you would record the wind direction as _____.

A. 000°
B. 090°
C. 180°
D. 270°

1040. An occluded front is usually caused by a _____.

A. cold front becoming stationary
B. warm front becoming stationary
C. cold front overtaking a warm front
D. warm front dissipating

1041. You are steaming along the coast of Ireland in the Irish Sea. You sight a lighted buoy with a white flashing light showing a group of two flashes. The buoy indicates you _____.

A. must pass south of the buoy
B. must pass north of the buoy
C. should pass well clear on either side of the buoy

D. must pass the buoy close to starboard

1042. What is the approximate geographic range of Shinnecock Light, NY, if your height of eye is 24 feet (7.3 meters)? Refer to Re-prints from the Light Lists and Coast Pilots.

A. 8.7 nm
B. 9.9 nm
C. 14.4 nm
D. 15.9 nm

1043. You are about to go to sea and adjust the magnetic compass. To expedite the adjustment at sea, in what order should the following dockside adjustments be made?

A. Flinders bar first, then the heeling magnet and spheres
B. Heeling magnet first, then the Flinders bar and spheres
C. Flinders bar first, then the spheres and heeling magnet
D. Spheres first, then the Flinders bar and heeling magnet

1044. The dry-bulb temperature is 78°F and the wet-bulb temperature is 62°F. What is the relative humidity?

A. 16%
B. 24%
C. 39%
D. 79%

1045. The Light List shows that a navigational light has a nominal range of 15 miles and a height above water of 40 feet (12.2 meters). Your height of eye is 25 feet (7.6 meters) and the visibility is 5 miles. At about what range will you FIRST sight the light?

A. 6.2 miles
B. 9.5 miles
C. 12.9 miles
D. 14.2 miles

1046. The probability of a sudden wind may be foretold by _____.

A. a partly cloudy sky
B. an overcast sky
C. a fast approaching line of dark clouds
D. the formation of cumulus clouds in the sky

1047. Which is NOT a contributing cause of ocean currents?

A. Surface winds
B. Density differences in the water
C. Underwater topography
D. Gravitational effects of celestial bodies

1048. The velocity of the current in large coastal harbors is _____.

A. unpredictable
B. generally too weak to be of concern
C. predicted in Tidal Current Tables
D. generally constant

1049. At 0000 you fix your position and change course to 270°T. At 0030 you again fix your position, and it is 0.5 mile east of your DR. Which statement is TRUE?

A. The set is 090°, drift 0.5 knot.
B. The set is 090°, drift 1.0 knot.
C. The set is 270°, drift 0.5 knot.
D. The set is 270°, drift 1.0 knot.

1050. The passing of a low pressure system can be determined by periodically checking the _____.

A. thermometer
B. hygrometer
C. barometer
D. anemometer

1051. Under the IALA Buoyage Systems, a cardinal mark may NOT be used to _____.

A. indicate that the deepest water in an area is on the named side of the mark
B. indicate the safe side on which to pass a danger
C. draw attention to a feature in the channel such as a bend, junction, bifurcation, or end of a shoal
D. indicate the port and starboard sides of well-defined channels

1052. What is the approximate geographic range of Southwest Ledge Light, Connecticut, if your height of eye is 32 feet (9.8 meters)? Refer to Reprints from the Light Lists and Coast Pilots.

A. 15.5 nm
B. 13.4 nm
C. 8.7 nm
D. 6.9 nm

1053. Before a magnetic compass is adjusted certain correctors must be checked to ensure that they are free of permanent magnetism. These correctors are the _____.

A. fore-and-aft and athwartships magnets
B. dip needle and heeling magnet
C. heeling magnet and Flinders bar
D. Flinders bar and quadrantal spheres

1054. The dry-bulb temperature is 78°F (26°C) and the wet-bulb temperature is 68°F (20°C). What is the relative humidity?

A. 10%
B. 24%
C. 56%
D. 60%

1056. The steepness of a cold front depends on _____.

A. the direction of wind around the front
B. its velocity
C. the temperature of the air behind the front
D. the precipitation generated by the front

1057. One of the causes of ocean currents is density differences in the water. This is true because _____.

A. in an area of high density the water's surface is lower than in an area of low density
B. surface water flows from an area of high density to one of low density
C. the lesser the density gradient the freer the water is to move
D. it is the density differences that cause the currents to stay in the troughs

1059. The Light List shows that a navigational light has a nominal range of 17 miles and a height above water of 28 feet (8.5 meters). Your height of eye is 32 feet (9.8 meters) and the visibility is 11.0 miles. At what approximate range will you first sight the light?

A. 11.0 miles
B. 12.6 miles
C. 15.7 miles
D. 18.0 miles

1060. Isobars on a weather map are useful in predicting _____.

A. temperature
B. dew point
C. wind velocity
D. relative humidity

1061. In waters where the cardinal system is used you would expect to find danger _____.

A. lying to the south of an eastern quadrant buoy
B. lying to the south of a northern quadrant buoy
C. lying to the east of an eastern quadrant buoy
D. beneath or directly adjacent to the buoy

1062. What is the approximate geographic range of Horton Point Light, NY, if your height of eye is 40 feet (12.2 meters)? Refer to Reprints from the Light Lists and Coast Pilots.

A. 18.8 nm
B. 19.3 nm
C. 20.3 nm
D. 24.8 nm

1063. When adjusting a magnetic compass using the fore-and-aft permanent magnets, you should _____.

A. use the magnets one at a time, putting one in one side and then one on the opposite side, one step higher.
B. use the magnets in pairs, starting at the top, with trays at the highest point of travel
C. use the magnets in pairs, from the bottom up, with the trays at the lowest point of travel
D. fill all the trays with magnets, then remove them one by one until the deviation is removed

1064. The dew point temperature is _____.

A. always higher than the air temperature
B. always lower than the air temperature
C. equal to the difference between the wet and dry bulb temperatures
D. the temperature at which the air is saturated with water vapor

1065. You are in the Northern Hemisphere and a tropical wave is located 200 miles due east of your position. Where will the wave be located 12 hours later?

A. Farther away to the east
B. In the same position
C. Nearby to the east
D. Farther away to the west

1066. The slope of a warm front is about _____.

A. 1 mile vertically to 10 miles horizontally
B. 1 mile vertically to 50 miles horizontally
C. 1 mile vertically to 150 miles horizontally
D. 1 mile vertically to 500 miles horizontally

1067. The two most effective generating forces of surface ocean currents are _____.

A. temperature and salinity differences in the water
B. wind and density differences in the water
C. water depth and underwater topography
D. rotation of the Earth and continental interference

1068. A vessel sighting a northern right whale dead ahead should _____.

A. maintain course and speed
B. alter course to give a wide clearance
C. report the whale's position to the Canadian Coast Guard
D. All of the above

1069. What do the numbers on isobars indicate?

A. barometric pressure
B. temperature
C. rain in inches
D. wind speed

1070. Chart legends which indicate a conspicuous landmark are printed in _____.

A. underlined letters
B. capital letters
C. italics
D. boldface print

1071. A cardinal mark showing an uninterrupted quick-flashing white light indicates the deepest water in the area is on the _____.

A. north side of the mark
B. west side of the mark
C. east side of the mark
D. south side of the mark

1072. What is the approximate geographic range of Assateague Light, VA, if your height of eye is 52 feet (15.8 meters)? Refer to Reprints from the Light Lists and Coast Pilots.

A. 14.1 nm

B. 21.8 nm
C. 23.0 nm
D. 50.2 nm

1073. Chart legends printed in capital letters show that the associated landmark is _____.

A. inconspicuous
B. a radio transmitter
C. conspicuous
D. a government facility or station

1074. As the temperature for a given mass of air increases, the _____.

A. dew point increases
B. dew point decreases
C. relative humidity increases
D. relative humidity decreases

1075. The expression first magnitude is usually used to refer only to bodies of magnitude _____.

A. 1.5 and greater
B. 1.25 and greater
C. 1.0 and greater
D. 0.5 and greater

1076. Which is TRUE concerning the speed of fronts?

A. Cold fronts move faster than warm fronts.
B. Cold fronts move slower than warm fronts.
C. Cold fronts and warm fronts move with equal speed.
D. Cold fronts move slower at the northern end and faster at the southern end.

1077. A current will develop between areas of different density in ocean waters. If you face in the same direction the current is flowing, the water of _____.

A. high density will be on the left in the Northern Hemisphere
B. high density will be on the right in the Southern Hemisphere
C. low density will be on the left in the Northern Hemisphere
D. low density will be on the left in the Southern Hemisphere

1078. The description "Racon" beside an illustration on a chart would mean a _____.

A. radar conspicuous beacon
B. radar transponder beacon
C. radar calibration beacon
D. circular radiobeacon

1080. Information on northern right whales can be found in _____.

A. the Coast Pilot
B. HO 229
C. the Nautical Almanac
D. Ship's Medicine Chest and Medical Aid at Sea

1081. D026NG. On a voyage along the coast of France, you sight a buoy with the top marks as shown. You are required to steer _____.

A. west of the buoy
B. east of the buoy
C. south of the buoy
D. north of the buoy

1082. Northern right whales can be identified by _____.

A. whitish patches of skin on top of the head
B. V-shaped blow easily visible from ahead or behind
C. no dorsal fin on the back
D. All of the above

1083. Magnets are placed in horizontal trays in the compass binnacle to compensate for the _____.

A. induced magnetism in the vessel's horizontal soft iron
B. change in the magnetic field when the vessel inclines from vertical
C. permanent magnetism of the vessel
D. magnetic fields caused by electrical currents in the vicinity

1084. As the temperature of an air mass decreases, the _____.

A. absolute humidity decreases
B. relative humidity increases
C. specific humidity decreases
D. dew point rises

1085. A chart position enclosed by a semicircle is a(n) _____.

A. fix
B. estimated position

C. dead reckoning position
D. running fix

1086. When crossing a front isobars tend to _____.

A. change from smooth curves within the air mass to sharp bends at the front
B. change from sharp bends within the air mass to smooth curves at the front
C. pass smoothly across the front with no change
D. become closer together at the front and pass through in straight lines

1087. The velocity of a rotary tidal current will increase when the Moon is _____.

A. new
B. full
C. at perigee
D. All of the above

1088. Which statement about an estimated position is TRUE?

A. It is more reliable than a fix based on radar bearings.
B. It may be based on a single LOP or questionable data.
C. When a 3-LOP fix plots in a triangle, the center of the triangle is the estimated position.
D. It is usually based on soundings.

1089. You are enroute to assist vessel A. Vessel A is underway at 5.5 knots on course 033°T, and bears 248°T at 64 miles from you. What is the course to steer at 13 knots to intercept vessel A?

A. 262°
B. 269°
C. 276°
D. 281°

1090. D049NG. What weather conditions would you expect to find at position A?

A. Winds NW-W at 15 knots, partly cloudy, and slight seas
B. winds SW-S at 20 knots, heavy rain, and rough seas
C. Winds calm, light rain, and calm seas
D. Winds NE-E at 20 knots, heavy rain, and rough seas

1091. The cardinal mark topmark shown in illustration D024NG represents which quadrant?

A. Northern
B. Eastern
C. Southern
D. Western

1092. The wind velocity is higher in the dangerous semicircle of a tropical cyclone because of the _____.

A. extension of the low pressure ridge
B. wind circulation and forward motion of the storm
C. recurvature effect
D. direction of circulation and pressure gradient

1093. The Flinders bar on a magnetic compass compensates for the _____.

A. induced magnetism in vertical soft iron
B. induced magnetism in horizontal soft iron
C. permanent magnetism in ship's steel
D. vessel's inclination from the vertical

1094. A light, feathery deposit of ice caused by the sublimation of water vapor directly into the crystalline form, on objects whose temperatures are below freezing, is called _____.

A. dew
B. frost
C. glaze
D. snow

1096. With the passage of an occluded front the temperature _____.

A. rises rapidly
B. remains about the same
C. drops rapidly
D. depends on whether warm type or cold type occlusion

1097. The velocity of a rotary tidal current will be decreased when the Moon is _____.

A. at apogee
B. new
C. full
D. All of the above

1098. A chart position enclosed by a square is a(n) _____.

A. fix
B. estimated position
C. dead reckoning position
D. running fix

1099. You are enroute to assist vessel A. Vessel A is underway at 6 knots on course 133°T, and bears 343°T at 92 miles from you. What is the course to steer at 9 knots to intercept vessel A?

A. 356°
B. 003°
C. 022°
D. 038°

1101. D031NG. In the North Sea area, you sight a buoy showing an uninterrupted quick-flashing white light. Which of the four topmarks shown will this buoy be fitted with under the IALA Buoyage system?

A. A
B. B
C. C
D. D

1102. What is the approximate geographic range of Race Rock Light, NY, if your height of eye is 27 feet (8.2 meters)? Refer to Reprints from the Light Lists and Coast Pilots.

A. 9.9 nm
B. 14.3 nm
C. 15.7 nm
D. 17.4 nm

1103. The vertical component of the Earth's magnetic field causes induced magnetism in vertical soft iron. This changes with latitude. What corrects for this coefficient of the deviation?

A. The Flinders bar
B. The heeling magnet
C. Quadrantal soft iron spheres
D. Bar magnets in the binnacle

1104. Which condition(s) is(are) necessary for the formation of dew?

A. Clear skies
B. Calm air
C. Earth's surface cooler than the dew point of the air
D. All of the above

1105. The Light List shows that a navigational light has a nominal range of 22 miles and a height above water of 48 feet (14.6 meters). Your height of eye is 35 feet (10.7 meters) and the visibility is 20.0 miles. At what approximate range will you first sight the light?

A. 10.5 nm
B. 13.2 nm
C. 14.7 nm
D. 32.0 nm

1106. The legend/symbol which designates an occluded front is represented by a _____.

A. red line
B. purple line
C. blue line
D. dashed blue line

1107. A rotary current sets through all directions of the compass. The time it takes to complete one of these cycles is approximately _____.

A. 2-1/2 hours
B. 3-1/2 hours
C. 6-1/2 hours
D. 12-1/2 hours

1108. Preferred channel buoys indicate the preferred channel to transit by _____.

A. odd or even numbers
B. the color of their top band
C. the location of the buoy in the channel junction
D. the buoy's light rhythms

1110. To make sure of getting the full advantage of a favorable current, you should reach an entrance or strait at what time in relation to the predicted time of the favorable current?

A. At the predicted time
B. 30 minutes before the predicted time
C. One hour after the predicted time
D. 30 minutes before flood, one hour after an ebb

1111. D030NG. Black double-cone topmarks are the most important feature, by day, of cardinal marks. Which of the four topmarks shown indicates the best navigable water lies to the west of the buoy?

A. A
B. B
C. C
D. D

1112. Considering the general circulation of the atmosphere, the wind system between latitudes 30°N and 60°N is commonly called the _____.

A. prevailing westerlies
B. horse latitudes
C. tradewinds
D. subpolar low pressure belts

1113. A single vertical magnet placed underneath the compass in the binnacle is used to compensate for _____.

A. the horizontal component of the permanent magnetism
B. deviation caused by the vessel's inclination from the vertical
C. induced magnetism in the horizontal soft iron
D. induced magnetism in the vertical soft iron

1114. Mechanical lifting of air by the upslope slant of the terrain is called _____.

A. vertical lifting
B. convective lifting
C. advective lifting
D. topographic lifting

1115. Which light characteristic may be used on a special purpose mark?

A. Flashing
B. Occulting
C. Equal interval
D. Quick flashing

1116. When a cold air mass and a warm air mass meet, and there is no horizontal motion of either air mass, it is called a(n) _____.

A. cold front
B. occluded front
C. stationary front
D. warm front

1117. A rotary current sets through all directions of the compass. The time it takes to complete one of these cycles is approximately _____.

A. 3 hours
B. 6-1/2 hours
C. 12-1/2 hours
D. 25 hours

1118. When entering from seaward, a buoy displaying a single-flashing red light indicates _____.

A. a junction with the preferred channel to the left

B. the starboard side of the channel
C. a sharp turn in the channel to the right
D. a wreck to be left on the vessel's port side

1119. D051NG. The position labeled D was plotted because _____.

A. the vessel's speed changed at 1125
B. a dead reckoning position is plotted withen 30 minutes of a running fix
C. a dead reckoning position is plotted for each course change
D. All of the above

1121. The articulated light is superior to other types of buoys because _____.

A. the radar reflectors reflect better signals
B. fog horn signals travel farther to sea
C. it is equipped with strobe lights
D. it has a reduced watch circle

1122. A barometer showing falling pressure indicates the approach of a _____.

A. high pressure system
B. low pressure system
C. high dew point
D. low dew point

1123. What are the only magnetic compass correctors that correct for both permanent and induced effects of magnetism?

A. Quadrantal spheres
B. Heeling magnets
C. Athwartships magnets
D. Fore-and-aft magnets

1124. The region containing 3/4 of the mass of the atmosphere and the region to which are confined such phenomena as clouds, storms, precipitation and changing weather conditions is called _____.

A. stratosphere
B. troposphere
C. stratopause
D. tropopause

1125. The Light List shows that a navigational light has a nominal range of 19 miles and a height above water of 52 feet (15.8 meters). Your height of eye is 42 feet (12.8 meters) and the visibility is 10.0 miles. At what approximate range will you first sight the light?

A. 10.0 miles

B. 16.0 miles
C. 17.3 miles
D. 19.0 miles

1126. When a warm air mass is adjacent to a cold air mass, the separation line between the two is called a(n) _____.

A. front
B. isobar
C. isotherm
D. equipotential line

1127. In a river subject to tidal currents, the best time to dock a ship without the assistance of tugs is _____.

A. at slack water
B. at flood tide
C. when there is a following current
D. at high water

1130. During daylight savings time the meridian used for determining the time is located farther _____.

A. west in west longitude and east in east longitude
B. east in west longitude and west in east longitude
C. west
D. east

1131. On navigational aids, what does the light characteristic Fl(2+1) mean?

A. A flashing light combined with a fixed light of greater brightness
B. Light flashes combined in groups, with a different number of flashes in each group
C. A light showing groups of two or more flashes at regular intervals
D. A fixed light varied at regular intervals by groups of two or more flashes of greater brightness

1132. On charts of U.S. waters, a magenta marking is NOT used for marking a _____.

A. radiobeacon
B. 5-fathom curve
C. prohibited area
D. lighted buoy

1133. Which compensates for errors introduced when the vessel heels over?

A. The soft iron spheres on the arms of the binnacle

B. Magnets placed in trays inside the binnacle
C. A single vertical magnet beneath the compass
D. The Flinders bar

1134. The Earth's irregular heating is caused by _____.

A. the time of day
B. the seasons
C. geography
D. All of the above

1136. When a warm air mass overtakes and replaces a cold air mass, the contact surface is called a(n)_____.

A. warm front
B. cold front
C. line squall
D. occluded front

1137. When the declination of the Moon is 0°12.5'S, you can expect some tidal currents in Gulf Coast ports to _____.

A. become weak and variable
B. exceed the predicted velocities
C. become reversing currents
D. have either a double ebb or a double flood

1138. On approaching the English Channel on course 080°T, you note the symbol YBY near a charted buoy. You must pass _____.

A. northward of the buoy
B. southward of the buoy
C. eastward of the buoy
D. westward of the buoy

1140. What is the light characteristic of a lighted, preferred-channel buoy?

A. Group flashing
B. Composite group flashing
C. Interrupted quick flashing
D. Fixed and flashing

1141. What is characteristic of an isophase light?

A. 4 sec. flash, 2 sec. eclipse, 3 sec. flash, 2 sec. eclipse
B. 2 sec. flash, 5 sec. eclipse
C. 1 sec. flash, 1 sec. eclipse
D. 6 sec. flash, 3 sec. eclipse

1142. D049NG. Which weather conditions would you expect to find 100 miles East of position B?

A. Winds NW at 20.5 knots, steady warm temperature, high seas
B. Winds calm, falling temperature, clear skies, high seas
C. Winds WSW, steady temperature, scattered clouds, moderate seas
D. None of the above

1143. What is used to correct for both induced and permanent magnetism, and consequently must be readjusted with radical changes in latitude?

A. Flinders bar
B. Soft iron spheres
C. Fore-and-aft permanent magnets in their trays
D. Heeling magnet

1144. Freezing salt water spray should be anticipated when the air temperature drops below what temperature?

A. 32°F (0.0°C)
B. 28°F (−2.2°C)
C. 0°F (−17.8°C)
D. −40°F (−28.9°C)

1146. What is true about a front?

A. It is a boundary between two air masses.
B. There are temperature differences on opposite sides of a front.
C. There are abrupt pressure differences across a front.
D. All of the above

1147. To make sure of getting the full advantage of a favorable current, you should reach an entrance or strait at which time in relation to the predicted time of the favorable current?

A. One hour after
B. At the predicted time
C. 30 minutes before
D. 30 minutes before flood, one hour after an ebb

1148. The numeral in the center of a wind rose circle on a pilot chart indicates the _____.

A. total number of observations
B. average wind force on the Beaufort scale
C. average wind force in knots

D. percentage of calms

1149. D047NG. You are entering port and have been instructed to anchor, as your berth is not yet available. You are on a SW'ly heading, preparing to drop anchor, when you observe the range lights, as shown, on your starboard beam. You should _____.

A. ensure your ship will NOT block the channel or obstruct the range while at anchor
B. drop the anchor immediately as the range lights mark an area free of obstructions
C. drop the anchor immediately as a change in the position of the range lights will be an indication of dragging anchor
D. NOT drop the anchor until the lights are in line

1151. Buoys are marked with reflective material to assist in their detection by searchlight. Which statement is TRUE?

A. A safe-water buoy will display red and white vertical stripes of reflective material.
B. All reflective material is white because it is the most visible at night.
C. A special-purpose mark will display either red or green reflective material to agree with its shape.
D. A preferred-channel buoy displays either red or green reflective material to agree with the top band of color.

1152. When using GPS (Global Positioning System) you may expect your position to be accurate 95% of the time to within _____.

A. 1 to 3 meters
B. 10 to 20 meters
C. 50 to 100 meters
D. 100 to 200 meters

1153. Heeling error is defined as the change of deviation for a heel of _____.

A. 2° while the vessel is on an intercardinal heading
B. 1° while the vessel is on a compass heading of 000°
C. 2° and is constant on all headings
D. 1° while the vessel is on a compass heading of 180°

1154. The speed at which an ocean wave system advances is called _____.

A. wave length
B. ripple length
C. group velocity
D. wave velocity

1155. Which aid is NOT marked on a chart with a magenta circle?

A. Radar station
B. Aero light
C. Radiobeacon
D. Radar transponder beacon

1156. When cold air displaces warm air you have a(n) _____.

A. cold front
B. occluded front
C. stationary front
D. warm front

1157. How many slack tidal currents usually occur each day on the east coast of the United States?

A. One
B. Two
C. Three
D. Four

1158. What type of cloud is indicated by the number 5 in illustration D039NG?

A. Cirrostratus
B. Cirrocumulus
C. Altocumulus
D. Nimbostratus

1159. Two navigational hazards are located near to each other, but each is marked by an individual cardinal buoyage system. The buoys of one cardinal system may be identified from the other system by _____.

A. the differing light colors
B. one system having odd numbers while the other system has even numbers
C. one system using horizontal bands while the other system uses vertical stripes
D. the difference in the periods of the light

1160. What will be the velocity of the tidal current at 0.2 mile SSW of Clason Point, NY, at 1125 on 17 April 1983?

A. 0.5 knot
B. 0.8 knot
C. 1.1 knots
D. 1.9 knots

1161. What is characteristic of an occulting light?

A. 1 sec. flash, 2 sec. eclipse, 1 sec. flash, 5 sec. eclipse
B. 5 sec. flash, 5 sec. eclipse
C. 4 sec. flash, 2 sec. eclipse, 3 sec. flash, 2 sec. eclipse
D. 6 sec. flash, 6 sec. eclipse

1162. A line connecting all possible positions of your vessel at any given time is a _____.

A. longitude line
B. latitude line
C. line of position
D. fix

1163. The total magnetic effects which cause deviation of a vessel's compass can be broken down into a series of components which are referred to as _____.

A. divisional parts
B. coefficients
C. fractional parts
D. equations

1164. The largest waves (heaviest chop) will usually develop where the wind blows _____.

A. at right angles to the flow of the current
B. against the flow of the current
C. in the same direction as the flow of the current
D. over slack water

1165. Which statement concerning the chartlet in illustration D010NG is TRUE? (Soundings and heights are in meters.)

A. Maury lightship is visible for 17 miles.
B. There is a dangerous eddy southeast of Beito Island.
C. There is a 12-meter deep hole west of Beito Island and inside the 5-meter line.
D. The bottom to the south-southeast of the lightship is soft coral.

1166. A series of brief showers accompanied by strong, shifting winds may occur along or some distance ahead of a(n) _____.

A. upper front aloft
B. cyclone
C. occluded front
D. cold front

1167. The velocity of the current in large coastal harbors is _____.

A. unpredictable
B. predicted in Tidal Current Tables
C. generally constant
D. generally too weak to be of concern

1168. D039NG. Which type of cloud is indicated by the number 4?

A. Altocumulus
B. Cirrostratus
C. Cumulus
D. Altostratus

1169. D042NG. The symbols shown are used on radiofacsimile weather charts. The symbol indicated at letter O represents _____.

A. sandstorms
B. thunderstorms
C. snow
D. rain showers

1170. Which statement concerning illustration D010NG is correct? (Soundings and heights are in meters.)

A. Maury Lightship swings about her anchor on a circle with a 21-meter diameter.
B. The sunken wreck southwest of Beito Island shows the hull or superstructure above the sounding datum.
C. There is a 12-meter deep hole inside the 5-meter curve just west of Beito Island.
D. The position of the lightship is indicated by the center of the star on the symbol's mast.

1171. A light that has a light period shorter than its dark period is described as _____.

A. flashing
B. pulsating
C. occulting
D. alternating

1172. Which position on illustration D049NG would likely have stratus or stratocumulus clouds, occasional light drizzle, steady westerlies around 10 knots, and steady temperatures?

A. B
B. C
C. D
D. E

1173. When adjusting a magnetic compass for error, a deviation table should be made _____.

A. before correcting for any deviation
B. after correcting for variation
C. after adjusting the fore-and-aft and athwartships permanent magnets
D. before the quadrantal correctors are placed on the compass

1174. D013NG. Your vessel is enroute from Japan to Seattle and is located at position I on the weather map. You should experience which weather condition?

A. Clear skies with warm temperatures
B. Steady precipitation
C. Overcast skies with rising temperature
D. Thundershowers

1175. Solid green arrows on the main body of a pilot chart indicate _____.

A. prevailing wind directions
B. prevailing ocean current directions
C. probable surface current flow
D. shortest great circle routes

1176. After a cold front passes, the barometric pressure _____.

A. drops, and the temperature drops
B. drops, and the temperature rises
C. rises, and the temperature drops
D. rises, and the temperature rises

1178. The range of tide is the _____.

A. distance the tide moves out from the shore
B. difference between the heights of high and low tide
C. duration of time between the high and low tide
D. maximum depth of the water at high tide

1179. D039NG. Which type of cloud is indicated by the number 3?

A. Cirrocumulus
B. Altocumulus
C. Nimbostratus
D. Cumulus

1181. An occulting light is one in which _____.

A. the period of darkness exceeds the period of light
B. there is only a partial eclipse of the light
C. the periods of light and darkness are equal
D. the period of light exceeds the period of darkness

1182. Referring to illustration D049NG, which wind speed is reported in position C?

A. 3 knots
B. 10 knots
C. 20 knots
D. 30 knots

1183. The principal purpose of magnetic compass adjustment is to _____.

A. reduce the variation as much as possible
B. reduce the deviation as much as possible
C. reduce the magnetic dip as much as possible
D. allow the compass bowl to swing freely on its gimbals

1184. D009NG. Your position X is at LAT 35°S. Which winds are you experiencing?

A. Northeasterly
B. Northwesterly
C. Southeasterly
D. Southwesterly

1185. An orange and white buoy with a rectangle on it displays _____.

A. directions
B. distances
C. locations
D. All of the above

1186. As a cold front passes an observer, pressure _____.

A. drops and winds become variable
B. rises and winds become gusty
C. drops and winds become gusty
D. rises and winds become variable

1187. Off Barnegat, NJ, with the wind coming out of the east, the wind-driven current will be flowing approximately _____.

A. 016°
B. 106°
C. 254°
D. 286°

1190. D039NG. Which type of cloud is indicated by the number 2?

A. Cumulus
B. Cirrostratus
C. Stratocumulus
D. Altostratus

1191. You plot a fix using three lines of position and find they intersect in a triangle. The actual position of the vessel _____.

A. is outside of the triangle
B. may be anywhere in the triangle
C. may be inside or outside of the triangle
D. is the geometric center of the triangle

1192. You are enroute to assist vessel A. Vessel A is underway at 5.5 knots on course 033°T, and bears 284°T at 43 miles from you. What is the course to steer at 16 knots to intercept vessel A?

A. 284°
B. 303°
C. 329°
D. 342°

1193. If a ship is proceeding towards the magnetic equator, the uncorrected deviation due to permanent magnetism _____.

A. increases
B. remains the same
C. decreases
D. is unimportant and may be neglected

1194. D014NG. In the Northern Hemisphere, an observer at point II in the weather system should experience a wind shift from the _____.

A. southwest, clockwise to northwest
B. northeast, clockwise to west-southwest
C. northeast, counterclockwise to northwest
D. east, counterclockwise to south-southwest

1195. A position that is obtained by applying estimated current and wind to your vessel's course and speed is a(n) _____.

A. dead reckoning position
B. fix
C. estimated position
D. None of the above

1196. In the Northern Hemisphere, gusty winds shifting clockwise, a rapid drop in temperature, thunderstorms or rain squalls in summer (frequent rain/snow squalls in winter) then a rise in pressure followed by clearing skies, indicate the passage of a(n) _____.

A. warm front
B. tropical cyclone
C. anticyclone
D. cold front

1197. Off Fire Island, NY, with winds from the southwest, the average wind-driven current flows in a direction of _____.

A. 014°
B. 076°
C. 170°
D. 256°

1198. D042NG. The Illustration shows the symbols used on radiofacsimile weather charts. Which of these symbols indicates a dust storm?

A. I
B. H
C. O
D. P

1199. The Sailing Directions (Enroute) contain information on _____.

A. well-charted inner dangers
B. port facilities
C. coastal anchorages
D. offshore traffic separation schemes

1200. You want to transit Pollock Rip Channel, MA, on 6 April 1983. What is the period of time around the 0955 (ZD +5) slack in which the current does not exceed 0.3 knot?

A. 0911 to 0955
B. 0940 to 1010
C. 0955 to 1044
D. 0935 to 1017

1201. What is NOT true concerning color sectors of lights?

A. Color sectors are expressed in degrees from the light toward the vessel.
B. Color sectors may indicate dangerous waters.
C. Color sectors may indicate the best water across a shoal.
D. Color sectors may indicate a turning point in a channel.

1202. Referring to illustration D049NG, which wind speeds are reported at position A?

A. 10 knots
B. 15 knots
C. 20 knots
D. 25 knots

1203. If the compass heading and the magnetic heading are the same then _____.

A. the deviation has been offset by the variation
B. there is something wrong with the compass
C. the compass is being influenced by nearby metals
D. there is no deviation on that heading

1204. Which of the symbols in illustration D018NG designates a stationary front?

A. A
B. B
C. C
D. D

1205. How is the annual rate of change for magnetic variation shown on a pilot chart?

A. Gray lines on the uppermost inset chart
B. Red lines on the main body of the chart
C. In parenthesis on the lines of equal magnetic variation
D. Annual rate of change is not shown.

1206. Brief, violent showers frequently accompanied by thunder and lightning are usually associated with _____.

A. passage of a warm front
B. passage of a cold front
C. winds shifting counterclockwise in the Northern Hemisphere
D. stationary high pressure systems

1207. What will be the velocity of the tidal current at New London Harbor Entrance, CT, at 1615 EST (ZD +5) on 26 December 1983?

A. 0.2 knot
B. 0.4 knot
C. 0.7 knot
D. 0.9 knot

1208. D039NG. Which type of cloud is indicated by the number 1?

A. Cirrus
B. Altostratus
C. Altocumulus
D. Nimbostratus

1210. D047NG. You are inbound in a channel marked by a range. The range line is 309°T. You are steering 306°T and have the range in sight as shown. The range continues to open. What action should you take?

A. Alter course to the right to 309°T or more to bring the range in line.
B. Maintain course as it is normal for the range to open as you get close.
C. Alter course to the left until the range closes, then steer to the left of 306°T.
D. Alter course to the left to close the range, then alter course to 309°T.

1211. Red sectors of navigation lights warn mariners of _____.

A. floating debris
B. heavily trafficked areas
C. recently sunken vessels
D. shoals or nearby land

1213. If the magnetic heading is greater than the compass heading, the deviation is _____.

A. east
B. west
C. north
D. south

1215. Daylight savings time is a form of zone time that adopts the time_____.

A. two zones to the east
B. two zones to the west
C. one zone to the east
D. one zone to the west

1216. In the Northern Hemisphere, winds veering sharply to the west or northwest with increasing speed are indications that a _____.

A. cold front has passed
B. low pressure center is approaching
C. stationary front exists
D. high pressure center has passed

1217. What will be the velocity and direction of the tidal current at Old Ferry Point, NY, at 1340 EST (ZD +5) on 5 February 1983?

A. 0.8 knot at 060°T
B. 0.8 knot at 240°T
C. 1.0 knot at 076°T
D. 1.4 knots at 076°T

1218. If your position is LAT 25°N, LONG 35°W, what correction should be applied to an RDF bearing received from a transmitting station in LAT 30°N, LONG 40°W?

A. −1.3°
B. +1.3°
C. −2.1°
D. +2.1°

1220. Under the U.S. Aids to Navigation System, a lighted buoy with a spherical topmark marks _____.

A. the position of underwater cables
B. a hazard to navigation
C. the port side of the channel
D. safe water

1221. On a chart, the characteristic of the light on a lighthouse is shown as flashing white with a red sector. The red sector _____.

A. indicates the limits of the navigable channel
B. indicates a danger area
C. is used to identify the characteristics of the light
D. serves no significant purpose

1222. On entering from seaward, a starboard side daymark will_____.

A. show a fixed red light if lighted
B. show a Morse (A) white light
C. be square in shape
D. have an even number if numbered

1223. The difference between magnetic heading and compass heading is called _____.

A. variation
B. deviation
C. compass error
D. drift

1224. NIMA charts are adopting the metric system. In order to change a charted depth in meters to feet you may use the conversion table found _____.

A. in the Light List
B. in Bowditch Vol. II

C. on the chart
D. All of the above

1225. The term Western Rivers, when it refers to regulations requiring towing vessels to carry navigational-safety equipment, charts or maps, and publications, includes the _____ .

A. Mississippi River and its tributaries
B. Port Allen–Morgan City Alternate Rt.
C. Red River and the Old River
D. All of the above

1226. Cumulonimbus clouds are most likely to accompany a(n) _____.

A. high pressure system
B. cold front
C. warm front
D. occluded front

1227. What will be the direction and velocity of the tidal current at Provincetown Harbor, MA, at 1405 DST (ZD +4) on 5 May 1983?

A. 0.0 knot at 135°T
B. 0.2 knot at 135°T
C. 0.4 knot at 315°T
D. 0.6 knot at 315°T

1228. An electronic or electric device that indicates the rate of turn of a vessel defines a/an _____ .

A. magnetic compass
B. gyrocompass
C. swing meter
D. odometer

1229. The initial great circle course angle between LAT 23°00′S, LONG 42°00′W and LAT 34°00′S, LONG 18°00′E is 063.8°. What is the true course?

A. 063.8°T
B. 116.2°T
C. 243.8°T
D. 296.2°T

1231. Some lights used as aids to marine navigation have a red sector to indicate a danger area. How are the limits of a colored sector of light listed in the Light List?

A. Geographical positions outlining the area of the sector
B. True bearings as observed from the light toward a vessel

C. True bearings as observed from a vessel toward the light
D. Bearings given in the Light List are always magnetic

1232. Entering from seaward, triangular-shaped daymarks are used to mark _____.

A. the starboard side of the channel
B. the centerline of the channel
C. an obstruction where the preferred channel is to starboard
D. special purpose areas

1233. Deviation is the angle between the _____.

A. true meridian and the axis of the compass card
B. true meridian and the magnetic meridian
C. magnetic meridian and the axis of the compass card
D. axis of the compass card and the degaussing meridian

1234. Which information does the outer ring of a compass rose on a nautical chart provide?

A. Variation
B. True directions
C. Magnetic directions
D. Annual rate of variation change

1236. After the passage of a cold front the visibility_____.

A. does not change
B. improves rapidly
C. improves only slightly
D. becomes poor

1237. What will be the velocity of the tidal current at Port Royal, VA, at 1505 DST (ZD +4) on 4 June 1983?

A. 0.0 knot
B. 0.1 knot
C. 0.4 knot
D. 0.7 knot

1238. What will be the height of tide at Three Mile Harbor Entrance, Gardiners Bay, NY, at 0700 (ZD +5) on 14 Nov 1983?

A. 1.1 feet (0.3 meters)
B. 1.7 feet (0.5 meters)
C. 1.9 feet (0.6 meters)
D. 2.2 feet (0.7 meters)

1239. While taking weather observations, you determine that the wind is blowing from the northeast. You would record the wind direction in the weather log as _____.

A. 045°
B. 090°
C. 135°
D. 225°

1240. Weather information is available from _____.

A. commercial radio broadcasts
B. the Coast Guard on scheduled marine information broadcasts
C. VHF-FM continuous marine weather broadcasts provided by the National Weather Service
D. all of the above

1241. Which picture in illustration D034NG shows a fixed and flashing light?

A. A
B. B
C. C
D. D

1242. Daymarks marking the starboard side of the channel when going towards the sea are _____.

A. green squares
B. green triangles
C. red squares
D. red triangles

1243. Magnetic heading differs from compass heading by _____.

A. compass error
B. true heading
C. variation
D. deviation

1245. You can follow the approach of a dangerous cyclonic storm by inspecting _____.

A. a newspaper, a weather map, a weather fax, or a weather forecast
B. the National Weather Service Observing Handbook No.1, Marine Surface Observations
C. the Coast Pilot or Sailing Directions
D. the sky overhead

1246. What weather change accompanies the passage of a cold front in the Northern Hemisphere?

A. Wind shift from northeast clockwise to southwest
B. Steady dropping of barometric pressure
C. Steady precipitation, gradually increasing in intensity
D. A line of cumulonimbus clouds

1247. What is the predicted velocity of the tidal current 2 miles west of Southwest Ledge for 2330 DST (ZD +4) on 7 September 1983?

A. 1.3 knots
B. 1.6 knots
C. 1.9 knots
D. 2.2 knots

1248. On 6 July 1983, at 1520 DST (ZD +4) what will be the predicted height of tide at Newburgh, NY?

A. 2.1 feet
B. 1.7 feet
C. 1.2 feet
D. 0.6 foot

1249. What is the light characteristic of a lighted, preferred-channel buoy?

A. Fixed and flashing
B. Continuous quick
C. Isophase
D. Composite group-flashing

1250. Daylight savings time is a form of zone time that adopts the time _____.

A. one zone to the east
B. one zone to the west
C. two zones to the east
D. two zones to the west

1251. A List of Lights entry (L Fl) is a single flashing light which shows a long flash of not less than _____.

A. 1.0 second duration
B. 1.5 seconds duration
C. 2.0 seconds duration
D. 3.0 seconds duration

1252. Port side daymarks may be _____.

A. numbered
B. octagonal
C. black and white
D. of any shape

1253. The horizontal angle between the magnetic meridian and the north-south line of the magnetic compass is _____.

A. deviation
B. variation
C. compass error
D. dip

1254. Lighted white and orange buoys must show which color light?

A. Orange
B. White
C. Red
D. Alternating yellow and white

1255. The wind velocity is higher in the dangerous semicircle of a tropical cyclone because of the _____.

A. extension of the low pressure ridge
B. direction of circulation and pressure gradient
C. recurvature effect
D. the wind circulation and forward motion of the storm

1256. A cold front moving in from the northwest can produce _____.

A. thunderstorms, hail, and then rapid clearing
B. increasing cloud cover lasting for several days
C. lengthy wet weather
D. low ceilings with thick cirrus clouds

1257. What will be the velocity of the tidal current 1.0 mile southwest of Lewis Pt., RI, at 1501 EST (ZD +5) on 4 April 1983?

A. 0.7 knot
B. 1.4 knots
C. 1.6 knots
D. 1.9 knots

1258. You should log all barometer readings taken at sea _____.

A. regularly
B. at least once during each watch
C. more often under changeable weather conditions
D. all of the above

1259. General information on enroute weather and climate is found in _____.

A. the Sailing Directions and the Coast Pilot
B. a weather fax
C. the Local Notice to Mariners
D. the Light List

1260. On 26 February 1983, at 1750 EST (ZD +5) what will be the predicted height of tide at New Haven (city dock), CT?

A. –0.3 foot (–0.1 meter)
B. –0.6 foot (–0.2 meter)
C. 1.3 feet (0.4 meter)
D. 1.6 feet (0.5 meter)

1261. A light having characteristics which include color variations is defined as _____.

A. switching
B. alternating
C. oscillating
D. fluctuating

1262. A safe water daymark has what shape?

A. Triangular
B. Diamond
C. Circular
D. Octagonal

1263. The compass deviation changes as the vessel changes _____.

A. geographical position
B. speed
C. heading
D. longitude

1264. You take an RDF bearing on a vessel requiring assistance. The position of the vessel requiring assistance is LAT 30°00'N, LONG 140°00'W. Your position is LAT 25°00'N, LONG 135°00'W. What is the conversion angle you must apply to the RDF bearing to convert it to a Mercator course?

A. –1.0°
B. +1.0°
C. –1.3°
D. +1.3°

1265. When reporting wind direction, you should give the direction in _____.

A. true degrees
B. magnetic compass degrees
C. relative degrees
D. isobaric degrees

1266. A line of clouds, sharp changes in

wind direction, and squalls are most frequently associated with a(n) _____.

A. occluded front
B. warm front
C. cold front
D. warm sector

1267. What will be the velocity of the tidal current at Coxsackie, NY, at 0945 EST (ZD +5) on 11 March 1983?

A. 0.3 knot
B. 0.7 knot
C. 1.2 knots
D. 1.9 knots

1268. On a nautical chart, the inner ring of a compass rose indicates _____.

A. true directions
B. compass error
C. deviation
D. magnetic directions

1269. The Light List indicates that a light has a nominal range of 14 miles and is 42 feet (12.7 m) high. If the visibility is 16 miles and your height of eye is 20 feet (6.1 m), at which approximate distance will you sight the light?

A. 20.1 miles
B. 16.0 miles
C. 12.8 miles
D. 7.6 miles

1271. Which word indicates color variation in the characteristics of a light?

A. Opposing
B. Changing
C. Reversing
D. Alternating

1272. What are the colors of a midchannel daymark?

A. Black and red
B. Red and white
C. Green and red
D. Green and white

1273. Deviation changes with a change in _____.

A. latitude
B. heading
C. longitude
D. sea conditions

1274. D042NG. The Illustration shows the symbols used on radiofacsimile weather charts. Which of these symbols indicates a sandstorm?

A. H
B. O
C. P
D. K

1275. How is variation indicated on a small-scale nautical chart?

A. Magnetic compass table
B. Magnetic meridians
C. Isogonic lines
D. Variation is not indicated on small-scale nautical charts.

1276. Which weather change accompanies the passage of a cold front in the Northern Hemisphere?

A. Wind shift from NE, clockwise to SW
B. Steady dropping of barometric pressure
C. Steady precipitation, gradually increasing in intensity
D. A line of cumulonimbus clouds

1277. The velocity and direction of the tidal current at Port Morris, NY, at 1135 DST (ZD +4) on 13 May 1983 will be _____.

A. negligible at 220°T
B. 3.1 knots at 045°T
C. 1.2 knots at 220°T
D. 1.0 knot at 045°T

1278. The difference between the heights of low and high tide is the _____.

A. depth
B. distance
C. range
D. period

1279. For 3 November 1983, at 0830 EST (ZD +5) at Catskill, NY, what is the predicted height of tide?

A. +0.1 foot (+0.0 m)
B. –0.6 foot (–0.2 m)
C. +0.9 foot (+0.3 m)
D. –1.3 feet (–0.4 m)

1280. A current perpendicular to a vessel's track has the greatest effect on the vessel's course made good _____.

A. at high vessel speeds

B. at low vessel speeds
C. in shallow water
D. in deep water

1281. The time required for a lighted aid to complete a full cycle of light changes is listed in the Light List as the _____.

A. set
B. frequency
C. period
D. function

1282. Entering from sea, a daymark on the port side of the channel would be indicated on a chart by a _____.

A. red triangle with the letter R
B. white triangle with the letters RG
C. green square with the letter G
D. white square with the letters GR

1283. The error in a magnetic compass caused by the vessel's magnetism is called _____.

A. variation
B. deviation
C. compass error
D. bearing error

1284. The Sailing Directions (Enroute) contain information on all of the following EXCEPT _____.

A. ocean currents
B. outer dangers to navigation
C. tidal currents
D. major port anchorages

1285. You are enroute to assist vessel A. Vessel A is underway at 5.5 knots on course 033°T, and bears 248°T at 64 miles from you. What is the time to intercept if you make 13 knots?

A. 4h 55m
B. 4h 36m
C. 3h 59m
D. 3h 44m

1286. Which condition will occur after a cold front passes?

A. Temperature rises
B. Stratus clouds form
C. Pressure decreases
D. Humidity decreases

1287. What will be the velocity of the tidal

current 4.5 miles east of Smith Point, VA, at 0630 DST (ZD +4) on 6 May 1983?

A. 0.3 knot
B. 0.5 knot
C. 0.7 knot
D. 1.0 knot

1288. Your vessel will be docking at Chester, PA, during the evening of 22 April 1983. The chart shows a depth of 20 feet (6.1 meters) at the pier. What will be the depth of water available at 2310 EST (ZD +5)?

A. 19.2 feet (5.9 meters)
B. 20.8 feet (6.3 meters)
C. 24.7 feet (7.5 meters)
D. 25.8 feet (7.9 meters).

1290. In addition to the National Weather Service, what agency provides plain-language radio weather advisories for the coastal waters of the United States?

A. National Imagery and Mapping Agency
B. U.S. Hydrological Survey
C. U.S. Coast Guard
D. American Meteorological Service

1291. The period of a lighted aid to navigation refers to the _____.

A. date of construction or establishment
B. length of time between flashes of the light
C. time required for the longest flash of each cycle
D. time required for the light to complete each cycle

1292. A triangular daymark would be colored _____.

A. red
B. red and white
C. green
D. green and white

1293. Deviation is caused by _____.

A. changes in the earth's magnetic field
B. nearby magnetic land masses or mineral deposits
C. magnetic influence inherent to that particular vessel
D. the magnetic lines of force not coinciding with the lines of longitude

1295. The best estimate of the wind direc-

tion at sea level can be obtained from observing the direction of the _____.

A. cloud movement
B. vessel heading
C. waves
D. swells

1296. After a cold front passes the barometric pressure usually _____.

A. fluctuates
B. remains the same
C. remains the same, with clouds forming rapidly
D. rises, often quite rapidly, with clearing skies

1297. What will be the velocity of the tidal current at Bournedale, MA, at 1135 DST (ZD +4) on 3 May 1983?

A. 1.1 knots
B. 2.3 knots
C. 3.0 knots
D. 3.6 knots

1298. The vertex of a great circle track is in LONG 109°E. An eastbound vessel would cross the equator in LONG _____.

A. 161°W
B. 161°E
C. 19°E
D. 19°W

1299. What will be the time (ZD +5) of the second high tide at Weymouth Fore River Bridge, MA, on 12 November 1983?

A. 1639
B. 1643
C. 1647
D. 1650

1300. You are approaching a sea buoy which emits a racon signal. This signal is triggered by which type of radar?

A. 3 cm
B. 10 cm
C. Both 3 cm and 10 cm
D. Signal does not depend on radar type.

1301. The four standard light colors used for lighted aids to navigation are red, green, white, and _____.

A. purple
B. orange

C. blue
D. yellow

1302. What feature(s) of a daymark is (are) used to identify the beacon upon which it is mounted?

A. Color and shape
B. Size
C. Method of construction
D. Signal characteristics

1303. Compass deviation is caused by _____.

A. magnetism from the earth's magnetic field
B. misalignment of the compass
C. magnetism within the vessel
D. a dirty compass housing

1304. The distance to the nearest vertex from any point on a great circle track cannot exceed _____.

A. 5400 nautical miles
B. 5840 nautical miles
C. 6080 nautical miles
D. 10,800 nautical miles

1306. What type of clouds are associated with a cold front?

A. Altostratus and fracto-cumulus
B. Altostratus and cirrus
C. Cirrus and cirrostratus
D. Cumulus and cumulonimbus

1307. What will be the velocity of the tidal current southwest of Hunts Point, NY, at 0932 EST (ZD +5) on 16 March 1983?

A. 0.9 knot
B. 1.5 knots
C. 1.8 knots
D. 2.3 knots

1308. On a voyage from Capetown to London, the favorable ocean current off the coast of Africa is the _____.

A. Canary Current
B. Benguela Current
C. Agulhas Current
D. South Atlantic Current

1309. When recording the wind direction in the weather log, you would report the _____.

A. direction the wind is blowing toward
B. direction the wind is blowing from
C. duration of the maximum gust of wind
D. wind chill factor

1310. An urgent marine storm warning message would be broadcast on_____.

A. 2670 kHz
B. 156.80 MHz (VHF-FM Ch. 16)
C. 157.10 MHz (VHF-FM Ch. 22A)
D. None of the above

1311. What is the characteristic of a quick light?

A. Shows groups of 2 or more flashes at regular intervals
B. Durations of light and darkness are equal
C. Shows not less than 60 flashes per minute
D. Shows quick flashes for about 5 seconds followed by a 1 second dark period

1312. Which factor(s) determine(s) the charted visibility of a lighthouse's light in clear visibility?

A. Height and intensity of the light
B. Height of the light and the observer
C. Height of the observer and the intensity of the light
D. Height of the light only

1313. Variation in a compass is caused by _____.

A. worn gears in the compass housing
B. magnetism from the earth's magnetic field
C. magnetism within the vessel
D. lack of oil in the compass bearings

1314. D042NG. The Illustration shows the symbols used on radiofacsimile weather charts. Which of these symbols indicates hail?

A. N
B. H
C. Q
D. F

1315. What is a lighted safe water mark fitted with to aid in its identification?

A. Red and white retroreflective material
B. A sequential number
C. A spherical topmark
D. A red and white octagon

1316. When a warm air mass overtakes a cold air mass, the contact surface is called a _____.

A. line squall
B. water spout
C. cold front
D. warm front

1317. What will be the velocity and direction of the tidal current at Mobile River Entrance, AL, at 0915 CDT (ZD +5) on 13 May 1983?

A. 0.1 knot at 333°T
B. 0.3 knot at 333°T
C. 0.7 knot at 151°T
D. 1.8 knots at 025°T

1318. You are to sail from Elizabethport, N.J., on 17 November 1983 with a maximum draft of 27 feet. You will pass over an obstruction in the channel near Sandy Hook that has a depth of 25.5 feet. The steaming time from Elizabethport to the obstruction is 1h 50m. What is the earliest time (ZD +5) you can sail on 17 November and pass over the obstruction with 2 feet of clearance?

A. 59
B. 128
C. 159
D. 221

1319. The Sailing Directions (Planning Guide) contain information on all of the following EXCEPT _____.

A. coastal features
B. ocean basin environment
C. ocean routes
D. military operating areas

1320. You are enroute to Savannah, GA, from Recife, Brazil. There is a strong N'ly wind blowing. As you cross the axis of the Gulf Stream you would expect to encounter _____.

A. steeper waves, closer together
B. smoother seas and warmer water
C. cirrus clouds
D. long swells

1321. A lighthouse can be identified by its _____.

A. painted color
B. light color and phase characteristic

C. type of structure
D. All of the above

1322. What will be the velocity of the tidal current at Grant's Tomb, 123rd Street, NY, NY, at 1412 EST (ZD +5) on 22 March 1983?

A. 0.5 knot
B. 0.8 knot
C. 1.1 knots
D. 1.3 knots

1323. The magnetic compass error which changes with the geographical location of your vessel is called _____.

A. deviation
B. variation
C. compensation
D. differentiation

1324. When daylight savings time is kept, the time of tide and current calculations must be adjusted. One way of doing this is to _____.

A. add one hour to the times listed under the reference stations
B. subtract one hour from the time differences listed for the subordinate stations
C. apply no correction as the times in the reference stations are adjusted for daylight savings time
D. add 15° to the standard meridian when calculating the time difference

1325. D047NG. You change course entering port and steady up on a range with the lights in line. After a few minutes you observe the range lights as shown. You should alter your heading to the _____.

A. left, and when the range lights are in line again, resume your original heading
B. right, and when the range lights are in line again, steer to keep them dead ahead
C. left, and when the range lights are in line again, steer to keep them in line fine on the starboard bow
D. right, and when the range lights are in line again, steer to keep them in line fine on the port bow

1326. A cloud sequence of cirrus, cirrostratus, and altostratus clouds followed by rain usually signifies the approach of a(n) _____.

A. occluded front
B. stationary front

C. warm front
D. cold front

1328. What will be the velocity of the tidal current in Bolivar Roads, Texas, at a point 0.5 mile north of Ft. Point, on 23 November 1983 at 0330 CST (ZD +6)?

A. Slack water
B. 0.8 kt
C. 1.2 kts
D. 3.4 kts

1330. You are located within a stationary high pressure area. Your aneroid barometer is falling very slowly. This indicates a(n) _____.

A. wind shift of 180°
B. large increase in wind velocity
C. decrease in the intensity of the system
D. increase in the intensity of the system

1331. When trying to sight a lighthouse you notice a glare from a town in the background. The range at which the light may be sighted due to this glare is _____.

A. considerably reduced
B. increased slightly due to extra lighting
C. unchanged
D. increased if the light is red or green due to contrast with the glare

1332. The longitude of the upper vertex of a great circle track is 169°E. What is the longitude of the lower vertex?

A. 076°E
B. 169°W
C. 101°W
D. 011°W

1333. If a magnetic compass is not affected by any magnetic field other than the Earth's, which statement is TRUE?

A. Compass error and variation are equal.
B. Compass north will be true north.
C. Variation will equal deviation.
D. There will be no compass error.

1334. D042NG. The Illustration shows the symbols used on radiofacsimile weather charts. The symbol indicated at letter H represents _____.

A. ice
B. snow
C. rain
D. hail

1335. Plain language is usually used on marine weather _____.

A. forecasts
B. observations
C. analyses
D. reports

1336. On the approach of a warm front, barometric pressure usually _____.

A. falls
B. is steady
C. is uncertain
D. rises

1337. What will be the time of maximum flood current at Sagamore Bridge on the Cape Cod Canal during the morning of 6 December 1983 (ZD +5)?

A. 0708
B. 0712
C. 0716
D. 1020

1338. D039NG. Which type of cloud is indicated by the number 6?

A. Altocumulus
B. Stratocumulus
C. Altostratus
D. Cirrus

1340. The annual change in variation for an area can be found in_____.

A. the handbook for Magnetic Compass Adjustment, Pub 226
B. the center of the compass rose on a chart of the area
C. the compass deviation table
D. Variation does not change.

1341. The height of a light is measured from which reference plane?

A. Mean low water
B. Mean high water
C. Average water level
D. Geographical sea level

1342. An occluded front on a weather map is a colored _____.

A. blue line
B. purple line
C. dashed blue line
D. alternate red and blue line

1343. Variation is a compass error that you _____.

A. can correct by adjusting the compass card
B. can correct by adjusting the compensating magnets
C. can correct by changing the vessel's heading
D. cannot correct

1344. Which buoy symbol in illustration D032NG indicates a safe water mark?

A. D
B. C
C. B
D. A

1345. A large automated navigational buoy, such as those that have replaced some lightships, would be shown on a chart by which symbol in illustration D015NG?

A. D
B. C
C. B
D. A

1346. Cirrus clouds followed by cirrostratus then altostratus, stratus, and occasionally nimbostratus indicate the approach of a(n) _____.

A. cold front
B. warm front
C. tropical front
D. occluded front

1347. What will be the velocity of the tidal current south of Doubling Point, ME, at 1357 EST (ZD +5) on 3 April 1983?

A. 0.9 knot
B. 1.3 knots
C. 2.0 knots
D. 2.6 knots

1348. Vessels required to have an Automatic Radar Plotting Aid must have a device to indicate the _____.

A. speed of the vessel over the ground or through the water
B. distance to the next port
C. time of the next navigational satellite pass
D. None of the above

1349. D042NG. The symbols shown are used on radiofacsimile weather charts. Which of these symbols indicates a severe squall line?

A. F
B. I
C. G
D. H

1350. You are running parallel to the coast and plotting running fixes using bearings of the same object. You are making more speed than assumed for the running fix. In relation to the position indicated by the fix you will be _____.

A. closer to the coast
B. farther from the coast
C. on the track line ahead of the fix
D. on the track line behind the fix

1351. Luminous range is the _____.

A. maximum distance at which a light may be seen in clear weather
B. maximum distance at which a light may be seen under existing visibility conditions
C. maximum distance at which a light may be seen considering the height of the light and the height of the observer
D. average distance of visibility of the light

1352. Weather observations provided by each weather station include all of the following except _____.

A. temperature
B. visibility
C. predicted weather for the next 12 hours
D. barometric pressure and change in the last three hours

1353. The difference in degrees between true north and magnetic north is called _____.

A. variation
B. deviation
C. drift
D. compass error

1354. A ship is in longitude 54°00'W on a true course of 090°. The ship's clocks are on the proper time zone. At what longitude should the clocks be changed to maintain the proper zone time?

A. 45°00'W
B. 52°30'W

C. 60°00'W
D. 67°30'W

1356. The first indications a mariner will have of the approach of a warm front will be _____.

A. large cumulonimbus (thunderclouds) building up
B. high cirrus clouds gradually changing to cirrostratus and then to altostratus
C. fog caused by the warm air passing over the cooler water
D. low dark clouds accompanied by intermittent rain

1357. You will transit the Cape Cod Canal on 7 November 1983. If you arrive at the R R Bridge at 1655 EST (ZD +5), for what period of time during your transit will you have currents of not more than 0.5 knot?

A. 1631 to 1719
B. 1638 to 1655
C. 1648 to 1702
D. 1655 to 1709

1358. Despite weather predictions for continued good weather, a prudent mariner should be alert for all of the following, EXCEPT a sudden _____.

A. drop in barometric pressure
B. drop in temperature
C. wind shift
D. squall line

1359. The distance in longitude from the intersection of a great circle and the equator to the lower vertex is how many degrees of longitude?

A. 45°
B. 90°
C. 135°
D. 180°

1360. Which type of cloud is composed entirely of ice crystals and is found at very high altitudes?

A. Cumulus
B. Cirrus
C. Stratus
D. Nimbostratus

1361. The luminous range of a light takes into account the _____.

A. glare from background lighting

B. existing visibility conditions
C. elevation of the light
D. observer's height of eye

1362. Which type of cloud is indicated by the number 7 in illustration D039NG?

A. Cirrostratus
B. Altocumulus
C. Cumulus
D. Cumulonimbus

1363. True heading differs from magnetic heading by _____.

A. deviation
B. variation
C. compass error
D. northerly error

1364. The Sailing Directions are published in the Enroute format and the _____.

A. Coastal editions
B. World Port Index
C. Pilot format
D. Planning Guide

1366. Clouds appearing in the following order: cirrus, cirrostratus, altostratus, stratus, and nimbostratus usually indicate the approach of a(n) _____.

A. warm front
B. occluded front
C. medium front
D. cold front

1367. You want to transit Hell Gate, NY, on 23 July 1983. What is the period of time around the AM (ZD +4) slack before ebb when the current will be less than 0.3 knot?

A. 0939 to 0957
B. 0943 to 0953
C. 0844 to 0852
D. 0348 to 0356

1368. What area of the earth cannot be shown on a standard Mercator chart?

A. Equator
B. Areas including both N and S latitudes
C. North and South Poles
D. A narrow band along the central meridian.

1369. Which of the following is the most useful factor for predicting weather?

A. the present reading of the barometer
B. the previous reading of the barometer
C. the difference in the barometric readings within the past 24 hours
D. the rate and direction of change of barometric readings

1372. You are enroute to Jacksonville, FL, from San Juan, P.R. There is a fresh N'ly wind blowing. As you cross the axis of the Gulf Stream you would expect to encounter _____.

A. cirrus clouds
B. long swells
C. smoother seas and warmer water
D. steeper waves, closer together

1373. The reaction of a gyrocompass to an applied force is known as _____.

A. precession
B. earth rate
C. gyroscopic inertia
D. gravity effect

1374. On a working copy of a weather map, a warm front is represented by what color line?

A. Red
B. Blue
C. Alternating red and blue
D. Purple

1376. What is typical of warm front weather conditions?

A. An increase in pressure
B. A wind shift from SW to NW
C. Scattered cumulus clouds
D. Steady precipitation

1377. What is the velocity of the tidal current at the east end of Pollock Rip Channel at 1700 DST (ZD +4) on 23 July 1983?

A. 0.6 knot ebbing
B. 0.8 knot flooding
C. 1.5 knots flooding
D. 1.9 knots flooding

1378. The latitude of the upper vertex of a great circle is 36°N. What is the latitude of the lower vertex?

A. 36°N
B. 0°
C. 36°S

D. Cannot be determined from the information given

1379. The lubber's line on a magnetic compass indicates _____.

A. compass north
B. the direction of the vessel's head
C. magnetic north
D. a relative bearing taken with an azimuth circle

1380. Which type of weather could you expect soon after seeing hook or comma shaped cirrus clouds?

A. Rain with the approach of a warm front
B. Clearing with the approach of a cold front
C. Continuing fog and rain
D. The formation of a tropical depression

1381. Geographic range is the maximum distance at which a light may be seen under _____.

A. existing visibility conditions, limited only by the curvature of the Earth
B. perfect visibility conditions, limited only by the curvature of the Earth
C. existing visibility conditions, limited only by the intensity of the light
D. perfect visibility conditions, limited only by interference from background lighting

1382. The chart indicates the variation was 3°45'W in 1988, and the annual change is increasing 6'. If you use the chart in 1991 how much variation should you apply?

A. 3°27'W
B. 3°27'E
C. 4°03'W
D. 4°03'E

1383. The spin axis of a gyroscope tends to remain fixed in space in the direction in which it is started. How does this gyroscope become north seeking so that it can be used as a compass?

A. By mechanically or electrically applying forces to precess the gyroscope
B. By starting the compass with the spin axis in a north/south position
C. By taking advantage of the property of gyroscopic inertia
D. The rotation of the Earth (Earth rate) automatically aligns the gyroscope with north, except for speed errors

1384. D039NG. Which type of cloud is indicated by number 9?

A. Cumulus
B. Cumulonimbus
C. Altostratus
D. Stratocumulus

1385. What is the length of the lunar day?

A. 24h 50m 00s
B. 24h 00m 00s
C. 23h 56m 04s
D. 23h 03m 56s

1386. The FIRST indications a mariner will have of the approach of a warm front will be _____.

A. large cumulonimbus clouds building up
B. low dark clouds with intermittent rain
C. fog caused by the warm air passing over the cooler water
D. high clouds gradually followed by lower thicker clouds

1387. You will be entering the Mystic River in Connecticut. What is the current at the Highway Bridge at 1900 EST (ZD +5) on 24 January 1983?

A. 2.2 knots flooding
B. Slack water
C. Slight ebb
D. 2.5 knots ebbing

1388. If you observe a rapid fall of barometric pressure you should _____.

A. call the Coast Guard to verify the change
B. know the barometer is not working properly
C. contact the NWS or a local radio station
D. prepare for the onset of stormy weather with strong winds

1389. A boundary between two air masses is a(n) _____.

A. lapse rate
B. isobar
C. front
D. continent

1390. The fog most commonly encountered at sea is called _____.

A. conduction fog
B. radiation fog
C. frontal fog
D. advection fog

1391. When a light is first seen on the horizon it will disappear again if the height of eye is immediately lowered several feet. When the eye is raised to its former height the light will again be visible. This process is called _____.

A. checking a light
B. raising a light
C. obscuring a light
D. bobbing a light

1392. D039NG. Cumulonimbus clouds are indicated by which number?

A. 9
B. 7
C. 5
D. 3

1393. The directive force of a gyrocompass _____.

A. increases with latitude, being maximum at the geographic poles
B. decreases with latitude, being maximum at the geographic equator
C. is greatest when a vessel is near the Earth's magnetic equator
D. remains the same at all latitudes

1394. A great circle crosses the equator at 17°W. It will also cross the equator at what other longitude?

A. 173°W
B. 117°W
C. 163°E
D. 17°E

1395. The lunar day is _____.

A. longer than a solar day
B. shorter than a solar day
C. the same length as the solar day
D. longer than a solar day during the summer months and shorter in winter months

1396. On the approach of a warm front the barometric pressure usually _____.

A. falls
B. rises
C. is steady
D. is unreliable

1397. What will be the velocity of the tidal current at Port Jefferson Harbor Entrance, NY, at 1600 EST (ZD +5) on 23 December 1983?

A. 0.9 knot
B. 1.1 knots
C. 1.6 knots
D. 2.0 knots

1398. Nimbostratus clouds are indicated by what number in illustration D039NG?

A. 8
B. 6
C. 4
D. 1

1399. You are bound for Baltimore via Cape Henry on a 15 knot ship. If the flood at Chesapeake Bay entrance begins at 1800 EST (ZD +5), at what time would you depart from the Chesapeake Bay entrance to have the most favorable current?

A. 1700 hours
B. 1800 hours
C. 1900 hours
D. 2030 hours

1400. Which type of cloud is among the most dependable for giving an indication of an approaching weather system?

A. Cumulus
B. Altostratus
C. Cumulostratus
D. Nimbus

1401. The maximum distance at which a light may be seen under existing visibility conditions is called _____.

A. nominal range
B. luminous range
C. charted range
D. geographic range

1402. As a vessel changes course to starboard, the compass card in a magnetic compass _____.

A. first turns to starboard then counterclockwise to port
B. also turns to starboard
C. turns counterclockwise to port
D. remains aligned with compass north

1403. Which statement about the gyrocompass is FALSE?

A. Its accuracy remains the same at all latitudes.
B. It seeks the true meridian.
C. It can be used near the Earth's magnetic poles.
D. If an error exists, it is the same on all headings.

1404. A great circle will intersect the equator at how many degrees of longitude apart?

A. 0°
B. 45°
C. 90°
D. 180°

1406. What will act to dissipate fog?

A. Upwelling cold water
B. Advection of warm air over a colder surface
C. Rain that is warmer than air
D. Downslope motion of an air mass along a coast

1408. An occluded front is caused by a(n) _____.

A. low pressure area
B. high pressure area
C. area of calm air
D. cold front overtaking a warm front

1410. A white buoy marked with an orange rectangle indicates _____.

A. a fish net area
B. general information
C. an anchorage
D. midchannel

1411. The nominal range of a light may be accurately defined as the maximum distance at which a light may be seen _____.

A. under existing visibility conditions
B. under perfect visibility
C. with ten miles visibility
D. with fifteen miles visibility

1412. The distance between the surface of the water and the tidal datum is the _____.

A. actual water depth
B. range of tide
C. charted depth
D. height of tide

1413. The gyrocompass error resulting from your vessel's movement in OTHER than an east-west direction is called _____.

A. damping error
B. ballistic deflection
C. quadrantal error
D. speed error

1414. You are planning a voyage from New York to Norway via the English Channel. Which publication contains information on the dangers to navigation in the English Channel?

A. Channel Pilot's Guide
B. World Port Index
C. Coast Pilot
D. Sailing Directions (Enroute)

1415. Planetary aberration is due, in part, to _____.

A. refraction of light as it enters the Earth's atmosphere
B. rotation of the Earth on its axis
C. the body's orbital motion during the time required for its light to reach Earth
D. a false horizon

1416. Radiation fog _____.

A. always forms over water
B. is formed by a temperature inversion
C. is thinnest at the surface
D. dissipates during the evening

1417. Determine the first time after 1200 EST (ZD +5) when the velocity of the current will be 0.5 knot on 18 November 1983, at Marcus Hook, PA.

A. 1221
B. 1226
C. 1239
D. 1312

1418. Static on your AM radio may be _____.

A. an indication of nearby thunderstorm activity
B. an indication of clearing weather
C. of no meteorological significance
D. a sign of strong winds

1419. The MOST important feature of the material used for making the binnacle of a standard magnetic compass is that it is _____.

A. nonmagnetic
B. weatherproof
C. corrosion resistant
D. capable of being permanently affixed to the vessel

1420. D051NG. The position labeled E was plotted because _____.

A. the vessel's position was fixed at 1145
B. a dead reckoning position is plotted within a half-hour of each course change
C. the position is a running fix
D. a dead reckoning position is plotted for each speed change

1421. What is the approximate geographic visibility of an object with a height above the water of 70 feet, for an observer with a height of eye of 65 feet?

A. 16.8 nm
B. 19.0 nm
C. 20.6 nm
D. 22.4 nm

1423. Quadrantal error in a gyrocompass has its GREATEST effect _____.

A. in high latitudes
B. near the equator
C. on north or south headings
D. on intercardinal headings

1424. Except for N-S courses, and E-W courses on the equator, a great circle track between two points, when compared to a rhumb line track between the same two points, will _____.

A. always be nearer to the equator
B. always be nearer to the elevated pole
C. be nearer to the pole in the Northern Hemisphere and nearer to the equator in the Southern Hemisphere
D. be nearer to the pole or the equator depending on the latitudes of the arrival and departure positions

1426. Fog is most commonly associated with a(n) _____.

A. warm front at night
B. low pressure area
C. anticyclone
D. cold front in the spring

1427. Determine the duration of the first PM slack water on 3 March 1983, east of the Statue of Liberty, when the current is less than 0.1 knot?

A. 10 minutes
B. 13 minutes
C. 16 minutes
D. 19 minutes

1428. The speed of sound in water is approximately _____.

A. 1.5 times its speed in air
B. 2.5 times its speed in air
C. 3.5 times its speed in air
D. 4.5 times its speed in air

1430. The Light List indicates that a light has a nominal range of 14 miles and is 42 feet high (12.8 meters). If the visibility is 6 miles and your height of eye is 20 feet (6.1 meters), at what approximate distance will you sight the light?

A. 20.1 miles
B. 10.0 miles
C. 7.6 miles
D. 6.0 miles

1431. A lighthouse is 120 feet (36.6 meters) high and the light has a nominal range of 18 miles. Your height of eye is 42 feet (12.8). If the visibility is 11 miles, approximately how far off the light will you be when the light becomes visible?

A. 12.5 miles
B. 16.0 miles
C. 19.0 miles
D. 23.5 miles

1432. What benefit is a weather bulletin to a mariner?

A. It provides a legal reason to cancel a projected voyage.
B. It allows the mariner to make long term weather forecasts.
C. It is of little benefit since the weather changes frequently and rapidly.
D. It gives the mariner time to prepare for weather changes.

1433. A system of reservoirs and connecting tubes in a gyrocompass is called a _____.

A. spider element
B. mercury ballistic

C. gyrotron
D. rotor

1434. What is NOT a characteristic of cardinal marks?

A. Yellow and black bands
B. White lights
C. Square or triangular topmarks
D. Directional orientation to a hazard

1436. Fog forms when the air_____.

A. is 50% water saturated
B. is 90% water saturated
C. temperature is greater than the dew point temperature
D. temperature is equal to or below the dew point temperature

1437. Determine the time after 0300 CST (ZD +6) when the velocity of the tidal current will be 0.5 knot on 16 April 1983, at Port Arthur Canal Entrance, TX.

A. 0436
B. 0507
C. 0538
D. 0554

1438. In the Northern Hemisphere you are caught in the dangerous semicircle of a storm with plenty of sea room available. The best course of action is to bring the wind on the _____.

A. port quarter and make as much headway as possible
B. starboard quarter and make as much headway as possible
C. starboard bow and make as much headway as possible
D. port bow and make as much headway as possible

1439. D042NG. The symbols shown are used on radiofacsimile weather charts. The symbol indicated at letter G represents a _____.

A. weather boundary
B. thunderstorm
C. widespread sandstorm
D. severe, line squall

1440. A mercurial barometer at sea is subject to rapid variations in height (pumping) due to the pitch and roll of the vessel. To avoid this error, measurements of atmo-

spheric pressure at sea are usually measured with a(n) _____.

A. syphon barometer
B. cistern barometer
C. aneroid barometer
D. fortin barometer

1441. Your height of eye is 40 feet (12.2 meters). What is the approximate geographical distance at which Ambrose Light, NY, could be visible? Refer to Reprints from the Light Lists and Coast Pilots.

A. 18.3 nm
B. 19.5 nm
C. 21.0 nm
D. 22.8 nm

1442. A great circle track provides the maximum saving in distance on _____.

A. easterly courses in high latitudes
B. southerly courses in high latitudes
C. westerly courses in low latitudes
D. easterly courses in low latitudes that cross the equator

1443. At the master gyrocompass, the compass card is attached to the _____.

A. spider element
B. sensitive element
C. link arm
D. pickup transformer

1444. D039NG. Stratocumulus clouds are indicated by which number?

A. 1
B. 4
C. 6
D. 7

1446. When compared to air temperature, which factor is most useful in predicting fog?

A. Vapor pressure
B. Dew point
C. Barometric pressure
D. Absolute humidity

1447. What will be the velocity of the tidal current 6 miles south of Shoal Point, NY, at 1850 DST (ZD +4) on 9 July 1983?

A. –0.2 knot
B. 0.2 knot
C. 1.2 knots
D. 1.4 knots

1448. Spring tides occur when the _____.

A. Moon is in its first quarter or third quarter phase
B. Sun and Moon are in quadrature
C. Moon's declination is maximum and opposite to that of the Sun
D. Moon is new or full

1449. The presence of stratus clouds and a dying wind will usually result in _____.

A. heavy rain
B. heavy snow
C. thick fog
D. clearing skies

1450. The distance between the surface of the water and the tidal datum is the _____ .

A. range of tide
B. charted depth
C. height of tide
D. actual water depth

1452. When is the rhumb line distance the same as the great circle distance?

A. Course 090°T in high latitudes
B. Course 180°T when you cross the equator
C. Course 045°T in low latitudes
D. The rhumb line distance is always longer than the great circle distance.

1453. Indications of the master gyrocompass are sent to remote repeaters by the _____.

A. follow-up system
B. transmitter
C. phantom element
D. azimuth motor

1454. Atmospheric pressure may be measured with a(n) _____.

A. barograph
B. aneroid barometer
C. mercurial barometer
D. all of the above

1456. The fog produced by warm moist air passing over a cold surface is called _____.

A. conduction fog
B. radiation fog
C. frontal fog
D. advection fog

1457. What is the period of time from around 1008 DST (ZD +4) at Canapitsit Channel, MA, on 7 August 1983, in which the current does not exceed 0.4 knot?

A. 0945 to 1031
B. 0950 to 1026
C. 0955 to 1021
D. 1000 to 1024

1458. When navigating coastwise and hurricane warnings are received, you should _____.

A. call the Coast Guard to request further information
B. call the NWS for further information
C. just begin to react and make plans
D. have battened down and be heading for the nearest port of refuge

1459. In a tropical cyclone, in the Northern Hemisphere, a vessel hove to with the wind shifting counterclockwise is _____.

A. ahead of the storm center
B. in the dangerous semicircle
C. in the navigable semicircle
D. directly in the approach path of the storm

1460. What is the major advantage of a rhumb line track?

A. The vessel can steam on a constant heading (disregarding wind, current, etc.).
B. The rhumb line is the shortest distance between the arrival and departure points.
C. It is easily plotted on a gnomonic chart for comparison with a great circle course.
D. It approximates a great circle on east-west courses in high latitudes.

1461. The chart indicates the variation was 3°45'W in 1988, and the annual change is decreasing 6'. If you use the chart in 1991 how much variation should you apply?

A. 3°27'W
B. 3°27'E
C. 4°03'W
D. 4°03'E

1463. If the gyrocompass error is east, what describes the error and the correction to be made to gyrocompass headings to obtain true headings?

A. The readings are too low (small numeri-

cally) and the amount of the error must be added to the compass to obtain true
B. The readings are too low and the amount of the error must be subtracted from the compass to obtain true
C. The readings are too high (large numerically) and the amount of the error must be added to the compass to obtain true
D. The readings are too high and the amount of the error must be subtracted from the compass to obtain true

1464. A line of position derived from a loran reading is a section of a(n) _____.

A. straight line
B. arc
C. parabola
D. hyperbola

1466. Advection fog is most commonly caused by _____.

A. air being warmed above the dew point
B. saturation of cold air by rain
C. a rapid cooling of the air near the surface of the Earth at night
D. warm moist air being blown over a colder surface

1467. Determine the time after 0730 EST (ZD +5) when the velocity of the current will be 2.1 knots on 26 March 1983, at Fort Pulaski, GA.

A. 0802
B. 0812
C. 0821
D. 0840

1468. What is NOT an advantage of the rhumb line track over a great circle track?

A. Easily plotted on a Mercator chart
B. Negligible increase in distance on east-west courses near the equator
C. Does not require constant course changes
D. Plots as a straight line on Lambert conformal charts

1469. The charted channel depth at Eastport, ME, is 28 feet. You are drawing 31.5 feet and wish 2 feet clearance under the keel. What is the earliest time after 1700 (ZD +4) on 6 September 1983 that you can enter the channel?

A. 1805
B. 1840

C. 1925
D. 2000

1470. D042NG. The Illustration shows the symbols used on radiofacsimile weather charts. Which symbol indicates a hurricane?

A. M
B. I
C. L
D. K

1471. A mountain peak charted at 700 feet breaks the horizon, and your height of eye is 12 feet. What is your approximate distance off (choose closest answer)?

A. 34.7 nm
B. 40.3 nm
C. 55.3 nm
D. 61.6 nm

1473. Which statement about gyrocompass error is TRUE?

A. The amount of the error and the sign will generally be the same on all headings.
B. The sign (E or W) of the error will change with different headings of the ship.
C. Any error will remain constant unless the compass is stopped and restarted.
D. Any error shown by a gyro repeater will be the same as the error of the master compass.

1475. Which type of cloud is the classic thunderhead?

A. Cumulonimbus
B. Stratus
C. Cirrus
D. Altostratus

1476. When warm moist air blows over a colder surface and is cooled below its dew point, the result is _____.

A. radiation fog
B. ice fog
C. advection fog
D. frost smoke

1477. The wind in the vicinity of Nantucket Shoals Light has been southerly at an average speed of 23 knots. The predicted set and drift of the rotary tidal current are 225° at 0.8 knot. What are the set and drift of the current you can expect at Nantucket Shoals Light?

A. 025° at 1.8 knots
B. 218° at 1.1 knots
C. 235° at 0.5 knot
D. 247° at 0.7 knot

1479. A microbarograph is a precision instrument that provides a _____.

A. charted record of atmospheric temperature over time
B. charted record of atmospheric pressure over time
C. graphic record of combustible gases measured in an atmosphere
D. graphic record of vapor pressure from a flammable/combustible liquid

1480. What is the definition of height of tide?

A. The vertical difference between the heights of low and high water
B. The vertical difference between a datum plane and the ocean bottom
C. The vertical distance from the surface of the water to the ocean floor
D. The vertical distance from the tidal datum to the level of the water at any time

1481. What is the approximate geographic range of Fenwick Island Light, Delaware, if your height of eye is 42 feet (12.8 meters)? Refer to Reprints from the Light Lists and Coast Pilots.

A. 18.3 nm
B. 15.4 nm
C. 13.1 nm
D. 10.3 nm

1482. Which statement concerning current is TRUE?

A. Current can be determined by measuring the direction and distance between simultaneous EP and DR positions.
B. The drift of the current should be averaged out on a one-hour basis.
C. After the current is determined, it should not be used for further plotting because it is an unknown variable.
D. The distance between a simultaneous DR position and fix is equal to the drift of the current.

1483. The most accurate method of determining gyrocompass error while underway is by _____.

A. comparing the gyro azimuth of a celestial body with the computed azimuth of the body
B. comparing the gyro heading with the magnetic compass heading
C. determining from the chart the course made good between celestial fixes
D. It cannot be determined accurately at sea due to drift of unknown currents.

1484. You should plot your dead-reckoning position at _____.

A. every fix or running fix
B. every course change
C. every speed change
D. All of the above are correct.

1485. The safest and most prudent procedure to follow while navigating in the vicinity of a tropical cyclone is to _____.

A. take positive steps to avoid it if possible
B. batten down and prepare to ride out the storm
C. continue to navigate farther from the coast
D. always navigate towards the coast by the most direct route

1486. Which condition would most likely result in fog?

A. Warm moist air blowing over cold water
B. Airborne dust particles
C. Warm moist air blowing over warm water
D. Dew point falling below the air temperature

1487. At the approaches to Savannah, GA, with the wind coming out of the west, the wind-driven current will be flowing approximately _____.

A. 080°
B. 100°
C. 260°
D. 280°

1488. What defines a great circle?

A. A curved line drawn on a Mercator Chart
B. A course line that inscribes a loxodromic curve
C. The shortest distance between any two points on the earth
D. The smallest circle that can be drawn on the face of a sphere

1489. Cumulonimbus clouds can produce _____.

A. dense fog and high humidity
B. gusty winds, thunder, rain or hail, and lightning
C. clear skies with the approach of a cold front
D. a rapid drop in barometric pressure followed by darkness

1490. In the IALA Buoyage System, preferred-channel-to-port or preferred-channel-to-starboard buoys, when fitted with lights, will show a _____.

A. quick-flashing light
B. long-flashing light
C. composite group-flashing (2 + 1) light
D. group flashing

1492. You are planning a voyage from San Francisco to Japan. Which publication contains information on the ocean routes?

A. Coast Pilot
B. Sailing Directions (Planning Guide)
C. Sailing Directions (Enroute)
D. World Port Index

1493. You are running parallel to the coast and estimate that the current is against you. In plotting a running fix using bearings from the same object on the coast, the greatest safety margin from inshore dangers will result if what speed is used to determine the fix?

A. Minimum speed estimate
B. Maximum speed estimate
C. Average speed estimate
D. A running fix should not be used under these conditions.

1494. D039NG. Cirrocumulus clouds are indicated by which number?

A. 7
B. 5
C. 3
D. 1

1495. A great circle crosses the equator at 157°W. It will also cross the equator at what other longitude?

A. 157°E
B. 57°E
C. 23°E
D. 57°W

1496. In a microbarograph, the pen should be checked and the inkwell filled _____.

A. each time the chart is changed
B. once per month
C. once per week
D. daily

1497. When drawing a weather map and an isobar crosses a front, the isobar is drawn _____.

A. perpendicular to the front
B. kinked and pointing away from the low
C. kinked and pointing towards the low
D. kinked and pointing towards the high for a warm front only

1498. A true bearing of a charted object, when plotted on a chart, will establish a _____.

A. fix
B. line of position
C. relative bearing
D. range

1499. You are scanning the radar screen for a buoy fitted with racon. How should this signal appear on the PPI display?

A. Starting with a dash and extending radially outward from the target
B. As a broken line from center of PPI to the target
C. Starting with a dot and extending radially inward from the target
D. Starting with a dash and extending to the right of the target

1501. What is the distance from the bottom of a wave trough to the top of a wave crest?

A. Wave length
B. Wave height
C. Wave breadth
D. Wave depth

1502. You are running parallel to the coast and take a running fix using bearings of the same object. If you are making less speed than used for the running fix, in relation to the position indicated by the fix, you will be _____.

A. closer to the coast
B. farther from the coast
C. on the track line ahead of the fix
D. on the track line behind the fix

1503. A radar range to a small, charted object such as a light will provide a line of position in which form?

A. Straight line
B. Arc
C. Parabola
D. Hyperbola

1504. The time meridian used when computing the height of tide for Pensacola Bay, FL, is _____.

A. 75°00′W
B. 82°30′W
C. 90°00′W
D. 97°30′W

1505. At 0000 you fix your position and change course to 090°T. At 0030 you again fix your position and it is 0.5 mile east of your DR. Which statement is TRUE?

A. The current is easterly.
B. The drift is 0.5 knot.
C. You should alter course to the right to regain the track line.
D. The current is perpendicular to your track line.

1506. You are steaming southward along the west coast of the United States when you sight a buoy showing a flashing green light. How should you pass this buoy?

A. Leave it to your port.
B. Leave it to your starboard.
C. Pass it close aboard on either side.
D. Pass it on either side but well clear of it.

1507. When you are steering on a pair of range lights and find the upper light is above the lower light you should _____.

A. come right
B. come left
C. wait until the lights are no longer in a vertical line
D. continue on the present course

1508. A line of position is _____.

A. a line connecting two charted objects
B. a line on some point of which the vessel may be presumed to be located
C. the position of your vessel
D. not used in a running fix

1509. Your facsimile prognostic chart indicates that you will cross the cold front of a low pressure system in about 24 hours. You should _____.

A. expect to see cirrus clouds followed by altostratus and nimbostratus clouds
B. alter course to remain in the navigable semicircle
C. prepare for gusty winds, thunderstorms, and a sudden wind shift
D. expect clear weather, with steady winds and pressure, until the front passes

1510. During daylight savings time the meridian used for determining the time is located farther _____.

A. west
B. east
C. east in west longitude and west in east longitude
D. west in west longitude and east in east longitude

1511. A vessel encountering hurricane or typhoon conditions is required to transmit reports to the closest meteorological service every _____.

A. 8 hours
B. 6 hours
C. 3 hours
D. hour

1512. You are plotting a running fix. The LOP to be run forward is an arc from a radar range; what technique should be used?

A. The arc should be converted into a straight line using offsets and then run forward.
B. An arc should never be run forward.
C. The position of the object observed should be advanced to the new time and a new arc swung using the radius of the old arc.
D. The distance between LOP's should be added to the radar range and a new arc swung.

1513. Scales on aneroid barometers are usually graduated in inches of mercury in the general range of _____.

A. 26 to 29 inches
B. 28 to 31 inches
C. 30 to 33 inches
D. 32 to 35 inches

1514. The compass error of a magnetic compass that has no deviation is _____.

A. zero
B. equal to variation
C. eliminated by adjusting the compass
D. constant at any geographical location

1515. An aneroid barometer on a boat should always be _____.

A. located in an air-conditioned area
B. mounted in the passenger compartment
C. protected by a collision bulkhead
D. permanently mounted

1516. Which correction(s) must be applied to an aneroid barometer?

A. instrument error and height error
B. instrument error only
C. height error only
D. instrument error and latitude correction

1518. Which publication requires infrequent corrections?

A. List of Lights
B. Coast Pilot
C. Sailing Directions (Planning Guide)
D. Radio Navigational Aids

1520. The diurnal inequality of the tides is caused by _____.

A. the declination of the Moon
B. changing weather conditions
C. the Moon being at apogee
D. the Moon being at perigee

1521. To avoid error you should read the scale of an aneroid barometer with your eye placed _____.

A. to the right of the pointer
B. to the left of the pointer
C. directly in front of the pointer
D. slightly above the meniscus

1522. The pressure-sensitive element of an aneroid barometer is called a _____.

A. pressure bellows
B. sylphon cell
C. column of mercury
D. constant pressure capsule

1523. Which is a characteristic of the weather preceding an approaching warm front?

A. Gusty winds
B. Steadily falling barometric pressure

C. Decreasing relative humidity
D. Clearing skies

1527. Your vessel is on course 270°T, speed 10 knots. The apparent wind is from 10° off the port bow, speed 30 knots. From which direction is the true wind?

A. 345°T
B. 255°T
C. 165°T
D. 075°T

1529. Widely spaced isobars on a weather map indicate _____.

A. high winds
B. gentle breezes
C. ice, snow or frozen rain
D. probability of tornados

1530. In shallow water, waves that are too steep to be stable, causing the crests to move forward faster than the rest of the wave, are called _____.

A. rollers
B. breakers
C. white caps
D. surfers

1532. D051NG. The position labeled E was plotted because _____.

A. a dead-reckoning position is plotted for each speed change
B. a dead-reckoning position is plotted within a half-hour of each course change
C. the position is a running fix
D. the vessel's position was fixed at 1145

1533. Lighted information markers show _____.

A. white lights
B. green lights
C. yellow lights
D. red lights

1535. When observing a rapid rise in barometric pressure, you may expect _____.

A. clear weather with no wind, but the possibility of rain or snow within 24 hours
B. deteriorating weather with rain or snow
C. heavy rain or severe thundershowers
D. clearing weather, possibly accompanied by high winds

1536. What will NOT induce errors into a Doppler sonar log?

A. Increased draft
B. Pitch
C. Roll
D. Change in trim

1538. The winds of the roaring forties are strongest near _____.

A. 40°N
B. 50°N
C. 40°S
D. 50°S

1539. You are steaming in the open ocean of the North Pacific between the Aleutian Chain and Hawaii. A warning broadcast indicates that an earthquake has occurred in the Aleutians and has generated a tsunami that is predicted to hit Hawaii. What action is necessary for the ship's safety?

A. Calculate the tsunami's ETA at your position and turn to a course that will head into the tsunami.
B. Securely stow all loose gear, check deck lashings, and prepare for extreme rolls.
C. No special action as tsunamis are inconspicuous in the open ocean
D. Prepare for sudden, high-velocity wind gusts from rapidly changing directions.

1540. You are sailing south on the Intracoastal Waterway (ICW) when you sight a green can buoy with a yellow square painted on it. Which of the following is TRUE?

A. You should pass the buoy close aboard on either side.
B. The buoy marks the end of the ICW in that area.
C. You should leave the buoy to port.
D. The yellow square is retroreflective material used to assist in sighting the buoy at night.

1542. To find a magnetic course from a true course you must apply _____.

A. magnetic anomalies (local disturbances)
B. deviation
C. variation
D. deviation and variation

1543. The distance between the surface of the water and the tidal datum is the _____.

A. height of tide
B. charted depth
C. actual water depth
D. range of tide

1544. The height of a tide can be increased by _____.

A. a storm surge
B. a high pressure area
C. the jet stream
D. a cold front

1546. You are sailing south on the Intracoastal Waterway (ICW) when you sight a red nun buoy with a yellow triangle painted on it. Which statement is TRUE?

A. Geometric symbols such as squares and triangles replace letters and numbers on ICW aids to navigation.
B. The ICW and another waterway coincide in this geographical area.
C. The yellow triangle identifies a sharp turn (over 60°) in the channel.
D. This is an information or regulatory buoy that also has lateral significance.

1547. Which light combination does NOT indicate a navigational channel passing under a fixed bridge?

A. Red lights on the LDB and green lights on the RDB
B. Three white lights in a vertical line
C. Two green lights in a range under the span
D. A fixed red light on each pier at the channel edge

1548. D042NG. The illustration shows the symbols used on radiofacsimile weather charts. The symbol indicated at letter K represents a _____.

A. hurricane
B. thunderstorm
C. convergence zone
D. convergence line

1550. D039NG. Cirrus clouds are indicated by which number?

A. 1
B. 4
C. 5
D. 7

1551. In order to get the maximum benefit from the Gulf Stream, on a voyage between Houston and Philadelphia, you should navigate _____.

A. about 75 miles east of Ormond Beach, FL
B. close inshore between Jupiter Inlet and Fowey Rocks, FL
C. along the 50-fathom curve while off the east coast of Florida
D. about 10 miles east of Cape Canaveral, FL

1552. Which sextant in illustration D043NG reads 30°42.5'?

A. A
B. B
C. C
D. D

1554. A slow rise in the barometric pressure forecasts _____.

A. rainy weather for the next 48 hours
B. high seas
C. improving weather conditions
D. deteriorating weather conditions

1555. Under the U.S. Aids to Navigation System, a yellow buoy is a _____.

A. safe water buoy
B. junction buoy
C. cardinal mark
D. special-purpose mark

1556. The vertical distance from the tidal datum to the level of the water is the _____.

A. range of tide
B. charted depth
C. height of tide
D. actual water depth

1557. A Doppler log in the volume reverberation mode indicates _____.

A. speed being made good
B. speed through the water
C. the set of the current
D. the depth of the water

1558. As a high pressure system approaches, the barometer reading _____.

A. stays the same
B. falls

C. rises
D. falls rapidly

1559. You are underway in the North Sea on course 216°T when you sight a buoy bearing 021° relative. Under the IALA Buoyage System, you are in the best navigable water if the buoy _____.

A. has a light characteristic of Q(6) + L Fl 15s
B. is horizontally banded yellow, black, yellow
C. has a double cone topmark with both points up
D. has a continuous very quick light

1560. Under the IALA-A and B Buoyage Systems, a buoy with alternating red and white vertical stripes indicates _____.

A. that there is navigable water all around
B. an isolated danger exists
C. that the preferred channel is to port
D. that the preferred channel is to starboard

1561. You are sailing south on the Intracoastal Waterway (ICW) when you sight a red nun buoy with a yellow square painted on it. Which statement is TRUE?

A. The buoy is off station and should be ignored as a navigational mark.
B. The waterway in that area has shoaled and the available depth of water is less than the project depth.
C. ICW traffic should not proceed beyond the buoy unless the crossing waterway is clear of all traffic.
D. You should leave the buoy to port.

1563. Neap tides occur only _____.

A. at a new or full Moon
B. when the Sun, Moon, and Earth are in line
C. at approximately 28-day intervals
D. when the Moon is at quadrature

1564. What is a characteristic of cardinal marks?

A. Light rhythms indicating directional orientation
B. Vertical stripes
C. Square or triangular topmarks
D. Number-letter combinations for identification

1565. Determine the approximate geographic visibility of an object, with a height above the water of 85 feet (25.9 meters), for an observer with a height of eye of 60 feet (18.3 meters).

A. 18.4 nm
B. 19.9 nm
C. 20.8 nm
D. 21.5 nm

1566. D042NG. The illustration shows the symbols used on radiofacsimile weather charts. Which of these symbols indicates thunderstorms?

A. I
B. K
C. L
D. M

1567. Buoys and day beacons exhibiting a yellow triangle or square painted on them are used _____.

A. in minor harbors where the controlling depth is 10 feet (3 meters) or less
B. on isolated stretches of the ICW to mark undredged areas
C. where the ICW and other waterways coincide
D. at particularly hazardous turns of the channel

1568. You are approaching a vertical lift bridge. You know the span is fully open when _____.

A. three white lights in a vertical line are lit
B. a red light starts to flash at about 60 times a minute
C. a yellow light is illuminated on the bridge pier
D. there is a range of green lights under the lift span

1569. Three or four feet of the total height of a storm surge in a hurricane can be attributed to _____.

A. an increase in temperature
B. an increase in the wave period
C. the wind velocity
D. the decrease in atmospheric pressure

1572. Generally speaking, in the Northern Hemisphere, when winds are blowing from between SE and SW the barometric reading _____.

A. makes no change at all
B. is somewhat lower than it would be for winds from a northern quadrant
C. is uncertain and may fluctuate by increasing and decreasing
D. is somewhat higher than it would be for winds from the northern quadrant

1574. Information about currents around Pacific Coast ports of the U.S. is found in the _____.

A. Nautical Almanac
B. Tide Tables
C. Tidal Current Tables
D. Ocean Current Tables

1576. You are entering an east coast port and see a buoy with a yellow triangle painted on it. This indicates_____.

A. you are in the vicinity of the ICW
B. the buoy is a special mark
C. the buoy is off station
D. the buoy designates a sharp turn in the channel

1579. You get underway from the oil terminal at Marcus Hook, PA, at 0815 ZT (ZD +5) on 20 February 1983, enroute to sea. You will be turning for 11 knots. What is the approximate current when you are abreast Reedy Island?

A. Slack
B. 2.0 knots ebbing
C. 1.5 knots flooding
D. 0.5 knot flooding

1581. D042NG. Shown are the symbols used on radiofacsimile weather charts. The symbol indicated at letter I represents _____.

A. rain showers
B. thunderstorms
C. snow storms
D. sand storms

1584. A decrease in barometric pressure is associated with all of the following except _____.

A. rising warm air
B. proximity to a low pressure area
C. inward spiraling circulation
D. clear dry weather

1586. A green buoy has a yellow triangle on it. This is a(n) _____.

A. information or regulatory buoy that has lateral significance
B. buoy that is off-station and is marked to warn mariners of its wrong position
C. dual purpose marking used where the ICW and other waterways coincide
D. buoy that was set in error and will be replaced with a red nun buoy

1589. You are enroute to Savannah, GA, from Recife, Brazil. There is a strong N'ly wind blowing. As you cross the axis of the Gulf Stream you would expect to encounter _____.

A. smoother seas and warmer water
B. steeper waves, closer together
C. long swells
D. cirrus clouds

1592. A white buoy marked with an orange rectangle indicates _____.

A. an anchorage
B. a fish net area
C. midchannel
D. general information

1594. D042NG. The Illustration shows the symbols used on radiofacsimile weather charts. The symbol indicated at letter P represents _____.

A. snow
B. hail
C. freezing rain
D. sleet

1595. The Light List indicates that a light has a nominal range of 8 miles and is 48 feet (14.6 meters) high. If the visibility is 6 miles and your height of eye is 35 feet (10.7 meters), at what approximate distance will you sight the light?

A. 15.0 nm
B. 12.4 nm
C. 8.0 nm
D. 5.9 nm

1596. You are sailing south on the Intracoastal Waterway (ICW) when you sight a red nun buoy with a yellow square painted on it. Which of the following is TRUE?

A. You should leave the buoy on your port hand.
B. This buoy marks the end of the ICW in that geographic area.

C. The yellow is retroreflective material used to assist in sighting the buoy at night.
D. The yellow square is in error and it should be a yellow triangle.

1597. The dense black cumulonimbus clouds surrounding the eye of a hurricane are called _____.

A. spiral rainbands
B. cloud walls
C. funnel clouds
D. cyclonic spirals

1599. The time interval between successive wave crests is called the _____.

A. trough
B. period
C. frequency
D. epoch

1602. Most modern Loran-C receivers automatically detect secondary station blink which _____.

A. indicates the station is transmitting normally
B. automatically shuts down the receiver
C. triggers alarm indicators to warn the operator
D. causes the receiver to shift automatically to another Loran chain

1603. A position that is obtained by using two or more intersecting lines of position, taken at nearly the same time, is a(n) _____.

A. estimated position
B. fix
C. running fix
D. dead-reckoning position

1604. D042NG. The Illustration shows the symbols used on radiofacsimile weather charts. Which of these symbols indicates freezing rain?

A. M
B. N
C. O
D. P

1606. Aids to navigation marking the Intracoastal Waterway can be identified by _____.

A. the letters ICW after the aid's number or letter

B. yellow stripes, squares, or triangles marked on them
C. white retroreflective material
D. the light characteristic and color for lighted aids

1607. When your barometer reading changes from 30.25 to 30.05 in a 12-hour period it indicates _____.

A. rapidly changing weather
B. improving weather
C. high winds within the next 6 hours
D. little or no immediate change

1608. When using a buoy as an aid to navigation which of the following should be considered?

A. If the light is flashing the buoy should be considered to be in the charted location.
B. The buoy may not be in the charted position.
C. The buoy should be considered to be in the charted position if it has been freshly painted.
D. The buoy should be considered to always be in the charted position.

1609. A rapid rise or fall of the barometer indicates _____.

A. heavy rain within 6 hours
B. a decrease in wind velocity
C. a change in the present conditions
D. that fog will soon set in

1610. When the navigational channel passes under a fixed bridge, the edges of the channel are marked on the bridge with what lights?

A. Red lights
B. Three white lights in a vertical line
C. Red lights on the LDB and green lights on the RDB
D. Yellow lights

1611. What indicates a dual-purpose buoy?

A. Red buoy with a horizontal yellow band
B. Red and white vertically striped buoy with a vertical yellow stripe
C. Red and white vertically striped buoy with a red spherical topmark
D. Green buoy with a yellow square

1612. The strongest winds and heaviest rains in a hurricane are found in the _____.

A. outer bands
B. eye
C. cloud walls
D. spiral rainbands

1613. Where would you find information concerning the duration of slack water?

A. Tide Tables
B. Tidal Current Tables
C. American Practical Navigator
D. Sailing Directions

1614. Hot air can hold _____.

A. less moisture than cold air
B. more moisture than cold air
C. the same amount of moisture as cold air
D. moisture independent of air temperature

1615. D042NG. The Illustration shows the symbols used on radiofacsimile weather charts. Which symbol indicates snow?

A. G
B. H
C. M
D. N

1616. Which picture in illustration D034NG shows a Morse (A) light?

A. A
B. B
C. C
D. D

1617. The inner cloud bands of a hurricane, when viewed from a distance, form a mass of dense, black cumulonimbus clouds called the _____.

A. bar of the storm
B. eye of the storm
C. funnel
D. front

1618. The Light List indicates that a light has a nominal range of 14 miles and is 26 feet high. If the visibility is 4 miles and your height of eye is 20 feet, at what approximate distance will you sight the light?

A. 7.5 miles
B. 9.6 miles
C. 11.2 miles
D. 14.0 miles

1620. You are at anchor in the anchorage at the entrance to Delaware Bay. If you weigh

anchor at 1445 DST (ZD +4) on 24 July 1983 and proceed northbound enroute to Philadelphia at a speed of 10 knots, you will have _____.

A. a flood current the entire trip
B. a flood current from Ship John Shoal Lt. to Philadelphia
C. an ebb current north of New Castle, DE
D. a weak flood between Reedy Island and Edgemoore

1623. Which of the following statements is FALSE?

A. an anemometer measures wind speed.
B. a barometer measures atmospheric pressure.
C. a thermometer measures temperature.
D. a psychrometer measures wind pressure.

1624. A psychrometer has two thermometers that provide dry bulb and wet bulb temperatures. By comparing these two temperature readings with a set of tables you can determine the _____.

A. atmospheric pressure
B. wind speed
C. relative humidity and dew point
D. wind chill factor

1625. A sling psychrometer is used to measure_____.

A. seawater temperature
B. engine temperature
C. dry bulb and wet bulb temperatures
D. barometric pressure

1626. Which instrument is used to measure the relative humidity of the air?

A. hydrometer
B. hygrometer
C. spectrometer
D. barograph

1627. An instrument that maintains a continuous record of humidity changes is called a _____.

A. thermometer
B. barometer
C. hygrograph
D. thermograph

1628. As the temperature of the air reaches the dew point, _____.

A. rain must develop
B. fog may form
C. it begins to snow
D. water freezes

1629. Air temperature varies with _____.

A. altitude above sea level
B. season of the year
C. latitude or distance from the equator
D. all of the above

1631. Which picture in illustration D034NG shows an occulting light?

A. A
B. B
C. C
D. D

1632. Lighted white and orange buoys must show which color light?

A. Orange
B. Red
C. White
D. Alternating yellow and white

1633. To find a magnetic compass course from a true course you must apply _____.

A. deviation and variation
B. deviation
C. variation
D. magnetic anomalies (local disturbances)

1634. A lighted buoy to be left to starboard, when entering a U.S. port from seaward, shall have a _____.

A. red light
B. white light
C. green light
D. light characteristic of Morse (A)

1635. An isotherm is_____.

A. a line on a weather map connecting equal points of both temperature and pressure
B. an instrument that measures the climatological effects of temperature
C. a line connecting points of equal barometric pressure on a weather map
D. a line connecting points of equal temperature on a weather map

1636. A type of precipitation that occurs only in thunderstorms with strong convection currents that convey raindrops above

and below the freezing level is known as
_____.

A. sleet
B. hail
C. freezing rain
D. rime

1637. Which of the following is NOT a form of precipitation?

A. rain
B. frost
C. sleet
D. snow

1638. Clouds form _____.

A. as a mass of warm, humid air rises into the atmosphere and cools, condensing moisture into small droplets
B. as winds blow across bodies of water, the sun causes the moisture to be absorbed and move upward forming clouds
C. as dry air compresses moisture from the atmosphere into clouds
D. when the relative humidity of the atmosphere is low

1640. Clouds with the prefix "nimbo" in their name _____.

A. are sheet or layer clouds
B. have undergone great vertical development
C. are middle or high altitude clouds
D. are rain clouds

1641. The low, dark, sheet-like cloud which is associated with continuous precipitation for many hours is a _____.

A. cirrus cloud
B. cumulus cloud
C. cumulonimbus cloud
D. nimbostratus cloud

1642. Which type of cloud formation should be of immediate concern to small craft operators?

A. cirrus
B. altostratus
C. nimbostratus
D. cumulonimbus

1643. Cumulus clouds that have undergone vertical development and have become cumulonimbus in form, indicate _____.

A. clearing weather
B. that a warm front has passed
C. probable thunderstorm activity
D. an approaching hurricane or typhoon

1644. Which scale is used to estimate wind speed by observing sea conditions _____.

A. metric scale
B. wind scale
C. Coriolis scale
D. Beaufort scale

1646. Which picture in illustration D034NG shows a flashing light?

A. A
B. B
C. C
D. D

1647. Cumulonimbus clouds are formed by _____.

A. vertical air movements
B. heavy rainstorms
C. horizontal air movements
D. any movement of moist air

1648. A sign of thunderstorm development is a cumulus cloud _____.

A. darkening, growing in size and forming an anvil top
B. that shows extensive vertical development
C. creating cold downdrafts that are felt on the ground
D. all of the above

1649. If you count 20 seconds between seeing lightning and hearing the thunder, how far is the storm away from you?

A. 2 miles
B. 4 miles
C. 6 miles
D. 8 miles

1651. From which type of cloud can a tornado or waterspout develop?

A. nimbostratus
B. altostratus
C. cumulonimbus
D. cirrus

1652. Small, visible mound-like protuberances on the bottom of cumulonimbus clouds, that are potential breeding

grounds for waterspouts and tornadoes, are called_____.

A. thunderheads
B. mamma
C. rime
D. ice prisms

1653. In a weather report, the term "visibility" expresses _____.

A. how far you can see with the "naked eye"
B. how far you can see with a telescope or binoculars
C. how well you can identify an object at night
D. the distance in miles at which prominent objects are identifiable

1654. Which weather element cannot be measured accurately while on board a moving vessel?

A. visibility
B. temperature
C. wind direction
D. atmospheric pressure

1655. Yesterday your chronometer read 11h 59m 59s at the 1200 GMT time tick. Today the chronometer reads 11h 59m 57s at the 1200 time tick. What is the

chronometer rate?
A. +2s
B. −2s
C. −3s
D. +3s

1656. Which instrument is most useful in forecasting fog?

A. barometer
B. anemometer
C. sling psychrometer
D. pyrometer

1657. Fog is formed when _____.

A. the moisture in the air is condensed into small droplets
B. air is cooled to its dew point
C. the base of a cloud is on the ground
D. all of the above

1658. Fog forms when the air temperature is at or below _____.

A. 32° F
B. the wet bulb temperature
C. the dew point
D. the dry bulb temperature

1659. The type of fog that occurs on clear nights with very light breezes and forms when the earth cools rapidly by radiation is known as _____.

A. radiation fog
B. frontal fog
C. convection fog
D. advection fog

1660. Which of the following is TRUE of advection fog?

A. It commonly occurs on coastal waters during cold seasons.
B. It moves in a bank or dense cloud.
C. It is caused by warmer air moving to a cooler location.
D. all of the above

1661. Advection fog may be formed by warm moist air passing over a_____.

A. warmer sea surface
B. cooler sea surface
C. dry coastal plain
D. polar land mass

1662. Fog generally clears when the _____.

A. wind speed increases
B. wind direction changes
C. temperature increases
D. all of the above

1663. What is the primary source of the earth's weather?

A. the oceans
B. the moon
C. the sun
D. the solar system

1664. Ascending and descending air masses with different temperatures is part of an important heat transmitting process in our atmosphere called _____.

A. conduction
B. radiation
C. convection
D. barometric inversion

1665. Air circulation is caused or affected by _____.

A. the rotation of the earth on its axis
B. convection currents caused by differences in radiant heating between equatorial and polar regions
C. mountain ranges
D. all of the above

1666. The process by which the temperature and/or moisture characteristics of an air mass changes is called _____.

A. sublimation or condensation
B. modification
C. consolidation
D. association

1667. Air masses near the earth's surface _____.

A. move from areas of high pressure to areas of low pressure
B. are deflected by the earth's rotation in both hemispheres
C. are deflected by the Coriolis effect
D. all of the above

1671. Cirrus clouds are composed primarily of _____.

A. ice crystals
B. water droplets
C. snow crystals
D. nitrogen

1672. Data relating to the direction and velocity of rotary tidal currents can be found in the _____.

A. Mariner's Guide
B. Tidal Current Tables
C. Nautical Almanac
D. Tide Tables

1673. Information about currents on the Pacific Coast of the U.S. is found in the _____.

A. Nautical Almanac
B. Tidal Current Tables
C. Ocean Current Tables
D. Tide Tables

1675. D047NG. You are entering port and have been instructed to anchor, as your berth is not yet available. You are on a SW'ly heading, preparing to drop anchor, when you observe the range lights as shown on your starboard beam. You should _____.

A. NOT drop the anchor until the lights are in line
B. ensure your ship will NOT block the channel or obstruct the range while at anchor
C. drop the anchor immediately as the range lights mark an area free of obstructions
D. drop the anchor immediately as a change in the position of the range lights will always be an indication of dragging anchor

1676. Lighted information markers show _____.

A. green lights
B. white lights
C. yellow lights
D. red lights

1677. D051NG. The position labeled E was plotted because _____.

A. a dead-reckoning position is plotted within a half-hour of each course change
B. a dead-reckoning position is plotted for each speed change
C. the position is a running fix at 1125
D. the vessel's position was fixed at 1145

1680. A weather front exists when _____.

A. air masses of the same temperature meet
B. air masses of different temperatures meet
C. many clouds create a differential in air density
D. two lows are separated by a ridge of higher pressure

1681. You can expect frontal activity when two air masses collide and _____.

A. their barometric pressures and temperatures are the same
B. there are differences in how they track along the jet stream
C. there are no significant differences between their temperatures and moisture content
D. there are significant differences between the temperature of each air mass

1682. Which of the listed properties does warm air possess?

A. It rises above cooler air and cools as it rises.

B. Atmospheric pressure drops as warm air rises.
C. Moisture in warm air condenses as the air is cooled.
D. All of the above

1683. As it approaches, a typical warm front will bring _____.

A. rising temperatures and falling barometric pressure
B. falling temperature and pressure
C. falling temperatures and rising pressure
D. rising barometric pressure and temperatures

1684. Which type of frontal passage is associated with a relatively narrow band of precipitation?

A. a cold front
B. a warm front
C. a stationary front
D. none of the above

1685. Squall lines with an almost unbroken line of threatening dark clouds and sharp changes in wind direction generally precede a(n) _____.

A. slow-moving warm front
B. fast-moving cold front
C. stationary front
D. occluded front

1686. Which of the following statements concerning frontal movements is TRUE?

A. The temperature rises after a cold front passes.
B. The barometric pressure rises when a warm front passes.
C. A cold front generally passes faster than a warm front.
D. A warm front usually has more violent weather associated with it than a cold front.

1687. Which statement is TRUE when comparing cold and warm fronts?

A. Cold fronts are more violent and of shorter duration.
B. Cold fronts are milder and last longer.
C. They are very similar with the exception of wind direction.
D. Warm fronts are more violent and of longer duration.

1688. Which type of front forms when a cold front overtakes and forces a warm front upwards?

A. cold front
B. occluded front
C. warm front
D. stationary front

1689. The horse latitudes are regions of _____.

A. brisk prevailing winds
B. light airs and calms
C. abundant blue sea grass vegetation
D. none of the above

1690. In regions near the poles, the winds are generally described as _____.

A. westerlies
B. easterlies
C. northerlies
D. southerlies

1691. Which of the following is associated with consistently high barometric pressure?

A. the horse latitudes
B. the doldrums
C. the prevailing westerlies
D. the trade winds

1692. The force resulting from the earth's rotation that causes winds to deflect to the right in the Northern Hemisphere and to the left in the Southern Hemisphere is called _____.

A. pressure gradient
B. Coriolis effect
C. aurora borealis
D. ballistic deflection

1693. A phenomenon where the atmospheric pressure is higher than that of other surrounding regions is called _____.

A. the "trade winds"
B. a low front or an occluded front
C. a high pressure area; an anticyclone; or a "high"
D. the "doldrums"

1694. In the Southern Hemisphere the wind circulation in a high pressure system rotates _____.

A. clockwise and inward

B. clockwise and outward
C. counterclockwise and outward
D. counterclockwise and inward

1695. Compared to a low pressure system, generally the air in a high is _____.

A. warmer, less dense, and less stable
B. cool, more dense, and drier
C. muggy and cloudy
D. extremely moist with high relative humidity

1696. Two well-developed high pressure areas may be separated by a _____.

A. hill of low pressure
B. trough of low pressure
C. valley of low pressure
D. ridge of low pressure

1697. In the Northern Hemisphere, if the center of a high pressure area is due west of you, what wind direction would you expect?

A. south to west
B. south to east
C. north to west
D. north to east

1698. When a high pressure system is centered north of your vessel in the Northern Hemisphere _____.

A. you should experience hot, moist, clear weather
B. the wind direction is generally easterly
C. the winds should be from the southwest at your location
D. the winds should be brisk

1699. In the Northern Hemisphere, when the center of a high pressure system is due east of your position, you can expect winds from the _____.

A. south to west
B. south to east
C. north to west
D. north to east

1700. Generally speaking, you should expect to find low atmospheric pressure prevailing in the earth's _____.

A. equatorial area
B. polar regions
C. mid-latitudes
D. all of the above

1701. Which general weather conditions should you expect to find in a low pressure system?

A. fair weather
B. precipitation and cloudiness
C. scattered clouds at high elevations
D. gradual clearing and cooler temperatures

1702. In a cyclone the lowest pressure is found in the _____.

A. center
B. outer edge
C. warm front
D. cold front

1703. In the Northern Hemisphere, when the wind at your location is northerly, the low pressure center causing the wind is located to your _____.

A. NNW
B. WSW
C. ESE
D. SSW

1704. If the center of low pressure is due west of you in the Northern Hemisphere, which wind direction should you expect?

A. south to west
B. south to east
C. west to north
D. north to east

1705. Two well-developed low pressure areas may be separated by a _____.

A. trough of higher pressure
B. hill of higher pressure
C. ridge of higher pressure
D. valley of higher pressure

1706. In the Northern Hemisphere a wind is said to veer when the wind _____.

A. changes direction clockwise, as from north to east, etc.
B. changes direction violently and erratically
C. remains constant in direction and speed
D. changes direction counterclockwise, as from south to east, etc.

1707. "Surface circulation" is another term for _____.

A. cyclones
B. air in motion at all levels of the atmosphere
C. wind in the lower troposphere
D. ocean currents

1708. What generally occurs when the land is cooler than the nearby water?

A. a land breeze
B. a sea breeze
C. a norther
D. a prevailing westerly

1709. The Beaufort scale is used to estimate the _____.

A. wind direction
B. percentage of cloud cover
C. wind speed
D. barometric pressure

1710. A gale is characterized by a wind speed of _____.

A. 10 to 20 knots
B. 34 to 47 knots
C. 48 to 63 knots
D. 64 to 83 knots

1711. An instrument that indicates wind direction is known as a(n) _____.

A. weather vane, wind vane or wind sock
B. hydrometer
C. hygrometer
D. sling psychrometer

1712. Tornados are often associated with _____.

A. winds in the warm sector ahead of a cold front and travel from southwest towards the east or northeast
B. squall lines and very heavy thunderstorm activity
C. winds that may be in excess of 200 knots and destructive funnel clouds
D. all of the above

1713. When a tornado moves over the water from land it is called a _____.

A. tornado
B. waterspout
C. hurricane
D. cyclone

1714. Which statement concerning storm surges on the Great Lakes is FALSE?

A. They are common along the deeper areas of the lakes.
B. They cause rapid differences in levels between one end of the lake and the other.
C. The greatest water level difference occurs when the wind is blowing along the longitudinal axis of the lake.
D. If the wind subsides rapidly, a seiche effect will most likely occur.

1715. The hurricane season generally occurs from _____.

A. August to January
B. July to December
C. June to November
D. January to June

1716. The hurricane season in the North Atlantic Ocean reaches its peak during the month of _____.

A. June
B. September
C. November
D. July

1717. A tropical storm is a tropical cyclone that generates winds of _____.

A. between 20 and 33 knots
B. between 34 and 63 knots
C. over 63 knots
D. none of the above

1718. A hurricane is characterized by winds of _____.

A. up to 33 knots
B. 34 to 47 knots
C. 48 to 63 knots
D. 64 knots or greater

1719. What is the direction of rotation of tropical cyclones, tropical storms and hurricanes in the Northern Hemisphere?

A. clockwise and outward
B. counterclockwise and inward
C. counterclockwise and outward
D. clockwise and inward

1720. In the Southern Hemisphere winds in a low pressure system rotate in a _____.

A. clockwise direction

B. northeasterly direction
C. northerly direction
D. counterclockwise direction

1721. A storm's track is characterized by all of the following except _____.

A. the direction the storm has come from
B. the direction in which the storm is moving
C. the speed at which the storm is moving
D. the path taken by the storm

1722. Hurricanes may move in any direction. However, it is rare and generally of short duration when a hurricane in the Northern Hemisphere moves toward the _____.

A. west or northwest
B. northeast
C. southeast
D. north

1723. The intensity of a hurricane as it reaches higher latitudes and cooler waters _____.

A. increases
B. remains the same
C. decreases
D. none of the above

1724. What is the first visible indication of the presence of a tropical cyclone or hurricane?

A. stratocumulus clouds or strange birds
B. rain and increasing winds
C. an exceptionally long swell
D. dark clouds and the "bar" of the storm

1725. Your present weather is sunny with a steady barometer. A low swell approaches your vessel from the south with crests passing at relatively long periods of about four per minute. This usually indicates _____.

A. a warm front from the south
B. a tropical cyclone south of your vessel
C. a hurricane about 100 miles south of your vessel and heading in your direction
D. an extra-tropical cyclone

1726. How can you estimate the position of a tropical storm's center?

A. with a radio weather bulletin or weather-fax
B. using shipboard radar

C. observe the wind direction and apply Buys Ballot's law
D. all of the above

1727. What enables you to estimate the bearing of a storm's center?

A. Buys Ballot's Law
B. an educated guess
C. Pascal's Law
D. the left-hand rule

1728. If a hurricane several hundred miles away is moving in your general direction your barometer would _____.

A. start to rise rapidly
B. start to fall gradually
C. rise slowly, begin "pumping" and then start a slow, steady fall
D. remain steady

1729. The first cloud formations you can use to indicate the bearing of the center of a hurricane or tropical storm are _____.

A. the point of convergence of the cirrus clouds
B. the direction of movement of thunderstorms on radar
C. the darkest point of the clouds in the "bar" of the storm
D. the point of origin of the altostratus clouds

1730. If you observe the point of cloud convergence shifting to the right and the "bar" of the storm appears to move along the horizon _____.

A. the center of the storm will bypass you
B. the storm will strike you on the starboard side
C. you are in the direct path of the storm and should take immediate steps to batten down loose gear
D. the storm is starting to break up

1731. When your vessel is on or near the path of an approaching tropical storm the _____.

A. wind direction remains steady
B. wind speed increases
C. barometer falls
D. all of the above

1732. The eye of a hurricane is surrounded by dense black cumulonimbus clouds which are called the _____.

A. wall cloud
B. nimbostratus cloud
C. bar
D. funnel

1733. An instrument which maintains a continuous record of temperature changes is called a _____.

A. thermometer
B. barometer
C. thermograph
D. hygrograph

1734. The eye of the hurricane has _____.

A. very high barometric pressure
B. average barometric pressure
C. the lowest barometric pressure
D. no change in barometric pressure

1735. A vessel entering the eye of a hurricane should expect _____.

A. moderating winds and heavy confused seas to strike his vessel from all directions
B. the winds to increase to hurricane force and strike from a different direction as the eye passes
C. the barometer to reach the lowest point
D. all of the above

1736. Which statement is FALSE concerning the dangerous semicircle of a hurricane?

A. The actual wind speed is increased by the forward movement of the storm along its track
B. The direction of the wind and the sea might carry a vessel directly into the storm's path
C. The seas are higher
D. The rain is heavier

1737. You can determine if your vessel's position is in the dangerous or navigable semicircle of a hurricane by _____.

A. observing whether the wind is veering or backing
B. plotting two or more recent storm positions from weather bulletins
C. both A and B
D. neither A nor B.

1738. In the Northern Hemisphere, the right half of the storm is known as the dangerous semicircle because _____.

A. the wind speed is greater here since the wind is traveling in the same general direction as the storm's track
B. the direction of the wind and seas might carry a vessel into the path of the storm
C. the seas are higher because of greater wind speed
D. all of the above

1739. Which condition indicates that you are in a hurricane's dangerous semicircle in the Northern hemisphere?

A. a backing wind
B. a veering wind
C. a norther
D. a strong, gusty wind

1740. If you are in the dangerous semicircle of a hurricane you can expect all of the following except _____.

A. backing winds
B. high seas
C. high winds
D. veering winds

1741. The left half of the storm is called the navigable semicircle because _____.

A. the wind speed is decreased by the storm's forward motion
B. the wind tends to blow vessels away from the storms track
C. both A and B
D. neither A nor B.

1742. In the Northern Hemisphere which semicircle of a hurricane is the navigable semicircle?

A. left
B. right
C. front
D. back

1743. In the Northern Hemisphere, if your vessel is in a hurricane's navigable semicircle it should be positioned with the wind on the _____.

A. starboard quarter, hold course and make as much speed as possible
B. port bow, hold course and make as much speed as possible until the hurricane has passed
C. port quarter, maintain course and make as much speed as possible
D. starboard bow and heave to until the hurricane has passed

1744. Which condition suggests that your present position lies in the navigable semicircle of a tropical storm?

A. a backing wind
B. a veering wind
C. sustained gale force winds
D. a strong wind that maintains a constant speed and direction

1745. When your vessel is on the storm track but behind the storm's center the

_____.

A. wind direction remains steady
B. wind speed decreases
C. barometer rises
D. all of the above

1746. Swells that have outrun the storm are produced in the _____.

A. left front quadrant
B. right front quadrant
C. rear
D. directly ahead on the storms projected track

1749. If the current and wind are in opposite directions, the sea surface represents

_____.

A. a greatly reduced wind speed
B. a higher wind speed than what really exists
C. a lower wind speed than what really exists
D. more turbulent winds

1750. Clearance gauges at bridges indicate

_____.

A. the height of the tide
B. depth of water under the bridge
C. charted vertical clearance at mean low water
D. distance from the water to low steel of the bridge

1751. A tsunami is caused by a(n) _____.

A. tidal wave
B. storm surge caused by a hurricane or tropical storm
C. earthquake on the ocean's floor
D. tornado

1753. On a weather map, a large letter "H" means _____.

A. a high pressure area with cool, dry air, and fair weather
B. a high pressure area with warm, moist air, and inclement weather
C. horse latitudes, with rough seas and strong winds
D. a heavy squall line near the "H"

1754. The dumping of refuse in a lock is permitted _____.

A. when approved by the lockmaster
B. when locking downbound
C. at no time
D. during high water only

1755. Which weather system produces strong cold winds called "Northers" during the winter months in the Gulf of Mexico?

A. an anticyclone
B. a high pressure system
C. a cyclone
D. both A and B.

1756. Where would you expect to find climatological and meteorological tables for the Gulf Coast area?

A. In the publication entitled Radio Aids to Navigation
B. In the back of Coast Pilot #5
C. In any Coast Pilot volume
D. Only at the National Weather Service office

1757. Where would you obtain data on currents for areas of the world not covered by the U.S. National Ocean Service?

A. In the Coast Pilot
B. In the Nautical Almanac
C. In the List of Lights
D. In the Sailing Directions

1758. The climate of the eastern Gulf Coast _____.

A. is humid and subtropical through the year
B. has an east coast marine type of climate
C. has a Mediterranean type of climate
D. varies from warm to subtropical

1759. Which magnetic compass corrector(s) can be set while the vessel is on a heading of magnetic north or magnetic south?

A. Quadrantal spheres

B. Heeling magnets
C. Flinders bar
D. Fore-and-aft magnets

1760. A Doppler log in the bottom return mode indicates the _____.

A. velocity of the current
B. bottom characteristics
C. depth of the water
D. speed over the ground

1761. Chart legends which indicate a conspicuous landmark are printed in _____.

A. italics
B. underlined letters
C. capital letters
D. boldfaced print

1763. Weather patterns in the Gulf Coast area of the United States are _____.

A. those of a transition zone between tropical and a temperate area
B. those of a tropical region
C. extremely hot in summer
D. tropical over Florida and subtropical over the rest of the Gulf Coast area

1764. What natural feature is responsible for the rather even climate found on the Florida peninsula throughout the year?

A. strong masses of continental air
B. the Gulf Stream
C. the Bermuda high
D. the cool waters of the Sargasso sea

1765. Which meteorological feature controls the climate of the Gulf and the Gulf Coast area during late spring and summer?

A. the Bermuda High
B. the doldrums
C. the horse latitudes
D. tropical cyclones

1766. You are approaching a lock and see a flashing amber light located on the lock wall. You should _____.

A. stand clear of the lock entrance
B. approach the lock under full control
C. enter the lock as quickly as possible
D. hang off your tow on the lock wall

1767. Which statement describes the prevailing wind direction in mid-winter in the Gulf Coast area?

A. 30% to 40% of midwinter winds are from a northern quadrant.
B. 40% to 50% of midwinter winds are from a southern quadrant.
C. the winds are variable in speed, but strongest in March.
D. none of the above

1768. A flashing red light displayed at a single lock means that the lock_____.

A. is ready to use but vessels must stand clear
B. is ready to use and vessels may approach
C. cannot be made ready immediately and vessels shall stand clear
D. cannot be made ready immediately but vessels may approach

1769. Under the numbering system used by NIMA, a three digit number may be used for _____.

A. a small scale chart depicting a major portion of an ocean basin or a position plotting sheet
B. non-navigational materials such as radar plotting sheets
C. products issued periodically such as the Notice to Mariners
D. large scale charts of areas that are infrequently used for navigation such as the headwaters of rivers

1770. A Doppler speed log indicates speed over ground _____.

A. at all times
B. in the bottom return mode
C. in the volume reverberation mode
D. only when there is no current

1771. Which type of precipitation is a product of the violent convection found in thunderstorms?

A. Snow
B. Freezing Rain
C. Hail
D. Sleet

1773. A "Norther" in the Gulf of Mexico is _____.

A. a wind shift to the north accompanied by a drop in temperature
B. a forcible northerly wind of at least 20 knots
C. a strong northerly wind that generally occurs between November and March
D. all of the above

1774. Restricted areas at locks and dams are indicated by _____.

A. flashing red lights upstream and fixed red lights downstream
B. yellow unlighted buoys
C. signs and/or flashing red lights
D. red daymarks upstream and green daymarks downstream

1776. A vessel operating on the Great Lakes, and whose position is southeast of an eastward-moving storm center, would NOT experience _____.

A. a falling barometer
B. lowering clouds and drizzle
C. a northeast wind
D. rain or snow

1777. If the current and wind are in the same direction, the sea surface represents a wind speed _____.

A. lower than actually exists
B. higher than actually exists
C. that actually exists
D. that has no proportional relationship

1779. The Light List indicates that a light has a nominal range of 14 miles and is 26 feet high. If the visibility is 14 miles and your height of eye is 20 feet, at which approximate distance will you sight the light?

A. 7.5 miles
B. 11.2 miles
C. 14.0 miles
D. 18.1 miles

1780. While in port, you can follow the approach of a dangerous cyclonic storm by inspecting _____.

A. the Coast Pilot or Sailing Directions
B. the National Weather Service Observing Handbook No.1, Marine Surface Observations
C. a newspaper
D. the sky overhead

1781. While in port, you can follow the approach of a dangerous cyclonic storm by inspecting _____.

A. the sky overhead
B. the National Weathe Service Observing Handbook No.1, Marine Surface Observations
C. the Coast Pilot or Sailing Directions
D. a weather map

1782. You are on course 027°T and take a relative bearing to a lighthouse of 220°. What is the true bearing to the lighthouse?

A. 113°
B. 193°
C. 247°
D. 279°

1783. You can follow the approach of a dangerous cyclonic storm by inspecting _____.

A. the National Weather Service Observing Handbook No.1, Marine Surface Observations
B. a weather fax
C. the Coast Pilot or Sailing Directions
D. the sky overhead

1784. If your vessel were proceeding down river (descending), a green square marker with a green reflector border on the right bank would be a _____.

A. mile board
B. dredging mark
C. passing daymark
D. crossing daymark

1785. Which factor(s) is/are used to develop the charted information of a lighthouse?

A. height of the light and the observer
B. height and brightness of the light
C. brightness of the light and height of the observer
D. height of the light only

1786. You are downbound approaching a lock and see 3 green lights in a vertical line. This indicates _____.

A. that the lock chamber is open and ready to receive your tow
B. that you should hold up until the signal changes to 2 green lights
C. the upstream end of the river wall
D. the upstream end of the land wall

1787. What indicates that a tropical cyclone may be within 500 to 1,000 miles of your position?

A. a pumping of the barometer up and down a few millibars
B. a sudden wind shift from southwest to northwest followed by steadily increasing winds

C. the normal swell pattern becoming confused, with the length of the swell increasing
D. an overcast sky with steadily increasing rain from nimbostratus clouds

1788. You can follow the approach of a dangerous cyclonic storm by inspecting _____.

A. the Coast Pilot or Sailing Directions
B. the National Weather Service Observing Handbook No.1, Marine Surface Observations
C. a weather forecast
D. the sky overhead

1790. A Doppler speed log indicates speed through the water _____.

A. at all times
B. in the bottom return mode
C. in the volume reverberation mode
D. only when there is no current

1793. Which weather element cannot be measured accurately while on board a moving vessel?

A. relative humidity
B. temperature
C. true wind speed
D. atmospheric pressure

1795. Which weather element cannot be measured accurately while on board a moving vessel?

A. relative humidity
B. cloud base height
C. temperature
D. atmospheric pressure

1796. Which weather element cannot be measured accurately while on board a moving vessel?

A. relative humidity
B. atmospheric pressure
C. temperature
D. wave period

1797. A phenomenon where the atmospheric pressure is higher than that of other surrounding regions is called _____.

A. a high pressure area
B. a low front or an occluded front
C. the trade winds
D. the doldrums

1798. The climate of the northern Gulf Coast _____.

A. is humid and subtropical through the year
B. has an east coast marine type of climate
C. is a warm marine type of climate
D. varies from warm to subtropical

1800. In order to insure that a RACON signal is displayed on the radar, you should _____.

A. increase the brilliance of the PPI scope
B. turn off the interference controls on the radar
C. use the maximum available range setting
D. increase the radar signal output

1801. A phenomenon where the atmospheric pressure is higher than that of other surrounding regions is called _____.

A. the trade winds
B. an anticyclone
C. a low front or an occluded front
D. the doldrums

1803. The difference between the DR position and a fix, both of which have the same time, is known as _____.

A. the estimated position
B. set
C. current
D. leeway

1804. Magnetic information on a chart may be _____.

A. found in the center(s) of the compass rose(s)
B. indicated by isogonic lines
C. found in a note on the chart
D. All of the above

1805. A phenomenon where the atmospheric pressure is higher than that of other surrounding regions is called _____.

A. the trade winds
B. a low front or an occluded front
C. the doldrums
D. a high

1806. Sometimes foreign charts are reproduced by NIMA. On such a chart a wire dragged (swept) area may be shown in purple or _____.

A. green
B. red
C. magenta
D. yellow

1807. Which weather system produces strong cold winds called "Northers" during the winter months in the Gulf of Mexico?

A. a polar maritime air mass
B. a high pressure system
C. a cyclone
D. a low pressure system

1808. A white buoy with an open-faced orange diamond on it indicates _____.

A. danger
B. vessels are excluded from the area
C. the buoy is a mooring buoy
D. operating restrictions are in effect

1809. What occurs when rising air cools to the dew point?

A. Advection fog forms
B. Humidity decreases
C. Winds increase
D. Clouds form

1810. Where will you find information about the duration of slack water?

A. Tide Tables
B. Sailing Directions
C. Tidal Current Tables
D. American Practical Navigator

1811. To find a magnetic compass course from a true course you must apply _____.

A. deviation
B. deviation and variation
C. variation
D. magnetic anomalies (local disturbances)

1816. A white buoy with an orange circle marked on it indicates_____.

A. danger
B. vessels are excluded from the area
C. a mooring buoy
D. operating restrictions are in effect

1818. In order to utilize the capacity of a lock to its maximum, pleasure craft are locked through with all of the following EXCEPT _____.

A. coal barges

B. oil barges
C. sand barges
D. cement barges

1820. Information on the operating times and characteristics of foreign radiobeacons can be found in which publication?

A. List of Lights
B. Coast Pilot
C. Sailing Directions
D. List of Radiobeacons

1822. What is the relative bearing of an object broad on the port bow?

A. 315°
B. 330°
C. 345°
D. 360°

1826. Illustration D036NG represents a fixed C of E lock and dam. What navigational light(s) is(are) exhibited at the position indicated by the letter D in the illustration?

A. One red light
B. Two green lights
C. Three green lights
D. No light

1827. D051NG. The position labeled D was plotted because _____.

A. a dead-reckoning position is plotted within 30 minutes of a running fix
B. a dead-reckoning position is plotted for each course change
C. the vessel's speed changed at 1125
D. All of the above

1828. When entering from seaward, a buoy displaying a single-flashing red light indicates _____.

A. a junction with the preferred channel to the left
B. a wreck to be left on the vessel's port side
C. a sharp turn in the channel to the right
D. the starboard side of the channel

1830. A vessel heading NNW is on a course of _____.

A. 274.5°
B. 292.0°
C. 315.5°
D. 337.5°

1831. In Region A of the IALA Buoyage System, when entering from seaward, the port side of a channel would be marked by a _____.

A. red conical buoy
B. black can buoy
C. red can buoy
D. black conical buoy

1832. Which magnetic compass corrector(s) can be set while the vessel is on a heading of magnetic northeast or magnetic southeast?

A. Flinders bar
B. Heeling magnets
C. Fore-and-aft magnets
D. Quadrantal spheres

1838. The Light List shows a lighted aid to navigation on the left bank. This means that the light can be seen on the starboard side of a vessel_____.

A. ascending the river
B. descending the river
C. crossing the river
D. proceeding towards sea

1840. A vessel heading NW is on a course of _____.

A. 274.5°
B. 292.5°
C. 315.0°
D. 337.5°

1844. What is the relative bearing of an object sighted dead ahead?

A. 180°
B. 090°
C. 015°
D. 000°

1848. The buoy symbol printed on your chart is leaning to the northeast. This indicates _____.

A. you should stay to the north or east of the buoy
B. you should stay to the west or south of the buoy
C. the buoy is a major lighted buoy
D. nothing special for navigational purposes

1850. A vessel heading WNW is on a course of _____.

A. 270.0°
B. 292.5°
C. 315.0°
D. 337.5°

1858. A white buoy with an orange cross within a diamond marked on it indicates _____.

A. danger
B. vessels are excluded from the area
C. an anchorage area
D. operating restrictions are in effect

1859. While proceeding downriver (descending) you sight a red diamond-shaped panel with small, red reflector squares in each corner on the left bank. Under the U.S. Aids to Navigation System on the Western Rivers this is a _____.

A. special-purpose signal
B. passing daymark
C. crossing daymark
D. cable crossing

1860. A vessel heading WSW is on a course of _____.

A. 202.5°
B. 225.0°
C. 247.5°
D. 271.0°

1862. What is the relative bearing of an object broad on the starboard quarter?

A. 090°
B. 105°
C. 135°
D. 150°

1866. What term is used to describe a tank barge constructed with the structural framing inside the cargo tank and the side shell plating containing the cargo?

A. Single hull
B. Shell plated
C. Hopper type
D. Independent tank

1870. A vessel heading SW is on a course of _____.

A. 202.5°
B. 225.0°

C. 247.5°
D. 270.0°

1871. A lighted buoy to be left to starboard, when entering a U.S. port from seaward, shall have a _____.

A. green light
B. white light
C. red light
D. light characteristic of Morse (A)

1872. To find a magnetic compass course from a true course you must apply _____.

A. deviation
B. variation
C. deviation and variation
D. magnetic anomalies (local disturbances)

1873. Lighted information markers show _____.

A. green lights
B. red lights
C. yellow lights
D. white lights

1874. Lighted white and orange buoys must show which color light?

A. Orange
B. Red
C. Alternating yellow and white
D. White

1875. D051NG. The position labeled E was plotted because _____.

A. a dead-reckoning position is plotted within a half-hour of each course change
B. the position is a running fix
C. a dead-reckoning position is plotted for each speed change
D. the vessel position was fixed at 1145

1880. A vessel heading SSW is on a course of _____.

A. 202.5°
B. 225.0°
C. 247.5°
D. 270.0°

1883. Pressure gradient is a measure of _____.

A. a high-pressure area
B. pressure difference over horizontal distance

C. pressure difference over time
D. vertical pressure variation

1884. If a sound signal is emitted from the oscillator of a fathometer, and two seconds elapse before the returning signal is picked up, what depth of water is indicated?

A. 1648 fathoms
B. 1248 fathoms
C. 1048 fathoms
D. 824 fathoms

1885. Under the Uniform State Waterway Marking System a mooring buoy is painted _____.

A. white with a blue band
B. yellow
C. any color that does not conflict with the lateral system
D. white with a green top

1886. What is the relative bearing of an object dead astern?

A. 000°
B. 090°
C. 180°
D. 270°

1887. The Light List indicates that a light has a nominal range of 10 miles and is 11 feet high. If the visibility is 15 miles and your height of eye is 20 feet, at what approximate distance will you sight the light?

A. 12.0 miles
B. 11.0 miles
C. 10.0 miles
D. 9.0 miles

1888. What is the relative bearing of an object broad on the starboard bow?

A. 030°
B. 045°
C. 060°
D. 075°

1890. A vessel heading SSE is on a course of _____.

A. 112.5°
B. 135.0°
C. 157.5°
D. 180.0°

1892. The shoreline shown on nautical charts of areas affected by large tidal fluctuations is usually the line of mean _____.

A. lower low water
B. low water
C. tide level
D. high water

1898. The subregions of the United States Gulf and East Coasts are numbered 11, 12 and 13 within the chart numbering system. Which chart number indicates a chart for either the Gulf or East coast?

A. 14312
B. 25134
C. 21105
D. 11032

1899. What is the relative bearing of an object broad on the starboard beam?

A. 045°
B. 060°
C. 075°
D. 090°

1902. Under the numbering system used by NIMA, a four digit number is used for _____.

A. large scale charts of infrequently navigated areas such as the polar regions
B. charts of rivers or canal systems such as the Ohio River or Erie Canal
C. non-navigational materials, such as a chart correction template or maneuvering board
D. foreign charts reproduced by NIMA

1905. In order to insure that the racon signal is visible on your 3 cm radar, the _____.

A. 10 cm radar should be placed on stand-by or turned off
B. gain control should be turned to maximum
C. radar should be stabilized, head up
D. rain clutter control should be off but, if necessary, may be on low

1906. In the horizon system of coordinates what is equivalent to latitude on the Earth?

A. Altitude
B. Zenith
C. Declination
D. Zenith distance

1907. Information about direction and velocity of rotary tidal currents is found in the _____.

A. Tide Tables
B. Nautical Almanac
C. Tidal Current Tables
D. Mariner's Guide

1909. In the horizon system of coordinates what is equivalent to the equator on the Earth?

A. Prime vertical circle
B. Principal vertical circle
C. Parallels of altitude
D. Horizon

1914. In the horizon system of coordinates what is equivalent to longitude on the Earth?

A. Altitude
B. Azimuth angle
C. Horizon
D. Zenith distance

1922. In the North Sea area, you sight a buoy showing a quick white light with 9 flashes every 15 seconds. Which of the four topmarks shown in illustration D030NG would be fitted to the buoy?

A. A
B. B
C. C
D. D

1923. Little or no change in the barometric reading over a twelve hour period indicates _____.

A. stormy weather is imminent
B. that present weather conditions will continue
C. a defect in the barometer
D. increasing wind strength

1925. Above-normal tides near the center of a hurricane may be caused by the _____.

A. high barometric pressure
B. jet stream
C. storm surge
D. torrential rains

1936. The parallel of latitude at 66°33'N is the _____.

A. Tropic of Cancer
B. Tropic of Capricorn
C. Arctic Circle
D. ecliptic

1941. In Region A of the IALA Buoyage System, when entering from seaward, the starboard side of a channel would be marked by a _____.

A. red can buoy
B. red conical buoy
C. green can buoy
D. green conical buoy

1946. When making landfall at night, you can determine if a light is a major light or an offshore buoy by_____.

A. the intensity of the light
B. checking the period and characteristics against the Light List
C. the color, because the buoy will have only a red or a green light
D. Any of the above can be used to identify the light.

1951. Spring tides occur _____.

A. when the moon is new or full
B. when the moon and sun have declination of the same name
C. only when the moon and sun are on the same sides of the earth
D. at the beginning of spring when the sun is over the equator

1956. In the North Sea area, you sight a buoy showing a quick white light with 6 flashes, followed by one long flash at 15 second intervals. Which of the four topmarks shown in illustration D030NG would be fitted to this buoy?

A. A
B. B
C. C
D. D

1961. What kind of pressure systems travel in tropical waves?

A. Subsurface pressure
B. Terrastatic pressure
C. High pressure
D. Low pressure

1962. When outbound from a U.S. port, a buoy displaying a flashing red light indicates _____.

A. the port side of the channel
B. a sharp turn in the channel to the right
C. a junction with the preferred channel to the left
D. a wreck to be left on the vessel's starboard side

1968. The Earth has the shape of a(n) _____.

A. sphere
B. oblate spheroid
C. spheroid of revolution
D. oblate eggoid

1974. Ocean currents are well defined and _____.

A. create large waves in the direction of the current
B. change direction 360° during a 24-hour period
C. remain fairly constant in direction and velocity throughout the year
D. are characterized by a light green color

1976. The Moon is nearest to the Earth at _____.

A. perigee
B. the vernal equinox
C. the new Moon
D. the full Moon

1984. When a dual purpose marking is used, the mariner following the Intracoastal Waterway should be guided by the _____.

A. color of the aid
B. shape of the aid
C. color of the top band
D. shape of the yellow mark

1986. The Moon is farthest from the Earth at _____.

A. the full Moon
B. apogee
C. the lunar solstice
D. quadrature

1987. An instrument useful in predicting fog is the _____.

A. sling psychrometer
B. microbarograph
C. anemometer
D. aneroid barometer

1988. The parallel of latitude at 23°27'N is the _____.

A. Tropic of Cancer
B. Tropic of Capricorn
C. Arctic Circle
D. ecliptic

1992. The parallel of latitude at 23°27'S is the _____.

A. Tropic of Cancer
B. Tropic of Capricorn
C. Arctic Circle
D. ecliptic

1996. When approaching a lock entrance, the visual signal displayed when a single lock is ready for entrance is a flashing _____.

A. red light
B. green light
C. amber light
D. white light

2000. A vessel heading SE is on a course of _____.

A. 112.5°
B. 135.0°
C. 157.5°
D. 180.0°

2001. You have changed course and steadied up on a range. Your heading is 285°T, same as the charted range, and it appears as in illustration D048NG. After several minutes the range appears as in illustration D047NG and your heading is still 285°T. This indicates a _____.

A. south-setting current
B. north-setting current
C. leeway caused by a NE'ly wind
D. course made good to the left of the DR track

2002. What term is used to describe a river barge designed to carry coal or any similar cargo not requiring weather protection?

A. Single skin
B. Double skin
C. Open hopper
D. Deck barge

2004. The velocity of the wind, its steady direction, and the amount of time it has

blown determines a wind driven current's _____.

A. temperature
B. density
C. deflection
D. speed

2006. What is the relative bearing of an object broad on the port beam?

A. 315°
B. 300°
C. 270°
D. 235°

2007. Information about the direction and velocity of rotary tidal currents is found in the _____.

A. Mariner's Guide
B. Tidal Current Tables
C. Nautical Almanac
D. Tide Tables

2008. What term is used to describe a tank barge constructed with the structural framing outside the cargo tank and the cargo tank plating separated from the shell plating?

A. Shell plated
B. Double hull
C. Hopper type
D. Independent tank

2010. A vessel heading ESE is on a course of _____.

A. 112.5°
B. 135.0°
C. 157.5°
D. 180.0°

2014. Which stock number indicates a NIMA chart designed for navigation outside of outlying reefs and shoals?

A. 19BCO19243
B. WOPGN530
C. LCORR5873
D. 14XCO14902

2016. Which statement about the Flinders bar of the magnetic compass is CORRECT?

A. It compensates for the error caused by the vertical component of the Earth's magnetic field.

B. It compensates for error caused by the heeling of a vessel.

C. It compensates for quadrantal deviation.

D. It is only needed in equatorial waters.

2018. Which magnetic compass corrector(s) can be set while the vessel is on a heading of magnetic east or magnetic west?

A. Quadrantal spheres
B. Heeling magnet
C. Flinders bar
D. Athwartships magnets

2020. A vessel heading ENE is on a course of _____.

A. 022.5°
B. 045.0°
C. 067.5°
D. 090.0°

2021. While on watch, you notice that the air temperature is dropping and is approaching the dew point. Which type of weather should be forecasted?

A. Hail
B. Heavy rain
C. Sleet
D. Fog

2024. In the North Sea area, you sight a buoy with a quick light showing 3 flashes every 10 seconds. Which topmark in illustration D030NG would be fitted to this buoy under the IALA Buoyage Systems?

A. A
B. B
C. C
D. D

2028. Which stock number indicates a NIMA chart designed for navigation and anchorage in a small waterway?

A. WOAZC17
B. LCORR5876
C. 15XHA15883
D. PILOT55

2030. A vessel heading NE is on a course of _____.

A. 022.5°
B. 045.0°
C. 067.5°
D. 090.0°

2040. A vessel heading NNE is on a course of _____.

A. 022.5°
B. 045.0°
C. 067.5°
D. 090.0°

2043. Stormy weather is usually associated with regions of _____.

A. changing barometric pressure
B. high barometric pressure
C. steady barometric pressure
D. low barometric pressure

2044. What is the relative bearing of an object broad on the port quarter?

A. 195°
B. 225°
C. 240°
D. 265°

2048. You are upbound approaching a lock and dam and see two green lights in a vertical line. This indicates _____.

A. the downstream end of an intermediate wall
B. that a double lockage is in progress
C. the downstream end of the land wall
D. the navigable pass of a fixed weir dam

2050. The point where the vertical rise or fall of tide has stopped is referred to as _____.

A. slack water
B. the rip tide
C. the stand of the tide
D. the reverse of the tide

2052. Under the chart numbering system used by NIMA, the first digit of a multi-digit number indicates _____.

A. the general geographic area
B. the general scale of the chart
C. whether it is a major or minor chart
D. the projection used to construct the chart

2053. When outbound from a U.S. port, a buoy displaying a flashing red light indicates _____.

A. a sharp turn in the channel to the right
B. the port side of the channel

C. a junction with the preferred channel to the left
D. a wreck to be left on the vessel's starboard side

2060. What is the relative bearing of an object broad on the starboard quarter?

A. 045°
B. 090°
C. 135°
D. 225°

2061. Fog is likely to occur when there is little difference between the dew point and the _____.

A. relative humidity
B. air temperature
C. barometric pressure
D. absolute humidity

2067. The Light List indicates that a light has a nominal range of 10 miles and is 11 feet high. If the visibility is 5 miles and your height of eye is 20 feet, at what approximate distance will you sight the light?

A. 6.3 miles
B. 7.4 miles
C. 8.4 miles
D. 9.0 miles

2068. Diagram D037NG represents a movable dam. If there is high water and the wickets are down so that there is an unobstructed navigable pass through the dam, what light(s) will be shown at D if the lock walls and piers are not awash?

A. One red light
B. Two red lights
C. Three red lights
D. One amber light

2070. What is the relative bearing of an object on the port beam?

A. 045°
B. 090°
C. 180°
D. 270°

2073. Chart legends printed in capital letters show that the associated landmark is _____.

A. a radio transmitter
B. a government facility or station
C. inconspicuous
D. conspicuous

2074. When approaching a lock and at a distance of not more than a mile, vessels desiring a single lockage shall sound which signal?

A. One long blast followed by one short blast
B. One short blast followed by one long blast
C. Two short blasts
D. Two long blasts

2075. Information about major breakdowns, repairs, or other emergency operations with regard to weirs and (or) wicket dams, on the Western Rivers, may be obtained by consulting the _____.

A. Light List Vol. V
B. U.S. Coast Pilot
C. Broadcast Notice to Mariners
D. Sailing Directions

2076. You should plot your dead reckoning position _____.

A. from every fix or running fix
B. from every estimated position
C. every three minutes in pilotage waters
D. only in pilotage waters

2078. If a towboat requires a double lockage it shall give which sound signal at a distance of not more than one mile from the lock?

A. One short blast followed by two long blasts
B. One long blast followed by one short blast
C. Two long blasts followed by one short blast
D. One long blast followed by two short blasts

2079. Permission to enter the riverward chamber of twin locks is given by the lockmaster and consists of which sound signal?

A. One short blast
B. Two short blasts
C. One long blast
D. Two long blasts

2080. You are on course 030°T. The relative bearing of a lighthouse is 45°. What is the true bearing?

A. 015°
B. 075°

C. 255°
D. 345°

2081. You are taking bearings on two known objects ashore. The BEST fix is obtained when the angle between the lines of position is _____.

A. 30°
B. 45°
C. 60°
D. 90°

2082. You are holding position above Gallipolis Lock and Dam when you hear two long blasts of the horn from the lock. This indicates that you should _____.

A. enter the riverward lock
B. hold position until two more upbound tows have locked through
C. enter the landward lock
D. hold position until the lower gates are closed

2083. Information about major breakdowns, repairs, or other emergency operations with regard to weirs and (or) wicket dams, on the Western Rivers, may be obtained by consulting the _____.

A. U.S. Coast Pilot
B. Broadcast Notice to Mariners
C. Sailing Directions
D. Light List Vol. V

2084. You are approaching Gallipolis Lock and Dam. The traffic signal light is flashing red. You should _____.

A. hold your position and not attempt to enter the lock
B. approach the lock slowly under full control
C. proceed at normal speed to enter the lock
D. None of the above

2085. Information about major breakdowns, repairs, or other emergency operations with regard to weirs and (or) wicket dams, on the western rivers, may be obtained from the _____.

A. Broadcast Notice to Mariners
B. Light List Vol. V
C. U.S. Coast Pilot
D. Sailing Directions

2086. You are downbound on the Ohio River locking through Greenup. The chamber has been emptied and the lower gates are open. You hear one short blast of the whistle from the lock. You should _____.

A. leave the lock
B. hold up until another tow enters the adjacent lock
C. tie off to the guide wall until the river is clear of traffic
D. hold in the lock chamber due to a malfunction with the gate

2087. The Light List indicates that a light has a nominal range of 20 miles and is 52 feet (16 meters) high. If the visibility is 20 miles and your height of eye is 20 feet (6 meters), at what approximate distance will you sight the light?

A. 33.0 nm
B. 20.0 nm
C. 13.5 nm
D. 8.5 nm

2088. Information about major breakdowns, repairs, or other emergency operations with regard to weirs and (or) wicket dams, on the Western Rivers, may be obtained by consulting the _____.

A. Sailing Directions
B. Light List Vol. V
C. U.S. Coast Pilot
D. Broadcast Notice to Mariners

2089. Permission to leave the riverward chamber of twin locks is given by the lockmaster and consists of which sound signal?

A. One short blast
B. Two short blasts
C. One long blast
D. Two long blasts

2090. You are underway in an area where the charted depth is 8 fathoms. You compute the height of tide to be –4.0 feet. The draft of your vessel is 5.0 feet (1.52 meters). You determine the depth of the water beneath your keel to be _____.

A. 39 feet (11.9 meters)
B. 43 feet (13.1 meters)
C. 47 feet (14.3 meters)
D. 57 feet (17.4 meters)

2091. The velocity of the current in large coastal harbors is _____.

A. unpredictable
B. generally constant
C. generally too weak to be of concern
D. predicted in Tidal Current Tables

2092. Descending boats, while awaiting their turn to enter a lock, shall NOT block traffic from the lock. They shall be above the lock by at LEAST _____.

A. 100 feet
B. 200 feet
C. 300 feet
D. 400 feet

2093. Information about major breakdowns, repairs, or other emergency operations with regard to weirs and (or) wicket dams, on the Western Rivers, may be obtained from the _____.

A. Light List Vol. V
B. List of Lights
C. Broadcast Notice to Mariners
D. Sailing Directions

2097. Information about major breakdowns, repairs, or other emergency operations with regard to weirs and (or) wicket dams, on the Western Rivers, may be obtained by consulting the _____.

A. Sailing Directions
B. Broadcast Notice to Mariners
C. Light List Vol. V
D. None of the above

2098. Which magnetic compass corrector(s) can be set while the vessel is on a heading of magnetic east or magnetic west?

A. Quadrantal spheres
B. Heeling magnets
C. Fore-and-aft magnets
D. Athwartships magnets

2099. D047NG. You are inbound in a channel marked by a range. The range line is 309°T. You are steering 306°T. The range appears as shown and is closing. Which action should you take?

A. Continue on the present heading until the range is in line, then alter course to the left.
B. Continue on course until the range is closed, then alter course to the right.
C. Immediately alter course to the right to bring the range in line.

D. Immediately alter course to 309°T.

2100. You are underway in a vessel with a draft of 7.0 feet (2.1 meters). The charted depth for your position is 9 fathoms. You compute the height of tide to be +3.0 feet (0.9 meters). You determine the depth of the water beneath your keel to be _____.

A. 32 feet (9.8 meters)
B. 41 feet (12.6 meters)
C. 50 feet (15.3 meters)
D. 64 feet (19.6 meters)

2101. Information about major breakdowns, repairs, or other emergency operations with regard to weirs and (or) wicket dams, on the Western Rivers, may be obtained by consulting the _____.

A. Broadcast Notice to Mariners
B. Light List Vol. V
C. U.S. Coast Pilot
D. All of the above

2102. The subregions of the United States Gulf and East Coasts are numbered 11, 12 and 13 within the chart numbering system. Which chart number indicates a chart for either the Gulf or East Coast?

A. 21214
B. 11314
C. 14313
D. 14114

2103. The description "Racon" beside an illustration on a chart would mean a _____.

A. radar calibration beacon
B. circular radiobeacon
C. radar conspicuous beacon
D. radar transponder beacon

2104. A white buoy marked with an orange rectangle indicates _____.

A. mid-channel
B. a fish net area
C. general information
D. an anchorage

2110. You are underway in a vessel with a draft of 6.0 feet. You are in an area where the charted depth of the water is 4 fathoms. You would expect the depth of water beneath your keel to be approximately _____.

A. 12 feet

B. 18 feet
C. 24 feet
D. 30 feet

2111. Vessels regularly navigating Ohio and Mississippi rivers above Cairo, Illinois, and their tributaries, shall at all times have on board a copy of _____.

A. Tide Tables
B. U.S. Coast Pilot
C. U.S. Army Corps of Engineers Navigation Regulations (Blue Book)
D. Sailing Directions

2112. Vessels regularly navigating rivers above Cairo, Illinois, shall at all times have on board a copy of _____.

A. U.S. Coast Pilot
B. U.S. Army Corps of Engineers Regulations (Blue Book)
C. Nautical Almanac for the year
D. Light List Vol. V

2113. Vessels regularly navigating rivers above Cairo, Illinois, shall at all times have on board a copy of _____.

A. U.S. Army Corps of Engineers Regulations (Blue Book)
B. Nautical Almanac for the year
C. Sailing Directions
D. Light List Vol. V

2114. Vessels regularly navigating rivers above Cairo, Illinois, shall at all times have on board a copy of_____.

A. Sailing Directions
B. Nautical Almanac for the year
C. U.S. Coast Pilot
D. U.S. Army Corps of Engineers Regulations (Blue Book)

2115. Vessels regularly navigating rivers above Cairo, Illinois, shall at all times have on board a copy of_____.

A. U.S. Army Corps of Engineers Regulations (Blue Book)
B. Light List Vol. V
C. U.S. Coast Pilot
D. None of the above

2116. Vessels regularly navigating rivers above Cairo, Illinois, shall at all times have on board a copy of the _____.

A. Nautical Almanac for the year

B. U.S. Army Corps of Engineers Regulations (Blue Book)
C. Sailing Directions
D. All of the above

2119. Which stock number indicates a NIMA chart designed for fixing positions at sea and DR plotting while on a long voyage?

A. WOAGN520
B. PILOT16
C. 16BCO16212
D. WOPZC5245

2120. If a chart indicates the depth of water to be 6 fathoms and your draft is 6.0 feet, what is the depth of the water under your keel? (Assume the actual depth and charted depth to be the same.)

A. 6.0 feet
B. 26.5 feet
C. 30.0 feet
D. 56.5 feet

2121. In plotting a running fix, how many fixed objects are needed to take your lines of position from?

A. Three
B. Two
C. One
D. None

2122. A position that is obtained by using two or more intersecting lines of position taken at nearly the same time, is a(n) _____.

A. fix
B. running fix
C. estimated position
D. dead-reckoning position

2125. On charts of U.S. waters, a magenta marking is NOT used for marking a _____.

A. radiobeacon
B. lighted buoy
C. 5-fathom curve
D. prohibited area

2126. Your chart indicates that there is an isolated rock and names the rock using vertical letters. This indicates the _____.

A. rock is visible at low water springs only
B. rock is a hazard to deep draft vessels only
C. rock is dry at high water

D. exact position of the rock is doubtful

2130. You are underway and pass by a lighthouse. Its light, which was white since you first sighted it, changes to red. This means _____.

A. the light is characterized as alternately flashing
B. the lighthouse has lost power and has switched to emergency lighting
C. it is the identifying light characteristic of the lighthouse
D. you have entered an area of shoal water or other hazard

2131. The white lights in a vertical line on a multiple-span bridge indicate _____.

A. the main channel
B. the draw span is inoperable
C. the river is obstructed under that span
D. scaffolding under the span is reducing the vertical clearance

2132. What is the definition of height of tide?

A. The vertical difference between the heights of low and high water
B. The vertical difference between a datum plane and the ocean bottom
C. The vertical distance from the tidal datum to the level of the water at any time
D. The vertical distance from the surface of the water to the ocean floor

2140. The visible range marked on charts for lights is the _____.

A. minimum distance at which the light may be seen with infinite visibility
B. minimum distance at which the light may be seen based on a 12 mile distance to visible horizon
C. maximum distance the light may be seen restricted by the height of the light and the curvature of the earth
D. maximum distance at which a light may be seen in clear weather with 10 miles visibility

2141. What lights would you see on the Illinois waterway when any wickets of the dam or bear traps are open, or partially open, which may cause a set in the current conditions in the upper lock approach?

A. Red over green
B. Green over red

C. Red over amber (yellow)
D. Green over amber (yellow)

2142. Which lights would you see on the Illinois waterway when any wickets of the dam or bear traps are open, or partially open, which may cause a set in the current conditions in the upper lock approach?

A. Green over amber (yellow)
B. Red over amber (yellow)
C. Red over blue
D. Green over red

2143. What lights would you see on the Illinois waterway when any wickets of the dam or bear traps are open, or partially open, which may cause a set in the current conditions in the upper lock approach?

A. Red over amber (yellow)
B. Green over amber (yellow)
C. Red over Green
D. Green over Red

2145. What lights would you see on the Illinois waterway when any wickets of the dam or bear traps are open, or partially open, which may cause a set in the current conditions in the upper lock approach?

A. Green over red
B. Red over blue
C. Green over amber (yellow)
D. Red over amber (yellow)

2146. What lights would you see on the Illinois waterway when any wickets of the dam or bear traps are open, or partially open, which may cause a set in the current conditions in the upper lock approach?

A. Green over red
B. Red over blue
C. Red over amber (yellow)
D. None of the above

2147. What lights would you see on the Illinois waterway when any wickets of the dam or bear traps are open, or partially open, which may cause a set in the current conditions in the upper lock approach?

A. Green over blue
B. Red over amber (yellow)
C. Red over green
D. None of the above

2150. On a Mercator chart, 1 nautical mile is equal to _____.

A. 1 minute of longitude
B. 1 degree of longitude
C. 1 minute of latitude
D. 1 degree of latitude

2152. Permanent magnetism is found in _____.

A. hard iron
B. soft iron
C. vertical iron only
D. horizontal iron only

2158. Permanent magnetism is caused by _____.

A. operation of electrical equipment and generators on board ship
B. the earth's magnetic field affecting the ship's hard iron during construction
C. the horizontal component of the earth's magnetic field acting on the horizontal soft iron
D. the vertical component of the earth's magnetic field acting on the vertical soft iron

2159. Induced magnetism is found in _____.

A. hard iron
B. soft iron
C. vertical iron only
D. horizontal iron only

2160. Information for updating nautical charts is primarily found in the_____.

A. Notice to Mariners
B. Coast Pilots
C. nautical chart catalogs
D. Sailing Directions

2162. The new Moon cannot be seen because the Moon is _____.

A. in the opposite direction of the Sun
B. below the horizon
C. between the Earth and the Sun
D. at quadrature

2164. The line connecting the points of the earth's surface where there is no dip is the _____.

A. agonic line
B. magnetic equator
C. isodynamic
D. isopor

2165. Diagram D037NG represents a movable dam. If there is high water and the wickets are down so that there is an unobstructed navigable pass through the dam, what light(s) will be shown at B if the lock walls and piers are not awash?

A. Three red lights
B. Two red lights
C. One red light
D. One amber light

2168. By convention, the north pole of a magnet is painted _____.

A. red
B. blue
C. white
D. black

2169. To make sure of getting the full advantage of a favorable current, you should reach an entrance or strait at what time in relation to the predicted time of the favorable current?

A. 30 minutes before the predicted time
B. One hour after the predicted time
C. At the predicted time
D. 30 minutes before flood, one hour after ebb

2170. The temperature at which the air is saturated with water vapor and below which condensation of water vapor will occur is referred to as the _____.

A. precipitation point
B. vapor point
C. dew point
D. absolute humidity

2174. By convention, the Earth's north magnetic pole is colored _____.

A. red
B. white
C. blue
D. black

2176. Diagram D037NG represents a movable dam. If there is high water and the wickets are down so that there is an unobstructed navigable pass through the dam, what light(s) will be shown at D if the lock walls and piers are not awash?

A. Three red lights
B. Two red lights

C. One red light
D. One amber light

2177. Diagram D037NG represents a movable dam. If there is high water and the wickets are down so that there is an unobstructed navigable pass through the dam, what light(s) will be shown at D if the lock walls and piers are not awash?

A. One amber light
B. Three red lights
C. Two red lights
D. One red light

2178. The Flinders bar and the quadrantal spheres should be tested for permanent magnetism at what interval?

A. They are not subject to permanent magnetism; no check is necessary.
B. Semiannually
C. Annually
D. Every five years

2180. Relative humidity is defined as _____.

A. the maximum vapor content the air is capable of holding
B. the minimum vapor content the air is capable of holding
C. the ratio of the actual vapor content at the current temperature to the air's vapor holding capability
D. the relation of the moisture content of the air to barometric pressure

2184. By convention, the south seeking ends of a compass's magnets are colored _____.

A. blue
B. red
C. white
D. black

2187. Diagram D037NG represents a movable dam. If there is high water and the wickets are down so that there is an unobstructed navigable pass through the dam, what light(s) will be shown at D if the lock walls and piers are not awash?

A. No lights
B. Three red lights
C. Two red lights
D. One red lights

2190. Clouds are classified according to their _____.

A. size
B. moisture content
C. altitude and how they were formed
D. location in a front

2191. The chart indicates the variation was 3°45'E in 1988, and the annual change is increasing 6'. If you use the chart in 1991 how much variation should you apply?

A. 3°27'E
B. 3°27'W
C. 3°45'E
D. 4°03'E

2192. Off Fire Island, NY, with winds from the southwest, the average wind-driven current flows in a direction of _____.

A. 256°
B. 170°
C. 076°
D. 014°

2198. Opposition occurs when _____.

A. the Sun, Earth, and Moon are at right angles
B. the Sun's declination is 0° and is moving south
C. an inferior planet is at the maximum angle to the line of sight to the Sun
D. the Earth is between a planet and the Sun

2199. Denebola is found in what constellation?

A. Hydrus
B. Leo
C. Centaurus
D. Aquila

2200. Cloud formations are minimal when the _____.

A. surface temperature and temperature aloft are equal
B. surface temperature and temperature aloft differ greatly
C. barometric pressure is very low
D. relative humidity is very high

2203. You get underway from the shipyard in Chester, PA, at 1515 DST (ZD +4) on 6 August 1983, enroute to sea. You will be turning for eight knots. What current can you expect at Fourteen Foot Bank Light?

A. Slack
B. 1.3 knots ebbing
C. 1.7 knots ebbing
D. 0.5 knot ebbing

2209. You have completed the magnetic compass adjustments on magnetic east and magnetic south. The vessel is now steady on magnetic west but the compass reads 266°. You should now adjust the compass until it reads _____.

A. 268°
B. 270°
C. 274°
D. Do not adjust the compass; just record the error.

2210. A dead-reckoning (DR) plot _____.

A. ignores the effect of surface currents
B. is most useful when in sight of land
C. must be plotted using magnetic courses
D. may be started at an assumed position

2211. What is the length of a nautical mile?

A. 1,850 meters
B. 6,076 feet
C. 5,280 feet
D. 2,000 yards

2212. Which information is found in the chart title?

A. Number of the chart
B. Edition date
C. Variation information
D. Survey information

2214. By convention, the Earth's south magnetic pole is colored _____.

A. blue
B. black
C. white
D. red

2215. You are required to enter a lock on your voyage. Information on the lock regulations, signals, and radio communications can be found in _____.

A. the publication "Key to the Locks"
B. Bowditch
C. Corps of Engineers Information Bulletin
D. Coast Pilot

2220. A dead-reckoning (DR) plot_____.

A. must utilize magnetic courses
B. must take set and drift into account
C. should be replotted hourly
D. should be started each time the vessel's position is fixed

2222. By convention, the south pole of a magnet is painted _____.

A. red
B. blue
C. white
D. black

2224. By convention, the north-seeking ends of a compass's magnets are colored _____.

A. black
B. blue
C. red
D. white

2230. A nautical mile is a distance of approximately how much greater than or less than a statute mile?

A. 1/4 less
B. 1/7 less
C. 1/4 greater
D. 1/7 greater

2234. A vessel is heading magnetic north and its magnetic compass indicates a heading of 003°. What action should be taken to remove this error during compass adjustment?

A. Move the quadrantal spheres closer to the compass
B. Raise the heeling magnet if the red end is up
C. Remove some of the Flinders bar
D. Raise or lower the athwartships magnets

2236. Which is TRUE of a downbound power-driven vessel, when meeting an up-bound vessel on the Western Rivers?

A. She has the right of way.
B. She shall propose the manner of passage.
C. She shall initiate the maneuvering signals.
D. All of the above

2239. A flashing green light displayed at a single lock means that the lock is _____.

A. ready for entrance
B. ready for entrance, but gates cannot be closed completely
C. being made ready for entrance
D. not ready for entrance

2240. If you observe a buoy off station you should _____.

A. fill out and mail CG Form 2692 to the nearest Coast Guard office
B. appear in person at the nearest Coast Guard office
C. notify Coast Guard Headquarters in Washington, DC
D. immediately contact the nearest Coast Guard office by radiotelephone

2243. Which aid is NOT marked on a chart with a magenta circle?

A. Radar station
B. Radar transponder beacon
C. Aero light
D. Radiobeacon

2244. Capella is found in what constellation?

A. Gemini
B. Auriga
C. Libra
D. Crab

2246. The speed of an ocean current is dependent on _____.

A. the density of the water
B. the air temperature
C. the presence of a high pressure area near it
D. underwater soil conditions

2250. The most important information to be obtained from a barometer is the _____.

A. difference between the reading of the two pointers, which shows wind direction
B. last two figures of the reading of the pointer, such as 0.87, 0.76, or 0.92
C. present reading of the pressure, combined with the changes in pressure observed in the recent past
D. weather indications printed on the dial (such as cold, wet, etc.) under the pointer

2251. Which statement concerning the chartlet in illustration D010NG is TRUE? (Soundings and heights are in m.)

A. Maury lightship is visible for 17 miles.
B. The bottom to the south-southeast of the lightship is soft coral.
C. There is a dangerous eddy southeast of Beito Island.
D. There is a 12-meter deep hole west of Beito Island and inside the 5-meter line.

2252. The vertical angle between the horizontal and the magnetic line of force is the _____.

A. elevation
B. magnetic angle
C. vertical angle
D. dip

2254. A rock and sand structure extending from the bank of the river toward the channel is known as a _____.

A. wingdam
B. towhead
C. cutoff
D. landwall

2255. The height of tide is the _____.

A. depth of water at a specific time due to tidal effect
B. difference between the depth of the water at high tide and the depth of the water at low tide
C. difference between the depth of the water and the high water tidal level
D. difference between the depth of the water and the area's tidal datum

2256. The constellation that contains Polaris is _____.

A. Orion
B. Cassiopeia
C. Ursa Minor
D. Corona Borealis

2261. You determine your vessel's position by taking a range and bearing to a buoy. Your position will be plotted as a(n) _____.

A. running fix
B. fix
C. dead-reckoning position
D. estimated position

2262. The Milky Way is an example of a _____.

A. cluster
B. galaxy
C. nova
D. nebula

2264. The revision date of a chart is printed on which area of the chart?

A. Top center
B. Lower-left corner
C. Part of the chart title
D. Any clear area around the neat line

2268. What condition exists at perigee?

A. The Earth is farthest from the Sun.
B. The Earth, Sun, and Moon are in line.
C. The Earth, Sun, and Moon are at right angles.
D. The Moon is closest to the Earth.

2269. One of the factors which affects the circulation of ocean currents is _____.

A. humidity
B. varying densities of water
C. vessel traffic
D. the jet stream

2270. The lubber's line of a magnetic compass _____.

A. always shows true north direction
B. indicates the vessel's heading
C. is always parallel to the vessel's transom
D. is located on the compass card

2271. What is the definition of height of tide?

A. The vertical distance from the surface of the water to the ocean floor
B. The vertical distance from the tidal datum to the level of the water at any time
C. The vertical difference between a datum plane and the ocean bottom
D. The vertical difference between the heights of low and high water

2277. The Light List indicates that a light has a nominal range of 20 miles and is 52 feet high. If the visibility is 12.0 miles and your height of eye is 20 feet, at what approximate distance will you sight the light?

A. 21.5 miles
B. 20.0 miles
C. 13.7 miles
D. 12.0 miles

2280. Which would influence a magnetic compass?

A. Electrical wiring
B. Iron pipe
C. Radio
D. All of the above

2282. You have completed the magnetic compass adjustments on magnetic east and magnetic south. The vessel is now steady on magnetic west but the compass reads 276°. You should now adjust the compass until it reads _____.

A. 264°
B. 270°
C. 273°
D. Do not adjust the compass; just record the error.

2286. Which light signal indicates that you have permission to enter a lock on the Ohio River?

A. Steady red
B. Flashing amber
C. Steady green
D. Flashing green

2290. Magnets in the binnacles of magnetic compasses are used to reduce the effect of _____.

A. deviation
B. variation
C. local attraction
D. All of the above

2292. The points on the earth's surface where the magnetic dip is 90° are _____.

A. along the magnetic equator
B. connected by the isoclinal line
C. the isopors
D. the magnetic poles

2298. The period of rotation of the Moon on its axis is _____.

A. about 19 years
B. 365 days
C. about 27.3 days
D. 24 hours

2299. What condition exists at apogee?

A. The Earth is closest to the Sun.
B. The Moon is farthest from the Sun.
C. The Earth is farthest from the Moon.

D. The Moon is between the Earth and the Sun.

2300. When a magnetic compass is not in use for a prolonged period of time it should _____.

A. be shielded from direct sunlight
B. be locked into a constant heading
C. have any air bubbles replaced with nitrogen
D. have the compensating magnets removed

2306. In the North Sea area, you sight a buoy showing a quick white light with 9 flashes every 15 seconds. Which of the four topmarks shown in illustration D031NG would be fitted to the buoy?

A. A
B. B
C. C
D. D

2308. The points where the Sun is at 0° declination are known as _____.

A. solstices
B. equinoxes
C. perigee
D. apogee

2310. Which weather instrument measures atmospheric pressure?

A. Beaufort scale
B. Anemometer
C. Sling psychrometer
D. Barometer

2317. The Light List indicates that a light has a nominal range of 13 miles and is 36 feet high (11.0 meters). If the visibility is 7.0 miles and your height of eye is 25 feet (7.6 meters), at what approximate distance will you sight the light?

A. 10.0 miles
B. 12.9 miles
C. 14.2 miles
D. 17.0 miles

2318. Miaplacidus is found in what constellation?

A. Puppis
B. Hydrus
C. Centaurus
D. Carina

2320. The type of current which will have the greatest effect on the course made good for your vessel is _____.

A. one flowing in the same direction as your course steered
B. one flowing in the opposite direction as your course steered
C. one that flows at nearly right angles to your course steered
D. a rotary current in which the direction of current flow constantly changes

2328. Universal time (UTI) is another name for _____.

A. sidereal time
B. Greenwich mean time
C. ephemeris time
D. atomic time

2330. You are heading in a northerly direction when you come across an easterly current. Your vessel will_____.

A. be pushed to starboard
B. be pushed to port
C. decrease in engine speed
D. remain on course

2332. Magnetic dip is a measurement of the angle between the_____.

A. geographic pole and the magnetic pole
B. lubber's line and true north
C. horizontal and the magnetic line of force
D. compass heading and the magnetic heading

2335. The Light List indicates that a light has a nominal range of 13 miles and is 36 feet high. If the visibility is 17 miles and your height of eye is 25 feet, at what approximate distance will you sight the light?

A. 10.0 miles
B. 12.9 miles
C. 14.2 miles
D. 17.0 miles

2336. The period of revolution of the Moon is _____.

A. 24 hours
B. about 27.3 days
C. 365 days
D. about 19 years

2338. A group of stars which appear close together and form a striking configuration such as a person or animal is a _____.

A. cluster
B. shower
C. constellation
D. galaxy

2340. What is a Special Warning?

A. An urgent message concerning a vessel in distress
B. A weather advisory about unusual meteorological or oceanographic phenomena hazardous to vessels
C. A broadcast disseminating an official government proclamation affecting shipping
D. A radio navigational warning concerning a particularly hazardous condition affecting navigation

2345. You should plot your dead reckoning position _____.

A. from every estimated position
B. every three minutes in pilotage waters
C. only in pilotage waters
D. from every fix or running fix

2346. The first point of Aries is the point where the Sun is at _____.

A. maximum declination north
B. maximum declination south
C. 0° declination going to northerly declinations
D. 0° declination going to southerly declinations

2348. Under the IALA cardinal system, a mark with a quick light showing 9 flashes every 15 seconds indicates that the safest water is on the _____.

A. north side of the mark
B. west side of the mark
C. east side of the mark
D. south side of the mark

2349. The summer solstice is the point where the Sun is at _____.

A. maximum declination north
B. maximum declination south
C. 0° declination going to northerly declinations
D. 0° declination going to southerly declinations

2350. The principal advantage of NAVTEX radio warnings is that_____.

A. they can be used by mariners who do not know Morse code
B. only an ordinary FM radio is necessary to receive these warnings
C. information on a given topic is only broadcast at specified times
D. they cover a broad spectrum of the radio band allowing reception on almost any type of receiver

2351. A position obtained by applying ONLY your vessel's course and speed to a known position is a _____.

A. running fix
B. probable position
C. fix
D. dead-reckoning position

2353. A single line of position combined with a dead-reckoning position results in a(n) _____.

A. estimated position
B. assumed position
C. fix
D. running fix

2360. What U.S. agency is responsible for NAVAREA warnings?

A. Coast Guard
B. National Oceanic and Atmospheric Administration
C. National Ocean Service
D. National Geospatial-Intelligence Agency

2361. The range of tide is the _____.

A. maximum depth of the water at high tide
B. duration between high and low tide
C. distance the tide moves from the shore
D. difference between the heights of high and low tide

2362. You have completed the magnetic compass adjustments on magnetic east and magnetic south. The vessel is now steady on magnetic north but the compass reads 004°. Which action should be taken?

A. Use the Flinders bar and adjust the compass until it reads 002°.
B. Use the fore-and-aft magnets and adjust the compass until it reads 000°.

C. Use the athwartships magnets and adjust the compass until it reads 002°.
D. Use the athwartships magnets and adjust the compass until it reads 000°.

2363. In illustration D051NG, the position labeled C was plotted because _____.

A. the vessel's speed changed
B. the vessel's course changed form due North to due East
C. running fixes are better estimates of true position than dead-reckoning positions
D. All of the above are correct

2369. Which magnetic compass corrector(s) CANNOT be set on a heading of magnetic east or magnetic west?

A. Heeling magnet
B. Flinders bar
C. Fore-and-aft magnets
D. All of the above can be set on magnetic east or magnetic west headings.

2370. In the United States, short-range radio navigational warnings are broadcast by the _____.

A. Coast Guard
B. Corps of Engineers
C. NOAA
D. harbor master of the nearest port

2372. In the North Sea area, you sight a buoy showing a quick white light showing 6 flashes followed by one long flash at 15 second intervals. Which of the four topmarks illustrated in diagram D031NG would be fitted to this buoy?

A. A
B. B
C. C
D. D

2373. The vertical distance from the tidal datum to the level of the water is the _____.

A. actual water depth
B. range of tide
C. charted depth
D. height of tide

2375. The shortest distance between any two points on earth defines a _____.

A. small circle
B. great circle

C. rhumb line
D. hyperbola

2378. Which light signal indicates that you may approach the lock?

A. Flashing red
B. Flashing amber
C. Steady amber
D. Steady green

2379. The winter solstice is the point where the Sun is at _____.

A. maximum declination north
B. maximum declination south
C. 0° declination going to northerly declinations
D. 0° declination going to southerly declinations

2380. The navigation regulations applicable to a U.S. inland waterway can be found in the _____.

A. Notices to Mariners
B. Channel Reports
C. Sailing Directions
D. Coast Pilots

2381. The difference between the heights of low and high tide is the _____.

A. period
B. distance
C. depth
D. range

2384. On U.S. charts, you can tell if a named feature such as a rock (i.e., Great Eastern Rock in Block Island Sound) is submerged by the _____.

A. color of ink used to print the name
B. style of type used to print the name
C. dashed circle around the feature
D. magenta circle around the feature

2387. You are on a voyage from New Orleans to Boston and navigating off the Florida coast. You will get the greatest benefit from the Gulf Stream if you navigate _____.

A. about 5 miles east of Cape Canaveral
B. about 15 miles east of Daytona
C. along the 50-fathom curve
D. about 20 miles east of Jupiter Inlet

2388. The reference point for determination of GMT is the passage of the mean sun over what line?

A. First point of Aries
B. Observer's meridian
C. 0° longitude
D. 180° longitude

2389. The autumnal equinox is the point where the Sun is at _____.

A. maximum declination north
B. maximum declination south
C. 0° declination going to northerly declinations
D. 0° declination going to southerly declinations

2390. You are in a channel in U.S. waters near an industrial plant with a load/discharge facility for barges. You hear a siren being sounded at the facility. What does this indicate?

A. There is danger at the facility due to a fire or cargo release.
B. A towboat with a hazardous cargo barge is being moved to or from the facility.
C. The facility is warning a barge to shut down transfer operations due to weather conditions (electrical storms, tornado, etc.).
D. A barge at the facility has commenced loading or discharging operations.

2392. The point where the Sun is at maximum declination north or south is _____.

A. aphelion
B. perihelion
C. an equinox
D. a solstice

2394. A vessel is heading magnetic east and its magnetic compass indicates a heading of 093°. What action should be taken to remove this error during compass adjustment?

A. If the red ends of the magnets are aft, and the fore-and-aft tray is at the top, you should remove some magnets.
B. If the red ends of the magnet are aft, and the fore-and-aft tray is at the bottom, you should reverse the magnets.
C. If the red ends of the magnets are aft you should raise the fore-and-aft tray.
D. If the blue ends of the magnets are forward you should remove some magnets from the fore-and-aft tray.

2396. Perihelion is the point where the Sun _____.

A. is nearest to the Earth
B. is farthest from the Earth
C. is on the opposite side of the Earth from the Moon
D. and Moon and Earth are in line

2400. You are in a channel in U.S. waters near an industrial plant with a load/discharge facility for barges. You see an emergency rotating flashing light on the facility light up. What does this indicate?

A. A barge at the facility has commenced transferring a hazardous cargo.
B. A barge carrying a hazardous cargo is mooring or unmooring at the facility.
C. The facility is warning a barge to shut down transfer operations due to weather conditions (electrical storm, tornado, hurricane, etc.).
D. There is danger at the facility due to a fire or cargo release.

2402. You have completed the magnetic compass adjustments on magnetic east and magnetic south. The vessel is now steady on magnetic north but the compass reads 356°. You should now adjust the compass until it reads _____.

A. 358°
B. 000°
C. 002°
D. 004°

2404. The dividing meridian between zone descriptions +7 and +8 is _____.

A. 105°00'W
B. 112°30'W
C. 117°00'W
D. 120°30'W

2406. The dividing meridian between zone descriptions +4 and +5 is _____.

A. 67°30'W
B. 90°00'W
C. 67°30'E
D. 75°00'E

2408. What is the equivalent of 42 min. 48 sec. in arc units?

A. 21°24'
B. 18°16'
C. 11°19'
D. 10°42'

2409. You are approaching the first of two drawbridges that span a narrow channel. The second drawbridge is close to the first. Which signals should you sound?

A. Sound the request-for-opening signal for the first bridge only, who will notify the second bridge of your approach
B. Sound the request-for-opening signal twice in succession to indicate you must pass through both bridges
C. Sound the request-for-opening signal, pause for about 10 seconds, then sound two prolonged blasts.
D. Sound the request-for-opening signal and, after the bridge acknowledges it, sound the request-for-opening signal for the second bridge.

2410. A facility used for the discharge of a cargo of a particular hazard, such as chlorine, butane or ethane, must have what to warn water traffic of an immediate danger during fire or cargo release?

A. An emergency boat and crew
B. A siren or rotating flashing light
C. Flashing red lights located one-half mile upstream and downstream of the facility
D. Buoys with flashing lights controlled from shore, located one-half mile upstream and downstream of the facility

2412. The permanent magnetism of a vessel may change in polarity due to _____.

A. being moored for a long time on one heading
B. being struck by lighting
C. steaming from the north magnetic hemisphere to the south magnetic hemisphere
D. loading a homogenous magnetic cargo such as steel plate, iron bars, etc.

2416. An orange and white buoy indicating a vessel-exclusion area will be marked with what symbol?

A. Open-faced diamond
B. Diamond with a cross
C. Circle
D. Square

2418. While proceeding downriver, you sight a red triangular-shaped daymark on the left bank. Under the U.S. Aids to Navigation System on the Western Rivers this is a _____.

A. special purpose signal
B. passing daymark
C. mark with no lateral significance
D. crossing daymark

2419. A backlash below a lock is defined as a _____.

A. current setting your vessel on the wall
B. current setting into the lock chamber
C. an eddy working along the lower guide wall
D. current setting counterclockwise

2420. You are on course 355°T and take a relative bearing of a lighthouse of 275°. What is the true bearing of the lighthouse?

A. 080°
B. 085°
C. 280°
D. 270°

2423. In Region A of the IALA Buoyage System, when entering from seaward, the starboard side of a channel would be marked by a _____.

A. red conical buoy
B. green conical buoy
C. red can buoy
D. green can buoy

2424. Under the IALA-B Buoyage System, when entering from seaward a lateral system buoy to be left to starboard may display which topmark in illustration D046NG?

A. A
B. B
C. C
D. D

2425. A vessel's position should be plotted using bearings of _____.

A. fixed objects on shore
B. buoys at a distance
C. buoys close by
D. All of the above

2426. You are in charge of a power-driven vessel crossing a river on the Western Rivers. You must keep out of the way of _____.

A. a sail vessel descending the river
B. a power-driven vessel ascending the river

C. a vessel restricted in its ability to maneuver crossing the river
D. All of the above

2428. If your vessel were proceeding up river (ascending), the port side of the channel would be marked according to the U. S. Aids to Navigation System on the Western Rivers by_____.

A. green can buoys
B. red can buoys
C. green nun buoys
D. red nun buoys

2429. The lock chamber is 600 feet X 110 feet. Your towboat is 150 feet X 35 feet. Which of these tows will require a double lockage?

A. A set-over single
B. 4 standard barges abreast next to your boat's head and 3 jumbo abreast in the lead
C. 6 jumbo (3 abreast and 2 long) with a standard on each side of your boat
D. 9 jumbo barges

2430. You are on course 222°T and take a relative bearing of a lighthouse of 025°. What is the true bearing to the lighthouse?

A. 197°
B. 247°
C. 315°
D. 335°

2434. A vessel is heading magnetic east and its magnetic compass indicates a heading of 093°. What action should be taken to remove this error during compass adjustment?

A. If the red ends of the magnets are aft you should lower the fore-and-aft tray.
B. If the red ends of the magnets are forward, and the fore-and-aft tray is at the bottom, you should remove some magnets.
C. If the red ends of the magnets are to port you should raise the athwartships tray.
D. If the red ends of the magnets are to port, and the athwartships tray is at the top, you should reverse the magnets.

2435. What is a lighted safe water mark fitted with to aid in its identification?

A. A red and white octagon
B. Red and white retroreflective material

C. A sequential number
D. A spherical topmark

2437. When daylight savings time is kept, the times of tide and current calculations must be adjusted. One way of doing this is to _____.

A. add 15° to the standard meridian when calculating the time differences
B. apply no correction as the times at the reference stations are adjusted for daylight savings time
C. add one hour to the times listed for the reference stations
D. subtract one hour from the times listed for the subordinate stations

2438. The radar control that reduces weak echoes out to a limited distance from the ship is the _____.

A. sensitivity time control (sea-clutter control)
B. receiver gain control
C. brilliance control
D. fast time constant (differentiator)

2440. You are on course 357°T and take a relative bearing of a lighthouse of 180°. What is the true bearing to the lighthouse?

A. 003°
B. 227°
C. 177°
D. 363°

2442. You have completed the magnetic compass adjustments on magnetic east and magnetic south. The vessel is now steady on magnetic north but the compass reads 004°. You should now adjust the compass until it reads _____.

A. 356°
B. 358°
C. 000°
D. 002°

2444. What is the equivalent of 0°48′ in time units?

A. 2 min. 12 sec.
B. 2 min. 42 sec.
C. 3 min. 02 sec.
D. 3 min. 12 sec.

2446. What is the equivalent of 47 min. 20 sec. in arc units?

A. 8°27′
B. 11°50′
C. 13°42′
D. 13°56′

2448. What is the equivalent of 37 min. 32 sec. in arc units?

A. 4°47′
B. 6°38′
C. 7°41′
D. 9°23′

2450. You are on course 180°T and take a relative bearing of a lighthouse of 225°. What is the true bearing of the lighthouse?

A. 045°
B. 135°
C. 180°
D. 270°

2452. The permanent magnetism of a vessel may change in strength due to _____.

A. the nature of the cargo being carried
B. changes in heading
C. major structural repair
D. All of the above

2454. Illustration D037NG represents a movable dam. If the wickets are down and there are open weirs due to high water, what light(s) will be shown at C if the lock walls and piers are not awash?

A. One red light
B. Two red lights
C. Three red lights
D. One amber light

2456. An orange and white buoy marking an area where operating restrictions are in effect will be marked with which symbol?

A. Open-faced diamond
B. Diamond with a cross
C. Circle
D. Rectangle

2458. In the U.S. Aids to Navigation System on the Western Rivers, the light characteristic of group flashing (2) is used for lights on _____.

A. the right descending bank
B. the left descending bank
C. preferred channel buoys
D. daymarks with no lateral significance

2459. The controlling depth of the river is _____.

A. the minimum depth of the river prescribed in the channel maintenance program
B. the edge of a dredged channel
C. the highest level to which the river may rise without flooding
D. the least available water in a channel which limits the draft of boats and tows

2460. You are on course 344°T and take a relative bearing of a lighthouse of 270°. What is the true bearing to the lighthouse?

A. 016°
B. 074°
C. 090°
D. 254°

2464. Under the IALA-A Buoyage System, when entering from seaward a lateral system buoy to be left to port may display which topmark in illustration D046NG?

A. A
B. B
C. C
D. D

2466. On the Western Rivers, a vessel crossing a river must _____.

A. only keep out of the way of a power-driven vessel descending the river
B. keep out of the way of any vessel descending the river
C. keep out of the way of a power-driven vessel ascending or descending the river
D. keep out of the way of any vessel ascending or descending the river

2468. Under the U.S. Aids to Navigation System on the Western Rivers, the buoys marking the starboard side of the channel when going upstream will be _____.

A. black
B. red
C. green
D. yellow

2469. A tow that is properly aligned to pass through a narrow opening between two bridge piers is _____.

A. on course
B. headed fair

C. holding on
D. in shape

2470. You are on course 344°T and take a relative bearing of a lighthouse of 090°. What is the true bearing to the lighthouse?

A. 016°
B. 074°
C. 254°
D. 270°

2472. The Sun is closest to the Earth in what month?

A. October
B. July
C. April
D. January

2480. You are on course 277°T and take a relative bearing of a lighthouse of 045°. What is the true bearing to the lighthouse?

A. 038°
B. 232°
C. 315°
D. 322°

2482. When a vessel changes course from one cardinal heading to another cardinal heading while adjusting the compass, which action should be taken?

A. The course change should be made rapidly to prevent transient induced magnetism while passing the intercardinal headings.
B. After the new heading is reached, the vessel should steam on that course for at least two minutes before the adjustment.
C. During the course change, you should gently tap the compass to remove any error caused by friction on the pivot bearing.
D. After steadying on the new heading, the compass card should be slewed by a magnet and allowed to oscillate freely to remove any gaussin error.

2483. A white buoy with an orange rectangle on it is used to indicate_____.

A. general information
B. an exclusion area
C. danger
D. a controlled area

2484. What is the equivalent of 1°53' in time units?

A. 3 min. 16 sec.
B. 5 min. 28 sec.
C. 6 min. 43 sec.
D. 7 min. 32 sec.

2486. What is the equivalent of 23 min. 20 sec. in arc units?

A. 16°40'
B. 12°32'
C. 9°28'
D. 5°50'

2488. In which publication could you find information concerning the minimum lighting required for bridges on U.S. waters?

A. Chart No. 1.
B. Code of Federal Regulations
C. Mississippi River Systems Light List
D. Notice to Mariners

2489. You are approaching a drawbridge and must pass through during a scheduled closure period. What signal should you sound?

A. Five short blasts
B. Two prolonged, two short blasts
C. Three prolonged blasts
D. Three short blasts, two prolonged blasts

2496. An orange and white buoy marking a danger area will have what symbol on it?

A. Open-faced diamond
B. Diamond with a cross
C. Circle
D. Square

2498. The light characteristic of flashing is used in the Aids to Navigation System on the Western Rivers for lights on _____.

A. the right descending bank
B. the left descending bank
C. preferred channel buoys
D. daymarks with no lateral significance

2499. The head of the bend is the _____.

A. top or upstream beginning of a bend
B. bottom or downstream beginning of a bend
C. midpoint or center radius of a bend
D. center line or apex of a bend

2504. Under the IALA-A Buoyage System, when entering from seaward a lateral system buoy to be left to starboard may display which topmark in illustration D046NG?

A. A
B. B
C. C
D. D

2505. At the approaches to Savannah, GA, with the wind coming out of the west, the wind-driven current will be flowing approximately _____.

A. 280°
B. 260°
C. 100°
D. 080°

2506. Which is TRUE on the Western Rivers when a vessel downbound with a following current is meeting an upbound vessel?

A. She has the right of way only if she is a power-driven vessel.
B. She has the right of way only if she has a tow.
C. She does not have the right of way, since the other vessel is not crossing the river.
D. She must wait for a whistle signal from the upbound vessel.

2508. Normal pool elevation is the height in feet of the section of river above a dam. This height is measured from _____.

A. low steel on the Huey P. Long Bridge
B. mean sea level
C. the local water table
D. the minimum dam control level

2509. All persons or vessels within the lock area, including the lock approach channels, come under the authority of the _____.

A. dockmaster
B. dock captain
C. lockmaster
D. lock foreman

2510. When correcting apparent altitude to observed altitude, you do NOT apply a correction for _____.

A. the equivalent reading to the center of the body
B. the equivalent reading from the center of the Earth

C. the bending of the rays of light from the body
D. inaccuracies in the reference level

2519. The standard time meridian for zone description –12 is _____.

A. 165.0°E
B. 172.5°E
C. 180.0°
D. 172.5°W

2524. What is the equivalent of 2°35' in time units?

A. 10 min. 20 sec.
B. 9 min. 10 sec.
C. 7 min. 06 sec.
D. 6 min. 43 sec.

2525. Daylight savings time is a form of zone time that adopts the time_____.

A. two zones to the west
B. two zones to the east
C. one zone to the west
D. one zone to the east

2526. What is the equivalent of 10 min. 52 sec. in arc units?

A. 0°47'
B. 1°12'
C. 2°43'
D. 3°52'

2527. In the doldrums you can expect _____.

A. steady, constant winds
B. frequent rain showers and thunderstorms
C. steep pressure gradients
D. low relative humidity

2529. A bridge over a navigable waterway is being repaired. There is a traveller platform under the bridge's deck that significantly reduces the vertical clearance. If required by the CG district commander, how will this be indicated at night?

A. Illumination by flood lights
B. A quick flashing red light at each lower corner
C. A strobe light visible both up and downstream
D. Fixed amber lights under the extreme outer edges of the traveller

2530. The distance between any two meridians measured along a parallel of latitude _____.

A. increases in north latitude and decreases in south latitude
B. decreases as DLO increases
C. increases with increased latitude
D. decreases with increased latitude

2536. A revised print of a chart is made _____.

A. after every major hydrographic survey of the area covered by the chart
B. when there are numerous corrections to be made or the corrections are extensive
C. when a low-stock situation occurs and minor corrections are made
D. every two years to update the magnetic variation information

2538. The light characteristic of composite group flashing (2 + 1) is used in the Aids to Navigation System on the Western Rivers for lights on_____.

A. the right descending bank
B. the left descending bank
C. preferred-channel buoys
D. daymarks with no lateral significance

2539. Under the IALA cardinal system, a mark with quick white light showing 3 flashes every 10 seconds indicates that the safest water in the area is on the _____.

A. north side of the mark
B. west side of the mark
C. east side of the mark
D. south side of the mark

2540. The distance between any two meridians measured along a parallel of latitude and expressed in miles is the _____.

A. difference in longitude
B. mid-longitude
C. departure
D. meridian angle

2542. Which magnetic compass corrector(s) CANNOT be set while the vessel is on a heading of magnetic north or magnetic south?

A. Athwartships magnets
B. Heeling magnet
C. Flinders bar
D. All of the above can be set on magnetic north or magnetic south headings.

2544. At McAlpine L & D, normal upper pool elevation is 420.0 feet MSL, equal to 12.0 feet on the upper gauge. The vertical clearance at the Clark Memorial Highway bridge is 72.6 feet above normal pool. What is the clearance if the gauge reads 27.2 feet?

A. 25.4 feet
B. 57.4 feet
C. 60.6 feet
D. 72.6 feet

2546. A structure, usually made of stone or cement pilings which extends from the bank at approximately right angles to the current is called a _____.

A. dike
B. revetment
C. cutoff
D. crib

2548. On the Mississippi River, gauge zero is the gauge reading measured from the _____.

A. National Geodetic Vertical Datum
B. low water reference plane
C. the lowest recorded river depth
D. the highest recorded river depth

2560. A plane that cuts the Earth's surface at any angle and passes through the center will always form _____.

A. the equator
B. a great circle
C. a small circle
D. a meridian

2567. When outbound from a U.S. port, a buoy displaying a flashing red light indicates _____.

A. a sharp turn in the channel to the right
B. a wreck to be left on the vessel's starboard side
C. a junction with the preferred channel to the left
D. the port side of the channel

2570. A plane that cuts the Earth's surface and passes through the poles will always form _____.

A. the equator
B. a loxodromic curve
C. a small circle
D. a meridian

2572. The dividing meridian between zone descriptions –4 and –5 is _____.

A. 60°00'E
B. 67°30'E
C. 75°00'E
D. 60°00'W

2574. What is the equivalent of 2°52' in time units?

A. 9 min. 23 sec.
B. 11 min. 28 sec.
C. 11 min. 56 sec.
D. 12 min. 18 sec.

2576. What is the equivalent of 8 min. 56 sec. in arc units?

A. 0°28'
B. 0°46'
C. 1°12'
D. 2°14'

2580. The angle at the pole measured through 180° from the prime meridian to the meridian of a point is known as _____.

A. the departure
B. the polar arc
C. longitude
D. Greenwich hour angle

2583. You are in the Northern Hemisphere and a tropical wave is located 200 miles due west of your position. Where will the wave be located 24 hours later?

A. In the same place
B. Closer and to the west
C. Closer and to the east
D. Farther away to the west

2586. A chart has extensive corrections to be made to it. When these are made and the chart is again printed, the chart issue is a _____.

A. first edition
B. new edition
C. revised edition
D. reprint

2588. You are approaching an open drawbridge and sound the proper signal. You receive no acknowledgment from the bridge. Which action should you take?

A. Approach with caution and proceed through the open draw.

B. Approach under full control to a position no closer than 400 yards from the bridge and await a signal from the bridge.
C. Hold in the channel as a vessel is closing the bridge from the other direction.
D. Resound the opening signal and do not pass through the bridge until signals have been exchanged.

2589. Under the IALA cardinal system, a mark with a quick white light showing 6 flashes followed by one long flash indicates that the safest water is on the _____.

A. north side of the mark
B. west side of the mark
C. east side of the mark
D. south side of the mark

2590. A plane perpendicular to the polar axis will never form what line on the Earth's surface?

A. Great circle
B. Equator
C. Small circle
D. Meridian

2592. A deadhead is a(n) _____.

A. tree or log awash in a nearly vertical position
B. crew member who refuses to work
C. upstream end of a land wall
D. buoy that is adrift

2594. At McAlpine L & D, normal upper pool elevation is 420.0 feet (130.8 meters) MSL, equal to 12.0 feet (3.7 meters) on the upper gauge. The vertical clearance at the Clark Memorial Highway bridge is 72.6 feet (22.1 meters) above normal pool. What is the clearance if the gauge reads 10.6 feet (3.2 meters)?

A. 84.6 feet (25.8 meters)
B. 83.2 feet (25.4 meters)
C. 74.0 feet (22.6 meters)
D. 62.0 feet (18.9 meters)

2596. The abbreviation L.W.R.P. on the navigation maps means _____.

A. low water reference plane
B. low winter runoff point
C. least water river plane
D. land wall reference point

2597. You determine your vessel's position by taking a range and bearing to a buoy.

Your position will be plotted as a(n) _____.

A. fix
B. running fix
C. estimated position
D. dead-reckoning position

2598. A vessel is proceeding downstream in a narrow channel on the Western Rivers when another vessel is sighted moving upstream. Which vessel has the right of way?

A. The vessel moving upstream against the current
B. The vessel moving downstream with a following current
C. The vessel located more towards the channel centerline
D. The vessel with the least amount of maneuverability

2600. A parallel of latitude other than the equator is a _____.

A. great circle
B. loxodromic curve
C. small circle
D. gnomonic curve

2602. The lunar day is also known as the _____.

A. lunitidal interval
B. vulgar establishment of the port
C. nodal day
D. tidal day

2608. You should plot your dead-reckoning position _____.

A. from every estimated position
B. every three minutes in pilotage waters
C. from every fix or running fix
D. only in pilotage waters

2610. A line on the Earth parallel to the equator is a _____.

A. gnomonic curve
B. small circle
C. meridian
D. great circle

2612. The dividing meridian between zone descriptions –7 and –8 is _____.

A. 112°30'E
B. 118°30'E
C. 120°00'E
D. 116°30'W

2614. What is the equivalent of 4°36' in time units?

A. 9 min. 12 sec.
B. 14 min. 36 sec.
C. 15 min. 36 sec.
D. 18 min. 24 sec.

2616. What is the equivalent of 4 min. 04 sec. in arc units?

A. 60°16'
B. 8°08'
C. 2°08'
D. 1°01'

2625. Stormy weather is usually associated with regions of _____.

A. high barometric pressure
B. changing barometric pressure
C. low barometric pressure
D. steady barometric pressure

2626. What information is found in the chart title?

A. Date of the first edition
B. Date of the edition and, if applicable, the revision
C. Information on the sounding datum
D. Information on which IALA buoyage system applies

2627. Stormy weather is usually associated with regions of _____.

A. high barometric pressure
B. low barometric pressure
C. steady barometric pressure
D. changing barometric pressure

2628. A drawbridge may use visual signals to acknowledge a vessel's request to open the draw. Which signal indicates that the draw will NOT be opened immediately?

A. A flashing amber light
B. A fixed red light
C. A white flag raised and lowered vertically
D. A flashing white light

2629. D022NG. In both regions of the IALA buoyage system, which topmark is used on a special mark?

A. A
B. B
C. C
D. D

2632. A section of the river that is narrower than usual and is often navigable from bank to bank is a _____.

A. chute
B. stabilized channel
C. slough
D. navigable pass

2634. Under the U.S. Aids to Navigation System on the Western Rivers, a preferred-channel buoy is _____.

A. horizontally banded red and green
B. vertically striped red and white
C. solid red
D. solid green

2636. You are ascending a river and exchanging navigational information via radiotelephone with a descending vessel. If the descending vessel advises you to watch for the set above point X, what would you expect to encounter above point X?

A. An increase in current velocity
B. Slack water
C. Shallow water
D. A sideways movement of your vessel

2638. A vessel crossing a river on the Western Rivers has the right of way over _____.

A. vessels ascending the river
B. vessels descending the river
C. all vessels ascending and descending the river
D. None of the above

2639. Under the U.S. Aids to Navigation System used on the Western Rivers, aids to navigation lights on the right descending bank show _____.

A. white or green lights
B. white or red lights
C. green lights only
D. white lights only

2646. During daylight savings time the meridian used for determining the time is located farther _____.

A. east
B. west
C. east in west longitude and west in east longitude
D. west in west longitude and east in east longitude

2648. The 3 cm radar as compared to a 10 cm radar with similar specifications will _____.

A. give better range performance in rain, hail, etc.
B. display small targets in a mass of dense sea clutter at a greater range
C. have less sea return in choppy rough seas
D. display a more maplike presentation for inshore navigation

2651. Low pressure disturbances which travel along the intertropical convergence zone are called _____.

A. tropical waves
B. tropical disturbances
C. permanent waves
D. tidal waves

2652. The dividing meridian between zone descriptions –10 and –11 is _____.

A. 135°30'E
B. 145°00'E
C. 150°00'E
D. 157°30'E

2654. What is the equivalent of 5°54' in time units?

A. 20 min. 16 sec.
B. 23 min. 36 sec.
C. 25 min. 54 sec.
D. 30 min. 27 sec.

2656. What is the equivalent of 0 min. 16 sec. in arc units?

A. 0°32'
B. 0°16'
C. 0°04'
D. 0°01'

2659. In Region A of the IALA Buoyage System, when entering from seaward, the port side of a channel would be marked by a _____.

A. black can buoy
B. red conical buoy
C. black conical buoy
D. red can buoy

2664. The Light List shows a lighted aid to navigation on the right bank. This means that the light can be seen on the port side of a vessel _____.

A. crossing the river
B. descending the river
C. ascending the river
D. proceeding towards sea

2666. The following boats are approaching a lock. Which has priority for locking?

A. An 85-foot yacht
B. Corps of Engineer towboat running empty-headed
C. Delta Queen (passenger vessel)
D. An integrated chemical tow

2668. You are approaching a drawbridge and have sounded the request-for-opening signal. The bridge has responded with five short blasts. What reply should you sound?

A. None; no reply is required
B. Five short blasts
C. Two prolonged blasts
D. One prolonged, one short blast

2669. Under the IALA Buoyage System, which topmark in illustration D023NG will be displayed on a safe water mark?

A. A
B. B
C. C
D. D

2672. When you are steering on a pair of range lights and find the upper light is in line above the lower light, you should _____.

A. continue on the present course
B. come left
C. come right
D. wait until the lights are no longer in a vertical line

2673. A bluff bar is a bar _____.

A. extending out from a bluff alongside the river
B. that tends to give a false indication of its position
C. that has a sharp dropoff into deep water
D. that is perpendicular to the current

2674. In the U.S. Aids to Navigation System on the Western Rivers, a preferred channel buoy to be left to port while proceeding downstream will _____.

A. have the upper band red
B. show a red light if lighted

C. have a characteristic of composite group flashing if lighted
D. All of the above

2675. When you are steering on a pair of range lights and find the upper light is in line above the lower light, you should _____.

A. come left
B. continue on the present course
C. come right
D. wait until the lights are no longer in a vertical line

2676. The place where a channel moves from along one bank of the river over to the other bank of the river is called a _____.

A. draft
B. cutoff
C. draw
D. crossing

2678. A vessel crossing a river on the Western Rivers, must keep out of the way of a power-driven vessel _____.

A. descending the river with a tow
B. ascending the river with a tow
C. ascending the river without a tow
D. All of the above

2679. Under the U.S. Aids to Navigation System on the Western Rivers a daymark on the right descending bank will _____.

A. be green
B. have an odd number
C. indicate the gauge reading
D. have yellow retroreflective markings

2683. A vessel's position should be plotted using bearings of _____.

A. buoys close at hand
B. fixed known objects on shore
C. fixed objects
D. All of the above

2686. The standard time meridian for description +12 is _____.

A. 172.5°E
B. 180.0°
C. 172.5°W
D. 165.0°W

2688. The 10 cm radar as compared to a 3 cm radar of similar specifications will _____.

A. be more suitable for river and harbor navigation
B. provide better range performance on low-lying targets during good weather and calm seas
C. have a wider horizontal beam width
D. have more sea return during rough sea conditions

2695. You are plotting a running fix in an area where there is a determinable current. How should this current be treated in determining the position?

A. The drift should be added to the ship's speed.
B. The current should be ignored.
C. The course and speed made good should be determined and used to advance the LOP.
D. The set should be applied to the second bearing.

2704. The Light List shows a lighted aid to navigation on the right bank. This means that the light can be seen on the starboard side of a vessel _____.

A. proceeding from seaward
B. crossing the river
C. ascending the river
D. descending the river

2705. Information about the direction and velocity of rotary tidal currents is found in the _____.

A. Tidal Current Tables
B. Mariner's Guide
C. Tide Tables
D. Nautical Almanac

2706. The following types of vessels are awaiting lockage on the upper Mississippi. Which type of vessel is normally passed through the lock first?

A. Pleasure craft
B. Commercial towboats
C. Commercial passenger vessels
D. Commercial fishing vessels

2707. You will find information about the duration of slack water in the _____.

A. Tidal Current Tables
B. Tide Tables
C. American Practical Navigator
D. Sailing Directions

2708. You are approaching a drawbridge and have sounded the proper whistle signal requesting it to open. You hear a signal of one prolonged and one short blast from the bridge. Which action should you take?

A. Anchor or use an alternate route because the bridge is out of service for an extended period of time.
B. Approach to a point not closer than 400 yards (360 meters) from the bridge and await further signals.
C. Hold in the channel as the bridge will open within 15 minutes.
D. Approach under full control to pass through the bridge.

2709. Under the IALA-B Buoyage System, when entering from seaward a lateral system buoy to be left to port may display which topmark in illustration D046NG?

A. A
B. B
C. C
D. D

2711. Information about currents on the Pacific Coast of the U.S. are found in the _____.

A. Tidal Current Tables
B. Nautical Almanac
C. Tide Tables
D. Ocean Current Tables

2712. A bold reef is a reef _____.

A. with part of it extending above the water
B. that can be detected by water turbulence
C. that drops off sharply
D. perpendicular to the current

2714. A current moving across a lock entrance toward the river or toward the dam is called a(n) _____.

A. cutoff
B. outdraft
C. lockwash
D. springpool

2716. Under the U.S. Aids to Navigation System on the Western Rivers, passing daymarks on the left descending bank are _____.

A. green squares
B. green diamonds
C. red diamonds
D. red triangles

2718. A power-driven vessel operating in a narrow channel with a following current, on the Western Rivers, is meeting an upbound vessel. Which statement is TRUE?

A. The downbound vessel has the right-of-way.
B. The downbound vessel must initiate the required maneuvering signals.
C. The downbound vessel must propose the manner and place of passage.
D. All of the above

2719. Under the U.S. Aids to Navigation System on the Western Rivers, passing daymarks on the right descending bank are _____.

A. red diamond-shaped panels with red reflector borders
B. red triangular-shaped panels with red reflector borders
C. green square-shaped panels with green reflector borders
D. green triangular-shaped panels with green reflector borders

2720. When pushing barges ahead close to a steep revetment where there is no current, what is MOST likely to occur?

A. The stern of the towboat will tend to sheer away from the revetment.
B. Your speed over the ground will increase.
C. The head of the tow will tend to sheer away from the revetment.
D. All of the above

2721. You are plotting a running fix. How many fixed objects are needed to take your lines of position from?

A. One
B. Two
C. Three
D. None

2722. The paths of intended travel between three or more points is the _____.

A. course
B. track
C. bearing
D. course over the ground

2724. Which condition indicates that your radar needs maintenance?

A. Serrated range rings
B. Indirect echoes
C. Multiple echoes
D. Blind sector

2725. A position that is obtained by using two or more intersecting lines of position taken at nearly the same time, is a(n) _____.

A. estimated position
B. dead-reckoning position
C. running fix
D. fix

2726. A daymark used as a special mark is indicated by what letter in illustration D045NG?

A. A
B. B
C. C
D. D

2729. While navigating in fog off a coastline of steep cliffs, you hear the echo of the ship's foghorn 5.5 seconds after the signal was sounded. What is the distance to the shore?

A. 3825 ft. (1166 meters)
B. 3450 ft. (1052 meters)
C. 3072 ft. (936 meters)
D. 2475 ft. (754 meters)

2730. When attempting an upstream landing while pushing empty barges ahead in a hard onshore wind, the approach is best made _____.

A. with bow out, stern in
B. with bow in, stern out
C. parallel to the dock, as close in as possible
D. parallel to the dock, as far out as possible

2737. A lateral system buoy displaying a quick light _____.

A. should be passed close aboard on either side
B. indicates that special caution is required
C. is used at a channel bifurcation or junction
D. is painted with red and white vertical stripes

2738. While navigating in fog off a coastline of steep cliffs, you hear the echo of the ship's foghorn 3 seconds after the signal was sounded. What is the distance to the shore?

A. 1100 yards
B. 872 yards
C. 550 yards
D. 792 yards

2739. A daymark used to indicate the starboard side of the channel when approaching from seaward will have the shape indicated by what letter in illustration D045NG?

A. A
B. B
C. C
D. D

2740. When one upbound vessel is overtaking another vessel and both are pushing a tow ahead, what reaction may you expect?

A. Both towheads will tend to drift apart, and the overtaking vessel will be slowed down.
B. Both towheads will tend to drift together, and the overtaking vessel will be slowed down.
C. Both towheads will tend to drift apart, and the overtaken vessel will be slowed down.
D. Both towheads will tend to drift together, and the overtaken vessel will be slowed down.

2741. A general chart could have a scale of _____.

A. 1:200,000
B. 1:1,000,000
C. 1:50,000
D. not more than 1:25,000

2742. A white diamond daymark with an orange border is a(n) _____.

A. special mark
B. information or regulatory mark

C. lateral aid on the intracoastal waterway
D. safe water mark

2744. The standard atmospheric pressure measured in inches of mercury is _____.

A. 29.92
B. 500
C. 760
D. 1013.2

2746. What is used to measure wind velocity?

A. Psychrometer
B. Barometer
C. Wind sock
D. Anemometer

2750. When pushing a tow and approaching barges tied off to the shore, you should _____.

A. increase speed so you will pass faster
B. decrease speed while passing so you won't create a suction
C. do nothing different as the barges should be tied off properly
D. move to the opposite side of the channel from the barges and increase speed

2752. A daymark used to indicate the safe water in a channel will have the shape indicated by which letter in illustration D045NG?

A. A
B. B
C. C
D. D

2760. You are pushing a tow ahead, at high speed, near the right hand bank of a canal. The forces affecting your towboat and tow will tend to_____.

A. push both the head of the tow and the stern of the towboat away from the right hand bank
B. push the head of the tow away from, and pull the stern of the towboat into, the right hand bank
C. pull both the head of the tow and the stern of the towboat into the right hand bank
D. pull the head of the tow into, and push the stern of the towboat away from, the right hand bank

2762. You take a bearing of 176° of a lighthouse. Which bearing of another object would give the best fix?

A. 079°
B. 151°
C. 176°
D. 292°

2764. You are in a channel inbound from sea. A daymark used to mark a channel junction when the preferred channel is to port will have the shape indicated by what letter in illustration D045NG?

A. A
B. B
C. C
D. D

2766. In low latitudes, the high(s) of the diurnal variation of pressure occur(s) at _____.

A. noon
B. noon and midnight
C. 1000 and 2200
D. 1600

2768. Which type of daymark is used to mark the starboard side of the channel when entering from sea?

A. Red and white octagon
B. Black and white diamond
C. Red triangle
D. Green square

2769. If your vessel must pass through a draw during a scheduled closure period, what signal should you sound to request the opening of the draw?

A. One prolonged blast followed by one short blast
B. Three short blasts
C. One prolonged blast followed by three short blasts
D. Five short blasts

2770. What is most likely to happen when you push a multiple tow into a countercurrent?

A. Going upstream you will make better speed with no danger involved.
B. Going downstream you will be slowed down but will keep control of the tow.
C. There is a good chance you will break up the tow.

D. No danger exists as long as you steer a straight course through the eddy.

2772. The direction in which a vessel should be steered between two points is the _____.

A. course
B. heading
C. bearing
D. course over the ground

2774. Your radar is set on a true motion display. Which of the following will NOT appear to move across the PPI scope?

A. Echoes from a buoy
B. Own ship's marker
C. Echo from a ship on the same course at the same speed
D. Echo from a ship on a reciprocal course at the same speed

2777. A sailing chart could have a scale of _____.

A. not more than 1:25,000
B. 1:35,000
C. 1:100,000
D. 1:700,000

2778. A special daymark is a_____.

A. red-and-white octagon
B. daymark with a yellow stripe on it
C. green square
D. yellow diamond

2780. You are pushing a tow ahead and passing close to another towboat which is pushing ahead in the same direction (you are overtaking). After the towheads pass close alongside _____.

A. you will gain speed
B. both boats will gain speed
C. the tows will tend to drift apart
D. the tows will tend to drift together

2782. Your radar is set on a true motion display. Which of the following will appear to move across the PPI scope?

A. Own ship's marker
B. Echo from a ship at anchor
C. Echoes from land masses
D. All of the above

2788. The Light List indicates that a dayboard is a type KGW. You should _____.

A. see a green and white diamond
B. leave it to port when southbound on the Atlantic Coast ICW
C. pass it close aboard on either side
D. look for another daymark to form the range

2790. A towboat has the same draft as the barges it is pushing ahead. If the distance from the stern of the towboat to the head of the tow is 800 feet, where is the approximate location of the pivot point of the unit?

A. At the head of the tow
B. 250 feet from the head of the tow
C. 400 feet from the head of the tow
D. 600 feet from the head of the tow

2792. You take a bearing of 142° and 259° of two objects. Which bearing of a third object will give the best fix?

A. 081°
B. 238°
C. 201°
D. 234°

2794. The standard atmospheric pressure in millibars is _____.

A. 760
B. 938.9
C. 1000
D. 1013.2

2798. A can buoy is indicated by which letter in illustration D044NG?

A. A
B. B
C. C
D. D

2800. Where is the pivot point of a towboat with a tow ahead?

A. One-third the length of the combined unit forward of the towboat
B. One-third the length of the combined unit back from the head
C. At the head of the towboat
D. One-half the length of the combined unit

2801. Mean high water is used _____.

A. as the reference for soundings on the Gulf Coast of the U.S.

B. to indicate the shoreline where there is a large tidal fluctuation
C. as the reference plane for bottom contour lines
D. as the sounding datum for rivers, lakes, etc., regulated by locks

2803. Some locations maintain a zone time of −13. What are the Greenwich time and date if the zone time and date are 0152, 10 January?

A. 1252, 9 January
B. 1452, 9 January
C. 0052, 11 January
D. 1452, 11 January

2804. The altitude at LAN may be observed by starting several minutes in advance and continuing until a maximum altitude occurs. This procedure should not be used _____.

A. when the declination and latitude are of different names
B. when the declination is greater than and the same name as the latitude
C. if the vessel is stopped or making bare steerageway
D. on a fast vessel on northerly or southerly headings

2805. D047NG. You are entering port and have been instructed to anchor, as your berth is not yet available. You are on a SW'ly heading, preparing to drop anchor, when you observe the range as shown on your starboard beam. You should _____.

A. drop the anchor immediately as the range lights mark an area free of obstructions
B. drop the anchor immediately as a change in the position of the range lights will be an indication of dragging anchor
C. NOT drop the anchor until the lights are in line
D. ensure your ship will NOT block the channel or obstruct the range while at anchor

2809. The diurnal variation of pressure is not visible in the middle latitudes in winter because _____.

A. it is masked by the pressure changes of moving weather systems
B. the decreased gravitational effect from the sun causes the variation to fade

C. the decreased average temperature is less than the critical temperature

D. the increased Coriolis force disperses the pressure variation

2810. When steering a tow downstream around the shape of a sand bar, and staying on the proper side of the buoys, an operator should be cautious of _____.

A. eddies under the bar
B. swift current under the bar causing loss of control
C. cross-currents pushing the tow away from the bar
D. cross-currents pushing the tow into the bar

2814. In low latitudes the range of the diurnal variation of pressure is up to _____.

A. 0.5 millibar
B. 3.0 millibars
C. 6.0 millibars
D. 10.0 millibars

2816. The length of a wave is the length _____.

A. of the wave's crest
B. of the wave's trough
C. measured from crest to trough
D. measured from crest to crest

2818. You take bearings of 313°T and 076°T on two objects. Which bearing of a third object will give the best fix?

A. 048°T
B. 101°T
C. 142°T
D. 187°T

2819. The time interval between successive wave crests is called _____.

A. wave period
B. wavelength
C. frequency
D. significant wave height

2820. A towboat is pushing barges ahead at a dangerously fast speed when _____.

A. the towboat vibrates when backing down
B. the roostertail exceeds the height of the main deck
C. a strain is placed on the face wires

D. water comes over the foredeck of the lead barges

2821. The height of tide is the _____.

A. difference between the depth of the water at high tide and the depth of the water at low tide
B. depth of water at a specific time due to tidal effect
C. difference between the depth of the water and the area's tidal datum
D. difference between the depth of the water and the high water tidal level

2822. While navigating in fog off a coastline of steep cliffs, you hear the echo of the ships' foghorn 2 seconds after the signal was sounded. What is the distance to the shore?

A. 360 yards
B. 320 yards
C. 280 yards
D. 140 yards

2824. When you turn on the fast time constant (differentiator) control of a radar it will _____.

A. enhance weak target echoes and brighten them on the PPI
B. reduce clutter over the entire PPI by shortening the echoes
C. only suppress weak targets to a limited distance from the ship (sea clutter)
D. reduce the beam width to provide a map-like presentation for navigation

2826. You take a bearing of 043° and 169° of two objects. What bearing of a third object will give the best fix?

A. 356°
B. 102°
C. 144°
D. 201°

2828. The daily recurring pattern of pressure changes most noticeable in low latitudes is the _____.

A. daily lapse reading
B. diurnal variation of pressure
C. pressure tendency
D. synoptic pressure

2830. The proper way to approach a downstream lock where there is an outdraft is to be _____.

A. wide out from the land wall, keeping the stern in at all times
B. wide out from the land wall, keeping the stern out at all times
C. close in to the land wall, keeping the stern in at all times
D. close in to the land wall, keeping the stern out at all times

2831. A coastal chart could have a scale of _____.

A. not more than 1:25,000
B. 1:35,000
C. 1:100,000
D. 1:500,000

2832. The Light List indicates that a dayboard is a type MR. You should _____.

A. leave it on either side
B. look for the other dayboard forming the range
C. look for an all red daymark
D. check to enter the correct channel at this junction daymark

2838. You take a bearing of 191° and 313° to two objects. Which bearing of a third object will give the best fix?

A. 001°
B. 069°
C. 209°
D. 356°

2839. Privately maintained aids to navigation included in the Light List _____.

A. are painted white and must use a white light if lighted
B. must be conspicuously marked by a signboard with the words "PRIVATE AID"
C. must conform to the standards of the U.S. Aids to Navigation System
D. are not permitted in or along first-class waterways and may be authorized for second- and third-class waterways

2840. The lockmaster has given you permission to tie off on the lower guide wall to wait your turn to lock through. What should you be most concerned with?

A. A downbound vessel
B. An upbound vessel
C. Current reaction when the lock chamber is being emptied
D. Current reaction when the lock chamber is being filled

2841. You are required to enter a lock on your voyage. Information on the lock regulations, signals, and radio communications can be found in _____.

A. Coast Pilot
B. Corps of Engineer Information Bulletin
C. Bowditch
D. the publication "Key to the Locks"

2842. The drawspan of a floating drawbridge may be marked with _____.

A. two white lights
B. a yellow diamond
C. flashing blue lights
D. three red lights on each side of the draw

2843. A position obtained by applying ONLY your vessel's course and speed to a known position is a _____.

A. fix
B. running fix
C. dead-reckoning position
D. probable position

2844. The signal from a ramark will show on the PPI as a _____.

A. coded signal on the same bearing and at a greater range than the transponder
B. circle surrounding the transponder
C. radial line from the transponder to the center of the PPI
D. dashed circle at the same range as the transponder

2846. Which type of daymark is used to mark the port side of the channel when entering from sea?

A. Red and white octagon
B. Black and white diamond
C. Red triangle
D. Green square

2848. While navigating in fog off a coastline of steep cliffs, you hear the echo of the ship's foghorn 6 seconds after the signal was sounded. What is the distance to the shore?

A. 1200 yards
B. 1100 yards
C. 1000 yards
D. 900 yards

2849. You take a bearing of 086° of a light-house. What bearing of another object would give the best fix?

A. 000°
B. 066°
C. 112°
D. 271°

2850. What is used to help prevent damage to barges, locks, and landings when you are locking or landing a tow?

A. Dock cushions
B. Springers
C. Landing bars
D. Bumpers (fenders)

2851. You determine your vessel's position by taking a range and bearing to a buoy. Your position will be plotted as a(n) _____.

A. dead-reckoning position
B. estimated position
C. running fix
D. fix

2852. A daymark warning of a danger will have the shape indicated by what letter in illustration D045NG?

A. A
B. B
C. C
D. D

2858. While navigating in fog off a coastline of steep cliffs, you hear the echo of the ship's foghorn 2-1/2 seconds after the signal was sounded. What is the distance to the shore?

A. 225 yards
B. 460 yards
C. 750 yards
D. 910 yards

2860. On the Mississippi and Ohio Rivers, there is a special type of fog known as steam fog. It is caused by _____.

A. warm air passing over much colder water
B. cold air passing over much warmer water
C. a rapid cooling of the ground on a clear night
D. rain coming out of a warm air mass aloft

2862. When slanted letters are used to spell the name of a charted object you know the _____.

A. object is only a hazard to vessels drawing in excess of 20 feet
B. position is approximate or doubtful
C. object is always visible
D. object may cover and uncover with the tide

2866. Some locations maintain a zone time of −13. What are the zone time and date if the Greenwich time and date are 2152, 10 January?

A. 1052, 9 January
B. 0852, 10 January
C. 1052, 10 January
D. 1052, 11 January

2868. D048NG. You are inbound in a channel marked by a range. The range line is 309°T. You are steering 306°T and have the range in sight as shown. Which action should you take?

A. Continue on the present heading until the range is in line then alter course to the right.
B. Immediately alter course to the right to bring the range in line.
C. Immediately alter course to the left to bring the range in line.
D. Immediately alter course to 309°T if the range is closing.

2869. A pillar buoy is indicated by which letter in illustration D044NG?

A. A
B. B
C. C
D. D

2870. Steam fog is most likely to occur on the Mississippi and Ohio Rivers in _____.

A. spring, around late evening
B. spring, around early evening
C. fall, around early morning
D. fall, around midday

2874. What daymark has NO lateral significance?

A. Red triangle
B. Red triangle with a green horizontal stripe
C. Green and white diamond
D. Green square

2875. A harbor chart could have a scale of _____.

A. not more than 1:25,000
B. 1:35,000
C. 1:150,000
D. not less than 1:500,000

2877. Class I and II private aids to navigation in or along navigable waters of the United States are listed in the _____.

A. Sailing Directions
B. Light List
C. List of Private Aids
D. Aids to Navigation Manual

2880. While upbound through Memphis, the weather report on the TV news indicates that a cold front will cross western Kentucky and Tennessee the next morning. What weather should accompany this front?

A. Light, southerly winds; high humidity and possibly fog
B. Overcast with steady, light rain or drizzle
C. Gusting winds shifting to the northwest with thunderstorms
D. Scattered clouds with light to moderate southeasterly winds and possibly fog

2882. While upbound through Memphis, the weather report on TV news indicates that a warm front is stationary over the Kentucky–Missouri–Tennessee areas. What weather conditions should you expect?

A. Strong, gusting winds from the NW with thundershowers
B. Light winds from the northeast with clear skies
C. A blue norther
D. Southerly winds with steady rain; fog or overcast

2884. D011NG. The pictures shown represent the geographic location of a vessel and the radar presentation at the same time. Which statement is TRUE?

A. Ship No. 1 does not appear as an individual target due to the effect of beam width.
B. Small island is not detected due to the multiple echo effect from the mountain.
C. A tangent bearing of the headland to the south-southeast is corrected by subtracting one-half of the beam width.
D. Ship No. 2 is not detected due to the side lobe effect of radar reflecting from the mountain.

2886. On mid-ocean waters, the height of a wind-generated wave is not affected by the _____.

A. water depth exceeding 100 feet
B. fetch
C. wind's velocity
D. duration of the wind

2890. While passing through Memphis, the weather report on the TV news indicates that a cold front is crossing western Kentucky and Tennessee. Tomorrow's weather will be dominated by a high pressure area. What weather should you expect tomorrow?

A. Light, southerly winds; high humidity and possibly fog
B. Moderate winds from the northwest, clear visibility and cooler temperatures
C. Low overcast; mild temperatures with light, steady rain or drizzle
D. Scattered clouds with light, southeasterly winds; high humidity and possibly fog

2891. Twenty-three meters equals_____.

A. 17.50 feet
B. 75.46 feet
C. 96.00 feet
D. 104.99 feet

2892. The Light List indicates that a dayboard is a type NB. You should _____.

A. see a black triangle
B. look for another daymark forming a range
C. expect a daymark of no lateral significance
D. check to enter the correct channel at the junction daymark

2894. Fetch is the _____.

A. distance a wave travels between formation and decay
B. stretch of water over which a wave-forming wind blows
C. time in seconds required for two crests to pass a given point
D. measurement of a wave's steepness

2895. A white buoy with an orange rectangle on it is a(n) _____.

A. junction buoy
B. safe water buoy
C. informational buoy
D. All of the above

2896. You are navigating in pilotage waters. The maximum time between fixes should be about _____.

A. 5 minutes
B. 30 minutes
C. 1 hour
D. 4 hours

2899. You take a bearing of 043° and 169° of two objects. What bearing of a third object will give the best fix?

A. 356°
B. 073°
C. 192°
D. 309°

2900. Who should be consulted for changing conditions of controlling depths in major channels?

A. U.S. Coast Guard
B. National Imagery and Mapping Agency
C. National Ocean Service
D. U.S. Army Corps of Engineers

2902. The direction a vessel is pointed at any given time is the_____.

A. course
B. track
C. heading
D. course over the ground

2904. Your radar displays your ship off center. As you proceed on your course, your ship's marker moves on the PPI scope while echoes from land masses remain stationary. What is this display called?

A. Off center
B. True motion
C. Stabilized
D. Head up

2909. A nun buoy is indicated by which letter in illustration D044NG?

A. A
B. B
C. C
D. D

2910. You are taking bearings on two known objects ashore. The BEST fix is obtained when the angle between the lines of position is _____.

A. 60°
B. 45°
C. 90°
D. 30°

2913. The Daily Memorandum contains information on _____.

A. active weather disturbances such as hurricanes or tropical storms
B. the latest navigational warnings
C. scheduled vessel arrivals and departures for a 24-hour period
D. water levels at river ports where run-off affects tidal heights

2916. You take a bearing of 191° and 313° to two objects. Which bearing of a third object will give the best fix?

A. 022°
B. 131°
C. 211°
D. 249°

2918. Which agency maintains federal aids to navigation?

A. Corps of Engineers
B. Coast Guard
C. National Ocean Service
D. Maritime Administration

2920. Navigation charts of the Upper Mississippi River are published by _____.

A. National Ocean Service
B. Lake Survey
C. Corps of Engineers, U.S. Army
D. U.S. Coast Guard

2922. The Light List indicates that a dayboard is a type TR-SY. You should _____.

A. look for a dayboard of type TR-TY to form a range
B. leave it to port when southbound on the Atlantic portions of the ICW
C. pass it close aboard on either side
D. expect a daymark with no lateral significance

2923. You should plot your dead reckoning position _____.

A. from every estimated position
B. from every fix or running fix
C. every three minutes in pilotage waters
D. only in pilotage waters

2925. A single line of position combined with a dead-reckoning position results in a(n) _____.

A. running fix
B. fix
C. assumed position
D. estimated position

2926. You are inbound in a channel marked by a range. The range line is 309°T. You are steering 306°T and have the range in sight as indicated in illustration D047NG. The range continues to open. Which action should you take?

A. Come left until the range closes then steer to the left of 306°T.
B. Alter course to the right to 309°T or more to bring the range in line.
C. Continue on course but be prepared to come right if the range continues to open.
D. Alter course to the left to close the range, then alter course to 309°T.

2927. In illustration D051NG, the position labeled C was plotted because _____.

A. the vessel's course changed from due North to due East
B. running fixes are better estimates of true position than dead-reckoning positions
C. the vessel's speed changed
D. All of the above are correct

2928. You are in a buoyed channel at night and pass a lighted buoy with an irregular characteristic. You should report this to the _____.

A. Coast Guard
B. harbor master
C. Corps of Engineers
D. National Ocean Service

2930. How is a navigation light identified on an Army Corps of Engineers navigation map?

A. Name and light characteristic
B. Name and miles from a reference point
C. Light characteristic and miles A.H.P.
D. None of the above

2931. The vertical distance from the tidal datum to the level of the water is the _____.

A. range of tide
B. height of tide
C. actual water depth
D. charted depth

2932. If the main channel under a bridge is marked with lights of the lateral system the adjacent bridge piers should be marked with _____.

A. occulting white lights
B. fixed yellow lights
C. fixed white lights
D. flashing yellow lights

2936. Information on search and rescue procedures and special, local communications used in Mexican waters will be found in the _____.

A. World Port Index
B. International Code of Signals (Pub 102)
C. Sailing Directions (Planning Guides)
D. International Aeronautical and Maritime Search and Rescue Manual

2937. The depth of the water is indicated on a chart as 32 meters. This is equal to _____.

A. 11.50 fathoms
B. 12.62 fathoms
C. 17.50 fathoms
D. 104.99 fathoms

2938. You take a bearing of 176° of a lighthouse. What bearing of another object would give the best fix?

A. 000°
B. 021°
C. 189°
D. 272°

2939. The buoy indicated by the letter D in illustration D044NG is a _____.

A. nun
B. can
C. spar
D. pillar

2940. On the Corps of Engineer's Navigation Maps, the channel is _____.

A. midway between the banks
B. indicated by depths (in feet)

C. indicated by a broken line
D. not indicated

2941. During daylight savings time the meridian used for determining the time is located farther _____.

A. west in west longitude and east in east longitude
B. east in west longitude and west in east longitude
C. east
D. west

2944. The height of a wave is the vertical distance _____.

A. from the still water plane to the crest
B. from the still water plane to the trough
C. from crest to trough
D. between water levels at one-quarter of the wave's length

2945. A position that is obtained by applying estimated current and wind to your vessel's course and speed is a(n) _____.

A. estimated position
B. dead reckoning position
C. fix
D. None of the above

2947. A position obtained by crossing lines of position taken at different times and advanced to a common time is a(n) _____.

A. fix
B. dead-reckoning position
C. running fix
D. estimated position

2950. On an Army Corps of Engineers navigation map, each mile A.H.P. on the Lower Mississippi River is marked by a _____.

A. dashed red line
B. number showing mileage
C. navigation light
D. red circle

2952. The channel under a bridge is marked with lights of the lateral system. The centerline of the channel shall be marked on the bridge by _____.

A. an occulting white light
B. a yellow light
C. three fixed white lights
D. a flashing blue light

2954. D047NG. You are inbound in a channel marked by a range. The range line is 309°T. You are steering 306°T. The range appears as shown and is closing. Which action should you take?

A. Continue on the present heading until the range is in line then alter course to the left.
B. Immediately alter course to the right to bring the range in line.
C. Continue on course until the range is closed, then alter course to the right.
D. Immediately alter course to 309°T.

2958. Drawbridges equipped with radiotelephones display a _____.

A. day signal of a yellow diamond marked with the call sign
B. white sign with the number 16 and the call sign on it
C. black and white diamond marked with "RT 16"
D. blue and white sign showing the radio's channels

2959. Vessels required to have an Automatic Radar Plotting Aid must have a device to indicate the_____.

A. time of the next navigational satellite
B. distance to the next port
C. speed of the vessel over the ground or through the water
D. None of the above

2960. What is NOT found in the Mississippi River System Light List?

A. Distance that a lighted aid to navigation can be seen at night
B. Distance between major points on the Mississippi River
C. A color plate showing the details of the aids to navigation used on the Mississippi River
D. Times of Coast Guard broadcasts concerning river stages

2961. Which position includes the effects of wind and current?

A. Dead reckoning positions
B. Estimated positions
C. Leeway position
D. Set position

2962. While navigating in fog off a coastline of steep cliffs, you hear the echo of the ship's foghorn 4-1/2 seconds after the sig-

nal was sounded. What is the distance to the shore?

A. 405 yards
B. 628 yards
C. 730 yards
D. 825 yards

2964. D011NG. The pictures shown represent the geographic location of a vessel and the radar presentation at the same time. Which statement is TRUE?

A. Ship No. 1 does not paint as an individual target due to the side lobe affect.
B. The small island is not detected due to the limitation caused by the pulse length.
C. A tangent bearing of the headland to the south-southeast is corrected by subtracting one-half of the beam width.
D. Ship No. 2 is not detected due to the combined affects of beam width and pulse length.

2965. Which symbol represents a 10-fathom curve?

A. _____ _____ _____
B. ... _____ ... _____
C. _____ . _____ . _____ . _____
D. ....

2966. You take a bearing of 264° of a lighthouse. Which bearing of another object would give the best fix?

A. 291°
B. 059°
C. 182°
D. 239°

2968. Some locations maintain a zone time of −13. What are the zone time and date if the Greenwich time and date are 0152, 10 January?

A. 0052, 9 January
B. 0258, 9 January
C. 1452, 10 January
D. 0052, 11 January

2969. A red triangular daymark marks

_____.

A. the centerline of a navigable channel
B. the starboard side of a channel
C. a prominent object of navigational interest that has no lateral significance
D. an area of a channel where passing another vessel is permitted

2970. The Light List shows a lighted aid to navigation on the left bank. This means that the light can be seen on the port side of a vessel _____.

A. ascending the river
B. descending the river
C. crossing the river
D. proceeding from seaward

2972. You are in a channel inbound from sea. A daymark used to mark a channel junction when the preferred channel is to starboard will have the shape indicated by what letter in illustration D045NG?

A. A
B. B
C. C
D. D

2973. You should plot a dead reckoning position after every _____.

A. course change
B. speed change
C. fix or running fix
D. All of the above

2974. What daymark shape is used in the lateral system?

A. Semicircle
B. Triangle
C. Pentagon
D. Diamond

2977. Which symbol represents a 2-fathom curve?

A. — — —
B. .. _____ .. _____ .. _____
C. _____ . _____ . _____ .
D. ... .

2979. You take a bearing of 356° of a lighthouse. What bearing of another object would give the best fix?

A. 013°
B. 082°
C. 176°
D. 201°

2980. What volume of the Coast Guard Light List is used for the Mississippi River system?

A. I
B. II

C. IV
D. V

2981. The maritime radio system consisting of a series of coast stations transmitting coastal warnings is called _____.

A. NAVTEX
B. HYDROLANT/HYDROPAC
C. NAVAREA
D. SAFESEA

2982. You take a bearing of 142° and 259° of two objects. What bearing of a third object will give the best fix?

A. 019°
B. 084°
C. 166°
D. 281°

2984. What two shapes indicated in illustration D045NG are used to indicate a preferred channel?

A. A and B
B. B and C
C. C and D
D. A and D

2986. Some places maintain a zone time of –13. What are the time and date at Greenwich if the zone time and date are 2152, 10 January?

A. 1052, 9 January
B. 0852, 10 January
C. 1052, 10 January
D. 1052, 11 January

2988. The buoy indicated by the letter A in illustration D044NG is a _____.

A. nun
B. can
C. spar
D. pillar

2990. In which source could you find the vertical clearance of a bridge on the Ohio River?

A. Notice to Mariners
B. Light List of the Mississippi River System
C. Great Lakes Pilot
D. Coast Pilot of the Gulf of Mexico

2991. When using a radar in an unstabilized mode, fixes are determined most easily from _____.

A. objects that are close aboard
B. ranges
C. tangent bearings
D. center bearings

2994. You take a bearing of 313° and 076° of two objects. Which bearing of a third object will give the best fix?

A. 014°
B. 133°
C. 255°
D. 339°

2998. While navigating in fog off a coastline of steep cliffs, you hear the echo of the ship's foghorn 3-1/2 seconds after the signal was sounded. What is the distance to the shore?

A. 640 yards
B. 480 yards
C. 315 yards
D. 143 yards

2999. When entering a channel from seaward, the numbers on buoys _____.

A. are the same as their Light List number
B. are marked in 6 inch figures with retroreflective material
C. increase with the even numbers to starboard
D. decrease with the odd numbers to starboard

3000. All aids to navigation listed in the Mississippi River System Light List are shown as miles from a reference point and on the _____.

A. east or west bank
B. left or right descending bank
C. port or starboard side of the vessel
D. left or right ascending bank

3002. The diurnal variation of pressure is most noticeable _____.

A. above the polar circles
B. in a low pressure area
C. during periods of low temperatures
D. in the doldrums

3003. The height of tide is the _____.

A. difference between the depth of the water and the area's tidal datum
B. depth of water at a specific time due to tidal effect

C. difference between the depth of the water and the high water tidal level
D. difference between the depth of the water at high tide and the depth of the water at low tide

3004. While navigating in fog off a coastline of steep cliffs, you hear the echo of the ship's foghorn 4 seconds after the signal was sounded. What is the distance to the shore?

A. 209 yards
B. 363 yards
C. 480 yards
D. 730 yards

3005. The agonic line on an isomagnetic chart indicates the _____.

A. magnetic equator
B. magnetic longitude reference line
C. points where there is no variation
D. points where there is no annual change in variation

3006. D047NG. You are outbound in a channel marked by a range astern. The range line is 309°T. You are steering 127°T and have the range in sight as shown. What action should you take?

A. Come right to 129°T.
B. Come left until the range comes in line then alter course to 129°T.
C. Come left until the range comes in line then alter course to 125°T.
D. Come right to close the range then when on the range steer 129°T.

3007. A rotary current sets through all directions of the compass. The time it takes to complete one of these cycles, in a locale off the East coast of the US, is approximately _____.

A. 2-1/2 hours
B. 3-1/2 hours
C. 6-1/4 hours
D. 12-1/2 hours

3008. You take a bearing of 086° of a lighthouse. Which bearing of another object would give the best fix?

A. 291°
B. 261°
C. 242°
D. 196°

3009. Proceeding from seaward for the purpose of the direction of buoying offshore, lateral system buoys would be proceeding _____.

A. northerly on the Atlantic Coast
B. easterly on the Gulf Coast
C. northerly on the Pacific Coast
D. None of the above

3010. A white buoy with a blue band is _____.

A. an isolated danger mark
B. a hydrographic data collection buoy
C. a mooring buoy
D. marking a restricted area

3011. The survey information upon which a chart is based is found _____.

A. at the top center of the next line
B. near the chart title
C. at the lower left corner
D. at any convenient location

3012. The drawspan of a floating drawbridge may be marked with _____.

A. a yellow light showing Morse Code (B)
B. a yellow and white diamond
C. flashing blue lights
D. three red lights on each side of the draw

3016. The radar control that shortens all echoes on the display and reduces clutter caused by rain or snow is the _____.

A. sensitivity time control (sea clutter control)
B. receiver gain control
C. brilliance control
D. fast time constant (differentiator)

3017. A rotary current sets through all directions of the compass. The time it takes to complete one of these cycles, in a locale off the East coast of the US, is approximately _____.

A. 3 hours
B. 6-1/4 hours
C. 12-1/2 hours
D. 18-3/4 hours

3018. You take a bearing of 356° of a lighthouse. Which bearing of another object would give the best fix?

A. 013°
B. 178°
C. 256°
D. 342°

3019. Where would you find information about the time of high tide at a specific location on a particular day of the year?

A. Tide Tables
B. Tidal Current Tables
C. Coast Pilot
D. Nautical Almanac

3020. A mooring buoy, if lighted, shows which color light?

A. Yellow
B. White
C. Blue
D. Any color except red or green

3021. Which information is found in the chart title?

A. Chart number
B. Chart sounding datum
C. Revision and edition date
D. Variation information

3022. D045NG. A green-and-red banded daymark, green band uppermost, will have the shape shown at letter _____.

A. A
B. B
C. C
D. D

3023. D047NG. You have steadied up on a range dead ahead in line with your keel. After a few minutes the range, still dead ahead, appears as shown. Which action do you take?

A. Alter heading to the left
B. Alter heading to the right
C. Increase speed
D. Maintain heading, keeping the range dead ahead

3025. You determine your vessel's position by taking a range and bearing to a buoy. Your position will be plotted as a(n) _____.

A. estimated position
B. dead-reckoning position
C. fix
D. running fix

3026. A compass card without north-seeking capability that is used for relative bearings is a(n) _____.

A. bearing circle
B. pelorus
C. bearing bar
D. alidade

3030. Isogonic lines are lines on a chart indicating _____.

A. points of equal variation
B. points of zero variation
C. the magnetic latitude
D. magnetic dip

3031. Which symbol in illustration D015NG would indicate a large automated navigational buoy, such as those that have replaced some lightships?

A. A
B. B
C. C
D. D

3032. The direction in which a vessel is steered is the course. The path actually followed is the _____.

A. route
B. track
C. heading
D. course over the ground

3033. A navigator fixing a vessel's position by radar _____.

A. can use radar information from one object to fix the position
B. should never use radar bearings
C. should only use radar bearings when the range exceeds the distance to the horizon
D. must use information from targets forward of the beam

3035. A major advantage of the NAVTEX system when compared to other systems is that _____.

A. the information can be received on an ordinary FM radio
B. warnings are printed out for reading when convenient
C. broadcasts are at scheduled times
D. a low frequency band is used for long distance transmission

3036. Which daymark has no lateral significance?

A. Square; top half green and bottom half red
B. Black and white diamond
C. Red triangle
D. Green square

3038. In low latitudes, the low(s) of the diurnal variation of pressure occur(s) at _____.

A. noon
B. noon and midnight
C. 1000 and 2200
D. 0400 and 1600

3039. As you enter a U.S. channel from seaward the numbers on the buoys _____.

A. increase with the can buoys being even numbered
B. increase with the can buoys being odd numbered
C. decrease with the can buoys being even numbered
D. increase in channels going to the north or west, and decrease in channels going to the south or east

3040. Which instrument is used to predict the approach of a low pressure system?

A. Anemometer
B. Fathometer
C. Barometer
D. Thermometer

3042. How long would a steady wind need to blow in order to create a wind driven current?

A. 2 hours
B. 6 hours
C. 12 hours
D. 18 hours

3052. The Sailing Directions contain information on _____.

A. required navigation lights
B. lifesaving equipment standards
C. casualty reporting procedures
D. currents in various locations

3053. The vertical distance from the tidal datum to the level of the water is the _____.

A. height of tide
B. range of tide
C. actual water depth
D. charted depth

3054. In illustration D051NG, the position labeled C was plotted because _____.

A. running fixes are better estimates of true position than dead-reckoning positions are
B. the vessel's course changed from due North to due East
C. the vessel's speed changed
D. All of the above are correct

3055. A single line of position combined with a dead-reckoning position results in a(n) _____.

A. running fix
B. fix
C. estimated position
D. assumed position

3056. A position obtained by applying ONLY your vessel's course and speed to a known position is a _____.

A. fix
B. dead-reckoning position
C. running fix
D. probable position

3057. In Region A of the IALA Buoyage System, when entering from seaward, the starboard side of a channel would be marked by a _____.

A. green conical buoy
B. green can buoy
C. red can buoy
D. red conical buoy

3060. What information is NOT found in the chart title?

A. Survey information
B. Scale
C. Date of first edition
D. Projection

3061. In a river subject to tidal currents, the best time to dock a ship without the assistance of tugs is _____.

A. at flood tide
B. at high water
C. when there is a following current
D. at slack water

NAVIGATION GENERAL ANSWERS

NAVIGATION GENERAL ANSWERS

NBR	ANS	NBR	ANS	NBR	ANS	NBR	ANS	NBR	ANS	NBR	ANS	NBR	ANS	NBR	ANS
1	B	67	A	134	B	207	D	276	B	351	B	423	B	489	A
2	D	68	D	135	C	208	D	277	B	352	D	424	D	490	B
3	C	70	C	136	C	209	A	278	D	355	C	426	C	491	D
4	B	71	A	137	D	210	B	279	A	356	D	427	C	492	B
5	B	72	B	138	B	211	D	280	B	357	B	428	B	493	C
6	B	74	D	140	C	212	D	281	B	358	B	429	B	494	D
7	C	76	B	141	C	213	C	282	D	359	D	430	D	496	D
8	C	77	B	142	B	216	B	283	A	360	B	431	D	497	B
9	A	78	B	143	D	217	B	285	C	361	B	432	B	498	C
10	A	80	C	144	B	218	D	286	D	362	D	433	A	499	D
11	B	81	A	145	D	219	D	287	D	363	D	434	B	500	B
12	D	82	D	146	A	220	D	288	C	365	A	436	C	501	D
13	B	83	B	147	C	221	B	289	A	366	B	437	B	502	A
14	A	84	A	148	B	222	D	290	D	367	C	438	C	503	D
15	C	86	B	149	B	223	B	291	A	368	A	439	A	504	A
16	C	87	A	150	B	226	D	292	C	369	D	440	D	506	D
17	A	88	C	151	B	227	D	293	C	370	D	441	B	507	A
18	B	90	B	152	B	228	D	296	A	371	C	442	D	508	A
19	D	91	D	153	C	229	A	297	C	372	A	443	D	509	B
20	A	92	C	154	D	230	A	298	A	373	B	444	B	510	A
21	B	93	A	155	A	231	B	299	B	376	D	446	B	511	D
22	A	94	A	156	A	232	D	300	C	377	B	447	A	512	C
23	A	95	C	157	A	234	D	301	D	378	B	448	C	513	B
24	D	96	A	158	C	236	C	302	A	379	C	449	D	514	D
25	A	97	B	159	B	237	A	305	A	380	B	450	C	516	D
26	D	98	B	161	D	238	B	306	A	381	B	451	A	517	A
27	A	99	B	162	C	239	D	307	C	382	A	452	A	518	A
28	C	100	B	163	B	240	C	308	B	386	B	453	B	519	B
29	C	101	C	166	D	241	B	309	C	388	D	454	A	520	A
31	A	102	C	167	C	242	A	311	B	389	A	456	D	522	D
32	B	103	B	168	C	243	A	312	B	390	A	457	D	523	B
34	B	104	B	169	A	244	D	313	C	391	C	458	A	524	A
35	D	105	D	170	A	246	C	316	A	392	B	459	D	526	B
36	B	106	D	171	A	247	C	317	C	393	A	460	D	527	B
37	B	107	D	172	A	249	D	318	B	394	C	461	A	528	B
38	D	108	C	176	C	250	A	319	B	396	C	462	A	529	B
40	C	109	C	177	B	251	B	320	C	397	D	463	D	530	C
41	B	110	C	178	A	252	B	321	B	398	B	464	C	531	C
42	C	111	A	179	C	253	D	323	B	399	D	466	C	532	B
43	C	112	D	180	A	254	A	326	A	400	D	467	C	533	A
44	A	113	C	181	B	255	C	327	B	401	A	468	B	534	C
46	A	114	B	182	C	256	A	328	C	402	D	469	C	536	A
47	C	116	C	185	D	257	D	329	D	404	B	470	C	537	B
48	D	117	D	186	C	258	D	330	A	406	D	471	A	538	A
49	A	118	C	187	D	259	C	331	D	407	B	472	B	539	A
50	B	119	C	188	B	260	B	333	B	408	C	473	D	540	D
51	D	120	A	190	A	261	D	336	D	409	A	474	B	541	C
52	B	121	D	191	C	262	D	337	B	410	B	476	A	542	B
56	A	122	A	192	C	263	B	338	C	411	C	477	C	543	C
57	B	123	A	193	B	265	C	339	C	412	A	478	D	544	B
58	D	124	B	194	A	266	A	340	D	413	A	479	A	546	D
59	D	125	B	196	C	267	B	341	C	414	D	480	B	547	A
60	A	126	C	197	A	268	D	342	D	416	B	481	A	548	C
61	A	127	C	198	C	269	D	345	C	417	D	482	D	549	D
62	B	128	A	200	A	270	C	346	C	418	A	483	A	550	A
63	D	130	B	201	B	271	D	347	A	419	B	484	A	551	C
64	C	131	D	202	D	272	B	348	D	420	A	486	D	552	A
66	A	132	B	203	B	273	A	349	C	421	B	487	D	553	C
		133	B	206	C	275	A	350	C	422	B	488	B	554	C

No.	Ans	No.	Ans	No.	Ans	No.	Ans	No.	Ans	No.	Ans	No.	Ans	No.	Ans
556	A	631	C	709	B	778	D	847	B	913	D	982	A	1048	C
557	A	632	B	710	B	780	C	848	D	914	C	983	D	1049	B
558	A	633	A	711	A	781	C	849	B	916	A	984	B	1050	C
559	D	635	B	712	D	782	A	850	C	917	A	986	A	1051	D
561	B	636	B	713	C	783	B	851	B	918	B	987	C	1052	A
562	A	637	D	716	C	784	C	852	A	919	B	988	C	1053	D
563	C	638	B	717	A	786	C	853	A	920	B	989	D	1054	D
564	D	639	A	718	A	787	A	854	A	921	A	990	D	1056	B
566	D	641	A	720	A	788	A	855	C	922	C	991	D	1057	B
567	C	642	C	721	B	789	A	856	B	923	C	992	A	1058	C
568	A	643	C	722	C	791	C	857	A	924	C	993	B	1059	B
569	B	646	D	723	C	792	C	858	A	926	B	994	B	1060	C
570	B	647	C	724	C	793	D	859	D	927	B	996	B	1061	B
571	C	648	B	726	D	794	B	860	A	928	A	997	B	1062	B
572	B	650	C	727	C	796	B	861	C	929	C	998	D	1063	C
573	B	651	B	729	B	797	D	862	A	931	C	999	D	1064	D
574	B	652	A	730	C	799	C	863	A	932	B	1000	A	1065	C
576	D	653	B	731	C	800	A	864	A	933	A	1001	A	1066	C
577	C	656	A	732	B	801	A	865	A	934	D	1002	A	1067	B
579	C	657	B	733	D	802	B	866	A	935	B	1003	A	1068	B
581	D	658	C	734	B	803	C	867	A	936	C	1004	C	1069	A
582	A	660	D	736	C	804	D	869	A	937	D	1005	B	1070	B
583	B	661	D	737	C	806	B	870	C	938	B	1006	B	1071	A
584	A	662	A	738	C	807	C	871	B	939	D	1007	B	1072	C
586	B	663	A	739	A	808	C	872	A	940	A	1008	C	1073	C
587	B	665	C	740	A	809	B	873	C	941	B	1009	C	1074	D
588	C	666	B	741	D	810	C	874	B	942	D	1010	C	1075	A
591	C	667	B	742	C	811	A	876	A	943	C	1011	D	1076	A
592	C	668	D	743	C	812	D	877	D	944	B	1012	A	1077	C
593	B	669	B	744	D	813	C	878	C	946	D	1013	D	1078	B
594	B	671	C	746	C	814	A	879	A	947	B	1014	B	1080	A
596	D	672	C	747	B	815	A	880	B	949	B	1016	B	1081	C
597	B	673	D	748	B	816	B	881	C	950	A	1017	C	1082	D
598	D	675	B	749	B	817	D	882	B	951	C	1018	A	1083	C
599	B	676	C	750	B	818	D	883	C	952	C	1019	D	1084	B
600	C	677	A	751	D	820	B	884	D	953	C	1020	C	1085	C
601	A	679	B	752	D	821	C	886	A	954	D	1021	D	1086	A
602	B	680	D	754	D	822	C	887	A	956	B	1022	B	1087	D
603	A	681	D	756	B	823	D	888	A	957	A	1023	A	1088	B
606	A	682	B	757	A	824	B	889	B	960	B	1024	D	1089	A
607	D	683	C	758	B	826	A	890	C	961	A	1026	B	1090	A
608	B	685	D	759	B	827	C	891	D	962	D	1027	A	1091	D
609	A	686	B	760	C	828	A	892	A	963	C	1028	D	1092	B
610	C	687	B	761	D	829	D	893	B	964	A	1031	B	1093	A
611	C	688	A	762	D	830	C	894	A	966	B	1032	C	1094	B
612	B	690	C	763	D	831	A	896	C	967	C	1033	D	1096	D
613	B	691	A	764	D	832	B	897	D	968	B	1034	A	1097	A
615	B	692	C	765	B	833	D	900	A	969	A	1036	C	1098	B
617	A	693	B	766	D	834	A	901	D	970	B	1037	B	1099	B
619	B	696	D	767	B	836	D	902	C	971	C	1038	B	1101	B
620	A	697	D	768	A	837	B	903	B	972	B	1039	D	1102	C
621	B	698	A	769	B	838	D	904	A	973	C	1040	C	1103	A
622	A	700	C	770	A	839	A	906	A	974	A	1041	C	1104	D
623	B	701	C	771	A	840	A	907	C	976	A	1042	D	1105	C
625	C	702	A	772	D	841	B	908	C	977	A	1043	C	1106	B
626	D	703	D	773	A	842	B	909	C	978	C	1044	C	1107	D
627	C	705	B	774	C	843	B	910	C	979	A	1045	B	1108	B
629	D	706	C	776	C	844	D	911	A	980	B	1046	C	1110	B
630	A	707	D	777	A	846	C	912	B	981	A	1047	D	1111	C

1112 A	1178 B	1247 A	1309 B	1376 D	1442 A	1512 C	1603 B
1113 B	1179 A	1248 D	1310 C	1377 C	1443 B	1513 B	1604 D
1114 D	1181 D	1249 D	1311 C	1378 C	1444 C	1514 B	1606 B
1115 A	1182 D	1250 A	1312 A	1379 B	1446 B	1515 D	1607 D
1116 C	1183 B	1251 C	1313 B	1380 A	1447 B	1516 A	1608 B
1117 C	1184 A	1252 A	1314 B	1381 B	1448 D	1518 C	1609 C
1118 B	1185 D	1253 A	1315 C	1382 C	1449 C	1520 A	1610 A
1119 C	1186 B	1254 B	1316 D	1383 A	1450 C	1521 C	1611 D
1120 B	1187 C	1255 D	1317 B	1384 B	1452 B	1522 B	1612 C
1121 D	1190 B	1256 A	1318 B	1385 A	1453 B	1523 B	1613 B
1122 B	1191 C	1257 A	1319 A	1386 D	1454 D	1527 B	1614 B
1123 B	1192 B	1258 D	1320 A	1387 C	1456 D	1529 B	1615 C
1124 B	1193 C	1259 A	1321 D	1388 D	1457 C	1530 B	1616 D
1125 B	1194 A	1260 B	1322 C	1389 C	1458 D	1532 A	1617 A
1126 A	1195 C	1261 B	1323 B	1390 D	1459 C	1533 A	1618 A
1127 A	1196 D	1262 D	1324 A	1391 D	1460 A	1535 D	1620 D
1130 D	1197 B	1263 C	1325 C	1392 A	1461 A	1536 A	1623 D
1131 B	1198 C	1264 C	1326 C	1393 B	1463 A	1538 D	1624 C
1132 B	1199 C	1265 A	1328 A	1394 C	1464 D	1539 C	1625 C
1133 C	1200 D	1266 C	1330 C	1395 A	1466 D	1540 C	1626 B
1134 D	1201 A	1267 B	1331 A	1396 A	1467 D	1542 C	1627 C
1136 A	1202 B	1268 D	1332 D	1397 B	1468 D	1543 A	1628 B
1137 A	1203 D	1269 C	1333 A	1398 A	1469 C	1544 A	1629 D
1138 D	1204 A	1271 D	1334 D	1399 D	1470 D	1546 B	1631 B
1140 B	1205 A	1272 B	1335 A	1400 B	1471 A	1547 A	1632 C
1141 C	1206 B	1273 B	1336 A	1401 B	1473 A	1548 A	1633 A
1142 C	1207 A	1274 B	1337 A	1402 D	1475 A	1550 A	1634 A
1143 D	1208 A	1275 C	1338 B	1403 A	1476 C	1551 A	1635 D
1144 B	1210 C	1276 D	1340 B	1404 D	1477 C	1552 B	1636 B
1146 D	1211 D	1277 A	1341 B	1406 D	1479 B	1554 C	1637 B
1147 C	1213 A	1278 C	1342 B	1408 D	1480 D	1555 D	1638 A
1148 D	1215 C	1279 B	1343 D	1410 B	1481 A	1556 C	1640 D
1149 A	1216 A	1280 B	1344 A	1411 C	1482 B	1557 B	1641 D
1151 D	1217 D	1281 C	1345 C	1412 D	1483 A	1558 C	1642 D
1152 B	1218 A	1282 C	1346 B	1413 D	1484 D	1559 A	1643 C
1153 B	1220 D	1283 B	1347 C	1414 D	1485 A	1560 A	1644 D
1154 C	1221 B	1284 A	1348 A	1415 C	1486 A	1561 D	1646 C
1155 B	1222 D	1285 D	1349 C	1416 B	1487 A	1563 D	1647 A
1156 A	1223 B	1286 D	1350 B	1417 C	1488 C	1564 A	1648 D
1157 D	1224 D	1287 A	1351 B	1418 A	1489 B	1565 B	1649 B
1158 C	1225 D	1288 C	1352 C	1419 A	1490 C	1566 A	1651 C
1159 D	1226 B	1290 C	1353 A	1420 D	1492 B	1567 C	1652 B
1160 C	1227 C	1291 D	1354 B	1421 B	1493 A	1568 D	1653 D
1161 C	1228 C	1292 A	1356 B	1423 D	1495 C	1569 D	1654 A
1162 C	1229 B	1293 C	1357 C	1424 B	1496 A	1572 B	1655 B
1163 B	1231 C	1295 C	1358 B	1426 A	1497 B	1574 C	1656 D
1164 B	1232 A	1296 D	1359 B	1427 B	1498 B	1576 A	1657 C
1165 B	1233 C	1297 C	1360 B	1428 D	1499 A	1579 B	1658 A
1166 D	1234 B	1298 A	1361 B	1430 B	1501 B	1581 B	1659 A
1167 B	1236 B	1299 D	1362 C	1431 C	1502 A	1584 D	1660 D
1168 D	1237 C	1300 A	1363 B	1432 D	1503 B	1586 C	1661 B
1169 A	1238 B	1301 D	1364 D	1433 B	1504 C	1589 B	1662 D
1170 B	1239 A	1302 A	1366 A	1434 C	1505 A	1592 D	1663 C
1171 A	1240 D	1303 C	1367 B	1436 D	1506 B	1594 C	1664 C
1172 C	1241 A	1304 A	1368 C	1437 B	1507 D	1595 D	1665 D
1173 C	1242 A	1305 A	1369 D	1438 C	1508 B	1596 A	1666 B
1174 D	1243 D	1306 D	1372 D	1439 D	1509 C	1597 B	1667 D
1175 B	1245 A	1307 B	1373 A	1440 C	1510 B	1599 B	1671 A
1176 C	1246 D	1308 B	1374 A	1441 C	1511 C	1602 C	1672 B

1673 B	1735 D	1807 B	1974 C	2100 C	2220 D	2372 C	2486 D
1675 B	1736 D	1808 A	1976 A	2101 A	2222 B	2373 D	2488 B
1676 B	1737 C	1809 D	1984 D	2102 B	2224 C	2375 B	2489 A
1677 B	1738 D	1810 C	1986 B	2103 D	2230 D	2378 B	2496 A
1680 B	1739 B	1811 B	1987 A	2104 C	2234 D	2379 B	2498 A
1681 D	1740 A	1816 D	1988 A	2110 B	2236 D	2380 D	2499 A
1682 D	1741 C	1818 B	1992 B	2111 C	2239 A	2381 D	2504 C
1683 A	1742 A	1820 A	1996 B	2112 B	2240 D	2384 B	2505 D
1684 A	1743 A	1822 A	2000 B	2113 A	2243 C	2387 D	2506 A
1685 B	1744 A	1826 B	2001 B	2114 D	2244 B	2388 D	2508 B
1686 C	1745 D	1827 B	2002 C	2115 A	2246 A	2389 D	2509 C
1687 A	1746 B	1828 D	2004 D	2116 B	2250 C	2390 A	2510 D
1688 B	1749 B	1830 D	2006 C	2119 A	2251 C	2392 D	2519 C
1689 B	1750 D	1831 C	2007 B	2120 C	2252 D	2394 C	2524 A
1690 B	1751 C	1832 D	2008 B	2121 C	2254 A	2396 A	2525 D
1691 A	1753 A	1838 A	2010 A	2122 A	2255 D	2400 D	2526 C
1692 B	1754 C	1840 C	2014 B	2125 C	2256 C	2402 A	2527 B
1693 C	1755 D	1844 D	2016 A	2126 C	2261 D	2404 B	2529 B
1694 C	1756 B	1848 D	2018 C	2130 D	2262 B	2406 A	2530 D
1695 B	1757 D	1850 B	2020 C	2131 A	2264 B	2408 D	2536 C
1696 B	1758 D	1858 B	2021 D	2132 C	2268 D	2409 D	2538 C
1697 C	1759 B	1859 C	2024 D	2140 D	2269 B	2410 B	2539 C
1698 B	1760 D	1860 C	2028 C	2141 C	2270 B	2412 B	2540 C
1699 B	1761 C	1862 C	2030 B	2142 B	2271 B	2416 B	2542 C
1700 A	1763 A	1866 A	2040 A	2143 A	2277 C	2418 B	2544 B
1701 B	1764 B	1870 B	2043 D	2145 D	2280 D	2419 C	2546 A
1702 A	1765 A	1871 C	2044 B	2146 C	2282 C	2420 D	2548 A
1703 C	1766 B	1872 C	2048 A	2147 B	2286 D	2423 B	2560 B
1704 B	1767 A	1873 D	2050 C	2150 C	2290 A	2424 A	2567 D
1705 C	1768 C	1874 D	2052 A	2152 A	2292 D	2425 A	2570 D
1706 A	1769 A	1875 C	2053 B	2158 B	2298 C	2426 D	2572 B
1707 C	1770 B	1880 A	2060 C	2159 B	2299 C	2428 A	2574 B
1708 A	1771 C	1883 B	2061 B	2160 A	2300 A	2429 D	2576 D
1709 C	1773 D	1884 D	2067 A	2162 C	2306 A	2430 B	2580 C
1710 B	1774 C	1885 A	2068 A	2164 B	2308 B	2434 B	2583 D
1711 A	1776 C	1886 C	2070 D	2165 A	2310 D	2435 D	2586 B
1712 D	1777 A	1887 D	2073 D	2168 A	2317 A	2437 C	2588 A
1713 B	1779 B	1888 B	2074 A	2169 A	2318 D	2438 A	2589 D
1714 A	1780 C	1890 C	2075 C	2170 C	2320 C	2440 C	2590 D
1715 C	1781 D	1892 D	2076 A	2174 C	2328 B	2442 D	2592 A
1716 B	1782 C	1898 D	2078 D	2176 C	2330 A	2444 D	2594 C
1717 B	1783 B	1899 D	2079 D	2177 D	2332 C	2446 B	2596 A
1718 D	1784 C	1902 C	2080 B	2178 C	2335 B	2448 D	2597 C
1719 B	1785 B	1905 D	2081 D	2180 C	2336 B	2450 A	2598 B
1720 A	1786 C	1906 A	2082 A	2184 A	2338 C	2452 C	2600 C
1721 C	1787 A	1907 C	2083 B	2187 D	2340 C	2456 C	2602 D
1722 C	1788 C	1909 D	2084 A	2190 C	2345 D	2458 B	2608 C
1723 C	1790 C	1914 B	2085 A	2191 D	2346 C	2459 D	2610 B
1724 C	1793 C	1922 C	2086 A	2192 C	2348 B	2460 D	2612 A
1725 B	1795 B	1923 B	2087 C	2198 D	2349 A	2464 B	2614 D
1726 D	1796 D	1925 C	2088 D	2199 B	2350 A	2466 C	2616 D
1727 A	1797 A	1936 C	2089 B	2200 A	2351 D	2468 B	2625 C
1728 B	1798 C	1941 D	2090 A	2203 B	2353 A	2469 D	2626 C
1729 A	1800 B	1946 B	2091 D	2209 A	2360 D	2470 B	2627 B
1730 A	1801 B	1951 A	2092 D	2210 A	2361 D	2472 D	2628 B
1731 D	1803 C	1956 A	2093 C	2211 B	2362 C	2480 D	2629 D
1732 A	1804 D	1961 D	2097 B	2212 D	2363 C	2482 B	2632 A
1733 C	1805 D	1962 A	2098 C	2214 D	2369 A	2483 A	2634 A
1734 C	1806 A	1968 B	2099 B	2215 D	2370 A	2484 D	2636 D

2638 D	2768 C	2884 A	2986 B
2639 A	2769 D	2886 A	2988 B
2646 A	2770 C	2890 B	2990 B
2648 D	2772 A	2891 B	2991 B
2651 A	2774 A	2892 C	2994 A
2652 D	2777 D	2894 B	2998 A
2654 B	2778 D	2895 C	2999 C
2656 C	2780 D	2896 B	3000 B
2659 D	2782 A	2899 D	3002 D
2664 C	2788 D	2900 D	3003 A
2666 B	2790 B	2902 C	3004 D
2668 B	2792 C	2904 B	3005 C
2669 A	2794 D	2909 D	3006 D
2672 A	2798 A	2910 C	3007 D
2673 C	2800 B	2913 B	3008 D
2674 D	2801 B	2916 D	3009 C
2675 B	2803 A	2918 B	3010 C
2676 D	2804 D	2920 C	3011 B
2678 D	2805 D	2922 B	3012 A
2679 A	2809 A	2923 B	3016 D
2683 B	2810 A	2925 D	3017 C
2686 B	2814 B	2926 A	3018 C
2688 C	2816 D	2927 B	3019 A
2694 C	2818 D	2928 A	3020 B
2695 C	2819 A	2930 B	3021 B
2704 D	2820 D	2931 B	3022 A
2705 A	2821 C	2932 B	3023 A
2706 C	2822 A	2936 C	3025 A
2707 A	2824 B	2937 C	3026 B
2708 D	2826 B	2938 D	3030 A
2709 D	2828 B	2939 A	3031 B
2711 A	2830 C	2940 C	3032 D
2712 B	2831 C	2941 C	3033 A
2714 B	2832 A	2944 C	3035 B
2716 D	2838 B	2945 A	3036 B
2718 D	2839 C	2947 C	3038 D
2719 C	2840 C	2950 D	3039 B
2720 C	2841 A	2952 A	3040 C
2721 A	2842 B	2954 C	3042 C
2722 B	2843 C	2958 D	3052 D
2724 A	2844 C	2959 C	3053 A
2725 D	2846 D	2960 A	3054 A
2726 B	2848 B	2961 B	3055 C
2729 C	2849 A	2962 D	3056 B
2730 A	2850 D	2964 D	3057 A
2737 B	2851 B	2965 C	3060 C
2738 C	2852 B	2966 C	3061 D
2739 D	2858 B	2968 C	
2740 C	2860 B	2969 B	
2741 A	2862 D	2970 B	
2742 B	2866 D	2972 A	
2744 A	2868 B	2973 D	
2746 D	2869 C	2974 B	
2750 B	2870 C	2977 D	
2752 C	2874 C	2979 B	
2760 B	2875 B	2980 D	
2762 A	2877 B	2981 A	
2764 D	2880 C	2982 A	
2766 C	2882 D	2984 D	

SAFETY

EMERGENCIES

Emergencies fall into two categories: those involving personnel, and those involving the vessel. The overriding consideration is always preservation of life, and all attempts to save equipment or the vessel is toward that end.

Emergency Signals

The following signals are given both on the ship's whistle (horn) and the general alarm:

- *Abandon ship*—seven or more short blasts followed by a long blast
- *Fire/emergency*—continuous whistle for at least 10 seconds
- *Man overboard (MOB)*—three prolonged blasts (Morse for "O") plus hoist of "Oscar" flag
- *Lower all boats*—one short blast
- *Stop lowering all boats*—two short blasts
- *Dismissed from fire/emergency stations*—three short blasts

Station Bill

A station bill details:

- place of assignment
- action to be taken
- equipment responsibilities
- chain of command at each emergency station
- appropriate on ship's whistle and general alarm

In summary, the *whistle and general alarm* will signal the problem and the *station bill* specifies who's to go where, what they're to do when they get there, and who's in charge.

The station bill is the Master's responsibility, and his signature attests to the fact that he has both reviewed and approved it. It must be posted so as to be available and conspicuous to both crew and passengers. An important part of crew indoctrination is to ensure that the crew is familiar with and understands the Bill.

Passengers must be made aware of proper abandon ship procedures, life jacket use, route to and location of their abandon ship stations. The Bill also specifies who or what department is responsible for passenger guidance.

Emergency Check-Off Lists

In addition to the above, emergency check-off lists are required to be posted on both inspected and uninspected vessels of <100T. The lists detail the actions to be taken in case of:

- rough weather or crossing hazardous bars
- man overboard
- fire at sea

Emergency Drills

Fire and boat drills are to be conducted at least once a week. They must also be held within 24 hours of an international voyage or if new crew in excess of 25% is involved. If the voyage is to be in excess of one week, the first drill must be held prior to departure.

The drills are to be conducted as if the event were actually occurring, i.e., hoses led out and charged, watertight doors secured, boats swung out and lowered, etc. Passengers are to be directed to their assigned abandon-ship stations, instructed, and don life jackets.

Helicopter Transfers

Transfer of a victim by helicopter requires a fine degree of coordination between the aircraft crew and the vessel, as it is an operation involving risks to all, including the person being transferred.

First, establish communication on either VHF 156.8 mHz (CH 16) or SSB 2182 kHz. If another frequency is requested, advise whether you have or don't have the frequency.

When requesting a transfer, provide information as to the nature of the emergency, condition of the victim, vessel position, etc. If possible, alter course toward the station where the flight will originate. Advise the base or aircraft of your course and speed so that the aircraft can plot an intercept.

At night train a searchlight vertically to act as a beacon, but secure it when the aircraft arrives in the area. Do not train the light at the aircraft, as it may blind the pilot.

Put the apparent wind 30 degrees on your port bow and fly a flag to assist the pilot in wind evaluation. Provide a hoist area of 50-foot radius, if possible, with all lines, cables and loose gear secured and cargo booms topped along their masts.

Sailboats should assume port tack on jib only with the boom lashed to the starboard shrouds.

Do not touch either the cable or the basket until they have been grounded. Dangerous static voltages will have built up on the aircraft.

Do not secure either cable or basket to anything on the vessel that might tether the aircraft and bring it down. If necessary to remove the basket from the pick-up area, detach it from the cable. The helicopter may retract the cable and re-lower it when the basket is ready. *The cable will again require grounding before being touched.*

Man Overboard
Action of the Crew

The person who observes a man-overboard incident should shout, "Man overboard (starboard or port) side!" and immediately throw a life ring or PFD toward the victim. This will mark the location, as well as provide assurance to the victim. The crew should then point continuously toward the person in the water. If there is another person on board, he/she can be designated to point, as well, while the crew dons a life vest and lifeline.

Upon hearing the man-overboard cry, the helmsman should immediately put the helm hard to the same side as the victim in order to swing the stern away from the victim, then initiate a turn to retrieve the victim as quickly as possible. At the same time a PAN-PAN should be sent on VHF CH 16, giving the vessel location to all other vessels in the area.

The choice of turns depends on whether the victim is in sight, the victim's capabilities, and the maneuvering characteristics of the vessel:

- The *single (round) turn* is the quickest, but will not result in a good approach to the victim unless the vessel is small and extremely maneuverable.

- If the victim is still visible, the quickest turn for a larger vessel is the *racetrack*.

- If the location of the victim is unknown, the *Scharnow turn* (turn until headed 240° from the original course, then swing back until headed 180° from the original course) should

be executed in order to most quickly retrace the original track to where the victim is most likely to be found.

- The *Williamson turn* (turn until headed 60° from the original course, then swing back until headed 180° from the original course) is similar to the Scharnow in returning to the original track, but takes slightly longer to execute.

Generally, the victim should be taken aboard midships on the leeward side. This will keep the victim away from the propellers, give the victim some protection from waves and ensure that the vessel will not be blown out of reach. A stepladder is the best way to retrieve the victim, with a life-jacketed and tethered crew in the water to assist, if necessary.

Action of the Victim

If the boat trails a pick-up line, the victim should swim across the wake. In a heavy wind/sea, the line will be to leeward of the wake. If in boots, get them off immediately. If not in a PFD and there will be a long wait, take off trousers, knot the leg ends, grasp by the waist and bring over the head forcefully to below the water surface in order to trap air in the legs. Believe it or not, the pant legs will hold air and provide buoyancy. Repeat as necessary.

Don't panic, and don't try to chase the vessel; it will waste valuable energy and sap body heat much faster. Don't drink salt water. If in a jacket, use the (hopefully) attached whistle, light and/or mirror to attract attention.

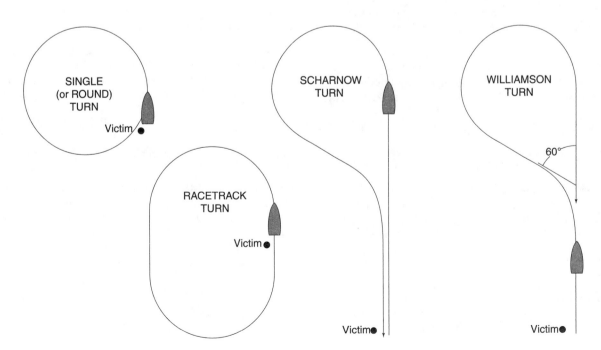

Vessel Emergencies
Heavy Weather
The first principle regarding heavy weather is to avoid it. This requires attention to radio, weatherfax and local observations. If in port and the weather is questionable, it very well may worsen. "If in doubt, don't," is a good maxim to follow, but if caught out:

- Maintain a plot and be able to quickly transmit your position in an emergency. Know where you are relative to a lee shore.

- If involved with a hurricane, determine its center and your position relative to the dangerous/navigable semicircles. See Deck General, Hurricanes for a discussion of these as well as recommended evasive maneuvers.

- Rig inboard lifelines.

- On deck, don life jackets and safety harnesses.

- If sailing and questioning whether it's time to shorten sail, it is . . . or was!

- Clear the bilges and pressure up tanks to eliminate free surface (see Deck General, Stability).

Taking the wind on the bow may be needed in a lee shore situation.

Running downwind (either quarter) is generally preferred, sea room allowing, due to less strain on vessel and crew, but it does introduce the possibility of pooping (taking a wave over the stern) and/or pitchpoling (end-over-end, bow first). If accelerating too much and in danger of overrunning a crest (thus plunging into the trough, tripping and pitchpoling), bear off and let the crest get ahead a little. Trailing a drogue/warps helps control heading and speed.

Heaving-to (storm jib sheeted to windward, trysail amidships and rudder to windward) is a good option for sailing vessels. The action (with occasional use of a sea anchor) holds the vessel's head about 45 degrees off the wind, while jogging to windward.

Animal or vegetable oil (not mineral) released slowly overboard has been known to help.

Loss of Steering
Advise other vessels in vicinity and the Coast Guard by both radio and proper light/day shapes (see "Not Under Command" in Rules of the Road, Lights).

Slow, or stop, depending on the situation, and consider anchoring.

In a single-screw vessel, use a bow thruster, if available. In twin-screw vessels, set one to moderate rpm, and use the other for directional control.

Loss of Propulsion
Advise other vessels in the vicinity and the Coast Guard by both radio (*Securité*) and proper light/day shapes (see "Not Under Command" in Rules of the Road, Lights).

Anchor if being blown onto a lee shore or into a channel.

Grounding
Priority remains the safety of personnel. Prudence dictates requesting help early in any situation which is potentially serious. Remember the appropriate day-shape/lights for grounded vessel (see Rules of the Road, Lights).

If the stability or the integrity of the hull is in doubt, follow the procedures for abandon ship until the situation becomes clear. This includes calls to the Coast Guard and vessels in the vicinity. All personnel should don life jackets, etc., and passengers should go to their assigned stations.

Check the watertight integrity of the hull. Close all watertight doors. Take soundings to determine the depth of water around the vessel, particularly in the direction of the channel.

Lead a kedge anchor to deep water to prevent going further aground. Ballast, if necessary, to prevent further wave-induced creep. If one end of the vessel is in deep water and the other aground, ballasting the afloat end may help in freeing the vessel.

In towing situations, the towing vessel will likely back in, with or without having placed an anchor with considerable scope. With an offshore wind the towing vessel may come in bow-first.

The towing hawser should not be secured at the bow or stern of the towing vessel as this greatly impairs rudder control. If towing from astern it should be led to, and secured forward of, the rudder post.

In a cross-wind, approach from upwind, and set a course approximately 30–40 degrees off the wind in order to drift past the stranded vessel and be in position to receive her line.

Be aware of the tide. If on the rise, be prepared to take a tow or to kedge off with engine assist (if able to do so without fouling your cooling water intake). On a falling tide a small craft can wait it out without serious consequences. A large vessel, however, must consider the loss of stability inherent in grounding, since there is generally a "virtual rise" in the center of gravity, with a consequent reduction of GM. (See Deck General, Stability.)

Collision

This unpleasant subject can be approached from three directions: how to prevent the situation from developing, what to do when a collision is imminent, and what to do after it happens.

Preventing the Situation. Two vessels arriving at the same point at the same time are most often both at fault (but not necessarily to the same degree). The burdened vessel obviously didn't know (or ignored) the Rules of the Road. The privileged vessel was compelled to take action when she realized that a collision was likely. Changes in heading should be made early enough and of sufficient magnitude to be obvious, particularly at night. It is not unknown for two vessels to indulge in "radar-guided-collisions" (*Andrea Doria* and *Stockholm*).

Collision Imminent. Sound the alarm and secure watertight doors, hatches, and ports. If inevitable, collision damage should be minimized by reversing engines and maneuvering for a glancing blow.

After It Happens. Your three priorities are:

- preservation of life
- hull integrity and stability
- fulfilling legal obligations

Notify the Coast Guard immediately. Perform a medical assessment and administer first aid as necessary. If required, prepare for a transfer by helicopter.

If either vessel is impaled by the other, do not pull apart until inspection deems that watertight integrity is not jeopardized in either vessel. The impaling vessel may be plugging a large hole.

It is a legal—not to mention moral—requirement to assist any vessel or person in trouble ". . . insofar as it can be done without risk of incurring serious danger to crew or vessel. . . . " Failing to do so may incur a $1000 fine and/or a two-year prison term. Ancillary fines are also possible for discharge of oil, violation of the Rules of the Road, negligent operation, etc. It is also a requirement to exchange appropriate information with the Master of the other vessel.

Abandon Ship

The governing principle is that one abandons ship only when there is no obvious way of saving the vessel. However, the decision to abandon ship should be made in sufficient time to allow preparation of the crew and passengers, avoiding panic, etc.

Your initial Mayday call is critical as it may be the only one you will be able to get off. Within 20 nm of shore, use VHF CH 16. Beyond 20 nm, use both VHF and SSB 2182 kHz.

Your first transmission should include:
- *who you are (vessel name)*
- *where you are (lat/lon or chart reference)*
- *your problem (fire, explosion, sinking)*

Subsequent transmissions should include:
- number aboard
- life jacket status
- injuries
- type of vessel (sail vs. power)
- hull/canvas colors
- any other identifiers

The abandon-ship signal is seven or more short blasts followed by a long blast on both ship's whistle and general alarm. After leaving the vessel stay together and near the vessel (if afloat and possible) as this dramatically increases the chances of being seen by rescue craft.

If the vessel is large enough to have lifeboats, they should be lowered to embarkation points for boarding and the vessel stopped. Personnel should wear both life jackets and warm clothing and, if possible, avoid water entry to avoid hypothermia.

Lifeboat signals are:

- 1 blast—lower boats
- 2 blasts—stop lowering boats
- 3 blasts—secure from lifeboat (drills)

If water entry proves necessary, several factors should be considered. If the vessel is drifting downwind at a good rate, or there is burning oil in the water, departure should be to windward. In rough weather, however, raft and boat damage is more likely on the windward side. If going into burning oil is necessary, go feet first, ankles crossed, one hand holding down the life jacket and the other pinching the nose. (In WWII, sailors sometimes had to doff their jackets to swim under the oil and then spread the oil with hands as they surfaced for air in prep for the next dive.)

Each crew member (not passenger) should have personal equipment with him at all times, including a knife and a waterproof flashlight—both on lanyards.

In drilling for an abandon-ship situation, it should always be assumed that it could happen at any time. Passengers and crew should not only be drilled in the proper donning of life jackets, where their stations are, and how to get there. They should take it upon themselves to walk the route daily. Shuffling through a drill in a well-lit, calm vessel in a party atmosphere is far removed from doing it in a black-smoke-filled passageway on a listing vessel with screaming, panicked, shoving people.

LIFE RAFTS AND FLOATS

Inflatable Life Rafts

The cradle-mounted white cylinder seen on many passenger vessels, fishing vessels, and offshore sailboats contains a self-inflating life raft. A tie-down strap holds the cylinder in the cradle and is fitted with a *hydrostatic release* triggered to free the cylinder when the vessel sinks below approximately 10 feet. Attached to the cylinder is an *operating cord (sea painter)*, the other end being attached to the vessel. As the vessel sinks the cylinder (having been released at about 10 feet) is still tethered to the vessel by the operating cord. When the sinking vessel reaches about 100 feet (the length of the operating cord), the cord pulls on a CO_2 inflation mechanism, causing the raft to inflate. Inflation snaps the cylinder packing bands and frees the raft from its container. At the same time an inside light comes on and a canopy and sea anchor are deployed.

Should the vessel sink to a depth less than 100 feet (leaving the cylinder afloat but raft not released), a manual pull on the operating cord will trigger the CO_2 mechanism.

Alternatively, the raft can be launched by activating the *quick-release button,* which will open the hydrostatic release, freeing the cylinder from the tie-down strap. Pulling on the cord will then inflate the raft, snapping the packing bands. Make sure the operating cord is still attached to the vessel, however, so the inflated raft doesn't get blown away from the vessel before boarding.

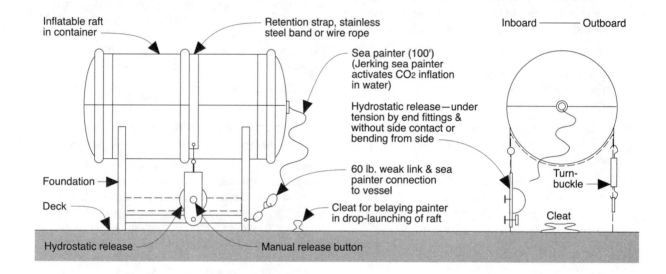

Inflatable raft in container — Retention strap, stainless steel band or wire rope — Inboard ——— Outboard

Sea painter (100') (Jerking sea painter activates CO2 inflation in water)

Hydrostatic release—under tension by end fittings & without side contact or bending from side

Foundation — 60 lb. weak link & sea painter connection to vessel — Turn-buckle

Deck — Cleat for belaying painter in drop-launching of raft — Cleat

Hydrostatic release — Manual release button

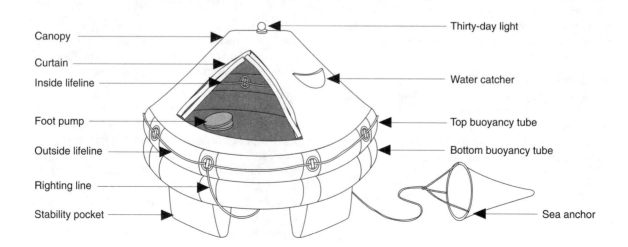

Canopy — Thirty-day light

Curtain

Inside lifeline — Water catcher

Foot pump — Top buoyancy tube

Outside lifeline — Bottom buoyancy tube

Righting line

Stability pocket — Sea anchor

Required raft equipment includes:
- 100 feet of line
- 2 paddles
- orange smoke signals
- 6 handheld red flares
- 2 handheld red parachute flares
- sea dye packets
- jackknife
- sealing (emergency) repair clamps
- sealant for permanent repairs
- hand inflation pump
- light and switch
- 1 lb. food and 1.5 qt. water/person
- signal mirror
- first aid kit
- fishing kit
- sponges and bailers

A hissing sound is normal venting of excess pressure. Ignore the sound unless the raft is obviously deflating from a leak. Temporary (emergency) leak repairs can be made with the repair clamps. Make permanent repairs with the sealant kit, and give the sealant 24 hours to cure before fully reinflating the raft.

After boarding a life raft, take seasickness pills immediately—even if you have never been seasick—because dehydration is your greatest peril.

To conserve on rations, don't take any food or water during the first 24 hours, then 1/3 pint of water three times per day. Never drink sea water, as it will dehydrate you further.

Before a helicopter rescue, deflate the raft so it isn't capsized by the copter's prop wash.

Lifeboats

You are unlikely to encounter lifeboat questions. Just in case, however, here are the names of the various lines involved in handling/launching a lifeboat:

- *Gripes*—wires used to secure boats at sea. Slack in the gripes is taken up with turnbuckles.

- *Tricing pendants*—lines which hold the lifeboat against the vessel's side after the gripes have been removed and the boat lowered (with the boat falls) to the embarkation position.

- *Frapping lines*—lines passing around the boat falls and tended from the vessel after the tricing pennants are released. These steady the boat as it is lowered from the embarkation level to the water.

- *Sea painter*—the line led from the bow of the lifeboat forward to the deck of the vessel.

- *Boat falls*—the blocks and tackle used to lower a lifeboat.

Personal Flotation Devices (PFDs)

Type	Buoyancy	Comment
I	20 lb.	Turn unconscious victim face up Required on T-boats
II	15.5 lb.	Turn unconscious victim face up More comfortable than Type I
III	15.5 lb.	Won't turn unconscious victim
IV	16.5 lb.	Throwable ring or cushion
V	—	Special-purpose device, such as a work vest

- *Uninspected vessels:* 1 Type I, II, III, or V PFD for each person aboard. The Type V must be worn to count.

- *Inspected vessels:* 1 Type I for each person aboard, plus child-size PFDs for 10% of the vessel capacity. In any case, child-size PFDs must be provided for every child aboard. All PFDs must be marked with the vessel name.

Approved PFDs must be International Orange in color and labeled with type, size (adult or child), manufacturer's name and address, and CG approval number. A "child" is any person weighing less than 90 lb.

Ring Buoys

All inspected passenger-carrying vessels must carry at least one throwable ring buoy:

≤65'   one 24" life ring buoy

>65'   three 24" life ring buoys

At least one ring buoy must have a 60' line of 5/16", buoyant, non-kinking, and dark/UV-resistant material.

Life Floats

The number and sizes of life floats for inspected vessels depend on the vessel's operating area, water temperature, and construction. However, all life floats must be readily accessible, be both manually and automatically deployable on sinking and include a lifeline, pendant, painter, two paddles and a floating light.

Life Rafts

Wood inspected vessels with no subdivision operating coastwise routes must have inflatable buoyant apparatus (life rafts) for 67% of capacity.

All inspected vessels operating warm-water ocean routes must have inflatable buoyant apparatus for 67% of capacity.

All vessels with no subdivision operating cold-water ocean routes must have inflatable buoyant apparatus for 100% of capacity.

VHF Radio

Required Licenses

An FCC ship station radio license is required for any vessel required to carry a marine radio, on an international voyage, or carrying an HF single sideband radiotelephone or marine satellite terminal. FCC license forms, including applications for ship and land station radio licenses, can now be downloaded from the Internet. The ship station radio license is no longer required for vessels traveling in U.S. waters, using VHF, radar or EPIRB, which are *not* required to carry radio equipment, i.e., recreational boats.

T-boats operating outside of the headlands are required to have an FCC Safety Radio Telephone Certificate and a Radio Operator's License. Note that the Radio Operator's License requires an exam and is not the same as the Restricted Radiotelephone Operator Permit formerly required to operate radios on recreational vessels. The inspection interval for the Safety Radio Telephone Certificate is five years.

The Vessel Bridge-to-Bridge Act

Vessels over 100 tons carrying one or more passengers, vessels over 300 tons, commercial tugs over 26', dredges and floating power plants in inland waters are required to monitor CH 13 (one watt maximum transmit) whenever underway. Transmissions are exclusively for vessel bridge-to-bridge conversations regarding maneuvering and for communication with operable bridges.

Radio Logs Required

Every inspected vessel is required to maintain a radio log listing hours of operation, operating condition of the radio, any radio checks performed, all radio tests and maintenance performed by a licensed radio technician, all MAYDAY messages received and all MAYDAY, PAN-PAN or SECURITÉ messages sent.

Entries in the log may never be erased. If a change is required, the error should be crossed out and accompanied by the initials of the person making the correction.

Maintenance and repair performed by a licensed radio technician not part of the crew must be logged with the repair person's name, license number and issue date of the license.

Priority Messages

There are three levels of radio traffic that have priority over ordinary traffic. In decreasing order:

- *MAYDAY*—a vessel in immediate danger (fire, sinking, grounded and breaking up, etc.).

- *PAN-PAN*—urgent situation requiring assistance (man overboard, medivac required, etc.).

- *SECURITÉ*—information regarding vessel movement, navigation safety, or severe weather warning (examples: large tug and tow in narrow channel, missing navigation aid, tornado warning).

VHF Protocol

- *Priority Messages.* Call and remain on CH 16, unless directed by the Coast Guard to CH 22A. No other vessel should use CH 16 while the emergency exists. A vessel receiving a distress signal should respond, "Received" or "Romeo, Romeo, Romeo." If the vessel in distress or the Coast Guard is having difficulty with interfering traffic, either may transmit a "Seelonce distress" message, which should silence all other traffic until the rescinding "Seelonce fini" is given.

- *Non-Priority Messages.* Initiate contact on CH 9 (some areas CH 16). Upon contact, immediately switch to a working channel. Limit all calls to two minutes. A marine radio is not a telephone!

VHF Channel Allocations
Source: 47 CFR 80.371(c) and 47 CFR 80.373(f)

Distress safety and calling	16
Intership safety	6
Coast Guard liaison	22
Noncommercial working	9,68,69,71,72,78–80
Commercial working	7–11,18,19,67,79,80
Marine operator	24–28, 84–88
Port operations	12,14,20,65,66,73,74,77
Bridge-to-bridge	13,67
Maritime control	17
Digital selective calling	70
NOAA weather	Wx-1,Wx-2,Wx-3

	Range, ship-to-ship	Power	Distress Frequency	Calling Frequency	Bridge-to-Bridge
VHF	line-of-sight (20–30 nm)	low 1 Watt high 25 Watt	CH 16 156.8 MHz	CH 9	CH 13 1 Watt maximum
SSB	up to 10,000 nm	150 Watt	2,182 kHz	any	NA

Distress Signals
Flares and Smoke Signals Required for:
Uninspected Vessels:

- *Day:*   3 floating orange smoke, or

  3 handheld orange smoke, or

  1 orange flag with black square and circle

- *Day* and *Night:*   3 rocket parachute red flares, or

  3 aerial pyrotechnic red flares, or

  3 handheld red flares

Inspected Vessels—Lakes, Bays, Sounds & Rivers:

- *Day:*   3 handheld orange smoke and

  3 handheld red flares, or

  3 rocket parachute red flares

- *Night*   3 handheld red flares, or

  3 rocket parachute red flares

Inspected Vessels—Oceans and Coastwise:

- *Day:*   6 handheld orange smoke and

  6 handheld red flares, or

  6 rocket parachute red flares

- *Night:*   6 handheld red flares, or

  6 rocket parachute red flares

Official COLREGS 72 Distress Signals

| Red star shells | Fog horn continuous sounding | Flames on a vessel | Black square and ball on orange flag |

| Wave arms vertically | Parachute red flare | Smoke | MAYDAY by radio |

| Dye marker (any color) | Code flags November & Charlie | Square flag and ball | Gun fired at 1 minute intervals |

| Radiotelegraph alarm signal | Radiotelephone alarm signal | EPIRB | Morse code SOS |

EPIRBS
121.5/243 MHz EPIRBS
These earlier models generate position accurate to about 15 nm, and broadcast no identifying signal. They are no longer available and will not be recognized by satellite after February 1, 2009.

Class A	float free
	manual or automatic activation
Class B	manual activation only

406 MHz EPIRBS
These newer units transmit an identifier code, allowing vessel and owner identification, as well as prosecution information for misuse. They also broadcast a 121.5 MHz homing signal for rescue craft, as well as a strobe light. Accuracy is 3 nm.

Category I	float free
	manual or automatic activation
Category II	manual activation only

Inspected vessels and uninspected commercial vessels ≥ 36 feet, operating on the high seas or that operate beyond three miles of the Great Lakes coastline, and fishing industry vessels ≥ 36 feet operating beyond three miles from shore, must carry a Category I 406 MHz EPIRB.

Uninspected commercial and fishing vessels <36 feet are required to carry at least a Category II 406 MHz EPIRB.

Uninspected passenger vessels are not required to carry an EPIRB.

Testing must be performed and logged monthly by using the integrated test circuit and output indicator. The battery must be replaced after use or before the date required by the FCC, whichever is earlier. All testing must be performed between 00 and 05 minutes past the hour.

Table of Lifesaving Signals

The signals shown are taken from Pub. 102,
International Code of Signals for Visual, Sound, and Radio Communications, 1969 Edition (Revised 1993).

I Landing signals for the guidance of small boats with crews or persons in distress

	MANUAL SIGNALS	LIGHT SIGNALS	OTHER SIGNALS	SIGNIFICATION
Day signals	**Vertical** motion of a white flag or of the arms	or firing of a green star signal	or code letter **K** given by light or sound-signal apparatus	This is the best place to land
Night signals	**Vertical** motion of a white light or flare	or firing of a green star signal	or code letter **K** given by light or sound-signal apparatus	

A range (indication of direction) may be given by placing a steady white light or flare at a lower level and in line with the observer

	MANUAL SIGNALS	LIGHT SIGNALS	OTHER SIGNALS	SIGNIFICATION
Day signals	**Horizontal** motion of a white flag or of the arms extended horizontally	or firing of a red star signal	or code letter **S** given by light or sound-signal apparatus	Landing here highly dangerous
Night signals	**Horizontal** motion of a light or flare	or firing of a red star signal	or code letter **S** given by light or sound-signal apparatus	
Day signals	1 Horizontal motion of a white flag, followed by 2 the placing of the white flag in the ground and 3 by the carrying of another white flag in the direction to be indicated	1 or firing of a red star signal vertically and 2 a white star signal in the direction toward the better landing place	1 or signaling the code letter **S** (. . .) followed by the code letter **R** (. _ .) if a better landing place for the craft in distress is located more to the *right* in the direction of approach 2 or signaling the code letter **S** (. . .) followed by the code letter **L** (. _ . .) if a better landing place for the craft in distress is located more to the *left* in the direction of approach	Landing here highly dangerous. A more favorable location for landing is in the direction indicated.
Night signals	1 Horizontal motion of a white light or flare followed by 2 the placing of the white light or flare on the ground and 3 the carrying of another white light or flare in the direction to be indicated	1 or firing of a red star signal vertically and a 2 white star signal in the direction toward the better landing place	1 or signaling the code letter **S** (. . .) followed by the code letter **R** (. _ .) if a better landing place for the craft in distress is located more to the *right* in the direction of approach 2 or signaling the code letter **S** (. . .) followed by the code letter **L** (. _ . .) if a better landing place for the craft in distress is located more to the *left* in the direction of approach	

II Signals to be employed in connection with the use of shore lifesaving apparatus

	MANUAL SIGNALS	LIGHT SIGNALS	OTHER SIGNALS	SIGNIFICATION
Day signals	 **Vertical** motion of a white flag or of the arms	 or firing of a green star signal		In general: Affirmative Specifically: Rocket line is held – Tail block is made fast – Man is in the breeches buoy – Haul away
Night signals	 **Vertical** motion of a white light or flare	 or firing of a green star signal		
Day signals	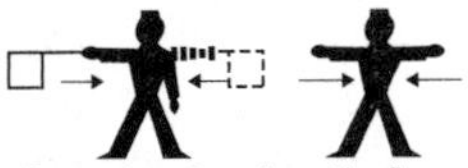 **Horizontal** motion of a white flag or of the arms extended horizontally	 or firing of a red star signal		In general: Negative Specifically: Slack away Avast hauling
Night signals	 **Horizontal** motion of a white light or flare	 or firing of a red star signal		

III Replies from lifesaving stations or maritime rescue units to distress signals made by ship or person

Day signals	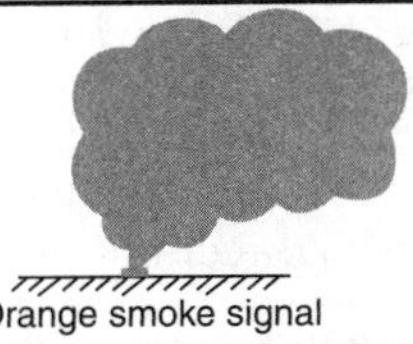 Orange smoke signal	 or combined light and sound signal (thunder-light) consisting of 3 single signals fired at intervals of one minute	You are seen – assistance will be given as soon as possible (Repetition of such signal shall have same meaning)
Night signals	 White star rocket consisting of 3 single signals fired at intervals of one minute		You are seen – assistance will be given as soon as possible (Repetition of such signal shall have same meaning)

III Air-to-surface visual signals

Signals used by aircraft engaged in search and rescue operations to direct ships toward an aircraft, ship or person in distress

PROCEDURES PERFORMED IN SEQUENCE BY AN AIRCRAFT			SIGNIFICATION
 1. CIRCLE the vessel at least once.	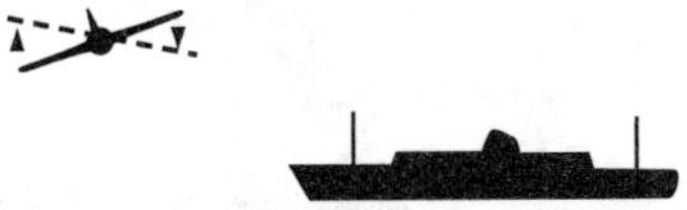 2. CROSS the vessel's projected course close AHEAD at a low altitude ROCKING wings.	 3. HEAD in the direction the vessel is to be directed.	You are seen – assistance will be given as soon as possible (Repetition of such signal shall have same meaning)
 4. CROSS the vessel's wake close ASTERN at low altitude while ROCKING wings. Note–opening and closing throttle or changing propeller pitch is an alternative. Rocking wings is preferred due to noise level on ship.			The assistance of the vessel is no longer required.

RESPONSE OF VESSEL TO SIGNALING AIRCRAFT

Hoist "Code and Answering" pendant Close up; or	Change vessel heading to the required direction; or	— Flash Morse Code "T" by lamp	Acknowledges receipt of aircraft's signal
Hoist international flag "N" (NOVEMBER); or		— • Flash Morse Code "N" by lamp	Indicates inability to comply

FIRE FIGHTING

Definitions

Blowback—situation occurring when a direct attack forces combustible vapors, smoke into a pocket (closed passageway, compartment, etc). Building pressure suddenly expands outward toward its only egress—where the firefighters are.

Conduction—heat spread by contact

Convection—heat spread by moving air or water

Fire Point—lowest temperature at which combustion will be maintained in a vapor-emitting fuel. Is slightly above Flash Point.

Fire Triangle—the three necessary ingredients for fire. Lacking one it can't start; remove one and it can't be sustained . . . Oxygen . . . Heat . . . Fuel.

Flammable (Explosive) Range—range of fuel vapor mix which can be ignited, bounded by the Lower Explosive Limit (LEL) and Upper Explosive Limit (UEL). Below the LEL (mixture too lean) and above the UEL (mixture too rich) ignition cannot occur. (Range is 1 to 6% for petroleum vapor.)

Flash Point—the temperature at which fuel emits sufficient vapor to be ignitable momentarily if an ignition source is present. It will sustain combustion only if the Fire Point is reached.

Fuel—anything capable of burning

Ignition Temperature—lowest temperature at which a fuel's vapor ignites without any outside source of ignition. It is above the Fire Point.

Jacket—canvas cover of a fire hose

Lower Explosive Limit (LEL)—minimum ratio of fuel vapor to air which can be ignited. Below LEL, there is too little fuel vapor.

Oxidation—chemical process by which oxygen unites with fuel vapor which, upon ignition, releases heat and light.

Overhaul—breaking up a fire source; searching for burning or smoldering area

Radiation—heat spread by infra-red radiation

Spanner—a C-shaped wrench used to secure hose to hydrant

Spontaneous Combustion—process by which an inflammable material in the presence of oxygen, but without adequate ventilation, builds up sufficient heat to allow the material to ignite

Upper Explosive Limit (UEL)—maximum ratio of fuel vapor/air which can be ignited. Above UEL, the mixture has too little oxygen.

Fire Classes

Fires are grouped into four classes depending on the type of fuel. It is important to identify the class because both extinguishing agent and firefighting technique depend on it. The classes are:

- *Class A*—wood, cloth, paper, rubber, plastics.
- *Class B*—petroleum products, alcohols, paints.
- *Class C*—energized electrical components.
- *Class D*—combustible metals such as magnesium.

The Fire Triangle

Fires always involve three elements. Remove any one of the three and the fire goes out. *This is the basic principle of fire fighting*. To illustrate the point, the three elements are often presented as a triangle (below). If any of the triangle's legs (the three elements) are removed, the triangle collapses (the fire goes out). The three elements are:

- *Fuel*—any combustible material, such as wood, paper, oil, plastic, rubber, gasoline, paint, electrical insulation, and certain metals.
- *Oxygen*—a minimum of 16% by volume of air (normal concentration of oxygen in air is 21%).
- *Heat*—temperature high enough to ignite the fuel.

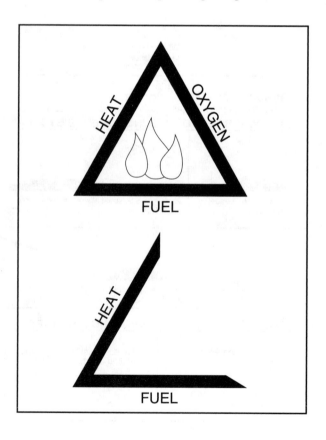

Extinguishing Agents

Water

The agent, water, includes the *solid streams* and *fog* (high and low velocity). It acts mainly by cooling but, as a result of steam formation, has a smothering (oxygen blocking) effect as well.

Solid streams tend to break up burning material, getting to underlying hot embers. A precaution with solid streams is the effect on vessel stability of a large volume of water. Water is the agent of choice on Class A fires. Low velocity fog can be used on Class B fires for its smothering effect, but foam and/or CO_2 are preferred. A solid stream or high velocity fog could spread/scatter/float a Class B fire. Water (including fog and foam) is never used on Class C or D fires due to the risk of electrocution in the former and violent reaction in the latter.

Fog, delivered via the combination nozzle as either high or low velocity, has a greater cooling effect than a solid stream because the fine droplets present a greater surface area. In general approach a fire from downwind if using high velocity fog and upwind if using low velocity fog. A danger with high velocity fog is the possibility of blowback resulting from trapped gases, smoke and heat. Ventilating the area reduces this hazard. Low velocity fog can be used on a Class B fire for its smothering and cooling effects, although either foam or CO_2 is preferred. See below for operation of the combination nozzle.

Water is delivered via fixed fire mains (ship's piping), auto or manual sprinklers and hoses. Hoses are of 50′ length in two diameters: 1-1/2″ and 2-1/2″. Manning requirements are two for 1-1/2″, three for 2-1/2″. The combination nozzle (below) discharges a solid stream with the handle back, high velocity fog with the handle straight up, and is off with the handle forward. To generate low velocity fog, the high velocity fog tip is replaced by a low velocity fog applicator in two sizes: 10′ with a 90° bend and 4′ with a 60° bend.

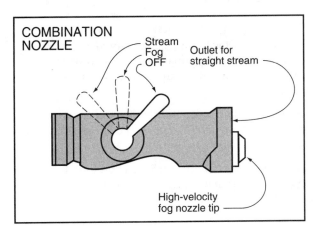

COMBINATION NOZZLE
Stream
Fog
OFF
Outlet for straight stream
High-velocity fog nozzle tip

Foam

Foams contain water and are thus unsuitable for Class C and D fires. The foam may be generated either chemically or mechanically. All foams work by smothering (separating oxygen and fuel) and, to a lesser degree, cooling. They are the preferred agents for Class B fires and can be effective on Class A fires as well. The foam is generally applied by bouncing it off a bulkhead to avoid splattering the fuel. Two concentrations of foam are available:

High Expansion (100/1 to 1,000/1): dryer, lighter, less heat resistant, clings to vertical surfaces.

Low Expansion (<100/1): wetter, heavier, more resistant to evaporation, less cling.

Carbon Dioxide (CO_2)

A colorless, odorless, heavier-than-air gas, CO_2 is used in Class B and C fires. It is non-conductive and leaves no residue (an advantage over dry chemicals). It extinguishes by smothering but is not effective on combustible metals. Due to its gaseous nature, it is most effective in a confined space, so securing (closing) the ventilation is critical. Fixed CO_2 systems in closed spaces require an evacuation alarm giving crew a 20-second warning before release. Problems and limitations include:

- possible death by suffocation
- little cooling effect
- possibility of re-ignition requires standing by with other agents

Halon

This colorless, odorless, residue-free gas acts as a chain-breaker. It is used in a fashion similar to CO_2 and, like the latter, can cause suffocation. Halon production in the U.S. has been terminated because of ozone depletion, but remaining stocks can be used. Pending development of a Halon replacement, some vessels are replacing it with CO_2.

Dry Chemicals (not Dry Powder)

Extinguishing action is by smothering and preventing oxidation of the fuel. Dry chemicals are generally approved for A, B and C fires but cool little, so have limited effect on A fires. Pros and cons include:

- range greater than that of CO_2
- residue
- flashback possible with Class B fires
- not effective on D fires

Dry Powder

This agent is specific to Class D fires, which include burning sodium, potassium, lithium, magnesium, titanium, and zirconium. The powder extinguishes by fusing over the metal and cutting off oxygen.

Methods of Attack
Direct
Advance to the area with the equipment and agent(s) dictated by the class of fire. If there is danger of combustible gas accumulating around or ahead of personnel, ventilate the fire to avoid blowback.

Indirect
Evacuate the space containing the fire, secure (close off) all ventilation, and flood the space with the chosen extinguishing agent. Remember that reflash can occur if the space is unsealed too quickly and resupplied with O_2.

Prevention and Detection
Prevention
Shipboard fires are easier to prevent than to put out. Cleanliness, proper storage of flammables, and elimination of sources of spontaneous combustion, bilge vapors, and cigarette hazards all help to prevent fires. Automatic fire dampers closed by melted fusible links prevent fire spread by convection.

Detection
Automatic fire detection systems activated by temperature rise in a compartment should be checked weekly and repaired immediately if defective.

Fire alarms should be sounded immediately—not after an attempt to extinguish has failed. Fire and boat drills must include fire pump startup, deployment of all safety and rescue equipment from lockers, and demonstrations of their uses.

Compartment Testing
Before entering a compartment suspected of an accumulation of explosive vapors and/or a lack of oxygen, it is critical to check for both. A spark in the former could result in loss of the vessel; entering the latter could result in death.

Instruments used for testing are:

- Oxygen Indicator
- Flame Safety Lamp
- Combustible Gas Indicator

Oxygen Indicator
An oxygen indicator measures the concentration of O_2 in the atmosphere. Testing should be performed before any personnel enter a questionable space. The test is performed by squeezing an aspirating bulb, which draws a sample through a tube extended into the space to be tested. All levels of the space should be sampled. An oxygen test should also be performed prior to use of a combustible gas indicator since the latter is inaccurate if the oxygen level is deficient.

Clean the oxygen indicator and tubing after each use by drawing fresh air (purging) through the tube several times. Some gases (such as flue gas, CO_2, halogens, nitrogen and sulfur oxides) affect the accuracy of the test.

Flame Safety Lamp
The flame safety lamp tests for the presence of oxygen in an atmosphere by its effect on a flame, rather than by a meter. The reaction of the flame can also suggest the presence of a combustible gas. The lamp is designed to be safe in the presence of combustible gas but, if defective, an explosion could result. Therefore, use the flame safety lamp only to test for oxygen in a space free of combustible gas.

Oxygen percentages:

- normal oxygen concentration is 21%
- flame extinguishes at about 16%
- person becomes unconscious between 16% and 10%

Reading the flame:

- flame flares up—gases are present but below the lower explosive level (LEL)
- flame pops—gas concentration is between LEL and upper explosive limit (UEL)
- flame flares then goes out—gases above the UEL

Combustible Gas Indicator
A meter indicates the concentration of explosive gases as a percentage of the LEL. An aspirated sample drawn through a tube passes over an energized platinum wire, and the degree to which the wire heats is reflected in its resistance. The meter is calibrated such that the needle deflection indicates percent of LEL of the atmosphere tested.

Warning: continued sampling of atmospheres above the UEL will cause the wire to overheat and possibly burn out. The instrument functions poorly if the oxygen concentration is below 10% or above 25%.

Recharging CO_2 Extinguishers
CO_2 extinguishers must be recharged either by the manufacturer or by a manufacturer-certified repair facility when the weight of CO_2 drops by 10 percent or more.

Example: when will a B-II (15 lb.) CO_2 extinguisher require recharging if the gross weight (weight of equipment plus CO_2) is 42 lb.?

Answer: 10% of 15 lb. is 1.5 lb. Therefore, the extinguisher will require recharging when its gross weight drops to 42.0 lb. – 1.5 lb. = 40.5 lb.

Fire Extinguisher Characteristics

Type	Fire Class	How It Works	Comments
Water	A	Direct stream from comb. nozzle Removes heat by vaporization	Conducts electricity (not for Class C)
Fog	AB	From comb. nozzle/applicator High velocity from comb. nozzle Low velocity from nozzle/applicator	Conducts electricity (not for Class C) High velocity fog range 25–35 feet Low velocity fog range 5 feet
Foam	AB	From portable foam extinguisher Cuts off oxygen supply Removes heat by vaporization	Conducts electricity (not for Class C) High expansion clings Low expansion resists heat better
CO_2	ABC	From portable foam extinguisher Displaces oxygen	Doesn't lower temperature, so fire can reignite. Easily dissipated by wind. Suffocating to personnel.
Halon	ABC	From portable and fixed system Displaces oxygen	Discontinued due to ozone depletion Good for Class C (electrical) fires
Dry Chemical	ABC BC	Reacts with fuel/inhibits combustion	Powder residue harmful to engines and electronics.
Dry Powder	D	Powder fuses to isolate metal from oxygen	Powder may be metal-specific

Required Contents of Fire Extinguishers

Extinguisher Class	CO_2, lb.	Halon, lb.	Dry Chemical, lb.	Foam, gal.
B-I	4	2.5	2	1.25
B-II	15	10	10	2.5

Coast Guard Requirements

Boat Size	Fire Extinguishers Required	Extinguishers Required if Fixed Extinguisher in Engine Space
Under 26′	(1) B-I, unless construction does not allow	Not applicable
26′ to <40′	(2) B-I or (1) B-II	(1) B-I
40′ to 65′	(3) B-I, or (1) B-I plus (1) B-II	(2) B-I or (1) B-II

FIRST AID

Wounds
Types

• *Punctures* are holes produced by pointed objects such as bullets, nails, or sharp sticks. Surface bleeding may be minor, but hidden, internal bleeding may occur if the puncture is deep. Infection is a major concern since the wound is not easily cleaned.

• *Incisions* are cuts such as would be produced by a knife or broken glass. Arteries and veins may be severed, so bleeding can be extensive. Extensive incisions require stitches to close the wound.

• *Abrasions* are a wearing away of the skin, as by sandpaper. Bleeding is usually a minor oozing, but the wound should be thoroughly cleaned because the skin's primary defensive layer has been worn away.

• *Lacerations* are irregular breaks in the skin—as opposed to incisions. Tissue damage is often greater than with incisions. Lacerations should be thoroughly cleansed and usually require stitches.

• *Avulsions* are a tearing away of the flesh, such as a torn ear or severed limb. Bleeding is extensive when veins and arteries are severed as well.

Stopping Bleeding

• *Direct pressure* is the preferred blood-stopping method for a nonprofessional. The object is to slow blood flow enough for clotting to take place by compressing the veins and arteries against muscle or bone. The wound should be covered with a sterile bandage or clean cloth if possible, while the pressure is being applied. Even if the bandage becomes soaked, do not remove the pressure until bleeding stops.

• *Elevation* of the wounded part reduces the blood pressure and rate of bleeding. It is not a substitute for direct pressure.

• *Arterial pressure* is pressure applied directly to an artery where it passes over a bone. The *brachial pressure point* is inside the upper arm, midway between shoulder and elbow, and between the biceps and triceps muscles. The *femoral pressure point* is inside the thigh at the middle of the crease of the groin. Since pressure at these points cuts off blood flow to the entire arm or leg, it should be used only when direct pressure and elevation prove insufficient.

• *Tourniquets* are bands of cloth tightened around a limb just above a wound to stop all blood flow. Releasing pressure on a tourniquet resumes blood flow and may actually increase the chances of shock and death. They are, thus, last resort measures where the decision is to risk losing the limb to save the life.

Removing Foreign Objects

• *Splinters* are normally more irritants than dangers. Remove shallow splinters with sterilized—held over an open flame or boiled—tweezers or needles. Deep splinters should be removed only by a doctor.

• *Fish hooks* may be simply backed out if the barb has not engaged. If the barb is deep, however, the least damage is usually caused by pushing it out the other side, clipping it off, then backing the hook out. A tetanus shot should be given for the latter case.

• *Large objects* that are deeply embedded—even knives—should not be removed! While in place they likely minimize internal bleeding. Immobilize the object and rush the victim to the hospital.

Preventing Infection

• *Cleansing* the wound is the most important step in preventing infection. Antibacterial agents may be used but are not required. Simply wash your hands and the skin area around the wound with soap and water. Flush the wound—opening it wide—with running tap water. Blot the wound dry with sterile gauze and cover with a sterile bandage.

• *Symptoms* of an infected wound include: redness (particularly if the redness spreads), swelling of the area, tenderness or pain, pus draining from the wound and elevated temperature (fever).

• *Infected wounds* require the attention of a doctor. Until then, immobilize and elevate the wound and apply dry or wet heat to the area, 30 minutes on and 30 minutes off.

Bones and Joints
Fractures

• *Simple fractures* are those where the bone is not exposed.

• *Compound fractures* are those where the fracture is compounded by the bone being exposed. The wound is usually caused by the jagged edge of the broken bone. Compound fractures are more serious due to the likelihood of infection.

- *Symptoms* of a fracture include: an audible snap, difficulty moving the member, pain or tenderness at the fracture location, asymmetry (difference in length or shape between like members), swelling and discoloration and an obvious crookedness.

- *First aid* consists of immobilizing the fractured member to prevent further damage before being attended by a doctor. If the wait will be long, apply a splint.

Joints

- *Sprains* are damage to tendons, ligaments and blood vessels due to overextension of a joint. Severe sprains should be x-rayed to see if a fracture is also involved. First aid consists of immobilization, elevation and the application of ice packs over several days.

- *Strains* are damage to muscles due to overexertion. The muscles are stretched and may be partially torn. First aid consists of rest and application of moist heat.

- *Dislocation* is the separation of a joint. Reduction—restoring the bones to their proper places—should not be attempted except by a doctor or other trained person, due to the possibility of further damage to the joint. First aid until the doctor attends is immobilization.

Shock
Definition and Causes
Traumatic shock, as opposed to electrical or insulin shock, is a depression of the body's vital functions (principally blood flow and respiration) as a result of injury. If untreated, it often leads to death even when the injury itself is not life-threatening. The causes are many, including: loss of blood, loss of body fluids other than blood, chemical poisoning, anaphylaxis (allergic reaction) and respiratory difficulty.

Symptoms

- *Early* signs of traumatic shock include: pale, cool, and possibly clammy skin, dizziness, faint rapid pulse and abnormal breathing.

- *Late (advanced)* signs include apathy, mottled skin and, especially, wide dilation of the pupils of the eye.

First Aid

- *Improve circulation.* Blood pressure and flow to the head are most important and are improved by laying the victim flat on the ground and raising the feet. A single exception to the feet-up rule is the case of a victim with a head injury, where increased blood pressure to the brain may prove dangerous.

- *Aid respiration.* If the victim is having difficulty breathing, make sure the airway is clear, then place him on his back with the chest and head slightly elevated.

- *Regulate temperature.* Make sure the victim is neither too cold nor too hot.

- *Administer fluids.* If and only if: 1) medical assistance will be delayed for more than an hour; 2) the victim is fully conscious and having no respiratory problem; and 3) there is no likelihood of head injury. Fluids may be given orally. The recommended fluid is room-temperature water with one teaspoon of salt per quart, administered at the rate of one half cup (4 oz.) every 15 minutes.

Respiratory Failure
The ABCs
The three critical requirements to get oxygen to the brain are the ABCs:

- *(A)irway*—unobstructed mouth and throat.

- *(B)reathing*—air heard or felt flowing in and out of the mouth or nose.

- *(C)irculation*—flow of blood, evidenced by a pulse felt at the carotid artery beside the Adam's apple.

Cardiopulmonary Resuscitation (CPR)
To administer CPR to a victim:

1. Check the ABCs.

2. Clean the mouth of any obstruction.

3. Raise the chin and pinch the nose shut.

4. Place your mouth over the victim's and give two breaths.

5. Place the heel of one hand 2″ above the bottom of the breastbone and the other hand on top of the bottom hand, and depress the chest 1-1/2″ to 2″ for 1/2 second. Repeat 15 times at the rate of 80-100 compressions per minute.

6. Repeat Steps 4 and 5 until victim resumes breathing. Check the ABCs every two minutes.

7. If two people are available to administer CPR, one gives one breath, the other gives five compressions, etc.

The Heimlich Maneuver

To clear an airway obstruction when it cannot be reached through the mouth:

1. Stand behind the victim.

2. Hold arms around the victim below the rib cage.

3. Make a fist with one hand and grip the fist with your other hand. Place the thumb of the fist against the chest hollow just below the ribs and thrust it rapidly and forcefully up against the chest up to four times.

4. If the victim is already unconscious, lay him flat on his back and apply the chest thrusts from the front. Be prepared to remove whatever comes up.

5. If the obstruction is dislodged, start CPR.

Burns
Degrees

• *First degree*—skin is red.

• *Second degree*—skin red and blistered.

• *Third degree*—skin charred (brown or black).

First Aid

1. Check breathing. Apply CPR, if necessary.

2. Apply cold, wet cloths for 5–10 minutes.

3. Administer strong pain medication.

4. Flush the burned area with fresh water (salt water, if fresh is not available) for a full 30 minutes. DO NOT apply Vaseline or any type of cooking oil or butter.

5. DO apply an antibacterial ointment, if available.

6. Cover with a loose sterile bandage. Do not puncture blisters.

Poisoning
Ingested

• *Corrosive substances* such as acids, alkalis, ammonia and petroleum distillates (gasoline, diesel fuel, paint thinner, etc.) typically burn the lips, mouth and throat and lead to breathing difficulty. Do NOT induce vomiting, as this will just lead to further exposure of the esophagus to corrosion. All you can do is dilute the substance with several glasses of milk.

• *Noncorrosive substances* should be gotten up as soon as possible. Induce vomiting by sticking the finger down the throat or by swallowing 30 cc syrup of Ipecac diluted with four glasses of water.

• *Bacterial food* results in abdominal pain, vomiting and diarrhea. If vomiting has not yet occurred, hasten it with the finger or syrup of Ipecac. Fluids will be helpful, but only well after vomiting has ceased.

Inhaled

Carbon monoxide and the fumes of many petroleum distillates may cause headaches, dizziness and disorientation. Treatment consists of fresh air. Administer CPR, if necessary.

Contact with Skin

Poisons, such as acids and alkalis, on the skin or in the eyes should be flushed with plenty of fresh water.

Heat Effects
Heatstroke (Sunstroke)

• *Symptoms* include red, hot and dry skin, strong and rapid pulse and very high body temperature.

• *Treatment* consists of lowering the body temperature by immersion in cold water (not ice), or sponging with a cold, wet towel or rubbing alcohol until the temperature drops to less than 102°F.

Heat Exhaustion

• *Symptoms* include pale, cool and clammy skin, dizziness, nausea and sometimes cramps.

• *Treatment* consists of laying the victim down with feet elevated and giving salted water (1 teaspoon per quart) at the rate of 8 ounces every 15 minutes for one hour.

Heat Cramps

• *Symptoms* include cramping of legs and abdomen.

• *Treatment* consists of giving salted water (1 teaspoon per quart) at the rate of 8 ounces every 15 minutes for one hour, and gentle massage of the cramped muscles.

Cold Effects
Frostbite

• *Symptoms* include glossy, white skin that is hard on the surface but soft underneath. In extreme cases, large blisters may appear.

• *Treatment* consists of rapid warming in running or circulating warm water (102–105°F). Do not massage frozen area. Discontinue warming as soon as color returns. If frozen area is a limb or member, exercise it gently.

Hypothermia

- *Symptoms* include shivering, muscular weakness and numbness and low body temperature. In extreme cases, the victim becomes unconscious.

- *Treatment* consists of warming the entire body quickly. Remove clothing and immerse the victim fully in water at 102–105°F. If the victim is conscious, give him hot liquids, but not alcohol. Discontinue treatment as soon as body temperature returns to normal.

Sudden Illness
Heart Attack

- *Symptoms* include pain described as pressure on the chest, pain radiating to the neck, shoulders and possibly down one or both arms, shortness of breath, sweating, nausea and mild indigestion.

- *Treatment* consists of 1) calling for an ambulance, 2) CPR if necessary, 3) loosening clothing, having victim sit quietly in a comfortable position, and administering three nitroglycerine tablets, if available, under the tongue at 10-minute intervals.

Stroke

- *Symptoms of a major stroke* include unconsciousness, paralysis or weakness on one side of the body, unequal pupil size, slurred speech, respiratory difficulty and loss of bowel and/or bladder control.

- *Symptoms of a minor stroke* include headache, dizziness, confusion, weakness in an arm or leg, some memory and speech loss and personality change.

- *Treatment* consists of 1) calling for an ambulance, 2) CPR if necessary, and 3) placing the victim on his side to maintain an open airway.

Fainting

- *Symptoms* include paleness, sweating, dizziness, coldness of the skin and unconsciousness.

- *Treatment* consists of laying victim down and loosening clothing. If victim recovers consciousness quickly, give him fluids. If recovery is not quick, call for an ambulance.

Seizure (Convulsions)

- *Symptoms* include unconsciousness and convulsions.

- *Treatment* consists of protecting the victim from injuring himself until the seizure passes. Insert a padded stick—not your fingers—between the teeth to prevent biting of the tongue and remove furniture or otherwise protect the victim's head from injury. When victim recovers, encourage rest.

Hyperglycemia (Excess Blood Sugar)

- *Symptoms* include drowsiness, confusion and a fruity breath odor.

- *Treatment* consists of immediate hospitalization.

Hypoglycemia (Insulin Shock or Insufficient Blood Sugar)

- *Symptoms* include gnawing hunger, dizziness, weakness, cold sweat, tremor and ultimately unconsciousness.

- *Treatment (conscious victim)* consists of increasing the victim's blood sugar content by administering candy, fruit juice, a soft drink or anything that contains real sugar.

- *Treatment (unconscious victim)* consists of taking the patient to the emergency room ASAP for intravenous dextrose.

Anaphylactic Shock (Severe Allergic Reaction)

- *Symptoms* include respiratory distress (the most dangerous aspect), burning and itching of the skin, particularly around head and neck, possible nausea, vomiting and/or diarrhea.

- *Treatment* consists of injecting epinephrine (every vessel should carry a kit). If epinephrine is not available, administer an antihistamine such as Benadryl.

SMALL ENGINE OPERATION

Gasoline Engines

Principle

Fuel is brought to the carburetor from the fuel tank by a fuel pump. On the intake stroke of a piston, air and vaporized fuel are drawn through the intake valve into the cylinder. On the compression stroke, the air/fuel mixture is compressed to about 1/8 of its original volume (compression ratio of eight). Near the top of the compression stroke a spark, induced across the gap of the spark plug, ignites the air/fuel mixture. The combustion and expansion of gas forces the piston down in a power stroke. In the following exhaust stroke, the combustion gases are vented out through the exhaust valve.

Troubleshooting

If a gasoline engine won't start, it probably isn't getting one of two things:

1. Fuel—check in order:

   • Is there fuel in the tank?

   • Is the fuel shutoff valve open?

   • Is fuel getting to the carburetor?

   • Is the choke in the proper position (on, or closed, if the engine is cold/off if warm)?

2. Spark—remove a spark plug and, holding the threaded portion against the engine, see if a blue spark jumps the gap as the engine is cranked. If not, check the distributor, coil, and power to the coil.

Ventilation

Gasoline engines and fuel tank spaces must be positively ventilated. The blower should be wired so that the engine can't be started until the blower has run. The engine space must be equipped with a flammable vapor detector that operates 30 seconds before engine startup and while the engine is running.

Diesel Engines

Principle

Fuel is pulled through a fuel filter (usually primary and secondary fuel filters) to remove particulates and water. From the fuel filter the fuel enters an injection pump that increases the fuel pressure to thousands of pounds per square inch and delivers a timed pulse of fuel to each of the fuel injectors in turn.

On the intake stroke, air is drawn through the intake valve, filling the cylinder. On the compression stroke, the air is compressed to about 1/20 of its original volume (compression ratio of 20), which heats the air to about 1,000°F. The fuel injector then delivers a fine spray of diesel fuel which ignites, since its ignition temperature is around 750°F. The controlled injection/burn results in a power stroke. When the piston returns on its exhaust stroke, the combustion gases are flushed out through the exhaust valve.

Troubleshooting

Since the diesel fuel is ignited simply by the high temperature resulting from the high compression, a diesel engine has no electrical ignition system, making it much more reliable in the marine environment. If a diesel engine won't start, it probably isn't getting fuel (air in the fuel line is a likely reason).

Check in order:

   • Is there fuel in the tank?

   • Is the fuel shutoff valve open?

   • Is the primary fuel filter clogged or full of water?

   • Is there fuel at the outlet of the fuel pump?

   • With the engine cranking, does clear fuel (no bubbles) flow from the injection pump bleed screw(s), indicating air in the line?

Both Gasoline and Diesel Engines

Engine Cooling

Both gasoline and diesel propulsion engines must be water cooled. The engine head, block, and exhaust manifold must be water jacketed and cooled by water from a pump that operates whenever the engine is running. Fresh water systems (with heat exchangers) may also be used.

Outboard engines and auxiliary engines with self-contained fuel systems may be air cooled, if they are installed on an open deck.

Fuel Shutoff Valves

Fuel supply lines must have fuel shutoff valves—one at the tank connection, and one at the engine end of the fuel line. The shutoff valve at the tank must be manually operable from outside the compartment in which the valve is located, preferably from the weather deck.

If suitably protected from flames, the valve handle may be located so that the operator doesn't have to reach more than 12″ into the valve space.

SAFETY
QUESTIONS

The illustrations cited in the questions are shown on page 812.

2. An airplane wants a vessel to change course and proceed towards a vessel in distress. The actions of the aircraft to convey this message will NOT include _____.

A. circling the vessel at least once
B. heading in the direction of the distress location
C. flashing the navigation lights on and off
D. crossing ahead and rocking the wings.

3. To turn over an inflatable life raft that is upside down, you should pull on the _____.

A. canopy
B. manropes
C. sea painter
D. righting strap

4. A green signal, floating in the air from a parachute, about 300 feet above the water, indicates that a submarine _____.

A. has fired a torpedo during a drill
B. will be coming to the surface
C. is on the bottom in distress
D. is in distress and will try to surface

5. Pollution of the waterways may result from the discharge of _____.

A. sewage
B. the galley trash can
C. an oily mixture of one part per million
D. All of the above

8. You are alone and administering CPR to an adult victim. How many chest compressions and how many inflations should you administer in each sequence?

A. 5 compressions then 1 inflation
B. 15 compressions then 2 inflations
C. 20 compressions then 3 inflations
D. 30 compressions then 4 inflations

9. The International Regulations for Preventing Collisions at Sea contain the requirements for _____.

A. signals that must be sounded when being towed in restricted visibility
B. minimum hawser lengths when being towed
C. lights that must be displayed on anchor buoys
D. mooring procedures for support vessels when transferring cargo

10. What is the definition of transverse metacenter?

A. The distance between the actual center of gravity and the maximum center of gravity that will still allow a positive stability.
B. The point to which G may rise and still permit the vessel to possess positive stability.
C. The sum of the center of buoyancy and the center of gravity.
D. The transverse shift of the center of buoyancy as a vessel rolls.

11. A patient in shock should NOT be placed in which position?

A. On their side if unconscious
B. Head down and feet up, no injuries to face or head
C. Flat on their back with head and feet at the same level
D. Arms above their head

13. Your life raft is to leeward of a fire on the water and riding to its sea anchor. You should FIRST _____.

A. boat the sea anchor
B. paddle away from the fire
C. splash water over the life raft to cool it
D. get out of the raft and swim to safety

14. A yellow signal floating in the air from a small parachute, about 300 feet above the water, would indicate that a submarine _____.

A. has fired a torpedo during a drill
B. is about to rise to periscope depth
C. is on the bottom in distress
D. is disabled and unable to surface

15. In reference to accidental oil pollution, the most critical time during bunkering is when _____.

A. you first start to receive fuel
B. hoses are being blown down
C. final topping off is occurring
D. hoses are being disconnected

18. When giving mouth-to-mouth rescue breathing to an adult, you should breathe at the rate of how many breaths per minute?

A. 4
B. 8

C. 12
D. 20

19. The operator of the ship's radio-telephone, if the radiotelephone is carried voluntarily, must hold at least a _____.

A. mate's license
B. restricted radiotelephone operator permit
C. second-class radio operator's license
D. seaman's document

20. If the vertical center of gravity (VCG) of a ship rises, the righting arm (GZ) for the various angles of inclination will _____.

A. decrease
B. increase
C. remain unchanged
D. be changed by the amount of GG' x cosine of the angle

21. Coast Guard regulations require that all of the following emergencies be covered at the periodic drills on a fishing vessel EXCEPT _____.

A. minimizing the affects of unintentional flooding
B. fire on board
C. rescuing an individual from the water
D. emergency towing

23. Your ship is sinking rapidly. A container containing an inflatable life raft has bobbed to the surface upon functioning of the hydrostatic release. Which action should you take?

A. Cut the painter line so it will not pull the life raft container down.
B. Swim away from the container so you will not be in danger as it goes down.
C. Take no action because the painter will cause the life raft to inflate and open the container.
D. Manually open the container and inflate the life raft with the hand pump.

24. Which single-letter sound signal may be made only in compliance with the International Rules of the Road?

A. D
B. F
C. Q
D. U

28. The rescuer can best provide an airtight seal during mouth-to-mouth resuscitation by pinching the victim's nostrils and _____.

A. cupping a hand around the patient's mouth
B. keeping the head elevated
C. applying his mouth tightly over the victim's mouth
D. holding the jaw down firmly

29. In order to discharge a CO_2 portable fire extinguisher, the operator must FIRST _____.

A. invert the CO_2 extinguisher
B. squeeze the two trigger handles together
C. remove the locking pin
D. open the discharge valve

30. Transverse stability calculations require the use of _____.

A. hog or sag calculations or tables
B. hydrostatic curves
C. general arrangement plans
D. cross-sectional views of the vessel

31. All of the following are part of the fire triangle EXCEPT _____.

A. electricity
B. fuel
C. oxygen
D. heat

33. Inflatable life rafts are less maneuverable than lifeboats due to their _____.

A. shape
B. shallow draft
C. large sail area
D. All of the above

34. Which single-letter sound signal(s) may only be made in compliance with the Rules of the Road?

A. D
B. E
C. S
D. All of the above

35. Which statement is TRUE of a gasoline spill?

A. It is visible for a shorter time than a fuel oil spill.
B. It is not covered by the pollution laws.
C. It does little harm to marine life.

D. It will sink more rapidly than crude oil.

36. The number and type of hand portable fire extinguishers required outside and in the vicinity of the paint locker exit is _____.

A. one A-I
B. two A-IIs
C. one B-II
D. one C-II

38. When applying chest compressions on an adult victim during CPR, the sternum should be depressed about _____.

A. 1/2 inch or less
B. 1/2 to 1 inch
C. 1 to 1-1/2 inches
D. 1-1/2 to 2 inches

39. A flame screen _____.

A. permits the passage of vapor but not of flame
B. prevents the passage of flammable vapors
C. prevents inert gas from leaving a tank
D. permits vapors to exit but not enter a tank

40. Regardless of local requirements/regulations, when in a U.S. port, all oil spills must be reported to _____.

A. Environmental Protection Agency
B. Minerals Management Service
C. National Response Center (USCG)
D. All of the Above

41. Before using a fixed CO_2 system to fight an engine room fire, you must _____.

A. secure the engine room ventilation
B. secure the machinery in the engine room
C. evacuate all engine room personnel
D. All of the above

43. If an inflatable life raft is overturned, it may be righted by _____.

A. filling the stabilizers on one side with water
B. releasing the CO_2 cylinder
C. pushing up from under one end
D. standing on the inflating cylinder and pulling on the straps on the underside of the raft

44. The spread of fire is prevented by _____.

A. heating surfaces adjacent to the fire
B. removing combustibles from the endangered area
C. increasing the oxygen supply
D. All of the above

45. Which statement is TRUE concerning small oil spills?

A. They usually disappear quickly.
B. They usually stay in a small area.
C. They may cause serious pollution as the effect tends to be cumulative.
D. A small spill is not dangerous to sea life in the area.

48. You are administering chest compressions during CPR. Where on the victim's body should the pressure be applied?

A. Lower half of the sternum
B. Tip of the sternum
C. Top half of the sternum
D. Left chest over the heart

49. You are fighting a fire in the electrical switchboard in the engine room. You should secure the power, then _____.

A. use a portable foam extinguisher
B. use a low-velocity fog adapter with the fire hose
C. use a portable CO_2 extinguisher
D. determine the cause of the fire

53. If an inflatable life raft inflates upside down, you can right it by _____.

A. pushing up on one side
B. standing on the CO_2 bottle, holding the bottom straps, and throwing your weight backwards
C. getting at least three or four men to push down on the side containing the CO_2 cylinder
D. doing nothing; it will right itself after the canopy supports inflate

55. Most minor spills of oil products are caused by _____.

A. equipment failure
B. human error
C. major casualties
D. unforeseeable circumstances

57. The minimum concentration of a vapor in air which can form an explosive mixture is called the _____.

A. auto-ignition point
B. flash point
C. lower explosive limit (LEL)
D. threshold limit value (TLV)

58. Changing rescuers while carrying out artificial respiration should be done _____.

A. without losing the rhythm of respiration
B. only with the help of two other people
C. by not stopping the respiration for more than 5 minutes
D. at ten-minute intervals

60. Your vessel rolls slowly and sluggishly. This indicates that the vessel _____.

A. has offcenter weights
B. is taking on water
C. has a greater draft forward than aft
D. has poor stability

63. You have abandoned ship and are in an inflatable raft that has just inflated. You hear a continuous hissing coming from a fitting in a buoyancy tube. What is the cause of this?

A. The saltwater is activating the batteries of the marker lights on the canopy.
B. The inflation pump is in automatic operation to keep the tubes fully inflated.
C. A deflation plug is partially open allowing the escape of CO_2.
D. Excess inflation pressure is bleeding off and should soon stop.

65. The most serious effect of trapped air in a diesel engine jacket water cooling system is that it _____.

A. accelerates erosion
B. reduces the effectiveness of chromate additives
C. can form pockets of high chemical concentrates
D. accelerates formation of sludge deposits

68. The MOST important element in administering CPR is _____.

A. having the proper equipment for the process
B. starting the treatment quickly
C. administering of oxygen
D. treating for traumatic shock

69. Fire hose couplings _____.

A. are made of bronze, brass, or soft alloy metals
B. should be painted red in order to identify hose lengths
C. are specially hardened to prevent crushing
D. should be greased frequently

70. (Ill. D001SA) What represents the center of gravity?

A. GZ
B. M
C. B
D. G

71. Each hand portable fire extinguisher must be marked with _____.

A. the name of the vessel on which it is located
B. the date that it was installed
C. the names of the individuals qualified to use it
D. an identification number

73. A life raft which has inflated bottom-up on the water _____.

A. should be righted by standing on the carbon dioxide cylinder, holding the righting straps, and leaning backwards
B. should be righted by standing on the lifeline, holding the righting straps, and leaning backwards
C. will right itself when the canopy tubes inflate
D. must be cleared of the buoyant equipment before it will right itself

74. Outlets in gasoline fuel lines are _____.

A. prohibited
B. permitted for draining fuel from lines
C. permitted for drawing fuel samples
D. permitted for bleeding air from lines

77. Normally, the percentage of oxygen in air is _____.

A. 16%
B. 18%
C. 21%
D. 25%

78. Before CPR is started, you should _____.

A. establish an open airway
B. treat any bleeding wounds

C. insure the victim is conscious
D. make the victim comfortable

79. A squeeze-grip type carbon dioxide portable fire extinguisher has been partially discharged. It should be _____.

A. labeled empty and recharged as soon as possible
B. replaced in its proper location if weight loss is no more than 25%
C. replaced in its proper location regardless of weight
D. replaced in its proper location if weight loss is no more than 15%

80. (Ill. D001SA) What represents the metacentric height?

A. M
B. GM
C. BM
D. GZ

81. Which extinguishing agent is most likely to allow reflash as a result of not cooling the fuel below its ignition temperature?

A. CO_2
B. Water stream
C. Water spray
D. Foam

82. You are fighting a class "B" fire with a portable dry chemical extinguisher. The discharge should be directed _____.

A. to bank off a bulkhead onto the fire
B. at the seat of the fire, starting at the near edge
C. over the top of the fire
D. at the main body of the fire

83. If more than one raft is manned after the vessel has sunk, you should _____.

A. go in a different direction in search of land
B. spread out to increase the possibility of a search aircraft finding you
C. reduce the number of rafts by getting as many people as possible into as few rafts as possible
D. tie the rafts together and try to stay in a single group

84. After using a CO_2 portable extinguisher, it should be _____.

A. put back in service if some CO_2 remains

B. hydrostatically tested
C. retagged
D. recharged

85. To prevent the spread of fire by convection you should _____.

A. shut off all electrical power
B. remove combustibles from direct exposure
C. cool the bulkhead around the fire
D. close all openings to the area

88. You are attempting to administer CPR to a victim. When you blow into his mouth it is apparent that no air is getting into the lungs. What should you do?

A. Blow harder to force the air past the tongue.
B. Raise the victim's head higher than his feet.
C. Press on the victim's lungs so that air pressure will blow out any obstruction.
D. Re-tip the head and try again.

89. To determine what navigation lights and dayshapes must be displayed on mobile offshore drilling units under tow, you should check the _____.

A. American Bureau of Shipping classification rules
B. International Regulations for Preventing Collisions at Sea
C. Safety of Life at Sea Convention
D. Minerals Management Service rules

90. Refer to illustration D001SA. Which represents the righting arm?

A. GM
B. GZ
C. BM
D. Angle MGZ

91. Except in rare cases, it is impossible to extinguish a shipboard fire by _____.

A. removing the fuel
B. interrupting the chain reaction
C. removing the oxygen
D. removing the heat

93. If, for any reason, it is necessary to abandon ship while far out at sea, it is important that the crew members should _____.

A. separate from each other as this will increase the chances of being rescued
B. get away from the area because sharks will be attracted to the vessel
C. immediately head for the nearest land
D. remain together in the area because rescuers will start searching at the vessel's last known position

94. If you desired to communicate with another station that your navigation lights were not functioning, you would send _____.

A. PB
B. PD1
C. MJ
D. LN1

95. A spark arrestor _____.

A. keeps sparks from falling into an open tank
B. secures covers on ullage openings
C. prevents sparks from getting out of an engine's exhaust system
D. grounds static electricity

96. A B-III foam extinguisher contains _____.

A. 2-1/2 gallons of foam
B. 8 gallons of foam
C. 10 gallons of foam
D. 12 gallons of foam

98. Two people are administering CPR to a victim. How many times per minute should the chest be compressed?

A. 30
B. 45
C. 60
D. 80

99. Annex V to MARPOL 73/78 contains requirements pertaining to the discharge into the marine environment of _____.

A. oil
B. garbage
C. noxious liquid substances
D. None of the above

100. When a vessel has positive stability, the distance between the line of force through B and the line of force through G is called the _____.

A. metacentric height

B. righting arm
C. righting moment
D. metacentric radius

102. You are underway when a fire breaks out in the forward part of your vessel. If possible, you should _____.

A. put the vessel's stern into the wind
B. abandon ship to windward
C. call for assistance
D. keep going at half speed

103. You have just abandoned ship and boarded a raft. After the raft is completely inflated you hear a whistling noise coming from a safety valve. You should _____.

A. not become alarmed unless it continues for a long period of time
B. plug the safety valve
C. unscrew the deflation plugs
D. remove the safety valve and replace it with a soft patch

105. The International Regulations for Preventing Collisions at Sea contain the requirements for _____.

A. lights that must be displayed on anchor buoys
B. the display of load line markings
C. minimum horsepower for tugs involved in rig moves
D. lighting of mobile offshore drilling units being towed

106. A B-II fire extinguisher has a minimum capacity of _____.

A. 3 gallons of foam
B. 20 pounds of CO_2
C. 10 pounds of dry chemical
D. All of the above

108. Antiseptics are used principally to _____.

A. speed healing
B. prevent infection
C. reduce inflammation
D. increase blood circulation

109. Your vessel has a displacement of 10,000 tons. It is 350 feet long and has a beam of 55 feet. You have timed its full rolling period to be 15.0 seconds. What is your vessel's approximate GM?

A. 1.18 feet
B. 1.83 feet

C. 2.60 feet
D. 3.36 feet

110. A vertical shift of weight to a position above the vessel's center of gravity will _____.

A. increase reserve buoyancy
B. decrease the righting moments
C. decrease KG
D. increase KM

112. Your small vessel is broken down and rolling in heavy seas. You can reduce the possibility of capsizing by _____.

A. rigging a sea anchor
B. constantly shifting the rudder
C. moving all personnel forward and low
D. moving all personnel aft

113. You hear air escaping from the life raft just after it has inflated. You should _____.

A. quickly hunt for the hole before the raft deflates
B. check the sea anchor line attachment for a tear if the seas are rough
C. check the painter line attachment for a tear caused by the initial opening
D. not panic since the safety valves allow excess pressure to escape

115. Which is TRUE concerning immersion suits and their use?

A. Only a light layer of clothing may be worn underneath.
B. They provide sufficient flotation to do away with the necessity of wearing a life jacket.
C. They should be tight fitting.
D. A puncture in the suit will not appreciably reduce its value.

116. What is classified as a B-II fire extinguisher?

A. A 2-1/2 gallon soda acid and water
B. A 1-1/4 gallon foam
C. A 2-1/2 gallon foam
D. A 20 pound dry chemical

118. A tourniquet should be used to control bleeding ONLY _____.

A. with puncture wounds
B. when all other means have failed
C. when the victim is unconscious
D. to prevent bleeding from minor wounds

119. What would be considered a vessel under the International Rules of the Road?

A. A jack-up rig under tow
B. A semisubmersible drilling rig under tow
C. A semisubmersible drilling rig drifting after breaking a tow line
D. All of the above

120. The point to which your vessel's center of gravity (G) may rise and still permit the vessel to have positive stability is called the _____.

A. metacentric point
B. metacenter
C. metacentric radius
D. tipping center

122. A negative metacentric height _____.

A. will always cause a vessel to capsize
B. should always be immediately corrected
C. always results from off-center weights
D. All of the above are correct

125. Addition of weight to a vessel will ALWAYS _____.

A. reduce reserve buoyancy
B. increase righting moments
C. increase GM
D. All of the above

126. Which portable fire extinguisher is classified as a type B-III extinguisher?

A. 12 gallon soda acid
B. 20 gallon foam
C. 30 pound carbon dioxide
D. 20 pound dry chemical

128. A seaman has a small, gaping laceration of the arm that is not bleeding excessively. What can be done as an alternative to suturing to close the wound?

A. Wrap a tight bandage around the wound.
B. Apply a compression bandage.
C. Use temporary stitches of sail twine.
D. Apply butterfly strips, then a sterile dressing.

129. A life float on a fishing vessel must be equipped with _____.

A. a righting line
B. red hand flares

C. pendants
D. drinking water

130. When making a turn (course change) on most merchant ships, the vessel will heel outwards if _____.

A. the vessel has very little draft
B. G is above the center of lateral resistance
C. G is below the center of lateral resistance
D. the vessel is deeply laden

133. You have abandoned ship and are in charge of a life raft. How much water per day should you permit each occupant to drink after the first 24 hours?

A. 1 can
B. 1 pint
C. 1 quart
D. 1 gallon

135. Which statement concerning an accidental oil spill in the navigable waters of the U.S. is FALSE?

A. The person in charge must report the spill to the Coast Guard.
B. Failure to report the spill may result in a fine.
C. The company can be fined for the spill.
D. The Corps of Engineers is responsible for the clean up of the spill.

136. Which item is NOT required to be marked with the vessel's name?

A. Hand-portable fire extinguisher
B. Life preserver
C. Immersion suit
D. Lifeboat oar

138. A person reports to you with a fishhook in his thumb. To remove it you should _____.

A. pull it out with pliers
B. cut the skin from around the hook
C. push the barb through, cut it off, then remove the hook
D. have a surgeon remove it

139. When fighting a fire in an enclosed space, the hose team should crouch as low as possible to _____.

A. protect themselves from smoke
B. obtain the best available air
C. allow the heat and steam to pass overhead

D. All of the above

140. Which statement is TRUE of a stiff vessel?

A. She will have a large metacentric height.
B. Her period of roll will be large due to her large metacentric height.
C. She will have an unusually high center of gravity.
D. She will pitch heavily.

141. Which emergency is required to be covered at the required periodic drills on a fishing vessel?

A. Recovering an individual from the water
B. Steering casualty
C. Emergency towing
D. Loss of propulsion power

142. You are in the Baltic Sea which is a special area listed in ANNEX V of MARPOL. How many miles from land must you be to discharge ground rags, glass, and bottles into the sea?

A. 3
B. 12
C. 25
D. Must be retained aboard

143. You have abandoned ship in tropical waters. Which procedure(s) should be used during a prolonged period in a raft?

A. Wet clothes during the day to decrease perspiration.
B. Get plenty of rest.
C. Keep the entrance curtains open.
D. All of the above

144. The unit of duration of a dash in Morse Code is _____.

A. one and one-half times the length of a dot
B. twice the length of a dot
C. three times the length of a dot
D. four times the length of a dot

145. Which statement concerning an accidental oil spill in the navigable waters of the U.S. is TRUE?

A. The Corps of Engineers is responsible for the clean up of the spill.
B. The Department of Interior is responsible for the clean up of the spill.
C. A warning broadcast must be made by radiotelephone.

D. The person in charge must report the spill to the Coast Guard.

148. First aid treatment for small cuts and open wounds is to _____.

A. lay the patient down and cover the wound when the bleeding stops
B. stop the bleeding, clean, medicate, and cover the wound
C. apply an ice pack to the wound and cover it when the bleeding stops
D. apply a hot towel to purge the wound, then medicate and cover it

152. What is the function of the bypass valve on the self-contained breathing apparatus?

A. The valve opens in excessive heat to release the oxygen in the bottle and prevent the bottle from exploding.
B. In the event of a malfunction in the equipment, the valve can be operated manually to give the wearer air.
C. When pressure in the apparatus exceeds 7 psi above atmospheric pressure, the valve opens to release pressure.
D. The valve reduces the high pressure in the bottle to about 3 psi above atmospheric pressure.

153. If you reach shore in a life raft, the first thing to do is _____.

A. drag the raft ashore and lash it down for a shelter
B. find some wood for a fire
C. get the provisions out of the raft
D. set the raft back out to sea so someone may spot it

155. When oil is accidentally discharged into the water, what should you do after reporting the discharge?

A. Contain the oil and remove as much of it as possible from the water
B. Throw chemical agents on the water to disperse the oil
C. Throw sand on the water to sink the oil
D. Obtain your permit from the Corps of Engineers

156. The Coast Guard determines how many passengers are permitted on a "T-Boat" by applying the _____.

A. "Length of Rail" criteria, allowing 30

inches of rail space along the vessel's sides and transom for each passenger
B. "Deck Area" criteria that permits one passenger for every 10 square feet of deck space available for passenger use
C. "Fixed Seating" criteria that allocates 18 inches of space for each passenger to rest his/her buttocks upon
D. Any or a combination of the above criteria

158. A person has suffered a laceration of the arm. Severe bleeding has been controlled by using a sterile dressing and direct pressure. What should you do next?

A. Apply a tourniquet to prevent the bleeding from restarting.
B. Apply a pressure bandage over the dressing.
C. Remove any small foreign matter and apply antiseptic.
D. Administer fluids to assist the body in replacing the lost blood.

162. The function of the bypass valve on the self-contained breathing apparatus is to _____.

A. control the pressure of the oxygen as it enters the body
B. allow the wearer to manually give himself oxygen
C. release excess heat which would otherwise cause the bottle to explode
D. allow exhaled gases to pass outside the bottle

163. You are at sea in an inflatable life raft. In high latitutes, the greatest danger is _____.

A. asphyxiation due to keeping the canopy closed
B. hypothermia caused by cold temperature
C. collapse of the raft due to cold temperatures
D. starvation

165. Which statement is FALSE regarding Halon as a fire extinguishing agent?

A. It is more effective than CO_2.
B. It leaves no residue.
C. It is noncorrosive.
D. It is always non-toxic.

168. In all but the most severe cases, bleeding from a wound should be controlled by _____.

A. applying direct pressure to the wound
B. submerging the wound in lukewarm water
C. cooling the wound with ice
D. applying a tourniquet

171. You are underway when a fire breaks out in the forward part of your vessel. If possible you should _____.

A. call for assistance
B. abandon ship to windward
C. put the vessel's stern into the wind
D. keep going at half speed

172. As Master of an inspected small passenger vessel, you have a question regarding a proposed modification to a watertight bulkhead. In which subchapter of title 46 of the Code of Federal Regulations would you find the answer?

A. Subchapter B
B. Subchapter S
C. Subchapter T
D. Subchapter F

173. While adrift in an inflatable life raft in hot, tropical weather _____.

A. the canopy should be deflated so that it will not block cooling breezes
B. the pressure valve may be periodically opened to prevent excessive air pressure
C. deflating the floor panels may help to cool personnel
D. the entrance curtains should never be opened

175. According to 46 CFR Subchapter T, a stability test may be dispensed with if the _____.

A. Coast Guard has the approved stability test results of a sister vessel
B. projected cost is unreasonable
C. Coast Guard does not have a qualified inspector available
D. vessel is of a proven design

177. Before taking drinking water on board in the U.S. or its possessions, the responsible person from the vessel should determine that the source _____.

A. is used by a city
B. has been treated with chlorine
C. is approved by the Public Health Service
D. is not from surface water

178. Bleeding from a vein may be ordinarily controlled by _____.

A. applying direct pressure to the wound
B. heavy application of a disinfectant
C. pouring ice water directly onto the wound
D. pinching the wound closed

180. Which is TRUE of a "stiff" vessel?

A. It has a small GM.
B. It pitches heavily.
C. It has an unusually high center of gravity.
D. Its period of roll is short.

182. Which abbreviation refers to the horizontal distance between perpendiculars taken at the forward-most and the after-most points on a small passenger vessel's waterline at her deepest operating draft?

A. LBP
B. LOA
C. LWL
D. LLL

183. Which statement is TRUE concerning an inflatable life raft?

A. The floor may be inflated for insulation from cold water.
B. Crew members can jump into the raft without damaging it.
C. The raft may be boarded before it is fully inflated.
D. All of the above

185. Which substance is NOT considered to be "Oil" under the pollution prevention regulations?

A. Petroleum and fuel oil
B. Sludge
C. Oil mixed with dredge spoil
D. Oil refuse and oil mixed with wastes

186. Fire hose stations shall be marked in red letters and figures such as Fire Station No. "1", "2", "3", etc. The height of the letters and figures must be at least _____.

A. 1/2 inch
B. 1 inch
C. 1-1/2 inches
D. 2 inches

187. What represents poor sanitary procedures?

A. Keep and use a separate filling hose for potable (drinking) water.
B. Locate potable (drinking) water tanks as low as possible in the bilge.
C. Eliminate enclosed spaces in which trash, food particles, dirt may gather.
D. After washing dishes with soap and warm water, sterilize them in water of at least 170°F (76.7°C).

188. The preferred method of controlling external bleeding is by _____.

A. direct pressure on the wound
B. elevating the wounded area
C. pressure on a pressure point
D. a tourniquet above the wound

189. The purpose of the inclining experiment is to _____.

A. determine the location of the metacenter
B. determine the lightweight center of gravity location
C. verify the hydrostatic data
D. verify data in the vessel's operating manual

190. Which technique could be used to give a more comfortable roll to a stiff vessel?

A. Concentrate weights in the upper tween-deck wings
B. Add weight near the centerline of the lower hold
C. Move weights lower in the ship
D. Ballast the peak tanks

191. Where will you find the requirements for the lights that must be displayed on a mobile offshore drilling unit that is being towed?

A. Notice to Mariners
B. COLREGS
C. Coast Pilot
D. Light List

195. As soon as the officer in charge of the vessel has taken steps to stop the discharge of oil or oily mixture into a U.S. harbor, what must he do FIRST?

A. Rig a boom for recovery.
B. Call the Coast Guard.
C. Alert the fire department.
D. Inform the Environmental Protection Agency.

196. The term "gross tonnage" refers to
_____.

A. the weight of the vessel measured in long tons
B. the weight of a vessel with all tanks full
C. the weight of a grossly overloaded vessel
D. the vessel's approximate volume including all enclosed spaces less certain exempt spaces

197. Normally, potable water systems are connected directly to the _____.

A. fire-main system
B. feed-water system
C. freshwater sanitary system
D. domestic water tank

198. A person suffering from possible broken bones and internal injuries should
_____.

A. be assisted in walking around
B. be examined then walked to a bunk
C. not be moved but made comfortable until medical assistance arrives
D. not be allowed to lie down where injured but moved to a chair or bunk

200. Which statement is TRUE of a tender vessel?

A. It has a large GM.
B. Its period of roll is long.
C. It has a very low center of gravity.
D. It has a good transverse stability.

205. When a vessel violates the oil pollution laws, who may be held responsible?

A. Master only
B. Owners only
C. Licensed officers only
D. Any individual connected with the vessel involved in the operation

207. Which chemical is used to treat water in order to ensure its safety for drinking?

A. Nitrogen
B. Chlorine
C. Carbon
D. Oxygen

208. What is the primary purpose of a splint applied in first aid?

A. Control bleeding
B. Reduce pain

C. Immobilize a fracture
D. Reset the bone

210. Metacentric height is an indication of a vessel's stability _____.

A. for all angles of inclination
B. for large angles of inclination
C. for small angles of inclination
D. in no case

212. In the navigable waters of the United States, Annex V to MARPOL 73/78 is NOT applicable to a(n) _____.

A. recreational yacht
B. uninspected towing vessel
C. uninspected passenger vessel under 100 GT
D. U.S. government vessel in non-commercial service

217. Which item do you NOT have to provide for the Coast Guard representative at the time of a stability test?

A. A stability letter.
B. Tank sounding tables and draft mark locations.
C. Capacity plans showing the vertical and longitudinal centers of gravity of stowage spaces and tanks.
D. General arrangement plans of decks; holds and inner bottoms.

218. A compound fracture is a fracture in which _____.

A. more than one bone is broken
B. the same bone is broken in more than one place
C. there is never any internal bleeding
D. the bone may be visible

219. For the purposes of the International Rules of the Road, a non-self-propelled mobile offshore drilling unit under tow is considered to be a _____.

A. non-displacement vessel
B. limited vessel
C. power-driven vessel
D. vessel

220. Metacentric height is a measure of
_____.

A. initial stability only
B. stability through all angles
C. maximum righting arm

D. All of the above

221. Which statement about the free surface effect is TRUE?

A. It increases in direct proportion to the length of the tank times the breadth squared.
B. It decreases at increased angles of heel due to pocketing when a tank is 90% full.
C. It decreases in direct proportion to increasing specific gravity of the liquid in the tank.
D. In practice, the correction is considered to be a virtual reduction of KG.

228. Which is the most serious type of fracture?

A. Compound
B. Greenstick
C. Closed
D. Crack

229. Fuel oil tank vents are fitted with a screen which will stop _____.

A. oil from flowing out of the tank vent
B. air from entering the tank vent
C. vapors from leaving the tank vent
D. flames on deck from entering the tank vent

230. Initial stability of a vessel may be improved by _____.

A. removing loose water
B. adding weight low in the vessel
C. closing crossover valves between partly filled double bottom tanks
D. All of the above

231. The Coast Guard inspection required before a Certificate of Ispection can be issued is conducted _____.

A. when deemed necessary by the Regional Inspection Center
B. after you apply in writing to the nearest Officer in Charge of Marine Inspection (OCMI)
C. at random from a Coast Guard patrol boat
D. after a formal complaint is filed with the OCMI

238. Unless there is danger of further injury, a person with a compound fracture should not be moved until bleeding is controlled and _____.

A. the bone has been set
B. the fracture is immobilized
C. radio advice has been obtained
D. the wound has been washed

240. According to 46 CFR Subchapter T the definition of a ferry includes vessels that _____.

A. operate in other than ocean or coastwise service
B. have provisions only for deck passengers, vehicles, or both
C. operate on a short run on a frequent schedule between two points over the most direct water route
D. All of the above

245. Storage batteries should be charged in a well ventilated area because _____.

A. they generate heat
B. they emit hydrogen
C. of the toxic fumes they emit
D. they recharge faster in a well ventilated space

247. During a stability test on a small passenger vessel _____.

A. the vessel must be moored snugly
B. each tank must be partially full to show it does not leak
C. all dunnage, tools, and extraneous items are secured
D. water under vessel must be deep enough to prevent grounding

248. You are treating a shipmate with a compound fracture of the lower arm. Which action should you take?

A. Apply a tourniquet to control bleeding then align the bones and splint.
B. Apply traction to the hand to keep the bones in line, splint, and apply a pressure dressing.
C. Force the ends of the bones back into line, treat the bleeding, and splint.
D. Apply a bulky, sterile, pressure dressing to control bleeding, then apply a temporary splint, and obtain medical advice.

250. Which will be a result of removing on-deck containers?

A. KG will increase
B. Metacentric height will increase
C. KB will increase
D. Reserve buoyancy will decrease

251. Free communication effect is in direct proportion to _____.

A. length and width of space
B. length of space only
C. width of space only
D. neither length nor width

252. What, when removed, will result in the extinguishment of a fire?

A. Nitrogen
B. Sodium
C. Oxygen
D. Carbon dioxide

257. Which vessel greater than 100 GT is NOT required to have an EPIRB?

A. A sailing vessel
B. A fishing vessel
C. A non-self-propelled vessel in tow
D. A towing vessel

258. In any major injury to a person, first aid includes the treatment for the injury and _____.

A. application of CPR
B. removal of any foreign objects
C. administration of oxygen
D. for traumatic shock

259. What does NOT affect the value of the free surface correction?

A. Width of the tank
B. Length of the tank
C. Registered tonnage
D. Specific gravity of the liquid in the tank

261. A person who willfully violates safety regulations may be fined up to $5,000 and _____.

A. imprisoned for up to a year
B. imprisoned for up to five years
C. forbidden to work in the fishing industry
D. no other penalty may be applied

262. Which fire detection system is actuated by sensing a heat rise in a compartment?

A. Manual fire detection system
B. Automatic fire detection system
C. Smoke detection system
D. Watchman's supervisory system

265. The term "discharge," as it applies to the pollution regulations, means _____.

A. spilling
B. leaking
C. pumping
D. All of the above

267. Which type of EPIRB must each ocean-going ship carry?

A. Class A
B. Class B
C. Class C
D. Category 1

268. What is NOT a treatment for traumatic shock?

A. Keep the patient warm but not hot.
B. Have the injured person lie down.
C. Massage the arms and legs to restore circulation.
D. Relieve the pain of the injury.

269. To remedy a leaking fire hose connection at the hydrant, secure the valve and _____.

A. replace the gasket in the male coupling
B. reduce fire pump pressure
C. replace the gasket in the female coupling
D. rethread the male coupling

270. When cargo is shifted from the lower hold to the main deck the _____.

A. center of gravity will move upward
B. GM will increase
C. center of buoyancy will move downward
D. All of the above

271. A fishing vessel casualty must be reported to the Coast Guard if it involves _____.

A. loss of life
B. an injury requiring only first aid
C. $10,000 in property damage
D. loss of equipment which doesn't reduce the vessel's maneuverability

272. Fire alarm system thermostats are actuated by _____.

A. smoke sensors
B. the difference in thermal expansion of two dissimilar metals
C. pressure loss due to air being heated

D. an electric eye which actuates when smoke interferes with the beam

275. When cleaning up an oil spill in U.S. waters you must obtain the approval of the Federal On-Scene Coordinator before using _____.

A. skimmers
B. straw
C. chemical agents
D. sawdust

277. The vessel's Emergency Position Indicating Radiobeacon (EPIRB) must be tested _____.

A. weekly
B. monthly
C. every 2 months
D. every 3 months

278. What is a treatment for traumatic shock?

A. Administer CPR.
B. Administer fluids.
C. Open clothing to allow cooling of the body.
D. Keep the victim in a sitting position.

280. In the regulations that apply to small passenger vessels an "open boat" is a vessel _____.

A. that is used for charter fishing or tours and is open to the public
B. on which gambling and consumption of alcoholic beverages is permitted
C. that is docked and open for visitors
D. that is not protected from entry of water by means of a complete weathertight deck

281. The gross weight of a fully charged CO_2 bottle in a fixed CO_2 system is 220 lbs. When the bottle is empty it weighs 110 lbs. What is the minimum acceptable gross weight of the CO_2 bottle before it should be recharged by the manufacturer?

A. 200 lbs
B. 205 lbs
C. 210 lbs
D. 220 lbs

282. The difference in water spray pattern between the high-velocity tip and low-velocity applicator used with the all-purpose nozzle is due to _____.

A. a difference in water pressure
B. the method of breaking up the water stream
C. the length of the applicator
D. All of the above

283. Spreading oil on the open sea has the effect of _____.

A. diminishing the height of the seas
B. lengthening the distance between successive crests
C. increasing the height of the seas
D. preventing the wave crests from breaking

285. The use of sinking and dispersing chemical agents for removal of surface oil is _____.

A. the most common method used in the United States
B. too expensive for common use
C. generally safe to sea life
D. authorized only with prior approval of the Federal On-Scene Coordinator

287. The Master shall insure that the Emergency Position Indicating Radiobeacon (EPIRB) is _____.

A. secured inside the wheelhouse
B. tested annually
C. tested monthly
D. secured in the emergency locker

288. A negative metacentric height _____.

A. will always cause a vessel to capsize
B. always results from off-center weights
C. should always be immediately corrected
D. All of the above are correct

289. You are at the helm of a sailing vessel under sail on the starboard tack, close hauled, and you are instructed to "head up." You should _____.

A. turn the wheel to port if you are steering with a wheel
B. push the tiller to starboard if you are steering with a tiller
C. turn the rudder to starboard
D. All of the above are correct

290. What will happen when cargo is shifted from the main deck into the lower hold of a vessel?

A. The GM will increase.
B. The metacenter will move upward.
C. The center of buoyancy will move upward.
D. All of the above

291. A Certificate of Inspection issued to a small passenger vessel describes _____.

A. the mimimum fire extinguishing equipment, life jackets, survival and rescue craft she must carry
B. the name of the managing operator
C. any special conditions or restrictions on her operation
D. All the above

292. High-velocity fog _____.

A. is a finer, more diffuse water spray than low-velocity fog
B. requires that the water pressure be no greater than 60 psi
C. produces an effective fog pattern no more than 6 feet beyond the nozzle
D. extinguishes a fire by absorbing heat and reducing the supply of oxygen

293. Which statement is TRUE concerning life jackets which are severely damaged?

A. They should be replaced.
B. They must be tested for buoyancy before being continued in use.
C. They can be repaired by a reliable seamstress.
D. They can be used for children.

295. The preferred type of pollution control for oil spills on the water is(are) _____.

A. straw
B. booms
C. skimmers
D. chemical dispersants

296. In weighing CO_2 cylinders, they must be recharged if weight loss exceeds _____.

A. 10% of weight of full bottle
B. 15% of weight of full bottle
C. 20% of weight of charge
D. 10% of weight of charge

297. Which information is NOT required to be posted in or near the wheelhouse?

A. Stopping time and distance from full speed while maintaining course with minimum rudder

B. A diagram of advance and transfer for turns of 30°, 60°, 90° and 120° at full speed with maximum rudder and constant power
C. For vessels with a fixed propeller, a table of shaft RPMs for a representative range of speeds
D. Operating instructions for change-over procedures for remote steering gear systems

298. Which is NOT a symptom of traumatic shock?

A. Slow, deep breathing
B. Pale, cold skin
C. Weak, rapid pulse
D. Restlessness and anxiety

300. In the small passenger vessel regulations a coastwise route is defined as one that is _____.

A. not more than 50 statute miles from shore in the Gulf of Mexico
B. on ocean waters more than 200 nautical miles from shore in the Gulf of Alaska
C. not more than 20 statute miles from the nearest safe harbor in the Pacific Ocean
D. not more than 20 nautical miles offshore in the ocean

301. Which factor has the greatest effect on the value of the free surface correction?

A. The width of the tank
B. The length of the tank
C. The draft of the vessel
D. The specific gravity of the liquid in the tank

302. If you are fighting a fire below the main deck of your vessel, which action is most important concerning the stability of the vessel?

A. Shutting off electricity to damaged cables
B. Pumping fire-fighting water overboard
C. Maneuvering the vessel so the fire is on the lee side
D. Removing burned debris from the cargo hold

303. Plastic material may be thrown overboard from a vessel which is _____.

A. 25 miles from shore
B. 12 miles from shore
C. 3 miles from shore

D. None of the above are correct.

305. It is generally NOT allowed to clean up an oil spill by using _____.

A. a boom
B. suction equipment
C. chemical agents
D. skimmers

308. A person being treated for shock should be wrapped in warm coverings to _____.

A. increase body heat
B. preserve body heat
C. avoid self-inflicted wounds caused by spastic movement
D. protect the person from injury during transportation

311. Spontaneous ignition can result from _____.

A. an unprotected drop-light bulb
B. careless disposal or storage of material
C. smoking in bed
D. worn electrical wires on power tools

312. The spray of water in low-velocity fog will have _____.

A. greater range than high-velocity fog
B. lesser range than high-velocity fog
C. about the same range as high-velocity fog
D. greater range than a solid stream

313. Kapok life jackets should NOT be _____.

A. stowed near open flame or where smoking is permitted
B. used as seats, pillows, or foot rests
C. left on open decks
D. All of the above

315. The maximum number of passengers a "T-Boat" may carry _____.

A. is stated on the vessel's Certificate of Inspection
B. is the number authorized in the Navigation Rules
C. depends on the number of life jackets you carry
D. is the number authorized by your license

316. The space containing the cylinders for the carbon dioxide (CO_2) fire extinguishing system must be designed to preclude an anticipated ambient temperature over _____.

A. 80°F
B. 95°F
C. 130°F
D. 150°F

317. Your vessel will be entering the navigable waters of the United States. You are required by regulations to _____.

A. test the primary and secondary steering systems no more than 8 hours before entering
B. correct the charts of the area to be transited using the Notice(s) to Mariners or foreign equivalent reasonably available
C. have a copy of Radio Navigational Aids
D. check the magnetic compass for the correct deviation

318. The best treatment for preventing traumatic shock after an accident is to _____.

A. have the victim exercise to increase circulation
B. keep the victim from electrical equipment
C. keep the victim warm and dry while lying down
D. apply ice packs and avoid excitement

319. Foam is effective in combating which class(es) of fire?

A. A
B. B
C. A and B
D. B and C

320. As the displacement of a vessel increases, the detrimental effect of free surface _____.

A. increases
B. decreases
C. remains the same
D. may increase or decrease depending on the fineness of the vessel's form

322. A definite advantage of using water as a fire extinguishing agent is its characteristic of _____.

A. alternate expansion and contraction as water in a liquid state becomes a vapor
B. absorption of smoke and gases as water is converted from a liquid to a vapor
C. rapid contraction as water is converted from a liquid to a vapor
D. rapid expansion as water absorbs heat and changes to steam

323. You must make a written application to obtain or renew your "T" boat's Certificate of Inspection _____.

A. on form CG-835
B. at the shipyard where you are hauled out
C. on form CG-3752
D. everytime your boat is hauled out

324. The national distress, safety, and calling frequency is channel _____.

A. 13
B. 16
C. 18
D. 22

326. CO_2 cylinders, which protect the small space in which they are stored, must _____.

A. NOT contain more than 200 pounds of CO_2
B. be automatically operated by a heat actuator
C. have an audible alarm
D. All of the above

327. The maneuvering information required to be posted in the wheelhouse must be based on certain conditions. Which of the following is NOT one of these conditions?

A. The hull must be clean.
B. There must be calm weather-wind 10 knots or less and a calm sea.
C. There must be no current.
D. The depth of the water must be at least one and one-half times the draft.

328. A man has suffered a burn on the arm. There is extensive damage to the skin with charring present. How is this injury classified using standard medical terminology?

A. Dermal burn
B. Third-degree burn
C. Major burn
D. Lethal burn

329. Which statement about the free surface effect is TRUE?

A. It has the same affect on initial stability whether the tank is 75% full or 25% full.
B. The free surface effect usually increases at angles of heel above 25°.
C. The effect increases if the tank is off the centerline.
D. The effect can be reduced by shifting weights vertically.

331. One of the limitations of foam as an extinguishing agent is that foam _____.

A. cannot be made with salt water
B. is heavier than oil and sinks below its surface
C. is corrosive and a hazard to fire fighters
D. conducts electricity

332. When using a high-velocity fog stream in a passageway, the possibility of a blow back must be guarded against. Blow back is most likely to occur when _____.

A. pressure builds up in the nozzle which causes a surge of water
B. the only opening in a passageway is the one from which the nozzle is being advanced
C. pressure in the fire hose drops below 100 psi
D. a bulkhead collapses due to heat and pressure

333. Which statement is TRUE concerning life preservers (Type I personal flotation devices)?

A. Buoyant vests may be substituted for life jackets.
B. Life preservers are designed to turn an unconscious person's face clear of the water.
C. Life preservers must always be worn with the same side facing outwards to float properly.
D. Lightly stained or faded life jackets will fail in the water and should not be used.

338. A man has a burn on his arm. There is reddening of the skin, blistering, and swelling. Using standard medical terminology this is a _____.

A. major burn
B. secondary burn
C. second-degree burn
D. blister burn

339. If a fire-fighting situation calls for low-velocity fog you would _____.

A. order the engine room to reduce pressure on the fire pump
B. put the lever on an all-purpose fire nozzle all the way forward
C. attach a low-velocity fog applicator with the nozzle shut down
D. put the lever on an all-purpose fire nozzle all the way back

340. Which statement about the free surface correction is TRUE?

A. It is added to the uncorrected GM to arrive at the corrected available GM.
B. It is obtained by dividing the free surface moments by 12 times the volume of displacement.
C. It is obtained by dividing the total free surface by the total vertical moments.
D. It is subtracted from the total longitudinal moments before dividing by displacement to find LCG.

341. The Master or other vessel representative must contact the nearest Coast Guard Marine Safety Office within five days of a(n) _____.

A. grounding
B. injury which requires first aid
C. accident which requires $2500 of repairs
D. All of the above are correct.

342. Every injury aboard a commercial fishing industry vessel must be reported to the _____.

A. Coast Guard
B. vessel owner or owner's agent
C. Occupational Safety and Health Administration
D. National Fisheries Service

343. An emergency sea anchor may be constructed by using _____.

A. a boat bucket
B. an air tank filled with water
C. an oar and canvas weighted down
D. All of the above

345. A 100 GT vessel, constructed before July 1,1974, is loading diesel fuel. What is the minimum capacity of the drip pans required for placement under or around each fuel tank vent, overflow, and fill pipe?

A. 1 gallon
B. 5 gallons
C. 1 barrel
D. 2 barrels

348. A man has suffered a burn on the arm. There is a reddening of the skin but no other apparent damage. Using standard MEDICAL terminology, this is a _____.

A. Minor burn
B. Superficial burn
C. Extremity burn
D. First-degree burn

349. A marine radar system for surface navigation must be fitted on all ocean or coastwise vessels of over _____.

A. 1,400 GT
B. 1,500 GT
C. 1,600 GT
D. 1,700 GT

350. The most detrimental effect on initial stability is a result of liquids _____.

A. flowing from side to side within the vessel
B. flowing from fore to aft within a vessel
C. flowing in and out of a holed wing tank
D. pocketing in a slack tank as a vessel heels

352. What is an advantage of water fog or water spray over a straight stream of water in fighting an oil fire?

A. It has a smothering effect on the fire.
B. It requires less water to remove the same amount of heat.
C. It gives more protection to fire fighting personnel.
D. All of the above

353. When a sea anchor is used in landing stern first in a heavy surf, headway is checked by _____.

A. slacking the tripping line and towing the sea anchor from the stern
B. slacking the tripping line and towing the sea anchor by the holding line
C. towing with the tripping line and leaving the holding line slack
D. towing the apex end forward with the tripping line

354. The distress message of a ship should include considerable information which

might facilitate the rescue. This information should _____.

A. ALWAYS be included in the initial distress message
B. be sent to a Coast Guard station FIRST
C. be transmitted as a series of short messages, if time allows
D. include the vessel's draft

355. The center of flotation of a vessel is the point in the waterplane _____.

A. about which the vessel lists and trims
B. which coincides with the center of buoyancy
C. which, in the absence of external forces, is always vertically aligned with the center of gravity
D. which is shown in the hydrostatic tables as VCB

357. The operator of a vessel's radiotelephone must hold at least a _____.

A. third class radiotelegraph operator certificate
B. restricted radiotelephone operator permit
C. general radiotelephone operator license
D. mate's license

358. When treating a person for third-degree burns, you should _____.

A. submerge the burn area in cold water
B. make the person stand up and walk to increase circulation
C. cover the burns with thick, sterile dressings
D. break blisters and remove dead tissue

360. The greatest effect on stability occurs from loose liquids flowing _____.

A. from side to side in the tanks of the vessel
B. from fore to aft in the tanks of a vessel
C. in and out of a vessel that is holed in a wing tank
D. in and out of a vessel that is holed in a peak tank

361. What can be used to measure the percentage of oxygen inside a chain locker?

A. Flame safety lamp
B. Combustible gas indicator
C. Oxygen indicator
D. H_2S meter

362. Water fog from an all-purpose nozzle may be used to _____.

A. fight an electrical fire
B. fight a magnesium fire
C. eliminate smoke from a compartment
D. All of the above

365. What is the minimum fuel-oil discharge-containment needed for a 100 gross ton vessel constructed after June 30, 1974?

A. At least 5 gallons
B. At least 1 barrel
C. At least 2 barrels
D. At least 3 barrels

367. A ship's radiotelephone station license is issued by the _____.

A. U.S. Coast Guard
B. Federal Communications Commission
C. Radio Technical Commission for Marine Services
D. Maritime Mobile Service Commission

370. What is the principal danger from the liquid in a half full tank onboard a vessel?

A. Corrosion from the shifting liquid
B. Rupturing of bulkheads from the shifting liquid
C. Loss of stability from free surface effect
D. Holing of the tank bottom from the weight of the shifting liquid

373. Your vessel is broken down and rolling in heavy seas. You can reduce the possibility of capsizing by _____.

A. shifting the rudder constantly
B. moving all personnel forward and low
C. moving all personnel aft
D. rigging a sea anchor

374. A vessel operating outside of coastal waters must carry an automatically activated Emergency Position Indicating Radiobeacon (EPIRB) if she _____.

A. does not have berthing facilities
B. has berthing and galley facilities
C. is a workboat and her mothership carries an EPIRB
D. None of the above are correct.

375. Fueling results in the collection of waste oil in drip pans and containers. Which is an approved method of disposing

of the waste oil?

A. Draining it overboard when the vessel gets underway
B. Placing it in proper disposal facilities
C. Adding sinking agents and discharging it into the water
D. Mixing it with dispersants before draining it overboard

377. The regulations governing the frequencies of the bridge-to-bridge radiotelephone are issued by the _____.

A. Department of Transportation
B. Federal Communications Commission
C. U.S. Coast Guard
D. Department of Defense

378. The FIRST treatment for a surface burn is to _____.

A. wash the burned area with a warm soap and water solution
B. flood, bathe, or immerse the burned area in cold water
C. cover the burned area with talcum powder and bandage it tightly
D. leave the burned area exposed to the atmosphere

379. Plastic material may be discharged overboard from a vessel if it is _____.

A. 3 miles from shore
B. 12 miles from shore
C. 25 miles from shore
D. None of the above

382. A damaged "T-Boat" that is unable to meet the requirements of its Certificate of Inspection but is able to travel to a shipyard under its own power should _____.

A. make the trip only after obtaining a "Permit to Proceed to Another Port for Repair," Form CG-948
B. get underway as soon as possible
C. hire a tug and pilot instead
D. request an Expiration Certificate if the vessel displays a tendency to sink

383. The purpose of the tripping line on a sea anchor is to _____.

A. aid in casting off
B. direct the drift of the vessel
C. aid in its recovery
D. maintain maximum resistance to broaching

385. You are operating a non-oceangoing vessel, how much of the accumulated oily waste must you be able to retain on board?

A. 25%
B. 50%
C. 75%
D. 100%

386. On vessels subject to 46 CFR Subchapter T, Certification Expiration Date Stickers _____.

A. are issued along with a valid Certificate of Inspection (COI) to indicate the date the COI expires
B. must be readily visible to each passenger prior to boarding and to patrolling Coast Guard law enforcement personnel
C. must be placed on glass or other smooth surface where they may be removed without damage to the vessel
D. All of the above

387. If your vessel is equipped with a radiotelephone, what must also be aboard?

A. Certificate of Inspection
B. List of ship stations
C. Copy of ship to shore channels
D. Radio station license

388. A victim has suffered a second-degree burn to a small area of the lower arm. What is the proper treatment for this injury?

A. Immerse the arm in cold water for 1 to 2 hours, apply burn ointment, and bandage.
B. Open any blisters with a sterile needle, apply burn ointment and bandage.
C. Apply burn ointment, remove any foreign material and insure that nothing is in contact with the burn.
D. Immerse the arm in cold water for 1 to 2 hours, open any blisters and apply burn ointment.

390. A tank which carries liquid is dangerous to the stability of a vessel when it is _____.

A. low in the vessel
B. completely empty
C. completely full
D. slack

391. Foam is a very effective smothering agent and _____.

A. it provides cooling as a secondary effect

B. works well on extinguishing electrical fires
C. can be used to combat combustible metal fires
D. All of the above

393. A sea anchor is _____.

A. a heavy anchor with an extra long line used to anchor in deep water
B. a cone-shaped bag used to slow down the wind drift effect
C. a padeye to which the sea painter is made fast
D. made of wood if it is of an approved type

394. If you are transmitting a distress message by radiotelephone you should _____.

A. use English language
B. always use the International Code
C. preface it by the word "interco"
D. follow the transmission with the radio alarm signal

398. For small, first-degree burns the quickest method to relieve pain is to _____.

A. immerse the burn in cold water
B. administer aspirin
C. apply petroleum jelly
D. apply a bandage to exclude air

399. What is the minimum number of people required to safely handle a 2-1/2 inch fire hose?

A. 1
B. 2
C. 3
D. 4

400. Whenever a "T-Boat" is hauled out for repairs or alterations affecting its safety you must _____.

A. provide a complete set of plans to the Commandant for review
B. notify the cognizant OCMI
C. schedule a full safety equipment inspection
D. Both B and C

402. To lubricate the swivel or remove corrosion from a fire hose coupling, you should use _____.

A. glycerine
B. graphite

C. kerosene
D. fresh water and soap

403. Due to the shape of the sea anchor, the best way to haul it back aboard is by _____.

A. hauling in on the anchor line as you would any anchor
B. getting all hands to assist
C. its trip line
D. cutting the line, as you cannot haul it back in

406. A SOLAS passenger ship safety certificate is required on all _____.

A. T-Boats carrying more than 49 passengers for hire
B. T-Boats that carry more than 12 passengers on an international voyage
C. T-Boats carrying more than 150 passengers for hire
D. large excursion vessels on lakes, bays, sounds, and river routes

407. Any person maintaining a listening watch on a bridge-to-bridge radiotelephone must be able to _____.

A. speak English
B. repair the unit
C. send Morse Code
D. speak a language the vessel's crew will understand

408. If a person is unconscious from electric shock, you should first remove him from the electrical source and then _____.

A. administer ammonia smelling salts
B. check for serious burns on the body
C. determine if he is breathing
D. massage vigorously to restore circulation

410. The effect of free surface on initial stability depends upon _____.

A. the amount of liquid in the compartment
B. the dimensions of the liquid surface and the vessel's displacement
C. only the length of the compartment
D. the vertical position of the liquid in the vessel

411. Under Annex V to MARPOL 73/78, garbage discharged from vessels that are located between 3 and 12 nautical miles

from nearest land must be ground to less than _____.

A. 1"
B. 1-1/4"
C. 1-1/2"
D. 2"

412. To get low-velocity fog from an all-purpose nozzle, you would _____.

A. attach the bronze nozzle tip to the fog outlet of the nozzle
B. attach an applicator to the nozzle in place of the bronze nozzle tip
C. attach an applicator to the solid stream outlet on the nozzle
D. simply move the handle to the vertical position on the nozzle

413. Paint and oil lockers on small passenger vessels must be constructed of or lined with _____.

A. steel or equivalent material
B. fiberglass
C. sheetrock, asbestos, or other material that retards the spread of fire
D. marine plywood

414. A vessel in distress should send by radiotelephone the two-tone alarm signal followed immediately by the _____.

A. distress position
B. spoken words "Mayday, Mayday, Mayday"
C. ship's name
D. ship's call letters

417. By regulation, you MUST keep a record of the use of your radiotelephone for at least _____.

A. one month
B. four months
C. six months
D. one year

418. Treatments of heat exhaustion consist of _____.

A. moving to a shaded area and lying down
B. bathing with rubbing alcohol
C. placing the patient in a tub of cold water
D. All of the above

422. The all-purpose nozzle will produce a fog spray when you _____.

A. pull the nozzle handle all the way back toward the operator
B. pull the nozzle handle back to a position where the handle is perpendicular to the plane of the nozzle
C. push the nozzle handle forward as far as it will go
D. insert a fog applicator between the fire hose and nozzle

423. When you stream a sea anchor, you should make sure that the holding line is _____.

A. long enough to cause the pull to be more horizontal than downward
B. long enough to reach bottom
C. short enough to cause the pull to be downward
D. short enough to avoid tangling

424. What would be used to call all stations in your vicinity by radiotelephone?

A. Calling all stations
B. Charlie Quebec
C. Alpha Alpha
D. Kilo

425. If you must pump bilges while a vessel is in port, you should pump only _____.

A. if discharge is led to a shore tank or barge
B. during the hours of darkness
C. on the outgoing tide
D. as much as is necessary

427. Radio station logs involving communications during a disaster shall be kept by the station licensee for at least _____.

A. 4 years from date of entry
B. 3 years from date of entry
C. 2 years from date of entry
D. 1 year from date of entry

428. Physical exertion on the part of a person who has fallen into cold water would _____.

A. be the best thing to try if there was no rescue in sight
B. increase survival time in the water
C. increase the rate of heat loss from the body
D. not affect the heat loss from the body

429. You are at sea and not in a special area as defined in ANNEX V of MARPOL. How many nautical miles from land must you be to discharge ground garbage that will pass through a one-inch (25 mm) screen into the sea?

A. 3 nm
B. 6 nm
C. 12 nm
D. 25 nm

430. The effects of free surface on a vessel's initial stability do NOT depend upon the _____.

A. volume of displacement of the vessel
B. dimensions of the surface of the liquid
C. amount of liquid in slack tanks
D. specific gravity of the liquid in the tank

432. One advantage of the all-purpose nozzle is that it _____.

A. can fit any size hose
B. converts a stream of water into a fog
C. increases the amount of water reaching the fire
D. can spray two streams of water at the same time

433. If passengers are on board when an abandon ship drill is carried out, they should _____.

A. take part
B. watch
C. go to their quarters
D. stay out of the way and do what they want

434. You are underway in the Gulf of Mexico when you hear a distress message over the VHF radio. The position of the sender is about 20 miles south of Galveston, TX, and you are about 80 miles ESE of Galveston. What action should you take?

A. Immediately acknowledge receipt of the distress message
B. Defer acknowledgment for a short interval so that a coast station may acknowledge receipt
C. Do not acknowledge receipt until other ships nearer to the distress have acknowledged
D. Do not acknowledge receipt because you are too far away to take action

437. On small passenger vessels bunks installed in overnight passenger accommodation spaces _____.

A. must be no less than 74" long and 24" wide with 24" of clear space above
B. must not be located more than 3 high, fitted with a suitable aid to access bunks more than 5' above deck
C. must be immediately adjacent to an aisle leading to a means of escape
D. All of the above

438. A crew member has suffered frostbite to the toes of both feet. You should _____.

A. immerse the feet in warm water
B. warm the feet with a heat lamp
C. warm the feet at room temperature
D. rub the feet

439. Fixed CO_2 systems would not be used on crew's quarters or _____.

A. the paint locker
B. spaces open to the atmosphere
C. cargo holds
D. the engine room

441. Your vessel is broken down and rolling in heavy seas. You can reduce the possibility of capsizing by _____.

A. moving all personnel aft
B. constantly shifting the rudder
C. rigging a sea anchor
D. moving all personnel forward and low

442. On the all-purpose nozzle, the position of the valve when the handle is all the way forward is _____.

A. shut
B. fog
C. solid stream
D. spray

444. A call between any two ship stations on an intership working frequency shall have a maximum duration of _____.

A. 2 minutes
B. 3 minutes
C. 4 minutes
D. 5 minutes

447. According to the "Vessel Bridge-to-Bridge Radiotelephone Act," what is NOT required in the radiotelephone log?

A. Distress and alarm signals transmitted or intercepted
B. Times of beginning and end of watch period
C. Routine navigational traffic
D. Daily statement about the condition of the required radiotelephone equipment

448. Treatment of frostbite includes _____.

A. rubbing affected area with ice or snow
B. rubbing affected area briskly to restore circulation
C. wrapping area tightly in warm cloths
D. warming exposed parts rapidly

450. Which type of portable fire extinguisher is best suited for putting out a Class D fire?

A. Dry chemical
B. CO_2
C. Foam
D. Dry powder

452. When the handle of an all-purpose nozzle is in the forward position, the nozzle will _____.

A. produce high-velocity fog
B. produce low-velocity fog
C. produce a straight stream
D. shut off the water

453. You must shift a weight from the upper tween deck to the lower hold. This shift will _____.

A. make the vessel more tender
B. make the vessel stiffer
C. increase the rolling period
D. decrease the metacentric height

454. Marine Operators, when calling a ship on VHF-FM radiotelephone, normally call on channel _____.

A. 13
B. 16
C. 19
D. 23

457. According to the "Vessel Bridge-to-Bridge Radiotelephone Act," your radiotelephone log must contain _____.

A. a record of all routine calls
B. a record of your transmissions only
C. the home address of the vessel's Master or owner

D. a summary of all distress calls and messages

459. What is the minimum number of people required to safely handle a 1-1/2 inch fire hose?

A. 1
B. 2
C. 3
D. 4

460. A vessel of not more than 65 feet in length must have a collision bulkhead if it carries more than _____.

A. 6 passengers
B. 12 passengers
C. 36 passengers
D. 49 passengers

461. Which statement about transmitting distress messages by radiotelephone is INCORRECT?

A. It is advisable to follow a distress message on 2182 kHz by two dashes of 10 to 15 seconds duration.
B. Channel 16 (156.8 MHz) may be used for distress messages.
C. If no answer is received on the designated distress frequencies, repeat the distress call on any frequency available.
D. Distress messages should first be transmitted on 2182 kHz.

462. When the handle of an all-purpose nozzle is in the vertical position and without an applicator, the all-purpose nozzle will _____.

A. produce high-velocity fog
B. produce low-velocity fog
C. produce a straight stream
D. shut off the water

463. When water-cooled engines are installed on small passenger vessels, the cooling system _____.

A. pump must operate whenever the engine is operating
B. must have a suitable hull strainer in the raw water intake
C. may use a closed fresh water system
D. All of the above

464. You are making a telephone call ship-to-shore using the VHF-FM service. You can tell that the working channel is busy if you

hear _____.

A. speech
B. signaling tones
C. a busy signal
D. All of the above

467. Which is the required location of the radiotelephone station aboard a vessel to which the "Vessel Bridge-to-Bridge Radiotelephone Act" applies?

A. On the bridge or in the wheelhouse
B. In a separate radio compartment
C. Adjacent to the main power source
D. As high as possible on the vessel

470. A squeeze-grip type carbon-dioxide portable fire extinguisher has been partially discharged. It should be _____.

A. replaced in its proper location if weight loss is no more than 15%
B. labeled empty and recharged as soon as possible
C. replaced in its proper location regardless of weight
D. replaced in its proper location if weight loss is no more than 25%

472. When the handle of an all-purpose nozzle is pulled all the way back, it will _____.

A. produce high-velocity fog
B. produce low-velocity fog
C. produce a straight stream
D. shut off the water

473. Each small passenger vessel that operates on the high seas or beyond 3 miles from the coastline of the Great Lakes must have a Category 1 406 MHz EPIRB that _____.

A. is in good operating condition and is stowed near its charger
B. will float free and clear of a sinking vessel and automatically activate
C. is protected against all physical hazards
D. All of the above

474. You are making ship-to-shore telephone calls on VHF. You should use the _____.

A. VHF-FM service
B. coastal harbor service
C. high seas service
D. emergency broadcast service

477. The radiotelephone required by the "Vessel Bridge-to-Bridge Radiotelephone Act" is for the exclusive use of _____.

A. the Master or person in charge of the vessel
B. a person designated by the Master
C. a person on board to pilot the vessel
D. All of the above

478. A crew member is unconscious and the face is flushed. You should _____.

A. lay the crew member down with the head and shoulders slightly raised
B. administer a liquid stimulant
C. lay the crew member down with the head lower than the feet
D. attempt to stand the crew member upright to restore consciousness

481. How should the letter "D" be pronounced when spoken on the radiotelephone?

A. DUKE
B. DA VID
C. DOG
D. DELL TAH

482. The high-velocity fog tip used with the all-purpose fire fighting nozzle should always be _____.

A. attached by a chain
B. coated with heavy grease to prevent corrosion
C. painted red for identity as emergency equipment
D. stored in the clip at each fire station

484. A message warning of a tropical storm should be sent as a(n) _____.

A. routine message
B. urgent message
C. distress message
D. safety message

487. Which statement is TRUE concerning radiotelephones on board towing vessels?

A. There cannot be a radiotelephone located anywhere except in the wheelhouse.
B. The officer in charge of the wheelhouse is considered to have the radiotelephone watch.
C. Only distress messages may be transmitted over channel 13.

D. Only the Master of the vessel is allowed to speak over the radiotelephone.

488. A rescuer can most easily determine whether or not an adult victim has a pulse by checking the pulse at the _____.

A. carotid artery in the neck
B. femoral artery in the groin
C. brachial artery in the arm
D. radial artery in the wrist

489. An extinguisher with 15 lbs. of CO_2 or 10 lbs. of dry chemical is a size _____.

A. I
B. II
C. III
D. IV

492. The spray of water produced by using the high-velocity fog position on an all-purpose nozzle will have _____.

A. greater range than low-velocity fog
B. lesser range than low-velocity fog
C. about the same range as low-velocity fog
D. greater range than a solid stream

494. A message giving warning of a hurricane should have which prefix when sent by radiotelephone?

A. Pan-Pan (3 times)
B. Securité Securité Securité
C. TTT TTT TTT
D. No special prefix

497. The Coast Guard broadcasts routine weather reports on channels _____.

A. 13 or 14
B. 16 or 17
C. 21A or 22A
D. 44 or 45

498. An unconscious person should NOT be _____.

A. placed in a position with the head lower than the body
B. given an inhalation stimulant
C. given something to drink
D. treated for injuries until conscious

500. Safety shackles are fitted with _____.

A. a threaded bolt
B. a round pin, with a cotter pin

C. a threaded bolt, locknuts, and cotter pins
D. round pins and locknuts

502. Penetrations and openings in watertight bulkheads in a small passenger vessel less than 100 gross tons must _____.

A. be kept as high and as far inboard as possible
B. not contain sluice valves that allow water to flow freely from one watertight compartment to another
C. have some means to make them watertight
D. All of the above

504. If you wished to transmit a message by voice concerning the safety of navigation, you would preface it by the word _____.

A. Mayday
B. Pan-Pan
C. Securité
D. Safety

506. The capacity of any life raft on board a vessel can be determined by _____.

A. examining the Certificate of Inspection
B. examining the plate on the outside of the raft container
C. referring to the station bill
D. referring to the shipping articles

507. While underway, if you are required to have a radiotelephone, you must maintain a continuous listening watch on channel _____.

A. 6 (156.3 MHz)
B. 12 (156.6 MHz)
C. 14 (156.7 MHz)
D. 16 (156.8 MHz)

508. Which should NOT be a treatment for a person who has received a head injury and is groggy or unconscious?

A. Give a stimulant.
B. Elevate his head.
C. Stop severe bleeding.
D. Treat for shock.

509. Placing a lashing across a hook to prevent a fitting from slipping out of the hook is called _____.

A. faking
B. flemishing down

C. mousing
D. worming

510. A new crew member aboard your fishing vessel, who has not received any safety instructions or participated in any drills, reports on board. The Master must provide a safety orientation _____.

A. within one week
B. within 24 hours
C. on reporting day if it occurs within normal work hours
D. before sailing

514. You hear on the radiotelephone the word "Securité" spoken three times. This indicates that _____.

A. a message about the safety of navigation will follow
B. a message of an urgent nature about the safety of a ship will follow
C. the sender is in distress and requests immediate assistance
D. you should secure your radiotelephone

515. Which statement is TRUE concerning the placard entitled "Discharge of Oil Prohibited"?

A. It is required on all vessels.
B. It may be located in a conspicuous place in the wheelhouse.
C. It may be located at the bilge and ballast pump control station.
D. All of the above

516. Which toxic gas is a product of incomplete combustion, and is often present when a fire burns in a closed compartment?

A. Carbon dioxide
B. Hydrogen sulfide
C. Carbon monoxide
D. Nitric oxide

517. The VHF radiotelephone calling/safety/distress frequency is_____.

A. 156.8 MHz (channel 16)
B. 156.7 MHz (channel 14)
C. 156.65 MHz (channel 13)
D. 156.6 MHz (channel 12)

518. A person who gets battery acid in an eye should IMMEDIATELY wash the eye with _____.

A. boric acid solution

479

B. water
C. baking soda solution
D. ammonia

520. What is the displacement of a barge which measures 85' x 46' x 13' and is floating in salt water with a draft of ten feet?

A. 1117 tons
B. 1452 tons
C. 500 tons
D. 17.5 tons

522. A spanner is a _____.

A. cross connection line between two main fire lines
B. special wrench for tightening couplings in a fire hose line
C. tackle rigged to support a fire hose
D. None of the above

524. The radiotelephone safety message urgently concerned with safety of a person would be prefixed by the word _____.

A. Mayday
B. Pan
C. Safety
D. Interco

527. The VHF radiotelephone frequency designated to be used only to transmit or receive information pertaining to the safe navigation of a vessel is _____.

A. 156.8 MHz (channel 16)
B. 156.7 MHz (channel 14)
C. 156.65 MHz (channel 13)
D. 156.6 MHz (channel 12)

528. If a person gets something in his or her eye and you see that it is not embedded, you can _____.

A. get them to rub their eye until the object is gone
B. remove it with a match or toothpick
C. remove it with a piece of dry sterile cotton
D. remove it with a moist, cotton-tipped applicator

529. You are ordering ship's stores. Which statement is TRUE?

A. Up to five gallons of a flammable liquid may be stowed in the engine room.
B. All stores of line, rags, linens and other

similar type stores must be certified by UL as being fire retardant.
C. Cylinders containing compressed gasses must be constructed and tested in accordance with the Bureau of Standards.
D. All distress flares when received must be stored in the portable magazine chest.

531. A CO_2 portable extinguisher is annually checked by _____.

A. reading the gauge pressure
B. weighing the extinguisher
C. discharging a small amount of CO_2
D. seeing if the seal has been broken

532. Fire hose should be washed with_____.

A. salt water and a wire brush
B. caustic soap
C. mild soap and fresh water
D. a holystone

533. What is the purpose of limber holes?

A. To allow for air circulation
B. To allow for stress and strain in rough waters
C. To allow water in the boat to drain overboard
D. To allow water in the bilge to get to the boat drain

534. Your vessel has been damaged and is taking on water, but you do not require immediate assistance. You would preface a message advising other vessels of your situation with _____.

A. Mayday-Mayday-Mayday
B. Pan-Pan (3 times)
C. Securité-Securité-Securité
D. SOS-SOS-SOS

537. What frequency has the FCC designated for the use of bridge-to-bridge radiotelephone communications?

A. 156.275 MHz channel 65
B. 156.650 MHz channel 13
C. 157.000 MHz channel 28
D. 157.000 MHz channel 20

538. A victim is coughing and wheezing from a partial obstruction of the airway. An observer should _____.

A. perform the Heimlich maneuver

B. immediately start CPR
C. give back blows and something to drink
D. allow the person to continue coughing and dislodge the obstruction on his own

542. (Ill. D004SA) Before inserting a low-velocity fog applicator into an all-purpose nozzle, you must _____.

A. install the high-velocity nozzle tip
B. move the handle to position 2
C. move the handle to position 1
D. remove the high-velocity nozzle tip

544. In radiotelephone communications, the prefix PAN-PAN indicates that _____.

A. a ship is threatened by grave and imminent danger and requests immediate assistance
B. a calling station has an urgent message about the safety of a person
C. the message following the prefix will be about the safety of navigation
D. the message following is a meteorological warning

547. Channel 13 (156.65 MHz), the designated bridge-to-bridge channel, may NOT be used to _____.

A. exchange navigational information between vessels
B. exchange navigational information between a vessel and a shore station
C. conduct necessary tests
D. exchange operating schedules with company dispatcher

548. A shipmate chokes suddenly, cannot speak, and starts to turn blue. You should _____.

A. perform the Heimlich maneuver
B. make the victim lie down with the feet elevated to get blood to the brain
C. immediately administer CPR
D. do nothing until the victim becomes unconscious

549. If a vessel takes a sudden, severe list or trim from an unknown cause, you should FIRST _____.

A. determine the cause before taking countermeasures
B. assume the shift is due to off-center loading
C. counterflood

D. assume the cause is environmental forces

554. When using the International Code of Signals to communicate, the end of a radiotelephone transmission is indicated by the signal _____.

A. YZ
B. CQ
C. WA
D. AR

555. The transfer procedures for oil products are required to be posted _____.

A. in the pilothouse
B. in the officer's lounge
C. in the upper pumproom flat
D. where they can be easily seen or readily available

557. Under the "Vessel Bridge-to-Bridge Radiotelephone Act" the frequency for bridge-to-bridge communications is 156.65 MHz or channel _____.

A. 12
B. 13
C. 14
D. 16

558. A small passenger vessel operating on exposed or partially protected waters may not have a port light below the weather deck unless _____.

A. its sill is at least 30 inches above the deepest load waterline
B. it opens and has a solid, inside, hinged cover
C. it is made of thick transparent plastic
D. it is sealed shut

560. On small passenger vessels each inlet or discharge pipe penetrating the hull less than six inches above the deepest load waterline _____.

A. must have a check valve to prevent water from entering
B. except for engine exhausts must have a means to prevent water from entering the vessel if the pipe fails
C. must be fitted with a gate valve
D. must be sealed

561. The 12-foot low-velocity fog applicator _____.

A. has a spray pattern 12 feet in diameter
B. can be used in conjunction with both 1-1/2 inch and 2-1/2 inch all-purpose nozzles
C. has a 90° bend at its discharge end
D. has a screw thread end which connects to the all-purpose nozzle

562. One gallon of high expansion foam solution will produce _____.

A. 8 to 10 gallons of foam
B. 25 to 50 gallons of foam
C. 100 to 200 gallons of foam
D. 500 to 1000 gallons of foam

565. Small oil spills on deck can be kept from going overboard by _____.

A. driving wooden plugs into the vents
B. closing the lids on the vents
C. plugging the scuppers
D. plugging the sounding pipes

566. Which statement is TRUE concerning a motor lifeboat?

A. It is propelled by engine or hand-propelling gear.
B. It has a sufficient fuel capacity, if motorized, for 48 hours of operation.
C. It must be able to maintain a loaded speed of 6 knots.
D. All of the above

567. On small passenger vessels if an item of lifesaving equipment is carried but not required _____.

A. the equipment must be approved by the Commandant
B. it must be removed from the vessel as excess equipment
C. it may remain aboard the vessel as excess equipment regardless of its condition
D. it must be destroyed in the presence of a marine inspector

568. On a small passenger vessel, if an inlet or discharge pipe is not accessible, its shut off valve _____.

A. must be operable from the weather deck
B. may be operable from any accessible location above the bulkhead deck
C. must be labeled at its operating point to show its identity and direction of closing
D. All of the above

571. To increase the extent of flooding your vessel can suffer without sinking, you could _____.

A. ballast the vessel
B. increase reserve buoyancy
C. lower the center of gravity
D. raise the center of gravity

575. Pollution regulations require that each scupper in an enclosed deck area have a _____.

A. wooden plug
B. soft rubber plug
C. two-piece soft patch
D. mechanical means of closing

578. When fighting fires in spaces containing bottles of LPG (liquefied petroleum gas), you should _____.

A. attempt to isolate the fire from the LPG
B. cool the bottles or remove them from the fire area
C. see that the valves on all LPG bottles are closed
D. place insulating material over the bottles

579. The letter R followed by one or more numbers indicates _____.

A. a vessel's identity
B. bearing
C. visibility
D. distance

580. Freeboard is measured from the upper edge of the _____.

A. bulwark
B. deck line
C. gunwale bar
D. sheer strake

585. How long must a "Declaration of Inspection" be kept on board?

A. One week
B. Two weeks
C. One month
D. Three months

586. On small passenger vessels, which material must not be used in a valve or fitting for a hull penetration?

A. Cast bronze
B. Plastic

C. Cast iron
D. Stainless steel

587. Which vessel is NOT required to have a radiotelephone?

A. A 34-foot vessel engaged in towing
B. A dredge operating in a channel
C. A vessel of 100 GT carrying 50 passengers for hire
D. A 12-meter private yacht

589. Fires are grouped into what categories?

A. Class A, B, C, and D
B. Type 1, 2, 3, and 4
C. Combustible solids, liquids, and gases
D. Flammable solids, liquids, and gases

590. The distance between the waterline of a vessel and the main deck is called _____.

A. draft
B. freeboard
C. buoyancy
D. camber

592. A foam-type portable fire extinguisher would be most useful in combating a fire in _____.

A. solid materials such as wood or bales of fiber
B. flammable liquids
C. a piece of electrical equipment
D. combustible metallic solids

597. The "Vessel Bridge-to-Bridge Radiotelephone Act" applies to _____.

A. every towing vessel of 16 feet or over in length while navigating
B. every vessel of 50 GT and upward, carrying one or more persons for hire
C. all aircraft operating on the water
D. every power-driven vessel of 20 meters and upward while navigating

598. A fire must be ventilated _____.

A. when using an indirect attack on the fire such as flooding with water
B. to prevent the gases of combustion from surrounding the firefighters
C. to minimize heat buildup in adjacent compartments
D. if compressed gas cylinders are stowed in the compartment on fire

599. When starting CPR on a drowning victim, you should _____.

A. start chest compressions before the victim is removed from the water
B. drain water from the lungs before ventilating
C. begin mouth-to-mouth ventilations as soon as possible
D. do not tilt the head back since it may cause vomiting

600. The amount of freeboard which a ship possesses has a tremendous effect on its _____.

A. initial stability
B. free surface
C. stability at large angles of inclination
D. permeability

602. What does EPIRB stand for?

A. Emergency Position Indicating Radar Buoy
B. Electronic Pulse Indicating Radiobeacon
C. Emergency Position Indicating Radiobeacon
D. None of the above

604. To prevent loss of stability from free communication flooding you should _____.

A. close the cross-connection valve between the off-center tanks
B. completely flood high center tanks
C. ballast double bottom wing tanks
D. close any opening to the sea in an off-center tank

605. The operator of a vessel subject to the pollution regulations shall keep a written record available for inspection by the COPT or OCMI containing _____.

A. the name of each person currently designated as a person in charge
B. the date and result of the most recent test on the system relief valves
C. hose information including the minimum design burst pressure for each hose
D. All of the above

607. The "Vessel Bridge-to-Bridge Radiotelephone Act" applies to which towboat?

A. A 100 GT towboat, 24 feet in length
B. A 90-foot towboat tied to the pier

C. A 60-foot towboat towing by pushing ahead
D. A 400 GT towboat anchored

608. A fire of escaping liquefied flammable gas is best extinguished by _____.

A. cooling the gas below the ignition point
B. cutting off the supply of oxygen
C. stopping the flow of gas
D. interrupting the chain reaction

609. Which small passenger vessel(s) is/are NOT required to carry a Category 1 406 MHz EPIRB?

A. A coastwise vesssel whose route does not take it more than three miles from shore
B. A vessel operating on lakes, bays, sounds, and rivers
C. A vessel operating within three miles from the coastline of the Great Lakes
D. All of the above

610. The amount of freeboard which a ship possesses has a tremendous effect on its _____.

A. initial stability
B. free surface
C. permeability
D. stability at large angles of inclination

611. The maximum mean draft to which a vessel may be safely loaded is called _____.

A. mean draft
B. calculated draft
C. deep draft
D. load line draft

612. The service life of distress signals must be not more than _____.

A. forty-two months from the date of manufacture
B. thirty-six months from the date of the last inspection
C. twenty-four months from the date of approval
D. twelve months from the date of purchase

614. Your vessel is damaged and listing to port. There is a short rolling period around the angle of list. The portside freeboard is reduced to 1 foot. There is no trim and the weather is calm. You should FIRST _____.

A. press up a slack double bottom tank on the port side
B. fill an empty centerline double bottom tank
C. pump out a slack marine portable tank located on the portside amidships
D. jettison the anchors and anchor cables

615. The operator of each vessel subject to the pollution regulations is NOT required to keep written records of _____.

A. the name of each person designated as a person in charge
B. the date and results of the most recent equipment inspection
C. cargoes carried and dates delivered, including destinations
D. hose information not marked on the hose

617. For the purposes of distress signaling, small passenger vessels that operate on runs of more than 30 minutes duration on lakes, bays and sounds, and river routes must carry _____.

A. A radiotelephone
B. Three hand red flare distress signals, and three hand orange smoke distress signals
C. A "Very" pistol and flare kit
D. An approved noise-making device

619. A fire in the galley ALWAYS poses the additional threat of _____.

A. contaminating food with extinguishing agent
B. spreading through the engineering space
C. causing loss of stability
D. a grease fire in the ventilation system

621. The color of the signal flare sent up by a submarine about to surface because of an emergency on board is _____.

A. white
B. green
C. yellow
D. red

625. When the Captain of the Port or Officer in Charge, Marine Inspection, issues an order of suspension to the operator of a vessel concerning oil transfer operations, it _____.

A. is always effective immediately

B. includes a statement of each condition requiring corrective action
C. must be in writing before it takes effect
D. All of the above

627. Distress flares and smoke signals for small passenger vessels _____.

A. are not required aboard vessels on runs of less than 30 minutes duration
B. must be Coast Guard approved and stowed in a portable, watertight container
C. must be marked with an expiration date not more than 42 months from the date of manufacture
D. All of the above

629. Sign(s) of respiratory arrest requiring artificial respiration is(are) _____.

A. vomiting
B. blue color and lack of breathing
C. irregular breathing
D. unconsciousness

630. Reserve buoyancy is _____.

A. also called GM
B. the void portion of the ship below the waterline which is enclosed and watertight
C. affected by the number of transverse watertight bulkheads
D. the watertight portion of a vessel above the waterline

632. Portable foam type fire extinguishers are most effective on _____.

A. mattress fires
B. oil fires
C. wood fires
D. All of the above

633. A sweep oar is an oar that is _____.

A. generally shorter than the others and is used to steer with
B. is longer than the others and is used as the stroke oar
C. raised in the bow of the boat for the steersman to steer by
D. longer than the others used for steering

634. You are fighting a fire in a watertight compartment using hoses and salt water. Stability may be reduced because of_____.

A. progressive downflooding
B. reduction of water in the storage tanks

C. increase in free surface which reduces the metacentric height
D. reduction of KG to the minimum allowable

637. The date and time kept in the radiotelephone log shall commence at _____.

A. midnight
B. noon
C. beginning of the watch
D. any convenient time

640. The volume of a vessel's intact watertight space above the waterline is its_____.

A. free surface
B. marginal stability
C. reserve buoyancy
D. freeboard

642. As an extinguishing agent, foam_____.

A. conducts electricity
B. should be directed at the base of the fire
C. is most effective on burning gases which are flowing
D. extinguishes by cooling oil fires below ignition temperature

644. The difference between the forward and aft drafts is _____.

A. list
B. heel
C. trim
D. flotation

647. Under the "Vessel Bridge-to-Bridge Radiotelephone Act," the maximum power of all transmitters used shall be not more than _____.

A. 25 watts
B. 50 watts
C. 75 watts
D. 100 watts

648. Ring life buoys used aboard a small passenger vessels on oceans or coastwise routes are required to be what color?

A. White
B. White or international orange
C. Orange
D. Any highly visible color easily seen from the air

649. The lifeline of a life float or buoyant apparatus shall _____.

A. be at least 3/8 inch diameter and properly secured around the sides and ends of the device
B. be festooned in bights not longer than three feet long
C. have a seine float in each bight unless the line is an inherently buoyant material
D. All of the above

650. Which is an indication of reserve buoyancy?

A. Metacentric height
B. Righting moment
C. Rolling period
D. Freeboard

651. Small passenger vessels not limited to service during daylight hours must carry _____.

A. a radar maintained in good operating condition
B. a collision bulkhead
C. a white 20-point anchor light
D. at least one floating water light

652. How does foam extinguish an oil fire?

A. By cooling the oil below the ignition temperature
B. By removing the fuel source from the fire
C. By excluding the oxygen from the fire
D. By increasing the weight of the oil

654. Which of the following statements about transmitting distress messages by radiotelephone is INCORRECT?

A. Distress messages should first be transmitted on 2182 kHz.
B. Channel 16 (156.8 MHz) may be used for distress messages.
C. If no answer is received on the designated distress frequencies, repeat the distress call on any frequency available.
D. It is advisable to follow a distress message on 2182 kHz by two dashes of 10 to 15 seconds duration.

655. The spread of fire is NOT prevented by _____.

A. shutting off the oxygen supply
B. cooling surfaces adjacent to the fire
C. removing combustibles from the endangered area
D. removing smoke and toxic gases by ensuring adequate ventilation

657. What is the normal operating power for ship-to-ship communications on channel 13?

A. 1 watt or less
B. 5 watts
C. 10 watts
D. 20 watts

658. The ventilation system of your ship has fire dampers restrained by fusible links. Which statement is TRUE?

A. A fusible link will automatically open after a fire is extinguished and reset the damper.
B. Fusible links must be replaced at every inspection for certification.
C. Fusible links are tested by applying a source of heat to them.
D. Fusible links must be replaced if a damper is activated.

660. Reserve buoyancy is _____.

A. the watertight part of a vessel above the waterline
B. the void portion of the ship below the waterline which is enclosed and watertight
C. transverse watertight bulkheads
D. a measure of metacentric height

661. The Master of a fishing vessel must ensure that each crew member participates in at least one fire drill every _____.

A. day
B. week
C. month
D. 3 months

662. Foam extinguishes a fire mainly by _____.

A. cooling
B. chemical action
C. smothering
D. inerting the air

664. Your vessel is in distress and you have made radiotelephone contact with a U.S. Coast Guard vessel. The Coast Guard vessel requests that you give him a long count. This indicates that _____.

A. your radio transmitter is not working properly
B. the Coast Guard vessel is testing its receiver

C. the Coast Guard vessel is taking a radio direction finder bearing on your vessel
D. the Coast Guard vessel is requesting your position in latitude and longitude

667. Failure to comply with, or enforce, the provisions of the "Vessel Bridge-to-Bridge Radiotelephone Act" can result in a_____.

A. $500 civil penalty charged against the person in charge of the vessel
B. $1500 civil penalty charged against the person in charge of the vessel
C. $500 criminal penalty charged against the Master
D. $1500 criminal penalty charged against the Master

670. Which action will affect the trim of a vessel?

A. Moving high weights lower
B. Adding weight at the tipping center
C. Moving a weight forward
D. All of the above

672. A foam-type portable fire extinguisher is most useful in fighting a fire in _____.

A. generators
B. oil drums
C. the bridge controls
D. combustible metals

674. A distress frequency used on radiotelephone is _____.

A. 400 kilohertz
B. 2182 kilohertz
C. 2728 kilohertz
D. 8221 kilohertz

677. A vessel which violates the "Vessel Bridge-to-Bridge Radiotelephone Act" may be fined up to _____.

A. $100
B. $500
C. $1,000
D. $1,500

678. Fire may be spread by which means?

A. Conduction of heat to adjacent surfaces
B. Direct radiation
C. Convection
D. All of the above

679. All of the following are part of the fire triangle EXCEPT _____.

A. heat
B. oxygen
C. electricity
D. fuel

681. Size III, IV, and V extinguishers are considered _____.

A. hand portable
B. all purpose
C. fixed extinguishers
D. semi-portable

682. How are lifelines attached to a life float?

A. By serving
B. By splicing one end of the line around the apparatus
C. Securely attached around the outside in bights no longer than three feet
D. With an approved safety hook or shackle

684. The Coast Guard emergency radiotelephone frequency is _____.

A. 2132 kilohertz
B. 2182 kilohertz
C. 2670 kilohertz
D. 2750 kilohertz

685. The operator of each vessel engaged in a vessel-to-vessel oil transfer operation must keep a signed copy of the declaration of inspection for _____.

A. 10 days
B. 1 month
C. 6 months
D. 1 year

686. You should be most concerned about a possible explosion or fire in fuel tanks_____.

A. during fueling when the fuel first strikes the tank bottom
B. during fueling when the fuel strikes fuel already in the tank
C. when underway as the fuel is moved by wave action
D. shortly after fueling when fuel vapors gather

687. The Master or person in charge of a vessel subject to the "Vessel Bridge-to-Bridge Radiotelephone Act" who fails to comply with the Act or the regulations thereunder may be fined not more than _____.

A. $2,000
B. $1,500
C. $1,000
D. $500

688. Which may ignite fuel vapors?

A. Static electricity
B. An open and running motor
C. Loose wiring
D. All of the above

689. After a person has been revived by artificial respiration, he should be _____.

A. walked around until he is back to normal
B. given several shots of whiskey
C. kept lying down and warm
D. allowed to do as he wishes

692. Why should foam be banked off a bulkhead when extinguishing an oil fire?

A. To coat the surrounding bulkheads with foam in case the fire spreads
B. To cool the bulkhead closest to the fire
C. To prevent any oil on the bulkheads from igniting
D. To prevent agitation of the oil and spreading the fire

693. You are operating a fire hose with an applicator attached. If you put the handle of the nozzle in the vertical position you will _____.

A. produce high-velocity fog
B. produce low-velocity fog
C. produce a straight stream
D. shut off the water

694. What is the international distress frequency for radiotelephones?

A. 500 kHz
B. 1347 kHz
C. 2182 kHz
D. 2738 kHz

697. A violation of the "Vessel Bridge-to-Bridge Radiotelephone Act" may result in a _____.

A. civil penalty of $500 against the Master or person in charge of a vessel
B. civil penalty of $1,000 against the vessel itself
C. suspension and/or revocation of an operator's FCC license
D. All of the above

698. The spread of fire is prevented by _____.

A. cooling surfaces adjacent to the fire
B. removing combustibles from the endangered area
C. shutting off the oxygen supply
D. All of the above

699. What is the minimum length of a life float's paddle on a small passenger vessel?

A. Three feet
B. Four feet
C. Five feet
D. Six feet

700. Intact buoyancy is a term used to describe _____.

A. the volume of all intact spaces above the waterline
B. an intact space below the surface of a flooded area
C. an intact space which can be flooded without causing a ship to sink
D. the space at which all the vertical upward forces of buoyancy are considered to be concentrated

702. Which statement about firefighting foam is TRUE?

A. Foam conducts electricity.
B. To be most effective, foam should be directed at the base of the fire.
C. Foam is most effective on burning liquids which are flowing.
D. Foam can ONLY be used to extinguish class A fires.

704. Which radiotelephone transmission may be sent over channel 16?

A. Distress signal MAYDAY
B. Call to a particular station
C. A meteorological warning
D. All of the above

706. The painter on a life float or buoyant apparatus shall _____.

A. have a minimum breaking strength of 3,000 lbs. if the capacity of the lifesaving gear is 50 persons or greater
B. be resistant to ultraviolet sunlight deterioration
C. be stowed to pay out freely if the vessel sinks
D. All of the above

707. If your bridge-to-bridge radio-telephone ceases to operate, you must _____.

A. immediately anchor your vessel and arrange for repairs to the system
B. moor your vessel at the nearest dock available and arrange for repairs to the system
C. arrange for the repair of the system to be completed within 48 hours
D. exercise due diligence to restore the system at the earliest practicable time

708. Removing which will extinguish a fire?

A. Nitrogen
B. Carbon dioxide
C. Sodium
D. Oxygen

710. Buoyancy is a measure of the ship's _____.

A. ability to float
B. deadweight
C. freeboard
D. midships strength

711. When administering artificial respiration to an adult, the breathing cycle should be repeated about _____.

A. 12 to 15 times per minute
B. 18 to 20 times per minute
C. 20 to 25 times per minute
D. as fast as possible

712. Which statement is TRUE concerning the application of foam on an oil fire?

A. It cools the surface of the liquid.
B. It gives protection to fire fighting personnel against the heat of the fire.
C. It forms a smothering blanket on the surface of the oil.
D. It should be used at the same time a solid stream of water is being applied.

714. A Coast Guard radiotelephone message about an aid to navigation that is off station is preceded by the word _____.

A. "PAN-PAN"
B. "MAYDAY"
C. "SOS"
D. "SECURITé"

715. Your vessel is taking on fuel when a small leak develops in the hose. You order

the pumping stopped. Before you resume pumping, you should _____.

A. notify the terminal superintendent
B. place a large drip pan under the leak and plug the scuppers
C. repair the hose with a patch
D. replace the hose

717. If your radiotelephone fails while underway, _____.

A. you must visually signal oncoming vessels
B. you must immediately tie up in the nearest port until the radiotelephone is repaired
C. you must anchor until the radio-telephone is repaired
D. the loss of the radiotelephone must be considered in navigating the vessel

718. Painters fitted to life floats and buoyant apparatus with a capacity of 49 or less persons must _____.

A. be of manila rope or equivalent, not less than two inches in circumference and not less than four fathoms long
B. be 100 feet long and have a breaking strength of at least 1500 lbs.
C. be at least 100 feet long and have a breaking strength of 3,000 lbs.
D. be made of 90 feet of 3/8" nylon

719. A fire hose has a _____.

A. male coupling at both ends
B. female coupling at both ends
C. female coupling at the nozzle end and a male coupling at the hydrant end
D. male coupling at the nozzle end and a female coupling at the hydrant end

720. The center of volume of the immersed portion of the hull is called the _____.

A. center of buoyancy
B. center of flotation
C. center of gravity
D. tipping center

721. Forces within a vessel have caused a difference between the starboard and port drafts. This difference is called _____.

A. list
B. heel
C. trim
D. flotation

723. The color of the signal flare sent up by a submarine to indicate an emergency condition within the submarine is _____.

A. red
B. white
C. yellow
D. green

724. Messages concerning weather conditions transmitted by radiotelephone are preceded by _____.

A. MAYDAY
B. PAN-PAN
C. SECURITé
D. SOS

725. You notice oil on the water near your vessel while taking on fuel. You should FIRST _____.

A. stop fueling
B. notify the senior deck officer
C. notify the terminal superintendent
D. determine whether your vessel is the source

727. Under the "Vessel Bridge-to-Bridge Radiotelephone Act," failure of a vessel's radiotelephone equipment _____.

A. constitutes a violation of the Act
B. obligates the operator to moor or anchor the vessel immediately
C. requires immediate, emergency repairs
D. does not, in itself, constitute a violation of the Act

728. When water is used to fight a fire on board a ship, the effect of the weight of the water must be taken into account. How much sea water will increase the weight displacement by one ton?

A. 64 cubic feet
B. 35 cubic feet
C. 100 gallons
D. 500 liters

729. At what rate would you render mouth to mouth or mouth to nose artificial respiration to an adult?

A. 4 to 6 times per minute
B. 12 to 15 times per minute
C. 20 to 30 times per minute
D. At least 30 times per minute

730. The percentage of the total surface area or volume of a flooded compartment that can be occupied by water caused by damage is known as _____.

A. one compartment standard
B. center of flotation
C. permeability
D. form gain

731. If Annex V to MARPOL 73/78 applies to your vessel, you will not be able to discharge _____ anywhere at sea.

A. plastic
B. metal
C. glass
D. paper

732. Which statement(s) is(are) TRUE concerning the use of dry chemical extinguishers?

A. You should direct the spray at the base of the fire.
B. You should direct the spray directly into the fire.
C. You should direct the spray at a vertical bulkhead and allow it to flow over the fire.
D. All of the above

734. On small passenger vessels painters fitted to life floats shall be at least _____.

A. 20.0 meters (65.5 feet) in length
B. 30.5 meters (100 feet) in length
C. 10 fathoms (60 feet) in length
D. 90 feet (27.5 meters) in length

735. You are fueling your vessel when you notice oil in the water around your vessel. You should immediately stop fueling and _____.

A. begin cleanup operations
B. notify the U.S. Coast Guard
C. leave the area
D. notify the Corps of Engineers

738. There is a fire aft aboard your vessel. To help fight the fire, you should _____.

A. put the wind off either beam
B. head the bow into the wind and decrease speed
C. put the stern into the wind and increase speed
D. put the stern into the wind and decrease speed

740. What is NOT a motion of the vessel?

A. Pitch
B. Roll
C. Trim
D. Yaw

742. An advantage of an ABC dry chemical over a carbon dioxide extinguisher is _____.

A. lack of toxicity
B. the multipurpose extinguishing ability
C. burn-back protection
D. cooling ability

744. You are using VHF channel 16 (156.8 MHz) or 2182 kHz. You need help but are not in danger. You should use the urgent signal _____.

A. "ASSISTANCE NEEDED"
B. "PAN-PAN"
C. "MAYDAY"
D. "SECURITé"

748. A fire has broken out on the stern of your vessel. You should maneuver your vessel so the wind _____.

A. blows the fire back toward the vessel
B. comes over the bow
C. comes over the stern
D. comes over either beam

749. Small passenger vessels on river routes in cold water must be provided with lifefloats of an aggregate capacity to accommodate _____.

A. at least 50% of all persons on board or meet certain construction standards
B. 100% of the crew and 50% of all passengers allowed to be carried
C. not less than 50% of all passengers on board at the time
D. All persons on board (100% of all passengers and crew)

750. The center of flotation of a vessel is _____.

A. the center of volume of the immersed portion of the vessel
B. the center of gravity of the water plane
C. that point at which all the vertical downward forces of weight are considered to be concentrated
D. that point at which all the vertical

upward forces of buoyancy are considered to be concentrated

752. Which statement describes the primary process by which fires are extinguished by dry chemical?

A. The stream of dry chemical powder cools the fire.
B. The dry chemical powder attacks the fuel and oxygen chain reaction.
C. The powder forms a solid coating over the surface.
D. The dry chemical smothers the fire.

753. How should signal flares be used after you have abandoned ship and are adrift in a life raft?

A. Immediately use all the signals at once.
B. Use all the signals during the first night.
C. Employ a signal every hour after abandoning ship until they are gone.
D. Use them only when you are aware of a ship or plane in the area.

754. "PAN-PAN" repeated three times over the radiotelephone indicates which type of message will follow?

A. Distress
B. Safety
C. All clear
D. Urgency

755. While your vessel is taking on fuel you notice oil on the water around the vessel. What should you do FIRST?

A. Stop the fueling.
B. Notify the Coast Guard.
C. Notify the terminal superintendent.
D. Determine the source of the oil.

758. A fire is discovered in the forepeak of a vessel at sea. The wind is from ahead at 35 knots. You should _____.

A. remain on course and hold speed
B. change course and put the stern to the wind
C. change course to put the wind on either beam and increase speed
D. remain on course but slack the speed

760. With certain exceptions a suitable rescue boat is required _____.

A. on most "T-Boats" more than 65 feet in length
B. on most "T-Boats" regardless of length
C. only on "K-Boats"
D. None of the above

761. Which when removed will result in the extinguishment of a fire?

A. Oxygen
B. Carbon dioxide
C. Sodium
D. Nitrogen

762. The most effective extinguishing action of dry chemical is _____.

A. breaking the chain reaction
B. the CO_2 that is formed by heat
C. smothering
D. shielding of radiant heat

764. Which word is an international distress signal when transmitted by radiotelephone?

A. Securité
B. Mayday
C. Breaker
D. Pan

767. On every vessel, distress signals must be stowed _____.

A. on or near the navigating bridge
B. on the flying bridge not closer than 15 feet to any bulkhead
C. above the freeboard deck away from heat
D. in an enclosed space below the freeboard deck away from heat

768. Which statement is TRUE concerning carbon dioxide?

A. It is heavier than air.
B. It is non-conductive.
C. It is used on class B and C fires.
D. All of the above are true.

769. A life float on a fishing vessel must be equipped with _____.

A. a painter
B. red smoke flares
C. a jacknife
D. a signal mirror

770. A vessel is described as a two compartment vessel when it _____.

A. has no more than two compartments
B. has two compartments in addition to the engine room
C. will sink if any two compartments are flooded
D. will float if any two adjacent compartments are flooded

772. What do the small passenger vessel regulations require when installing a hydraulic accumulator or other unfired pressure vessel?

A. It be operated at one and one half times normal operating pressure for ten minutes.
B. Safety and/or relief valves settings be checked at two and one half times normal operating pressures.
C. It be installed to the satisfaction of the cognizant OCMI
D. All of the above

776. When dry chemical extinguishers are used to put out class B fires, there is a danger of reflash because dry chemical _____.

A. is not an effective agent on Class B fires
B. does little or no cooling
C. dissipates quickly
D. is rapidly absorbed by the liquid

777. On small passenger vessels a gasoline engine must be fitted with _____.

A. A means of backfire flame control
B. A lubricating oil pressure gauge and a tachometer
C. Jacket water discharge temperature gauges
D. All of the above

778. An aluminum powder fire is classified as class _____.

A. A
B. B
C. C
D. D

781. How is the external flotation bladder of an immersion suit inflated?

A. It is inflated by a small CO_2 bottle that is automatically tripped when the front zipper is at the top of the zipper track.
B. It is inflated by a small CO_2 bottle that is manually tripped.

C. It is inflated by blowing through an inflation tube.
D. It inflates by sea water bleeding into the flotation bladder and reacting with a chemical therein.

782. On small passenger vessels what device must you install under carburetors, other than the downdraft type, to allow ready removal of fuel leakage?

A. A drip collector
B. A funnel and a tin can
C. A sponge
D. Suitable absorbent material

785. 33 CFR 156 deals with matters concerning _____.

A. oil and hazardous material transfer operations
B. vessel construction and design
C. operation of nautical schoolships
D. lifesaving and firefighting equipment

788. Fires of which class would most likely occur in the engine room of a vessel?

A. Classes A and B
B. Classes B and C
C. Classes C and D
D. Classes A and D

789. An inflatable life raft equipped with a SOLAS B pack must be stowed _____.

A. so as to float free
B. with the vessel's emergency equipment
C. near the wheelhouse
D. as far forward as possible

790. Which would NOT provide extra buoyancy for a vessel with no sheer?

A. Lighter draft
B. Raised fo'c'sle head
C. Raised poop
D. Higher bulwark

791. During a training exercise a submarine indicating that a torpedo has been fired will send up smoke from a float. The smoke's color will be _____.

A. black
B. red
C. orange
D. yellow

792. What is an advantage of a dry chemi-

cal extinguisher as compared to a carbon dioxide extinguisher?

A. It has a greater duration.
B. It provides a heat shield for the operator.
C. It is nontoxic.
D. It offers lasting, effective protection against burn-back.

796. When discharging a portable CO_2 fire extinguisher, you should NOT hold the horn of the extinguisher because the horn _____.

A. becomes extremely hot
B. becomes extremely cold
C. could come off in your hands
D. is placed directly in the flames

798. A fire starts in a switchboard due to a short circuit. This is which class of fire?

A. A
B. B
C. C
D. D

799. Lines or gear NOT in use should be _____.

A. conspicuously marked
B. stowed anywhere
C. left on deck
D. secured or stowed out of the way

800. The "trimming arm" of a vessel is the horizontal distance between the _____.

A. LCB and LCF
B. LCF and LCB
C. forward perpendicular and LCG
D. LCB and LCG

801. No person on board any vessel to which Annex V to MARPOL 73/78 applies may discharge garbage of any type when _____.

A. less than 12 nautical miles from the United States
B. less than 12 nautical miles from nearest land
C. in the navigable waters of the United States
D. less than 25 nautical miles from nearest land

802. A portable dry chemical fire extinguisher discharges by _____.

A. gravity when the extinguisher is turned upside down
B. pressure from a small CO_2 cartridge on the extinguisher
C. air pressure from the hand pump attached to the extinguisher
D. pressure from the reaction when water is mixed with the chemical

803. The abandon-ship signal on the ship's whistle is _____.

A. 6 short blasts and 1 long blast
B. more than 6 short blasts
C. more than 6 short blasts and 1 long
D. 1 long blast of at least 10 seconds

806. On small passenger vessels electrical equipment in spaces that contain gasoline powered machinery must be _____.

A. explosion-proof
B. intrinsically safe
C. ignition protected for use in a gasoline atmosphere
D. All of the above

807. The space containing carbon dioxide cylinders shall be properly ventilated and designed to prevent an ambient temperature in excess of _____.

A. 75°F
B. 100°F
C. 130°F
D. 165°F

808. A fire in a pile of canvas is classified as class _____.

A. A
B. B
C. C
D. D

809. If the patient vomits during mouth-to-mouth resuscitation, the rescuer should FIRST _____.

A. ignore it and continue mouth-to-mouth ventilation
B. pause for a moment until the patient appears quiet again, then resume ventilation mouth-to-mouth
C. switch to mouth-to-nose ventilation
D. turn the patient's body to the side, sweep out the mouth and resume mouth-to-mouth ventilation

810. When a vessel's LCG is aft of her LCB, the vessel will _____.

A. trim by the stern
B. trim by the head
C. be on an even keel
D. be tender

811. Your vessel is broken down and rolling in heavy seas. You can reduce the possibility of capsizing by _____.

A. constantly shifting the rudder
B. rigging a sea anchor
C. moving all personnel aft
D. moving all personnel forward and low

812. You are fighting a class B fire with a portable dry chemical extinguisher. The discharge should be directed _____.

A. at the seat of the fire, starting at the near edge
B. to bank off a bulkhead onto the fire
C. over the top of the fire
D. at the main body of the fire

813. You hear the general alarm and ship's whistle sound for over 10 seconds. Traditionally, this is the signal for _____.

A. abandon ship
B. dismissal from fire and emergency stations
C. fire and emergency
D. man overboard

818. A fire in a transformer terminal would be classified as class _____.

A. A
B. B
C. C
D. D

819. Providing you are not in a special area, such as the Mediterranean or Red Sea, how many nautical miles from land must you be to throw wooden dunnage into the sea?

A. 25 nm
B. 12 nm
C. 6 nm
D. 3 nm

820. The two points that act together to trim a ship are the _____.

A. LCF and LCB
B. LCG and LCB

C. metacenter and LCG
D. VCG and LCG

821. Bleeding from a vein is _____.

A. dark red and has a steady flow
B. bright red and slow
C. bright red and spurting
D. dark red and spurting

822. When electrical equipment is involved in a fire, the stream of dry chemicals should be _____.

A. aimed at the source of the flames
B. fogged above the equipment
C. shot off a flat surface onto the flames
D. used to shield against electrical shock

823. Traditionally, the signal for fire aboard ship is _____.

A. more than 6 short blasts and 1 long blast on the whistle, and the same signal on the general alarm
B. continuous sounding of the ship's whistle and the general alarm for at least 10 seconds
C. 1 short blast on the whistle
D. alternating short and long blasts on the ship's whistle

825. ABYC equipment standards are published by the _____.

A. Association of Boat and Yacht Classifiers
B. American Boat and Yacht Council
C. American Boat and Yacht Convention 1991
D. American Boat and Yacht Club

827. A small passenger vessel's Official Number must be marked _____.

A. in block type Arabic numerals not less than 3 inches high
B. or mounted so that any alteration, removal, or replacement would be obvious
C. on some clearly visible interior structural hull part
D. All of the above

828. A fire in a pile of dunnage would be classified as class _____.

A. A
B. B
C. C
D. D

829. A fire starting by spontaneous combustion can be expected in which condition?

A. Paints, varnish, or other liquid flammables are stowed in a dry stores locker.
B. Inert cargoes such as pig iron are loaded in a wet condition.
C. Oily rags are stowed in a metal pail.
D. Clean mattresses are stored in contact with an electric light bulb.

831. The spread of fire is prevented by _____.

A. heating surfaces adjacent to the fire
B. leaving combustibles in the endangered area
C. shutting off the oxygen supply
D. All of the above

832. Which statement is TRUE concerning the use of a dry chemical extinguisher?

A. You should direct the stream at the base of the fire.
B. You should direct the stream directly into the fire.
C. You should direct the stream at a vertical bulkhead and allow it to flow over the fire.
D. All of the above

833. While reading the muster list you see that "3 short blasts on the whistle and 3 short rings on the general alarm bells" is the signal for _____.

A. abandon ship
B. dismissal from fire and emergency stations
C. fire and emergency
D. man overboard

838. A class C fire would be burning _____.

A. fuel oil
B. wood
C. celluloid
D. electrical insulation

839. A small passenger vessel's Official Number must be marked _____.

A. in block type Arabic numerals not less than 1-1/2 inch high
B. or mounted so its alteration, removal, or replacement would be obvious
C. on some clearly visible exterior structural hull part
D. All of the above

840. If a vessel is sagging, what kind of stress is placed on the sheer strake?

A. Compression
B. Tension
C. Thrust
D. Racking

841. Blood flowing from a cut artery appears _____.

A. dark red with a steady flow
B. bright red with a steady flow
C. bright red and in spurts
D. dark red and in spurts

842. As compared to carbon dioxide, dry chemical has which advantage?

A. Cleaner
B. Effective on metal fires
C. Greater range
D. More cooling effect

845. Each pressure gauge used in an oil transfer operation must be accurate to within _____.

A. 1 percent
B. 3 percent
C. 5 percent
D. 10 percent

848. The class of fire on which a blanketing effect is essential is class _____.

A. A
B. B
C. C
D. D

849. You are testing the external inflation bladder on an immersion suit and find it has a very slow leak. Which action should be taken?

A. Replace the suit.
B. Replace the inflation bladder.
C. Take it out of service and repair in accordance with the manufacturer's instructions.
D. Some leakage should be expected and a topping off tube is provided; no other action is necessary.

850. When a vessel is stationary and in a hogging condition, the main deck is under _____.

A. compression stress
B. tension stress

C. shear stress
D. racking stress

851. The preferred agent used in fighting a helicopter crash fire is _____.

A. CO_2
B. dry chemical
C. water
D. foam

852. Which statement concerning the application of dry chemical powder is FALSE?

A. At temperatures of less than 32°F, the extinguisher must be recharged more often.
B. When possible, the fire should be attacked from windward.
C. The stream should be directed at the base of the fire.
D. Directing the stream into burning flammable liquid may cause splashing.

856. Which statement about immersion suits is TRUE?

A. Immersion suits should be worn during routine work on deck to provide maximum protection.
B. After purchasing, the suit should be removed from its storage bag and hung on a hanger where readily accessible.
C. Immersion suits must have a PFD light attached to the front shoulder area.
D. Small leaks or tears may be repaired using the repair kit packed with the suit.

858. A fire in trash and paper waste is classified as class _____.

A. A
B. B
C. C
D. D

862. Dry chemical extinguishers extinguish class B fires to the greatest extent by _____.

A. cooling
B. smothering
C. oxygen dilution
D. breaking the chain reaction

865. On board a small passenger vessel, fuel tank vents should _____.

A. be connected at the highest point in the tank

B. terminate in a U-bend fitted with a single corrosion resistant wire screen of at least 30x30 mesh
C. be installed with an upward gradient to prevent fuel from being trapped in the line
D. All of the above

868. Burning wood is which class of fire?

A. A
B. B
C. C
D. D

869. As a last resort, a tourniquet can be used to _____.

A. hold a victim in a stretcher
B. stop uncontrolled bleeding
C. hold a large bandage in place
D. restrain a delirious victim

870. The forward draft of your ship is 27'-11" and the after draft is 29'-03". The draft amidships is 28'-05". Your vessel is

_____.

A. hogged
B. sagged
C. listed
D. trimmed by the head

871. The bilge pump on a fishing vessel

_____.

A. must be fixed if the vessel exceeds 12 meters in length
B. may be used as a fire pump
C. must be portable if there are more than 4 watertight compartments
D. must be capable of pumping at least 450 gpm

873. On small passenger vessels which parts of a water-cooled gasoline or diesel engine must be water-jacketed and cooled?

A. The engine's head
B. The block
C. The exhaust manifold
D. All of the above

878. A fire in a pile of linen is a class _____.

A. A
B. B
C. C
D. D

879. To operate a portable CO_2 extinguisher continuously in the discharge mode _____.

A. slip the "D yoke" ring in the lower handle over the upper handle
B. reinsert the locking pin
C. open the discharge valve
D. invert the CO_2 extinguisher

880. A ship's forward draft is 22'-04" and its after draft is 23'-00". The draft amidships is 23'-04". This indicates a concentration of weight _____.

A. at the bow
B. in the lower holds
C. amidships
D. at the ends

881. You should FIRST treat a simple fracture by _____.

A. attempting to set the fracture
B. preventing further movement of the bone
C. applying a tourniquet
D. alternately applying hot and cold compresses

882. Fire in an engine compartment is best extinguished with carbon dioxide gas (CO_2) and by _____.

A. closing the compartment except for the ventilators
B. completely closing the compartment
C. leaving the compartment open to the air
D. increasing the air flow to the compartment by blowers

885. Which type of marine sanitation device (MSD) is used solely for the storage of sewage and flushwater at ambient air pressure and temperature?

A. Type I
B. Type II
C. Type III
D. Type IV

887. Carbon dioxide as a fire fighting agent has which advantage over other agents?

A. It causes minimal damage.
B. It is safer for personnel.
C. It is cheaper.
D. It is most effective on a per unit basis.

888. An oil fire is classified as class _____.

A. A
B. B
C. C
D. D

889. Small quantities of flammable liquids needed at a work site should be _____.

A. used only under the supervision and direction of a ship's officer
B. tightly capped and stowed with other tools near the job site when securing at the end of the day
C. used only when a pressurized fire hose is laid out ready for immediate use
D. in a metal container with a tight cap

891. On small passenger vessels, cooling water for the exhaust lines from an internal combustion engine must be _____.

A. obtained from the engine's cooling water system or from a separate engine-driven pump
B. chemically treated to prevent corrosion
C. flushed and changed periodically
D. obtained from a fresh water storage tank or an expansion tank

892. While you are working in a space, the fixed CO_2 system is accidentally activated. You should _____.

A. secure the applicators to preserve the charge in the cylinders
B. continue with your work as there is nothing you can do to stop the flow of CO_2
C. retreat to fresh air and ventilate the compartment before returning
D. make sure all doors and vents are secured

895. Air-cooled gasoline auxiliary engines are allowed on vessels not more than 65 feet in length, carrying not more than 12 passengers if _____.

A. it is not practicable to supply water to the engine
B. they have a self-contained fuel system and are installed on an open deck
C. they are rated at not more than 4.5 horsepower
D. All of the above

897. Which statement is TRUE concerning carbon dioxide?

A. It is lighter than air.
B. It is an inert gas.
C. It is used mostly on class A fires.
D. All of the above

898. A galley grease fire would be classified as which class of fire?

A. A
B. B
C. C
D. D

899. EXCEPT when suffering from a head or chest injury a patient in shock should be placed in which position?

A. Head up and feet down
B. Head down and feet up
C. Flat on back with head and feet elevated
D. Arms above the head

901. A squeeze-grip type carbon dioxide portable fire extinguisher has been partially discharged. It should be _____.

A. replaced in its proper location if weight loss is no more than 15%
B. replaced in its proper location if weight loss is no more than 25%
C. labeled empty and recharged as soon as possible
D. labeled empty and replaced in its proper location regardless of weight

902. Your vessel is equipped with a fixed CO_2 system and a fire main system. In the event of an electrical fire in the engine room what is the correct procedure for fighting the fire?

A. Use the CO_2 system and evacuate the engine room.
B. Use the fire main system and evacuate the engine room.
C. Evacuate the engine room and use the CO_2 system.
D. Evacuate the engine room and use the fire main system.

904. If you are on the beach and are signaling to a small boat in distress that your present location is dangerous and they should land to the left, you would _____.

A. fire a green star to the left
B. send the letter K by light and point to the left
C. place an orange signal to your left as you signal with a white light
D. send the code signal S followed by L

905. The color of the signal flare sent up by a submarine coming to periscope depth is _____.

A. white
B. green
C. yellow
D. red

906. Inflatable life rafts shall be serviced at an approved servicing facility every 12 months or not later than the next vessel inspection for certification. However, the total elapsed time between servicing cannot exceed _____.

A. 12 months
B. 15 months
C. 17 months
D. 18 months

907. An advantage of a dry chemical over a carbon dioxide fire extinguisher is its _____.

A. greater range
B. effectiveness on all types of fires
C. cleanliness
D. All of the above

908. If ignited, which material would be a class B fire?

A. Magnesium
B. Paper
C. Wood
D. Diesel Oil

912. A "fifteen-pound" CO_2 extinguisher is so called because _____.

A. there are fifteen pounds of CO_2 in the container
B. the container, when full, weighs fifteen pounds
C. the pressure at the discharge nozzle is 15 psi
D. the empty container weighs fifteen pounds

914. What is the lifesaving signal for "You are seen—Assistance will be given as soon as possible"?

A. Red star rocket
B. Orange smoke signal

C. Green star rocket
D. Vertical motion of a flag

915. Which is/are required for engine exhaust pipe installations on small passenger vessels?

A. Protection where people or equipment can contact the pipe.
B. Piping must be arranged so that water backflow cannot reach the engine exhaust ports
C. Dry exhaust pipe ending at the transom should be located as far outboard as possible
D. All of the above

917. Foam-type portable fire extinguishers are most useful in combating fires involving _____.

A. solid materials such as wood or bales of fiber
B. flammable liquids
C. electrical equipment
D. metallic solids

918. Fires which occur in energized electrical equipment, such as switchboard insulation, are class _____.

A. A
B. B
C. C
D. D

919. After an accident the victim may go into shock and die. What should be done to help prevent shock?

A. Slightly elevate the head and feet.
B. Keep the person awake.
C. Keep the person lying down and at a comfortable temperature.
D. Give the person a stimulant to increase blood flow.

920. If a vessel lists to port, the center of buoyancy will _____.

A. move to port
B. move to starboard
C. move directly down
D. stay in the same position

921. You can determine that a CO_2 fire extinguisher is fully charged by _____.

A. looking at the gauge
B. checking the nameplate data

C. weighing by hand
D. weighing on a properly calibrated scale

922. An upright vessel has negative GM. GM becomes positive at the angle of loll because the _____.

A. free-surface effects are reduced due to pocketing
B. KG is reduced as the vessel seeks the angle of loll
C. effective beam is increased causing BM to increase
D. underwater volume of the hull is increased

923. You are at sea on a vessel whose beam is 60 feet and full period of roll is 20 seconds. What is the estimated metacentric height of the vessel?

A. 1.3 ft
B. 1.5 ft
C. 1.7 ft
D. 1.9 ft

924. What is the lifesaving signal for "You are seen—Assistance will be given as soon as possible"?

A. 3 white star signals
B. Horizontal motion with a white flag
C. Vertical motion of a white light
D. Code letter "K" by blinker light

925. The center of flotation of a vessel is the geometric center of the _____.

A. underwater volume
B. above water volume
C. amidships section
D. waterplane area

926. Inflatable life rafts must be overhauled and inspected at a U.S. Coast Guard approved service facility every _____.

A. six months
B. twelve months
C. eighteen months
D. twenty-four months

927. The extinguishing agent most effective for combating wood fires is _____.

A. water
B. carbon dioxide
C. foam
D. dry chemical

928. A fire in the radio transmitter would be of what class?

A. A
B. B
C. C
D. D

929. According to Annex V to MARPOL 73/78, garbage containing plastic is permitted to be disposed of by _____.

A. incinerating offshore
B. discharging when at least 12 nautical miles from nearest land
C. grinding to less than 1" and discharging at least 12 nautical miles from nearest land
D. grinding to less than 1" and discharging at least 25 nautical miles from nearest land

930. Semi-portable extinguishers used on inspected vessels are sizes _____.

A. II, III, and IV
B. I, II, and III
C. III, IV, and V
D. IV and V

931. The major cause of shock in burn victims is the _____.

A. high level of pain
B. emotional stress
C. increase in body temperature and pulse rate
D. massive loss of fluid through the burned area

932. Portable CO_2 fire extinguishers should NOT be used to inert a space containing flammable liquids due to the danger of _____.

A. the CO_2 being inhaled by personnel
B. reflash of burning liquids
C. vapor condensation on the extinguisher
D. the discharge causing a static spark

933. You are at sea on a vessel whose beam is 40 feet and the full rolling period is 20 seconds. What is the estimated metacentric height of the vessel?

A. 0.3 ft.
B. 0.5 ft.
C. 0.8 ft.
D. 1.1 ft.

934. The signal used with shore lifesaving equipment to indicate "Affirmative" is _____.

A. vertical motion of the arms
B. code signal "C" sent by light or sound signaling apparatus
C. firing of a red star signal
D. None of the above

935. If an airplane circles a vessel 3 times, crosses the vessel's course close ahead while rocking the wings, and heads off in a certain direction, what does this indicate?

A. The plane is in distress and will have to ditch.
B. The plane is going to drop a package and wishes the vessel to recover it.
C. Someone is in distress in that direction and the vessel should follow and assist.
D. There is danger ahead and the best course is indicated by the direction of the aircraft.

936. If your vessel is equipped with inflatable life rafts, how should they be maintained?

A. Have your crew check them annually.
B. They do not need any maintenance.
C. Have them sent ashore to an approved maintenance facility annually.
D. Have them serviced by the shipyard annually.

937. On a class B fire, which portable fire extinguisher would be the LEAST desirable?

A. Carbon dioxide
B. Water (stored pressure)
C. Dry chemical
D. Foam

938. A magnesium fire is classified as class _____.

A. A
B. B
C. C
D. D

939. CO_2 cylinders forming part of a fixed fire extinguishing system must be pressure tested at least every _____.

A. year
B. 2 years
C. 6 years
D. 12 years

940. When a vessel is inclined by an external force, the _____.

A. shape of the vessel's underwater hull remains the same
B. vessel's center of gravity shifts to the center of the vessel's underwater hull
C. vessel's center of buoyancy shifts to the center of the vessel's underwater hull
D. vessel's mean draft increases

942. A fifteen-pound CO_2 extinguisher _____.

A. contains 15 pounds of CO_2
B. weighs 15 pounds when full of CO_2
C. has 15 pounds of pressure at the nozzle
D. weighs 15 pounds when empty

943. You are at sea on a vessel that has a beam of 60 feet, and you calculate the period of roll to be 25 seconds. What is the vessel's metacentric height?

A. 0.8 ft.
B. 1.1 ft.
C. 1.4 ft.
D. 1.6 ft.

945. The color of rockets, shells, or rocket parachute flares used to indicate that the vessel is in distress and requires immediate assistance is _____.

A. white
B. green
C. red
D. yellow

947. When fighting an oil or gasoline fire in the bilge, which of the following should NOT be used?

A. Foam
B. Solid stream water nozzle
C. All-purpose nozzle
D. Carbon dioxide

948. Fires in combustible metals, such as sodium or magnesium, are classified as class _____.

A. A
B. B
C. C
D. D

950. Your vessel has taken a slight list from off-center loading of material on deck. The _____.

A. list should be easily removed
B. mean draft is affected
C. vessel may flop
D. vessel is trimmed

951. If a crewman suffers a second-degree burn on the arm, you should _____.

A. drain any blisters
B. apply antiseptic ointment
C. scrub the arm thoroughly to prevent infection
D. immerse the arm in cold water

952. Which is the proper method of determining whether a portable CO_2 fire extinguisher needs recharging?

A. Check the tag to see when the extinguisher was last charged.
B. Release a small amount of CO_2; if the CO_2 discharges, the extinguisher is acceptable.
C. Weigh the extinguisher and compare the weight against that stamped on the valve.
D. Recharge the extinguisher at least once each year.

953. You are at sea on a vessel that has a beam of 50 feet, and you calculate the period of roll to be 22 seconds. What is the vessel's metacentric height?

A. 0.8 ft.
B. 1.0 ft.
C. 1.2 ft.
D. 1.4 ft.

954. Which is the lifesaving signal for "This is the best place to land"?

A. Red star rocket
B. Orange smoke signal
C. Green star rocket
D. Horizontal motion of a flag

957. An engine compartment gasoline fire requires which type of extinguisher?

A. Carbon dioxide
B. Dry chemical
C. Foam
D. All of the above

958. Which substance might be subject to spontaneous combustion?

A. Coal
B. Scrap rubber
C. Leather
D. All of the above

960. Your vessel has just finished bunkering and has a small list due to improper distribution of the fuel oil. This list will cause _____.

A. a decrease in reserve buoyancy
B. a decrease in the maximum draft
C. the vessel to flop to port and starboard
D. None of the above

961. Safety is increased if _____.

A. extra line and wire are laid out on deck for emergency use
B. all lashings are made up, and the decks are clean and clear
C. power tools are kept plugged in for immediate use
D. spare parts are kept on deck for ready access

962. A carbon dioxide fire extinguisher should be recharged _____.

A. at least annually
B. whenever it is below its required weight
C. only if the extinguisher has been used
D. before every safety inspection

963. Your vessel has a displacement of 19,800 tons. It is 464 feet long, and has a beam of 64 feet. You have timed its full rolling period to be 21.0 seconds. What is your vessel's approximate GM?

A. 1.1 ft.
B. 1.3 ft.
C. 1.6 ft.
D. 1.8 ft.

965. What statement about immersion suits is TRUE?

A. Immersion suits should be worn while performing routine work on deck.
B. No stowage container for immersion suits may be capable of being locked.
C. During the annual maintenance, the front zipper should be lubricated using light machine oil or mineral oil.
D. Any tear or leak will render the suit unserviceable and it must be replaced.

967. Gasoline fuel tanks on small passenger vessels must be installed _____.

A. independent of the hull
B. on a level higher than the engine
C. in a cool and insulated place

D. so the fuel line to the engine leads from a shut-off valve at the bottom of the tank

968. Which condition is necessary for a substance to burn?

A. The temperature of the substance must be equal to or above its fire point.
B. The air must contain oxygen in sufficient quantity.
C. The mixture of vapors with air must be within the "explosive range."
D. All of the above

969. That center around which a vessel trims is called the _____.

A. tipping center
B. center of buoyancy
C. center of gravity
D. turning center

971. When should you first have any food or water after boarding a lifeboat or life raft?

A. After 12 hours
B. After 24 hours
C. Within 48 hours
D. Some food and water should be consumed immediately and then not until 48 hours later

972. Which statement concerning carbon dioxide is FALSE?

A. It displaces the oxygen in the air.
B. It cannot be seen.
C. It cannot be smelled.
D. It is safe to use near personnel in a confined space.

973. You are on a vessel that has a metacentric height of 1.0 foot and a beam of 40 feet. What can you expect the rolling period of the vessel to be?

A. 15.2 seconds
B. 15.9 seconds
C. 17.0 seconds
D. 17.6 seconds

974. On board small passenger vessels the minimum fill pipe size for a gasoline or diesel tank is _____.

A. 2-1/2 inches nominal pipe size
B. 1-1/2 inches nominal pipe size
C. Not specified by the Regulations

D. Large enough so it does not cause back-pressure and fuel spillage

976. Inflatable life rafts carried on passenger vessels must be annually _____.

A. overhauled by the ship's crew
B. sent to the Coast Guard for servicing
C. sent to the steamship company shore repair facility
D. sent to a Coast Guard approved service facility

977. Which type of fire is the foam (stored-pressure type) fire extinguisher effective on?

A. Classes A & B
B. Classes A & C
C. Classes B & C
D. All of the above

979. When should you first have any food or water after boarding a lifeboat or life raft?

A. After 12 hours
B. After 24 hours
C. Within 48 hours
D. Some food and water should be consumed immediately and then not until 48 hours later.

980. Assuming an even transverse distribution of weight in a vessel, which condition could cause a list?

A. Empty double bottoms and lower holds, and a heavy deck cargo
B. Flooding the forepeak to correct the vessel's trim
C. Having KG smaller than KM
D. Having a small positive righting arm

981. Oily rags stored in a pile that is open to the atmosphere are a hazard because they may _____.

A. deteriorate and give off noxious gasses
B. spontaneously heat and catch fire
C. attract lice and other vermin and serve as a breeding ground
D. None of the above

982. In continuous operation, the effective range of the 15 pound CO_2 extinguisher is limited to _____.

A. 2 to 4 feet
B. 3 to 8 feet

C. 9 to 12 feet
D. 10 to 15 feet

983. Your vessel has a metacentric height of 1.12 feet and a beam of 60 feet. Your average rolling period will be _____.

A. 20 seconds
B. 23 seconds
C. 25 seconds
D. 35 seconds

984. The lifesaving signal indicated by a horizontal motion of a white light or white flare means _____.

A. "Landing here highly dangerous"
B. "Negative"
C. "Avast hauling"
D. All of the above

986. According to Coast Guard Regulations (CFR 33), the shipboard Oil Pollution Emergency Plan must include _____.

A. all information ordinarily provided in the Oil Record Book
B. an explanation and purpose of the plan
C. a one-line schematic of the plan to be implemented
D. the operating instructions for any and all oily-water separators installed aboard the vessel

988. Which portable fire extinguisher should be used on a class C fire on board a vessel?

A. Carbon dioxide
B. Water (stored pressure)
C. Foam
D. Carbon tetrachloride

989. First-, second-, and third-degree burns are classified according to the _____.

A. area of the body burned
B. source of heat causing the burn
C. layers of skin affected
D. size of the burned area

990. If your vessel will list with equal readiness to either side, the list is most likely caused by _____.

A. negative GM
B. off-center weight
C. pocketing of free surface
D. excessive freeboard

991. Fire extinguishing agents used on Class C fires must be _____.

A. able to absorb heat
B. water based
C. nonconducting
D. nontoxic

992. On small passenger vessels gasoline tanks must be _____.

A. electrically bonded to a common ground
B. fitted with vertical baffle plates if the tank is longer than 30 inches in any horizontal dimension
C. built without flanged-up top edges
D. All of the above

993. If your vessel has a GM of one foot and a breadth of 50 feet, what will be your full rolling period?

A. 11 seconds
B. 15 seconds
C. 20 seconds
D. 22 seconds

994. The signal to guide vessels in distress which indicates "This is the best place to land" is the _____.

A. horizontal motion of a white flag
B. letter K in Morse code given by light
C. code flag S as a hoist
D. firing of a white star signal

996. What is the penalty for failure to enforce, or comply with, the vessel bridge-to-bridge radiotelephone regulations?

A. Civil penalty of no more than $500
B. Civil penalty of no more than $5,000
C. $5,000 fine and imprisonment for not more than one year, or both
D. $1,000 fine or imprisonment for not more than two years

997. Which fire-fighting agent is most effective at removing heat?

A. Water spray
B. Foam
C. Carbon dioxide
D. Dry chemical

998. Fire extinguishers of sizes III, IV, and V are designated as _____.

A. portable
B. semi-portable

C. fixed
D. disposable

1000. A vessel continually lists to one side and has a normal rolling period. Which statement is TRUE?

A. The vessel has negative GM.
B. The center of gravity is on the centerline.
C. The list can be corrected by reducing KM.
D. The vessel has asymmetrical weight distribution.

1002. How do you operate a portable CO_2 fire extinguisher?

A. Point the horn down.
B. Turn cylinder upside-down.
C. Break the rupture disc.
D. Pull pin, squeeze grip.

1003. You are on a vessel that has a metacentric height of 4 feet, and a beam of 50 feet. What can you expect the rolling period of the vessel to be?

A. 10.0 seconds
B. 10.5 seconds
C. 11.0 seconds
D. 11.5 seconds

1004. The lifesaving signal used to indicate "Landing here highly dangerous" is _____.

A. firing of a white star signal
B. firing of a red star signal
C. vertical motion of a red light
D. code letter "K" given by light or sound signaling apparatus

1006. An immersion suit must be equipped with a(n) _____.

A. air bottle for breathing
B. orange smoke canister
C. whistle, light and retroreflective material
D. sea dye marker

1007. What is the BEST conductor of electricity?

A. Carbon dioxide
B. Distilled water
C. Fresh water
D. Salt water

1008. A minor heat burn of the eye should be treated by _____.

A. gently flooding with water
B. warming the eye with moist warm packs
C. laying the person flat on his back
D. mineral oil drops directly on the eye

1011. Which vessel(s) is(are) required to comply with the vessel bridge-to-bridge radiotelephone regulations while navigating?

A. All towing vessels 25 feet or less in length
B. All passenger vessels of 50 gross tons or less, carrying one or more passengers
C. Power-driven vessels 20 meters in length or longer
D. An intermittently manned floating plant under the control of a dredge

1012. The discharge from a carbon dioxide fire extinguisher should be directed _____.

A. at the base of the flames
B. at the center of the flames
C. to the lee side of the flames
D. over the tops of the flames

1013. If it is impractical to use the fill line to sound the fuel tank, then the tank should be fitted with _____. (Small Passenger Vessel Regulations.)

A. a separate sounding tube or an installed marine type fuel gauge
B. An extra five-gallon tank for reserve fuel
C. A good air vent of sufficient diameter
D. A glass tube to visually observe the fuel

1014. Which signal would be used by a shore rescue unit to indicate "Landing here highly dangerous"?

A. The firing of a white star signal
B. Horizontal motion with a white flag
C. Vertical motion of a white light
D. Code letter "K" by blinker light

1016. What is the maximum length of time that distress flares are approved for?

A. 1-1/2 years
B. 2 years
C. 3-1/2 years
D. 5 years

1017. The extinguishing agent most likely to allow reignition of a fire is _____.

A. carbon dioxide
B. foam

C. water fog
D. water stream

1019. You are operating 10 miles offshore with three people aboard. What kind of survival craft must you carry?

A. An inflatable life raft with a coastal pack
B. A life float
C. An inflatable buoyant apparatus
D. No survival craft is required.

1020. Which vessels must comply with the vessel bridge-to-bridge radiotelephone regulations while navigating?

A. Towing vessels 25 feet in length or less
B. Passenger vessels of 100 gross tons or greater, carrying one or more passengers for hire
C. Power-driven vessels 12 meters or less in length
D. All of the above

1021. Which vessel(s) is(are) required to comply with the vessel bridge-to-bridge radiotelephone regulations while navigating?

A. Towing vessel 25 feet or less in length
B. Passenger vessel of 50 GT or less, carrying one or more passengers for hire
C. Power-driven vessels 12 meters or less in length, operating on inland waters
D. Dredges engaged in operations likely to restrict navigation of other vessels in or near a channel or fairway

1022. When fighting a fire on a bulkhead using a portable carbon dioxide extinguisher, the stream should be directed at the _____.

A. base of the flames, moving the horn from side to side, following the flames upward as they diminish
B. top of the flaming area, moving the horn from side to side, following the flames downward as they diminish
C. center of the flaming area, moving the horn vertically from top to bottom
D. bottom of the flaming area, moving the horn vertically to the top following the flames upward as they diminish

1023. Providing you are not in a special area, such as the Mediterranean or Red Sea, how many nautical miles from land must you be to throw packing materials that will float into the sea?

A. 3 nm
B. 6 nm
C. 12 nm
D. 25 nm

1024. The firing of a red star signal may mean _____.

A. "This is the best place to land"
B. "You are seen—assistance will be given as soon as possible"
C. "Tail block is made fast"
D. "Slack away"

1027. What is the most important characteristic of the extinguishing agent in fighting a class C fire?

A. Weight
B. Temperature
C. Electrical nonconductivity
D. Cost

1028. Symptoms of heat stroke are _____.

A. cold and moist skin, high body temperature
B. cold and dry skin, low body temperature
C. hot and moist skin, high body temperature
D. hot and dry skin, high body temperature

1029. Which vessel(s) is(are) required to comply with the vessel bridge-to-bridge radiotelephone regulations while navigating?

A. Towing vessel 26 feet in length or greater
B. Passenger vessels of 100 gross tons or greater, carrying one or more passengers for hire
C. Power-driven vessels 20 meters in length or greater
D. All of the above

1030. Which vessel(s) is(are) required to comply with the "Vessel Bridge-to-Bridge Radiotelephone Regulations" while navigating?

A. Towing vessels 25 feet or less in length, engaged in towing operations
B. Passenger vessel 50 gross tons or less, carrying passengers for hire
C. Dredges engaged in operations likely to restrict navigation of other vessels in or near a channel or fairway
D. An intermittently manned floating plant under the control of a dredge

1032. When used to fight fire, carbon dioxide _____.

A. is effective if used promptly on an oil fire
B. has a greater cooling effect than water
C. is lighter than air
D. is harmless to cargo and crew

1033. Your vessel has been in a collision. After assessing the damage, you begin down flooding. This will cause the KB to do what?

A. Fall
B. Remain stationary
C. Rise
D. Shift to the high side

1034. Which vessels must comply with the vessel bridge-to-bridge radiotelephone regulations while navigating?

A. All towing vessels 26 feet in length or greater
B. All passenger vessels less than 100 gross tons
C. All power-driven vessels 12 meters or less in length
D. All of the above

1036. Life preservers must be marked with the _____.

A. stowage space assigned
B. vessel's name
C. vessel's home port
D. maximum weight allowed

1037. What is the minimum size power-driven vessel, not engaged in towing, required to comply with the vessel bridge-to-bridge radiotelephone regulations?

A. 50 meters
B. 25 meters
C. 20 meters
D. 12 meters

1038. You are piloting a vessel, which is required to have a radiotelephone, on the navigable waters of the United States. You must _____.

A. maintain a listening watch and communicate in English
B. use the bridge-to-bridge VHF-FM designated frequency only to exchange navigational information or necessary tests
C. have on board an operator who holds a restricted radiotelephone operator permit

or higher license, as well as a FCC ship station license
D. All of the above

1039. On board small passenger vessels, fill lines and sounding pipes of gasoline tanks must extend directly_____.

A. to within one-half of their diameter from the bottom of the tank
B. To within one-half foot from the bottom of the tank
C. To the tank top
D. Midway between the top and bottom of the tank

1040. General requirements for a vessel's radiotelephone station log are that _____.

A. logs must be kept in an orderly manner
B. erasures are not allowed
C. it must identify the vessel's name and official number
D. All of the above

1042. Which danger exists to people when CO_2 is discharged into a small enclosed space?

A. Damaged eardrums
B. Electric shock
C. Frostbite
D. Respiratory arrest

1044. What is the lifesaving signal for "You are seen—Assistance will be given as soon as possible"?

A. Green star rocket
B. Red star rocket
C. Orange smoke signal
D. Horizontal motion of a flag

1046. On small passenger vessels a gasoline tank vent pipe must _____.

A. have a cross sectional area not less than that of 19 millimeters OD tubing.
B. be connected to the tank at its highest point
C. terminate in a U-bend as high above the weather deck as practicable
D. All of the above

1047. The main advantage of a steady stream of water on a class A fire is that it _____.

A. breaks up and cools the fire
B. protects the firefighting crew

C. removes the oxygen
D. washes the fire away

1050. A gasoline fuel tank vent on a small passenger vessel should terminate _____.

A. As close to the deck plates as possible
B. Below the waterline to eliminate the accumulation of explosive vapors
C. Midway between the fuel tank and the engine
D. On the hull exterior as high above the waterline as practicable and remote from any hull opening

1051. The fresh air intake of the inert gas system _____.

A. prevents the flue gas from falling below an oxygen content of 3%
B. allows the inert gas piping to be used for gas freeing the tanks
C. opens when there is excessive vacuum on the deck water seal
D. enables outside air to mix with and to cool the hot flue gasses

1052. The danger associated with using carbon dioxide in an enclosed space is _____.

A. frostbite
B. skin burns
C. asphyxiation
D. an explosive reaction

1053. Your vessel is damaged and listing to port. The rolling period is long, and the vessel will occasionally assume a starboard list. Which action should you take FIRST?

A. Fill an empty double bottom tank on the starboard side
B. Transfer all possible movable weights from port to starboard
C. Pump out ballast from the port and starboard double bottom tanks
D. Press up a slack centerline double bottom tank

1054. By day, the signal meaning "This is the best place to land" is a _____.

A. vertical motion of a red flag
B. vertical motion of a white flag or the arms
C. white smoke signal
D. white star rocket

1056. U.S.C.G. approved buoyant work

vests are considered to be items of safety equipment and may be worn by members of the crew _____.

A. in lieu of life preservers during fire drills
B. in lieu of life preservers during boat drills
C. in lieu of life preservers during an actual emergency
D. when carrying out duties near a weather deck's edge

1057. The primary method by which water spray puts out fires is by _____.

A. removing the oxygen
B. cooling the fire below the ignition temperature
C. removing combustible material
D. diluting combustible vapors

1059. Provided every effort is made to preserve body moisture content by avoiding perspiration, how long is it normally possible to survive without water?

A. Up to 3 days
B. 8 to 14 days
C. 15 to 20 days
D. 25 to 30 days

1061. What are the symptoms of sunstroke?

A. Temperature falls below normal, pulse is rapid and feeble, skin is cold and clammy.
B. Temperature is high, pulse is strong and rapid, skin is hot and dry.
C. Temperature is high, pulse is slow and feeble, skin is clammy.
D. Temperature falls below normal, pulse is rapid, skin is clammy.

1062. Weight is considered during the periodic required inspection and servicing of _____.

A. CO$_2$ (carbon dioxide) fire extinguishers
B. foam fire extinguishers
C. water (stored pressure) fire extinguishers
D. All of the above

1063. Gasoline tank vent lines on board small passenger vessels must be fitted with removable flame screens _____.

A. and 30 square inches of louvers
B. three inches in diameter with a check valve to prevent water from entering in heavy weather

C. three inches in circumference inside the fill pipe
D. consisting of a single screen of at least 30 X 30 mesh, corrosion resistant wire

1064. By day, the horizontal motion of a white flag, or arms extended horizontally, by a person on the beach indicates _____.

A. "Haul away"
B. "Tail block is made fast"
C. "Negative"
D. "Affirmative"

1066. Coast Guard approved buoyant work vests _____.

A. may be substituted for 10 percent of the required life preservers
B. should be stowed adjacent to lifeboats and emergency stations
C. may be used by boat crews and line handlers during lifeboat drills
D. should be used when carrying out duties near a weather deck's edge

1067. A large oil fire on the deck of a ship can be fought most effectively with _____.

A. dry chemical
B. foam
C. high-velocity fog
D. Water (cartridge-operated)

1068. The "flammable limits" of an atmosphere are the _____.

A. two temperatures between which an atmosphere will self-ignite
B. upper and lower percentage of vapor concentrations in an atmosphere which will burn if an ignition source is present
C. upper and lower pressures between which an atmosphere will not burn
D. two temperatures between which an atmosphere will burn if an ignition source is present

1070. On small passenger vessels, fuel lines may be made of _____.

A. plastic, rubber, or seamless steel tubing
B. stainless steel, iron, or brass
C. copper, plastic, stainless steel, or galvanized iron
D. annealed tubing of copper, nickel-copper, or copper nickel

1071. Aboard small passenger vessels, which material may be used for diesel fuel

line installations but not for gasoline fuel lines?

A. Annealed copper tubing
B. Nickel-copper tubing
C. Copper-nickel tubing
D. Seamless steel pipe or tubing

1074. Which one of the following signals is made at night by a lifesaving station to indicate "Landing here highly dangerous"?

A. Horizontal motion of a white light or flare
B. Vertical motion of a white light or flare
C. White star rocket
D. Vertical motion of a red light or flare

1076. The life jackets on all vessels shall be _____.

A. inspected weekly
B. worn at all times
C. readily available
D. tested yearly

1077. A vessel's KG is determined by _____.

A. dividing the total longitudinal moment summation by displacement
B. dividing the total vertical moment summation by displacement
C. multiplying the MT1 by the longitudinal moments
D. subtracting LCF from LCB

1080. A vessel to which Annex V to MARPOL 73/78 applies is located in a MARPOL designated special area, 14 nautical miles from nearest land. What type of garbage is permitted to be discharged?

A. Paper products
B. Glass ground to less than 1"
C. Metal ground to less than 1"
D. Food waste

1081. All of the following are part of the fire triangle EXCEPT _____.

A. heat
B. oxygen
C. fuel
D. electricity

1083. On board small passenger vessels, fittings used in a gasoline supply line must be _____.

A. made of non-ferrous metal, and be a flare or non-bite flareless type
B. an interlocking type
C. a silver-soldered type
D. an asbestos covered type

1084. On small passenger vessels, what type of devices are required at both the tank and engine connections of all internal combustion engine fuel lines?

A. Clean-out plates
B. Fuel gauges
C. Drain valves
D. Shut-off valves

1086. Required lifesaving equipment on existing vessels may be continued in use on the vessel if _____.

A. kept on board no more than 2 years
B. inspected and serviced every 6 months
C. destroyed if more than 5 years old
D. maintained in good and serviceable condition

1087. A combination or all-purpose nozzle produces _____.

A. low-velocity fog only
B. a solid stream only
C. a solid stream and foam
D. a solid stream and fog

1088. The flash point of a liquid means the temperature _____.

A. at which a liquid will give off flammable vapors
B. at which a liquid will burn steadily
C. at which a liquid will explode
D. that a liquid must reach before it will flow readily

1089. During counterflooding to correct a severe list aggravated by an off-center load, your vessel suddenly takes a list or trim to the opposite side. You should _____.

A. continue counterflooding in the same direction
B. continue counterflooding, but in the opposite direction
C. immediately stop counterflooding
D. deballast from the low side

1093. On small passenger vessels, which device(s) must be fitted to a fuel line's tank connection?

A. A fuel strainer
B. A shut-off valve
C. A tubular glass gauge to indicate the fuel level
D. All of the above

1094. A small craft advisory forecasts winds of up to what speed?

A. 16 kts.
B. 24 kts.
C. 33 kts.
D. 48 kts.

1097. Foam extinguishes a fire by _____.

A. shutting off the air supply
B. cooling the fuel to below ignition temperature
C. dispersing the fuel
D. removing the source of ignition

1098. Which statement is TRUE concerning the "flash point" of a substance?

A. It is lower than the ignition temperature.
B. It is the temperature at which a substance will spontaneously ignite.
C. It is the temperature at which a substance, when ignited, will continue to burn.
D. It is the temperature at which the released vapors will fall within the explosive range.

1099. On small passenger vessels, shut-off valves must be installed on both gasoline and diesel fuel supply lines _____.

A. at the tank and the engine end of the fuel line
B. outside the engineroom on the fill and vent lines
C. only at the tank end of the fuel line
D. only at the engine end of the fuel line

1101. A crew member has suffered frostbite to the toes of the right foot. Which is NOT an acceptable first aid measure?

A. Rub the toes briskly.
B. Elevate the foot slightly.
C. Rewarm rapidly.
D. Give aspirin or other medication for pain if necessary.

1103. A vessel is "listed" when it is _____.

A. inclined due to an off-center weight
B. inclined due to the wind
C. down by the head

D. down by the stern

1104. When there is a small craft advisory winds are predicted up to _____.

A. 15 knots
B. 24 knots
C. 33 knots
D. 42 knots

1106. On small passenger vessels, when may a flexible hose be used in gasoline or diesel fuel lines?

A. In diesel installations only
B. In gasoline installations only
C. In both diesel and gasoline installations
D. In neither diesel nor gasoline installations

1107. In the production of chemical foam by a continuous-type generator _____.

A. the maximum water pressure to be used is 50 psi
B. the speed of foam production is slower at lower water temperatures
C. each pound of foam powder produces about 800 gallons of chemical foam
D. fresh water only should be used

1108. The vapor pressure of a substance _____.

A. increases with the temperature
B. decreases as temperature increases
C. is not affected by temperature
D. may increase or decrease as the temperature rises

1109. On small passenger vessels, drains or outlets for drawing off diesel fuel from water traps or strainers _____.

A. must be located at the lowest portion of the tank
B. must have only a gravity-forced flow
C. must be extended to an external area of the hull
D. are permitted

1111. On small passenger vessels, outlets in fuel lines are permitted _____.

A. to tap fuel for cleaning parts and engine wash down
B. for inspection purposes only
C. to bleed fuel lines
D. under no circumstances in gasoline installations

1114. The National Weather Service differentiates between small craft, gale, whole gale, and hurricane warnings by the _____.

A. amount of rain forecasted
B. wave heights forecasted
C. amount of cloud cover forecasted
D. wind speed forecasted

1117. Production of mechanical foam by a portable in-line foam proportioner _____.

A. increases the size of foam bubbles formed
B. increases the rate of foam production
C. improves the extinguishing properties of foam
D. gives the nozzleman more freedom of movement, since it can be placed anywhere in the hose line

1118. The volatility of a flammable liquid is indicated by its _____.

A. ignition temperature
B. flash point
C. flammable range
D. conversion index

1119. A fill pipe for a gasoline tank on board a small passenger vessel must be _____.

A. arranged so neither liquid gasoline nor its vapors can overflow or escape inside the vessel
B. terminated on the weather deck and extend to within one-half of its diameter from the bottom of the tank
C. fitted with a suitably marked watertight deckplate or screw cap
D. All of the above

1123. On small passenger vessels, all spaces containing gasoline-powered machinery or gasoline storage tanks must be ventilated with _____.

A. mechanical air supply fans and natural exhaust
B. natural air supply and mechanical exhaust fans
C. cowls and scoops which can be closed during foul weather
D. air conditioning to control moisture

1124. Spaces containing gasoline-powered machinery or gasoline storage tanks on small passenger vessels should have ventilator ducts that extend to the bilges

because _____.

A. air is heavier than gas fumes
B. oil and water mix there
C. it prevents air from entering or leaving the space
D. Gasoline vapors are heavier than air, tend to settle in the bilges, and create an explosion hazard

1126. Aboard small passenger vessels which type(s) of ventilation must be provided for enclosed spaces containing gasoline engines or gasoline fuel tanks?

A. Natural supply and mechanical exhaust
B. At least one opening to the exterior of the hull
C. Mechanical supply and natural exhaust
D. Any of the above

1127. Compared to the amount of concentrated foam liquid used, the amount of low expansion mechanical foam produced is

_____.

A. 97 times greater
B. 94 times greater
C. 10 times greater
D. 2 times greater

1128. Most small passenger vessels have an auxiliary steering arrangement. According to the regulations, which is acceptable as a substitute for the auxiliary steering system?

A. A threefold purchase, rove to advantage
B. A spare rudder, stowed so it can be readily mounted
C. A suitable hand tiller, approved by the OCMI
D. All of the above

1131. If you observe any situation which presents a safety or pollution hazard during fuel transfer operations, what action should you take FIRST?

A. Close the valves at the transfer manifold
B. Notify the person in charge of the shore facility
C. Shut down the transfer operation
D. Sound the fire alarm

1132. According to 46 CFR Subchapter T, how long should exhaust blowers be operated in enclosed spaces containing gasoline powered machinery before starting the engine?

A. For at least four to five minutes
B. Long enough to achieve a minimum of two complete air changes
C. Long enough to achieve at least one complete change of air
D. No fixed amount, but the blower should run until you don't smell any gas

1133. If you must enter water on which there is an oil fire, you should _____.

A. protect your life preserver by holding it above your head
B. enter the water on the windward side of the vessel
C. keep both hands in front of your face to break the water surface when diving head first
D. wear very light clothing

1134. On board small passenger vessels, ducts for compartments which contain gasoline powered machinery or gasoline storage tanks _____.

A. must not allow any appreciable vapor flow except through their normal openings
B. must be of rigid, permanent construction
C. must lead as directly as possible and be properly fastened and supported
D. All of the above

1135. Which statement about the bilge piping system of "T-Boats" that are more than 26 feet in length is NOT correct?

A. Each watertight compartment must have its own bilge suction line or pump
B. Each space's bilge suction connection to a manifold must have stop and check valves, or a stop-check valve
C. All bilge piping must be at least 2" inside-diameter brass pipe
D. Bilge suction strainers must have an open area not less than three times the area of the bilge pipe

1137. One gallon of low expansion foam solution will produce about _____.

A. 10 gallons of foam
B. 25 gallons of foam
C. 100 gallons of foam
D. 500 gallons of foam

1138. What is LEAST likely to cause ignition of fuel vapors?

A. Static electricity
B. An open running electric motor

C. Loose wiring
D. Explosion proof lights

1139. You are at the helm of a sloop-rigged sailing vessel under sail on the port tack, on a beam reach, with all appropriate sails set and properly trimmed. You are instructed to "head up quickly." To utilize your sails to assist with the turn, you should _____.

A. slack the main sheet
B. slack the main outhaul
C. trim the foreguy
D. slack the jib sheet

1143. For pumping the bilges, a 54 foot long "T-Boat," which is not a ferry, but is certificated to carry 30 passengers, must be fitted with at least _____.

A. one fixed power pump and one portable hand pump
B. one fixed hand pump and one portable hand pump
C. two portable hand pumps
D. either "A" or "B"

1144. Aboard a 60 foot long small passenger vessel (other than a ferry) which is certificated to carry 33 persons, the minimum capacity required per bilge pump is _____.

A. 10 gallons per minute
B. 19 gallons per minute
C. 38 gallons per minute
D. 50 gallons per minute

1147. In addition to a portable hand-operated bilge pump, a 55 foot long ferry must have a fixed power operated bilge pump capable of pumping at least _____.

A. 5 GPM
B. 10 GPM
C. 25 GPM
D. 50 GPM

1148. Spontaneous combustion is most likely to occur in _____.

A. rags soaked in linseed oil
B. overloaded electrical circuits
C. dirty swabs and cleaning gear
D. partially loaded fuel tanks

1149. If the metacentric height is small, a vessel will _____.

A. be tender

B. have a quick and rapid motion
C. be stiff
D. yaw

1151. Treatment of sunstroke consists principally of _____.

A. cooling, removing to shaded area, and lying down
B. bathing with rubbing alcohol
C. drinking ice water
D. All of the above

1152. Hand tillers are only accepted as an auxiliary means of steering if _____.

A. they are at least 6 feet long
B. they are not operated through a reduction gear
C. they are found satisfactory by the cognizant OCMI
D. Both A and C above

1153. According to 46 CFR Subchapter T, rigid plastic and other non-metallic piping materials _____.

A. may replace metal pipe or tubing in any installation
B. may not be used on inspected vessels
C. may only be used in non-vital systems
D. are preferable to steel pipe

1154. On a small passenger vessel, backfire flame arrestors are installed on a/an _____.

A. oil fired turbine or reciprocating steam engine
B. turbocharged diesel engine
C. natural gas (propane) engine
D. gasoline powered engine

1158. Spontaneous combustion is caused by _____.

A. an outside heat source heating a substance until it ignites
B. conduction of heat through a wall of material to the substance
C. chemical action within a substance
D. All of the above

1161. You are approaching another vessel and see that she has the signal flag "A" hoisted. What should you do?

A. Give the vessel a wide berth as she is carrying dangerous goods.

B. Attempt to call the vessel on VHF radiotelephone because she is disabled.
C. Stop your vessel instantly.
D. Slow your vessel and keep well clear because she has a diver down.

1163. Individual wires, used in systems greater than 50 volts, _____.

A. should be supported at 24 inch intervals with plastic tie wraps
B. should never be located in a tank
C. must be installed in conduit
D. All of the above

1168. What is the maximum oxygen content below which flaming combustion will no longer occur?

A. 1%
B. 10%
C. 15%
D. 21%

1173. On small passenger vessels all connections to electrical conductors MUST be _____.

A. made within enclosures
B. served and parcelled with the lay, turned and wormed the other way
C. installed only by a licensed marine electrician
D. inspected annually by the USCG

1174. In general, batteries aboard small passenger vessels should be _____.

A. as high above the bilge as practicable
B. stowed in well-ventilated spaces to allow dissipation of any gases generated
C. accessible for maintenance and removal
D. All of the above

1178. The lowest temperature required to cause self-sustained combustion of a substance independent of any outside source of ignition is called _____.

A. explosive range
B. flash point
C. ignition temperature
D. combustion temperature

1184. If an inflatable life raft is to be released manually, where should the operating cord be attached before throwing the raft overboard?

A. Do not attach the cord to anything but throw it overboard with the raft container.
B. Attach the cord to a fixed object on the ship.
C. You should stand on the cord.
D. Attach the cord to the special padeye on the "raft davit launcher."

1187. A self-contained breathing apparatus is used to _____.

A. make underwater repairs to barges
B. determine if the air in a tank is safe for men
C. enter areas that may contain dangerous fumes or lack oxygen
D. resuscitate an unconscious person

1188. The most effective way to apply a foam stream if the fire is on deck or is a running fire, is to direct the stream _____.

A. onto the surface of the burning liquid
B. ahead of the burning liquid and bounce it on the fire
C. at the base of the burning liquid in a sweeping motion
D. just above the surface of the burning liquid

1191. According to the T-Boat regulations the reason for providing adequate ventilation for a battery storage area is to prevent _____.

A. accumulation of carbon dioxide gas that chokes the battery
B. accumulation of explosive and toxic gases the battery can generate
C. mildew or dry rot in the battery box
D. battery failure including battery case meltdown caused by excessive heat

1193. On small passenger vessels, spaces containing batteries require good ventilation because it _____.

A. adds as much as 2 volts to battery performance
B. supplies extra nitrogen for the battery
C. helps dissipate flammable gas accumulations
D. allows less soda water to be used in the diodes

1194. Which operation should be done when launching an inflatable life raft by hand?

A. Open the life raft casing.
B. Turn the valve on the CO_2 cylinder to start inflation.
C. Make sure the operating cord is secured to the vessel before throwing it over the side.
D. After inflation, detach operating cord from life raft.

1196. The knife on an inflatable life raft will always be located _____.

A. in one of the equipment bags
B. in a special pocket near the forward entrance
C. on a cord hanging from the canopy
D. in a pocket on the first aid kit

1197. A squeeze-grip type carbon-dioxide portable fire-extinguisher has been partially discharged. It should be _____.

A. replaced in its proper location if weight loss is no more than 15%
B. replaced in its proper location if weight loss is no more than 25%
C. replaced in its proper location regardless of weight
D. labeled empty and recharged as soon as possible

1198. Lead-acid batteries used aboard "T-Boats" must have terminal connections that are _____.

A. the spring slip style
B. a permanent type
C. located so as to be easily greased
D. temporarily clamped on the top of the battery

1199. To prevent damage by and to storage batteries aboard small passenger vessels they should be located _____.

A. in trays constructed of material that is resistant to the electrolyte
B. so as to prevent movement when the vessel pitches and rolls
C. in a well-ventilated area
D. All of the above

1201. While taking on fuel oil, the transfer hose leaks causing a sheen on the water. You should _____.

A. apply dispersants to the sheen
B. repair the leak with duct tape
C. reduce the rate of transfer

D. shut down operations

1204. Generally, when lifting an inflatable life raft back aboard ship you would use the _____.

A. towing bridle
B. main weather cover
C. external lifelines
D. righting strap

1205. On board small passenger vessels, storage batteries containing an electrolyte must be set in trays constructed of _____.

A. a fireproof material
B. a material resistant to damage by the electrolyte
C. a porous material that permits drainage of any acid overflow
D. suitably strong to hold the weight of the batteries

1206. Inflatable life rafts are provided with a _____.

A. knife
B. towing connection
C. lifeline
D. All of the above

1207. Which extinguishing agent is most effective on a mattress fire?

A. CO_2
B. Foam
C. Dry Chemical
D. Water

1208. A vessel aground may have negative GM since the _____.

A. decrease in KM is equal to the loss of draft
B. virtual rise of G is directly proportional to the remaining draft
C. lost buoyancy method is used to calculate KM, and KB is reduced
D. displacement lost acts at the point where the ship is aground

1209. According to 46 CFR Subchapter T the purpose of fuses in electric wiring is to _____.

A. allow for cutting out branch circuits
B. prevent overloading the circuits
C. reduce voltage to the branch circuits
D. permit the use of smaller wiring for lighting circuits

1211. A crew member suffering from hypothermia should be given _____.

A. a small dose of alcohol
B. treatment for shock
C. a large meal
D. a brisk rub down

1212. Ambient air, which you normally breathe, contains what percent of oxygen?

A. 6%
B. 10%
C. 15%
D. 21%

1213. When a wind force causes a vessel to heel to a static angle, the _____.

A. centers of buoyancy and gravity are in the same vertical line
B. righting moment equals the wind-heeling moment
C. center of buoyancy remains the same
D. deck-edge immersion occurs

1214. An inflatable life raft should be lifted back aboard the ship by using _____.

A. the single hook at the top of the raft
B. two lines passed under the raft
C. the towing bridle
D. All of the above

1215. According to the regulations for small passenger vessels, fuses and circuit breakers are used in electrical circuits to _____.

A. keep equipment from shutting off unexpectedly
B. prevent voltage fluctuations
C. keep the circuit from becoming overloaded or overheated
D. make the operator inspect his wiring periodically after the fuses blow

1216. After launching, an inflatable raft should be kept dry inside by _____.

A. opening the automatic drain plugs
B. draining the water pockets
C. using the electric bilge pump
D. using the bailers and cellulose sponge

1217. Which types of portable fire extinguishers are designed for use on electrical fires?

A. Dry chemical and carbon dioxide

B. Foam (stored pressure) and soda-acid
C. Carbon dioxide and foam (stored pressure)
D. Dry chemical and soda-acid

1218. To safely enter a compartment where CO_2 has been released from a fixed extinguishing system, you should _____.

A. wear a canister type gas mask
B. test the air with an Orsat apparatus
C. test the air with a pure air indicator
D. wear a self-contained breathing apparatus

1219. 46 CFR Subchapter T requires that rigid plastic or other non-metallic piping _____.

A. only be used in non-vital systems
B. not be used in gasoline or diesel fuel systems
C. have approved metallic fittings and cut-off valves where it penetrates a watertight deck or bulkhead
D. All of the above

1223. The survival craft carried aboard a commercial fishing vessel must safely accommodate _____.

A. all of the people aboard
B. the number of people required by the certificate of inspection
C. the entire crew
D. None of the above are correct.

1224. In order to retrieve an inflatable life raft and place it on deck, you should heave on the _____.

A. lifelines
B. righting strap
C. sea anchor
D. towing bridle

1226. For what purpose may gasoline be used on small passenger vessels?

A. Heating
B. Lighting
C. Cooking
D. None of the above

1227. Which type of portable fire extinguishers is NOT designed for use on flammable liquid fires?

A. Foam (stored-pressure)
B. Water (cartridge-operated)

C. Dry chemical
D. Carbon dioxide

1228. When approaching a fire from leeward, you should shield firefighters from the fire by using _____.

A. low-velocity fog
B. high-velocity fog
C. a straight stream of water
D. foam spray

1229. Which T-Boat must be fitted with a suitable compass?

A. A vessel in river service
B. A vessel operating on a short, restricted route on lakes, bays, and sounds
C. A vessel engaged in ocean or coastwise service
D. The regulations do not require a compass on any vessel

1231. A "T-Boat" accident resulting in loss of life, serious injury or more than $25,000 property damage must be reported to _____.

A. the Maritime Administration (MARAD)
B. the Coast Guard
C. the owner or his insurance agent
D. All of the above

1233. The owner, agent, Master or person-in-charge of a small passenger vessel involved in a marine casualty is NOT required to notify the Coast Guard in cases where there is _____.

A. property damage less than $25,000
B. no injury which requires more than first aid treatment
C. death or injury to a shipyard worker or harbor worker not resulting from the vessel casualty
D. All of the above

1235. Which procedure should NOT be done for a person who has fainted?

A. Revive the person with smelling salts.
B. Loosen the clothing.
C. Lay the person horizontally.
D. Give pain reliever.

1236. Inflatable life rafts are provided with _____.

A. a portable radio
B. an oil lantern

C. canned milk
D. a towing connection

1237. Portable-foam fire extinguishers are designed for use on what classes of fires?

A. A and B
B. A and C
C. B and C
D. A, B, and C

1238. When attempting to enter a compartment containing a fire, which method of applying water is best?

A. High-velocity fog stream directed toward the overhead
B. Straight stream directed into the center of the fire
C. Sweeping the compartment with a fog stream
D. Solid stream directed toward the overhead

1242. The bosun has thrown the life raft into the water before abandoning the vessel. The operating cord _____.

A. serves as a sea painter
B. detaches from the life raft automatically
C. is used to rig the boarding ladder
D. is cut immediately as it is of no further use

1244. The painter on a rigid life raft must have a length sufficient to reach the lightest waterline plus an additional _____.

A. 5 meters (16 feet)
B. 10 meters (31 feet)
C. 15 meters (50 feet)
D. 20 meters (66 feet)

1245. The Master of a small passenger vessel fitted with loading doors must ensure that the doors are closed, watertight and secured _____.

A. at all times when underway unless operating on protected or partially protected waters
B. when leaving the dock
C. when loading cargo
D. at all times, at the dock or underway when the loading door is not actually being used for passage

1246. Inflatable life rafts are provided with _____.

A. a Very pistol
B. a towing connection
C. a portable radio
D. canned milk

1247. The BEST method of applying foam to a fire is to _____.

A. spray directly on the base of the fire
B. flow the foam down a nearby vertical surface
C. sweep the fire with the foam
D. spray directly on the surface of the fire

1248. In the event of fire in a machinery space, _____.

A. the fixed carbon dioxide system should be used only when all other means of extinguishment have failed
B. the fixed carbon dioxide system should be used immediately, as it is the most efficient means of extinguishment
C. water in any form should not be used as it will spread the fire
D. the space should be opened 5 minutes after flooding CO_2 to prevent injury to personnel

1249. Which area is designated a special area by Annex V to MARPOL 73/78?

A. Gulf of Saint Lawrence
B. Sargasso Sea
C. Red Sea
D. Great Lakes

1251. The proper stimulant for an unconscious person is _____.

A. tea
B. coffee
C. whiskey and water
D. ammonia inhalant

1252. When fighting a fire with a portable dry chemical fire extinguisher, the stream should be directed _____.

A. over the top of the flames
B. off a bulkhead into the fire
C. in front of the fire
D. at the base of the fire

1255. The color of the signal flare sent up by a submarine indicating that a torpedo has been fired in a training exercise is _____.

A. white

B. green
C. yellow
D. red

1256. The water pockets located on the underside of inflatable life rafts _____.

A. stow rainwater; these 4 spaces do not take up valuable space
B. act as stabilizers by filling with sea water as soon as the raft is inflated and upright
C. hold the freshwater required by regulation to be provided in the raft when packed
D. None of the above

1257. Providing you are not sailing in the Red Sea or another special area as listed in ANNEX V of MARPOL, how many miles from land must you be to throw garbage including bottles, rags, and glass that has not been ground up into the sea?

A. 3 nm
B. 6 nm
C. 12 nm
D. 25 nm

1259. When an autopilot is being used aboard small passenger vessels, who must make or supervise the changeover from automatic to manual steering and vice versa?

A. A licensed state or federal pilot
B. A certified quartermaster
C. The Master or Mate on watch
D. A qualified Engineer

1261. On small passenger vessels, when must watchmen patrol throughout the vessel to guard against and give alarm in case of fire or other danger?

A. At all times outside normal work hours
B. At all times when the vessel is underway
C. During the nighttime when the vessel carries overnight passengers
D. When the rest of the crew is asleep

1262. Which portable fire extinguisher is normally recharged in a shore facility?

A. Dry chemical (cartridge-operated)
B. Water (cartridge-operated)
C. Water (pump tank)
D. Carbon dioxide

1263. When chipping rust on a vessel, the MOST important piece of safety gear is _____.

A. a hard hat
B. gloves
C. goggles
D. a long sleeve shirt

1264. The operating cord on an inflatable life raft should be renewed by _____.

A. removing the top half of the shell, cutting the line at its source, and renewing completely
B. cutting the line where it enters the case and replacing that portion
C. leaving the original line and tying another one to it so the two lines will take the strain
D. an approved servicing facility ashore

1265. The Master of a small passenger vessel must conduct sufficient drills and give sufficient instruction as necessary _____.

A. At each crew change
B. Every week
C. Every month
D. To ensure that all crew members are familiar with their duties during emergencies

1266. A lifeline must be connected to the life raft _____.

A. at the bow
B. at the stern
C. in the middle
D. all around

1268. Where must the draft marks be placed on a small passenger vessel?

A. On each side of the stem
B. Near the stern post or rudder post
C. At each end of the vessel
D. All of the above

1269. Life floats and buoyant apparatus used aboard small passenger vessels shall be marked in clearly legible letters and numbers _____.

A. with the parent vessels name in 3" high letters and the number of persons allowed with 1-1/2" high numbers
B. by a Coast Guard inspector after inspecting the equipment
C. by the American Bureau of Shipping (ABS), another recognized, authorized classification society or the vessel's underwriters
D. by all of the above

1272. When approaching a fire from windward, you should shield firefighters from the fire by using _____.

A. low-velocity fog
B. high-velocity fog
C. a straight stream of water
D. foam spray

1274. On inflatable life rafts, the operating cord should be renewed by _____.

A. cutting the old line off and renewing same
B. an approved servicing facility ashore
C. opening the case and replacing the entire line
D. one of the ship's officers

1275. A documented vessel's name is marked on a clearly visible exterior area of both sides of the bow and on the stern in block letters not less than _____.

A. 6 inches in height
B. 5 inches in height
C. 4 inches in height
D. 3 inches in height

1276. The lights on the outside of the canopy on an inflatable life raft operate _____.

A. by turning the globe clockwise
B. by a switch at each light
C. by a light sensor
D. automatically when the raft is inflated

1277. When possible, what is the FIRST step in fighting an engine fuel-pump fire which results from a broken fuel line?

A. Secure all engine room doors, hatches, and vents.
B. Close the fuel line valve.
C. Check the spread of the fire with foam.
D. Cast the barge off the wharf.

1278. An extinguishing agent which effectively cools, dilutes combustible vapors, removes oxygen, and provides a heat and smoke screen is _____.

A. carbon dioxide
B. Halon 1301
C. dry chemical
D. water fog

1279. On a documented small passenger vessel, what information must be permanently affixed in block-type letters and/or

numerals to the main beam or other clearly visible interior structural part of the hull?

A. The vessel's name and gross tonnage
B. The vessel's official number
C. Draft markings
D. The vessel's name and home port

1281. You are in the process of righting an inflatable life raft that has inflated in an upside down position. Which statement is TRUE?

A. As the raft flips to the upright position, you will be thrown clear.
B. After the raft is in the upright position on top of you, dive down to prevent your life preservers from fouling as you come out.
C. Swim out from under the raft in a face up position to keep your life preservers clear of the raft.
D. You should remove your life preservers before attempting to right an inflatable raft.

1282. When approaching a fire from leeward you should shield fire fighters from the fire by using _____.

A. a straight stream of water
B. foam spray
C. high-velocity fog
D. low-velocity fog

1284. The operating cord on an inflatable life raft also serves as a _____.

A. lifeline
B. painter
C. drogue
D. marker

1286. The inside light in an inflatable life raft is turned on _____.

A. automatically as the life raft inflates
B. with a switch near the boarding handle
C. at night because the light has a photo-sensitive switch
D. by screwing the bulb in after the raft is inflated

1288. Which extinguishing agent is the best for use on electrical fires?

A. Foam
B. CO_2
C. Dry chemical
D. Water fog

1289. An undocumented vessel with 10 people aboard and operating 25 miles off the seacoast must carry a survival craft of the _____.

A. inflatable buoyant apparatus type
B. buoyant apparatus type
C. life float type
D. Any of the above types are acceptable.

1292. What is the MOST important consideration when determining how to fight an electrical fire?

A. Whether the fire is in machinery or passenger spaces
B. Danger of shock to personnel
C. The amount of toxic fumes created by the extinguisher
D. Maintaining electrical power

1294. According to the "T-Boat" regulations, the permanent marks placed on each side of a vessel forward, aft, and amidships to indicate the maximum allowable draft and trim are called _____.

A. loading marks
B. the air draft
C. depth marks
D. Plimsoll marks

1296. Hand holds or straps on the underside of an inflatable life raft are provided _____.

A. to right the raft if it capsizes
B. to carry the raft around on deck
C. for crewmen to hang on to
D. to hang the raft for drying

1297. A small passenger vessel of not more than 65 feet in length must have a collision bulkhead if it _____.

A. operates on exposed waters
B. carries more than 49 passengers
C. is more than 40 feet in length and operates on partially exposed waters
D. All of the above

1298. If a powdered aluminum fire is being fought, the correct extinguishing agent would be _____.

A. dry powder
B. water fog
C. CO_2
D. steam

1299. In reviving a person who has been overcome by gas fumes, what would you AVOID doing?

A. Giving stimulants
B. Prompt removal of the patient from the suffocating atmosphere
C. Applying artificial respiration and massage
D. Keeping the patient warm and comfortable

1301. A vessel to which Annex V to MARPOL 73/78 applies is 24 nautical miles from the nearest land. Which type of garbage is prohibited from being discharged?

A. Glass
B. Crockery
C. Metal
D. Dunnage

1302. A class B fire is most successfully fought by _____.

A. preventing oxygen from reaching the burning material
B. cooling the burning material below its ignition temperature
C. using the extinguishing agent to make the burning material fire-resistant
D. using the extinguishing agent to absorb the heat

1303. According to 46 CFR Subchapter T, where practicable carburetor drip collectors should drain to _____.

A. the engine air intakes
B. the fuel tanks
C. a separate pipe leading to the bilges
D. a suitable absorbant material

1304. The painter of an inflatable life raft should be _____.

A. free running on the deck
B. faked out next to the case
C. secured to a permanent object on deck
D. stowed near the raft

1306. Water pockets on the underside of an inflatable life raft are for _____.

A. catching rain water
B. stability
C. easy drainage
D. maneuverability

1307. Firefighting foam is only effective when the foam _____.

A. penetrates to the bottom of the fire
B. is kept saturated with low-velocity water fog
C. mixes with the burning fuel oil
D. completely covers the top of the burning liquid

1308. What would be the most effective agent to use to extinguish a fire in drums of flammable liquids stowed on the weather deck of a vessel?

A. Carbon dioxide
B. Foam
C. Steam
D. Water fog

1309. On small passenger vessels which type of internal combustion engine carburetor does not require a drip collector?

A. Updraft
B. Two barrel
C. Four barrel
D. Downdraft

1311. Which statement about pneumatic chipping tools is TRUE?

A. The operator must wear safety goggles or glasses.
B. The equipment must be grounded to prevent shock hazard.
C. The chipping mechanism is made of a non-sparking material that is safe to use near explosive atmospheres.
D. The needles of the needle-type chipping gun must be replaced when they have been blunted more than 1/2 of their diameter.

1312. The best method of extinguishing a class A fire is to _____.

A. remove oxygen from the area
B. cool fuel below ignition temperature
C. smother with CO_2
D. smother fire with foam

1314. Under normal conditions a life raft is released from its cradle by _____.

A. cutting the restraining strap
B. unscrewing the turnbuckle on the back of the cradle
C. lifting one end of the raft
D. pushing the plunger on the center of the hydrostatic release

1317. The most effective way of applying carbon dioxide from a portable extinguisher to a fire is by _____.

A. forming a cloud cover over the flames
B. directing the gas at the base of the flames in a slow sweeping motion
C. discharging the carbon dioxide into the heart of the flames
D. bouncing the discharge off an adjacent bulkhead just above the burning surface

1318. The most effective fire extinguishing agent to use on burning linen is _____.

A. water
B. carbon dioxide
C. dry chemical
D. foam

1319. Where should muster lists be posted?

A. In crew's accommodation spaces
B. On the navigating bridge
C. In the engine room
D. All of the above

1320. Fire extinguishers on inspected vessels are numbered by size I through V, with I being _____.

A. used for electrical fires only
B. the smallest
C. the most accessible
D. the most effective

1324. A hydrostatic release mechanism for a life raft _____.

A. must be wet before it will release
B. should be kept in a watertight cover except in an emergency
C. will inflate the raft in its cradle if operated manually
D. must be submerged to a certain depth to release automatically

1326. All inflatable life rafts have _____.

A. safety straps from the overhead
B. built in seats
C. releasing hooks at each end
D. water stabilizing pockets

1327. If you are forced to abandon ship in a life raft, your course of action should be to _____.

A. remain in the immediate vicinity
B. head for the nearest land

C. head for the closest sea-lanes
D. let the persons in the boat vote on what to do

1328. Any extinguishing agent used on a Class C fire must have which important property?

A. Cooling ability
B. Leaves no residue
C. Penetrating power
D. Nonconductivity

1332. An important step in fighting any electrical fire is to _____.

A. stop ventilation
B. stop the vessel
C. de-energize the circuit
D. apply water to extinguish the fire

1334. An inflatable life raft should be manually released from its cradle by _____.

A. cutting the straps that enclose the container
B. removing the rubber sealing strip from the container
C. loosening the turnbuckle on the securing strap
D. pushing the button on the hydrostatic release

1335. What prevents an inflated life raft from being pulled under by a vessel which sinks in water over 100 feet in depth?

A. The hydrostatic release
B. Nothing
C. A Rottmer release
D. The weak link in the painter line

1336. A feature of an inflatable raft which helps keep people stationary in rough weather is _____.

A. lashings on the floor of the raft for the passenger's feet
B. straps from the overhead
C. lifelines on the inside of the raft
D. ridges in the floor of the raft

1337. It is desirable to have screens on the vents of potable water tanks to _____.

A. filter the incoming air
B. prevent explosions
C. prevent backups
D. stop insects from entering

1338. Regular foam can be used on all but which flammable liquid?

A. Motor gasoline
B. Jet fuel
C. Crude petroleum
D. Alcohol

1340. When compared to a high-expansion foam, a low-expansion foam will _____.

A. be dryer
B. be lighter
C. be less heat resistant
D. not cling to vertical surfaces

1341. Persons who have swallowed a non-petroleum based poison are given large quantities of warm soapy water or warm salt water to _____.

A. induce vomiting
B. absorb the poison from the blood
C. neutralize the poison in the blood
D. increase the digestive process and eliminate the poison

1342. If there's a fire aboard your vessel, you should FIRST _____.

A. notify the Coast Guard
B. sound the alarm
C. have passengers put on life preservers
D. cut off air supply to the fire

1344. What is the purpose of the hydrostatic release on an inflatable life raft?

A. To release the raft from the cradle automatically as the ship sinks
B. To inflate the raft automatically
C. To test the rafts hydrostatically
D. None of the above

1345. An inflatable life raft can be launched by _____.

A. the float-free method ONLY
B. breaking the weak link on the painter
C. throwing the entire container overboard and then pulling on the operating cord to inflate the raft
D. removing the securing straps

1346. The canopy of an inflatable life raft should _____.

A. go into place as the raft is inflated
B. be put up after everyone is aboard
C. be put up only in severe weather

D. be used as a sail if the wind is blowing

1347. A quick and rapid motion of a vessel in a seaway is an indication of a(n) _____.

A. large GM
B. high center of gravity
C. excessive free surface
D. small GZ

1348. Dry chemical fire extinguishers are effective on which type(s) of fire?

A. Burning oil
B. Electrical
C. Paint
D. All of the above

1352. If you have a fire in the engine room, your FIRST act should be to _____.

A. discharge the fixed CO_2 system into the engine room
B. secure the fuel supply and ventilation to the engine room
C. maneuver your vessel into the wind
D. have all of your crew get into the life raft

1354. If the hydrostatic release mechanism for an inflatable life raft is not periodically serviced and becomes inoperative, it will NOT _____.

A. set the water lights on immersion
B. release the dye-marker from the life raft
C. free the life raft from a sinking vessel
D. break the seal on the carbon dioxide cylinder

1355. As a vessel sinks to a depth of 15 feet, the hydrostatic trip releases the life raft container from its cradle by _____.

A. breaking the weak link
B. releasing the tie-down strap
C. pulling the operating cord
D. releasing the CO_2 canister

1356. What is placed on the under side of an inflatable life raft to help prevent it from being skidded by the wind or overturned?

A. Water pockets
B. A keel
C. Strikes
D. Sea anchor

1358. Which extinguishing agent is best for use on a magnesium fire?

A. Water
B. Sand
C. CO_2
D. Dry chemical

1361. What is the minimum diameter allowed for bilge piping on small passenger vessels which are more than 65 feet in length?

A. 1"
B. 1-1/2"
C. 2"
D. 2-1/2"

1362. On small passenger vessels, backfire flame arrestors are installed on _____.

A. all electric motors
B. turbocharged diesel engines
C. gasoline engines
D. both A and C

1363. Before entering the chain locker, you should _____.

A. have someone standing by
B. make sure there is sufficient air within the locker
C. de-energize the windlass
D. All of the above

1364. Signaling devices required on inflatable life rafts include a(n) _____.

A. Very pistol
B. orange smoke signal
C. air horn
D. lantern

1365. The most important thing to remember when launching an inflatable life raft by hand is to _____.

A. open the CO_2 inflation valve
B. open the raft container
C. ensure that the operating cord is secured to the vessel
D. inflate the raft on the vessel, then lower it over the side

1366. The air spaces in the floor of an inflatable life raft will provide protection against _____.

A. asphyxiation from CO_2
B. loss of air in the sides of the raft
C. rough seas
D. cold water temperatures

1368. A fire in electrical equipment should be extinguished by using _____.

A. salt water
B. foam
C. low-velocity fog
D. CO_2

1371. Which statement about immersion suits is TRUE?

A. The suit's oil resistance is such that it will be serviceable after exposure to gasoline or mineral spirits.
B. The suit seals in body heat and provides protection against hypothermia indefinitely.
C. The suit is flameproof and provides protection to the wearer while swimming through burning oil.
D. All models will automatically turn an unconscious person face-up in the water.

1372. It is necessary to secure the forced ventilation to a compartment where there is a fire to _____.

A. allow the exhaust fans to remove smoke
B. extinguish the fire by carbon monoxide smothering
C. prevent additional oxygen from reaching the fire
D. protect fire fighting personnel from smoke

1373. You are reading draft marks on a vessel. The water level is halfway between the bottom of the number 5 and the top of the number 5. What is the draft of the vessel?

A. 4'-09"
B. 5'-09"
C. 5'-03"
D. 5'-06"

1374. Puncture leaks in the lower tubes or bottom of an inflatable life raft should FIRST be stopped by using _____.

A. sealing clamps
B. repair tape
C. a tube patch
D. sail twine and vulcanizing kit

1375. To launch a life raft by hand you should _____.

A. cut the casing bands, throw the life raft over the side, and it will then inflate

B. detach the operating cord, throw the raft over the side, and it will then inflate
C. cut the casing bands, throw the raft over the side, and pull the operating cord
D. throw the life raft over the side and pull the operating cord

1376. Which distress signal is required for a life raft in ocean service and could be effectively used to attract the attention of aircraft at night?

A. The water light
B. Smoke marker
C. Red flares
D. Orange dye marker

1378. The most effective cooling agent among those normally used to fight fires is _____.

A. water fog or spray
B. chemical foam
C. mechanical foam
D. carbon dioxide

1381. Large volumes of carbon dioxide are safe and effective for fighting fires in enclosed spaces, such as in a pumproom, provided that the _____.

A. persons in the space wear gas masks
B. persons in the space wear damp cloths over their mouths and nostrils
C. ventilation system is secured and all persons leave the space
D. ventilation system is kept operating

1382. Ventilation systems connected to a compartment in which a fire is burning are normally closed to prevent the rapid spread of the fire by _____.

A. convection
B. conduction
C. radiation
D. spontaneous combustion

1384. According to 46 CFR Subchapter T, rigid plastic or other non-metallic piping _____.

A. may only be used for gasoline fuel piping
B. may only be used for diesel fuel piping
C. may not be used for diesel or gasoline fuel piping
D. may be used for gasoline or diesel fuel piping

1385. An inflatable life raft is hand-launched by _____.

A. pulling a cord
B. cutting the wire restraining bands
C. removing the rubber packing strip
D. throwing the entire container overboard

1386. If the metacentric height is large, a vessel will _____.

A. be tender
B. have a slow and easy motion
C. be stiff
D. have a tendency to yaw

1388. Which extinguishing agent will absorb the most heat?

A. CO_2
B. Foam
C. Water
D. Dry chemical

1391. Halon extinguishes fire primarily by _____.

A. cooling
B. smothering
C. shielding of radiant heat
D. breaking the chain reaction

1392. Except in rare cases, it is impossible to extinguish a shipboard fire by _____.

A. removing the heat
B. removing the oxygen
C. removing the fuel
D. interrupting the chain reaction

1393. You are reading the draft marks. The water level is about 4 inches below the bottom of the number 11. What is the draft?

A. 10'-08"
B. 10'-10"
C. 11'-04"
D. 11'-08"

1394. In each inflatable life raft, what equipment is provided to make quick, emergency, temporary repairs to large holes in the raft?

A. No equipment is provided.
B. Glue and rubber patches
C. Several various-sized sealing clamps
D. Self-adhesive rubberized canvas patches

1395. After you have thrown the life raft and stowage container into the water, you inflate the life raft by _____.

A. pulling on the painter line
B. forcing open the container which operates the CO_2
C. hitting the hydrostatic release
D. using the hand pump provided

1396. If you find an inflatable life raft container with steel bands around the case, you should _____.

A. tell the Master
B. leave the bands in place
C. tell the Mate
D. remove the bands yourself

1397. To reduce mild fever the MOST useful drug is _____.

A. bicarbonate of soda
B. paregoric
C. aspirin
D. aromatic spirits of ammonia

1401. Which statement about transmitting distress messages by radiotelephone is INCORRECT?

A. Distress messages should first be transmitted on 2182 kHz.
B. It is advisable to follow a distress message on 2182 kHz by two dashes of 10 to 15 seconds duration.
C. If no answer is received on the designated distress frequencies, repeat the distress call on any frequency available.
D. Channel 16 (156.8 MHz) may be used for distress messages.

1402. When using carbon dioxide to fight a fire on a bulkhead, the CO_2 should be applied _____.

A. first to the bottom of the flaming area, sweeping from side to side, and following the flames upward
B. in a circular motion from the middle of the bulkhead outward
C. to the top of the flaming area, sweeping from side to side, and working toward the bottom
D. in an up-and-down motion from one side of the bulkhead to the other

1404. Signaling devices which are required on inflatable life rafts include _____.

A. a rocket shoulder rifle
B. an oil lantern
C. red flares
D. an air horn

1405. When launching an inflatable life raft, you should make sure that the operating cord is _____.

A. fastened to some substantial part of the vessel
B. not fastened to anything
C. secured to the hydrostatic release
D. fastened to the raft container

1406. The principal danger from ice collecting on a vessel is the _____.

A. decrease in capabilities of radar
B. decrease in displacement
C. adverse effect on trim
D. loss of stability

1408. What is NOT a characteristic of carbon dioxide fire-extinguishing agents?

A. Effective even if ventilation is not shut down
B. Will not deteriorate in storage
C. Non-corrosive
D. Effective on electrical equipment

1410. Which statement about immersion suits is TRUE?

A. Prior to abandonment, the suit allows body movement such as walking, climbing a ladder and picking up small objects.
B. The immersion suit seals in body heat and provides protection against hypothermia for weeks.
C. The suit is flameproof and provides protection to the wearer while swimming through burning oil.
D. The wearer of the suit is severely restricted in body movement, and the suit should not be donned until abandonment is imminent.

1411. Which statement about entry into a space that has been sealed for a long time is TRUE?

A. A tank that has been used to carry hazardous liquids should be tested for oxygen content, toxicity, and explosive gases.
B. You can safely enter the space without a breathing apparatus if the oxygen content exceeds 14%.

C. The natural ventilation through the installed vents is sufficient to provide the proper oxygen content.
D. The heat of the sun on upper ballast tanks, such as in a bulk carrier, may generate carbon monoxide.

1413. Your vessel is damaged, and there is no list or trim. The rolling period is short. The freeboard before the damage was 12'02" (3.7 meters). It is now reduced to 3'00" (1 meter). Which action would you take FIRST?

A. Press up a slack centerline double bottom tank
B. Pump out an amidships centerline ballast tank
C. Transfer ballast from the peak tanks to an amidships centerline tank
D. Pump out the marine potable tank located on the starboard side amidships

1416. You will extinguish a fire when you remove _____.

A. nitrogen
B. oxygen
C. sodium
D. carbon dioxide

1417. A vessel is "listed" when it is _____.

A. down by the head
B. down by the stern
C. inclined due to off-center weight
D. inclined due to wind

1419. Your vessel is listing 4° to port and has a short rolling period. There is loose firefighting water in the hull. The ship is trimmed down by the head with one foot of freeboard at the bow. Which action should you take FIRST?

A. Press up the slack No. 1 starboard double bottom tank.
B. Pump out the forepeak tank.
C. Eliminate the water in the tween decks aft.
D. Jettison stores out of the paint locker in the fo'c'sle.

1422. Mechanical gearing of deck machinery such as the windlass or boat hoists should _____.

A. be open to view so, if a foreign object

gets in the gearing, the operator can immediately stop the machinery
B. have a guard over the gearing
C. be painted a contrasting color from the base color in order to call attention to the gearing
D. not be operated if there is any crew within 10 feet of the machinery

1424. Halon gas will decompose and may form very hazardous toxic fumes when discharged _____.

A. directly on flames
B. at room temperature
C. in an extremely cold climate
D. None of the above

1425. Which advantage does dry chemical have over carbon dioxide (CO_2) in firefighting?

A. Compatible with all foam agents
B. Cleaner
C. More protective against re-flash
D. All of the above

1426. A vessel aground may have negative GM since the _____.

A. decrease in KM is equal to the loss of draft
B. virtual rise of G is directly proportional to the remaining draft
C. displacement lost acts at the point where the ship is aground
D. lost buoyancy method is used to calculate KM, and KB is reduced

1428. A Halon 1301 cylinder contains 100 pounds of liquid at 360 psi. It must be recharged when the pressure drops below how many psi?

A. 360
B. 352
C. 336
D. 324

1429. When collecting condensation for drinking water, _____.

A. a sponge used to mop up and store condensation must be kept salt free
B. only condensation on the bottom of the canopy should be collected
C. it should be strained through a finely woven cloth

D. chlorine tablets should be used to make it drinkable

1431. Which statement is FALSE regarding Halon 1301?

A. It is colorless.
B. It is sweet smelling.
C. It may cause dizziness when inhaled.
D. It does not conduct electricity.

1433. You should NOT use a power tool if _____.

A. it has a three-prong plug
B. the insulation of the power wires is worn
C. hand tools can be used instead
D. the power source is alternating current

1434. Halon fire extinguishers are NOT effective when used on which types of fires?

A. Fires in electrical equipment
B. Flammable oils and greases
C. Class "A" fires in ordinary combustibles
D. Materials containing their own oxygen

1438. The color of the signal flare sent up by a submarine to indicate an emergency condition within the submarine is _____.

A. white
B. green
C. yellow
D. red

1439. Safety goggles or glasses are NOT normally worn when _____.

A. using a rotary grinder with an installed shield
B. letting go the anchor
C. handling wire rope or natural fiber line
D. painting with a spray gun

1440. A ship is inclined by moving a weight of 30 tons a distance of 30 ft. from the centerline. A 28-foot pendulum shows a deflection of 12 inches. Displacement including weight moved is 4,000 tons. KM is 27.64 feet. What is the KG?

A. 21.34 feet
B. 22.06 feet
C. 22.76 feet
D. 23.21 feet

1441. On small passenger vessels, how many supply and exhaust ducts are required in each enclosed space containing gasoline powered machinery or gasoline fuel tanks?

A. 1 of each
B. 2 of each
C. 3 of each
D. 4 of each

1442. If the cause of severe list or trim is off-center ballast, counterflooding into empty tanks will _____.

A. increase the righting moment
B. increase the righting arm
C. increase list or trim
D. decrease list or trim

1443. When jumping into water upon which there is an oil fire, you should _____.

A. break the water surface with your hands when diving head-first
B. use your hands to hold your knees to your chest
C. cover your eyes with one hand while pinching your nose shut and covering your mouth with the other
D. enter the water at the bow or stern on the windward side of the vessel

1444. A stored-pressure water extinguisher is most effective against fires of class _____.

A. A
B. B
C. C
D. D

1445. When instructing a crew member concerning the right way to lift a weight, you would instruct him to_____.

A. arch the back to add strength to the muscles
B. bend his knees and lift with his legs
C. bend his back and stoop
D. bend his back and stoop with arms straight

1447. Why is carbon dioxide (CO_2) better than dry chemical for fighting a class "C" fire?

A. The dry chemical is a conductor.
B. The dry chemical leaves a residue.
C. CO_2 will not dissipate in air.
D. It takes smaller amounts of CO_2 to cover the same area.

1448. After making the required notification that a large oil spill into the water has occurred, the FIRST action should be to _____.

A. apply straw or sawdust on the oil
B. contain the spread of the oil
C. throw grains of sand into the oil
D. have the vessel move out of the spill area

1449. A vessel to which Annex V to MARPOL 73/78 applies is located 10 nautical miles from the nearest land. Which type of garbage is prohibited from being discharged?

A. Food waste
B. Rags ground to less than 1"
C. Paper ground to less than 1"
D. None of the above

1450. When a vessel is stationary and in a hogging condition, the main deck is under _____.

A. compression stress
B. racking stress
C. shear stress
D. tension stress

1451. Before counterflooding to correct a list, you must be sure the list is due to _____.

A. negative GM
B. flooding
C. off-center weight
D. reserve buoyancy

1452. First aid means _____.

A. medical treatment of accident
B. setting of broken bones
C. emergency treatment at the scene of the injury
D. dosage of medications

1453. The hoods over galley ranges present what major hazard?

A. Grease collects in the duct and filter and if it catches fire is difficult to extinguish.
B. In order to effectively draw off cooking heat they present a head-injury hazard to a person of average or more height.
C. They inhibit the effective operation of fire fighting systems in combatting deep fat fryer or range fires.
D. They concentrate the heat of cooking and may raise surrounding flammable material to the ignition point.

1457. When choosing extinguishers to fight a Class B fire do NOT use _____.

A. carbon dioxide
B. dry chemical
C. foam (stored-pressure type)
D. water (cartridge-operated)

1458. Your vessel displaces 14,500 tons, with a longitudinal CG 247.5 ft. aft of the FP. If you pump 80 tons of ballast from forward to aft through a distance of 480 feet, your new CG will be _____.

A. 244.85 feet aft of FP
B. 246.22 feet aft of FP
C. 248.87 feet aft of FP
D. 250.15 feet aft of FP

1462. When authorized to use chemical agents on an oil spill they would _____.

A. absorb the oil for easy removal
B. dissolve the oil in the water
C. facilitate the removal of the pollutant from the water
D. sink the oil

1463. To prevent the spread of fire by convection you should _____.

A. cool the bulkhead around the fire
B. close all openings to the area
C. shut off all electrical power
D. remove combustibles from direct exposure

1466. You used a carbon dioxide (CO_2) fire extinguisher but did not empty the extinguisher. You must have it recharged if the weight loss exceeds _____.

A. one percent of the weight of the charge
B. five percent of the weight of the charge
C. seven percent of the weight of the charge

D. ten percent of the weight of the charge

1469. Which statement about immersion suits is TRUE?

A. The primary color of the suit's exterior may be red, orange or yellow.
B. All models will automatically turn an unconscious person face-up in the water.
C. The suit is flameproof and provides protection to a wearer swimming in burning oil.
D. The suit may be stored in a machinery space where the ambient temperature is 160°F.

1471. What do regulations allow to be marked with EITHER the name of the fishing vessel OR the name of the person to whom it is assigned?

A. Immersion suit
B. Buoyant apparatus
C. Ring buoy
D. Life float

1474. In cleaning up an oil spill, straw is an example of a _____.

A. Chemical agent
B. Blocker
C. Sorbent
D. None of the above

1475. You need to pull the sea anchor back aboard your life raft. What part of the anchor do you pull on?

A. Drag line
B. Bridle
C. Trip line
D. Iron ring

1477. A fire starts on your vessel while refueling. You should FIRST _____.

A. stop the ventilation
B. sound the general alarm
C. determine the source of the fire
D. attempt to extinguish the fire

1478. There is a fire in the crew's quarters of your vessel. You should _____.

A. ventilate the quarters as much as possible
B. prepare to abandon ship

C. close all ventilation to the quarters if possible
D. attempt to put the fire out yourself before sounding the alarm

1479. If your vessel is aground at the bow, it would be preferable that any weight removals be made from the _____.

A. bow
B. mid-section
C. stern
D. All of the above

1485. Which statement about immersion suits is TRUE?

A. All models will automatically turn an unconscious person face-up in the water.
B. The immersion suit seals in body heat and provides protection against hypothermia for weeks.
C. The suit will still be serviceable after a brief (2–6 minutes) exposure to flame and burning.
D. The collar must be inflated before abandoning ship.

1487. A vessel's heavy displacement is 24,500 tons with light displacement of 13,300 tons. Fully loaded it carries 300 tons of fuel and stores. What is the vessel's deadweight?

A. 10,900 tons
B. 11,200 tons
C. 13,000 tons
D. 24,200 tons

1488. When compared to a high-expansion foam, a low-expansion foam will _____.

A. be dryer
B. be lighter
C. be more heat resistant
D. cling to vertical surfaces

1492. You have abandoned ship. There are several rafts in the water. One of the FIRST things to do is _____.

A. separate the rafts as much as possible to increase chances of detection
B. transfer all supplies to one raft
C. transfer all the injured to one raft
D. secure the rafts together to keep them from drifting apart

1493. A new life raft has been installed on your vessel. The operating cord should be _____.

A. attached to the raft stowage cradle or to a secure object nearby with a weak link
B. checked to see that it's unattached
C. coiled neatly on the raft container
D. faked on deck and lead through a chock

1498. The spread of fire is prevented by _____.

A. cooling surfaces adjacent to the fire
B. leaving combustibles in the endangered area
C. increasing the oxygen supply
D. All of the above

1502. A portable foam (stored-pressure type) fire extinguisher would be most useful in combating a fire in _____.

A. generators
B. oil drums
C. the bridge controls
D. combustible metals

1503. If you have to jump in the water when abandoning ship, your legs should be _____.

A. spread apart as far as possible
B. held as tightly against your chest as possible
C. in a kneeling position
D. extended straight down and crossed at the ankles

1505. What is one of the FIRST things you would do on boarding an inflatable life raft?

A. Open equipment pack.
B. Post a lookout.
C. Issue anti-seasickness medicine.
D. Pick up other survivors.

1507. A thrust block is designed to _____.

A. absorb the shock of wave pressure at the bow
B. be placed between the engines and the foundation to absorb the vibration
C. transmit the thrust of the engine to the propeller
D. transmit the thrust of the propeller to the vessel

1508. Portable foam fire-extinguishers are designed for use on class _____.

A. A and class B fires
B. A and class C fires
C. B and class C fires
D. A, class B, and class C fires

1511. Which step should normally be taken FIRST by those who have boarded a life raft in an emergency?

A. Ration food and water supplies.
B. Take anti-seasickness pills, if available.
C. Determine position and closest point of land.
D. Check pyrotechnic supplies.

1512. Where are the draft marks required to be displayed on a ship?

A. Deep tanks
B. Voids
C. Midships near the waterline
D. Area of water line near stem and stern

1513. Limit switches, winches, falls, etc., must be thoroughly inspected at least every _____.

A. 2 months
B. 4 months
C. 6 months
D. year

1519. All oil spills must be reported to the _____.

A. U.S. Corps of Engineers
B. U.S. Coast Guard
C. local police
D. local fire department

1522. The pollution prevention regulations in MARPOL apply to U.S. flag vessels _____.

A. only on the Great Lakes and international waters
B. only on the Western Rivers and international waters
C. on international voyages outside U.S. territorial waters
D. on all international and inland waters

1523. The term "oil" as used in the Oil Pollution Regulations means _____.

A. fuel oil
B. sludge
C. oil refuse
D. All of the above

1524. A U.S. merchant vessel in ocean service is NOT subject to the requirements of Annex V to MARPOL 73/78 _____.

A. outside of 25 nautical miles from nearest land
B. outside of the navigable waters of the United States
C. in the waters of those countries not signatory to MARPOL
D. A U.S. vessel in ocean service is ALWAYS subject to MARPOL.

1526. Which type of portable fire extinguishers is NOT designed for use on flammable liquid fires?

A. Foam
B. Dry chemical
C. Water (cartridge-operated)
D. Carbon dioxide

1527. You discharge garbage overboard at sea. When recording your vessel's position as required, you must include _____.

A. latitude, longitude and approximate depth of water
B. latitude, longitude, course, speed, and a copy of that day's noon position slip
C. latitude, longitude, and estimated distance from shore
D. latitude and longitude only

1528. You are offloading garbage to another ship. Your records must identify that ship by name and show her _____.

A. home port
B. next port-of-call
C. official number
D. Master

1529. Under the Pollution Regulations, garbage disposal records must be kept _____.

A. until the end of the voyage
B. until the next Coast Guard inspection
C. one year
D. two years

1530. Which vessel in ocean service is not subject to Annex V of MARPOL 73/79?

A. A 20-foot sailing vessel
B. A 26-foot tug and tow
C. An uninspected 35-foot passenger vessel
D. A Navy Destroyer

1531. You intend to discharge medical or hazardous wastes ashore. MARPOL Annex V requires you to notify a receiving port or terminal in advance. How much advance notice is required?

A. 12 hours
B. 24 hours
C. 48 hours
D. Advance notification is not required.

1533. Which statement is TRUE?

A. You need not keep a record of ground garbage dumped into the sea more than 25 miles offshore.
B. You need not keep a record of garbage incinerated on the ship.
C. You must keep a record of the approximate weight of the garbage dumped.
D. You must keep a record of garbage discharged in port to a shore facility.

1534. Which statement is TRUE?

A. You must keep a record of garbage discharged in port to a shore facility.
B. You need not keep a record of dumping ground garbage in to the sea more than 25 miles offshore.
C. You must keep a record of the approximate weight of the garbage dumped.
D. You need not keep a record of garbage incinerated on the ship.

1536. Which types of portable fire extinguishers are designed for putting out electrical fires?

A. Foam and water (stored pressure)
B. Foam and carbon dioxide
C. Foam and dry chemical
D. Dry chemical and carbon dioxide

1540. Which statement concerning the sources of drinking water is FALSE?

A. Fresh water may be obtained from fish.
B. Lifeboat covers or canopies should be washed with rain before drinking water is collected.

C. Fresh water may be collected from condensation inside the life raft.
D. Seawater should never be consumed.

1541. Which would be considered pollution under the U.S. water pollution laws?

A. Garbage
B. Hazardous substances
C. Oil
D. All of the above

1543. The ship station license for your radiotelephone is valid for _____.

A. one year
B. two years
C. ten years
D. the life of the vessel

1546. What are the most important reasons for using water fog to fight fires?

A. Smothers burning surfaces, organically destroys fuel
B. Cools fire and adjacent surfaces, provides protective barrier
C. Reaches areas not protected by steam or CO_2 smothering systems
D. Allows fire to be attacked from leeward, saturates liquid surfaces

1547. If you must swim through an oil fire, you should NOT _____.

A. wear as much clothing as possible
B. enter the water feet first
C. swim with the wind
D. cover eyes with one hand when entering the water

1548. You have abandoned your vessel. You are in a life raft and have cleared away from your vessel. One of your FIRST actions should be to _____.

A. take measures to maintain morale
B. prepare and use radio equipment
C. identify the person in charge of life raft
D. search for survivors

1549. You are sailing in a strong wind and may accidentally jibe when _____.

A. reaching
B. tacking
C. running-free
D. in irons

1553. What is an advantage of using foam in fire fighting?

A. It is effective in controlling fire in flowing oil such as coming from a broken fuel line.
B. It absorbs heat from materials that could cause reignition.
C. Most foams can be used jointly with dry chemical extinguishing agents to attack a fire by two methods of extinguishment.
D. Once the surface is blanketed with foam and the fire is extinguished, no further foam is required.

1555. Seawater may be used for drinking _____.

A. at a maximum rate of two ounces per day
B. after mixing with an equal quantity of fresh water
C. if gathered during or immediately after a hard rain
D. under no conditions

1556. Which fire extinguishing agent has the greatest capacity for absorbing heat?

A. Water
B. Foam
C. Dry chemical
D. Carbon dioxide

1558. A Halon 1301 cylinder is periodically tested for weight loss and pressure loss. What minimum percentage of the full pressure can be lost before the cylinder must be recharged?

A. 3%
B. 5%
C. 10%
D. 15%

1560. The most important reason for taking anti-seasickness pills as soon as possible after entering a life raft is to_____.

A. assist in sleeping
B. reduce appetite by decreasing nausea
C. prevent loss of body moisture by vomiting
D. prevent impaired judgement due to motion-induced deliriousness

1561. Which is NOT a mandatory part of the shipboard Oil Pollution Emergency Plan?

A. Reporting requirements
B. Diagrams

C. Steps to control a discharge
D. National and local coordination

1562. Drinking salt water will _____.

A. protect against heat camps
B. prevent seasickness
C. be safe if mixed with fresh water
D. dehydrate you

1563. Who should inspect and test an inflatable life raft?

A. The person in charge
B. An approved servicing facility
C. Shipyard personnel
D. A certificated lifeboatman

1564. Which action is routinely performed at the annual servicing and inspection of a dry-chemical cartridge-operated portable fire extinguisher?

A. Insure the chemical is powdery.
B. Replace the cartridge.
C. Pressure test the discharge hose.
D. Test the pressure gauge for proper operation.

1566. CO_2 extinguishes a fire by _____.

A. cooling
B. smothering
C. chemical action
D. All of the above

1570. Which is a mandatory section of the shipboard Oil Pollution Emergency Plan?

A. Reporting requirements
B. Removal equipment list
C. Planned exercises
D. List of individuals required to respond

1571. A Halon 1301 cylinder is periodically tested for weight loss and pressure loss. It must be recharged if it has lost more than what minimum percentage of its weight?

A. 3%
B. 5%
C. 10%
D. 15%

1575. Foam extinguishes a fire by _____.

A. smothering the burning material

B. chemical combination with burning material
C. absorbing the burning material
D. organic destruction of the burning material

1580. Which statement is TRUE concerning the placard entitled "Discharge of Oil Prohibited"?

A. It is required on all vessels.
B. It is only required in the wheelhouse.
C. It may be located at the bilge and ballast pump control station.
D. All of the above

1582. You are off the coast of South Africa when a seaman is injured. What indicator should be used in a message requesting medical advice from a South African station?

A. DH MEDICO
B. XXX RADIOMEDICAL
C. MEDRAD
D. PORT HEALTH

1583. You are having a Coast Guard inspection. All carbon dioxide fire extinguishers aboard will be _____.

A. weighed
B. discharged and recharged
C. checked for pressure loss
D. sent ashore to an approved service facility

1586. The success of an indirect attack on a fire depends on the _____.

A. size of the fire when initially observed
B. complete containment of the fire
C. cooling ability of the firefighting agent
D. class of the fire

1596. By regulation, orange smoke distress signals will expire not more than how many months from the date of manufacture?

A. 24 months
B. 36 months
C. 42 months
D. 54 months

1597. Which characteristic is an advantage of Halon as a fire extinguishing medium?

A. Electrically non-conductive
B. Relatively inexpensive
C. Effective against chemicals containing an oxidizer
D. All of the above

1598. On board a small passenger vessel connections to electric conductors MUST be _____.

A. made within enclosures
B. served and parcelled
C. installed only by a licensed marine electrician
D. inspected annually

1599. All self-propelled vessels on an international voyage must be equipped with how many Emergency Position Indicating Radiobeacons (EPIRB)?

A. One approved Category 1 EPIRB
B. Three approved Category 1 EPIRBs
C. One approved Class B EPIRB
D. Two approved Class B EPIRBs

1601. Channel 13 is primarily used for ship to ship communication. Channel 13 is also authorized for _____.

A. coast to aircraft operational communications
B. aircraft to ship operational communications
C. lock & bridge communications
D. aircraft to ship navigational communications

1607. A bilge suction line, in a fishing vessel with more than 16 individuals aboard, must have a strainer with an open area not less than how many times the open area of the suction line?

A. one
B. two
C. three
D. four

1610. An "ABC" dry chemical fire extinguisher would be LEAST effective against a fire in _____.

A. a mattress
B. spilled liquids such as oil or paint
C. high voltage electrical gear
D. a trash can

1612. Which action is routinely performed at the annual servicing and inspection of a dry-chemical cartridge-operated portable fire extinguisher?

A. Test the pressure gauge for correct reading.
B. Weigh the cartridge.
C. Replace the dry chemical.
D. Pressure test the discharge hose.

1614. You may have to give artificial respiration after a/an _____.

A. drowning
B. electrocution
C. poisoning
D. All of the above

1615. When administering artificial respiration, it is MOST important to _____.

A. monitor blood pressure
B. clear airways
C. use the rhythmic pressure method
D. know all approved methods

1616. As Master of an inspected small passenger vessel of 90 gross tons, you have a question regarding a proposed modification to a watertight bulkhead. In which subchapter of title 46 of the Code of Federal Regulations would you find the answer?

A. Subchapter F
B. Subchapter T
C. Subchapter S
D. Subchapter B

1617. When compared to low-expansion foam, a high-expansion foam will _____.

A. be wetter
B. be lighter
C. be more heat resistant
D. not cling to vertical surfaces

1618. Which characteristic of Halon is a disadvantage when it is used as a fire extinguishing medium?

A. Leaves a residue
B. Cost, relative to other agents
C. Breaks down while under prolonged storage
D. Conducts electricity

1619. A conscious victim who has suffered a blow to the head has symptoms that indicate the possibility of concussion. If the patient feels no indication of neck or spine injury, recommended treatment would include _____.

A. turning the victim's head to the side to keep his airway open
B. positioning the victim so the head is lower than the body
C. giving the victim water if he is thirsty, but no food
D. elevating the head and shoulders slightly with a pillow

1620. One disadvantage of using regular dry chemical (sodium bicarbonate) in firefighting is that _____.

A. it can break down under high heat and emit noxious fumes
B. it will decompose under prolonged storage and lose its effectiveness
C. fire has been known to flash back over the surface of an oil fire
D. it is ineffective in fighting fires in high-voltage electrical equipment

1621. Why is spare fire hose rolled for storage?

A. Water in the hose is forced out the end in the rolling process.
B. The threads on the male end are protected by the hose.
C. Rolling provides maximum protection against entry of foreign objects into the couplings.
D. Rolling provides maximum protection to the outer covering of the hose.

1624. A sail plan, including the vessel's itinerary, name, number, and persons aboard, should be filed with _____.

A. the FAA
B. the Coast Guard
C. U.S. Customs
D. a responsible person

1625. A shipmate suffers a heart attack and stops breathing. You must _____.

A. immediately give a stimulant, by force if necessary
B. make the victim comfortable in a bunk
C. administer oxygen

D. immediately start CPR

1626. A shipmate suffers a heart attack and stops breathing. You must _____.

A. administer oxygen
B. immediately check his pulse and start CPR
C. make the victim comfortable in a bunk
D. immediately give a stimulant, by force if necesssary

1627. The canvas covering of fire hose is called the _____.

A. casing
B. outer hose
C. line cover
D. jacket

1629. Which statement is TRUE about fire fighting foam?

A. The air bubbles in foam act as an insulator in fighting a class C fire.
B. The effectiveness of foam in forming a blanket over a burning liquid increases as the temperature of the liquid increases.
C. Foam can be used to control gases escaping from compressed gas cylinders.
D. Foam sets up a vapor barrier over a flammable liquid preventing flammable gases from rising.

1632. When joining the female coupling of the fire hose to the male outlet of the hydrant, you should make sure that the

_____.

A. threads are lubricated
B. nozzle is attached to the hose
C. female coupling has a gasket
D. hose is led out

1634. To prevent the spread of fire by convection you should _____.

A. close all openings to the area
B. shut off all electrical power
C. remove combustibles from direct exposure
D. cool the bulkhead around the fire

1635. Which firefighting method is an example of an indirect attack on a fire?

A. Bouncing a straight stream of water off the overhead to create spray effect

B. Spraying foam on a bulkhead and letting it flow down and over a pool of burning oil
C. Flooding a paint locker with CO_2 and sealing the compartment
D. Cooling adjacent bulkheads with water to prevent the spread of the fire by conduction

1637. Which is a disadvantage of Halon as a fire extinguishing medium?

A. Conducts electricity
B. Difficult to store
C. Large volume necessary to be effective
D. Ineffective in powdered metal fires

1638. As Master of a small passenger vessel, you have a question regarding a proposed modification to a watertight bulkhead. In which subchapter of title 46 of the Code of Federal Regulations would you find the answer?

A. Subchapter S
B. Subchapter B
C. Subchapter T
D. Subchapter F

1640. A Halon 1301 cylinder contains 100 pounds of liquid at 360 psi. It must be recharged when the weight drops below how many pounds of liquid?

A. 90
B. 92
C. 95
D. 98

1641. The most serious effect of air trapped in a non-treated diesel engine jacket water cooling system is that it _____.

A. causes corrosion
B. reduces the ability of the system to cool the engine
C. can form pockets which block the flow of coolant through the system
D. accelerates formation of metal plating

1647. Electrical wiring on all "T-Boats" must be _____.

A. concealed to prevent mechanical damage
B. concealed so the boat can be maintained more easily
C. protected from the weather
D. in an accessible place behind the ceiling

1648. What is an advantage of using foam

in fire fighting?

A. It is MOST effective on very hot oil fires where the temperatures of the liquid exceed 100°C (212°F).
B. Most foams can be used with dry chemicals to attack a fire by two methods.
C. Foam is effective on combustible metal fires.
D. Foam can be made with seawater or fresh water.

1650. When compared to low-expansion foam, a high-expansion foam will _____.

A. be drier
B. be heavier
C. be more heat resistant
D. not cling to vertical surfaces

1664. The number of fire extinguishers required on an uninspected "motor vessel" is based on the vessel's _____.

A. length
B. gross tonnage
C. draft
D. crew list

1665. Which statement about stowing spare hose is TRUE?

A. Fold the hose so that the male coupling is about 4 feet from the female coupling, then roll it up.
B. Roll the hose starting at the female end.
C. Roll the hose starting at the male end.
D. Fold the hose into lengths about 6 feet long and then lash the folds together.

1667. A shipmate suffers a heart attack and stops breathing. You must _____.

A. immediately give a stimulant, by force if necessary
B. make the victim comfortable in a bunk
C. immediately start CPR
D. administer oxygen

1669. You have abandoned ship and after two days in a life raft you can see an aircraft near the horizon apparently carrying out a search pattern. You should _____.

A. switch the EPIRB to the homing signal mode
B. use the voice transmission capability of the EPIRB to guide the aircraft to your raft
C. turn on the strobe light on the top of the EPIRB

D. use visual distress signals in conjunction with the EPIRB

1676. Before you start an engine in a compartment, it's MOST important to _____.

A. check the flame arrester
B. check the fuel tank
C. check the battery
D. ventilate the bilges

1677. After an engine is started you should _____.

A. increase engine speed to insure adequate flow of oil to all parts of the engine
B. pay no attention unless there are unusual noises from the engine
C. check operating pressures and temperatures, and check for leaks
D. run the engine at idle until the temperature has increased

1678. Your vessel is 79 feet long with 20 people aboard. The coaming of a deck above the lowest weather deck (except an exposed forecastle deck) must be at least _____.

A. 6" high
B. 12" high
C. 24" high
D. Not required

1679. You are on a 92-foot fishing vessel with 35 individuals on board. Which one of the following items are you NOT required to have on board?

A. Gyrocompass
B. Magnetic compass
C. Electronic positon fixing device
D. VHF radiotelephone

1681. An LWT anchor often has difficulty tripping in _____.

A. sand
B. soft soil
C. stiff clay
D. heterogeneous soil

1682. Which radio call-in plan is the most prudent?

A. There must be a designated responsible person who will be available to receive your call at anytime.
B. There must be specific instructions for the designated responsible person to

follow if your call does not come in on schedule.

C. The designated responsible person must be instructed to call the Coast Guard search and rescue authorities immediately if your call does not come in on schedule.

D. The designated responsible person should be over 18 years of age.

1685. A storm is forecast for the area where your vessel is moored. For its safety you should put _____.

A. more slack in the mooring lines
B. a strain on the mooring lines
C. chafing gear on the mooring lines
D. grease on the mooring lines

1687. The old sailor's admonition "Beware the lee shore" warns of the danger due to _____.

A. the wind blowing stronger at this location
B. the ground swell making it difficult to tack off
C. the current flowing directly on shore
D. there being less wind in the lee of the shore

1688. Each commercial fishing vessel must have at least one immersion suit, exposure suit, or life preserver for each _____.

A. person aboard
B. person working on deck
C. crew member
D. None of the above are correct.

1689. You must pick up an individual who has fallen overboard from a sailboat. The final approach should be _____.

A. upwind
B. downwind
C. on a close reach
D. on a broad reach

1692. You are preparing for what promises to be a rough ocean passage. Your 120-foot schooner carries a yard on the foremast, about 50 feet above the water. The yard weighs about 1000 pounds. If you take the yard down and stow it on deck for the trip, you will _____.

A. increase your vessel's GM
B. decrease the metacentric height
C. give the vessel a gentler roll
D. increase the reserve bouyancy

1695. In order to prevent galvanic corrosion, an aluminum boat must be insulated from the davits and gripes. Which of the following is acceptable as an insulator?

A. Hard rubber
B. Canvas
C. Leather
D. Sponge rubber

1698. To prevent a wooden hull from leaking you caulk it _____.

A. after drydocking, while the hull is moist
B. after drydocking, and the hull has dried
C. afloat, where it is leaking
D. afloat, in all accessible areas

1699. On small sailing vessels, the PRIMARY reason for using nylon in a combination chain-nylon anchor line is to _____.

A. provide elasticity
B. increase the strength
C. reduce the cost
D. reduce the weight

1701. Movement of liquid in a tank when a vessel inclines causes an increase in _____.

A. righting arm
B. metacentric height
C. height of the uncorrected KG
D. natural rolling period

1708. A chemical additive to LPG gives it a characteristic _____.

A. odor
B. color
C. pressure
D. density

1712. The gross weight of a fully charged CO_2 cylinder is 80 lbs. When the bottle is empty it weighs 60 lbs. What is the minimum acceptable gross weight of the CO_2 bottle before it should be recharged by the manufacturer?

A. 55 lbs.
B. 68 lbs.
C. 74 lbs.
D. 82 lbs.

1714. The painter of a rigid life raft must have a minimum length of _____.

A. 36 feet
B. 50 feet

C. 200 feet
D. 300 feet

1723. The regulations that were passed to implement MARPOL 73/78 concerning oil pollution apply to a U.S. flag vessel that sails on which waters?

A. Inland waters only
B. Great Lakes only
C. International waters
D. All of the above

1725. The most effective treatment for warming a crew member suffering from hypothermia is _____.

A. running or jumping to increase circulation
B. raising body temperature rapidly by placing hands and feet in hot water
C. bundling the body in blankets to rewarm gradually
D. laying prone under heat lamps to rewarm rapidly

1734. Which procedure should be followed when individuals are rescued in cold climates and suffer from hypothermia?

A. Give them brandy or other alcoholic stimulation to promote a return to an acceptable body temperature.
B. Move them to a warm room to gradually raise their body temperature.
C. Keep them moving to stimulate circulation to raise their body temperature.
D. Warm them under an electric blanket to rapidly regain normal body temperature.

1756. Under federal regulations, what minimum level of Blood Alcohol Content (BAC) constitutes a violation of the laws prohibiting Boating Under the Influence of Alcohol (BUI) on commercial vessels?

A. 0.18% BAC
B. 0.16% BAC
C. 0.12% BAC
D. 0.10% BAC

1772. The definition of "partially protected waters," as used in the Regulations does not include _____.

A. harbors, lakes and similar waters determined by the OCMI to be protected waters
B. waters within 20 nautical miles from the mouth of a harbor of safe refuge

519

C. the Great Lakes during the summer season

D. sheltered waters presenting no special hazard

1773. What must Inland vessels of 100 GT and over be fitted with for oily mixtures?

A. A fixed system to discharge the slops overboard
B. A fixed system to discharge oily mixtures to a reception facility
C. A portable system to discharge the slops overboard
D. A portable system to discharge oily mixtures to a reception facility

1822. Which hazard probably would NOT be encountered when entering an empty but uncleaned fish hold?

A. Lack of oxygen
B. Methane gas
C. Hydrogen sulfide gas
D. Carbon monoxide

1823. What is the MINIMUM distance a vessel subject to the requirements of Annex V to MARPOL 73/78 must be located from nearest land to legally discharge paper trash?

A. 5 nautical miles
B. 10 nautical miles
C. 12 nautical miles
D. 25 nautical miles

1831. A slow and easy motion of a vessel in a seaway is an indication of a _____.

A. small GM
B. low center of gravity
C. stiff vessel
D. large GZ

1837. Each life raft, which does not have an indicated maximum stowage height indicated on the life raft, must be _____.

A. limited to carry no more than 10 persons
B. stowed not more than 59 feet above the lightest waterline
C. stowed in quick release racks
D. inspected every six months

1854. How is the Master or operator of a vessel required to keep the crew informed of the regulations concerning the discharging of garbage overboard?

A. Give each crewmember a copy of ANNEX V of MARPOL.
B. Call an all hands meeting before sailing.
C. Keep placards prominently posted.
D. Have each person read and sign a copy of the regulations.

1860. You are underway at sea when a fire is reported in the forward part of the vessel. The wind is from dead ahead at 20 knots. You should _____.

A. remain on course and hold speed
B. change course to put the wind on either beam and increase speed
C. change course and put the stern to the wind
D. remain on course but decrease speed

1862. All electrical appliances aboard a vessel should be grounded to _____.

A. prevent them from falling when the vessel rolls
B. protect personnel from electrical shock
C. increase their operating efficiency
D. prevent unauthorized personnel from operating them

1867. Under the Pollution Regulations, when you dump garbage in to the sea you must _____.

A. notify the U.S. Coast Guard
B. make an entry in the Official Logbook
C. keep a record for two years
D. No action is required if you are more than 25 miles from land and no plastic materials are dumped.

1870. When should a fire be ventilated?

A. When attacking the fire directly
B. When using a steam smothering system
C. When using the fixed CO_2 system
D. All of the above

1871. If the cause of a sudden severe list is negative initial stability, counterflooding into empty tanks may _____.

A. increase the righting moment
B. cause an increase in the righting arm
C. bring the vessel to an upright equilibrium position
D. cause the vessel to flop to a greater angle

1875. After abandoning ship which action should be taken IMMEDIATELY upon enter-

ing a life raft?

A. Open equipment pack.
B. Issue anti-seasickness medicine.
C. Cut painter and clear the ship.
D. Dry the life raft floor and inflate.

1879. Your vessel measures 127 feet long by 17 feet in beam. If the natural rolling period at a draft of 7' 10" is 5 seconds, what is the GM?

A. 1.96 feet
B. 2.24 feet
C. 2.45 feet
D. 2.68 feet

1880. The primary reason for placing covers over storage batteries is to _____.

A. prevent the accumulation of explosive gases
B. protect the hull from leaking electrolyte
C. prevent movement of the battery in rough waters
D. protect against accidental shorting across terminals

1890. Spaces containing batteries require good ventilation because _____.

A. ventilation avoids CO_2 build up
B. ventilation supplies extra oxygen for charging the battery
C. ventilation avoids flammable gas accumulation
D. less electrolyte is required to maintain the batteries' charge

1900. The accumulation of dangerous fumes generated by the storage batteries is best prevented by _____.

A. covering the batteries in a nonconducting, solid enclosure
B. mounting the batteries in a position as high as possible
C. natural or mechanical ventilation
D. securing the batteries to vibration reducing mounting brackets

1907. The color of the signal flare sent up by a submarine to indicate an emergency condition within the submarine is _____.

A. yellow
B. red
C. green
D. white

1909. On a passenger vessel, the vessel's name must appear on _____.

A. ring life buoy
B. lifeboats
C. lifeboat oars
D. All of the above

1910. Which visual distress signal is acceptable for daylight use only?

A. Hand-held red flare
B. Self-contained rocket-propelled parachute red flare
C. Hand-held orange smoke distress flare
D. Red aerial pyrotechnic flare

1920. Which statement is TRUE concerning life preservers?

A. Buoyant vests may be substituted for life preservers.
B. Kapok life preservers must have vinyl-covered pad inserts.
C. Life preservers must always be worn with the same side facing outwards.
D. Life preservers are not designed to turn a person's face clear of the water when unconscious.

1930. You must ensure that lifesaving equipment is _____.

A. locked up
B. readily accessible for use
C. inaccessible to passengers
D. on the topmost deck of the vessel at all times

1938. A wobbling tail shaft is an indication of _____.

A. shallow water
B. an engine that is misfiring
C. a tight tail shaft gland
D. worn stern bearing or misalignment

1940. Life jackets should be stowed in _____.

A. survival craft
B. messrooms
C. readily accessible locations
D. locked watertight containers

1942. Which EPIRB transmits a distress alert that is received and relayed by an INMARSAT satellite?

A. Class A EPIRBs

B. Class B EPIRBs
C. L-Band EPIRBs
D. Category I EPIRBs

1943. Which statement concerning satellite EPIRBs is TRUE?

A. Once activated, these EPIRBs continuously send up a signal for use in identifying the vessel and for determining the position of the beacon.
B. The coded signal identifies the nature of the distress situation.
C. The coded signal only identifies the vessel's name and port of registry.
D. If the GMDSS Radio Operator does not program the EPIRB, it will transmit default information such as the follow-on communications frequency and mode.

1949. What is meant by "CES"?

A. Coast Earth Satellite
B. Coast Earth Station
C. Central Equatorial Station
D. Coastal Equivalent Station

1950. The lifesaving equipment on all vessels shall be _____.

A. inspected weekly
B. stowed in locked compartments
C. readily accessible
D. tested yearly

1951. If you must jump from a vessel, the correct posture includes_____.

A. holding down the life preserver against the chest with one arm crossing the other, covering the mouth and nose with a hand, and feet together
B. knees bent and held close to the body with both arms around legs
C. body straight and arms held tightly at the sides for feet first entry into the water
D. both hands holding the life preserver below the chin with knees bent and legs crossed

1964. When crossing a bar in rough weather, you should enter on a(n) _____.

A. tidal bore
B. ebbing current
C. flood current
D. All of the above

1967. Define the acronym MSI.

A. Maritime Safety Information
B. Maritime Shipping Index
C. Maritime Satellite Indicator
D. Mariner Safety Intelligence

1975. On a commercial fishing vessel, a wearable personal flotation device must be marked with the name of the _____.

A. vessel
B. assigned individual
C. owner of the device
D. Any of the above

1979. A documented oceangoing fishing vessel is required to have emergency instructions posted if it _____.

A. exceeds 49 feet in length
B. is over 25 gross tons
C. carries more than 16 persons
D. has sleeping accommodations

1983. What is required in addition to the heat, fuel, and oxygen of the fire triangle to have a fire?

A. Electricity
B. Chain reaction
C. Pressure
D. Smoke

1986. Which statement is TRUE?

A. You need not keep a record of ground garbage dumped into the sea more than 25 miles offshore.
B. You must keep a record of garbage discharged in port to a shore facility.
C. You need not keep a record of garbage incinerated on the ship.
D. You must keep a record of the approximate weight of the garbage dumped.

1997. Vessels to which Annex V to MARPOL 73/78 applies may discharge garbage containing plastics _____.

A. 5 nautical miles from nearest land
B. 12 nautical miles from nearest land
C. 25 nautical miles from nearest land
D. None of the above

2008. Your vessel measures 119 feet long by 17 feet in beam. If the natural rolling period at a draft of 5' 05" is 6 seconds, what is the GM?

A. 1.14 feet
B. 1.36 feet

C. 1.55 feet
D. 1.96 feet

2009. Your vessel measures 114 feet long by 16 feet in beam. If the natural rolling period at a draft of 5' 06" is 6 seconds, what is the GM?

A. 1.38 feet
B. 1.53 feet
C. 1.76 feet
D. 1.98 feet

2010. Your vessel measures 128 feet long by 21 feet in beam. If the natural rolling period at a draft of 7' 06" is 6 seconds, what is the GM?

A. 1.56 feet
B. 2.37 feet
C. 2.55 feet
D. 2.74 feet

2014. Your vessel measures 131 feet long by 20 feet in beam. If the natural rolling period at a draft of 8' 03" is 6 seconds, what is the GM?

A. 1.26 feet
B. 1.74 feet
C. 1.93 feet
D. 2.15 feet

2016. Your vessel measures 125 feet long by 17 feet in beam. If the natural rolling period at a draft of 7' 09" is 6 seconds, what is the GM?

A. 0.95 foot
B. 1.25 feet
C. 1.55 feet
D. 1.78 feet

2018. When can routine communications be resumed on a frequency or channel on which radio silence has been imposed?

A. After determining that the frequency or channel appears to be no longer in use
B. After determining that geographic distance from the distress situation will prohibit any other signal from interfering with emergency communications
C. After the Rescue Coordination Center transmits a message on the frequency or channel being used for emergency communications stating that such traffic has concluded
D. Routine communications can resume if, in the Master's opinion, communications on that frequency or channel will not interfere with emergency communications.

2020. Free communication will adversely affect transverse stability only when the flooded space is _____.

A. offcenter
B. on the centerline
C. completely flooded
D. open to the sea above and below the waterline

2027. Who is responsible for transmitting a message stating that distress communications have ceased?

A. The Rescue Coordination Center (RCC) controlling the distress communications
B. The vessel providing the initial communications with the distressed vessel
C. The Coast Radio Station (CRS) that was first contacted concerning the distress situation
D. No formal message must be transmitted as long as no distress-related communications have occurred after reasonable time.

2031. Which condition is NOT necessary for a combustible liquid to burn?

A. The temperature of the substance must be equal to or above its fire point.
B. The air must contain oxygen in sufficient quantity.
C. The mixture of vapors with air must be within the "explosive range."
D. All of the above are necessary for a combustible liquid to burn.

2032. What is the primary hazard, other than fire damage, associated with a class C fire?

A. Possibility of reflash
B. Electrocution or shock
C. Explosion
D. Flashover

2033. How is "radio silence" imposed?

A. By the Rescue Coordination Center (RCC) controlling the distress communications on that frequency or channel
B. By the Coast Earth Station (CES) controlling the distress communications on that frequency or channel
C. By the Public Correspondence Station (PCS), controlling the distress communications on that frequency or channel
D. By the High Seas Service (HSS) controlling the distress communications on that frequency or channel.

2043. How does a coast radio station communicating by HF radio normally identify itself?

A. By its subscriber number
B. By its call sign
C. By its MMSI
D. By its MID

2045. How often does a coast radio station that regularly broadcasts traffic lists transmit the list?

A. As often as is deemed necessary to effect delivery
B. No less often than every four hours
C. Only on an as-needed basis
D. Once per 24-hour period

2051. You are standing a radio watch aboard the rig. A crew boat calls you on VHF channel 16. When you reply with your vessel name and call letters, you should request the crew boat to switch to an intership channel such as channel _____.

A. 6
B. 10
C. 12
D. 14

2052. Which radio call-in plan is the most prudent?

A. The designated responsible person must be instructed to call the Coast Guard search and rescue authorities immediately if your call does not come in on schedule.
B. There must be a designated responsible person available at all times to receive your call.
C. There must be a designated responsible person who knows they are expecting your call at a certain time.
D. Two responsible persons should be designated so that one can relieve the other as necessary.

2053. What is the international calling and distress channel found on all VHF-FM equipped drilling rigs?

A. Channel 1
B. Channel 10
C. Channel 16
D. Channel 68

2054. Your vessel measures 126 feet (38 meters) long by 21 feet (6 meters) in beam. If the natural rolling period at a draft of 8 feet (2 meters) is 6 seconds, what is the GM?

A. 2.4 feet (0.70 meter)
B. 2.8 feet (0.85 meter)
C. 3.0 feet (0.90 meter)
D. 3.2 feet (0.98 meter)

2057. You cannot operate a VHF or SSB radiotelephone aboard a rig unless that station is licensed by the _____.

A. Federal Communications Commission
B. U.S. Coast Guard
C. Minerals Management Service
D. Department of Energy

2061. Where would you find the "call sign" or "call letters" of the radio station on your rig?

A. In the rig safety manual
B. On the Certificate of Inspection
C. On the Ship Station License
D. On the rig Watch Bill

2063. If there are a number of survivors in the water after abandoning ship, they should _____.

A. tie themselves to the unit so they won't drift with the current
B. form a small circular group to create a warmer pocket of water in the center of the circle
C. send the strongest swimmer to shore for assistance
D. form a raft by lashing their life preservers together

2071. The generators on your rig have shut down, leaving you without navigation lights. Which emergency signal would you transmit over the VHF radio to alert vessels in the area of your predicament?

A. Mayday, Mayday, Mayday
B. Pan, Pan, Pan
C. Securité, Securité, Securité
D. Lights out, Lights out, Lights out

2073. If your rig is equipped with a SSB radio, what frequency would you use to initiate a distress call?

A. 1982 kHz
B. 2082 kHz

C. 2182 kHz
D. 2282 kHz

2078. A device fitted over the discharge opening on a relief valve consisting of one or two woven wire fabrics is called a flame _____.

A. stopper
B. screen
C. filter
D. restrictor

2086. A partially full tank causes a virtual rise in the height of the _____.

A. metacenter
B. center of buoyancy
C. center of flotation
D. center of gravity

2094. Your vessel measures 122 feet long by 18 feet in beam. If the natural rolling period at a draft of 6' 09" is 5 seconds, what is the GM?

A. 1.4 feet
B. 2.1 feet
C. 2.5 feet
D. 2.9 feet

2109. A fire is discovered in the forepeak of a vessel at sea. The wind is from ahead at 35 knots. You should _____.

A. change course and put the stern to the wind
B. remain on course and hold speed
C. change course to put the wind on either beam and increase speed
D. remain on course but slack the speed

2112. You are sailing the navigable waters of the United States. You must have a currently corrected copy (or extract) of the _____.

A. List of Lights
B. Tide Tables
C. Sailing Directions
D. H.O. 249 Sight Reduction Tables

2114. You have hand launched an inflatable life raft. What should be one of your FIRST actions upon boarding the life raft?

A. Open the equipment pack.
B. Inflate the life raft floor.

C. Decide on food and water rations.
D. Cut the sea painter and clear the vessel.

2119. Your vessel displaces 475 tons. The existing deck cargo has a center of gravity of 2.6 feet above the deck and weighs 22 tons. If you load 16 tons of ground tackle with an estimated center of gravity of 8 inches above the deck, what is the final height of the CG of the deck cargo?

A. 1.64 feet
B. 1.79 feet
C. 1.96 feet
D. 2.14 feet

2121. A life float on a fishing vessel must be equipped with _____.

A. smoke flares
B. a lifeline
C. a hydrostatic release
D. a signal mirror

2131. When a person is in shock, their skin will be _____.

A. warm and dry
B. warm and damp
C. cold and dry
D. cold and damp

2133. If a vessel is sagging, which kind of stress is placed on the sheer strake?

A. Compression
B. Racking
C. Tension
D. Thrust

2137. Where would you find the FCC authorization for transmitting on your rig's EPIRB?

A. On the Ship Station License
B. On the side of the EPIRB transmitter
C. In the radio log
D. On the Certificate of Inspection

2142. What is meant by the term "overhaul" in firefighting?

A. Slow down the spread of fire by cooling adjacent structures
B. Cover the fire with foam
C. Smother the fire with a blanket or similar object
D. Break up solid objects to ensure that any deep seated fires are extinguished

2146. Aboard damaged vessels, the MOST important consideration is preserving _____.

A. bilge pumping capacity
B. reserve buoyancy
C. level attitude
D. instability

2147. Each life preserver must be readily accessible to the person for whom it is intended while he or she is _____.

A. at work, only
B. in his or her berthing area, only
C. BOTH at work and in his or her berthing area
D. None of the above

2150. You have approximately 6 tons of fish on deck. What will be the shift in the center of gravity after you shift the fish to the fish hold, a vertical distance of 7 feet? (Total displacement is 422 tons.)

A. 0.1 foot
B. 0.3 foot
C. 0.5 foot
D. 0.9 foot

2158. You have approximately 15 tons of fish on deck. What will be the shift in the center of gravity after you shift the fish to the fish hold, a vertical distance of 8 feet? (Total displacement is 300 tons.)

A. 0.1 foot
B. 0.2 foot
C. 0.3 foot
D. 0.4 foot

2159. Your vessel displaces 528 tons. The existing cargo has a center of gravity of 2.9 feet above the deck and weighs 28 tons. If you load 14 tons of ground tackle with an estimated center of gravity of 9 inches above the deck, what is the final height of the CG of the deck cargo?

A. 1.76 feet
B. 1.93 feet
C. 2.18 feet
D. 2.43 feet

2160. You have approximately 29 tons of fish on deck. What will be the shift in the center of gravity after you shift the fish to the fish hold, a vertical distance of 5 feet? (Total displacement is 483 tons.)

A. 0.3 foot
B. 0.4 foot
C. 0.5 foot
D. 0.6 foot

2163. You are approaching a small vessel and see that it has the signal flag "T" hoisted. What should you do?

A. Proceed on present course and speed since the vessel is stopped and making no way through the water.
B. Keep clear of the vessel because it is engauged in pair trawling.
C. Attempt to call the vessel on VHF radiotelephone because it requires assistance.
D. Keep clear of the vessel because it has a diver down.

2164. Your vessel is damaged, listing to port and on occasion flopping to the same angle to starboard. It has a long, slow, sluggish roll around the angle of list. There is excessive trim by the stern with little freeboard aft. What action should you take FIRST to correct this situation?

A. Jettison any off-center topside weights to lower GM and correct the list.
B. Pump out any slack after double-bottom tanks to reduce free surface and increase freeboard aft.
C. Pump out the after peak and fill the forepeak to change the trim.
D. Press up any slack double-bottom tanks forward of the tipping center, then fill the forepeak if empty.

2167. The color of the signal flare sent up by a submarine about to surface is _____.

A. red
B. yellow
C. green
D. white

2168. When a vessel is stationary and in a hogging condition, the main deck is under which type of stress?

A. compression
B. tension
C. shear
D. racking

2170. You have approximately 60 tons of fish on deck. What will be the shift in the center of gravity after you shift the fish to the fish hold, a vertical distance of 8 feet?

(Total displacement is 960 tons.)

A. 0.6 foot
B. 0.5 foot
C. 0.4 foot
D. 0.3 foot

2171. The approval period for a shipboard Oil Pollution Emergency Plan expires after _____.

A. two years
B. three years
C. four years
D. five years

2172. Your vessel displaces 560 tons. The existing deck cargo has a center of gravity of 4.5 feet above the deck and weighs 34 tons. If you load 10 tons of ground tackle with an estimated center of gravity of 2.8 feet above the deck, what is the final height of the CG of the deck cargo?

A. 4.11 feet
B. 4.36 feet
C. 4.57 feet
D. 4.78 feet

2175. To keep injured survivors warm in the water after abandoning ship, they should _____.

A. be placed in the middle of a small circle formed by the other survivors in the water
B. float on their backs with their arms extended for maximum exposure to the air
C. remove their life preservers and hold on to the uninjured survivors
D. sip water at intervals of 15 minutes

2179. If a vessel is sagging, what kind of stress is placed on the sheer strake?

A. Compression
B. Tension
C. Thrust
D. Racking

2180. You have approximately 16 tons of fish on deck. What will be the shift in the center of gravity after you shift the fish to the fish hold, a vertical distance of 8 feet? (Total displacement is 640 tons.)

A. 0.1 foot
B. 0.2 foot
C. 0.3 foot
D. 0.4 foot

2181. To prevent the spread of fire by conduction you should _____.

A. shut off all electrical power
B. close all openings to the area
C. remove combustibles from direct exposure
D. cool the bulkheads around the fire

2184. Your vessel is damaged and is listing to port. The rolling period is short. There is sufficient freeboard so that deck edge submersion is not a problem. What corrective action should be taken FIRST in regard to the vessel's stability?

A. Press up any slack double-bottom tanks to eliminate free surface
B. Flood any empty double-bottom tanks to add weight low and down
C. Jettison topside weights to reduce KG and KB
D. Shift any off-center weights from port to starboard

2190. You have approximately 24 tons of fish on deck. What will be the shift in the center of gravity after you shift the fish to the fish hold, a vertical distance of 8 feet? (Total displacement is 540 tons.)

A. 0.14 foot
B. 0.23 foot
C. 0.36 foot
D. 0.44 foot

2192. Your vessel displaces 689 tons and measures 123'L x 31'B. You ship a large wave on the after deck which measures 65'L x 31'B. The weight of the water is estimated at 62 tons. What is the reduction in GM due to free surface before the water drains overboard?

A. 5.51 feet
B. 5.67 feet
C. 5.89 feet
D. 6.14 feet

2194. Your vessel is damaged with no list, but down by the stern. There is progressive flooding and trim by the stern is increasing. What is the effect on transverse stability after the deck edge at the stern is submerged?

A. KB increases, increasing BM and therefore GM
B. KG increases due to the weight of the added water on deck

C. BM decreases from loss of water plane and greater volume.
D. There is no effect on transverse stability.

2199. Your vessel displaces 564 tons. The existing deck cargo has a center of gravity of 1.5 feet above the deck and weighs 41 tons. If you load 22 tons of ground tackle with an estimated center of gravity of 2.5 feet above the deck, what is the final height of the CG of the deck cargo?

A. 1.62 feet
B. 1.85 feet
C. 2.10 feet
D. 2.46 feet

2201. The name of the fishing vessel is NOT required to be marked on a(n) _____.

A. EPIRB
B. inflatable life raft
C. lifefloat
D. buoyant apparatus

2202. Which approved lifesaving device is required for each person on board a motor vessel carrying passengers?

A. Buoyant cushion
B. Buoyant vest
C. Life jacket
D. Ring life buoy

2205. You board an inflatable life raft that has been hand launched from a sinking vessel. What should you do FIRST after everyone is onboard the life raft?

A. Cut the painter.
B. Operate the radio equipment.
C. Open the equipment pack.
D. Ventilate the life raft of CO_2.

2207. You are keeping the required garbage disposal records. The amount of garbage disposed must be stated in _____.

A. both cubic meters and cubic feet
B. cubic meters
C. both kilos and pounds
D. barrels of 55 gallon capacity

2211. You discharge garbage overboard at sea. When recording your vessel's position as required, you must include _____.

A. latitude, longitude and estimated distance from shore

B. latitude, longitude and approximate depth of water
C. latitude, longitude, course, speed, and a copy of that day's noon position slip
D. Latitude and longitude only

2219. Each buoyant work vest must be _____.

A. U.S. Coast Guard approved
B. marked with the name of the vessel
C. equipped with a water light
D. All of the above

2225. Which system is least likely to be affected by atmospheric disturbances?

A. NAVTEX
B. INMARSAT
C. MF NBDP
D. HF NBDP

2233. You are underway when a fire breaks out in the forward part of your vessel. If possible, you should _____.

A. call for assistance
B. abandon ship to windward
C. keep going at half speed
D. put the vessel's stern into the wind

2234. As a vessel falls off the wind from close-hauled to a beam reach, the tendency for the vessel to move sideways through the water will _____.

A. increase
B. decrease
C. change only if the vessel comes about on the opposite tack
D. not change

2235. You are aboard a vessel which is near a platform engaged in oil exploration. Under U.S. pollution regulations, you may NOT discharge garbage if you are within

_____.
A. 1650 feet (500 meters)
B. 1750 feet (533 meters)
C. 1970 feet (600 meters)
D. 2500 feet (762 meters)

2237. Topside icing decreases vessel stability because it increases _____.

A. displacement
B. free surface
C. draft
D. KG

2238. Which system has the least effective radius of operation?

A. HF SITOR
B. MF SITOR
C. VHF DSC
D. NAVTEX

2240. What is classified as a combustible liquid?

A. Acetaldehyde
B. Ethyl alcohol
C. Carbon tetrachloride
D. Tetraethylene glycol

2251. What will NOT decrease the stability of a vessel?

A. Topside icing
B. Running with a following sea
C. Using 35% of the fuel in a full tank
D. Lowering a weight suspended by a boom onto the deck

2264. Where a propeller shaft passes through the hull, water is prevented from entering by means of a _____.

A. stuffing box
B. propeller boss
C. seacock
D. stop-water

2266. Which fire extinguishing agent can NOT be used on an ethylenediamine?

A. Water foam
B. Dry chemical powder
C. Water fog
D. Alcohol foam

2270. When a vessel is inclined at a small angle the center of buoyancy will _____.

A. remain stationary
B. move toward the low side
C. move toward the high side
D. move to the height of the metacenter

2274. A virtual rise in the center of gravity may be caused by _____.

A. filling a partially filled tank
B. using an onboard crane to lift a freely swinging heavy object
C. emptying a partially filled tank
D. transferring ballast from the forepeak to the after peak

2307. Why does a centrifugal bilge pump require priming?

A. To lubricate shaft seals
B. Lack of ability to lift water level to impellers
C. Head pressure must equal discharge pressure
D. To overcome resistance of water in the discharge line

2320. You are attempting to recover a mooring buoy. If you approach the object on the port tack, how would you slow the vessel as you draw near?

A. Quickly change to a starboard tack as you reach the object.
B. Shift the rudder from port to starboard several times as you reach the object.
C. Bring the wind so that it comes over the stern and ease all the sheets.
D. Bring the wind directly over the bow and allow the sails to luff.

2327. How many B-II fire extinguishers must be in the machinery space of a 75-foot long fishing vessel propelled by engines with 600 brake horsepower?

A. 5
B. 4
C. 3
D. 2

2335. What is required in addition to the heat, fuel, and oxygen of the fire triangle to have a fire?

A. Chain reaction
B. Electricity
C. Pressure
D. Smoke

2343. A marker pole, with a horseshoe buoy and a sea anchor attached, should be used to _____.

A. mark the position of a lost mooring
B. determine your vessel's sideslip under-way
C. determine your speed through the water
D. indicate location of a man overboard

2345. During an annual FCC inspection _____.

A. all required documents and publications may have to be produced

B. licensed GMDSS radio operators may be required to demonstrate equipment competencies
C. all required equipment must be fully operational
D. All of the above

2351. How many B-II fire extinguishers must be in the machinery space of a 75-foot long fishing vessel propelled by engines with 2200 brake horsepower?

A. 5
B. 4
C. 3
D. 2

2371. What does the term "head" mean when applied to a fire pump?

A. Length of the discharge pipe
B. Height of the discharge pipe
C. Difference between the discharge and suction pressures
D. Sum of discharge and suction pressures

2387. A magnetic compass card is marked in how many degrees?

A. 90
B. 180
C. 360
D. 400

2395. A negative metacentric height _____.

A. should always be immediately corrected
B. will always cause a vessel to capsize
C. always results from off-center weights
D. All of the above are correct

2421. How many degrees are there on a compass card?

A. 360°
B. 380°
C. 390°
D. 420°

2424. Which statement pertaining to log keeping is TRUE?

A. Entries relating to pre-voyage, pre-departure and daily tests are required
B. Both A and C
C. All distress, urgent and safety communications must be logged
D. Routine daily MF-HF and INMARSAT-C transmissions do not have to be logged

2425. Every seaman injured on a fishing vessel must report the injury to the Master, individual in charge, or other agent of the employer _____.

A. before the end of the voyage
B. no later than 24 hours after the vessel docks
C. no later than 7 days after the injury occurred
D. only if the injury prevents him from working

2429. A vessel trimmed by the stern has a _____.

A. list
B. drag
C. set
D. sheer

2457. What is a grooved pulley?

A. Sheave
B. Slip
C. Block
D. Reeve

2475. Your fishing vessel is required to have a compass. It must also have a(n) _____.

A. deviation table
B. radar reflector
C. electronic position-fixing device
D. copy of the Sailing Directions

2504. A reinspection of the vessel shall be made between which of the following months while the Certificate of Inspection is valid?

A. 8–12 months
B. 10–12 months
C. 10–14 months
D. 12–14 months

2507. When using a crane for transferring personnel in a basket, the load hook must be equipped with a _____.

A. moused shackle
B. safety latch
C. safety belt for each rider
D. quick-release device

2511. When lowering a personnel net to pick up personnel from a boat, the personnel basket should be _____.

A. lowered over open water
B. tied to the vessel with a tag line
C. dropped in the water
D. tied to the rig with a tag line

2523. How many B-II fire extinguishers must be in the machinery space of a 75-foot long fishing vessel propelled by engines with 2000 brake horsepower?

A. 2
B. 3
C. 4
D. 5

2528. Which action should you take after sending a false distress alert on VHF?

A. Send a DSC cancellation message on CH 70.
B. Make a voice announcement to cancel the alert on CH 16.
C. Make a voice announcement to cancel the alert on CH 13.
D. Make a voice announcement to cancel the alert on CH 22A.

2531. What is the fundamental purpose for imposing radio silence?

A. To ensure that interference to proprietary communications is minimized
B. To ensure that only voice communications can be effected on the distress frequency or channel
C. To ensure that a distressed vessel will have a "window" twice each hour for transmitting routine messages
D. To ensure that interference on a particular frequency or channel to communications concerning emergency traffic is minimized

2536. To prevent the spread of fire by conduction you should _____.

A. shut off all electrical power
B. close all openings to the area
C. cool the bulkheads around the fire
D. remove combustibles from direct exposure

2549. Vessels A and B are identical; however, A is more tender than B. This means that A relative to B has a _____.

A. lower KG
B. smaller GM
C. smaller roll angle
D. larger GZ

2552. When can routine communications be resumed when radio silence has been imposed?

A. After determining that the frequency or channel appears to be no longer in use
B. After determining that geographic distance from the distress situation will prohibit any other signal from interfering with emergency communications
C. Routine communications can resume after the Rescue Coordination Center transmits a message on the frequency or channel being used for emergency communications stating that such traffic has concluded.
D. If, in the Master's opinion, communications on that frequency will interfere with emergency communications

2553. What is meant by the term "radio silence"?

A. Stations not directly involved with the on-going distress communications may not transmit on the distress frequency or channel
B. Stations remaining off the air to safeguard proprietary information
C. Two three-minute silent periods, at 15 and 45 minutes after the hour, that provide a transmitting "window" for distressed vessels to transmit distress alerts using J3E
D. Communications on a distress frequency or channel is banned for 24 hours following the cessation of the distress traffic

2554. How is "radio silence" imposed?

A. By the On Scene Coordinator (OSC)
B. By the Coast Earth Station (CES) controlling the distress communications on that frequency
C. It is imposed by the Public Correspondence Station (PCS) controlling the distress communications on that frequency or channel
D. It is imposed by the High Seas Service (HSS) controlling the distress communications on that frequency or channel

2571. You have abandoned ship in rough weather. After picking up other survivors in your life raft, what should you do next?

A. Close up the entrances.
B. Top up the bouyancy tubes.
C. Prepare for the arrival of rescue units.
D. Decide on food and water rations.

2572. The radiotelephone urgency signal is
_____.

A. mayday
B. pan pan
C. securité
D. seelonce feenee

2575. The "urgent" priority should be used
for messages _____.

A. concerning the Safety of Life at Sea
(SOLAS)
B. detailing important navigational warn-
ings
C. containing information concerning the
safety of a mobile unit or person
D. concerning on-scene communications

2577. The radiotelephone safety signal is
_____.

A. "securité" repeated 3 times
B. "safety" repeated 3 times
C. "pan pan" repeated 3 times
D. "securité securité" repeated 3 times

2582. When the height of the metacenter is
the same as the height of the center of
gravity, the metacentric height is equal to
_____.

A. the height of the metacenter
B. the height of the center of gravity
C. half the height of the metacenter
D. zero

2596. Drinking salt water will _____.

A. dehydrate you
B. prevent seasickness
C. be safe if mixed with fresh water
D. protect against heat cramps

2599. Oil fires are best extinguished by
_____.

A. cutting off the supply of oxygen
B. removing the fuel
C. cooling below the ignition temperature
D. spraying with water

2613. What is required in addition to the
heat, fuel, and oxygen of the fire triangle to
have a fire?

A. Smoke
B. Electricity
C. Chain reaction

D. Pressure

2614. What is required in addition to the
heat, fuel, and oxygen of the fire triangle to
have a fire?

A. Smoke
B. Electricity
C. Pressure
D. Chain reaction

2617. Which is an exception to the garbage
discharge requirements in Annex V to
MARPOL 73/78?

A. The garbage to be discharged will sink.
B. Garbage accumulation on board has ex-
ceeded storage space.
C. A person falls overboard, and a plastic
ice chest is thrown for flotation.
D. The destination port or terminal cannot
receive garbage.

2636. When providing first aid to a victim of
gas poisoning, the MOST important symptom to check for is _____.

A. suspension of breathing
B. unconsciousness
C. slow and weak pulse
D. cold and moist skin

2652. Which vessel is required to carry an
efficient daylight signaling lamp? (Uninspected Vessel Regulations.)

A. 99 GT towing vessel on Inland Waters
B. 199 GT towing vessel on a coastwise voyage
C. 299 GT towing vessel on a coastwise voyage
D. 199 GT towing vessel on an international
voyage

2658. As a vessel changes course to
starboard, the compass card in a magnetic
compass _____.

A. first turns to starboard then counter-
clockwise to port
B. also turns to starboard
C. turns counterclockwise to port
D. remains aligned with compass north

2662. A vessel with a large GM will _____.

A. have a small amplitude of roll in heavy
weather

B. tend to ship water on deck in heavy
weather
C. be subject to severe racking stresses
D. be less likely to have cargo shift

2664. Gasoline fumes tend to _____.

A. settle near the bottom of the bilge
B. settle near the top of the bilge
C. settle evenly throughout all levels of the
bilge by mixing with air
D. disperse to atmosphere

2668. As a vessel changes course to
starboard, the compass card in a magnetic
compass _____.

A. remains aligned with compass north
B. also turns to starboard
C. first turns to starboard then counter-
clockwise to port
D. turns counterclockwise to port

2676. A safe fuel system must _____.

A. prevent engine overheating
B. have proper air/gasoline fuel mixture
ratio
C. be liquid- and vapor-tight
D. supply sufficient air to the intake mani-
fold

2681. You are offloading garbage to another ship. Your records must identify that ship
by name and show her _____.

A. official number
B. home port
C. Master
D. next port of call

2682. The purpose of fuses in electric
wiring is to _____.

A. allow for cutting out branch circuits
B. prevent overloading the circuits
C. reduce voltage to the branch circuits
D. permit the use of smaller wiring for light-
ing circuits

2687. As a vessel changes course to
starboard, the compass card in a magnetic
compass _____.

A. first turns to starboard then
counterclockwise to port
B. also turns to starboard
C. remains aligned with compass north
D. turns counterclockwise to port

2689. A vessel with a large GM will _____.

A. have more resistance to listing in case of damage
B. have less tendency to have synchronous rolling
C. be less likely to have cargo shift
D. ride more comfortably

2690. Heavy fuel oils when spilled are _____.

A. more harmful to sea life than lighter oils
B. easier to clean up than lighter refined oils
C. less harmful to sea life than lighter oils
D. not a real threat to marine life

2694. The heading of a vessel is indicated by what part of the compass?

A. Card
B. Needle
C. Lubber's line
D. Gimbals

2729. You are approaching another vessel and see that it has the signal flag "O" hoisted. What is your next action?

A. Proceed on present course and speed since the vessel is requesting a pilot.
B. Attempt to call the vessel on VHF radiotelephone and begin a search because the vessel has a man overboard.
C. Attempt to call the vessel on VHF radiotelephone because it is disabled.
D. Approach with caution because the vessel is stopped and making no way through the water.

2742. A vessel with a small GM will _____.

A. have a large amplitude of roll
B. provide a comfortable ride for the crew and passengers
C. have drier decks in heavy weather
D. be likely to have cargo shift in heavy weather

2744. Radar reflectors are required for _____.

A. all fishing vessels over 39 feet in length
B. sail-propelled fishing vessels
C. all fishing vessels of less than 200 GT
D. wooden hull fishing vessels with a poor radar echo

2754. Which lifesaving equipment must be tested monthly?

A. Inflatable PFDs
B. EPIRB
C. Hydrostatic releases
D. Dated batteries

2764. If you wear extra clothing when entering the water after abandoning ship it will _____.

A. weigh you down
B. preserve body heat
C. reduce your body heat
D. make it more difficult to breathe

2766. How do you know how many passengers you may carry? (Small Passenger Vessel Regulations)

A. As many as possible
B. The amount on the Certificate of Inspection
C. Use your own judgment
D. No more than 40 passengers

2768. Small passenger vessels of less than 100 gross registered tons must be inspected by the Coast Guard when they carry more than _____. (Small Passenger Vessel Regulations.)

A. 12 passengers
B. 50 passengers
C. 6 passengers
D. 1 passenger

2769. Starting motors, generators, and any other spark producing devices shall be _____. (Small Passenger Vessel Regulations.)

A. of the alternating current type
B. mounted as high as practicable above the bilges
C. rated for at least 12 volts
D. All of the above

2776. The lubber's line of a magnetic compass _____.

A. always shows true north direction
B. indicates the vessel's heading
C. is always parallel to the vessel's transom
D. is located on the compass card

2777. The lubber's line on a magnetic compass indicates _____.

A. compass north
B. the direction of the vessel's head
C. magnetic north
D. a relative bearing taken with azimuth circle

2779. Error may be introduced into a magnetic compass by _____.

A. making a structural change to the vessel
B. a short circuit near the compass
C. belt buckles
D. All of the above

2784. When abandoning ship and jumping into the water from a substantial height without a life jacket, you should _____.

A. dive head first, using your hands to break the surface of the water
B. hold your arms firmly at your sides and jump feet first
C. jump feet first, covering your nose and mouth with one hand and grasping the opposing upper arm with the other
D. jump feet first, holding your knees to your chest

2786. Certain equipment aboard vessels, inspected under the small passenger vessel regulations, is required to be marked with the vessel's name. This includes _____. (Small Passenger Vessel Regulations.)

A. bunks, silverware, china, and glassware
B. anchors, line, paint cans, and fuel drums
C. life jackets, life floats and paddles
D. whistles, searchlights, navigation lights, and ship's bell

2787. You are on a commercial fishing vessel 78 feet long. At least one of your ring buoys or throwable flotation devices must have a line of what minimum length attatched?

A. 60 feet
B. 70 feet
C. 80 feet
D. 90 feet

2789. As appropriate for the voyage, all vessels must carry adequate and up-to-date _____. (Small Passenger Vessel Regulations.)

A. charts
B. Coast Pilots
C. Light Lists
D. All of the above

2790. The weight of liquefied petroleum gas vapors as compared to air is _____.

A. variable
B. the same
C. lighter
D. heavier

2791. Seawater may be used for drinking _____.

A. under no conditions
B. at a maximum rate of two ounces per day
C. if gathered during or immediately after a hard rain
D. after mixing with an equal quantity of fresh water

2794. Which would influence a magnetic compass?

A. Electrical wiring
B. Iron pipe
C. Radio
D. All of the above

2796. On small passenger vessels cooking and heating equipment _____.

A. shall be suitable for marine use
B. may use liquefied petroleum gas
C. cannot use gasoline
D. All of the above

2801. How many B-II fire extinguishers must be in the machinery space of a 175-foot long fishing vessel propelled by engines with 2000 brake horsepower?

A. 2
B. 3
C. 4
D. 5

2803. When a magnetic compass is not in use for a prolonged period of time it should _____.

A. be shielded from direct sunlight
B. be locked into a constant heading
C. have any air bubbles replaced with nitrogen
D. have the compensating magnets removed

2805. A vessel heading NNW is on a course of _____.

A. 274.5°
B. 292.0°

C. 315.5°
D. 337.5°

2806. A vessel heading NW is on a course of _____.

A. 274.5°
B. 292.5°
C. 315.0°
D. 337.5°

2807. A vessel heading SSW is on a course of _____.

A. 202.5°
B. 225.0°
C. 247.5°
D. 270.0°

2811. A vessel heading SW is on a course of _____.

A. 202.5°
B. 225.0°
C. 247.5°
D. 270.0°

2812. What is correct with respect to required watertight bulkheads on small passenger vessels less than 100 GT?

A. Penetrations are prohibited.
B. Sluice valves are not permitted.
C. Each bulkhead must be stepped at its midpoint.
D. All of the above

2813. A vessel heading WSW is on a course of _____.

A. 202.5°
B. 225.0°
C. 247.5°
D. 271.0°

2815. A vessel heading WNW is on a course of _____.

A. 270.0°
B. 292.5°
C. 315.0°
D. 337.5°

2816. When a lifeline is required to be attached to a ring life buoy

it must be at least _____. (Small Passenger Vessel Regulations.)
A. 30 feet long
B. 60 feet long

C. 90 feet long
D. 120 feet long

2817. A vessel heading SSE is on a course of _____.

A. 112.5°
B. 135.0°
C. 157.5°
D. 180.0°

2819. Distress flares and smoke signals are not required on vessels operating on short runs. A "short run" is limited to _____. (Small Passenger Vessel Regulations.)

A. water of less than 20 feet in depth
B. where land is always in sight
C. no more than 5 miles
D. about 30 minutes away from the dock

2821. A vessel heading SE is on a course of _____.

A. 112.5°
B. 135.0°
C. 157.5°
D. 180.0°

2822. Survival craft required on a steel small passenger vessel operating in cold water must _____.

A. have sufficient capacity for all persons on board the vessel in ocean service.
B. have sufficient capacity for at least 50% of all persons on board for vessels in ocean service
C. be only inflatable life rafts
D. international orange in color only for vessels in lakes, bays and sounds service

2823. A vessel heading ESE is on a course of _____.

A. 112.5°
B. 135.0°
C. 157.5°
D. 180.0°

2825. The purpose of the inclining experiment is to _____.

A. determine the location of the metacenter
B. determine the lightweight center of gravity location
C. verify the hydrostatic data
D. verify data in the vessel's operating manual

2826. To prevent the spread of fire by convection you should _____.

A. cool the bulkhead around the fire
B. remove combustibles from direct exposure
C. close all openings to the area
D. shut off all electrical power

2828. On board small passenger vessels, how often shall the Master test the steering gear?

A. Once a week
B. Once a month
C. Every 72 operating hours while underway
D. Before getting underway for the day's operations

2829. Aboard small passenger vessels the steering gear, signaling whistle, controls, and communication system shall be tested by the Master _____.

A. once a week
B. before getting underway for the day's operation
C. at every inspection and reinspection
D. at least once in every 48 hours

2831. A vessel heading ENE is on a course of _____.

A. 022.5°
B. 045.0°
C. 067.5°
D. 090.0°

2832. Which fuel cannot be used for cooking on vessels carrying passengers for hire? (Small Passenger Vessel Regulations.)

A. Kerosene
B. Coal
C. Wood
D. Gasoline

2833. A vessel heading NE is on a course of _____.

A. 022.5°
B. 045.0°
C. 067.5°
D. 090.0°

2835. A vessel heading NNE is on a course of _____.

A. 022.5°

B. 045.0°
C. 067.5°
D. 090.0°

2836. The remote control for a fixed fire extinguishing system should be _____. (Uninspected Vessel Regulations.)

A. painted red and labeled
B. concealed from the crew
C. protected by plexiglas
D. padlocked

2838. How many B-II hand portable fire extinguishers are required in the machinery space of a 260 GT tow vessel with 2400 B.H.P.? (Uninspected Vessel Regulations.)

A. 6
B. 5
C. 3
D. 2

2839. What type of cooking equipment may NOT be used aboard vessels subject to The Rules and Regulations for Small Passenger Vessels?

A. Gasoline
B. Propane
C. Butane
D. LPG

2842. No "T-boat," however propelled, may operate with more than six passengers onboard _____.

A. unless the operator has a Coast Guard license
B. unless the vessel has a valid Permit to Proceed
C. until the Boarding Officer has checked the papers
D. until a permit is obtained from the Collector of Customs

2843. Under the Pollution Regulations, garbage disposal records must be kept _____.

A. two years
B. one year
C. until the next Coast Guard inspection
D. until the end of the voyage

2846. A small passenger vessel engaging in international voyages must be drydocked at least once every _____.

A. 6 months

B. 12 months
C. 36 months
D. 60 months

2849. A vessel would be referred to as "stiff" when the weight of the cargo is _____.

A. evenly distributed vertically and the double bottoms are full
B. concentrated low and the double bottoms are empty
C. concentrated low and the double bottoms are full
D. concentrated high and the double bottoms are empty

2852. You are fighting a fire in a watertight compartment using hoses and river water. Stability may be reduced because of _____.

A. progressive downflooding
B. reduction of water in the storage tanks
C. increase in free surface which reduces the metacentric height
D. reduction of KG to the minimum allowable

2856. Which vessel is NOT required to have a Pollution Placard posted on board?

A. 215-foot naval auxiliary vessel
B. 75-foot towing vessel
C. 50-foot cabin cruiser used for pleasure only
D. 150-foot unmanned tank barge

2858. A 50-foot passenger vessel not limited to daylight operation is required to be equipped with at least _____.

A. 1 ring life buoy with a water light
B. 2 ring life buoys with a water light
C. 2 ring life buoys with 2 water lights
D. 3 ring life buoys with 2 water lights

2859. For emergency communications, vessels operating on oceans, coastwise, or Great Lakes routes, on runs of more than 30 minutes shall carry in a portable watertight container at or near the operating station _____. (Small Passenger Vessel Regulations.)

A. six orange hand smoke distress signals
B. six red hand flare distress signals
C. one 3-cell flashlight
D. six red hand flare distress signals and six orange hand smoke distress signals

531

2861. What is the minimum number of portable fire extinguishers required on board a 35-foot towing vessel having a fixed fire system on board? (Uninspected Vessel Regulations.)

A. 1 B-I
B. 2 B-I
C. 3 B-I
D. 4 B-I

2862. A wooden small passenger vessel operating on a coastwise route in cold water shall carry sufficient inflatable buoyant apparatus for _____ or meet alternate requirements regarding collision bulkhead standards and the provision of life floats. (Small Passenger Vessel Regulations.)

A. all persons aboard
B. 67% of the total number of persons permitted on board.
C. 50% of all persons aboard
D. 30% of all persons aboard

2865. Which statement about the free surface correction is TRUE?

A. It is added to GM at light drafts and subtracted at deep drafts.
B. It is increased if the slack tank is not on the centerline.
C. It is decreased if the slack tank is below the KG of the vessel.
D. The correction decreases as the draft increases

2866. If a vessel is not equipped with an automatically activated emergency lighting system, the vessel must be _____. (Small Passenger Vessel Regulations.)

A. operated only in daylight hours
B. provided with gasoline or kerosene lights
C. equipped with luminous tape markings on emergency equipment
D. equipped with individual battery-powered lights

2869. Mechanical gearing of deck machinery such as the windlass or towing engine should _____.

A. be open to view so, if a foreign object gets in the gearing, the operator can immediately stop the machinery
B. have a guard over the gearing
C. be painted a contrasting color from the base color in order to call attention to the gearing
D. not be operated if there is any crew within 10 feet of the machinery

2876. The minimum number of portable B-II fire extinguishers required in the machinery space of a 199 GT motor towing vessel of 8000 B.H.P. is _____. (Uninspected Vessel Regulations.)

A. 3
B. 6
C. 8
D. 9

2878. To prevent the spread of fire by conduction you should _____.

A. remove combustibles from direct exposure
B. cool the bulkheads around the fire
C. close all openings to the area
D. shut off all electrical power

2881. How many type B-II hand portable fire extinguishers are required in the machinery space of an uninspected towing vessel with 1,400 B.H.P.? (Uninspected Vessel Regulations.)

A. 2
B. 3
C. 4
D. 5

2882. Whenever an inspected vessel is drydocked for major repairs, the person in charge of the vessel, the owner or the agent should report this to the _____. (Small Passenger Vessel Regulations.)

A. Officer in Charge, Marine Inspection
B. National Cargo Bureau, Inc.
C. American Boat and Yacht Council, Inc.
D. All of the above

2883. Life jackets should be stowed in _____.

A. survival craft
B. messrooms
C. readily accessible locations
D. locked watertight containers

2886. A small passenger vessel, operating only on domestic routes, which is operated in salt water for more than three months in a year must undergo a drydock and internal structural examination at least once every _____.

A. 2 years
B. 3 years
C. 4 years
D. 5 years

2887. Seawater may be used for drinking _____.

A. at a maximum rate of two ounces per day
B. under no conditions
C. after mixing with an equal quantity of fresh water
D. if gathered during or immediately after a hard rain

2889. Switchboards shall be _____. (Small Passenger Vessel Regulations.)

A. Watertight
B. Grounded to the main engine on a wooden hulled boat
C. The dead-front type, totally enclosed
D. Equipped with switch locks

2892. Regulations define the bulkhead deck as _____. (Subdivision and Stability Regulations.)

A. any deck extending from stem to stern
B. the uppermost deck to which transverse watertight bulkheads extend
C. the lowermost deck to which transverse watertight bulkheads extend
D. the uppermost complete deck

2896. Your vessel is certificated to carry 50 persons. You are required to have _____. (Small Passenger Vessel Regulations.)

A. 50 adult life jackets
B. 40 adult life jackets and 10 child life jackets
C. 50 adult life jackets and 5 child life jackets
D. 50 adult life jackets and 2 child life jackets

2897. If the result of loading a vessel is an increase in the height of the center of gravity, there will always be an increase in the _____.

A. metacentric height
B. righting arm
C. righting moment
D. vertical moments

2898. Painters on life floats shall be not less than _____. (Small Passenger Vessel Regulations.)

A. 20 feet in length
B. 30 feet in length
C. 70 feet in length
D. 100 feet in length

2899. All small passenger vessels operating on lakes, bays, sounds, or river routes on runs of more than 30 minutes are required to carry _____. (Small Passenger Vessel Regulations.)

A. 3 red hand flare distress signals and 3 orange smoke hand distress signals
B. 8 red hand flare distress signals and 8 orange smoke hand distress signals
C. 6 red hand flare distress signals and 6 orange smoke hand distress signals
D. None of the above

2901. What is one of the FIRST actions you should take after abandoning and clearing away from a vessel?

A. Identify the person in charge.
B. Gather up useful floating objects.
C. Prepare for arrival of rescue units.
D. Arrange watches and duties.

2902. Vessels in ocean service shall carry sufficient life floats for _____. (Small Passenger Vessel Regulations.)

A. 25% of all persons on board
B. 50% of all persons on board
C. 75% of all persons on board
D. 100% of all persons on board

2903. Life jackets should be marked with the _____.

A. maximum weight allowed
B. stowage space assigned
C. vessel's home port
D. vessel's name

2905. Each emergency light must be marked with _____.

A. the letter "E"
B. an arrow pointing to the nearest exit
C. a no-smoking symbol
D. the word "DANGER"

2906. Which vessel must carry a compass on board? (Small Passenger Vessel Regulations.)

A. A non-self-propelled vessel
B. A vessel operating in protected waters with a short restricted route
C. A vessel operating on the Ohio River
D. A vessel operating on the Gulf of Mexico

2908. How many months after its expiration date may a Coast Guard license be renewed without retaking the complete exam?

A. 1 month
B. 6 months
C. 12 months
D. 24 months

2909. Following a collision or accident, the Master of each vessel involved must render assistance to persons affected by the collision or accident _____.

A. if he can do so without any risk to his vessel
B. if he can do so without undue delay
C. if he can do so without serious danger to his vessel or to individuals on board
D. without regard to any danger to his vessel

2919. All of the following are part of the fire triangle EXCEPT _____.

A. fuel
B. electricity
C. oxygen
D. heat

2922. Whenever practicable, the Certificate of Inspection must be posted _____. (Small Passenger Vessel Regulations.)

A. as high as feasible in the pilot house
B. near the area where passengers embark
C. in any location desired
D. in a conspicuous place where it will most likely be observed by the passengers

2928. It is recommended that drip collectors required on all updraft carburetors be drained by _____.

(Small Passenger Vessel Regulations.)
A. a device to automatically return all drip to the engine air intakes
B. no means whatsoever

C. a separate pipe leading to the bilges
D. a pump leading to a point outside the hull

2932. What is FALSE concerning the use of unicellular plastic foam work vests on small passenger vessels? (Small Passenger Vessel Regulations.)

A. They may be substituted for up to 50% of the required life jackets.
B. They shall be of an approved type.
C. They shall be stowed separately from required lifesaving equipment.
D. They may be worn by crew members when working near or over the water.

2935. Which statement is TRUE concerning life jackets which are severely damaged?

A. They should be replaced.
B. They must be tested for buoyancy before being continued in use.
C. They can be repaired by a reliable seamstress.
D. They can be used for children.

2938. What equipment must be on a life float? (Small Passenger Vessel Regulations.)

A. Two paddles, a light, painter, lifeline and pendants
B. Water light, painter, and signal mirror
C. Water light and painter only
D. Two paddles, painter, and six red flares

2939. How many distress flares and smoke signals are small pssenger vessels on oceans, coastwise or Great Lakes routes required to carry?

A. Six red hand flares and six orange smoke signals in a watertight container
B. Two ring life buoys with attached water lights
C. A battery operated red-flasher lantern
D. All of the above

2942. Vessels in ocean service shall carry _____.

(Small Passenger Vessel Regulations.)
A. lifefloats for 50% of all persons on board
B. buoyant apparatus for all persons on board
C. sufficient inflatable buoyant apparatus for all persons on board
D. life jackets for 50% of all persons on board

2948. Licenses are issued for _____.

A. 3 years
B. 5 years
C. 1 year
D. 2 years

2949. Which information are you required to report to the Coast Guard when an accident occurs in which loss of life results? (Small Passenger Vessel Regulations.)

A. Location of the occurrence
B. Number and name of vessel
C. Names of owners
D. All of the above

2953. When the height of the metacenter has the same value as the height of the center of gravity, the metacentric height is equal to _____.

A. the height of the metacenter
B. the height of the center of gravity
C. the same as half the height of the metacenter
D. zero

2958. The discharge side of every fire pump must be equipped with a _____.

A. gate valve
B. pressure gauge
C. check valve
D. strainer

2960. As Master of a small passenger vessel, you have a question regarding a proposed modification to a watertight bulkhead. In which subchapter of title 46 of the Code of Federal Regulations will you find the answer?

A. Subchapter B
B. Subchapter T
C. Subchapter F
D. Subchapter S

2961. The Certificate of Inspection issued to a vessel carrying more than six passengers must be _____. (Small Passenger Vessel Regulations.)

A. posted on board under glass, if practical
B. posted on the dock where passengers are embarked
C. retained at the owner's principal place of business
D. kept on file by the Collector of Customs

2963. Which of the following statements about transmitting distress messages by radiotelephone is INCORRECT?

A. If no answer is received on the designated distress frequencies, repeat the distress call on any frequency available.
B. Channel 16 (156.8) may be used for distress messages.
C. It is advisable to follow a distress message on 2182 kHz by two dashes of 10 to 15 seconds duration.
D. Distress messages should first be transmitted on 2182 kHz.

2965. Which is TRUE concerning immersion suits and their use?

A. Only a light layer of clothing may be worn underneath.
B. They provide sufficient flotation to do away with the necessity of wearing a life jacket.
C. They should be tight fitting.
D. A puncture in the suit will not appreciably reduce its value.

2966. Each vessel shall be dry-docked or hauled out at intervals not to exceed 2 years if operated in salt water for a total of more than _____. (Small Passenger Vessel Regulations.)

A. 3 months in any 12 month period since it was last hauled out
B. 6 months in the 3 year period since it was last hauled out
C. 12 months in the 5 year period since it was last hauled out
D. whenever ownership or management changes

2968. Air-cooled radiators for gasoline propulsion engine cooling _____. (Small Passenger Vessel Regulations.)

A. must be approved for marine use
B. must have a double fan installation
C. must be filled with fresh water
D. are permitted on vessels less than 65 feet carrying not more than 12 passengers

2969. All inlet and discharge fittings below the waterline shall have _____. (Small Passenger Vessel Regulations.)

A. cast-iron shut-off valves
B. a wooden plug with a 36 inch lanyard
C. an efficient and accessible means of closing

D. a blank-off flange of similar material

2970. An immersion suit must be equipped with a/an _____.

A. air bottle for breathing
B. orange smoke canister
C. whistle, light and retroreflective material
D. sea dye marker

2971. Which statement about immersion suits is TRUE?

A. The suit's oil resistance is such that it will be serviceable after exposure to gasoline or mineral spirits.
B. The immersion suit seals in body heat and provides protection against hypothermia indefinitely.
C. The suit is flameproof and provides protection to the wearer while swimming through burning oil.
D. All models will automatically turn an unconscious person face-up in the water.

2972. Regulations require that approved buoyant work vests _____. (Small Passenger Vessel Regulations.)

A. may not be carried on inspected vessels
B. may be substituted for 10% of the required life jackets
C. shall be stowed in a place inaccessible to passengers
D. shall be stowed separately from the required life jackets

2973. Which statement about immersion suits is TRUE?

A. All models will automatically turn an unconscious person face-up in the water.
B. The immersion suit seals in body heat and provides protection against hypothermia for weeks.
C. The suit will still be serviceable after a brief (2–6 minutes) exposure to flame and burning.
D. The collar must be inflated before abandoning ship.

2976. Aboard small passenger vessels the number of childrens' life jackets carried must be at least what percentage of the total number of persons aboard?

A. 4%
B. 7.50%
C. 10%
D. 15%

2978. Which equipment is not required for a life float? (Small Passenger Vessel Regulations.)

A. Paddles
B. Light
C. Painter
D. Compass

2979. Which vessel is required to carry a Category I, 406 MHz EPIRB installed to automatically float free and activate? (Small Passenger Vessel Regulations.)

A. A vessel operating exclusively on inland waters.
B. A vessel limited to 20 miles offshore, which carries a radiotelephone on board.
C. A vessel limited to 100 miles offshore.
D. Each vessel operating on the high seas or beyond three miles from the coastline of the Great Lakes.

2980. Which statement about immersion suits is TRUE?

A. The primary color of the suit's exterior may be red, orange or yellow.
B. All models will automatically turn an unconscious person face-up in the water.
C. The suit is flameproof and provides protection to a wearer swimming in burning oil.
D. The suit may be stored in a machinery space where the ambient temperature is 160°F.

2983. The height of the metacenter above the keel will vary depending on the _____.

A. draft and beam of the drilling unit
B. displacement and deadweight of the drilling unit
C. buoyancy and trim of the drilling unit
D. tonnage and deadweight of the drilling unit

2986. What must be mounted at a small passenger vessel's operating station for use by the Master and crew?

A. Emergency Instructions
B. A tide table for the area
C. Instructions on artificial respiration
D. The location of the first aid kit

2988. No person whose license has been revoked shall be issued another license except upon _____.

A. approval of the Commandant
B. taking a new examination
C. approval of the Officer-in-Charge, Marine Inspection
D. approval of an administrative law judge

2989. When would it NOT be necessary to immediately notify the U.S. Coast Guard? (Small Passenger Vessel Regulations.)

A. Loss of life
B. Major damage affecting the seaworthiness of a vessel
C. Damage amounting to $2,000
D. Injury to a person which requires medical treatment beyond first aid

2991. Which statement about immersion suits is TRUE?

A. Prior to abandonment, the suit allows body movement such as walking, climbing a ladder and picking up small objects.
B. The immersion suit seals in body heat and provides protection against hypothermia for weeks.
C. The suit is flameproof and provides protection to the wearer while swimming through burning oil.
D. The wearer of the suit is severely restricted in body movement, and the suit should not be donned until abandonment is imminent.

2992. A 98 GT uninspected towing vessel with a 1500 B.H.P. engine capability would be required to carry how many type B-II hand portable fire extinguishers on board? (Uninspected Vessel Regulations.)

A. 2
B. 4
C. 6
D. 8

2993. Convection spreads a fire by _____.

A. the transfer of heat across an unobstructed space
B. burning liquids flowing into another space
C. transmitting the heat of a fire through the ship's metal
D. heated gases flowing through ventilation systems

2995. On a rigid life raft which is equipped with all of the required equipment you may NOT find a _____.

A. boathook
B. fishing kit
C. lifeline or grab rail
D. sea painter

2999. The use of portable electrical equipment in the pumproom on tank barges is prohibited unless _____.

A. the pumproom is gas-free
B. spaces with bulkheads common to the pumproom are either gas-free, inert, filled with water, or contain grade E liquid
C. all other compartments in which flammable vapors and gases may exist are closed and secured
D. All of the above

3000. A rigid lifesaving device ONLY designed for survivors to hold on to while in the water is known as a _____.

A. life raft
B. life float
C. life preserver
D. buoyant apparatus

3001. Which statement concerning immersion suits is TRUE?

A. Immersion suits should be worn during routine work on deck to provide maximum protection.
B. After purchasing, the suit should be removed from its storage bag and hung on a hanger where it will be readily accessible.
C. During the annual maintenance the front zipper should be lubricated with paraffin or beeswax.
D. Small leaks or tears may be repaired using the repair kit packed with the suit.

3002. A vessel's Certificate of Inspection will show the _____. (Small Passenger Vessel Regulations.)

A. crew requirements
B. minimum fire fighting and lifesaving equipment
C. route permitted
D. All of the above

3003. How is the external flotation bladder of an immersion suit inflated?

A. It is inflated by a small CO_2 bottle that is automatically tripped when the front zipper is at the top of the zipper track.

B. It is inflated by a small CO_2 bottle that is manually tripped.
C. It is inflated by blowing through an inflation tube.
D. It inflates by seawater bleeding into the inflation bladder and reacting with a chemical.

3005. All vessels having a Certificate of Inspection and operating exclusively in salt water shall be dry-docked or hauled out _____. (Small Passenger Vessel Regulations.)

A. once in each calendar year
B. once in each fiscal year
C. at the time of each inspection
D. at intervals not to exceed 2 years

3009. Which type of ventilation is required for enclosed spaces containing gasoline, machinery, or fuel tanks? (Small Passenger Vessel Regulations.)

A. Natural supply and mechanical exhaust
B. Mechanical supply and natural exhaust
C. Mechanical supply and mechanical exhaust
D. Natural supply and natural exhaust

3016. Hand held red flares expire 42 months from the date of manufacture. Floating orange smoke distress signals expire after how many months?

A. 18 months
B. 24 months
C. 42 months
D. 60 months

3018. Each lifefloat on an inspected vessel shall be fitted and equipped with _____. (Small Passenger Vessel Regulations.)

A. a lifeline, a painter, and one paddle
B. a lifeline, a painter, and a water light
C. two paddles, a light, and a lifeline
D. two paddles, a light, a lifeline, a painter and pendants

3019. All vessels not limited to daylight service shall be fitted with a ring life buoy _____. (Small Passenger Vessel Regulations.)

A. on the stern of the vessel
B. with a twenty fathom line attached
C. with no line attached
D. with a water light to be attached during nighttime operation

3022. Vessels operating in warm water whose routes are restricted to 20 miles from a harbor of safe refuge shall carry life floats or buoyant apparatus for not less than _____. (Small Passenger Vessel Regulations.)

A. 25% of all persons on board
B. 50% of all persons on board
C. 75% of all persons on board
D. 100% of all persons on board

3026. Who is required to prepare and post Emergency Instructions in a conspicuous place accessible to crew and passengers? (Small Passenger Vessel Regulations.)

A. The buider of the vessel
B. The owner or Master of the vessel
C. The U.S. Coast Guard
D. The classification society

3028. While serving as Master on board your vessel, your license must be _____. (Small Passenger Vessel Regulations.)

A. displayed in the company office on shore
B. displayed in your home
C. in your possession on board the vessel
D. kept in the Coast Guard office where you sat for your license

3032. Controls for a fixed carbon dioxide system shall be mounted _____. Uninspected Vessel Regulations.)

A. directly outside the space protected by the system
B. as near the gas cylinders as possible
C. in the pilothouse
D. on the main deck near the bow

3033. The effects of free surface on initial stability depend upon the dimensions of the surface of the free liquids and the _____.

A. volume of liquid in the tank
B. volume of displacement of the vessel
C. location of the tank in the vessel
D. height of the center of gravity of the vessel

3035. The external inflation bladder on an immersion suit should be inflated _____.

A. before you enter the water
B. after you enter the water

C. after one hour in the water
D. after you notice that your suit is losing buoyancy

3037. An immersion suit should be equipped with a/an _____.

A. air bottle for breathing
B. whistle and hand held flare
C. whistle, strobe light and reflective tape
D. whistle, hand held flare and sea dye marker

3041. Under the Pollution Regulations, garbage disposal records must be kept _____.

A. one year
B. two years
C. until the end of the voyage
D. until the next Coast Guard inspection

3045. You are testing the external flotation bladder of an immersion suit and find it has a very slow leak. Which action should be taken?

A. Replace the suit.
B. Replace the inflation bladder.
C. Contact the manufacturer for repair instructions.
D. Some leakage should be expected and a topping off tube is provided; no other action is necessary.

3046. How long is the Certificate of Inspection issued to a 50 gross ton, passenger carrying vessel which is 60 feet (18 meters) in length valid? (Small Passenger Vessel Regulations.)

A. One year
B. Two years
C. Three years
D. Four years

3047. Automatic fire dampers in ventilation systems are operated by use of _____.

A. remotely operated valves
B. fusible links
C. CO_2 system pressure switches
D. heat or smoke detectors

3048. What is required for a dry exhaust pipe? (Small Passenger Vessel Regulations.)

A. Noncombustible hangers and supports
B. Insulation from combustible material
C. An automatic damper

D. A rain spray and spray cap

3051. The external flotation bladder on an immersion suit should be inflated _____.

A. only after two hours in the water
B. only after four hours in the water
C. before entry into the water
D. upon entry into the water

3052. Which statement is TRUE concerning work vests on a small passenger vessel?

A. They may be worn during drills
B. They may be substituted for up to 10% of the required life jackets on board
C. They need not be an approved type
D. They must be stowed separately from approved life jackets

3055. Which statement is TRUE concerning life jackets?

A. Buoyant vests may be substituted for life jackets.
B. Life jackets are designed to turn an unconscious person's face clear of the water.
C. Life jackets must always be worn with the same side facing outwards to float properly.
D. Lightly stained or faded life jackets will fail in the water and should not be used.

3056. The service use of pyrotechnic distress signals measured from the date of manufacture shall be limited to a period of _____.

A. 24 months
B. 36 months
C. 42 months
D. 60 months

3057. Each buoyant work vest on an OSV must be _____.

A. Coast Guard Approved
B. marked with the name of the unit
C. equipped with a waterlight
D. All of the above

3058. Life floats and buoyant apparatus shall be marked _____. (Small Passenger Vessel Regulations.)

A. with the vessel's name in 3" letters
B. conspicuously in 1-1/2" letters with the number of persons allowed
C. with the vessel's name on all paddles
D. All of the above

3059. How many ring life buoys must a small passenger vessel, of less than 65 feet in length, carry?

A. 1
B. 2
C. 3
D. 4

3061. When transferring survivors from a survival craft to a rescue vessel, personnel on board the craft should _____.

A. remove their life jackets to make it easier to climb on board the rescue vessel
B. climb on top of the survival craft while waiting their turn to transfer to the rescue vessel
C. remain seated inside the survival craft and make the transfer one person at a time
D. enter the water and swim over to the rescue vessel

3062. The Master of a vessel shall make sure the EPIRB is tested _____. (Small Passenger Vessel Regulations.)

A. daily
B. weekly
C. every two weeks
D. monthly

3066. Prior to getting underway for the day's operations, every small passenger vessel shall have its steering gear tested by _____.

A. the Mate on watch
B. the Master
C. a Mate or Designated Duty Engineer
D. a licensed Engineer

3067. The canopy of your life raft should _____.

A. go into place as your life raft is inflated
B. be put up after everyone is aboard
C. be put up only in severe weather
D. be used as a sail if the wind is blowing

3069. Unless otherwise stated, the term "approved" applied to a vessel's equipment, means approved by the _____. (Small Passenger Vessel Regulations.)

A. American Bureau of Shipping
B. Congress of the United States
C. Commandant of the Coast Guard
D. Board of Fire Underwriters

3078. If you see an individual fall overboard, you should _____.

A. throw him/her a life buoy
B. hail "man overboard"
C. pass the word to the bridge
D. All of the above

3082. On vessels subject to the provisions of 46 CFR Subchapter T, life jackets shall be _____.

A. kept locked up at all times when underway
B. stored in convenient places throughout the accommodation spaces
C. inaccessible to passengers
D. on the topmost deck of the vessel at all times

3084. All lifefloats and buoyant apparatus shall be clearly and legibly marked or painted with the _____. (Small Passenger Vessel Regulations.)

A. manufacturer's price, stock number, and inspection date
B. vessel's name, tonnage, and horsepower
C. vessel's name in 3" letters
D. vessel's name, and number of persons allowed, all in at least 3" high letters and numbers

3091. When will the float-free emergency position indicating radiobeacon be activated after abandoning ship?

A. Immediately after floating free
B. After about one hour when the salt water activates the battery
C. Only when keyed by the radar of another vessel
D. Only when daylight activates the photovoltaic cell

3092. Why is it necessary to extend ventilators of gasoline powered vessels to the bilges?

A. To keep them dry, thus easier to clean
B. To remove fuel vapors which are heavier than air
C. To provide adequate air to the engines
D. To cool the machinery areas

3094. A type B-III CO_2 extinguisher has a rated capacity of _____.

A. 15 lbs.
B. 25 lbs.

C. 35 lbs.
D. 45 lbs.

3096. The shutoff valve at the gasoline tank which can be operated from outside the tank space _____.

A. controls the amount of gasoline to the engine
B. shuts off the gasoline supply at the tank
C. is used if the gasoline tank leaks
D. All of the above

3102. Which type of fixed fire-extinguishing system is approved for use on board uninspected vessels? (Uninspected Vessel Regulations.)

A. Carbon dioxide
B. Steam smothering
C. Chemical foam
D. All of the above

3104. An emergency check-off list is required on vessels carrying six or fewer passengers for hire. The list must contain information on all of the following EXCEPT _____. (Uninspected Vessel Regulations.)

A. precautions for rough weather
B. actions required in the event of accident
C. procedures for man overboard emergencies
D. emergency procedures for fire at sea

3108. A CO_2 extinguisher which has lost 10% of its charge must be _____.

A. used at the earliest opportunity
B. hydrotested
C. recharged
D. weighed again in one month

3110. When a vessel is not in compliance with its Certificate of Inspection, which certificate may be issued to allow its movement to a repair facility? (Small Passenger Vessel Regulations.)

A. Change of Employment
B. Permit to Proceed
C. Application for Inspection
D. Temporary Certificate of Inspection

3112. An 85 foot uninspected towing vessel with a crew of ten (10) persons on board must carry at LEAST _____. (Uninspected Vessel Regulations.)

A. 10 approved ring life buoys and 10 approved life preservers
B. 10 approved work vests
C. 10 approved life jackets and 1 approved ring life buoy
D. 11 approved life preservers

3116. According the Lifesaving regulations in Subchapter W, fire and abandon ship drills must be held within 24 hours of leaving port if the percentage of the crew that has not participated in drills aboard that particular vessel in the prior month exceeds _____.

A. 5%
B. 10%
C. 25%
D. 40%

3119. Life floats and buoyant apparatus may be stowed in tiers, one above the other, to a height of not more than _____. (Small Passenger Vessel Regulations.)

A. 3 feet
B. 4 feet
C. 5 feet
D. 6 feet

3120. Before issuing an initial Certificate of Inspection, the construction arrangement and equipment of a vessel must be acceptable to the _____. (Small Passenger Vessel Regulations.)

A. American Bureau of Shipping Surveyor
B. U.S. Salvage Marine Surveyor
C. Officer in Charge, Marine Inspection
D. U.S. Customs Collector

3121. To prevent the spread of fire by conduction you should _____.

A. cool the bulkheads around the fire
B. remove combustibles from direct exposure
C. close all openings to the area
D. shut off all electric power

3122. All life jackets carried on board small passenger vessels are required to be marked _____. (Small Passenger Vessel Regulations.)

A. with the vessel's name
B. with the vessel's official number
C. with the maximum weight to be held by the life preserver

D. with the maximum serviceable life of the life preserver

3123. You are monitoring VHF Channel 16 when you receive a call to your vessel, TEXAS PRIDE. What is the proper way to answer this call?

A. "This is TEXAS PRIDE. Pick a channel."

B. "This is TEXAS PRIDE on Channel 16. Come back."

C. "This is TEXAS PRIDE, WSR 1234, reply Channel 10."
D. "Please stand by. We're busy right now."

3124. On a life float or buoyant apparatus, the lifeline is _____. (Small Passenger Vessel Regulations.)

A. secured around the sides and ends in bights of not longer than three feet
B. woven into a net and secured in the center of the float
C. used for securing unconscious persons to the sides
D. the lanyard for securing provisions

3127. Automatic fire dampers in ventilation systems are operated by use of a _____.

A. fusible link
B. remote operated valve
C. CO_2 system pressure switch
D. heat or smoke detector

3130. What is the minimum height of rails on passenger decks of ferryboats, excursion vessels, and vessels of a similar type? (Small Passenger Vessel Regulations.)

A. 18 inches (0.5 m) high
B. 24 inches (0.6 m) high
C. 39-1/2 inches (1 m) high
D. 42 inches (1.1 m) high

3134. Which is a B-II fire extinguisher? (Uninspected Vessel Regulations.)

A. A 2-1/2 gallon water (stored pressure) extinguisher
B. A 15 lb. CO_2 extinguisher
C. A 2 lb. dry chemical extinguisher
D. A 1-1/4 gallon foam extinguisher

3136. Where should the tops of vents from gasoline tanks terminate?

A. In open air
B. Inside cabins near the overhead
C. In the machinery space near the engine air intake
D. Underwater

3137. With damaged floating vessels, the most important consideration is the preservation of _____.

A. bilge pumping capacity
B. reserve buoyancy
C. level attitude
D. instability

3140. Hatches on small passenger vessels operating on exposed waters and exposed to the weather _____.

A. must be watertight
B. must be open at all times
C. need not be watertight
D. None of the above

3142. In the machinery space of all uninspected motor vessels, there must be one type B-II hand portable fire extinguisher for every _____. (Uninspected Vessel Regulations.)

A. 500 S.H.P. of the main engines
B. 1000 S.H.P. of the main engines
C. 500 B.H.P. of the main engines
D. 1000 B.H.P. of the main engines

3149. To find the cause of a gasoline engine's failure to start, you should _____.

A. break the joint in the fuel line at the engine and let the gas run in the bilges
B. disconnect the wires at the spark plugs and make the spark jump the gap
C. prime the engine with ether through spark plug openings
D. ventilate the space, then check the battery, spark plugs, carburetor, and fuel line

3150. Your vessel must have a B-II fire extinguisher. Which extinguisher fulfills this requirement? (Small Passenger Vessel Regulations.)

A. 4 lb. carbon dioxide
B. 4 lb. dry chemical
C. 15 lb. carbon dioxide
D. 12 gallon foam

3152. U.S. Coast Guard approved work vests may be substituted life jackets _____. (Uninspected Vessel Regulations.)

A. aboard work vessels
B. aboard towing vessels
C. aboard sailing vessels
D. under no circumstances

3154. How many escape routes must normally exist from all general areas accessible to the passengers or where the crew may be quartered or normally employed? (Small Passenger Vessel Regulations.)

A. Two
B. Three
C. Four
D. Five

3156. Lifesaving regulations in Subchapter W require that a fire drill include _____.

A. starting the fire pumps
B. checking the operation of watertight doors
C. checking arrangements for abandon ship
D. All of the above

3158. Electric generators can be protected against overload _____.

A. with switches
B. with a governor on the engine
C. with fuses or circuit breakers
D. by using heavy wire

3159. Fusible-link fire dampers are operated by _____.

A. a break-glass and pull-cable system
B. electrical controls on the bridge
C. a mechanical arm outside the vent duct
D. the heat of a fire melting the link

3160. Fixed ballast, if used, may be _____. (Small Passenger Vessel Regulations.)

A. discharged or moved at any time
B. moved temporarily for examination or repair of the vessel, when done under the supervision of an inspector
C. moved under the supervision of the owner, Master or shipyard
D. moved under any condition except extreme emergency

3161. The wooden plug fitted tightly in the vent of a damaged tank may prevent the tank from _____.

A. filling completely
B. developing free surfaces
C. developing free surface moments
D. collapsing

3162. All life jackets and life buoys shall be marked with the vessel's name in letters at least _____. (Small Passenger Vessel Regulations.)

A. 1/2 inch high
B. 1 inch high
C. Height not specified
D. 1-1/2 inches high

3167. Topside icing that blocks freeing ports and scuppers _____.

A. is usually below the center of gravity and has little effect on stability
B. will cause water on deck to pocket and increase stability
C. may decrease stability by increasing free-surface effect due to water on deck
D. increases the effective freeboard and increases the wind-heel affect

3170. What would be an example of a B-I extinguisher? (Small Passenger Vessel Regulations.)

A. 2.5 gallon foam
B. 10 pound carbon dioxide
C. 2 pound dry chemical
D. 5 pound foam

3171. Automatic fire dampers in ventilation systems are operated by use of _____.

A. fusible links
B. remotely operated valves
C. CO_2 system pressure switches
D. heat or smoke detectors

3172. Your vessel has a gasoline engine and a mechanical exhaust ventilation system. BEFORE starting the engine, the exhaust blower should be run long enough to _____.

A. warm up the exhaust blower motor
B. provide a proper supply of fresh air for the engine(s)
C. see the system is in good operating condition
D. insure at least one complete change of air in the compartments concerned

3173. What is considered to be a B-II portable fire extinguisher?

A. 2 pound dry chemical
B. 2-1/2 gallon foam
C. 4 pound carbon dioxide
D. All of the above

3174. What is considered to be a B-II portable fire extinguisher?

A. 2-1/2 gallon foam
B. 4 pound carbon dioxide
C. 2 pound dry chemical
D. All of the above

3176. The tops of vents from gasoline tanks should terminate _____.

A. in open air
B. inside cabins
C. in machinery space
D. underwater

3182. What is the minimum number of portable fire extinguishers required on board a 35-foot motorboat having a fixed fire system on board? (Uninspected Vessel Regulations.)

A. 1 B-I
B. 2 B-I
C. 3 B-I
D. 4 B-I

3184. The center of buoyancy and the metacenter are in the line of action of the buoyant force _____.

A. only when there is positive stability
B. only when there is negative stability
C. only when there is neutral stability
D. at all times

3186. Using a sea anchor will _____.

A. reduce the drift rate of the life raft
B. keep the life raft from turning over
C. aid in recovering the life raft
D. increase your visibility

3188. The air spaces in the floor of an inflatable life raft will provide protection against _____.

A. asphyxiation from CO_2
B. loss of air in the sides of the raft

C. rough seas
D. cold water temperatures

3189. If a gasoline engine turns over freely but will not start, the cause is generally _____.

A. a defective ignition system
B. low lube oil level
C. weak valve springs
D. too heavy a load

3192. Which statement is FALSE concerning the use of approved buoyant work vests on board uninspected towboats? (Uninspected Vessel Regulations.)

A. They may be substituted for up to 50% of the required life preservers.
B. They shall be of an approved type.
C. They shall be stowed separately from required lifesaving equipment.
D. They may be worn by crew members when working near or over the water.

3194. Generally, what is used to inflate life rafts?

A. Non-toxic gas
B. Oxygen
C. Hydrogen
D. Helium

3198. Starting motors, generators, and other spark producing devices should be mounted as high above the bilges as possible to _____.

A. keep them dry when the bilges are full of water
B. keep them cool when the vessel is underway
C. make them more accessible for repairs
D. prevent accidental ignition of any gasoline vapors that may have accumulated in the bilges

3200. Which circumstance concerning an inspected passenger vessel would require knowledge and approval of the Officer in Charge, Marine Inspection? (Small Passenger Vessel Regulations.)

A. The removal of a watertight bulkhead
B. A minor overhaul of the propulsion machinery

C. Renewal of a FCC Certificate for a radiotelephone
D. All of the above

3201. The stamped full weight of a 100-lb. CO_2 bottle is 314 lbs. What is the minimum weight of the bottle before it has to be recharged?

A. 282 lbs.
B. 294 lbs.
C. 300 lbs.
D. 304 lbs.

3202. Which of these approved lifesaving devices must a small passenger vessel carrying passengers for hire carry for each person on board? (Small Passenger Vessel Regulations.)

A. Buoyant cushion
B. Life jacket
C. Ring buoy
D. Buoyant vest

3203. The inside light in an inflatable life-raft is turned on _____.

A. automatically as the life raft inflates
B. with a switch near the boarding handle
C. at night because the light has a photosensitive switch
D. by screwing the bulb in after the raft inflates

3204. On most makes of inflatable life rafts, the batteries to operate the light on the inside of rafts can be made to last longer by _____.

A. unscrewing the bulb during the daylight
B. operating the switch for the light
C. taking no action as there is no way on saving power
D. taking no action as they shut off automatically in daylight

3207. The lights on the outside of the canopy of an inflatable life raft operate _____.

A. by turning the globe clockwise
B. by a switch at the light
C. by a light sensor
D. automatically when the raft is inflated

3208. Water pockets on the underside of an inflatable life raft are for _____.

A. catching rain water
B. stability
C. easy drainage
D. maneuverability

3210. On a small passenger vessel, 58 feet in length, carrying 52 passengers the fire pump shall have a minimum pumping capacity of _____.

A. 10 gallons per minute
B. 25 gallons per minute
C. 50 gallons per minute
D. 100 gallons per minute

3211. What is placed on the underside of an inflatable life raft to help prevent it from being skidded by the wind or overturned?

A. Ballast bags
B. A keel
C. Strikes
D. Sea anchor

3212. Before starting a gasoline engine on a motorboat, you should make sure for safety that _____.

A. the gasoline tank is full
B. the bilges, cabins, etc., are thoroughly ventilated
C. you have fresh water on board
D. Each of the above is followed

3213. A safety feature provided on all inflatable life rafts is _____.

A. overhead safety straps
B. built in seats
C. internal releasing hooks
D. water stabilizing pockets

3214. What does the "B" on a B-II fire extinguisher refer to? (Uninspected Vessel Regulations.)

A. Size of the applicator
B. Size of the nozzle
C. Size of the extinguisher
D. Class of fire that the extinguisher should be used on

3215. The jackknife stored on an inflatable life raft will always be located _____.

A. in one of the equipment bags
B. in a special pocket near the forward entrance
C. on a cord hanging from the canopy

D. in a pocket on the first aid kit

3216. Gasoline fuel tank vents should terminate _____.

A. in the engine compartment
B. in the fuel tank space
C. above or outside the hull
D. at the most convenient location

3217. Which of the devices listed will prevent an inflated life raft from being pulled under by a vessel which sinks in water over 100 feet deep?

A. The hydrostatic release
B. A shear pin
C. A rottmer release
D. A weak link in the painter

3220. All vessels not required to have a power driven fire pump shall carry _____. (Small Passenger Vessel Regulations.)

A. a suitable, detachable pump usable for fire fighting purposes
B. at least three 2-1/2 gallon fire buckets
C. an emergency hand fire and bilge pump
D. not less than three hand fire pumps

3222. Either one type B-III semi-portable fire-extinguishing system or a fixed fire-extinguishing system shall be fitted in the machinery space on vessels of over _____. (Uninspected Vessel Regulations.)

A. 100 GT
B. 200 GT
C. 300 GT
D. 400 GT

3223. After 1 September 1992, in the North Pacific area, a documented 75-foot fishing vessel operating in cold waters 25 miles off the coast must have at least a(n) _____.

A. buoyant cushion for each person on board
B. inflatable life raft with a SOLAS pack
C. inflatable buoyant apparatus with EPIRB attached
D. approved rescue boat

3228. A fuel line breaks, sprays fuel on the hot exhaust manifold, and catches fire. Your FIRST action should be to _____.

A. batten down the engine room
B. start the fire pump

C. apply carbon dioxide to the fire
D. shut off the fuel supply

3229. The engine head, block, and exhaust manifold shall be _____. (Small Passenger Vessel Regulations.)

A. water jacketed
B. air cooled
C. preheated prior to starting
D. drained weekly

3230. Which statement is TRUE concerning a power driven fire pump on board a small passenger vessel?

A. The hand fire pump shall be located adjacent to the main engine spaces.
B. It shall be of at least 2 gallons per minute capacity.
C. It shall be painted red.
D. It may also serve as a bilge pump.

3231. A lifeline must be connected to the life raft _____.

A. at the bow
B. at the stern
C. in the middle
D. all around

3232. Which statement is TRUE concerning work vests aboard a vessel? (Uninspected Vessel Regulations.)

A. They may be worn during drills.
B. They may be substituted for up to 10% of the required lifesaving gear aboard.
C. They need not be of an approved type.
D. They must be stowed separately from approved life preservers.

3233. The color of the signal flare sent up by a submarine about to surface is _____.

A. red
B. yellow
C. white
D. green

3234. The abandon ship signal is _____.

A. a continuous ringing of general alarm bells for at least 10 seconds
B. a continuous ringing of the general alarm, and sounding of the ship's whistle

C. more than 6 short blasts and 1 long blast of the ship's whistle and the same signal on the general alarm bells
D. a continuous sounding of the ship's whistle

3238. During fueling, all doors, hatches, and ports _____.

A. to windward should be opened and the ones to leeward should be closed
B. to leeward should be opened and the ones to windward should be closed
C. should be opened
D. should be closed

3240. When a vessel is required to have a power-driven fire pump, the pump may also be used for _____. (Small Passenger Vessel Regulations.)

A. the drinking water supply system
B. the bilge pump
C. engine cooling water
D. None of the above

3242. A vessel carrying passengers for hire shall have on board an approved life jacket _____. (Small Passenger Vessel Regulations.)

A. for every passenger on board
B. for every person on board, plus 10% children's life jackets
C. for every person on board, plus 10% additional on upper deck in box
D. or buoyant cushion for every person on board plus 10% for children

3243. If there's a fire aboard your vessel, you should FIRST _____.

A. notify the Coast Guard
B. cut off air supply to the fire
C. have passengers put on life preservers
D. sound the alarm

3250. Which statement is TRUE concerning fire hose on a small passenger vessel?

A. Fire hose shall be at least 3/4" outside diameter.
B. One length of fire hose shall be provided for every two fire hydrants.
C. All fittings on hoses shall be of steel or other ferrous metal.
D. A length of hose with nozzle attached shall be attached to each fire hydrant at all times.

3251. A hydrostatic release mechanism for a life raft _____.

A. must be wet before it will release
B. should be kept in a watertight cover except in an emergency
C. will inflate the raft in its cradle if operated manually
D. must be submerged to a certain depth to release automatically

3252. Before any machinery is put in operation, you should _____.

A. ventilate all compartments, see that the machinery is clean and there are no obstructions
B. just turn the key and start up
C. take for granted that there are no fuel leaks
D. assume there are no volatile fumes in the engine space

3254. All uninspected motor vessels constructed after 25 April 1940, which use fuel with a flash point of 110°F (43°C) or less, shall have at least what number of ventilator ducts for the removal of explosive or flammable gases from every engine and fuel tank compartment? (Uninspected Vessel Regulations.)

A. 1
B. 2
C. 3
D. 4

3256. Gasoline vapor tends to collect _____.

A. above the floor plates of the bilges
B. above the carburetor level
C. at the lowest point of the bilge areas
D. at no particular level

3260. A length of fire hose shall be _____. (Small Passenger Vessel Regulations.)

A. attached to each fire hydrant at all times
B. equipped with a rotary sprinkler head
C. marked with the lot number and wholesale price
D. not more than 10 feet in length

3268. Diesel engines are considered safer than gasoline engines because _____.

A. they are more heavily built
B. the fuel used is less volatile

C. they can be easily reversed
D. they operate at a lower speed

3269. What is the purpose of the life raft's hydrostatic release?

A. To release raft automatically as the ship sinks
B. To inflate the raft automatically
C. To test rafts hydrostatically
D. None of the above

3270. Which portable fire extinguisher is required just outside the exit of the propulsion machinery space of a 75-ton passenger vessel?

A. 2-1/2 gallon foam extinguisher
B. 15 lb. CO_2 extinguisher
C. 2 lb. dry chemical extinguisher
D. None of the above

3272. Where should life jackets be stowed? (Small Passenger Vessel Regulations.)

A. In the forepeak
B. In the wheelhouse
C. Throughout the accommodation spaces
D. In locked watertight and fireproof containers on or above the main deck

3274. Vessels required to be equipped with an approved backfire flame arrester are _____.

A. those with diesel engines
B. all those with gasoline engines
C. those with large engines only
D. None of the above

3278. Gasoline tanks should be filled _____.

A. to the top to expel all vapors from the tanks
B. to the top so the operator is certain how much fuel he has aboard
C. with only sufficient fuel for the planned trip so excess gasoline is not carried
D. to near the top with some space allowed for gasoline expansion

3280. Which type of fire extinguishers are permitted on inspected vessels? (Small Passenger Vessel Regulations.)

A. Foam
B. Carbon dioxide
C. Dry chemical
D. All of the above

3284. Unless the COI is endorsed for adults only, there shall be provided a number of approved life jackets suitable for children equal to at least _____. (Small Passenger Vessel Regulations.)

A. 20% of the passengers carried
B. 10% of the total number of persons carried
C. 10% of the passengers carried
D. 20% of the total number of persons carried

3290. On vessels that are required to have fixed carbon dioxide fire extinguishing systems, the controls to operate the system shall be installed in an accessible location _____. (Small Passenger Vessel Regulations.)

A. outside the space protected
B. inside the space protected
C. at the carbon dioxide cylinders
D. in a padlocked waterproof metal box

3292. Upon completion of fueling a gasoline-driven vessel it is necessary to _____.

A. keep ports, doors, windows, and hatches closed
B. start engines immediately
C. ventilate before starting engine
D. None of the above

3294. What is the purpose of the life raft hydrostatic release?

A. To release the life raft from the cradle automatically as the ship sinks
B. To inflate the raft automatically
C. To test rafts hydrostatically
D. None of the above

3296. Which statement is TRUE concerning fuel vapors on a vessel?

A. Fuel vapors gather in the lowest portions of the vessel.
B. Fuel vapors can only be ignited by an open flame.
C. Vent outlets should be located above the level of the carburetor air intake.
D. None of the above

3300. How many portable fire extinguishers are required to be located inside the machinery space of a small passenger vessel?

A. None are required
B. One B-I, C-I
C. One B-II, C-II
D. One B-II

3302. What is the minimum number of Type B-II hand portable fire extinguishers required to be aboard a 3,000 BHP, 99 GT harbor tug? (Uninspected Vessel Regulations.)

A. 2
B. 3
C. 5
D. 6

3304. If your passenger vessel has been issued a stability letter, it must be _____.

A. filed in the ship's office
B. posted in a passenger area
C. posted adjacent to the Certificate of Inspection
D. posted in the pilothouse

3308. The quickest method to stop a small diesel engine whose throttle or governor has become stuck open is to _____.

A. drain the fuel tank
B. turn off the ignition switch
C. close the fuel supply valve
D. apply the shaft brake

3309. The exhaust pipe must be gas tight throughout its entire length otherwise _____.

A. bilge water may enter the exhaust pipe
B. entry of air may cause vapor lock
C. carbon monoxide may enter the interior of the vessel
D. the joint gaskets may be blown

3310. Fixed carbon dioxide fire extinguishing systems shall be installed to protect enclosed machinery and fuel tank spaces of all vessels using gasoline or other fuel having a flash point of _____. (Small Passenger Vessel Regulations.)

A. 0°F or lower
B. 75°F or lower
C. 90°F or lower
D. 110°F or lower

3312. By regulation, life preservers aboard an uninspected towing vessel must be _____. (Uninspected Vessel Regulations.)

A. readily accessible
B. securely stowed
C. stored in sealed containers
D. stowed with the emergency provisions

3313. If the hydrostatic release mechanism for an inflatable life raft is not periodically serviced and becomes inoperable, it will fail to _____.

A. set the water lights on immersion
B. release the dye marker from the life raft
C. free the life raft from the vessel
D. break the seal on the carbon dioxide cylinder

3314. Which device is required to be installed under the carburetor of a gasoline engine? (Small Passenger Vessel Regulations.)

A. Box of sawdust
B. Drip collector
C. Vent
D. Flame arrestor ONLY

3316. When supplemented by a comparable signal on the general alarm, what is the signal for boat stations or boat drill?

A. More than six short blasts followed by one long blast of the whistle
B. A continuous blast of the whistle for a period of not less than 10 seconds
C. One long blast followed by three short blasts of the whistle
D. Three short blasts of the whistle

3318. You discover a leak in the fuel line to the engine. You should FIRST _____.

A. activate the CO_2 system
B. make a temporary repair with canvas or tape
C. start the bilge pump
D. close the fuel valve at the tank

3320. If your vessel is required to have a fire ax on board, where should it be located? (Small Passenger Vessel Regulations.)

A. In or adjacent to the primary operating station
B. In below-decks passenger accommodations
C. Just outside the engine room access
D. In the galley near the stove

3322. If your vessel is certificated to carry 10 persons, including both adults and children, how many life jackets are you required to carry on board? (Small Passenger Vessel Regulations.)

A. 11 adult
B. 10 adult and 1 child
C. 10 adult and 5 child
D. 10 adult

3326. The nozzle of a gasoline hose or can should be kept _____.

A. in contact with the fill opening to guard against static spark
B. from making contact with the fill opening to guard against static spark
C. in contact with the fill opening to allow proper venting
D. None of the above

3329. A fire is discovered in the forepeak of a vessel at sea. The wind is from ahead at 35 knots. You should _____.

A. remain on course and hold speed
B. remain on course but slack the speed
C. change course and put the stern to the wind
D. change course to put the wind on either beam and increase speed

3330. A carbon dioxide fire extinguisher is required to be recharged if the weight loss exceeds what percentage of the weight of the charge? (Small Passenger Vessel Regulations.)

A. One percent
B. Five percent
C. Seven percent
D. Ten percent

3331. The stability which remains after a compartment is flooded is called _____.

A. intact stability
B. initial stability
C. immersion stability
D. damage stability

3332. When fueling has been completed _____.

A. the fuel tank fill pipe should be left open to allow vapors to vent from the tank
B. the engine should be started immediately to prevent vapor lock in the fuel line

C. all hatches should be opened and all compartments should be ventilated
D. open the fuel line and drain a small amount of gasoline into the bilge to clear the line of sediment

3334. Inflatable life rafts are provided with _____.

A. a portable radio
B. an oil lantern
C. canned milk
D. a towing bridle

3335. Inflatable life rafts are provided with a _____.

A. jackknife
B. towing connection
C. lifeline
D. All of the above

3336. Which statement is TRUE concerning gasoline vapors on board a vessel?

A. They are heavier than air and will settle in the lowest part of the vessel.
B. They are lighter than air and will settle in the highest part of the vessel.
C. They should be vented into the engine to improve combustion.
D. They should be vented into the wheelhouse.

3339. What is acceptable flame screening?

A. A fitted single brass screen of 10 x 10 mesh
B. A fitted stainless steel screen of 30 x 30 mesh
C. A fitted single stainless steel screen of 15 x 15 mesh
D. Two fitted brass screens of 10 x 15 mesh spaced 1/2 inch apart

3341. Inflatable life rafts are provided with a _____.

A. Very pistol
B. towing connection
C. portable radio
D. canned milk

3345. When launching an inflatable life raft, you should make sure that the operating cord is _____.

A. fastened to some substantial part of the vessel

B. not fastened to anything
C. secured to the hydrostatic release
D. fastened to the raft container

3346. An inflatable life raft is thrown into the water from a sinking vessel. Which action occurs automatically after the painter trips the CO_2 bottles to inflate the raft?

A. The sea anchor is deployed.
B. The floor inflates.
C. If upside down, the raft will right itself.
D. The painter detaches from the raft.

3348. Generally speaking, the fuel injected into a marine diesel engine combustion chamber is ignited by _____.

A. spark plugs
B. glow plugs
C. heat of compression
D. a magneto

3349. Which device is required in the fuel supply line at the engine?

A. Flow meter
B. Shut-off valve
C. Pressure gauge
D. Filter

3350. Which statement is TRUE concerning the number of portable fire extinguishers required at the operating station of a small passenger vessel? (Small Passenger Vessel Regulations.)

A. None are required.
B. One B-I extinguisher is required.
C. One B-II extinguisher is required.
D. Two B-I extinguishers are required.

3351. You should deploy the sea anchor from the life raft to _____.

A. keep the life raft from capsizing
B. navigate against the current
C. keep personnel from getting seasick
D. stay in the general location

3352. Which personal lifesaving device(s) is(are) approved for use on a towboat 150 feet in length? (Uninspected Vessel Regulations.)

A. Life preserver
B. Buoyant vest or cushion
C. Special purpose safety device
D. All of the above

3353. An inflatable life raft can be launched by _____.

A. the float free method only
B. kicking the hydrostatic release
C. throwing the entire container overboard, then pulling on the operating cord to inflate the raft
D. removing the securing straps

3354. Backfire flame arrestors are installed on _____.

A. fuel tanks
B. spark plugs
C. carburetors
D. distributors

3355. The sea painter of an inflatable life raft should be _____.

A. free running on deck
B. faked out next to the case
C. secured to a permanent object on deck via a weak link
D. stowed near the raft

3357. What must be carried out in order to launch and inflate an inflatable life raft?

A. Pull on the hydrostatic release, pull on the sea painter.
B. Push on the hydrostatic release, pull on the sea painter.
C. Push on the hydrostatic release, push on the sea painter.
D. Pull on the hydrostatic release, push on the sea painter.

3358. Spaces containing batteries require good ventilation because _____.

A. ventilation avoids CO_2 buildup
B. ventilation supplies extra oxygen for the battery
C. ventilation avoids flammable gas accumulation
D. less water would be used

3360. The premixed foam agent in fixed and semiportable fire extinguishing systems should be replaced _____. (Small Passenger Vessel Regulations.)

A. every 12 months
B. every 18 months
C. every 36 months
D. only when used

3361. The moment created by a force of 12,000 tons and a moment arm of 0.25 foot is _____.

A. 48,000 ft.-tons
B. 6,000 ft.-tons
C. 3,000 ft.-tons
D. 0 ft.-tons

3362. The number of approved adult life jackets that shall be carried is equal to _____. (Small Passenger Vessel Regulations.)

A. the number of persons listed in the vessel's Certificate of Inspection
B. 50% of the number of persons listed in the vessel's Certificate of Inspection
C. the number of persons on board at the time
D. 50% of the number of persons on board at the time

3363. What must be carried out in order to manually launch an inflatable life raft not designed for float-free operation?

A. It will be easily launched by simply breaking the weak link.
B. Depress the hydrostatic release button.
C. It is easily launched by cutting the container securing straps.
D. It is only necessary to attach the weak link to the vessel.

3366. An inflatable life raft is floating in its container, attached to the ship by its painter, as the ship is sinking rapidly. Which action should be taken with respect to the life raft container?

A. Cut the painter line so that it will not pull the life raft container down.
B. Swim away from the container so that you will not be in danger as it goes down.
C. Take no action as the pull on the painter will cause the life raft to inflate and open the container.
D. Manually open the container and inflate the life raft with the hand pump.

3367. After a life raft is launched, the operating cord _____.

A. serves as a sea painter
B. detaches automatically
C. is used to rig the boarding ladder
D. is cut immediately as it is of no further use

3370. The carbon dioxide cylinders of all fixed fire extinguishing systems shall be retested and remarked whenever a cylinder remains in place on a vessel for _____. (Small Passenger Vessel Regulations.)

A. 5 years from the latest test date stamped on the cylinder
B. 7 years from the latest test date stamped on the cylinder
C. 10 years from the latest test date stamped on the cylinder
D. 12 years from the latest test date stamped on the cylinder

3372. Which statement is FALSE concerning precautions during fueling operations?

A. All engines, motors, fans, etc., should be shut down when fueling.
B. All windows, doors, hatches, etc., should be closed.
C. A fire extinguisher should be kept nearby.
D. Fuel tanks should be topped off with no room for expansion.

3374. What is NOT listed on the metallic name plate required to be attached to hand portable fire extinguishers? (Uninspected Vessel Regulations.)

A. The rated capacity in gallons, quarts, or pounds
B. The hydrostatic test date of the cylinder
C. The name of the item
D. An identifying mark of the actual manufacturer

3376. Outlets in gasoline fuel lines are _____.

A. permitted for drawing fuel samples
B. permitted for draining fuel from lines
C. permitted for bleeding air from lines
D. prohibited

3386. While proceeding towards a distress site you hear the message PRU-DONCE over the radiotelephone. Which action should you take?

A. Advise the sender of your course, speed, position, and ETA at the distress site.
B. Resume base course and speed because the distress is terminated.
C. Shift your radio guard to the working frequency that will be indicated in the message.
D. Use that frequency only for restricted working communications.

3388. A carburetor is required to have a safety device called a(n) _____.

A. pressure release
B. backfire flame arrestor
C. automatic shutoff
D. flow valve

3390. Aboard small passenger vessels non-required items of lifesaving equipment on existing vessels _____.

A. must be removed from the vessel when carrying passengers
B. are carried as additional equipment and must be of an approved type
C. may be carried as a substitute of not more than 5% of the required life jackets
D. may be carried regardless of approval or condition if in excess of required lifesaving equipment

3394. The carburetor is placed on the engine to _____.

A. distribute the gasoline
B. mix the fuel and air
C. properly lubricate the engine
D. assist in priming the cylinders

3398. Before starting any diesel or gasoline engine, which of the following must be checked?

A. Oil level
B. Flow of cooling water
C. Exhaust discharge
D. All of the above

3399. Which sizes of fire extinguishers are considered to be semi-portable? (Uninspected Vessel Regulations.)

A. I, II, III, IV, and V
B. I, II, and III only
C. II, III, and IV only
D. III, IV, and V only

3400. How should the number "9" be pronounced when spoken on the radiotelephone?

A. NEW-MER-AL-NINER
B. NUM-BER-NINE
C. NO-VAY-NINER
D. OK-TOH-NINE

3404. Convection spreads a fire by _____.

A. transmitting the heat of a fire through the ship's metal
B. heated gases flowing through ventilation systems
C. burning liquids flowing into another space
D. the transfer of heat across an unobstructed space

3407. The most important thing to remember when launching an inflatable life raft by hand is to _____.

A. open the CO_2 inflation valve
B. open the raft container
C. ensure that the operating cord is secured to the vessel
D. inflate the raft on the vessel, then lower it over the side

3409. To launch a life raft by hand, you should _____.

A. cut the casing bands, throw the raft over the side and it will inflate by itself
B. detach the operating cord, throw the life raft over the side and it will then inflate
C. cut the casing bands, throw the raft over the side and pull the operating cord
D. throw the life raft over the side and pull the operating cord

3410. How should the letter "I" be pronounced when spoken on the radiotelephone?

A. IN DEE GO
B. IN DEE AH
C. I EE
D. I VAN HO

3414. A rigid lifesaving device designed to support survivors in the water is a _____.

A. rigid life raft
B. life float
C. inflatable life raft
D. survival capsule

3415. A vessel has a strong wind on the port beam. This has the same affect on stability as _____.

A. weight that is off-center to starboard
B. increasing the draft
C. reducing the freeboard
D. increasing the trim

3417. Which statement is TRUE concerning an inflatable life raft?

A. The floor may be inflated for insulation from cold water.
B. Crew members may jump into the raft without damaging it.
C. The raft may be boarded before it is fully inflated.
D. All of the above

3420. How should the number "1" be pronounced when spoken on the radiotelephone?

A. OO-NO
B. OO-NAH-WUN
C. NUM-EV-WUN
D. NEW-MAL-WON

3421. In order to retrieve an inflatable life raft and place it on deck, you should heave on the _____.

A. lifelines
B. righting strap
C. sea anchor
D. towing bridle

3428. Which river passenger vessel must have a copy of the vessel's plans permanently displayed?

A. A 200 GT vessel carrying more than 50 passengers
B. A 325 GT vessel on a voyage in excess of 8 hours
C. A 550 GT vessel with sleeping accommodations
D. A 1100 GT vessel making daylight excursion trips only

3430. How should the letter "Q" be pronounced when spoken on the radio-telephone?

A. QWE BEC
B. QUE BACH
C. KEH BECK
D. QU UE

3433. An inflatable life raft should be lifted back aboard ship by using _____.

A. the single hook at the top of the raft
B. two line passed under the raft
C. the towing bridle
D. All of the above

3435. Small wooden hull passenger vessels, whose routes are limited to coastwise warm water routes on the high seas, must

carry approved lifefloats or buoyant apparatus _____.

A. for all persons on board
B. for not less than 67% of all persons per-
mitted on board
C. for not less than 100% of all persons per-
mitted on board
D. in place of ring life buoys

3436. After launching, an inflatable raft
should be kept dry inside by _____.

A. opening the automatic drain plugs
B. draining the water pockets
C. using the electric bilge pump
D. using the bailers and cellulose sponge

3438. Generally, when lifting an inflatable
life raft back aboard ship, you would use
the _____.

A. towing bridle
B. main weather cover
C. external lifelines
D. righting strap

3439. An inflatable life raft should be manually released from its cradle by _____.

A. cutting the straps that enclose the container
B. removing the rubber sealing strip from
the container
C. loosening the turnbuckle on the securing strap
D. pushing the button on the hydrostatic
release

3440. How should the number "7" be pronounced when spoken on the
radiotelephone?

A. SAY-TAY-SEVEN
B. SEE-ETA-SEVEN
C. NUM-BER-SEVEN
D. NEW-MER-AL-SEVEN

3444. The nautical term "lee shore" refers to
the _____.

A. shore on the lee side of the vessel
B. shore that is in the lee
C. western shore of the Lesser Antilles
D. shore in a harbor of refuge

3457. Using a sea anchor will _____.

A. reduce your drift rate
B. keep the life raft from turning over

C. aid in recovering the life raft
D. increase your visibility

3460. How should the letter "T" be
pronounced when spoken on the
radiotelephone?

A. TEE
B. TA HO
C. TANG GO
D. TU TU

3462. A rigid lifesaving device only
designed for survivors to hold on to while
in the water is known as a _____.

A. life raft
B. life float
C. life preserver
D. buoyant apparatus

3465. The free-surface effects of a partially
full liquid tank decrease with increased
_____.

A. density of the liquid
B. placement of the tank above the keel
C. displacement volume of the vessel
D. size of the surface area in the tank

3466. A sea anchor is _____.

A. a heavy metal anchor with an extra long
line used to anchor in deep water
B. a cone shaped bag used to slow down
the wind drift effect
C. a padeye to which the sea painter is
made fast
D. made of wood if it is of an approved
type

3467. An emergency sea anchor may be
constructed by using _____.

A. a boat bucket
B. an air tank filled with water
C. an oar and canvas weighted down
D. All of the above

3468. Handholds or straps on the
underside of an inflatable life raft are
provided _____.

A. to right the raft if it capsizes
B. to carry the raft around on deck
C. for crewmen to hang on to
D. to hang the raft for drying

3469. The knife on an inflatable life raft will
always be located _____.

A. in one of the equipment bags
B. in a special pocket on the exterior of the
canopy
C. on a cord hanging from the canopy
D. in a pocket on the first aid kit

3471. Every fishing vessel required to have
a general alarm system must test it _____.

A. once every day that the vessel is
operated
B. once every week that the vessel is oper-
ated
C. prior to operation of the vessel
D. Both B and C

3472. If you find an inflatable life raft container with the steel bands still in place
around its case, you should _____.

A. tell the Master
B. leave the bands in place
C. tell the Mate
D. remove the bands yourself

3473. In each inflatable rescue boat, what
piece of equipment is provided to make
quick, emergency, temporary repairs to a
large hole in a raft?

A. No equipment is provided.
B. Glue and rubber patches
C. Several various-sized sealing clamps
D. Self-adhesive rubberized canvas patches

3478. Puncture leaks in the lower tubes or
bottom of an inflatable life raft should
FIRST be stopped by using _____.

A. sealing clamps
B. repair tape
C. a tube patch
D. sail twine and vulcanizing kit

3479. A feature of an inflatable raft which
helps keep people stationary in rough
weather is _____.

A. lashings on the floor of the raft for the
passenger's feet
B. straps from the overhead
C. lifelines on the inside of the raft
D. ridges in the floor of the raft

3480. How should the number "6" be pronounced when spoken on the
radiotelephone?

A. SOX-SIX
B. NUM-BER-SIX
C. SOK-SEE-SIX
D. NEW-MER-AL-SIX

3487. Generally, what is used to inflate life rafts?

A. Non-toxic inert gas
B. Oxygen
C. Hydrogen
D. Carbon monoxide

3488. Who should inspect and test an inflatable life raft?

A. The person in charge
B. An approved servicing facility
C. Shipyard personnel
D. A certificated lifeboatman

3489. If the hydrostatic release mechanism for an inflatable life raft is not periodically serviced and becomes inoperative, it will NOT _____.

A. set the water lights on immersion
B. release the dye-marker from the life raft
C. free the life raft from a sinking vessel
D. break the seal on the carbon dioxide cylinder

3494. A passenger vessel in river service which operates in fresh water at least 6 out of every 12 months since the last drydock examination must be dry-docked at intervals not to exceed _____.

A. 12 months
B. 24 months
C. 48 months
D. 60 months

3496. In general, how often are sanitary inspections of passenger and crew quarters made aboard passenger vessels in river service?

A. Once each day
B. Once each week
C. Once each month
D. Once each trip

3497. What is the purpose of the hydrostatic release on an inflatable life raft?

A. To release the raft from the cradle automatically as the ship sinks
B. To inflate the raft automatically
C. To test the rafts hydrostatically

D. None of the above

3498. Your passenger vessel is 130 feet (40 m) long and is alternatively equipped for operating in river service. The number of ring life buoys required for the vessel is _____.

A. 2
B. 4
C. 6
D. 8

3500. How should the letter "Z" be pronounced when spoken on the radiotelephone?

A. ZEE BR AH
B. ZEE ZE
C. ZE HE
D. ZOO LOO

3508. Except in rare cases, it is impossible to extinguish a shipboard fire by _____.

A. interrupting the chain reaction
B. removing the heat
C. removing the oxygen
D. removing the fuel

3512. You have sent a visual signal to an aircraft. The aircraft then flies over your position on a straight course and level altitude. What should you do?

A. Repeat your signal.
B. Send any more signals necessary.
C. Change course to follow the airplane.
D. Prepare for a helicopter pickup.

3516. Drinking salt water will _____.

A. will protect against heat cramps
B. dehydrate you
C. be safe if mixed with fresh water
D. prevent seasickness

3520. How should the number "5" be pronounced when spoken on the radio?

A. FIVE-ER
B. NEW-MARL-FIVE
C. NUM-ERL-FIVE
D. PAN-TAH-FIVE

3536. There are two disadvantages to CO_2 as a firefighting agent. One of these is the limited quantity available, and the other is _____.

A. the lack of cooling effect on heated materials
B. that it cannot be used in a dead ship situation with no electrical power to the CO_2 pump
C. that it breaks down under extreme heat to form poisonous gases
D. there is no effect on a class A fire even in an enclosed space

3540. How should the letter "R" be pronounced when spoken on the radiotelephone?

A. ROW ME OH
B. AR AH
C. ROA MA O
D. AR EE

3542. An aircraft has indicated that he wants you to change course and follow him. You cannot comply because of an emergency on board. Which signal should you make?

A. Fire a red flare at night or a red smoke signal by day
B. Send the Morse signal "N" by flashing light
C. Make a round turn (360°) and resume course
D. Make an "S" turn (hard right then hard left) and resume course

3546. According to the regulations for passenger vessels, a "motor vessel" is one which is propelled by machinery other than steam and is more than _____.

A. 16 ft. in length
B. 34 ft. in length
C. 45 ft. in length
D. 65 ft. in length

3551. Which toxic gas is a product of incomplete combustion, and is often present when a fire burns in a closed compartment?

A. Carbon monoxide
B. Carbon dioxide
C. Hydrogen sulfide
D. Nitric oxide

3552. You are communicating by radiotelephone using the International Code of Signals. What is the correct method of sending the group 1.3?

A. "Wun point tree"

B. "Unaone point tercetree"
C. "Unaone decimal terrathree"
D. "One decimal three"

3554. You are underway in mid-ocean, when you hear a distress message over the VHF radio. The position of the sender is 20 miles away. What action should you take?

A. Immediately acknowledge receipt of the distress message.
B. Defer acknowledgment for a short interval so that a coast station may acknowledge receipt.
C. Do not acknowledge receipt until other ships nearer to the distress have acknowledged.
D. Do not acknowledge because you are too far away to take action.

3556. The normal equipment of every rescue boat shall include _____.

A. compass
B. one 50 meter line
C. one can opener
D. All of the above

3560. How should the number "4" be pronounced when spoken on the radiotelephone?

A. QUAD-ROS-FOOR
B. NUM-ERL-FOUR
C. NUMB-ER-FOWER
D. KAR-TAY-FOWER

3580. How should the letter "V" be pronounced when spoken on the radiotelephone?

A. VIK TAH
B. VIC TO RE
C. VIX TOO RE
D. VEE

3585. When a man who has fallen overboard is being picked up by a rescue boat, the boat should normally approach with the wind _____.

A. astern and the victim just off the bow
B. ahead and the victim just off the bow
C. just off the bow and the victim to windward
D. just off the bow and the victim to leeward

3586. A person has fallen overboard and is being picked up with a rescue boat. If the person appears in danger of drowning, the

rescue boat should be maneuvered to make _____.

A. an approach from leeward
B. an approach from windward
C. the most direct approach
D. an approach across the wind

3587. A person has fallen overboard and is being picked up with a rescue boat. If the person appears in danger of drowning, the rescue boat should be maneuvered to make_____.

A. an approach from leeward
B. an approach from windward
C. an approach across the wind
D. the most direct approach

3590. The patrolman, while on duty on a passenger vessel, must have in his possession a(n) _____.

A. nightstick
B. flashlight
C. passenger list showing assigned berths
D. A-I fire extinguisher

3594. After having activated the emergency position indicating radio beacon, you should _____.

A. turn it off for 5 minutes every half-hour
B. turn it off and on at 5 minute intervals
C. turn it off during daylight hours
D. leave it on continuously

3596. The light on a life jacket must be replaced _____.

A. when the power source is replaced
B. each year after installation
C. every six months
D. when it is no longer serviceable

3598. If you have to abandon ship, the EPIRB can be used to _____.

A. hold the survival craft's head up into the seas
B. generate orange smoke
C. seal leaks in rubber rafts
D. send radio homing signals to searching aircraft

3599. What should you do with your emergency position indicating radio beacon if you are in a lifeboat during storm conditions?

A. Bring it inside the life raft and leave it on.

B. Bring it inside the life raft and turn it off until the storm passes.
C. Leave it outside the life raft and leave it on.
D. Leave it outside the life raft and turn it off.

3600. How should the number "3" be pronounced when spoken on the radiotelephone?

A. TAY-RAH-TREE
B. BEES-SOH-THREE
C. NUM-ERL-THREE
D. TRIC-THREE

3604. You are the first vessel to arrive at the scene of a distress. Due to the volume of traffic on the radio, you are unable to communicate with the vessel in distress. Which action should you take?

A. Switch to flag hoists.
B. Broadcast "Seelonce Distress."
C. Broadcast "Charlie Quebec-Mayday-Quiet".
D. Key the microphone three times in quick succession.

3606. Which radiotelephone signal indicates receipt of a distress message?

A. Roger wilco
B. Romeo, romeo, romeo
C. SOS acknowledged
D. Mayday roger

3608. A fire has broken out on the stern of your vessel. You should maneuver your vessel so the wind _____.

A. comes over the bow
B. blows the fire back toward the vessel
C. comes over the stern
D. comes over either beam

3609. General arrangement plans shall be permanently exhibited on all passenger vessels of at least _____.

A. 200 GT and over
B. 500 GT and over
C. 1000 GT and over
D. 1500 GT and over

3610. A passenger vessel is underway. When may passengers visit the pilothouse?

A. Passengers are excluded from the pilothouse while underway.

B. Passengers are permitted in the pilothouse during daylight hours only.

C. Passengers are permitted to visit the pilothouse when authorized by the Master and officer of the watch.

D. Passengers are permitted in the pilothouse when they are escorted by a ship's officer.

3611. Each life jacket light that has a non-replaceable power source must be replaced _____.

A. every 6 months after initial installation
B. every 12 months after initial installation
C. every 24 months after initial installation
D. on or before the expiration date of the power source

3613. You are in a survival craft broadcasting a distress message. What information would be essential to your rescuers?

A. The nature of the distress
B. The time of day
C. Your radio call sign
D. Your position by latitude and longitude

3614. While proceeding towards a distress site you hear the message "Seelonce Feenee" over the radiotelephone. Which action should you take?

A. Resume base course and speed because the distress situation is over.
B. Do not transmit over the radiotelephone.
C. Relay the initial distress message to the nearest shore station.
D. Resume normal communications on the guarded frequency.

3616. Which radiotelephone signal indicates receipt of a distress message?

A. Received Mayday
B. Roger wilco
C. Seelonce
D. Mayday wilco

3620. How should the letter "O" be pronounced when spoken on the radiotelephone?

A. OCK TOW BER
B. O RI AN
C. OSS CAH
D. OA KAM

3623. You wish to communicate by radiotelephone with a foreign vessel using

the International Code of Signals. This is indicated by the signal _____.

A. "Charlie Quebec"
B. "Code"
C. "Kilo"
D. "Interco"

3626. When personnel are lifted by a helicopter from an inflatable life raft, the personnel on the raft should _____.

A. deflate the floor of the raft to reduce the danger of capsizing
B. inflate the floor of the raft to provide for additional stability
C. remove their life jackets to prepare for the transfer
D. take in the sea anchor to prevent fouling of the rescue sling

3628. Each vessel in ocean and coastwise service must have an approved EPIRB. An EPIRB _____.

A. must be stowed in a manner so that it will float free if the vessel sinks
B. must be stowed where it is readily accessible for testing and use
C. is a devise that transmits a radio signal
D. All of the above

3629. When a helicopter is lifting personnel from a rescue boat, the other individuals in the boat should _____.

A. enter the water in case the person being lifted slips from the sling
B. stand on the outside of the boat to assist the person being lifted
C. remove their life jackets to prepare for their transfer to the helicopter
D. remain seated inside to provide body weight for stability

3630. A passenger vessel is required to have a supervised patrol when _____.

A. there are passengers berthed on board
B. navigating in excess of eight hours
C. the vessel has substantial wood in its construction
D. there is no automatic fire-detection system installed

3632. When using a handheld smoke signal in a life raft, you should activate the signal _____.

A. on the upwind side

B. inside the boat
C. at the stern
D. on the downwind side

3634. You are underway in mid-ocean when you hear a distress message. The position of the sender is 150 miles away. No other vessel has acknowledged the distress. Your maximum speed is 5 knots and due to the seriousness of the distress, you cannot arrive on scene to provide effective assistance. What action should you take?

A. Do not acknowledge the distress message.
B. Send an urgency message about the distress.
C. Use the signal MAYDAY RELAY and transmit the distress message.
D. Transmit a message as though your vessel was in distress.

3638. When using a handheld smoke signal in a life raft, you should activate the signal _____.

A. on the downwind side
B. inside the boat
C. at the stern
D. on the upwind side

3639. Which condition represents the appropriate time for setting off distress flares and rockets?

A. Only when there is a chance of their being seen by rescue vessels
B. At half hour intervals
C. At one hour intervals
D. Immediately upon abandoning the vessel

3640. How should the number "2" be pronounced when spoken on the radiotelephone?

A. NUM-BER-TOO
B. BEES-SOH-TOO
C. DOS-SOH-TU
D. NEM-MARL-TWO

3641. Signaling devices required on inflatable life rafts include a(n)_____.

A. Very pistol
B. orange smoke signal
C. air horn
D. lantern

3642. When communicating on the radiotelephone using plain English, what procedure word indicates the end of my transmission and that a response is necessary?

A. Out
B. Over
C. Roger
D. Wilco

3644. When should distress flares and rockets be used?

A. Immediately upon abandoning the vessel
B. Only when there is a chance of their being seen by a rescue vessel
C. At one hour intervals
D. At half hour intervals

3645. Signaling devices required on inflatable life rafts include _____.

A. a rocket shoulder rifle
B. an oil lantern
C. red flares
D. an air horn

3646. One of the signals, other than a distress signal, that can be used by a rescue boat to attract attention is a/an _____.

A. red star shell
B. searchlight
C. burning barrel
D. orange smoke signal

3647. A distress signal _____.

A. consists of 5 or more short blasts of the fog signal apparatus
B. consists of the raising and lowering of a large white flag
C. may be used individually or in conjunction with other distress signals
D. is used to indicate doubt about another vessel's intentions

3648. All of the following are recognized distress signals under the Navigation Rules EXCEPT _____.

A. a green star signal
B. orange-colored smoke
C. red flares
D. the repeated raising and lowering of outstretched arms

3649. A man aboard a vessel, signaling by raising and lowering his outstretched arms

to each side, is indicating _____.

A. danger, stay away
B. all is clear, it is safe to pass
C. all is clear, it is safe to approach
D. a distress signal

3650. If your passenger vessel is fitted with a loudspeaker system, it must be tested at least once _____.

A. every week
B. a day
C. every trip
D. a watch or once a trip, whichever is shorter

3651. Distress signals may be _____.

A. red flares
B. smoke signals
C. sound signals
D. Any of the above

3653. When a vessel signals her distress by means of a gun or other explosive signal, the firing should be at intervals of approximately _____.

A. 10 minutes
B. 1 minute
C. 1 hour
D. 3 minutes

3654. You are communicating on the radiotelephone using plain English. Which procedural word (proword) indicates that you have received another vessel's transmission?

A. Out
B. Over
C. Roger
D. Wilco

3655. You can indicate that your vessel is in distress by _____.

A. displaying a large red flag
B. displaying three black balls in a vertical line
C. sounding five or more short and rapid blasts on the whistle
D. continuously sounding the fog whistle

3660. How should the letter "W" be pronounced when spoken on the radiotelephone?

A. DUB A U

B. WISS KEY
C. WI NE
D. WOO LF

3666. When you are firing a pyrotechnic distress signal, it should be aimed at _____.

A. straight overhead
B. at the vessel whose attention you are trying to get
C. into the wind
D. about 60 degrees above the horizon

3669. The free surface corrections depend upon the dimensions of the surface of the free liquids and the _____.

A. volume of liquid in the tank
B. displacement of the vessel
C. location of the tank in the vessel
D. height of the center of gravity of the vessel

3672. Which item of the listed survival craft equipment would be the most suitable for night signaling to a ship on the horizon?

A. A red parachute flare
B. A red handheld flare
C. An orange smoke flare
D. A flashlight

3674. Which condition represents the appropriate time for setting off distress flares and rockets?

A. At one hour intervals
B. At half hour intervals
C. Only when there is a chance of their being seen by rescue vessels
D. Immediately upon abandoning the vessel

3676. You have abandoned ship and after two days in a life raft you can see an aircraft near the horizon apparently carrying out a search pattern. You should _____.

A. switch the EPIRB to the homing signal mode
B. use the voice transmission capability of the EPIRB to guide the aircraft to your raft
C. turn on the strobe light on the top of the EPIRB
D. use visual distress signals in conjunction with the EPIRB

3678. When giving mouth-to-mouth rescue breathing to an adult, you should breathe at the rate of how many breaths per minute?

A. 4
B. 8
C. 12
D. 20

3679. You are alone and administering CPR to an adult victim. How many chest compressions and how many inflations should you administer in each sequence?

A. 5 compressions then 1 inflation
B. 15 compressions then 2 inflations
C. 20 compressions then 3 inflations
D. 30 compressions then 4 inflations

3680. When administering artificial respiration to an adult, the breathing cycle should be repeated about _____.

A. 12 to 15 times per minute
B. 18 to 20 times per minute
C. 20 to 25 times per minute
D. as fast as possible

3682. At what rate would you render mouth to mouth or mouth to nose artificial respiration to an adult?

A. 4 to 6 times per minute
B. 12 to 15 times per minute
C. 20 to 30 times per minute
D. At least 30 times per minute

3684. The rescuer can best provide an airtight seal during mouth-to-mouth resuscitation by pinching the victim's nostrils and _____.

A. cupping a hand around the patient's mouth
B. keeping the head elevated
C. applying his mouth tightly over the victim's mouth
D. holding the jaw down firmly

3686. When applying chest compressions on an adult victim during CPR, the sternum should be depressed about _____.

A. 1/2 inch or less
B. 1/2 to 1 inch
C. 1 to 1-1/2 inches
D. 1-1/2 to 2 inches

3688. You are administering chest compressions during CPR. Where on the victim's body should the pressure be applied?

A. Lower half of the sternum

B. Tip of the sternum
C. Top half of the sternum
D. Left chest over the heart

3689. Changing rescuers while carrying out artificial respiration should be done _____.

A. without losing the rhythm of respiration
B. only with the help of two other people
C. by not stopping the respiration for more than 5 minutes
D. at ten-minute intervals

3690. The MOST important element in administering CPR is _____.

A. having the proper equipment for the process
B. starting the treatment quickly
C. administering of oxygen
D. treating for traumatic shock

3692. Before CPR is started, you should _____.

A. establish an open airway
B. treat any bleeding wounds
C. insure the victim is conscious
D. make the victim comfortable

3694. When administering artificial respiration, it is MOST important to _____.

A. monitor blood pressure
B. clear airways
C. use the rhythmic pressure method
D. know all approved methods

3698. You are attempting to administer CPR to a victim. When you blow into his mouth it is apparent that no air is getting into the lungs. What should you do?

A. Blow harder to force the air past the tongue.
B. Raise the victim's head higher than his feet.
C. Press on the victim's lungs so that air pressure will blow out any obstruction.
D. Re-tip the head and try again.

3699. Two people are administering CPR to a victim. How many times per minute should the chest be compressed?

A. 30
B. 45
C. 60
D. 80

3700. Sign(s) of respiratory arrest requiring artificial respiration is(are) _____.

A. vomiting
B. blue color and lack of breathing
C. irregular breathing
D. unconsciousness

3704. After a person has been revived by artificial respiration, he should be _____.

A. walked around until he is back to normal
B. given several shots of whiskey
C. kept lying down and warm
D. allowed to do as he wishes

3706. You are in charge of a fishing vessel with 18 individuals on board. You are required to conduct drills and give safety instruction at least once _____.

A. every week
B. every 15 days
C. every month
D. before you begin fishing

3708. If the patient vomits during mouth-to-mouth resuscitation, the rescuer should FIRST _____.

A. ignore it and continue mouth-to-mouth ventilation
B. pause for a moment until the patient appears quiet again, then resume ventilation mouth-to-mouth
C. switch to mouth-to-nose ventilation
D. turn the patient's body to the side, sweep out the mouth and resume mouth-to-mouth ventilation

3709. When starting CPR on a drowning victim, you should _____.

A. start chest compressions before the victim is removed from the water
B. drain water from the lungs before ventilating
C. begin mouth-to-mouth ventilations as soon as possible
D. do not tilt the head back since it may cause vomiting

3710. Which statement is CORRECT with respect to inserting an airway tube?

A. Only a trained person should attempt to insert an airway tube.
B. A size 2 airway tube is the correct size for an adult.

C. The airway tube will not damage the victim's throat.
D. Inserting the airway tube will prevent vomiting.

3711. Changing rescuers while carrying out artificial respiration should be done _____.

A. without losing the rhythm of respiration
B. only with the help of two other people
C. by not stopping the respiration for more than 5 minutes
D. at ten minute intervals

3712. The rescuer can best provide an airtight seal during mouth to mouth ventilation by pinching the victim's nostrils and _____.

A. cupping a hand around the patient's mouth
B. keeping the head elevated
C. applying his mouth tightly over the victim's mouth
D. holding the jaw down firmly

3714. If someone suffers a heart attack and has ceased breathing, you should _____.

A. immediately give a stimulant, by force if necessary
B. make the victim comfortable in a bunk
C. immediately start CPR
D. administer oxygen

3715. The necessity for administering artificial respiration may be recognized by the victim's _____.

A. vomiting
B. blue color and lack of breathing
C. irregular breathing
D. unconscious condition

3716. In order to initiate CPR on a drowning victim, _____.

A. start chest compressions before the victim is removed from the water
B. drain water from the lungs before ventilating
C. begin mouth-to-mouth ventilations
D. do not tilt the head back since it may cause vomiting

3718. Treatments of heat exhaustion consist of _____.

A. moving to a shaded area and lying down
B. bathing with rubbing alcohol
C. placing the patient in a tub of cold water
D. All of the above

3719. Symptoms of heat stroke are _____.

A. cold and moist skin, high body temperature
B. cold and dry skin, low body temperature
C. hot and moist skin, high body temperature
D. hot and dry skin, high body temperature

3723. A patient suffering from heat exhaustion should be _____.

A. moved to a cool room and told to lie down
B. kept standing and encouraged to walk slowly and continuously
C. given a glass of water and told to return to work after 15 minutes of rest
D. None of the above is correct.

3724. Physical exertion on the part of a person who has fallen into cold water would _____.

A. be the best thing to try if there was no rescue in sight
B. increase survival time in the water
C. increase the rate of heat loss from the body
D. not affect the heat loss from the body

3725. A crew member has suffered frostbite to the toes of both feet. You should _____.

A. immerse the feet in warm water
B. warm the feet with a heat lamp
C. warm the feet at room temperature
D. rub the feet

3726. Treatment of frostbite includes _____.

A. rubbing affected area with ice or snow
B. rubbing affected area briskly to restore circulation
C. wrapping area tightly in warm cloths
D. warming exposed parts rapidly

3728. A crew member has suffered frostbite to the toes of the right foot. Which is NOT an acceptable first aid measure?

A. Rub the toes briskly.
B. Elevate the foot slightly.

C. Rewarm rapidly.
D. Give aspirin or other medication for pain if necessary.

3729. A crew member suffering from hypothermia should be given _____.

A. a small dose of alcohol
B. treatment for shock
C. a large meal
D. a brisk rub down

3730. The symptoms of heat exhaustion are _____.

A. slow and strong pulse
B. flushed and dry skin
C. slow and deep breathing
D. pale and clammy skin

3732. Heat exhaustion is caused by excessive _____.

A. loss of body temperature
B. loss of water and salt from the body
C. gain in body temperature
D. intake of water when working or exercising

3734. Which procedure should be followed when individuals are rescued in cold climates and suffer from hypothermia?

A. Give them brandy or other alcoholic stimulation to promote a return to an acceptable body temperature.
B. Move them to a warm room to gradually raise their body temperature.
C. Keep them moving to stimulate circulation to raise their body temperature.
D. Warm them under an electric blanket to rapidly regain normal body temperature.

3736. The most effective treatment for warming a crew member suffering from hypothermia is _____.

A. running or jumping to increase circulation
B. raising body temperature rapidly by placing hands and feet in hot water
C. bundling the body in blankets to rewarm gradually
D. lying prone under heat lamps to rewarm rapidly

3737. The most important consideration in the event the Deep Driller suffers damage is _____.

A. preserve reserve buoyancy
B. advise authorities
C. pump from adjacent undamaged compartments
D. counterflood on the opposite corner

3738. A crew member is unconscious and the face is flushed. You should _____.

A. lay the crew member down with the head and shoulders slightly raised
B. administer a liquid stimulant
C. lay the crew member down with the head lower than the feet
D. attempt to stand the crew member upright to restore consciousness

3739. Which procedure should NOT be done for a person who has fainted?

A. Revive the person with smelling salts.
B. Loosen the clothing.
C. Lay the person horizontally.
D. Give pain reliever.

3740. The proper stimulant for an unconscious person is _____.

A. tea
B. coffee
C. whiskey and water
D. ammonia inhalant

3742. A rescuer can most easily determine whether or not an adult victim has a pulse by checking the pulse at the _____.

A. carotid artery in the neck
B. femoral artery in the groin
C. brachial artery in the arm
D. radial artery in the wrist

3743. An unconscious person should NOT be _____.

A. placed in a position with the head lower than the body
B. given an inhalation stimulant
C. given something to drink
D. treated for injuries until conscious

3744. Which should NOT be a treatment for a person who has received a head injury and is groggy or unconscious?

A. Give a stimulant.
B. Elevate his head.
C. Stop severe bleeding.
D. Treat for shock.

3745. In reviving a person who has been overcome by gas fumes, what would you AVOID doing?

A. Giving stimulants
B. Prompt removal of the patient from the suffocating atmosphere
C. Applying artificial respiration and massage
D. Keeping the patient warm and comfortable

3746. A conscious victim who has suffered a blow to the head has symptoms that indicate the possibility of concussion. If the patient feels no indication of neck or spine injury, recommended treatment would include _____.

A. turning the victim's head to the side to keep his airway open
B. positioning the victim so the head is lower than the body
C. giving the victim water if he is thirsty, but no food
D. elevating the head and shoulders slightly with a pillow

3747. A person who gets battery acid in an eye should IMMEDIATELY wash the eye with _____.

A. boric acid solution
B. water
C. baking soda solution
D. ammonia

3748. A victim is coughing and wheezing from a partial obstruction of the airway. An observer should _____.

A. perform the Heimlich maneuver
B. immediately start CPR
C. give back blows and something to drink
D. allow the person to continue coughing and dislodge the obstruction on his own

3749. If a person gets something in his or her eye and you see that it is not embedded, you can _____.

A. get them to rub their eye until the object is gone
B. remove it with a match or toothpick
C. remove it with a piece of dry sterile cotton
D. remove it with a moist, cotton-tipped applicator

3750. While providing assistance to a vic-

tim of an epileptic seizure, it is most important to _____.

A. give artificial respiration
B. prevent patient from hurting himself
C. keep the patient awake and make him/her walk if necessary to keep him/her awake
D. remove any soiled clothing and put the patient in a clean bed

3751. A shipmate chokes suddenly, cannot speak, and starts to turn blue. You should _____.

A. perform the Heimlich maneuver
B. make the victim lie down with the feet elevated to get blood to the brain
C. immediately administer CPR
D. do nothing until the victim becomes unconscious

3752. A shipmate suffers a heart attack and stops breathing. You must _____.

A. administer oxygen
B. immediately check his pulse and start CPR
C. make the victim comfortable in a bunk
D. immediately give a stimulant, by force if necessary

3753. A shipmate suffers a heart attack and stops breathing. You must _____.

A. immediately give a stimulant, by force if necessary
B. make the victim comfortable in a bunk
C. administer oxygen
D. immediately start CPR

3754. First aid means _____.

A. medical treatment of accident
B. setting of broken bones
C. emergency treatment at the scene of the injury
D. dosage of medications

3755. To reduce mild fever the MOST useful drug is _____.

A. bicarbonate of soda
B. paregoric
C. aspirin
D. aromatic spirits of ammonia

3756. Treatment of sunstroke consists principally of _____.

A. cooling, removing to shaded area, and lying down
B. bathing with rubbing alcohol
C. drinking ice water
D. All of the above

3757. What are the symptoms of sun stroke?

A. Temperature falls below normal, pulse is rapid and feeble, skin is cold and clammy.
B. Temperature is high, pulse is strong and rapid, skin is hot and dry.
C. Temperature is high, pulse is slow and feeble, skin is clammy.
D. Temperature falls below normal, pulse is rapid, skin is clammy.

3758. To treat a person suffering from heat exhaustion, you should _____.

A. administer artificial respiration
B. put him in a tub of ice water
C. give him sips of cool water
D. cover him with a light cloth

3759. Seasickness is caused by rolling or rocking motions which affect fluids in the _____.

A. stomach
B. lower intestines
C. inner ear
D. bladder

3760. Symptoms of sea sickness include _____.

A. fever and thirst
B. nausea and dizziness
C. stomach cramps and diarrhea
D. reddening of skin and hives

3761. Symptoms of sugar diabetes include _____.

A. increased appetite and thirst
B. decreased appetite and thirst
C. gain in weight
D. elevated temperature

3762. The symptoms of a fractured back are _____.

A. leg cramps in the muscles in one or both legs
B. pain and uncontrolled jerking of the legs and arms
C. vomiting and involuntary urination or bowel movement

D. pain at the site of the fracture and possible numbness or paralysis below the injury

3763. What is the procedure for checking for spinal cord damage in an unconscious patient?

A. Beginning at the back of the neck, and proceeding to the buttocks, press the spine to find where it hurts
B. Prick the skin of the hands and the soles of the feet with a sharp object to check for reaction
C. Selectively raise each arm and each leg and watch patient's face to see if he registers pain
D. Roll patient onto his stomach and prick along the length of his spine to check reaction

3764. What are symptom(s) of a ruptured appendix?

A. Dilated pupils and shallow breathing
B. Diarrhea and frequent urination
C. Muscle tenseness in almost the entire abdomen
D. Extreme sweating and reddening skin

3765. When administering first aid you should avoid _____.

A. any conversation with the patient
B. instructing bystanders
C. unnecessary haste and appearance of uncertainty
D. touching the patient before washing your hands

3766. The primary concern in aiding a back injury patient is _____.

A. relieving the patient's pain by giving aspirin or stronger medication
B. avoiding possible injury to the spinal cord by incorrect handling
C. preventing convulsions and muscle spasms caused by the pain
D. providing enough fluids to prevent dehydration

3768. What is one of the FIRST actions you should take after abandoning and clearing away from a vessel?

A. Identify the person in charge.
B. Gather up useful floating objects.
C. Prepare for arrival of rescue units.
D. Arrange watches and duties.

3769. You hear the general alarm and ship's whistle sound for over 10 seconds. Traditionally, this is the signal for _____.

A. abandon ship
B. dismissal from fire and emergency stations
C. fire and emergency
D. man overboard

3770. The abandon ship signal is _____.

A. a continuous ringing of general alarm bells for at least 10 seconds
B. a continuous ringing of the general alarm, and sounding of the ship's whistle
C. more than 6 short blasts and 1 long blast of the ship's whistle and the same signal on the general alarm bells
D. a continuous sounding of the ship's whistle

3772. The abandon ship signal sounded by the vessel's whistle is _____.

A. 6 short blasts and 1 long blast
B. more than 6 short blasts
C. more than 6 short and 1 long blast
D. 1 long blast of at least 10 seconds

3776. If you continue to wear extra clothing when entering the water after abandoning your vessel, it will _____.

A. weigh you down
B. preserve body heat
C. reduce your body heat
D. make it more difficult to breathe

3778. When a ship is abandoned and there are several life rafts in the water, one of the FIRST things to be done is _____.

A. separate the rafts as much as possible to increase chances of detection
B. transfer all supplies to one raft
C. transfer all the injured to one raft
D. secure the rafts together to keep them from drifting apart

3780. One of the first actions to be taken by survivors when they have boarded an inflatable life raft is to _____.

A. stream the sea anchor
B. take an anti-seasickness pill
C. open the pressure relief valve
D. drink at least one can of water

3782. You have abandoned ship in tropical waters. Which procedure should be used during a prolonged period in a life raft?

A. Wet clothes during the day to decrease perspiration.
B. Get plenty of rest.
C. Keep the entrance curtains open.
D. All of the above

3786. When using the rainwater collection tubes of a life raft, the FIRST collection should be _____.

A. passed around so all can drink
B. poured overboard because of salt washed off the canopy
C. saved to be used at a later time
D. used to boil food

3788. When you hear three short blasts on the ship's whistle and the same signal on the general alarm bells, you _____.

A. are required to be at your life raft
B. are dismissed from drills
C. should point to the man overboard
D. should start the fire pump

3790. While reading the muster list you see that "3 short blasts on the whistle and three short rings on the general alarm bell bells" is the signal for _____.

A. abandon ship
B. dismissal from fire and emergency stations
C. fire and emergency
D. man overboard

3796. Which of the following steps should normally be taken first by those who have boarded a life raft in an emergency situation?

A. Ration food and water supplies
B. Search for survivors
C. Determine position and closest point of land
D. Check pyrotechnic supplies

3798. After having thrown the life raft and stowage container into the water, the life raft is inflated by _____.

A. pulling on the painter line
B. forcing open the container which operates the CO_2
C. hitting the hydrostatic release
D. using the hand pump provided

3800. If you have to jump in the water when abandoning ship, your legs should be _____.

A. spread apart as far as possible
B. held as tightly against your chest as possible
C. in a kneeling position
D. extended straight down and crossed at the ankles

3806. A life raft which has inflated bottom-up on the water _____.

A. should be righted by standing on the carbon dioxide cylinder, holding the righting straps and leaning backwards
B. should be righted by standing on the lifeline, holding the righting straps leaning backward
C. will right itself when the canopy tube inflates
D. must be cleared of the buoyant eqipment before it will right itself

3809. Provided every effort is used to produce, as well as preserve body moisture content by avoiding perspiration, how long is it normally possible to survive without stored quantities of water?

A. Up to 3 days
B. 8 to 14 days
C. 15 to 20 days
D. 25 to 30 days

3812. If you have to abandon ship, and enter a life raft, your main course of action should be to _____.

A. remain in the vicinity of the sinking vessel
B. head for the closest land
C. head for the closest sea-lanes
D. get a majority opinion

3814. If you are forced to abandon ship in a rescue boat, you should _____.

A. remain in the immediate vicinity
B. head for the nearest land
C. head for the closest sea-lanes
D. vote on what to do, so all hands will have a part in the decision

3820. Once the daily ration of drinking water in a survival situation has been established, the drinking routine should include _____.

A. small sips at regular intervals during the day
B. a complete daily ration at one time during the day
C. one-half the daily ration twice during the day
D. small sips only after sunset

3822. In the first 24 hours after abandoning a vessel, water should be given only to personnel who are _____.

A. thirsty
B. sick or injured
C. wet
D. awake

3824. After abandoning a vessel, water consumed within the first 24 hours _____.

A. will pass through the body with very little being absorbed by the system
B. will help prevent fatigue
C. will quench thirst for only two hours
D. help prevent seasickness

3826. You have abandoned ship and are in charge of a life raft or survival craft. How much water per day should you permit each person to have after the first 24 hours?

A. 1 can
B. 1 pint
C. 1 quart
D. 1 gallon

3829. Inflatable life rafts shall be serviced at an approved servicing facility every 12 months or not later than the next vessel inspection for certification. However, the total elapsed time between servicing cannot exceed _____.

A. 12 months
B. 15 months
C. 17 months
D. 18 months

3830. Inflatable life rafts must be overhauled and inspected at a U.S. Coast Guard approved service facility every _____.

A. six months
B. twelve months
C. eighteen months
D. twenty-four months

3834. Who should inspect and test an inflatable life raft?

A. The Chief Mate
B. An approved servicing facility
C. Shipyard personnel
D. A certificated lifeboatman

3838. Fire dampers prevent the spread of fire by _____.

A. convection
B. conduction
C. radiation
D. direct contact

3839. The painter on a rigid life raft must have a length sufficient to reach the lightest waterline plus an additional _____.

A. 5 meters (16 feet)
B. 10 meters (31 feet)
C. 15 meters (50 feet)
D. 20 meters (66 feet)

3840. The painter of the inflatable life raft has a length of _____.

A. 25 feet
B. 100 feet
C. 200 feet
D. 400 feet

3842. You must ensure that lifesaving equipment is _____.

A. locked up
B. readily accessible for use
C. inaccessible to passengers
D. on the topmost deck of the vessel at all times

3849. The capacity of any life raft on board a vessel can be determined by _____.

A. examining the Certificate of Inspection
B. examining the plate on the outside of the raft container
C. referring to the station bill
D. referring to the shipping articles

3853. Coast Guard Regulations (46 CFR) require inflatable life rafts to be equipped with _____.

A. a first aid kit
B. an instruction manual
C. a sea anchor
D. All of the above

3854. According to the regulations, the capacity of a life raft is required to be marked _____.

A. on the station bill
B. at the life raft stowage location
C. on the Certificate of Inspection
D. in the Operations Manual

3855. Which document will describe lifesaving equipment located aboard your vessel?

A. Station Bill
B. Certificate of Inspection
C. Forecastle Card
D. Clearance Papers

3857. Where would you find a list of the lifesaving equipment onboard your supply boat?

A. Ship's Articles
B. Station Bill
C. Certificate of Inspection
D. U.S. Coast Guard Regulations

3858. Lifesaving equipment shall be stowed so that it will be _____.

A. locked up
B. readily accessible for use
C. inaccessible to passengers
D. on the topmost deck of the vessel at all times

3859. When can a work vest be substituted for a life jacket in the total count of the required lifesaving gear?

A. When it is approved by the Coast Guard
B. When working near or over the water
C. When stowed away from the ring buoys
D. A work vest may never be counted as a life jacket.

3860. Life jackets should be stowed in _____.

A. the forepeaks
B. the pumproom
C. readily accessible spaces
D. locked watertight containers

3861. Coast Guard Regulations (46 CFR) require that life jackets shall be _____.

A. provided for each person onboard
B. provided for all personnel of watch

C. readily accessible to persons in the engine room
D. All of the above

3862. In accordance with Coast Guard Regulations, Coast Guard approved buoyant work vests _____.

A. should be stowed in engineering spaces in lieu of approved life jackets because they are less bulky and permit free movement in confined spaces
B. may be used as a substitute for approved life preservers during routine drills, but never during an emergency
C. should not be stowed where they could be confused with life jackets in an emergency
D. All of the above

3866. Each distress signal and self-activated smoke signal must be replaced not later than the marked date of expiration, or not more than how many months from the date of manufacture?

A. 12
B. 24
C. 36
D. 42

3887. The Master shall insure that the Emergency Position Indicating Radiobeacon (EPIRB) is _____.

A. secured inside the wheelhouse
B. tested annually
C. tested monthly
D. secured in the emergency locker

3888. Category I EPIRB's transmit on frequencies that are monitored by _____.

A. orbiting satellites in space
B. commercial radio stations
C. private, commercial, and military aircraft
D. Both A & C

3891. Which statement is TRUE concerning distress signals in a survival craft?

A. Handheld flares and orange smoke signals are required.
B. If handheld rocket-propelled parachute flares are provided, they are the only distress signals required.
C. Two handheld smoke signals shall be provided.
D. A Very pistol with twelve flares is required.

3892. By regulation, orange smoke distress signals will expire not more than how many months from the date of manufacture?

A. 24 months
B. 36 months
C. 42 months
D. 54 months

3894. A life raft with a capacity of 8 people used in ocean service is required by regulations to carry _____.

A. 8 litres of fresh water
B. 12 units of provisions
C. 12 litres of fresh water
D. 24 units of provisions

3896. Life preservers must be marked with the _____.

A. stowage space assigned
B. vessel's name
C. vessel's home port
D. maximum weight allowed

3897. What is the maximum time that distress flares are approved for?

A. 1-1/2 years
B. 2 years
C. 3-1/2 years
D. 5 years

3900. The life jackets on all vessels shall be _____.

A. inspected weekly
B. worn at all times
C. readily available
D. tested yearly

3904. The light on a life jacket must be replaced _____.

A. when the power source is replaced
B. each year after installation
C. every six months
D. when it is no longer serviceable

3906. When a lifeline is required to be attached to a ring life buoy it must be at least _____.

A. 30 feet long
B. 60 feet long
C. 90 feet long
D. 120 feet long

3912. If you must enter water on which there is an oil fire, you should _____.

A. protect your life preserver by holding it above your head
B. enter the water on the windward side of the vessel
C. keep both hands in front of your face to break the water surface when diving head first
D. wear very light clothing

3914. If you must jump from a vessel, the correct posture includes _____.

A. holding down the life preserver against the chest with one arm crossing the other, covering the mouth and nose with a hand, and feet together
B. knees bent and held close to the body with both arms around legs
C. body straight and arms held tightly at the sides for feet first entry into the water
D. both hands holding the life preserver below the chin with knees bent and legs crossed

3916. If an inflatable life raft inflates upside down, you can right it by _____.

A. pushing up on one side
B. standing on the CO_2 bottle, holding the bottom straps, and throwing your weight backwards
C. getting at least three or four men to push down on the side containing the CO_2 cylinder
D. doing nothing; it will right itself after the canopy supports inflate

3918. If your life raft is to leeward of a fire on the water, you should FIRST _____.

A. cut the line to the sea anchor
B. paddle away from the fire
C. splash water over the life raft to cool it
D. get out of the raft and swim to safety

3920. Inflatable life rafts are less maneuverable than lifeboats due to their _____.

A. shape
B. shallow draft
C. large sail area
D. All of the above

3922. You have abandoned ship and are in an inflatable raft that has just inflated. You hear a continuous hissing coming from a fitting in a buoyancy tube. What is the cause of this?

A. The salt water is activating the batteries of the marker lights on the canopy.
B. The inflation pump is in automatic operation to keep the tubes fully inflated.
C. A deflation plug is partially open allowing the escape of CO_2.
D. Excess inflation pressure is bleeding off and should soon stop.

3924. If you are forced to abandon ship in a life raft, your course of action should be to _____.

A. remain in the immediate vicinity
B. head for the nearest land
C. head for the closest sea-lanes
D. let the persons in the boat vote on what to do

3926. To keep injured survivors warm in the water after abandoning ship, they should _____.

A. be placed in the middle of a small circle formed by the other survivors in the water
B. float on their backs with their arms extended for maximum exposure to the air
C. remove their life preservers and hold on to the uninjured survivors
D. sip water at intervals of fifteen minutes

3928. Immediately after abandoning a vessel, lookouts should be posted aboard life rafts to look for _____.

A. survivors in the water
B. food and water
C. land
D. bad weather

3929. What is one of the FIRST things you would do on boarding an inflatable life-raft?

A. Open equipment pack.
B. Post a lookout.
C. Issue anti-seasickness medicine.
D. Pick up other survivors.

3930. You have abandoned your vessel. You are in a life raft and have cleared away from your vessel. One of your FIRST actions should be to _____.

A. take measures to maintain morale
B. prepare and use radio equipment
C. identify the person in charge of life raft
D. search for survivors

3932. You have hand launched an inflatable life raft. What should be one of your FIRST actions upon boarding the life raft?

A. Open the equipment pack.
B. Inflate the life raft floor.
C. Decide on food and water rations.
D. Cut the sea painter and clear the vessel.

3936. After abandoning ship which action should be taken IMMEDIATELY upon entering a life raft?

A. Open equipment pack.
B. Issue anti-seasickness medicine.
C. Cut painter and clear the ship.
D. Dry the life raft floor and inflate.

3938. You have abandoned ship in rough weather. After picking up other survivors in your life raft, what should you do next?

A. Close up the entrances.
B. Top up the buoyancy tubes.
C. Prepare for the arrival of rescue units.
D. Decide on food and water rations.

3939. You board an inflatable life raft that has been hand launched from a sinking vessel. What should you do FIRST after everyone is onboard the life raft?

A. Cut the painter.
B. Operate the radio equipment.
C. Open the equipment pack.
D. Ventilate the life raft of CO_2.

3940. If you must swim through an oil fire, you should NOT _____.

A. wear as much clothing as possible
B. enter the water feet first
C. swim with the wind
D. cover eyes with one hand when entering the water

3942. You have abandoned ship in tropical waters. Which procedure(s) should be used during a prolonged period in a raft?

A. Wet clothes during the day to decrease perspiration.
B. Get plenty of rest.
C. Keep the entrance curtains open.
D. All of the above

3944. What is the most vulnerable part of the fire main system?

A. The fire pump

B. Exposed hard piping
C. The hydrant valve
D. The fire hose

3946. Fusible-link fire dampers are operated by _____.

A. a mechanical arm outside the vent duct
B. the heat of a fire melting the link
C. electrical controls on the bridge
D. a break-glass and pull-cable system

3948. While adrift in an inflatable life raft in hot, tropical weather _____.

A. the canopy should be deflated so that it will not block cooling breezes
B. the pressure valve may be periodically opened to prevent excessive air pressure
C. deflating the floor panels may help to cool personnel
D. the entrance curtains should never be opened

3949. When should you first have any food or water after boarding a lifeboat or life raft?

A. After 12 hours
B. After 24 hours
C. Within 48 hours
D. Some food and water should be consumed immediately and then not until 48 hours later

3950. You are picking up a conscious person that has fallen overboard. Recovery is easier if you approach with the _____.

A. victim to leeward
B. victim to windward
C. wind on your port side
D. wind on your starboard side

3951. All personnel on board a vessel should be familiar with the rescue boat's _____.

A. boarding and operating procedure
B. maintenance schedules
C. navigational systems
D. fuel consumption rates

3952. If an inflatable life raft is overturned, it may be righted by _____.

A. filling the stabilizers on one side with water
B. releasing the CO_2 cylinder
C. pushing up from under one end

D. standing on the inflating cylinder and pulling on the straps on the underside of the raft

3953. To turn over a life raft that is floating upside down, you should pull on the _____.

A. canopy
B. manropes
C. sea painter
D. righting lines

3954. The float free link attached to a sea painter on an inflatable life raft has a breaking strength of _____.

A. 100–134 lbs. for buoyant apparatus with a capacity of 10 persons or less
B. 200–268 lbs. for buoyant apparatus with a capacity of 11 to 20 persons
C. 400–536 lbs. for buoyant apparatus with a capacity of 21 persons or more
D. All of the above

3956. Your ship is sinking rapidly. A container containing an inflatable life raft has bobbed to the surface upon functioning of the hydrostatic release. Which action should you take?

A. Cut the painter line so it will not pull the life raft container down.
B. Swim away from the container so you will not be in danger as it goes down.
C. Take no action because the painter will cause the life raft to inflate and open the container.
D. Manually open the container and inflate the life raft with the hand pump.

3958. If there's a fire aboard your vessel, you should FIRST _____.

A. notify the Coast Guard
B. have passengers put on life preservers
C. sound the alarm
D. cut off air supply to the fire

3960. A rigid lifesaving device designed to support survivors in the water is a _____.

A. rigid life raft
B. life float
C. inflatable life raft
D. survival capsule

3962. When should food or water be provided to survivors after boarding a life raft?

A. After 12 hours
B. After 24 hours
C. After 48 hours
D. Some food and water should be consumed immediately and then not until 48 hours later

3964. Paints and solvents on a vessel should be _____.

A. stored safely in a cool dark non-ventilated area until work is completed
B. resealed and returned to a well ventilated area after each use
C. covered at all times to protect from ignition sources
D. stored in a suitable gear locker

3986. A fire is discovered in the bow of your vessel while making way. The wind is from ahead at 35 knots. You should _____.

A. remain on course and hold speed
B. remain on course but slack the speed
C. change course to put the wind on either beam and increase speed
D. change course and put the stern to the wind

3989. Inflatable life rafts on vessels on an international voyage must be able to carry at least _____.

A. 2 persons
B. 4 persons
C. 6 persons
D. 8 persons

3992. How many B-II fire extinguishers must be in the machinery space of a 175-foot long fishing vessel propelled by engines with 3300 brake horsepower?

A. 2
B. 3
C. 4
D. 5

3994. The color of the signal flare sent up by a submarine about to surface is _____.

A. green
B. white
C. red
D. yellow

4010. A ship that, at any time, operates seaward of the outermost boundary of the territorial sea is required to prepare, submit, and maintain a(n) _____.

A. synthetic plastic discharge plan
B. oil discharge plan
C. shipboard oil pollution emergency plan
D. vapor recovery procedures plan

4011. If you fail to notify the Coast Guard of an oil spill, you may be imprisoned up to _____.

A. 1 year
B. 2 years
C. 3 years
D. 5 years

4012. The Federal Water Pollution Control Act requires the person in charge of a vessel to immediately notify the Coast Guard as soon as he knows of any oil discharge. Failure to notify the Coast Guard can lead to a monetary fine and imprisonment up to _____.

A. 5 years
B. 3 years
C. 2 years
D. 1 years

4017. Towing vessel fire protection regulations define a "fixed fire-extinguishing system" to include all of the following EXCEPT a _____.

A. carbon-dioxide system
B. halon system
C. manually operated clean-agent system
D. manually operated water-mist system

4018. Towing vessel fire protection regulations distinguish between "new" and "existing" towing vessels. A "new" towing vessel is one that was _____.

A. built within the last three years
B. contracted for on or after January 1, 1999
C. contracted for on or after January 18, 2000
D. not previously owned

4019. The regulations for a general alarm system on a towing vessel require all of the following EXCEPT that it _____.

A. be capable of notifying persons in any accomodation, work space and the engine room

B. have a contact maker at the operating station
C. have a flashing red light in areas that have high background noise
D. be used instead of the public address system

4020. The control panel of a fire detection system must have all of the following EXCEPT _____.

A. a power-available light
B. an audible alarm to notify the crew and identify the origin of the fire
C. a means to silence audible alarms while maintaining visible alarm lights
D. a way to bypass the entire panel if it malfunctions

4021. A towing vessel's fire detection system may be certified to comply with the Coast Guard's towing vessel fire protection regulations by _____.

A. a Coast Guard inspector
B. a registered professional engineer
C. the owner or Master of the vessel
D. a licensed electrician

4022. Which towing vessels are NOT required to have an internal communication system between the engine room and the operating station?

A. Twin-screw vessels that have operating station control for both engines
B. Vessels on limited routes
C. Fleet boats making or breaking tows
D. Vessels serving a single company or facility

4023. Which devices may be used as part of an internal communication system on a towing vessel?

A. Sound-powered telephones
B. Portable radios
C. Either fixed or portable equipment
D. All of the above

4024. In the towing vessel fire protection regulations, all of the following are fire detection requirements, EXCEPT that _____.

A. the control panel must have labels for all switches and indicator lights
B. the detection system must be powered from two sources, with the switchover being either manual or automatic

C. there must be a circuit-fault detector test-switch in the control panel
D. none of the above

4025. When is direct voice communication allowed in place of an internal communication system on a towing vessel?

A. When the vessel is less than 20 meters in length
B. When the vessel is ruled to be an "existing vessel"
C. When the controls at the operation station are within 3 meters (10 feet) of the engine room access
D. When it is easier to shout than use a radio or telephone

4026. When do the towing vessel fire protection regulations allow a new towing vessel to carry portable fuel systems on board?

A. When used for outboard engines
B. When permanently attached to portable equipment such as bilge and fire pumps
C. If the portable tanks used for portable equipment meet published safety standards
D. All of the above

4028. Fire protection regulations for towing vessels allow all of these types of fuel piping, EXCEPT _____ .

A. steel
B. aluminum in an aluminum-hulled vessel
C. schedule 80 fire resistant plastic pipe
D. nickel-copper, copper-nickel or annealed copper

4029. Fire protection regulations for towing vessels allow you to use a nonmetallic flexible hose in fuel line installations under all of the following conditions EXCEPT when _____ .

A. used in lengths of not more than 30 inches
B. reinforced with wire braid
C. visible and easily accessible
D. fitted with Coast Guard approved garden hose fittings

4030. Fire protection regulations for towing vessels require any fuel line subject to internal head pressure from fuel in the tank to _____ .

A. be fitted with a positive fuel shut-off valve located at the tank
B. have a shut-off valve at the top of the tank
C. have a gate valve easily accessible in the space where the tank is located
D. have a drain cock at the lowest point in the fuel line

4032. Towing vessel fire protection regulations require that all fuel tank vent pipes comply with all of the following provisions EXCEPT that the vent _____ .

A. connects to the highest point of the tank
B. system discharges on a weather deck through a U-shaped 180 degree pipe bend
C. be fitted with a 30-by-30 corrosion resistant flame screen
D. must have a positive-acting shut-off valve to prevent water from entering the tank in heavy weather

4034. When a standard in the fire protection regulations for towing vessels is "incorporated by reference," it means that the

_____ .

A. Coast Guard accepts a commercial or military standard as part of a specific regulation
B. standard is readily available to the public
C. standard, and where it can be obtained or referred to, are listed in the Code of Federal Regulations
D. All of the above

4036. Fire protection regulations for towing vessels require that all crew members participate in drills and receive instruction at least once a month. Who is responsible for ensuring it takes place?

A. The Officer in Charge, Marine Inspection
B. The Master, or person in charge of the vessel
C. The vessel's owner or manager
D. The company's port captain or port engineer

4038. Fire protection regulations for towing vessels require all crew members to know how to perform each of these tasks EXCEPT _____ .

A. start the mechanical ventilation system for the engine room

B. operate the fuel shut-off for the engine room
C. operate all fire extinguishing equipment aboard the vessel on board the vessel, including starting the fire pump
D. All of the above

4039. Do the fire protection regulations for "existing" towing vessels require that the crew of existing vessels be trained for fire and other emergencies with drills and safety orientations?

A. Yes, if the vessel is greater than 100 gross tons.
B. Yes, as stated in the regulations.
C. No, the rules only apply to "new" towing vessels.
D. No, if your license or MMD was grandfathered.

4040. Fire protection regulations for towing vessels require training in all of the following, EXCEPT _____ .

A. putting on a fireman's outfit, if the vesel is so equipped
B. donning a self-contained breathing apparatus, if the vessel is so equipped
C. activating the general alarm and reporting inoperative alarm systems and fire-detection systems
D. refilling and servicing all expended fire extinguishing equipment

4042. How many B-II fire extinguishers must be in the machinery space of a 75-foot long fishing vessel propelled by engines with 1200 brake horsepower?

A. 1
B. 2
C. 3
D. 4

4044. Convection spreads a fire by _____.

A. heated gases flowing through ventilation systems
B. the transfer of heat across an unobstructed space
C. burning liquids flowing into another space
D. transmitting the heat of a fire through the ship's metal

4046. Fire protection regulations for towing vessels require that drills be conducted on board the vessel as if there were an actual emergency. Drills include all of the following, EXCEPT _____ .

A. testing all alarm and detection systems
B. breaking out and using the vessel's emergency equipment
C. participation by selected crew members
D. one person putting on protective clothing, if the vessel is so equipped

4048. Fire protection and manning regulations for towing vessels state that the Master or person in charge must ensure that all crew members who have not participated in the drills or received the safety orientation _____ .

A. receive a safety orientation before the vessel gets underway
B. receive a safety orientation within 48 hours of reporting for duty
C. become familiar with relevant characteristics of the vessel before assuming their duties
D. All of the above

4049. The owner or Master of a towing vessel shall ensure that all tests and inspections of gear take place and are logged _____ .

A. on each watch, immediately before being relieved
B. before embarking on a voyage of more than 24 hours
C. daily, at 1200 local zone time
D. weekly, before 0000 Sunday

4050. The owner or Master of a towing vessel shall ensure that all tests and inspections of gear take place and are logged _____ .

A. when a new Master assumes command
B. daily, at 0800 local zone time
C. weekly, before 2400 Saturday
D. immediately after assuming the watch

4052. The test of a towing vessel's steering gear control system includes each item EXCEPT _____ .

A. a test from the alternative power supply, if installed
B. timing the movement of the rudder from hard over to hard over
C. verification that the rudder angle indicator shows the actual position of the rudder(s)
D. visual inspection of the steering linkage

4054. Which navigational equipment is required to be tested and logged before a towing vessel embarks on a voyage of more than 24 hours?

A. Compass and/or swing meter
B. Radar(s) and VHF radio(s)
C. LORAN-C and/or GPS receiver(s)
D. All required navigational equipment, without exception

4056. Which installed equipment must be tested and logged when a new Master assumes command?

A. Internal communications, including sound-powered telephones
B. Navigational lights and search lights
C. Vessel control alarms
D. All of the above must be tested

4059. What must the owner or Master do if any of the towing vessel's required navigational safety equipment fails during a voyage?

A. Repair it at the earliest practicable time
B. Enter its failure in the log or other on board record
C. Consider the state of the equipment in deciding whether it is safe for the vessel to proceed
D. All of the above

4060. After an item of required safety equipment on a towing vessel fails, the owner or Master must consider all of these factors before continuing the voyage, EXCEPT the _____ .

A. weather conditions, including visibility
B. estimated time of arrival promised to the customer
C. safety of the vessel, considering the other traffic in the area
D. dictates of good seamanship

4062. The owner or Master of a towing vessel that is operating within a Vessel Traffic Service (VTS) area must report all of the following to VTS as soon as practicable EXCEPT _____ .

A. any malfunction of propulsion machinery, steering gear, radar, gyrocompass or depth-sounder, if installed
B. shortage of personnel, lack of charts, maps or other required publications
C. the type of license he/she holds and its serial number
D. any characteristics of the vessel that affect its maneuverability

4064. If you are the Master of a towing vessel whose only working radar no longer functions, what must you do?

A. Notify the Captain of the Port (COTP) if you cannot repair it within 96 hours.
B. Notify the Officer in Charge of Marine Inspection (OCMI) if you cannot repair it within 48 hours.
C. Moor the vessel until it is repaired.
D. Anchor the vessel until it is repaired.

4066. The most important concern in treating a person with extensive burns is _____ .

A. reducing disfigurement
B. preventing infection
C. cooling with ice water
D. reducing swelling

4078. When shifting to a course where the wind comes more from astern, easing the mainsheet will _____ .

A. bring the boom more fore and aft
B. decrease the force needed to haul on the mainsheet
C. bring the head of the sail down from the top of the mast
D. allow the sail to catch more wind

4079. Your cargo vessel's Certification of Inspection expires 30 April 2002. One of your inflatable life rafts was last serviced in January 2002. The raft must be reinspected no later than _____ .

A. Jan-03
B. Jun-03
C. Apr-04
D. Jan-07

4082. A towing vessel is NOT required to be fitted with radar if it is _____ .

A. used solely for assistance towing
B. under 65 feet in length
C. used exclusively on the Western Rivers
D. pushing ahead

4084. A towing vessel is NOT required to be fitted with radar if it is _____ .

A. used occasionally to assist vessels in distress
B. used solely for pollution response
C. less than 49 feet in length
D. towing alongside

4086. What signal flag is the "Pilot Flag" ("I have a pilot on board")?

A. "P"
B. "C"
C. "H"
D. "Z"

4088. Which towing vessel(s) is/are exempt from carrying radar?

A. A vessel used solely in a limited area, such as a barge fleeting area.
B. A vessel exempted, in writing, by the Captain of the Port.
C. A vessel used solely for pollution response or assistance towing.
D. All of the above

4089. Which piece of navigational safety equipment is NOT required on towing vessels over 12 meters in length, provided that the vessel remains within the navigable waters of the U.S.?

A. VHF-FM radio(s)
B. LORAN-C or GPS receiver
C. Charts or maps of the areas to be transited
D. Searchlight

4090. Which instrument may a towing vessel, engaged in towing exclusively on the Western Rivers, use in place of a magnetic compass?

A. Gyrocompass
B. Illuminated Swing Meter
C. LORAN-C Receiver
D. GPS Receiver

4092. On which route is a towing vessel over 39.4 feet in length NOT required to carry an echo-sounding device?

A. Great Lakes
B. Inland Waters, other than the Western Rivers
C. Western Rivers
D. Coastwise Routes

4093. Towing vessels of more than 39.4 feet in length must carry charts or maps _____.

A. of the area to be navigated
B. with enough detail to make safe navigation possible
C. of the current edition or currently corrected edition
D. All of the above

4096. Which statement(s) is/are TRUE concerning radio equipment on towing vessels of 26 feet or more in length?

A. The vessel must have a ship-radio-station license issued by the FCC.
B. Each radio operator must hold an FCC-issued restricted operator's license, or higher.
C. Maintain a continuous listening watch on VHF channel 16 and the bridge-to-bridge channel.
D. All of the above.

4098. Which publication(s) must a towing vessel of 12 meters or more in length carry when operating on U.S. waters other than the Western Rivers?

A. US Coast Pilot(s)
B. Tide Tables and Tidal Current Tables
C. Notice to Mariners
D. All of the above

4102. The center of the underwater volume of a floating vessel is the _____.

A. center of buoyancy
B. center of flotation
C. uncorrected height of the center of gravity of the vessel
D. center of gravity of the vessel corrected for free surface effects

4112. A fire is discovered in the forepeak of a vessel at sea. The wind is from ahead at 35 knots. You should _____.

A. remain on course and hold speed
B. remain on course but slack the speed
C. change course to put the wind on either beam and increase speed
D. change course and put the stern to the wind

4115. The inspection of a 50 ft. vessel of 65 gross tons carrying more than twelve passengers on an international voyage is required by the Coast Guard once in every _____. (Small Passenger Vessel Regulations.)

A. four years with a minimum of three reinspections during the four year period
B. three years with a minimum of two reinspections during the three year period
C. two years
D. year

4138. Multiple fire pumps may be used for other purposes provided that one pump is _____.

A. on line to the fire main
B. kept available for use on the fire main at all times
C. capable of being connected to the fire main
D. rated at or above 125 psi

4142. You are underway at sea when a fire is reported in the forward part of the vessel. The wind is from dead ahead at 20 knots. You should _____.

A. change course and put the stern to the wind
B. change course to put the wind on either beam and increase speed
C. remain on course and hold speed
D. remain on course but decrease speed

4174. Each EPIRB shall be tested using the integrated test circuit and output indicator every _____.

A. week
B. two weeks
C. month
D. quarter

4246. Radiation spreads a fire by _____.

A. transferring heat across an unobstructed space
B. heated gases flowing through ventilation systems
C. burning liquids flowing into another space
D. transmitting the heat of a fire through the ship's metal

4346. The EPIRB on board your vessel is required to be tested _____.

A. weekly
B. monthly
C. quarterly
D. yearly

4362. The free-surface effects of a partially full tank in a vessel increase with the _____.

A. surface area of the fluid in the tank
B. displacement volume of the vessel
C. draft of the vessel
D. height of the tank above the keel

4404. The letter and number symbols, such as B-II, used to classify portable fire extinguishers indicate the _____.

A. class of fire and size of the extinguisher
B. class of fire and location aboard vessel
C. extinguishing agent and relative size of the extinguisher
D. extinguishing agent and location aboard vessel

4416. The color of the signal flare sent up by a submarine indicating that a torpedo has been fired in a training exercise is _____.

A. white
B. yellow
C. red
D. green

4458. Any firefighting equipment that is carried in addition to the minimum required must _____.

A. meet the applicable standards
B. be marked as additional equipment
C. be stowed in a separate area
D. All of the above

4486. The international body responsible for drafting the convention prohibiting marine pollution (MARPOL) is the _____.

A. Maritime Advisory Council
B. International Maritime Organization
C. International Association of Shipping
D. Association of Seafaring Nations

4546. Fire dampers prevent the spread of fire by _____.

A. direct contact
B. radiation
C. conduction
D. convection

4572. You are underway at sea. A fire is reported in the forward part of the vessel. The wind is from dead ahead at 20 knots. You should _____.

A. remain on course and hold speed
B. change course and put the stern to the wind

C. change course to put the wind on either beam and increase speed
D. remain on course but decrease speed

4701. After you activate your emergency position indicating radiobeacon, you should _____.

A. turn it off for five minutes every half-hour
B. turn it off and on at five-minute intervals
C. turn it off during daylight hours
D. leave it on continuously

4734. Seawater may be used for drinking _____.

A. if gathered during or immediately after a hard rain
B. at a maximum rate of two ounces per day
C. under no conditions
D. after mixing with an equal quantity of fresh water

4784. If there's a fire aboard your vessel, you should FIRST _____.

A. sound the alarm
B. notify the Coast Guard
C. have passengers put on life preservers
D. cut off air supply to the fire

4785. What should you do with your emergency position indicating radiobeacon if you are in a life raft in a storm?

A. Bring it inside the life raft and leave it on.
B. Bring it inside the life raft and turn it off until the storm passes.
C. Leave it outside the life raft and leave it on.
D. Leave it outside the life raft but turn it off.

5031. For the purposes of the International Rules of the Road, a jack-up drilling rig under tow is considered to be a _____.

A. vessel
B. non-displacement vessel
C. power-driven vessel
D. limited vessel

5033. For the purposes of the International Rules of the Road, a non-self-propelled, semisubmersible drilling unit under tow is considered to be a _____.

A. power-driven vessel

B. limited vessel
C. non-displacement vessel
D. vessel

5037. Where will you find the requirements for the signals that must be sounded by a mobile offshore drilling unit that is being towed through an area of restricted visibility?

A. COLREGS
B. MMS Rules
C. SOLAS Convention
D. Coast Pilot

5192. There is a fire aft aboard your vessel. To help fight the fire, you should _____.

A. put the wind off either beam
B. put the stern into the wind and decrease speed
C. put the stern into the wind and increase speed
D. head the bow into the wind and decrease speed

5225. If the cause of a sudden severe list or trim is negative initial stability, counterflooding into empty tanks may _____.

A. increase the righting moment
B. cause an increase in the righting arm
C. bring the unit to an upright equilibrium position
D. cause the unit to flop to a greater angle

5231. If the cause of severe list or trim is off-center ballast, counterflooding into empty tanks will _____.

A. increase the righting moment
B. increase the righting arm
C. increase list or trim
D. decrease list or trim

5232. Fusible-link fire dampers are operated by _____.

A. a mechanical arm outside the vent duct
B. electrical controls on the bridge
C. the heat of a fire melting the link
D. a break-glass and pull-cable system

5286. A vessel is inclined at an angle of loll. In the absence of external forces, the righting arm (GZ) is _____.

A. positive
B. negative
C. zero

D. vertical

5386. Which toxic gas is a product of incomplete combustion, and is often present when a fire burns in a closed compartment?

A. Carbon dioxide
B. Carbon monoxide
C. Nitric oxide
D. Hydrogen sulfide

5387. Which toxic gas is a product of incomplete combustion, and is often present when a fire burns in a closed compartment?

A. Nitric oxide
B. Carbon dioxide
C. Hydrogen sulfide
D. Carbon monoxide

5408. One of the first actions to be taken by survivors when they have boarded an inflatable life raft is to _____.

A. stream the sea anchor
B. take an anti-seasickness pill
C. open the pressure relief valve
D. drink at least one can of water

5418. Small passenger vessels in coastwise service must carry approved _____.

A. life floats
B. inflatable buoyant apparatus
C. inflatable life rafts
D. Any of the above

5455. What percentage of the breaking strength is the generally accepted safe operating load of an anchor cable?

A. 10%
B. 25%
C. 35%
D. 50%

5457. The only wire rope termination which may be made in the field is _____.

A. swaged socket
B. thimbled mechanical splice
C. hand splice
D. spelter poured and resin sockets

5461. Thirty-five percent of the breaking strength of an anchor cable is generally accepted as the _____.

A. safe operating load
B. normal operating tension
C. emergency working load
D. allowable storm load

5463. A common class of wire rope used for mooring is the 6 x19 class. What does the 6 represent?

A. Factor of safety
B. Number of wires per strand
C. Number of strands per wire rope
D. Number of wires in the core

5465. A common class of wire rope used for mooring is the 6 x 37 class. What does the 37 represent?

A. Number of wires in the inner core
B. Number of strands per wire rope
C. Tensile strength of the wire
D. Number of wires per strand

5467. What is an advantage of the 6 x19 class of wire rope over the 6 x 37 class of wire rope of the same diameter?

A. Greater holding power
B. Better fatigue life
C. Resistance to elongation
D. Resistance to corrosion

5471. What is an advantage of the 6 x 37 class of wire rope over the 6 x 19 class of wire rope of the same diameter?

A. Flexibility
B. Resistance to corrosion
C. Resistance to elongation
D. Lower weight per foot

5473. Where do fatigue failures of wire rope mooring lines usually occur?

A. In the middle part of the line length
B. Near the socketed end fitting adjacent to the anchor
C. At the point where the line touches the bottom
D. At the place the anchor buoy is attached to the line

5475. The primary purpose for using stud link chain in a mooring system on a rig is the _____.

A. stud link is more economical
B. stud keeps the chain from kinking
C. stud link chain is the lightest night design

D. stud link improves the anchor's holding power

5479. The purpose of the inclining experiment on a vessel is to determine the _____.

A. location of the center of gravity of the light ship
B. position of the center of buoyancy
C. position of the metacenter
D. maximum load line

5481. A common means of connecting shots of anchor chain in the field is to use a _____.

A. sprocket
B. Kenter link
C. swivel
D. end shackle

5485. The maximum angular tolerance for a bent link of an anchor chain is _____.

A. 1 degree
B. 3 degrees
C. 5 degrees
D. 7 degrees

5487. A measurement device for inspecting anchor chain is the _____.

A. slide rule
B. go-no-go gauge
C. derrick tape
D. amp probe

5495. Extended cyclical variations in tensions will cause an anchor chain to break due to _____.

A. fatigue
B. corrosion
C. distortion
D. abrasion

5505. Which problem is virtually impossible to detect during an in-service inspection of used mooring chain?

A. Cracks
B. Elongation
C. Loose studs
D. Fatigue

5513. A link on an anchor chain should be replaced when wear or grinding of surface cracks has reduced the cross section area by _____.

A. 4%
B. 6%
C. 8%
D. 10%

5515. What should be done after repairing a surface crack on a link of anchor chain by grinding?

A. Examine the area by magnetic particle inspection
B. Replace the chain in service
C. Galvanize the area
D. Post heat the area

5517. Grinding to eliminate shallow surface defects should be done _____.

A. parallel to the longitudinal direction of the chain
B. perpendicular to the direction of the anchor chain
C. diagonally across the link of the anchor chain
D. around the circumference of the chain link

5521. Prior to magnetic particle inspection of anchor chain, the chain should be _____.

A. degaussed
B. demagnetized
C. soaked
D. sandblasted

5522. Radiation spreads a fire by _____.

A. transmitting the heat of a fire through the ship's metal
B. transferring heat across an unobstructed space
C. burning liquids flowing into another space
D. heated gases flowing through ventilation systems

5523. Before being certified by the American Bureau of Shipping, anchor chain must undergo _____.

A. USCG inspection
B. a breaking test
C. x-ray inspection
D. spectroanalysis

5525. What does the proof test load of an anchor chain demonstrate?

A. The breaking strength of the anchor chain
B. Strength of the anchor chain to a specified limit
C. Adequate holding power for new bottom conditions
D. Safe working load of the anchor chain

5527. With adaptor blocks/chocks in place on an LWT stock anchor, the trip angle will be _____.

A. 20°
B. 30°
C. 40°
D. 50°

5531. With adaptor blocks/chocks removed from an LWT stock anchor, the trip angle will be _____.

A. 20°
B. 30°
C. 40°
D. 50°

5533. Connecting elements of a mooring system should be fabricated from _____.

A. cast iron
B. forged steel
C. stainless steel
D. cast steel

5535. What effect is achieved from soaking an anchor?

A. It allows the bottom soil to consolidate.
B. It gives the palms time to trip the anchor.
C. It stabilizes the mooring system.
D. It lubricates the anchor for better tripping.

5537. Why should you soak an anchor?

A. It can prevent the anchor from slipping during pretensioning.
B. It will lubricate all the moving parts of a stock anchor.
C. It will increase the maximum breaking strength of the anchor chain.
D. It will make it easier to disassemble the anchor for repair.

5541. What is the "holding power ratio" of an anchor?

A. Maximum mooring line tension divided by the anchor's weight in air
B. Anchor's weight in air divided by the maximum mooring line tension
C. Preloading tension divided by the anchor's weight in air
D. Operating tension divided by the anchor's weight in air

5543. What happens to the efficiency of an anchor when it is moved from sand to mud?

A. The efficiency increases.
B. The efficiency decreases.
C. The efficiency remains the same.
D. The efficiency cannot be determined.

5545. When a combination chain and wire rope mooring line is used, the chain is deployed _____.

A. at the anchor end of the line
B. at the wildcat end of the line
C. midway between the anchor and the wildcat
D. through the anchor buoy

5547. In a combination chain and wire rope mooring system, the chain is deployed at the anchor end of the line to _____.

A. increase fatigue life
B. eliminate the need for mooring buoys
C. prevent the anchor from fouling
D. increase the catenary

5551. Anchor shackles should have a breaking strength that is _____.

A. equal to the chains they are connecting
B. 25% more than the chains they are connecting
C. 50% more than the chains they are connecting
D. 100% more than the chains they are connecting

5553. The angle between the flukes and the shank of an anchor is called the _____.

A. holding angle
B. fleet angle
C. fluke angle
D. shank angle

5555. The fluke angle of an anchor system is the angle between the _____.

A. flukes and the shank
B. shank and the sea bottom
C. mooring line and the sea bottom
D. flukes and the shackle

557. The holding power of an anchor is the _____.

A. maximum sustained vertical load an anchor will resist before dragging
B. maximum sustained horizontal load an anchor will resist before dragging
C. maximum sustained vertical load an anchor will resist before the mooring line breaks
D. maximum sustained horizontal load an anchor will resist before the mooring line breaks

5561. What line receives the hardest service in the mooring system?

A. Guy wire
B. Joining pendant
C. Wildcat leader
D. Anchor pendant

5563. Most large anchors are manufactured with a _____.

A. bow type shackle
B. D-type shackle
C. U-type shackle
D. Kenter shackle

5565. What is the bow type anchor shackle primarily used for?

A. Chain to chain connections
B. Chain to anchor connections
C. Kenter link to anchor connections
D. Wire rope connections

5567. What is the most important difference between the bow type anchor shackle and the D-type anchor shackle?

A. The bow type shackle provides a superior connection.
B. The D-type shackle is weaker than the bow type.
C. The bow type shackle is weaker than the D-type.
D. The D-type shackle provides an inferior connection.

5571. Which two components pass through the shank of an LWT anchor?

A. Anchor shackle and stock
B. Tripping palm and flukes
C. Crown and chocks
D. Swivel and stabilizer bar

5573. To develop maximum anchor holding power, the optimum angle between the anchor's shank and the mooring lines is _____.

A. 0 degrees
B. 10 degrees
C. 20 degrees
D. 30 degrees

5575. Increasing the area of the anchor flukes will _____.

A. increase holding power
B. decrease holding power
C. make penetration more complete
D. not effect holding power

5577. What is the advantage of a single streamlined fluke anchor over a double fluked anchor of similar weight?

A. It has multiple fluke angle settings.
B. It has increased holding power.
C. It holds well with either side down.
D. It is easier to handle on an anchor boat.

5591. The major cause of anchor buoy pendant wire failures is _____.

A. corrosion
B. rough weather
C. defective sockets
D. mishandling

5595. An anchor winch should be equipped with mechanical brakes capable of holding _____.

A. half the breaking strength of the mooring line
B. the full breaking strength of the mooring line
C. the maximum expected tension of the mooring line
D. 50% over the working tension of the mooring line

5597. A chain stripper is used to _____.

A. prevent chain from clinging to the wildcat
B. clean the marine debris from the chain

C. flake chain from a boat's chain locker
D. clean chain prior to an x-ray inspection

5598. Fire dampers prevent the spread of fire by _____.

A. direct contact
B. radiation
C. convection
D. conduction

5648. The hydrostatic release on the inflatable life rafts on a fishing vessel must be _____.

A. replaced annually
B. tested monthly
C. serviced annually
D. overhauled quarterly

5655. When the air temperature is just below 32°F, snow FIRST adheres to _____.

A. surfaces near the waterline
B. vertical surfaces
C. horizontal surfaces
D. leeward surfaces

5697. The motion that can significantly increase mooring line tension is _____.

A. pitch
B. roll
C. yaw
D. sway

5711. Installing tandem anchors on the same mooring line is referred to as _____.

A. doubling
B. pretensioning
C. piggybacking
D. paralleling

5715. What can cause a lack of oxygen in a chain locker?

A. Absorption
B. Osmosis
C. Evaporation
D. Oxidation

5753. The length of chain between the anchor and the end of the pendant line is called the _____.

A. pigtail chain
B. thrash chain

C. crown chain
D. wear chain

5763. What is the purpose of a chain stopper?

A. Stops the chain during pay out
B. Secures the chain after is has been stopped
C. Stops off a 6 foot section for inspection
D. Hydraulically cuts anchor chain

5806. Damage stability is the stability _____.

A. which exists when the wind speed is less than 50 knots
B. before collision
C. after flooding
D. at the maximum load

5824. The vertical distance between G and M is used as a measure of _____.

A. stability at all angles of inclination
B. initial stability
C. stability at angles less than the limit of positive stability
D. stability at angles less than the downflooding angle

5825. The tension on an anchor cable increases so that the angle of the catenary to the seabed at the anchor reaches 10 degrees. How will this affect the anchor in sandy soil?

A. It will have no effect.
B. It will increase the holding power.
C. It will reduce the holding power.
D. It will cause the anchor to snag.

5845. Yawing can be described as _____.

A. jumping on the tow line as the rig pitches
B. jumping on the tow line as the rig slams into waves
C. veering from side to side on the end of the tow line
D. corkscrew motion due to wave action

5953. The stamped full weight of a 100 lb. CO_2 bottle is 314 lbs. What is the minimum weight of the bottle before it has to be recharged?

A. 282 lbs.
B. 294 lbs.
C. 300 lbs.

D. 304 lbs.

6005. Fire extinguishers of sizes III, IV, and V are designated as _____.

A. portable
B. semi-portable
C. fixed
D. disposable

6049. While proceeding to a distress site, you hear the words "Seelonce mayday" on the radiotelephone. Which action should you take?

A. Resume base course and speed as your assistance is no longer required.
B. Acknowledge receipt and advise your course, speed, and ETA.
C. Relay the original distress message as no other vessel has acknowledged it.
D. Monitor the radiotelephone but do not transmit.

6073. Before releasing the CO_2 into the space, the alarm for a fixed CO_2 system must sound for at least _____.

A. 20 seconds
B. 30 seconds
C. 40 seconds
D. 60 seconds

6077. Operation of the valve control release on a fixed CO_2 system must immediately _____.

A. release CO_2 to the protected space
B. secure all mechanical ventilation in the protected space
C. sound the rig's general alarm signal for a fire
D. sound an alarm in the ballast control room

6246. The ventilation system of your ship has fire dampers restrained by fusible links. Which statement is TRUE?

A. A fusible link will automatically open after a fire is extinguished and reset the damper.
B. Fusible links must be replaced at every inspection for certification.
C. Fusible links must be replaced if a damper is activated.
D. Fusible links are tested by applying a source of heat to them.

6249. Automatic fire dampers in ventilation

systems are operated by use of _____.

A. heat or smoke detectors
B. CO_2 system pressure switches
C. remotely operated valves
D. fusible links

6253. The Coast Guard requires machinery spaces and enclosed mud handling spaces to have _____.

A. remote ventilation shutdowns
B. remote pump shutdowns
C. alternative control stations
D. a smoke and/or fire detection system

6273. During a storm, the chance of fatigue failure of a mooring line will increase as _____.

A. vessel motions increase
B. mooring tensions decrease
C. KG increases
D. KG decreases

6274. You are fighting a class B fire with a portable dry chemical extinguisher. The discharge should be directed _____.

A. at the main body of the fire
B. to bank off a bulkhead onto the fire
C. over the top of the fire
D. at the seat of the fire, starting at the near edge

6291. When dragging of an anchor occurs, you must either reposition it at greater range or _____.

A. adjust the tensiometer
B. reduce the conductor tension
C. use a piggyback (backing) anchor
D. increase the riser tension

6303. The most doubtful and unpredictable factor in a mooring system is the _____.

A. ability of the anchors to hold in a seabed
B. anchor chain catenary length
C. variability of the fairlead
D. angle of the flukes

6305. When dragging of an anchor occurs, you must back it up with a piggyback (backing) anchor or _____.

A. reduce the riser tension
B. reposition it at a greater range
C. change the winch
D. change the anchor heading

6306. An inflatable life raft is thrown into the water from a sinking vessel. What occurs automatically after the painter trips the CO_2 bottles to inflate the raft?

A. The sea anchor deploys.
B. The floor inflates.
C. If upside down, the craft rights itself.
D. The painter detaches from the raft.

6307. Using high working tensions in the mooring system reduces the _____.

A. hook load at drilling depths over 10,000 feet
B. possibility of dragging anchors
C. allowable deck load at operating draft
D. margin between working tension and breaking strength

6308. You are underway at sea when a fire is reported in the forward part of the vessel. The wind is from dead ahead at 20 knots. You should _____.

A. remain on course and hold speed
B. change course to put the wind on either beam and increase speed
C. remain on course but decrease speed
D. change course and put the stern to the wind

6313. The holding power of an anchor increases when the _____.

A. amount of chain lying along the bottom increases
B. length of the catenary is reduced
C. mooring line tension is increased
D. amount of chain lying along the bottom decreases

6402. Small passenger vessels in cold water ocean routes, that do not meet the standards for collision bulkheads or subdivision in subchapter S, must carry _____. (Small Passenger Vessel Regulations.)

A. 100% inflatable buoyant apparatus
B. at least one hand fire pump
C. at least two EPIRBs
D. All of the above.

6594. How many B-II fire extinguishers must be in the machinery space of a 175-foot long fishing vessel propelled by engines with 2500 brake horsepower?

A. 2
B. 3

C. 4
D. 5

6604. Fusible-link fire dampers are operated by _____.

A. the heat of a fire melting the link
B. a break-glass and pull-cable system
C. electrical controls on the bridge
D. a mechanical arm outside the vent duct

6624. The color of the signal flare sent up by a submarine indicating that a torpedo has been fired in a training exercise is _____.

A. red
B. white
C. green
D. red

6631. All portable fire extinguishers must be capable of being _____.

A. carried by hand to a fire
B. carried or rolled to a fire
C. recharged in the field
D. used on class "B" fires

6646. Fire in an engine compartment is best extinguished with carbon dioxide gas (CO_2) and by _____.

A. closing the compartment except for the ventilators
B. increasing the air flow to the compartment by blowers
C. leaving the compartment open to the air
D. completely closing the compartment

6742. With an approved combination nozzle, low-velocity fog is produced by _____.

A. inserting an applicator in the nozzle
B. putting the handle of the nozzle in the forward position
C. directing a straight stream of water against the ship's structure
D. the combination nozzle only when the water pressure exceeds 125 psi

6761. Each distress signal and self-activated smoke signal must be replaced not later than the marked date of expiration, or, from the date of manufacture, not later than _____.

A. 6 months
B. 12 months
C. 24 months

D. 42 months

6786. The color of the signal flare sent up by a submarine to indicate an emergency is _____.

A. white
B. yellow
C. red
D. green

6792. All portable fire extinguishers must be capable of being _____.

A. carried by hand to a fire
B. carried or rolled to a fire
C. recharged in the field
D. used on class B fires

6806. A fire has broken out on the stern of your vessel. You should maneuver your vessel so the wind _____.

A. blows the fire back toward the vessel
B. comes over the stern
C. comes over the bow
D. comes over either beam

6856. Fire dampers prevent the spread of fire by _____.

A. conduction
B. convection
C. radiation
D. direct contact

6917. Injuries resulting in loss of life or incapacitation, aboard vessels, must be reported to the _____.

A. Minerals Management Service
B. American Petroleum Institute
C. U.S. Coast Guard
D. International Association of Drilling Contractors

6987. Severe airway burns can cause _____.

A. nausea
B. reddening of cheeks
C. complete obstruction of respiratory passages
D. nosebleed

6991. The FIRST treatment of a person suspected of having airway burns is to _____.

A. move him to a cool location
B. maintain an open airway

C. apply a cool damp dressing to his neck
D. have him drink cool liquids

7003. When treating a chemical burn, you should flood the burned area for at least _____.

A. five minutes
B. ten minutes
C. fifteen minutes
D. twenty minutes

7005. Chemical burns are caused by the skin coming in contact with _____.

A. acids or alkalies
B. diesel oil
C. acids, but not alkalies
D. alkalies, but not acids

7007. What precaution should be taken when treating burns caused by contact with dry lime?

A. Water should be applied in a fine spray.
B. The burned area should be immersed in water.
C. The entire burn area should be covered with ointment.
D. Before washing, the lime should be brushed away gently.

7021. The symptoms of heat exhaustion are _____.

A. slow and strong pulse
B. flushed and dry skin
C. slow and deep breathing
D. pale and clammy skin

7023. Heat exhaustion is caused by excessive _____.

A. loss of body temperature
B. loss of water and salt from the body
C. gain in body temperature
D. intake of water when working or exercising

7025. A patient suffering from heat exhaustion should be _____.

A. moved to a cool room and told to lie down
B. kept standing and encouraged to walk slowly and continuously
C. given a glass of water and told to return to work after 15 minutes of rest
D. None of the above are correct

7027. To treat a person suffering from heat exhaustion, you should _____.

A. administer artificial respiration
B. put him in a tub of ice water
C. give him sips of cool water
D. cover him with a light cloth

7031. Symptoms of sugar diabetes include _____.

A. increased appetite and thirst
B. decreased appetite and thirst
C. gain in weight
D. elevated temperature

7032. Overspeed of the diesel engine driving an electric generator could cause _____.

A. low voltage trip
B. reverse power trip
C. damage to windings
D. excessive exhaust temperatures

7033. A person with diabetes has received a minor leg injury. The symptoms of the onset of a diabetic coma may include _____.

A. reduced appetite and thirst
B. sneezing and coughing
C. only a low grade fever
D. slurred speech and loss of coordination

7035. If a diabetic suffers an insulin reaction and is conscious, he should be given _____.

A. soda crackers and water
B. orange juice
C. an ounce of whiskey
D. a glass of milk

7037. Epilepsy is a chronic nervous disorder characterized by _____.

A. severe nausea and cramps
B. muscular convulsions with partial or complete loss of consciousness
C. sudden thirst and craving for candy
D. severe agitation and desire to get out of closed spaces

7041. A crew member is having an epileptic convulsion. You should _____.

A. give the victim artificial respiration
B. completely restrain the victim
C. give the victim one 30 mg tablet of phenobarbital

D. keep the victim from injuring him or herself

7043. While providing assistance to a victim of an epileptic seizure, it is most important to _____.

A. give artificial respiration
B. prevent the patient from hurting himself
C. keep the patient awake and make him/her walk if necessary to keep him/her awake
D. remove any soiled clothing and put the patient in a clean bed

7046. A fire has broken out on the stern of your vessel. You should maneuver your vessel so the wind _____.

A. blows the fire back toward the vessel
B. comes over either beam
C. comes over the stern
D. comes over the bow

7047. What are symptom(s) of a ruptured appendix?

A. Dilated pupils and shallow breathing
B. Diarrhea and frequent urination
C. Muscle tenseness in almost the entire abdomen
D. Extreme sweating and reddening skin

7051. When a patient is suspected of having appendicitis, the primary action is to _____.

A. give the patient a laxative to relieve pain
B. give the patient morphine sulfate to relieve pain
C. confine to bed until helicopter arrives
D. give the patient aspirin with a glass of water

7053. When a patient is suspected of having appendicitis, the pain should be relieved by _____.

A. keeping an ice bag over the appendix area
B. giving the patient a laxative
C. giving the patient morphine sulfate
D. giving the patient aspirin with a glass of water

7055. Seasickness is caused by rolling or rocking motions which affect fluids in the _____.

A. stomach

B. lower intestines
C. inner ear
D. bladder

7057. Symptoms of seasickness include
_____.

A. fever and thirst
B. nausea and dizziness
C. stomach cramps and diarrhea
D. reddening of skin and hives

7058. Blocking open or removing fire dampers can cause _____.

A. fixed foam systems to be ineffective
B. faster cooling of the fire
C. the accumulation of explosive gases
D. the fire to spread through the ventilation system

7061. The primary concern in aiding a back injury patient is _____.

A. relieving the patient's pain by giving aspirin or stronger medication
B. avoiding possible injury to the spinal cord by incorrect handling
C. preventing convulsions and muscle spasms caused by the pain
D. providing enough fluids to prevent dehydration

7062. You are aboard a life raft in a storm. What should you do with your Emergency Position Indicating Radiobeacon?

A. Bring it inside the life raft and leave it on.
B. Bring it inside the life raft and turn it off until the storm passes.
C. Leave it outside the life raft and leave it on.
D. Leave it outside the life raft but turn it off.

7063. The symptoms of a fractured back are _____.

A. leg cramps in the muscles in one or both legs
B. pain and uncontrolled jerking of the legs and arms
C. vomiting and involuntary urination or bowel movement
D. pain at the site of the fracture and possible numbness or paralysis below the injury

7065. What is the procedure for checking for spinal cord damage in an unconscious patient?

A. Beginning at the back of the neck, and proceeding to the buttocks, press the spine to find where it hurts
B. Prick the skin of the hands and the soles of the feet with a sharp object to check for reaction
C. Selectively raise each arm and each leg and watch patient's face to see if he registers pain
D. Roll patient onto his stomach and prick along the length of his spine to check reaction

7067. An effective method for moving patients with spinal injuries onto a spine board is known as the _____.

A. pack-strap carry
B. two man extremities carry
C. fireman's drag
D. four man log roll

7068. Deballasting a double bottom has what affect on KG?

A. KG is increased.
B. KG is decreased.
C. KG is not affected.
D. KG increases at light drafts and decreases at deep drafts.

7071. The sorting of accident victims according to the severity of their injuries is called _____.

A. evaluation
B. triage
C. surveying
D. prioritizing

7073. Where there are multiple accident victims, which condition should be the first to receive emergency treatment?

A. Back injuries
B. Major multiple fractures
C. Suspension of breathing
D. Burns

7075. Where there are multiple accident victims, which injuries should be the FIRST to receive emergency treatment?

A. Major multiple fractures
B. Eye injuries
C. Back injuries with spinal-cord damage
D. Airway and breathing difficulties

7077. Where there are multiple accident victims, which type of injury should be the first to receive emergency treatment?

A. Severe shock
B. Eye injuries
C. Burns
D. Major multiple fractures

7081. In managing a situation involving multiple injuries, the rescuer must be able to _____.

A. provide the necessary medication
B. rapidly evaluate the seriousness of obvious injuries
C. accurately diagnose the ailment or injury
D. prescribe treatment for the victim

7083. What can be determined about an injury from examining the condition of a victim's pupils?

A. The degree of pain being suffered
B. The degree of vision impairment
C. Whether or not the brain is functioning properly
D. Whether or not the victim's blood pressure is normal

7093. Normal mouth temperature is _____.

A. 96.4°F
B. 97.5°F
C. 98.6°F
D. 99.7°F

7096. Convection spreads a fire by _____.

A. transmitting the heat of a fire through the ship's metal
B. burning liquids flowing into another space
C. heated gases flowing through ventilation systems
D. the transfer of heat across an unobstructed space

7097. What is a convenient and effective system of examining the body of an injury victim?

A. Check the corresponding (left versus right) parts of the body.
B. Watch the patient's eyes as you probe parts of the body.
C. Look for discoloration of the patient's skin.
D. Look for uncontrolled vibration or twitching of parts of the body.

7121. CO_2 cylinders equipped with pressure actuated discharge heads will discharge automatically when _____.

A. the discharge valve is open
B. the control box glass is broken
C. pressure from the control cylinders is detected
D. the control cylinders have been completely discharged

7127. Spaces protected by a fixed CO_2 system must be equipped with an alarm which sounds _____.

A. for the first 20 seconds CO_2 is being released into the space
B. for at least 20 seconds prior to release of CO_2
C. during the entire period that CO_2 is being released
D. if all doors and ventilation are not secured

7131. A safety outlet is provided on the CO_2 discharge piping to prevent _____.

A. overpressurization of the space being flooded
B. rupture of cylinder due to temperature increase
C. overpressurization of the CO_2 discharge piping
D. flooding of a space where personnel are present

7143. Actuating the CO_2 fixed system causes the shutdown of the _____.

A. fuel supply
B. exhaust ventilation
C. supply and exhaust ventilation
D. mechanical and natural ventilation

7147. What should you do if you have transmitted a distress call a number of times on channel 16 and have received no reply?

A. Repeat the message using any other channel on which you might attract attention.
B. Key the microphone several times before transmitting again.
C. Turn up the volume on the receiver before transmitting again.
D. Report the problem to the head electrician.

7305. If you use obscene, indecent, or pro-

fane language over the radiotelephone, you can be _____.

A. assessed a fine of up to $5,000, imprisonment of up to three years, or both
B. assessed a fine not to exceed $10,000, imprisonment of not more than two years, or both
C. assessed a fine not to exceed $20,000
D. imprisoned up to five years

7307. All VHF marine band radios operate in the simplex mode, which means that _____.

A. only one person may talk at a time
B. only two persons may talk at the same time
C. the radio only transmits
D. the radio only receives

7311. What is the calling and distress frequency on a single side band (SSB) marine radiotelephone?

A. 1492 kHz
B. 1892 kHz
C. 2082 kHz
D. 2182 kHz

7313. What is the MOST important thing you should do before transmitting on a marine radio?

A. Ask for permission.
B. Record the time in your radio log.
C. Press the "push to talk" button three times.
D. Monitor the channel to insure that it is clear.

7317. When sending and receiving messages on the marine radio, confusion over unusual words can be avoided by using the _____.

A. delimiter switch
B. standard phonetic alphabet
C. low power switch
D. high power switch

7318. A cabinet or space containing the controls or valves for the fixed firefighting system must be _____.

A. posted with instructions on the operation of the system
B. ventilated and equipped with explosion-proof switches

C. painted with red and black diagonal stripes
D. equipped with a battery powered source of emergency lighting

7321. The reception of weak radio signals may be improved by "opening up" the squelch control. What is the normal setting of the squelch control?

A. Just past the point where background noise is cut off
B. Completely closed with the volume at the highest level
C. Completely open with the volume at the lowest level
D. None of the above

7323. Whenever your marine radio is on, FCC Rules require you to monitor _____.

A. a commercial ship-to-ship channel
B. the last frequency that was used
C. the distress and calling frequency
D. the radio only if expecting a call

7325. One method of reducing the length of radio transmissions without distorting the meaning of your words is by using _____.

A. slang
B. secret codes
C. procedure words
D. analogies

7331. Routine radio communications should be no more than _____.

A. one minute
B. three minutes
C. five minutes
D. eight minutes

7333. You have just tried calling another vessel on the VHF and they have not replied. How long should you wait before calling that station again?

A. One minute
B. Two minutes
C. Five minutes
D. Seven minutes

7335. When making VHF radio calls to nearby stations, what level of transmitting power should you use?

A. Low power
B. Medium power

C. High power
D. Extra high power

7337. If you log a distress message, it must include the _____.

A. sea state
B. names of witnesses
C. time of its occurrence
D. wind direction and velocity

7341. If you know that the vessel you are about to call on the VHF radio maintains a radio watch on both the working and the calling frequencies, which frequency should you call on?

A. Calling frequency
B. Distress frequency
C. Urgency frequency
D. Working frequency

7343. What is maximum power allowed by the FCC for VHF-FM radio transmissions?

A. One watt
B. Five watts
C. 15 watts
D. 25 watts

7345. What is the average range of vessel-to-vessel VHF-FM radio communications?

A. 15 to 20 miles
B. 60 to 90 miles
C. 90 to 120 miles
D. 120 to 150 miles

7351. The range of a SSB transmission is MOST affected by _____.

A. atmospheric noise and radiated power
B. the frequency band selected and time of day or night
C. interference and position of the moon
D. radiated power and nearness to shore

7353. The height of a VHF radio antenna is more important than the power output wattage of the radio because _____.

A. VHF communications are basically "line of sight"
B. the air is more dense the higher you go
C. salt water is a poor conductor of sound
D. sea water absorbs the radiated energy

7355. When do you use your FCC call sign when transmitting on channel 16?

A. Only at the beginning of a transmission
B. Only in an emergency
C. Only if asked by the U.S. Coast Guard
D. Always at the beginning and ending of a transmission

7388. All marine low-speed diesels are of what design?

A. Four-stroke
B. Two-stroke
C. Electronic ignition
D. Forced exhaust

7405. VHF Channel 6 is used exclusively for what kind of communications?

A. Radio checks and time checks
B. Inter-vessel safety and search and rescue
C. Working with helicopters
D. Radio direction finding

7407. Which VHF channel should you avoid using as a working channel?

A. 7A
B. 8
C. 9
D. 16

7411. What is the spoken emergency signal for a distress signal over a VHF radio?

A. Red Alert
B. Securité
C. Mayday
D. Pan

7412. In the event of a fire, the doors to a stairtower must be closed to prevent the spread of fire by _____.

A. ventilation
B. radiation
C. convection
D. conduction

7413. Which spoken emergency signal would you use to call a boat to come assist a man overboard?

A. Distress signal
B. Urgency signal
C. Safety signal
D. None of the above

7415. What is the spoken emergency signal for a "man overboard" on the VHF radio?

A. Man Overboard
B. Securité
C. Mayday
D. Pan-Pan

7417. You receive a call from the U.S. Coast Guard addressed to all stations. The call begins with the words "Pan-Pan" (3 times). Which type of emergency signal would this be?

A. Safety signal
B. Urgency signal
C. Distress signal
D. Red alert signal

7421. After receiving your distress call, the U.S.C.G. will ask you to switch to which SSB frequency?

A. 2570
B. 2670
C. 2770
D. 2870

7427. What is the expected range of a VHF radio transmission from a vessel to a shore station?

A. About 20 miles
B. 50–100 miles
C. 100–150 miles
D. 150–200 miles

7431. What time would an SSB radio have the longest transmitting range?

A. Daylight before noon
B. At noon
C. Daylight after noon
D. During darkness

7575. The upward pressure of displaced water is called _____.

A. buoyancy
B. deadweight
C. draft
D. freeboard

7577. The value of the maximum righting arm depends on the position of the center of buoyancy and the _____.

A. longitudinal center of gravity
B. transverse center of gravity
C. downflooding angle
D. vertical location of the center of gravity

7581. For a given displacement, the righting arm has its maximum value when _____.

A. KG is minimum
B. angle of inclination is a maximum
C. small-angle stability applies
D. KM is a minimum

7583. Stability is determined by the relationship of the center of gravity and the _____.

A. water depth
B. keel
C. center of flotation
D. center of buoyancy

7587. The geometric center of the underwater volume is known as the _____.

A. center of flotation
B. tipping center
C. center of gravity
D. center of buoyancy

7591. Stability is determined principally by the location of the center of gravity and the _____.

A. aft perpendicular
B. center of buoyancy
C. keel
D. center of flotation

7593. The horizontal distance between the vertical lines of action of gravity and the buoyant forces is called the _____.

A. righting arm
B. metacentric height
C. metacentric radius
D. height of the center of buoyancy

7595. For a vessel inclined by the wind, multiplying the buoyant force by the horizontal distance between the lines of action of the buoyant and gravity forces gives the _____.

A. righting moment
B. vertical moment
C. longitudinal moment
D. transverse moment

7597. In small-angle stability theory, the metacenter is located at the intersection of the inclined vertical centerline and a vertical line through _____.

A. G
B. F
C. B
D. K

7601. At all angles of inclination, the true measure of a vessel's stability is the _____.

A. metacentric height
B. displacement
C. righting moment
D. inclining moment

7603. Initial stability refers to stability _____.

A. at small angles of inclination
B. when loaded with minimum deck load
C. when at transit draft
D. when GZ is zero

7605. For small angles of inclination, if the KG were equal to the KM, then the vessel would have _____.

A. positive stability
B. negative stability
C. neutral stability
D. maximum stability

7607. The difference between the height of the metacenter and the metacentric height is known as _____.

A. righting arm
B. metacentric radius
C. height of the center of buoyancy
D. height of the center of gravity

7613. GM cannot be used as an indicator of stability at all angles of inclination because _____.

A. M is not fixed at large angles
B. there is no M at large angles
C. G is not fixed at large angles
D. there is no G at large angles

7621. Which statement is TRUE about metacentric height?

A. It is a measure of initial stability.
B. It is located above the center of buoyancy.
C. It is measured vertically above the center of buoyancy.
D. Its determination is the objective of the inclining experiment.

7623. The weight of the liquid displaced by a vessel floating in sea water is equal to the _____.

A. weight required to sink the vessel
B. total weight of the vessel
C. displaced volume
D. reserve buoyancy

7625. The original equilibrium position is always unstable when _____.

A. metacentric height is negative
B. KM is higher than KG
C. KG exceeds maximum allowable limits
D. free surfaces are excessive

7631. At an angle of loll, the capsizing moment is _____.

A. maximum
B. negative
C. positive
D. zero

7635. At an angle of loll, the righting arm (GZ) is _____.

A. maximum
B. negative
C. positive, but reflexive
D. zero

7641. In small-angle stability, when external forces exist, the buoyant force is assumed to act vertically upwards through the center of buoyancy and through the _____.

A. center of gravity
B. center of flotation
C. metacenter
D. metacentric height

7643. When a vessel is floating upright, the distance from the keel to the metacenter is called the _____.

A. metacentric radius
B. height of the baseline
C. height of the metacenter
D. righting arm

7645. What abbreviation represents the height of the center of buoyancy?

A. BK
B. KB
C. CB
D. BM

7647. The abbreviation GM is used to represent the _____.

A. height of the metacenter
B. righting arm
C. righting moment
D. metacentric height

7648. Buoyant apparatus are required to be fitted or equipped with all of the following equipment EXCEPT _____. (Small Passenger Vessel Regulations.)

A. lifelines
B. paddles
C. water lights
D. painters

7651. When positive stability exists, GZ represents the _____.

A. righting moment
B. center of gravity
C. righting arm
D. metacentric height

7655. In small-angle stability, the metacentric height _____.

A. is found in the hydrostatic tables for a level vessel
B. multiplied by the displacement yields the righting moment
C. is always positive
D. is calculated by subtracting KG from KM

7657. The righting moment can be determined by multiplying the displacement by the _____.

A. vertical center of gravity (KG)
B. longitudinal center of gravity (LCG)
C. righting arm (GZ)
D. center of gravity (CG)

7663. Subtracting KG from KM yields _____.

A. BM
B. GM
C. GZ
D. KG

7665. Subtracting KG from KM yields _____.

A. BL
B. GM
C. FS
D. KG

7667. Subtracting GM from KM yields _____.

A. BL
B. GM

C. FS
D. KG

7677. Reducing free surfaces has the effect of lowering the _____.

A. uncorrected KG
B. virtual height of the center of gravity
C. metacenter
D. metacentric height

7683. Increasing free surfaces has the effect of raising the _____.

A. uncorrected KG
B. virtual height of the center of gravity
C. metacenter
D. metacentric height

7697. The distance between the bottom of the hull and the waterline is called _____.

A. tonnage
B. reserve buoyancy
C. draft
D. freeboard

7701. After transferring a weight forward on a vessel, the draft at the center of flotation will _____.

A. change, depending on the location of the LCG
B. increase
C. decrease
D. remain constant

7703. The average of the forward and after drafts is the _____.

A. mean draft
B. true mean draft
C. mean of the calculated drafts
D. draft at the center of flotation

7713. Your vessel is listing because of a negative GM. To lower G below M, you should _____.

A. deballast
B. transfer weight to the high side
C. ballast on the high side
D. add weight symmetrically below G

7725. Reserve buoyancy is the _____.

A. unoccupied space below the waterline
B. volume of intact space above the waterline
C. excess of the buoyant force over the gravity force

D. difference in the buoyant force in salt and fresh waters

7727. When flooding occurs in a damaged vessel, reserve buoyancy _____.

A. decreases
B. remains the same
C. increases
D. shifts to the low side

7737. The geometric center of the waterplane area is called the _____.

A. center of buoyancy
B. center of gravity
C. metacenter
D. center of flotation

7747. In the absence of external forces, the center of gravity of a floating vessel is located directly above the _____.

A. metacenter
B. amidships
C. center of flotation
D. geometric center of the displaced volume

7785. The result of multiplying a weight by a distance is a _____.

A. moment
B. force
C. couple
D. center of gravity location

7786. The straight stream capability of an all-purpose nozzle is used in fighting a class A fire to _____.

A. shield fire fighters from radiant heat
B. break up burning material
C. get the most water possible on the fire
D. drive heat and smoke ahead of the fire fighters

7787. A moment is obtained by multiplying a force by its _____.

A. couple
B. lever arm
C. moment of inertia
D. point of application

7805. A tank with internal dimensions of 40 feet X 20 feet X 12 feet is pressed with fuel oil weighing 54 pounds per cubic foot. What is the weight, in short tons, of the liquid?

A. 518.4 short tons
B. 259.2 short tons
C. 135.0 short tons
D. 11.3 short tons

7841. In a combination chain and wire rope mooring system, the anchor chain is deployed at the anchor end of the line to _____.

A. increase fatigue life of the system
B. reduce the time to retrieve the line
C. increase the holding power
D. reduce the catenary

7977. Overspeed of the diesel engine driving an electric generator could cause _____.

A. low voltage trip
B. reverse power trip
C. damage to windings
D. excessive exhaust temperatures

8036. Radiation spreads a fire by _____.

A. transmitting the heat of a fire through the ship's metal
B. burning liquids flowing into another space
C. transferring heat across an unobstructed space
D. heated gases flowing through ventilation systems

8045. At an angle of loll, the righting moment is _____.

A. maximum
B. negative
C. positive
D. zero

8054. A thrust block is designed to _____.

A. transmit the thrust of the engine to the propeller
B. transmit the thrust of the propeller to the vessel
C. absorb the shock of wave pressure at the bow
D. be placed between the engines and the foundation to absorb the vibration

8155. The moment created by a force of 12,000 tons and a moment arm of 0.25 foot is _____.

A. 48,000 ft-tons
B. 6,000 ft-tons

C. 3,000 ft-tons
D. 0 ft-tons

8156. Category 1 EPIRBs are required to be carried on board _____.

A. small passenger vessels on the Great Lakes
B. all deep draft vessels
C. fishing industry vessels
D. small passenger vessels

8157. A moment of 300 ft-tons is created by a force of 15,000 tons. What is the moment arm?

A. 50.00 feet
B. 25.00 feet
C. 0.04 foot
D. 0.02 foot

8222. Which will improve stability?

A. Closing watertight doors
B. Pumping the bilges
C. Loading cargo on deck
D. Consuming fuel from a full tank

8223. What is the purpose of a check valve?

A. Passes air but not liquid
B. Regulates liquid flow
C. Permits flow in one direction only
D. Passes liquid but not air

8225. On what type of pump would you find an impeller?

A. Centrifugal
B. Gear
C. Piston
D. Vane

8235. What is the proper direction of flow through a globe valve when the valve is installed to be in a normally open position?

A. Direction is unimportant
B. Depends on seat configuration
C. From below the seat
D. From above the seat

8275. In a wire rope mooring system, the fairlead sheave should be a minimum of _____.

A. 10–18 times the diameter of the wire rope
B. 18–36 times the diameter of the wire rope

C. 36–50 times the diameter of the wire rope
D. 50–75 times the diameter of the wire rope

8287. Automatic mechanical ventilation shutdown is required for CO_2 systems protecting the _____.

A. machinery spaces
B. cargo compartments
C. living quarters
D. galley

8337. What is the percentage of oxygen in a typical sample of uncontaminated air?

A. 12 percent
B. 15 percent
C. 18 percent
D. 21 percent

8342. Blocking open or removing fire dampers can cause _____.

A. the accumulation of explosive gases
B. the fire to spread through the ventilation system
C. faster cooling of the fire
D. fixed foam systems to be ineffective

8347. All diesel engines are classified as _____.

A. four cycle
B. compression ignition
C. vacuum ignition
D. external combustion

8353. What power source actuates a solenoid valve?

A. Air pressure
B. Hydraulic pressure
C. Electric current
D. Mechanical force

8355. What quality of a diesel fuel is most significant for efficient combustion?

A. Volatility
B. Viscosity
C. Flash point
D. Specific heat

8361. What is the effect of heated intake air on a diesel engine?

A. Increases efficiency
B. Increases engine horsepower

C. Increases engine life
D. Reduces engine horsepower

8363. Lubricating oil should be changed on a heavy duty diesel engine when _____.

A. it gets dark in color
B. a sample rubbed between fingers feels thin
C. it has been in use for a specified interval
D. it no longer supports combustion

8365. How should you warm up a diesel engine that has not been run for some time?

A. Run it at minimum speed for a period of time.
B. Run it at half speed for a period of time.
C. Bring it to top speed immediately.
D. Inject ether into the air intake.

8367. How would the exhaust of a properly operating diesel engine appear?

A. Light blue haze
B. Light brown haze
C. Light gray haze
D. Perfectly clear

8371. Each cylinder in a two-stroke cycle engine experiences combustion _____.

A. once each crankshaft revolution
B. twice each crankshaft revolution
C. every other crankshaft revolution
D. every fourth stroke

8373. How does combustion air enter the cylinder of a two-cycle diesel engine?

A. Cylinder head valves
B. Ports
C. Turbo chargers
D. Bleeder valves

8375. Maintaining the close tolerances in diesel fuel pumps and injectors requires the use of _____.

A. fuel/water separators
B. day tanks
C. injector test stand
D. fuel filters

8377. What factor is essential to the proper operation of a radiator-cooled engine?

A. Cooling water pressure
B. Jacket water treatment
C. Air flow through the radiator
D. Low heat of combustion

8381. What are the three basic types of engine starters?

A. Air, water, electric
B. Air, hydraulic, electric
C. Metered, hydraulic, automatic
D. Air, emergency, hydraulic

8383. What does a pyrometer measure on a diesel engine?

A. Water temperature
B. Water pressure
C. Exhaust temperature
D. Air box pressure

8384. A moment of 300 ft.-tons is created by a force of 15,000 tons. What is the moment arm?

A. 50.00 feet
B. 25.00 feet
C. 0.04 foot
D. 0.02 foot

8385. What condition will result in the automatic shutdown of a diesel engine?

A. High jacket water pressure
B. High lube oil pressure
C. Low lube oil pressure
D. Excessive turbocharger speed

8391. What monitoring device best indicates the load being carried by a diesel engine?

A. Lube oil pressure gauge
B. Jacket water temperature gauge
C. Tachometer
D. Exhaust pyrometer

8392. You are preparing for what promises to be a rough ocean passage. Your 120-foot schooner carries a yard on the foremast about 50 feet above the water. The yard weighs about 1000 pounds. If you take the yard down and stow it on deck for the trip, you will _____.

A. decrease the GM
B. give the vessel a gentler roll
C. increase the metacentric height
D. decrease the reserve bouyancy

8393. Diesel engines obtain combustion air through turbo chargers, blowers, or _____.

A. air starters
B. carburetors

C. natural aspiration
D. air receivers

8395. What is the purpose of the intake/exhaust valves in a diesel engine?

A. They regulate the combustion cycle.
B. They supply cooling water.
C. They synchronize the ignition spark.
D. They supply and regulate the lubricant flow.

8397. What is the best indication of the loading of a diesel engine?

A. Oil temperature
B. Manifold pressure
C. Exhaust gas temperature
D. Fuel consumption

8403. What is the most probable cause of reduced capacity in a reciprocating air compressor?

A. Carbon on cylinder heads
B. Faulty unloader
C. Leaking air valves
D. Plugged air cooler

8405. The most serious effect of oxygen retained in a diesel engine jacket water cooling system is that it _____.

A. causes corrosion
B. reduces the effectiveness of the coolant
C. can form air pockets which exclude coolant contact with hot surfaces
D. accelerates formation of hydrogen peroxide deposits

8407. If you are unable to stop a diesel engine by any other means, you should _____.

A. discharge a CO_2 extinguisher in the air inlet
B. pull off the distributor cap
C. secure the jacket water
D. secure the starting air supply valve

8411. What is one effect of running a diesel engine at too cool a temperature?

A. Buildup of sludge in the lubricating system
B. Excessive fuel consumption
C. Severe heat stresses on mechanical parts
D. Foaming of the lubricating oil

8412. When abandoning ship and jumping into the water from a substantial height, you should _____.

A. dive head first using your hands to break the surface of the water
B. hold your arms firmly at your sides and jump feet first
C. throw your life jacket into the water first and then jump feet first into the water next to it
D. jump feet first, holding onto your life jacket with one hand while covering your nose and mouth with the other

8413. What would white exhaust smoke from a diesel engine probably mean?

A. Late fuel injection
B. Excess combustion air
C. Dribbling injector tips
D. Excessive lube oil consumption

8415. The three conditions which cause engine shutdown are overspeed, low lube oil pressure, and _____.

A. high lube oil pressure
B. high jacket water pressure
C. high jacket water temperature
D. low jacket water pressure

8417. Sudden unloading of a diesel engine can cause _____.

A. decreased fuel efficiency
B. increased exhaust temperature
C. black smoke
D. overspeed trip

8421. If an engine shuts down due to high jacket water temperature, what action should be taken?

A. Open crankcase explosion covers
B. Allow engine to cool gradually
C. Slowly add cool water to the expansion tank
D. Back flush the cooling water system

8440. Addition of weight above the center of gravity of a vessel will ALWAYS _____.

A. reduce initial stability
B. increase righting moments
C. increase GM
D. All of the above

8541. The process of waiting a period of time before pretensioning an anchor is known as _____.

A. soaking
B. settling
C. sinking
D. bedding in

8547. What does the term "head" mean when applied to a pump?

A. Length of its discharge pipe
B. Height of its discharge pipe
C. Difference between the discharge and suction pressures
D. Sum of discharge and suction pressures

8555. The discharge side of every fire pump must be equipped with a _____

A. gate valve
B. pressure gauge
C. check valve
D. strainer

8563. How often must CO_2 systems be inspected to confirm cylinders are within 10% of the stamped full weight of the charge?

A. quarterly
B. semiannually
C. annually
D. biannually

8575. If a man falls overboard from a rig under tow, you should FIRST _____.

A. notify the tug
B. deploy life buoys
C. launch a boat
D. sound the general alarm

8576. The ventilation system of your ship has fire dampers restrained by fusible links. Which statement is TRUE?

A. A fusible link will automatically open after a fire is extinguished and reset the damper.
B. Fusible links must be replaced if a damper is activated.
C. Fusible links are tested by applying a source of heat to them.
D. Fusible links must be replaced at every inspection for certification.

8577. The indication of a slipping anchor is a(n) _____.

A. decrease in mooring line length
B. increase in the opposite amperage
C. increase in the opposite line tension
D. decrease in mooring line tension and amperage

8615. The LWT anchor has two angular positions for the flukes. These are _____.

A. 30° and 40°
B. 30° and 50°
C. 30° and 60°
D. 40° and 60°

8635. A weight of 1,000 kips is equivalent to _____.

A. 1,000 pounds
B. 2,000 short tons
C. 2,240 pounds
D. 500 short tons

8662. When may a work vest be substituted for a required life preserver?

A. To replace a damaged life preserver
B. For use during fire drills
C. For use during boat drills
D. At no time

8702. An oil fire is classified as class _____.

A. D
B. C
C. B
D. A

8712. Jettisoning weight from topside _____.

A. returns the vessel to an even keel
B. reduces free surface effect
C. lowers the center of gravity
D. raises the center of buoyancy

8782. Control of fire should be addressed _____.

A. immediately after restoring vital services
B. immediately
C. following control of flooding
D. following establishment of fire boundaries

8807. The prohibition against displaying lights which may be confused with required navigation lights applies _____.

A. from sunset to sunrise and during restricted visibility
B. only when other vessels are in the area
C. only when operating in a traffic separation scheme
D. only when under tow

8897. The international body responsible for drafting the convention prohibiting marine pollution (MARPOL) is the _____.

A. Maritime Advisory Council
B. International Maritime Organization
C. International Association of Shipping
D. Association of Seafaring Nations

8901. The Safety of Life at Sea Convention was developed by the _____.

A. U.S. Coast Guard
B. American Bureau of Shipping
C. International Maritime Organization
D. American Institute of Maritime Shipping

8903. The most effective first aid treatment for chemical burns is to immediately _____.

A. apply ointment to the burned area
B. flood the affected area with water
C. wrap the burn with sterile dressing
D. apply an ice pack to the burned area

8905. When it is necessary to remove a victim from a life threatening situation, the person giving first aid must _____.

A. pull the victim by the feet
B. avoid subjecting the victim to any unnecessary disturbance
C. carry the victim to a location where injuries can be assessed
D. place the victim on a stretcher before attempting removal

8907. When giving first aid, you should understand how to conduct primary and secondary surveys and know _____.

A. which medications to prescribe
B. how to diagnose an illness from symptoms
C. the limits of your capabilities
D. how to set broken bones

8911. If a victim is unconscious, you should first look for evidence of _____.

A. high fever
B. head injury

C. broken limbs
D. irregular breathing

8925. A vessel behaves as if all of its weight is acting downward through the center of gravity, and all its support is acting upward through the _____.

A. keel
B. center of buoyancy
C. tipping center
D. amidships section

8973. For a floating vessel, the result of subtracting KG from KM is the _____.

A. height of the metacenter
B. height of the righting arm
C. height of the center of buoyancy
D. metacentric height

8977. The important stability parameter, KG, is defined as the _____.

A. metacentric height
B. height of the metacenter above the keel
C. height of the center of buoyancy above the keel
D. height of the center of gravity above the keel

8981. The important initial stability parameter, GM, is the _____.

A. metacentric height
B. height of the metacenter above the keel
C. height of the center of buoyancy above the keel
D. height of the center of gravity above the keel

8983. The time required to incline from port to starboard and back to port again is called _____.

A. initial stability
B. range of stability
C. inclining moment
D. rolling period

8985. The time required to incline from bow down to stern down and return to bow down again is called _____.

A. rolling period
B. amplitude moment
C. inclining moment
D. pitching period

8987. The tendency of a vessel to return to its original trim after being inclined by an external force is _____.

A. equilibrium
B. buoyancy
C. transverse stability
D. longitudinal stability

8991. The enclosed area defined as the intersection of the surface of the water and the hull of a vessel is the _____.

A. amidships plane
B. longitudinal reference plane
C. baseline
D. waterplane

8993. The waterplane area is described as the intersection of the surface of the water in which a vessel floats and the _____.

A. baseline
B. vertical reference plane
C. hull
D. horizontal reference plane

8994. Two types of anchor shackles which are currently available are _____.

A. U-Type and posilok shackles
B. C-Type and wedge shackles
C. D-Type and bow shackles
D. wedge and kenter shackles

8997. Aboard a vessel, multiplying a load's weight by the distance of the load's center of gravity from the centerline results in the load's _____.

A. TCG
B. transverse moment
C. righting moment
D. transverse free surface moment

9001. The difference between the starboard and port drafts caused by shifting a weight transversely is _____.

A. list
B. heel
C. trim
D. flotation

9021. Aboard a vessel, dividing the sum of the longitudinal moments by the total weight yields the vessel's _____.

A. inclining moments
B. righting moments

C. vertical moments
D. longitudinal position of the center of gravity

9067. The TCG of a vessel may be found by dividing the displacement of the vessel into the _____.

A. transverse center of gravity of the vessel
B. sum of the vertical moments of the vessel
C. sum of the transverse moments of the vessel
D. transverse baseline of the vessel

9087. No outlet on a fire hydrant may point above the horizontal in order to _____.

A. avoid kinking the hose
B. avoid personal injury during connection
C. make connecting easier
D. prevent spray on electrical equipment

9091. The outlet at a fire hydrant may be positioned anywhere from horizontal to pointing _____.

A. 45° upward
B. vertically upward
C. vertically downward
D. all of the above

9093. In addition to weighing the cartridge, which other maintenance is required for a cartridge-operated dry chemical extinguisher?

A. Weigh the powder in the canister.
B. Discharge a small amount to see that it works.
C. Check the hose and nozzle for clogs.
D. Check the external pressure gauge.

9097. When must a dry chemical fire extinguisher be recharged?

A. After each use
B. When the air temperature exceeds 90°F
C. Every 6 months
D. Every 12 months

9101. Recharging a previously used cartridge-operated dry-chemical extinguisher is accomplished by _____.

A. authorized fire equipment servicing personnel only
B. replacing the propellant cartridge and refilling with powder

C. puncturing the cartridge seal after installation
D. recharging the cartridge and refilling it with powder

9107. The amount of Halon remaining in an extinguisher is determined by _____.

A. internal inspection
B. checking the gauge
C. weighing the cylinder
D. checking the tag

9111. Inspection of a Halon extinguisher involves checking the hose, handle, nozzle, and _____.

A. sight glass
B. weighing the extinguisher
C. service technician's report
D. last date it was charged

9113. After using a Halon extinguisher, it should be _____.

A. put back in service if more than 50% of the charge remains
B. repainted
C. discarded
D. recharged

9115. An airplane should NOT send which signal in reply to a surface craft?

A. Opening and closing the throttle
B. Rocking the wings
C. Flashing the navigational lights off and on
D. Flashing Morse T

9121. The blocking or absence of fire dampers can cause _____.

A. the accumulation of explosive gases
B. faster cooling of the fire
C. the fire to spread through the ventilation system
D. fixed foam systems to be ineffective

9125. Automatic fire dampers in ventilation systems are operated by a _____.

A. remote operated valve
B. fusible link
C. CO_2 system pressure switch
D. heat or smoke detector

9129. Automatic fire dampers in ventilation systems are operated by use of a _____.

A. heat or smoke detector
B. fusible link
C. remote operated valve
D. CO_2 system pressure switch

9130. When administering first aid you should avoid _____.

A. any conversation with the patient
B. instructing bystanders
C. unnecessary haste and appearance of uncertainty
D. touching the patient before washing your hands

9137. Fighting a fire in the galley poses the additional threat of _____.

A. contaminating food with extinguishing agent
B. spreading through the engineering space
C. loss of stability
D. a grease fire in the ventilation system

9191. After abandoning a vessel, water that is consumed within the first 24 hours will _____.

A. pass through the body with little absorbed by the system
B. help to prevent fatigue
C. quench thirst for only 2 hours
D. help to prevent seasickness

9193. Drinking salt water will _____.

A. be safe if mixed with fresh water
B. prevent seasickness
C. dehydrate you
D. protect against heat cramps

9195. When using the rain water collection tubes on a life raft, the first collection should be _____.

A. passed around so all can drink
B. poured overboard because of salt washed off the canopy
C. saved to be used at a later time
D. used to boil food

9197. In the first 24 hours after abandoning a vessel, water should be given only to personnel who are _____.

A. thirsty
B. sick or injured
C. wet
D. awake

9205. When you are firing a pyrotechnic distress signal, it should be aimed _____.

A. horizontally and directly abeam of your vessel
B. at the vessel whose attention you want to attract
C. into the wind
D. at greater than 60 degrees above the horizon

9276. You are underway when a fire breaks out in the forward part of your vessel. If possible, you should _____.

A. call for assistance
B. put the vessel's stern into the wind
C. abandon ship to windward
D. keep going at half speed

9282. There is a fire aft aboard your vessel. To help fight the fire, you should put the _____.

A. wind off either beam
B. stern into the wind and increase speed
C. bow into the wind and decrease speed
D. stern into the wind and decrease speed

9303. When displacement increases, the free surface corrections for slack tanks _____.

A. increase
B. decrease
C. are directly proportional
D. remain unchanged

9307. When a rescuer finds an electrical burn victim in the vicinity of live electrical equipment or wiring, his first step is to _____.

A. flush water over any burned area of the patient
B. apply ointment to the burned areas on the patient
C. get assistance to shut down electrical power in the area
D. remove the patient from the vicinity of the live electrical equipment or wiring

9311. Basic emergency care for third degree electrical burn is to _____.

A. flood the burned area with warm water for two minutes
B. brush away the charred skin and wrap the burned area
C. cover the burned area with a clean cloth

and transport the patient to a medical facility
D. apply ointment or spray to the burned area and wrap with a clean cloth

9313. When a patient has an electrical burn, it is important to _____.

A. look for a second burn, which may have been caused by the current passing through the body
B. locate the nearest water source and flood the burn with water for five minutes
C. remove any dirt or charred skin from the area of the burn
D. apply ointment to the burn area and wrap with clean cloth

9315. Since electrical burn victims may be in shock, the FIRST medical response is to check for _____.

A. indication of broken bones
B. breathing and heartbeat
C. symptoms of concussion
D. bleeding injuries

9317. Which statement is CORRECT with respect to inserting an airway tube?

A. Only a trained person should attempt to insert an airway tube.
B. A size 2 airway tube is the correct size for an adult.
C. The airway tube will not damage the victim's throat.
D. Inserting the airway tube will prevent vomiting.

9321. In battery charging rooms, exhaust ventilation should be provided _____.

A. at the lowest point
B. near the batteries
C. at the highest point
D. only when charging is in progress

9323. A fuel-air mixture below the lower explosive limit is too _____.

A. rich to burn
B. lean to burn
C. cool to burn
D. dense to burn

9325. Good housekeeping on a vessel prevents fires by _____.

A. allowing better access in an emergency
B. eliminating potential fuel sources
C. eliminating trip hazards

D. improving personnel qualifications

9327. Accumulations of oily rags should be _____.

A. kept in nonmetal containers
B. discarded as soon as possible
C. cleaned thoroughly for reuse
D. kept in the paint locker

9331. Paints and solvents on a vessel should be _____.

A. stored safely at the work site until work is completed
B. returned to the paint locker after each use
C. covered at all times to protect from ignition sources
D. stored in a suitable gear locker

9333. After extinguishing a fire with CO_2, it is advisable to _____.

A. use all CO_2 available to cool the surrounding area
B. stand by with water or other agents
C. thoroughly ventilate the space of CO_2
D. jettison all burning materials

9335. The disadvantage of using CO_2 is that the _____.

A. CO_2 does not cool the fire
B. cylinders are regulated pressure vessels
C. CO_2 is not effective on class "B" fires
D. CO_2 is not effective on class "C" fires

9337. Size I and II fire extinguishers are designated as _____.

A. portable
B. semi-portable
C. fixed
D. compact

9341. Dry chemical extinguishers may be used on what class of fires?

A. A only
B. B only
C. B and C only
D. A, B or C as marked on the extinguisher

9342. The ventilation system of your ship has fire dampers restrained by fusible links. Which statement is TRUE?

A. Fusible links must be replaced if a damper is activated.

581

B. Fusible links are tested by applying a source of heat to them.
C. Fusible links must be replaced at every inspection for certification.
D. A fusible link will automatically open after a fire is extinguished and reset the damper.

9347. CO_2 cylinders must be recharged when the weight of the charge in the cylinder is less than what percent of the stamped full weight of the charge?

A. 80%
B. 85%
C. 90%
D. 95%

9351. Halon from extinguishers used on a class B fire should be directed _____.

A. at the top of the flames
B. at the base of the fire near the edge
C. in short quick bursts
D. toward the upwind side of the fire

9357. Halon extinguishers used on a class C fire should be directed at the _____.

A. base of the equipment
B. top of the equipment
C. power source
D. source of the fire

9361. The principal personnel hazard unique to Halon extinguishers is _____.

A. displacement of oxygen
B. skin irritation
C. inhaling toxic vapors
D. eye irritation

9362. You are releasing carbon dioxide gas (CO_2) into an engine compartment to extinguish a fire. The CO_2 will be most effective if the _____.

A. compartment is closed and ventilators are opened
B. compartment is left open to the air
C. compartment is closed and airtight
D. air flow to the compartment is increased with blowers

9363. The primary function(s) of an automatic sprinkler system is(are) to _____.

A. extinguish the fire which triggers it
B. limit the spread of fire and control the amount of heat produced

C. protect people in the areas which have sprinkler heads
D. alert the crew to the fire

9365. When flammable liquids are handled in a compartment on a vessel, the ventilation for that area should be _____.

A. operated continuously while vapors may be present
B. operated intermittently to remove vapors
C. available on standby for immediate use
D. shut down if an explosive mixture is present

9367. A galley grease fire on the stove may be extinguished using _____.

A. water
B. foam
C. the range hood extinguishing system
D. fire dampers

9371. Overhauling a fire in the living quarters on a vessel must include _____.

A. opening dead spaces to check for heat or fire
B. evacuation of the vessel
C. sounding the "all clear" signal
D. operation of the emergency generator

9373. If heavy smoke is coming from the paint locker, the FIRST firefighting response should be to _____.

A. release the CO_2 flooding system
B. open the door to evaluate the extent of the fire
C. enter and use a portable extinguisher
D. secure the ventilation

9375. After extinguishing a paint locker fire using the fixed CO_2 system, the next action is to have the space _____.

A. opened and burned material removed
B. left closed with vents off until all boundaries are cool
C. checked for oxygen content
D. doused with water to prevent reflash

9377. After abandoning ship, you should deploy the sea anchor from a life raft to _____.

A. keep the life raft from capsizing
B. navigate against the current
C. keep personnel from getting seasick

D. stay in the general location

9381. If the life raft capsizes, all personnel should leave the raft and _____.

A. climb onto the bottom
B. swim away from the raft
C. right the raft using the righting strap
D. inflate the righting bag

9382. Fire in an engine compartment is best extinguished with carbon dioxide gas (CO_2) and by _____.

A. completely closing the compartment
B. closing the compartment except for the ventilators
C. leaving the compartment open to the air
D. increasing the air flow to the compartment by blowers

9383. Immediately after abandoning a vessel, lookouts should be posted aboard life rafts to look for _____.

A. survivors in the water
B. food and water
C. land
D. bad weather

9385. When personnel are lifted by a helicopter from an inflatable life raft, the personnel on the raft should _____.

A. deflate the floor of the raft to reduce the danger of the raft overturning
B. inflate the floor of the raft to provide for additional stability
C. remove their life preservers to prepare for the transfer
D. take in the sea anchor to prevent fouling of the rescue sling

9387. When should you use distress flares and rockets?

A. Only when there is a chance of their being seen by rescue vessels
B. At half-hour intervals
C. At one-hour intervals
D. Immediately upon abandoning the vessel

9391. Once you have established the daily ration of drinking water in a survival situation, how should you drink it?

A. Small sips at regular intervals during the day

B. The complete daily ration at one time during the day
C. One-third the daily ration three times daily
D. Small sips only after sunset

9397. Category I EPIRBs transmit on frequencies that are monitored by _____.

A. orbiting satellites in space
B. commercial radio stations
C. private, commercial, and military aircraft
D. Both A & C

9411. When anchoring in an area with a soft bottom, the fluke angle of an anchor should be set at _____.

A. 20°
B. 30°
C. 40°
D. 50°

9412. Radiation spreads a fire by _____.

A. transmitting the heat of a fire through the ship's metal
B. burning liquids flowing into another space
C. heated gases flowing through ventilation systems
D. the transfer of heat across an unobstructed space

9413. When anchoring in an area with a hard bottom, the fluke angle of an anchor should be set at _____.

A. 20°
B. 30°
C. 40°
D. 50°

9414. Blocking open or removing fire dampers can cause _____.

A. the fire to spread through the ventilation system
B. fixed foam systems to be ineffective
C. faster cooling of the fire
D. the accumulation of explosive gases

9415. A solution to overcome tripping defects is an arrangement of special plates on either side of the flukes, designed to set them in the correct tripping position. These special plates are called _____.

A. trippers
B. stocks

C. stabilizers
D. palms

9425. Which formula can be used to calculate metacentric height?

A. KM + GM
B. KM – GM
C. KM – KG
D. KB + BM

9427. In the absence of external forces, adding weight on one side of a floating vessel causes the vessel to _____.

A. heel until the angle of loll is reached
B. list until the center of buoyancy is aligned vertically with the center of gravity
C. trim to the side opposite TCG until all moments are equal
D. decrease draft at the center of flotation

9432. The color of the signal flare sent up by a submarine indicating that a torpedo has been fired in a training exercise is

_____.

A. green
B. white
C. red
D. yellow

9435. For an upright vessel, draft is the vertical distance between the keel and the

_____.

A. waterline
B. freeboard deck
C. plimsoll mark
D. amidships section

9437. A wind has caused a difference between drafts starboard and port. This difference is _____.

A. list
B. heel
C. trim
D. flotation

9441. The moment of a force is a measure of the _____.

A. turning effect of the force about a point
B. instantaneous value of the force
C. stability characteristics of the vessel
D. center of gravity location

9443. The magnitude of a moment is the product of the force and _____.

A. time
B. lever arm
C. displacement
D. angle of inclination

9445. The difference between the height of the metacenter and the height of the center of gravity is known as the _____.

A. metacentric height
B. height of the righting arm
C. fore and aft perpendicular
D. height of the center of buoyancy

9447. When initial stability applies, the height of the center of gravity plus the metacentric height equals the _____.

A. free-surface moments
B. righting arm
C. height of the metacenter
D. corrected height of the center of gravity

9451. Initial stability is indicated by _____.

A. GM
B. KM
C. Deck load
D. Maximum allowed KG

9453. At all angles of inclination, the metacenter is _____.

A. vertically above the center of buoyancy
B. vertically above the center of gravity
C. at the intersection of the upright vertical centerline and the line of action of the buoyant force
D. at the geometric center of the underwater volume

9455. The original equilibrium position is stable when _____.

A. metacentric height is positive
B. metacentric radius is positive
C. KG exceeds maximum allowable limits
D. free surfaces are excessive

9457. The center of buoyancy is located at the _____.

A. geometric center of the waterplane area
B. intersection of the vertical centerline and line of action of the buoyant force
C. center of gravity of the vessel corrected for free surface effects
D. geometric center of the displaced volume

9463. The value of the righting arm at an angle of loll is _____.

A. negative
B. zero
C. positive
D. equal to GM

9465. When inclined to an angle of list, the value of the righting arm is _____.

A. negative
B. zero
C. positive
D. maximum

9467. When inclined to an angle of list, the value of the righting moment is _____.

A. negative
B. zero
C. positive
D. maximum

9471. What is used as an indicator of initial stability?

A. GM
B. KG
C. KM
D. GZ

9473. What is the stability term for the distance from the center of gravity (G) to the metacenter (M), when small-angle stability applies?

A. metacentric height
B. metacentric radius
C. height of the metacenter
D. righting arm

9477. The water in which a vessel floats provides vertical upward support. The point through which this support is assumed to act is known as the center of _____.

A. effort
B. flotation
C. gravity
D. buoyancy

9481. The difference between the initial trim and the trim after loading is known as _____.

A. trim
B. change of trim
C. final trim

D. change of draft

9483. A tank which is NOT completely full or empty is called _____.

A. pressed
B. slack
C. inertial
D. elemental

9485. The difference between the starboard and port drafts due to wind or seas is called _____.

A. list
B. heel
C. trim
D. flotation

9487. The geometric center of the underwater volume of a floating vessel is the center of _____.

A. hydrodynamic forces
B. flotation
C. gravity
D. buoyancy

9491. The difference between the height of the metacenter and the height of the center of gravity is _____.

A. KB
B. KG
C. KM
D. GM

9493. On a vessel, multiplying a load's weight by the distance of the load's center of gravity above the baseline results in a(n) _____.

A. transverse moment
B. vertical moment
C. righting moment
D. inclining moment

9495. Reducing the liquid free surfaces in a vessel reduces the _____.

A. roll period
B. metacentric height
C. waterplane area
D. vessel's draft

9497. Stability is determined principally by the location of the point of application of two forces: the upward-acting buoyant force and the _____.

A. upward-acting weight force
B. downward-acting weight force
C. downward-acting buoyant force
D. environmental force

9501. Stability is determined principally by the location of the point of application of two forces: the downward-acting gravity force and the _____.

A. upward-acting weight force
B. downward-acting weight force
C. upward-acting buoyant force
D. environmental force

9503. Stability is determined principally by the location of two points in a vessel: the center of buoyancy and the _____.

A. metacenter
B. geometric center of the waterplane area
C. center of gravity
D. center of flotation

9505. With no environmental forces acting on the vessel, the center of gravity of an inclined vessel is vertically aligned with the _____.

A. longitudinal centerline
B. center of flotation
C. original vertical centerline
D. metacenter

9507. With no environmental forces, the center of gravity of an inclined vessel is vertically aligned with the _____.

A. longitudinal centerline
B. center of flotation
C. original vertical centerline
D. center of buoyancy

9511. In the absence of external forces, the center of buoyancy of an inclined vessel is vertically aligned directly below the _____.

A. center of gravity
B. amidships station
C. center of flotation
D. geometric center of the waterplane area

9513. In the presence of external forces, the center of buoyancy of an inclined vessel is vertically aligned with the _____.

A. center of gravity
B. metacenter
C. center of flotation
D. keel

9515. With no environmental forces, the center of gravity of an inclined vessel is vertically aligned directly above the _____.

A. longitudinal centerline
B. center of buoyancy
C. original vertical centerline
D. center of flotation

9517. Aboard a vessel, dividing the sum of the transverse moments by the total weight yields the vessel's _____.

A. vertical moments
B. transverse position of the center of gravity
C. inclining moments
D. righting moments

9521. Aboard a vessel, dividing the sum of the vertical moments by the total weight yields the vessel's _____.

A. height of the center of gravity
B. vertical moments
C. righting moments
D. inclining moments

9523. When the height of the metacenter is the same as the height of the center of gravity, the upright equilibrium position is _____.

A. stable
B. neutral
C. unstable
D. negative

9525. When the height of the metacenter is greater than the height of the center of gravity a vessel has which type of stability?

A. Stable
B. Neutral
C. Unstable
D. Negative

9527. When the height of the metacenter is less than the height of the center of gravity, a vessel has which type of stability?

A. Stable
B. Neutral
C. Negative
D. Positive

9528. You are in Inland Waters of the United States. You may discharge overboard _____.

A. bottles
B. metal
C. dunnage
D. None of the above

9531. When the height of the metacenter is greater than the height of the center of gravity, the upright equilibrium position is stable and stability is _____.

A. unstable
B. neutral
C. negative
D. positive

9533. Unstable equilibrium exists at small angles of inclination when _____.

A. G is above M
B. G is off the centerline
C. B is off the centerline
D. B is above G

9535. When stability of a vessel is neutral, the value of GM _____.

A. only depends on the height of the center of gravity
B. only depends on the height of the metacenter
C. is greater when G is low
D. is zero

9537. When the height of the metacenter is less than the height of the center of gravity of a vessel, the upright equilibrium position is _____.

A. stable
B. neutral
C. unstable
D. negative

9541. When the height of the metacenter is the same as the height of the center of gravity of a vessel, the upright equilibrium position is _____.

A. stable
B. neutral
C. unstable
D. negative

9543. Stable equilibrium for a vessel means that the metacenter is _____.

A. at a lower level than the baseline
B. on the longitudinal centerline
C. higher than the center of gravity
D. at amidships

9545. An unstable upright equilibrium position on a vessel means that the metacenter is _____.

A. lower than the center of gravity
B. at the same height as the center of gravity
C. higher than the baseline
D. on the longitudinal centerline

9547. A neutral equilibrium position for a vessel means that the metacenter is _____.

A. lower than the keel
B. at the same height as the center of gravity
C. exactly at midships
D. at the center of the waterplane area

9551. When the height of the metacenter is less than the height of the center of gravity, a vessel has which type of stability?

A. Stable
B. Neutral
C. Unstable
D. Positive

9553. When the height of the metacenter is greater than the height of the center of gravity, a vessel is in _____.

A. stable equilibrium
B. neutral equilibrium
C. unstable equilibrium
D. negative equilibrium

9563. The KG of a vessel is found by dividing the displacement into the _____.

A. height of the center of gravity of the vessel
B. sum of the vertical moments of the vessel
C. sum of the free surface moments of the vessel
D. sum of the longitudinal moments of the vessel

9564. Automatic fire dampers in ventilation systems are operated by use of _____.

A. remotely operated valves
B. CO_2 system pressure switches
C. fusible links
D. heat or smoke detectors

9565. The LCG of a vessel may be found by dividing displacement into the _____.

585

A. longitudinal center of gravity of the vessel
B. sum of the vertical moments of the vessel
C. sum of the longitudinal moments of the vessel
D. longitudinal baseline of the vessel

9567. The correction to KG for transverse free surface effects may be found by dividing the vessel's displacement into the _____.

A. transverse free surface correction for the vessel
B. sum of the vertical moments of the vessel
C. sum of the transverse free surface moments of the vessel
D. transverse baseline of the vessel

9571. The correction to KG for longitudinal free surface effects for a vessel can be found by dividing the vessel's displacement into the _____.

A. transverse free surface correction for the vessel
B. sum of the vertical moments of the vessel
C. sum of the longitudinal free surface moments of the vessel
D. longitudinal centerline of the vessel

9573. A floating vessel will behave as if all of its weight is acting downward through the _____.

A. center of gravity
B. center of buoyancy
C. center of flotation
D. metacenter

9581. The CO_2 flooding system is actuated by a sequence of steps which are _____.

A. break glass, pull valve, break glass, pull cylinder control
B. sound evacuation alarm, pull handle
C. open bypass valve, break glass, pull handle
D. open stop valve, open control valve, trip alarm

9604. Except in rare cases, it is impossible to extinguish a shipboard fire by _____.

A. removing the oxygen
B. removing the fuel
C. interrupting the chain reaction
D. removing the heat

9606. You are fighting a Class B fire with a portable dry chemical extinguisher. The discharge should be directed _____.

A. over the top of the fire
B. to bank off a bulkhead onto the fire

C. at the seat of the fire, starting at the near edge
D. at the main body of the fire

9607. There is a fire aft aboard your vessel. To help fight the fire, you should _____.

A. head the bow into the wind and decrease speed
B. put the wind off either beam
C. put the stern into the wind and increase speed
D. put the stern into the wind and decrease speed

9608. On small passenger vessels how many supply and exhaust ducts are required in each enclosed space containing gasoline powered machinery or gasoline fuel tanks?

A. 4 of each
B. 3 of each
C. 2 of each
D. 1 of each

9700. The regulations governing the sleeping accommodations of a cargo vessel are found in _____.

A. 46 CFR subchapter S
B. 46 CFR subchapter T
C. 46 CFR subchapter B
D. 46 CFR subchapter I

SAFETY
ANSWERS

SAFETY ANSWERS

NBR	ANS														
2	C	90	B	185	C	292	D	382	A	474	A	585	C	685	B
3	D	91	A	186	D	293	A	383	C	477	D	586	C	686	A
4	A	93	D	187	B	295	B	385	D	478	A	587	D	687	D
5	D	94	B	188	A	296	D	386	D	481	D	589	A	688	D
8	B	95	C	189	B	297	B	387	D	482	A	590	B	689	C
9	A	96	D	190	A	298	A	388	A	484	D	592	B	692	D
10	B	98	C	191	B	300	D	390	D	487	B	597	D	693	B
11	D	99	B	195	B	301	A	391	A	488	A	598	B	694	C
13	A	100	B	196	D	302	B	393	B	489	B	599	C	697	A
14	B	102	A	197	D	303	D	394	A	492	A	600	C	698	D
15	C	103	A	198	C	305	C	398	A	494	B	602	C	699	B
18	C	105	D	200	B	308	B	399	C	497	C	604	D	700	B
19	B	106	C	205	D	311	B	400	B	498	C	605	D	702	A
20	A	108	B	207	B	312	B	402	D	500	C	607	C	704	D
21	D	109	C	208	C	313	D	403	C	502	D	608	D	706	D
23	C	110	B	210	C	315	A	406	B	504	C	609	D	707	D
24	A	112	A	212	D	316	C	407	A	506	B	610	D	708	D
28	C	113	D	217	A	317	B	408	A	507	D	611	D	710	A
29	C	115	B	218	D	318	C	410	B	508	A	612	A	711	A
30	B	116	C	219	D	319	C	411	A	509	C	614	C	712	C
31	A	118	B	220	A	320	B	412	B	510	D	615	C	714	D
33	D	119	D	221	B	322	D	413	A	514	A	617	B	715	D
34	D	120	B	228	A	323	C	414	B	515	C	619	D	717	D
35	A	122	B	229	D	324	B	417	D	516	C	621	D	718	B
36	C	125	A	230	D	326	B	418	A	517	A	625	B	719	D
38	D	126	D	231	B	327	D	422	B	518	B	627	D	720	A
39	A	128	D	238	B	328	B	423	A	520	A	629	B	721	A
40	C	129	C	240	D	329	A	424	B	522	B	630	D	723	A
41	D	130	B	245	B	331	D	425	A	524	B	632	B	724	C
43	D	133	B	247	D	332	B	427	B	527	C	633	D	725	A
44	B	135	D	248	D	333	B	428	C	528	D	634	C	727	D
45	C	136	A	250	B	338	C	429	A	529	A	637	A	728	B
48	A	138	C	251	A	339	C	430	C	531	B	640	C	729	B
49	C	139	D	252	C	340	B	432	B	532	C	642	A	730	C
53	B	140	A	257	C	341	A	433	A	533	D	644	C	731	A
55	B	141	A	258	D	342	B	434	B	534	B	647	A	732	A
57	C	142	D	259	C	343	D	437	D	537	B	648	C	734	B
58	A	143	D	261	A	345	B	438	A	538	D	649	D	735	B
60	D	144	C	262	B	348	D	439	B	542	D	650	D	738	B
63	D	145	D	265	D	349	C	441	C	544	B	651	D	740	C
65	A	148	B	267	D	350	C	442	A	547	D	652	C	742	B
68	B	152	B	268	C	352	D	444	B	548	A	654	D	744	B
69	A	153	A	269	C	353	B	447	C	549	A	655	D	748	B
70	D	155	A	270	A	354	C	448	D	554	D	657	A	749	A
71	D	156	D	271	A	355	A	450	D	555	D	658	D	750	B
73	A	158	B	272	B	357	B	452	D	557	B	660	A	752	B
74	A	162	B	275	C	358	C	453	B	558	A	661	C	753	D
77	C	163	B	277	B	360	C	454	B	560	B	662	C	754	D
78	A	165	D	278	B	361	C	457	D	561	C	664	C	755	A
79	A	168	A	280	D	362	C	459	B	562	D	667	A	758	B
80	B	171	C	281	C	365	A	460	D	565	C	670	C	760	A
81	A	172	B	282	B	367	B	461	A	566	C	672	B	761	A
82	B	173	C	283	D	370	C	462	A	567	A	674	B	762	A
83	D	175	A	285	D	373	D	463	D	568	D	677	B	764	B
84	D	177	C	287	C	374	B	464	D	571	B	678	D	767	A
85	D	178	A	288	C	375	B	467	A	575	D	679	C	768	D
88	D	180	D	289	C	377	B	470	B	578	B	681	D	769	A
89	B	182	A	290	A	378	B	472	C	579	D	682	C	770	D
		183	D	291	D	379	D	473	B	580	B	684	B	772	C

776 B	878 A	957 D	1036 B	1131 C	1236 D	1326 D	1416 B
777 D	879 A	958 D	1037 C	1132 C	1237 A	1327 A	1417 C
778 D	880 C	960 D	1038 D	1133 B	1238 C	1328 D	1419 B
781 C	881 B	961 B	1039 A	1134 D	1242 A	1332 C	1422 B
782 A	882 B	962 B	1040 D	1135 C	1244 D	1334 D	1424 A
785 A	885 C	963 D	1042 D	1137 A	1245 A	1335 D	1425 C
788 B	887 A	965 B	1044 C	1138 D	1246 B	1336 C	1426 C
789 A	888 B	967 A	1046 D	1139 D	1247 B	1337 D	1428 D
790 D	889 D	968 D	1047 A	1143 D	1248 A	1338 D	1429 A
791 A	891 A	969 A	1050 D	1144 A	1249 C	1340 D	1431 B
792 D	892 C	971 B	1051 B	1147 C	1251 D	1341 A	1432 B
796 B	895 B	972 D	1052 C	1148 A	1252 D	1342 B	1433 B
798 C	897 B	973 D	1053 D	1149 A	1255 B	1344 A	1434 D
799 D	898 B	974 B	1054 B	1151 A	1256 B	1345 C	1438 D
800 D	899 B	976 D	1056 D	1152 C	1257 C	1346 A	1439 C
801 C	901 C	977 A	1057 B	1153 C	1259 C	1347 A	1440 A
802 B	902 C	979 B	1059 B	1154 D	1261 C	1348 D	1441 B
803 C	904 D	980 A	1061 B	1158 C	1262 D	1352 B	1442 D
806 D	905 C	981 B	1062 A	1161 D	1263 C	1354 C	1443 D
807 C	906 C	982 B	1063 D	1163 C	1264 D	1355 B	1444 A
808 A	907 A	983 C	1064 C	1168 C	1265 D	1356 A	1445 B
809 D	908 D	984 D	1066 D	1173 A	1266 D	1358 B	1447 B
810 A	912 A	986 B	1067 B	1174 D	1268 D	1361 B	1448 B
811 B	914 B	988 A	1068 B	1178 C	1269 A	1362 C	1449 A
812 A	915 D	989 C	1070 D	1184 B	1272 A	1363 D	1450 D
813 C	917 B	990 A	1071 D	1187 C	1274 B	1364 B	1451 C
818 C	918 C	991 C	1074 A	1188 B	1275 C	1365 C	1452 C
819 A	919 C	992 D	1076 C	1191 B	1276 D	1366 D	1453 A
820 B	920 A	993 D	1077 B	1193 C	1277 B	1368 D	1456 B
821 A	921 D	994 B	1080 D	1194 C	1278 D	1371 D	1457 D
822 A	922 C	996 A	1081 D	1196 B	1279 B	1372 C	1458 D
823 B	923 C	997 A	1083 A	1197 D	1281 C	1373 C	1462 C
825 B	924 A	998 B	1084 D	1198 B	1282 C	1374 A	1463 B
827 D	925 D	1000 D	1086 D	1199 D	1284 B	1375 D	1466 D
828 A	926 B	1002 D	1087 D	1201 D	1286 A	1376 C	1469 B
829 C	927 A	1003 C	1088 A	1204 A	1288 B	1378 A	1471 A
831 C	928 C	1004 B	1089 C	1205 B	1289 A	1381 C	1472 D
832 A	929 A	1006 C	1093 B	1206 D	1292 B	1382 A	1474 C
833 B	930 C	1007 D	1094 C	1207 D	1294 A	1384 C	1475 C
838 D	931 D	1008 A	1097 A	1208 D	1296 A	1385 D	1477 B
839 B	932 D	1011 C	1098 A	1209 B	1297 D	1386 C	1478 C
840 A	933 C	1012 A	1099 A	1211 B	1298 A	1388 C	1479 A
841 C	934 A	1013 A	1101 A	1212 D	1299 A	1391 D	1481 D
842 C	935 C	1014 B	1103 A	1213 B	1301 D	1392 C	1485 A
845 D	936 C	1016 C	1104 C	1214 C	1302 A	1393 A	1487 B
848 B	937 B	1017 A	1106 C	1215 C	1303 A	1394 C	1488 C
849 C	938 D	1019 D	1107 B	1216 D	1304 C	1395 A	1490 C
850 B	939 D	1020 B	1108 A	1217 A	1306 B	1396 B	1492 D
851 D	940 C	1021 D	1109 D	1218 D	1307 D	1397 C	1493 A
852 A	942 A	1022 A	1111 D	1219 D	1308 B	1401 B	1498 A
856 C	943 B	1023 D	1114 D	1223 A	1309 D	1402 A	1502 B
858 A	945 C	1024 D	1117 D	1224 D	1311 A	1404 C	1503 D
862 D	947 B	1027 C	1118 B	1226 D	1312 B	1405 A	1504 C
865 D	948 D	1028 D	1119 D	1227 B	1314 D	1406 D	1505 D
868 A	950 A	1029 D	1123 B	1228 B	1317 B	1408 A	1507 D
869 B	951 D	1030 C	1124 D	1229 C	1318 A	1410 A	1508 A
870 A	952 C	1032 A	1126 A	1231 B	1319 D	1411 A	1511 B
871 A	953 B	1033 C	1127 C	1233 D	1320 B	1413 B	1512 D
873 D	954 C	1034 A	1128 C	1235 D	1324 D	1415 A	1513 D

1519 B	1632 C	1938 D	2171 D	2582 D	2833 B	2972 D	3112 C
1522 D	1634 A	1940 C	2172 A	2596 A	2835 A	2973 A	3116 C
1523 D	1635 C	1942 C	2175 A	2599 A	2836 A	2976 C	3119 B
1524 D	1637 D	1943 A	2179 A	2613 C	2838 C	2978 D	3120 C
1525 C	1638 A	1949 B	2180 B	2614 D	2839 A	2979 C	3121 A
1526 C	1640 C	1950 C	2181 D	2617 C	2842 A	2980 B	3122 A
1527 C	1641 A	1951 A	2184 D	2636 A	2843 A	2983 A	3123 C
1528 C	1647 C	1964 C	2190 C	2652 D	2846 B	2986 A	3124 A
1529 D	1648 D	1967 A	2192 D	2658 D	2849 C	2988 A	3127 A
1530 D	1650 A	1975 D	2194 C	2662 C	2852 C	2989 C	3130 C
1531 B	1664 B	1979 C	2199 B	2664 A	2856 A	2991 A	3134 B
1533 D	1665 A	1983 B	2201 B	2668 A	2858 A	2992 B	3136 A
1534 A	1667 C	1986 B	2202 C	2676 C	2859 D	2993 D	3137 B
1536 D	1669 D	1997 D	2205 A	2681 A	2861 B	2995 B	3140 A
1540 A	1676 D	2008 C	2207 B	2682 B	2862 B	2999 B	3142 D
1541 D	1677 C	2009 A	2211 A	2687 C	2865 D	3000 D	3149 B
1543 C	1678 D	2010 B	2219 A	2689 A	2866 D	3001 C	3150 C
1546 B	1679 A	2014 D	2225 B	2690 C	2869 B	3002 D	3152 B
1547 C	1681 B	2016 C	2233 D	2694 C	2876 B	3003 C	3154 A
1548 D	1682 B	2018 C	2235 A	2729 B	2878 B	3005 D	3156 D
1549 C	1685 C	2020 A	2237 D	2742 B	2881 A	3009 A	3158 C
1553 B	1687 B	2027 A	2238 C	2744 D	2882 A	3016 C	3159 D
1555 D	1688 A	2031 D	2240 D	2754 B	2883 C	3018 D	3160 B
1556 A	1689 C	2032 B	2251 D	2764 B	2886 A	3019 D	3161 A
1558 C	1692 A	2033 A	2264 A	2766 B	2887 B	3022 B	3162 C
1560 C	1695 A	2043 B	2266 A	2768 C	2889 C	3026 B	3167 C
1561 B	1698 B	2045 B	2270 B	2769 B	2892 B	3028 C	3170 C
1562 D	1699 A	2051 B	2274 B	2776 B	2896 C	3032 A	3171 A
1563 B	1701 D	2052 C	2307 B	2777 B	2897 D	3033 B	3172 D
1564 A	1708 A	2053 C	2320 D	2779 D	2898 D	3035 B	3173 B
1566 B	1712 C	2054 A	2327 D	2784 C	2899 A	3037 C	3174 A
1570 A	1714 B	2057 A	2335 A	2786 C	2901 A	3041 B	3176 A
1571 B	1723 C	2061 C	2343 D	2787 D	2902 D	3045 C	3182 B
1575 A	1725 C	2063 B	2345 D	2789 D	2903 D	3046 C	3184 D
1580 C	1734 B	2071 C	2351 C	2790 D	2905 A	3047 B	3186 A
1582 D	1756 D	2073 C	2371 C	2791 A	2906 D	3048 A	3188 D
1583 A	1772 D	2078 B	2387 C	2794 D	2908 C	3051 D	3189 A
1586 B	1773 B	2086 D	2395 A	2796 D	2909 C	3052 D	3192 A
1596 C	1811 A	2094 C	2421 A	2801 A	2919 B	3055 B	3194 A
1597 A	1822 D	2109 A	2424 B	2803 A	2922 D	3056 C	3198 D
1598 A	1823 C	2112 B	2425 C	2805 D	2928 A	3057 A	3200 A
1599 A	1831 A	2114 D	2429 B	2806 C	2932 A	3058 D	3201 D
1601 C	1837 B	2119 B	2457 A	2807 A	2935 A	3059 A	3202 B
1607 C	1854 C	2121 B	2475 A	2811 B	2938 A	3061 C	3203 A
1610 A	1860 C	2131 D	2504 C	2812 B	2939 A	3062 D	3204 B
1612 B	1862 B	2133 A	2507 B	2813 C	2942 C	3066 B	3207 D
1614 D	1867 C	2137 A	2511 A	2815 B	2948 B	3067 A	3208 B
1615 B	1870 A	2142 D	2523 A	2816 B	2949 D	3069 C	3210 C
1616 C	1871 D	2146 B	2528 B	2817 C	2953 D	3078 D	3211 A
1617 B	1875 C	2147 C	2531 D	2819 D	2958 B	3082 B	3212 B
1618 B	1879 B	2150 A	2536 C	2821 B	2960 D	3084 C	3213 D
1619 D	1880 D	2158 D	2549 B	2822 A	2961 A	3091 A	3214 D
1620 C	1890 C	2159 C	2552 C	2823 A	2963 C	3092 B	3215 B
1621 B	1900 C	2160 A	2553 A	2825 B	2965 B	3094 C	3216 C
1624 D	1907 B	2163 B	2554 A	2826 C	2966 A	3096 B	3217 D
1625 D	1909 D	2164 D	2571 A	2828 D	2968 D	3102 A	3220 B
1626 B	1910 C	2167 D	2572 B	2829 B	2969 C	3104 B	3222 C
1627 D	1920 B	2168 B	2575 C	2831 C	2970 C	3108 C	3223 B
1629 D	1930 B	2170 B	2577 A	2832 D	2971 D	3110 B	3228 D

3229 A	3354 C	3498 B	3666 D	3756 A	3904 D	4026 D	5033 D
3230 D	3355 C	3500 D	3669 B	3757 B	3906 B	4028 C	5037 A
3231 D	3357 B	3508 D	3672 A	3758 C	3912 B	4029 D	5154 D
3232 D	3358 C	3512 A	3674 C	3759 C	3914 A	4030 A	5192 D
3233 C	3360 C	3516 B	3676 D	3760 B	3916 B	4032 D	5225 D
3234 C	3361 C	3520 D	3678 C	3761 A	3918 A	4034 D	5231 D
3238 D	3362 A	3536 A	3679 B	3762 D	3920 D	4036 B	5232 C
3240 B	3363 B	3540 A	3680 A	3763 B	3922 D	4038 A	5286 C
3242 B	3366 C	3542 B	3682 B	3764 C	3924 A	4039 B	5386 B
3243 D	3367 A	3546 D	3684 C	3765 C	3926 A	4040 D	5387 D
3250 D	3370 D	3551 A	3686 D	3766 B	3928 A	4042 B	5408 B
3251 D	3372 D	3552 C	3688 A	3768 A	3929 D	4044 A	5418 D
3252 A	3374 B	3554 A	3689 A	3769 C	3930 D	4046 C	5455 C
3254 B	3376 D	3556 A	3690 B	3770 C	3932 D	4048 C	5457 D
3256 C	3386 D	3560 D	3692 A	3772 C	3936 C	4049 B	5461 A
3260 A	3388 B	3580 A	3694 B	3776 B	3938 A	4050 A	5463 C
3268 B	3390 B	3585 D	3698 D	3778 D	3939 A	4052 B	5465 D
3269 A	3394 B	3586 C	3699 C	3780 B	3940 C	4054 D	5467 D
3270 B	3398 A	3587 D	3700 B	3782 D	3942 D	4056 D	5471 A
3272 C	3399 D	3590 B	3704 C	3786 B	3944 D	4059 D	5473 B
3274 B	3400 C	3594 D	3706 C	3788 B	3946 B	4060 B	5475 B
3278 D	3404 B	3596 D	3708 D	3790 B	3948 C	4062 C	5479 A
3280 D	3407 C	3598 D	3709 C	3796 B	3949 B	4064 A	5481 B
3284 B	3409 D	3599 A	3710 A	3798 A	3950 A	4066 B	5485 B
3290 A	3410 B	3600 A	3711 A	3800 D	3951 A	4069 C	5487 B
3292 C	3414 B	3604 B	3712 C	3806 A	3952 D	4076 D	5495 A
3294 A	3415 A	3606 B	3714 C	3809 B	3953 D	4078 D	5505 D
3296 A	3417 D	3608 A	3715 B	3812 A	3954 D	4079 A	5513 D
3300 A	3420 B	3609 C	3716 C	3814 A	3956 C	4082 A	5515 A
3302 C	3421 D	3610 A	3718 A	3820 C	3958 C	4084 B	5517 A
3304 D	3428 D	3611 D	3719 D	3822 B	3960 B	4086 C	5521 D
3308 C	3430 C	3613 D	3723 A	3824 A	3962 B	4088 D	5522 B
3309 C	3433 C	3614 D	3724 C	3826 B	3964 B	4089 B	5523 B
3310 D	3435 C	3616 A	3725 A	3829 C	3966 D	4090 B	5525 B
3312 A	3436 D	3620 C	3726 D	3830 B	3969 D	4092 C	5527 B
3313 C	3438 A	3623 D	3728 A	3834 B	3972 C	4093 D	5531 D
3314 B	3439 D	3626 A	3729 B	3838 A	3974 D	4096 D	5533 B
3316 A	3440 A	3628 D	3730 D	3839 D	3976 C	4098 D	5535 A
3318 D	3444 A	3629 D	3732 B	3840 B	3979 A	4102 A	5537 A
3320 A	3457 A	3630 A	3734 B	3842 B	3980 B	4112 D	5541 A
3322 B	3460 C	3632 D	3736 C	3849 B	3982 C	4115 D	5543 B
3326 A	3462 D	3634 C	3737 A	3853 D	3984 B	4138 B	5545 A
3329 C	3465 C	3638 A	3738 A	3854 B	3986 D	4142 A	5547 D
3330 D	3466 B	3639 A	3739 D	3855 B	3988 A	4174 C	5551 A
3331 D	3467 D	3640 B	3740 D	3857 C	3989 C	4246 A	5553 C
3332 C	3468 A	3641 B	3742 A	3858 B	3992 C	4346 B	5555 A
3334 D	3469 B	3642 B	3743 C	3859 D	3994 B	4362 A	5557 B
3335 D	3471 D	3644 B	3744 A	3860 C	4010 C	4404 A	5561 D
3336 A	3472 B	3645 C	3745 A	3861 D	4011 D	4416 D	5563 B
3339 B	3473 C	3646 B	3746 D	3862 C	4012 A	4458 A	5565 D
3341 B	3478 A	3647 C	3747 B	3866 B	4017 B	4486 B	5567 C
3345 A	3479 C	3648 A	3748 D	3887 C	4018 C	4546 D	5571 A
3346 A	3480 C	3649 D	3749 D	3888 A	4019 D	4572 B	5573 A
3348 C	3487 A	3650 A	3750 B	3891 A	4020 D	4701 D	5575 A
3349 B	3488 B	3651 D	3751 A	3892 C	4021 B	4734 C	5577 B
3350 B	3489 C	3653 B	3752 B	3894 C	4022 A	4784 A	5591 B
3351 D	3494 D	3654 C	3753 D	3896 B	4023 D	4785 A	5595 B
3352 A	3496 C	3655 D	3754 C	3897 C	4024 D	4786 B	5597 A
3353 C	3497 A	3660 B	3755 C	3900 C	4025 C	5031 A	5598 C

5648 C	7051 C	7587 D	8361 D	9021 D	9412 D	9573 A
5655 C	7053 A	7591 B	8363 C	9067 C	9413 B	9581 A
5697 D	7055 C	7593 A	8365 B	9087 A	9414 A	9604 B
5711 C	7057 B	7595 A	8367 D	9091 C	9415 D	9606 C
5715 D	7058 D	7597 C	8371 A	9093 C	9425 C	9607 A
5753 C	7061 B	7601 C	8373 B	9097 A	9427 B	9608 C
5763 B	7062 A	7603 A	8375 D	9101 B	9432 A	9700 D
5806 C	7063 D	7605 C	8377 C	9107 C	9435 A	
5824 B	7065 B	7607 D	8381 B	9111 B	9437 B	
5825 C	7067 D	7613 A	8383 C	9113 D	9441 A	
5845 C	7068 A	7621 A	8384 D	9115 A	9443 B	
5953 D	7071 B	7623 B	8385 C	9121 C	9445 A	
6005 B	7073 C	7625 A	8391 D	9125 B	9447 C	
6049 D	7075 D	7631 D	8392 C	9129 B	9451 A	
6073 A	7077 A	7635 D	8393 C	9130 C	9453 A	
6077 B	7081 B	7641 C	8395 A	9137 D	9455 A	
6246 C	7083 C	7643 C	8397 C	9191 A	9457 D	
6249 D	7093 C	7645 B	8403 C	9193 C	9463 B	
6253 A	7096 C	7647 D	8405 A	9195 B	9465 B	
6273 A	7097 A	7648 B	8407 A	9197 B	9467 B	
6274 D	7121 C	7651 C	8411 A	9205 D	9471 A	
6291 C	7127 B	7655 D	8412 D	9276 B	9473 A	
6303 A	7131 C	7657 C	8413 A	9282 C	9477 D	
6305 B	7143 C	7663 B	8415 C	9303 B	9481 B	
6306 A	7147 A	7665 B	8417 D	9307 C	9483 B	
6307 D	7305 B	7667 D	8421 B	9311 C	9485 B	
6308 D	7307 A	7677 B	8440 A	9313 A	9487 D	
6313 A	7311 D	7683 B	8541 A	9315 B	9491 D	
6402 A	7313 D	7697 C	8547 C	9317 A	9493 B	
6594 B	7317 B	7701 D	8555 B	9321 C	9495 A	
6604 A	7318 A	7703 A	8563 C	9323 B	9497 B	
6624 C	7321 A	7713 D	8575 B	9325 B	9501 C	
6631 A	7323 C	7725 B	8576 B	9327 B	9503 C	
6646 D	7325 C	7727 A	8577 D	9331 B	9505 D	
6742 A	7331 B	7737 D	8615 B	9333 B	9507 D	
6761 D	7333 B	7747 D	8635 D	9335 A	9511 A	
6786 C	7335 A	7785 A	8662 D	9337 A	9513 B	
6792 A	7337 C	7786 B	8702 C	9341 D	9515 B	
6806 C	7341 D	7787 B	8712 C	9342 A	9517 B	
6856 B	7343 D	7805 B	8782 B	9347 C	9521 A	
6917 C	7345 A	7841 C	8807 A	9351 B	9523 B	
6987 C	7351 B	7977 C	8897 B	9357 D	9525 A	
6991 B	7353 A	8036 C	8901 C	9361 C	9527 C	
7003 A	7355 D	8045 D	8903 B	9362 C	9528 D	
7005 A	7388 B	8054 B	8905 B	9363 B	9531 D	
7007 D	7405 B	8155 C	8907 C	9365 A	9533 A	
7021 D	7407 D	8156 C	8911 D	9367 C	9535 D	
7023 B	7411 C	8157 D	8925 B	9371 A	9537 C	
7025 A	7412 C	8222 B	8973 D	9373 D	9541 B	
7027 C	7413 B	8223 C	8977 D	9375 B	9543 C	
7031 A	7415 D	8225 A	8981 A	9377 D	9545 A	
7032 C	7417 B	8235 C	8983 D	9381 C	9547 B	
7033 D	7421 B	8275 B	8985 D	9382 A	9551 C	
7035 B	7427 A	8287 A	8987 D	9383 A	9553 A	
7037 B	7431 D	8337 D	8991 D	9385 A	9563 B	
7041 D	7575 A	8342 B	8993 C	9387 A	9564 C	
7043 B	7577 D	8347 B	8994 C	9391 C	9565 C	
7046 D	7581 A	8353 C	8997 B	9397 A	9567 C	
7047 C	7583 D	8355 A	9001 A	9411 D	9571 C	

NAVIGATION PROBLEMS

LATITUDE, LONGITUDE, DISTANCE AND COURSE

Latitude and Longitude

The earth approximates a sphere. Ignoring topography and irregularities due to density differences in the crust, the earth is actually an *oblate spheroid*, meaning that it is slightly fat around its middle. Leaving the fine points of the earth's shape and dimensions to cartographers, we will assume that the earth is a sphere.

A position on a flat piece of paper can be specified by its vertical distance from a horizontal edge of the paper and its horizontal distance from a vertical edge. Likewise, a position on a sphere can be specified by the vertical angle (latitude) from a horizontal reference plane through the sphere and the horizontal angle (longitude) from a vertical reference plane through the sphere.

Latitude is the distance in degrees North or South of the Equator. *Longitude* is the distance in degrees East or West of the Prime Meridian (also known as the Greenwich Meridian because it passes through Greenwich, England).

The length of one degree of latitude is approximately the circumference of the earth around a meridian, divided by 360. The nautical mile (nm) was chosen to be the length of one minute of latitude (1′ = 1/60°). At the Equator, where the earth's horizontal circumference approximately equals its vertical circumference, the lengths of latitude and longitude degrees are nearly the same. At any other latitude, however, the length of a degree of longitude is less than that of a degree of latitude, and diminishes to zero at the poles.

Most charts used for coastal navigation are Mercator projections—what the earth would look like if projected from the center of the earth (imagine a tiny light at the center of a transparent earth) onto a cylinder tangent to the earth at the Equator. Since most charts cover a small area (typically a degree or less), the longitudinal distortion is tolerable. If you compare the lengths of latitude (vertical scale) and longitude (horizontal scale) minutes on the chart on the facing page, you will find that the longitude minute is shorter.

Find the latitude of a point by placing the points of a pair of dividers on the point and on the nearest horizontal reference (the top or bottom of the chart or an intermediate latitude line). Without changing the spread of the dividers, move them laterally to either edge of the chart and read degrees, minutes, and tenths of minutes. Longitude is found in the same manner, substituting the horizontal scale for the vertical. Do this to confirm that the position of buoy "A" in the chart on the facing page is: Latitude 44° 13.8′N and Longitude 70° 07.5′W.

Distance

As pointed out above, distances on a nautical chart are usually measured in nautical miles (nm), where 1 nm equates to 1′ of latitude. (Inland and Waterway charts are most often in statute miles, requiring the use of distance scales printed on the charts.) In the Mercator projection, the horizontal scale is adjusted so that all *distances*, regardless of direction, can be measured off the vertical latitude scale. On small-scale charts covering very large areas, the latitude scale does vary a small amount, so it is a good idea to use the portion of the latitude scale centered on where you are measuring.

To measure the *distance between two points,* hold your dividers to the vertical scale and adjust the points to exactly 1 nm (or other convenient exact distance, such as 2, 5, 10, etc., nm), then "walk" the dividers from point A to point B, counting as you go. When you get to the point where the remaining distance is less than the span of the dividers, adjust the dividers down to the remaining span, then measure the smaller span against the latitude scale to get the fraction of a nm. The total distance is the number of full steps plus the fraction.

Practice this technique to confirm the distances, D, plotted on the chart. For example, the distance between buoys "A" and "B" measures 5.3′ of latitude on the latitude scale along the right edge of the chart. The distance, D, is therefore 5.3 nm. It is customary to write the distance under the course.

Course

Charts are overprinted with one or more compass roses. The compass rose shows two sets of directions:

True—direction relative to the direction to the Geographic North Pole, indicated by the outer circle.

Magnetic—direction relative to the local lines of magnetic force, indicated by the inner circle.

Converting from magnetic to true and the reverse is covered in the chapter Navigation General. In this chapter we will use only true directions.

Course is the direction you intend to steer, in degrees clockwise from north. First draw a course line from a fix, or other position, in the direction you intend to steer. Using parallel rules, transfer the course line to the center of the nearest compass rose and read the direction in degrees. Write the course above the course line, as shown, preceded by C and followed by T (true) or M (magnetic). Do this to confirm that the course from buoy "A" to buoy "B" in the chart on the facing page is 082°T (or 093°M).

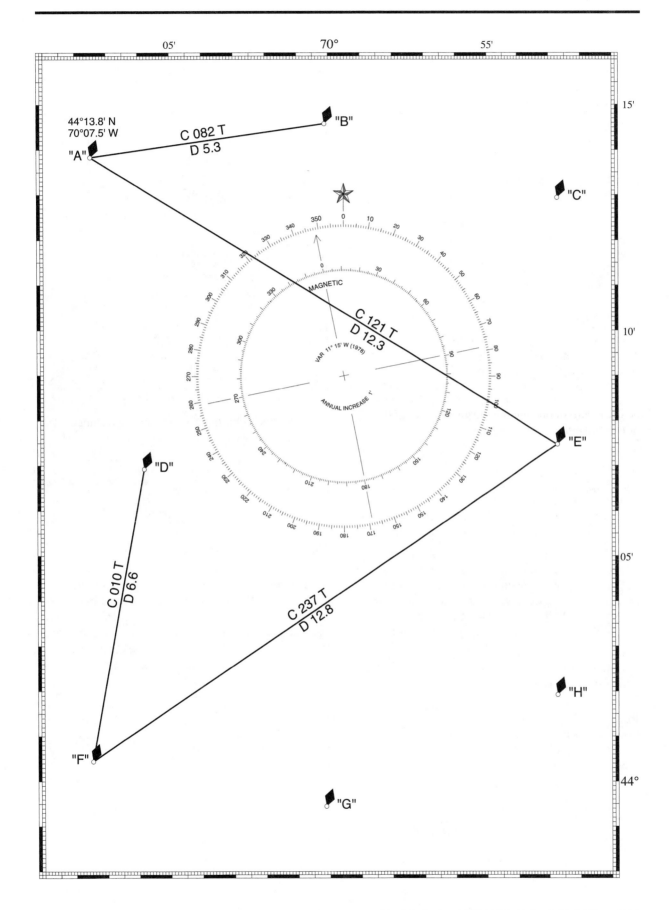

DEAD RECKONING

Dead (from "deduced") reckoning is the projection of courses and speeds from a known position. The projected position is estimated, as opposed to fixed, because it doesn't take account of current, leeway, helmsman error, or unknown compass errors.

The dead-reckoning (DR) plot should be drawn on a chart with pencil and updated:

- at least once per hour
- at every change of course or speed
- after any plotted line of position

Constructing a Dead Reckoning Plot

Draw a course line from the point of departure in the direction to be steered. Write the course above the course line, starting with the letter C, followed by the number of degrees, followed by T or M. Place the letter S and the speed in knots below the course line.

Indicate the point of departure by a small circle and dot (indicating certainty of position)—unless the point is a buoy or other obvious point on the chart. Note the time horizontally with four digits. Time can be either local or Universal (formerly known as GMT). Indicate a fix from two or more lines of position (explained later in this chapter) by a similar circle and dot and the time horizontally.

Determine the first DR position by multiplying the speed by the time elapsed since departure (see box, above right). Transfer this distance from the latitude scale to the course line. Indicate the relative uncertainty of this DR position by a small semicircle and dot, labeled with the four-digit time diagonally.

If the course changes at this point, draw a new course line in the new direction. Otherwise, extend the original course line in the same direction. Repeat the process, from DR to DR, each time using the speed and time elapsed since the previous DR to calculate the incremental distance traveled.

Indicate an estimated position (explained later in this chapter) by a small square and dot, also labeled with a diagonal time.

Practice Problem

Copy the blank plotting sheet on page 608 and use the following information to plot the DR shown in the chart on the next page:

0800 Depart Buoy "F" at Course 090T, Speed 10 kn
0816 Change Course to 028T, Speed to 8.5 kn
0841 Change Course to 090T, Speed to 10 kn
0904 Change Course to 042T, Speed to 8.5 kn
0929 Plot DR position

Speed, Distance and Time

Some navigators find the relationship between (S)peed, (D)istance and (T)ime obvious. For those not so blessed, try the following trick: Remember the term DTs, then picture the D over the TS:

$$\frac{D}{TS}$$

To find one quantity from the other two, cover up the one you seek and what remains will give the answer. To find D, for example, cover the D and see the answer: TS.

$$D = TS$$

To find elapsed time, T, cover T and see: D/S

$$T = D/S$$

Remember to always convert a fractional hour to a decimal value by dividing minutes by 60 before using it in a calculation. For example:

$$37 \text{ min} = 37/60 = 0.62 \text{ hr}$$

$$1 \text{ hr } 37 \text{ min} = 1 + 37/60 = 1.62 \text{ hr}$$

Example: At 7.8 kn (nm/hr), what distance will you travel in 1 hr 37 min.?

Answer: $D = TS$

$$= 1.62 \text{ hr} * 7.8 \text{ nm/hr}$$

$$= 12.64 \text{ nm}$$

Transfer and Advance

The distance a large vessel travels *during* a change of course can be so great it must be figured into the DR plot. The transfer and advance characteristics of a vessel are determined and recorded by sea trial and then used in maneuvering. You will probably not see such questions, but just in case, here is the geometry.

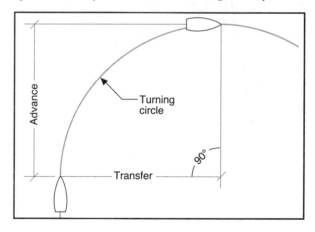

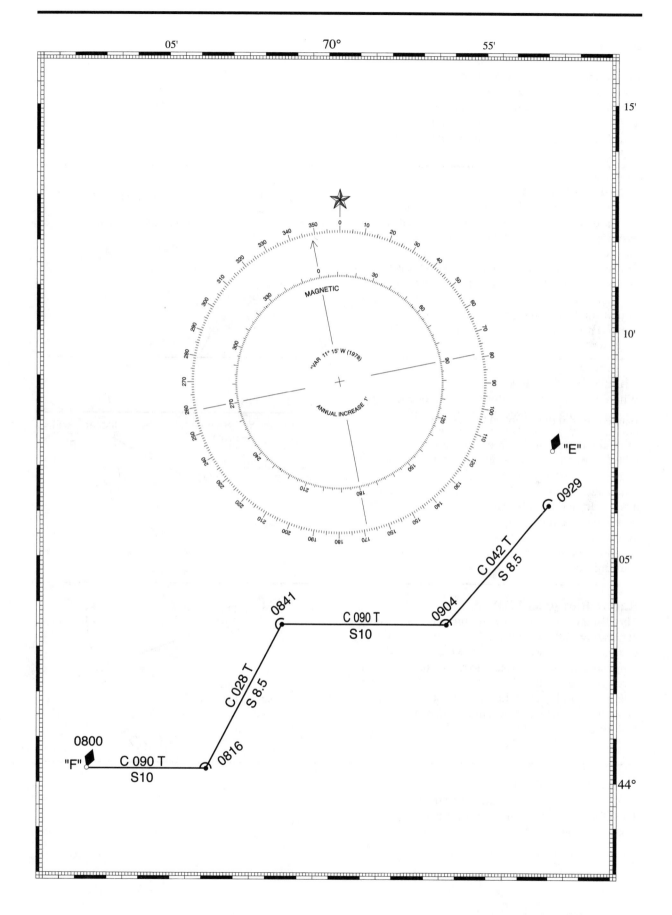

FIXES BY BEARINGS

Single Bearing

A bearing is the direction *from a vessel* to an object of known position, measured in degrees clockwise from north. Since there is only one line with that bearing which can be drawn through the known object, the vessel must be somewhere along the bearing line. The bearing line is, therefore, a line of position (LOP).

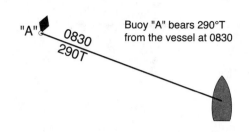

Buoy "A" bears 290°T from the vessel at 0830

Two-Bearing Fix

When you have two different LOPs, obtained by taking simultaneous (as nearly as possible) bearings on two objects of known position, you know that you must be on both LOPs at the same time, i.e., at their intersection. The intersection of two LOPs is known as a two-bearing fix. We indicate the certainty of such a fix with a small circle and dot at the intersection of the LOPs. Since this is a fix—not a DR or estimated position—we label it with the four-digit time, written horizontally.

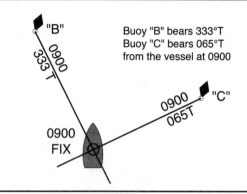

Buoy "B" bears 333°T
Buoy "C" bears 065°T
from the vessel at 0900

Three-Bearing Fix

When you have three different LOPs, obtained by taking bearings on three different objects of known positions, you know that you should be at the intersection of all three LOPs. Since bearings taken from a vessel underway are subject to a few degrees uncertainty, however, the "intersection" will usually be a triangle (sometimes referred to as a "cocked hat") formed by the three LOPs. In this case we place the circle and dot at the geometric center of the triangle, this being the most likely position. Again, label the fix with a horizontal, four-digit time.

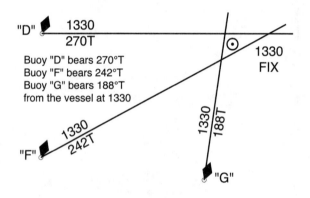

Buoy "D" bears 270°T
Buoy "F" bears 242°T
Buoy "G" bears 188°T
from the vessel at 1330

Radar Range as LOP

The distance, or range, to an object is easily and accurately obtained with radar. With this known distance from vessel to object, we can turn the range around and use it as the radius of an arc centered on the known object. Circular LOPs may be combined with each other or with straight-line LOPs from bearings to obtain two-LOP and three-LOP fixes.

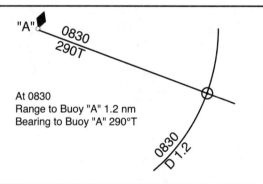

At 0830
Range to Buoy "A" 1.2 nm
Bearing to Buoy "A" 290°T

Practice Problem

Find the latitudes and longitudes of the 0900 and 1000 fixes shown on the chart on the next page. You should get, ±0.1′:

0900	44° 12.5′N	069° 55.8′W
1000	44° 03.1′N	069° 59.0′W

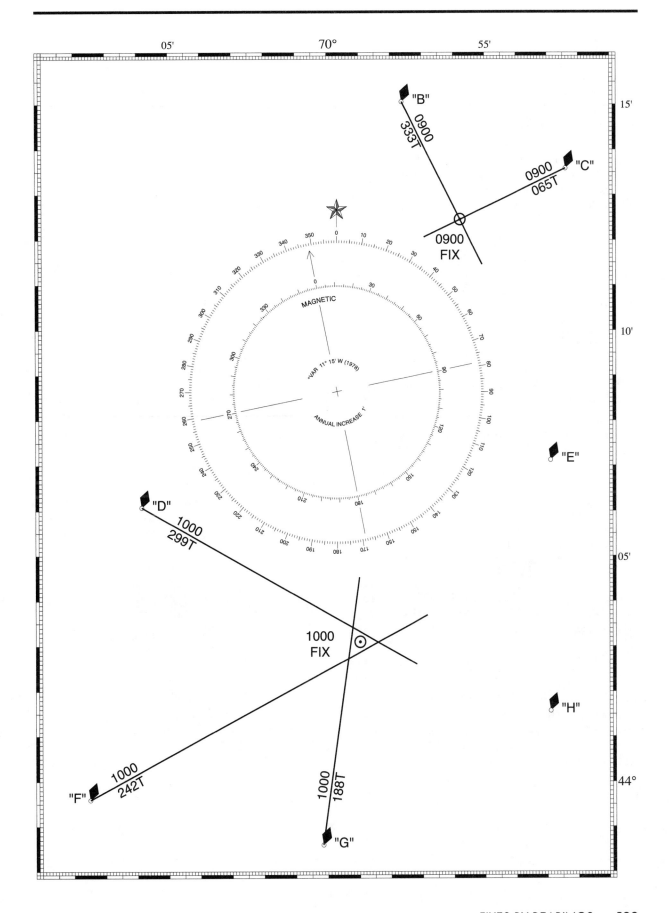

05'   70°   55'

"B"
0900
333T

0900
065T
"C"

0900
FIX

★
MAGNETIC
"VAR 11° 15' W (1978)
ANNUAL INCREASE 1'

"E"

"D"
1000
299T

1000
FIX

"H"

1000
242T
"F"

1000
188T
"G"

15'

10'

05'

44°

A running fix is a two-bearing fix except that the two bearings are taken on the same body at different times. The first bearing is taken, then advanced by DR to the time of the second bearing. Since the position of the advanced bearing is subject to the uncertainties of leeway and current during the elapsed time, the accuracy of the running fix is somewhat less than that of a simultaneous-bearing fix.

Plotting a Running Fix

In the illustration at right a bearing of 050°T is taken from the vessel to the buoy at 0900. At 0915 a bearing of 100°T is taken on the same buoy. During the time between bearing sights (0900 to 0915), the vessel remains on course 020°T at speed 6.0 knots.

To plot the fix:

• Plot the first bearing; label it with bearing and time.

• Calculate the advance of the vessel in the time elapsed between the first and second bearings (D = S * T = 6.0 * 15/60 = 1.5 nm).

• Advance the first bearing 1.5 nm along the vessel's course—not at right angles to the bearing! Label the advanced bearing with both times.

• Plot the second bearing and label it with bearing and the second time.

• The fix is the intersection of the advanced bearing and the second bearings. Indicate the fix with a circle and dot, accompanied by "R FIX" and the four-digit time.

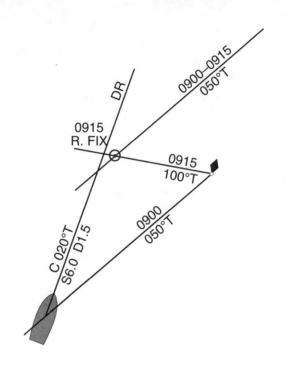

Track Not Important

One of the reasons a running fix is considered a fix, rather than a DR position or estimated position, is that the precise location of the vessel's track doesn't matter.

In the illustration at right two parallel DR tracks are plotted. It makes no difference to the final solution which track—DR1 or DR2—we use to advance bearing 1. Only the direction of bearing 1 is important to the solution.

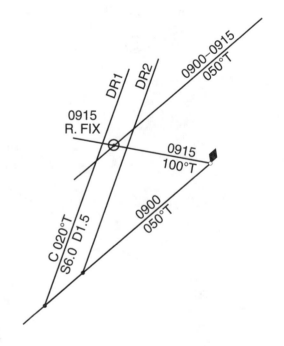

A Practice Problem

Find the latitudes and longitudes of the 0900 and 1000 fixes shown on the chart on the next page. You should get, ±0.1':

0411/1440	44° 13.0'N	070° 03.6'W
0630/0707	43° 59.6'N	069° 58.7'W

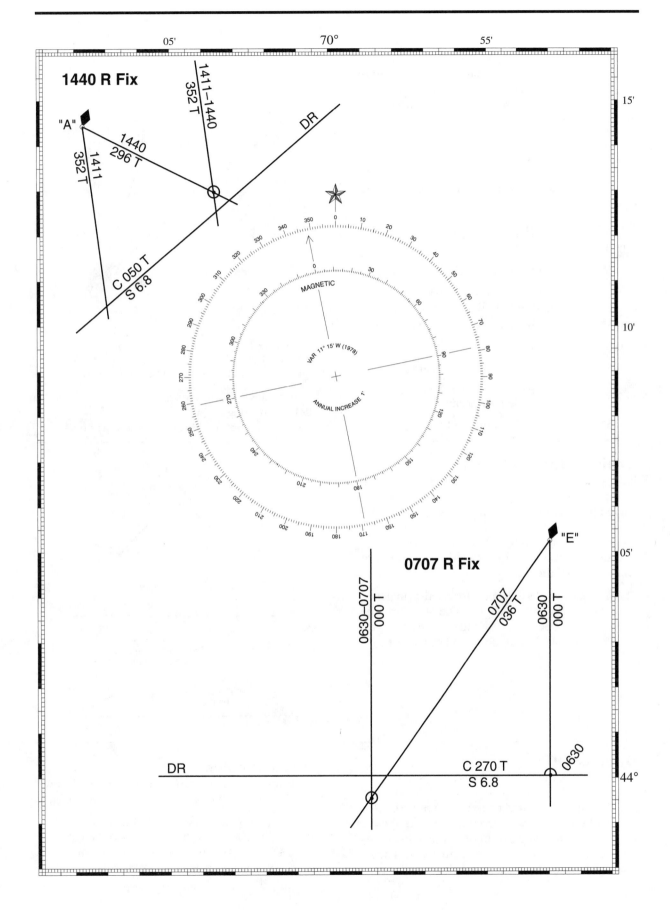

1440 R Fix

1411-1440
352 T

"A"

1440
296 T

DR

1411
352 T

C 050 T
S 6.8

MAGNETIC

VAR 11° 15' W (1978)

ANNUAL INCREASE 1'

"E"

0707 R Fix

0630-0707
000 T

0707
036 T

0630
000 T

0630

DR

C 270 T
S 6.8

RELATIVE BEARINGS AND DISTANCE OFF

Relative Angles/Relative Bearings

Courses and bearings are measured clockwise, 0–360°, from True North or Magnetic North. *Relative angles* and *relative bearings* are taken relative to the course or the vessel's fore-and-aft line. *Relative angles* are expressed as 0–180° port or starboard. *Relative bearings* are 0–360° clockwise from the bow.

When the precision of a relative bearing is not very important, it is traditional to refer to the bearing relative to the bow, beam, and stern of the observing vessel. These terms are:

Bearing	Descriptive Term
000°	Dead ahead
045°	Broad on the starboard bow
090°	Broad on the starboard beam, or on the starboard beam
135°	Broad on the starboard quarter
180°	Dead astern
225°	Broad on the port quarter
270°	Broad on the port beam, or on the port beam
315°	Broad on the port bow

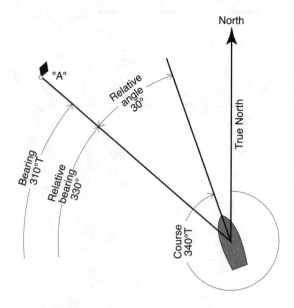

In the illustration above:
Course 340°T; buoy "A" is at a bearing of 310°T

Relative angle = 30° to port
Relative bearing = 330°
Closest Descriptor = "broad on the port bow"

Doubling the Angle on the Bow

Relative angles have a valuable property. If a vessel maintains a steady course, and the relative angle to a fixed point doubles, then the distance from the vessel to the point at the time of the second sight equals the distance traveled between first and second sights. This piloting trick works for all relative angles from 0° through 90°.

The trick also works in reverse for relative angles from 90° to 180°, where the distance off is from the first sight. The special case of the relative angle pair of 45°/90° is called taking "bow-and-beam bearings."

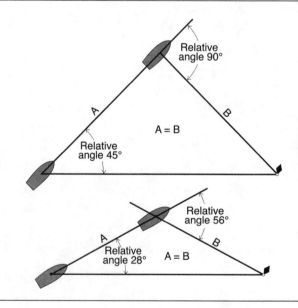

Distance Off

Distance off is the distance from the vessel to a fixed object. Most "distance off" problems are really nothing more than running fixes (see previous page) where the distance from the sighted object is measured with dividers from the fix position or at right angles from the extended course line. The practice problem offers an example.

Practice Problem

Use a blank plotting sheet to solve the problem below. The solution is shown on the chart on the next page.

Your vessel is on a course of 297°T at 11 knots. At 0019 a light bears 274.5°T, and at 0048 the light bears 252°T. At what time and at what distance off will your vessel be when abeam of the light?

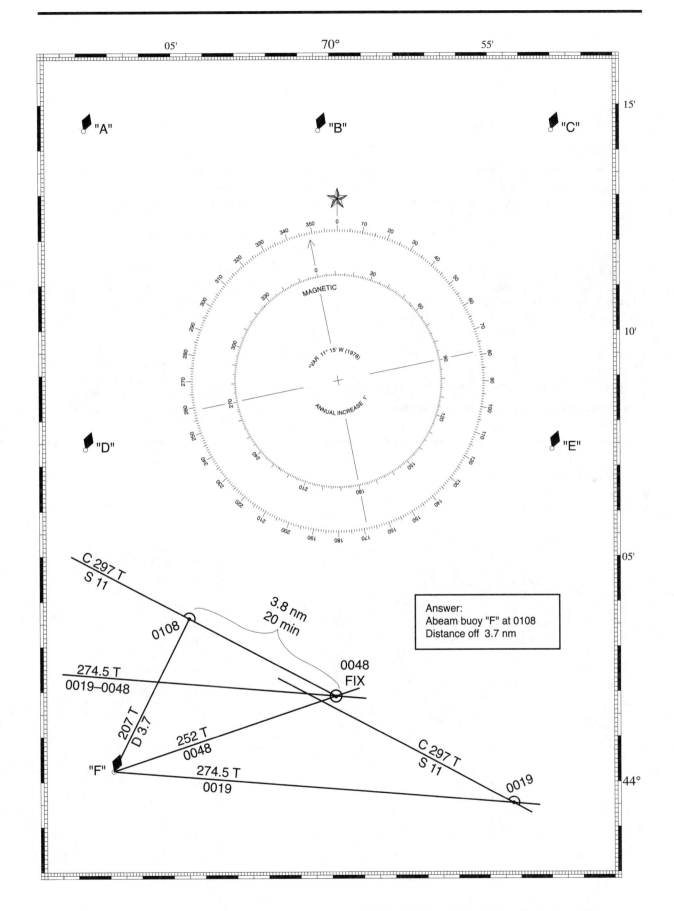

Answer:
Abeam buoy "F" at 0108
Distance off 3.7 nm

CURRENT SET AND DRIFT

Current is a horizontal flow of water. In bays and estuaries, current is most often tidal; offshore it is caused by the tide (rotary tidal current) and steady winds. Current is described by two terms:

- *Set* is the direction toward which it is flowing, i.e., a set of 090°T is "setting to the east."

- *Drift* is the speed of the flow over the bottom.

A vessel has course and speed. A current has set and drift. The motion of the water can be calculated in the very same way as the motion of a vessel. The resulting motion of the vessel over the ground is thus the motion of the vessel through the water *plus* the motion of the water over the ground.

When a vessel's course is parallel to the current's set, calculating vessel speed over the ground (SOG) is simple: just add or subtract current drift to or from vessel speed, depending on whether the current is with or against the vessel.

Example: A vessel is on course 270°T at 10 knots. There is a current setting 090°T at 2 knots. The vessel's SOG is thus 10 knots – 2 knots = 8 knots.

The illustration below shows the general effects of current on a vessel's track.

Quantities having both magnitude and direction are called *vectors*. Both vessel speed and current are vectors. The wonderful thing about vectors is that they can be added by drawing them head-to-tail.

The top example on the chart on the next page demonstrates the concept. A vessel departs buoy "A" at 1330 on course 082°T at speed 9.8 knots. At 1417 (47 minutes after departure) the vessel has advanced 9.8 × 47/60 = 7.7 nm along the course line. During the same 47 minutes the current has been setting 135°T at 2.0 knots. The water has thus shifted 2.0 × 47/60 = 1.6 nm on a course of 135°T. The net effect is exactly as if the vessel had sailed both legs, and the problem is solved in the same manner.

The bottom example turns the problem around to determine the set and drift of a current that would cause the observed offset between a DR position and a fix. The vessel departs buoy "F" at 1330 on course 082°T at speed 9.8 knots. At 1417 (47 minutes after departure) the vessel has advanced 9.8 × 47/60 = 7.7 nm through the water. At the same time a fix is obtained from bearings on buoys "G" and "H." The set is measured to be 339°T; the drift is calculated as distance/time, 2.0 nm/(47/60 hr) = 2.6 knots.

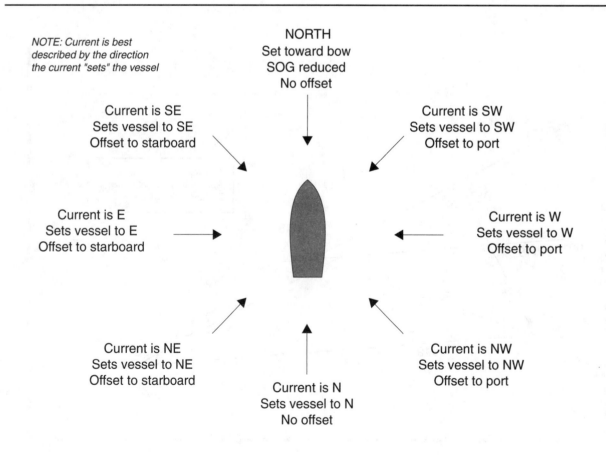

NOTE: Current is best described by the direction the current "sets" the vessel

NORTH
Set toward bow
SOG reduced
No offset

Current is SE
Sets vessel to SE
Offset to starboard

Current is SW
Sets vessel to SW
Offset to port

Current is E
Sets vessel to E
Offset to starboard

Current is W
Sets vessel to W
Offset to port

Current is NE
Sets vessel to NE
Offset to starboard

Current is N
Sets vessel to N
No offset

Current is NW
Sets vessel to NW
Offset to port

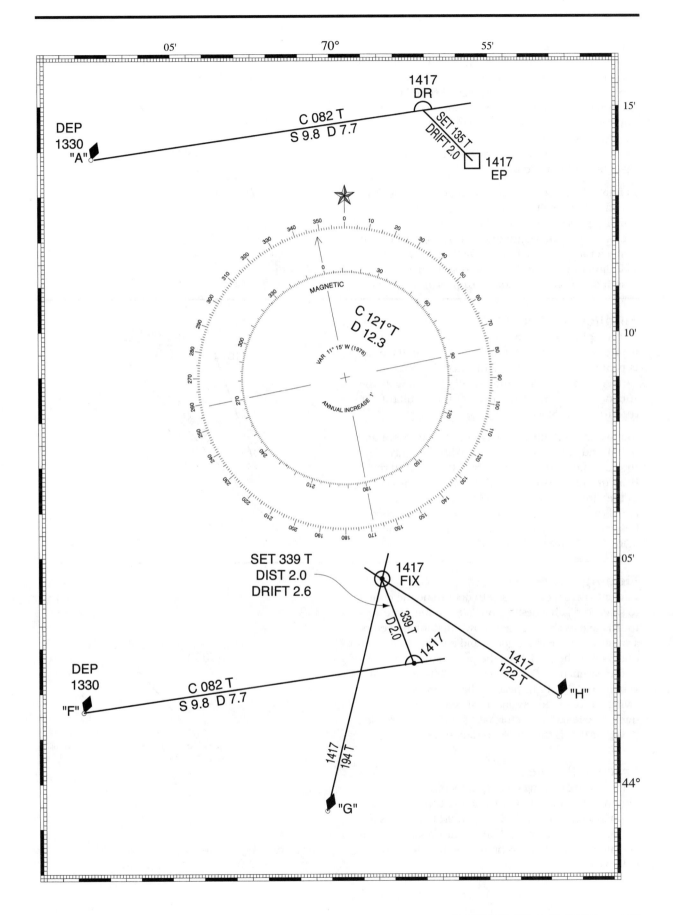

CURRENT VECTORS AND COURSE TO STEER

Current Vectors

As we saw in the previous section, any motion that can be specified by a speed and a direction can be represented as a vector. Both vessel speed through the water and current are such motions. Here we will refine the concept by adding arrow heads to the vectors to show their directions and to remind us that vectors are drawn, tail-to-head, to find the resulting motion vector.

In illustration 1 a vessel is steering course 020°T at speed 5.0 knots. It is subject to a current of set 082°T and drift 2.9 knots. The resultant motion over the bottom is the vector drawn from the tail of the first vector, A, to the head of the second vector, C. The direction of line AC is the vessel's *track*. The length of line AC is the *speed over ground* (SOG).

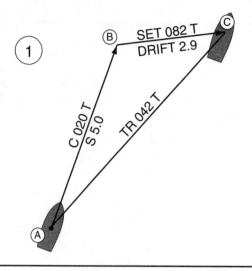

Finding Track and SOG

The simplest way to determine the track and SOG is to plot the motion for one hour. Since distance is proportional to speed, and since the distance advanced in one hour is numerically the same as the speed, we can read the length of the resultant vector directly as SOG.

In illustration 2 draw the vessel's course vector at 020°T and of length equal to the distance travelled through the water in one hour, 5.0 nm. From the head of the course vector, draw the current vector in the direction of the set, 082°T, and of length equal to the drift, 2.9 nm. Find the resultant vector between points A and C and read the track and SOG, 042°T and 6.8 knots.

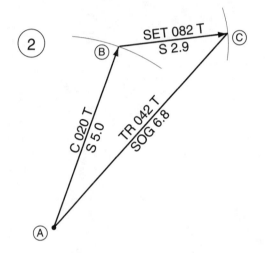

Finding Course to Steer

Current vectors can be used to determine the course to steer to reach a destination. We use the same vector triangle as above except now the known vectors are track (course made good) and current. In illustration 3 draw the track from the point of departure, A, to the destination, D. Next draw the 1-hour current vector, A–B. From the head of the current vector, B, swing an arc of radius equal to speed to intersect the track. The length of vector A–C is SOG. The direction of vector B–C is the course to steer (CTS).

Practice Problem

Using a blank plotting sheet (photocopy the blank plotting sheet on page 608), find the course to steer through a current of set 114°T and drift 2.9 knots if the destination bears 073°T and your vessel's speed is 5.0 knots. Our solution is plotted on the chart on the next page.

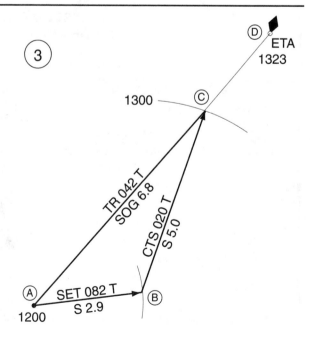

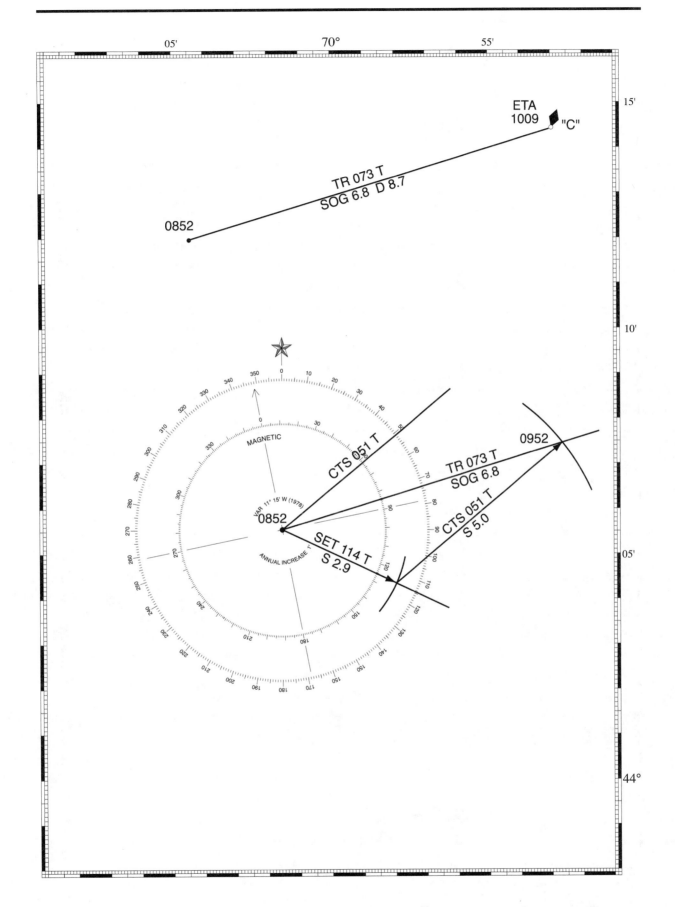

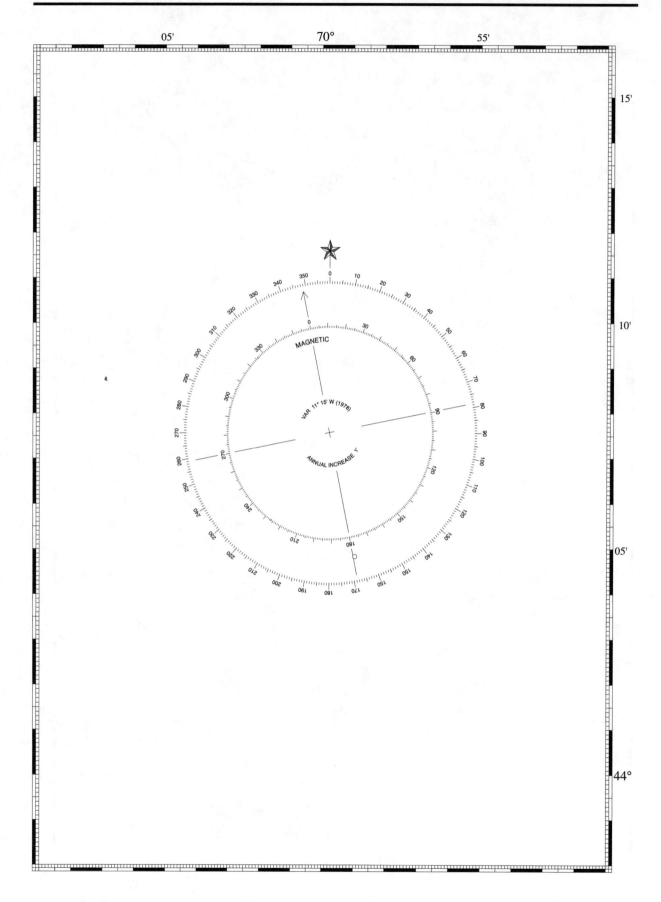

CHART PRACTICE PROBLEMS

In the Navigation Problem section of the exam you will be asked a number of questions which will put you through the paces exactly as if you were piloting a vessel through one of the areas:

Chesapeake Bay Entrance (Chart 12221)

Long Island Sound—Eastern Part (Chart 12354)

Block Island Sound and Approaches (Chart 13205)

Columbia River (Chart 18531)

The questions will test your abilities to:

- find information of all sorts on a nautical chart
- find information in the related Coast Pilot
- find positions and plot DR courses

Here is a series of 10 problems to be solved using Chart 13205, *Block Island Sound and Approaches; Coast Pilot, Volume 2;* and *Light List, Volume 1*—all are available in the exam room.

Question 1
517. BLOCK ISLAND SOUND
At 0520, you take the following observations: Point Judith Light 032°pgc; Point Judith Harbor of Refuge Main Breakwater Center Light 308°pgc. What is the position of your 0520 fix?

A. LAT 41°20.8′N, Long 71°29.7′W
B. LAT 41°20.6′N, Long 71°30.4′W
C. LAT 41°20.6′N, Long 71°30.0′W
D. LAT 41°20.5′N, Long 71°29.4′W

Solution:
Since no gyro error was given, the per gyrocompass bearings (pgc) are True bearings. We are given two bearings, separated by 84°—a nearly ideal spread. Find your 0520 position using the 2-bearing fix, as shown on page 598. Correct answer: A.

Question 2
518. BLOCK ISLAND SOUND
Point Judith Harbor of Refuge _____.

A. is used mostly by towing vessels
B. has a maximum depth of 14 feet at MHW
C. is entered through the East Gap or the West Gap
D. is easily accessible in heavy southerly seas

Solution:
Some of the possible answers cannot be gotten from the chart, so we turn to *Coast Pilot, Vol. 2.* In the index of that book, Point Judith Harbor of Refuge is described on page 177. Correct answer: C.

Question 3
519. BLOCK ISLAND SOUND
At 0520 you are on course 243°pgc at 12 knots. What is the course per standard magnetic compass?

A. 227°psc
B. 233°psc
C. 258°psc
D. 262°psc

Solution:
From the compass rose on the chart we find the local variation to be 14°45′W. Assuming no gyro error, the question gives us a True course (pgc) of 243°. Going from True to Magnetic is uncorrecting, so we use the inverse of the rule "Correct Add East." We "Uncorrect Add West": 243° + 15° = 258°. Correct answer: C.

Question 4
521. BLOCK ISLAND SOUND
The coastline between Point Judith and Watch Hill is

_____.

A. steep with rocky bluffs
B. sandy and broken by rocky points
C. low and marshy
D. heavily forested

Solution:
Looking at the stretch from Point Judith to Watch Hill on the chart, we see a fairly smooth shoreline with what appear to be a series of closely spaced periods. Looking in *Chart No. 1*, we find on page 14 that the symbol indicates "Sandy shore." Correct answer: B

Question 5
522. BLOCK ISLAND SOUND
In clear weather, how far away will you sight Point Judith Light?

A. 14.0 nm
B. 12.3 nm
C. 10.6 nm
D. 9.2 nm

Solution:
First we look in the index of *Light List, Vol. 1* and find Pt. Judith Light, #19450. Using the light number, we find the light listed on page 159. Its nominal range, assuming meteorological visibility of 10 nm, is given in column 6 as 16 nm. Next we enter the Luminous Range Diagram (*Light List*, page xxxii) with nominal range 16 nm, run vertically to the intercept (interpolated) with visibility 7, then across to a luminous range of approximately 15 nm. Correct answer: A.

Question 6

523. BLOCK ISLAND SOUND
At what time will you cross the 60 foot curve if you make good 12 knots?

A. 0544
B. 0541
C. 0534
D. 0528

Solution:

Using the compass rose, align the parallel rule with your course, 243°T. Walk the rule over to your 0520 fix (circle with dot), and draw a course line. Set the points of the divider on the center of the fix and the intersection of your course line and the 60-foot depth curve. Now measure the distance by placing the dividers on the nm scale at the top of the chart. The distance is 1.6 nm.

To find the time, use D/TS. Covering up T, we see:

$$T = D/S = 1.6 \text{ nm}/12.0 \text{ kt} = 0.133 \text{ hr}$$
$$1.33 \text{ hr.} \times 60 \text{ min./hr} = 8 \text{ minutes}$$

We will cross the 60-foot line at 0520 + 08 = 0528. Correct answer: D.

Question 7

524. BLOCK ISLAND SOUND
The two wavy magenta lines running to Green Hill Point represent _____.

A. recommended approaches to Green Hill Point
B. areas of unreliable loran readings
C. submarine cables
D. prohibited fishing areas

Solution:

The wavy magenta lines are labeled "cable area" right on the chart. In case of doubt, *Chart No. 1* identifies the symbol on page 48. Correct answer: C.

Question 8

525. BLOCK ISLAND SOUND
At 0600 your loran reads: 9960-W-14542.5; 9960-X-25909.5; 9960-Y-43950.0. What is your 0600 position?

A. LAT 41°18.3'N, LONG 71°38.7'W
B. LAT 41°18.4'N, LONG 71°38.0'W
C. LAT 41°18.5'N, LONG 72°38.1'W
D. LAT 41°18.7'N, LONG 71°38.9'W

Solution:

Chart 13205 is overprinted with the three sets of GRI 9960 curves: W (cyan), X (magenta), and Y (black). Plotting the three TD LOPs gives us a small cocked hat, the center of which is at 41°18.3'N and 71°38.7'W. Correct answer: A.

Question 9

544. BLOCK ISLAND SOUND
From your 0600 position, what is the course per gyrocompass to leave Watch Hill Light abeam to starboard at 2.0 miles if a southerly wind is producing 3° of leeway?

A. 262°pgc
B. 258°pgc
C. 256°pgc
D. 252°pgc

Solution:

Using the scale at the top or bottom of the chart, set the points of your dividers at 2.0 nm. With one divider point on the light, trace a 2.0 nm arc outward from the light. From your 0600 fix (small circle with dot) at 41°18.3'N, 71°38.7'W, draw a light pencil line so that it is tangent to the arc. This will be your track, or course over the ground. Using the parallel rule, transfer this line to the compass rose and read a True course of 255°T. Since the southerly (from the south) wind is pushing you 3° degrees off course to the north, you should steer 3° to the south, or 252°T. Correct answer: D.

Question 10

545. BLOCK ISLAND SOUND
At 0645, Watch Hill Point (left tangent) bears 314.5°T at 2.75 miles. What was the speed made good between 0600 and 0645?

A. 11.4 knots
B. 10.7 knots
C. 9.8 knots
D. 8.1 knots

Solution:

We are given a single-bearing fix. Using the parallel rule and compass rose for the bearing, and the dividers for the distance, plot the 0645 position. Set your dividers at 1.0 nm on the nm scale at the top of the chart, and walk off the distance between the 0600 and 0645 fixes. The number of whole steps (8) is the whole number of nm. (If there were a remaining small distance, you would reset the dividers to the remaining fractional distance and take the dividers back to the chart scale to read the fraction of a nm.) So you traveled a distance (D) of 8.0 nm in time (T) of 45 minutes. Convert T to decimal hours:

$$45 \text{ min.}/60 \text{ min.} = 0.75 \text{ hr}$$

Finally use D/TS: cover the value you want to compute (S) and read D/T.

$$S = D/T = 8.0/0.75 = 10.7 \text{ knots.}$$

Correct answer: B.

NAVIGATION PROBLEMS— QUESTIONS

In order to work these questions you will need the following charts:

12221 TR *Chesapeake Bay Entrance*
12354 TR *Long Island Sound—Eastern Part*
13205 TR *Block Island Sound and Approaches*
18531 *Columbia River*

The training (TR) charts are available through the mail for $3.50 each at many websites, including Blue Water Books (*www.bluewaterweb.com*) and Landfall Navigation (*www.landfallnavigation.com*). Chart 18531 can be purchased from any NOAA chart seller.

Questions involving the Mississippi River require the publication *Flood Control and Navigation Maps Mississippi River Below Hannibal, Missouri to the Gulf of Mexico, 1998.* The maps are available for purchase in hardcopy ($20) and on CD-ROM ($5) from Vicksburg District Map Sales, (601) 631-5042. They are also available for free in PDF format for viewing, printing and downloading at: *http://www.mvd.usace.army. mil/Gis/navbook/html/instruct.htm.*

The following questions are based on the C of E Mississippi River Maps (Cairo to the Gulf) and the Light List. On 16 October, you depart the Formosa Plastics mooring facility at mile 233.5 AHP with six loaded tankbarges enroute to to the Agrico Chemical dock, Herculaneum, MO (mile 153.4 UMR). Your engines are making turns for 6.5 mph in still water.

33. What is the total length of the trip?

A. 873.7 miles
B. 900.7 miles
C. 901.4 miles
D. 910.6 miles

34. You estimate the current at 3.0 mph. What is the speed over the ground?

A. 9.5 mph
B. 7.5 mph
C. 4.5 mph
D. 3.5 mph

35. What are the dimensions of the channel maintained at Baton Rouge, LA?

A. 30 feet × 300 feet
B. 40 feet × 500 feet
C. 30 feet × 500 feet
D. 40 feet × 300 feet

36. You pass Springfield Bend Lt. (244.8 AHP) at 1242, on 17 October, and estimate the current will average 2.5 mph for the remainder of your trip. What is your ETA at the mouth of the Ohio River if you are making turns for 10.5 mph?

A. 1905, 19 October
B. 2122, 19 October
C. 0232, 21 October
D. 0519, 21 October

37. As you pass under the Natchez–Vidalia Dual Bridge, the gauge on the bridge reads -3.6. If the highest point on your vessel is 62 ft. above the water, what is your vertical clearance?

A. 122.0 feet
B. 67.2 feet
C. 63.6 feet
D. 60.0 feet

38. What are the color and shape of Sunnyside Daymark at mile 530.6 AHP?

A. Green - Square
B. Green - Diamond
C. Red - Triangle
D. Red - Square0

39. At 1227, on 19 October, you pass under the Greenville Highway Bridge (mile 531.3 AHP). What speed must you average to arrive at Jimmy Hawken Light (mile 663.5 AHP) at 0930 the following day?

A. 6.3 mph
B. 5.9 mph
C. 5.6 mph
D. 5.2 mph

40. Which of the following statements regarding aids to navigation in the Corps of Engineers map book is TRUE?

A. The U.S. Army Corp. of Engineers is responsible for placing and maintaining all aids to navigation.
B. Buoy positions as shown on the chart are exact.
C. Buoys should always be given as wide a berth as possible.
D. Lights and daymarks are always shown in their exact location.

41. The Delta-Friar Point revetment on the LMR extends from mile _____.

A. 648.5 – 645.5 LDB
B. 652.8 – 649.6 RDB
C. 657.3 – 652.2 LDB
D. 645.6 – 641.4 RDB

42. What is the distance from Greenville, MS, to St. Louis, MO, on the Mississippi River System?

A. 832 miles
B. 733 miles
C. 597 miles
D. 566 miles

The following questions are based on the C of E Mississippi River Maps (Cairo to the Gulf) and the Light List. At 1745, on 25 August, you depart Memphis Harbor, McKellar Lake (mile 726.0 AHP - LMR) enroute to to Baton Rouge, LA, with a tow of twelve empty gasoline barges.

43. You have received orders to proceed to the Amoco Pipeline Co. (253.6 AHP) above Baton Rouge. If your vessel is making turns for 9 mph with an estimated average current of 1.5 mph, what is your ETA at the Amoco docks?

A. 0844, 28 Aug
B. 1454, 28 Aug
C. 1444, 27 Aug
D. 2214, 27 Aug

44. The highest point on your towboat is 52 feet above the water, and the Helena Gauge reads +9.6 feet. What is the vertical clearance when you pass under the A-span of the Helena Highway Bridge?

A. 73.1 feet
B. 58.0 feet
C. 53.9 feet
D. 49.8 feet

45. You are in charge of a vessel that damages an aid to navigation established and maintained by the United States. Which statement is TRUE?

A. You must take the aid in tow and deliver it to the nearest Coast Guard, Marine Safety Office.
B. You must report the accident to the nearest Officer in Charge, Marine Inspection.
C. You may wait until you reach your destination before reporting the collision to the U.S. Coast Guard.
D. You must report the collision to the nearest Corps of Engineers office

46. At 2342, on 25 August, you pass under the Helena Highway Bridge (661.7 AHP). What has been the average speed of the current since departing Memphis Harbor, McKellar Lake, if you have been making turns for 9 mph?

A. 5.6 mph
B. 4.4 mph
C. 2.1 mph
D. 1.8 mph

47. What is the distance in river miles, from the new mouth of the White River to the RR and Hwy bridge at Baton Rouge, LA?

A. 384 miles
B. 370 miles
C. 365 miles
D. 358 miles

48. The Clinch River empties into which river?

A. Arkansas
B. Mississippi
C. Tennessee
D. Ohio

49. As you pass under the Greenville Highway Bridge, you estimate the current as 4.5 mph. What is the speed over the ground, if your vessel is making turns for 9 mph?

A. 13.5 mph
B. 14.5 mph
C. 15.5 mph
D. 16.5 mph

51. As you approach Cottonwood Chute Light (mile 530.5 AHP), which type of daymark would you see on the light structure?

A. Red triangle
B. Red diamond
C. Green square
D. Green diamond

53. What are the dimensions of Old River Lock, on the Lower Mississippi River?

A. 1185 feet × 75 feet
B. 1045 feet × 75 feet
C. 760 feet × 75 feet
D. 425 feet × 75 feet

The following questions are based on the C of E Mississippi River Maps (Cairo to the Gulf) and the Light List. At 1707, on 23 May, you get underway from mile 234.2 AHP enroute to to Louisville, KY (mile 612.6 OR).

54. What is the length of the trip?

A. 1566.4 miles
B. 1334.6 miles
C. 1332.2 miles
D. 1088.0 miles

55. After you get underway, what is the first river gauge you will pass?

A. Bayou Sara
B. Baton Rouge
C. Head of Passes
D. Red River Landing

56. The Red River Landing gauge reads 5.2 feet. Which of the following statements is TRUE?

A. The depth over revetment at Old River is 25.2 feet.
B. River level is below the Low Water Reference Plane.
C. The depth over Old River Lock sill is greater than 11 ft.
D. This gauge reading is at a higher elevation than the same reading on the gauge at Head of Passes.

57. At 0922, on 24 May, you are abreast the St. Catherine Bar Lt. (mile 348.6 AHP). If you are turning for 8.0 mph, what is the current?

A. 7.0 mph
B. 2.0 mph
C. 1.4 mph
D. 1.0 mph

58. What daymark will you see as you approach Warnicott Bar Lt. (mile 351.3 AHP)?

A. Red diamond
B. Red triangle
C. White square
D. Green square

59. You pass Warnicott Bar Lt. at 1146, 24 May. What is your ETA off the Mhoon Landing gauge if you average 6.5 mph?

A. 0909, 27 May
B. 1528, 26 May
C. 0426, 26 May
D. 0152, 26 May

60. What town is located at mile 389.8 AHP?

A. Whitehall
B. Belmont
C. Rodney
D. St. James

62. The Greenville gauge reads 10.6 feet. The high point of your towboat is 54 feet above water. What is the vertical clearance as you pass under the Greenville Highway Bridge?

A. 75.4 feet
B. 65.5 feet
C. 54.2 feet
D. 44.4 feet

63. In addition to the C of E maps, data on bridge clearances may be found in the _____.

A. Light List
B. Waterways Journal
C. C of E Regulations
D. Channel Report

The following questions are based on the C of E Mississippi River Maps (Cairo to the Gulf) and the Light List. On 3 January, you get underway from Morganza, LA (mile 278.3 AHP) enroute to to the Eagle Marine Docks, LDB, in St. Louis.

64. What is the length of the trip?

A. 726.0 miles
B. 851.9 miles
C. 878.9 miles
D. 879.6 miles

65. What are the dimensions of the Old River Lock on the lower Old River (304 AHP)?

A. 1202 × 84 feet
B. 1200 × 75 feet
C. 1195 × 75 feet
D. 1185 × 75 feet

66. At 2126, you pass Morganza Bend Light (mile 278.4 AHP). At 0122, 4 January, you pass Red River Landing Gauge (302.4 AHP). You have been turning for 7.5 mph. What is the current?

A. 6.2 MPH
B. 2.7 MPH
C. 1.8 MPH
D. 1.4 MPH

67. The gauge at Red River Landing reads 22.2 feet. How many feet is this above the low water reference plane?

A. 32.8 ft.
B. 22.2 ft.
C. 11.6 ft.
D. 10.6 ft.

68. The river will be temporarily closed to navigation at mile 531.3 AHP due to repairs to the bridge. This will occur at 1300, 5 January, and last for six hours. What minimum speed over the ground must you make from Red River Landing Gauge in order not to be delayed?

A. 7.3 mph
B. 6.8 mph
C. 6.4 mph
D. 6.0 mph

69. What type of daymark will you see as you approach Joe Pierce Light (mile 334.4 AHP)?

A. Red triangle
B. Red square
C. Red diamond
D. Private aid—no daymark

70. What is the vertical clearance of the Natchez Highway Bridge (westbound) when the river level is the same as the Low Water Reference Plane?

A. 125.6 ft
B. 119.5 ft
C. 108.3 ft
D. 102.2 ft

71. The Natchez gauge reads 20.6 feet. The high point on your towboat is 47 feet above the water. What is the vertical clearance as you pass under the Natchez Highway Bridge?

A. 78.6 feet
B. 72.5 feet
C. 64.1 feet
D. 58.0 feet

72. In order to determine what buoys, if any, are in place at Concordia Bar crossing (mile 596.0 AHP), what should you check?

A. Channel Report
B. Waterways Journal
C. Bulletin Board at the Rosedale Gauge
D. Light List

73. The area between Island 67 Upper Light (mile 623.1 AHP) and Sunflower Cut-Off Foot Light (mile 624.8 AHP) is known as a _____.

A. crossing
B. chute
C. transit
D. slough

The following questions are based on the C of E Mississippi River Maps (Cairo to the Gulf) and the Light List. On 21 September, you are making up your tow at the fleeting area in Cairo, IL, (mile 980.6 Ohio River). You get underway at 0952 enroute to to New Orleans with a mixed tow.

74. You are turning for 7.8 mph and estimate the current at 1.0 mph. What is your speed over the ground?

A. 6.8 mph
B. 7.8 mph
C. 7.9 mph
D. 8.8 mph

75. What is your ETA at the Memphis–Arkansas Highway Bridge?

A. 1813, 22 Sept
B. 1405, 22 Sept
C. 1052, 22 Sept
D. 0828, 22 Sept

76. What daymark should you see as you approach Parker Landing Light (mile 924.6 AHP)?

A. Green square
B. Green diamond
C. Red and green rectangle
D. Green triangle

77. You pass Morrison Towhead Light (mile 890.5 AHP) at 1723. What was your average speed since leaving Cairo?

A. 8.8 mph
B. 8.5 mph
C. 7.8 mph
D. 7.5 mph

78. At 1723 you increase speed to make good 9.2 mph. At 1937 you have a daymark on your port beam. What daymark is this?

A. Tiptonville Ferry Landing Daymark
B. Tiptonville Light
C. Alaska Light and Daymark
D. Merriwether Bend Light and Daymark

79. The map shows a circle with two black quadrants located at mile 846.4 AHP. What does this indicate?

A. A gauge
B. A bulletin board
C. The grain elevator at Bunge Grain
D. A culvert with a sluice gate

80. The Helena gauge reads 9.4 feet. The high point on your towboat is 46 feet above water. What is the vertical clearance when you pass under the Helena Highway Bridge?

A. 106.1 feet
B. 79.5 feet
C. 64.2 feet
D. 56.0 feet

81. What company does NOT have a marine facility along the river bank in Helena (mile 658 to 665 AHP)?

A. Riceland Food Corp.
B. Helena Marine Services, Inc.
C. Helena Grain Co.
D. Texas Eastern Pipeline Co.

82. If the Rosedale gauge reads –0.5 feet, what is the water level in relation to the low water reference plane?

A. 3.5 feet below the plane
B. 2.5 feet above the plane
C. 0.5 feet above the plane
D. 0.5 feet below the plane

The following questions are based on the C of E Mississippi River Maps (Cairo to the Gulf) and the Light List. At 1015, on 16 April, you are at the Amoco Pipeline Co. Docks (253.6 AHP), when you get underway, enroute to Institute, WV with a tow of eight barges carrying molten sulphur.

84. What is the distance from the Amoco Docks at Baton Rouge, LA, to the mouth of the Ohio River?

A. 981.5 miles
B. 953.5 miles
C. 727.9 miles
D. 700.2 miles

85. You are turning for 10 mph, approaching Angola, LA. Angola reports that the current at Red River Landing is estimated at 4.5 MPH. Which of the following statements is TRUE?

A. You should expect to encounter vessels crossing the river at mile 300.5 AHP
B. You are making 14.5 mph over the ground.
C. You would expect to find a more favorable current near the broken red line in the river.
D. Hog Pt. Light and Hog Pt. Lower Light may be used as range lights when entering Shreves cut-off.

86. As you approach Shreves cut-off you see Red River Landing Gauge (302.4 AHP) which reads 6.2 feet. Which of the following statements is TRUE?

A. This reading is 6.2 feet above the Low Water Reference Plane.
B. This reading is at the same elevation as the 6.2 ft. mark on the gauge at Head of Passes.
C. The depth of water at Red River Landing is 6.2 ft.
D. A vessel drawing 7 ft. would be able to pass through the locks at Lower Old River.

87. You pass Red River Gauge at 2015 on 16 April and estimate the current will average

3.5 mph for the remainder of the time on the Mississippi River. What is your ETA at the mouth of the Ohio River if you continue to turn for 10 mph?

A. 0821, 21 April
B. 0028, 21 April
C. 1830, 20 April
D. 1445, 20 April

88. What is the vertical clearance between the highest point of your towboat, if it is 58 feet above the water, and if the Natchez Gauge reads 28.13 feet when passing under the Natchez Upper Highway Bridge?

A. 45.4 feet
B. 39.3 feet
C. 33.2 feet
D. 15.9 feet

89. In high water conditions, which publication would you consult for the latest information on buoys between Baton Rouge and Cairo?

A. C of E Navigation Chart
B. U.S.C.G. Light List
C. U.S.C.G. Notice to Mariners Channel Report
D. List of Buoys and Daymarks

90. As you approach Giles Bend Cutoff Light (mile 367.7 LDB), what type of daymark would you see on the light structure?

A. None
B. Red triangle
C. Red square
D. Red diamond

91. At 0305 on 18 April, you pass under the Greenville Bridge (mile 531.3 AHP). What was your average speed since departing Amoco Pipeline Co. Docks (253.6 AHP)?

A. 7.2 mph
B. 6.8 mph
C. 6.5 mph
D. 6.2 mph

92. A stretch where the channel changes from one side of the river to the other is called a _____.

A. crossing
B. transit
C. transfer
D. passing

93. After you enter the Ohio River at Cairo, which span of the Illinois Central RR Bridge would you select to pass under?

A. Any span is navigable
B. Northbank or Southbank
C. Southbank span only
D. Northbank span only

The following questions are based on the C of E Mississippi River Maps (Cairo to the Gulf) and the Light List. At 1835, on 10 August, you are downbound on the Upper Mississsippi River at St. Louis, MO (mile 184.0 UMR), with a mixed tow of 6 loaded, covered hopper barges, 2 loaded tank barges, and 2 empty hopper barges.

94. You have orders to drop off the empties at the fleeting area in Cairo and add five loaded barges to your tow. If you are turning for 8 mph and estimate the current at 0.5 mph, what is your ETA at Cairo?

A. 1928, 11 Aug
B. 1614, 11 Aug
C. 1327, 11 Aug
D. 2352, 10 Aug

95. You complete changing out your tow and get underway enroute to Memphis, Tennessee to deliver 2 tank barges. What is the distance you must travel from Cairo Point Light to the Lion Oil Refining Co. Docks in Memphis?

A. 180.3 miles
B. 220.2 miles
C. 246.5 miles
D. 734.3 miles

96. As you approach Kate Aubrey Bar Light (mile 788 AHP), your searchlight will show what type of marking at the light?

A. Green square
B. Red and green banded square
C. Green triangle
D. Green diamond

97. The highest point on your towboat is 57 feet above the water, and the Memphis Gauge reads +1.3 feet. What is the vertical clearance when you pass under the Memphis–Arkansas Highway Bridge in Memphis?

A. 112.7 feet
B. 55.7 feet

C. 54.5 feet
D. 51.8 feet

98. At 0230 on 13 August, you are at mile 610.5 AHP when you see about a mile ahead two separate white lights on the water near the left bank. There is a red light on the bank in the same vicinity. What can you expect to see when you come abreast of these lights?

A. Privately maintained buoys at a yacht club
B. Government buoys marking the Hurricane Point dikes
C. Barges moored at the River Grain Co.
D. A pipeline discharging dredge spoil

99. What is the milepoint of the Rosedale Gauge?

A. 598 AHP
B. 592 AHP
C. 587 AHP
D. 554 AHP

100. Which of the following statements concerning the buoys on the Mississippi River is TRUE?

A. Buoy locations may be changed to indicate the channel for the existing river stage.
B. The buoys are maintained on station year round.
C. Buoys have permanent moorings on the river bottom and will not shift position.
D. The position of river buoys can be determined by consulting the latest Light List, Vol. V.

101. At 1430 on 13 August, you pass Carolina Landing Light (508.8 AHP). What has been the average current since 0230, 13 August if you have been making turns for 8.0 mph?

A. 8.5 mph
B. 5.7 mph
C. 1.5 mph
D. 0.5 mph

102. The latest available information on the channel conditions above Baton Rouge that includes recommended course and the latest buoy information is found in the _____.

A. Channel Report
B. Waterways Journal
C. Sailing Directions
D. Corps of Engineers maps

103. You are approaching the Old River Control Structure (mile 314.5 AHP). The structure is in operation. Which of the following statements is TRUE?

A. The maximum speeds permitted when passing the channel are 10 mph downbound and 7.5 mph upbound.
B. Tows must be no more than 110 feet wide when passing the inflow channel.
C. You should navigate as close to the left descending bank of the Mississippi River as safety permits.
D. Tow length should not exceed 850 feet when passing the inflow channel.

The following questions are based on the C of E Mississippi River Maps (Hannibal, Missouri, to the Gulf of Mexico) and the Light List. At 0815, on the 16 of April, you depart the Exxon Refinery Docks (mile 232 AHP) bound for the fleeting area at Sycamore Chute Light (740.3 AHP).

108. The horizontal clearance of the center span on the Baton Rouge RR and Highway 190 Bridge is _____.

A. 443
B. 500
C. 623
D. 748

110. You have passed Ben Burman Lt. (mile 235.0 AHP) and see on the map a dark purplish area extending past Bayou Baton Rouge. This indicates a _____.

A. revetment
B. dredge material
C. dike
D. fleeting area

111. As you pass Solitude Lt. (mile 249.0 AHP) which dayboard would you see?

A. green diamond
B. green square
C. red triangle
D. red diamond

112. Which of the following statements regarding buoys on the Mississippi River is TRUE?

A. Buoys should be given as wide a berth as possible in passing.
B. Buoy positions on the chart are exact.
C. The buoys are maintained on station year round.

D. The buoys do not shift positions due to permanent moorings.

113. What is indicated by the two light gray shaded areas that cross the river above False River Lt. (mile 251.0 AHP)?

A. ferry crossings
B. utility crossings
C. aerial cable crossings
D. bridge construction

114. What are the light characteristics of Greenwood Light (mile 288.6 AHP)?

A. fixed red light
B. 1 red flash every 4 seconds
C. 2 red flashes every 5 seconds
D. 2 white flashes every 4 seconds

115. After passing Wilkinson Lt. (mile 310.0 AHP) you see a flashing amber light on the right descending bank ahead. The flashing light indicates that you should _____.

A. stay in the deepest water
B. slow down due to dredging operations
C. keep as close to the right descending bank as safety permits
D. keep as close to the left descending bank as safety permits

116. At which of the following times would you be able to listen to lower Mississippi River conditions on VHF Channel 22.

A. 0900 hours
B. 1100 hours
C. 1300 hours
D. 1700 hours

117. At 0645, on the 17th of April, you pass Hole in the Wall Lt. (mile 373.4 AHP). What has been your average speed since departing the Exxon Refinery?

A. 5.8 mph
B. 6.3 mph
C. 6.7 mph
D. 7.1 mph

118. Your company wants to know at what time you will be arriving at the fleeting area at Sycamore Chute Light (mile 740.3 AHP) in Memphis, Tenn. You are making turns for 9.0 mph and you estimate the average current at 2.2 mph. Figuring the distance and time from Hole in the Wall Lt. (mile 373.4 AHP), what is your ETA at Sycamore Chute Lt.?

A. 0557, April 19th
B. 1045, April 19th
C. 1242, April 19th
D. 1733, April 19th

The following questions are based on the C of E Mississippi River Maps (Hannibal, Missouri, to the Gulf of Mexico) and the Light List. On the 10th of May at 1130, you leave the fleeting area at Gartness Lt. (mile 227.8 AHP) bound for the Monsanto Terminal in St. Louis (mile 178.0 UMR). Your engines turn for 8.5 mph in still water.

119. What is the length of the trip?

A. 405.8 miles
B. 553.0 miles
C. 904.0 miles
D. 1136.8 miles

120. You estimate the current as 2.5 mph. What is the speed over the ground?

A. 5.5 mph
B. 6.0 mph
C. 8.0 mph
D. 11.0 mph

121. As you approach Casting Yard Dock Lt. (mile 265.4 AHP) you notice on the map a circle with 2 black sectors. This symbol indicates a _____.

A. lock
B. warning sign
C. mooring buoy
D. river gauge

122. From Baton Rouge to Cairo, what is the maintained minimum channel depth during low water?

A. 6 feet
B. 9 feet
C. 12 feet
D. 30 feet

123. On which map would you find Redman Point, Arkansas?

A. 57
B. 60
C. 66
D. 74

124. At 1000, on May 11th, you are passing George Prince Lt. (mile 364.1 AHP) in Natchez, Mississippi and must send an ETA to the Monsanto Terminal in St. Louis (mile

178.0 UMR). Your engines are still turning for 8.5 mph and you estimate the current at 2.5 mph. What will be your arrival time in St. Louis?

A. 1919 on 15 May
B. 2344 on 15 May
C. 1757 on 16 May
D. 2236 on 16 May

125. As you approach Ashland Light (mile 378.1 AHP) which daymark would you see?

A. red triangle
B. red diamond
C. green square
D. green diamond

126. What is your clearance as you pass under the Vicksburg Highway 80 Bridge (mile 437.8 AHP) if the Vicksburg gauge reads 14.8 feet and the highest point on your tow boat is 44.5 feet?

A. 36 feet
B. 42 feet
C. 57 feet
D. 66 feet

127. After entering Milliken Bend (mile 455 AHP) you wish to locate the river service in Madison Parish, Louisiana. The river service is indicated by the square containing which number?

A. 2
B. 3
C. 4
D. 5

128. At Filter Point Light (mile 475 AHP) there are 3 close straight dashed lines on the map passing through the black dot below the number 475. What do these lines represent?

A. submerged oil pipelines
B. submerged telephone cables
C. submerged gas pipelines
D. aerial power cables

The following questions are based on the C of E Mississippi River Maps (Hannibal, Missouri, to the Gulf of Mexico) and the Light List. At 1400, 12 January, you are downbound on the Upper Mississippi River at St. Louis, MO (mile 181.0 UMR) bound for the River Cement Co. in Natchez, MS.

129. When you pass under the Jefferson Barracks Highway Bridge (mile 168.6 UMR) what will be your vertical clearance if the highest point on your towboat is 55 feet and the St. Louis Gauge reads 21 feet?

A. 11.8 feet
B. 14.6 feet
C. 19.7 feet
D. 25.8 feet

130. You are on map #13. What is the mile point of the facility known as Slay Warehousing, Inc.?

A. mile 169 UMR
B. mile 170 UMR
C. mile 172 UMR
D. mile 174 UMR

131. Which light characteristics does Foster Light have?

A. 1 green flash every 4 seconds
B. 1 red flash every 4 seconds
C. 2 white flashes every 5 seconds
D. 2 red flashes every 5 seconds

132. At 2100, January 12, you are passing Cherokee Landing Lt. (mile 112.5 UMR). What has been your speed over the ground since leaving St. Louis, MO (mile 181 UMR)?

A. 10.4 mph
B. 9.8 mph
C. 9.2 mph
D. 8.8 mph

133. You are turning for 7.5 mph and estimate the current at 3.0 mph. What is your ETA at the River Cement Co. in Natchez considering that you passed Cherokee Landing Lt. at 2100?

A. 1605 on 15 January
B. 0355 on 16 January
C. 1244 on 16 January
D. 1922 on 16 January

134. You are passing Goose Island Lt. (mile 34.4 UMR). The brown shaded areas alongside the river represent _____.

A. levees
B. revetments
C. dikes
D. dredged material

135. At 1030, 13 January, you are passing Columbus Point Lt. (mile 936.1 AHP). What

has been your average speed since leaving St. Louis (mile 181 UMR) on the 12th of January at 1400 hours?

A. 10.4 mph
B. 9.7 mph
C. 9.4 mph
D. 9.1 mph

136. What is the mile point of Hickman, KY gauge?

A. 846.4 AHP
B. 889.0 AHP
C. 922.0 AHP
D. 937.2 AHP

137. Which daymark would you see at Shields Bar Lt. (mile 882.2 AHP)?

A. red triangle
B. green triangle
C. red diamond
D. green square

138. You are passing Eastwood Lt. (mile 849.3 AHP) and the map indicates that Bunge Grain facility would be located at the square with number _____.

A. 2
B. 4
C. 6
D. 8

139. What is the distance to Caruthersville Gauge from Cape Girardeau?

A. 54.4 miles
B. 160.4 miles
C. 793.4 miles
D. 899.4 miles

140. If the highest point on your towboat is 52 feet and the West Memphis gauge reads 26 feet what is the vertical clearance when you pass under the Hernando Desoto Bridge (736.6 AHP)?

A. 25.8 feet
B. 30.7 feet
C. 42.6 feet
D. 56.7 feet

141. Your vessel is making turns for 9.5 mph and you estimate the average current for the trip will be 2.5 mph. What will be your ETA Donaldsonville, LA?

A. 1222 on 7 October
B. 1823 on 7 October
C. 0443 on 8 October
D. 1033 on 8 October

142. As you approach West Memphis Lt. (mile 727.4 AHP) you notice on the map a dashed line crossing the river. This line indicates a _____.

A. submerged oil pipeline
B. submerged gas pipeline
C. aerial tramway
D. aerial transmission line

143. At 1609, on October 5, you are abeam of Star Landing Lt. (mile 707.2 AHP) . You calculate your speed since you departed Sycamore Chute fleeting area. If you are turning for 9.5 mph what was the current?

A. 1.0 mph
B. 1.5 mph
C. 2.0 mph
D. 2.5 mph

144. What is the distance from the Arkansas River mouth to the Ohio River mouth in river miles?

A. 594 miles
B. 546 miles
C. 422 miles
D. 372 miles

145. As you approach Joseph Henry Light (mile 445.2 AHP) which daymark would you see?

A. red triangle
B. red square
C. green diamond
D. green square

146. On which river is Dover, KY, located?

A. Mississippi
B. Tennessee
C. Ohio
D. Missouri

147. After passing Oak Bend Lt. (mile 425.6 AHP) you see a light gray shaded area extending into the river shown on the map. This indicates a _____.

A. fleeting area
B. weir
C. dike
D. revetment

The following questions are based on the C of E Mississippi River Maps (Hannibal, MO, to the Gulf of Mexico) and the Light List. At 0620 on 25 November, you depart Cape Girardeau fleeting area (mile 53.0 UMR) bound for the Gold Bond Building Products Wharf in New Orleans, LA (mile 102.0 AHP).

149. Your engines are turning for 8.2 mph. You estimate the current at 1.5 mph. What is your speed over the ground?

A. 9.7 mph
B. 8.8 mph
C. 8.2 mph
D. 6.7 mph

150. Which dayboard would you see on Putney Light (mile 943.6 AHP)?

A. green square
B. green triangle
C. red diamond
D. red triangle

151. What is the distance from the Memphis gauge to the Gold Bond Building Products Wharf in New Orleans, LA?

A. 460 miles
B. 503 miles
C. 588 miles
D. 633 miles

152. How long will it take you to go from the Memphis gauge to your destination in New Orleans, LA, if you estimate the average current on this segment of the route to be 2.0 mph and you increase the engine turns to 8.5 mph.

A. 1 day 20 hours 33 minutes
B. 2 days 6 hours 24 minutes
C. 2 days 12 hours 15 minutes
D. 3 days 4 hours 11 minutes

153. What is the minimum maintained depth of the channel from Cairo to Baton Rouge during low water?

A. 9 feet
B. 12 feet
C. 15 feet
D. 18 feet

154. You see a buoy with red and green bands. This buoy marks _____.

A. the center of the channel
B. the preferred channel

C. a channel crossing
D. an isolated danger

155. As you approach Old River Control Structure Light you see a flashing amber light. You should _____.

A. navigate as close to the left descending bank as safety permits
B. navigate as close to the right descending bank as safety permits
C. turn into the inflow channel as the bypass is now open
D. slow your engine speed to not more than 5 mph

156. What are the dimensions of the Old River Lock?

A. 110ft × 1190ft
B. 100ft × 990ft
C. 75ft × 1000ft
D. 75ft × 1190ft

157. At 1710 on 27 November, you are abeam of Kings Point Lt. (mile 439.8 AHP). At this time you receive a message that there will no be space for you at the Gold Bond Building Products wharf until after 1200 on the 29 November. What speed over the ground will you have to slow to so as not to arrive before this time?

A. 5.4 mph
B. 6.1 mph
C. 6.9 mph
D. 7.9 mph

158. Which daymark should you see as you approach French Point Light (mile 915.4 AHP)?

A. red triangle
B. green square
C. red and green rectangle
D. green diamond

The following questions are based on the C of E Mississippi River Maps (Hannibal, MO, to the Gulf of Mexico) and the Light List. You are making up your tow at the fleeting area at Cairo Point, IL (mile 980.8 Ohio River). At 0952, on 21 September, you get underway enroute to to New Orleans with a mixed tow.

159. You are turning for 6.8 mph and estimate the current at 1.0 mph. What is your speed over the ground?

A. 8.8 mph
B. 8.2 mph
C. 7.8 mph
D. 6.8 mph

160. How far is it to the Hernando Desoto Bridge in Memphis, TN?

A. 980.8 miles
B. 736.6 miles
C. 218.1 miles
D. 202.4 miles

161. At 1923, on September 21, you pass Bixby Towhead Light (mile 873.7 AHP). What was your average speed since leaving Cairo?

A. 7.8 mph
B. 8.5 mph
C. 8.8 mph
D. 9.2 mph

162. At 1923, you increase speed to make good 9.2 mph. What is the first gauge you will pass after your speed change?

A. Cottonwood Point
B. New Madrid
C. Fulton
D. Tiptonville

163. Which light will you be passing at 0059, on 22 September, if you make good 9.2 mph?

A. Kate Aubrey Lt.
B. Obion Bar Lt.
C. Trotter Lt.
D. Quaker Oats Lt

164. The Helena gauge reads 9.4 feet. The high point on your towboat is 42 feet above water. What is the vertical clearance when you pass under the Helena Highway Bridge?

A. 53.0 feet
B. 64.2 feet
C. 68.0 feet
D. 110.0 feet

165. Which company does NOT have a marine facility along the river bank in Helena (mile 661 to 665 AHP)?

A. Helena Grain, Inc.
B. Helena Marine Services, Inc.
C. Quincy Grain Co.
D. Texas Eastern Pipeline Co.

166. If the Bayou Sara gauge reads –0.5 feet, what is the water level in relation to the low water reference plane?

A. 0.5 foot below the plane
B. 0.5 foot above the plane
C. 5.25 feet above the plane
D. 5.75 feet below the plane

167. The Arkansas City Yellow Bend revetment on the LMR extends from mile _____.

A. 555.5-549.7 RDB
B. 549.0-548.5 RDB
C. 556.9-554.9 LDB
D. 548.5-546.5 LDB

The following questions are based on chart 12221TR, Chesapeake Bay Entrance, and the supporting publications. Your vessel has a draft of 10 feet (3 meters), and your height of eye is 20 feet (6.1 meters). Use 10°W variation where required. The gyro error is 3°E. The deviation table is:

HDG.	M.DEV.	HDG.	M.DEV.	HDG.	M.DEV.
000°	0°	120°	2°W	240°	3°E
030°	1°W	150°	1°W	270°	3°E
060°	2°W	180°	1°E	300°	2°E
090°	4°W	210°	2°E	330°	1°E

181. You are on course 192° pgc at 12 knots. You obtain a loran fix at 1900 using the following information: 9960-X-27120; 9960-Y-41623; 9960-Z-58729. What is your latitude and longitude at 1900?

A. LAT 37°21.5'N, LONG 75°34.8'W
B. LAT 37°22.0'N, LONG 75°34.9'W
C. LAT 37°22.2'N, LONG 75°35.0'W
D. LAT 37°22.6'N, LONG 75°35.7'W

182. What course should you steer using the standard magnetic compass (psc) to make good the course of 192° pgc?

A. 188° psc
B. 203° psc
C. 205° psc
D. 208° psc

183. At 1920, the buoy off your starboard bow is _____.

A. Sand Shoal Inlet Lighted Buoy A
B. Hog Island Lighted Bell Buoy
C. South Light Buoy
D. an interrupted quick-flashing buoy

184. At 1930, your position is LAT 37°16.7'N,

LONG 75°37.7'W. The depth of water is approximately _____.

A. 40 feet (12.2 meters)
B. 50 feet (15.2 meters)
C. 60 feet (18.3 meters)
D. 70 feet (23.2 meters)

185. At 1950, your position is LAT 37°12.3'N, LONG 75°38.6'W. The set and drift from 1930 to 1950 were_____.

A. 150°T at 1.6 knots
B. 150°T at 0.6 knot
C. 330°T at 0.6 knot
D. 330°T at 1.6 knots

186. Assume set and drift have no effect on your vessel. If you change course to 187° pgc from your 1950 position, how close will you pass Cape Charles Lighted Bell Buoy 14?

A. 0.1 mile
B. 0.5 mile
C. 0.8 mile
D. 1.1 miles

187. At 2020, you obtain a fix using the following information: 9960-X-27112; 9960-Y-41432; Cape Charles Lighted Bell Buoy 14 bears 333° pgc. Your longitude is _____.

A. 75°38.9'W
B. 75°39.1'W
C. 75°40.5'W
D. 75°41.4'W

188. At 2020, what is the course to steer to enter the inbound lane of North Chesapeake Entrance traffic separation scheme if a northwestly wind causes 3° of leeway?

A. 227° pgc
B. 221° pgc
C. 218° pgc
D. 215° pgc

189. At 0645, Watch Hill Point (left tangent) bears 316.5° pgc at 2.75 miles. What was the speed made good between 0600 and 0645?

A. 8.1 knots
B. 9.8 knots
C. 10.3 knots
D. 11.4 knots

191. If you make good 12 knots, what is the

ETA at North Chesapeake Channel Entrance Buoy NCA (LL #375)?

A. 2121
B. 2116
C. 2111
D. 2101

192. At 2100, Cape Charles Light bears 321° pgc, and Cape Henry Light bears 247° pgc. Your latitude is _____.

A. 37°00.6'N
B. 37°00.0'N
C. 36°59.7'N
D. 36°59.4'N

193. If the visibility is 3 miles, at what range will you lose sight of Chesapeake Light?

A. The light has never been visible.
B. 4.6 miles
C. 6.4 miles
D. 8.3 miles

194. At 2100, you alter course to 250°T and reduce speed to 7 knots. You enter the traffic separation scheme on the inbound side. At 2200, your fix shows you crossing a broken purple line on the chart, and you observe North Chesapeake Entrance Lighted Gong Buoy NCD to port. This area is _____.

A. an area with local magnetic disturbances
B. a pilotage area
C. a precautionary area centered on buoy CBJ
D. in inland waters

196. What course per standard magnetic compass (psc) is the same as 247° pgc?

A. 257° psc
B. 260° psc
C. 262° psc
D. 265° psc

197. At 2215, Cape Henry Light bears 242° pgc, Cape Charles Light bears 010.5° pgc, and Chesapeake Channel Tunnel North Light bears 319° pgc. You are heading 271° pgc. What is the relative bearing of Thimble Shoal Light?

A. 014°
B. 017°
C. 280°
D. 332°

198. While navigating inbound Thimble Shoal Channel system you must _____.

A. navigate in the main channel when between Trestles A & B
B. use the north auxiliary channel
C. remain 1500 yards (1360 meters) from large naval vessels
D. maintain a speed of six knots

The following questions should be answered using chart number 13205TR, Block Island and Approaches, and supporting publications. You are steering a westerly course and approaching Block Island Sound. The variation for the area is 15°W. The gyro error is 2°E. The deviation table is:

HDG.	M.DEV.	HDG.	M.DEV.	HDG.	M.DEV.
000°	0.0°	120°	1.0°W	240°	2.0°E
030°	1.0°W	150°	0.0°	270°	1.5°E
060°	3.0°W	180°	0.0°	300°	1.0°E
090°	2.0°W	210°	1.0°E	330°	0.0°

199. You are underway in the vicinity of Block Island and obtain the following lines of position: Montauk Point Light, 263° pgc; Block Island Southeast Light, 026° pgc; Radar Bearing to Block Island Southwest Point, 348° pgc. What is your position at the time of these sightings?

A. LAT 41°05.0'N, LONG 71°36.2'W
B. LAT 41°05.3'N, LONG 71°35.8'W
C. LAT 41°05.3'N, LONG 71°35.1'W
D. LAT 41°05.4'N, LONG 71°35.0'W

201. What course should you steer by your standard magnetic compass to make good a course of 280°T?

A. 294° psc
B. 290° psc
C. 272° psc
D. 266° psc

202. Which statement concerning Montauk Point Light is TRUE?

A. The light comes on at sunset.
B. There is an emergency light if the main light is extinguished.
C. The height of the light is 24 feet.
D. The tower is painted with black and white stripes.

203. At 1800, your position is LAT 41°06.5'N, LONG 71°43.5'W. How would the buoy which bears 030°T from your position at a range of approximately 0.5 mile be painted?

A. Horizontally banded, red over green
B. Horizontally banded, green over red
C. Vertically striped, red and green
D. Solid green with red letters BIS

204. From your 1800 position you steer a course of 350° psc at a speed of 10.0 knots. At 1830, your position is LAT 41°11.7'N, LONG 71°45.8'W. What are the set and drift of the current?

A. 029°T, 1.4 knots
B. 029°T, 0.7 knot
C. 209°T, 0.7 knot
D. 209°T, 1.4 knots

205. From your 1830 fix, you come left to a course of 290°T. Which of the following statements concerning Watch Hill Light is FALSE?

A. The nominal range of its white light is 15 miles.
B. It displays both red and white lights.
C. Its geographic range is 18.5 miles at a 35 foot (10.7 meter) height of eye.
D. Its horn blasts every 30 seconds in fog.

206. At 1850, you obtain the following bearings and distances: Montauk Point 189° pgc 8.7 miles; Watch Hill Light 340° pgc 5.7 miles. What true course did you make good between 1830 and 1850?

A. 293°T
B. 297°T
C. 299°T
D. 305°T

207. If your height of eye is 35 feet (10.7 meters), what is the approximate geographic range of Block Island North Light?

A. 7.4 nm
B. 13.0 nm
C. 15.8 nm
D. 17.5 nm

208. From your 1850 fix, you come left to a course of 280°T while maintaining a speed of 10 knots. Which of the following combinations of available Loran-C lines would be best for position determination?

A. 9960-X and 9960-Y
B. 9960-Y and 9960-W
C. 9960-W and 9960-X
D. All are equally good.

209. At 0705, you take the following bearings: Watch Hill Light, 034.5° pgc; Latimer Reef Light, 338.0° pgc; Race Rock Light, 268.0° pgc. What was the true course made good between 0645 and 0705?

A. 253°T
B. 256°T
C. 263°T
D. 266°T

211. You decide to use the 9960-Y and 9960-W rates. At 1915, you obtain the following readings: 9960-Y-43936.0; 9960-W-14653.3. What is your 1915 position?

A. LAT 41°13.0'N, LONG 71°54.1'W
B. LAT 41°13.0'N, LONG 71°53.9'W
C. LAT 41°13.2'N, LONG 71°53.7'W
D. LAT 41°13.4'N, LONG 71°53.4'W

212. If you were to head into Fishers Island Sound, which of the following charts would you switch to for better detail of Mystic and Mystic Harbor?

A. 13209
B. 13212
C. 13214
D. 13215

213. From your 1915 position, you come left and set a course for Gardiners Point. At 1930, your position is LAT 41°12.7'N, LONG 71°56.8'W. What type of bottom is charted at this position?

A. Blue mud, gritty shells
B. Buried mussels, gritty shells
C. Bumpy muck with grainy surface
D. Blue mud, gray sand

214. From your 1930 position, you plot a course to pass 0.5 mile due south of Race Rock Light. If your vessel's speed is 10.0 knots, the current's set and drift are 040°T at 1.8 knots, and a north wind produces a 3° leeway, what true course should you steer to make good your desired course?

A. 300°T
B. 295°T
C. 290°T
D. 280°T

215. As an option to heading into Long Island Sound, you consider anchoring in the vicinity of the Gardiners Point Ruins at the north end of Gardiners Island. What is the minimum recommended distance from the ruins for fishing, trawling, or anchoring?

A. 1.0 mile
B. 0.8 mile
C. 0.5 mile
D. 300 yards (91 meters)

216. NOAA VHF-FM weather broadcasts from New London, CT, are on _____.

A. 162.55 MHz
B. 162.40 MHz
C. 162.30 MHz
D. 162.25 MHz

The following questions are to be answered by using chart 12221TR, Chesapeake Bay Entrance, and the supporting publications. Your draft is 14 feet (4.2 meters). Use 10°W for variation where required. The gyro error is 3°E. The deviation table is:

HDG.	M.DEV.	HDG.	M.DEV.	HDG.	M.DEV.
000°	2.0°E	120°	1.0°W	240°	0.5°W
030°	1.0°E	150°	2.0°W	270°	0.5°E
060°	0.0°	180°	2.0°W	300°	1.5°E
090°	0.5°W	210°	1.0°W	330°	2.5°E

217. Your 1600 position is LAT 37°22.5'N, LONG 75°32.3'W. The depth of water under the keel is about _____.

A. 59 feet (17.3 meters)
B. 52 feet (15.8 meters)
C. 45 feet (13.6 meters)
D. 38 feet (11.5 meters)

218. If there is no current, what is the course per gyro compass from your 1600 position to point A located 0.5 mile due east of Hog Island Lighted Bell Buoy 12?

A. 199° pgc
B. 196° pgc
C. 193° pgc
D. 190° pgc

219. At 1630, you reach point A and come right to 204°T. Your engine speed is 12 knots. Your 1715, position is LAT 37°09.8'N, LONG 75°37.4'W. The current was _____.

A. 067°T at 1.4 knots
B. 246°T at 1.0 knot
C. 067°T at 1.0 knot
D. 246°T at 1.4 knots

220. From your 1715 fix, you steer 214°T at 12 knots. At 1800, you take a fix using the following Loran-C readings: 9960-X-27116.8; 9960-Y-41386.0; 996-Z-58620.6. Your 1800 position is _____.

A. LAT 37°02.7'N, LONG 75°42.7'W
B. LAT 37°02.9'N, LONG 75°43.1'W
C. LAT 37°03.0'N, LONG 75°43.3'W
D. LAT 37°03.1'N, LONG 75°42.8'W

221. At 1815, your position is LAT 37°01.0'N, LONG 75°42.7'W. If there is no current, what is the course per standard magnetic compass to arrive at a point 0.3 mile due north of North Chesapeake Entrance Lighted Whistle Buoy NCA (LL#375)?

A. 257.0°
B. 255.5°
C. 251.0°
D. 249.0°

222. From your 1815 position, you want to make good a course of 263°T. Your engines are turning RPMs for 12 knots. The current is 050°T at 1.9 knots. Adjusting your course for set and drift, at what time should you expect to enter the red sector of Cape Henry Light?

A. 1904
B. 1859
C. 1854
D. 1849

223. At 1920, Cape Henry Light bears 225° pgc, and Chesapeake Channel Tunnel North Light bears 288° pgc. If your heading is 268°T, what is the relative bearing of Chesapeake Light?

A. 206°
B. 213°
C. 215°
D. 220°

224. Which statement concerning your 1920 position is TRUE?

A. You are governed by the Inland Rules of the Road.
B. You are entering a restricted area.
C. You are within the Chesapeake Bay Entrance traffic separation scheme.
D. You can expect differences of as much as 6° from the normal magnetic variation of the area.

225. From your 1920 position, you change course to enter Chesapeake Channel between buoys 9 and 10. What is the course per standard magnetic compass (psc)?

A. 274° psc
B. 280° psc

C. 283° psc
D. 286° psc

226. At 2000, your position is LAT 37°04.1'N, LONG 76°05.6'W. You change course for the Eastern Shore. At 2037, Old Plantation Flats Light bears 033° pgc, and York Spit Light bears 282° pgc. The course made good from your 2000 position is _____.

A. 020°T
B. 014°T
C. 006°T
D. 359°T

227. At 2037, you change course to make good a course of 016°T. There is no current, but a westerly wind is causing 3° leeway. What course per standard magnetic compass (psc) should you steer to make good the course 016°T?

A. 022° psc
B. 025° psc
C. 028° psc
D. 031° psc

228. Your height of eye is 25 feet (7.6 meters). If the visibility is 5.5 nautical miles, what is the luminous range of Wolf Trap Light?

A. 17.0 miles
B. 16.0 miles
C. 12.0 miles
D. 7.5 miles

229. If you want a more detailed chart of the area at your 2115 DR position, which chart should you use?

A. 12222
B. 12225
C. 12224
D. 12222

230. At 2123, your position is LAT 37°20.0'N, LONG 76°03.0'W. What is your distance offshore of Savage Neck?

A. 1.7 miles
B. 2.6 miles
C. 3.4 miles
D. 4.6 miles

231. From your 2123 position, you are approximately 42 miles from Crisfield, MD. If you are making good a speed of 13 knots, at what time should you arrive at Crisfield, MD?

A. 0148
B. 0112
C. 0037
D. 2359

The following questions are to be answered by using chart 12354TR, Long Island Sound - Eastern Part, and supporting publications. Your draft is 11 feet (3.3 meters). Use 14°W for variation where required. The gyro error is 3°E. The deviation table is:

HDG.	M.DEV.	HDG.	M.DEV.	HDG.	M.DEV.
000°	2.0°E	120°	1.0°W	240°	–
030°	1.0°E	150°	2.0°W	270°	0.5°E
060°	0.5°W	180°	2.0°W	300°	1.5°E
090°	–	210°	1.0°W	330°	2.5°E

232. At 0700, Stratford Shoal Middle Ground Light bears 137° pgc. From your radar, you get a bearing of 007° pgc to the south tip of Stratford Point with a range of 4.5 miles. What is your 0700 position?

A. LAT 41°04.6'N, LONG 73°07.0'W
B. LAT 41°04.6'N, LONG 73°06.6'W
C. LAT 41°04.6'N, LONG 73°07.4'W
D. LAT 41°04.6'N, LONG 73°07.2'W

233. At 0725, you are heading 054°T, and Stratford Point Light is abeam to port at 3.1 miles. The current is 135°T at 1.8 knots. If you make turns for an engine speed of 8 knots, which course must you steer to make good 048°T?

A. 055°T
B. 047°T
C. 042°T
D. 035°T

234. Which structure should you look for while trying to locate Southwest Ledge Light?

A. White octagonal house on a cylindrical pier
B. White conical tower with a brown band midway of height
C. Conical tower, upper half white, lower half brown
D. Black skeleton tower on a granite dwelling

235. At 0830, you obtained the following Loran-C readings: 9960-X-26562.5; 9960-Y-44028.1. What is your vessel's position?

A. LAT 41°12.4'N, LONG 73°56.0'W
B. LAT 40°17.4'N, LONG 73°54.0'W

C. LAT 41°12.4'N, LONG 72°53.8'W
D. LAT 41°13.4'N, LONG 72°53.8'W

236. From your 0830 position, you wish to make good 097°T. There is no current, but a southerly wind is producing 3° leeway. What course should you steer per standard magnetic compass in order to make good your true course?

A. 109° psc
B. 112° psc
C. 115° psc
D. 118° psc

237. At 0845, you are on a course of 097°T, and Townshend Ledge Buoy 10A is close abeam to port. With a westerly current of 1.2 knots, what speed will you have to turn for from your 0845 position in order to arrive abeam of Six Mile Reef Buoy 8C at 1030?

A. 12.1 knots
B. 10.9 knots
C. 9.7 knots
D. 8.5 knots

238. At 0910, your DR position is LAT 41°11.9'N, LONG 72°47.8'W. Your vessel is on course 097°T at 9.5 knots, and the weather is foggy. At 0915, Branford Reef Light is sighted through a break in the fog bearing 318°T. At 0945, Falkner Island Light is sighted bearing 042°T. What is your 0945 running fix position?

A. LAT 41°11.1'N, LONG 72°41.2'W
B. LAT 41°11.3'N, LONG 72°41.3'W
C. LAT 41°11.5'N, LONG 72°40.7'W
D. LAT 41°11.8'N, LONG 72°40.2'W

239. What do the dotted lines around Goose Island and Kimberly Reef represent?

A. Depth contours
B. Breakers
C. Limiting danger
D. Tide rips

240. At 1100, your position is LAT 41°11.3'N, LONG 72°28.0'W. You are steering a course of 069°T to leave Black Point one mile off your port beam. It has been reported that the Long Sand Shoal Buoys and Hatchett Reef Buoys are off station. Which of the following will serve as a line marking the hazards and keep your vessel in safe water?

A. A bearing to Little Gull Island Light of not less than 090°
B. A Loran reading of more than 9960-Y-43985.0
C. Danger bearing to Black Point of not more than 064°T
D. A distance to Saybrook Breakwater Light of not less than 1.3 miles

241. Little Gull Island Light is _____.

A. lighted only during daytime when the sound signal is in operation
B. lighted throughout 24 hours
C. maintained only from May 1 to Oct 1
D. obscured by trees from 253°to 352°

242. At 1210, you are in position LAT 41°14.3'N, LONG 72°16.5'W. What is the depth of water below your keel?

A. 92 feet (28.0 meters)
B. 97 feet (29.4 meters)
C. 108 feet (32.7 meters)
D. 115 feet (35.0 meters)

243. From your 1210 position, you are making good a course of 083°T. Your engines are turning RPMs for 10 knots. The set and drift of the current are 310° at 1.7 knots. At what time should you expect to enter the red sector of New London Harbor Light?

A. 1243
B. 1254
C. 1259
D. 1305

244. Your vessel is entering New London Harbor Channel. If there is no current, what should you steer per gyrocompass to stay on the range?

A. 006°
B. 357°
C. 354°
D. 351°

245. On chart 12354, the datum from which heights of objects are taken is _____.

A. lowest low water
B. mean low water
C. mean high water
D. mean lower low water

246. The red sector of New London Harbor Light covers from _____.

A. 040°–310°
B. 000°–031°
C. 208°–220°
D. 000°–041°

The following questions are based on chart 12354TR, Long Island Sound - Eastern Part, and supporting publications. Your vessel has a draft of 8.5 feet (2.6 meters). Use 14°W variation where required. The deviation table is:

HDG.	M.DEV.	HDG.	M.DEV.	HDG.	M.DEV.
000°	0°	120°	2°W	240°	3°E
030°	1°W	150°	1°W	270°	3°E
060°	2°W	180°	1°E	300°	2°E
090°	4°W	210°	2°E	330°	1°E

247. What type of bottom is found at Long Sand Shoal?

A. Rocky
B. Muddy
C. Hard
D. Sandy

248. You are southeast of Saybrook Breakwater Light passing Saybrook Bar Lighted Bell Buoy 8. This buoy marks _____.

A. a sunken wreck
B. a bifurcation
C. the junction with the Connecticut River
D. shoal water

249. At 0005, on 26 January, your position is LAT 41°11.8'N, LONG 72°20.5'W. From this position, you plot a course to steer to Mattituck Breakwater Light MI with an engine speed of 9.0 knots. If there are no set and drift, what course should you steer?

A. 225.0° psc
B. 230.5° psc
C. 233.0° psc
D. 236.0° psc

250. At 0045, you obtain the following information: Radar range to Inlet Point is 1.4 miles; Radar range to Rocky Point is 2.8 miles; Radar range to Horton Point is 2.8 miles. What were the set and drift between 0005 and 0045?

A. 275° true, 0.9 knot
B. 275° true, 1.4 knots
C. 095° true, 1.4 knots
D. 095° true, 0.9 knot

251. You alter course from your 0045 position to head for Mattituck Breakwater Light MI. If the visibility is 10 miles and you make good 9 knots, at what time will you lose sight of Saybrook Breakwater Light?

A. 0100
B. 0123
C. 0131
D. The light is visible all the way to Mattituck Inlet

252. At 0100, you obtain the following radar ranges: Inlet Point—2.7 miles; Rocky Point—4.5 miles; Horton Point—1.0 mile. What was the speed made good between 0045 and 0100?

A. 6.7 knots
B. 7.2 knots
C. 8.0 knots
D. 8.7 knots

253. According to the DR track line from your 0100 position, how far off Roanoke Point Shoal Buoy 5 should you be when the buoy is abeam?

A. 1.8 miles
B. 1.3 miles
C. 0.8 mile
D. 0.2 mile

254. At 0130, you obtain the following radar ranges: Horton Point Light—4.3 miles; Mattituck Breakwater Light—3.45 miles; Duck Pond Point—2.0 miles. What were the course and speed made good between 0100 and 0130?

A. 236°T at 9.4 knots
B. 246°T at 9.8 knots
C. 259°T at 9.8 knots
D. 267°T at 9.4 knots

255. From your 0130 position, you change course to adjust for set and drift, and you later obtain the following loran lines of position: 9960-W-14975; 9960-X-26412; 9960-Y-43919. What is the latitude and longitude of the loran fix?

A. LAT 41°00.8'N, LONG 72°40.8'W
B. LAT 41°01.2'N, LONG 72°40.4'W
C. LAT 41°02.0'N, LONG 72°39.5'W
D. LAT 41°02.6'N, LONG 72°39.0'W

256. At 0209, your position is LAT 41°01.8'N, LONG 72°40.8'W. What course should you steer per standard magnetic compass to make good 278°magnetic? (assume no set and drift)

A. 262.0° psc
B. 265.0° psc
C. 270.5° psc
D. 275.5° psc

257. At 0705, you change course to head for The Race. You wish to leave Race Rock Light bearing due north at 0.4 mile. If the current is 110°T, at 2.8 knots, and you are turning for 12.0 knots, what course (pgc) should you steer?

A. 252° pgc
B. 257° pgc
C. 265° pgc
D. 271° pgc

259. The south coast of Long Island Sound between Mattituck Inlet and Port Jefferson is _____.

A. composed of high rocky bluffs
B. a high, flat plateau with sheer cliffs
C. low and marshy with isolated beaches
D. fringed by rocky shoals

260. At 0300, your position is LAT 41°01.7'N, LONG 72°55.1'W. From this position you steer a course of 289° per standard magnetic compass at an engine speed of 10.0 knots. At what time can you first expect to see Stratford Shoal Middle Ground Light if the luminous range is 8.0 miles?

A. 0318
B. 0312
C. 0309
D. 0303

261. You must arrive at your final destination by 0800. The distance from your 0300 position to the final destination is 40.5 miles. What minimum speed must be made good to arrive on time?

A. 9.6 knots
B. 9.3 knots
C. 8.5 knots
D. 8.1 knots

262. You are northwest of Port Jefferson Harbor steering 242° per standard magnetic compass. As you continue westward, you see that the Port Jefferson Range Front Light and Rear Light come into line. If the deviation table is correct, the bearing of the range should be _____.

A. 157° psc
B. 160° psc
C. 163° psc
D. 166° psc

The following questions should be answered using chart number 12354TR, Long Island Sound - Eastern Part, and the supporting publications. Your vessel has a draft of 9 feet (2.7 meters). You are turning for 7.5 knots. Your height of eye is 25 feet (7.6 meters). The variation for the area is 14°W. The deviation table is:

HDG.	M.DEV.	HDG.	M.DEV.	HDG.	M.DEV.
000°	0°	120°	1.0°W	240°	2.0°E
030°	1.0°W	150°	0.0°	270°	1.5°E
060°	3.0°W	180°	0.0°	300°	1.0°E
090°	2.0°W	210°	1.0°E	330°	0.0°

263. As you enter the New Haven Outer Channel, you sight the range markers in line directly over the stern. Your heading at the time is 155.5° per gyrocompass. What is the gyro error?

A. 1.0°E
B. 1.0°W
C. 2.0°E
D. 2.0°W

264. At 0720, you are in the outer channel between buoy 1 and buoy 2 and change course to pass Townshend Ledge Lighted Bell Buoy 10A abeam to port at 200 yards. What is your ETA off the buoy?

A. 0745
B. 0741
C. 0738
D. 0734

265. At 0740, you plot a loran fix from the following readings: 9960-X-26542.0; 9960-Y-44023.0; 9960-W-15027.0. What is your position?

A. LAT 41°12.4'N, LONG 72°51.5'W
B. LAT 41°12.6'N, LONG 72°51.8'W
C. LAT 41°12.7'N, LONG 72°51.9'W
D. LAT 41°12.2'N, LONG 72°52.0'W

266. From your 0740 position, you change course to pass 1.1 miles north of Falkner Island Light. What loran reading will ensure that you will remain clear of the 18' shoal located 1 mile NW of Falkner Island Light?

A. 9960 Y: not less than 44014
B. 9960 X: not more than 26452
C. 9960 W: not less than 14942
D. None of the above

267. At 0802, Branford Reef Light bears 348°T at 0.75 mile, and the north point of Falkner Island bears 088°T at 6.7 miles. What were the set and drift since 0740?

A. Set 040°T, drift 0.2 knot
B. Set 220°T, drift 0.2 knot
C. Set 220°T, drift 0.6 knot
D. You are making good your intended course and speed.

268. What publication contains information on the navigational hazards in the vicinity of Falkner Island?

A. The navigational regulations in Title 46, Code of Federal Regulations
B. U.S. Coast Pilot
C. U.S. Coast Guard Light List
D. Inland Navigation Rules

269. If there is no current, what is the course per standard magnetic compass from your 0802 fix to the position 1.1 miles north of Falkner Island Light?

A. 099°
B. 095°
C. 068°
D. 064°

270. At 0830, you wish to get the latest weather forecasts for the Falkner Island area. On what frequency would you set your FM radio for this information?

A. 2181 kHz
B. 162.40 MHz
C. 156.80 MHz
D. 156.65 MHz

271. At 0844, the range to the north end of Falkner Island is 2.0 miles and the left tangent bearing is 102°T. What is the approximate charted depth of the water?

A. 29 ft. (8.8 meters)
B. 22 ft. (6.7 meters)
C. 19 ft. (5.8 meters)
D. 14 ft. (4.2 meters)

272. At 0925, you plot the following loran fix: 9960-W-14931.5; 9960-X-26418.2; 9960-Y-44006.5. If you correct for a current setting 215°T at 0.5 knot, what course will you

steer from the 0925 position to arrive at a position 0.5 mile south of Long Sand Shoal West End Horn Buoy W?

A. 102°T
B. 096°T
C. 093°T
D. 089°T

273. If you correct for the current in the previous question (215°T at 0.5 knot) and maintain an engine speed of 7.5 knots, what is your ETA 0.5 mile south of buoy W?

A. 1014
B. 1018
C. 1021
D. 1026

274. At what approximate distance would you expect Bartlett Reef Light to break the horizon, if the visibility is 27 nautical miles?

A. 12.8 nm
B. 12.0 nm
C. 6.9 nm
D. 5.9 nm

275. At 1038, you are 0.4 mile south of Long Sand Shoal Buoy 8A on course 090°T when visibility is reduced to 1 mile in rain and haze. You intend to stay on 090°T until your Loran shows a reading that you can safely follow to the approaches of New London. Which of the following Loran readings will you look for?

A. 9960-Y-43980
B. 9960-X-26290
C. 9960-W-14730
D. 9960-W-14810

276. At 1200, your position is 2.0 miles southwest of Bartlett Reef Light. Your heading is 075°T. Visibility is less than 0.2 mile in fog and rain. Which of the following signals is most likely to be from another vessel?

A. Whistle from 125° relative
B. Bell from 350° relative
C. Whistle from 075° relative
D. Horn from 330° relative

277. What chart should you use after you enter New London Harbor?

A. 13211
B. 13214
C. 13213
D. 13272

The following questions are based on chart 12221TR, Chesapeake Bay Entrance, and the supporting publications. Your height of eye is 25 feet (7.6 meters). Use 10°W variation where required. The gyro error is 3°E. The deviation table is:

HDG.	M.DEV.	HDG.	M.DEV.	HDG.	M.DEV.
000°	0.0°	120°	2°W	240°	3°E
030°	1°W	150°	1°W	270°	3°E
060°	2°W	180°	1°E	300°	2°E
090°	4°W	210°	2°E	330°	1°E

278. The National Weather Service provides 24 hour weather broadcasts to vessels transiting the Chesapeake Bay Bridge Tunnel area on which frequency?

A. 162.55 MHz
B. 162.85 MHz
C. 181.15 MHz
D. 202.35 MHz

279. At 1752, your position is LAT 37°04.3'N, LONG 76°06.4'W. On a flood current you should expect to be set to the _____.

A. south southeast
B. south southwest
C. east southeast
D. north northwest

280. Your 1752 position places you _____.

A. less than 0.5 mile eastward of York Spit Channel
B. less than 0.5 mile westward of York Spit Channel
C. greater than 0.5 mile westward of York Spit Channel
D. greater than 0.5 mile eastward of York Spit Channel

281. What is the average velocity of the maximum flood current at the Tail of the Horseshoe?

A. 1.6 knots
B. 1.3 knots
C. 0.9 knot
D. 0.6 knot

282. From your 1752 position, you steer 307° pgc at 9 knots. At 1805, you obtain the visual bearings. What are the latitude and longitude of your 1805 position? Old Pt. Comfort Light 232° pgc. Chesapeake Bay Tunnel North Light 130° pgc.

A. LAT 37°05.9'N, LONG 76°08.0'W

B. LAT 37°06.0'N, LONG 76°08.4'W
C. LAT 37°05.9'N, LONG 76°07.7'W
D. LAT 37°06.1'N, LONG 76°07.5'W

283. At 1810, you sight a buoy on your starboard side labeled 19. This buoy marks_____.

A. the side of York Spit Channel
B. the visibility limit of the red sector of Cape Henry Light
C. the end of York Spit Channel
D. the junction of the York Spit and York River Entrance Channels

284. Based on a DR, at approximately 1817 you would expect to _____.

A. enter a traffic separation zone
B. cross a submerged pipeline
C. depart a regulated area
D. depart a restricted area

285. At 1845, you obtain a loran fix using the following information: 9960-X-27252.0; 9960-Y-41432.0; 9960-Z-58537.5. Your latitude is _____.

A. 37°10.7'N
B. 37°10.9'N
C. 37°11.2'N
D. 37°11.6'N

286. Your 1900 position is LAT 37°12.9'N, LONG 76°13.5'W. You change course to 317° pgc and slow to 8.0 knots. What is the course per standard magnetic compass?

A. 329° psc
B. 319° psc
C. 311° psc
D. 309° psc

287. If the visibility is 11 miles, what is the luminous range of New Point Comfort Spit Light 4?

A. 6.5 miles
B. 5.0 miles
C. 3.3 miles
D. 2.0 miles

288. According to your track line, how far off New Point Comfort Spit Light 4 will you be when abeam of this light?

A. 0.5 mile
B. 0.9 mile
C. 1.5 miles
D. 1.8 miles

289. At 1930, you take a fix using the following radar ranges: York Spit Light—3.6 miles; New Point Comfort Spit Light 2—2.0 miles; York Spit Swash Channel Light 3—2.5 miles. Your longitude is _____.

A. 76°16.2'W
B. 76°16.5'W
C. 76°16.8'W
D. 76°17.2'W

290. What was the speed made good from 1845 to 1930?

A. 6.2 knots
B. 6.8 knots
C. 7.5 knots
D. 8.3 knots

291. What is the height above water of Davis Creek Channel Light 1?

A. 15 feet (4.6 meters)
B. 17 feet (5.2 meters)
C. 19 feet (5.8 meters)
D. 24 feet (7.3 meters)

292. If you have 17.3 miles to reach your destination from your 2000 position and want to be there at 2230, what speed should you make good?

A. 6.9 knots
B. 6.5 knots
C. 6.1 knots
D. 5.7 knots

The following questions are based on chart 12221TR, Chesapeake Bay Entrance, and the supporting publications. Your vessel has a draft of 8.0 feet (2.4 meters). Use 10°W variation where required. The gyro error is 2°W. The deviation table is:

HDG.	M.DEV.	HDG.	M.DEV.	HDG.	M.DEV.
000°	0°	120°	2°W	240°	3°E
030°	1°W	150°	1°W	270°	3°E
060°	2°W	180°	1°E	300°	2°E
090°	4°W	210°	2°E	330°	1°E

293. At 1730, your position is LAT 37°13.9'N, LONG 76°26.4'W. You are steering course 088° per standard magnetic compass (psc) at an engine speed of 8.0 knots. What is your distance off Tue Marshes Light at 1730?

A. 3.2 miles
B. 3.0 miles

C. 2.8 miles
D. 2.6 miles

294. What is the maximum allowable speed of vessels underway up river from Tue Marshes Light?

A. 12 knots
B. 10 knots
C. 8 knots
D. 6 knots

295. At 1750, your position is LAT 37°14.5'N, LONG 76°22.9'W. What was the course made good between 1730 and 1750?

A. 081°T
B. 078°T
C. 075°T
D. 072°T

296. At 1800, Tue Marshes Light bears 264.5° pgc, York Spit Swash Channel Light 3 bears 007° pgc. Your position is _____.

A. LAT 37°15.5'N, LONG 76°19.8'W
B. LAT 37°15.2'N, LONG 76°20.3'W
C. LAT 37°14.5'N, LONG 76°20.1'W
D. LAT 37°15.0'N, LONG 76°20.4'W

297. What course should you steer per standard magnetic compass in order to navigate down the center of York River Entrance Channel (ignore set and drift)?

A. 149° psc
B. 145° psc
C. 141° psc
D. 139° psc

298. You have just passed York River Entrance Channel Lighted Buoys 13 and 14. The chart shows a light approximately 1.0 mile off your port beam with a light characteristic Fl 6 sec. What is the name of this light?

A. York Spit Light
B. New Point Comfort Shoal Light
C. Mobjack Bay Entrance Light
D. York River Entrance Channel Light 1

299. At 1930, your vessel is between York River Entrance Channel Lighted Buoys 1YR and 2. From this position, you change course to 142° pgc at an engine speed of 8.0 knots. At 2001, you obtain the following information: Chesapeake Channel Tunnel North Light—131° pgc; Thimble Shoal

Light—248° pgc. What were the set and drift between 1930 and 2001?

A. 127° at 0.5 knot
B. 127° at 1.1 knots
C. 307° at 1.1 knots
D. 307° at 0.5 knot

The following questions are based on chart 12221TR, Chesapeake Bay Entrance, and the supporting publications. Your vessel has a draft of 9.0 feet (2.7 meters). Your height of eye is 15 feet (4.6 meters). Use 10°W variation where required. The gyro error is 2°W. The deviation table is:

HDG.	M.DEV.	HDG.	M.DEV.	HDG.	M.DEV.
000°	0°	120°	2°W	240°	3°E
030°	1°W	150°	1°W	270°	3°E
060°	2°W	180°	1°E	300°	2°E
090°	4°W	210°	2°E	330°	1°E

313. At 1400, your position is LAT 37°14.7'N, LONG 76°22.3'W. From this position, you head for the York River Entrance Channel Buoy 17. What should you steer per standard magnetic compass for this heading?

A. 125° psc
B. 122° psc
C. 119° psc
D. 108° psc

314. At 1430, your position is LAT 37°12.8'N, LONG 76°17.7'W. At this time, you come left and steer 045°T. This course will lead you through a channel bordered by yellow buoys. The dashed magenta lines between the buoys mark _____.

A. York River Entrance Channel
B. Fish trap areas
C. The piloting channel for Mobjack Bay
D. New Point Comfort shoal area

315. From your 1430 fix, you order turns for 8 knots. You steer 045°T and experience no set and drift. At what time would you expect to have New Point Comfort Spit Light 4 abeam?

A. 1510
B. 1504
C. 1458
D. 1452

316. From your 1830 fix, you continue south on a course of 150°T turning RPMs for 6 knots. You encounter a flood current

in the direction of 330°T at 2 knots. Adjusting your course for set and drift, which course would you steer to make good a course of 150°T while turning RPMs for 6 knots?

A. 162°T
B. 158°T
C. 150°T
D. 144°T

317. Determine your 1915 position using the following information obtained at 1915. Visual bearings: Cape Charles Light—107° pgc; Cape Henry Light—172° pgc. Radar Bearing and Range: Chesapeake Channel Tunnel South Light—189° pgc at 7.2 miles.

A. LAT 37°03.5'N, LONG 76°05.9'W
B. LAT 37°03.5'N, LONG 76°09.3'W
C. LAT 37°09.3'N, LONG 76°03.1'W
D. LAT 37°09.8'N, LONG 76°04.1'W

318. From your 1915 fix you come right and steer a course of 200°T. At 2000, your position is LAT 37°05.5'N, LONG 76°07.0'W. Your intention is to pass through Chesapeake Channel. If there are no set and drift, what course would you steer per standard magnetic compass to make good a course of 145°T?

A. 156°
B. 151°
C. 139°
D. 134°

319. At 2100, you have passed through the Chesapeake Bay Bridge and Tunnel and determine your position to be LAT 37°01.3'N, LONG 76°03.0'W. The current is flooding in a direction of 303°T at 2.5 knots. Adjusting your course for set and drift, which course would you steer while turning RPMs for 6 knots to make good a course of 175°T?

A. 190°T
B. 183°T
C. 164°T
D. 156°T

320. At 2150, your position is LAT 36°57.2'N, LONG 76°01.3'W. In this position on the chart, you note a light magenta line running in a direction of 030°T. This line indicates the limits of _____.

A. a pilotage area
B. a precautionary area

C. the Cape Henry Light red sector
D. chart 12222

321. At 2200, you are in position LAT 36°57.5'N, LONG 76°02.5'W. You intend to travel up the Thimble Shoals auxiliary Channel to Hampton Roads. According to the Coast Pilot, what is the depth of the auxiliary channel on either side of the main channel?

A. 45 feet (13.7 meters)
B. 36 feet (11.0 meters)
C. 32 feet (9.8 meters)
D. 28 feet (8.5 meters)

322. From your 2200 fix, you steer course 288°T to travel up the Thimble Shoal North Auxiliary Channel. If you are making good 6.0 knots, at what time would you expect to pass buoy 18 at the west end of the channel? (There are no set and drift.)

A. 2355
B. 2344
C. 2335
D. 2324

323. At 2205, you are in Thimble Shoal North Auxiliary Channel abeam of lighted gong buoy 4. At this time the visibiliy decreases to 5 miles. You continue to turn RPMs for 6 knots and experience no set and drift. What time would you expect Old Point Comfort Light (white sector) to become visible?

A. 2258
B. 2246
C. 2240
D. 2230

324. The mean high water level at Old Point Comfort is _____.

A. 3.3 feet (1.1 meters)
B. 2.6 feet (0.8 meter)
C. 1.2 feet (0.4 meter)
D. 0

325. You are entering Norfolk Harbor and have just passed Craney Island. Which chart should you use for your final approach into Norfolk Harbor?

A. 12263
B. 12253
C. 12248
D. 12238

The following questions are based on chart 12221TR, Chesapeake Bay Entrance, and the supporting publications. The draft of your tow is 27 feet (8.2 meters). Use 10°W variation where required. There is no gyro error. The deviation table is:

HDG.	M.DEV.	HDG.	M.DEV.	HDG.	M.DEV.
000°	0°	120°	2°W	240°	3°E
030°	1°W	150°	1°W	270°	3°E
060°	2°W	180°	1°E	300°	2°E
090°	4°W	210°	2°E	330°	1°E

326. Your 0200 position is LAT 37°23.5'N, LONG 76°09.2'W. Your speed is 8 knots, and your course is 095°T. Which statement is TRUE?

A. The depth of the water in your vicinity is about 38 to 40 fathoms (69.1 meters to 72.7 meters).
B. The closest major aid to navigation is New Point Comfort.
C. You are less than a mile from a sunken wreck which could interfere with your tow.
D. You will pass through a disposal area on your present course.

327. At 0315, you obtain the following loran readings: 9960-Y-41588.0; 9960-X-27240.0. What is the true course from this position to the entrance of York Spit Channel?

A. 217°
B. 211°
C. 208°
D. 203°

328. From your 0315 position, what time can you expect to reach York Spit Channel Buoys 37 and 38?

A. 0423
B. 0417
C. 0412
D. 0405

329. The engineer has advised that it will be necessary to secure the gyrocompass and the electronic equipment. From your 0315 position, what is your course per standard magnetic compass to York Spit Channel Buoy 38, if there is no current?

A. 218° psc
B. 216° psc
C. 214° psc
D. 212° psc

330. Which chart could you use for greater detail of the area at the south end of York Spit Channel?

A. 12254
B. 12226
C. 12224
D. 12222

331. You leave York Spit Channel at buoy 14 at 0600 with an engine speed of 12 knots. You receive orders to rendezvous with the tug Quicksilver and her tow at Hog Island Bell Buoy 12. What is your ETA at the rendezvous point, if you pass through Chesapeake Channel to buoy CBJ, through the outbound traffic separation lane to buoy NCA (LL# 375), and then to the rendezvous point?

A. 0935
B. 0910
C. 0850
D. 0830

332. You arrive at the rendezvous point, secure the tow, and head back southward. At 1200, you take the following loran readings: 9960-Y-41534; 9960-X-27114; 9960-Z-58691. What is your 1200 position?

A. LAT 37°15.0′N, LONG 75°37.5′W
B. LAT 37°16.0′N, LONG 75°38.0′W
C. LAT 37°17.0′N, LONG 75°39.5′W
D. LAT 37°19.0′N, LONG 75°40.5′W

333. From your noon position, if there is no set and drift, what is your course per standard magnetic compass to the NCA (LL #375) buoy?

A. 221° psc
B. 219° psc
C. 217° psc
D. 215° psc

334. Your gyro and electronic gear are again operating. At 1710, Chesapeake Light bears 137° pgc at 6.6 miles. The current is setting 160°T at 2 knots. At your speed of 6 knots, what is your true course to steer to remain in the inbound traffic lane?

A. 250°
B. 261°
C. 265°
D. 269°

335. At 1810, you obtain the following loran readings: 9960-X-27158.0; 9960-Y-

41292.5; 9960-Z-58546.9. What is your position?

A. LAT 36°56.0′N, LONG 75°58.5′W
B. LAT 36°55.4′N, LONG 75°56.0′W
C. LAT 36°56.8′N, LONG 75°55.6′W
D. LAT 36°57.4′N, LONG 75°54.6′W

336. What speed have you made good from 1710 to 1810?

A. 6.3 knots
B. 5.5 knots
C. 4.9 knots
D. 4.2 knots

337. If you make good a speed of 6.0 knots from your 1810 position, what is your ETA at Chesapeake Channel Lighted Bell Buoy 2C?

A. 1900
B. 1855
C. 1845
D. 1833

338. You passed Cape Henry Light at 0730 outbound at maximum flood. What approximate current can you expect on entering Chesapeake Channel?

A. Slack before ebb
B. Slack before flood
C. Flood current
D. Ebb current

339. The coastline by Cape Henry is best described as _____.

A. rocky with pine scrubs
B. low wetlands
C. sandy hills about eighty feet high
D. low and thinly wooded with many beach houses

340. Inbound, the color of Cape Henry Light will _____.

A. alternate regardless of your position
B. change after you reach Chesapeake Channel Lighted Bell Buoy 2C
C. remain the same
D. change before you reach Chesapeake Channel Lighted Bell Buoy 2C

The following questions are based on chart 12354TR, Long Island Sound - Eastern Part, and the supporting publications. Your vessel has a draft of 12 feet (3.6 meters). Your height of eye is 16 feet (4.8 meters). The gyro error is

2°E. Use 14°W variation where required. The deviation table is:

HDG.	M.DEV.	HDG.	M.DEV.	HDG.	M.DEV.
000°	0°	120°	2°W	240°	3°E
030°	1°W	150°	1°W	270°	3°E
060°	2°W	180°	1°E	300°	2°E
090°	4°W	210°	2°E	330°	1°E

341. You are on course 082°T, and the engines are turning for 8 knots. At 0352, you take the following bearings: Stratford Point Light—016° pgc, Stratford Shoal (Middle Ground) Light—137° pgc. What is your 0352 position?

A. LAT 41°05.2′N, LONG 73°07.8′W
B. LAT 41°05.4′N, LONG 73°07.3′W
C. LAT 41°05.3′N, LONG 73°07.5′W
D. LAT 41°05.4′N, LONG 73°07.7′W

342. If the visibility is 11 miles, what is the earliest time you can expect to see New Haven Light?

A. The light is visible at 0352.
B. 443
C. 414
D. You will not sight the light.

343. While on a heading of 082°T, you sight Middle Ground Light in line with Old Field Point Light bearing 206° per standard magnetic compass. From this you can determine the _____.

A. deviation table is correct for that heading
B. variation
C. compass error is 17.5°E
D. deviation is 3.5°E for a bearing of 206° per standard magnetic compass

344. The maximum ebb current at a location 4.3 miles south of Stratford Point will occur at 0413. The predicted current will be 1.0 knot at 075°. What will be your course made good if you steer 082°T at 8 knots?

A. 087°T
B. 085°T
C. 083°T
D. 081°T

345. The characteristic of Branford Reef Light is _____.

A. flashing red every 4 seconds
B. flashing red every 3 seconds
C. flashing yellow every 4 seconds
D. flashing white every 6 seconds

346. At 0415, you take the following bearings: Stratford Point Light—329.5° pgc; Middle Ground Light—223.5° pgc; Old Field Point Light—199.5° pgc. Which statement is TRUE?

A. The current's drift is greater than predicted.
B. You are to the right of your intended track line.
C. The course made good since 0452 is 081°T.
D. Your fathometer reads about 76 fathoms.

347. If you change course at 0420, what is the course to make good to leave Twenty Eight Foot Shoal Lighted Buoy abeam to port at 1 mile?

A. 086°T
B. 084°T
C. 082°T
D. 079°T

348. At 0430, you take the following loran readings: 9960-X-26605.5; 9960-Y-43985.0. What is your 0430 position?

A. LAT 41°08.9'N, LONG 73°00.0'W
B. LAT 41°05.0'N, LONG 73°01.1'W
C. LAT 41°05.8'N, LONG 73°00.8'W
D. LAT 41°06.5'N, LONG 73°01.4'W

349. From your 0430 position, what is the course per standard magnetic compass to a position where Twenty-Eight Foot Shoal lighted buoy TE is abeam to port at 1 mile?

A. 101.5°
B. 098.0°
C. 086.0°
D. 082.5°

350. By 0430, the wind has increased, and the visibility cleared due to passage of a front. You estimate 3° leeway due to NW'ly winds. What is the course per gyrocompass to pass 1.2 miles due south of Twenty-Eight Foot Shoal Lighted Buoy TE?

A. 090°
B. 086°
C. 083°
D. 080°

351. At 0430, you change course and speed to make good 090°T at 10 knots. At 0433, you slow due to an engineering casualty and estimate you are making good 5.5 knots. At what time will Branford Reef Light bear 000°T?

A. 0624
B. 0620
C. 0609
D. 0601

352. What is the approximate distance to New Bedford, MA, from your 0530 DR position, if your 0352 position was 7 miles from Bridgeport, CT?

A. 122 miles
B. 115 miles
C. 104 miles
D. 95 miles

353. At 0550, engineering repairs are complete and speed is increased to 9.6 knots. At 0630, Falkner Island Light bears 023° pgc and Horton Point Light bears 097° pgc. From your 0630 fix you steer to make good a course of 086°T while turning for 9.6 knots. At 0700, Falkner Island Light bears 336.0° pgc and Horton Point Light bears 105.5° pgc. The radar range to the south tip of Falkner Island is 5.7 miles. Which statement is TRUE?

A. Your course made good from 0630 to 0700 was 082°T.
B. The speed made good from 0630 to 0700 was 10.1 knots.
C. You are making good your intended speed.
D. The current from 0630 to 0700 was 279°T at 0.6 knot.

354. The south shore of Long Island Sound from Horton Point to Orient Point is _____.

A. bluff and rocky
B. low and marshy
C. marked by sandy beaches and wooded uplands
D. bound by gradual shoaling

355. If visibility permits, Orient Point Light will break the horizon at a range of about _____.

A. 9.3 miles
B. 10.8 miles

C. 12.1 miles
D. 13.9 miles

The following questions are based on chart 12221TR, Chesapeake Bay Entrance, and the supporting publications. Your vessel draws 11 feet (3.3 meters), and your height of eye is 24 feet (7.3 meters). Use variation 10°W where necessary. The gyro error is 2°W. The deviation table is:

HDG.	M.DEV.	HDG.	M.DEV.	HDG.	M.DEV.
000°	1.5°E	120°	2.0°E	240°	0.0°
030°	1.5°E	150°	1.0°W	270°	0.0°
060°	3.0°E	180°	3.0°W	300°	1.0°E
090°	2.5°E	210°	1.0°W	330°	1.0°E

356. At 0410, you take the following bearings: New Point Comfort Light 2—242°T; Wolf Trap Light—313°T; Horn Harbor Entrance Light HH—262°T. What is your 0410 position?

A. LAT 37°20.9'N, LONG 76°07.7'W
B. LAT 37°21.0'N, LONG 76°08.1'W
C. LAT 37°21.1'N, LONG 76°07.9'W
D. LAT 37°21.2'N, LONG 76°08.2'W

357. If the visibility is 5 miles and you are in the red sector, at what distance off should you sight Cape Henry Light?

A. 9 miles
B. 11 miles
C. 13 miles
D. 15 miles

358. From your 0410 fix, what is the course per standard magnetic compass to the entrance to York Spit Channel between buoys 37 and 38?

A. 152°
B. 156°
C. 176°
D. 178°

359. You are turning for 9 knots, a westerly wind is causing 3° of leeway, and the current is 320°T at 1.2 knots. What true course should you steer to remain in the northern leg of York Spit Channel?

A. 203°T
B. 197°T
C. 194°T
D. 191°T

629

360. If you are making 8.3 knots over the ground, what is your ETA at the first turning point in York Spit Channel between buoys 29 and 30?

A. 0522
B. 0508
C. 0456
D. 0448

361. Which publication contains the specific information about navigating in York Spit Channel?

A. Coast Pilot
B. Light List
C. Chesapeake Bay Harbormaster's Regulations Manual
D. Navigator's Manual—Chesapeake Bay

362. At 0530, the Coast Guard announces that Chesapeake Channel is closed indefinitely due to a collision occurring in the channel between Trestle B and C of the Chesapeake Bay Bridge and Tunnel. You exit York Spit Channel, leaving buoy 20 abeam to port at 0.1 mile, and alter course to leave Horseshoe Crossing Lighted Bell Buoy abeam to port at 0.2 mile. What is the course per gyrocompass?

A. 193° pgc
B. 190° pgc
C. 187° pgc
D. 185° pgc

363. After you enter Thimble Shoal Channel, you will alter course to pass between Trestle A and B. Which channel should you use?

A. Thimble Shoal Main Channel or the South Auxiliary Channel
B. Any of the channels but keep to the right hand side
C. Thimble Shoal Main Channel
D. The South Auxiliary Channel

364. As you pass through the Chesapeake Bay Bridge and Tunnel, you sight Trestle A in line bearing 198° pgc. What is the gyro error?

A. 2°E
B. 0°E
C. 1°W
D. 2°W

365. You sighted Trestle A in line at 0707 and are steering 108°T. At 0731, Cape

Henry Light bears 136°T; Cape Charles Light bears 032.5°T; and Thimble Shoal Tunnel South Light bears 282°T. What was the speed made good between 0707 and 0731?

A. 9.4 knots
B. 9.2 knots
C. 8.8 knots
D. 8.3 knots

366. At 0731, approximately how much water is under your keel?

A. 26 feet (7.9 meters)
B. 31 feet (9.4 meters)
C. 48 feet (14.5 meters)
D. 54 feet (16.4 meters)

367. What is the distance from your 0731 fix to Wilmington, N.C. (LAT 34°14.0'N, LONG 77°57.0'W)?

A. 486 miles
B. 402 miles
C. 363 miles
D. 339 miles

368. You will enter waters governed by the International Rules when _____.

A. you cross the territorial sea boundary line
B. abeam of buoy CBJ
C. Cape Charles Light bears 022°T
D. you cross the boundary of the continuous zone

369. At 0812, you take the following loran readings: 9960-X-27155.2; 9960-Y-41267.9; 9960-Z-58537.8. What is your 0812 position?

A. LAT 36°53.7'N, LONG 75°56.0'W
B. LAT 36°53.8'N, LONG 75°56.1'W
C. LAT 36°54.6'N, LONG 75°55.8'W
D. LAT 36°55.2'N, LONG 75°55.4'W

370. At 0812, you are on course 132°T. The standard magnetic compass reads 135°. What should you conclude?

A. The deviation table is correct for that heading.
B. You should adjust the magnetic compass.
C. The deviation is increasing as you go south.
D. Your compass may be influenced by a local magnetic disturbance.

The following questions are based on chart 12354TR, Long Island Sound - Eastern Part, and the supporting publications. Your vessel has a draft of 10 feet (3.1 meters). Your height of eye is 35 feet (10.6 meters). Use 14°W variation where required. The deviation table is:

HDG.	M.DEV.	HDG.	M.DEV.	HDG.	M.DEV.
000°	0°	120°	2°W	240°	3°E
030°	1°W	150°	1°W	270°	3°E
060°	2°W	180°	1°E	300°	2°E
090°	4°W	210°	2°E	330°	1°E

425. At 0730, your position is LAT 41°10.5'N, LONG 72°32.2'W. From this position you steer course 286° psc with an engine speed of 9.0 knots. What is the approximate depth of water under your keel?

A. 67 feet (20.3 meters)
B. 62 feet (18.8 meters)
C. 57 feet (17.3 meters)
D. 52 feet (15.8 meters)

426. The broken magenta line which runs parallel to the shore between Roanoke Point and Mattituck Inlet marks a _____.

A. fish trap area
B. pipeline
C. demarcation line
D. cable area

427. Assuming no current, at what time can you expect to be abeam of Townshend Ledge Lighted Buoy?

A. 0910
B. 0905
C. 0902
D. 0859

428. At 0730, visibility is 5.5 miles. At what time will you lose sight of Horton Point Light?

A. It is not visible at 0730
B. 0733
C. 0751
D. 0812

429. At 0820, you take the following Loran-C readings: 9960-W-14978.0; 9960-Y-43993.5; 9960-X-26464.1. What are the set and drift since 0730?

A. Set 052°T, drift 1.1 knots
B. Set 052°T, drift 1.3 knots
C. Set 232°T, drift 1.3 knots
D. Set 232°T, drift 1.1 knots

430. At 0820, you change course to 301° psc and reduce speed to 7.5 knots. At 0900, you take the following visual bearings: Branford Reef Light—023° psc; New Haven Light—293° psc; Tweed Airport Aerobeacon—332° psc. Your 0900 position is _____.

A. LAT 41°11.9'N, LONG 72°50.6'W
B. LAT 41°12.1'N, LONG 72°48.6'W
C. LAT 41°12.3'N, LONG 72°47.7'W
D. LAT 41°12.5'N, LONG 72°44.3'W

431. At 0900, the current is flooding in a direction of 350°T at 1.2 knots. If your engines are turning RPMs for 9 knots, which course should you steer per standard magnetic compass to make good a course of 297° true?

A. 319° psc
B. 317° psc
C. 311° psc
D. 302° psc

432. Which chart would you use for more detailed information on New Haven Harbor?

A. 12371
B. 12370
C. 12372
D. 12373

433. What true course and speed did you make good between 0730 and 0900?

A. 271°T, 8.9 knots
B. 273°T, 8.7 knots
C. 277°T, 8.4 knots
D. 284°T, 7.5 knots

434. As you enter the New Haven Outer Channel, you sight the outer range markers in line directly ahead. Your heading at this time is 347° psc. What is your compass deviation by observation?

A. 4.5°West
B. 3.5°West
C. 3.0°East
D. 0.5°East

435. Which course should you change to per standard magnetic compass as you pass SW Ledge Light to remain in the channel?

A. 026° psc
B. 022° psc
C. 014° psc
D. 007° psc

The following questions are based on chart 13205TR, Block Island Sound, and the supporting publications. Your vessel has a draft of 11 feet (3.4 meters). Your height of eye is 32 feet (9.7 meters). The gyro error is 2°W. Use 15°W variation where required. The deviation table is:

HDG.	M.DEV.	HDG.	M.DEV.	HDG.	M.DEV.
000°	0°	120°	2°W	240°	3°E
030°	1°W	150°	1°W	270°	3°E
060°	2°W	180°	1°E	300°	2°E
090°	4°W	210°	2°E	330°	1°E

436. At 0227, you take the following radar ranges and bearings: Bartlett Reef Light—359°T at 2.4 miles, Race Rock Light—083°T at 4.1 miles. What is your 0227 position?

A. LAT 41°14.5'N, LONG 72°08.0'W
B. LAT 41°14.1'N, LONG 72°08.2'W
C. LAT 41°14.0'N, LONG 72°08.5'W
D. LAT 41°14.3'N, LONG 72°08.5'W

437. At 0227, you are on course 087°T at 10 knots. What course per standard magnetic compass should you steer to make good your true course?

A. 109° psc
B. 105° psc
C. 102° psc
D. 099° psc

438. You estimate that you are making 9.3 knots over the ground. At what time will you enter waters governed by the COLREGS?

A. 0258
B. 0255
C. 0251
D. 0247

439. At 0337, fog closes in and you anchor under the following radar ranges or bearing: South tip of Watch Hill Point—3.0 miles; East point of Fishers Island—1.4 miles; Latimer Reef Light—331°T. What is the approximate depth of water at your anchorage?

A. 135 feet (40.9 meters)
B. 120 feet (36.4 meters)
C. 100 feet (30.3 meters)
D. 83 feet (25.2 meters)

440. By 1015, visibility has increased to 5.0 miles and you can see Fishers Island. Fishers Island has _____.

A. sparsely wooded hills and is fringed with shoals to the south
B. sheer cliffs rising from the sea to a high, flat plateau
C. barren, rocky hills with prominent sandy beaches
D. low and sandy beaches with salt ponds and marsh grass

441. You get underway at 1030. The wind is out of the SSE and you estimate 3° leeway. What course should you steer per gyrocompass to make good a desired course of 075°T?

A. 080° pgc
B. 078° pgc
C. 076° pgc
D. 074° pgc

442. Shortly after getting underway, you sight Stonington Outer Breakwater Light in line with Stonington Inner Breakwater Light bearing 000° per gyrocompass. Which statement is TRUE?

A. The deviation is 2°W
B. The variation is 2°E.
C. The compass error is 16°W.
D. The gyro error is 2.5°W

443. At 1104, Watch Hill Point Light is in line with Stonington Outer Breakwater Light, the range to the south tip of Watch Hill Point is 2.6 miles and the range to the beach is 1.9 miles. You are steering to make good 075°T, speed 10.0 knots. At 1110, you change course to head for a position of LAT 41°05.0'N, LONG 71°50.0'W. What is the true course?

A. 193°
B. 190°
C. 187°
D. 185°

444. At 1110, you increase speed to 12 knots. What is your ETA at the new position?

A. 1220
B. 1215
C. 1208
D. 1157

445. You can follow what loran reading between your two positions?

A. There is no loran reading to follow.
B. 9960-Y-43958
C. 9960-X-25982
D. 9960-W-14655

446. At 1345, you depart from a position 1 mile due east of Montauk Point Light and set course for Block Island Southeast Light at 9 knots. At 1430, you take the following loran readings: 9960-W-14600.8; 9960-Y-43866.3; 9960-X-25912.3. What was the current encountered since 1345?

A. Set 015°, drift 0.5 knot
B. Set 195°, drift 0.7 knot
C. Set 015°, drift 0.7 knot
D. Set 195°, drift 0.5 knot

447. You are encountering heavy weather. What action should you take based on your 1430 fix?

A. Continue on the same course but increase speed.
B. Continue on the same course at the same speed.
C. Slow to 8.3 knots to compensate for the current.
D. Alter course to the right, to pass well clear of Southwest Ledge

448. At 2100, you set course of 000°T, speed 10 knots from LAT 41°07.0'N, LONG 71°30.0'W. Visibility is 5.5 nm. What is the earliest time you can expect to sight Point Judith Light? (Use charted range of 20 miles as nominal range.)

A. The light is visible at 2100.
B. 2106
C. 2111
D. 2123

449. You estimate the current to be 160°T at 1.2 knots. What should your course and speed be in order to make good 000°T at 10 knots?

A. 358°T at 09.8 knots
B. 358°T at 11.1 knots
C. 002°T at 11.2 knots
D. 002°T at 09.9 knots

450. If you want to put into Point Judith Harbor of Refuge, what chart should you use?

A. 13219
B. 13217
C. 13209
D. 13205

The following questions are based on chart 13205TR, Block Island Sound, and the supporting publications. Your vessel draws

8 feet (2.4 meters), and the height of eye is 20 feet (6.1 meters). Use 15°W variation where required. The gyro error is 3°E. The deviation table is:

HDG.	M.DEV.	HDG.	M.DEV.	HDG.	M.DEV.
000°	1.5°E	120°	1.0°W	240°	1.5°E
030°	2.5°W	150°	0.5°W	270°	2.0°E
060°	2.5°W	180°	0.0°	300°	1.0°E
090°	2.0°W	210°	1.0°E	330°	0.5°W

456. At 0630, you pass Buoy "PI" close abeam on the starboard side. You are steering 078°T and are headed directly toward Race Rock Light. At 0654, Little Gull Island Light is bearing 207°T and Race Rock Light is bearing 072°T. What is your 0654 position?

A. LAT 41°13.6'N, LONG 72°03.3'W
B. LAT 41°14.0'N, LONG 72°05.3'W
C. LAT 41°14.7'N, LONG 72°06.8'W
D. LAT 41°19.0'N, LONG 72°05.2'W

486. What is your speed from your 0630 position, with Buoy PI close abeam, to your 0654 position?

A. 11.4 knots
B. 10.5 knots
C. 9.3 knots
D. 8.2 knots

487. At 0700, your gyro alarm sounds. What course should you steer by the standard magnetic compass in order to maintain your original heading of 078°T?

A. 095° psc
B. 090° psc
C. 080° psc
D. 062° psc

488. At 0705, with your gyro again functioning properly, you change course to 096°T. At this time Race Rock Light is bearing 000°T at 0.35 mile. You are now governed by which Navigation Rules?

A. International Rules
B. Local Pilot Rules
C. Inland Rules
D. Coastal Fishery Rules

489. At 0728, Race Rock Light is bearing 282°T at 3.8 miles, and the closest point on Fishers Island is at a radar range of 2.1 miles. What speed have you been making since you changed course at 0705?

A. 11.4 knots
B. 10.6 knots
C. 9.9 knots
D. 9.2 knots

490. At 0728, you change course to 080°T. When steady on course, the standard magnetic compass reads 097°. Which statement is TRUE?

A. The magnetic compass error is 17°W.
B. The magnetic heading is 090°.
C. The deviation is 1.0°E.
D. The gyro course is 083° pgc.

491. At 0748, you take the following Loran-C readings: 9960-W-14651.0; 9960-X-26034.8; 9960-Y-43943.8. What is the approximate depth of water at this position?

A. 104 feet
B. 130 feet
C. 175 feet
D. 325 feet

492. At 0748, you change course to 160°T. What loran reading can you follow to remain on this course?

A. 9960-W-14660.0
B. 9960-W-14651.0
C. 9960-Y-43943.8
D. 9960-Y-43852.0

493. At 0815, Montauk Pt. Light House is bearing 167°T, Shagwong Pt. has a radar range of 4.5 miles, and Cerberus Shoal 9 Buoy is bearing 284°T. If the engine is making turns for 10 knots, what was the set and drift of the current since 0748?

A. Set 065°T, drift 1.1 knots
B. Set 065°T, drift 2.4 knots
C. Set 245°T, drift 2.4 knots
D. Set 245°T, drift 1.1 knots

494. What action should you take to compensate for the above current?

A. Continue on the same course and speed.
B. Alter your course to the right.
C. Slow to 8.5 knots.
D. Alter your course to the left.

495. At 0815, visibility is excellent and you can see Montauk Point. Montauk Point is _____.

A. low and rocky with scattered small pine trees
B. a low lying wetland
C. a high sandy bluff
D. a flat wooded plain

496. At 0815, you change course to 079°T and head for the entrance of Great Salt Pond on Block Island. To compensate for a northerly wind, you estimate a 5° leeway is necessary. What course should you steer per gyrocompass to make good 079°T?

A. 071° pgc
B. 074° pgc
C. 076° pgc
D. 079° pgc

497. At 0845, Montauk Pt. Light is bearing 205°T at a radar distance of 6.6 miles. What is your speed made good from your 0815 position?

A. 10.5 knots
B. 10.0 knots
C. 9.2 knots
D. 8.4 knots

498. As you head toward Great Salt Pond, visibility is unlimited. At what time will you lose sight of Montauk Pt. Light?

A. 905
B. 928
C. 950
D. It will remain visible to Great Salt Pond.

499. Which chart should you use to enter Great Salt Pond?

A. 13205
B. 13207
C. 13214
D. 13217

The following questions are based on chart 12354TR, Long Island Sound - Eastern Part, and the supporting publications. Your vessel has a draft of 12 feet (3.7 meters). Your height of eye is 24 feet (7.3 meters). Use 14°W variation where required. The deviation table is:

HDG.	M.DEV.	HDG.	M.DEV.	HDG.	M.DEV.
000°	0°	120°	2°W	240°	3°E
030°	1°W	150°	1°W	270°	3°E
060°	2°W	180°	1°E	300°	2°E
090°	4°W	210°	2°E	330°	1°E

500. Your position is LAT 40°59.0'N, LONG 73°06.2'W. What is the course per standard magnetic compass to New Haven Harbor Lighted Whistle Buoy NH?

A. 052°
B. 049°
C. 046°
D. 035°

501. You depart from the position in the previous question at 2114 and make good 12 knots on a course of 040°T. At what time will you sight New Haven Light if the visibility is 11 miles?

A. The light is visible at 2114.
B. 2152
C. 2159
D. 2166

502. At 2142, you take the following bearings: Stratford Point Light—331°T; Stratford Shoal Middle Ground Light—280°T; Old Field Point Light—223°T. What is your 2142 position?

A. LAT 41°02.7'N, LONG 73°01.2'W
B. LAT 41°03.0'N, LONG 73°01.7'W
C. LAT 41°03.1'N, LONG 73°01.3'W
D. LAT 41°03.3'N, LONG 73°01.9'W

503. What was the speed made good between 2114 and 2142?

A. 11.4 knots
B. 11.7 knots
C. 12.0 knots
D. 12.3 knots

504. At 2142, you change course to make good 030°T and increase speed to 14 knots. You rendezvous with another vessel and receive fresh supplies while off New Haven Harbor Lighted Whistle Buoy NH. What is the light characteristic of this buoy?

A. — .
B. — —
C. . . .
D. . —

505. At 0109 you get underway, and at 0112 you take the following Loran-C readings: 9960-W-15026.9; 9960-X-26536.9; 9960-Y-44015.7. What is your 0112 position?

A. LAT 41°11.0'N, LONG 72°51.0'W
B. LAT 41°11.4'N, LONG 72°51.3'W
C. LAT 41°11.6'N, LONG 72°51.6'W
D. LAT 41°11.8'N, LONG 72°51.8'W

506. At 0112, what is the approximate depth under the keel?

A. 57 feet (17.3 meters)
B. 51 feet (15.5 meters)
C. 47 feet (14.2 meters)
D. 38 feet (11.5 meters)

507. At 0112, you are on course 124°T and turning for 12.0 knots. What course will you make good if the current is 255°T at 1.2 knots?

A. 118°
B. 120°
C. 129°
D. 132°

508. Branford reef is _____.

A. a hard sand shoal marked with a light
B. completely submerged at all stages of the tide
C. surrounded by rocks awash at low water spring tides
D. a small, low, sandy islet surrounded by shoal water

509. At 0112, the radar range to Branford Reef Light is 2.9 miles. At 0125, the range is 3.6 miles. What is the position of your 0125 running fix if you are steering 124°T at 12 knots?`

A. LAT 41°09.3'N, LONG 72°48.7'W
B. LAT 41°09.7'N, LONG 72°48.1'W
C. LAT 41°09.8'N, LONG 72°47.2'W
D. LAT 41°10.2'N, LONG 72°47.7'W

511. At 0130, your position is LAT 41°09.3'N, LONG 72°46.9'W when you change course to 086°T. If you make good 086°T, what is the closest point of approach to Twenty-Eight Foot Shoal Lighted Buoy?

A. 1.2 miles
B. 1.1 miles
C. 0.9 mile
D. 0.7 mile

512. At 0200, you take the following bearings: Falkner Island Light—004.5°T; Kelsey Pt. Breakwater Lt.—054.0°T; Horton Point Light—115.0°T. What were the set and drift from 0130?

A. 260° at 1.0 knot
B. 080° at 0.5 knot
C. 260° at 0.5 knot
D. There is no current.

513. What is the distance from your 0200 position to the point where Twenty-Eight Foot Shoal Lighted Buoy is abeam to starboard?

A. 7.3 miles
B. 7.1 miles
C. 6.9 miles
D. 6.6 miles

514. The shoreline along Rocky Point should give a good radar return because _____.

A. the shore is bluff and rocky
B. of offshore exposed rocks
C. submerged reefs cause prominent breakers
D. the lookout tower is marked with radar reflectors

515. You depart LAT 50°06.0'N, LONG 153°06.0'E and steam 879 miles on course 090°. What is the LONG of arrival?

A. 175°56.0'E
B. 177°24.0'E
C. 178°36.0'W
D. 175°04.0'W

516. You sight Bartlett Reef Light in line with New London Harbor Light bearing 043° pgc. You are heading 088° pgc and 098.5° per standard magnetic compass at the time of the observation. Which statement is TRUE?

A. The true heading at the observation was 090°.
B. The gyro error is 2°E.
C. The magnetic compass error is 9.5°W.
D. The deviation is 1.5°E by observation.

The following questions are based on chart 13205TR, Block Island Sound, and the supporting publications. Your vessel has a draft of 12 feet (3.7 meters). Your height of eye is 16 feet (4.8 meters). The gyro error is 2°E. Use 15°W variation where required. The deviation table is:

HDG.	M.DEV.	HDG.	M.DEV.	HDG.	M.DEV.
000°	2.0°E	120°	1.0°E	240°	3.0°W
030°	3.0°E	150°	1.0°W	270°	3.5°W
060°	4.0°E	180°	2.0°W	300°	0.0°
090°	2.0°E	210°	3.5°W	330°	1.5°E

517. At 0520, you take the following observations: Point Judith Light—032° pgc; Point Judith Harbor of Refuge Main Breakwater Center Light—308° pgc. What is the position of your 0520 fix?

A. LAT 41°20.8'N, Long 71°29.7'W
B. LAT 41°20.6'N, Long 71°30.4'W
C. LAT 41°20.6'N, Long 71°30.0'W
D. LAT 41°20.5'N, Long 71°29.4'W

518. Point Judith Harbor of Refuge _____.

A. is used mostly by towing vessels
B. has a maximum depth of 14 feet at MHW
C. is entered through the East Gap or the West Gap
D. is easily accessible in heavy southerly seas

519. At 0520 you are on course 243° pgc at 12 knots. What is the course per standard magnetic compass?

A. 227° psc
B. 233° psc
C. 258° psc
D. 262° psc

521. The coastline between Point Judith and Watch Hill is _____.

A. steep with rocky bluffs
B. sandy and broken by rocky points
C. low and marshy
D. heavily forested

522. In clear weather, how far away will you sight Point Judith Light?

A. 14.0 nm
B. 12.3 nm
C. 10.6 nm
D. 9.2 nm

523. At what time will you cross the 60 foot curve if you make good 12 knots?

A. 0544
B. 0541
C. 0534
D. 0528

524. The two wavy magenta lines running to Green Hill Point represent _____.

A. recommended approaches to Green Hill Point
B. areas of unreliable loran readings

C. submarine cables
D. prohibited fishing areas

525. At 0600 your loran reads: 9960-W-14542.5; 9960-X-25909.5; 9960-Y-43950.0. What is your 0600 position?

A. LAT 41°18.3'N, LONG 71°38.7'W
B. LAT 41°18.4'N, LONG 71°38.0'W
C. LAT 41°18.5'N, LONG 72°38.1'W
D. LAT 41°18.7'N, LONG 71°38.9'W

544. From your 0600 position, what is the course per gyrocompass to leave Watch Hill Light abeam to starboard at 2.0 miles if a southerly wind is producing 3° of leeway?

A. 262° pgc
B. 258° pgc
C. 256° pgc
D. 252° pgc

545. At 0645, Watch Hill Point (left tangent) bears 314.5°T at 2.75 miles. What was the speed made good between 0600 and 0645?

A. 11.4 knots
B. 10.7 knots
C. 9.8 knots
D. 8.1 knots

546. At 0705, you take the following bearings: Watch Hill Light—030.5° pgc; Latimer Reef Light—329.0° pgc; Race Rock Light—262.0° pgc. What was the true course made good between 0645 and 0705?

A. 266°T
B. 263°T
C. 256°T
D. 252°T

547. At 0705, you change course to head for The Race. You wish to leave Race Rock Light bearing due north at 0.4 mile. If the current is 100°T, at 2.8 knots, and you are turning for 12.0 knots, what course (pgc) should you steer?

A. 267° pgc
B. 263° pgc
C. 255° pgc
D. 250° pgc

548. You are bound for New London. Where will you cross the demarcation line and be governed by the Inland Rules of the Road?

A. You are already governed by the Inland Rules.
B. Above the Thames River Bridge
C. In the Race
D. You will not be governed by the Rules.

549. In order to check your compasses, you sight North Dumpling Island Light in line with Latimer Reef Light bearing 074° pgc. The helmsman was steering 303° pgc and 315° per standard magnetic compass at the time. Which of the following is TRUE?

A. The true line of the range is 072°.
B. The deviation based on the observation is 15°W.
C. The magnetic compass error is 12°W.
D. The gyro error is still 2°E.

The following questions should be answered using chart 12354TR, Long Island Sound - Eastern Part, and the supporting publications. The draft of your vessel is 12 feet (3.6 meters) and your height of eye is 16 feet (4.8 meters). Gyro error is 2°W. "Per standard magnetic compass" is abbreviated "psc." Use a variation of 14°W for the entire plot. The deviation table is:

HDG.	M.DEV.	HDG.	M.DEV.	HDG.	M.DEV.
000°	0°	120°	2°W	240°	3°E
030°	1°W	150°	1°W	270°	3°E
060°	2°W	180°	1°E	300°	2°E
090°	4°W	210°	2°E	330°	1°E

551. You are on course 092°T, and the engines are turning for 8 knots. At 0452, you take the following bearings: Stratford Point Light—020° pgc; Stratford Shoal (Middle Ground) Light—141° pgc. What is your 0452 position?

A. LAT 41°05.2'N, LONG 73°07.8'W
B. LAT 41°05.0'N, LONG 73°07.5'W
C. LAT 41°05.0'N, LONG 73°07.3'W
D. LAT 41°04.8'N, LONG 73°07.3'W

552. If the visibility is 10 miles, what is the earliest time you can expect to see New Haven Light?

A. 0500
B. 0508
C. 0514
D. You will not sight the light.

553. At 0507, Stratford Shoal Middle Ground Light bears 208° pgc. What is the position of your 0507 running fix?

A. LAT 41°04.6'N, LONG 73°04.7'W
B. LAT 41°04.8'N, LONG 73°04.8'W
C. LAT 41°04.8'N, LONG 73°04.9'W
D. LAT 41°05.1'N, LONG 73°05.1'W

554. Based on your running fix, you _____.

A. have a following current
B. have a head current
C. are being set to the north
D. are not affected by a current

555. Your 0507 position is about 7 miles from Bridgeport, CT. What is the distance from this position to Newport, RI?

A. 114 miles
B. 101 miles
C. 95 miles
D. 88 miles

556. Your 0530 position is LAT 41°04.9'N, LONG 73°01.1'W. What is the course per standard magnetic compass to a position 1.0 mile south of Twenty Eight Foot Shoal TE buoy?

A. 099.5° psc
B. 096.0° psc
C. 092.5° psc
D. 082.0° psc

557. The south shore of Long Island Sound near your position is _____.

A. high with numerous cliffs
B. fringed with rock shoals
C. backed by marshes and wooded uplands
D. low and marshy

558. At 0530, you change course to 090°T and increase speed to 8.5 knots. What is the course to steer per gyrocompass if northerly winds are causing 2° of leeway?

A. 094° pgc
B. 092° pgc
C. 090° pgc
D. 088° pgc

559. At 0615, Stratford Point Light bears 292° pgc, Falkner Island Light bears 052° pgc, and Branford Reef Light bears 018° pgc. What was the current since 0530?

A. 083° at 0.9 knot
B. 083° at 1.2 knots
C. 263° at 1.2 knots
D. 263° at 0.9 knot

560. Which loran line can you follow to remain clear of all danger until south of New London?

A. 9960-Y-43960
B. 9960-X-26450
C. 9960-W-14900
D. 9960-W-15000

561. At 0615 you change course to 078°T. If there is no current, when will Falkner Island Light be abeam?

A. 0730
B. 0735
C. 0743
D. 0750

562. At 0700, Falkner Island Light bears 023° pgc, and the range to the south tip of Falkner Island is 7.1 miles. What was the course made good since 0615?

A. 087°T
B. 084°T
C. 081°T
D. 078°T

563. At 0705, the gyro loses power. At 0715, you are on course 092° per standard magnetic compass (psc) when you take the following bearings: Falkner Light bears 356° psc, Horton Point Light bears 123° psc, and Kelsey Point Breakwater Light bears 048° psc. What is the position of your 0715 fix?

A. LAT 41°06.7'N, LONG 72°36.0'W
B. LAT 41°07.0'N, LONG 72°36.2'W
C. LAT 41°07.2'N, LONG 72°36.4'W
D. LAT 41°07.4'N, LONG 72°36.4'W

564. Horton Point Light _____.

A. is 14 feet above sea level
B. has a fixed green light
C. is shown from a white square tower
D. is sychronized with a radiobeacon

565. If visibility permits, Little Gull Island Light will break the horizon at a range of approximately _____.

A. 18.0 miles
B. 15.6 miles
C. 12.8 miles
D. 11.1 miles

The following questions should be answered using chart 12221TR, and the supporting publications. The height of eye is 29 feet (8.8 meters). Your draft is 11 feet (3.4 meters). The gyro error is 2°W. "Per standard magnetic compass" is abbreviated "psc." Use a variation of 10°W for the entire plot. The deviation table is:

HDG.	M.DEV.	HDG.	M.DEV.	HDG.	M.DEV.
000°	0°	120°	2°W	240°	3°E
030°	1°W	150°	1°W	270°	3°E
060°	2°W	180°	1°E	300°	2°E
090°	4°W	210°	2°E	330°	1°E

566. Your cargo vessel is berthed near Lamberts Point in Norfolk. You are on a voyage to Baltimore, Maryland. Which larger scale chart should you use to show the area from Lamberts Point to Hampton Roads?

A. 12224
B. 12241
C. 12245
D. 12256

567. What is the distance from Lamberts Point to abeam of Thimble Shoal Lt. following the navigable channel?

A. 11.2 miles
B. 10.6 miles
C. 9.8 miles
D. 9.0 miles

568. You are delayed in sailing due to engineering problems. You get underway at 0630. A Coast Guard radio broadcast advises that an aircraft carrier will transit the Elizabeth River enroute to Norfolk Naval Shipyard and a safety zone is in effect. Further information on how far you must remain from the carrier found is in _____.

A. Pub. 117
B. Coast Pilot
C. Light List
D. Chart Number 1

569. At 0823, Old Point Comfort Light bears 000°T at 0.6 mile. What is your 0823 position?

A. LAT 36°59.8'N, LONG 76°18.0'W
B. LAT 36°59.5'N, LONG 76°18.4'W
C. LAT 36°59.0'N, LONG 76°19.6'W
D. LAT 36°55.5'N, LONG 76°18.6'W

571. At 0845, you are approaching the entrances to Thimble Shoal Channel. What channel must you use?

A. The South Auxiliary Channel or Thimble Shoal Channel, but you must remain on the right hand side of the channel.
B. The South Auxiliary Channel since your draft is less than 25 feet (7.6 meters) and you are not a passenger vessel.
C. The North Auxiliary Channel since you are going to turn to a northerly heading near buoy 12.
D. You are not permitted to use any of the channels, but must remain outside the buoyed channel line.

572. At 0908, you change course to 010°T. What course should you steer per standard magnetic compass?

A. 359°
B. 021°
C. 017°
D. 003°

573. Visibility has decreased to 1 mile in haze. At 0948, you take the following radar ranges: Thimble Shoal Light—5.9 miles; South end of trestle C of the Chesapeake Bay Bridge and Tunnel—3.8 miles; South end of trestle B of the Chesapeake Bay Bridge and Tunnel —5.4 miles. What course should you steer from this fix to the York Spit channel between buoys 19 and 20?

A. 010° pgc
B. 008° pgc
C. 004° pgc
D. 001° pgc

574. If you are making 10 knots, what is your ETA at York Spit Channel Buoys 19 and 20?

A. 0959
B. 1002
C. 1004
D. 1006

575. What is the course per standard magnetic compass on the southern leg of York Spit Channel between buoys 15 and 23?

A. 341°
B. 339°
C. 322°
D. 319°

576. What is indicated by the dashed magenta line crossing York Spit Channel between buoys 20 and 22?

A. You are crossing the demarcation line between the COLREGS and the Inland Rules.
B. The line indicates a submarine cable, and you should not anchor in the area.
C. The line marks the limits of a regulated area.
D. It marks the range between Ft. Wool Light and Cape Charles Harbor Range, Rear Light.

577. At 1015, you estimate you have 139 miles to complete the voyage. If you average 9.5 knots, you will complete the voyage in _____.

A. 14 hours 44 minutes
B. 14 hours 38 minutes
C. 14 hours 30 minutes
D. 14 hours 22 minutes

578. At 1008, you are entering York Spit Channel and buoy 19 is abeam to your starboard. What speed are you making good?

A. 9.9 knots
B. 9.7 knots
C. 9.0 knots
D. 8.4 knots

579. Which loran line of positon will serve as a danger reading on the loran to keep you west of the submerged obstruction at LAT 37°24.2'N, LONG 76°03.7'W, after you leave York Spit Channel?

A. Not less than 9960-X-27246
B. Not more than 9960-Y-41595
C. Not less than 9960-Y-41595
D. Not less than 9960-Z-58622

580. At 1037, you are on course 010°T at 10 knots, when you take the following loran readings: 9960-X-27243.8; 9960-Y-41497.6; 9960-Z-58575.9. What is your 1037 position?

A. LAT 37°15.9'N, LONG 76°07.9'W
B. LAT 37°15.9'N, LONG 76°07.7'W
C. LAT 37°16.1'N, LONG 76°07.4'W
D. LAT 37°16.3'N, LONG 76°07.2'W

581. At 1119, Wolf Trap Light bears 268°T at 4.4 miles by radar. What were the set and drift since your 1037 fix?

A. 358°, 0.7 knot
B. 358°, 0.5 knot
C. 178°, 0.7 knot
D. 178°, 0.5 knot

The following questions are based on the C of E Mississippi River Maps (Hannibal, MO, to the Gulf of Mexico) and the Light List. At 1215, on July 23, you get underway from the First Nitrogen Barge dock at mile 173.6 AHP enroute to to Racine, OH (mile 241.6 OR).

593. What is the length of the trip?

A. 1195.4 miles
B. 1223.1 miles
C. 1520.1 miles
D. 1657.8 miles

594. After you get underway, what is the first river gauge you will pass?

A. Head of Passes
B. Donaldsonville
C. Baton Rouge
D. Red River Landing

595. You are passing the Bayou Sara gauge which reads 3.9 feet. Which of the following statements is TRUE?

A. The river level is above the Low Water Reference Plane.
B. Red Store Landing Revetment is ahead on your starboard side
C. This gauge reading is at a lower elevation than the same reading on the gauge at Head of Passes.
D. None of the above.

596. At 0921, on 24 July, you are abreast the St. Catherine Bar Lt. (mile 348.6 AHP). If you are turning for 10.0 mph, what was the current since departure?

A. 1.4 mph
B. 1.7 mph
C. 2.0 mph
D. 7.0 mph

597. Which daymark will you see as you approach Natchez Beam Lt. (mile 364.8 AHP)?

A. red diamond
B. white square
C. green square
D. red triangle

598. At 1132, 24 July, you pass Natchez Beam Lt. (364.8 AHP). What is your ETA off the Memphis Gauge if you average 8.0 mph?

A. 2345, 25 July
B. 0525, 26 July
C. 0947, 26 July
D. 2215, 26 July

599. Which town is located at mile 663.5 AHP?

A. Helena
B. Friers Point
C. St. Francis
D. Rodney

600. What is the brown colored tint shown at Bordeaux Point Dykes (681.0 AHP)?

A. river gauge
B. fish hatchery
C. levee
D. dredge material

632. The Memphis gauge reads 18.4 feet. The high point of your towboat is 48 feet above water. What is the vertical clearance as you pass under the Memphis Highway Bridge?

A. 46.4 feet
B. 53.8 feet
C. 66.4 feet
D. 75.4 feet

633. The Linwood Bend revetment on the LMR extends from mile _____.

A. 828.1-823.1 RDB
B. 831.7-829.4 RDB
C. 841.3-838.0 LDB
D. 845.4-842.5 LDB

The following questions are based on the C of E Mississippi River Maps (Hannibal to the Gulf of Mexico) and the Light List. At 1914, on 21 June, you depart the Alton Barge Docks at Alton, IL (Mile 202.0 UMR), with a mixed tow of 6 loaded covered hopper barges, 2 loaded tank barges, and 2 empty hopper barges.

634. You have orders to drop off the empties at the fleeting area at Cairo Point and add five loaded tank barges to your tow. If you are turning for 9 mph and estimate the current at 1.5 mph, what is your ETA at Cairo?

A. 1031, 22 June
B. 1423, 22 June
C. 1741, 22 June
D. 2210, 22 June

635. You complete changing out your tow and get underway enroute to Ark City Tank Storage (mile 554.0 AHP) to deliver the tank barges. What is the distance you must travel from Cairo Point Light?

A. 606.8 miles
B. 554.0 miles
C. 400.7 miles
D. 202.1 miles

636. As you approach Dean Island Light (mile 755.7 AHP), which type of daymark will be observed at the light?

A. green triangle
B. red and green banded square
C. green square daymark
D. diamond-shaped green daymark

637. The highest point on your towboat is 48 feet above the water, and the Memphis Gauge reads +7.5 feet. What is the vertical clearance when you pass under the Hernando Desoto Bridge in Memphis?

A. 48.0 feet
B. 53.2 feet
C. 68.2 feet
D. 116.0 feet

638. What is the mile point of the Fulton Gauge?

A. 778 AHP
B. 687 AHP
C. 632 AHP
D. 598 AHP

640. Which of the following statements concerning the buoys on the Mississippi River is TRUE?

A. The position of river buoys can be determined by consulting the latest Light List - Vol. V.
B. A preferred channel mark is a lateral mark indicating a channel junction which must always be passed to starboard.
C. Setting a buoy is the act of placing a buoy on assigned position in the water.
D. None of the above.

641. At 1032 on 24 June, you pass Carolina Landing Light (508.8 AHP). What has been the average current since 2350, 23 June, if you have been making turns for 9.0 mph?

A. 0.5 mph
B. 1.5 mph
C. 5.7 mph
D. 8.5 mph

642. Where can scheduled broadcast times of river stages be found?

A. Sailing Directions
B. Light List
C. List of Lights
D. Coast Pilot

643. Which company does NOT have a marine facility in Rosedale harbor (mile 585 AHP)?

A. Sanders Elevator Corp
B. Rosedale-Bolivar County Port Commission
C. T.L. James
D. Cives Steel Company

The following questions are based on the C of E Mississippi River Maps (Hannibal, MO, to the Gulf of Mexico) and the Light List. At 0825 on 08 March, you get underway from the River Cement Co. (173.0 AHP), enroute to the Slay Warehousing docks (179.0 UMR) in St. Louis, MO, with a tow of eight barges carrying cement.

644. What is the distance from the River Cement Co. Dock to the mouth of the Ohio River?

A. 780.8 miles
B. 871.9 miles
C. 953.5 miles
D. 981.5 miles

645. As you pass under the Baton Rouge R.R. and Hwy 190 Bridge (233.9 AHP), the Ingram Aggregates facility is indicated by which numbered box?

A. 3
B. 8
C. 11
D. 15

646. You are turning for 9 mph, approaching Fort Adams Lt. (311.4 AHP) and it is reported that the current at Knox Landing is estimated at 4.5 MPH. Which of the following statements is TRUE?

A. You are making 13.5 mph over the ground.
B. The inflow channel is a navigable channel for any vessel.

C. Tows and other vessels should navigate as close to the left descending bank as safety will permit.
D. Old River Control Structure Light and Fort Adams Light may be used as range lights when entering the outflow channel.

647. At 0715, on March 9, you pass Knox Landing Gauge (313.8 AHP) and estimate the current will average 3.5 mph for the remainder of the time on the Mississippi River. What is your ETA at the mouth of the Ohio River if you increase speed to turn for 10 mph?

A. 0640, 11 March
B. 0554, 12 March
C. 1830, 12 March
D. 0943, 13 March

648. What is the vertical clearance between the highest point of your towboat, if it is 45 feet above the water, and if the Natchez Gauge reads 23.4 feet when passing under the Natchez-Vidalia Westbound Highway Bridge?

A. 45.0 feet
B. 52.2 feet
C. 57.1 feet
D. 67.5 feet

649. In high water conditions, which publication would you consult for the latest information on buoys between Baton Rouge and Cairo?

A. List of Buoys and Daymarks
B. U.S.C.G. Notice to Mariners Channel
C. Report C of E Navigation Chart
D. none of the above

650. As you approach Giles Bend Cut-off Light (367.7 AHP), which type of daymark would you see on the light structure?

A. green diamond
B. green triangle
C. red diamond
D. red square

663. At 1019, on 10 March, you pass under the Greenville Bridge (mile 531.3 AHP). What was your average speed since departing River Cement Co. Dock?

A. 6.2 mph
B. 6.5 mph
C. 6.8 mph
D. 7.2 mph

664. As you approach the Cahokia Marine Terminal Lights, you notice on the map a dashed line crossing the river at mile 178.3 UMR. This line indicates _____.

A. aerial crossings
B. 16 submarine power cables
C. 2 sub tel cables
D. 2-10′ gas pipelines

665. On which river is New Providence, TN, located?

A. Allegheny
B. Upper Mississippi
C. Cumberland
D. Ohio

The following questions are based on the C of E Mississippi River Maps (Hannibal, MO, to the Gulf of Mexico) and the Light List. On 9 September, you depart the Formosa Plastics mooring facility at mile 233.5 AHP with six loaded tank barges enroute to to the Alton Barge Terminal, Alton, IL, (mile 202.0 UMR). Your engines are making turns for 7.5 mph in still water.

672. What is the total length of the trip?

A. 922.3 miles
B. 985.3 miles
C. 1155.8 miles
D. 1187.3 miles

673. You estimate the current at 2.0 mph. What is the speed over the ground?

A. 3.5 mph
B. 4.5 mph
C. 5.5 mph
D. 9.5 mph

674. What are the dimensions of the Port Allen Lock at Baton Rouge, LA?

A. 75 feet × 1188 feet
B. 84 feet × 1188 feet
C. 84 feet × 1180 feet
D. 75 feet × 1180 feet

681. At 0119, on 10 September, you pass Springfield Bend Lt. (244.8 AHP) and estimate the current will average 2.5 mph for the remainder of your trip. What is your ETA at the mouth of the Ohio River if you are making turns for 8.5 mph?

A. 1746, 12 September
B. 1244, 13 September

C. 1244, 14 September
D. 2329, 14 September

682. As you pass under the Natchez-Vidalia Dual Bridge, the gauge on the bridge reads 8.9 ft. If the highest point on your vessel is 54 ft. above the water, what is your vertical clearance?

A. 60.0 feet
B. 62.6 feet
C. 67.2 feet
D. 122.0 feet

683. Which type of daymark would you see on the Belle Island Corner Lt. at mile 458.6 AHP?

A. green - diamond
B. green - square
C. red - triangle
D. red - diamond

684. At 1814, on 11 September, you pass under the Greenville Highway Bridge (mile 531.3 AHP). What speed must you average to arrive at Jimmy Hawken Light (mile 663.5 AHP) at 0930 the following day?

A. 8.9 mph
B. 8.7 mph
C. 6.3 mph
D. 5.6 mph

685. What company does NOT have a marine facility along the river bank in Madison Parish (mile 457.0 AHP)?

A. Complex Chemical Co.
B. Delta Southern Railroads
C. Baxter Wilson Steam plant
D. Scott Petroleum

686. The Vaucluse Trench fill revetment on the LMR extends from mile _____.

A. 534.3 - 532.6 RDB
B. 535.9 - 534.3 RDB
C. 535.9 - 534.3 LDB
D. 534.3 - 532.6 LDB

687. What is the distance from Greenville, MS, to Oquaka, IL, on the Mississippi River System?

A. 832 miles
B. 733 miles
C. 597 miles
D. 537 miles

The following questions are based on the C of E Mississippi River Maps (Hannibal, MO, to the Gulf of Mexico) and the Light List. At 1515, on 23 May, you get underway from the Amoco Pipeline Co. docks (253.6 AHP), enroute to to Pittsburgh, PA, with a tow of six barges carrying asphalt.

688. What is the distance from the Amoco Docks at Baton Rouge, LA, to Pittsburgh, PA?

A. 727.9 miles
B. 981.5 miles
C. 1575.3 miles
D. 1681.7 miles

689. You are turning for 10 mph and passing Hog Point, LA (mile 297.5 AHP). Angola reports that the current at Red River Landing is 4.5 mph. Which statement is TRUE?

A. The main channel lies on the south side of the island you see ahead.
B. You are making 14.5 mph over the ground.
C. An underwater stone dike has been constructed 0.5 miles upstream of Miles Bar Towhead.
D. You would expect to find the more favorable current near the broken red line in the river.

The following questions are based on the C of E Mississippi River Maps (Hannibal, MO, to the Gulf of Mexico) and the Light List. At 2345, on 25 December, you depart Vulcan Chemicals, Memphis Harbor, McKellar Lake (mile 726.0 AHP - LMR) enroute to to the Petroleum Fuel & Terminal Co. (144.6 AHP) in Angelina, LA, with a tow of eight full gasoline barges.

690. If your vessel is making turns for 7.5 mph with an estimated average current of 1.5 mph, what is your ETA at the dock in Angelina, LA?

A. 0516, 28 Dec
B. 1621, 28 Dec
C. 0516, 29 Dec
D. 1621, 29 Dec

691. The highest point on your towboat is 67 feet above the water, and the Helena Gauge reads +22.3 feet. What is the vertical clearance when you pass under the A-span of the Helena Highway Bridge?

A. 30.1 feet
B. 49.8 feet
C. 52.4 feet
D. 74.7 feet

692. Which of the following statements are TRUE?

A. Oil well structures are listed in the Light List.
B. All aids to navigation with lights have lateral significance.
C. On the Western Rivers, crossing marks may exhibit white lights.
D. all of the above.

693. At 0509, on 26 December, you pass under the Helena Highway Bridge (661.7 AHP). What has been the average speed of the current since departing Memphis Harbor, McKellar Lake, if you have been making turns for 7.5 mph?

A. 1.8 mph
B. 2.1 mph
C. 4.4 mph
D. 5.6 mph

694. What is the distance in river miles, from the new mouth of the White River to the Petroleum Fuel & Terminal Co. (144.6 AHP)?

A. 370 miles
B. 384 miles
C. 447 miles
D. 454 miles

695. The Platte River empties into which river?

A. Mississippi
B. Missouri
C. Ohio
D. Tennessee

696. You are downbound, passing by Warfield Point Lt. (mile 537 AHP), when you observe on your Mississippi River map a green diamond with an "SD" inside on the left bank below the light. This indicates a _____.

A. fleeting area
B. location for obtaining the latest safety directions
C. warning sign to downbound traffic that the channel soon crosses very close to the right bank
D. none of the above

697. As you pass under the Vicksburg Bridges, you estimate the current as 3.0 mph. What is the speed over the ground, if your vessel is making turns for 10.5 mph?

A. 7.5 mph
B. 10.5 mph
C. 13.5 mph
D. 16.5 mph

698. As you approach Buckridge Light (mile 411.5 AHP), which type of daymark would you see on the light structure?

A. red diamond
B. red triangle
C. green square
D. green diamond

699. The lighted mooring buoy at mile 228.7 AHP is a facility for which company?

A. Luhr Brothers
B. Cargo Carriers
C. National Marine, Inc.
D. International Marine Terminals

700. Which facility is located on the right descending bank at mile 363.6 AHP?

A. River Cement Corp.
B. Vidalia Dock and Storage Co.
C. T.L. James
D. Bunge Corp.

701. At 1118, on 24 May, you pass Natchez Gauge and estimate the current will average 3.0 mph for the remainder of the time on the Mississippi River. What is your ETA at Cairo, IL, if you continue to turn for 10 mph?

A. 0840, 26 May
B. 2218, 26 May
C. 2218, 27 May
D. 2339, 27 May

702. If the highest point of your towboat is 54 feet above the water and the Natchez Gauge reads 24.8 feet, what will be your vertical clearance when passing under the Natchez-Vidalia westbound Highway Bridge?

A. 35.9 feet
B. 43.2 feet
C. 46.7 feet
D. 57.5 feet

703. In high water conditions, which publication would you consult for the latest information on buoys between Baton Rouge and Cairo?

A. List of Buoys and Daymarks
B. U.S.C.G. Light List
C. C of E Navigation Chart
D. none of the above

704. As you approach Giles Bend Cut-off Light (367.7 AHP), which type of daymark would you see on the light structure?

A. green square
B. green triangle
C. red diamond
D. red square

705. At 1554, on 25 May, you pass Huntington Point Light (mile 555.2 AHP). What was your average speed since departing Amoco Pipeline Co. Docks (253.6 AHP)?

A. 6.2 mph
B. 5.2 mph
C. 4.8 mph
D. 4.3 mph

706. The solid lines extending into the channel at mile 948 AHP are _____.

A. revetments
B. dikes
C. spoil areas
D. Westvaco Service Facilities

707. What is the width of the widest span of the Cairo Highway Bridge (Upper Mississippi River mile 1.3)?

A. 503 feet
B. 625 feet
C. 675 feet
D. 800 feet

The following questions are based on the C of E Mississippi River Maps (Hannibal, MO, to the Gulf of Mexico) and the Light List. On 3 January you get underway from Hall-Buck Coke Terminal Dock, Baton Rouge, LA (mile 233.0 AHP) enroute to to the Mobile Oil Docks (east side), (mile 176.4 UMR), in St. Louis.

1117. What is the length of the trip?

A. 720.8 miles
B. 777.4 miles
C. 897.2 miles
D. 906.3 miles

1118. What are the dimensions of the Old River Lock on the Lower Old River (304 AHP)?

A. 1190 X 75 feet
B. 1185 X 84 feet
C. 1190 X 84 feet
D. 1185 X 75 feet

1119. At 2142, on January 3, you pass Sebastapol Light (mile 283.3 AHP). At 0137, January 4, you pass Fort Adams Light (311.4 AHP). You have been turning for 9.0 mph. What was the current?

A. 4.2 mph
B. 3.3 mph
C. 2.7 mph
D. 1.8 mph

1120. At 0850, 4 January, you pass the gauge at Natchez, MS, which reads 26.8 feet. How many feet is this above the low water reference plane?

A. 10.6 ft
B. 20.7 ft
C. 23.9 ft
D. 26.8 ft

1122. Which type of daymark will you see as you approach Old Levee Light (mile 385.2 AHP)?

A. green diamond
B. red square
C. green square
D. private aid - no daymark

1123. What is the vertical clearance of the Vicksburg Highway 80 Bridge when the river level is the same as the Low Water Reference Plane?

A. 128.3 ft
B. 125.6 ft
C. 119.5 ft
D. 116.1 ft

1124. The Vicksburg gauge reads 31.9 feet. The high point on your towboat is 43 feet above the water. What is the vertical clearance as you pass under the Vicksburg Highway 80 Bridge?

A. 36.2 feet
B. 41.3 feet
C. 58.0 feet
D. 84.3 feet

1125. Where would you find out which buoys, if any, are in place at Concordia Bar crossing (mile 596.0 AHP)?

A. Notice to Mariners
B. Bulletin board at the Rosedale gauge
C. Waterways Journal
D. none of the above

1126. Which type utility crossing is at mile 529.7 AHP?

A. 1-36" sub gas pipeline
B. 4-16" sub gas pipelines
C. 2-36" sub gas pipeline
D. 2-20" sub gas pipelines

The following questions are based on the C of E Mississippi River Maps (Hannibal, MO, to the Gulf of Mexico) and the Light List.
You are making up your tow at the fleeting area at Cairo Point, IL (mile 980.8 Ohio River). At 0952, on 21 September, you get underway enroute to to New Orleans with a mixed tow.

1127. You are turning for 6.8 mph and estimate the current at 1.0 mph. What is your speed over the ground?

A. 6.8 mph
B. 7.8 mph
C. 8.8 mph
D. 9.4 mph

1128. How far is it to the Hernando Desoto Bridge in Memphis, TN?

A. 980.8 miles
B. 736.6 miles
C. 312.3 miles
D. 218.1 miles

1129. Which daymark should you see as you approach French Point Light (mile 915.4 AHP)?

A. red diamond
B. green square
C. red triangle
D. green diamond

1130. At 1923, on September 21, you pass Bixby Towhead Light (mile 873.7 AHP). What was your average speed since leaving Cairo?

A. 9.2 mph
B. 8.8 mph
C. 8.5 mph
D. 7.2 mph

1131. At 1923, you increase speed to make good 9.2 mph. What is the first gauge you will pass after your speed change?

A. Cottonwood Point
B. Tiptonville
C. Fulton
D. New Madrid

1132. Which light will you be passing at 0059, on 22 September, if you make good 9.2 knots?

A. Obion Bar Lt.
B. Kate Aubrey Lt.
C. Trotter Lt.
D. Quaker Oats Lt

1133. The Helena gauge reads 9.4 feet. The high point on your towboat is 42 feet above water. What is the vertical clearance when you pass under the Helena Highway Bridge?

A. 53.0 feet
B. 62.6 feet
C. 64.2 feet
D. 68.0 feet

1134. What company does NOT have a marine facility along the river bank in Helena (mile 661 to 665 AHP)?

A. Helena Marine Services, Inc.
B. Riceland Food Corp.
C. Quincy Grain Co.
D. Texas Eastern Pipeline Co.

1135. If the Bayou Sara gauge reads –0.5 feet, what is the water level in relation to the low water reference plane?

A. 4.75 feet above the plane
B. 5.75 feet above the plane
C. 5.75 feet below the plane
D. 4.75 feet below the plane

1136. The Arkansas City Yellow Bend revetment on the LMR extends from mile _____.

A. 555.5-549.7 RDB
B. 549.0-548.5 RDB
C. 556.9-554.9 LDB
D. 548.5-546.5 LDB

The following questions are based on the C of E Mississippi River Maps (Hannibal, MO, to the Gulf of Mexico) and the Light List. At 1215, on May 23, you get underway from The First

Nitrogen Barge dock at mile 173.6 AHP enroute to to Racine, OH (mile 241.6 OR).

1137. What is the length of the trip?

A. 1195.4 miles
B. 1223.1 miles
C. 1464.8 miles
D. 1520.1 miles

1138. After you get underway, what is the first river gauge you will pass?

A. Donaldsonville
B. Head of Passes
C. Baton Rouge
D. Red River Landing

1139. You are passing the Bayou Sara gauge which reads 3.9 feet. Which of the following statements is TRUE?

A. The river level is above the Low Water Reference Plane.
B. Red Store Landing Revetment is ahead on your starboard side.
C. This gauge reading is at a lower elevation than the same reading on the gauge at Head of Passes.
D. none of the above.

1140. At 0921, on 24 May, you are abreast the St. Catherine Bar Lt. (mile 348.6 AHP). If you are turning for 10.0 mph, what was the current since departure?

A. 3.4 mph
B. 2.0 mph
C. 1.7 mph
D. 1.4 mph

1141. Which daymark will you see as you approach Natchez Beam Lt. (mile 364.8 AHP)?

A. red triangle
B. white square
C. green square
D. red diamond

1142. At 1132, 24 May, you pass Natchez Beam Lt. (364.8 AHP). What is your ETA off the Memphis Gauge if you average 8.0 mph?

A. 2345, 25 May
B. 0947, 26 May
C. 1525, 26 May
D. 2215, 26 May

1143. Which town is located at mile 663.5 AHP?

A. Friers Point
B. Helena
C. St. Francis
D. Rodney

1144. What is the brown colored tint shown at Bordeaux Point Dykes (681.0 AHP)?

A. river gauge
B. fish hatchery
C. dredge material
D. levee

1145. The Memphis gauge reads 18.4 feet. The high point of your towboat is 48 feet above water. What is the vertical clearance as you pass under the Memphis Highway Bridge?

A. 75.4 feet
B. 66.4 feet
C. 53.8 feet
D. 46.4 feet

1146. The Linwood Bend revetment on the LMR extends from mile _____.

A. 828.1-823.1 RDB
B. 831.7-829.4 RDB
C. 845.4-842.5 LDB
D. 841.3-838.0 LDB

The following questions are based on the C of E Mississippi River Maps (Hannibal to the Gulf of Mexico) and the Light List. At 1914, on 21 June, you depart the Alton Barge Docks at Alton, IL (mile 202.0 UMR), with a mixed tow of 6 loaded covered hopper barges, 2 loaded tank barges, and 2 empty hopper barges.

1147. You have orders to drop off the empties at the fleeting area at Cairo Point and add five loaded tank barges to your tow. If you are turning for 9 mph and estimate the current at 1.5 mph, what is your ETA at Cairo?

A. 2210, 22 June
B. 1741, 22 June
C. 1423, 22 June
D. 1031, 22 June

1148. You complete changing out your tow and get underway enroute to Ark City Tank Storage (mile 554.0 AHP) to deliver the tank barges. What is the distance you must travel from Cairo Point Light?

A. 202.1 miles
B. 400.7 miles
C. 554.2 miles
D. 605.8 miles

1149. As you approach Dean Island Light (mile 755.7 AHP), which type of daymark will be observed at the light?

A. green triangle
B. green diamond
C. green square
D. red-and-green banded square

1150. The highest point on your towboat is 48 feet above the water, and the Memphis Gauge reads +7.5 feet. What is the vertical clearance when you pass under the Hernando Desoto Bridge in Memphis?

A. 53.2 feet
B. 58.1 feet
C. 68.2 feet
D. 96.3 feet

1163. What is the mile point of the Fulton Gauge?

A. 598 AHP
B. 632 AHP
C. 687 AHP
D. 778 AHP

1164. At 0230 on 13 August, you are at mile 610.5 AHP when you see about a mile ahead lights on the water near the left bank. What might you see when you come abreast of these lights?

A. privately maintained buoys at a yacht club
B. government buoys marking the Hurricane Point dikes
C. barges moored at the Dennis Landing Terminal
D. a pipeline discharging dredge spoil

1165. Which of the following statements concerning the buoys on the Mississippi River is TRUE?

A. The position of river buoys can be determined by consulting the latest Light List - Vol. V.
B. A preferred channel mark is a lateral mark indicating a channel junction which must always be passed to starboard.
C. Buoys should be passed as close as possible.
D. Setting a buoy is the act of placing a buoy on assigned position in the water.

1166. At 1032 on 24 June, you pass Carolina Landing Light (508.8 AHP). What has been the average current since 2350, 23 June, if you have been making turns for 9.0 mph?

A. 8.5 mph
B. 5.7 mph
C. 1.5 mph
D. 0.5 mph

1167. Where can scheduled broadcast times of river stages be found?

A. Sailing Directions
B. List of Lights
C. Light List
D. Coast Pilot

1168. Which company does NOT have a marine facility in Rosedale harbor (mile 585 AHP)?

A. T.L. James
B. Rosedale-Bolivar County Port
C. Commission Cives Steel Company
D. Sanders Elevator Corp

The following questions are based on the C of E Mississippi River Maps (Hannibal, MO, to the Gulf of Mexico) and the Light List. At 0825 on 08 March, you get underway from the River Cement Co. (173.0 AHP), enroute to The Slay Warehousing docks (179.0 UMR) in St. Louis, MO, with a tow of eight barges carrying cement.

1169. What is the distance from the River Cement Co. Dock to the mouth of the Ohio River?

A. 718.8 miles
B. 780.8 miles
C. 953.5 miles
D. 981.5 miles

1170. As you pass under the Baton Rouge R.R. and Hwy 190 Bridge (233.9 AHP), you find that the Ingram Aggregates facility is indicated by which numbered box?

A. 8
B. 6
C. 5
D. 2

1171. You are turning for 9 mph, approaching Fort Adams Lt (311.4 AHP) and it is reported that the current at Knox Landing is estimated at 4.5 MPH. Which of the following statements is TRUE?

A. Tows and other vessels should navigate as close to the left descending bank as safety will permit.
B. The inflow channel is a navigable channel for any vessel.
C. You are making 13.5 mph over the ground.
D. Old River Control Structure Light and Fort Adams Light may be used as range lights when entering the outflow channel.

1172. At 0715, on March 9, you pass Knox Landing Gauge (313.8 AHP) and estimate the current will average 3.5 mph for the remainder of the time on the Mississippi River. What is your ETA at the mouth of the Ohio River if you increase speed to turn for 10 mph?

A. 0640, 11 March
B. 0554, 12 March
C. 0943, 13 March
D. 1242, 13 March

1173. What is the vertical clearance between the highest point of your towboat, if it is 45 feet above the water, and if the Natchez Gauge reads 23.4 feet when passing under the Natchez-Vidalia Westbound Highway Bridge?

A. 67.5 feet
B. 57.1 feet
C. 52.2 feet
D. 45.2 feet

1174. In high water conditions, which publication would you consult for the latest information on buoys between Baton Rouge and Cairo?

A. List of Buoys and Daymarks
B. Coast Pilot
C. C of E Navigation Chart
D. U.S.C.G. Notice to Mariners

1219. As you approach Buckridge Light (mile 411.5 AHP), which type of daymark would you see on the light structure?

A. red square
B. green triangle
C. red diamond
D. green diamond

1220. Anchorage regulations for this area may be obtained from _____.

A. Chesapeake Bay Port Authority, Hampton, VA
B. Virginia–Maryland Pilots Association

C. Office of the Commander 5th Coast Guard District
D. Commanding General, Corps of Engineers, Washington, D.C.

1221. At 1019, on 10 March, you pass under the Greenville Bridge (mile 531.3 AHP). What was your average speed since departing River Cement Co. Dock?

A. 7.2 mph
B. 6.8 mph
C. 6.5 mph
D. 6.2 mph

1222. As you approach the Cahokia Marine Terminal Lights, you notice on the map a dashed line crossing the river at mile 178.3 UMR. This line indicates _____.

A. aerial crossings
B. 2 sub tel cables
C. 16 submarine power cables
D. 2-10′ gas pipelines

1223. On which river is New Providence, TN, located?

A. Allegheny
B. Upper Mississippi
C. Ohio
D. Cumberland

The following questions are based on the C of E Mississippi River Maps (Hannibal, MO, to the Gulf of Mexico) and the Light List. On 9 September, you depart the Formosa Plastics mooring facility at mile 233.5 AHP with six loaded tank barges enroute to to the Alton Barge Terminal, Alton, IL, (mile 202.0 UMR). Your engines are making turns for 7.5 mph in still water.

1224. What is the total length of the trip?

A. 906.3 miles
B. 922.3 miles
C. 1155.8 miles
D. 1187.3 miles

1225. You estimate the current at 2.0 mph. What is the speed over the ground?

A. 9.5 mph
B. 5.5 mph
C. 5.0 mph
D. 4.5 mph

1226. What are the dimensions of the Port Allen Lock at Baton Rouge, LA?

A. 75 feet × 1188 feet
B. 84 feet × 1180feet
C. 84 feet × 1188 feet
D. 75 feet × 1180 feet

1227. At 0119, on 10 September, you pass Springfield Bend Lt. (244.8 AHP) and estimate the current will average 2.5 mph for the remainder of your trip. What is your ETA at the mouth of the Ohio River if you are making turns for 8.5 mph?

A. 1746, 12 September
B. 1244, 13 September
C. 2329, 14 September
D. 0210, 15 September

1228. As you pass under the Natchez-Vidalia Dual Bridge, the gauge on

the bridge reads 8.9 ft. If the highest point on your vessel is 54 ft. above the water, what is your vertical clearance?
A. 62.6 feet
B. 65.3 feet
C. 67.2 feet
D. 122.0 feet

1229. Which type of daymark would you see on the Belle Island Corner Lt. at mile 458.6 AHP?

A. green - diamond
B. B. green - square
C. red - diamond
D. red - triangle

1230. At 1814, on 11 September, you pass under the Greenville Highway Bridge (mile 531.3 AHP). What speed must you average to arrive at Jimmy Hawken Light (mile 663.5 AHP) at 0930 the following day?

A. 8.7 mph
B. 7.7 mph
C. 6.3 mph
D. 5.6 mph

1231. Which company does NOT have a marine facility along the river bank in Madison Parish (mile 457.0 AHP)?

A. Complex Chemical Co.
B. Delta Southern Railroads
C. Scott Petroleum
D. Baxter Wilson Steam plant

1232. The Vaucluse Trench fill revetment on the LMR extends from mile _____.

A. 524.3–522.6 RDB
B. 534.3–532.6 RDB
C. 535.9–534.3 LDB
D. 534.3–532.6 LDB

1233. What is the distance from Greenville, MS, to Oquawka, IL, on the Mississippi River System?

A. 537 miles
B. 597 miles
C. 733 miles
D. 832 miles

The following questions are based on the C of E Mississippi River Maps (Hannibal, MO, to the Gulf of Mexico) and the Light List. At 1515, on 23 May, you get underway from the Amoco Pipeline Co. docks (253.6 AHP), enroute to to Pittsburgh, PA, with a tow of six barges carrying asphalt.

1234. What is the distance from the Amoco Docks at Baton Rouge, LA, to Pittsburgh, PA?

A. 1681.7 miles
B. 1575.3 miles
C. 981.7 miles
D. 727.9 miles

1235. You are turning for 10 mph and passing Hog Point, LA (mile 297.5 AHP). Angola reports that the current at Red River Landing is 4.5 mph. Which statement is TRUE?

A. The main channel lies on the south side of the island you see ahead.
B. You are making 14.5 mph over the ground.
C. An underwater stone dike has been constructed 0.5 miles upstream of Miles Bar Towhead.
D. You would expect to find the more favorable current near the broken red line in the river.

1236. Which facility is located on the right descending bank at mile 363.6 AHP?

A. River Cement Corp.
B. Bunge Corp.
C. T.L. James
D. Vidalia Dock and Storage Co.

1237. At 1118, on 24 May, you pass Natchez Gauge and estimate the current will average 3.0 mph for the remainder of the time on the Mississippi River. What is your ETA at

Cairo, IL, if you continue to turn for 10 mph?

A. 0840, 26 May
B. 2218, 26 May
C. 2339, 27 May
D. 0339, 28 May

1238. If the highest point of your towboat is 54 feet above the water and the Natchez Gauge reads 24.8 feet, what will be your vertical clearance when passing under the Natchez-Vidalia westbound Highway Bridge?

A. 35.9 feet
B. 46.7 feet
C. 49.6 feet
D. 57.5 feet

1239. In high water conditions, which publication would you consult for the latest information on buoys between Baton Rouge and Cairo?

A. List of Buoys and Daymarks
B. U.S.C.G. Light List
C. C of E Navigation Chart
D. none of the above

1240. As you approach Ashland Light (mile 378.1 AHP), which type of daymark would you see on the light structure?

A. green square
B. green triangle
C. red square
D. red triangle

1241. At 1554, on 25 May, you pass Huntington Point Light (mile 555.2 AHP). What was your average speed since departing Amoco Pipeline Co. Docks (253.6 AHP)?

A. 6.9 mph
B. 6.2 mph
C. 4.8 mph
D. 4.3 mph

1242. The solid lines extending into the channel at mile 948 AHP are _____.

A. dikes
B. revetments
C. spoil areas
D. Westvaco Service Facilities

1243. What is the width of the widest span of the Cairo Highway Bridge (Upper Mississippi River mile 1.3)?

A. 800 feet
B. 675 feet
C. 625 feet
D. 503 feet

The following questions are based on the C of E Mississippi River Maps (Hannibal, MO, to the Gulf of Mexico) and the Light List. At 2345, on 25 December, you depart Vulcan Chemicals, Memphis Harbor, McKellar Lake (mile 726.0 AHP - LMR) enroute to to the Petroleum Fuel & Terminal Co. (144.6 AHP) in Angelina, LA, with a tow of eight full gasoline barges.

1244. If your vessel is making turns for 7.5 mph with an estimated average current of 1.5 mph, what is your ETA at the dock in Angelina, LA?

A. 1621, 28 Dec
B. 2203, 28 Dec
C. 0516, 29 Dec
D. 1621, 29 Dec

1245. The highest point on your towboat is 67 feet above the water, and the Helena Gauge reads +22.3 feet. What is the vertical clearance when you pass under the A-span of the Helena Highway Bridge?

A. 74.7 feet
B. 52.4 feet
C. 49.8 feet
D. 30.1 feet

1246. Which of the following statements is TRUE?

A. Oil well structures are listed in the Light List.
B. All aids to navigation with lights have lateral significance.
C. On the Western Rivers, crossing marks may exhibit white lights.
D. none of the above.

1247. At 0509, on 26 December, you pass under the Helena Highway Bridge (661.7 AHP). What has been the average speed of the current since departing Memphis Harbor, McKellar Lake, if you have been making turns for 7.5 mph?

A. 5.6 mph
B. 4.4 mph
C. 2.1 mph
D. 1.8 mph

248. What is the distance in river miles, from the new mouth of the White River to the Petroleum Fuel & Terminal Co. (144.6 AHP)?

A. 454 miles
B. 447 miles
C. 384 miles
D. 370 miles

1249. The Platte River empties into which river?

A. Mississippi
B. Ohio
C. Missouri
D. Tennessee

1250. You are downbound, passing by Warfield Point Lt. (mile 537 AHP), when you observe on your Mississippi River map a green diamond with an "SD" inside on the left bank below the light. This indicates a _____.

A. fleeting area
B. location for obtaining thr latest safety directions
C. warning sign to downbound traffic that the channel soon crosses very close to the right bank
D. none of the above

1286. As you pass under the Vicksburg Bridges, you estimate the current as 3.0 mph. What is the speed over the ground, if your vessel is making turns for 10.5 mph?

A. 16.5 mph
B. 13.5 mph
C. 10.5 mph
D. 7.5 mph

1287. As you approach Buckridge Light (mile 411.5 AHP), which type of daymark would you see on the light structure?

A. red diamond
B. red triangle
C. green diamond
D. green square

1288. The lighted mooring buoy at mile 228.7 AHP is a facility for which company?

A. Luhr Brothers
B. Cargo Carriers
C. International Marine Terminals
D. National Marine Inc.

The following questions are based on the C of E Mississippi River Maps (Hannibal, MO, to the Gulf of Mexico) and the Light List. At 0815, on the 16 of April, you depart the Exxon Refinery Docks (mile 232 AHP) bound for the fleeting area at Sycamore Chute Light (740.3 AHP).

1289. The horizontal clearance of the center span on the Baton Rouge RR and Highway 190 Bridge is _____.

A. 443
B. 500
C. 575
D. 623

1290. You have passed Ben Burman Lt. (mile 235.0 AHP) and see on the map a dark purplish area extending past Bayou Baton Rouge. This indicates a _____.

A. revetment
B. dredge material
C. fleeting area
D. dike

1291. As you pass Solitude Lt. (mile 249.0 AHP) which dayboard would you see?

A. green square
B. green diamond
C. red triangle
D. red diamond

1292. Which of the following statements regarding buoys on the Mississippi River is TRUE?

A. Buoy positions on the chart are exact.
B. Buoys should be given as wide a berth as possible in passing.
C. The buoys are maintained on station year round.
D. The buoys do not shift positions due to permanent moorings.

1293. What is indicated by the two light gray shaded areas that cross the river above False River Lt. (mile 251.0 AHP)?

A. utility crossings
B. ferry crossings
C. aerial cable crossings
D. bridge construction

1294. What are the light characteristics of Greenwood Light (mile 288.6 AHP)?

A. fixed red light
B. 2 red flashes every 5 seconds
C. 1 red flash every 4 seconds
D. 2 white flashes every 4 seconds

1295. After passing Wilkinson Lt. you see a flashing amber light on the right descending bank ahead. The flashing light indicates that you should _____.

A. stay in the deepest water
B. slow down due to dredging operations
C. keep as close to the left descending bank as safety permits
D. keep as close to the right descending bank as safety permits

1296. At which of the following times would you be able to listen to lower Mississippi River conditions on VHF Channel 22?

A. 0900 hours
B. 1100 hours
C. 1200 hours
D. 1300 hours

1297. At 0645, on the 17th of April, you pass Hole in the Wall Lt. (mile 373.4 AHP). What has been your average speed since departing the Exxon Refinery?

A. 8.8 mph
B. 7.3 mph
C. 6.8 mph
D. 6.3 mph

1298. Your company wants to know at what time you will be arriving at the fleeting area at Sycamore Chute Light (mile 740.3 AHP) in Memphis, Tenn. You are making turns for 9.0 mph and you estimate the average current at 2.2 mph. Figuring the distance and time from Hole in the Wall Lt. (mile 373.4 AHP), what is your ETA at Sycamore Chute Lt.?

A. 1242, April 19th
B. 1645, April 19th
C. 2242, April 19th
D. 2333, April 19th

The following questions are based on the C of E Mississippi River Maps (Hannibal, MO, to the Gulf of Mexico) and the Light List. On the 10th of May at 1130, you leave the fleeting area at Gartness Lt. (mile 227.8 AHP) bound for the Monsanto Terminal in St. Louis (mile 178.0 UMR). Your engines turn for 8.5 mph in still water.

1299. What is the length of the trip?

A. 405.8 miles
B. 904.0 miles
C. 1002.0 miles
D. 1136.8 miles

1300. You estimate the current as 2.5 mph. What is the speed over the ground?

A. 11.0 mph
B. 8.0 mph
C. 6.0 mph
D. 5.5 mph

1301. As you approach Casting Yard Dock Lt (mile 265.4 AHP) you notice on the map a circle with 2 black sectors. This symbol indicates a _____.

A. lock
B. warning sign
C. river gauge
D. mooring buoy

1302. From Baton Rouge to Cairo, what is the maintained minimum channel depth during low water?

A. 9 feet
B. 12 feet
C. 15 feet
D. 30 feet

1303. On which map would you find Redman Point, Arkansas?

A. 60
B. 57
C. 45
D. 38

1304. At 1000, on May 11th, you are passing George Prince Lt. (mile 364.1 AHP) in Natchez, Mississippi, and must send an ETA to the Monsanto Terminal in St. Louis (mile 178.0 UMR). Your engines are still turning for 8.5 mph and you estimate the current at 2.5 mph. What will be your arrival time in St. Louis?

A. 1919 on 15 May
B. 2344 on 15 May
C. 1113 on 16 May
D. 1757 on 16 May

1305. As you approach Ashland Light (mile 378.1 AHP) which daymark would you see?

A. red diamond
B. red triangle
C. green square
D. green diamond

1306. What is your clearance as you pass under the Vicksburg Highway 80 Bridge (mile 437.8 AHP) if the Vicksburg gauge reads 14.8 feet and the highest point on your tow boat is 44.5 feet?

A. 36 feet
B. 42 feet
C. 48 feet
D. 57 feet

1307. After entering Milliken Bend (mile 455 AHP) you wish to locate the river service in Madison Parish, Louisiana. The river service is indicated by the square containing which number?

A. 5
B. 4
C. 3
D. 2

1308. At Filter Point Light (mile 475 AHP) there are 3 close straight dashed lines on the map passing through the black dot below the number 475. What do these lines represent?

A. submerged oil pipelines
B. submerged gas pipelines
C. submerged telephone cables
D. aerial power cables

The following questions are based on the C of E Mississippi River Maps (Hannibal, MO, to the Gulf of Mexico) and the Light List. At 1400, 12 January, you are downbound on the Upper Mississippi River at St. Louis, MO (mile 181.0 UMR), bound for the River Cement Co. in Natchez, MI.

1309. When you pass under the Jefferson Barracks Highway Bridge (mile 168.6 UMR) what will be your vertical clearance if the highest point on your towboat is 55 feet and the St. Louis Gauge reads 21 feet?

A. 25.8 feet
B. 19.6 feet
C. 14.7 feet
D. 11.8 feet

1310. You are on map #13. What is the mile point of the facility known as Slay Warehousing, Inc.?

A. mile 174 UMR
B. mile 173 UMR
C. mile 172 UMR
D. mile 171 UMR

1311. Which light characteristics does Foster Light (mile 157.7 AHP) have?

A. 1 green flash every 4 seconds
B. 2 white flashes every 5 seconds
C. 1 red flash every 4 second
D. 2 red flashes every 5 seconds

1312. At 2100, January 12, you are passing Cherokee Landing Lt. (mile 112.5 UMR). What has been your speed over the ground since leaving St. Louis, MO (mile 181 UMR)?

A. 8.8 mph
B. 9.2 mph
C. 9.8 mph
D. 10.4 mph

1313. You are turning for 7.5 mph and estimate the current at 3.0 mph. What is your ETA at the River Cement Co. in Natchez considering that you passed Cherokee Landing Lt. at 2100?

A. 1243 on 15 January
B. 1605 on 15 January
C. 1244 on 16 January
D. 1922 on 16 January

1314. You are passing Goose Island Lt. (mile 34.4 UMR). The brown shaded areas alongside the river represent _____.

A. levees
B. revetments
C. dredged material
D. dikes

1315. At 1030, 13 January, you are passing Columbus Point Lt. (mile 936.1 AHP). What has been your average speed since leaving St. Louis (mile 181 UMR) on the 12th of January at 1400 hours?

A. 9.1 mph
B. 9.4 mph
C. 9.7 mph
D. 10.4 mph

1316. What is the mile point of Hickman, KY, gauge?

A. 922.0 AHP
B. 889.0 AHP

C. 865.0 AHP
D. 837.2 AHP

1317. Which daymark would you see at Shields Bar Lt. (mile 882.2 AHP)?

A. red triangle
B. green triangle
C. green square
D. red diamond

1318. You are passing Eastwood Lt. (mile 849.3 AHP) and the map indicates that Bunge Grain facility would be located at the square with number _____.

A. 8
B. 6
C. 4
D. 2

1339. At 1300, 5 January, the river will be temporarily closed to navigation for six hours at mile 531.3 AHP due to repairs to a bridge. What minimum speed over the ground must you make from Natchez Gauge in order not to be delayed?

A. 5.7 mph
B. 6.0 mph
C. 6.8 mph
D. 7.3 mph

The following questions are based on the C of E Mississippi River Maps (Hannibal, MO, to the Gulf of Mexico) and the Light List. At 1515, on 23 May, you get underway from the Amoco Pipeline Co. docks (253.6 AHP), enroute to to Pittsburgh, PA, with a tow of six barges carrying asphalt.

1410. What is the distance from the Amoco Docks at Baton Rouge, LA, to Pittsburgh, PA?

A. 1681.7 miles
B. 1575.3 miles
C. 981.7 miles
D. 727.9 miles

1411. After you get underway, what is the first river gauge you will pass?

A. Head of Passes
B. Baton Rouge
C. Bayou Sara
D. Red River Landing

1412. At Filter Point Light (mile 475 AHP) there are 3 close straight dashed lines on the map passing through the black dot below the number 475. What do these lines represent?

A. submerged oil pipelines
B. submerged gas pipelines
C. submerged telephone cables
D. aerial power cables

1413. You complete changing out your tow and get underway enroute to Ark City Tank Storage (mile 554.0 AHP) to deliver the tank barges. What is the distance you must travel from Cairo Point Light?

A. 202.1 miles
B. 400.7 miles
C. 554.2 miles
D. 605.8 miles

1414. What is the mile point of the Fulton Gauge?

A. 598 AHP
B. 632 AHP
C. 687 AHP
D. 778 AHP

1415. The highest point on your towboat is 52 feet above the water, and the Helena Gauge reads +9.6 feet. What will be the vertical clearance when you pass under the A-span of the Helena Highway Bridge?

A. 49.8 feet
B. 53.9 feet
C. 58.0 feet
D. 73.1 feet

1416. Which company does NOT have a marine facility along the river bank in Madison Parish (mile 457.0 AHP)?

A. Complex Chemical Co.
B. Delta Southern Railroads
C. Scott Petroleum
D. Baxter Wilson Steam plant

1417. What is the distance from Greenville, MS, to Oquawka, IL, on the Mississippi River System?

A. 537 miles
B. 597 miles
C. 733 miles
D. 832 miles

1418. How far is it to the Hernando Desoto Bridge in Memphis, TN?

A. 980.8 miles
B. 736.6 miles
C. 312.3 miles
D. 218.1 miles

1419. Which light will you be passing at 0059, on 22 September, if you make good 9.2 knots?

A. Obion Bar Lt.
B. Kate Aubrey Lt.
C. Trotter Lt.
D. Quaker Oats Lt

1420. What company does NOT have a marine facility along the river bank in Helena (mile 661 to 665 AHP)?

A. Helena Marine Services, Inc.
B. Riceland Food Corp.
C. Quincy Grain Co.
D. Texas Eastern Pipeline Co.

1421. What is your ETA at the Helena Highway Bridge?

A. 1335, 24 Sept
B. 1109, 24 Sept
C. 0926, 24 Sept
D. 0458, 24 Sept

1422. What organization has an installation at the uppermost end of Carthage Revetment?

A. City of Natchez (waterfront)
B. U.S. Coast Guard
C. U.S. Army Corps of Engineers
D. International Paper Co.

1423. You pass Ratcliff Light (mile 289.8) at 1650. What was your average speed since leaving Baton Rouge?

A. 7.3 mph
B. 7.6 mph
C. 8.0 mph
D. 8.3 mph

1424. You pass Springfield Bend Lt. (244.8 AHP) at 1242, on 17 October, and estimate the current will average 2.5 mph for the remainder of your trip. What is your ETA at the mouth of the Ohio River if you are making turns for 10.5 mph?

A. 1905, 19 October
B. 2122, 19 October
C. 0519, 21 October
D. 0847, 21 October

1425. At 1227, on 19 October, you pass under the Greenville Highway Bridge (mile 531.3 AHP). What speed must you average to arrive at Jimmy Hawken Light (mile 663.5 AHP) at 0930 the following day?

A. 5.2 mph
B. 5.6 mph
C. 5.9 mph
D. 6.3 mph

The following questions are based on the C of E Mississippi River Maps (Cairo to the Gulf) and the Light List.
On 16 October, you depart the Formosa Plastics mooring facility at mile 233.5 AHP with six loaded tank barges enroute to to the Agrico Chemical dock, Herculaneum, MO (mile153.4 UMR). Your engines are making turns for 6.5 mph in still water.

1426. What is the total length of the trip?

A. 910.6 miles
B. 901.4 miles
C. 900.7 miles
D. 873.7 miles

1427. What is the distance to Caruthersville Gauge from Cape Girardeau?

A. 54.4 miles
B. 160.4 miles
C. 793.4 miles
D. 899.4 miles

1428. At 1710 on 27 November, you are abeam of Kings Point Lt. (mile 439.8 AHP). At this time you receive a message that there will no be space for you at the Gold Bond Building Products wharf until after 1200 on the 29 November. What speed over the ground will you have to slow to so as not to arrive before this time?

A. 5.4 mph
B. 6.1 mph
C. 6.9 mph
D. 7.9 mph

1429. What is the distance from the Memphis gauge to the Gold Bond Building Products Wharf in New Orleans, LA?

A. 460 miles
B. 503 miles
C. 588 miles
D. 633 miles

1430. Which dayboard would you see on Putney Light (mile 943.6 AHP)?

A. green square
B. green triangle
C. red diamond
D. red triangle

1431. As you pass under the Greenville Highway Bridge, you estimate the current as 4.5 mph. What is the speed over the ground, if your vessel is making turns for 9 mph?

A. 9.5 mph
B. 13.5 mph
C. 14.5 mph
D. 16.5 mph

1432. As you approach Joseph Henry Light (mile 445.2 AHP) which daymark would you see?

A. Red square
B. Red triangle
C. Green diamond
D. Green square

1433. Your vessel is making turns for 9.5 mph and you estimate the average current for the trip will be 2.5 mph. What will be your ETA Donaldsonville, LA?

A. 1044 on 7 October
B. 1222 on 7 October
C. 0443 on 8 October
D. 1033 on 8 October

1434. You are passing Eastwood Lt. (mile 849.3 AHP) and the map indicates that Bunge Grain facility would be located at the square with number _____.

A. 8
B. 6
C. 4
D. 2

1435. When you pass under the Jefferson Barracks Highway Bridge (mile 168.6 UMR) what will be your vertical clearance if the highest point on your towboat is 55 feet and the St. Louis Gauge reads 21 feet?

A. 25.8 feet
B. 19.6 feet
C. 14.7 feet
D. 11.8 feet

1436. At which of the following times would you be able to listen to lower Mississippi River conditions on VHF Channel 22A?

A. 0900 hours
B. 1100 hours
C. 1200 hours
D. 1500 hours

1437. What is indicated by the two light grey shaded areas that cross the river above False River Light (mile 251.0 AHP)?

A. Utility crossings
B. Ferry crossings
C. Aerial cable crossings
D. Bridge construction

1438. The lighted mooring buoy at mile 228.7 AHP is a facility for which company?

A. Luhr Brothers
B. Cargo Carriers
C. International Marine Terminals
D. National Marine Inc.

1439. You are turning for 10 mph and passing Hog Point, LA (mile 297.5 AHP). Angola reports that the current at Red River Landing is 4.5 mph. Which statement is TRUE?

A. The main channel lies on the south side of the island you see ahead.
B. You are making 14.5 mph over the ground.
C. An underwater stone dike has been constructed 0.5 miles upstream of Miles Bar Towhead.
D. You would expect to find the more favorable current near the broken red line in the river.

1440. Where can scheduled broadcast times of river stages be found?

A. Sailing Directions
B. List of Lights
C. Light List
D. Coast Pilot

1441. You complete changing out your tow and get underway enroute to Ark City Tank Storage (mile 554.0 AHP) to deliver the tank barges. What is the distance you must travel from Cairo Point Light?

A. 202.1 miles
B. 400.7 miles
C. 554.2 miles
D. 605.8 miles

1442. What is the brown colored tint shown at Bordeaux Point Dykes (681.0 AHP)?

A. river gauge
B. fish hatchery
C. dredge material
D. levee

1443. How far is it to the Hernando Desoto Bridge in Memphis, TN?

A. 980.8 miles
B. 736.6 miles
C. 312.3 miles
D. 218.1 miles

1444. What is the distance from the Arkansas River mouth to the Ohio River mouth in river miles?

A. 594 miles
B. 546 miles
C. 422 miles
D. 372 miles

1445. What is the milepoint of Hickman, KY, gauge?

A. 846.4 AHP
B. 889.0 AHP
C. 922.0 AHP
D. 937.2 AHP

1446. At 2100, January 12, you are passing Cherokee Landing Lt. (mile 112.5 UMR). What has been your speed over the ground since leaving St. Louis, MO (mile 181 UMR)?

A. 10.4 mph
B. 9.8 mph
C. 9.2 mph
D. 8.8 mph

1447. As you approach Casting Yard Dock Lt. (mile 265.4 AHP) you notice on the map a circle with 2 black sectors. This symbol indicates a _____.

A. lock
B. warning sign
C. mooring buoy
D. river gauge

1448. Your company wants to know at what time you will be arriving at the fleeting area at Sycamore Chute Light (mile 740.3 AHP) in Memphis, Tenn. You are making turns for 9.0 mph and you estimate the average current at 2.2 mph. Figuring the

distance and time from Hole in the Wall Lt. (mile 373.4 AHP), what is your ETA at Sycamore Chute Lt.?

A. 0557, April 19th
B. 1045, April 19th
C. 1242, April 19th
D. 1733, April 19th

1506. At 0850, 4 January, you pass the gauge at Natchez, MS, which reads 26.8 feet. How many feet is this above the low water reference plane?

A. 10.6 ft.
B. 11.6 ft.
C. 20.7 ft.
D. 26.8 ft.

1507. At 1300, 5 January, the river will be temporarily closed to navigation for six hours at mile 531.3 AHP due to repairs to a bridge. What minimum speed over the ground must you make from Natchez Gauge in order not to be delayed?

A. 6.0 mph
B. 6.4 mph
C. 6.8 mph
D. 7.3 mph

1508. Which light will you be passing at 0059, on 22 September, if you make good 9.2 mph?

A. Kate Aubrey Lt.
B. Obion Bar Lt.
C. Trotter Lt.
D. Quaker Oats Lt.

1509. The Arkansas City Yellow Bend revetment on the LMR extends from mile _____.

A. 555.5–549.7 RDB
B. 549.0–548.5 RDB
C. 556.9–554.9 LDB
D. 548.5–546.5 LDB

1510. At 1132, 24 May, you pass Natchez Beam Lt. (364.8 AHP). What is your ETA off the Memphis Gauge if you average 8.0 mph?

A. 2345, 25 May
B. 0525, 26 May
C. 0947, 26 May
D. 2215, 26 May

1511. Which company does NOT have a marine facility in Rosedale harbor (mile 585 AHP)?

A. Sanders Elevator Corp
B. Rosedale-Boliver County Port Commission
C. T.L. James
D. Cives Steel Company

1512. What is the vertical clearance between the highest point of your towboat, if it is 45 feet above the water, and if the Natchez Gauge reads 23.4 feet when passing under the Natchez–Vidalia Westbound Highway Bridge?

A. 45.0 feet
B. 52.2 feet
C. 57.1 feet
D. 67.5 feet

1513. Which facility is located on the right descending bank at mile 363.6 AHP?

A. River Cement Corp.
B. Vidalia Dock and Storage Co.
C. T.L. James
D. Bunge Corp.

1514. You are downbound, passing by Warfield Point Lt. (mile 537 AHP), when you observe on your Mississippi River map a green diamond with an "SD" inside on the left bank below the light. This indicates a _____.

A. fleeting area
B. location for obtaining the latest safety directions
C. warning sign to downbound traffic that the channel soon crosses very close to the right bank
D. none of the above

1515. What are the light characteristics of Greenwood Light (mile 288.6 AHP)?

A. Fixed red light
B. 1 red flash every 4 seconds
C. 2 red flashes every 5 seconds
D. 2 white flashes every 4 seconds

1516. On which map would you find Redman Point, Arkansas?

A. 57
B. 60
C. 66
D. 74

1517. Which daymark would you see at Shields Bar Lt. (mile 882.2 AHP)?

A. Red triangle
B. Green triangle
C. Red diamond
D. Green square

1518. Your engines are turning for 8.2 mph. You estimate the current at 1.5 mph. What is your speed over the ground?

A. 9.7 mph
B. 8.8 mph
C. 8.2 mph
D. 6.7 mph

1519. At 1710 on 27 November, you are abeam of Kings Point Lt. (mile 439.8 AHP). At this time you receive a message that there will no be space for you at the Gold Bond Building Products wharf until after 1200 on the 29 November. What speed over the ground will you have to slow to so as not to arrive before this time?

A. 5.4 mph
B. 6.1 mph
C. 6.9 mph
D. 7.9 mph

1520. What are the dimensions of the Old River Lock on the Lower Old River (304 AHP)?

A. 1190 X 75 feet
B. 1185 X 84 feet
C. 1190 X 84 feet
D. 1185 X 75 feet

1521. At 0850, 4 January, you pass the gauge at Natchez, MS, which reads 26.8 feet. How many feet is this above the low water reference plane?

A. 10.6 ft
B. 20.7 ft
C. 23.9 ft
D. 26.8 ft

1522. At 1923, on September 21, you pass Bixby Towhead Light (mile 873.7 AHP). What was your average speed since leaving Cairo?

A. 9.2 mph
B. 8.8 mph
C. 8.5 mph
D. 7.2 mph

1523. What company does NOT have a marine facility along the river bank in Helena (mile 661 to 665 AHP)?

A. Helena Marine Services, Inc.
B. Riceland Food Corp.
C. Quincy Grain Co.
D. Texas Eastern Pipeline Co.

1524. After you get underway, what is the first river gauge you will pass?

A. Donaldsonville
B. Head of Passes
C. Baton Rouge
D. Red River Landing

1525. At 2350, on 23 June, you are at mile 610.5 AHP when you see about a mile ahead two separate white lights on the water near the left bank. There is a red light on the bank in the same vicinity. What can you expect to see when you come abreast of these lights?

A. privately maintained buoys at a yacht club
B. government buoys marking the Hurricane Point dikes
C. a pipeline discharging dredge spoil
D. none of the above

1526. As you approach Dean Island Light (mile 755.7 AHP), which type of daymark will be observed at the light?

A. Green triangle
B. Green diamond
C. Green square
D. Red-and-green banded square

1527. As you pass under the Baton Rouge RR and Hwy 190 Bridge (233.9 AHP), the Ingram Aggregates facility is indicated by which numbered box?

A. 8
B. 6
C. 5
D. 2

1528. As you approach Gibson Light (mile 371.2 AHP), which type of daymark would you see on the light structure?

A. Red square
B. Green triangle
C. Red diamond
D. Green diamond

1529. Which type of daymark would you see on the Belle Island Corner Lt. at mile 458.6 AHP?

A. Green - Diamond
B. Green - Square
C. Red - Diamond
D. Red - Triangle

1530. The Platte River empties into which river?

A. Mississippi
B. Ohio
C. Missouri
D. Tennessee

1531. The horizontal clearance of the center span on the Baton Rouge RR and Highway 190 Bridge is _____.

A. 443
B. 500
C. 575
D. 623

1532. As you pass Solitude Lt. (mile 249.0 AHP) which dayboard would you see?

A. Green square
B. Green diamond
C. Red triangle
D. Red diamond

1533. Your company wants to know at what time you will be arriving at the fleeting area at Sycamore Chute Light (mile 740.3 AHP) in Memphis, Tenn. You are making turns for 9.0 mph and you estimate the average current at 2.2 mph. Figuring the distance and time from Hole in the Wall Lt. (mile 373.4 AHP), what is your ETA at Sycamore Chute Lt.?

A. 1242, April 19th
B. 1645, April 19th
C. 2242, April 19th
D. 2333, April 19th

1534. At 1609, on October 5, you are abeam of Star Landing Lt. (mile 707.2 AHP). You calculate your speed since you departed Sycamore Chute fleeting area. If you are turning for 9.5 mph what was the current?

A. 2.5 mph
B. 2.0 mph
C. 1.5 mph
D. 1.0 mph

1535. The Red River Landing gauge reads 5.2 feet. Which of the following statements is TRUE?

A. River level is below the Low Water Reference Plane.
B. The depth over revetment at Old River is 25.2 ft.
C. The depth over Old River Lock sill is greater than 11 ft.
D. This gauge reading is at a higher elevation than the same reading on the gauge at Head of Passes.

1536. As you approach Casting Yard Dock Lt. (mile 265.4 AHP) you notice on the map a circle with 2 black sectors. This symbol indicates a _____.

A. lock
B. warning sign
C. river gauge
D. mooring buoy

1537. What is your clearance as you pass under the Vicksburg Highway 80 Bridge (mile 437.8 AHP) if the Vicksburg gauge reads 14.8 feet and the highest point on your tow boat is 44.5 feet?

A. 36 feet
B. 42 feet
C. 48 feet
D. 57 feet

1538. At 1032 on 24 June, you pass Carolina Landing Light (508.8 AHP). What has been the average current since 2350, 23 June, if you have been making turns for 9.0 mph?

A. 8.5 mph
B. 5.7 mph
C. 1.5 mph
D. 0.5 mph

1539. As you approach Cottonwood Chute Light (mile 530.5 AHP), which type of daymark would you see on the light structure?

A. red diamond
B. red triangle
C. green square
D. green diamond

1540. You estimate the current at 2.0 mph. What is the speed over the ground?

A. 9.5 mph
B. 5.5 mph
C. 5.0 mph
D. 4.5 mph

1541. At 0119, on 10 September, you pass Springfield Bend Lt. (244.8 AHP) and estimate the current will average 2.5 mph for the remainder of your trip. What is your ETA at the mouth of the Ohio River if you are making turns for 8.5 mph?

A. 1746, 12 September
B. 1244, 13 September
C. 2329, 14 September
D. 0210, 15 September

The following questions are based on the C of E Mississippi River Maps (Hannibal, MO, to the Gulf of Mexico) and the Light List. You are making up your tow at the fleeting area at Cairo Point, IL (mile 980.8 Ohio River). At 0952, on 21 September, you get underway enroute to to New Orleans with a mixed tow.

1542. You are turning for 6.8 mph and estimate the current at 1.0 mph. What is your speed over the ground?

A. 6.8 mph
B. 7.8 mph
C. 8.8 mph
D. 9.4 mph

1543. As you pass under the Natchez-Vidalia Dual Bridge, the gauge on the bridge reads –3.6. If the highest point on your vessel is 62 ft. above the water, what is your vertical clearance?

A. 60.0 feet
B. 63.6 feet
C. 67.2 feet
D. 122.0 feet

1544. What is the distance in river miles, from the new mouth of the White River to the Petroleum Fuel & Terminal Co. (144.6 AHP)?

A. 370 miles
B. 384 miles
C. 447 miles
D. 454 miles

1545. You are downbound, passing by Warfield Point Lt. (mile 537 AHP), when you observe on your Mississippi River map a green diamond with an "SD" inside on the left bank below the light. This indicates a _____.

A. fleeting area
B. location for obtaining the latest safety directions
C. warning sign to downbound traffic that the channel soon crosses very close to the right bank
D. none of the above

1546. As you pass under the Vicksburg Bridges, you estimate the current as 3.0 mph. What is the speed over the ground, if your vessel is making turns for 10.5 mph?

A. 7.5 mph
B. 10.5 mph
C. 13.5 mph
D. 16.5 mph

1547. At 0509, on 26 December, you pass under the Helena Highway Bridge (661.7 AHP). What has been the average speed of the current since departing Memphis Harbor, McKellar Lake, if you have been making turns for 7.5 mph?

A. 5.6 mph
B. 4.4 mph
C. 2.1 mph
D. 1.8 mph

1548. As you approach Buckridge Light (mile 411.5 AHP), which type of daymark would you see on the light structure?

A. red diamond
B. red triangle
C. green diamond
D. green square

1549. Your vessel is making turns for 9.5 mph and you estimate the average current for the trip will be 2.5 mph. What will be your ETA at Donaldsonville, LA?

A. 1222 on 7 October
B. 1823 on 7 October
C. 0443 on 8 October
D. 1033 on 8 October

1550. Which numbered box indicates the Exxon Terminal in Baton Rouge?

A. 3
B. 6
C. 8
D. 10

1551. What daymark should you see as you approach Lobdell Light (mile 238.1 AHP)?

A. green diamond
B. green square
C. green triangle
D. red square

1552. Which light will you be passing at 0059, on 22 September, if you make good 9.2 mph?

A. Kate Aubrey Lt.
B. Obion Bar Lt.
C. Trotter Lt.
D. Quaker Oats Lt

1553. The Arkansas City Yellow Bend revetment on the LMR extends from mile _____.

A. 555.5-549.7 RDB
B. 549.0-548.5 RDB
C. 556.9-554.9 LDB
D. 548.5-546.5 LDB

1554. After you get underway, what is the first river gauge you will pass?

A. Donaldsonville
B. Head of Passes
C. Baton Rouge
D. Red River Landing

1555. Which town is located at mile 663.5 AHP?

A. Helena
B. Friers Point
C. St. Francis
D. Rodney

1556. At 1118, on 24 May, you pass Natchez Gauge and estimate the current will average 3.0 mph for the remainder of the time on the Mississippi River. What is your ETA at Cairo, IL, if you continue to turn for 10 mph?

A. 0840, 26 May
B. 2218, 26 May
C. 2218, 27 May
D. 2339, 27 May

1557. What is the width of the widest span of the Cairo Highway Bridge (Upper Mississippi River mile 1.3)?

A. 503 feet
B. 625 feet
C. 675 feet
D. 800 feet

1558. At 0715, on March 9, you pass Knox Landing Gauge (313.8 AHP) and estimate the current will average 3.5 mph for the remainder of the time on the Mississippi River. What is your ETA at the mouth of the Ohio River if you increase speed to turn for 10 mph?

A. 0640, 11 March
B. 0554, 12 March
C. 1830, 12 March
D. 0943, 13 March

The following questions are based on the C of E Mississippi River Maps (Hannibal, MO, to the Gulf of Mexico) and the Light List. At 0815, on the 16 of April, you depart the Exxon Refinery Docks (mile 232 AHP) bound for the fleeting area at Sycamore Chute Light (740.3 AHP).

1559. The horizontal clearance of the center span on the Baton Rouge RR and Highway 190 Bridge is _____.

A. 443 feet
B. 500 feet
C. 575 feet
D. 623 feet

1560. What is indicated by the two light gray shaded areas that cross the river above False River Lt. (mile 251.0 AHP)?

A. utility crossings
B. ferry crossings
C. aerial cable crossings
D. bridge construction

1561. You are turning for 10 mph, approaching Angola, LA. Angola reports that the current at Red River Landing is estimated at 4.5 MPH. Which of the following statements is TRUE?

A. You are making 14.5 mph over the ground.
B. You should expect to encounter vessels crossing the river at mile 300.5 AHP.
C. You would expect to find more favorable current near the broken red line in the river.
D. Hog Pt. Light and Hog Pt. Lower Light may be used as range lights when entering Shreves cut-off.

1562. From Baton Rouge to Cairo, what is the maintained minimum channel depth during low water?

A. 6 feet
B. 9 feet
C. 12 feet
D. 30 feet

1563. At 1000, on May 11th, you are passing George Prince Lt. (mile 364.1 AHP) in Natchez, Mississippi, and must send an ETA to the Monsanto Terminal in St. Louis (mile 178.0 UMR). Your engines are still turning for 8.5 mph and you estimate the current at 2.5 mph. What will be your arrival time in St. Louis?

A. 1919 on 15 May
B. 2344 on 15 May
C. 1757 on 16 May
D. 2236 on 16 May

1564. As you approach Dean Island Light (mile 755.7 AHP), which type of daymark will be observed at the light?

A. green triangle
B. red and green banded square
C. green square daymark
D. diamond-shaped green daymark

1565. Which of the following statements concerning the buoys on the Mississippi River is TRUE?

A. The position of river buoys can be determined by consulting the latest Light List - Vol. V.
B. A preferred channel mark is a lateral mark indicating a channel junction which must always be passed to starboard.
C. Setting a buoy is the act of placing a buoy on assigned position in the water.
D. none of the above.

1566. You estimate the current at 2.0 mph. What is the speed over the ground?

A. 3.5 mph
B. 4.5 mph
C. 5.5 mph
D. 9.5 mph

1567. The Vaucluse Trench fill revetment on the LMR extends from mile _____.

A. 534.3 - 532.6 RDB
B. 535.9 - 534.3 RDB
C. 535.9 - 534.3 LDB
D. 534.3 - 532.6 LDB

1568. At 2100, January 12, you are passing Cherokee Landing Lt. (mile 112.5 UMR).

What has been your speed over the ground since leaving St. Louis, MO (mile 181 UMR)?

A. 8.8 mph
B. 9.2 mph
C. 9.8 mph
D. 10.4 mph

1569. What is the mile point of Hickman, KY, gauge?

A. 922.0 AHP
B. 889.0 AHP
C. 865.0 AHP
D. 837.2 AHP

1570. The charts show a circle with two black quadrants located at mile 846.0 AHP. What does this indicate?

A. hazardous chemical dock
B. bulletin board
C. Betz-Tipton Veneers Terminal
D. river gauge

1571. If the Rosedale gauge reads –0.5 feet, what is the water level in relation to the low water reference plane?

A. 0.5 foot below the plane
B. 0.5 foot above the plane
C. 2.5 feet above the plane
D. 3.5 feet below the plane

1622. Which of the following statements concerning the buoys on the Mississippi River is TRUE?

A. The position of river buoys can be determined by consulting the latest Light List - Vol. V.
B. A preferred channel mark is a lateral mark indicating a channel junction which must always be passed to starboard.
C. Buoys should be passed as close as possible.
D. Setting a buoy is the act of placing a buoy on assigned position in the water.

1623. How long will it take you to go from the Memphis gauge to your destination in New Orleans, LA, if you estimate the average current on this segment of the route to be 2.0 mph and you increase the engine turns to 8.5 mph?

A. 1 day 20 hours 33 minutes
B. 2 days 12 hours 15 minutes
C. 2 days 15 hours 12 minutes
D. 3 days 4 hours 11 minutes

1624. Your engines are turning for 8.2 mph. You estimate the current at 1.5 mph. What is your speed over the ground?

A. 6.7 mph
B. 8.2 mph
C. 8.8 mph
D. 9.7 mph

1625. At 1030, 13 January, you are passing Columbus Point Lt. (mile 936.1 AHP). What has been your average speed since leaving St. Louis (mile 181 UMR) on the 12th of January at 1400 hours?

A. 9.1 mph
B. 9.4 mph
C. 9.7 mph
D. 10.4 mph

1626. At 2100, January 12, you are passing Cherokee Landing Lt. (mile 112.5 UMR). What has been your speed over the ground since leaving St. Louis, MO (mile 181 UMR)?

A. 8.8 mph
B. 9.2 mph
C. 9.8 mph
D. 10.4 mph

1627. What is your clearance as you pass under the Vicksburg Highway 80 Bridge (mile 437.8 AHP) if the Vicksburg gauge reads 14.8 feet and the highest point on your tow boat is 44.5 feet?

A. 36 feet
B. 42 feet
C. 48 feet
D. 57 feet

1628. At 1554, on 25 May, you pass Huntington Point Light (mile 555.2 AHP). What was your average speed since departing Amoco Pipeline Co. Docks (253.6 AHP)?

A. 6.9 mph
B. 6.2 mph
C. 4.8 mph
D. 4.3 mph

1629. Which facility is located on the right descending bank at mile 363.6 AHP?

A. River Cement Corp.
B. Bunge Corp.
C. T.L. James
D. Vidalia Dock and Storage Co.

1630. As you pass under the

Natchez–Vidalia Dual Bridge, the gauge on the bridge reads 8.9 ft. If the highest point on your vessel is 54 ft. above the water, what is your vertical clearance?

A. 62.6 feet
B. 65.3 feet
C. 67.2 feet
D. 122.0 feet

The following questions are based on the C of E Mississippi River Maps (Hannibal, MO, to the Gulf of Mexico) and the Light List. On 9 September, you depart the Formosa Plastics mooring facility at mile 233.5 AHP with six loaded tank barges enroute to to the Alton Barge Terminal, Alton, IL, (mile 202.0 UMR). Your engines are making turns for 7.5 mph in still water.

1631. What is the total length of the trip?

A. 906.3 miles
B. 922.3 miles
C. 1155.8 miles
D. 1187.3 miles

1632. As you approach the Cahokia Marine Terminal Lights, you notice on the map a dashed line crossing the river at mile 178.3 UMR. This line indicates _____.

A. aerial crossings
B. 2 sub. tel. cables
C. 16 submarine power cables
D. 2 10' gas pipelines

1633. What is the vertical clearance between the highest point of your towboat if it is 45 feet above the water and if the Natchez Gauge reads 23.4 feet when passing under the Natchez–Vidalia Westbound Highway Bridge?

A. 67.5 feet
B. 57.1 feet
C. 52.2 feet
D. 45.2 feet

1634. Which type utility crossing is at mile 529.7 AHP?

A. 1 36 Sub Gas Pipeline
B. 4 16 Sub Gas Pipelines
C. 2 36 Sub Gas Pipelines
D. 2 20 Sub Gas Pipelines

1635. How long will it take you to go from the Memphis gauge to your destination in New Orleans, LA, if you estimate the average current on this segment of the route to be 2.0 mph and you increase the engine turns to 8.5 mph?

A. 1 day 20 hours 33 minutes
B. 2 days 6 hours 24 minutes
C. 2 days 12 hours 15 minutes
D. 3 days 4 hours 11 minutes

1636. At 1030, 13 January, you are passing Columbus Point Lt. (mile 936.1 AHP). What has been your average speed since leaving St. Louis (mile 181 UMR) on the 12th of January at 1400 hours?

A. 10.4 mph
B. 9.7 mph
C. 9.4 mph
D. 9.1 mph

1637. What is the width of the widest span of the Cairo Highway Bridge (Upper Mississippi River mile 1.3)?

A. 503 feet
B. 625 feet
C. 675 feet
D. 800 feet

1639. Which of the following statements concerning the buoys on the Mississippi River is TRUE?

A. The position of river buoys can be determined by consulting the latest Light List - Vol. V.
B. A preferred channel mark is a lateral mark indicating a channel junction which must always be passed to starboard.
C. Setting a buoy is the act of placing a buoy on assigned position in the water.
D. None of the above.

1640. Which town is located at mile 663.5 AHP?

A. Helena
B. Friers Point
C. St. Francis
D. Rodney

1642. From your 2129 position you reduce engine speed to 14 knots. What is the course to make good from your 2129 position to arrive 0.3 mile north of Lighted Whistle Buoy NCA (LL #375) assuming no set and drift?

A. 216°T
B. 219°T

C. 222°T
D. 225°T

1643. Which facility is located on the right descending bank at mile 363.6 AHP?

A. River Cement Corp.
B. Bunge Corp.
C. T.L. James
D. Vidalia Dock and Storage Co.

1644. From your 2207 position you adjust your course to arrive 0.3 mile north of Lighted Whistle Buoy NCA. If you make good 14 knots, at what time will Cape Charles Light be abeam?

A. 2242
B. 2245
C. 2247
D. 2250

1646. Where would you find out which buoys, if any, are in place at Concordia Bar crossing (mile 596.0 AHP)?

A. Channel Report
B. Bulletin board at the Rosedale gauge
C. Waterways Journal
D. None of the above

1647. In high water conditions, which publication would you consult for the latest information on buoys between Baton Rouge and Cairo?

A. List of Buoys and Daymarks
B. U.S.C.G. Notice to Mariners Channel Report
C. C of E Navigation Chart
D. None of the above

The following questions are based on the C of E Mississippi River Maps (Cairo to the Gulf) and the Light List. At 0630, on 15 March, you are upbound on the Lower Mississippi River passing Kaiser Aluminum & Chemical Corp. (mile 234.0 AHP).

1701. The latest available information on the channel conditions above Baton Rouge that includes the latest buoy information, as well as recommended courses, is found in the _____.

A. Corps of Engineers maps
B. Waterways Journal
C. Notice to Mariners Channel Report
D. Sailing Directions

1702. You are upbound approaching Springfield Lt. (mile 245.6 AHP), downriver from Profit Island. Which of the following statements is TRUE?

A. Profit Island Chute is closed to navigation.
B. Tow length must not exceed 600 feet to use Profit Island Chute.
C. Tows must navigate toward left ascending bank when passing Profit Island Chute.
D. Profit Island Chute is open to navigation and is a shortcut for single barge tows.

1703. At 1218, on 16 March, you are passing the Vicksburg gauge (mile 437.0 AHP). What has been the average current since 0630, 15 March, if you have been making turns for 8.0 mph?

A. 0.2 mph
B. 0.5 mph
C. 0.8 mph
D. 1.2 mph

1704. Which of the following statements regarding buoys on the Mississippi River is TRUE?

A. The positions of river buoys can be found in the latest edition of Light List-Vol. V.
B. The buoys are maintained on station year round.
C. Bouy positions on the chart are approximate.
D. The buoys do not shift positions due to permanent moorings.

1705. What is the mile point of the Rosedale, Miss., gauge?

A. 554.2 AHP
B. 592.2 AHP
C. 632.5 AHP
D. 663.0 AHP

1706. The highest point on your towboat is 53 feet above the water, and the Helena gauge (mile 663 AHP) reads 3.9 feet. What is the vertical clearance when you pass under the B-span of the Helena Highway Bridge in Helena?

A. 59.9 feet
B. 62.5 feet
C. 64.1 feet
D. 65.5 feet

1707. You are passing the Memphis gauge at 0405, 18 March. If you are turning for 8 mph and estimate the current at 2.3 mph, what is your ETA at Cairo Point, IL, (954.5 AHP)?

A. 0447, 19 Mar
B. 1052, 19 Mar
C. 1518, 19 Mar
D. 1839, 19 Mar

1708. At 0300 on 19 April, you pass under the Greenville Bridge (mile 531.3 AHP). What was your average speed since departing Amoco Pipeline Co. Docks (253.6 AHP)?

A. 6.2 mph
B. 5.2 mph
C. 4.8 mph
D. 4.3 mph

1709. A stretch where the channel changes from one side of the river to the other is called a _____.

A. bifurcation
B. transit
C. crossing
D. changeover

1710. Under which span of the Cairo Highway Bridge (Ohio River) would you find the deepest water?

A. East span
B. West span
C. Center span
D. all spans have equal depth

The following questions are based on the C of E Mississippi River Maps (Cairo to the Gulf) and the Light List. At 0519 on 23 May, you get underway from Baton Rouge, L (mile 231.8 AHP), bound for Louisville, KY (mile 610.1 OR).

1711. What is the length of the trip?

A. 722.0 miles
B. 953.8 miles
C. 1097.9 miles
D. 1332.1 miles

1712. What is the distance from Cairo Point, IL, to Arkansas City?

A. 28 miles
B. 110 miles
C. 218 miles
D. 400 miles

1716. What are the dimensions of the Old River Lock on the Lower Old River (304 AHP)?

A. 1185 X 75 feet
B. 1190 X 75 feet
C. 1190 X 84 feet
D. 1185 X 84 feet

1720. As you approach mile 427.6 AHP, you see on the right side a white buoy with orange bands and diamond. This buoy marks _____.

A. a cable crossing
B. a sunken barge
C. a submerged discharge pipe
D. the end of a wharf

The following questions are based on the C of E Mississippi River Maps (Cairo to the Gulf) and the Light List. On 25 March, you depart the Morganza, LA, Docks at mile 278.2 AHP with 12 barges enroute to to St. Louis, MO (mile 175UMR). Your engines are turning for 7.5 mph in still water.

1721. What is the total length of the trip?

A. 850.6 miles
B. 894.8 miles
C. 922.5 miles
D. 946.5 miles

1722. You estimate the current as 2.0 mph. What is the speed over the ground?

A. 4.5 mph
B. 5.5 mph
C. 7.5 mph
D. 9.5 mph

1723. You will pass the first gauge at _____.

A. Profit Island
B. Bayou Sara
C. Baton Rouge
D. Red River Landing

1724. What is the milepoint of the Natchez, Miss., gauge?

A. 228.4 AHP
B. 265.4 AHP
C. 302.4 AHP
D. 363.3 AHP

1725. As you pass Fort Adams (311.4 AHP) you observe a flashing amber light on the right descending bank ahead. This indicates that you should _____.

A. proceed with caution as there is construction work being done on the revetment
B. keep as close to the right descending bank as safety permits
C. keep as close to the left descending bank as safety permits
D. proceed with caution as the river is congested around the bend

1726. The highest point on your towboat is 57 feet above water. The Natchez gauge (mile 363.3 AHP) reads 16.7 feet. What is the vertical clearance when you pass under the Natchez (westbound) Hwy. Bridge?

A. 51.9 feet
B. 59.9 feet
C. 61.0 feet
D. 68.6 feet

1727. You pass under the Natchez bridge (363.3 AHP) at 1300, on 27 March, and estimate the current to be 3.3 mph. What is your ETA at St. Louis if you continue to turn for 7.5 mph?

A. 0617, 4 April
B. 0316, 4 April
C. 1153, 30 March
D. 1253, 31 April

1728. As you approach Cannon Point Light (mile 418.3 AHP), what daymark will you see on the light structure?

A. Green square
B. Green diamond
C. Red triangle
D. Red diamond

1729. The small red and white striped rectangle to the north of Oak Bend Lt. (425.6 AHP) indicates a _____.

A. river stage gauge
B. loading crane at the freight terminal
C. commercial dock
D. ferry landing

1730. What is the distance from Arkansas City, AR, to St. Louis, MO, on the Mississippi River System?

A. 584 miles
B. 597 miles
C. 733 miles
D. 832 miles

The following questions are based on the C of E Mississippi River Maps (Cairo to the Gulf) and the Light List. On 16 October, you depart the Formosa Plastics mooring facility at mile 233.5 AHP with six loaded tank barges enroute to to the Apex Oil dock, St. Louis, MO (mile180.9 UMR). Your engines are making turns for 6.5 mph in still water.

1731. What is the total length of the trip?

A. 910.6 miles
B. 901.2 miles
C. 900.3 miles
D. 873.7 miles

1732. You estimate the current at 2.0 mph. What is the speed over the ground?

A. 3.5 mph
B. 4.5 mph
C. 7.5 mph
D. 9.5 mph

1733. What are the dimensions of the channel maintained at Baton Rouge, LA?

A. 30 feet × 300 feet
B. 40 feet × 300 feet
C. 40 feet × 500 feet
D. 30 feet × 500 feet

1734. You pass Springfield Bend Lt. (244.8 AHP) at 1242, on 17 October, and estimate the current will average 2.5 mph for the remainder of your trip. What is your ETA at the mouth of the Ohio River if you are making turns for 10.5 mph?

A. 1905, 19 October
B. 0207, 21 October
C. 0519, 21 October
D. 0847, 21 October

1735. As you pass under the Natchez-Vidalia Dual Bridge, the gauge on the bridge reads 3.6 feet. If the highest point on your vessel is 62 ft. above the water, what is your vertical clearance?

A. 60.0 feet
B. 63.6 feet
C. 67.2 feet
D. 122.0 feet

1736. What are the color and shape of Joseph Henry Daymark at mile 445.2 AHP?

A. Red - Square
B. Green - Square
C. Green - Triangle
D. Red - Diamond

1737. At 1227, on 19 October, you pass under the Greenville Highway Bridge (mile 531.3 AHP). What speed must you average to arrive at Jimmy Hawken Light (mile 663.5 AHP) at 1045 the following day?

A. 5.2 mph
B. 5.6 mph
C. 5.9 mph
D. 6.3 mph

1738. Which of the following statements regarding aids to navigation shown in the Corps of Engineers map book is TRUE?

A. Buoys should always be given as wide a berth in passing as possible.
B. The U.S. Army Corp. of Engineers is responsible for placing and maintaining all aids to navigation.
C. Buoy positions as shown on the chart are exact.
D. Lights and daymarks are always shown in their exact location.

1739. The Delta-Friar Point revetment on the LMR extends from mile _____.

A. 645.6–641.4 RDB
B. 652.8–649.6 RDB
C. 648.5–645.5 LDB
D. 657.3–652.2 LDB

1740. On what river is Ghent, Kentucky, located?

A. Tennessee
B. Mississippi
C. Missouri
D. Ohio

The following questions are based on the C of E Mississippi River Maps (Cairo to the Gulf) and the Light List. At 1145, on 24 August, you depart Memphis Harbor, McKellar Lake (mile 726.0 AHP) enroute to to Baton Rouge, LA, with a tow of twelve empty gasoline barges.

1741. You have received orders to proceed to the Amoco Pipeline Co. (253.6 AHP) above Baton Rouge. If your vessel is making turns for 9 mph with an estimated average current of 1.5 mph, what is your ETA at the Amoco docks?

A. 2044, 25 Aug
B. 0214, 26 Aug
C. 0745, 26 Aug
D. 0845, 26 Aug

1742. The highest point on your towboat is 32 feet above the water, and the Helena Gauge reads +6.6 feet. What is the vertical clearance when you pass under the A-span of the Helena Highway Bridge?

A. 80.8 feet
B. 73.1 feet
C. 68.0 feet
D. 56.1 feet

1743. You are in charge of a vessel that damages an aid to navigation established and maintained by the United States. Which statement is TRUE?

A. You must take the aid in tow and deliver it to the nearest Coast Guard, Marine Safety Office.
B. You must report the allision to the nearest Corp. of Engineers Office.
C. You must report the accident to the nearest Officer in Charge, Marine Inspection.
D. You may wait until you reach your destination before reporting the allision to the U.S. Coast Guard.

1744. At 1727, on 24 August, you pass under the Helena Highway Bridge (661.7 AHP). What has been the average speed of the current since departing Memphis Harbor, McKellar Lake, if you have been making turns for 9 mph?

A. 1.8 mph
B. 2.3 mph
C. 2.8 mph
D. 3.6 mph

1745. What is the distance in river miles, from the mouth of the Yazoo Diversion Canal to the RR and Hwy. bridge at Baton Rouge, LA?

A. 365 miles
B. 310 miles
C. 265 miles
D. 203 miles

1746. The Crooked River empties into which river?

A. Missouri
B. Mississippi

C. Tennessee
D. Ohio

747. As you pass under the Greenville Highway Bridge, you estimate the current is 3.5 mph. What is the speed over the ground, if your vessel is making turns for 9 mph?

A. 14.5 mph
B. 13.5 mph
C. 12.5 mph
D. 11.5 mph

748. As you approach Walnut Point Light (mile 522.5 AHP), which type of daymark would you see on the light structure?

A. Red triangle
B. Green diamond
C. Green square
D. Red diamond

1750. In addition to the C of E maps, data on bridge clearances may be found in the _____.

A. C of E Regulations
B. Light List
C. Waterways Journal
D. Channel Report

1751. At 1118, on 24 May, you pass Natchez Gauge and estimate the current will average 3.0 mph for the remainder of the time on the Mississippi River. What is your ETA at Cairo, IL, if you continue to turn for 10 mph?

A. 0840, 26 May
B. 2218, 26 May
C. 2339, 27 May
D. 0339, 28 May

1752. After you get underway, what is the third river gauge you will pass?

A. Head of Passes
B. Natchez
C. Bayou Sara
D. Red River Landing

1753. The Bayou Sara gauge reads 5.25 feet. Which statement is TRUE?

A. This gauge reading is at a higher elevation than the same reading on the gauge at Head of Passes.
B. The depth over revetment at Old River is 25.2 ft.

C. The depth over Old River Lock sill is greater than 11 ft.
D. River level is at the Low Water Reference plane

1754. At 0715, on 24 May, you are abreast the St. Catherine Bar Lt. (mile 348.6 AHP). If you are turning for 8.0 mph, what has been the average current since you left Baton Rouge?

A. 1.0 mph
B. 1.4 mph
C. 3.8 mph
D. 4.4 mph

1756. You pass Hole in Wall Light at 1200, 24 May. What is your ETA off the Mhoon Landing gauge if you average 6.5 mph?

A. 0152, 26 May
B. 0426, 26 May
C. 1128, 26 May
D. 1221, 26 May

1757. What town is located at mile 395 AHP?

A. St. Joseph
B. Belmont
C. St. James
D. Rodney

1759. The Greenville gauge reads 1.6 feet. The high point of your towboat is 54 feet above water. What is the vertical clearance as you pass under the Greenville Highway Bridge?

A. 74.5 feet
B. 64.2 feet
C. 55.5 feet
D. 44.4 feet

1760. The area between Island 67 Upper Light (mile 623.1 AHP) and Sunflower Cut-Off Foot Light (mile 624.8 AHP) is known as a _____.

A. transit
B. crossing
C. chute
D. slough

The following questions are based on the C of E Mississippi River Maps (Cairo to the Gulf) and the Light List. On 3 January you get underway from Cambalick Dock, Morganza, LA (mile 278.3 AHP), enroute to to Portage, MO (UMR).

1761. What is the length of the trip?

A. 887.9 miles
B. 878.9 miles
C. 851.9 miles
D. 726.0 miles

1762. What are the dimensions of the Old River Lock on the lower Old River (304 AHP)?

A. 1175 × 75 feet
B. 1185 × 75 feet
C. 1195 × 84 feet
D. 1202 × 84 feet

1763. At 2126, you pass Morganza Bend Light (mile 278.4 AHP). At 0226, 4 January, you pass Red River Landing Gauge (302.4 AHP). You have been turning for 7.5 mph. What is the current?

A. 1.4 MPH
B. 1.8 MPH
C. 2.7 MPH
D. 6.2 MPH

1764. The gauge at Red River Landing reads 43.4 feet. How many feet is this above the low water reference plane?

A. 10.6 ft.
B. 11.6 ft.
C. 22.2 ft.
D. 32.8 ft.

1765. The river will be temporarily closed to navigation at mile 531.3 AHP due to repairs to the bridge. This will occur at 1530, 5 January, and last for six hours. What minimum speed over the ground must you make from Red River Landing Gauge in order not to be delayed?

A. 6.2 mph
B. 6.4 mph
C. 6.8 mph
D. 7.3 mph

1766. What type of daymark will you see as you approach Black Hills Light (mile 337.7 AHP)?

A. Private aid—no daymark
B. Red square
C. Red diamond
D. Red triangle

1767. What is the vertical clearance of the Natchez Highway Bridge when the Natchez Bridge Gauge reads 23.4 feet?

A. 102.2 ft.
B. 108.3 ft.
C. 119.5 ft.
D. 125.6 ft.

1768. The Natchez gauge reads 14.5 feet. The high point on your towboat is 47 feet above the water. What is the vertical clearance as you pass under the Natchez Highway Bridge?

A. 58.0 feet
B. 64.1 feet
C. 72.5 feet
D. 78.6 feet

1769. In order to determine what buoys, if any, are in place at Concordia Bar crossing (mile 596.0 AHP), what should you check?

A. Bulletin board at the Rosedale gauge
B. Waterways Journal
C. Light List
D. Channel Report

1770. Which of the following describes the DeSoto Terminal Co. facility at mile 570.6 AHP?

A. Mooring dolphins in midstream and a conveyor
B. A wingdam creating a sheltered mooring and two dolphins
C. Three mooring dolphins along the revetment and a conveyor on pilings
D. A submerged intake extending out 300 feet to mooring dolphins

The following questions are based on the C of E Mississippi River Maps (Cairo to the Gulf) and the Light List. On 11 September, you are making up your tow at the fleeting area in Cairo, IL, (mile 980.6 Ohio River). You get underway at 0600 enroute to to New Orleans with a mixed tow.

1771. You are turning for 7.8 mph and estimate the current at 1.0 mph. What is your speed over the ground?

A. 6.8 mph
B. 7.8 mph
C. 8.8 mph
D. 9.8 mph

1772. What is your ETA at the Fulton Gauge?

A. 1405, 12 Sept.
B. 1052, 12 Sept.
C. 0828, 12 Sept.
D. 0204, 12 Sept.

1773. What daymark should you see as you approach French Point Light (915.4 AHP)?

A. Red triangle
B. Green triangle
C. Red and green rectangle
D. Green diamond

1774. You pass New Madrid, MO (mile 889.0 AHP), at 1412. What was your average speed since leaving Cairo?

A. 8.0 mph
B. 7.8 mph
C. 7.6 mph
D. 7.3 mph

1775. At 1412 you increase speed to make good 10.2 mph. At 1506 you have a daymark on your port beam. Which daymark is this?

A. Bessie Daymark
B. Nolan Light
C. Everetts Light
D. Marr Towhead Light

1786. Which daymark should you see as you approach French Point Light (mile 915.4 AHP)?

A. Red triangle
B. Green square
C. Red and green rectangle
D. Green diamond

1787. The Linwood Bend revetment on the LMR extends from mile _____.

A. 828.1–823.1 RDB
B. 831.7–829.4 RDB
C. 841.3–838.0 LDB
D. 845.4–842.5 LDB

1788. What is the distance from the River Cement Co. Dock to the mouth of the Ohio River?

A. 780.8 miles
B. 871.9 miles
C. 953.5 miles
D. 981.5 miles

1789. You estimate the current at 2.0 mph. What is the speed over the ground?

A. 3.5 mph
B. 4.5 mph
C. 5.5 mph
D. 9.5 mph

1790. As you approach the Cahokia Marine Terminal Lights, you notice on the map a dashed line crossing the river at mile 178.3 UMR. This line indicates _____.

A. aerial crossings
B. 16 submarine power cables
C. 2 sub tel cables
D. 2 10' gas pipelines

1791. At 1032 on 24 June, you pass Carolina Landing Light (508.8 AHP). What has been the average current since 2350, 23 June, if you have been making turns for 9.0 mph?

A. 0.5 mph
B. 1.5 mph
C. 5.7 mph
D. 8.5 mph

1792. You have orders to drop off the empties at the fleeting area at Cairo Point and add five loaded tank barges to your tow. If you are turning for 9 mph and estimate the current at 1.5 mph, what is your ETA at Cairo?

A. 1031, 22 June
B. 1423, 22 June
C. 1741, 22 June
D. 2210, 22 June

1793. What is the brown colored tint shown at Bordeaux Point Dykes (681.0 AHP)?

A. river gauge
B. fish hatchery
C. levee
D. dredge material

1794. Which daymark will you see as you approach Natchez Beam Lt. (mile 364.8 AHP)?

A. Red diamond
B. White square
C. Green square
D. Red triangle

1795. You are passing the Bayou Sara gauge which reads 3.9 feet. Which of the following statements is TRUE?

A. The river level is above the Low Water Reference Plane.
B. Red Store Landing Revetment is ahead on your starboard side
C. This gauge reading is at a lower elevation than the same reading on the gauge at Head of Passes.
D. None of the above.

1796. What is the length of the trip?

A. 1195.4 miles
B. 1223.1 miles
C. 1520.1 miles
D. 1657.8 miles

1797. At 1923, on September 21, you pass Bixby Towhead Light (mile 873.7 AHP). What was your average speed since leaving Cairo?

A. 7.8 mph
B. 8.5 mph
C. 8.8 mph
D. 9.2 mph

1798. You are turning for 6.8 mph and estimate the current at 1.0 mph. What is your speed over the ground?

A. 8.8 mph
B. 8.2 mph
C. 7.8 mph
D. 6.8 mph

1799. Which type of daymark will you see as you approach Old Levee Light (mile 385.2 AHP)?

A. Green square
B. Red square
C. Green diamond
D. Private aid—no daymark

1800. At 2142, on January 3, you pass Sebastapol Light (mile 283.3 AHP). At 0137, January 4, you pass Fort Adams Light (311.4 AHP). You have been turning for 9.0 mph. What was the current?

A. 1.2 mph
B. 1.8 mph
C. 2.7 mph
D. 6.2 mph

The following questions are based on the C of E Mississippi River Maps (Cairo to the Gulf) and the Light List. At 1015, on 16 April, you are at the Amoco Pipeline Co. docks (253.6 AHP), when you get underway enroute to to Institute, WV, with a tow of eight barges carrying molten sulphur.

1801. What is the distance from the Amoco Docks at Baton Rouge, LA, to the new mouth of the White River?

A. 981.5 miles
B. 953.5 miles
C. 345.3 miles
D. 700.2 miles

1802. You are turning for 10 mph and passsing Hog Point, LA. Angola reports that the current at Red River Landing is 4.5 mph. Which statement is TRUE?

A. The main channel lies on the north side of the island you see ahead.
B. You are making 14.5 mph over the ground.
C. You would expect to find the more favorable current near the broken red line in the river.
D. You should expect to encounter vessels crossing the river at mile 300.5 AHP.

1803. As you approach Shreves cut-off you see Red River Landing Gauge (302.4 AHP) which reads 4.2 feet. Which of the following statements is TRUE?

A. This reading is at the same elevation as the 6.2 ft. mark on the gauge at Head of Passes.
B. A vessel drawing 8 ft. would be able to pass over the sill at Old River Lock
C. This reading is 6.4 feet below the Low Water Reference Plane.
D. A vessel drawing 7 ft. would be able to pass through the locks at Lower Old River.

1804. You pass Red River Gauge at 2015 on 16 April and estimate the current will average 3.0 mph for the remainder of the time on the Mississippi River. What is your ETA at the mouth of the Ohio River if you continue to turn for 10 mph?

A. 1718, 20 April
B. 1830, 20 April
C. 0028, 21 April
D. 0821, 21 April

1805. What is the vertical clearance between the highest point of your towboat, if it is 48 feet above the water, and if the Natchez Gauge reads 20.1 feet when passing under the Natchez Upper Highway Bridge?

A. 35.9 feet
B. 43.2 feet
C. 49.3 feet
D. 57.5 feet

1806. In high water conditions, which publication would you consult for the latest information on buoys between Baton Rouge and Cairo?

A. U.S.C.G. Light List
B. U.S.C.G. Notice to Mariners Channel Report
C. C of E Navigation Chart
D. List of Buoys and Daymarks

1807. As you approach Hole in Wall Light (mile 373.2 AHP), what type of daymark would you see on the light structure?

A. Green square
B. Green triangle
C. Red diamond
D. Red square

1808. You are on map #13. What is the mile point of the facility known as Slay Warehousing, Inc.?

A. mile 169 UMR
B. mile 170 UMR
C. mile 172 UMR
D. mile 173 UMR

1809. Which daymark would you see at Shields Bar Lt. (mile 882.2 AHP)?

A. Red triangle
B. Green triangle
C. Red diamond
D. Green square

1810. You are turning for 9 mph, approaching Fort Adams Lt. (311.4 AHP), and it is reported that the current at Knox Landing is estimated at 4.5 MPH. Which of the following statements is TRUE?

A. Tows and other vessels should navigate as close to the left descending bank as safety will permit.
B. The inflow channel is a navigable channel for any vessel.

C. You are making 13.5 mph over the ground.
D. Old River Control Structure Light and Fort Adams Light may be used as range lights when entering the outflow channel.

1811. Where would you find out which buoys, if any, are in place at Concordia Bar crossing (mile 596.0 AHP)?

A. Notice to Mariners
B. bulletin board at the Rosedale gauge
C. Waterways Journal
D. none of the above

1812. What are the dimensions of the Port Allen Lock at Baton Rouge, LA?

A. 75 feet × 1188 feet
B. 84 feet × 1188 feet
C. 84 feet × 1180 feet
D. 75 feet × 1180 feet

1813. Which type of daymark would you see on the Belle Island Corner Lt. at mile 458.6 AHP?

A. Green - Diamond
B. Green - Square
C. Red - Triangle
D. Red - Diamond

1814. What is the distance from Greenville, MS, to Oquaka, IL, on the Mississippi River System?

A. 832 miles
B. 733 miles
C. 597 miles
D. 537 miles

1815. At 1554, on 25 May, you pass Huntington Point Light (mile 555.2 AHP). What was your average speed since departing Amoco Pipeline Co. Docks (253.6 AHP)?

A. 6.2 mph
B. 5.2 mph
C. 4.8 mph
D. 4.3 mph

1816. What is the distance in river miles, from the new mouth of the White River to the Petro-leum Fuel & Terminal Co. (144.6 AHP)?

A. 370 miles
B. 384 miles
C. 447 miles
D. 454 miles

1817. The horizontal clearance of the center span on the Baton Rouge RR and Highway 190 Bridge is _____.

A. 443
B. 500
C. 623
D. 748

1818. At which of the following times would you be able to listen to lower Mississippi River conditions on VHF Channel 22A?

A. 0900 hours
B. 1100 hours
C. 1500 hours
D. 1700 hours

1819. You estimate the current as 2.5 mph. What is the speed over the ground?

A. 5.5 mph
B. 6.0 mph
C. 8.0 mph
D. 11.0 mph

1820. What is your clearance as you pass under the Vicksburg Highway 80 Bridge (mile 437.8 AHP) if the Vicksburg gauge reads 14.8 feet and the highest point on your tow boat is 44.5 feet?

A. 36 feet
B. 42 feet
C. 57 feet
D. 66 feet

1821. As you approach Joseph Henry Light (mile 445.2 AHP) which daymark would you see?

A. Red triangle
B. Red square
C. Green diamond
D. Green square

1822. You see a buoy with red and green bands. This buoy marks _____.

A. the center of the channel
B. the preferred channel
C. a channel crossing
D. an isolated danger

1823. The Vicksburg gauge reads 31.9 feet. The high point on your towboat is 43 feet above the water. What is the vertical clearance as you pass under the Vicksburg Highway 80 Bridge?

A. 36.2 feet
B. 41.3 feet
C. 58.0 feet
D. 84.3 feet

1824. At 1923, you increase speed to make good 9.2 mph. What is the first gauge you will pass after your speed change?

A. Cottonwood Point
B. Tiptonville
C. Fulton
D. New Madrid

1825. The Arkansas City Yellow Bend revetment on the LMR extends from mile _____.

A. 555.5-549.7 RDB
B. 549.0-548.5 RDB
C. 556.9-554.9 LDB
D. 548.5-546.5 LDB

1826. Which town is located at mile 663.5 AHP?

A. Friers Point
B. Helena
C. St. Francis
D. Rodney

1827. What is the distance in river miles, from the new mouth of the White River to the Petroleum Fuel & Terminal Co. (144.6 AHP)?

A. 454 miles
B. 447 miles
C. 384 miles
D. 370 miles

1828. You are downbound, passing by Warfield Point Lt. (mile 537 AHP), when you observe on your Mississippi River map a green diamond with an SD inside on the left bank below the light. This indicates a _____.

A. fleeting area
B. location for obtaining latest safety directions
C. warning sign to downbound traffic that the channel soon crosses very close to the right bank
D. none of the above

1829. You see a buoy with red and green bands. This buoy marks _____.

A. the center of the channel
B. a channel crossing
C. the preferred channel

D. an isolated danger

1830. At 1710 on 27 November, you are abeam of Kings Point Lt. (mile 439.8 AHP). At this time you receive a message that there will no be space for you at the Gold Bond Building Products wharf until after 1200 on the 29 November. What speed over the ground will you have to slow to so as not to arrive before this time?

A. 7.9 mph
B. 6.9 mph
C. 6.1 mph
D. 5.4 mph

1831. You pass Warnicott Bar Lt. at 1146, 24 May. What is your ETA off the Mhoon Landing gauge if you average 6.5 mph?

A. 0152, 26 May
B. 0426, 26 May
C. 1528, 26 May
D. 0909, 27 May

1832. Where can scheduled broadcast times of river stages be found?

A. Sailing Directions
B. List of Lights
C. Light List
D. Coast Pilot

1833. What are the dimensions of the Port Allen Lock at Baton Rouge, LA?

A. 75 feet × 1188 feet
B. 84 feet × 1180feet
C. 84 feet × 1188 feet
D. 75 feet × 1180 feet

1834. Which type of daymark would you see on the Belle Island Corner Lt. at mile 458.6 AHP?

A. green - diamond
B. green - square
C. red - diamond
D. red - triangle

1835. The Vaucluse Trench fill revetment on the LMR extends from mile _____.

A. 524.3 - 522.6 RDB
B. 534.3 - 532.6 RDB
C. 535.9 - 534.3 LDB
D. 534.3 - 532.6 LDB

1836. Which daymark should you see as you approach French Point Light (mile 915.4 AHP)?

A. red diamond
B. green square
C. red triangle
D. green diamond

1837. The Arkansas City Yellow Bend revetment on the LMR extends from mile _____.

A. 555.5-549.7 RDB
B. 549.0-548.5 RDB
C. 556.9-554.9 LDB
D. 548.5-546.5 LDB

1838. What is the distance from Greenville, MS, to St. Louis, MO, on the Mississippi River System?

A. 566 miles
B. 597 miles
C. 733 miles
D. 832 miles

1839. What are the dimensions of the channel maintained from Baton Rouge to New Orleans, LA?

A. 30 feet × 300 feet
B. 40 feet × 300 feet
C. 30 feet × 500 feet
D. 45 feet × 500 feet

1840. You see a buoy with red and green bands. This buoy marks _____.

A. the center of the channel
B. the preferred channel
C. a channel crossing
D. an isolated danger

1841. At 0509, on 26 December, you pass under the Helena Highway Bridge (661.7 AHP). What has been the average speed of the current since departing Memphis Harbor, McKellar Lake, if you have been making turns for 7.5 mph?

A. 1.8 mph
B. 2.1 mph
C. 4.4 mph
D. 5.6 mph

1842. What town is located at mile 389.8 AHP?

A. Whitehall
B. Belmont
C. St. James
D. Rodney

1843. As you approach Casting Yard Dock Lt. (mile 265.4 AHP) you notice on the map a circle with 2 black sectors. This symbol indicates a _____.

A. lock
B. warning sign
C. river gauge
D. mooring buoy

1844. You estimate the current at 2.0 mph. What is the speed over the ground?

A. 9.5 mph
B. 5.5 mph
C. 5.0 mph
D. 4.5 mph

1845. At 1032 on 24 June, you pass Carolina Landing Light (508.8 AHP). What has been the average current since 2350, 23 June, if you have been making turns for 9.0 mph?

A. 8.5 mph
B. 5.7 mph
C. 1.5 mph
D. 0.5 mph

1846. The Helena gauge reads 9.4 feet. The high point on your towboat is 42 feet above water. What is the vertical clearance when you pass under the Helena Highway Bridge?

A. 53.0 feet
B. 62.6 feet
C. 64.2 feet
D. 68.0 feet

1847. Which type of daymark will you see as you approach Old Levee Light (mile 385.2 AHP)?

A. Green diamond
B. Red square
C. Green square
D. Private aid—no daymark

1848. If the highest point on your towboat is 52 feet and the West Memphis gauge reads 26 feet what is the vertical clearance when you pass under the Hernando Desoto Bridge (736.6 AHP)?

A. 25.8 feet
B. 30.7 feet
C. 42.6 feet
D. 56.7 feet

1849. As you pass Solitude Lt. (mile 249.0 AHP) which dayboard would you see?

A. Green diamond
B. Green square
C. Red triangle
D. Red diamond

1850. At 0715, on March 9, you pass Knox Landing Gauge (313.8 AHP) and estimate the current will average 3.5 mph for the remainder of the time on the Mississippi River. What is your ETA at the mouth of the Ohio River if you increase speed to turn for 10 mph?

A. 0640, 11 March
B. 0554, 12 March
C. 1830, 12 March
D. 0943, 13 March

The following questions are based on the C of E Mississippi River Maps (Hannibal, MO, to the Gulf of Mexico) and the Light List. On 9 September, you depart the Formosa Plastics mooring facility at mile 233.5 AHP with six loaded tank barges enroute to to the Alton Barge Terminal, Alton, IL, (mile 202.0 UMR). Your engines are making turns for 7.5 mph in still water.

1931. What is the total length of the trip?

A. 922.3 miles
B. 985.3 miles
C. 1155.8 miles
D. 1187.3 miles

1932. What company does NOT have a marine facility along the river bank in Madison Parish (mile 457.0 AHP)?

A. Complex Chemical Co.
B. Delta Southern Railroads
C. Baxter Wilson Steamplant
D. Scott Petroleum

1933. You are turning for 10 mph and passing Hog Point, LA (mile 297.5 AHP). Angola reports that the current at Red River Landing is 4.5 mph. Which statement is TRUE?

A. The main channel lies on the south side of the island you see ahead.
B. You are making 14.5 mph over the ground.
C. An underwater stone dike has been constructed 0.5 miles upstream of Miles Bar Towhead.

D. You would expect to find the more favorable current near the broken red line in the river.

1934. Which of the following statements are TRUE?

A. Oil well structures are listed in the Light List.
B. All aids to navigation with lights have lateral significance.
C. On the Western Rivers, crossing marks may exhibit white lights.
D. All of the above.

1935. As you approach Buckridge Light (mile 411.5 AHP), which type of daymark would you see on the light structure?

A. Red diamond
B. Red triangle
C. Green square
D. Green diamond

1936. After passing Wilkinson Lt. you see a flashing amber light on the right descending bank ahead. The flashing light indicates that you should _____.

A. stay in the deepest water
B. slow down due to dredging operations
C. keep as close to the right descending bank as safety permits
D. keep as close to the left descending bank as safety permits

1937. At 0645, on the 17th of April, you pass Hole in the Wall Lt. (mile 373.4 AHP). What has been your average speed since departing the Exxon Refinery?

A. 5.8 mph
B. 6.3 mph
C. 6.7 mph
D. 7.1 mph

1938. As you approach West Memphis Lt. (mile 727.4 AHP) you notice on the map a dashed line crossing the river. This line indicates a _____.

A. submerged oil pipeline
B. submerged gas pipeline
C. aerial tramway
D. aerial transmission line

1939. At 1609, on October 5, you are abeam of Star Landing Lt. (mile 707.2 AHP). You calculate your speed since you departed Sycamore Chute fleeting area. If

you are turning for 9.5 mph what was the current?

A. 1.0 mph
B. 1.5 mph
C. 2.0 mph
D. 2.5 mph

1940. At 1300, 5 January, the river will be temporarily closed to navigation for six hours at mile 531.3 AHP due to repairs to a bridge. What minimum speed over the ground must you make from Natchez Gauge in order not to be delayed?

A. 5.7 mph
B. 6.0 mph
C. 6.8 mph
D. 7.3 mph

1941. The Linwood Bend revetment on the LMR extends from mile _____.

A. 828.1–823.1 RDB
B. 831.7–829.4 RDB
C. 845.4–842.5 LDB
D. 841.3–838.0 LDB

1942. What is the milepoint of the Fulton Gauge?

A. 598 AHP
B. 632 AHP
C. 687 AHP
D. 778 AHP

1943. At 0119, on 10 September, you pass Springfield Bend Lt. (244.8 AHP) and estimate the current will average 2.5 mph for the remainder of your trip. What is your ETA at the mouth of the Ohio River if you are making turns for 8.5 mph?

A. 1746, 12 September
B. 1244, 13 September
C. 2329, 14 September
D. 0210, 15 September

1944. The Vaucluse Trench fill revetment on the LMR extends from mile _____.

A. 524.3–522.6 RDB
B. 534.3–532.6 RDB
C. 535.9–534.3 LDB
D. 534.3–532.6 LDB

1945. In high water conditions, which publication would you consult for the latest information on buoys between Baton Rouge and Cairo?

A. List of Buoys and Daymarks
B. U.S.C.G. Light List
C. C of E Navigation Chart
D. None of the above

1946. As you approach Buckridge Light (mile 411.5 AHP), which type of daymark would you see on the light structure?

A. Red diamond
B. Red triangle
C. Green diamond
D. Green square

The following questions are based on the C of E Mississippi River Maps (Hannibal, MO, to the Gulf of Mexico) and the Light List. On the 10th of May at 1130, you leave the fleeting area at Gartness Lt. (mile 227.8 AHP) bound for the Monsanto Terminal in St. Louis (mile 178.0 UMR). Your engines turn for 8.5 mph in still water.

1947. What is the length of the trip?

A. 405.8 miles
B. 904.0 miles
C. 1002.0 miles
D. 1136.8 miles

1948. You are passing Goose Island Lt. (mile 34.4 UMR). The brown shaded areas alongside the river represent _____.

A. levees
B. revetments
C. dredged material
D. dikes

1949. The lake located near Grand Gulf Island Light (404.9 AHP) is called _____.

A. Gin Lake
B. Hamilton Lake
C. Coon Island Lake
D. Rock Lake

1950. The Greenville gauge reads 10.6 feet. The high point of your towboat is 54 feet above water. What is the vertical clearance as you pass under the Greenville Highway Bridge?

A. 44.4 feet
B. 54.2 feet
C. 65.5 feet
D. 75.4 feet

1951. As you approach Ashland Light (mile 378.1 AHP) which daymark would you see?

A. red diamond
B. red triangle
C. green square
D. green diamond

1952. As you approach Dean Island Light (mile 755.7 AHP), which type of daymark will be observed at the light?

A. green triangle
B. green diamond
C. green square
D. red-and-green banded square

1953. You are downbound when you observe on your Mississippi River map a diamond with an "SD" inside on the left bank. This indicates _____.

A. a location for obtaining latest "steering directions"
B. that there is a "sunken derelict" near bank
C. a "submerged danger" and that you should stay well clear of the bank
D. that you must "slow down" to prevent bank erosion ahead

The following questions are based on the C of E Mississippi River Maps (Cairo to the Gulf) and the Light List. At 1745, on 25 August, you depart Memphis Harbor, McKellar Lake (mile 726.0 AHP - LMR) enroute to to Baton Rouge, LA, with a tow of twelve empty gasoline barges.

1954. You have received orders to proceed to the Amoco Pipeline Co. (253.6 AHP) above Baton Rouge. If your vessel is making turns for 9 mph with an estimated average current of 1.5 mph, what is your ETA at the Amoco docks?

A. 1444, 27 Aug
B. 2214, 27 Aug
C. 0844, 28 Aug
D. 1454, 28 Aug

1955. At 1814, on 11 September, you pass under the Greenville Highway Bridge (mile 531.3 AHP). What speed must you average to arrive at Jimmy Hawken Light (mile 663.5 AHP) at 0930 the following day?

A. 8.7 mph
B. 7.7 mph
C. 6.3 mph
D. 5.6 mph

1956. At 1923, you increase speed to make

good 9.2 mph. What is the first gauge you will pass after your speed change?

A. Cottonwood Point
B. Tiptonville
C. Fulton
D. New Madrid

1957. At 1923, on September 21, you pass Bixby Towhead Light (mile 873.7 AHP). What was your average speed since leaving Cairo?

A. 9.2 mph
B. 8.8 mph
C. 8.5 mph
D. 7.2 mph

1958. Which daymark would you see as you approach Red Store Light (mile 269.5 AHP)?

A. green diamond
B. green triangle
C. green square
D. red square

1959. The charts show two dashed lines crossing the river just south of St. Catherine Bar Light. What does this indicate?

A. overhead power lines
B. Louisiana-Mississippi ferry crossings
C. two railroad trestles
D. two submerged oil pipelines

1960. If the gauge at the Greenville Highway Bridge reads 22.0 feet, what is the water level in relation to the low water reference plane (LWRP)?

A. 22.1 feet below the LWRP
B. 10.7 feet below the LWRP
C. 10.7 feet above the LWRP
D. 0.5 feet below the LWRP

1961. The Delta-Friar Point revetment on the LMR extends from mile _____.

A. 657.3 - 652.2 LDB
B. 652.8 - 649.6 RDB
C. 648.5 - 645.5 LDB
D. 645.6 - 641.4 RDB

1962. How long will it take you to go from the Memphis gauge to your destination in New Orleans, LA, if you estimate the average current on this segment of the route to be 2.0 mph and you increase the engine turns to 8.5 mph?

A. 1 day 20 hours 33 minutes
B. 2 days 6 hours 24 minutes
C. 2 days 12 hours 15 minutes
D. 3 days 4 hours 11 minutes

1963. Which of the following statements are TRUE?

A. Oil well structures are listed in the Light List.
B. All aids to navigation with lights have lateral significance.
C. On the Western Rivers, crossing marks may exhibit white lights.
D. All of the above.

1964. The Platte River empties into which river?

A. Mississippi
B. Missouri
C. Ohio
D. Tennessee

1965. As you approach West Memphis Lt. (mile 727.4 AHP) you notice on the map a dashed line crossing the river. This line indicates a _____.

A. submerged oil pipeline
B. submerged gas pipeline
C. aerial tramway
D. aerial transmission line

1966. After passing Oak Bend Lt. (mile 425.6 AHP) you see a light gray shaded area extending into the river shown on the map. This indicates a _____.

A. fleeting area
B. weir
C. dike
D. revetment

1967. On which river is Dover, KY, located?

A. Mississippi
B. Tennessee
C. Ohio
D. Missouri

1968. The Natchez gauge reads 8.6 feet. The high point on your towboat is 38 feet above water. What is the vertical clearance when you pass under the Natchez Highway Bridge?

A. 79.0 feet
B. 71.3 feet

C. 65.2 feet
D. 59.1 feet

1969. What does the green diamond with the letters "SD" indicate just below the entrance to Greenville Harbor (536.7 miles AHP)?

A. location of a sunken wreck
B. location where latest steering directions may be obtained
C. shoaling area
D. speed zone

1970. Which town is located at mile 663.5 AHP?

A. Friers Point
B. Helena
C. St. Francis
D. Rodney

1971. The Linwood Bend revetment on the LMR extends from mile _____.

A. 828.1-823.1 RDB
B. 831.7-829.4 RDB
C. 845.4-842.5 LDB
D. 841.3-838.0 LDB

1972. Which daymark will you see as you approach Natchez Beam Lt. (mile 364.8 AHP)?

A. red diamond
B. white square
C. green square
D. red triangle

1973. As you approach Giles Bend Cut-off Light (367.7 AHP), which type of daymark would you see on the light structure?

A. green square
B. green triangle
C. red diamond
D. red square

1974. As you approach Giles Bend Cut-off Light (367.7 AHP), which type of daymark would you see on the light structure?

A. green diamond
B. green triangle
C. red diamond
D. red square

1975. After passing Wilkinson Lt. you see a flashing amber light on the right descending bank ahead. The flashing light indicates that you should _____.

A. stay in the deepest water
B. slow down due to dredging operations
C. keep as close to the left descending bank as safety permits
D. keep as close to the right descending bank as safety permits

1976. At 0645, on the 17th of April, you pass Hole in the Wall Lt. (mile 373.4 AHP). What has been your average speed since departing the Exxon Refinery?

A. 8.8 mph
B. 7.3 mph
C. 6.8 mph
D. 6.3 mph

1977. As you approach Giles Bend Cutoff Light (mile 367.7 LDB), what type of daymark would you see on the light structure?

A. green diamond
B. green triangle
C. red diamond
D. red square

1978. After you enter the Ohio River at Cairo, the map shows that the deepest water under the Illinois Central RR Bridge would be found under which span?

A. right descending bank span
B. left descending bank span
C. center span
D. water is equal under all spans

The following questions are based on the C of E Mississippi River Maps (Hannibal, MO, to the Gulf of Mexico) and the Light List. On the 10th of May at 1130, you leave the fleeting area at Gartness Lt. (mile 227.8 AHP) bound for the Monsanto Terminal in St. Louis (mile 178.0 UMR). Your engines turn for 8.5 mph in still water.

1979. What is the length of the trip?

A. 405.8 miles
B. 553.0 miles
C. 904.0 miles
D. 1136.8 miles

1980. At Filter Point Light (mile 475 AHP) there are 3 close straight dashed lines on the map passing through the black dot below the number 475. What do these lines represent?

A. submerged oil pipelines
B. submerged telephone cables

C. submerged gas pipelines
D. aerial power cables

1981. Where can scheduled broadcast times of river stages be found?

A. Sailing Directions
B. Light List
C. List of Lights
D. Coast Pilot

1982. What are the dimensions of the Port Allen Lock at Baton Rouge, LA?

A. 75 feet × 1188 feet
B. 84 feet × 1188 feet
C. 84 feet × 1180 feet
D. 75 feet × 1180 feet

1983. As you pass under the Natchez-Vidalia Dual Bridge, the gauge on the bridge reads 8.9 ft. If the highest point on your vessel is 54 ft. above the water, what is your vertical clearance?

A. 60.0 feet
B. 62.6 feet
C. 67.2 feet
D. 122.0 feet

1984. What company does NOT have a marine facility along the river bank in Madison Parish (mile 457.0 AHP)?

A. Complex Chemical Co.
B. Delta Southern Railroads
C. Baxter Wilson Steam plant
D. Scott Petroleum

1985. Which light characteristics does Foster Light (mile 157.7 AHP) have?

A. 1 green flash every 4 seconds
B. 2 white flashes every 5 seconds
C. 1 red flash every 4 seconds
D. 2 red flashes every 5 seconds

1986. You are in charge of a vessel that damages an aid to navigation established and maintained by the United States. Which statement is TRUE?

A. You must take aid in tow and deliver it to the nearest Coast Guard, Marine Safety Office.
B. You must report the allision to the nearest Corp. of Engineers Office.
C. You may wait until you reach your destination before reporting the allision to the U.S. Coast Guard.

D. You must report the accident to the nearest Officer in Charge, Marine Inspection.

1987. As you approach Old River Control Structure Light you see a flashing amber light. You should _____.

A. navigate as close to the right descending bank as safety permits
B. navigate as close to the left descending bank as safety permits
C. turn into the inflow channel as the bypass is now open
D. slow your engine speed to not more than 5 mph

1988. As you approach West Memphis Lt. (mile 727.4 AHP) you notice on the map a dashed line crossing the river. This line indicates a _____.

A. submerged oil pipeline
B. submerged gas pipeline
C. aerial transmission line
D. aerial tramway

1989. What is the milepoint of Hickman, KY, gauge?

A. 922.0 AHP
B. 889.0 AHP
C. 865.0 AHP
D. 837.2 AHP

1990. At Filter Point Light (mile 475 AHP) there are 3 close straight dashed lines on the map passing through the black dot below the number 475. What do these lines represent?

A. Submerged oil pipelines
B. Submerged gas pipelines
C. Submerged telephone cables
D. Aerial power cables

1991. From Baton Rouge to Cairo, what is the maintained minimum channel depth during low water?

A. 9 feet
B. 12 feet
C. 15 feet
D. 30 feet

1992. What are the light characteristics of Greenwood Light (mile 288.6 AHP)?

A. Fixed red light
B. 2 red flashes every 5 seconds

C. 1 red flash every 4 seconds
D. 2 white flashes every 4 seconds

1993. The solid lines extending into the channel at mile 948 AHP are _____.

A. dikes
B. revetments
C. spoil areas
D. Westvaco Service Facilities

1994. At 0715, on March 9, you pass Knox Landing Gauge (313.8 AHP) and estimate the current will average 3.5 mph for the remainder of the time on the Mississippi River. What is your ETA at the mouth of the Ohio River if you increase speed to turn for 10 mph?

A. 0640, 11 March
B. 0554, 12 March
C. 0943, 13 March
D. 1242, 13 March

1995. Which company does NOT have a marine facility in Rosedale harbor (mile 585 AHP)?

A. T.L. James
B. Rosedale–Boliver County Port Commission
C. Cives Steel Company
D. Sanders Elevator Corp

1996. What is the distance from the Memphis gauge to the Gold Bond Building Products Wharf in New Orleans, LA?

A. 460 miles
B. 503 miles
C. 588 miles
D. 633 miles

1997. After passing Oak Bend Lt. (mile 425.6 AHP) you see a light grey shaded area extending into the river shown on the map. This indicates a _____.

A. fleeting area
B. weir
C. dike
D. revetment

1998. As you approach Ashland Light (mile 378.1 AHP) which daymark would you see?

A. Red triangle
B. Red diamond
C. Green square
D. Green diamond

1999. The lighted mooring buoy at mile 228.7 AHP is a facility for which company?

A. Luhr Brothers
B. Cargo Carriers
C. National Marine, Inc.
D. International Marine Terminals

The following questions are based on the C of E Mississippi River Maps (Hannibal, MO, to the Gulf of Mexico) and the Light List. On 3 January you get underway from Hall-Buck Coke Terminal Dock, Baton Rouge, LA (mile 233.0 AHP) enroute to to the Mobile Oil Docks (east side), (mile 176.4 UMR), in St. Louis.

2039. What is the length of the trip?

A. 720.8 miles
B. 777.4 miles
C. 897.2 miles
D. 906.3 miles

2040. The Memphis gauge reads 18.4 feet. The high point of your towboat is 48 feet above water. What is the vertical clearance as you pass under the Memphis Highway Bridge?

A. 75.4 feet
B. 66.4 feet
C. 53.8 feet
D. 46.4 feet

2041. You are turning for 9 mph, approaching Fort Adams Light (311.4 AHP) and it is reported that the current at Knox Landing is estimated at 4.5 mph. Which of the following statements is TRUE?

A. Tows and other vessels should navigate as close to the left descending bank as safety will permit.
B. The inflow channel is a navigable channel for any vessel.
C. You are making 13.5 mph over the ground.
D. Old River Control Structure Light and Fort Adams Light may be used as range lights when entering the outflow channel.

2042. Which of the following statements are TRUE?

A. Oil well structures are listed in the Light List.
B. All aids to navigation with lights have lateral significance.

C. On the Western Rivers, crossing marks may exhibit white lights.
D. None of the above.

2043. At 0509, on 26 December, you pass under the Helena Highway Bridge (661.7 AHP). What has been the average speed of the current since departing Memphis Harbor, McKellar Lake, if you have been making turns for 7.5 mph?

A. 5.6 mph
B. 4.4 mph
C. 2.1 mph
D. 1.8 mph

2044. At 1000, on May 11th, you are passing Prince George Lt. (mile 364.1 AHP) in Natchez, Mississippi, and must send an ETA to the Monsanto Terminal in St. Louis (mile 178.0 UMR). Your engines are still turning for 8.5 mph and you estimate the current at 2.5 mph. What will be your arrival time in St. Louis?

A. 1919 on 15 May
B. 2344 on 15 May
C. 1113 on 16 May
D. 1757 on 16 May

2045. You are turning for 8.2 mph and estimate the current at 1.5 mph. What is you speed over the ground?

A. 6.7
B. 8.2
C. 7.8
D. 9.7

2046. What is the distance from the Arkansas River mouth to the Ohio River mouth in river miles?

A. 372 miles
B. 422 miles
C. 546 miles
D. 594 miles

2047. What is the distance to Caruthersville Gauge from Cape Girardeau?

A. 899.4 miles
B. 793.4 miles
C. 160.4 miles
D. 54.4 miles

2048. What is the minimum maintained depth of the channel from Cairo to Baton Rouge during low water?

A. 18 feet
B. 15 feet
C. 12 feet
D. 9 feet

The following questions are based on the C of E Mississippi River Maps (Hannibal, MO, to the Gulf of Mexico) and the Light List. On the 10th of May at 1130, you leave the fleeting area at Gartness Lt. (mile 227.8 AHP) bound for the Monsanto Terminal in St. Louis (mile 178.0 UMR). Your engines turn for 8.5 mph in still water.

2049. What is the length of the trip?

A. 405.8 miles
B. 904.0 miles
C. 1002.0 miles
D. 1136.8 miles

2050. From Baton Rouge to Cairo, what is the maintained minimum channel depth during low water?

A. 9 feet
B. 12 feet
C. 15 feet
D. 30 feet

2051. On which map would you find Redman Point, Arkansas?

A. 60
B. 57
C. 45
D. 38

2052. The highest point on your towboat is 48 feet above the water, and the Memphis Gauge reads +7.5 feet. What is the vertical clearance when you pass under the Hernando Desoto Bridge in Memphis?

A. 53.2 feet
B. 58.1 feet
C. 68.2 feet
D. 96.3 feet

2053. At 2342, on 25 August, you pass under the Helena Highway Bridge (661.7 AHP). What has been the average speed of the current since departing Memphis Harbor, McKellar Lake, if you have been making turns for 9 mph?

A. 1.8 mph
B. 2.1 mph
C. 4.4 mph
D. 5.6 mph

2054. The Natchez gauge reads 16.3 feet. The high point on your towboat is 38 feet above water. What is the vertical clearance when you pass under the Natchez Highway Bridge?

A. 79.0 feet
B. 71.3 feet
C. 65.2 feet
D. 59.1 feet

2055. You estimate the current at 3.0 mph. What is the speed over the ground?

A. 3.5 mph
B. 4.5 mph
C. 7.5 mph
D. 9.5 mph

2056. What are the color and shape of Togo Island daymark at mile 415.0 AHP?

A. green - diamond
B. green - square
C. red - triangle
D. red - square

The following questions are based on the C of E Mississippi River Maps (Hannibal, MO, to the Gulf of Mexico) and the Light List. At 0620 on 25 November, you depart Cape Girardeau fleeting area (mile 53.0 UMR) bound for the Gold Bond Building Products Wharf in New Orleans, LA (mile 102.0 AHP).

2057. Your engines are turning for 8.2 mph. You estimate the current at 1.5 mph. What is your speed over the ground?

A. 9.7 mph
B. 8.8 mph
C. 8.2 mph
D. 6.7 mph

2058. As you approach Old River Control Structure Light you see a flashing amber light. You should _____.

A. navigate as close to the left descending bank as safety permits
B. navigate as close to the right descending bank as safety permits
C. turn into the inflow channel as the bypass is now open
D. slow your engine speed to not more than 5 mph

2059. What is the minimum maintained depth of the channel from Cairo to Baton Rouge during low water?

A. 9 feet
B. 12 feet
C. 15 feet
D. 18 feet

2060. The highest point on your towboat is 67 feet above the water, and the Helena Gauge reads +22.3 feet. What is the vertical clearance when you pass under the A-span of the Helena Highway Bridge?

A. 30.1 feet
B. 49.8 feet
C. 52.4 feet
D. 74.7 feet

2061. The lighted mooring buoy at mile 228.7 AHP is a facility for which company?

A. Luhr Brothers
B. Cargo Carriers
C. National Marine, Inc.
D. International Marine Terminals

2062. You are downbound, passing by Warfield Point Lt. (mile 537 AHP), when you observe on your Mississippi River map a green diamond with an "SD" inside on the left bank below the light. This indicates a _____.

A. fleeting area
B. location for obtaining the latest safety directions
C. warning sign to downbound traffic that the channel soon crosses very close to the right bank
D. none of the above

2063. At 1923, on September 21, you pass Bixby Towhead Light (mile 873.7 AHP). What was your average speed since leaving Cairo?

A. 7.8 mph
B. 8.5 mph
C. 8.8 mph
D. 9.2 mph

2064. At 1923, you increase speed to make good 9.2 mph. What is the first gauge you will pass after your speed change?

A. Cottonwood Point
B. New Madrid
C. Fulton
D. Tiptonville

2065. Which daymark will you see as you approach Natchez Beam Lt. (mile 364.8 AHP)?

A. red triangle
B. white square
C. green square
D. red diamond

2066. The Memphis gauge reads 18.4 feet. The high point of your towboat is 48 feet above water. What is the vertical clearance as you pass under the Memphis Highway Bridge?

A. 75.4 feet
B. 66.4 feet
C. 53.8 feet
D. 46.4 feet

2067. At 0921, on 24 July, you are abreast the St. Catherine Bar Lt. (mile 348.6 AHP). If you are turning for 10.0 mph, what was the current since departure?

A. 1.4 mph
B. 1.7 mph
C. 2.0 mph
D. 7.0 mph

2068. In high water conditions, which publication would you consult for the latest information on buoys between Baton Rouge and Cairo?

A. List of Buoys and Daymarks
B. U.S.C.G. Light List
C. C of E Navigation Chart
D. none of the above

2069. The solid lines extending into the channel at mile 948 AHP are _____.

A. revetments
B. dikes
C. spoil areas
D. Westvaco Service Facilities

The following questions are based on the C of E Mississippi River Maps (Hannibal, MO, to the Gulf of Mexico) and the Light List. At 0825 on 08 March, you get underway from the River Cement Co. (173.0 AHP), enroute to The Slay Warehousing docks (179.0 UMR) in St. Louis, MO, with a tow of eight barges carrying cement.

2070. What is the distance from the River Cement Co. Dock to the mouth of the Ohio River?

A. 780.8 miles
B. 871.9 miles
C. 953.5 miles
D. 981.5 miles

2071. As you approach the Cahokia Marine Terminal Lights, you notice on the map a dashed line crossing the river at mile 178.3 UMR. This line indicates _____.

A. aerial crossings
B. 16 submarine power cables
C. 2 sub tel cables
D. 2-10' gas pipelines

The following questions are based on the C of E Mississippi River Maps (Cairo to the Gulf) and the Light List. At 1015 on 16 April, you are at the Amoco Pipeline Co. Docks (253.6 AHP), when you get underway, enroute to Institute, WV, with a tow of eight barges carrying molten sulphur.

2072. What is the distance from the Amoco Docks at Baton Rouge, LA, to the mouth of the Ohio River?

A. 700.2 miles
B. 727.9 miles
C. 953.5 miles
D. 981.5 miles

2073. As you approach Casting Yard Dock Lt. (mile 265.4 AHP) you notice on the map a circle with 2 black sectors. This symbol indicates a _____.

A. lock
B. warning sign
C. mooring buoy
D. river gauge

2074. What is your clearance as you pass under the Vicksburg Highway 80 Bridge (mile 437.8 AHP) if the Vicksburg gauge reads 14.8 feet and the highest point on your tow boat is 44.5 feet?

A. 36 feet
B. 42 feet
C. 57 feet
D. 66 feet

2075. After entering Milliken Bend (mile 455 AHP) you wish to locate the river service in Madison Parish, Louisiana. The river service is indicated by the square containing which number?

A. 2
B. 3
C. 4
D. 5

2076. What is the mile point of the Fulton Gauge?

A. 778 AHP
B. 687 AHP
C. 632 AHP
D. 598 AHP

2077. At 0119, on 10 September, you pass Springfield Bend Lt. (244.8 AHP) and estimate the current will average 2.5 mph for the remainder of your trip. What is your ETA at the mouth of the Ohio River if you are making turns for 8.5 mph?

A. 1746, 12 September
B. 1244, 13 September
C. 1244, 14 September
D. 2329, 14 September

2078. You are turning for 7.5 mph and estimate the current at 3.0 mph. What is your ETA at the River Cement Co. in Natchez considering that you passed Cherokee Landing Lt. at 2100?

A. 1243 on 15 January
B. 1605 on 15 January
C. 1244 on 16 January
D. 1922 on 16 January

2079. At 1030, 13 January, you are passing Columbus Point Lt. (mile 936.1 AHP). What has been your average speed since leaving St. Louis (mile 181 UMR) on the 12th of January at 1400 hours?

A. 9.1 mph
B. 9.4 mph
C. 9.7 mph
D. 10.4 mph

The following questions are based on the C of E Mississippi River Maps (Cairo to the Gulf) and the Light List.
On 21 September, you are making up your tow at the fleeting area in Cairo, IL, (mile 980.6 Ohio River). You get underway at 0952 enroute to to New Orleans with a mixed tow.

2080. You are turning for 7.8 mph and estimate the current at 1.0 mph. What is your speed over the ground?

A. 8.8 mph
B. 7.9 mph
C. 7.8 mph
D. 6.8 mph

2081. You are steaming at 21 knots and burning 462 barrels of fuel per day. You must decrease your consumption to 221 barrels per day. What must you reduce your speed to in order to burn this amount of fuel?

A. 15.1 knots
B. 16.4 knots
C. 17.6 knots
D. 18.2 knots

2082. From your 0100 position, you change course to 258° per standard magnetic compass. Your engine speed is 10.0 knots. A short time later, your fathometer reads 51 feet (15.5 meters) under the keel. What is the water depth?

A. 42.5 feet (12.9 meters)
B. 51.0 feet (15.5 meters)
C. 59.5 feet (18.0 meters)
D. 60.4 feet (18.4 meters)

2083. You are steaming at 18 knots and burning 406 barrels of fuel per day. You must decrease your consumption to 221 barrels per day. What must you reduce your speed to in order to burn this amount of fuel?

A. 14.7 knots
B. 15.5 knots
C. 16.3 knots
D. 17.2 knots

2084. You are steaming at 16 knots and burning 326 barrels of fuel per day. You must decrease your consumption to 212 barrels per day. What must you reduce your speed to in order to burn this amount of fuel?

A. 15.2 knots
B. 14.8 knots
C. 14.4 knots
D. 13.9 knots

2085. At your current speed of 20 knots you only have enough fuel remaining to travel 360 miles. You must travel 440 miles to reach your destination. What should you reduce your speed to in order to reach your destination?

A. 18.1 knots
B. 17.5 knots
C. 16.9 knots
D. 16.3 knots

2086. At your current speed of 22 knots you only have enough fuel remaining to travel 440 miles. You must travel 618 miles to reach your destination. What should you reduce your speed to in order to reach your destination?

A. 17.8 knots
B. 18.6 knots
C. 19.4 knots
D. 20.2 knots

2087. At your current speed of 21 knots you only have enough fuel remaining to travel 404 miles. You must travel 731 miles to reach your destination. What should you reduce your speed to in order to reach your destination?

A. 18.9 knots
B. 17.8 knots
C. 16.7 knots
D. 15.6 knots

2088. At your current speed of 19 knots you only have enough fuel remaining to travel 265 miles. You must travel 731 miles to reach your destination. What should you reduce your speed to in order to reach your destination?

A. 13.8 knots
B. 12.6 knots
C. 11.4 knots
D. 10.2 knots

2089. At your current speed of 18 knots you only have enough fuel remaining to travel 316 miles. You must travel 731 miles to reach your destination. What should you reduce your speed to in order to reach your destination?

A. 10.4 knots
B. 11.8 knots
C. 13.2 knots
D. 14.6 knots

2090. At your current speed of 17 knots you only have enough fuel remaining to travel 316 miles. You must travel 622 miles to reach your destination. What should you reduce your speed to in order to reach your destination?

A. 12.1 knots
B. 13.3 knots
C. 14.5 knots
D. 15.7 knots

2091. At your current speed of 22 knots you only have enough fuel remaining to travel 422 miles. You must travel 844 miles to reach your destination. What should you reduce your speed to in order to reach your destination?

A. 19.8 knots
B. 18.4 knots
C. 17 knots
D. 15.6 knots

2092. At your current speed of 23 knots you only have enough fuel remaining to travel 386 miles. You must travel 785 miles to reach your destination. What should you reduce your speed to in order to reach your destination?

A. 19.3 knots
B. 17.7 knots
C. 16.1 knots
D. 14.5 knots

2093. At your current speed of 21 knots you only have enough fuel remaining to travel 435 miles. You must travel 755 miles to reach your destination. What should you reduce your speed to in order to reach your destination?

A. 15.9 knots
B. 17.1 knots
C. 18.3 knots
D. 19.5 knots

2094. At your current speed of 20 knots you only have enough fuel remaining to travel 218 miles. You must travel 395 miles to reach your destination. What should you reduce your speed to in order to reach your destination?

A. 17.4 knots
B. 16.2 knots
C. 14.9 knots
D. 13.7 knots

2095. You are steaming at 23 knots and burning 524 barrels of fuel per day. You must decrease your consumption to 260 barrels per day. What must you reduce your speed to in order to burn this amount of fuel?

A. 13.2 knots
B. 14.8 knots
C. 16.6 knots
D. 18.2 knots

2096. You are steaming at 22 knots and burning 618 barrels of fuel per day. You must decrease your consumption to 220 barrels per day. What must you reduce your speed to in order to burn this amount of fuel?

A. 14.2 knots
B. 15.6 knots
C. 17.0 knots
D. 18.4 knots

2097. You are steaming at 21 knots and burning 633 barrels of fuel per day. You must decrease your consumption to 410 barrels per day. What must you reduce your speed to in order to burn this amount of fuel?

A. 14.9 knots
B. 16.0 knots
C. 17.1 knots
D. 18.2 knots

2098. You are steaming at 20 knots and burning 568 barrels of fuel per day. You must decrease your consumption to 265 barrels per day. What must you reduce your speed to in order to burn this amount of fuel?

A. 14.7 knots
B. 15.5 knots
C. 16.3 knots
D. 17.1 knots

2099. You are steaming at 19 knots and burning 476 barrels of fuel per day. You must decrease your consumption to 185 barrels per day. What must you reduce your speed to in order to burn this amount of fuel?

A. 13.8 knots
B. 14.6 knots
C. 15.4 knots
D. 16.2 knots

2127. On which river is Dover, KY, located?

A. Mississippi
B. Tennessee
C. Missouri
D. Ohio

2128. You are on map #13. What is the mile point of the facility known as Slay Warehousing, Inc.?

A. mile 174 UMR
B. mile 173 UMR
C. mile 172 UMR
D. mile 171 UMR

2129. As you approach Ashland Light (mile 378.1 AHP) which daymark would you see?

A. Red diamond
B. Red triangle
C. Green square
D. Green diamond

2130. On which map would you find Redman Point, Arkansas?

A. 60
B. 57
C. 45
D. 38

2131. After passing Wilkinson Lt. you see a flashing amber light on the right descending bank ahead. The flashing light indicates that you should _____.

A. stay in the deepest water
B. slow down due to dredging operations
C. keep as close to the left descending bank as safety permits
D. keep as close to the right descending bank as safety permits

2132. What is the width of the widest span of the Cairo Highway Bridge (Upper Mississippi River mile 1.3)?

A. 800 feet
B. 675 feet
C. 625 feet
D. 503 feet

2133. As you approach Ashland Lower Light (mile 375.5 AHP), which type of daymark would you see on the light structure?

A. Green square
B. Green triangle
C. Red square
D. Red diamond

2134. At 1814, on 11 September, you pass under the Greenville Highway Bridge (mile 531.3 AHP). What speed must you average to arrive at Jimmy Hawken Light (mile 663.5 AHP) at 0930 the following day?

A. 8.7 mph
B. 7.7 mph

C. 6.3 mph
D. 5.6 mph

2135. In high water conditions, which publication would you consult for the latest information on buoys between Baton Rouge and Cairo?

A. List of Buoys and Daymarks
B. Coast Pilot
C. C of E Navigation Chart
D. U.S.C.G. Notice to Mariners Channel Report

2136. You have orders to drop off the empties at the fleeting area at Cairo Point and add five loaded tank barges to your tow. If you are turning for 9 mph and estimate the current at 1.5 mph, what is your ETA at Cairo?

A. 2210, 22 June
B. 1741, 22 June
C. 1423, 22 June
D. 1031, 22 June

2137. At 1132, 24 May, you pass Natchez Beam Lt. (364.8 AHP). What is your ETA off the Memphis Gauge if you average 8.0 mph?

A. 2345, 25 May
B. 0947, 26 May
C. 1525, 26 May
D. 2215, 26 May

2138. At 0921, on 24 May, you are abreast the St. Catherine Bar Lt. (mile 348.6 AHP). If you are turning for 10.0 mph, what was the current since departure?

A. 3.4 mph
B. 2.0 mph
C. 1.7 mph
D. 1.4 mph

2139. Which light will you be passing at 0059, on 22 September, if you make good 9.2 knots?

A. Obion Bar Lt.
B. Kate Aubrey Lt.
C. Trotter Lt.
D. Quaker Oats Lt.

2140. Which daymark should you see as you approach French Point Light (mile 915.4 AHP)?

A. Red diamond
B. Green square
C. Red triangle
D. Green diamond

2141. As you approach Old River Control Structure Light you see a flashing amber light. You should _____.

A. navigate as close to the left descending bank as safety permits
B. navigate as close to the right descending bank as safety permits
C. turn into the inflow channel as the bypass is now open
D. slow your engine speed to not more than 5 mph

2142. You are passing Eastwood Lt. (mile 849.3 AHP) and the map indicates that Bunge Grain facility would be located at the square with number _____.

A. 2
B. 4
C. 6
D. 8

2143. You are turning for 7.5 mph and estimate the current at 3.0 mph. What is your ETA at the River Cement Co. in Natchez considering that you passed Cherokee Landing Lt. at 2100?

A. 1605 on 15 January
B. 0355 on 16 January
C. 1244 on 16 January
D. 1922 on 16 January

2144. What light characteristics does Foster Light have?

A. 1 green flash every 4 seconds
B. 1 red flash every 4 seconds
C. 2 white flashes every 5 seconds
D. 2 red flashes every 5 seconds

2145. After entering Milliken Bend (mile 455 AHP) you wish to locate the river service in Madison Parish, Louisiana. The river service is indicated by the square containing which number?

A. 2
B. 3
C. 4
D. 5

2146. As you pass under the Vicksburg Bridges, you estimate the current as 3.0

mph. What is the speed over the ground, if your vessel is making turns for 10.5 mph?

A. 7.5 mph
B. 10.5 mph
C. 13.5 mph
D. 16.5 mph

2147. If your vessel is making turns for 7.5 mph with an estimated average current of 1.5 mph, what is your ETA at the dock in Angelina, LA?

A. 0516, 28 Dec.
B. 1621, 28 Dec.
C. 0516, 29 Dec.
D. 1621, 29 Dec.

2148. As you approach Ashland Lower Light (mile 375.5 AHP), which type of daymark would you see on the light structure?

A. Green square
B. Green triangle
C. Red diamond
D. Red square

2149. At 1118, on 24 May, you pass Natchez Gauge and estimate the current will average 3.0 mph for the remainder of the time on the Mississippi River. What is your ETA at Cairo, IL, if you continue to turn for 10 mph?

A. 0840, 26 May
B. 2218, 26 May
C. 2218, 27 May
D. 2339, 27 May

2150. As you pass under the Natchez–Vidalia Dual Bridge, the gauge on the bridge reads 8.9 ft. If the highest point on your vessel is 54 ft. above the water, what is your vertical clearance?

A. 60.0 feet
B. 62.6 feet
C. 67.2 feet
D. 122.0 feet

The following questions are based on the C of E Mississippi River Maps (Hannibal, MO, to the Gulf of Mexico) and the Light List. On the 10th of May at 1130, you leave the fleeting area at Gartness Lt. (mile 227.8 AHP) bound for the Monsanto Terminal in St. Louis (mile 178.0 UMR). Your engines turn for 8.5 mph in still water.

2188. What is the length of the trip?

A. 405.8 miles
B. 553.0 miles
C. 904.0 miles
D. 1136.8 miles

2189. At 1000, on May 11th, you are passing Prince George Lt. (mile 364.1 AHP) in Natchez, Mississippi, and must send an ETA to the Monsanto Terminal in St. Louis (mile 178.0 UMR). Your engines are still turning for 8.5 mph and you estimate the current at 2.5 mph. What will be your arrival time in St. Louis?

A. 1919 on 15 May
B. 2344 on 15 May
C. 1757 on 16 May
D. 2236 on 16 May

2190. You are turning for 8.2 mph and estimate the current at 1.5 mph. What is your speed over the ground?

A. 9.7
B. 8.2
C. 7.8
D. 6.7

2191. On which river is Dover, KY, located?

A. Mississippi
B. Tennessee
C. Ohio
D. Missouri

2192. You are turning for 6.8 mph and estimate the current at 1.0 mph. What is your speed over the ground?

A. 6.8 mph
B. 7.8 mph
C. 8.8 mph
D. 9.4 mph

2193. Which daymark will you see as you approach Natchez Beam Lt. (mile 364.8 AHP)?

A. Red triangle
B. White square
C. Green square
D. Red diamond

2194. What is the distance from the River Cement Co. Dock to the mouth of the Ohio River?

A. 718.8 miles
B. 780.8 miles

C. 953.5 miles
D. 981.5 miles

2195. What is the distance from the Amoco Docks at Baton Rouge, LA, to Pittsburgh, PA?

A. 1681.7 miles
B. 1575.3 miles
C. 981.7 miles
D. 727.9 miles

2196. If your vessel is making turns for 7.5 mph with an estimated average current of 1.5 mph, what is your ETA at the dock in Angelina, LA?

A. 1621, 28 Dec.
B. 2203, 28 Dec.
C. 0516, 29 Dec.
D. 1621, 29 Dec.

2197. You have passed Ben Burman Lt. (mile 235.0 AHP) and see on the map a dark purplish area extending past Bayou Baton Rouge. This indicates a _____.

A. revetment
B. dredge material
C. fleeting area
D. dike

2198. You estimate the current as 2.5 mph. What is the speed over the ground?

A. 11.0 mph
B. 8.0 mph
C. 6.0 mph
D. 5.5 mph

2199. After passing Oak Bend Lt. (mile 425.6 AHP) you see a light grey shaded area extending into the river shown on the map. This indicates a _____.

A. revetment
B. weir
C. dike
D. fleeting area

2200. Which dayboard would you see on Putney Light (mile 943.6 AHP)?

A. Green square
B. Green triangle
C. Red triangle
D. Red diamond

2201. At 1000, on May 11th, you are passing George Prince Lt. (mile 364.1 AHP) in

Natchez, Mississippi, and must send an ETA to the Monsanto Terminal in St. Louis (mile 178.0 UMR). Your engines are still turning for 8.5 mph and you estimate the current at 2.5 mph. What will be your arrival time in St. Louis?

A. 1919 on 15 May
B. 2344 on 15 May
C. 1113 on 16 May
D. 1757 on 16 May

2202. After entering Milliken Bend (mile 455 AHP) you wish to locate the river service in Madison Parish, Louisiana. The river service is indicated by the square containing which number?

A. 5
B. 4
C. 3
D. 2

The following questions are based on the C of E Mississippi River Maps (Hannibal to the Gulf of Mexico) and the Light List. At 1914, on 21 June, you depart the Alton Barge Docks at Alton, IL (Mile 202.0 UMR), with a mixed tow of 6 loaded covered hopper barges, 2 loaded tank barges, and 2 empty hopper barges.

2203. You have orders to drop off the empties at the fleeting area at Cairo Point and add five loaded tank barges to your tow. If you are turning for 9 mph and estimate the current at 1.5 mph, what is your ETA at Cairo?

A. 2210, 22 June
B. 1741, 22 June
C. 1423, 22 June
D. 1031, 22 June

2204. The Clinch River empties into which river?

A. Arkansas
B. Mississippi
C. Ohio
D. Tennessee

2205. What are the dimensions of Old River Lock, on the Lower Mississippi River?

A. 1202 feet × 84 feet
B. 1190 feet × 75 feet
C. 760 feet × 75 feet
D. 425 feet × 75 feet

2206. What is the distance in river miles, from the new mouth of the White River to the RR and Hwy bridge at Baton Rouge, LA?

A. 358 miles
B. 365 miles
C. 370 miles
D. 384 miles

2207. As you pass under the Natchez-Vidalia Dual Bridge, the gauge on the bridge reads 8.9 ft. If the highest point on your vessel is 54 ft. above the water, what is your vertical clearance?

A. 62.6 feet
B. 65.3 feet
C. 67.2 feet
D. 122.0 feet

The following questions are based on the C of E Mississippi River Maps (Hannibal, MO, to the Gulf of Mexico) and the Light List. On 9 September, you depart the Formosa Plastics mooring facility at mile 233.5 AHP with six loaded tank barges enroute to to the Alton Barge Terminal, Alton, IL (mile 202.0 UMR). Your engines are making turns for 7.5 mph in still water.

2208. What is the total length of the trip?

A. 906.3 miles
B. 922.3 miles
C. 1155.8 miles
D. 1187.3 miles

2209. The Helena gauge reads 9.4 feet. The high point on your towboat is 42 feet above water. What is the vertical clearance when you pass under the Helena Highway Bridge?

A. 53.0 feet
B. 62.6 feet
C. 64.2 feet
D. 68.0 feet

2210. If the Bayou Sara gauge reads −0.5 feet, what is the water level in relation to the low water reference plane?

A. 4.75 feet above the plane
B. 5.75 feet above the plane
C. 5.75 feet below the plane
D. 4.75 feet below the plane

The following questions are based on the C of E Mississippi River Maps (Cairo to the Gulf) and the Light List.

On 22 September, you are making up your tow at the Fleeting area in Baton Rouge, LA, near Gartness Light (mile 227.8 AHP). You get underway at 0842 enroute to to Cairo, IL, with a mixed tow.

2211. Your engine speed is 9.8 mph and you estimate the current at 1.6 mph. What is your speed over the ground?

A. 11.0 mph
B. 9.8 mph
C. 8.6 mph
D. 8.2 mph

2212. At 1650 you decrease speed to make good 7.1 mph. At 2020 you are _____.

A. abeam of the Old River Control Structure Light
B. entering the Vicksburg District of the U.S. Army Corps of Engineers
C. at Palmetto Point
D. at Latitude 31°10′N

2213. What does the green diamond with the letter "SD" indicate just below the entrance to Greenville Harbor (536.7 miles AHP)?

A. location where latest steering directions may be obtained
B. location of a sunken wreck
C. shoaling area
D. speed zone

2214. Which of the following statements regarding aids to navigation shown in the Corps of Engineers map book is TRUE?

A. The U.S. Army Corp. of Engineers is responsible for placing and maintaining all aids to navigation.
B. Buoys should always be given as wide a berth in passing as possible.
C. Buoy positions shown on chart are exact.
D. Lights and daymarks are always shown in their exact location.

2215. What are the dimensions of the Old River Lock?

A. 110ft × 1190ft
B. 100ft × 990ft
C. 75ft × 1000ft
D. 75ft × 1190ft

The following questions are based on the C of E Mississippi River Maps (Hannibal, MO, to the Gulf of Mexico) and the Light List.

At 2345, on 25 December, you depart Vulcan Chemicals, Memphis Harbor, McKellar Lake (mile 726.0 AHP - LMR) enroute to to the Petroleum Fuel & Terminal Co. (144.6 AHP) in Angelina, LA, with a tow of eight full gasoline barges.

2216. If your vessel is making turns for 7.5 mph with an estimated average current of 1.5 mph, what is your ETA at the dock in Angelina, LA?

A. 0516, 28 Dec
B. 1621, 28 Dec
C. 0516, 29 Dec
D. 1621, 29 Dec

2217. The highest point on your towboat is 67 feet above the water, and the Helena Gauge reads +22.3 feet. What is the vertical clearance when you pass under the A-span of the Helena Highway Bridge?

A. 74.7 feet
B. 52.4 feet
C. 49.8 feet
D. 30.1 feet

2218. If the highest point on your towboat is 52 feet and the West Memphis gauge reads 26 feet what is the vertical clearance when you pass under the Hernando Desoto Bridge (736.6 AHP)?

A. 25.8 feet
B. 30.7 feet
C. 42.6 feet
D. 56.7 feet

2219. You pass Ratcliff Light (mile 289.8) at 1612. What was your average speed since leaving Baton Rouge?

A. 7.3 mph
B. 7.6 mph
C. 8.0 mph
D. 8.3 mph

2220. The charts show two dashed lines crossing the river just south of St. Catherine Bar Light (348.6 AHP). What does this indicate?

A. overhead power lines
B. Louisiana Mississippi ferry crossings
C. two submerged oil pipelines
D. two railroad trestles

2221. Which daymark should you see as you approach French Point Light (mile 915.4 AHP)?

A. red triangle
B. green square
C. red and green rectangle
D. green diamond

2222. If the Bayou Sara gauge reads –0.5 feet, what is the water level in relation to the low water reference plane?

A. 0.5 foot below the plane
B. 0.5 foot above the plane
C. 5.25 feet above the plane
D. 5.75 feet below the plane

2223. What is the brown tint shown at Bordeaux Point Dykes (681.0 AHP)?

A. river gauge
B. fish hatchery
C. dredge material
D. levee

The following questions are based on the C of E Mississippi River Maps (Hannibal, MO, to the Gulf of Mexico) and the Light List. At 1215, on July 23, you get underway from the First Nitrogen Barge dock at mile 173.6 AHP enroute to to Racine, OH (mile 241.6 OR).

2224. What is the length of the trip?

A. 1195.4 miles
B. 1223.1 miles
C. 1520.1 miles
D. 1657.8 miles

2225. The Linwood Bend revetment on the LMR extends from mile _____.

A. 828.1-823.1 RDB
B. 831.7-829.4 RDB
C. 841.3-838.0 LDB
D. 845.4-842.5 LDB

2226. You are turning for 10 mph and passing Hog Point, LA (mile 297.5 AHP). Angola reports that the current at Red River Landing is 4.5 mph. Which statement is TRUE?

A. The main channel lies on the south side of the island you see ahead.
B. You are making 14.5 mph over ground.
C. An underwater stone dike has been constructed 0.5 miles upstream of Miles Bar Towhead.
D. You would expect to find the more

favorable current near the broken red line in the river.

2227. If the highest point of your towboat is 54 feet above the water and the Natchez Gauge reads 24.8 feet, what will be your vertical clearance when passing under the Natchez-Vidalia westbound Highway Bridge?

A. 35.9 feet
B. 43.2 feet
C. 46.7 feet
D. 57.5 feet

2228. As you pass under the Baton Rouge R.R. and Hwy 190 Bridge (233.9 AHP), the Ingram Aggregates facility is indicated by which numbered box?

A. 3
B. 8
C. 11
D. 15

2229. Which of the following statements regarding buoys on the Mississippi River is TRUE?

A. Buoy positions on the chart are exact.
B. Buoys should be given as wide a berth as possible in passing.
C. The buoys are maintained on station year round.
D. The buoys do not shift positions due to permanent moorings.

2230. What are the light characteristics of Greenwood Light (mile 288.6 AHP)?

A. fixed red light
B. 2 red flashes every 5 seconds
C. 1 red flash every 4 seconds
D. 2 white flashes every 4 seconds

2231. As you approach Shreves cut-off you see Red River Landing Gauge (302.4 AHP) which reads 6.2 feet. Which of the following statements is TRUE?

A. This reading is at the same elevation as the 6.2 ft. mark on the gauge at Head of Passes.
B. This reading is 6.2 ft. above the Low Water Reference Plane.
C. The depth of water at Red River Landing is 6.2 ft.
D. A vessel drawing 7 ft. would be able to pass through the locks at Lower Old River.

2232. What is the vertical clearance between the highest point of your towboat, if it is 58 feet above the water, and if the Natchez Gauge reads 28.13 feet when passing under the Natchez Upper Highway Bridge?

A. 15.9 feet
B. 33.2 feet
C. 39.3 feet
D. 45.4 feet

The following questions are based on the C of E Mississippi River Maps (Hannibal to the Gulf of Mexico) and the Light List. At 1914, on 21 June, you depart the Alton Barge Docks at Alton, IL (mile 202.0 UMR), with a mixed tow of 6 loaded covered hopper barges, 2 loaded tank barges, and 2 empty hopper barges.

2233. You have orders to drop off the empties at the fleeting area at Cairo Point and add five loaded tank barges to your tow. If you are turning for 9 mph and estimate the current at 1.5 mph, what is your ETA at Cairo?

A. 1031, 22 June
B. 1423, 22 June
C. 1741, 22 June
D. 2210, 22 June

2234. Which type of daymark would you see on the Belle Island Corner Lt. at mile 458.6 AHP?

A. green - diamond
B. green - square
C. red - triangle
D. red - diamond

The following questions are based on the C of E Mississippi River Maps (Hannibal, MO, to the Gulf of Mexico) and the Light List. At 1400, 12 January, you are downbound on the Upper Mississippi River at St. Louis, MO (mile 181.0 UMR), bound for the River Cement Co. in Natchez, MI.

2235. When you pass under the Jefferson Barracks Highway Bridge (mile 168.6 UMR) what will be your vertical clearance if the highest point on your towboat is 55 feet and the St. Louis Gauge reads 21 feet?

A. 25.8 feet
B. 19.6 feet
C. 14.7 feet
D. 11.8 feet

2236. What daymark should you see as you approach Parker Landing Light (mile 924.6 AHP)?

A. green square
B. green triangle
C. red and green rectangle
D. green diamond

2237. At 1723 you increase speed to make good 9.2 mph. At 1937 you have a daymark on your port beam. What daymark is this?

A. Tiptonville Ferry Landing Daymark
B. Tiptonville Light
C. Merriwether Bend Light and Daymark
D. Alaska Light and Daymark

2248. Which company does NOT have a marine facility in Rosedale harbor (mile 585 AHP)?

A. T.L. James
B. Rosedale-Bolivar County Port
C. Commission Cives Steel Company
D. Sanders Elevator Corp

2249. What are the dimensions of the Old River Lock?

A. 110ft × 1190 ft.
B. 100ft × 990 ft.
C. 75ft × 1190 ft.
D. 75ft × 1000 ft.

2250. What is the distance from the Memphis gauge to the Gold Bond Building Products Wharf in New Orleans, LA?

A. 633 miles
B. 588 miles
C. 503 miles
D. 460 miles

2251. If the highest point on your towboat is 52 feet and the West Memphis gauge reads 26 feet what is the vertical clearance when you pass under the Hernando Desoto Bridge (736.6 AHP)?

A. 56.7 feet
B. 42.6 feet
C. 30.7 feet
D. 25.8 feet

2252. Which daymark would you see at Shields Bar Lt. (mile 882.2 AHP)?

A. Red triangle
B. Green triangle

C. Green square
D. Red diamond

2253. You are turning for 7.5 mph and estimate the current at 3.0 mph. What is your ETA at the River Cement Co. in Natchez considering that you passed Cherokee Landing Lt. at 2100?

A. 1243 on 15 January
B. 1605 on 15 January
C. 1244 on 16 January
D. 1922 on 16 January

2254. After entering Milliken Bend (mile 455 AHP) you wish to locate the river service in Madison Parish, Louisiana. The river service is indicated by the square containing which number?

A. 5
B. 4
C. 3
D. 2

2255. At 0645, on the 17th of April, you pass Hole in the Wall Lt. (mile 373.4 AHP). What has been your average speed since departing the Exxon Refinery?

A. 8.8 mph
B. 7.3 mph
C. 6.8 mph
D. 6.3 mph

2256. Which of the following statements regarding buoys on the Mississippi River is TRUE?

A. Buoy positions on the chart are exact.
B. Buoys should be given as wide a berth as possible in passing.
C. The buoys are maintained on station year round.
D. The buoys do not shift positions due to permanent moorings.

2257. The highest point on your towboat is 67 feet above the water, and the Helena Gauge reads +22.3 feet. What is the vertical clearance when you pass under the A-span of the Helena Highway Bridge?

A. 74.7 feet
B. 52.4 feet
C. 49.8 feet
D. 30.1 feet

2258. If the highest point of your towboat is 54 feet above the water and the Natchez

Gauge reads 24.8 feet, what will be your vertical clearance when passing under the Natchez–Vidalia westbound Highway Bridge?

A. 35.9 feet
B. 46.7 feet
C. 49.6 feet
D. 57.5 feet

2259. What is the distance from Greenville, MS, to Oquawka, IL, on the Mississippi River System?

A. 537 miles
B. 597 miles
C. 733 miles
D. 832 miles

2260. What company does NOT have a marine facility along the river bank in Madison Parish (mile 457.0 AHP)?

A. Complex Chemical Co.
B. Delta Southern Railroads
C. Scott Petroleum
D. Baxter Wilson Steamplant

2261. What are the dimensions of the Port Allen Lock at Baton Rouge, LA?

A. 75 feet × 1188 feet
B. 84 feet × 1180 feet
C. 84 feet × 1188 feet
D. 75 feet × 1180 feet

2262. At 1019, on 10 March, you pass under the Greenville Bridge (mile 531.3 AHP). What was your average speed since departing River Cement Co. Dock?

A. 7.2 mph
B. 6.8 mph
C. 6.5 mph
D. 6.2 mph

2263. Which of the following statements concerning the buoys on the Mississippi River is TRUE?

A. The position of river buoys can be determined by consulting the latest Light List - Vol. V.
B. A preferred channel mark is a lateral mark indicating a channel junction which must always be passed to starboard.
C. Buoys should be passed as close as possible.
D. Setting a buoy is the act of placing a buoy on assigned position in the water.

2264. What is the length of the trip?

A. 1195.4 miles
B. 1223.1 miles
C. 1464.8 miles
D. 1520.1 miles

2265. If the Bayou Sara gauge reads –0.5 feet, what is the water level in relation to the low water reference plane?

A. 3.55 foot below the plane
B. 5.75 foot above the plane
C. 5.75 feet above the plane
D. 5.25 feet below the plane

2266. Where would you find out which buoys, if any, are in place at Concordia Bar crossing (mile 596.0 AHP)?

A. Channel Report
B. Bulletin board at the Rosedale gauge
C. Waterways Journal
D. None of the above

2267. At 2142, on January 3, you pass Sebastapol Light (mile 283.3 AHP). At 0137, January 4, you pass Fort Adams Light (311.4 AHP). You have been turning for 9.0 mph. What was the current?

A. 4.2 mph
B. 3.3 mph
C. 2.7 mph
D. 1.8 mph

2268. What is the minimum maintained depth of the channel from Cairo to Baton Rouge during low water?

A. 9 feet
B. 12 feet
C. 15 feet
D. 18 feet

2269. Which dayboard would you see on Putney Light (mile 943.6 AHP)?

A. Green square
B. Green triangle
C. Red diamond
D. Red triangle

2270. At Filter Point Light (mile 475 AHP) there are 3 close straight dashed lines on the map passing through the black dot below the number 475. What do these lines represent?

A. Submerged oil pipelines
B. Submerged telephone cables
C. Submerged gas pipelines
D. Aerial power cables

2271. From Baton Rouge to Cairo, what is the maintained minimum channel depth during low water?

A. 6 feet
B. 9 feet
C. 12 feet
D. 30 feet

2272 C As you approach Buckridge Light (mile 411.5 AHP), which type of daymark would you see on the light structure?
A. Red diamond
B. Red triangle
C. Green square
D. Green diamond

2273. What is indicated by the two light grey shaded areas that cross the river above False River Lt. (mile 251.0 AHP)?

A. Ferry crossings
B. Utility crossings
C. Aerial cable crossings
D. Bridge construction

2274. At 0509, on 26 December, you pass under the Helena Highway Bridge (661.7 AHP). What has been the average speed of the current since departing Memphis

Harbor, McKellar Lake, if you have been making turns for 7.5 mph?
A. 1.8 mph
B. 2.1 mph
C. 4.4 mph
D. 5.6 mph

The following questions are based on the C of E Mississippi River Maps (Hannibal, MO, to the Gulf of Mexico) and the Light List. At 2345, on 25 December, you depart Vulcan Chemicals, Memphis Harbor, McKellar Lake (mile 726.0 AHP - LMR) enroute to to the Petroleum Fuel & Terminal Co. (144.6 AHP) in Angelina, LA, with a tow of eight full gasoline barges.

2296. If your vessel is making turns for 7.5 mph with an estimated average current of 1.5 mph, what is your ETA at the dock in Angelina, LA?

A. 1621, 28 Dec
B. 2203, 28 Dec
C. 0516, 29 Dec
D. 1621, 29 Dec

2297. The Platte River empties into which river?

A. Mississippi
B. Ohio
C. Missouri
D. Tennessee

2298. What is the distance from the Arkansas River mouth to the Ohio River mouth in river miles?

A. 594 miles
B. 546 miles
C. 422 miles
D. 372 miles

2299. As you approach Joseph Henry Light (mile 445.2 AHP) which daymark would you see?

A. red triangle
B. red square
C. green diamond
D. green square

2300. What is your ETA at the Helena Highway Bridge?

A. 1344, 24 Sept
B. 1109, 24 Sept
C. 0926, 24 Sept
D. 0458, 24 Sept

2301. Which organization has an installation near the upper end of Carthage Revetment?

A. City of Natchez (waterfront)
B. International Paper Co.
C. U.S. Army Corps of Engineers
D. U.S. Coast Guard

2302. If the gauge at the Greenville Highway Bridge reads 10.8 feet, what is the water level in relation to the low water reference plane (LWRP)?

A. 0.5 feet below the LWRP
B. 10.8 feet below the LWRP
C. 10.8 feet above the LWRP
D. 22.1 feet above the LWRP

2303. How far is it to the Hernando Desoto Bridge in Memphis, TN?

A. 980.8 miles
B. 736.6 miles
C. 218.1 miles
D. 202.4 miles

2304. What company does NOT have a marine facility along the river bank in Helena (mile 661 to 665 AHP)?

A. Helena Grain, Inc.
B. Helena Marine Services, Inc.
C. Quincy Grain Co.
D. Texas Eastern Pipeline Co.

2305. You are passing the Bayou Sara gauge which reads 3.9 feet. Which of the following statements is TRUE?

A. The river level is above the Low Water Reference Plane.
B. Red Store Landing Revetment is ahead on your starboard side
C. This gauge reading is at a lower elevation than the same reading on the gauge at Head of Passes.
D. None of the above.

2306. At 0921, on 24 May, you are abreast the St. Catherine Bar Lt. (mile 348.6 AHP). If you are turning for 10.0 mph, what was the current since departure?
A. 3.4 mph
B. 2.0 mph
C. 1.7 mph
D. 1.4 mph

2307. At 1132, 24 May, you pass Natchez Beam Lt. (364.8 AHP). What is your ETA off the Memphis Gauge if you average 8.0 mph?

A. 2345, 25 May
B. 0947, 26 May
C. 1525, 26 May
D. 2215, 26 May

2308. You are passing the Bayou Sara gauge which reads 3.9 feet. Which of the following statements is TRUE?

A. The river level is above the Low Water Reference Plane.
B. Red Store Landing Revetment is ahead on your starboard side
C. This gauge reading is at a lower elevation than the same reading on the gauge at Head of Passes.
D. None of the above.

2309. What is the brown tint shown at Bordeaux Point Dykes (681.0 AHP)?

A. river gauge
B. fish hatchery

C. levee
D. dredge material

2310. The Memphis gauge reads 18.4 feet. The high point of your towboat is 48 feet above water. What is the vertical clearance as you pass under the Memphis Highway Bridge?

A. 46.4 feet
B. 53.8 feet
C. 66.4 feet
D. 75.4 feet

2311. Which facility is located on the right descending bank at mile 363.6 AHP?

A. River Cement Corp.
B. Vidalia Dock and Storage Co.
C. T.L. James
D. Bunge Corp.

2312. In high water conditions, which publication would you consult for the latest information on buoys between Baton Rouge and Cairo?

A. List of Buoys and Daymarks
B. U.S.C.G. Notice to Mariners
C. C of E Navigation Chart
D. none of the above

2313. On which river is New Providence, TN, located?

A. Allegheny
B. Upper Mississippi
C. Cumberland
D. Ohio

2314. You have passed Ben Burman Lt. (mile 235.0 AHP) and see on the map a dark purplish area extending past Bayou Baton Rouge. This indicates a _____.

A. revetment
B. dredge material
C. fleeting area
D. dike

2315. You pass Red River Gauge at 2015 on 16 April and estimate the current will average 3.5 mph for the remainder of the time on the Mississippi River. What is your ETA at the mouth of the Ohio River if you continue to turn for 10 mph?

A. 1445, 20 April
B. 1830, 20 April

C. 0028, 21 April
D. 0821, 21 April

2316. At 0305 on 18 April, you pass under the Greenville Bridge (mile 531.3 AHP). What was your average speed since departing Amoco Pipeline Co. Docks (253.6 AHP)?

A. 6.2 mph
B. 6.5 mph
C. 6.8 mph
D. 7.2 mph

2317. You estimate the current as 2.5 mph. What is the speed over the ground?

A. 5.5 mph
B. 6.0 mph
C. 8.0 mph
D. 11.0 mph

2318. As you approach Ashland Light (mile 378.1 AHP) which daymark would you see?

A. red triangle
B. red diamond
C. green square
D. green diamond

2319. You complete changing out your tow and get underway enroute to Ark City Tank Storage (mile 554.0 AHP) to deliver the

tank barges. What is the distance you must travel from Cairo Point Light?
A. 606.8 miles
B. 554.0 miles
C. 400.7 miles
D. 202.1 miles

2320. The highest point on your towboat is 48 feet above the water, and the Memphis Gauge reads +7.5 feet. What is the vertical clearance when you pass under the Hernando Desoto Bridge in Memphis?

A. 48.0 feet
B. 53.2 feet
C. 68.2 feet
D. 116.0 feet

2321. At 2350 on 23 June, you are at mile 610.5 AHP when you see about a mile ahead lights on the water near the left bank. What might you see when you come abreast of these lights?

A. privately maintained buoys at a yacht club

B. government buoys marking the Hurricane Point dikes
C. barges moored at the Dennis Landing Terminal
D. a pipeline discharging dredge spoil

2322. At 1032 on 24 June, you pass Carolina Landing Light (508.8 AHP). What has been the average current since 2350, 23 June, if you have been making turns for 9.0 mph?

A. 0.5 mph
B. 1.5 mph
C. 5.7 mph
D. 8.5 mph

The following questions are based on the C of E Mississippi River Maps (Hannibal, MO, to the Gulf of Mexico) and the Light List. At 1515, on 23 May, you get underway from the Amoco Pipeline Co. docks (253.6 AHP), enroute to to Pittsburgh, PA, with a tow of six barges carrying asphalt.

2381. What is the distance from the Amoco Docks at Baton Rouge, LA, to Pittsburgh, PA?

A. 727.9 miles
B. 981.5 miles
C. 1575.3 miles
D. 1681.7 miles

2382. At 1554, on 25 May, you pass Huntington Point Light (mile 555.2 AHP). What was your average speed since departing Amoco Pipeline Co. Docks (253.6 AHP)?

A. 6.2 mph
B. 5.2 mph
C. 4.8 mph
D. 4.3 mph

2383. You are turning for 9 mph, approaching Fort Adams Lt (311.4 AHP) and it is reported that the current at Knox Landing is estimated at 4.5 MPH. Which of the following statements is TRUE?

A. You are making 13.5 mph over ground.
B. The inflow channel is a navigable channel for any vessel.
C. Tows and other vessels should navigate as close to the left descending bank as safety will permit.
D. Old River Control Structure Light and Fort Adams Light may be used as range lights when entering the outflow channel.

2384. What is the vertical clearance between the highest point of your towboat, if it is 45 feet above the water, and if the Natchez Gauge reads 23.4 feet when passing under the Natchez-Vidalia Westbound Highway Bridge?

A. 45.0 feet
B. 52.2 feet
C. 57.1 feet
D. 67.5 feet

2385. At 1019, on 10 March, you pass under the Greenville Bridge (mile 531.3 AHP). What was your average speed since departing River Cement Co. Dock?

A. 6.2 mph
B. 6.5 mph
C. 6.8 mph
D. 7.2 mph

2386. As you pass Solitude Lt. (mile 249.0 AHP) which dayboard would you see?

A. green square
B. green diamond
C. red triangle
D. red diamond

2387. At which of the following times would you be able to listen to lower Mississippi River conditions on VHF Channel 22A?

A. 0900 hours
B. 1100 hours
C. 1200 hours
D. 1300 hours

2388. Your company wants to know at what time you will be arriving at the fleeting area at Sycamore Chute Light (mile 740.3 AHP) in Memphis, Tenn. You are making turns for 9.0 mph and you estimate the average current at 2.2 mph. Figuring the distance and time from Hole in the Wall Lt. (mile 373.4 AHP), what is your ETA at Sycamore Chute Lt.?

A. 1242, April 19th
B. 1645, April 19th
C. 2242, April 19th
D. 2333, April 19th

2389. In high water conditions, which publication would you consult for the latest information on buoys between Baton Rouge and Cairo?

A. U.S.C.G. Notice to Mariners
B. U.S.C.G. Light List
C. C of E Navigation Chart
D. List of Buoys and Daymarks

2390. A stretch where the channel changes from one side of the river to the other is called a _____.

A. passing
B. transit
C. transfer
D. crossing

2391. On which map would you find Redman Point, Arkansas?

A. 57
B. 60
C. 66
D. 74

2392. Which company does NOT have a marine facility in Rosedale harbor (mile 585 AHP)?

A. Sanders Elevator Corp
B. Rosedale-Bolivar County Port Commission
C. T.L. James
D. Cives Steel Company

2393. At 1814, on 11 September, you pass under the Greenville Highway Bridge (mile 531.3 AHP). What speed must you average to arrive at Jimmy Hawken Light (mile 663.5 AHP) at 0930 the following day?

A. 8.9 mph
B. 8.7 mph
C. 6.3 mph
D. 5.6 mph

2394. What is the distance from Greenville, MS, to Oquaka, IL, on the Mississippi River System?

A. 832 miles
B. 733 miles
C. 597 miles
D. 537 miles

2395. You are on map #13. What is the mile point of the facility known as Slay Warehousing, Inc.?

A. mile 174 UMR
B. mile 173 UMR
C. mile 172 UMR
D. mile 171 UMR

2396. You are passing Goose Island Lt. (mile 34.4 UMR). The brown shaded areas alongside the river represent _____.

A. levees
B. revetments
C. dredged material
D. dikes

2397. Which daymark would you see at Shields Bar Lt. (mile 882.2 AHP)?

A. red triangle
B. green triangle
C. green square
D. red diamond

2398. You pass Morrison Towhead Light (mile 890.5 AHP) at 1723. What was your average speed since leaving Cairo?

A. 7.5 mph
B. 7.8 mph
C. 8.5 mph
D. 8.8 mph

2399. The Helena gauge reads 9.4 feet. The high point on your towboat is 46 feet above water. What is the vertical clearance when you pass under the Helena Highway Bridge?

A. 56.0 feet
B. 64.2 feet
C. 79.5 feet
D. 106.1 feet

2400. What company does NOT have a marine facility along the river bank in Helena (mile 658 to 665 AHP)?

A. Helena Grain Co.
B. Helena Marine Services, Inc.
C. Riceland Food Corp.
D. Texas Eastern Pipeline Co.

2401. Which of the following describes the river at Cypress Bend, mile 569.0 AHP?

A. There are revetments on both banks.
B. The river is three tenths of a mile wide.
C. There is dredge spoil on both banks.
D. There is a turning basin located on the LDB.

2424. The lighted mooring buoy at mile 228.7 AHP is a facility for which company?

A. Luhr Brothers
B. Cargo Carriers

C. International Marine Terminals
D. National Marine Inc.

The following questions should be answered using chart 12354TR, Long Island Sound - Eastern Part, and the supporting publications. The draft of your vessel is 10 feet and your height of eye is 25 feet. Gyro error is 2°W. "Per standard magnetic compass" is abbreviated "psc." Use a variation of 14°W for the entire plot.The deviation table is:

HDG.	M.DEV.	HDG.	M.DEV.	HDG.	M.DEV.
000°	0°	120°	1.0°W	240°	2.0°E
030°	1°W	150°	0.0°	270°	1.5°E
060°	3.0°W	180°	0.0°	300°	1.0°E
090°	2.0°W	210°	1.0°E	330°	0.0°

On 04 December 1983, you are departing New London Harbor. At 1712, you are between buoys "1" and "2" on a course of 250° psc turning for 8.4 knots.

2581. At 1732, Bartlett Reef Lt. bears 016° psc. Race Rock Lt. bears 125.5° psc with a radar range of 4.4 miles. What is the set and drift?

A. 116°, 0.4 knot
B. 116°, 1.0 knot
C. 296°, 0.4 knot
D. 296°, 1.0 knot

2582. From your 1750 GPS position at LAT 41°15.6'N, LONG 072°11.5'W, you plot a course of 255°T at 8.5 kts. At what time would you see Falkner Island Light, if visibility is 10 miles?

A. 1819
B. 1850
C. 1910
D. 1917

2583. You lose GPS and are navigating solely on LORAN. What LORAN line would you follow to leave Six Mile Reef buoy "8C" abeam to port at 1.0 mile?

A. 9960-W-14885.0
B. 9960-Y-43980.5
C. 9960-Y-43982.0
D. 9960-Y-43983.5

2584. At 1930 you obtain two radar ranges: Hammonasset Point at 4.1 miles and the East side of Falkner Island at 7.6 miles. What is your position?

A. LAT 41°11.2'N, LONG 072°30.6'W
B. LAT 41°11.7'N, LONG 072°29.2'W
C. LAT 41°11.8'N, LONG 072°29.6'W
D. LAT 41°11.9'N, LONG 072°29.2'W

2585. At 2000 you plot your position as: LAT 41°11'N, LONG 072°35'W. The set and drift is 095°T at 0.8 knot. What course must you steer, and what engine speed must you turn, in order to make good 255°T at 8.5 knots?

A. 257°T, 9.3 knots
B. 253°T, 9.3 knots
C. 257°T, 7.7 knots
D. 253°T, 7.7 knots

2586. At 2100 Branford Reef Light bears 347° psc and Falkner Island Light bears 059° psc. You also get a radar range of 5.3 miles from Branford Reef Light. What are your LORAN readings?

A. 14994.0, 26473.0, 43982.0
B. 14994.5, 26482.0, 43982.0
C. 14996.0, 26477.5, 43981.0
D. 14997.5, 26479.5, 43981.0

2587. What VHF frequency would you use to listen to a weather forecast for the eastern part of Long Island Sound?

A. 156.65 MHz
B. 156.85 MHz
C. 162.475 MHz
D. 162.775 MHz

2588. At 2130 New Haven buoy "NH" bears 337° per gyro compass and Middle Ground Lt. bears 254° per gyro compass. You must arrive 0.3 miles off the Port Jefferson "PJ" buoy at 2300. What speed will you have to make good, for arrival at 2300?

A. 9.0 knots
B. 9.3 knots
C. 9.6 knots
D. 10.7 knots

2589. From the 2130 position, you steer 236°T at 10 knots. A strong northerly wind is causing 4° of leeway. What course must you steer per standard compass, to make good 236°T?

A. 232° psc
B. 240° psc
C. 244° psc
D. 252° psc

2590. You have maneuvered for traffic and at 2215 your LORAN readings are: 26567.5 and 15089.5. What course must you steer to arrive at buoy "PJ", passing 0.5 nm off "Mt Misery Shoal"?

A. 237° psc
B. 257° psc
C. 261° psc
D. 265° psc

2591. Which statement best describes the shoreline at Mount Misery?

A. wooded, barren hills with a rocky beach
B. low, rocky cliffs with heavily wooded hills inland
C. sand dunes and beaches with a mud and sand bottom
D. sand bluffs 60 feet high and banks dug out by sand and gravel companies

2592. What chart would you need to enter Port Jefferson Harbor?

A. 12362
B. 12364
C. 12369
D. 12370

2593. At 2315, you are notified that the Port Jefferson pilot will be delayed. Old Field Point Light bears 257°T, Stratford Shoal Middle Ground Light bears 355°T and Port Jefferson East Breakwater Light bears 171°T. What is the depth under the keel at this time on December 4, 1983?

A. 41 feet
B. 47 feet
C. 51 feet
D. 57 feet

2594. What will be the current at Port Jefferson entrance at 0130 on December 5, 1983?

A. 1.4 knots, flood
B. 1.4 knots, ebb
C. 0.8 knot, flood
D. 0.8 knot, ebb

2595. At 0145 you take on the pilot and are inbound Port Jefferson. The ship's heading is 147° pgc when lined up on the Port Jefferson range. What is your gyro error?

A. 1°W
B. 1°E

C. 2°E
D. 0°

2651. You are steering 246°T, and a light is picked up dead ahead at a distance of 14 miles at 1037. You change course to pass the light 2.5 miles off abeam to port. If you are making 12 knots, what is your ETA at the position 2.5 miles off the light?

A. 1143
B. 1146
C. 1149
D. 1152

2652. You are steering 163°T, and a light is picked up dead ahead at a distance of 11 miles at 0142. You change course to pass the light 2 miles off abeam to starboard. If you are making 13 knots, what is your ETA at the position 2 miles off the light?

A. 0226
B. 0229
C. 0232
D. 0235

2653. You are steering 019°T, and a light is picked up dead ahead at a distance of 11.6 miles at 0216. You change course to pass the light 3 miles off abeam to port. If you are making 14 knots, what is your ETA at the position 3 miles off the light?

A. 0258
B. 0301
C. 0304
D. 0307

2654. You are steering 231°T, and a light is picked up dead ahead at a distance of 12.3 miles at 0338. You change course to pass the light 4 miles off abeam to starboard. If you are making 16.5 knots, what is your ETA at the position 4 miles off the light?

A. 0420
B. 0423
C. 0426
D. 0429

2655. You are steering 078°T, and a light is picked up dead ahead at a distance of 15.6 miles at 2316. You change course to pass the light 4.5 miles off abeam to port. If you are making 17 knots, what is your ETA at the position 4.5 miles off the light?

A. 0006
B. 0009

C. 0012
D. 0015

2656. You are steering 257°T, and a light is picked up dead ahead at a distance of 13.3 miles at 2016. You change course to pass the light 4 miles off abeam to starboard. If you are making 18.5 knots, what is your ETA at the position 4 miles off the light?

A. 2057
B. 2100
C. 2103
D. 2113

2657. You are steering 349°T, and a light is picked up dead ahead at a distance of 17.2 miles at 2122. You change course to pass the light 4.5 miles off abeam to port. If you are making 19.5 knots, what is your ETA at the position 4.5 miles off the light?

A. 2207
B. 2210
C. 2213
D. 2216

2658. You are steering 202°T, and a light is picked up dead ahead at a distance of 14.6 miles at 2234. You change course to pass the light 5 miles off abeam to starboard. If you are making 21 knots, what is your ETA at the position 5 miles off the light?

A. 2310
B. 2313
C. 2316
D. 2319

2659. You are steering 115°T, and a light is picked up dead ahead at a distance of 16.7 miles at 0522. You change course to pass the light 3.5 miles off abeam to port. If you are making 12 knots, what is your ETA at the position 3.5 miles off the light?

A. 0644
B. 0647
C. 0650
D. 0653

2660. You are steering 287°T, and a light is picked up dead ahead at a distance of 19.4 miles at 0419. You change course to pass the light 4 miles off abeam to starboard. If you are making 13 knots, what is your ETA at the position 4 miles off the light?

A. 0541
B. 0544

C. 0547
D. 0550

2661. You are steering 143°T, and a light is picked up dead ahead at a distance of 18.2 miles at 2006. You change course to pass the light 5.5 miles off abeam to port. If you are making 14.5 knots, what is your ETA at the position 5.5 miles off the light?

A. 2115
B. 2118
C. 2121
D. 2124

2662. You are on course 006°T, speed 16.6 knots. At 0516 you see a light bearing 008°T at a range of 10.2. If you change course at 0528 to leave the light abeam to port at 1.0 mile, at what time will the light be abeam?

A. 0553
B. 0556
C. 0604
D. 0607

2663. You are on course 035°T, speed 18.3 knots. At 0719 you see a buoy bearing 036°T at a range of 4.1. If you change course at 0725 to leave the buoy abeam to port at 1.0 mile, at what time will the buoy be abeam?

A. 0740
B. 0738
C. 0735
D. 0732

2664. You are on course 061°T, at a speed of 12.4 knots. At 0839 you see a rock bearing 059°T at a range of 4.4 miles. If you change course at 0845 to leave the rock abeam to starboard at 1.5 miles, at what time will the rock be abeam?

A. 0854
B. 0859
C. 0903
D. 0906

2665. You are on course 079°T, speed 11.2 knots. At 0904 you see a daymark bearing 078°T at a range of 4.6. If you change course at 0910 to leave the daymark abeam to starboard at 0.5 mile, at what time will the daymark be abeam?

A. 0918
B. 0923

C. 0928
D. 0935

2666. You are on course 086°T, speed 11.7 knots. At 1013 you see a buoy bearing 088°T at a range of 4.8 miles. If you change course at 1019 to leave the buoy abeam to port at 1.0 mile, at what time will the buoy be abeam?

A. 1037
B. 1040
C. 1043
D. 1052

2667. Your vessel is on a course of 255°T, 14 knots. At 2126 a lighthouse is sighted dead ahead at a distance of 11 miles. You change course at this time to pass the lighthouse 3 miles abeam to port. What will be your ETA at this position off the lighthouse?

A. 2149
B. 2201
C. 2211
D. 2228

2668. Your vessel is on a course of 255°T, at 14 knots. At 2116 a lighthouse is sighted dead ahead at a distance of 11 miles. You change course at this time to pass the lighthouse 3 miles abeam to port. What will be your ETA at this position off the lighthouse?

A. 2149
B. 2201
C. 2212
D. 2228

2671. While on a course of 349°T, a light bears 13° on the starboard bow at a distance of 10.8 miles. What course should you steer to pass 2.5 miles abeam of the light leaving it to starboard?

A. 346°T
B. 349°T
C. 352°T
D. 355°T

2672. While on a course of 283° pgc, a light bears 10° on the port bow at a distance of 8.3 miles. What course should you steer to pass 3.5 miles abeam of the light leaving it to port?

A. 289° pgc
B. 294° pgc

C. 298° pgc
D. 302° pgc

2673. At 2221 your course is 222° pgc at a speed of 11.2 knots, when radar detects a buoy bearing 355° relative, at a range of 5.8 miles. The gyro error is 2°E. If you change course at 2226, what course should you steer to leave the buoy 1.0 mile abeam to port?

A. 206° pgc
B. 210° pgc
C. 228° pgc
D. 231° pgc

2674. You are steaming on course 126°T at 14.8 knots. At 1022 you sight a buoy bearing 128°T, at a range of 4.8 miles. If you change course at 1026, what true course will you steer to leave the buoy 0.5 mile abeam to port?

A. 136°
B. 133°
C. 122°
D. 119°

2675. At 1423 you are on course 072°T at 12.2 knots, when you sight a rock awash bearing 070°T at a range of 3.6 miles. If you change course at 1427, what course would you steer to leave the rock 1.0 mile abeam to port?

A. 049°
B. 054°
C. 086°
D. 091°

2676. While on a course of 019° pgc, a light bears 14° on the port bow at a distance of 15.3 miles. What course should you steer to pass 1.5 miles abeam of the light, leaving it to port?

A. 006° pgc
B. 011° pgc
C. 013° pgc
D. 015° pgc

2677. You sight a light 9° on your starboard bow at a distance of 21 miles. Assuming you make good your course, what will be your distance off the light when abeam?

A. 3.3 miles
B. 3.7 miles
C. 4.0 miles
D. 4.3 miles

2678. You are running coastwise on a course of 323°T, and you have a buoy bearing 11° on your port bow at a distance of 7 miles. You desire to leave the buoy abeam to port at a distance of 2.5 miles. What course should you steer?

A. 291°T
B. 312°T
C. 333°T
D. 344°T

2680. While on course 321° pgc with a 1°W gyro error, you pick up a buoy on radar bearing 001° relative at 5.2 miles. What will be the course to pass the buoy by 1 mile abeam to starboard, if you change course when the buoy is 4.5 miles away?

A. 305°T
B. 310° pgc
C. 316°T
D. 336° pgc

2681. Your vessel is on course 312° pgc and you sight a lighthouse dead ahead at a range of 10 miles. The gyro error is 3°E. What course would you steer to leave the lighthouse 1.5 miles abeam to starboard?

A. 309° pgc
B. 304° pgc
C. 309°T
D. 304°T

2682. While on a course of 066° pgc, a light bears 18° on the port bow at a distance of 12.3 miles. What course should you steer to leave the light 4 miles abeam to port?

A. 067° pgc
B. 072° pgc
C. 079° pgc
D. 085° pgc

2683. You are underway on a course of 135° pgc at 15 knots, and you sight a lighthouse dead ahead at a range of 12.5 miles at 1145. What course would you steer to leave the lighthouse 3.0 miles off your port beam?

A. 117° pgc
B. 121° pgc
C. 149° pgc
D. 154° pgc

2684. You are steering 173°T, and a light is picked up dead ahead at a distance of 13.9 miles at 0054. You change course to pass

the light 4.5 miles off abeam to port. If you are making 21 knots, what is your ETA at the position 4.5 miles off the light?

A. 0122
B. 0125
C. 0131
D. 0134

2685. You are steering 031°T, and a light is picked up dead ahead at a distance of 12.7 miles at 0017. You change course to pass the light 3.5 miles off abeam to starboard. If you are making 11 knots, what is your ETA at the position 3.5 miles off the light?

A. 0118
B. 0121
C. 0124
D. 0127

2686. While on a course of 034° pgc, a light bears 8° on the port bow at a distance of 8.8 miles. What course should you steer to pass 2.5 miles abeam of the light leaving it to port?

A. 035° pgc
B. 043° pgc
C. 051° pgc
D. 059° pgc

2687. While on a course of 321°T, a light bears 7° on the starboard bow at a distance of 9.7 miles. What course should you steer to pass 3.5 miles abeam of the light leaving it to starboard?

A. 297°T
B. 300°T
C. 303°T
D. 307°T

2688. While on a course of 214° pgc, a light bears 9° on the port bow at a distance of 7.4 miles. What course should you steer to pass 2 miles abeam of the light leaving it to port?

A. 189° pgc
B. 209° pgc
C. 221° pgc
D. 229° pgc

2689. You are steering 107°T, and a light is picked up dead ahead at a distance of 11 miles at 0847. You change course to leave the light 3 miles off to starboard. If you are making 15.5 knots, what is your ETA at the position 3 miles off the light?

A. 0928
B. 0931
C. 0934
D. 0937

2690. While on a course of 066° pgc, a light bears 13° on the port bow at a distance of 12.3 miles. What course should you steer to pass 4 miles abeam of the light leaving it to port?

A. 067° pgc
B. 072° pgc
C. 079° pgc
D. 085° pgc

2691. While on a course of 159°T, a light bears 11° on the starboard bow at a distance of 10.6 miles. What course should you steer to pass 2 miles abeam of the light leaving it to starboard?

A. 159°T
B. 163°T
C. 167°T
D. 171°T

2692. While on a course of 097° pgc, a light bears 8° on the port bow at a distance of 11.7 miles. What course should you steer to pass 3 miles abeam of the light leaving it to port?

A. 082° pgc
B. 091° pgc
C. 104° pgc
D. 112° pgc

2693. While on a course of 279°T, a light bears 12° on the starboard bow at a distance of 9.3 miles. What course should you steer to pass 4 miles abeam of the light leaving it to starboard?

A. 253°T
B. 265°T
C. 291°T
D. 305°T

2694. While on a course of 152°T, a light bears 9° on the port bow at a distance of 11.6 miles. What course should you steer to pass 3 miles abeam of the light leaving it to port?

A. 153°
B. 158°
C. 163°
D. 167°

2695. You are underway on course 017°T at a speed of 14.2 knots. You sight a buoy bearing 025°T at a radar range of 3.7 miles at 1947. If you change course at 1953, what is the course to steer to leave the buoy abeam to starboard at 0.1 mile?

A. 021°T
B. 024°T
C. 027°T
D. 030°T

2696. You are underway on course 059°T at a speed of 13.8 knots. You sight a light bearing 064°T at a radar range of 5.1 miles at 1839. If you change course at 1845, what is the course to steer to leave the light abeam to starboard at 1.0 mile?

A. 047°T
B. 050°T
C. 053°T
D. 058°T

2697. You are underway on course 106°T at a speed of 15.3 knots. You sight a buoy bearing 109°T at a radar range of 3.6 miles at 1725. If you change course at 1728, what is the course to steer to leave the buoy abeam to port at 0.5 mile?

A. 100°T
B. 117°T
C. 120°T
D. 125°T

2698. While on a course of 138°T, a light bears 14° on the starboard bow at a distance of 8.6 miles. What course should you steer to pass 3 miles abeam of the light leaving it to starboard?

A. 132°T
B. 135°T
C. 138°T
D. 141°T

2699. You are underway on course 137°T at a speed of 16.2 knots. You sight a rock bearing 134°T at a radar range of 4.6 miles at 1508. If you change course at 1514, what is the course to steer to leave the rock abeam to port at 1.5 miles?

A. 162°T
B. 158°T
C. 154°T
D. 151°T

2700. You are underway on course 163°T at a speed of 15.8 knots. You sight a buoy bearing 161°T at a radar range of 5.5 miles at 1319. If you change course at 1325, what is the course to steer to leave the buoy abeam to starboard at 1.0 mile?

A. 145°T
B. 148°T
C. 151°T
D. 175°T

2701. You are underway on course 204°T at a speed of 17.3 knots. You sight a light bearing 205°T at a radar range of 4.7 miles at 1222. If you change course at 1228, what is the course to steer to leave the light abeam to port at 1.5 miles?

A. 223°T
B. 229°T
C. 236°T
D. 240°T

2702. You are underway on course 241°T at a speed of 18.2 knots. You sight a daymark bearing 241°T at a radar range of 3.9 miles at 1006. If you change course at 1009, what is the course to steer to leave the daymark abeam to starboard at 1.0 mile?

A. 218°T
B. 222°T
C. 257°T
D. 260°T

2703. You are underway on course 254°T at a speed of 16.5 knots. You sight a rock bearing 255°T at a radar range of 6.1 miles at 0916. If you change course at 0922, what is the course to steer to leave the rock abeam to starboard at 1.5 miles?

A. 268°T
B. 239°T
C. 236°T
D. 233°T

2704. You are underway on course 340°T at a speed of 14.8 knots. You sight a buoy bearing 342°T at a radar range of 4.8 miles at 1422. If you change course at 1428, what is the true course to steer to leave the buoy abeam to port at 1.0 mile?

A. 327°T
B. 354°T
C. 357°T
D. 001°T

2705. While on a course of 192°T, a light bears 11° on the starboard bow at a distance of 12.7 miles. What course should you steer to pass 3 miles abeam of the light leaving it to starboard?

A. 167°T
B. 173°T
C. 185°T
D. 189°T

2706. While on a course of 216° pgc, a light bears 12° on the port bow at a distance of 11.2 miles. Which course should you steer to pass 2 miles abeam of the light leaving it to port?

A. 208° pgc
B. 210° pgc
C. 212° pgc
D. 214° pgc

2707. You are underway on course 128°T at a speed of 17.6 knots. You sight a daymark bearing 126°T at a radar range of 4.3 miles at 1649. If you change course at 1654, what is the course to steer to leave the daymark abeam to starboard at 0.5 mile?

A. 113°T
B. 116°T
C. 119°T
D. 136°T

2708. While on a course of 349°T, a light bears 13° on your starboard bow at a distance of 10.8 miles. What course should you steer to pass 2.5 miles abeam of the light, leaving it to starboard?

A. 323°
B. 336°
C. 349°
D. 002°

2851. Your vessel is on a course of 297°T at 11 knots. At 0019 a light bears 274.5°T, and at 0048 the light bears 252°T. At what time and at what distance off will your vessel be when abeam of the light?

A. 0102, 2.6 miles
B. 0108, 3.7 miles
C. 0057, 4.6 miles
D. 0117, 5.0 miles

2852. Your vessel is on a course of 129°T at 13 knots. At 1937 a light bears 151.5°T. At 2003 the light bears 174°T. At which time and distance off will your vessel be when abeam of this light?

A. 2016, 2.8 miles
B. 2016, 3.9 miles
C. 2021, 3.9 miles
D. 2021, 2.8 miles

2853. Your vessel is on a course of 343°T at 14 knots. At 2156 a light bears 320.5°T, and at 2217 the light bears 298°T. At what time and at what distance off will your vessel be when abeam of the light?

A. 2232, 3.4 miles
B. 2235, 4.3 miles
C. 2228, 4.9 miles
D. 2241, 6.9 miles

2854. Your vessel is on a course of 221°T at 15 knots. At 0319 a light bears 198.5°T, and at 0353 the light bears 176°T. At what time and at what distance off will your vessel be when abeam of the light?

A. 0407, 4.3 miles
B. 0410, 5.2 miles
C. 0417, 6.0 miles
D. 0427, 7.4 miles

2855. Your vessel is on a course of 107°T at 16 knots. At 0403 a light bears 129.5°T, and at 0426 the light bears 152°T. At what time and at what distance off will your vessel be when abeam of the light?

A. 0434, 3.2 miles
B. 0442, 4.3 miles
C. 0434, 4.3 miles
D. 0442, 3.4 miles

2856. Your vessel is on a course of 034°T at 17 knots. At 0551 a light bears 056.5°T, and at 0623 the light bears 079°T. At what time and at what distance off will your vessel be when abeam of the light?

A. 0636, 5.9 miles
B. 0646, 5.9 miles
C. 0636, 6.4 miles
D. 0646, 6.4 miles

2857. Your vessel is on a course of 253°T at 18 knots. At 2027 a light bears 275.5°T, and at 2055 the light bears 298°T. At what time and at what distance off will your vessel be when abeam of the light?

A. 2115, 5.9 miles
B. 2109, 6.4 miles

C. 2123, 7.3 miles
D. 2104, 7.7 miles

2858. Your vessel is on a course of 082°T at 19 knots. At 0255 a light bears 059.5°T, and at 0312 the light bears 037°T. At what time and at what distance off will your vessel be when abeam of the light?

A. 0333, 5.1 miles
B. 0321, 4.7 miles
C. 0327, 4.3 miles
D. 0324, 3.8 miles

2859. Your vessel is on a course of 307°T at 20 knots. At 0914 a light bears 284.5°T, and at 0937 the light bears 262°T. At what time and at what distance off will your vessel be when abeam of the light?

A. 0950, 4.4 miles
B. 0953, 5.4 miles
C. 0957, 6.6 miles
D. 1002, 7.1 miles

2860. Your vessel is on a course of 144°T at 16 knots. At 0126 a light bears 166.5°T, and at 0152 the light bears 189°T. At what time and at what distance off will your vessel be when abeam of the light?

A. 0205, 4.1 miles
B. 0210, 4.8 miles
C. 0215, 6.0 miles
D. 0220, 6.4 miles

2861. Your vessel is on a course of 196°T at 17 knots. At 0417 a light bears 218.5°T, and at 0442 the light bears 241°T. At what time and at what distance off will your vessel be when abeam of the light?

A. 0500, 5.0 miles
B. 0504, 6.2 miles
C. 0500, 6.2 miles
D. 0504, 5.0 miles

2862. Your are on course 317°T at 13 knots. A light is bearing 22.5° relative at 0640. At 0659 the same light is bearing 45° relative. At what time should the light be abeam?

A. 0709
B. 0712
C. 0718
D. 0721

2863. Your vessel is underway on a course of 115°T at 18 knots. At 1850 a lighthouse bears 137.5°T. At 1920, the same lighthouse bears 160°T. What time will the lighthouse pass abeam to starboard?

A. 1929
B. 1941
C. 1949
D. 1955

2864. You are steering a course of 316°T, and a light bears 34° on the port bow at 2053. At 2126 the same light bears 68° on the port bow, and you have run 5 miles since the first bearing. What is the ETA when the lighthouse is abeam?

A. 2139
B. 2143
C. 2149
D. 2159

2865. You are steering a course of 240°T, and a lighthouse bears 025° on the starboard bow at 2116. At 2144 the same lighthouse bears 050° on the starboard bow, and you have run 6 miles since the first bearing. What is the ETA when the lighthouse is abeam?

A. 2156
B. 2159
C. 2202
D. 2205

2866. Your vessel is on a course of 311°T at 21 knots. At 1957 a light bears 337.5°T, and at 2018 the light bears 356°T. At what time and at what distance off will your vessel be when abeam of the light?

A. 2027, 5.2 miles
B. 2033, 6.8 miles
C. 2039, 7.4 miles
D. 2043, 10.3 miles

2867. Your vessel is on a course of 144°T at 20 knots. At 0022 a light bears 117.5°T, and at 0035 the light bears 099°T. At what time and at what distance off will your vessel be when abeam of the light?

A. 0044, 3.2 miles
B. 0048, 4.3 miles
C. 0052, 5.1 miles
D. 0056, 6.0 miles

2868. Your vessel is on a course of 358°T at 19 knots. At 0316 a light bears 024.5°T, and at 0334 the light bears 043°T. At what time and at what distance off will your vessel be when abeam of the light?

A. 0352, 5.7 miles
B. 0355, 6.2 miles
C. 0359, 7.1 miles
D. 0403, 8.0 miles

2869. Your vessel is on a course of 237°T at 18 knots. At 0404 a light bears 263.5°T, and at 0430 the light bears 282°T. At what time and at what distance off will your vessel be when abeam of the light?

A. 0448, 6.8 miles
B. 0452, 7.2 miles
C. 0456, 7.8 miles
D. 0500, 8.4 miles

2870. Your vessel is on a course of 126°T at 17 knots. At 0251 a light bears 099.5°T, and at 0313 the light bears 081°T. At what time and at what distance off will your vessel be when abeam of the light?

A. 0327, 4.4 miles
B. 0335, 6.2 miles
C. 0345, 6.8 miles
D. 0351, 7.4 miles

2871. Your vessel is on a course of 052°T at 16 knots. At 0916 a light bears 078.5°T, and at 0927 the light bears 097°T. At what time and at what distance off will your vessel be when abeam of the light?

A. 0929, 2.0 miles
B. 0932, 2.3 miles
C. 0935, 2.6 miles
D. 0938, 2.9 miles

2872. Your vessel is on a course of 272°T at 15 knots. At 2113 a light bears 245.5°T, and at 2120 the light bears 227°T. At what time and at what distance off will your vessel be when abeam of the light?

A. 2124, 1.3 miles
B. 2127, 1.8 miles
C. 2131, 2.3 miles
D. 2135, 2.7 miles

2873. Your vessel is on a course of 103°T at 14 knots. At 1918 a light bears 129.5°T, and at 1937 the light bears 148°T. At what time and at what distance off will your vessel be when abeam of the light?

A. 1947, 2.8 miles
B. 1950, 3.2 miles
C. 1953, 3.8 miles
D. 1956, 4.4 miles

2874. Your vessel is on a course of 207°T at 13 knots. At 0539 a light bears 180.5°T, and at 0620 the light bears 162°T. At what time and at what distance off will your vessel be when abeam of the light?

A. 0633, 5.9 miles
B. 0641, 6.5 miles
C. 0653, 7.6 miles
D. 0701, 8.9 miles

2875. Your vessel is on a course of 316°T at 12 knots. At 2326 a light bears 289.5°T, and at 2354 the light bears 271°T. At what time and at what distance off will your vessel be when abeam of the light?

A. 0014, 4.8 miles
B. 0018, 5.2 miles
C. 0022, 5.6 miles
D. 0026, 6.4 miles

2877. Your vessel is steering 263°T at 22 knots. At 0413 a light bears 294°T, and at 0421 the same light bears 312°T. What will be your distance off abeam?

A. 3.4 miles
B. 3.7 miles
C. 4.3 miles
D. 4.9 miles

2878. Your vessel is steering 143°T at 16 knots. At 2147 a light bears 106°T, and at 2206 the same light bears 078°T. What will be your distance off abeam?

A. 5.1 miles
B. 5.4 miles
C. 5.9 miles
D. 6.5 miles

2879. Your vessel is steering 354°T at 14 knots. At 0317 a light bears 049°T, and at 0342 the same light bears 071°T. What will be your distance off abeam?

A. 12.4 miles
B. 12.7 miles
C. 13.0 miles
D. 13.3 miles

2880. Your vessel is steering 218°T at 19 knots. At 2223 a light bears 261°T, and at 2234 the same light bears 289°T. What will be your distance off abeam?

A. 4.5 miles
B. 4.9 miles

C. 5.3 miles
D. 5.7 miles

2881. Your vessel is steering 049°T at 15 knots. At 1914 a light bears 078°T, and at 1951 the same light bears 116°T. What will be your distance off abeam?

A. 6.7 miles
B. 7.1 miles
C. 7.5 miles
D. 8.3 miles

2882. Your vessel is steering 096°T at 17 knots. At 1847 light bears 057°T, and at 1916 the same light bears 033°T. What will be your distance off abeam?

A. 9.9 miles
B. 10.7 miles
C. 11.4 miles
D. 11.9 miles

2883. Your vessel is steering 157°T at 18 knots. At 2018 a light bears 208°T. At 2044 the same light bears 232°T. What will be your distance off when abeam?

A. 12.8 miles
B. 14.4 miles
C. 15.2 miles
D. 16.7 miles

2884. Your vessel is steering 238°T at 11 knots. At 2304 a light bears 176°T, and at 2323 the same light bears 155°T. What will be your distance off abeam?

A. 7.5 miles
B. 8.0 miles
C. 8.5 miles
D. 9.0 miles

2885. Your vessel is steering 194°T at 13 knots. At 0116 a light bears 243°T, and at 0147 the same light bears 267°T. What will be your distance off abeam?

A. 11.2 miles
B. 11.6 miles
C. 12.0 miles
D. 12.5 miles

2886. Your vessel is steering 074°T at 12 knots. At 0214 a light bears 115°T, and at 0223 the same light bears 135°T. What will be your distance off abeam?

A. 2.4 miles
B. 3.0 miles

C. 3.5 miles
D. 4.2 miles

2887. Your vessel is steering 283°T at 10 knots. At 0538 a light bears 350°T, and at 0552 the same light bears 002°T. What will be your distance off abeam?

A. 9.6 miles
B. 10.3 miles
C. 10.7 miles
D. 11.3 miles

2888. Your vessel is underway on a course of 323.5°T at a speed of 16 knots. At 1945 a light bears 350°T. At 2010 the light bears 008.5°T. What will be your distance off when abeam of the light?

A. 3.3 miles
B. 4.8 miles
C. 6.7 miles
D. 8.7 miles

2889. While underway you sight a light 11° on your port bow at a distance of 12 miles. Assuming you make good your course, what will be your distance off the light when abeam?

A. 2.3 miles
B. 3.1 miles
C. 3.9 miles
D. 4.5 miles

2890. You are steaming on a course of 084°T at a speed of 13 knots. At 1919 a lighthouse bears 106.5°T. At 1957 the same lighthouse bears 129°T. What will be your distance off the lighthouse when abeam?

A. 4.3 miles
B. 5.7 miles
C. 7.1 miles
D. 8.2 miles

2891. You are steaming on course 168°T at a speed of 18 knots. At 1426 you sight a buoy bearing 144°T. At 1435 you sight the same buoy bearing 116°T. What is your distance off at the second bearing and predicted distance when abeam?

A. 2.3 miles 2nd bearing, 1.8 miles abeam
B. 2.5 miles 2nd bearing, 2.8 miles abeam
C. 2.8 miles 2nd bearing, 1.8 miles abeam
D. 3.3 miles 2nd bearing, 2.8 miles abeam

2892. You are steaming on a course of 114°T at 17 knots. At 1122 you observe a

lighthouse bearing 077°T. At 1133 the lighthouse bears 051°T. What is your distance off at the second bearing?

A. 3.3 miles
B. 3.9 miles
C. 4.3 miles
D. 4.9 miles

2893. You are steaming on a course of 253°T at 14 knots. At 2329 you observe a lighthouse bearing 282°T. At 2345 the lighthouse bears 300°T. What is your distance off at the second bearing?

A. 3.7 miles
B. 4.3 miles
C. 5.2 miles
D. 5.9 miles

2894. You are steaming on a course of 071°T at 19 knots. At 1907 you observe a lighthouse bearing 122°T. At 1915 the lighthouse bears 154°T. What is your distance off at the second bearing?

A. 3.4 miles
B. 3.7 miles
C. 4.0 miles
D. 4.3 miles

2895. You are steaming on a course of 246°T at 17 knots. At 2107 you observe a lighthouse bearing 207°T. At 2119 the lighthouse bears 179°T. What is your distance off at the second bearing?

A. 3.9 miles
B. 4.2 miles
C. 4.6 miles
D. 5.1 miles

2896. You are steaming on a course of 133°T at 16 knots. At 2216 you observe a lighthouse bearing 086°T. At 2223 the lighthouse bears 054°T. What is your distance off at the second bearing?

A. 1.7 miles
B. 2.0 miles
C. 2.3 miles
D. 2.6 miles

2897. You are steaming on a course of 327°T at 13 knots. At 0207 you observe a lighthouse bearing 020°T. At 0226 the lighthouse bears 042°T. What is your distance off at the second bearing?

A. 8.5 miles
B. 8.9 miles
C. 9.2 miles
D. 9.7 miles

2898. You are steaming on a course of 267°T at 22 knots. At 0433 you observe a lighthouse bearing 290°T. At 0452 the lighthouse bears 328°T. What is your distance off at the second bearing?

A. 4.5 nm
B. 5.9 nm
C. 6.6 nm
D. 7.2 nm

2899. You are steaming on a course of 208°T at 21 knots. At 2019 you observe a lighthouse bearing 129°T. At 2030 the lighthouse bears 103°T. What is your distance off at the second bearing?

A. 8.2 miles
B. 8.6 miles
C. 8.9 miles
D. 9.3 miles

2900. You are steaming on a course of 167°T at 19.5 knots. At 1837 you observe a lighthouse bearing 224°T. At 1904 the lighthouse bears 268°T. What is your distance off at the second bearing?

A. 8.8 miles
B. 9.5 miles
C. 10.4 miles
D. 11.3 miles

2901. You are steaming on a course of 198°T at 18.5 knots. At 0316 you observe a lighthouse bearing 235°T. At 0348 the lighthouse bears 259°T. What is your distance off at the second bearing?

A. 14.8 miles
B. 15.3 miles
C. 15.8 miles
D. 16.3 miles

2902. You are steaming on a course of 058°T at 11.5 knots. At 0209 you observe a lighthouse bearing 129°T. At 0252 the lighthouse bears 173°T. What is your distance off at the second bearing?

A. 9.4 miles
B. 10.7 miles
C. 11.2 miles
D. 12.8 miles

2903. You are steaming on a course of 025°T at 15.5 knots. At 0645 you observe a lighthouse bearing 059°T. At 0655 the same lighthouse bears 075°T. What is your distance off at the second bearing?

A. 1.5 miles
B. 2.6 miles
C. 4.0 miles
D. 5.3 miles

2904. Your vessel is on course 093°T at 15 knots. At 1835 a light bears 136°T, and at 1857 the same light bears 170°T. What was your distance off the light at 1857?

A. 6.0 miles
B. 6.4 miles
C. 6.8 miles
D. 7.2 miles

2905. You are steaming on a course of 215°T at 14 knots. At 1841 you observe a lighthouse bearing 178°T. At 1904 the same lighthouse bears 156°T. What is your distance off at the second bearing?

A. 5.4 miles
B. 6.6 miles
C. 7.5 miles
D. 8.7 miles

2906. You are steaming on a course of 211°T at 17 knots. At 0417 a light bears 184°T, and at 0428 the same light bears 168°T. What is the distance off the light at 0428?

A. 3.4 miles
B. 4.6 miles
C. 5.1 miles
D. 5.6 miles

2907. You are running coastwise in hazy weather; the visibility improves just before you pass a lighthouse abeam. Your speed is 15 knots, and the lighthouse was abeam at 1015. At 1037 the lighthouse is 4 points abaft the beam. What is your distance off at the second bearing?

A. 3.9 miles
B. 5.5 miles
C. 6.6 miles
D. 7.8 miles

2908. Your vessel is on a course of 223°T at 17 knots. At 1323 a lighthouse bears 318° relative. At 1341 the same lighthouse bears 287° relative. What is your distance off the lighthouse at 1341?

A. 4.3 miles
B. 5.1 miles
C. 6.6 miles
D. 7.8 miles

2909. You are running coastwise at 14 knots. You sight a lighthouse abeam at 0912. At 0939 the lighthouse is 4 points abaft the beam. What is your distance off at the second bearing?

A. 5.5 miles
B. 6.3 miles
C. 7.8 miles
D. 8.9 miles

2910. Your vessel is steaming on a course of 140°T at 15 knots. At 1530 a lighthouse bears 200°T. At 1550 it bears 249°T. What is your distance from the lighthouse at 1550?

A. 1.15 miles
B. 4.60 miles
C. 5.45 miles
D. 5.75 miles

2911. What is indicated by the two light gray shaded areas that cross the river above False River Lt. (mile 251.0 AHP).

A. Ferry crossings
B. Utility crossings
C. Aerial cable crossings
D. Bridge construction

2912. Your vessel is on a course of 079°T at 11 knots. At 0152 a light bears 105.5°T, and at 0209 the light bears 124°T. At what time and at what distance off will your vessel be when abeam of the light?

A. 0219, 2.3 miles
B. 0226, 3.1 miles
C. 0233, 3.9 miles
D. 0242, 4.7 miles

2913. You are turning for 7.5 mph and estimate the current at 3.0 mph. What is your ETA at the River Cement Co. in Natchez considering that you passed Cherokee Landing Lt. at 2100?

A. 1605 on 15 January
B. 0355 on 16 January
C. 1244 on 16 January
D. 1922 on 16 January

050. The propeller on a vessel has a diameter of 23.7 feet and a pitch of 24.8 feet. What would be the apparent slip if the vessel cruised 442 miles in a 23 hour day (observed distance) at an average RPM of 89?

A. −7.60%
B. 7.60%
C. −11.80%
D. 11.80%

051. The propeller on a vessel has a diameter of 20.6 feet and a pitch of 23.4 feet. What would be the apparent slip if the vessel cruised 538 miles in a 24 hour day (observed distance) at an average RPM of 87?

A. −11.60%
B. 11.60%
C. −10.30%
D. 10.30%

3052. The propeller on a vessel has a diameter of 21.2 feet and a pitch of 20.0 feet. What would be the apparent slip if the vessel cruised 391 miles in a 24 hour day (observed distance) at an average RPM of 88?

A. −11.50%
B. 11.50%
C. −6.20%
D. 6.20%

3053. The propeller on a vessel has a diameter of 19.9 feet and a pitch of 21.6 feet. What would be the apparent slip if the vessel cruised 395 miles in a 23 hour day (observed distance) at an average RPM of 78?

A. −3.20%
B. 3.20%
C. −12.00%
D. 12.00%

3054. The propeller on a vessel has a diameter of 22.8 feet and a pitch of 19.3 feet. What would be the apparent slip if the vessel cruised 287 miles in a 24 hour day (observed distance) at an average RPM of 67?

A. −6.30%
B. 6.30%
C. −24.00%
D. 24.00%

3055. The propeller on a vessel has a diameter of 24.6 feet and a pitch of 26.1 feet. What would be the apparent slip if the vessel cruised 462 miles in a 24 hour day (observed distance) at an average RPM of 72?

A. −2.70%
B. 2.70%
C. −3.80%
D. 3.80%

3056. The propeller on a vessel has a diameter of 18.8 feet and a pitch of 21.4 feet. What would be the slip if the vessel cruised 378 miles in a 24 hour day (observed distance) at an average RPM of 76?

A. 1.90%
B. −1.90%
C. 4.70%
D. −4.70%

3057. The propeller on a vessel has a diameter of 25.3 feet and a pitch of 23.2 feet. What would be the apparent slip if the vessel cruised 515 miles in a 23 hour day (observed distance) at an average RPM of 93?

A. −3.60%
B. 3.60%
C. −5.20%
D. 5.20%

3058. The propeller on a vessel has a diameter of 20.9 feet and a pitch of 19.6 feet. What would be the apparent slip if the vessel cruised 447 miles in a 23 hour day (observed distance) at an average RPM of 108?

A. −5.60%
B. 5.60%
C. −7.00%
D. 7.00%

3059. The propeller on a vessel has a diameter of 21.5 feet and a pitch of 24.5 feet. What would be the apparent slip if the vessel cruised 458 miles in a 23 hour day (observed distance) at an average RPM of 78?

A. 5.60%
B. −5.60%
C. 12.30%
D. −12.30%

3060. The propeller on a vessel has a diameter of 24.0 feet and a pitch of 21.3 feet. What would be the slip if the vessel cruised 510 miles in a 24 hour day (observed distance) at an average RPM of 86?

A. −12.20%
B. 12.20%
C. −17.50%
D. 17.50%

3061. The propeller on a vessel has a diameter of 20.2 feet and a pitch of 19.0 feet. What would be the apparent slip if the vessel cruised 367 miles in a 24 hour day (observed distance) at an average RPM of 84?

A. 2.90%
B. −2.90%
C. 5.20%
D. −5.20%

3062. The propeller on your vessel has a pitch of 22.8 feet. From 0800, 18 April, to 1020, 19 April, you steamed an observed distance of 403.6 miles. If your average RPM was 74, what was the slip?

A. 7.00%
B. −7.00%
C. 8.00%
D. −8.00%

3063. The observed distance for a day's run was 302.7 miles. The propeller had a pitch of 20'06", and the average RPM was 67. What was the slip?

A. 0.70%
B. −0.70%
C. 7.00%
D. −7.00%

3064. The propeller of a vessel has a pitch of 19.0 feet. If the vessel traveled 183.5 miles (observed distance) in 24 hours at an average of 44 RPM, what was the slip?

A. 7.40%
B. −7.40%
C. 11.60%
D. −11.60%

3065. The propeller on your vessel has a pitch of 18'09". If the observed distance for a day's run was 399.4 miles and the average RPM was 86, which statement is TRUE?

A. The slip is a positive 5%.
B. The day's run by engine RPM was 404.5 miles.
C. The slip is a negative 5%.
D. The day's run by engine RPM was 390.6 miles.

3066. The observed noon to noon run for a 24 hour period is 489 miles. The average RPM for the day was 95. The pitch of the wheel is 22.5 feet. What is the slip of the wheel?

A. 3.20%
B. 3.40%
C. 3.70%
D. 3.90%

3067. From 1020, 3 March, to 1845, 5 March, your vessel steamed an observed distance of 845.6 miles. The average RPM was 78, and the pitch of the propeller was 20'03". What was the slip?

A. –4%
B. 4%
C. –8%
D. 8%

3068. Your vessel's propeller has a pitch of 22'06". From 0530, 19 March, to 1930, 20 March, the average RPM was 82. The distance run by observation was 721.5 miles. What was the slip?

A. 4%
B. –4%
C. 7%
D. –7%

3069. If the speed necessary for reaching port at a designated time is 18.5 knots and the pitch of the propeller is 21.7 feet, how many revolutions per minute will the shaft have to turn, assuming a 4% negative slip?

A. 83
B. 90
C. 97
D. 114

3070. If the speed necessary for reaching port at a designated time is 19.6 knots and the pitch of the propeller is 24.6 feet, how many revolutions per minute will the shaft have to turn, assuming a 5% positive slip?

A. 76
B. 85
C. 97
D. 106

3071. If the speed necessary for reaching port at a designated time is 20.7 knots and the pitch of the propeller is 23.8 feet, how many revolutions per minute will the shaft have to turn, assuming a 3% negative slip?

A. 74
B. 79
C. 86
D. 98

3072. If the speed necessary for reaching port at a designated time is 17.4 knots and the pitch of the propeller is 25.6 feet, how many revolutions per minute will the shaft have to turn, assuming a 3% positive slip?

A. 63
B. 67
C. 71
D. 75

3073. If the speed necessary for reaching port at a designated time is 16.8 knots and the pitch of the propeller is 22.3 feet, how many revolutions per minute will the shaft have to turn, assuming a 4% negative slip?

A. 61
B. 66
C. 73
D. 80

3074. If the speed necessary for reaching port at a designated time is 19.2 knots and the pitch of the propeller is 22.7 feet, how many revolutions per minute will the shaft have to turn, assuming a 4% positive slip?

A. 82
B. 89
C. 96
D. 103

3075. If the speed necessary for reaching port at a designated time is 15.7 knots and the pitch of the propeller is 23.4 feet, how many revolutions per minute will the shaft have to turn, assuming a 6% negative slip?

A. 64
B. 68
C. 72
D. 76

3076. If the speed necessary for reaching port at a designated time is 16.4 knots and the pitch of the propeller is 23.8 feet, how many revolutions per minute will the shaft have to turn, assuming a 6% positive slip?

A. 66
B. 74
C. 82
D. 90

3077. If the speed necessary for reaching port at a designated time is 23.7 knots and the pitch of the propeller is 20.8 feet, how many revolutions per minute will the shaft have to turn, assuming a 7% negative slip?

A. 108
B. 112
C. 116
D. 124

3078. If the speed necessary for reaching port at a designated time is 17.8 knots and the pitch of the propeller is 24.7 feet, how many revolutions per minute will the shaft have to turn, assuming a 7% positive slip?

A. 67
B. 71
C. 75
D. 79

3079. If the speed necessary for reaching port at a designated time is 18.2 knots and the pitch of the propeller is 23.9 feet, how many revolutions per minute will the shaft have to turn, assuming a 2% negative slip?

A. 70
B. 73
C. 76
D. 79

3080. If the speed necessary for reaching port at a designated time is 21.6 knots and the pitch of the propeller is 22.5 feet, how many revolutions per minute will the shaft have to turn, assuming a 2% positive slip?

A. 81
B. 87
C. 95
D. 99

3081. If the speed necessary for reaching port at a designated time is 12.6 knots and the pitch of the propeller is 13.6 feet, how many revolutions per minute will the shaft have to turn, assuming no slip?

A. 81
B. 85
C. 90
D. 94

3082. The speed of advance necessary to arrive in port at a designated time is 15.8 knots. The pitch of the propeller is 20.75 feet. You estimate 5% positive slip. How many RPM must you turn to make the necessary speed?

A. 73.5
B. 76.2
C. 79.9
D. 81.2

3083. The speed necessary to reach port at a designated time is 18.7 knots. The propeller pitch is 24'03", and you estimate 3% positive slip. How many RPMs will the shaft have to turn?

A. 81 RPM
B. 87 RPM
C. 98 RPM
D. 104 RPM

3084. If the speed necessary for reaching port at a designated time is 18.6 knots, and the pitch of the propeller is 26.2 feet, how many revolutions per minute will the shaft have to turn, assuming a 4% negative slip.

A. 69
B. 72
C. 75
D. 78

3085. You must average 16.25 knots to reach port at a designated time. Your propeller has a pitch of 21'08", and you estimate 4% negative slip. How many RPMs must you average to arrive on time?

A. 73 RPM
B. 77 RPM
C. 82 RPM
D. 88 RPM

3086. If the pitch of the propeller is 19.7 feet, and the revolutions per day are 86,178, calculate the day's run allowing 3% negative slip.

A. 279.2 miles
B. 287.6 miles
C. 311.4 miles
D. 326.2 miles

3087. If the pitch of the propeller is 20.6 feet, and the revolutions per day are 107,341, calculate the day's run allowing 3% positive slip.

A. 352.7 miles
B. 363.6 miles
C. 374.5 miles
D. 389.1 miles

3088. If the pitch of the propeller is 21.5 feet, and the revolutions per day are 96,666, calculate the day's run allowing 9% negative slip.

A. 311.1 miles
B. 341.8 miles

C. 357.9 miles
D. 372.6 miles

3089. If the pitch of the propeller is 22.4 feet, and the revolutions per day are 103,690, calculate the day's run allowing 9% positive slip.

A. 321.7 miles
B. 347.6 miles
C. 382.0 miles
D. 416.4 miles

3090. If the pitch of the propeller is 26.3 feet, and the revolutions per day are 87,421, calculate the day's run allowing 7% negative slip.

A. 351.7 miles
B. 378.1 miles
C. 404.6 miles
D. 419.3 miles

3091. If the pitch of the propeller is 25.1 feet, and the revolutions per day are 91,591, calculate the day's run allowing 7% positive slip.

A. 351.6 miles
B. 378.1 miles
C. 390.0 miles
D. 404.6 miles

3092. If the pitch of the propeller is 24.8 feet, and the revolutions per day are 93,373, calculate the day's run allowing 11% positive slip.

A. 307.3 miles
B. 339.0 miles
C. 380.9 miles
D. 422.8 miles

3093. If the pitch of the propeller is 23.2 feet, and the revolutions per day are 94,910, calculate the day's run allowing 11% negative slip.

A. 322.3 miles
B. 362.3 miles
C. 382.0 miles
D. 402.0 miles

3094. If the pitch of the propeller is 26.7 feet, and the revolutions per day are 131,717, calculate the day's run allowing 4% negative slip.

A. 555.2 miles
B. 578.4 miles

C. 601.6 miles
D. 649.4 miles

3095. If the pitch of the propeller is 21.3 feet, and the revolutions per day are 126,214, calculate the day's run allowing 4% positive slip.

A. 424.5 miles
B. 442.1 miles
C. 459.9 miles
D. 477.3 miles

3096. If the pitch of the propeller is 20.1 feet, and the revolutions per day are 118,178, calculate the day's run allowing 6% negative slip.

A. 367.2 miles
B. 381.6 miles
C. 398.4 miles
D. 414.1 miles

3097. If the pitch of the propeller is 19.4 feet, and the revolutions per day are 96,713, calculate the day's run allowing 6% positive slip.

A. 266.4 miles
B. 290.1 miles
C. 308.6 miles
D. 327.1 miles

3098. If the pitch of the propeller is 21.2 feet, and the revolutions per day are 93,660, calculate the day's run allowing 5% positive slip.

A. 163.3 miles
B. 217.8 miles
C. 310.3 miles
D. 342.9 miles

3099. The propellers on your twin screw vessel have a pitch of 16'04". What is the distance in a day's run if the average RPM is 94, and you estimate 7% positive slip?

A. 338.3 miles
B. 389.3 miles
C. 676.6 miles
D. 778.6 miles

3100. The pitch of the propeller on your vessel is 19'09". You estimate the slip at −3%. If you averaged 82 RPM for the day's run, how many miles did you steam?

A. 370.8
B. 373.6

C. 393.7
D. 395.3

3101. You are turning 100 RPM, with a propeller pitch of 25 feet, and an estimated slip of –5%. What is the speed of advance?

A. 24.7 knots
B. 23.5 knots
C. 25.9 knots
D. 22.3 knots

3102. You are turning 88 RPM, with a propeller pitch of 19 feet, and an estimated slip of 0%. What is the speed of advance?

A. 16.5 knots
B. 16.9 knots
C. 17.3 knots
D. 18.1 knots

3103. You are turning 93 RPM, with a propeller pitch of 25 feet, and an estimated slip of 0%. What is the speed of advance?

A. 20.2 knots
B. 21.9 knots
C. 22.4 knots
D. 22.9 knots

3104. You are turning 84 RPM, with a propeller pitch of 22 feet, and an estimated slip of 0%. What is the speed of advance?

A. 16.8 knots
B. 17.7 knots
C. 18.0 knots
D. 18.2 knots

3105. You are turning 82 RPM, with a propeller pitch of 23 feet, and an estimated slip of +6%. What is the speed of advance?

A. 17.5 knots
B. 17.9 knots
C. 18.4 knots
D. 19.7 knots

3106. You are turning 85 RPM, with a propeller pitch of 19 feet, and an estimated slip of +3%. What is the speed of advance?

A. 14.7 knots
B. 15.5 knots
C. 16.4 knots
D. 17.1 knots

3107. You are turning 68 RPM, with a propeller pitch of 18 feet, and an estimated slip of +2%. What is the speed of advance?

A. 10.7 knots
B. 11.5 knots
C. 11.8 knots
D. 12.3 knots

3108. You are turning 105 RPM, with a propeller pitch of 17 feet, and an estimated slip of –1%. What is the speed of advance?

A. 15.3 knots
B. 16.9 knots
C. 17.4 knots
D. 17.8 knots

3109. You are turning 90 RPM, with a propeller pitch of 24 feet, and an estimated slip of –3%. What is the speed of advance?

A. 18.8 knots
B. 19.2 knots
C. 20.6 knots
D. 21.9 knots

3110. You are turning 78 RPM, with a propeller pitch of 21 feet, and an estimated slip of –7%. What is the speed of advance?

A. 14.9 knots
B. 15.7 knots
C. 17.3 knots
D. 17.8 knots

3111. You are turning 100 RPM, with propeller pitch of 25 feet, and an estimated negative slip of 5%. What is the speed of advance?

A. 23.4 knots
B. 24.7 knots
C. 25.9 knots
D. 26.3 knots

3112. While enroute to from Montevideo to Walvis Bay a vessel's course is 116° psc. The variation for the locality is 25°W and the deviation is 6°W. What is the true course made good if a southerly wind produces 1° leeway?

A. 084°T
B. 086°T
C. 148°T
D. 085°T

3251. You have steamed 916 miles at 13 knots, and consumed 166 tons of fuel. If you have 203 tons of usable fuel remaining, how far can you steam at 14 knots?

A. 757 miles
B. 841 miles

C. 966 miles
D. 1108 miles

3252. You have steamed 803 miles at 13 knots, and consumed 179 tons of fuel. If you have 371 tons of usable fuel remaining how far can you steam at 16 knots?

A. 1099 miles
B. 1374 miles
C. 1833 miles
D. 2581 miles

3253. You have steamed 925 miles at 13.5 knots, and consumed 181 tons of fuel. If you have 259 tons of usable fuel remaining how far can you steam at 16 knots?

A. 795 miles
B. 942 miles
C. 1117 miles
D. 1409 miles

3254. You have steamed 746 miles at 14.0 knots, and consumed 152 tons of fuel. If you have 201 tons of usable fuel remaining how far can you steam at 10 knots?

A. 1381 miles
B. 1934 miles
C. 2263 miles
D. 2707 miles

3255. You have steamed 836 miles at 14.5 knots, and consumed 191 tons of fuel. If you have 310 tons of usable fuel remaining, how far can you steam at 17 knots?

A. 842 miles
B. 987 miles
C. 1157 miles
D. 1865 miles

3256. You have steamed 918 miles at 15.0 knots, and consumed 183 tons of fuel. If you have 200 tons of usable fuel remaining, how far can you steam at 12 knots?

A. 1021 miles
B. 1261 miles
C. 1568 miles
D. 1960 miles

3257. You have steamed 824 miles at 15.5 knots, and consumed 179 tons of fuel. If you have 221 tons of usable fuel remaining, how far can you steam at 18 knots?

A. 495 miles
B. 650 miles

C. 754 miles
D. 876 miles

3258. You have steamed 525 miles at 16.0 knots, and consumed 105 tons of fuel. If you have 308 tons of usable fuel remaining, how far can you steam at 19 knots?

A. 920 miles
B. 1092 miles
C. 1297 miles
D. 2172 miles

3259. You have steamed 607 miles at 17.0 knots, and consumed 121 tons of fuel. If you have 479 tons of usable fuel remaining, how far can you steam at 14.5 knots?

A. 1211 miles
B. 1748 miles
C. 2817 miles
D. 3303 miles

3260. You have steamed 726 miles at 17.5 knots, and consumed 138 tons of fuel. If you have 252 tons of usable fuel remaining, how far can you steam at 13.5 knots?

A. 789 miles
B. 1326 miles
C. 1719 miles
D. 2228 miles

3261. You have steamed 701 miles at 18.0 knots, and consumed 201 tons of fuel. If you have 259 tons of usable fuel remaining, how far can you steam at 14.5 knots?

A. 838 miles
B. 903 miles
C. 1392 miles
D. 1728 miles

3262. You have steamed 632 miles at 18.5 knots, and consumed 197 tons of fuel. If you have 278 tons of usable fuel remaining, how far can you steam at 15.0 knots?

A. 681 miles
B. 892 miles
C. 1100 miles
D. 1357 miles

3263. You have steamed 1124 miles at 21 knots, and consumed 326 tons of fuel. If you have 210 tons of usable fuel remaining, how far can you steam at 17 knots?

A. 1096 miles
B. 1105 miles

C. 1218 miles
D. 1304 miles

3264. You have steamed 1134 miles at 10 knots, and consumed 121 tons of fuel. If you have to steam 1522 miles to complete the voyage, how many tons of fuel will be consumed while steaming at 12 knots?

A. 146 tons
B. 189 tons
C. 200 tons
D. 234 tons

3265. You have steamed 1587 miles at 11.2 knots, and have consumed one-half of your total fuel capacity of 2840 bbls. What is the maximum speed you can steam to complete the remaining 1951 miles?

A. 9.1 knots
B. 9.9 knots
C. 10.1 knots
D. 11.6 knots

3266. Your vessel has consumed 1087 bbls of fuel after steaming 2210 miles at a speed of 10.75 kts. What is the maximum speed you can steam for the last 1000 miles of the voyage on the remaining 725 bbls, if you estimate 3% of the fuel is not usable?

A. 11.43 knots
B. 11.76 knots
C. 12.84 knots
D. 15.33 knots

3267. Your vessel arrives in port with sufficient fuel to steam 726 miles at 16 knots. If you are unable to take on bunkers, at what speed must you proceed to reach your next port, 873 miles distant?

A. 14.6 knots
B. 15.1 knots
C. 16.3 knots
D. 16.8 knots

3268. Your vessel arrives in port with sufficient fuel to steam 595 miles at 14 knots. If you are unable to take on bunkers, at what speed must you proceed to reach your next port, 707 miles distant?

A. 12.2 knots
B. 12.5 knots
C. 12.8 knots
D. 14.4 knots

3269. Your vessel arrives in port with sufficient fuel to steam 812 miles at 15 knots. If you are unable to take on bunkers, at what speed must you proceed to reach your next port, 928 miles distant?

A. 13.6 knots
B. 14.0 knots
C. 15.3 knots
D. 15.7 knots

3270. Your vessel arrives in port with sufficient fuel to steam 1260 miles at 18 knots. If you are unable to take on bunkers, at what speed must you proceed to reach your next port, 1423 miles distant?

A. 16.0 knots
B. 16.3 knots
C. 16.6 knots
D. 16.9 knots

3271. Your vessel arrives in port with sufficient fuel to steam 550 miles at 13 knots. If you are unable to take on bunkers, at what speed must you proceed to reach your next port, 683 miles distant?

A. 11.7 knots
B. 12.1 knots
C. 13.3 knots
D. 13.7 knots

3272. Your vessel arrives in port with sufficient fuel to steam 775 miles at 17 knots. If you are unable to take on bunkers, at what speed must you proceed to reach your next port, 977 miles distant?

A. 15.1 knots
B. 15.8 knots
C. 17.2 knots
D. 17.7 knots

3273. Your vessel arrives in port with sufficient fuel to steam 1175 miles at 19 knots. If you are unable to take on bunkers, at what speed must you proceed to reach your next port, 1341 miles distant?

A. 16.7 knots
B. 17.3 knots
C. 17.8 knots
D. 19.4 knots

3274. Your vessel arrives in port with sufficient fuel to steam 1066 miles at 21 knots. If you are unable to take on bunkers, at what speed must you proceed to reach your next port, 1251 miles distant?

A. 19.0 knots
B. 19.4 knots
C. 20.3 knots
D. 21.7 knots

3275. You have steamed 989 miles at 16.5 knots, and consumed 215 tons of fuel. If you have 345 tons of usable fuel remaining, how far can you steam at 13 knots?

A. 1025 miles
B. 1993 miles
C. 2557 miles
D. 3245 miles

3276. While steaming at 15 knots, your vessel burns 326 bbls of fuel per day. What will be the rate of fuel consumption if you decrease speed to 12.2 knots?

A. 178 bbls/day
B. 215 bbls/day
C. 277 bbls/day
D. 300 bbls/day

3277. While steaming at 12.3 knots, your vessel burns 168 bbls of fuel per day. What will be the rate of fuel consumption if you increase speed to 13.5 knots?

A. 192 bbls/day
B. 204 bbls/day
C. 222 bbls/day
D. 238 bbls/day

3278. While steaming at 14 knots, your vessel burns 276 bbls of fuel per day. What will be the rate of fuel consumption if you decrease speed to 11.7 knots?

A. 135 bbls/day
B. 160 bbls/day
C. 196 bbls/day
D. 245 bbls/day

3279. While steaming at 15.0 knots, your vessel consumes 326 barrels of fuel oil per day. In order to reduce consumption to 178 barrels of fuel oil per day, what is the maximum speed the vessel can turn for?

A. 8.1 knots
B. 8.5 knots
C. 11.1 knots
D. 12.2 knots

3280. While steaming at 14.5 knots, your vessel consumes 319 barrels of fuel oil per day. In order to reduce consumption to 217 barrels of fuel oil per day, what is the maximum speed the vessel can turn for?

A. 9.8 knots
B. 11.9 knots
C. 12.8 knots
D. 13.5 knots

3281. While steaming at 15.7 knots, your vessel consumes 329 barrels of fuel oil per day. In order to reduce consumption to 267 barrels of fuel oil per day, what is the maximum speed the vessel can turn for?

A. 12.7 knots
B. 13.5 knots
C. 14.6 knots
D. 15.5 knots

3282. While steaming at 16.3 knots, your vessel consumes 363 barrels of fuel oil per day. In order to reduce consumption to 298 barrels of fuel oil per day, what is the maximum speed the vessel can turn for?

A. 12.6 knots
B. 13.1 knots
C. 14.7 knots
D. 15.3 knots

3283. While steaming at 17.5 knots, your vessel consumes 378 barrels of fuel oil per day. In order to reduce consumption to 194 barrels of fuel oil per day, what is the maximum speed the vessel can turn for?

A. 12.5 knots
B. 14.0 knots
C. 15.5 knots
D. 16.8 knots

3284. While steaming at 18.9 knots, your vessel consumes 386 barrels of fuel oil per day. In order to reduce consumption to 251 barrels of fuel oil per day, what is the maximum speed the vessel can turn for?

A. 11.6 knots
B. 12.3 knots
C. 15.2 knots
D. 16.4 knots

3285. While steaming at 19.4 knots, your vessel consumes 392 barrels of fuel oil per day. In order to reduce consumption to 182 barrels of fuel oil per day, what is the maximum speed the vessel can turn for?

A. 13.2 knots
B. 15.0 knots
C. 17.4 knots
D. 18.2 knots

3286. While steaming at 14.5 knots, your vessel consumes 242 barrels of fuel oil per day. In order to reduce consumption to 15 barrels of fuel oil per day, what is the maximum speed the vessel can turn for?

A. 9.1 knots
B. 10.2 knots
C. 11.5 knots
D. 12.4 knots

3287. While steaming at 16.5 knots, your vessel consumes 349 barrels of fuel oil per day. In order to reduce consumption to 18 barrels of fuel oil per day, what is the maximum speed the vessel can turn for?

A. 12.1 knots
B. 13.5 knots
C. 14.6 knots
D. 15.4 knots

3288. While steaming at 13.5 knots, your vessel consumes 251 barrels of fuel oil per day. In order to reduce consumption to 12 barrels of fuel oil per day, what is the maximum speed the vessel can turn for?

A. 6.9 knots
B. 9.7 knots
C. 10.8 knots
D. 12.7 knots

3289. While steaming at 17.0 knots, your vessel consumes 382 barrels of fuel oil per day. In order to reduce consumption to 223 barrels of fuel oil per day, what is the maximum speed the vessel can turn for?

A. 9.9 knots
B. 11.8 knots
C. 13.0 knots
D. 14.2 knots

3290. While steaming at 15.5 knots, your vessel consumes 333 barrels of fuel oil per day. In order to reduce consumption to 176 barrels of fuel oil per day, what is the maximum speed the vessel can turn for?

A. 11.3 knots
B. 12.5 knots
C. 13.6 knots
D. 14.8 knots

3291. While steaming at 19.5 knots, your vessel burns 297 bbls of fuel per day. What will be the rate of fuel consumption if you decrease speed to 15 knots?

A. 135 bbls
B. 176 bbls
C. 229 bbls
D. 243 bbls

3292. Your vessel consumes 215 barrels of fuel per day at a speed of 18.0 knots. What will be the fuel consumption of your vessel at 14.0 knots?

A. 67 bbls
B. 101 bbls
C. 130 bbls
D. 167 bbls

3293. Your vessel consumes 274 barrels of fuel per day at a speed of 17.5 knots. What will be the fuel consumption of your vessel at 13.5 knots?

A. 126 bbls
B. 163 bbls
C. 211 bbls
D. 253 bbls

3294. Your vessel consumes 268 barrels of fuel per day at a speed of 19.0 knots. What will be the fuel consumption of your vessel at 15.0 knots?

A. 132 bbls
B. 167 bbls
C. 212 bbls
D. 243 bbls

3295. Your vessel consumes 178 barrels of fuel per day at a speed of 13.5 knots. What will be the fuel consumption of your vessel at 15.0 knots?

A. 172 bbls
B. 198 bbls
C. 219 bbls
D. 244 bbls

3296. Your vessel consumes 199 barrels of fuel per day at a speed of 14.5 knots. What will be the fuel consumption of your vessel at 10.0 knots?

A. 65 bbls
B. 95 bbls
C. 137 bbls
D. 148 bbls

3297. Your vessel consumes 236 barrels of fuel per day at a speed of 16.5 knots. What will be the fuel consumption of your vessel at 13.0 knots?

A. 102 bbls
B. 115 bbls
C. 147 bbls
D. 186 bbls

3298. Your vessel consumes 216 barrels of fuel per day at a speed of 15.0 knots. What will be the fuel consumption of your vessel at 17.5 knots?

A. 232 bbls
B. 252 bbls
C. 294 bbls
D. 343 bbls

3299. You have steamed 174 miles and consumed 18 tons of fuel. If you maintain the same speed, how many tons of fuel will you consume while steaming 416 miles?

A. 34.9 tons
B. 38.4 tons
C. 43.0 tons
D. 46.2 tons

3300. You have steamed 156 miles and consumed 19 tons of fuel. If you maintain the same speed, how many tons of fuel will you consume while steaming 273 miles?

A. 23.6 tons
B. 27.9 tons
C. 33.3 tons
D. 37.2 tons

3301. You have steamed 217 miles and consumed 23.0 tons of fuel. If you maintain the same speed, how many tons of fuel will you consume while steaming 362 miles?

A. 33.8 tons
B. 38.4 tons
C. 42.6 tons
D. 45.7 tons

3302. You have steamed 132 miles and consumed 14.0 tons of fuel. If you maintain the same speed, how many tons of fuel will you consume while steaming 289 miles?

A. 21.6 tons
B. 24.5 tons
C. 27.9 tons
D. 30.7 tons

3303. You have steamed 174 miles and consumed 18.0 tons of fuel. If you maintain the same speed, how many tons of fuel will you consume while steaming 416 miles?

A. 34.9 tons
B. 38.4 tons
C. 43.0 tons
D. 46.2 tons

3304. You have steamed 265 miles and consumed 25.0 tons of fuel. If you maintain the same speed, how many tons of fuel will you consume while steaming 346 miles?

A. 32.6 tons
B. 37.4 tons
C. 42.6 tons
D. 49.5 tons

3305. You have steamed 201 miles and consumed 18.0 tons of fuel. If you maintain the same speed, how many tons of fuel will you consume while steaming 482 miles?

A. 25.2 tons
B. 43.2 tons
C. 52.6 tons
D. 103.5 tons

3306. You have steamed 264 miles and consumed 22.0 tons of fuel. If you maintain the same speed, how many tons of fuel will you consume while steaming 521 miles?

A. 31.7 tons
B. 38.6 tons
C. 43.4 tons
D. 85.7 tons

3307. You have steamed 182 miles and consumed 16.0 tons of fuel. If you maintain the same speed, how many tons of fuel will you consume while steaming 392 miles?

A. 28.3 tons
B. 34.5 tons
C. 49.6 tons
D. 74.2 tons

3308. You have steamed 142 miles and consumed 21.0 tons of fuel. If you maintain the same speed, how many tons of fuel will you consume while steaming 465 miles?

A. 43.4 tons
B. 57.6 tons
C. 68.8 tons
D. 72.8 tons

3309. You have steamed 142 miles and consumed 15.0 tons of fuel. If you maintain the same speed, how many tons of fuel will you consume while steaming 472 miles?

A. 36.5 tons
B. 49.9 tons
C. 53.8 tons
D. 61.4 tons

3310. You have steamed 216 miles and consumed 19.0 tons of fuel. If you maintain the same speed, how many tons of fuel will you consume while steaming 315 miles?

A. 27.7 tons
B. 32.3 tons
C. 36.9 tons
D. 40.4 tons

3311. You have steamed 162 miles and consumed 14.0 tons of fuel. If you maintain the same speed, how many tons of fuel will you consume while steaming 285 miles?

A. 24.6 tons
B. 34.7 tons
C. 43.3 tons
D. 54.8 tons

3312. You have steamed 199 miles and consumed 23.0 tons of fuel. If you maintain the same speed, how many tons of fuel will you consume while steaming 410 miles?

A. 32.6 tons
B. 39.9 tons
C. 47.4 tons
D. 97.6 tons

3313. You have steamed 300 miles and consumed 34 tons of fuel. If you maintain the same speed, how many tons of fuel will you consume while steaming 700 miles?

A. 79.3 tons
B. 74.3 tons
C. 68.4 tons
D. 66.2 tons

3314. You have steamed 150 miles and consumed 17 tons of fuel. If you maintain the same speed, how many tons of fuel will you consume while steaming 350 miles?

A. 12.82 tons
B. 29.41 tons
C. 34.00 tons
D. 39.66 tons

3317. Your vessel consumes 156 barrels of fuel per day at a speed of 13.0 knots. What will be the fuel consumption of your vessel at 16.0 knots?

A. 192 bbls
B. 236 bbls
C. 291 bbls
D. 315 bbls

3318. While steaming at 12 knots, your vessel burns 45 tons of fuel per day. What will be the rate of fuel consumption if you decrease speed to 11.5 knots?

A. 31 tons/day
B. 36 tons/day
C. 40 tons/day
D. 43 tons/day

3451. You are underway and intend to make good a course of 040°T. You experience a current with a set and drift of 190°T at 1.4 knots, and a northwest wind produces a leeway of 3°. You adjust your course to compensate for the current and leeway, while maintaining an engine speed of 10 knots. What will be your speed made good over your intended course of 040°T?

A. 7.8 knots
B. 8.8 knots
C. 9.8 knots
D. 11.0 knots

3452. You wish to make good a course of 035°T while turning for an engine speed of 12 knots. The set is 340°T, and the drift is 2 knots. What course should you steer?

A. 027°T
B. 037°T
C. 044°T
D. 054°T

3453. You wish to make good a course of 350°T while turning for an engine speed of 10 knots. The set is 070°T, and the drift is 1.5 knots. What course should you steer?

A. 332°T
B. 341°T
C. 345°T
D. 359°T

3454. You wish to make good a course of 300°T while turning for an engine speed of 11 knots. The set is 350°T, and the drift is 2.1 knots. Which course should you steer?

A. 278°T
B. 288°T
C. 292°T
D. 308°T

3455. You wish to make good a course of 230°T while turning for an engine speed of 12.5 knots. The set is 180°T, and the drift is 1.7 knots. What course should you steer?

A. 244°T
B. 236°T
C. 231°T
D. 222°T

3456. You wish to make good a course of 053°T while turning for an engine speed of 16 knots. The set is 345°T, and the drift is 2.4 knots. What course should you steer?

A. 047°T
B. 051°T
C. 055°T
D. 061°T

3457. You wish to make good a course of 035°T while turning for an engine speed of 12 knots. The set is 340°T, and the drift is 2 knots. What speed will you make good along the track line?

A. 12.2 knots
B. 12.7 knots
C. 13.0 knots
D. 13.3 knots

3458. You wish to make good a course of 350°T while turning for an engine speed of 10 knots. The set is 070°T, and the drift is 1.5 knots. What speed will you make good along the track line?

A. 9.7 knots
B. 10.2 knots
C. 10.5 knots
D. 11.0 knots

3459. You wish to make good a course of 300°T while turning for an engine speed of 11 knots. The set is 350°T, and the drift is 2.1 knots. What speed will you make good along the track line?

A. 12.2 knots
B. 12.7 knots
C. 12.9 knots
D. 13.4 knots

3460. You wish to make good a course of 230°T while turning for an engine speed of 12.5 knots. The set is 180°T, and the drift is 1.7 knots. What speed will you make good along the track line?

A. 11.05 knots
B. 12.5 knots
C. 13.6 knots
D. 14.0 knots

3461. You wish to make good a course of 253°T while turning for an engine speed of 16 knots. The set is 345°T, and the drift is 2.4 knots. What speed will you make good along the track line?

A. 14.1 knots
B. 15.2 knots
C. 16.1 knots
D. 16.8 knots

3462. You are underway on course 160°T at 10 knots. The current is 210°T at 0.9 knots. What is the course made good?

A. 156°T
B. 160°T
C. 164°T
D. 169°T

3463. You are underway on course 215°T at 12 knots. The current is 000°T at 2.3 knots. What is the course made good?

A. 209°T
B. 217°T
C. 222°T
D. 232°T

3464. You are underway on course 315°T at 14 knots. The current is 135°T at 1.9 knots. What is the course being made good?

A. 130°T
B. 315°T
C. 317°T
D. 322°T

3465. You are underway on course 000°T at 9.5 knots. The current is 082°T at 1.1 knots. What is the course being made good?

A. 007°T
B. 009°T
C. 021°T
D. 353°T

3466. You are underway on course 172°T at 18.5 knots. The current is 078°T at 2.8 knots. What is the course made good?

A. 114°T
B. 163°T
C. 175°T
D. 181°T

3467. You are underway on course 160°T at 10 knots. The current is 210°T at 0.9 knots. What is the speed being made good?

A. 10.7 knots
B. 11.0 knots
C. 11.6 knots
D. 12.3 knots

3468. You are underway on course 215°T at 12 knots. The current is 000°T at 2.3 knots. What is the speed being made good?

A. 8.5 knots
B. 10.2 knots
C. 10.9 knots
D. 11.2 knots

3469. You are underway on course 315°T at 14 knots. The current is 135°T at 1.9 knots. What is the speed being made good?

A. 12.1 knots
B. 13.5 knots
C. 14.0 knots
D. 15.9 knots

3470. You are underway on course 000°T at 9.5 knots. The current is 082°T at 1.1 knots. What is the speed being made good?

A. 9.2 knots
B. 9.5 knots
C. 9.8 knots
D. 10.1 knots

3471. You are underway on course 172°T at 18.5 knots. The current is 078°T at 2.8 knots. What is the speed being made good?

A. 18.2 knots
B. 18.9 knots
C. 19.4 knots
D. 19.9 knots

3601. You are steering 142° pgc to make good your desired course. The gyro error is 1°E. The variation is 8°W. What should you steer by standard magnetic compass to make good the desired course?

DEVIATION TABLE

MAG HEADING	DEV.
120°	4°E
135°	2°E
150°	0°

A. 133° psc
B. 146° psc
C. 148° psc
D. 151° psc

3602. You are heading 328° pgc to make good a course of 332°T, allowing 3° leeway for westerly winds and 1°E gyro error. The variation is 17°E. What should your heading be by standard magnetic compass to make good 332°T?

DEVIATION TABLE

MAG HEADING	DEV.
345°	1°E
330°	1°W
315°	3°W

A. 315° psc
B. 318° psc
C. 343° psc
D. 345° psc

3603. You are steering 318° psc. A northeasterly wind causes 3° of leeway. The variation is 14°E and the deviation table is extracted below. What will be the true course made good?

DEVIATION TABLE

MAG HEADING	DEV.
300°	2°E
315°	0°
330°	2°W

A. 301°T
B. 303°T
C. 327°T
D. 329°T

3604. You wish to make good a course of 258°T, allowing 4° leeway for northerly winds. The variation is 21°W. What should you steer per standard magnetic compass to make good 258°T?

DEVIATION TABLE

MAG HDG	DEV.
285°	5°E
270°	3°E
255°	1°E
240°	1°W

A. 242° psc
B. 271° psc
C. 278° psc
D. 288° psc

3605. The true course from point A to point B is 317°. A SSW wind causes a 4° leeway, variation is 6°W and deviation is 1°E. What is the magnetic compass course to steer to make good the true course?

A. 326° psc
B. 318° psc
C. 313° psc
D. 308° psc

3606. You are steering 154° pgc. The wind is southwest causing 4° leeway. The gyro error is 3°E, variation is 11°W and deviation is 7°E. What is the true course made good?

A. 153°T
B. 158°T
C. 161°T
D. 164°T

3607. You desire to make good 152°T. The magnetic compass deviation is 4°E, the variation is 5°E, and the gyro error is 3°E. A southwesterly wind produces a 4° leeway. Which course would you steer per standard compass to make good the true course?

A. 137° psc
B. 141° psc
C. 143° psc
D. 147° psc

3608. You are steering 125° pgc. The wind is southwest by south causing a 3° leeway. The variation is 6°E, the deviation is 2°W, and the gyro error is 1°W. What is the true course made good?

A. 121°T
B. 123°T
C. 127°T
D. 129°T

3609. Enroute from Rio to Montevideo, the true course is 215°; the gyro error is 2° west. A north wind causes 3° leeway. What course would you steer per gyrocompass to make good the true course?

A. 220° pgc
B. 214° pgc
C. 216° pgc
D. 210° pgc

3610. While enroute to from Sydney to the Panama Canal a vessel's true course is 071°. Variation is 14°E. Deviation is 4°W. A northerly breeze causes 2° leeway. What course would you steer psc in order to make good the true course?

A. 059° psc
B. 061° psc
C. 063° psc
D. 079° psc

3611. The track line on the chart is 274°T. Variation is 4°E, and deviation is 2°E. The gyro error is 1.5°E. What course would be steered by gyrocompass to make good the desired course?

A. 280.5° pgc
B. 278.0° pgc
C. 275.5° pgc
D. 272.5° pgc

3612. Your vessel is steering 195° per standard magnetic compass. Variation for the area is 13°W, and the deviation is 4°E. The wind is from the west-southwest, producing a 2° leeway. Which true course are you making good?

A. 178°T
B. 180°T
C. 182°T
D. 184°T

3613. You are steering a magnetic compass course of 075°. The variation for the area is 10°W, and the compass deviation is 5°E. What is the true course you are steering?

A. 060°T
B. 070°T
C. 080°T
D. 090°T

3614. The true course between two points is 057°. Your gyrocompass has an error of 3° east and you make an allowance of 1° leeway for a north-northwest wind. Which gyro course should be steered to make the true course good?

A. 053° pgc
B. 056° pgc
C. 059° pgc
D. 060° pgc

3615. You want to make good a true course of 137°. A north-northeast wind produces a 3° leeway. The variation is 11° west, deviation is 5° east, and gyrocompass error is 2° east. What course must you steer per gyrocompass to make the true course good?

A. 132° pgc
B. 134° pgc
C. 136° pgc
D. 138° pgc

3616. You desire to make good a true course of 046°. The variation is 6°E, magnetic compass deviation is 12°W, and the gyrocompass error is 3°W. A northerly wind produces a 5° leeway. What is the course to steer per standard magnetic compass to make good the true course?

A. 047° psc
B. 049° psc

C. 052° psc
D. 057° psc

3617. Your vessel is steering course 299° psc, variation for the area is 7°W, and deviation is 4°W. The wind is from the southwest producing a 3° leeway. What true course are you making good?

A. 291°T
B. 296°T
C. 299°T
D. 313°T

3618. Your vessel is steering course 027° per standard magnetic compass (psc), variation for the area is 19°W, and deviation is 2°E. The wind is from the north-northwest, producing a 5° leeway. What true course are you making good?

A. 005°T
B. 015°T
C. 044°T
D. 049°T

3619. Your vessel is steering course 149° psc, variation for the area is 13°E, and deviation is 4°E. The wind is from the north, producing a 4° leeway. What true course are you making good?

A. 128°T
B. 136°T
C. 162°T
D. 170°T

3620. Your vessel is steering course 197° psc, variation for the area is 7°E, and deviation is 4°W. The wind is from the west, producing a 2° leeway. Which true course are you making good?

A. 192°T
B. 196°T
C. 198°T
D. 202°T

3621. Your vessel is steering course 216° per standard magnetic compass, variation for the area is 9°W, and deviation is 2°E. The wind is from the east, producing a 5° leeway. What true course are you making good?

A. 204°T
B. 214°T
C. 223°T
D. 227°T

3622. Your vessel is steering a course of 337° psc. Variation for the area is 13°W, and deviation is 4°E. The wind is from the south, producing a 3° leeway. Which true course are you making good?

A. 325°T
B. 328°T
C. 331°T
D. 349°T

3623. Your vessel is steering course 166° psc, variation for the area is 8°W, and deviation is 3°W. The wind is from the west-southwest, producing a 2° leeway. What true course are you making good?

A. 153°T
B. 157°T
C. 175°T
D. 179°T

3624. Your vessel is steering course 073° psc, variation for the area is 15°E, and deviation is 4°E. The wind is from the southeast, producing a 4° leeway. Which true course are you making good?

A. 050°T
B. 058°T
C. 088°T
D. 096°T

3625. Your vessel is steering course 111° psc, variation for the area is 5°E, and deviation is 3°W. The wind is from the northwest, producing a 1° leeway. What true course are you making good?

A. 108°T
B. 110°T
C. 112°T
D. 114°T

3626. Your vessel is steering course 284° psc, variation for the area is 6°W, and deviation is 3°E. The wind is from the north-northeast, producing a 3° leeway. What true course are you making good?

A. 275°T
B. 278°T
C. 284°T
D. 290°T

3627. Your vessel is steering course 243° psc. Variation for the area is 5°E, and deviation is 2°W. The wind is from the south-southeast, producing a 2° leeway. What true course are you making good?

A. 242°T
B. 244°T
C. 246°T
D. 248°T

3628. Your vessel is steering course 352° psc, variation for the area is 11°E, and deviation is 9°W. The wind is from the northeast, producing a 1° leeway. What true course are you making good?

A. 349°T
B. 351°T
C. 353°T
D. 355°T

3629. You desire to make good a true course of 129°. The variation is 7°E, magnetic compass deviation is 4°E, and gyrocompass error is 2°W. An easterly wind produces a 4° leeway. What is the course to steer per standard magnetic compass to make the true course good?

A. 114° psc
B. 116° psc
C. 122° psc
D. 126° psc

3630. You desire to make good a true course of 203°. The variation is 19°E, magnetic compass deviation is 2°W, and gyrocompass error is 1°E. A westerly wind produces a 3° leeway. What is the course to steer per standard magnetic compass to make the true course good?

A. 183° psc
B. 189° psc
C. 210° psc
D. 223° psc

3631. You desire to make good a true course of 329°. The variation is 13°W, magnetic compass deviation is 4°E, and gyrocompass error is 2°W. A southerly wind produces a 1° leeway. What is the course to steer per standard magnetic compass to make the true course good?

A. 319° psc
B. 321° psc
C. 337° psc
D. 339° psc

3632. You desire to make good a true course of 157°. The variation is 15°E, magnetic compass deviation is 9°W, and gyrocompass error is 3°E. A southwesterly wind produces a 2° leeway. What is the course to steer per standard magnetic compass to make the true course good?

A. 145° psc
B. 147° psc
C. 150° psc
D. 153° psc

3633. You desire to make good a true course of 067°. The variation is 11°W, magnetic compass deviation is 3°E, and gyrocompass error is 1°W. A northwesterly wind produces a 5° leeway. What is the course to steer per standard magnetic compass to make the true course good?

A. 054° psc
B. 064° psc
C. 070° psc
D. 074° psc

3634. You desire to make good a true course of 038°. The variation is 5°E, magnetic compass deviation is 4°W, and gyrocompass error is 4°W. A southeasterly wind produces a 4° leeway. What is the course to steer per standard magnetic compass to make the true course good?

A. 033° psc
B. 041° psc
C. 043° psc
D. 047° psc

3635. You desire to make good a true course of 236°. The variation is 8°E, magnetic compass deviation is 1°E, and gyrocompass error is 3°W. A south-southeasterly wind produces a 1° leeway. What is the course to steer per standard magnetic compass (psc) to make the true course good?

A. 226° psc
B. 228° psc
C. 244° psc
D. 246° psc

3636. You desire to make good a true course of 279°. The variation is 8°W, magnetic compass deviation is 3°E, and gyrocompass error is 1°E. A north-northwesterly wind produces 3° leeway. What is the course to steer per standard magnetic compass (psc) to make the true course good?

A. 281° psc
B. 284° psc
C. 287° psc
D. 290° psc

3637. You desire to make good a true course of 347°. The variation is 11°E, magnetic compass deviation is 7°W, and gyrocompass error is 4°W. A north by east wind produces a 4° leeway. What is the course to steer per standard magnetic compass to make the true course good?

A. 339° psc
B. 343° psc
C. 347° psc
D. 351° psc

3638. You desire to make good a true course of 007°. The variation is 5°E, magnetic compass deviation is 3°W, and gyrocompass error is 2°E. A southwest by west wind produces a 2° leeway. What is the course to steer per standard magnetic compass to make the true course good?

A. 003° psc
B. 005° psc
C. 007° psc
D. 009° psc

3639. You desire to make good a true course of 132°. The variation is 10°W, magnetic compass deviation is 5°E, and gyrocompass error is 5°W. A northeast by east wind produces a 5° leeway. What is the course to steer per standard magnetic compass to make the true course good?

A. 132° psc
B. 135° psc
C. 137° psc
D. 142° psc

3640. You desire to make good a true course of 223°. The variation is 2°E, magnetic compass deviation is 2°E, and gyrocompass error is 1°W. An east-southeast wind produces 3° leeway. What is the course to steer per standard magnetic compass to make the true course good?

A. 213° psc
B. 216° psc
C. 220° psc
D. 223° psc

3641. You desire to make good a true course of 174°. The variation is 17°W, magnetic compass deviation is 4°W, and gyrocompass error is 4°E. A west-southwest wind produces a 4° leeway. What is the course to steer per standard magnetic compass to make the true course good?

A. 195° psc
B. 197° psc
C. 199° psc
D. 203° psc

3642. You are steering 154° per gyrocompass. The wind is northeast by east, causing 4° leeway. The gyro error is 3° east, variation is 11° west, and deviation is 7°E. What is the true course made good?

A. 151°T
B. 158°T
C. 161°T
D. 164°T

3643. While enroute to from Montevideo to Walvis Bay a vessel's course is 116° psc. The variation for the locality is 25°W and the deviation is 6°W. What is the true course made good if a northerly wind produces 1° leeway?

A. 084°T
B. 086°T
C. 148°T
D. 085°T

3644. While enroute to from Capetown to Rio a vessel's course is 281° pgc. The variation for the locality is 24°W. The deviation is 4°E. The gyro error is 2°W. What is the true course made good?

A. 279°T
B. 261°T
C. 301°T
D. 283°T

3645. The true course between two points is 119°. Your gyrocompass has an error of 3°E. You allow of 4° leeway for a south-southwest wind. What gyro course should be steered to make the true course good?

A. 112° pgc
B. 118° pgc
C. 120° pgc
D. 126° pgc

3646. The true course between two points is 041°. Your gyrocompass has an error of 1°W. You make an allowance of 2° leeway for a east-southeast wind. What gyro course should be steered to make the true course good?

A. 040° pgc
B. 042° pgc
C. 043° pgc
D. 044° pgc

3647. The true course between two points is 220°. Your gyrocompass has an error of 1°E. You make an allowance of 1° leeway for a north-northwest wind. What gyro course should be steered to make the true course good?

A. 220° pgc
B. 221° pgc
C. 222° pgc
D. 223° pgc

3648. The true course between two points is 312°. Your gyrocompass has an error of 3°W. You make an allowance of 4° leeway for a west by south wind. What gyro course should be steered to make the true course good?

A. 305° pgc
B. 311° pgc
C. 315° pgc
D. 318° pgc

3649. The true course between two points is 078°. Your gyrocompass has an error of 2°E. You make an allowance of 3° leeway for a north wind. What gyro course should be steered to make the true course good?

A. 073° pgc
B. 075° pgc
C. 077° pgc
D. 079° pgc

3650. The true course between two points is 194°. Your gyrocompass has an error of 2°W and you make an allowance of 1° leeway for a southwest wind. What gyro course should you steer to make the true course good?

A. 193° pgc
B. 195° pgc
C. 197° pgc
D. 199° pgc

3651. The true course between two points is 337°. Your gyrocompass has an error of 3°E and you make an allowance of 5° leeway for a west wind. Which gyro course should be steered to make the true course good?

A. 329° pgc
B. 335° pgc
C. 339° pgc
D. 345° pgc

3652. The true course between two points is 023°T. Your gyrocompass has an error of

1°W and you make an allowance of 4° leeway for an east wind. What gyro course should be steered to make the true course good?

A. 020° pgc
B. 021° pgc
C. 026° pgc
D. 028° pgc

3653. The true course between two points is 106°. Your gyrocompass has an error of 2°E and you make an allowance of 2° leeway for a south wind. What gyro course should be steered to make the true course good?

A. 102° pgc
B. 104° pgc
C. 106° pgc
D. 108° pgc

3708. At what time would you listen to VHF Channel 22A (157.1 MHz) for information concerning the stage of the river between Memphis and Cairo?

A. 1300
B. 1435
C. 1620
D. 1815

3751. While proceeding up a channel on course 010° per gyrocompass, you notice a pair of range lights in alignment with the masts of your vessel when viewed forward. A check of the chart shows the range to be 009°T and the variation to be 15°W. If the ship's course is 026° psc, what is the deviation for the present heading?

A. 2°W
B. 2°E
C. 1°W
D. 1°E

3752. While your vessel is proceeding down a channel you notice a range of lights in line with your vessel's mast. If your vessel is on course 001° per gyrocompass and the charted value of the range of lights is 359°T, what is the gyrocompass error?

A. 2°W
B. 2°E
C. 1°E
D. 1°W

3753. Your vessel is proceeding up a channel, and you see a pair of range lights that

are in line dead ahead. The chart indicates that the direction of this pair of lights is 343°T, and the variation is 5° west. If the heading of your vessel at the time of the sighting is 344° per standard magnetic compass, what is the correct deviation?

A. 1°E
B. 1°W
C. 4°E
D. 4°W

3754. Your vessel is proceeding up a channel, and you see a pair of range lights that are in line ahead. The chart indicates that the direction of this pair of lights is 014°T, and the variation is 11°E. If the heading of your vessel at the time of the sighting is 009° per standard magnetic compass, what is the correct deviation?

A. 5°E
B. 5°W
C. 6°E
D. 6°W

3755. Your vessel is proceeding up a channel, and you see a pair of range lights that are in line ahead. The chart indicates that the direction of this pair of lights is 186°T, and the variation is 11°W. If the heading of your vessel at the time of the sighting is 193° per standard magnetic compass, what is the correct deviation?

A. 4°E
B. 4°W
C. 7°E
D. 7°W

3756. Your vessel is proceeding up a channel, and you see a pair of range lights that are in line dead ahead. The chart indicates that the direction of this pair of lights is 093°T, and the variation is 6°E. If the heading of your vessel at the time of the sighting is 097° per standard magnetic compass, what is the correct deviation?

A. 5°E
B. 5°W
C. 10°E
D. 10°W

3757. Your vessel is proceeding up a channel, and you see a pair of range lights that are in line ahead. The chart indicates that the direction of this pair of lights is 311°T, and the variation is 8°E. If the heading of your vessel at the time of the sighting is

305° per standard magnetic compass, what is the correct deviation?

A. 2°E
B. 2°W
C. 6°E
D. 6°W

3758. Your vessel is proceeding up a channel, and you see a pair of range lights that are in line ahead. The chart indicates that the direction of this pair of lights is 212°T, and the variation is 7°W. If the heading of your vessel at the time of the sighting is 208° per standard magnetic compass, what is the correct deviation?

A. 4°E
B. 4°W
C. 11°E
D. 11°W

3759. Your vessel is proceeding up a channel, and you see a pair of range lights that are in line ahead. The chart indicates that the direction of this pair of lights is 147°T, and the variation is 5°E. If the heading of your vessel at the time of the sighting is 148° per standard magnetic compass, what is the correct deviation?

A. 1°E
B. 1°W
C. 6°E
D. 6°W

3760. Your vessel is proceeding up a channel, and you see a pair of range lights that are in line ahead. The chart indicates that the direction of this pair of lights is 352°T, and the variation is 4°W. If the heading of your vessel at the time of the sighting is 359° per standard magnetic compass, what is the correct deviation?

A. 3°W
B. 7°E
C. 11°E
D. 11°W

3761. Your vessel is proceeding up a channel, and you see a pair of range lights that are in line dead ahead. The chart indicates that the direction of this pair of lights is 283°T, and the variation is 13°E. If the heading of your vessel at the time of the sighting is 278° per standard compass, what is the deviation?

A. 5°E
B. 5°W

C. 8°E
D. 8°W

3762. Your vessel is proceeding up a channel, and you see a pair of range lights that are in line ahead. The chart indicates that the direction of this pair of lights is 196°T, and the variation is 7°E. If the heading of your vessel at the time of the sighting is 192° per standard magnetic compass, what is the correct deviation?

A. 3°E
B. 3°W
C. 4°E
D. 4°W

3763. Your vessel is proceeding up a channel, and you see a pair of range lights that are in line dead ahead. The chart indicates that the direction of this pair of lights is 178°T, and the variation is 9°W. If the heading of your vessel at the time of the sighting is 180° per standard magnetic compass, what is the deviation?

A. 2°E
B. 2°W
C. 7°E
D. 7°W

3764. Your vessel is proceeding up a channel, and you see a pair of range lights that are in line ahead. The chart indicates that the direction of this pair of lights is 064°T, and the variation is 17°W. If the heading of your vessel at the time of the sighting is 094° per standard magnetic compass, what is the correct deviation?

A. 4°E
B. 4°W
C. 13°E
D. 13°W

3765. Your vessel is proceeding up a channel steering on a pair of range lights that are in line ahead. The chart indicates that the direction of this pair of lights is 249°T, and the variation is 14°E. If the heading of your vessel at the time of the sighting is 226° per standard magnetic compass, what is the correct deviation?

A. 5°E
B. 5°W
C. 9°E
D. 9°W

3766. Your vessel is proceeding down a channel, and you see a pair of range lights

that are in line dead ahead. The chart indicates that the direction of this pair of lights is 229°T, and variation is 6°W. If the heading of your vessel at the time of the sighting is 232° per standard magnetic compass, what is the correct deviation?

A. 3°E
B. 9°E
C. 3°W
D. 9°W

3767. You are on course 251° pgc and 241° per magnetic compass, when you observe a range in line bearing 192° pgc. The chart indicates that the range is in line on a bearing of 194°T. The variation is 16°E. What is the deviation of the magnetic compass?

A. 2°E
B. 2°W
C. 4°W
D. 10°W

3768. While entering a harbor on a course of 225° per gyrocompass, you take a bearing on a pair of range lights and get 220° per gyrocompass. The bearing on the chart is 217°T. The variation for the area is 6°W and deviation is 2°W. What course would you steer per gyrocompass to make good a true course of 232°?

A. 229° pgc
B. 243° pgc
C. 240° pgc
D. 235° pgc

3769. Entering a harbor, you take a bearing on a range and get 338° per gyrocompass (pgc). The true bearing from the chart is 340°T. Variation for the area is 14°E. Your course is 329° per standard magnetic compass (psc) and 338° pgc. The deviation on this heading is _____.

A. 3°E
B. 3°W
C. 5°E
D. 5°W

3770. You wish to check the deviation of your standard magnetic compass. You find a natural range that you steer for and note that the gyrocompass heading is 034°, and the heading by standard magnetic compass is 026°. The gyro error is 1°W. Variation is 9°E. What is the deviation for that heading?

A. 2°W
B. 0°
C. 2°E
D. 9°E

3771. Two beacons form a range in the direction of 221.5°T. The range is seen in line from your vessel bearing 223° per gyrocompass. The variation in the area is 4°E. What is the error of your gyrocompass?

A. 1.5°W
B. 2.5°W
C. 5.5°W
D. 2.5°E

3772. Your ship is entering port from sea, and you sight a pair of range lights. When in line, they bear 315° per standard magnetic compass. The chart shows that the range bearing is 312°T, and that variation is 6°W. What is the deviation of your compass at the time of the sighting?

A. 3°E
B. 3°W
C. 9°E
D. 9°W

4000. You swung ship and compared the magnetic compass against the gyrocompass to find deviation. Gyro error is 2°E. The variation is 8°W. Find the deviation on a magnetic compass heading of 057°.

HEADING

PSC	PGC
358.5°	350°
122.5°	110°
239.5°	230°
030.5°	020°
152.0°	140°
269.0°	260°
061.5°	050°
181.0°	170°
298.0°	290°
092.0°	080°
210.0°	200°
327.5°	320°

A. 1.0°E
B. 1.5°E
C. 1.5°W
D. 0.5°W

4001. You swung ship and compared the magnetic compass against the gyrocompass to find deviation. Gyro error is 2°E. The variation is 8°W. Find the deviation on a magnetic compass heading of 143°.

HEADING

PSC	PGC
358.5°	350°
122.5°	110°
239.5°	230°
030.5°	020°
152.0°	140°
269.0°	260°
061.5°	050°
181.0°	170°
298.0°	290°
092.0°	080°
210.0°	200°
327.5°	320°

A. 2.0°W
B. 1.5°W
C. 0.5°W
D. 0.0°

4002. You swung ship and compared the magnetic compass against the gyrocompass to find deviation. Gyro error is 2°E. The variation is 8°W. Find the deviation on a true heading of 258°.

HEADING

PSC	PGC
358.5°	350°
122.5°	110°
239.5°	230°
030.5°	020°
152.0°	140°
269.0°	260°
061.5°	050°
181.0°	170°
298.0°	290°
092.0°	080°
210.0°	200°
327.5°	320°

A. 0.5°W
B. 0.0°
C. 0.5°E
D. 1.0°E

4003. You swung ship and compared the magnetic compass against the gyrocompass to find deviation. Gyro error is 2°W. The variation is 8°W. Find the deviation on a gyro heading of 058°.

HEADING

PSC	PGC
358.5°	354°
122.5°	114°
239.5°	234°
030.5°	024°
152.0°	144°
269.0°	264°
061.5°	054°
181.0°	174°
298.0°	294°
092.0°	084°
210.0°	204°
327.5°	324°

A. 1.5°W
B. 1.0°W
C. 1.0°E
D. 0.5°W

4004. You swung ship and compared the magnetic compass against the gyrocompass to find deviation. Gyro error is 2°W. The variation is 8°W. Find the deviation on a magnetic compass heading of 166°.

HEADING

PSC	PGC
358.5°	354°
122.5°	114°
239.5°	234°
030.5°	024°
152.0°	144°
269.0°	264°
061.5°	054°
181.0°	174°
298.0°	294°
092.0°	084°
210.0°	204°
327.5°	324°

A. 2.0°W
B. 1.5°W
C. 1.0°W
D. 0.5°W

4005. You swung ship and compared the magnetic compass against the gyrocompass to find deviation. Gyro error is 2°W. The variation is 8°W. Find the deviation on a magnetic compass heading of 022°.

HEADING

PSC	PGC
358.5°	354°
122.5°	114°
239.5°	234°
030.5°	024°
152.0°	144°
269.0°	264°
061.5°	054°
181.0°	174°
298.0°	294°
092.0°	084°
210.0°	204°
327.5°	324°

A. 1.5°E
B. 0.5°E
C. 0.0°
D. 0.5°W

4006. You swung ship and compared the magnetic compass against the gyrocompass to find deviation. Gyro error is 2°W. The variation is 8°W. Find the deviation on a true heading of 236°.

HEADING

PSC	PGC
358.5°	354°
122.5°	114°
239.5°	234°
030.5°	024°
152.0°	144°
269.0°	264°
061.5°	054°
181.0°	174°
298.0°	294°
092.0°	084°
210.0°	204°
327.5°	324°

A. 1.0°W
B. 0.5°E
C. 1.5°E
D. 0.0°

4007. You swung ship and compared the magnetic compass against the gyrocompass to find deviation. Gyro error is 2°E. The variation is 8°W. Find the deviation on a gyro heading of 166°.

HEADING

PSC	PGC
358.5°	350°
122.5°	110°
239.5°	230°
030.5°	020°
152.0°	140°
269.0°	260°
061.5°	050°
181.0°	170°
298.0°	290°
092.0°	080°
210.0°	200°
327.5°	320°

A. 1.0°W
B. 1.0°E
C. 0.5°W
D. 0.5°E

4008. You swung ship and compared the magnetic compass against the gyrocompass to find deviation. Gyro error is 2°E. The variation is 8°W. Find the deviation on a gyro heading of 037°.

HEADING

PSC	PGC
358.5°	350°
122.5°	110°
239.5°	230°
030.5°	020°
152.0°	140°
269.0°	260°
061.5°	050°
181.0°	170°
298.0°	290°
092.0°	080°
210.0°	200°
327.5°	320°

A. 1.0°W
B. 1.5°W
C. 1.5°E
D. 2.0°E

4009. You swung ship and compared the magnetic compass against the gyrocompass to find deviation. Gyro error is 2°E. The variation is 8°W. Find the deviation on a true heading of 187°.

HEADING

PSC	PGC
358.5°	350°
122.5°	110°
239.5°	230°
030.5°	020°
152.0°	140°
269.0°	260°
061.5°	050°
181.0°	170°
298.0°	290°
092.0°	080°
210.0°	200°
327.5°	320°

A. 1.5°W
B. 0.5°W
C. 0.0°
D. 1.0°E

4010. You swung ship and compared the magnetic compass against the gyrocompass to find deviation. Gyro error is 2°E. The variation is 8°W. Find the deviation on a magnetic compass heading of 104°.

HEADING

PSC	PGC
358.5°	350°
122.5°	110°
239.5°	230°
030.5°	020°
152.0°	140°
269.0°	260°

061.5°	050°
181.0°	170°
298.0°	290°
092.0°	080°
210.0°	200°
327.5°	320°

A. 1.8°E
B. 2.6°E
C. 2.2°W
D. 2.7°W

4011. You swung ship and compared the magnetic compass against the gyrocompass to find deviation. Gyro error is 2°E. The variation is 8°W. Find the deviation on a magnetic compass heading of 234°.

HEADING

PSC	PGC
358.5°	350°
122.5°	110°
239.5°	230°
030.5°	020°
152.0°	140°
269.0°	260°
061.5°	050°
181.0°	170°
298.0°	290°
092.0°	080°
210.0°	200°
327.5°	320°

A. 2.5°W
B. 2.5°E
C. 1.0°W
D. 0.5°E

4012. You swung ship and compared the magnetic compass against the gyrocompass to find deviation. Gyro error is 2°W. The variation is 8°W. Find the deviation on a magnetic compass heading of 210°.

HEADING

PSC	PGC
358.5°	354°
122.5°	114°
239.5°	234°
030.5°	024°
152.0°	144°
269.0°	264°
061.5°	054°
181.0°	174°
298.0°	294°
092.0°	084°
210.0°	204°
327.5°	324°

A. 0.0°
B. 0.5°W

C. 0.5°E
D. 1.0°E

4013. You swung ship and compared the magnetic compass against the gyrocompass to find deviation. Gyro error is 2°W. The variation is 8°W. Find the deviation on a gyro heading of 039°.

HEADING

PSC	PGC
358.5°	354°
122.5°	114°
239.5°	234°
030.5°	024°
152.0°	144°
269.0°	264°
061.5°	054°
181.0°	174°
298.0°	294°
092.0°	084°
210.0°	204°
327.5°	324°

A. 0.8°E
B. 0.0°
C. 0.5°W
D. 1.0°W

4014. You swung ship and compared the magnetic compass against the gyrocompass to find deviation. Gyro error is 2°W. The variation is 8°W. Find the deviation on a true heading of 157°.

HEADING

PSC	PGC
358.5°	354°
122.5°	114°
239.5°	234°
030.5°	024°
152.0°	144°
269.0°	264°
061.5°	054°
181.0°	174°
298.0°	294°
092.0°	084°
210.0°	204°
327.5°	324°

A. 2.0°W
B. 1.5°W
C. 1.0°W
D. 0.0°

4015. You swung ship and compared the magnetic compass against the gyrocompass to find deviation. Gyro error is 2°W. The variation is 8°W. Find the deviation on a true heading of 319°.

HEADING

PSC	PGC
358.5°	354°
122.5°	114°
239.5°	234°
030.5°	024°
152.0°	144°
269.0°	264°
061.5°	054°
181.0°	174°
298.0°	294°
092.0°	084°
210.0°	204°
327.5°	324°

A. 0.5°E
B. 1.0°W
C. 2.5°E
D. 2.5°W

4016. You swung ship and compared the magnetic compass against the gyrocompass to find deviation. Gyro error is 2°W. The variation is 8°W. Find the deviation on a magnetic compass heading of 004°.

HEADING

PSC	PGC
358.5°	354°
122.5°	114°
239.5°	234°
030.5°	024°
152.0°	144°
269.0°	264°
061.5°	054°
181.0°	174°
298.0°	294°
092.0°	084°
210.0°	204°
327.5°	324°

A. 1.5°W
B. 0.5°W
C. 0.0°
D. 1.0°E

4017. You swung ship and compared the magnetic compass against the gyrocompass to find deviation. Gyro error is 2°E. The variation is 8°W. Find the deviation on a gyro heading of 196°.

HEADING

PSC	PGC
358.5°	350°
122.5°	110°
239.5°	230°
030.5°	020°
152.0°	140°
269.0°	260°
061.5°	050°
181.0°	170°
298.0°	290°
092.0°	080°
210.0°	200°
327.5°	320°

A. 2.0°E
B. 2.0°W
C. 1.0°W
D. 0.0°

The following questions are based on chart 12221TR, Chesapeake Bay Entrance, and the supporting publications.

10100. Your loran shows a position of LAT 36°59.0'N, LONG 75°48.6'W. What is the course per standard magnetic compass to a position one mile south of Cape Charles Buoy 14 (which is positioned at LAT 37°07.4'N, LONG 75°41.0'W)?

A. 045° psc
B. 049° psc
C. 053° psc
D. 057° psc

10101. Your loran shows a position of LAT 36°59.0'N, LONG 75°48.6'W. What is the course per standard magnetic compass to a position one mile east of Cape Charles Buoy 14 (LAT 37°07.4'N, LONG 75°41.0'W)?

A. 040° psc
B. 045° psc
C. 049° psc
D. 053° psc

10102. Your loran shows a position of LAT 37°07.5'N, LONG 75°39.1'W. What is the course per standard magnetic compass (psc) to a position 0.3 mile due north of North Chesapeake Entrance Buoy NCA (LL #375)?

A. 222° psc
B. 228° psc
C. 231° psc
D. 234° psc

10103. Your loran shows a position of LAT 37°01.5'N, LONG 75°31.7'W. What is the course per standard magnetic compass to Chesapeake Light?

A. 243°
B. 240°
C. 237°
D. 231°

10104. Your loran shows a position of LAT 36°55.2'N, LONG 75°33.1'W. What is the course per standard magnetic compass to Rudee Inlet (LAT 36°49.8'N, LONG 75°58.0'W)?

A. 246.0° psc
B. 254.5° psc
C. 261.0° psc
D. 265.5° psc

10105. What is the course psc from Chesapeake Light to North Chesapeake Entrance Buoy NCA?

A. 313° psc
B. 317° psc
C. 321° psc
D. 325° psc

10106. What is the course per standard magnetic compass from Chesapeake Light to North Chesapeake Entrance Lighted Whistle Buoy NCA?

A. 316° psc
B. 321° psc
C. 323° psc
D. 326° psc

10107. What is the first course per standard magnetic compass (psc) in the outbound southeasterly traffic lane of the Chesapeake Bay entrance traffic separation scheme?

A. 133° psc
B. 138° psc
C. 143° psc
D. 148° psc

10108. What is the base course per standard magnetic compass while southbound in the middle leg of York Spit Channel?

A. 161.0° psc
B. 165.5° psc
C. 180.0° psc
D. 184.0° psc

10109. What is the base course psc in the inbound northeasterly traffic lane of the Chesapeake Bay entrance traffic separation scheme?

A. 261° psc
B. 258° psc
C. 250° psc
D. 244° psc

The following questions are to be answered by using chart 12354TR, Long Island Sound - Eastern Part, and supporting publications.

10200. Your loran shows a fix position of LAT 41°10.0'N, LONG 72°52.5'W. What is the course per standard magnetic compass to a position one mile due south of Falkner Island Light?

A. 065° psc
B. 081° psc
C. 093° psc
D. 097° psc

10201. Your present position is LAT 41°05.5'N, LONG 72°38.0'W. Assuming that there are no set and drift, what course must you steer per standard magnetic compass (psc) to arrive at a position 0.5 mile due south of New Haven Lighted Whistle Buoy NH?

A. 111.5° psc
B. 210.5° psc
C. 294.3° psc
D. 310.5° psc

10202. Your present position is LAT 41°05.5'N, LONG 72°38.0'W. Assuming that there is no set and drift, what course must you steer per standard magnetic compass (psc) to arrive at a position midway between New Haven Harbor Channel buoys #1 and #2?

A. 137° psc
B. 309° psc
C. 315° psc
D. 319° psc

10203. Your present position is LAT 41°05.5'N, LONG 72°38.0'W. Assuming there is no set and drift, what course must you steer per standard magnetic compass (psc) to arrive at a position 3 miles due north of Horton Point Light?

A. 077° psc
B. 081° psc
C. 085° psc
D. 088° psc

10204. Your present position is LAT 41°05.5'N, LONG 72°38.0'W. Assuming that there is no set and drift, what course must you steer per standard magnetic compass (psc) to arrive at a position 5 miles due south of Saybrook Breakwater Light?

A. 089° psc
B. 080° psc
C. 077° psc
D. 066° psc

10205. Your present position is LAT 41°05.5'N, LONG 72°38.0'W. Assuming that there is no set and drift, what course must you steer per standard magnetic compass (psc) to arrive at a position 2 miles due west of Twenty-Eight Foot Shoal Lighted Buoy (LAT 41°09.3'N, LONG 72°30.5'W)?

A. 055° psc
B. 059° psc
C. 064° psc
D. 235° psc

10206. Your 2230 position is LAT 41°07.4'N, LONG 72°44.0'W. Assuming that there are no set and drift, what course must you steer per standard magnetic compass (psc) to leave Twenty-Eight Foot Shoal Lighted Buoy (LAT 41°09.3'N, LONG 72°30.4'W) 1 mile abeam to port?

A. 084° psc
B. 091° psc
C. 094° psc
D. 098° psc

10207. Your 2230 position is LAT 41°07.4'N, LONG 72°44.0'W. Assuming that there is no set and drift, what course must you steer per standard magnetic compass to leave Twenty-Eight Foot Shoal Lighted Buoy 1 mile abeam to starboard?

A. 086° psc
B. 091° psc
C. 094° psc
D. 098° psc

10208. A loran fix places your vessel at LAT 41°08.5'N, LONG 72°28.8'W. What course must you steer per standard magnetic compass (psc) to leave Cornfield Lighted Whistle Buoy CF 0.5 mile abeam to starboard?

A. 032° psc
B. 048° psc
C. 055° psc
D. 067° psc

10209. A loran fix places your vessel at LAT 41°08.5'N, LONG 72°28.8'W. What course must you steer per standard magnetic compass (psc) to leave Cornfield Lighted Whistle Buoy CF 0.5 mile abeam to port?

A. 064° psc
B. 077° psc
C. 088° psc
D. 092° psc

10210. Your present position is LAT 41°07.4'N, LONG 72°44.0'W. Assuming that there is no set and drift, what course must you steer per standard magnetic compass (psc) to a position of LAT 41°08.5'N, LONG 72°28.8'W?

A. 073° psc
B. 084° psc
C. 091° psc
D. 097° psc

The following questions should be answered using chart number 13205TR, Block Island and Approaches, and supporting publications.

10300. Determine the course per standard magnetic compass from the entrance to Quonochontaug Pond (LAT 41°19.8'N, LONG 71°43.2'W) to the entrance to Great Salt Pond on Block Island.

A. 129.5° psc
B. 134.0° psc
C. 157.5° psc
D. 160.5° psc

10301. Determine the course per standard magnetic compass from Cerberus Shoal Buoy 9 (LAT 41°10.4'N, LONG 71°57.1'W) to the entrance to Quonochontaug Pond (LAT 41°19.8'N, LONG 71°43.2'W).

A. 030° psc
B. 036° psc
C. 059° psc
D. 067° psc

10302. Determine the course per standard magnetic compass from Cerberus Shoal Buoy 9 (LAT 41°10.4'N, LONG 71°57.1'W) to a position 0.2 mile south of Race Rock Light (LAT 41°14.6'N, LONG 72°02.8'W).

A. 326.5° psc
B. 324.0° psc
C. 298.5° psc
D. 296.0° psc

10303. Determine the course per standard magnetic compass from 0.2 mile south of Race Rock Light (LAT 41°14.6'N, LONG 72°02.8'W) to the entrance of the channel to Lake Montauk (west of Montauk Point).

A. 137.0° psc
B. 152.0° psc
C. 165.5° psc
D. 168.5° psc

10304. Determine the course per standard magnetic compass from the entrance to Ninigret Pond (LAT 41°21.3'N, LONG 71°38.3'W) to the entrance to Great Salt Pond on Block Island.

A. 192.0° psc
B. 185.0° psc
C. 154.5° psc
D. 152.5° psc

10305. You are 3 miles due east of Montauk Point Light. What is the course per standard magnetic compass to a position one mile due south of Block Island Southeast Point Light?

A. 070.0°
B. 076.5°
C. 082.5°
D. 087.5°

10306. You are 3 miles due east of Montauk Point Light. What is the course per standard magnetic compass to LAT 41°00.0'N, LONG 71°40.0'W?

A. 145.5° psc
B. 142.5° psc
C. 138.5° psc
D. 127.0° psc

10307. You are 3 miles due east of Montauk Point Light. What is the course per standard magnetic compass to a position 0.5 mile due south of Race Rock Light?

A. 324° psc
B. 328° psc
C. 331° psc
D. 339° psc

10308. You are 3 miles due east of Montauk Point Light. What is the course per standard magnetic compass to a position 1.5 miles due east of Watch Hill Point Light?

A. 017° psc
B. 013° psc
C. 010° psc
D. 006° psc

10309. You are 3 miles due east of Montauk Point Light. What is the course per standard magnetic compass to LAT 41°00.0'N, LONG 71°30.0'W?

A. 108° psc
B. 122° psc
C. 124° psc
D. 130° psc

The following questions are based on chart 12221TR, Chesapeake Bay Entrance, and the supporting publications.

10500. At 1712 your loran set indicates a position of LAT 36°54.8'N, LONG 75°39.8'W. You are on course 319° per standard magnetic compass at a speed of 9.9 knots. At 1800 your loran set indicates your position at LAT 37°00.0'N, LONG 75°45.8'W. What were the set and drift?

A. 262°T at 0.9 knot
B. 267°T at 1.6 knots
C. 087°T at 1.5 knots
D. 093°T at 0.8 knot

10501. At 0939 your loran set indicates a position of LAT 36°57.0'N, LONG 75°41.0'W. You are on course 119° per standard magnetic compass at a speed of 12.8 knots. At 1017 your loran set indicates your position as LAT 36°54.2'N, LONG 75°33.1'W. What were the set and drift?

A. 280°T at 1.0 knot
B. 275°T at 2.0 knots
C. 091°T at 1.6 knots
D. 103°T at 1.1 knots

10502. At 1239 your loran set indicates a position of LAT 36°55.2'N, LONG 75°33.1'W. You are on course 281° per standard magnetic compass at a speed of 9.2 knots. At 1318 your loran set indicates your position as LAT 36°54.8'N, LONG 75°39.8'W. What were the set and drift?

A. 130°T at 1.2 knots
B. 156°T at 0.6 knot
C. 352°T at 1.3 knots
D. 335°T at 1.0 knot

10503. At 0817 your loran set indicates a position of LAT 37°01.6'N, LONG 75°31.7'W. You are on course 182° per standard magnetic compass at a speed of 9.2 knots. At 0913 your loran set indicates your position at LAT 36°52.3'N, LONG 75°30.8'W. What were the set and drift?

A. 121°T at 0.8 knot
B. 139°T at 1.1 knots
C. 219°T at 1.1 knots
D. 298°T at 0.7 knot

10504. At 1354 your loran set indicates a position of LAT 37°00.0'N, LONG 75°45.8'W. You are on course 088° per standard magnetic compass at a speed of 9.5 knots. At 1500 your loran set indicates your position as LAT 37°01.6'N, LONG 75°31.7'W. What were the set and drift?

A. 273°T at 0.8 knot
B. 241°T at 1.1 knots
C. 061°T at 1.3 knots
D. 092°T at 0.9 knot

10505. At 0919 your position is LAT 37°00.0'N, LONG 75°30.0'W. You are on course 270°T at 8.7 knots. At 1000 your position is LAT 36°59.5'N, LONG 75°37.0'W. What was the current?

A. 137° at 0.6 knot
B. 150° at 0.9 knot
C. 331° at 0.7 knot
D. 347° at 0.7 knot

10506. At 0919 your position is LAT 37°00.0'N, LONG 75°30.0'W. You are on course 270°T at 8.7 knots. At 1031 your position is LAT 36°59.5'N, LONG 75°44.9'W. What was the current?

A. 239° at 0.8 knot
B. 252° at 1.3 knots
C. 060° at 0.7 knot
D. 073° at 1.2 knots

10507. At 0919 your position is LAT 37°00.0'N, LONG 75°30.0'W. You are on course 270°T at 10.5 knots. At 1020 your position is LAT 36°59.5'N, LONG 75°44.9'W. What was the current?

A. 026° at 0.7 knot
B. 046° at 1.0 knot
C. 226° at 0.8 knot
D. 246° at 1.4 knots

10508. At 0919 your position is LAT 37°00.0'N, LONG 75°30.0'W. You are on course 270°T at 8.7 knots. At 1000 your position is LAT 37°00.5'N, LONG 75°37.0'W. What was the current?

A. 010° at 0.5 knot
B. 017° at 1.0 knot
C. 020° at 0.4 knot
D. 032° at 0.9 knot

10509. At 0919 your position is LAT 37°00.0'N, LONG 75°30.0'W. You are on course 270°T at 7.8 knots. At 1035 your position is LAT 37°00.5'N, LONG 75°43.8'W. What was the current?

A. 281° at 0.7 knot
B. 292° at 1.0 knot
C. 305° at 1.3 knots
D. 113° at 1.2 knots

The following questions are to be answered by using chart 12354TR, Long Island Sound - Eastern Part, and supporting publications.

10600. At 1620 your loran set indicates a position of LAT 41°09.0'N, LONG 72°40.0'W. You are on course 134° per standard magnetic compass at a speed of 10 knots. At 1700 your loran set indicates your position as LAT 41°05.3'N, LONG 72°33.7'W. What were the set and drift?

A. 067°T at 1.7 knots
B. 078°T at 1.1 knots
C. 243°T at 1.0 knot
D. 249°T at 1.6 knots

10601. At 1645 your loran set fixes your position at LAT 41°09.2'N, LONG 72°36.9'W. You are steering course 262° per standard magnetic compass at a speed of 12 knots. At 1721 you fix your position by plotting several compass bearings on nearby known fixed objects. These result in a position of LAT 41°07.2'N, LONG 72°44.9'W. What were your set and drift?

A. 040°T at 0.8 knot
B. 030°T at 1.7 knots
C. 225°T at 0.9 knot
D. 242°T at 1.1 knots

10602. At 1815 your loran set fixes your position at LAT 41°09.2'N, LONG 72°36.9'W. You are steering course 285° per standard magnetic compass at a speed of 16 knots. At 1909 you fix your position by plotting several compass bearings on nearby known fixed objects. These result in a position of LAT 41°08.5'N, LONG 72°53.7'W. What were your set and drift?

A. 292°T at 1.8 knots
B. 243°T at 1.0 knot
C. 118°T at 1.9 knots
D. 111°T at 2.1 knots

10603. At 1300 your loran set fixes your position at LAT 41°09.2' N, LONG 72°36.9'W. You are steering course 291° per standard magnetic compass at a speed of 8 knots. At 1345 you fix your position by plotting sev-

eral compass bearings on nearby known fixed objects. These result in a position of LAT 41°09.9'N, LONG 72°46.1'W. Which statement is TRUE with respect to the combined effects of wind and current experienced since 1300?

A. There has been no set and drift.
B. Set and drift are westerly at approximately 0.9 knot.
C. Your speed over the bottom is approximately 9.2 knots.
D. Set and drift are easterly at approximately 1.0 knot.

10604. At 2245 your loran set fixes your position at LAT 41°01.75'N, LONG 72°48.40'W. You are steering course 086° per standard magnetic compass at a speed of 6.0 knots. At 2400 you fix your position by plotting several compass bearings on nearby known fixed objects. These result in a position of LAT 41°04.20'N, LONG 72°38.85'W. What were your set and drift?

A. 162°T at 0.2 knot
B. 180°T at 0.4 knot
C. 339°T at 0.5 knot
D. 360°T at 0.3 knot

10605. At 0620 your loran set fixes your position at LAT 41°01.8'N, LONG 72°48.40'W. You are steering course 274° per standard magnetic compass at a speed of 10 knots. At 0735 you fix your position by plotting several compass bearings on nearby known fixed objects. These result in a position of LAT 40°59.50'N, LONG 73°06.50'W. What were your set and drift?

A. 304°T at 0.8 knot
B. 276°T at 1.2 knots
C. 099°T at 0.5 knot
D. 094°T at 1.3 knots

10606. At 0915 your loran set indicates a position of LAT 41°04.9'N, LONG 72°42.1'W. You are on course 085° per standard magnetic compass at a speed of 6 knots. At 1030 your loran set fixes your position at 0.5 mile due south of Twenty-Eight Foot Shoal Lighted Buoy TE. What were your set and drift?

A. 042°T at 2.4 knots
B. 045°T at 1.9 knots
C. 221°T at 2.0 knots
D. 225°T at 2.3 knots

10607. At 0912 your loran set indicates a position of LAT 41°04.9'N, LONG 72°42.1'W. You are on course 085° per standard magnetic compass at a speed of 6 knots. At 1052 your loran set fixes your position at 0.5 mile due south of Twenty-Eight Foot Shoal Lighted Buoy. What were your set and drift?

A. 145°T at 1.2 knots
B. 148°T at 0.9 knot
C. 322°T at 1.3 knots
D. 327°T at 0.7 knot

10608. At 1825 your loran set indicates a position of LAT 41°04.9'N, LONG 72°42.1'W. You are on course 085° per standard magnetic compass at a speed of 10 knots. At 1910 your loran set fixes your position at 1 mile due south of Twenty-Eight Foot Shoal Lighted Buoy. What were your set and drift?

A. 233°T at 2.9 knots
B. 227°T at 2.5 knots
C. 054°T at 2.8 knots
D. 051°T at 2.1 knots

10609. At 1922 your loran set indicates a position of LAT 41°04.9'N, LONG 72°42.1'W. You are on course 085° per standard magnetic compass at a speed of 10 knots. At 2019 your loran set fixes your position at 1 mile due south of Twenty-Eight Foot Shoal Lighted Buoy TE. What were your set and drift?

A. 345°T at 0.7 knot
B. 343°T at 1.2 knots
C. 164°T at 0.9 knot
D. 161°T at 1.1 knots

10610. At 1645 your loran set indicates a position of LAT 41°04.9'; N, LONG 72°42.1'W. You are on course 072° per standard magnetic compass at a speed of 14 knots. At 1727 another loran fix places your vessel 1 mile due north of Twenty-Eight Foot Shoal Lighted Buoy TE. What were your set and drift?

A. 032°T at 1.2 knot
B. 021°T at 1.0 knot
C. 207°T at 0.9 knot
D. 212°T at 1.2 knots

The following questions should be answered using chart number 13205TR, Block Island and Approaches, and supporting publications.

0700. At 1020 your position is LAT 41°11.0'N, LONG 71°50.0'W. You are on course 056° per standard magnetic compass at 9.2 knots. At 1112 your position is LAT 41°15.9'N, LONG 71°41.7'W. What were the set and drift?

A. 130°T at 0.9 knot
B. 141°T at 1.2 knots
C. 331°T at 0.8 knot
D. 346°T at 1.1 knots

0701. At 0947 your position is LAT 41°15.9'N, LONG 71°41.7'W. You are on course 182° per magnetic compass at 11.3 knots. At 1020 your position is LAT 41°09.2'N, LONG 71°40.6'W. What were the set and drift?

A. 211°T at 1.0 knot
B. 229°T at 2.0 knots
C. 058°T at 1.8 knots
D. 043°T at 1.1 knots

0702. At 1922 your position is LAT 41°09.2'N, LONG 71°40.6'W. You are on course 028° per standard magnetic compass at 6.4 knots. At 2046 your position is LAT 41°17.2'N, LONG 71°38.6'W. What were the set and drift?

A. 235°T at 0.8 knot
B. 247°T at 1.1 knots
C. 049°T at 0.7 knot
D. 062°T at 1.0 knots

0703. At 1516 your position is LAT 41°11.3'N, LONG 71°48.6'W. You are on course 300° per standard magnetic compass at 9.4 knots. At 1600 your position is LAT 41°14.0'N, LONG 71°58.1'W. What were the set and drift?

A. 142°T at 1.9 knots
B. 153°T at 1.4 knots
C. 332°T at 1.5 knots
D. 347°T at 1.1 knots

0704. At 2038 your position is LAT 41°09.2'N, LONG 71°40.6'W. You are on course 301° per standard magnetic compass at 7.2 knots. At 2152 your position is LAT 41°11.3'N, LONG 71°48.6'W. What were the set and drift?

A. 080°T at 1.0 knot
B. 096°T at 2.0 knots
C. 261°T at 1.2 knots
D. 277°T at 0.9 knot

10705. At 0726 you depart Lake Montauk with light 1 close aboard and set course 013.5° per standard magnetic compass at 7.6 knots. At 0812 your loran position is LAT 41°10.0'N, LONG 71°55.9'W. What is the current?

A. 151°T at 1.0 knot
B. 164°T at 0.7 knot
C. 334°T at 1.1 knots
D. 321°T at 0.8 knot

10706. At 0726 you depart Lake Montauk with light 1 close aboard and set course 310.5° per standard magnetic compass at 7.6 knots. At 0812 your loran position is LAT 41°08.1'N, LONG 72°03.7'W. What is the current?

A. 151°T at 1.0 knot
B. 164°T at 0.7 knot
C. 334°T at 1.4 knot
D. 321°T at 0.8 knot

10707. At 0726 you depart Lake Montauk with light 1 close aboard and set course 065° per standard magnetic compass at 6.7 knots. At 0912 your loran position is LAT 41°12.8'N, LONG 71°48.2'W. What is the current?

A. 151°T at 1.0 knot
B. 164°T at 0.7 knot
C. 287°T at 2.0 knots
D. 321°T at 0.8 knot

10708. At 0726 you depart Lake Montauk with light 1 close aboard and set course 309° per standard magnetic compass at 6.7 knots. At 0818 your loran position is LAT 41°07.1'N, LONG 72°02.6'W. What is the current?

A. 102°T at 0.6 knot
B. 164°T at 0.7 knot
C. 334°T at 0.9 knot
D. 321°T at 0.6 knot

10709. At 0726 you depart Lake Montauk with light 1 close aboard and set course 065° per standard magnetic compass at 6.7 knots. At 0912 your loran position is LAT 41°10.5'N, LONG 71°46.6'W. What is the current?

A. 151°T at 1.2 knots
B. 164°T at 0.7 knot
C. 227°T at 0.9 knot
D. 240°T at 1.4 knots

The following questions are based on chart 12221TR, Chesapeake Bay Entrance, and the supporting publications.

10900. The abandoned lighthouse west of Cape Henry Light is _____.

A. painted black and white
B. a low mound of rubble
C. a gray, pyramidal structure
D. a steel skeleton structure

10901. The area around Cape Charles is _____.

A. low and bare, but the land back of it is high and wooded
B. composed of low to medium rolling hills
C. well defined with rocky outcroppings
D. marked by high, barren hills

10902. Fishermans Island (LAT 37°05.0'N, LONG 75°57.7'W) is _____.

A. privately owned
B. sparsely wooded and awash at spring tides
C. a high rocky promontory with marshy backwater
D. a National Wildlife Refuge

10903. What is the distance from Norfolk to Philadelphia for a deep draft vessel via the Chesapeake Bay and C and D Canal ?

A. 209 miles
B. 245 miles
C. 286 miles
D. 302 miles

10904. What is the distance from Chesapeake Bay entrance to Baltimore?

A. 150 nm
B. 162 nm
C. 173 nm
D. 247 nm

10905. You wish to anchor and fish in the regulated navigation area in the vicinity of LAT 37°02'N, LONG 76°01'W. Which of the following statements is TRUE?

A. Anchoring is prohibited in this area due to the danger of unexploded mines on the bottom.
B. You may anchor in this area only in the event of an emergency such as loss of main propulsion.

C. You may anchor in this area if your vessel is less than 65 feet in length or if you have the Captain of the Port's permission.
D. Any vessel can anchor without restriction as the regulations only apply to vessels underway.

10906. What correction should be applied to the charted depths of the Poquoson River at York Point at the PM low water on 18 December 1983?

A. +1.9 feet
B. 0.1 foot
C. 0.4 foot
D. No correction is necessary

10907. What is the time (DST ZD +4) of the AM high tide at York Point, Poquoson River on 8 September 1983?

A. 0955
B. 1048
C. 1055
D. 1102

10908. What is the velocity of the first maximum flood current in Lynnhaven Roads on 23 July 1983?

A. 0.4 knot
B. 0.5 knot
C. 0.8 knot
D. 1.3 knots

10909. What will be the average direction of the current in Lynnhaven Roads at 1000 DST (ZD +4) on 23 July 1983?

A. 305°T
B. 125°T
C. 070°T
D. Almost slack water

The following questions are to be answered by using chart 12354TR, Long Island Sound - Eastern Part, and supporting publications.

11001. What time will high water occur at Saybrook Jetty on the morning of 29 October 1983?

A. 0145
B. 0255
C. 0405
D. 0920

11002. What was the height of the high water at Saybrook Jetty on the afternoon of 18 February 1983?

A. 1.4 ft.
B. 2.0 ft.
C. 2.4 ft.
D. 3.0 ft.

11003. What best describes the condition of the tidal current at New London Harbor Entrance, at 0945 on 3 March 1983?

A. It is slack water.
B. The current has reached its maximum flood velocity.
C. It has reached its maximum ebb velocity.
D. The current is approaching slack water.

11004. What is the maximum speed permitted on the Niantic River?

A. 4 mph
B. 6 mph
C. 8 mph
D. 10 mph

11005. What is the maximum speed permitted in the Main Entrance Channel to Port Jefferson Harbor?

A. 3 mph
B. 5 mph
C. 7 mph
D. 12 mph

11006. At what time will maximum flood occur 1 mile east of Old Field Point on 29 April 1983? (You are keeping daylight saving time ZD +4.)

A. 0957
B. 1059
C. 1328
D. 1423

11007. What will be the height of the high water at Mount Sinai Harbor on the morning of 26 August 1983?

A. 4.1 feet
B. 6.3 feet
C. 7.2 feet
D. 8.4 feet

11009. What best describes the structure from which Stratford Point Light is shown?

A. Brown conical tower with white horizontal band in center of light on black pier
B. Red conical tower on brown cylindrical pier
C. White octagonal house on brown cylindrical pier
D. White conical tower, with brown band midway of height

11010. What is the maximum speed permitted in Clinton Harbor?

A. 6 mph
B. 8 mph
C. 10 mph
D. 12 mph

11011. According to the U.S. Coast Pilot, what is the depth of the channel between State Pier No. 1 and the U.S. Navy Submarine Base in New London Harbor?

A. 40 feet (12.1 meters)
B. 38 feet (11.5 meters)
C. 36 feet (10.9 meters)
D. 34 feet (10.3 meters)

11012. Which statement is FALSE with regard to Plum Island Harbor West Dolphin Light?

A. The light is maintained from sundown to 0130 daily.
B. The light is white.
C. The light is maintained by the U.S. Dept. of Agriculture.
D. The light is located on a dolphin.

11013. What will be the height of the tide at Horton Pt., New York, on 16 June 1983, at 1845 DST (ZD +4)?

A. 0.2 foot
B. 2.7 feet
C. 4.1 feet
D. 5.5 feet

11014. What will be the velocity of the tidal current outside the breakwater at New Haven Hbr. entrance on 26 May 1983 at 1045 DST (ZD +4)?

A. 0.0 knot
B. 0.3 knot
C. 0.5 knot
D. 1.3 knots

The following questions should be answered using chart number 13205TR, Block Island and Approaches, and supporting publications.

11100. Block Island is _____.

A. surrounded by wide sandy beaches
B. a low, marshy island

C. hilly with elevations to 200 feet (60.5 m)
D. a national bird sanctuary

11101. Great Salt Pond on Block Island is
_____.

A. entered through a dredged cut
B. not accessible in easterly gales
C. available for vessels up to a maximum
draft of 8 feet (2.4 m)
D. not affected by the tide

11102. What is the velocity of the first PM
(Daylight Savings Time) maximum ebb current at Plum Gut on 10 August 1983?

A. 3.3 knots
B. 4.0 knots
C. 4.5 knots
D. 5.4 knots

11103. Point Judith Harbor of Refuge (LAT
41°22'N, LONG 71°30'W) _____.

A. is used only by tows
B. has moorings for small craft along the
breakwater
C. is easily entered in all sea conditions
D. is entered through either the East Gap or
the West Gap

11104. What is the time of the first PM
(Daylight Savings Time) maximum ebb current at Plum Gut on 10 August 1983?

A. 1231
B. 1249
C. 1340
D. 1445

11105. What is the height of the tide at
Great Salt Pond on Block Island at the afternoon high water (daylight savings time) on
1 July 1983?

A. 3.9 feet
B. 3.0 feet
C. 2.4 feet
D. 2.1 feet

11106. What is the height of the tide at
Great Salt Pond, on Block Island, at the
morning high water (daylight savings time)
on 1 July 1983?

A. 1.3 feet
B. 2.3 feet
C. 3.2 feet
D. There is no morning high water

11107. What is the time (Daylight Savings
Time) of the first high tide on 1 July 1983 at
Great Salt Pond on Block Island?

A. 0027
B. 0448
C. 1158
D. 1203

11108. The passage between Great Gull Island and Plum Island _____.

A. is subject to weak and variable tidal cur-
rents
B. uncovers at extreme low water
C. should be avoided
D. shows a whirlpool at maximum ebb cur-
rent when accompanied by NW gales

11109. What is the velocity of the
maximum ebb current approximately 1.1
miles ENE of Little Gull Island in the afternoon of 25 April 1983?

A. 5.5 knots
B. 4.7 knots
C. 4.2 knots
D. 1.3 knots

*The following questions are based on chart
12221TR, Chesapeake Bay Entrance, and the
supporting publications.*

11300. At 1256 your loran shows your position as LAT 36°57.0'N, LONG 75°41.0'W. At
1336 it shows your position as LAT
37°07.5'N, LONG 75°39.1'W. What was the
speed made good between the fixes?

A. 14.6 knots
B. 15.2 knots
C. 16.0 knots
D. 18.6 knots

11301. At 1256 your loran shows your position as LAT 36°57.0'N, LONG 75°41.0'W. At
1331 it shows your position at LAT
37°07.5'N, LONG 75°39.1'W. What was the
speed made good between the fixes?

A. 14.6 knots
B. 15.2 knots
C. 16.6 knots
D. 18.3 knots

11302. At 1614 your loran shows your position as LAT 37°01.6'N, LONG 75°31.7'W. At
1703 it shows your position as LAT
36°57.0'N, LONG 75°41.0'W. What was the
course made good between the fixes?

A. 238°T
B. 242°T
C. 247°T
D. 250°T

11303. At 0856 your loran shows your position as LAT 37°01.6'N, LONG 75°31.7'W. At
0945 it shows your position as LAT
36°57.0'N, LONG 75°41.0'W. What was the
speed made good between the fixes?

A. 8.4 knots
B. 8.9 knots
C. 9.6 knots
D. 10.7 knots

11304. At 1422 your loran shows your position as LAT 37°07.5'N, LONG 75°39.1'W. At
1549 it shows your position as LAT
36°57.0'N, LONG 75°41.0'W. What was the
course made good between the fixes?

A. 185°T
B. 188°T
C. 194°T
D. 198°T

11305. At 1919 your position is LAT
37°00.0'N, LONG 75°30.0'W. At 2000 your
position is LAT 36°59.5'N, LONG 75°37.0'W.
What was the speed made good?

A. 5.6 knots
B. 6.6 knots
C. 8.2 knots
D. 9.1 knots

11306. At 1919 your position is LAT
37°00.0'N, LONG 75°30.0'W. At 1950 your
position is LAT 36°59.5'N, LONG 75°37.0'W.
What is the speed made good?

A. 5.6 knots
B. 8.2 knots
C. 9.1 knots
D. 10.9 knots

11307. At 1919 your position is LAT
37°00.0'N, LONG 75°30.0'W. At 2031 your
position is LAT 36°59.5'N, LONG 75°44.9'W.
What was the speed made good?

A. 8.2 knots
B. 9.3 knots
C. 10.0 knots
D. 10.9 knots

11308. At 1919 your position is LAT
37°00.0'N, LONG 75°30.0'W. At 2011 your

position is LAT 36°59.5'N, LONG 75°44.9'W. What was the speed made good?

A. 13.7 knots
B. 12.0 knots
C. 11.6 knots
D. 10.9 knots

11309. At 1919 your position is LAT 37°00.5'N, LONG 75°43.8'W. At 2019 your position is LAT 37°00.0'N, LONG 75°30.0'W. What is the course made good?

A. 090°T
B. 093°T
C. 096°T
D. 099°T

The following questions are to be answered by using chart 12354TR, Long Island Sound - Eastern Part, and supporting publications.

11400. At 1035 your loran indicates a position of LAT 41°05.3'N, LONG 72°33.7'W. At 1103 your loran indicates a position of LAT 41°09.0'N, LONG 72°40.0'W. What was your speed made good?

A. 6.1 knots
B. 9.5 knots
C. 13.0 knots
D. 14.8 knots

11401. At 1520 your loran indicates a position of LAT 41°13.1'N, LONG 72°16.1'W. At 1630 another loran fix places your vessel at LAT 41°17.5'N, LONG 72°04.7'W. What were your true course and speed made good?

A. 344° at 8.2 knots
B. 077° at 9.5 knots
C. 063° at 8.3 knots
D. 059° at 8.1 knots

11402. At 1018 your loran indicates a position of LAT 41°14.4'N, LONG 72°07.2'W. At 1036 another loran fix places your vessel at LAT 41°13.1'N, LONG 72°16.1'W. What was your true course and speed made good?

A. 259° at 22.6 knots
B. 245° at 23.1 knots
C. 079° at 22.8 knots
D. 065° at 25.5 knots

11403. At 2115 your loran indicates a position of LAT 41°14.4'N, LONG 72°07.2'W. At 0015 another loran fix places your vessel at LAT 41°03.3'N, LONG 72°37.9'W. What was your true course made good?

A. 062°T
B. 076°T
C. 245°T
D. 259°T

11404. At 2115 your loran indicates a position of LAT 41°03.3'N, LONG 72°37.9'W. At 0027 another loran fix places your vessel at LAT 41°14.4'N, LONG 72°07.2'W. What was your speed made good?

A. 7.0 knots
B. 7.5 knots
C. 8.0 knots
D. 8.5 knots

11405. At 2125 your loran indicates a position of LAT 41°05.7'N, LONG 72°46.5'W. At 2208 another loran fix places your vessel at LAT 41°03.3'N, LONG 72°37.9'W. What was your course made good by standard magnetic compass?

A. 123° psc
B. 287° psc
C. 303° psc
D. 326° psc

11406. At 2021 a loran fix places your vessel at LAT 41°09.7'N, LONG 72°59.8'W. At 2057 another loran fix places your vessel at LAT 41°00.5'N, LONG 72°49.5'W. What are your true course and speed made good?

A. 140° at 20 knots
B. 145° at 18 knots
C. 316° at 19 knots
D. 320° at 17 knots

11407. At 1930 a loran fix places your vessel at LAT 41°00.5'N, LONG 72°49.5'W. At 2018 a loran fix places your vessel at LAT 41°08.6'N, LONG 72°41.6'W. What was your true course and speed made good?

A. 219° at 10.1 knots
B. 214° at 12.5 knots
C. 036° at 12.6 knots
D. 039° at 11.2 knots

11408. At 1930 a loran fix places your vessel at LAT 41°08.6'N, LONG 72°41.6'W. At 2024 another loran fix places your vessel at LAT 41°00.5'N, LONG 72°49.5'W. What is your true course and speed made good?

A. 219° at 10.1 knots
B. 216° at 11.2 knots
C. 039° at 9.9 knots
D. 036° at 11.1 knots

11409. At 0647 a loran fix places your vessel at LAT 41°08.6'N, LONG 72°41.6'W. At 0729 another loran fix places your vessel at LAT 41°10.3'N, LONG 72°29.2'W. What were your true course and speed made good?

A. 074° at 9.5 knots
B. 080° at 13.6 knots
C. 253° at 9.7 knots
D. 258° at 13.5 knots

11410. At 0647 a loran fix places your vessel 1 mile due south of buoy 8C (buoy position LAT 41°10.8'N, LONG 72°29.4'W). At 0753 another loran fix places your vessel at LAT 41°08.6'N, LONG 72°41.6'W. What were your true course and speed made good?

A. 088° at 9.6 knots
B. 192° at 8.8 knots
C. 263° at 8.5 knots
D. 268° at 9.1 knots

The following questions should be answered using chart number 13205TR, Block Island and Approaches, and supporting publications.

11500. At 2016 your loran position is LAT 41°07.6'N, LONG 71°37.8'W. At 2128 your position is LAT 41°00.4'N, LONG 71°29.4'W. What was the speed made good between the two positions?

A. 11.9 knots
B. 10.2 knots
C. 8.0 knots
D. 7.4 knots

11501. At 2016 your loran position is LAT 41°07.6'N, LONG 71°33.8'W. At 2128 your position is LAT 41°00.4'N, LONG 71°29.4'W. What was the speed made good between the two positions?

A. 11.9 knots
B. 10.2 knots
C. 8.9 knots
D. 6.7 knots

11502. At 1016 your loran position is LAT 41°07.6'N, LONG 71°38.5'W. At 1104 your position is LAT 41°00.4'N, LONG 71°29.4'W. What was the speed made good between the two positions?

A. 10.9 knots
B. 11.7 knots
C. 12.5 knots
D. 13.6 knots

11503. At 1016 your loran position is LAT 41°07.6'N, LONG 71°37.9'W. At 1104 your position is LAT 41°00.2'N, LONG 71°29.4'W. What was the true course made good between the two positions?

A. 134°T
B. 139°T
C. 143°T
D. 145°T

11504. At 1016 your loran position is LAT 41°07.6'N, LONG 71°38.5'W. At 1116 your position is LAT 41°01.4'N, LONG 71°29.4'N. What was the course made good between the two positions?

A. 132°T
B. 135°T
C. 140°T
D. 143°T

11505. At 1014 you depart the entrance to Lake Montauk with light 1 close aboard. Your course is 066° per standard magnetic compass, and the speed is 8.6 knots. At 1230 your position is LAT 41°20.0'N, LONG 71°40.0'W. What is the speed made good?

A. 8.0 knots
B. 8.3 knots
C. 8.6 knots
D. 8.9 knots

11506. At 1014 you depart the entrance to Lake Montauk with Light 1 close aboard. Your course is 066° per standard magnetic compass, and the speed is 8.6 knots. At 1238 your position is LAT 41°20.0'N, LONG 71°40.0'W. What is the speed made good?

A. 8.2 knots
B. 8.6 knots
C. 8.9 knots
D. 9.2 knots

11507. At 1014 you depart the entrance to Lake Montauk with light 1 close aboard. Your course is 066° per standard magnetic compass, and the speed is 8.6 knots. At 1222 your position is LAT 41°20.0'N, LONG 71°40.0'W. What is the speed made good?

A. 8.4 knots
B. 8.6 knots
C. 9.2 knots
D. 9.6 knots

11508. At 1014 you depart the entrance to Lake Montauk with light 1 close aboard.

Your course is 066° per standard magnetic compass, and the speed is 8.6 knots. At 1232 your position is LAT 41°20.0'N, LONG 71°40.0'W. What is the speed made good?

A. 8.2 knots
B. 8.5 knots
C. 8.9 knots
D. 9.2 knots

11509. At 1014 you depart the entrance to Lake Montauk with light 1 close aboard. Your course is 066° per standard magnetic compass, and the speed is 8.6 knots. At 1232 your position is LAT 41°20.0'N, 71°40.0'W. What is the course made good?

A. 036°T
B. 040°T
C. 044°T
D. 047°T

The following questions are based on chart 12221TR, Chesapeake Bay Entrance, and the supporting publications.

11700. What is the true heading to steer outbound in Thimble Shoal Channel if your engines are turning for 8.0 knots, the current is 050°T at 1.0 knot and a northerly wind causes 3° of leeway?

A. 111°T
B. 104°T
C. 101°T
D. 098°T

11701. What is the true heading to steer inbound in the York River Entrance Channel if your engines are turning for 9.5 knots, the current is 076°T at 1.2 knots, and a southwesterly wind causes 3° of leeway?

A. 313°T
B. 308°T
C. 303°T
D. 300°T

11702. You are eastbound in the Thimble Shoal Channel. What is the true heading to steer if the engines are turning for 9.5 knots, the current is 110°T at 1.2 knots, and a southerly wind causes 3° of leeway?

A. 111°
B. 108°
C. 105°
D. 100°

11703. What is the true heading to steer inbound in York River Entrance Channel if your engines are turning for 9.8 knots, the current is 220°T at 1.2 knots, and a northeasterly wind causes 3° of leeway?

A. 319°T
B. 315°T
C. 301°T
D. 298°T

11704. What is the true heading to steer in York River Entrance Channel if your engines are turning for 10.2 knots, the current is 220°T at 1.2 knots and a southwesterly wind causes 3° of leeway?

A. 316°T
B. 313°T
C. 309°T
D. 300°T

11705. Your position is LAT 37°00.0'N, LONG 75°30.0'W. What is the course to steer per standard magnetic compass to arrive at LAT 36°59.0'N, LONG 75°48.5'W, if the current is 043°T at 1.3 knots, a south-southeasterly wind is causing 3° of leeway, and you are turning for 8.7 knots?

A. 260.5° psc
B. 264.0° psc
C. 267.5° psc
D. 271.5° psc

11706. Your position is LAT 37°00.0'N, LONG 75°30.0'W. What is the course to steer per standard magnetic compass to arrive at LAT 36°59.0'N, LONG 75°48.5'W, if you are turning for 8.7 knots, the current is 039°T at 1.3 knots, and a northwesterly wind is causing 3° of leeway?

A. 264.0°
B. 267.5°
C. 270.0°
D. 273.0°

11707. Your position is LAT 37°00.0'N, LONG 75°30.0'W. What is the course to steer per standard magnetic compass to arrive at LAT 36°59.0'N, LONG 75°48.5'W, if you are turning for 7.8 knots, the current is 139°T at 1.3 knots, and a northwesterly wind is causing 3° of leeway?

A. 290.0° psc
B. 287.0° psc
C. 283.5° psc
D. 280.5° psc

11708. Your position is LAT 37°00.9'N, LONG 75°30.0'W. What is the course to steer per magnetic compass to arrive at LAT 36°59.0'N, LONG 75°48.5'W, if you are turning for 7.8 knots the current is 339°T at 1.3 knots, and a northwesterly wind is causing 3° of leeway?

A. 265° psc
B. 267° psc
C. 269° psc
D. 271° psc

11709. Your position is LAT 37°00.0'N, LONG 75°30.0'W. What is the course to steer per standard magnetic compass to arrive at LAT 36°59.0'N, LONG 75°48.5'W, if you are making 7.8 knots, the current is 239°T at 1.3 knots, and a southeasterly wind is causing 3° of leeway?

A. 271° psc
B. 274° psc
C. 278° psc
D. 282° psc

The following questions are to be answered by using chart 12354TR, Long Island Sound - Eastern Part, and supporting publications.

11800. What is the course to steer between Port Jefferson Approach buoy PJ and New Haven Lighted Buoy NH? Your engine speed is 12 knots and you allow for a current of 93°T at 0.8 knot. A NW'ly wind causes 3° leeway.

A. 031°T
B. 034°T
C. 037°T
D. 044°T

11801. What course should you steer by standard magnetic compass (psc) between Horton Pt. Light and Falkner Island Light, if the set and drift of the current are 040°T at 0.9 knot, and a westerly wind will cause 2° of leeway? Your engines are making turns for 10 knots.

A. 315.0° psc
B. 319.0° psc
C. 324.5° psc
D. 328.5° psc

11802. What course should you steer by your standard magnetic compass (psc), between New Haven Light and Stratford Pt. Light, if the set and drift of the current are 345°T at 3.0 knots, and a northerly wind will cause 1° of leeway? Your engines are making turns for 18.0 knots.

A. 245.0° psc
B. 247.0° psc
C. 264.0° psc
D. 266.5° psc

11803. What is the true course to steer between Falkner Island Light and Horton Point Light, if the set and drift of the current are 041° at 2.4 knots, and a northeasterly wind will cause 4° of leeway? Your engines are making turns for 15 knots.

A. 116°T
B. 124°T
C. 134°T
D. 142°T

11804. Your engines are making turns for 8 knots and a northerly wind is causing 3° of leeway. There is a current of 220°T at 1.5 knots. What is the course to steer between Branford Reef Light and Faulkner Island Light?

A. 084°T
B. 095°T
C. 102°T
D. 108°T

11805. What is the true course to steer between Stratford Shoal (Middle Ground Light) and New Haven Light, if the set and drift of the current are 048°T at 2 knots, and a southeasterly wind will cause 2° of leeway? Your engines are making turns for 10 knots.

A. 032°T
B. 037°T
C. 039°T
D. 041°T

11806. What course should you steer by standard magnetic compass between Mattituck Inlet and Branford Reef Light, if the set and drift of the current are 027° at 2.5 knots, and a northeasterly wind will cause 1° of leeway? Your engines are turning for 12 knots.

A. 295° psc
B. 305° psc
C. 318° psc
D. 321° psc

11807. What course should you steer by your standard magnetic compass (psc) be-tween Horton Pt. Light and a position 2 miles due south of Branford Reef Light, if the set and drift of the current are 111°T at 2.5 knots, and a southwesterly wind will cause 4° of leeway? (Your engines are turning for 18 knots.)

A. 306° psc
B. 301° psc
C. 295° psc
D. 275° psc

11808. What is the true course to steer from a position 2 miles due south of Bran-ford Reef Light to Horton Pt. Light, if the set and drift of the current are 247°T at 3 knots, and a southwesterly wind will cause 3° of leeway? (Your engines are making turns for 10 knots.)

A. 102°T
B. 098°T
C. 095°T
D. 087°T

11809. What course should you steer by your standard magnetic compass (psc) from a position 2 miles due south of Bran-ford Reef Light to Horton Pt. Light, if the set and drift of the current are 065°T at 2 knots, and a northerly wind will cause 2° of leeway. Your engines are turning for 14 knots.

A. 113° psc
B. 118° psc
C. 127° psc
D. 134° psc

11810. What is the true course to steer be-tween Horton Pt. Light and a position 2 miles due south of Branford Reef Light, if the set and drift of the current are 40°T at 1.5 knots, and an easterly wind will cause 3° of leeway? Your engines are making turns for 12 knots.

A. 271°T
B. 277°T
C. 283°T
D. 288°T

The following questions should be answered using chart number 13205TR, Block Island and Approaches, and supporting publications.

11900. What is the true course to steer be-tween the entrance to Great Salt Pond (LAT 41°12.0'N, LONG 71°35.6'W) and the

ntrance to Quonochontaug Pond (LAT
1°19.8'N, LONG 71°43.2'W), if you are turn-
ig for 8.5 knots, and you allow for a
urrent of 247°T at 1.2 knots, and an east-
rly wind is causing 2° of leeway?

A. 314°T
B. 320°T
C. 328°T
D. 333°T

1901. You are turning for 7.5 knots and a
westerly wind is causing 2° of leeway.
There is a current of 047°T at 1.2 knots.
What course should you steer between the
entrance to Quonochontaug Pond (LAT
41°19.8'N, LONG 71°43.2'W) and the
entrance to Great Salt Pond (LAT 41°12.0'N,
LONG 71°35.6'W)?

A. 157°T
B. 154°T
C. 144°T
D. 140°T

1902. What is the true course to steer between the entrance to Lake Montauk (LAT
41°04.8'N, LONG 71°56.3'W) and Winnapaug Pond entrance (LAT 41°19.6'N, LONG
71°45.8'W), if you are turning for 9.5 knots,
allow for a current of 075°T at 1.2 knots,
and a westerly wind is causing 3° of
leeway?

A. 020°T
B. 023°T
C. 026°T
D. 029°T

11903. What is the true course to steer
between the entrance to Winnapaug Pond
(LAT 41°19.6'N, LONG 71°45.8'W) and the
entrance to Lake Montauk (LAT 41°04.8'N,
LONG 71°56.3'W), if you are turning for 8.5
knots, allowing for a current of 095°T at 0.9
knot, and an easterly wind is causing 3° of
leeway?

A. 200°T
B. 208°T
C. 211°T
D. 214°T

11904. What is the true course to steer
between the entrance to Winnapaug Pond
(LAT 41°19.6'N, LONG 71°45.8'W) and the
entrance to Lake Montauk (LAT 41°04.8'N,
LONG 71°56.3'W), if you are turning for 6.5
knots, allow for a current of 295°T at 0.9
knot, and an easterly wind is causing 4° of
leeway?

A. 196°T
B. 200°T
C. 213°T
D. 217°T

11905. Your position is 3 miles due east of
Montauk Point Light. What is the course to
steer to arrive one mile due south of Block
Island Southeast Point Light, if you are
turning for 8.6 knots, the current is 130° at
1.2 knots, and a northerly wind causes 3° of
leeway?

A. 061°T
B. 064°T
C. 067°T
D. 070°T

11906. Your position is 3 miles due east of
Montauk Point Light. What is the course to
steer to arrive at LAT 41°00.0'N, LONG
71°30.0'W, if you are turning for 8.7 knots,
the current is 130° at 1.2 knots, and a
northerly wind causes 3° of leeway?

A. 112°T
B. 108°T
C. 105°T
D. 102°T

11907. Your position is 3 miles due east of
Montauk Point Light. What is the course to
steer to arrive at LAT 41°00.0'N, LONG
71°30.0'W, if you are turning for 7.8 knots,
the current is 130° at 1.2 knots, and a
southerly wind causes 3° of leeway?

A. 112°T
B. 108°T
C. 105°T
D. 102°T

11908. Your position is 3 miles due east of
Montauk Point Light. What is the course to
steer to arrive at LAT 41°00.0'N, LONG
71°30.0'W, if you are turning for 7.8 knots,
the current is 330° at 1.2 knots, and a
southerly wind causes 3° of leeway?

A. 117°T
B. 112°T
C. 104°T
D. 102°T

11909. Your position is 3 miles due east of
Montauk Point Light. What is the true
course to steer to arrive one mile due south
of Block Island Southeast Point Light, if you
are turning for 6.8 knots, the current is 330°
at 1.2 knots, and a southerly wind causes 3°
of leeway?

A. 081°T
B. 084°T
C. 087°T
D. 090°T

*The following questions are based on chart
12221TR, Chesapeake Bay Entrance, and the
supporting publications.*

12100. You sight Wolf Trap Light in line
with New Point Comfort Spit Light 2 bearing 040° per standard magnetic compass.
You are on course 319° per standard magnetic compass. Based on this, you _____.

A. know the compass error is 8°W
B. should apply 3° easterly deviation to the
bearing
C. know the deviation table is incorrect
D. should suspect the compass may be af-
fected by a local magnetic disturbance

12101. You sight Thimble Shoal Light in
line with Old Point Comfort Light bearing
267° per standard magnetic compass. You
are on course 182° psc. Based on this, you
know _____.

A. the existing deviation is correct for that
heading
B. you should adjust your compass
C. the compass error is 2°W
D. the variation is 11°W

12102. You sight Thimble Shoal Light in
line with Old Point Comfort Light bearing
265° per standard magnetic compass. You
are on course 135° psc. Based on this, you
know _____.

A. there is no compass error
B. there is a local magnetic disturbance
C. you should swing your vessel and check
the deviation table
D. the deviation is 0°

12103. You sight Wolf Trap Light in line
with New Point Comfort Spit Light 2 bearing 048° per standard magnetic compass.
You are on course 203° psc. Based on this,
you know _____.

A. the compass error is 12°W
B. the deviation is 9°W
C. that the deviation table is in error
D. the deviation is 3°E for bearings of 048°
per standard magnetic compass

12104. You sight Wolf Trap Light in line
with New Point Comfort Spit Light 2

bearing 234° per standard magnetic compass. You are on course 329° psc. Based on this, you _____.

A. know the compass error is 8°W
B. should swing the vessel to check the deviation table
C. know the deviation is 1°W
D. know the deviation table is accurate for that bearing

12105. While in the Back River, you sight the two tanks along the Northwest Branch (vicinity LAT 37°05.6'N, LONG 76°22.0'W) in line bearing 274° psc. If your vessel is heading 300° psc, what is TRUE?

A. There is no deviation.
B. The deviation is equal to the variation.
C. The deviation is 9°E.
D. The deviation is 0° only for a bearing of 274° psc.

12106. While in the Back River, you sight the two tanks along the Northwest Branch (vicinity LAT 37°05.6'N, LONG 76°22.0'W) in line bearing 277° per standard magnetic compass. If your vessel is heading 243° psc, what is TRUE?

A. There is no deviation.
B. The deviation table is incorrect.
C. The compass error is 12°W.
D. The deviation is 3°E for bearings of 277° psc.

12107. You sight Tue Marshes Light (LAT 37°14.1'N, LONG 76°23.2'W) in line with Goodwin Thorofare Light 16 (LAT 37°13.7'N, LONG 76°25.0'W) bearing 267° per standard magnetic compass. What is TRUE if your vessel's heading is 056° psc?

A. The compass error is 13°E.
B. The deviation table is in error and should be corrected.
C. The deviation is 4°E.
D. The deviation table is correct for a heading of 056° psc.

12108. You sight Tue Marshes Light (LAT 37°14.1'N, LONG 76°23.2'W) in line with Goodwin Thorofare Light 16 (LAT 37°13.7'N, LONG 76°25.0'W) bearing 262° per standard magnetic compass. What is TRUE if your vessel's heading is 119° psc?

A. The compass error is 10°W.
B. The deviation table must be corrected for the change in date.

C. The deviation is 1°W.
D. The deviation table is correct for a heading of 119° psc.

12109. You sight Tue Marshes Light (LAT 37°14.1'N, LONG 76°23.2'W) in line with Goodwin Thorofare Light 16 (LAT 37°13.7'N, LONG 76°25.0'W) dead ahead bearing 264° per standard magnetic compass. Which statement is TRUE?

A. The compass error is 11°W.
B. The deviation table must be corrected for the change in date.
C. The deviation is 1°W for a bearing of 264° only.
D. The variation is 9°W for a bearing of 264° only.

The following questions are to be answered by using chart 12354TR, Long Island Sound - Eastern Part, and supporting publications.

12200. You are on course 119° psc. You sight New Haven Outer Channel Range Rear Light in line with the Outer Channel Range Front Light bearing 346° per standard magnetic compass. This indicates that _____.

A. you should swing the vessel to determine the deviation
B. the existing deviation table is correct for that heading
C. your compass is affected by a local magnetic disturbance
D. the compass error is 16°W

12201. Your vessel is steady on a heading of 203° per standard magnetic compass when you sight New Haven Light and New Haven Outer Channel Range Front Light in line over the stern. This information indicates that the _____.

A. existing deviation table is correct for this heading
B. compass error is 17°W
C. deviation table is in error for this heading
D. deviation is 1°E

12203. Your vessel is steady on a heading of 310° per standard magnetic compass when you sight Stratford Point Light and Igor I. Sikorsky Airport Aero Beacon in line dead ahead. This information indicates that the _____.

A. existing deviation table is correct for this heading
B. deviation is 1°E
C. variation is 18°W for this area
D. compass error is 10°W

12204. You sight Stratford Shoal (Middle Ground) Light and Old Field Pt. Light in line and bearing 200° per standard magnetic compass. What is the deviation of the compass?

A. 7°E
B. 7°W
C. 3°E
D. 3°W

12205. Your vessel is steady on a heading of 160° per standard magnetic compass when you sight Southwest Ledge Light and New Haven Outer Channel Range Rear Light in line dead astern. What is the deviation of the compass based on this observation?

A. 2°E
B. 2°W
C. 5°E
D. 5°W

12206. You sight Bartlett Reef Light (LAT 41°16.5'N, LONG 72°08.2'W) in line with New London Harbor Light (LAT 41°19.0'N, LONG 72°05.4'W) and bearing 059° per standard magnetic compass. What is the compass deviation?

A. 4°E
B. 4°W
C. 10°E
D. 10°W

12207. You sight Stratford Pt. Light in line with the Igor I. Sikorsky Airport Aero Beacon bearing 319° per standard magnetic compass. What is the compass deviation?

A. 4°W
B. 4°E
C. 18°W
D. 18°E

12208. You sight Stratford Pt. Light in line with the Igor I. Sikorsky Airport Aero Beacon bearing 319° per standard magnetic compass. What is the compass error?

A. 4°E
B. 10°W
C. 14°E
D. 18°W

2209. You sight South West Ledge Light in line with New Haven Outer Channel Range Rear Light bearing 338.5° per standard magnetic compass. What is the deviation?

A. 3°E
B. 4°W
C. 6°E
D. 9°W

2210. You sight New Haven Outer Channel Range Rear Light in line with the Outer Channel Range Front Light bearing 343° per standard magnetic compass. What is your compass error?

A. 5°E
B. 5°W
C. 9°E
D. 9°W

The following questions should be answered using chart number 13205TR, Block Island and Approaches, and supporting publications.

12300. You are on course 244° per standard magnetic compass when you sight Block Island Southeast Point Light in line with Block Island Aero Beacon bearing 326° per standard magnetic compass. Based on this you _____.

A. should swing your vessel to check the deviation table
B. know the compass error is 12°W
C. should suspect that there is a local magnetic disturbance
D. should apply 3°W deviation to any bearing (psc) while on a heading of 244° psc

12301. You are on course 055° per standard magnetic compass when you sight Block Island Southeast Point Light in line with the Block Island Aero Beacon bearing 319° per standard magnetic compass. Based on this you _____.

A. should use 4°W deviation on true courses of 040°
B. know the compass error is 19°W
C. know the deviation table is correct for that heading
D. should apply 4°W deviation to all bearings

12302. You are on course 203° per standard magnetic compass when you sight Block Island North Light in line with the Block Island Aero Beacon bearing 194° per

standard magnetic compass. Based on this you _____.

A. know the correct deviation is 3°W
B. should swing your vessel to check the deviation table
C. should apply 15°W compass error to all compass readings
D. know you are steering a true course of 185°

12303. You are on course 056° per standard magnetic compass when you sight Block Island North Light in line with the Block Island Aero Beacon bearing 193° per standard magnetic compass. Based on this you _____.

A. know the compass error is 4°E
B. should swing your vessel to check for deviation
C. know the deviation table is correct for that heading
D. should use 3°W deviation on bearings of 193° psc

12304. You are on course 302° per standard magnetic compass when you sight Block Island Southeast Point Light in line with the Block Island Aero Beacon bearing 323° per standard magnetic compass. Based on this you _____.

A. know the deviation table is correct for that heading
B. know the deviation is 15°E
C. should swing your vessel to check the deviation table
D. know the deviation is equal to the variation

12305. You sight North Dumpling Island Light in line with Latimer Reef Light (LAT 41°18.2'N, LONG 71°56.0'W) bearing 095° per standard magnetic compass. If your vessel was heading 056° per standard magnetic compass at the time, which of the following is TRUE?

A. You should subtract 15° compass error for bearings of 095°.
B. The deviation table is correct for all bearings of 095°.
C. The vessel should be swung, and the deviation table checked.
D. The compass error is 19°W for all headings.

12306. You sight North Dumpling Island Light in line with Latimer Reef Light (LAT

41°18.2'N, LONG 71°56.0'W) bearing 093° per standard magnetic compass. If your vessel was heading 185° per standard magnetic compass at the time, which of the following is TRUE?

A. The compass error is 2°W.
B. The deviation is 17°W.
C. The deviation is 2°W for all bearings of 093°.
D. The deviation table is correct for that heading.

12307. You sight North Dumpling Island Light in line with Latimer Reef Light (LAT 41°18.2'N, LONG 71°56.0'W) bearing 091° per standard magnetic compass. If your vessel was heading 246° per standard magnetic compass at the time, which of the following is TRUE?

A. The deviation table is correct.
B. The compass error is 15°W for that heading.
C. The deviation is equal to the variation.
D. The deviation is equal to but of opposite sign to the variation.

12308. You sight North Dumpling Island Light in line with Latimer Reef Light (LAT 41°18.2'N, LONG 71°56.0'W) bearing 094° per standard magnetic compass. If your vessel was heading 207° per standard magnetic compass at the time, which of the following is TRUE?

A. The deviation table is correct for that heading.
B. The deviation by observation is 3°E.
C. The compass error is 12°W.
D. You should subtract 18° from all bearings of 094°.

12309. You sight North Dumpling Island Light in line with Latimer Reef Light (LAT 41°18.2'N, LONG 71°56.0'W) bearing 089° per standard magnetic compass. If your vessel was heading 297° per standard magnetic compass at the time, which of the following is TRUE?

A. The deviation table is correct for that heading.
B. The deviation equals the variation.
C. You should swing your vessel to check the deviation table.
D. The compass error is 13°W for all bearings of 089° psc.

12500. You are on course 135° per standard magnetic compass when you take the following bearings per standard magnetic compass: Cape Henry Light—266°, Cape Charles Light—353°, Chesapeake Light—124°. What is your position?

A. LAT 36°57.3'N, LONG 75°50.9'W
B. LAT 36°57.5'N, LONG 75°50.1'W
C. LAT 36°57.6'N, LONG 75°51.6'W
D. LAT 35°57.9'N, LONG 75°50.8'W

12501. You are on course 056° per standard magnetic compass when you take the following bearings: Cape Henry Light—262° psc, Cape Charles Light—344° psc, Chesapeake Light—125° psc. What is your position?

A. LAT 36°58.4'N, LONG 75°49.1'W
B. LAT 36°58.1'N, LONG 75°50.0'W
C. LAT 36°57.8'N, LONG 75°49.2'W
D. LAT 36°57.6'N, LONG 75°49.8'W

12502. You are on course 262° per standard magnetic compass when you take the following bearings: Cape Henry Light—252° psc, Cape Charles Light—003° psc, Chesapeake Light—131° psc. What is your position?

A. LAT 36°59.0'N, LONG 75°52.9'W
B. LAT 36°58.1'N, LONG 75°52.6'W
C. LAT 36°57.9'N, LONG 75°53.2'W
D. LAT 36°58.6'N, LONG 75°52.2'W

12505. You are on course 056° psc, when you take the following bearings: New Point Comfort Spit Light 2—260° psc, Horn Harbor Entrance Light HH—285° psc, Wolf Trap Light —336° psc. What is the position of the fix?

A. LAT 37°19.3'N, LONG 76°08.5'W
B. LAT 37°19.3'N, LONG 76°08.8'W
C. LAT 37°19.2'N, LONG 76°08.2'W
D. LAT 37°19.2'N, LONG 76°08.7'W

12506. You are on course 203° per standard magnetic compass when you take the following bearings: New Point Comfort Spit Light 2—267° psc, Horn Harbor Entrance Light HH—304° psc, Wolf Trap Light—006° psc. What is the position of the fix?

A. LAT 37°18.9'N, LONG 76°10.4'W
B. LAT 37°18.8'N, LONG 76°10.8'W
C. LAT 37°18.7'N, LONG 76°11.1'W
D. LAT 37°18.5'N, LONG 76°10.7'W

12507. You are on course 300° per standard magnetic compass (psc) when you take the following bearings: New Point Comfort Spit Light 2—240° psc, Horn Harbor Entrance Light HH—268° psc, Wolf Trap Light—003° psc. What is the position of the fix?

A. LAT 37°20.8'N, LONG 76°09.6'W
B. LAT 37°20.8'N, LONG 76°11.0'W
C. LAT 37°20.9'N, LONG 76°11.5'W
D. LAT 37°21.1'N, LONG 76°08.2'W

12508. You are on course 319° per standard magnetic compass when you take the following bearings: New Point Comfort Light 2—244° psc, Horn Harbor Entrance Light HH—267° psc, Wolf Trap Light—335° psc. What is the position of the fix?

A. LAT 37°20.9'N, LONG 76°09.7'W
B. LAT 37°21.0'N, LONG 76°09.2'W
C. LAT 37°21.0'N, LONG 76°09.9'W
D. LAT 37°21.1'N, LONG 76°09.5'W

12509. You are on course 027° per magnetic compass when you take the following bearings per magnetic compass: New Point Comfort Light 2—253°, Horn Harbor Entrance Light HH—282°, Wolf Trap Light—348°. What is the position of the fix?

A. LAT 37°19.4'N, LONG 76°09.5'W
B. LAT 37°19.4'N, LONG 76°09.8'W
C. LAT 37°19.7'N, LONG 76°10.3'W
D. LAT 37°19.7'N, LONG 76°09.9'W

The following questions are to be answered by using chart 12354TR, Long Island Sound - Eastern Part, and supporting publications.

12600. You are on course 243° per standard magnetic compass when you take the following bearings: Falkner Island Light—342° psc, Mattituck Inlet Light—207° psc, Horton Point Light—112° psc. What is your position?

A. LAT 41°05.9'N, LONG 72°32.7'W
B. LAT 41°05.7'N, LONG 72°31.8'W
C. LAT 41°05.5'N, LONG 72°32.6'W
D. LAT 41°05.3'N, LONG 72°31.9'W

12601. You are on course 062° per standard magnetic compass when you take the following bearings: Branford Reef Light—060°

psc, Stratford Point Light—272° psc, New Haven Light—324° psc. What is your position?

A. LAT 41°07.1'N, LONG 72°53.4'W
B. LAT 41°10.5'N, LONG 72°52.8'W
C. LAT 41°11.6'N, LONG 72°50.0'W
D. LAT 41°13.3'N, LONG 72°48.7'W

12602. You are on course 087° per standard magnetic compass (psc) when you take the following bearings: Falkner Island Light—022.0° psc, Horton Point Light—111.5° psc, Mt. Sinai Breakwater Light 254.0° psc. What is your position?

A. LAT 41°13.6'N, LONG 72°46.6'W
B. LAT 41°10.5'N, LONG 72°40.5'W
C. LAT 41°07.0'N, LONG 72°44.5'W
D. LAT 41°06.8'N, LONG 72°40.7'W

12603. You are on course 262° per standard magnetic compass when you take the following bearings: Saybrook Breakwater Light—338.5° psc, Little Gull Island Light—107.5° psc, Horton Point Light—240.0° psc. What is your position?

A. LAT 41°10.9'N, LONG 72°16.4'N
B. LAT 41°12.6'N, LONG 72°17.3'W
C. LAT 41°13.0'N, LONG 72Z°20.6'W
D. LAT 41°15.5'N, LONG 72°17.7'W

12604. You are on course 082° per standard magnetic compass (psc) when you take the following bearings: New London Ledge Light—036.5° psc, Little Gull Island Light—157.0° psc, Saybrook Breakwater Light—294.5° psc. What is your position?

A. LAT 41°02.3'N, LONG 72°04.5'W
B. LAT 41°09.5'N, LONG 72°07.1'W
C. LAT 41°13.6'N, LONG 72°07.5'W
D. LAT 41°14.1'N, LONG 72°12.8'W

12605. You are on course 209° per standard magnetic compass when you take the following bearings: New Haven Light—331.5° psc, Branford Reef Light—066.5° psc, Old Field Point Light—240.5° psc. What is your position?

A. LAT 41°10.5'N, LONG 72°52.8'W
B. LAT 41°11.3'N, LONG 72°49.9'W
C. LAT 41°13.6'N, LONG 72°53.0'W
D. LAT 41°14.5'N, LONG 72°48.8'W

12606. You are on course 242° per standard magnetic compass (psc) when you take the following bearings: Stratford Point Light—

325° psc, Old Field Point Light—239° psc, Middle Ground Light—270° psc. What is your position?

A. LAT 41°02.4'N, LONG 72°59.5'W
B. LAT 41°05.1'N, LONG 72°59.3'W
C. LAT 41°05.4'N, LONG 73°00.1'W
D. LAT 41°08.6'N, LONG 73°02.6'W

12607. You are on course 240° per standard magnetic compass when you take the following bearings: Old Field Point Light—253° psc, New Haven Light—357° psc, Mattituck Inlet Light—126° psc. What is your position?

A. LAT 41°04.5'N, LONG 72°49.2'W
B. LAT 41°05.7'N, LONG 72°50.2'W
C. LAT 41°05.9'N, LONG 72°53.1'W
D. LAT 41°08.6'N, LONG 72°53.5'W

12608. You are on course 083° per standard magnetic compass when you take the following bearings: Branford Reef Light—344.5° psc, Falkner Island Light—053.5° psc, Mattituck Inlet Light—141.5° psc. What is your position?

A. LAT 41°10.4'N, LONG 72°43.0'W
B. LAT 41°09.6'N, LONG 72°44.9'W
C. LAT 41°08.4'N, LONG 72°43.7'W
D. LAT 41°08.0'N, LONG 72°44.8'W

12609. You are on course 239° per standard magnetic compass when you take the following bearings: Falkner Island Light—314° psc, Duck Island West Breakwater Light 2DI—039° psc, Horton Point Light—157° psc. What is your position?

A. LAT 41°09.9'N, LONG 72°32.0'W
B. LAT 41°09.3'N, LONG 72°33.0'W
C. LAT 41°10.5'N, LONG 72°32.1'W
D. LAT 41°11.6'N, LONG 72°33.6'W

12610. You are on course 061° per standard magnetic compass when you take the following bearings: Bartlett Reef Light—070° psc, Saybrook Breakwater Light—010° psc, Horton Pt. Light—227° psc. What is your position?

A. LAT 41°10.4'N, LONG 72°19.6'W
B. LAT 41°11.2'N, LONG 72°20.6'W
C. LAT 41°13.7'N, LONG 72°23.9'W
D. LAT 41°15.4'N, LONG 72°24.3'W

The following questions should be answered using chart number 13205TR, Block Island

and Approaches, and supporting publications.

12700. You are on course 073° per standard magnetic compass when you take the following bearings: Watch Hill Point Light—037° psc, Montauk Point Light—179° psc, Race Rock Light—289° psc. What is your position?

A. LAT 41°13.6'N, LONG 71°54.6'W
B. LAT 41°13.7'N, LONG 71°53.8'W
C. LAT 41°13.7'N, LONG 71°54.9'W
D. LAT 41°13.8'N, LONG 71°54.3'W

12701. You are on course 298° per standard magnetic compass when you take the following bearings: Block Island Southeast Point Light—058° psc, Block Island Aero Beacon—005° psc, Montauk Point Light—268° psc. What is your position?

A. LAT 41°08.3'N, LONG 71°35.0'W
B. LAT 41°08.2'N, LONG 71°34.4'W
C. LAT 41°08.1'N, LONG 71°33.8'W
D. LAT 41°08.0'N, LONG 71°34.1'W

12702. You are on course 282° per standard magnetic compass when you take the following bearings: Point Judith Light—073° psc, Block Island North Light—156° psc, Watch Hill Point Light—293° psc. What is your position?

A. LAT 41°17.0'N, LONG 71°38.2'W
B. LAT 41°17.1'N, LONG 71°39.1'W
C. LAT 41°17.2'N, LONG 71°38.7'W
D. LAT 41°17.2'N, LONG 71°37.8'W

12703. You are on course 025° per standard magnetic compass when you take the following bearings: Point Judith Light—072° psc, Block Island North Point Light—116° psc, Watch Hill Light—306° psc. What is your position?

A. LAT 41°14.9'N, LONG 71°43.2'W
B. LAT 41°15.1'N, LONG 71°44.0'W
C. LAT 41°15.4'N, LONG 71°43.1'W
D. LAT 41°15.6'N, LONG 71°42.8'W

12704. You are on course 137° per standard magnetic compass when you take the following bearings: Watch Hill Point Light—051° psc, Montauk Point Light—184° psc, Race Rock Light—279° psc. What is your position?

A. LAT 41°15.2'N, LONG 71°54.4'W
B. LAT 41°15.1'N, LONG 71°53.8'W

C. LAT 41°15.1'N, LONG 71°54.9'W
D. LAT 41°15.0'N, LONG 71°53.7'W

12705. You are on course 087° per standard magnetic compass when you take the following bearings: Little Gull Island Light—277° psc, Race Rock Light—303° psc, Latimer Reef Light—025° psc. What is your position?

A. LAT 41°13.1'N, LONG 71°57.5'W
B. LAT 41°13.1'N, LONG 71°56.9'W
C. LAT 41°13.0'N, LONG 71°58.0'W
D. LAT 41°12.9'N, LONG 71°57.2'W

12706. You are on course 053° per standard magnetic compass when you take the following bearings: Little Gull Island Light—275° psc, Race Rock Light—296° psc, Latimer Reef Light—011° psc. What is your position?

A. LAT 41°12.9'N, LONG 71°56.3'W
B. LAT 41°13.2'N, LONG 71°56.0'W
C. LAT 41°13.4'N, LONG 71°55.5'W
D. LAT 41°13.8'N, LONG 71°56.1'W

12707. You are on course 246° per standard magnetic compass when you take the following bearings: Little Gull Island Light—286° psc, Race Rock Light—308° psc, Latimer Reef Light—018° psc. What is your position?

A. LAT 41°12.6'N, LONG 71°55.7'W
B. LAT 41°12.6'N, LONG 71°56.6'W
C. LAT 41°12.7'N, LONG 71°56.0'W
D. LAT 41°13.1'N, LONG 71°56.1'W

12708. You are on course 302° per standard magnetic compass when you take the following bearings: Little Gull Island Light—283° psc, Race Rock Light—311° psc, Latimer Reef Light—027° psc. What is your position?

A. LAT 41°12.2'N, LONG 71°57.6'W
B. LAT 41°12.4'N, LONG 71°57.4'W
C. LAT 41°12.4'N, LONG 71°57.9'W
D. LAT 41°12.7'N, LONG 71°57.7'W

12709. You are on course 157° per standard magnetic compass when you take the following bearings: Little Gull Island Light—277° psc, Race Rock Light—301° psc, Latimer Reef Light—028° psc. What is your position?

A. LAT 41°13.5'N, LONG 71°57.9'W
B. LAT 41°13.5'N, LONG 71°57.4'W

C. LAT 41°13.6'N, LONG 71°57.0'W
D. LAT 41°13.6'N, LONG 71°57.8'W

The following questions are based on chart 12221TR, Chesapeake Bay Entrance, and the supporting publications.

12900. Your 1302 position is LAT 37°14.7'N, LONG 76°22.7'W. You are turning for 9.6 knots. What is your ETA at Trestle C of the Chesapeake Bay Bridge and Tunnel if you follow York River Entrance Channel?

A. 1516
B. 1505
C. 1500
D. 1451

12901. Your 1152 position is LAT 37°23.9'N, LONG 76°05.5'W. You are turning for 10.3 knots. What is your ETA at Trestle C of the Chesapeake Bay Bridge and Tunnel if you follow York Spit Channel?

A. 1404
B. 1349
C. 1342
D. 1339

12902. Your 1312 position is LAT 37°10.9'N, LONG 75°29.6'W. You are turning for 8.3 knots. What is your ETA at LAT 37°21.9'N, LONG 75°42.6'W?

A. 1449
B. 1456
C. 1502
D. 1511

12903. Your 1426 position is LAT 37°10.9'N, LONG 75°29.6'W. You are turning for 9.3 knots. What is your ETA at Chesapeake Light?

A. 1616
B. 1621
C. 1626
D. 1633

12904. Your 0916 position is LAT 37°10.9'N, LONG 75°29.6'W. You are turning for 12.3 knots. What is your ETA at North Chesapeake Bay Entrance Buoy NCA?

A. 1035
B. 1043
C. 1051
D. 1101

12905. At 0919 you are in Chesapeake Channel between Trestle B and Trestle C of the Chesapeake Bay Bridge and Tunnel. What is your ETA to a point between York Spit Channel Buoys 35 and 36 if you are making 11.3 knots and follow the buoyed channel?

A. 1025
B. 1028
C. 1033
D. 1037

12906. At 0919 you are in Chesapeake Channel between Trestle B and Trestle C of the Chesapeake Bay Bridge and Tunnel. What is your ETA between York River Entrance Channel Buoys 17 and 18 if you are making 11.3 knots?

A. 1034
B. 1039
C. 1044
D. 1049

12907. At 0914 you are in Chesapeake Channel between Trestle B and Trestle C of the Chesapeake Bay Bridge and Tunnel. What is your ETA at North Chesapeake Entrance Buoy NCA if you are making good 10.9 knots? (Use the buoyed channel and appropriate sea lane.)

A. 1038
B. 1044
C. 1049
D. 1055

12908. At 0919 you are inbound, approximately 4 miles east of Cape Henry with buoy 15 close aboard to port. What is your ETA between Trestle B and Trestle C of the Chesapeake Bay Bridge and Tunnel if you are making 11.3 knots?

A. 1010
B. 1014
C. 1019
D. 1025

12909. At 0914 you are in Chesapeake Bay southeast inbound lane with buoy CBJ close aboard to port. What is your ETA at Thimble Shoal Channel Buoy 19 if you are making 10.9 knots?

A. 1034
B. 1038
C. 1046
D. 1042

The following questions are to be answered by using chart 12354TR, Long Island Sound - Eastern Part, and supporting publications.

13000. Your 2108 position is LAT 41°10.0'N, LONG 72°30.0'W. You are turning for 12.5 knots. What is your ETA at Buoy NH (LAT 41°12.1'N, LONG 72°53.8'W)?

A. 2133
B. 2227
C. 2235
D. 2248

13001. At 1222 your position is LAT 41°05.5'N, LONG 72°47.3'W. You are making turns for 14.5 knots. What is your ETA at Twenty-Eight Foot Shoal Lighted Buoy (LAT 41°09.3'N, LONG 72°30.5'W)?

A. 1309
B. 1317
C. 1321
D. 1328

13002. At 0829 your position is LAT 41°02.9'N, LONG 72°57.4'W. You are making turns for 8.5 knots. What is your ETA at a position midway between buoys 1 and 2 at the entrance of New Haven Outer Channel?

A. 0925
B. 0931
C. 0938
D. 0944

13003. At 2102 your position is LAT 41°02.9'N, LONG 72°57.4'W. You are making turns for 16 knots. What is your ETA at a position 5 miles due south of Falkner Island Light?

A. 2149
B. 2155
C. 2159
D. 2204

13004. At 1815 your position is LAT 41°05.5'N, LONG 72°47.3'W. You are making turns for 12.6 knots. What is your ETA at Plum Island Mid Channel Buoy PI (LAT 41°13.3'N, LONG 72°10.8'W)?

A. 2019
B. 2028
C. 2032
D. 2038

13005. At 1715 your position is LAT 41°00.0'N, LONG 72°40.0'W. You are making urns for 15.5 knots. What is your ETA at a osition 1.5 miles due south of Stratford hoal Middle Ground Light?

. 1820
. 1824
. 1828
. 1832

3006. Your 1600 position is LAT 41°08.0'N, ONG 72°44.8'W. You are making turns for 4 knots. What is your ETA at Mattituck nlet?

A. 1636
. 1643
. 1647
D. 1651

3007. Your 1600 position is LAT 41°08.0'N, ONG 72°44.8'W. You are making turns for 0 knots. What is your ETA at Twenty-Eight oot Shoal Lighted Buoy TE (LAT 41°09.3'N ONG 72°30.5'W)?

. 1647
. 1651
. 1702
. 1706

3008. Your 2215 position is LAT 41°05.4'N, ONG 72°59.4'W. You are making 15 knots. What is your ETA at Twenty-Eight Foot hoal Lighted Buoy (LAT 41°09.3'N, LONG 2°30.5'W)?

. 2338
. 2343
. 2349
. 2354

13009. Your 1830 position is LAT 41°05.4'N, ONG 72°59.4'W. You are making turns for 9 knots. What is your ETA at Mattituck nlet?

A. 2044
B. 2052
C. 2059
D. 2106

13010. Your 0620 position is LAT 40°59.5'N, LONG 73°00.5'W. You are making turns for 8 knots. What is your ETA at LAT 41°08.0'N, LONG 72°44.8'W?

A. 0748
B. 0802
C. 0809
D. 0814

The following questions should be answered using chart number 13205TR, Block Island and Approaches, and supporting publications.

13100. Your position is LAT 41°15.2'N, LONG 71°50.1'W at 1347. You are turning for 6.9 knots. What is your ETA at Shagwong Reef Buoy 7SR?

A. 1506
B. 1515
C. 1521
D. 1527

13101. At 1523 your position is LAT 41°08.2'N, LONG 71°34.4'W. You are turning for 8.7 knots. What is your ETA at Shagwong Reef Buoy 7SR?

A. 1653
B. 1700
C. 1711
D. 1718

13102. At 2330 your position is LAT 41°16.9'N, LONG 71°38.2'W. You are turning for 9.3 knots. What is your ETA at the entrance to Great Salt Pond on Block Island?

A. 2355
B. 0005
C. 0012
D. 0019

13104. At 0242 your position is LAT 41°16.8'N, LONG 71°39.9'W. You are turning for 9.3 knots. What is your ETA at the West Gap of Pt. Judith Harbor of Refuge?

A. 0319
B. 0325
C. 0329
D. 0336

13105. At 1048 you are in the entrance to Great Salt Pond on Block Island with buoy 5 close aboard. What is your ETA at the west gap of Point Judith Harbor of Refuge if you make good 8.3 knots?

A. 1149
B. 1154
C. 1158
D. 1203

13106. At 1048 you are in the entrance to Great Salt Pond on Block Island with buoy 5 close aboard. What is your ETA at the west

---

gap of Point Judith Harbor of Refuge if you make good 11.3 knots?

A. 1144
B. 1154
C. 1159
D. 1205

13107. At 1103 your position is LAT 41°12.5 N, LONG 71°37.4 W. What is your ETA at the west gap of Point Judith Harbor of Refuge if you make good 11.3 knots?

A. 1144
B. 1154
C. 1159
D. 1205

13108. At 1103 you are in the entrance to Great Salt Pond on Block Island with buoy 5 close aboard. What is your ETA at light 1 at the mouth of the approaches to Lake Montauk if you make good 8.2 knots?

A. 1249
B. 1254
C. 1259
D. 1310

13109. At 1113 you are in the entrance to Great Salt Pond on Block Island with buoy 5 close aboard. What is your ETA at light 1 at the mouth of the approaches to Lake Montauk if you make good 9.6 knots?

A. 1310
B. 1301
C. 1254
D. 1249

13210. At 0943, your position is LAT 41°14.8'N, LONG 71°54.3'W. You are turning for 12.2 knots. What is your ETA at the entrance to Great Salt Pond on Block Island?

A. 1054
B. 1048
C. 1040
D. 1032

The following questions are based on chart 12221TR, Chesapeake Bay Entrance, and the supporting publications.

13300. The soundings on this chart are measured in _____.

A. feet
B. yards

C. fathoms
D. meters

13301. The approach channel to the town of Cape Charles (LAT 37°16′N, LONG 76°01′W) has what controlling depth?

A. 9 feet
B. 17 feet
C. 20 feet
D. 40 feet

13302. The shoal spanned by Trestle B of the Chesapeake Bay Bridge and Tunnel is _____.

A. Chesapeake shoal
B. the Middle ground
C. Lynnhaven roads
D. the Tail of the Horseshoe

13303. You are considering anchoring a mile or two northeast of Chesapeake Light. After examining the chart you decide not to because of the _____.

A. large number of wrecks
B. coral being designated as a special protected area
C. danger of unexploded mines
D. area being designated as a National Marine Sanctuary

13305. What are the bottom characteristics of Nautilus Shoal (LAT 37°03′N, LONG 75°56′W)?

A. Sand and shells
B. Hard sand
C. Fine grey sand
D. Mud and sand

13306. In the northern quadrant of the circle surrounding Chesapeake Bay Entrance Junction Buoy CBJ the number 20 over a bracket appears 5 times. What do these indicate?

A. Markers or piles are 20 feet above mean low water.
B. The maximum draft permitted in this area is 20 feet.
C. Obstructions have been cleared by a wire drag to 20 feet.
D. Benchmarks used to measure channel depths while dredging.

13307. The soundings on the chart are based on the depth of water available at _____.

A. mean low water
B. mean lower low water
C. mean high water
D. mean high water springs

13308. You are navigating 1 mile north of Cape Henry Lighthouse at the southern entrance to Chesapeake Bay. You observe that this area is bounded on the chart by magenta bands. This indicates a (n) _____.

A. fish trap area
B. explosive anchorage
C. pilotage area
D. danger zone

13309. What type of bottom can be expected at the northern end of York Spit Channel?

A. Hard clay
B. Fine grey sand
C. Soft black mud
D. Mud and sand

The following questions are to be answered by using chart 12354TR, Long Island Sound - Eastern Part, and supporting publications.

13400. You are going to anchor at Gardiners Bay in LAT 41°04.5′N, LONG 72°13.0′W. What type of bottom should you expect?

A. Streaked mud
B. Sand
C. Hard rocks
D. Soft mud

13401. You are planning to anchor in Orient Harbor at LAT 41°07.9′N, LONG 72°18.5′W. Assuming that normal conditions exist, how much anchor cable should you put out?

A. 16 to 18 feet
B. 40 to 60 feet
C. 80 to 112 feet
D. 120 to 140 feet

13402. You are planning to anchor in Orient Harbor at LAT 41°07.9′N, LONG 72°18.5′W. What type of bottom should you expect?

A. Sticky
B. Soft
C. Stiff
D. Streaky

13403. Your vessel has become disabled and is dead in the water. Your loran set fixes your position at LAT 41°12.1′N, LONG 72°43.5′W. You decide to anchor at this position. Which type of bottom should you expect?

A. Soft clay and sand
B. Soft mud and shell
C. Hard sand and rocks
D. Blue mud and gray sand

13404. Your vessel has become disabled and is dead in the water. Your loran set fixes your position at LAT 41°12.1′N, LONG 72°43.5′W. You decide to anchor at this position. Under normal conditions, how much anchor chain should you expect to put out

A. 80 to 190 feet
B. 190 to 240 feet
C. 245 to 343 feet
D. 345 to 420 feet

13405. At 0400 your vessel is dead in the water and in heavy fog. Your loran set fixes your position at LAT 41°12.1′N, LONG 72°43.5′W. Bottom samples are taken and indicate a composition of soft mud and shell. Your fathometer reads 40 feet. If the vessel draws 9 feet of water, which of the following is TRUE?

A. The bottom samples and fathometer reading prove the loran fix is reliable.
B. The bottom samples and fathometer readings indicate that the loran fix is unreliable.
C. The information collected indicates that the fathometer may be in error.
D. The information collected indicates that the chart is most likely in error.

13406. You are planning to anchor your vessel at LAT 41°01.1′N, LONG 73°02.8′W. What type of bottom should you expect at this position?

A. Gray sand
B. Soft mud
C. Gray mud
D. Hard sand

13407. Your position is LAT 41°03.0′N, LONG 72°42.1′W. If your draft is 8 ft, what should your fathometer read at this position?

A. 80 ft.
B. 88 ft.

. 96 ft.

. 99 ft.

3409. You plan to anchor your vessel at LAT 1°00.5'N, LONG 73°02.8'W. What type of bottom should you expect at this position?

. Gray sand

. Soft mud

. Hard sand

. Gray mud

3410. You plan to anchor your vessel at AT 41°05.1'N, LONG 72°59.3'W. Assuming that normal conditions exist, how much anchor cable should you put out?

. 150 to 300 feet

. 300 to 440 feet

. 440 to 600 feet

. 640 to 750 feet

The following questions should be answered using chart number 13205TR, Block Island and Approaches, and supporting publications.

13500. The soundings on this chart are measured in _____.

. feet

. yards

. meters

. fathoms

13501. What type of bottom is found off the southern coast of Long Island?

. Blue Mud

. Shingle

. Brown Sand

. Shells

13502. The four soundings in the vicinity of LAT 41°12.2'N, LONG 71°33.0'W, that are underlined with a bracket indicate _____.

. that no bottom was found at the sounding depth indicated

. a submerged rock not dangerous to surface navigation

. the height a rock uncovers at low water springs

. a submerged danger that is cleared to the indicated depth by a wire drag

13503. You are proceeding from a point 4 miles due east of Montauk Point enroute to to Long Island Sound via The Race. You should expect the soundings to _____.

A. remain fairly constant
B. increase rapidly at first then remain constant until through the Race
C. start increasing when north of Montauk Point
D. be inaccurate due to sound absorption by the mud bottom

13504. A vessel anchoring in the middle of Cherry Harbor, 1 mile off Gardiner's Island, will find what type of bottom?

A. Rocky
B. Shells
C. Mud
D. Silt

13505. What soundings are indicated by a blue tint on this chart?

A. 30 fathoms or more
B. 30 feet or less
C. 30 feet or more
D. 30 fathoms or less

13506. The broken magenta lines starting at Montauk Point and running generally ENE to Block Island indicate _____.

A. recommended tracks to Block Island
B. a submerged cable area
C. a military exercise area
D. demarcation lines for application of the COLREGS

13507. Areas enclosed by a long and short dashed magenta line indicate _____.

A. cable areas
B. dumping grounds
C. fish trap areas
D. precautionary areas

13508. The bottom approximately three miles to the ESE of Block Island Southeast Point has _____.

A. gravel
B. shale
C. stones
D. grit

13509. Sounding contours in unshaded water areas are at what interval?

A. 10 foot up to 100 ft. depths then at 30 foot intervals
B. 30 foot intervals
C. 10 fathom intervals

D. The interval will vary to ensure any major underwater hazard is highlighted.

The following questions are based on chart 12221TR, Chesapeake Bay Entrance, and the supporting publications.

13700. Local magnetic disturbances of up to how many degrees have been noted from Cape Henry to Currituck Beach Light?

A. 2 degrees
B. 6 degrees
C. 11 degrees
D. 17 degrees

13701. Why are there no buoys charted at the approach to Sand Shoal Inlet (LAT 37°16'N, LONG 75°46'W)?

A. No buoys are stationed there.
B. They frequently shift position due to heavy weather.
C. They are frequently shifted to conform to the changing channel.
D. The buoys are being replaced with fixed lights.

13702. What chart should you use in Lynnhaven Bay (west of Cape Henry)?

A. 12221
B. 12256
C. 12205
D. 12254

13703. NOAA weather broadcasts can be received on what frequency while navigating off Cape Henry?

A. 162.45 MHz
B. 162.55 MHz
C. 162.65 MHz
D. 162.70 MHz

13705. The broken magenta lines (long and short dashes) in and around Mobjack Bay (LAT 37°20'N, LONG 76°22'W) indicate

_____.

A. amphibious training areas
B. grounds for dredge spoil
C. fishtrap areas
D. gunnery exercise areas

13706. What is the horizontal clearance of the navigation opening of Trestle B of the Chesapeake Bay Bridge and Tunnel?

A. 21 feet
B. 70 feet
C. 75 feet
D. 300 feet

13707. The level of mean high water at Old Point Comfort is how many feet above the sounding datum?

A. 1.5 feet
B. 2.2 feet
C. 2.5 feet
D. 3.5 feet

13708. A note on the chart indicates that currents in excess of how many knots can be expected in the vicinity of the Chesapeake Bay Bridge and Tunnel?

A. 3.00 knots
B. 2.20 knots
C. 1.75 knots
D. 1.50 knots

13709. Anchorage regulations for this area may be obtained from _____.

A. Office of the Commander 5th Coast Guard District
B. Commanding General, Corps of Engineers, Washington, D.C.
C. Virginia/Maryland Pilots Assoc.
D. Chesapeake Bay Port Authority, Hampton, VA

The following questions are to be answered by using chart 12354TR, Long Island Sound - Eastern Part, and supporting publications.

13801. You are operating in the area approximately 2 miles southeast of Kelsey Point when you realize that your vessel's intended track will carry you over the wreck charted at LAT 41°13.5′N, LONG 72°29.6′W. Which statement is TRUE?

A. The chart indicates the exact position of the wreck.
B. The wreck has been cleared by wire drag to a depth of 39 ft.
C. The wreck represents a danger to surface navigation.
D. The wreck is visible above the sounding datum.

13802. Which chart would you use for more detailed information on the Connecticut River?

A. 12354
B. 12370
C. 12371
D. 12375

13803. NOAA Weather Broadcasts for the New London area may be received by turning your radio to _____.

A. 162.550 MHz
B. 162.475 MHz
C. 162.400 MHz
D. 162.350 MHz

13804. What is the significance of the broken magenta lines which roughly parallel the shore between Roanoke Point and Orient Point on Long Island?

A. They mark the limits of breakers in that area.
B. These lines warn the mariner of submerged rocks.
C. They mark the boundary lines of fish trap areas.
D. These lines warn the mariner of submerged pipelines.

13805. What is the danger associated with anchoring your vessel within a 300 yard radius of Gardiners Point?

A. An unusually strong current exists in this area.
B. The bottom is not suitable for holding the anchor.
C. Submerged pilings may exist in this area.
D. Your anchor could become fouled on undetonated explosives.

13806. The chart symbol surrounding Saybrook Breakwater Light warns mariners that the navigational light structure is _____.

A. no longer maintained
B. protected by riprap
C. privately maintained
D. awash at high tide

13807. The chart symbol depicted at LAT 40°58.5′N, LONG 72°43.4′W indicates a (n) _____.

A. abandoned lighthouse
B. light ship
C. wreck with only its mast visible
D. wreck showing a portion of the hull above the sounding datum

13808. The chart symbol depicted at LAT 41°13.5′N, LONG 72°29.7′W indicates _____.

A. the exact position of a dangerous wreck
B. the approximate position of a wreck dangerous to surface navigation
C. a wreck cleared by wire drag to a depth of 39 feet
D. a wreck not dangerous to surface navigation

13809. Which chart, of the same scale, continues eastward from this chart?

A. 13205
B. 13212
C. 13214
D. 13216

13810. Which chart would you use if you planned to continue westward beyond the coverage of this chart?

A. 12363
B. 12373
C. 13205
D. 13218

The following questions should be answered using chart number 13205TR, Block Island and Approaches, and supporting publications.

13900. The trapezoidal shaped areas enclosed by a thin broken magenta line and located along the south coast of Long Island are _____.

A. designated training areas for Navy amphibious craft
B. disposal areas for unexploded munitions
C. fish trap areas
D. anchorage areas for small craft

13901. The precautionary area southeast of Block Island refers to a _____.

A. recommended traffic lane
B. military exercise area
C. national marine refuge
D. dumping ground for hazardous wastes

13902. A vessel enroute to to Long Island Sound from sea will enter waters governed by the Inland Rules of the Road_____.

A. when crossing the Territorial Sea boundary
B. between Montauk Point and Block Island

C. when north of latitude 41°10.0'N
D. when passing through The Race

13903. Your position is LAT 41°12.4'N, LONG 71°53.2'W. You are on course 163°T enroute to to sea. You can ensure that you will clear Montauk Point if your loran reading is always _____.

A. more than 9960-X-25990
B. less than 9960-W-14665
C. more than 9960-Y-43870
D. All of the above

13904. On the south and the east coasts of Block Island are circles with a dot in the center and labeled CUP. This is a _____.

A. conspicuous object
B. steep depression in the surrounding hills that resembles a cup
C. domed structure useful for navigation
D. calling-up-point used for traffic control

13905. The Ruins (LAT 41°08.5'N, LONG 72°08.8'W) is _____.

A. a classic example of 18th century military fortifications
B. in an area of unpredictable, treacherous currents
C. restricted to surface navigation due to fishery conservation projects nearby
D. prohibited to the public

13906. When approaching Block Island Sound from Long Island Sound, you will enter waters governed by the International Rules of the Road when you _____.

A. pass through The Race
B. cross the territorial sea boundary
C. exit Block Island Sound to the east or south
D. None of the above, as Long Island Sound is governed by the International Rules of the Road

13908. Montauk Point Light is 168 feet above what reference level?

A. Mean low water
B. Mean tide level
C. Ground level
D. Mean high water

13909. The irregular black line around a charted light such as Race Rock Light indicates that it is _____.

A. unwatched
B. surrounded by riprap
C. a minor light
D. constructed on an artificial island

The following questions should be answered using chart number 18531, Columbia River, and supporting publications.

14001. At 1745 Lady Island Range is in line dead ahead and Government Island Upper Range is in line on your starboard bow. Your vessel is steaming in a westerly direction. At 1851 you pass under the Interstate 5 highway bridge. What speed have you averaged?

A. 10 mph
B. 11 mph
C. 12 mph
D. 13 mph

14002. At 1630 your vessel exits Bonneville Lock steaming in a westerly direction. What speed must you average to arrive at the Interstate 5 highway bridge with an ETA of 2120?

A. 6 mph
B. 7 mph
C. 8 mph
D. 9 mph

14003. At 1430 your vessel passes under the Interstate 5 highway bridge eastbound. Your engines are making RPMs for 12 mph. If the current is a constant 3 mph, what is your ETA at Bonneville Lock?

A. 1744
B. 1753
C. 1834
D. 1848

14004. At 1745 Lady Island Upper Range is in line dead astern and Washougal Lower Range is in line on the starboard bow. You are steaming in an easterly direction. What speed must you average to arrive abeam of Cape Horn Light No. 67 at 1839?

A. 9.3 mph
B. 9.8 mph
C. 10.2 mph
D. 10.8 mph

14005. At 0800 your vessel is at mile 110 on the Columbia River. You are steaming in an easterly direction. At 0854 Lady Island Range is in line dead astern and Govern-

ment Island Upper Range is in line on your port quarter. What speed have you averaged?

A. 8.1 mph
B. 8.5 mph
C. 9.4 mph
D. 10.2 mph

14100. Your vessel is awaiting lockage at Bonneville Lock. The staff gauge on the guide wall reads 18'–06". What is the maximum vessel draft allowed to enter the lock?

A. 17'–00"
B. 17'–06"
C. 18'–00"
D. 18'–06"

14101. What signal is given by air horn to indicate that Bonneville Lock is ready for entrance?

A. two long blasts
B. two short blasts
C. one short blast
D. one long blast

14102. Your vessel is awaiting lockage at Bonneville Locks when you notice that the lock is displaying an amber signal light. What type of vessel is allowed to enter the chamber under this signal?

A. Vessels owned or operated by the United States
B. Passenger vessels
C. Commercial freight and log-tow vessels
D. All vessels

14103. You are approaching Bonneville Lock and Dam and desire lockage. Which call sign should you use to contact the lock?

A. WUJ 33
B. WUJ 34
C. WUJ 41
D. WUJ 45

14104. You are approaching Bonneville Lock and Dam. Which FM-radio channel should be used to communicate with the lockmaster?

A. 13
B. 14
C. 15
D. 16

14200. What is the length of the city wharf at The Dalles on the Columbia River?

A. 20 feet
B. over 1000 feet
C. 800 feet
D. 600 feet

14201. The draw of the Burlington Northern railroad bridge across the Columbia River at mile 328.0 shall be opened on signal, without prior notice, from _____.

A. 6:00 am to 6:00 pm
B. 6:00 pm to 6:00 am
C. 8:00 pm to 4:00 am
D. 8:00 am to 4:00 pm

14202. What is the minimum clearance for the bridge across the entrance to the Wind River at Home Valley, WA?

A. 14 feet
B. 26 feet
C. 34 feet
D. 38 feet

14203. What is the vertical clearance of the fixed bridge across the entrance to Rock Creek at Stevenson, Washington?

A. 18 feet
B. 36 feet
C. 54 feet
D. 70 feet

14204. The mooring float at Beacon Rock State Park is restricted to pleasure boats and to periods not to exceed _____.

A. 12 hours
B. 24 hours
C. 36 hours
D. 48 hours

14300. What is the height above the water of Government Island Upper Range, lower light?

A. 20 feet
B. 24 feet
C. 38 feet
D. 42 feet

14301. What are the characteristics of Washougal Light on the Columbia River?

A. Equal interval green, 6 seconds
B. Quick flashing red, 2 seconds
C. Flashing green, 4 seconds
D. Flashing red, 2.5 seconds

14302. What are the characteristics of the upper light of Government Island Lower Range, on the Columbia River?

A. Equal interval red, 6 seconds
B. Green group flashing, 6 seconds
C. Quick flashing red, 6 seconds
D. Equal interval green, 6 seconds

14303. What is the height above the water of light No. 84 on the Columbia River below Bonneville lock & dam?

A. 10 feet
B. 14 feet
C. 18 feet
D. 24 feet

14304. What is a characteristic of light No. 41 on the Columbia River above Bonneville Lock?

A. The light shows an isophase characteristic.
B. The light is 3 meters above the water.
C. The light is equipped with a radar reflector.
D. The light is red in color.

14401. You are underway and steaming in an easterly direction on the Columbia River. Your vessel is positioned in the middle half of Cape Horn Channel and is abeam of Cape Horn Light. What should your fathometer read at this position, if the staff gauge at Portland reads 0 feet?

A. 16 feet
B. 18 feet
C. 22 feet
D. 24 feet

14402. You are underway and proceeding in an easterly direction on the Columbia River. Your vessel is positioned in the right outside quarter of McGowans Channel and is abeam of light No. 88. What should your fathometer read at this position, if the staff gauge at Portland reads +15.0 feet?

A. 22 feet
B. 31 feet
C. 43 feet
D. 52 feet

14403. You are underway and steaming in an easterly direction on the Columbia River. After bringing Fisher Quarry Channel Range in line over your bow, you move to the left outside quarter of the channel. What should your fathometer read at this position, if the staff gauge at Portland reads +12.5 feet?

A. 7.5 feet
B. 32.5 feet
C. 41.5 feet
D. 51.5 feet

14404. You are underway and proceeding in an easterly direction on the Columbia River. You position your vessel in the middle of the channel and bring Government Island Lower Range in line over your bow. What should your fathometer read at this position, if the staff gauge at Portland reads 10.0 feet?

A. 15 feet
B. 24 feet
C. 28 feet
D. 31 feet

14500. Your vessel is at mile 170 on the Columbia River. You are proceeding in a westerly direction and are approaching the lift bridge at Hood River. The pool level of the Bonneville reservoir stands at 92 feet above MSL. If the highest point on your vessel is 52 feet above the water, which of the following statements is TRUE?

A. You may pass under the lift bridge, in the down position with a vertical clearance of 15 feet.
B. You may pass under the lift bridge in the up position with a clearance of 96 feet.
C. You may pass under the lift bridge, in the down position with a vertical clearance of 25 feet.
D. You may pass under the lift bridge, in the up position with a vertical clearance of 76 feet.

14501. You are proceeding in an easterly direction on the Columbia River. The pool level of the Bonneville Reservoir stands at 65 feet above MSL. If the highest point on your vessel is 54 feet above the water, what will be the vertical clearance as you pass under the overhead power cables at mile 186.2?

A. 94 feet
B. 101 feet
C. 108 feet
D. 117 feet

4502. You are proceeding in an easterly direction on the Columbia River. The pool level of the Bonneville reservoir stands at 74 feet above MSL. If the highest point on your vessel is 49 feet above the water, what will be the vertical clearance as you pass under the center of the Bridge of the Gods?

A. 74.0 feet
B. 86.0 feet
C. 97.5 feet
D. 123 feet

4503. You have just cleared Bonneville Lock and are proceeding in an easterly direction on the Columbia River. The pool level of the Bonneville reservoir stands at 78 feet above MSL. If the highest point on your vessel is 46 feet above the water, what will be the vertical clearance when you pass under the overhead power cables at mile 146.5?

A. 134 feet
B. 138 feet
C. 144 feet
D. 150 feet

4504. You are proceeding in a westerly direction on the Columbia River. The pool level of the Bonneville reservoir stands at 72 feet above MSL. If the highest point on your vessel is 44 feet above the water, what will be the vertical clearance as you pass under the overhead power cables at mile 173.8?

A. 43 feet
B. 68 feet
C. 111 feet
D. 115 feet

4600. What is the length of The Dalles Lock on the Columbia River?

A. 475 feet
B. 500 feet
C. 675 feet
D. 1200 feet

4601. Where would you look for information on the restricted areas shown on the chart immediately above and below the spillway at The Dalles Lock & Dam ?

A. Light List, Vol II
B. Coast Pilot 7, Chapter 2
C. Notice to Mariners
D. Sailing Directions

14602. Where would you tune your radio to receive a VHF-FM weather broadcast for the Columbia River in the vicinity of Government Island?

A. KIH-32, 162.40 MHz
B. KBA-99, 162.40 MHz
C. KEB-97, 162.55 MHz
D. KEC-62 162.55 MHz

14603. Clearances of bridges and overhead cables below Bonneville Dam refer to heights in feet above mean _____.

A. lower low water
B. high water
C. low water
D. sea level

14604. Contour elevations on this chart refer to heights in feet above mean _____.

A. lower low water
B. high water
C. low water
D. sea level

14700. How many nautical miles are between mile 105 and mile 234 on the Columbia River?

A. 112.1
B. 119.5
C. 129
D. 148.4

14701. How many nautical miles are between mile 44 and mile 163 on the Columbia River?

A. 98.6
B. 103.4
C. 119.5
D. 136.9

14702. At 2200 your vessel is at mile 95 proceeding in an easterly direction on the Columbia River. At 0400 the following morning, you pass the 125 mile mark. How many nautical miles have you traveled since 2200?

A. 22.6
B. 24.3
C. 26.1
D. 34.5

14703. At 0800 your vessel is at mile 110 proceeding in an easterly direction on the Columbia River. At 1030 Reed Island is

abeam to port as you pass the 125 mile mark. What has been your average speed in knots?

A. 4.3 knots
B. 5.2 knots
C. 8.7 knots
D. 10.0 knots

14704. At 0800 your vessel is at mile 110 on the Columbia River. Thirty minutes later your vessel is at mile 115. What is your speed in knots?

A. 4.3 knots
B. 5.7 knots
C. 7.8 knots
D. 8.7 knots

The following questions are to be answered using chart 12221 TR, Chesapeake Bay Entrance, and supporting publications. Your vessel is enroute to from New York, NY, to Baltimore, MD. Your vessel's draft is 29 feet, and your height of eye is 54 feet. Your present course is 206°T and your speed is 18 knots. Use 10°W variation where required.

15038. At 0705 you obtained the following Loran readings: 9960-X-27091.2; 9960-Y-41612.8; 9960-Z-58744.2. What is your vessel's position?

A. 37°20.4'N, 75°30.2'W
B. 37°20.8'N, 75°29.9'W
C. 37°21.3'N, 75°29.5'W
D. 37°21.2'N, 75°30.4'W

15039. At 0725 you determined your vessel's position to be 37°15.5'N, 75°33.2'W. Assuming that you make good your course of 206° true and a speed of 18 knots, at what time would you expect to be abeam of Cape Charles Lighted Bell Buoy 14?

A. 0750
B. 0754
C. 0758
D. 0802

15040. At about what time will you see Chesapeake Light if visibility is exceptionally clear?

A. 0729
B. 0733
C. 0738
D. 0742

15041. At 0741 you are still steering a course of 206° true, with a speed of 18 knots. At this time you observe Cape Charles Lighted Bell Buoy 14 bearing 222° true, Hog Island Lighted Bell Buoy 12 bearing 015° true and the Loran reading 9960-Z-58677.3. What were the set and drift experienced since 0725?

A. 259° true at 3.2 knots
B. 049° true at 2.5 knots
C. 240° true at 1.9 knots
D. 042° true at 3.3 knots

15042. From your 0741 position, you wish to change course in order to pass 2.2 miles easterly of Cape Charles Lighted Bell Buoy 14. Your engine speed is now 14.0 knots. You estimate the current to be 240° true at 1.8 knots. What is the true course to steer to make good the desired course?

A. 179° true
B. 185° true
C. 190° true
D. 197° true

15043. At 0811 your vessel's position is 37°04.9'N, 75°39.7'W. You are steering a course of 220° true at a speed of 14.0 knots. At what time would you expect the buoys in the northeasterly traffic scheme to line up, if you do not correct for a southwesterly current of 1.8 knots?

A. 0826
B. 0831
C. 0837
D. 0846

15044. At 0841 Chesapeake Light bears 164° true, Cape Charles Light bears 312° true, and Cape Henry Light bears 247° true. What was your course made good since 0811?

A. 226° true
B. 230° true
C. 233° true
D. 237° true

15045. From your 0841 position, you are steering a course of 241° true to the northeasterly inbound channel entrance, your speed is now 15 knots. What is your ETA abeam of buoy NCA (LL#375)?

A. 0850
B. 0855

C. 0901
D. 0911

15046. As you pass through the Chesapeake Bay Bridge and Tunnel, you take a bearing of 047° pgc along trestle C when it is in line. The helmsman reports the vessel's heading as 316° pgc and 329° psc. What is the deviation on that heading?

A. 3°E
B. 1°E
C. 1°W
D. 9°W

The following questions should be answered using chart 12354TR, Long Island Sound - Eastern Part, and supporting publications. The draft of your vessel is 12 feet (3.6 meters) and your height of eye is 25 feet (7.6 meters). Gyro error is 2°W. Your assumed speed is 7.5 knots. "Per standard magnetic compass" is abbreviated "psc." Use a variation of 14°W for the entire plot. The deviation table is:

HDG.	M.DEV.	HDG.	M.DEV.	HDG.	M.DEV.
000°	0°	120°	1.0°W	240°	2.0°E
030°	1°W	150°	0°	270°	1.5°E
060°	3.0°W	180°	0°	300°	1.0°E
090°	2.0°W	210°	1.0°E	330°	0°

15056. You are in New Haven Outer Channel and sight the range markers in line directly over the stern. Your heading at the time is 168° per standard magnetic compass. What is the magnetic compass error?

A. 15°W
B. 1°W
C. 1°E
D. 0°

15057. At 0720, you are in the outer channel between buoy 1 and buoy 2 and change course to pass Townshend Ledge Lighted Gong Buoy 10A abeam to port at 0.1 miles. What is the course to steer per gyrocompass if a northerly wind causes 2° of leeway?

A. 120° pgc
B. 118° pgc
C. 116° pgc
D. 114° pgc

15058. At 0740, you plot a loran fix from the following readings: 9960-X-26545.9; 9960-Y-44022.3; 9960-W-15030.3. What is your position?

A. LAT 41°12.0'N, LONG 72°51.3'W
B. LAT 41°12.0'N, LONG 72°51.8'W
C. LAT 41°12.1'N, LONG 72°51.5'W
D. LAT 41°12.1'N, LONG 72°52.0'W

15059. From your 0740 position, you change course to pass 0.8 miles north of Falkner Island Light. Which loran reading will ensure that you will remain clear of the 18' shoal located 1 mile NW of Falkner Island Light?

A. 9960 W: not less than 14942
B. 9960 X: not more than 26452
C. 9960 Y: not less than 44013
D. None of the above

15060. At 0802, the radar range and bearing to Branford Reef Light are 350° pgc at 0.8 mile, and the north point of Falkner Island are 090° pgc at 6.7 miles. What were the set and drift that you encountered since 0740?

A. Set 085°T, drift 0.2 knot
B. Set 085°T, drift 0.6 knot
C. Set 265°T, drift 0.2 knot
D. Set 265°T, drift 0.6 knot

15061. Falkner Island Light is shown _____

A. 46 feet (13.9 meters) above sea level
B. only from 1 June to 10 October
C. from a white octagonal tower
D. with a six-second period

15062. If there is no current, what is the course per standard magnetic compass from your 0802 fix to a position 1.1 miles north of Falkner Island Light?

A. 064° psc
B. 068° psc
C. 091° psc
D. 095° psc

15063. At 0830, you want the latest weather forecasts for the Falkner Island area. On what frequency do you set your FM radio for this information?

A. 2182 kHz
B. 162.80 MHz
C. 156.65 MHz
D. 162.55 MHz

15064. At 0844, the range to the north end of Falkner Island is 2.0 miles and the left tangent bearing is 102°T. If the height of the tide is +1.0 foot, what is the

approximate depth of the water under the
keel?

A. 14 ft. (4.2 meters)
B. 19 ft. (5.8 meters)
C. 22 ft. (6.7 meters)
D. 29 ft. (8.8 meters)

15065. At 0925, you plot the following
loran fix: 9960-W-14930.5; 9960-X-26417.0;
9960-Y-44006.5. If you correct for a current
setting 035°T at 0.5 knot, what true course
will you steer from the 0925 position to arrive at a position 0.5 mile south of Long
Sand Shoal West End Horn Buoy W?

A. 089°T
B. 092°T
C. 095°T
D. 102°T

15066. If you correct for the current in the
preceding question (035°T at 0.5 knot) and
maintain an engine speed of 7.5 knots,
what is your ETA 0.5 mile south of buoy W?

A. 1016
B. 1021
C. 1026
D. 1030

15067. At 0946, the radar range to
Hammonasset Point is 2.5 miles. The range
to the easternmost point of Falkner Island
is 3.3 miles, and the range to Horton Point
is 10.1 miles. What is your position at 0946?

A. LAT 41°13.1'N, LONG 72°34.8'W
B. LAT 41°13.0'N, LONG 72°34.5'W
C. LAT 41°12.8'N, LONG 72°35.1'W
D. LAT 41°12.8'N, LONG 72°34.4'W

15068. Long Sand Shoal _____.

A. shoals gradually on the north and south
sides
B. is hard and lumpy
C. shows breakers when northerly winds
exceed 10 knots
D. has grey sand with scattered shells

15069. During extreme low water, the
soundings near Saybrook may require corrections up to _____.

A. 1 foot (+ 0.3 meter)
B. 2 feet (–0.6 meter)
C. –3.5 feet (-1.1 meters)
D. The sounding datum is based on ex-

treme low water and no correction is necessary

15070. As you enter New London Harbor,
you are steering on the entrance range.
The lights are in line over the bow as you
are heading 352° pgc. What is the gyro
error?

A. 2°E
B. 0°
C. 1°W
D. 3°W

*The following questions are based on chart
12221TR, Chesapeake Bay Entrance, and the
supporting publications. Your height of eye is
25 feet (7.6 meters). Use 10°W variation
where required. The gyro error is 3°E. The deviation table is:*

HDG.	M.DEV.	HDG.	M.DEV.	HDG.	M.DEV.
000°	0°	120°	2°W	240°	3°E
030°	1°W	150°	1°W	270°	3°E
060°	2°W	180°	1°E	300°	2°E
090°	4°W	210°	2°E	330°	1°E

15106. The National Weather Service provides 24 hour weather broadcasts to vessels transiting the Chesapeake Bay Bridge
Tunnel area on which frequency?

A. 147.45 MHz
B. 162.55 MHz
C. 181.15 MHz
D. 202.35 MHz

15107. At 1752, your position is LAT
37°04.3'N, LONG 76°06.4'W. On a flood

current you should expect to be set to
the _____.
A. north-northwest
B. south-southwest
C. east-southeast
D. east

15108. Your 1752 position places you

_____.
A. less than 0.5 mile westward of York Spit
Channel
B. less than 0.5 mile eastward of York Spit
Channel
C. greater than 0.5 mile westward of York
Spit Channel
D. greater than 0.5 mile eastward of York
Spit Channel

15109. What is the average velocity of the
maximum flood current at the Tail of the
Horseshoe?

A. 0.6 knot
B. 0.9 knot
C. 1.3 knots
D. 1.6 knots

15110. From your 1752 position, you steer
307° pgc at 9 knots. At 1805, you obtain the
following visual bearings: Old Pt. Comfort
Light—232° pgc; Chesapeake Bay Tunnel
North Light—130° pgc. What are the latitude and longitude of your 1805 position?

A. LAT 37°06.1'N, LONG 76°08.1'W
B. LAT 37°06.0'N, LONG 76°08.4'W
C. LAT 37°05.9'N, LONG 76°07.7'W
D. LAT 37°05.9'N, LONG 76°08.0'W

15111. At 1810, you sight a buoy on your
starboard side labeled 19. This buoy marks
_____.

A. a submerged obstruction in York Spit
Channel
B. the visibility limit of the red sector of
Cape Henry Light
C. the side of York Spit Channel
D. the junction of the York Spit and York
River Entrance Channels

15112. Based on a DR, at approximately
1817 you would expect to _____.

A. enter a traffic separation zone
B. depart a regulated area
C. cross a submerged pipeline
D. depart a restricted area

15113. At 1845, you obtain a loran fix using
the following information: 9960-X-27252.0;
9960-Y-41432.0; 9960-Z-58537.5. Your latitude is _____.

A. 37°10.7'N
B. 37°10.9'N
C. 37°11.0'N
D. 37°11.2'N

15114. Your 1900 position is LAT 37°12.9'N,
LONG 76°13.5'W. You change course to
317° pgc and slow to 8.0 knots. What is the
course per standard magnetic compass?

A. 331° psc
B. 329° psc
C. 311° psc
D. 309° psc

15115. If the visibility is 11 miles, what is the luminous range of New Point Comfort Spit Light 4?

A. 0.5 mile
B. 3.8 miles
C. 4.3 miles
D. 5.0 miles

15116. According to your track line, how far off New Point Comfort Spit Light 4 will you be when abeam of this light?

A. 0.9 mile
B. 1.2 miles
C. 1.5 miles
D. 1.8 miles

15117. At 1930, you take a fix using the following radar ranges: York Spit Light—3.6 miles; New Point Comfort Spit Light 2—2.0 miles; York Spit Swash Channel Light 3—2.5 miles. Your longitude is _____.

A. 76°16.5'W
B. 76°16.8'W
C. 76°17.0'W
D. 76°17.2'W

15118. What was the speed made good from 1845 to 1930?

A. 6.2 knots
B. 7.5 knots
C. 8.3 knots
D. 9.4 knots

15119. What is the height above water of Davis Creek Channel Light 1?

A. 6 feet (1.8 meters)
B. 15 feet (4.6 meters)
C. 17 feet (5.2 meters)
D. 24 feet (7.3 meters)

15120. If you have 17.3 miles to reach your destination from your 2000 position and want to be there at 2230, what speed should you make good?

A. 5.7 knots
B. 6.1 knots
C. 6.5 knots
D. 6.9 knots

The following questions are to be answered using chart 13205 TR, Block Island Sound, and supporting publications. Your vessel is on a course of 048°T with a speed of 13.5 knots. Your draft is 39 feet and your height of eye is 58 feet.

15138. At 2045 you obtained the following Loran readings: 9960-W-14844.0; 9960-X-26128.0; 9960-Y-43712.5. What is your vessel's position?

A. 40°41.1'N, 72°10.5'W
B. 40°41.4'N, 72°10.7'W
C. 40°41.8'N, 72°10.8'W
D. 40°42.3'N, 72°11.3'W

15139. At what time would you expect to be abeam of Buoy MP?

A. 2240
B. 2244
C. 2248
D. 2252

15140. At 2100 your position is 40°44.1'N, 72°07.6'W. From this position, at which time will Montauk Point Light become visible if the luminous range of the light is 8 miles?

A. 2215
B. 2221
C. 2227
D. 2235

15141. At 2146 your position is 40°51.3'N, 71°59.2'W. If your engine speed has been 13 knots, what were the set and drift of the current you encountered since your 2100 position?

A. 115° true at 1.1 knots
B. 115° true at 1.5 knots
C. 295° true at 1.1 knots
D. 295° true at 1.5 knots

15142. At 2146 if your fathometer is set on feet, what should be the approximate reading on your fathometer?

A. 88 feet
B. 105 feet
C. 121 feet
D. 166 feet

15143. From your 2146 position, with a new engine speed of 12 knots, you wish to change course in order to pass southeast of Buoy MP at a distance of 2 miles. With a reported set of 320° true and a drift of 2 knots, which course should you steer to make good your desired course?

A. 055° true
B. 061° true
C. 066° true
D. 071° true

15144. At 2310 Buoy MP bears 305° true with a radar range of 2.5 miles, and you obtained a Loran reading of 9960-Y-43823.3. From this position you change course to 005° true. Without any set and drift, what would be your predicted distance off Southwest Ledge Buoy 2 when it is on your starboard beam?

A. 0.9 mile
B. 1.1 miles
C. 1.5 miles
D. 1.9 miles

15145. At 2357 your position is 41°09.0'N, 71°47.0'W and Montauk Point Light bears 216° true. You change to a course of 293° true and your speed is 14.5 knots. At 0012 Montauk Point Light bears 177° true. Which statement about your 0012 running fix is TRUE?

A. You are being set to the north.
B. The fathometer reading is about 14 fathoms.
C. You are governed by the Inland Rules of the Road.
D. The fathometer trace shows you passed over the 89 foot sounding.

15146. At 0016 your position is 41°10.3'N, 71°53.0'W. You are steering a course of 296° true with no set and drift. At 0049 Race Rock Light is on your starboard beam. What was your speed made good from your 0016 position?

A. 13.8 knots
B. 14.4 knots
C. 15.0 knots
D. 15.6 knots

The following questions should be answered using chart 12221TR, Chesapeake Bay Entrance, and the supporting publications. The draft of your vessel is 14 feet (4.2 meters). The gyro error is 3°W. "Per standard magnetic compass" is abbreviated "psc." Use a variation of 10°W for the entire plot. The deviation table is:

HDG.	M.DEV.	HDG.	M.DEV.	HDG.	M.DEV.
000°	2.0°E	120°	1.0°W	240°	0.5°W
030°	1.0°E	150°	2.0°W	270°	0.5°E
060°	0°	180°	2.0°W	300°	1.5°E
090°	0.5°W	210°	1.0°W	330°	2.5°E

15156. Your 1600 position is LAT 37°22.5'N, LONG 75°32.3'W. The depth of water is about _____.

A. 38 feet (11.5 meters)
B. 45 feet (13.6 meters)
C. 52 feet (15.8 meters)
D. 59 feet (17.3 meters)

15157. If there is no current, what is the course per gyrocompass from your 1600 position to point A located 0.5 mile due east of Hog Island Lighted Bell Buoy 12?

A. 190° pgc
B. 193° pgc
C. 196° pgc
D. 199° pgc

15158. At 1630, you reach point A and come right to 204°T. Your engine speed is 12 knots. Your 1715 position is LAT 37°09.8'N, LONG 75°37.4'W. The current was _____.

A. 067°T at 1.1 knots
B. 067°T at 1.5 knots
C. 247°T at 1.1 knots
D. 247°T at 1.6 knots

15159. From your 1715 fix you steer 214°T at 12 knots. At 1800 you take the following Loran-C readings: 9960-X-27116.8; 9960-Y-41386.0; 9960-Z-58620.6. Your 1800 position is _____.

A. LAT 37°02.8'N, LONG 75°43.9'W
B. LAT 37°02.9'N, LONG 75°43.1'W
C. LAT 37°03.0'N, LONG 75°43.3'W
D. LAT 37°03.1'N, LONG 75°42.8'W

15160. At 1815, your position is LAT 37°01.0'N, LONG 75°42.7'W. If there is no current, what is the course per standard magnetic compass to arrive at a point 0.3 mile due north of North Chesapeake Entrance Lighted Whistle Buoy NCA?

A. 249.0° psc
B. 251.5° psc
C. 255.0° psc
D. 257.0° psc

15161. From your 1815 position, you want to make good course 263°T. Your engines are turning RPMs for 12 knots. The current is 050°T at 1.9 knots. Adjusting your course for set and drift, at what time should you expect to enter the red sector of Cape Henry Light?

A. 1851
B. 1857
C. 1904
D. 1911

15162. At 1920, Cape Henry Light bears 231° pgc, and Chesapeake Channel Tunnel North Light bears 294° pgc. If your heading is 268°T, what is the relative bearing of Chesapeake Light?

A. 213°
B. 201°
C. 194°
D. 179°

15163. Which statement concerning your 1920 position is TRUE?

A. You are entering a restricted area.
B. You are governed by the Inland Rules of the Road.
C. You are within the Chesapeake Bay Entrance traffic separation scheme.
D. On your present course Trestle C of the Chesapeake Bay Bridge–Tunnel is dead ahead.

15164. From your 1920 position, you change course to enter Chesapeake Channel between buoys 9 and 10. What is the course per gyrocompass?

A. 271° pgc
B. 274° pgc
C. 277° pgc
D. 280° pgc

15165. At 2000, your position is LAT 37°04.1'N, LONG 76°05.6'W. You change course for the Eastern Shore. At 2037, Old Plantation Flats Light bears 033° pgc, and York Spit Light bears 282° pgc. The course made good from your 2000 position was

_____.

A. 006°T
B. 014°T
C. 020°T
D. 028°T

15166. At 2037, you change course and wish to make good a course of 016°T. There is no current, but an easterly wind is causing 3° leeway. What course per standard magnetic compass should you steer to make good the course 016°T?

A. 022° psc
B. 025° psc
C. 028° psc
D. 031° psc

15167. Your height of eye is 25 feet (7.6 meters). If the visibility is 11 nautical miles,

what is the luminous range of Wolf Trap Light?

A. 8.2 miles
B. 12.0 miles
C. 16.0 miles
D. 17.0 miles

15168. Which chart provides more detail of Cape Charles harbor and its approaches?

A. 12238
B. 12225
C. 12224
D. 12222

15169. At 2123, your position is LAT 37°20.0'N, LONG 76°03.0'W. What is your distance offshore of Savage Neck?

A. 1.7 miles
B. 2.5 miles
C. 3.6 miles
D. 10.9 miles

15170. From your 2123 position, you are approximately 42 miles from Crisfield, MD. If you are making good a speed of 11 knots, at what time should you arrive at Crisfield, MD?

A. 2359
B. 0037
C. 0112
D. 0149

The following questions are based on chart 12221TR, Chesapeake Bay Entrance, and the supporting publications. Your vessel has a draft of 8.0 feet (2.4 meters). Use 10°W variation where required. The gyro error is 2°W. Your height of eye is 26 feet. The deviation table is:

HDG.	M.DEV.	HDG.	M.DEV.	HDG.	M.DEV.
000°	0°	120°	2°W	240°	3°E
030°	1°W	150°	1°W	270°	3°E
060°	2°W	180°	1°E	300°	2°E
090°	4°W	210°	2°E	330°	1°E

15206. At 1730, your position is LAT 37°13.9'N, LONG 76°26.4'W. You are steering course 088° per standard magnetic compass (psc) at an engine speed of 8.0 knots. What is your distance off Tue Marshes Light at 1730?

A. 2.6 miles
B. 2.8 miles

C. 3.0 miles
D. 3.2 miles

15207. What is the maximum allowable speed of vessels underway up river from Tue Marshes Light?

A. 6 knots
B. 8 knots
C. 10 knots
D. 12 knots

15208. At 1750, your position is LAT 37°14.5'N, LONG 76°22.9'W. What was the course made good between 1730 and 1750?

A. 072°T
B. 075°T
C. 078°T
D. 080°T

15209. At 1800, Tue Marshes Light bears 264.5° pgc, York Spit Swash Channel Light 3 bears 007° pgc. Your position is _____.

A. LAT 37°15.5'N, LONG 76°19.8'W
B. LAT 37°15.2'N, LONG 76°20.3'W
C. LAT 37°15.0'N, LONG 76°20.0'W
D. LAT 37°14.5'N, LONG 76°20.1'W

15210. What course should you steer per standard magnetic compass in order to navigate down the center of York River Entrance Channel (ignore set and drift)?

A. 139° psc
B. 141° psc
C. 147° psc
D. 149° psc

15211. You have just passed York River Entrance Channel Lighted Buoys 13 and 14. The chart shows a light approximately

1.0 mile off your port beam with a light characteristic Fl 6 sec. What is the name of this light?
A. Mobjack Bay Entrance Light
B. New Point Comfort Shoal Light
C. York Spit Light
D. York River Entrance Channel Light 1

15212. At 1930, your vessel is between York River Entrance Channel Lighted Buoys 1YR and 2. From this position, you change course to 142° pgc at an engine speed of 8.0 knots. At 2001, you obtain the following information: Chesapeake Channel Tunnel North Light—131° pgc; Thimble Shoal

Light—248° pgc. What were the set and drift between 1930 and 2001?

A. 127° at 1.1 knots
B. 127° at 0.5 knot
C. 307° at 1.1 knots
D. 307° at 0.5 knot

15213. At 2015, your vessel is at the Chesapeake Bay Bridge and Tunnel midway between buoys 13 and 14. If the height of tide is –1 foot (–0.3 meter), what is the approximate depth of water?

A. 53 feet (15.5 meters)
B. 46 feet (13.9 meters)
C. 40 feet (12.1 meters)
D. 35 feet (10.6 meters)

15214. If you steer 143° pgc from your 2015 position at an engine speed of 8.0 knots, at what time would you reach a point midway between buoys 11 and 12 (ignore set and drift)?

A. 2023
B. 2029
C. 2032
D. 2037

15215. At 2015, you alter course to 154° pgc. What is the course per standard magnetic compass (psc)?

A. 162° psc
B. 157° psc
C. 152° psc
D. 142° psc

15216. Which of the following concerning Thimble Shoal Channel is TRUE?

A. Only deep-draft passenger ships and large naval vessels may use the main channel.
B. The channel is 14.5 miles in length.
C. A tow drawing 20 feet is excluded from the main channel.
D. Thimble Shoal Channel is in international waters.

15217. At 2118, you obtain the following bearings: Cape Henry Light—148° pgc; Cape Charles Light—033° pgc; Thimble Shoal Light—291° pgc. From this position, you proceed to Norfolk, VA, a distance of approximately 26.0 miles. To arrive at Norfolk at 0200 the next day, what is the speed to make good from your 2118 position to arrive at this time?

A. 5.0 knots
B. 5.5 knots
C. 6.0 knots
D. 6.5 knots

15218. What is your 2118 position?

A. LAT 36°57.0'N, LONG 76°01.5'W
B. LAT 36°57.4'N, LONG 76°01.9'W
C. LAT 36°57.8'N, LONG 76°01.5'W
D. LAT 36°58.2'N, LONG 76°02.4'W

15219. From your 2118 position, you steer a course of 288°T at an engine speed of 7.0 knots. At 2120 visibility is suddenly reduced to 2 miles. At what time can you expect to see Old Point Comfort Light?

A. 2136
B. 2143
C. 2202
D. 2228

15220. If the Old Point Comfort main light was inoperative what emergency light would be shown?

A. Flashing yellow
B. Alternating red and white
C. Light of reduced intensity
D. Strobe light

The following questions are to be answered using chart 12354 TR, Long Island Sound - Eastern Part, and supporting publications. Your vessel is enroute to to New Haven, CT. You are proceeding at a reduced speed of 9.8 knots on a course of 243°T. Your height of eye is 45 feet and your vessel's deep draft is 33 feet.

15238. At 0930 you obtain a position from the following information: Race Rock Light bears 110°T at a range of 1.4 miles, and Goshen Point bears 330°T at a range of 3.3 miles. What are your present latitude and longitude?

A. 41°16.0'N, 72°09.5'W
B. 41°15.1'N, 72°04.6'W
C. 41°17.4'N, 72°06.0'W
D. 41°14.6'N, 72°03.0'W

15239. At 1000 buoy PI is abeam to starboard a distance of 0.5 mile. From this position, with a set of 295°and a drift of 1.6 knots, what course must you steer to arrive at a point with Buoy TE one mile abeam to starboard?

A. 247°T
B. 249°T
C. 251°T
D. 253°T

15240. You take a Loran-C fix at 1130 using the following lines: 9960-X-26319; 9960-W-4880. The fathometer reads 81 ft. Your position is _____.

A. north of your intended track line
B. 41°09.4'N, 72°22.6'W
C. three miles southeast of Six Mile Reef Buoy 8A
D. 41°08.5'N, 72°27.3'W

15241. At 1155 your vessel's position is LAT 41°09.0'N, LONG 72°34.4'W. If you make good a course of 282°T and a speed of 10.0 knots, when will you arrive at New Haven Harbor Lighted Bell Buoy NH?

A. 1315
B. 1320
C. 1325
D. 1330

15242. From your 1155 position, you steer a course of 282°T at a speed of 9.5 knots. You obtain the following bearings: 1205—Falkner Island Light bears 318°T; 1225—Falkner Island Light bears 355°T. Your 1225 running fix is _____.

A. north of your intended track
B. 3.1 miles SSW of Falkner Island Light
C. ahead of the DR position
D. south of your intended track

15243. At 1245 the loran readings obtained show your position to be LAT 41°10.3'N, LONG 72°44.2'W. You are steering a course of 284°T at an engine speed of 13.0 knots. At what time would you expect the New Haven Harbor Outer Range to be in line if you have a current setting 112°T at 1.2 knots?

A. 1318
B. 1323
C. 1328
D. 1343

15244. At the time of your 1245 position, which statement is TRUE?

A. Your fathometer should indicate a reading of approximately 47 feet.
B. Bradford Reef is 5.7 miles on the starboard bow.

C. You are in a danger area.
D. You must follow the International Rules of the Road.

15245. After departing the New Haven terminals, your 1800 position puts the New Haven Harbor Lighted Bell Buoy NH bearing 130°T at a range of 0.2 mile. From this position you set a course to leave Stratford Shoal Middle Ground Light 1.0 mile off your starboard beam. Your speed is 12.5 knots. At 1845 you determine your position to be LAT 41°05.5'N; LONG 73°03.1'W. What were the set and drift of the current?

A. 294°T at 0.5 knot
B. 294°T at 0.8 knot
C. 114°T at 0.5 knot
D. 114°T at 0.8 knot

15246. From your 1845 position, you desire to leave Stratford Shoal Middle Ground Light 1.0 mile off your starboard beam at 1900. Which course and speed would you order if you allow for a 2.0 knot current with a set of 180°T?

A. 205°T at 9.2 knots
B. 208°T at 11.4 knots
C. 215°T at 9.2 knots
D. 225°T at 11.5 knots

The following questions should be answered using chart 12354TR, Long Island Sound - Eastern Part, and supporting publications. The draft of your vessel is 11 feet (3.3 meters). Gyro error is 3°W. "Per standard magnetic compass" is abbreviated "psc." Use a variation of 14°W for the entire plot. The deviation table is:

HDG.	M.DEV.	HDG.	M.DEV.	HDG.	M.DEV.
000°	2.0°E	120°	1.0°W	240°	0.5°W
030°	1.0°E	150°	2.0°W	270°	0.5°E
060°	0.0°	180°	2.0°W	300°	1.5°E
090°	0.5°W	210°	1.0°W	330°	2.5°E

15256. At 0700, Stratford Shoal Middle Ground Light bears 143° pgc at 1.8 miles. What is your 0700 position?

A. LAT 41°04.8'N, LONG 73°06.7'W
B. LAT 41°05.0'N, LONG 73°07.6'W
C. LAT 41°05.1'N, LONG 73°06.8'W
D. LAT 41°05.3'N, LONG 73°07.9'W

15257. At 0725, Stratford Point Light bears 327° pgc at 3.1 miles. At this time, you wish to change course to 048°T. The current is 135°T at 1.8 knots. Your engine speed is 8

knots. What course must you steer to make good 048°T?

A. 035°T
B. 038°T
C. 041°T
D. 044°T

15258. Which structure should you look for while trying to locate Stratford Point Light?

A. White conical tower with a brown band midway of height
B. White octagonal house on a cylindrical pier
C. Conical tower, upper half white, lower half brown
D. Black skeleton tower on a granite dwelling

15259. At 0830, you obtain the following Loran-C readings: 9960-W-15043.1; 9960-Y-44028.1. What is your vessel's position?

A. LAT 41°12.1'N, LONG 73°53.8'W
B. LAT 40°12.2'N, LONG 73°54.4'W
C. LAT 41°12.3'N, LONG 72°53.6'W
D. LAT 41°12.4'N, LONG 72°54.0'W

15260. From your 0830 position, you wish to make good 097°T. There is no current, but a southerly wind is producing 4° leeway. What course should you steer per standard magnetic compass in order to make good your true course?

A. 101° psc
B. 108° psc
C. 110° psc
D. 115° psc

15261. You make good 097°T from your 0830 fix. With a westerly current of 1.2 knots, what engine speed will you have to turn from your 0830 position in order to arrive abeam of Six Mile Reef Buoy 8C at 1030?

A. 9.7 knots
B. 10.5 knots
C. 10.9 knots
D. 12.1 knots

15262. At 0910, your DR position is LAT 41°11.9'N, LONG 72°47.8'W. Your vessel is on course 097°T at 9.5 knots, and the weather is foggy. At 0915, Branford Reef Light is sighted through a break in the fog bearing 318°T. At 0945, Falkner Island Light is sighted bearing 042°T. What is your 0945 running fix position?

A. LAT 41°11.3′N, LONG 72°41.2′W
B. LAT 41°11.3′N, LONG 72°41.0′W
C. LAT 41°11.5′N, LONG 72°40.7′W
D. LAT 41°11.6′N, LONG 72°41.0′W

15263. What do the dotted lines around Goose Island and Kimberly Reef represent?

A. Danger soundings
B. Breakers
C. Tide rips
D. Depth contours

15264. At 1100, your position is LAT 41°11.3′N, LONG 72°28.0′W. You are steering a course of 069°T to leave Black Point one mile off your port beam. It has been reported that the Long Sand Shoal Buoys and Hatchett Reef Buoys are off station. What will serve to keep your vessel in safe water and away from these hazards?

A. Danger bearing to Black Point of not less than 065°T
B. A Loran reading of not more than 9960-Y-43982.0
C. A bearing to Little Gull Island Light of not less than 090°
D. A distance to Saybrook Breakwater Light of not less than 1.3 miles

15265. Orient Point Light is _____.

A. lighted only during daytime when the sound signal is in operation
B. maintained only from May 1 to Oct. 1
C. 64 feet (19.4 meters) above mean low water
D. lighted throughout 24 hours

15266. At 1210, you are in position LAT 41°14.3′N, LONG 72°16.5′W. What is the charted depth of water?

A. 97 feet (29.4 meters)
B. 108 feet (32.7 meters)
C. 119 feet (36.1 meters)
D. 125 feet (37.9 meters)

15267. From your 1210 position, you are making good a course of 083°T. Your engines are turning RPMs for 10 knots. The set and drift of the current are 310° at 1.7 knots. At what time should you expect to enter the red sector of New London Harbor Light?

A. 1243
B. 1249
C. 1253
D. 1301

15268. Your vessel is proceeding up New London Harbor Channel, and you are in line with the range. What would be your course per standard magnetic compass?

A. 352°
B. 354°
C. 002°
D. 007°

15269. New London Harbor is _____.

A. limited to vessels drawing less than 36 feet (10.8 meters)
B. closed during the winter season
C. subject to dangerous freshets in the fall
D. difficult to enter at night

15270. The distance from New London to the east entrance of the Cape Cod Canal is _____.

A. 66 miles
B. 77 miles
C. 89 miles
D. 136 miles

The following questions are based on chart 12221TR, Chesapeake Bay Entrance, and the supporting publications. The draft of your tow is 27 feet (8.2 meters). Use 10°W variation where required. There is no gyro error. The deviation table is:

HDG.	M.DEV.	HDG.	M.DEV.	HDG.	M.DEV.
000°	0°	120°	2°W	240°	3°E
030°	1°W	150°	1°W	270°	3°E
060°	2°W	180°	1°E	300°	2°E
090°	4°W	210°	2°E	330°	1°E

15306. Your 0200 position is LAT 37°23.5′N, LONG 76°09.2′W. Your speed is 8 knots, and your course is 095°T. Which statement is TRUE?

A. The depth of the water in your vicinity is about 38 to 40 fathoms (69.1 meters to 72.7 meters).
B. You are less than a mile from a sunken wreck which could interfere with your tow.
C. The closest major aid to navigation is New Point Comfort Light.
D. You will pass through a disposal area on your present course.

15307. At 0315, you obtain the following loran readings: 9960-Y-41588.0; 9960-X-27240.0. What is the true course from this position to the entrance of York Spit Channel?

A. 203°
B. 208°
C. 211°
D. 217°

15308. From your 0315 position, what time can you expect to reach York Spit Channel Buoys 37 and 38?

A. 0405
B. 0412
C. 0417
D. 0423

15309. The engineer has advised that it will be necessary to secure the gyrocompass and the electronic equipment. From your 0315 position, what is your course per standard magnetic compass to York Spit Channel Buoy 38, if there is no current?

A. 212° psc
B. 214° psc
C. 216° psc
D. 218° psc

15310. Which chart could you use for greater detail of the area at the south end of York Spit Channel?

A. 12222
B. 12224
C. 12226
D. 12254

15311. You leave York Spit Channel at buoy 14 at 0600 with an engine speed of 12 knots. You receive orders to rendezvous with the tug Quicksilver and her tow at Hog Island Bell Buoy 12. What is your ETA at the rendezvous point, if you pass through Chesapeake Channel to buoy CBJ, through the outbound traffic separation lane to buoy NCA (LL#375), and then to the rendezvous point?

A. 0830
B. 0850
C. 0910
D. 0935

15312. You arrive at the rendezvous point, secure the tow, and head back southward. At 1200, you take the following loran readings: 9960-Y-41534; 9960-X-27114; 9960-Z-58691. What is your 1200 position?

A. LAT 37°10.5′N, LONG 75°33.0′W
B. LAT 37°12.0′N, LONG 75°35.0′W
C. LAT 37°15.0′N, LONG 75°37.5′W
D. LAT 37°19.0′N, LONG 75°40.5′W

15313. From your noon position, if there is no set and drift, what is your course per standard magnetic compass to the NCA (LL 375) buoy?

A. 215° psc
B. 217° psc
C. 219° psc
D. 221° psc

15314. Your gyro and electronic gear are again operating. At 1710, Chesapeake Light bears 137° pgc at 6.6 miles. The current is setting 160°T at 2 knots. At your speed of 6 knots, what is your true course to steer to remain in the inbound traffic lane?

A. 269°
B. 265°
C. 261°
D. 250°

15315. At 1810, you obtain the following loran readings: 9960-X-27158.0; 9960-Y-41292.5; 9960-Z-58546.9. What is your position?

A. LAT 36°56.0'N, LONG 75°58.5'W
B. LAT 36°55.4'N, LONG 75°56.0'W
C. LAT 36°54.9'N, LONG 75°53.8'W
D. LAT 36°56.8'N, LONG 75°55.6'W

15316. What speed have you made good from 1710 to 1810?

A. 4.2 knots
B. 4.9 knots
C. 5.5 knots
D. 6.3 knots

15317. If you make good a speed of 6.0 knots from your 1810 position, what is your ETA at Chesapeake Channel Lighted Bell Buoy 2C?

A. 1833
B. 1845
C. 1855
D. 1900

15318. You passed Cape Henry Light at 0730 outbound at maximum flood. What approximate current can you expect on entering Chesapeake Channel?

A. Slack before ebb
B. Slack before flood
C. Ebb current
D. Flood current

15319. The coastline by Cape Henry is best described as _____.

A. rocky with pine scrubs
B. sandy hills about eighty feet high
C. low wetlands
D. low and thinly wooded with many beach houses

15320. Inbound, the color of Cape Henry Light will _____.

A. change before you reach Chesapeake Channel Lighted Bell Buoy 2C
B. change after you reach Chesapeake Channel Lighted Bell Buoy 2C
C. remain the same
D. alternate regardless of your position

The following questions are to be answered using chart 13205 TR, Block Island Sound, and supporting publications. Your vessel is on a course of 090°T with a speed of 14 knots. Your draft is 37 feet and your height of eye is 56 feet.

15338. At 1705 Race Rock Light bears 099° true; Orient Point Light bears 176° true; Bartlett Reef Light bears 083° true. What is your vessel's position?

A. LAT 41°15.0'N, LONG 72°14.3'W
B. LAT 41°15.4'N, LONG 72°16.6'W
C. LAT 41°15.9'N, LONG 72°14.0'W
D. LAT 41°16.4'N, LONG 72°14.2'W

15339. If there is no set or drift, at what time would you be abeam of Bartlett Reef Light?

A. 1719
B. 1724
C. 1729
D. 1734

15340. At 1718, Bartlett Reef Light bears 050°T at a distance of 1.5 miles. From this position, you change course to 128°T. At 1750 Race Rock Light bears 336°T, Little Gull Island Light bears 285°T, and Montauk Point Light bears 134°T. What were the set and drift of the current you encountered since 1718?

A. 245°T at 0.9 knot
B. 245°T at 1.7 knots
C. 065°T at 1.7 knots
D. 065°T at 0.9 knot

15341. If your fathometer is set on fathoms, what should your fathometer read at 1750?

A. 8.5 fathoms
B. 10.2 fathoms
C. 14.7 fathoms
D. 51.0 fathoms

15342. At 1756 you determined your vessel's position to be 41°10.4'N, 71°59.2'W. From this position, you wish to change course to head for a point 5 miles west of Block Island North Light. With a reported set of 050°T, a drift of 2.0 knots and turning RPMs for 14 knots, which course should you steer to make good your desired course?

A. 070°T
B. 075°T
C. 080°T
D. 085°T

15343. At 1844 you obtained the following Loran readings: 9960-W-14607; 9960-X-25962; 9960-Y-43920. Which statement is TRUE?

A. Watch Hill Point is abeam.
B. You are governed by the Inland Rules of the Road.
C. You are to the left (north) of your desired course line.
D. Your vessel is approximately 8.7 miles off Sandy Point.

15344. From your 1850 position of 41°12.8'N, 71°44.1'W, you change course to 060°T. If you make the course good, what will be your predicted distance off Point Judith Light when the light bears 015°T?

A. 1.2 miles
B. 1.9 miles
C. 2.7 miles
D. 3.4 miles

15345. You are making good a course of 060°T at a speed of 13.5 knots. At 1855 Block Island North Light bears 086°T; at 1910 Block Island North Light bears 108°T; and at 1930 the same light bears 184°T. Which statement is TRUE about your 1930 running fix position?

A. You are on the edge of a cable area.
B. The bottom is mud, sand, and clay.
C. The wavy magenta lines to the north through east of your position are designated lobstering areas.

D. Following a Loran-C reading of 9960-Y-43941 or more will keep you to the south of Point Judith Buoy 2.

15346. At 1942 Point Judith bears 030°T and has a range of 3.6 miles and Sandy Point has a range of 5.3 miles. What was your speed made good from your 1850 position?

A. 12.5 knots
B. 13.4 knots
C. 14.0 knots
D. 14.5 knots

The following questions should be answered using chart 12354TR, Long Island Sound - Eastern Part, and supporting publications. The draft of your vessel is 12 feet (3.6 meters) and your height of eye is 16 feet (4.8 meters). Gyro error is 2°W. "Per standard magnetic compass" is abbreviated "psc." Use a variation of 14°W for the entire plot. The deviation table is:

HDG.	M.DEV.	HDG.	M.DEV.	HDG.	M.DEV.
000°	0°	120°	2°W	240°	3°E
030°	1°W	150°	1°W	270°	3°E
060°	2°W	180°	1°E	300°	2°E
090°	4°W	210°	2°E	330°	1°E

15356. You are on course 092°T, and the engines are turning for 8 knots. At 0452, you take the following bearings: Stratford Point Light—020° pgc; Stratford Shoal (Middle Ground) Light—141° pgc. What is your 0452 position?

A. LAT 41°05.4′N, LONG 73°07.7′W
B. LAT 41°05.2′N, LONG 73°07.8′W
C. LAT 41°05.2′N, LONG 73°07.5′W
D. LAT 41°05.1′N, LONG 73°07.7′W

15357. If the visibility is 10 miles, what is the earliest time you can expect to see New Haven Light?

A. The light is visible at 0452.
B. 0458
C. 0510
D. You will not sight the light.

15358. At 0507, Stratford Shoal Middle Ground Light bears 208° pgc. What is the position of your 0507 running fix?

A. LAT 41°04.8′N, LONG 73°05.0′W
B. LAT 41°04.9′N, LONG 73°04.8′W
C. LAT 41°05.1′N, LONG 73°05.1′W
D. LAT 41°05.3′N, LONG 73°04.8′W

15359. Based on your running fix, you _____.

A. have a head current
B. have a following current
C. are being set to the north
D. are not affected by a current

15360. Your 0507 position is about 7 miles from Bridgeport, CT. What is the distance from this position to Newport, RI?

A. 88 miles
B. 95 miles
C. 101 miles
D. 114 miles

15361. Your 0530 position is LAT 41°04.9′N, LONG 73°01.1′W. What is the course per standard magnetic compass to a position 1.0 mile south of Twenty Eight Foot Shoal TE buoy?

A. 082.0° psc
B. 092.5° psc
C. 096.0° psc
D. 099.5° psc

15362. The south shore of Long Island Sound near your position is _____.

A. marked by gradual shoaling
B. low and marshy
C. backed by marshes and wooded uplands
D. bluff and rocky

15363. At 0530, you change course to 090°T and increase speed to 8.5 knots. What is the course to steer per gyrocompass if northerly winds are causing 2° leeway?

A. 088° pgc
B. 090° pgc
C. 092° pgc
D. 094° pgc

15364. At 0615, Stratford Point Light bears 292° pgc, Falkner Island Light bears 052° pgc, and Branford Reef Light bears 018° pgc. What was the current since 0530?

A. 083° at 1.2 knots
B. 083° at 0.9 knot
C. 263° at 1.2 knots
D. 263° at 0.9 knot

15365. Which loran line can you follow to remain clear of all danger until south of New London?

A. 9960-W-15000
B. 9960-W-14900
C. 9960-X-26450
D. 9960-Y-43960

15366. At 0615 you change course to 078°T. If there is no current, when will Falkner Island Light be abeam?

A. 0750
B. 0743
C. 0735
D. 0730

15367. At 0700, Falkner Island Light bears 023° pgc, and the range to the south tip of Falkner Island is 7.1 miles. What was the course made good since 0615?

A. 078°T
B. 081°T
C. 084°T
D. 087°T

15368. At 0705, the gyro loses power. At 0730, you are on course 092° per standard magnetic compass (psc). Falkner Light bears 356° psc, Horton Point Light bears 123° psc, and Kelsey Point Breakwater Light bears 048° psc. What is the position of your 0730 fix?

A. LAT 41°06.7′N, LONG 72°36.1′W
B. LAT 41°06.8′N, LONG 72°36.0′W
C. LAT 41°07.0′N, LONG 72°36.2′W
D. LAT 41°07.2′N, LONG 72°36.1′W

15369. Horton Point Light _____.

A. is shown from a white square tower
B. has a fixed green light
C. is 14 feet above sea level
D. is sychronized with a radiobeacon

15370. If visibility permits, Little Gull Island Light will break the horizon at a range of approximately _____.

A. 11.1 miles
B. 12.8 miles
C. 15.6 miles
D. 18.0 miles

The following questions are based on chart 12221TR, Chesapeake Bay Entrance, and the supporting publications. Your vessel has a draft of 9.0 feet (2.7 meters). Your height of eye is 15 feet (4.6 meters). Use 10°W variation where required. The gyro error is 2°W. The deviation table is:

HDG.	M.DEV.	HDG.	M.DEV.	HDG.	M.DEV.
000°	0°	120°	2°W	240°	3°E
030°	1°W	150°	1°W	270°	3°E
060°	2°W	180°	1°E	300°	2°E
090°	4°W	210°	2°E	330°	1°E

15406. At 1400, your position is LAT 37°14.7'N, LONG 76°22.3'W. From this position, you head for the York River Entrance Channel Buoy 17. What should you steer per standard magnetic compass for this heading?

A. 108° psc
B. 119° psc
C. 122° psc
D. 125° psc

15407. At 1430, your position is LAT 37°12.8'N, LONG 76°17.7'W. At this time, you come left and steer 045°T. This course will lead you through a channel bordered by yellow buoys. The dashed magenta lines between the buoys mark _____.

A. York River Entrance Channel
B. New Point Comfort shoal area
C. the piloting channel for Mobjack Bay
D. the limits of fish trap areas

15408. From your 1430 fix, you order turns for 8 knots. You steer 045°T and experience no set and drift. At what time would you expect to have New Point Comfort Spit Light 4 abeam?

A. 1452
B. 1458
C. 1504
D. 1510

15409. At 1540, your position is LAT 37°18.4'N, LONG 76°10.5'W. Which course should you steer per gyrocompass to head for the entrance to Cape Charles City?

A. 109° pgc
B. 117° pgc
C. 123° pgc
D. 129° pgc

15410. You arrive at Cape Charles City at 1700 and depart at 1800. You are underway in Chesapeake Bay and encounter heavy fog. At 1830, you obtain the following Loran-C readings: 9960-X-27224; 9960-Y-41456; 9960-Z-58572. What is your 1830 position?

A. LAT 37°10.3'N, LONG 76°04.5'W
B. LAT 37°10.3'N, LONG 76°06.5'W
C. LAT 37°12.3'N, LONG 76°04.4'W
D. LAT 37°12.3'N, LONG 76°06.5'W

15411. From your 1830 fix, you continue south on a course of 150°T turning RPMs for 6 knots. You encounter a flood current in the direction of 330°T at 2 knots. Adjusting your course for set and drift, which course would you steer to make good a course of 150°T while turning RPMs for 6 knots?

A. 144°T
B. 150°T
C. 158°T
D. 162°T

15412. Determine your 1915 position using the following information obtained at 1915: Visual bearings—Cape Charles Light, 107° pgc; Cape Henry Light, 172° pgc. Radar Bearing and Range: Chesapeake Channel Tunnel South Light,189° pgc at 7.2 miles.

A. LAT 37°03.5'N, LONG 76°05.9'W
B. LAT 37°03.5'N, LONG 76°09.3'W
C. LAT 37°05.9'N, LONG 76°03.5'W
D. LAT 37°09.3'N, LONG 76°03.1'W

15413. From your 1915 fix you come right and steer a course of 200°T. At 2000, your position is LAT 37°05.5'N, LONG 76°07.0'W. Your intention is to pass through Chesapeake Channel. If there are no set and drift, what course would you steer per standard magnetic compass to make good a course of 145°T?

A. 134°
B. 139°
C. 151°
D. 156°

15414. At 2100, you have passed through the Chesapeake Bay Bridge and Tunnel and determine your position to be LAT 37°01.3'N, LONG 76°03.0'W. The current is flooding in a direction of 303°T at 2.5 knots. Adjusting your course for set and drift, which course would you steer while turning RPMs for 6 knots to make good a course of 175°T?

A. 156°T
B. 164°T
C. 183°T
D. 190°T

15416. At 2200, you are in position LAT 36°57.5'N, LONG 76°02.5'W. You intend to travel up the Thimble Shoals Auxiliary Channel to Hampton Roads. According to the Coast Pilot, what is the depth of the auxiliary channel on either side of the main channel?

A. 28 feet (8.5 meters)
B. 32 feet (9.8 meters)
C. 36 feet (11.0 meters)
D. 45 feet (13.7 meters)

15418. At 2205, you are in Thimble Shoal North Auxiliary Channel abeam of lighted gong buoy 4. At this time the visibility decreases to 5 miles. You continue to turn RPMs for 6 knots and experience no set and drift. What time would you expect Old Point Comfort Light (white sector) to become visible?

A. 2230
B. 2240
C. 2246
D. 2258

15419. The mean high water level at Old Point Comfort is _____.

A. 2.6 feet (0.8 meter)
B. 1.2 feet (0.4 meter)
C. 0.0 feet
D. –3.5 feet (-1.1 meters)

15420. You are entering Norfolk Harbor and have just passed Craney Island. Which chart should you use for your final approach into Norfolk Harbor?

A. 12223
B. 12238
C. 12248
D. 12253

The following questions are to be answered using chart 12221 TR, Chesapeake Bay Entrance, and supporting publications. It is July 13th and you are on a voyage to Baltimore. You are observing daylight savings time. You are turning for 9.8 knots. The maximum draft is 18 feet. The gyro error is 2°E. The visibility is obscured by patchy fog. Use 10°W variation where required.

HDG.	M.DEV.	HDG.	M.DEV.
315°	1.0°W	000°	2.0°E
330°	0.5°W	015°	3.0°E
345°	0.5°E	030°	1.5°E

15438. At 2038 you are on course 272°T when you take the following loran readings: 9960-X-27087.2; 9960-Y-41234.6; 9960-Z-58573.6. Based on this fix, which statement is TRUE?

A. You are inside a ten fathom depth curve.
B. You are less than five miles from Chesapeake Light.
C. You are 0.6 mile north of a wreck.
D. You are inside the contiguous zone.

15439. What is your ETA off Chesapeake Bay Entrance Buoy CB at the entrance to the inbound lane of the traffic separation scheme?

A. 2058
B. 2104
C. 2109
D. 2115

15440. Your ETA at Chesapeake Bay Bridge and Tunnel between trestles B and C is 2300. If your engine speed is 9.8 knots, what will be your approximate speed over the ground, at that time, allowing for the predicted current?

A. 7.0 knots
B. 8.2 knots
C. 11.4 knots
D. 12.5 knots

15441. At buoy CB you change course to follow the inbound traffic lane. What is the course to steer per gyrocompass if you correct your heading for a current of 315° at 1.0 knot and allow 3° leeway for northeasterly winds?

A. 297° pgc
B. 299° pgc
C. 302° pgc
D. 305° pgc

15442. At 2216 CBJ Buoy is close abeam to port. Your lookout reports several sound signals with their relative bearings. Which would you judge to be coming from a vessel?

A. A bell, broad on the port bow
B. A whistle, broad on the starboard beam
C. A bell, dead ahead
D. A gong, two points on the starboard quarter

15443. As you enter Chesapeake Bay, visibility improves. At 2235 you are between Chesapeake Channel Buoys 5 and 6 in the 41 foot dredged section of Chesapeake Channel. At that time, you change course to pass between buoys 9 and 10. If buoys 11 and 12 are extinguished, your best leading light to keep you in deep water in the Chesapeake Channel as you approach the Chesapeake Bay Bridge and Tunnel would be _____.

A. fixed red light on trestle C
B. fixed green light on trestle B
C. fixed red light on trestle B
D. Thimble Shoal Light

15444. At 2306, as you pass through Trestle C, you take a gyro bearing of the trestle when it is in line. The bearing is 049.5°. What is the gyro error?

A. 0°
B. 1.5°E
C. 1.0°W
D. 2.5°W

15445. As you proceed up York Spit Channel, what are the three base courses that you must steer to conform to the channel if steering by standard magnetic compass?

A. 337.5°, 359.5°, 028.0°
B. 337.5°, 357.5°, 026.0°
C. 324.0°, 352.5°, 009.5°
D. 340.0°, 000.5°, 025.0°

15446. You are abeam of buoy "18" at 2325. What is your ETA at Baltimore if you average 9.5 knots?

A. 1342
B. 1400
C. 1424
D. 1456

The following questions should be answered using chart 12221TR, and the supporting publications. The height of eye is 29 feet (8.8 meters). Your draft is 11 feet (3.4 meters). The gyro error is 2°W. "Per standard magnetic compass" is abbreviated "psc." Use a variation of 10°W for the entire plot. The deviation table is:

HDG.	M.DEV.	HDG.	M.DEV.	HDG.	M.DEV.
000°	0°	120°	2°W	240°	3°E
030°	1°W	150°	1°W	270°	3°E
060°	2°W	180°	1°E	300°	2°E
090°	4°W	210°	2°E	330°	1°E

15456. On 25 February, your vessel is berthed near Lamberts Point in Norfolk. You are preparing to sail for Baltimore and wish to be transiting York Spit Channel while the morning flood current is at its maximum speed. At what time should you be between buoys 33 and 34? And what will be the speed of the flood at this time?

A. 0513, 0.8 kt
B. 0810, 1.2 kts
C. 0810, 1.5 kts
D. 1124, 1.2 kts

15457. What is the distance from Lamberts Point to Thimble Shoal Lt.?

A. 9.0 miles
B. 9.8 miles
C. 10.6 miles
D. 11.2 miles

15458. You are delayed in sailing due to engineering problems. You get underway at 0630. A Coast Guard radio broadcast advises that an aircraft carrier will transit the Elizabeth River enroute to Norfolk Naval Shipyard and a safety zone is in effect. Further information on how far you must remain from the carrier found is in _____.

A. Pub. 117
B. Light List
C. Coast Pilot
D. Chart Number 1

15459. At 0823, Old Point Comfort Light bears 000°T at 0.6 mile. What is your 0823 position?

A. LAT 36°59.5'N, LONG 76°18.4'W
B. LAT 36°59.0'N, LONG 76°21.6'W
C. LAT 36°59.0'N, LONG 76°19.6'W
D. LAT 36°55.5'N, LONG 76°18.6'W

15460. At 0845, you are approaching the entrances to Thimble Shoal Channel. What channel must you use?

A. The South Auxiliary Channel since your draft is less than 25 feet (7.6 meters), and you are not a passenger vessel.
B. The South Auxiliary Channel or Thimble Shoal Channel, but you must remain on the right-hand side of the main channel.
C. The North Auxiliary Channel since you are going to turn to a northerly heading near buoy 12.

). You are not permitted to use any of the
hannels, but must remain outside the
•uoyed channel line.

5461. At 0908, you change course to
010°T. What course should you steer per
standard magnetic compass?

A. 003°
B. 017°
C. 021°
D. 359°

15462. Visibility has decreased to 1 mile in
haze. At 0948, you take the following radar
ranges. What course should you steer per
gyrocompass from this fix to enter the
channel between buoys 19 and 20? Thimble Shoal Light—5.9 miles; South end of
trestle C of the Chesapeake Bay Bridge and
Tunnel—3.8 miles; South end of trestle B of
the Chesapeake Bay Bridge and Tunnel—
5.4 miles.

A. 001° pgc
B. 004° pgc
C. 007° pgc
D. 010° pgc

15463. If you are making 10 knots, what is
your ETA at York Spit Channel Buoys 19
and 20?

A. 0959
B. 1002
C. 1006
D. 1011

15464. What is the course per standard
magnetic compass on the southern leg of
York Spit Channel between buoys 15 and
23?

A. 319°
B. 322°
C. 339°
D. 341°

15465. What is indicated by the dashed
magenta line crossing York Spit Channel
between buoys 20 and 22?

A. You are crossing the demarcation line
between the COLREGS and the Inland
Rules.
B. The line marks the limits of a regulated
area.
C. The line indicates a submarine cable, and
you should not anchor in the area.

D. It marks the range between Hampton
Roads and Cherrystone Channel.

15466. At 1015, you estimate you have 139
miles to complete the voyage. If you average 9.5 knots, you will complete the voyage in _____.

A. 14 hours 22 minutes
B. 14 hours 30 minutes
C. 14 hours 38 minutes
D. 14 hours 44 minutes

15467. At 1018, you are entering York Spit
Channel and buoy 19 is abeam to your starboard. At 1031, buoy 23 is abeam. What
speed are you making good?

A. 8.4 knots
B. 8.8 knots
C. 9.7 knots
D. 9.9 knots

15468. Which loran line of positon will
serve as a danger reading on the loran to
keep you west of the submerged obstruction at LAT 37°24.2'N, LONG 76°03.7'W,
after you leave York Spit Channel?

A. Not less than 9960-Z-58622
B. Not more than 9960-Y-41595
C. Not less than 9960-Y-41595
D. Not less than 9960-X-27246

15469. At 1037, you are on course 010°T at
10 knots, when you take the following
loran readings: 9960-X-27243.8; 9960-Y-
41497.6; 9960-Z-58575.9. What is your 1037
position?

A. LAT 37°15.9'N, LONG 76°07.1'W
B. LAT 37°16.1'N, LONG 76°07.4'W
C. LAT 37°16.2'N, LONG 76°07.8'W
D. LAT 37°16.3'N, LONG 76°07.2'W

15470. At 1119, Wolf Trap Light bears 268°T
at 4.4 miles by radar. What were the set and
drift since your 1037 fix?

A. 178°, 0.5 knot
B. 358°, 0.5 knot
C. 178°, 0.7 knot
D. 358°, 0.7 knot

*The following questions should be answered
using chart number 13205TR, Block Island
and Approaches, and supporting
publications. You are steering a westerly
course and approaching Block Island Sound.*

*The variation for the area is 15°W. The gyro
error is 2°E. The deviation table is:*

HDG.	M.DEV.	HDG.	M.DEV.	HDG.	M.DEV.
000°	0.0°	120°	1.0°W	240°	2.0°E
030°	1°W	150°	0.0°	270°	1.5°E
060°	3.0°W	180°	0.0°	300°	1.0°E
090°	2.0°W	210°	1.0°E	330°	0.0°

15506. You are underway in the vicinity of
Block Island and obtain the following lines
of position: Montauk Point Light—263°
pgc; Block Island Southeast Light—026°
pgc; Radar Bearing to Block Island Southwest Point—348° pgc. What is your
position at the time of these sightings?

A. LAT 41°05.0'N, LONG 71°36.2'W
B. LAT 41°05.1'N, LONG 71°36.0'W
C. LAT 41°05.3'N, LONG 71°35.8'W
D. LAT 41°05.4'N, LONG 71°35.5'W

15507. What course should you steer by
your standard magnetic compass to make
good a course of 280°T?

A. 266° psc
B. 272° psc
C. 290° psc
D. 294° psc

15508. From your position you observe a
rotating white and green light to the north.
This light is most likely _____.

A. from a submarine on the surface
B. the light at Southeast Point
C. at an airport
D. on a coastal patrol vessel

15509. At 1800, your position is LAT
41°06.5'N, LONG 71°43.5'W. How would the
buoy which bears approximately 040°T
from your position at a range of half a mile
be painted?

A. Horizontally banded, green over red,
with a green buoyancy chamber
B. Horizontally banded, red over green,
with a red buoyancy chamber
C. Vertically striped, red and green
D. Solid green with red letters BIS

15510. From your 1800 position you steer a
course of 350° psc at a speed of 10.0 knots.
At 1830, your position is LAT 41°11.7'N,
LONG 71°45.8'W. What are the set and drift
of the current?

A. 029°T, 0.7 knot
B. 029°T, 1.4 knots
C. 209°T, 0.7 knot
D. 209°T, 1.4 knots

15511. From your 1830 fix, you come left to a course of 290°T. Which of the following statements concerning Watch Hill Light is FALSE?

A. The nominal range of its white light is 15 miles.
B. It displays both red and white lights.
C. Its horn blasts every 30 seconds in fog.
D. Its geographic range is 18.5 miles at a 35 foot (10.7 meter) height of eye.

15512. At 1850, you obtain the following bearings and distances: Montauk Point—89° pgc, 8.7 miles; Watch Hill Light—340° pgc 5.7 miles. What true course did you make good between 1830 and 1850?

A. 289°T
B. 294°T
C. 299°T
D. 307°T

15513. If your height of eye is 35 feet (10.7 meters), what is the approximate geographic range of Block Island North Light?

A. 7.4 nm
B. 13.0 nm
C. 14.3 nm
D. 15.8 nm

15514. From your 1850 fix, you come left to a course of 280°T while maintaining a speed of 10 knots. Which of the following combinations of available Loran-C lines would give the best cross for position determining?

A. 9960-Y and 9960-W
B. 9960-X and 9960-Y
C. 9960-W and 9960-X
D. All are equally good.

15515. You decide to use the 9960-Y and 9960-W rates. At 1915, you obtain the following readings: 9960-Y-43936.0; 9960-W-14653.3. What is your 1915 position?

A. LAT 41°13.0'N, LONG 71°54.0'W
B. LAT 41°13.1'N, LONG 71°53.9'W
C. LAT 41°13.2'N, LONG 71°54.3'W
D. LAT 41°13.2'N, LONG 71°53.7'W

15516. If you were to head into Fishers Island Sound, which of the following charts would you switch to for better detail of Mystic and Mystic Harbor?

A. 13209
B. 13212
C. 13213
D. 13214

15517. From your 1915 position, you come left and set a course for Gardiners Point. At 1930, your position is LAT 41°12.7'N; LONG 71°56.8'W. What type of bottom is charted at this position?

A. Blue mud, gritty shells
B. Buried mussels, gritty shells
C. Blue mud, gray sand
D. Bumpy muck with grainy surface

15518. From your 1930 position, you plot a course to pass 0.5 mile due south of Race Rock Light. If your vessel's speed is 10.0 knots, the current's set and drift are 040°T at 1.8 knots, and a north wind produces a 3° leeway, what true course should you steer to make good your desired course?

A. 275°T
B. 280°T
C. 290°T
D. 294°T

15519. As an option to heading into Long Island Sound, you consider anchoring in the vicinity of the Gardiners Point Ruins approximately one mile off the north end of Gardiners Island. What is the minimum recommended distance from the ruins for fishing, trawling, or anchoring?

A. 300 yards (91 meters)
B. 1.0 mile
C. 0.5 mile
D. No distance is prescribed since any such activities in the area are prohibited.

15520. NOAA VHF-FM weather broadcasts from New London, CT, are on _____.

A. 162.25 MHz
B. 162.30 MHz
C. 162.40 MHz
D. 162.55 MHz

The following questions are to be answered using chart 12354 TR, Long Island Sound - Eastern Part, and supporting publications. You are turning for 12.7 knots. Your vessel's

deep draft is 16 feet. Gyro error is 2°W. Use 14°W variation where required.

HDG.	M.DEV.
045°	3.0°E
060°	3.0°E
075°	1.5°E
090°	0.5°W

15538. At 2127 you take the following round of bearings: Old Field Point Light—224.0° pgc; Middle Ground Light—320.5° pgc; Stratford Point Light—348.0° pgc. Based on the above fix, which statement is TRUE?

A. At 2127, your fathometer reads about 17 fathoms.
B. You are south of Mt. Misery Shoal.
C. By following loran line 9960-Y-43950, you will have safe water to the eastern tip of Great Gull Island.
D. You have lost sight of the red light at Old Field Point.

15539. At 2127 you are on course 076°T. What is your ETA at a position where Twenty Eight Foot Shoal Lighted Bell Buoy TE is abeam to port?

A. 2316
B. 2324
C. 2332
D. 2345

15540. At 2200 you take the following loran readings: 9960-W-15064.5; 9960-Y-43954.8. Which statement is TRUE?

A. The current is flooding.
B. You are being set to the left of the track.
C. The set is towards the southwest.
D. The drift is 0.6 knot.

15541. You alter course to make good 076°T from your 2200 fix and estimate you will make 13.6 knots over the ground. If the visibility is 5.5 miles, what is the earliest time you will sight Falkner Island Light (nominal range 13 miles)?

A. The light is visible at 2200
B. 2221
C. 2236
D. You will not sight the light

15542. At 2214 you receive a Securité call requesting you to remain at least 2 miles away from underwater work taking place at LAT 41°07.8'N, LONG 72°34.6'W. If you

hange course at 2220 and allow 3° leeway
or southerly winds which course will you
teer per gyrocompass to comply with this
equest? (No allowance made for current.)

. 079° pgc
. 083° pgc
. 086° pgc
. 089° pgc

5543. At 2236 you take the following loran
eadings: 9960-W-14994.6; 9960-X-26455.2;
960-Y-43949.0. What was the speed made
ood along the track line since your 2200
x?

. 12.7 knots
. 13.5 knots
. 13.9 knots
. 14.2 knots

5544. At 2310 your position is LAT
1°05.5'N, LONG 72°33.7'W and you change
ourse to make good 068°T. A radar speed
heck using Twenty Eight Foot Shoal Buoy
ndicates your speed over the ground is
3.6 knots. At 2325 Horton Point Light
ears 129°T. At 2341 the same light bears
94°T. What is the position of your 2341
unning fix?

. LAT 41°07.9'N, LONG 72°25.9'W
. LAT 41°08.3'N, LONG 72°25.8'W
. LAT 41°08.5'N, LONG 72°25.6'W
. LAT 41°08.8'N, LONG 72°25.2'W

15545. At 2342 the gyro alarm sounds and
you commence steering by standard magnetic compass. If you allow 3° leeway for
southerly winds and do not correct for any
existing current, what is the course to steer
by standard magnetic compass to make
good 068°T?

A. 054.0°
B. 079.5°
C. 081.0°
D. 084.5°

15546. At 2350 the gyro is restored to service. At 0016 the visibility improves. At
0028 you sight Bartlett Reef Light in line
with New London Harbor Light bearing
039° pgc. What is the gyro error?

A. 2°E
B. 0°
C. 2°W
D. 4°W

---

*The following questions are to be answered
by using chart 12221TR, Chesapeake Bay Entrance, and the supporting publications.
Your draft is 14 feet (4.2 meters). Use 10°W
variation where required. The gyro error is
3°E. The deviation table is:*

HDG.	M.DEV.	HDG.	M.DEV.	HDG.	M.DEV.
000°	2.0°E	120°	1.0°W	240°	0.5°W
030°	1.0°E	150°	2.0°W	270°	0.5°E
060°	0.0°	180°	2.0°W	300°	1.5°E
090°	0.5°W	210°	1.0°W	330°	2.5°E

15606. Your 1600 position is LAT 37°22.5'N,
LONG 75°32.3'W. The depth of water under
the keel is about _____.

A. 38 feet (11.5 meters)
B. 45 feet (13.6 meters)
C. 52 feet (15.8 meters)
D. 59 feet (17.3 meters)

15607. If there is no current, what is the
course per gyrocompass from your 1600
position to point A located 0.5 mile due
east of Hog Island Lighted Bell Buoy 12?

A. 190° pgc
B. 193° pgc
C. 196° pgc
D. 199° pgc

15608. At 1630, you reach point A and
come right to 204°T. Your engine speed is
12 knots. Your 1715 position is LAT
37°09.8'N, LONG 75°37.4'W. The current
was _____.

A. 067°T at 1.1 knots
B. 246°T at 1.1 knots
C. 067°T at 1.5 knots
D. 246°T at 1.5 knots

15609. From your 1715 fix, you steer 214°T
at 12 knots. At 1800 you take a fix using the
following Loran-C readings: 9960-X-
27116.8; 9960-Y-41386.0; 9960-Z-58620.6.
Your 1800 position is _____.

A. LAT 37°02.9'N, LONG 75°43.1'W
B. LAT 37°02.9'N, LONG 75°43.9'W
C. LAT 37°03.0'N, LONG 75°43.3'W
D. LAT 37°03.1'N, LONG 75°42.8'W

15610. At 1815, your position is LAT
37°01.0'N, LONG 75°42.7'W. If there is no
current, what is the course per standard
magnetic compass to arrive at a point 0.3
mile due north of North Chesapeake
Entrance Lighted Whistle Buoy NCA
(LL#375)?

A. 249.0°
B. 251.5°
C. 255.0°
D. 257.0°

15611. From your 1815 position, you want
to make good a course of 263°T. Your engines are turning RPMs for 12 knots. The
current is 050°T at 1.9 knots. Adjusting your
course for set and drift, at what time should
you expect to enter the red sector of Cape
Henry Light?

A. 1849
B. 1854
C. 1859
D. 1904

15612. At 1920, Cape Henry Light bears
225° pgc, and Chesapeake Channel Tunnel
North Light bears 288° pgc. If your heading
is 268°T, what is the relative bearing of
Chesapeake Light?

A. 194°
B. 205°
C. 213°
D. 220°

15613. Which statement concerning your
1920 position is TRUE?

A. You are entering a restricted area.
B. You are governed by the Inland Rules of
the Road.
C. You are within the Chesapeake Bay Entrance traffic separation scheme.
D. You can expect differences of as much as
6° from the normal magnetic variation of
the area.

15614. From your 1920 position, you
change course to enter Chesapeake Channel between buoys 9 and 10. What is the
course per standard magnetic compass
(psc)?

A. 286° psc
B. 283° psc
C. 280° psc
D. 274° psc

15615. At 2000, your position is LAT
37°04.1'N, LONG 76°05.6'W. You change
course for the Eastern Shore. At 2037, Old
Plantation Flats Light bears 033° pgc, and
York Spit Light bears 282° pgc. The course
made good from your 2000 position is

_____.

A. 359°T
B. 006°T
C. 014°T
D. 020°T

15616. At 2037, you change course to make good a course of 016°T. There is no current, but a westerly wind is causing 3° leeway. What course per standard magnetic compass (psc) should you steer to make good the course 016°T?

A. 031° psc
B. 028° psc
C. 025° psc
D. 022° psc

15617. Your height of eye is 25 feet (7.6 meters). If the visibility is 5.5 nautical miles, what is the luminous range of Wolf Trap Light?

A. 7.5 miles
B. 12.0 miles
C. 16.0 miles
D. 17.0 miles

15618. If you want a more detailed chart of the area at your 2115 DR position, which chart should you use?

A. 12222
B. 12224
C. 12225
D. 12238

15619. At 2123, your position is LAT 37°20.0'N, LONG 76°03.0'W. What is your distance offshore of Savage Neck?

A. 4.3 miles
B. 3.4 miles
C. 2.6 miles
D. 1.7 miles

15620. From your 2123 position, you are approximately 42 miles from Crisfield, MD. If you are making good a speed of 13 knots, at what time should you arrive at Crisfield, MD?

A. 2359
B. 0037
C. 0112
D. 0148

The following questions are based on the C of E Mississippi River Maps (Cairo to the Gulf) and the Light List. On 3 January you get underway from Cambalick Dock, Morganza,

LA (mile 278.3 AHP), enroute to to the Socony -Mobil Oil Docks (east side), LDB, in St. Louis.

15621. What is the length of the trip?

A. 879.6 miles
B. 878.9 miles
C. 851.9 miles
D. 726.0 miles

15622. What are the dimensions of the Old River Lock on the lower Old River (304 AHP)?

A. 1185 × 75 feet
B. 1195 × 75 feet
C. 1195 × 84 feet
D. 1202 × 84 feet

15623. At 2126, you pass Morganza Bend Light (mile 278.4 AHP). At 0122, 4 January, you pass Red River Landing Gauge (302.4 AHP). You have been turning for 7.5 mph. What is the current?

A. 1.4 MPH
B. 1.8 MPH
C. 2.7 MPH
D. 6.2 MPH

15624. The gauge at Red River Landing reads 22.2 feet. How many feet is this above the low water reference plane?

A. 10.6 ft.
B. 11.6 ft.
C. 22.2 ft.
D. 32.8 ft.

15625. The river will be temporarily closed to navigation at mile 531.3 AHP due to repairs to the bridge. This will occur at 1300, 5 January, and last for six hours. What minimum speed over the ground must you make from Red River Landing Gauge in order not to be delayed?

A. 6.0 mph
B. 6.4 mph
C. 6.8 mph
D. 7.3 mph

15626. What type of daymark will you see as you approach Joe Pierce Light (mile 334.4 AHP)?

A. Private aid—no daymark
B. Red square
C. Red diamond
D. Red triangle

15627. What is the vertical clearance of the Natchez Highway Bridge (westbound) when the river level is the same as the Low Water Reference Plane?

A. 102.2 ft.
B. 108.3 ft.
C. 119.5 ft.
D. 125.6 ft.

15628. The Natchez gauge reads 20.6 feet. The high point on your towboat is 47 feet above the water. What is the vertical clearance as you pass under the Natchez Highway Bridge?

A. 58.0 feet
B. 64.1 feet
C. 72.5 feet
D. 78.6 feet

15629. In order to determine what buoys, if any, are in place at Concordia Bar crossing (mile 596.0 AHP), what should you check?

A. Bulletin board at the Rosedale gauge
B. Waterways Journal
C. Channel Report
D. Light List

15630. The area between Island 67 Upper Light (mile 623.1 AHP) and Sunflower Cut-Off Foot Light (mile 624.8 AHP) is known as a _____.

A. transit
B. chute
C. crossing
D. slough

The following questions are to be answered using chart 13205 TR, Block Island Sound, and supporting publications. There are fog patches. You are turning for 12.1 knots. Your draft is 22 feet. The gyro error is 3°W. Use a variation of 14°W where required. The following tables are:

HDG.	M.DEV.
180°	2.5°E
195°	2.0°E
210°	1.0°E
225°	0.5°W

15638. At 2009 you are leaving New London Harbor with buoy 2 close abeam to port. What is the true course to the Race that will leave Race Rock Light 0.5 mile abeam to port?

A. 156°
B. 160°
C. 164°
D. 168°

15639. At 2016 you sight N. Dumpling Light in line with Latimer Reef Light (Fl 6 sec., 55 ft.) bearing 079° pgc. At the time of the bearing the helmsman reported he was steering 164° pgc and 172° per standard magnetic compass. What is the deviation for that heading?

A. 3°E
B. 1°E
C. 5°W
D. 2°W

15640. At which point in the voyage is your vessel bound by the International Rules of the Roads (COLREGS)?

A. At the mouth of New London Harbor
B. Upon entering
C. After crossing the line of the Territorial Sea
D. After passing between Montauk Point and Lewis Point on Block Island

15641. You will pass through the Race at approximately the time of maximum ebb current. As you APPROACH the Race from New London, you will be set _____.

A. to the left of the track line
B. to the right of the track line
C. forward along the track line
D. towards New London along the track line

15642. At 2030 you take the following radar ranges: Race Rock Light—2.1 miles; Latimer Reef Light—6.4 miles. If you estimate an average current of 080°T at 1.5 knots, which course will you steer per gyrocompass to leave Endeavor Shoals Gong Buoy bearing 270°T at 1.5 miles?
A. 115°
B. 118°
C. 124°
D. 127°

15643. The light on Block Island Sound South Entrance Obstruction Buoy BIS is reported extinguished. Which of the following will serve as a positive warning that you are being set onto the obstruction?

A. Radar ranges to Southwest Point of less than 7.9 miles
B. Soundings of less than 50 feet
C. Shagwong Reef Lighted Bell Bouy 7SR 3.1 miles off abeam
D. Race Rock Light bearing 299°T and decreasing

15644. At 2045 visibility decreases in fog, and at 2103 you take the following loran fix: 9960-W-14658; 9960-X-26012.5; 9960-Y-43904. Determine your 2103 fix.

A. LAT 41°09.2'N, LONG 71°52.5'W
B. LAT 41°09.1'N, LONG 71°52.2'W
C. LAT 41°09.0'N, LONG 71°52.9'W
D. LAT 41°08.8'N, LONG 71°52.5'W

15645. You round Montauk Point and steer to make good 206°T. Speed is increased to 13.0 knots. The current, if any, is unknown. The visibility has improved and is estimated to be 5 miles. At 2144 Montauk Point Light bears 273°T. At 2202 the same light bears 320°T. Which statement concerning your 2202 running fix is TRUE?

A. You are inside the lobster pot area.
B. The fathometer reads about 12 fathoms.
C. You are inside of the 90 foot curve.
D. You are outside the boundary of the Territorial Sea and Contiguous Zone.

15646. At 2229 the gyro fails. What is the course to steer per standard magnetic compass to make good 206°T, if you allow 3° leeway for southeasterly winds?

A. 187°
B. 191°
C. 217°
D. 220°

The following questions should be answered using chart 13205TR, Block Island Sound and Approaches, and supporting publications. Your draft is 18 feet (5.4 meters) and the height of eye is 20 feet (6.1 meters). Gyro error is 3°W. "Per standard magnetic compass" is abbreviated "psc." Use a variation of 15°W for the entire plot. The deviation table is:

HDG.	M.DEV.	HDG.	M.DEV.	HDG.	M.DEV.
000°	1.5°E	120°	1.0°W	240°	1.5°E
030°	2.5°W	150°	0.5°W	270°	2.0°E
060°	2.5°W	180°	0°	300°	1.0°E
090°	2.0°W	210°	1.0°E	330°	0.5°W

15656. At 0630, Buoy PI is close abeam on the starboard side. You are steering 078°T

and are headed directly toward Race Rock Light. At 0654, Little Gull Island Light is bearing 210° pgc and Race Rock Light is bearing 075° pgc. What is your 0654 position?

A. LAT 41°19.0'N, LONG 72°05.2'W
B. LAT 41°14.4'N, LONG 71°54.6'W
C. LAT 41°14.2'N, LONG 72°06.8'W
D. LAT 41°14.0'N, LONG 72°05.3'W

15657. What was the course made good from 0630 to 0654?

A. 078°T
B. 082°T
C. 086°T
D. 090°T

15658. What course should you steer by the standard magnetic compass in order to maintain a heading of 081° pgc?

A. 062° psc
B. 080° psc
C. 090° psc
D. 095° psc

15659. At 0705, you change course to 096°T. At this time, Race Rock Light is bearing 000°T at 0.35 mile. You are now governed by which Navigation Rules?

A. COLREGS
B. Local Pilot Rules
C. Inland Rules
D. Coastal Fishery Rules

15660. At 0728, Race Rock Light is bearing 282°T at 3.8 miles, and the closest point on Fishers Island has a radar range of 2.1 miles. What speed have you been making since you changed course at 0705?

A. 11.2 knots
B. 10.8 knots
C. 9.6 knots
D. 9.1 knots

15661. At 0727, the cupola on Fishers Island is in line with Latimer Reef Light bearing 024° pgc. Based on this, the gyro error is _____.

A. 2°E
B. 1°E
C. 0°
D. 3°W

15662. At 0748, you take the following Loran-C readings: 9960-W-14651.0; 9960-X-26034.8; 9960-Y-43943.8. What is the approximate depth of water under the keel at this position?

A. 325 feet (98.5 meters)
B. 175 feet (53.0 meters)
C. 130 feet (39.4 meters)
D. 112 feet (33.9 meters)

15663. At 0748, you change course to 160°T. Which loran reading will insure you clear Great Eastern Rock?

A. Nothing more than 9960-W-14645
B. Nothing more than 9960-X-25970
C. Nothing more than 9960-Y-43850
D. Nothing more than 9960-Y-43960

15664. At 0815, Montauk Pt. Light House is bearing 172°T; Shagwong Pt. has a radar range of 4.5 miles. If the engine was making turns for 10 knots, what was the current since 0748?

A. Set 040°T, drift 0.7 knot
B. Set 040°T, drift 1.6 knots
C. Set 220°T, drift 1.6 knots
D. Set 220°T, drift 0.7 knot

15665. Which action should you take to compensate for the above current?

A. Continue on the same course and speed.
B. Alter your course to the left.
C. Slow to 8.5 knots.
D. Alter your course to the right.

15666. At 0815, visibility is excellent and you can see Montauk Point. Montauk Point Light is _____.

A. shown from a brown tower
B. equipped with a fog diaphone
C. lighted 24 hours
D. is 79 feet (24 meters) high

15667. At 0815, you change course to 079°T. To compensate for a southerly wind, you estimate a 3° leeway is necessary. Which course should you steer per standard magnetic compass to make good 079°T?

A. 090° psc
B. 093° psc
C. 095° psc
D. 099° psc

15668. At 0839, Montauk Pt. Light is bearing 205°T at a radar distance of 6.6 miles. What is your speed made good from your 0815 position?

A. 8.2 knots
B. 9.2 knots
C. 10.0 knots
D. 10.5 knots

15669. The area between Block Island and Montauk Point that is bounded by dashed magenta lines is a _____.

A. naval exercise area
B. fish trap area
C. submerged cable area
D. restricted navigation area

15670. Which chart should you use to enter Great Salt Pond?

A. 13204
B. 13205
C. 13207
D. 13217

The following questions are to be answered by using chart 12354TR, Long Island Sound - Eastern Part, and supporting publications. Your draft is 11 feet (3.3 meters). Use 14°W for variation where required. The gyro error is 3°E. The deviation table is:

HDG.	M.DEV.	HDG.	M.DEV.	HDG.	M.DEV.
000°	2.0°E	120°	1.0°W	240°	0.5°W
030°	1.0°E	150°	2.0°W	270°	0.5°E
060°	0.5°W	180°	2.0°W	300°	1.5°E
090°	0.5°W	210°	1.0°W	330°	2.5°E

15706. At 0700, Stratford Shoal Middle Ground Light bears 137° pgc. From your radar, you get a bearing of 007° pgc to the south tip of Stratford Point with a range of 4.5 miles. What is your 0700 position?

A. LAT 41°04.6'N, LONG 73°07.0'W
B. LAT 41°04.6'N, LONG 73°07.4'W
C. LAT 41°04.7'N, LONG 73°07.2'W
D. LAT 41°04.8'N, LONG 73°07.0'W

15707. At 0725, you are heading 054°T, and Stratford Point Light is abeam to port at 3.1 miles. The current is 135°T at 1.8 knots. If you make turns for an engine speed of 8 knots, which course must you steer to make good 048°T?

A. 035°T
B. 042°T

C. 047°T
D. 055°T

15708. Which structure should you look for while trying to locate Southwest Ledge Light?

A. White conical tower with a brown band midway of height
B. White octagonal house on a cylindrical pier
C. Conical tower, upper half white, lower half brown
D. Black skeleton tower on a granite dwelling

15709. At 0830, you obtained the following Loran-C readings: 9960-X-26562.5; 9960-Y-44028.1. What is your vessel's position?

A. LAT 41°12.4'N, LONG 73°56.0'W
B. LAT 40°17.4'N, LONG 73°54.0'W
C. LAT 41°12.0'N, LONG 72°53.8'W
D. LAT 41°12.4'N, LONG 72°53.8'W

15710. From your 0830 position, you wish to make good 097°T. There is no current, but a southerly wind is producing 3° leeway. What course should you steer per standard magnetic compass in order to make good your true course?

A. 118° psc
B. 115° psc
C. 112° psc
D. 109° psc

15712. At 0910, your DR position is LAT 41°11.9'N, LONG 72°47.8'W. Your vessel is on course 097°T at 9.5 knots, and the weather is foggy. At 0915, Branford Reef Light is sighted through a break in the fog bearing 318°T. At 0945, Falkner Island Light is sighted bearing 042°T. What is your 0945 running fix position?

A. LAT 41°11.1'N, LONG 72°41.2'W
B. LAT 41°11.3'N, LONG 72°41.3'W
C. LAT 41°11.4'N, LONG 72°41.0'W
D. LAT 41°11.5'N, LONG 72°40.7'W

15713. What do the dotted lines around Goose Island and Kimberly Reef represent?

A. Limiting danger
B. Breakers
C. Depth contours
D. Tide rips

15714. At 1100, your position is LAT

41°11.3'N, LONG 72°28.0'W. You are steering a course of 069°T to leave Black Point one mile off your port beam. It has been reported that the Long Sand Shoal Buoys and Hatchett Reef Buoys are off station. Which of the following will serve as a line marking the hazards and keep your vessel in safe water?

A. Danger bearing to Black Point of not more than 064°T
B. A Loran reading of more than 9960-Y-43985.0
C. A bearing to Little Gull Island Light of not less than 090°
D. A distance to Saybrook Breakwater Light of not less than 1.3 miles

15715. Little Gull Island Light is _____.

A. lighted only during daytime when the sound signal is in operation
B. maintained only from May 1 to Oct. 1
C. lighted throughout 24 hours
D. obscured by trees from 253° to 352°

15716. At 1210, you are in position LAT 41°14.3'N, LONG 72°16.5'W. What is the depth of water below your keel?

A. 97 feet (29.4 meters)
B. 108 feet (32.7 meters)
C. 119 feet (36.1 meters)
D. 125 feet (37.9 meters)

15717. From your 1210 position, you are steering a course of 083°T. Your engines are turning RPMs for 10 knots. The set and drift of the current are 310° at 1.7 knots. At what time should you expect to enter the red sector of New London Harbor Light?

A. 1241
B. 1249
C. 1256
D. 1309

15718. Your vessel is entering New London Harbor Channel. If there is no current, what should you steer per gyrocompass to stay on the range?

A. 351°
B. 354°
C. 357°
D. 006°

15719. On chart 12354, the datum from which heights of objects are taken is _____.

A. mean high water
B. mean low water
C. lowest low water
D. mean lower low water

15720. The red sector of New London Harbor Light covers from _____.

A. 040°–310°
B. 000°–041°
C. 208°–220°
D. 204°–239°

The following questions are based on the C of E Mississippi River Maps (Cairo to the Gulf) and the Light List. On 21 September, you are making up your tow at the fleeting area in Cairo, IL, (mile 980.6 Ohio River). You get underway at 0952 enroute to to New Orleans with a mixed tow.

15721. You are turning for 7.8 mph and estimate the current at 1.0 mph. What is your speed over the ground?

A. 8.8 mph
B. 7.9 mph
C. 7.8 mph
D. 6.8 mph

15722. What is your ETA at the Memphis - Arkansas Highway Bridge?

A. 0828, 22 Sept
B. 1052, 22 Sept
C. 1405, 22 Sept
D. 1813, 22 Sept

15723. What daymark should you see as you approach Parker Landing Light (mile 924.6 AHP)?

A. green square
B. green triangle
C. red and green rectangle
D. green diamond

15724. You pass Morrison Towhead Light (mile 890.5 AHP) at 1723. What was your average speed since leaving Cairo?

A. 7.5 mph
B. 7.8 mph
C. 8.5 mph
D. 8.8 mph

15725. At 1723 you increase speed to make good 9.2 mph. At 1937 you have a daymark on your port beam. What daymark is this?

A. Tiptonville Ferry Landing Daymark
B. Tiptonville Light
C. Merriwether Bend Light and Daymark
D. Alaska Light and Daymark

15726. The charts show a circle with two black quadrants located at mile 846.0 AHP. What does this indicate?

A. hazardous chemical dock
B. bulletin board
C. Betz-Tipton Veneers Terminal
D. river gauge

15727. The Helena gauge reads 9.4 feet. The high point on your towboat is 46 feet above water. What is the vertical clearance when you pass under the Helena Highway Bridge?

A. 56.0 feet
B. 64.2 feet
C. 79.5 feet
D. 106.1 feet

15728. What company does NOT have a marine facility along the river bank in Helena (mile 658 to 665 AHP)?

A. Helena Grain Co.
B. Helena Marine Services, Inc.
C. Riceland Food Corp.
D. Texas Eastern Pipeline Co.

15729. If the Rosedale gauge reads –0.5 feet, what is the water level in relation to the low water reference plane?

A. 0.5 foot below the plane
B. 0.5 foot above the plane
C. 2.5 feet above the plane
D. 3.5 feet below the plane

The following questions are to be answered using chart 13205 TR, Block Island Sound, and supporting publications. On 7 September, you are approaching Block Island Sound from sea. Your vessel has a draft of 20 feet. Equipment on board your vessel includes gyrocompass, magnetic compass, depth finder, Loran-C and radar.

15738. At 1830 you obtained the following Loran-C readings: 9960-W-14820.0; 9960-X-26097.0; 9960-Y-43713.5. What is your vessel's position?

A. LAT 40°41.0'N, LONG 72°06.0'W
B. LAT 40°41.0'N, LONG 72°10.6'W
C. LAT 40°42.5'N, LONG 72°07.1'W
D. LAT 40°47.5'N, LONG 72°02.9'W

15739. Your 1900 position is LAT 40°45.5'N, LONG 72°03.0'W. Your course is 046°T, and your engines are turning RPMs for 9 knots. At your 1939 DR position, what is the expected relative bearing of Montauk Point Light on the port bow?

A. 024° relative
B. 028° relative
C. 032° relative
D. 036° relative

15740. At 2000 Montauk Point Light bears 010°T. At 2030 the loran reads 9960-Y-43785.7. Assuming that you are making good your course of 046°T and a speed of 9 knots, what is your 2030 running fix position?

A. LAT 40°53.9'N, LONG 71°51.3'W
B. LAT 40°54.2'N, LONG 71°50.2'W
C. LAT 40°55.9'N, LONG 71°49.0'W
D. LAT 40°56.7'N, LONG 71°48.1'W

15741. At 2050 you obtain the following Loran-C readings: 9960-X-25945; 9960-Y-43802; 9960-W-14662. From this position, you change course in order to pass 1 mile due east of Montauk Point Lighted Whistle Buoy MP. If there are no set and drift, what course must you steer?

A. 024°T
B. 028°T
C. 032°T
D. 036°T

15742. At 2100 your position is LAT 40°58.5'N, LONG 71°46.0'W. You are proceeding north. At 2131 Montauk Point Light has a radar range of 5.1 miles and bears 284°T. Block Island Southeast Light has a radar range of 10.8 miles. What was the course made good from your 2100 position?

A. 005°T
B. 011°T
C. 017°T
D. 025°T

15743. At 2155 Montauk Point Light bears 249°T, Watch Hill Point Light bears 335°T, and Block Island North Light bears 045°T. At this time, you wish to change course to 288°T. The current has a set of 355°T and a drift of 2.0 knots. If your vessel is turning RPMs for 9 knots, what course must you steer in order to make your desired course good?

A. 276°T
B. 280°T
C. 284°T
D. 288°T

15744. Montauk Point Light has a radar range of 4.0 miles and bears 173°T at 2232. What is the depth of water below your keel?

A. 32 feet
B. 47 feet
C. 52 feet
D. 60 feet

15745. Your 2239 position is LAT 41°08.5'N, LONG 71°53.3'W. You change course to 315°T, and you maintain RPMs for 9 knots. At 2329 Little Gull Island Light bears 253°T, Race Rock Light bears 309°T, and Watch Hill Point Light bears 058°T. What were the set and drift of the current you experienced from your 2239 position?

A. 076°T at 0.75 knot
B. 076°T at 0.90 knot
C. 256°T at 0.75 knot
D. 256°T at 0.90 knot

15746. Which nautical chart would you use to navigate into New London, CT?

A. 13209
B. 13211
C. 13212
D. 13214

The following questions should be answered using chart 13205TR, Block Island Sound and approaches, and supporting publications. Your vessel draws 8 feet (2.4 meters) and the height of eye is 24 feet (7.3 meters). Gyro error is 2°E. "Per standard magnetic compass" is abbreviated "psc." Use a variation of 15°W for the entire plot. The deviation table is:

HDG.	M.DEV.	HDG.	M.DEV.	HDG.	M.DEV.
000°	4.0°E	120°	3.0°W	240°	1.0°W
030°	3.0°E	150°	4.0°W	270°	1.0°E
060°	1.0°E	180°	4.0°W	300°	3.0°E
090°	1.0°W	210°	3.0°W	330°	4.0°E

15756. You are steering 087° pgc and turning for 6.8 knots. At 0600, you take the following loran readings: 9960-W-14784.4; 9960-X-26208.3; 9960-Y-43959.1. What is your 0600 position?

A. LAT 41°12.1'N, LONG 72°13.8'W
B. LAT 41°12.1'N, LONG 72°14.6'W
C. LAT 41°12.3'N, LONG 72°14.7'W
D. LAT 41°12.5'N, LONG 71°14.9'W

15757. If you change course at 0610, what is the course to steer per gyrocompass to a point where Little Gull Island Light bears 180°T at 0.7 mile (Point A)?

A. 072° pgc
B. 076° pgc
C. 080° pgc
D. 084° pgc

15758. What is your ETA at point A?

A. 0637
B. 0643
C. 0649
D. 0700

15759. You calculate that the current will be flooding at the Race at 0700. You should expect to be set in which general direction at the Race?

A. West
B. East
C. Northeast
D. Southwest

15760. As you near Little Gull Island, you use your loran to insure that you do not come within 0.5 mile of the island. Which loran reading will act as a danger line and keep you off Little Gull Island by a minimum of 0.5 mile?

A. Not more than 9960-W-14735.9
B. Not more than 9960-X-26149.0
C. Not less than 9960-X-26140.0
D. Not less than 9960-Y-43953.5

15761. From point A, you lay out an intended track line to a point where Block Island North Light bears 180°T at 2.9 miles (Point B). What is the length of this leg of the voyage?

A. 20.4 miles
B. 23.7 miles
C. 24.4 miles
D. 25.3 miles

15762. What is the course per standard magnetic compass between points A and B?

A. 090.5°
B. 093.0°
C. 095.5°
D. 098.5°

15763. At 0715, you take the following bearings: Race Rock Light—324° pgc; Little Gull Island Light—245° pgc; Mt. Prospect Antenna—034° pgc. Based on your 0715 fix, which statement is TRUE?

A. You are to the right of your track line.
B. The charted depth is about 265 feet (80.3 meters).
C. You are in a cable area.
D. You are governed by the Inland Rules.

15764. From your 0715 position, you set a course of 085°T. At 0745, you take the following bearings: Race Rock Light—274° pgc; Watch Hill Point Light—045° pgc; Fisher's Island East Harbor Cupola—006° pgc. What was the current encountered between 0715 and 0745?

A. Set 030°T, drift 0.4 knot
B. Set 070°T, drift 0.7 knot
C. Set 210°T, drift 0.8 knot
D. Set 238°T, drift 1.0 knot

15765. The wind is northerly, and you estimate 3° leeway. Allowing for leeway what is the course to steer per gyrocompass from your 0745 position to pass 1 mile south of Watch Hill Buoy WH?

A. 077° pgc
B. 082° pgc
C. 085° pgc
D. 087° pgc

15766. From your 0745 fix, you change course to pass 1.0 mile south of buoy WH and estimate your speed at 7 knots. If the visibility clears, what is the earliest time you can expect to see Block Island North Light tower?

A. The tower is in sight at 0745.
B. 0750
C. 0806
D. 0838

15767. Which statement describes the shore between Watch Hill Point and Point Judith?

A. Low, rocky cliffs with heavily wooded hills inland
B. Sandy beaches broken by rocky points
C. Sand dunes and beaches with a mud and sand bottom
D. Wooded, barren hills with isolated prominent buildings

15768. At 0830, Watch Hill Point bears 343°T at 3.5 miles by radar. What was the speed made good since 0745?

A. 7.1 knots
B. 6.7 knots
C. 5.8 knots
D. 5.4 knots

15769. At 0900, you take the following radar ranges: Watch Hill Point—5.4 miles; Block Island Grace Point—8.3 miles. Which statement is TRUE?

A. You are to the right of the track line.
B. The bottom in the area is sand and gravel.
C. You are inside of the Territorial Sea.
D. The fix is indeterminate.

15770. At 0930, your position is LAT 41°16.5'N, LONG 71°41.4'W, and you are turning for 7 knots. Allowing 3° leeway for northerly winds and estimating the current as 035° at 0.3 knot, what is the course to steer (pgc) to point B?

A. 084° pgc
B. 086° pgc
C. 091° pgc
D. 094° pgc

15799. At 0845, you are on a course of 097°T, and Townshend Ledge Buoy 10A is close abeam to port. With a westerly current of 1.2 knots, what speed will you have to turn for from your 0845 position in order to arrive abeam of Six Mile Reef Buoy 8C at 1030?

A. 8.5 knots
B. 9.7 knots
C. 10.9 knots
D. 12.1 knots

The following questions are based on chart 12354TR, Long Island Sound - Eastern Part, and the supporting publications. Your vessel has a draft of 8.5 feet (2.6 meters). Use 14°W variation where required. The deviation table is:

HDG.	M.DEV.	HDG.	M.DEV.	HDG.	M.DEV.
000°	0°	120°	2°W	240°	3°E
030°	1°W	150°	1°W	270°	3°E
060°	2°W	180°	1°E	300°	2°E
090°	4°W	210°	2°E	330°	1°E

15806. What type of bottom is found at Long Sand Shoal?

A. Rocky
B. Muddy
C. Sandy
D. Hard

15807. You are southeast of Saybrook Breakwater Light passing Saybrook Bar Lighted Bell Buoy 8. This buoy marks _____.

A. shoal water
B. a tide rips area
C. the junction with the Connecticut River
D. a sunken wreck

15808. At 0005, on 26 January, your position is LAT 41°11.8'N; LONG 72°20.5'W. From this position, you plot a course to steer to a point one half mile north of Mattituck Breakwater Light Ml with an engine speed of 9.0 knots. If there are no set and drift, what course should you steer?

A. 207° psc
B. 213° psc
C. 220° psc
D. 235° psc

15809. At 0045, you obtain the following bearings: Rocky Point lookout tower — 072°T; Horton Point lighthouse—213°T. What were the set and drift between 0005 and 0045?

A. 272° true, 0.9 knot
B. 272° true, 1.4 knots
C. 092° true, 0.9 knot
D. 092° true, 1.4 knots

15810. You alter course from your 0045 position to head for a point 0.5 mile north of Mattituck Breakwater Light Ml. If the visibility is 10 miles and you make good 9 knots,

at approximately what time will you lose sight of Saybrook Breakwater Light?
A. You have already lost sight at 0045
B. 0055
C. 0120
D. The light is visible all the way to Mattituck Inlet

15811. At 0100, you obtain the following bearings: Rocky Point Lookout Tower—062°T; Horton Point Lighthouse—189°T. What was the speed made good between 0045 and 0100?

A. 7.4 knots
B. 8.0 knots

C. 8.7 knots
D. 9.2 knots

15813. According to the DR track line from your 0100 position, how far off Roanoke Point Shoal Buoy 5 should you be when the buoy is abeam?

A. 0.2 mile
B. 0.8 mile
C. 1.3 miles
D. 1.8 miles

15814. At 0130, you obtain the following bearings: Horton Point Lighthouse—078°T; Mattituck Breakwater Light Tower—196°T. What were the course and speed made good between 0100 and 0130?

A. 246°T at 9.8 knots
B. 253°T at 9.4 knots
C. 259°T at 9.8 knots
D. 267°T at 9.4 knots

15815. From your 0130 position, you change course to adjust for set and drift, and you later obtain the following loran lines of position: 9960-W-14975; 9960-X-26412; 9960-Y-43919. What is the latitude and longitude of the loran fix?

A. LAT 41°00.8'N, LONG 72°40.8'W
B. LAT 41°01.2'N, LONG 72°40.4'W
C. LAT 41°01.6'N, LONG 72°40.0'W
D. LAT 41°02.0'N, LONG 72°39.5'W

15816. At 0209, your position is LAT 41°01.8'N, LONG 72°40.8'W. What course should you steer per standard magnetic compass to make good 278° magnetic? (assume no set and drift)

A. 262.0° psc
B. 265.0° psc
C. 275.5° psc
D. 280.5° psc

15817. The south coast of Long Island Sound between Mattituck Inlet and Port Jefferson is _____.

A. composed of high rocky bluffs
B. a high, flat plateau with sheer cliffs
C. fringed by rocky shoals
D. low and marshy with isolated beaches

15818. At 0300, your position is LAT 41°01.7'N, LONG 72°55.1'W. From this position you steer a course of 289° per standard magnetic compass at an engine speed of

10.0 knots. At what time can you first expect to see Stratford Shoal Middle Ground Light if the luminous range is 8.0 miles?

A. 0303
B. 0309
C. 0312
D. 0318

15819. You must arrive at your final destination by 0800. The distance from your 0300 position to the final destination is 40.5 miles. What minimum speed must be made good to arrive on time?

A. 8.1 knots
B. 8.5 knots
C. 9.3 knots
D. 9.6 knots

15820. You are northwest of Port Jefferson Harbor steering 242° per standard magnetic compass. As you continue westward you see that the Port Jefferson Range Front Light and Rear Light come into line. If the deviation table is correct, the bearing of the range should be _____.

A. 140° psc
B. 146° psc
C. 157° psc
D. 160° psc

The following questions are based on the C of E Mississippi River Maps (Cairo to the Gulf) and the Light List. At 1015 on 16 April, you are at the Amoco Pipeline Co. Docks (253.6 AHP), when you get underway, enroute to Institute, WV, with a tow of eight barges carrying molten sulphur.

15821. What is the distance from the Amoco Docks at Baton Rouge, LA, to the mouth of the Ohio River?

A. 700.2 miles
B. 727.9 miles
C. 953.5 miles
D. 981.5 miles

15822. You are turning for 10 mph, approaching Angola, LA. Angola reports that the current at Red River Landing is estimated at 4.5 MPH. Which of the following statements is TRUE?

A. You are making 14.5 mph over ground.
B. You should expect to encounter vessels crossing the river at mile 300.5 AHP.

C. You would expect to find a more favorable current near the broken red line in the river.
D. Hog Pt. Light and Hog Pt. Lower Light may be used as range lights when entering Shreves cut-off.

15823. As you approach Shreves cut-off you see Red River Landing Gauge (302.4 AHP) which reads 6.2 feet. Which of the following statements is TRUE?

A. This reading is at the same elevation as the 6.2 ft. mark on the gauge at Head of Passes.
B. This reading is 6.2 ft. above the Low Water Reference Plane.
C. The depth of water at Red River Landing is 6.2 ft.
D. A vessel drawing 7 ft. would be able to pass through the locks at Lower Old River.

15824. You pass Red River Gauge at 2015 on 16 April and estimate the current will average 3.5 mph for the remainder of the time on the Mississippi River. What is your ETA at the mouth of the Ohio River if you continue to turn for 10 mph?

A. 1445, 20 April
B. 1830, 20 April
C. 0028, 21 April
D. 0821, 21 April

15825. What is the vertical clearance between the highest point of your towboat, if it is 58 feet above the water, and if the Natchez Gauge reads 28.13 feet when passing under the Natchez Upper

Highway Bridge?
A. 15.9 feet
B. 33.2 feet
C. 39.3 feet
D. 45.4 feet

15826. In high water conditions, which publication would you consult for the latest information on buoys between Baton Rouge and Cairo?

A. U.S.C.G. Notice to Mariners
B. U.S.C.G. Light List
C. C of E Navigation Chart
D. List of Buoys and Daymarks

15827. As you approach Giles Bend Cutoff Light (mile 367.7 LDB), what type of daymark would you see on the light structure?

A. green diamond
B. green triangle
C. red diamond
D. red square

15828. At 0305 on 18 April, you pass under the Greenville Bridge (mile 531.3 AHP). What was your average speed since departing Amoco Pipeline Co. Docks (253.6 AHP)?

A. 6.2 mph
B. 6.5 mph
C. 6.8 mph
D. 7.2 mph

15829. A stretch where the channel changes from one side of the river to the other is called a _____.

A. passing
B. transit
C. transfer
D. crossing

15830. After you enter the Ohio River at Cairo, the map shows that the deepest water under the Illinois Central RR Bridge would be found under which span?

A. right descending bank span
B. left descending bank span
C. center span
D. water is equal under all spans

The following questions are to be answered using chart 12221 TR, Chesapeake Bay Entrance, and supporting publications. You are southbound along the coast on a course of 180°T and the engine speed is 14 knots. Your draft is 16 feet. Gyro error is 2°W. Use 10°W variation where required.

15838. At 2000 Loran readings give you the following information: 9960-X-27106; 9960-Y-41639; 9960-Z-58746. Your position is _____.

A. 37°35.0'N, 75°32.2'W
B. 37°23.5'N, 75°32.2'W
C. 37°03.5'N, 75°32.2'W
D. 37°03.5'N, 75°02.2'W

15839. From your 2000 position you change course to 206°T. What time would you expect to be abeam of Hog Island Buoy 12?

A. 2021
B. 2026
C. 2031
D. 2040

15840. You should expect to pass how far off buoy 12?

A. 0.8 mile
B. 1.2 miles
C. 1.7 miles
D. 2.1 miles

15841. At 2030 you take the following bearings: Sand Shoal Inlet South Light—275°T; Cape Charles Light—235°T. You also obtained a Loran-C reading of 9960-Z-58702. The set and drift from 2000 to 2030 are _____.

A. 088° at 0.7 knot
B. 088° at 1.4 knots
C. 268° at 0.7 knot
D. 268° at 1.4 knots

15842. From your 2030 fix you change course to 195°T, and leave the engine speed at 14 knots. At 2045, Sand Shoal Inlet Buoy A bears 318° true, and you obtain the following Loran-C readings: 9960-X-27114; 9960-Y-41516. Which statement is TRUE?

A. Cape Charles Light bears 050° relative.
B. Chesapeake Light bears 190° relative.
C. Your fathometer reading is approximately 40 fathoms.
D. Your vessel is located in a restricted area.

15843. You continue to steer 195°T. You pass Cape Charles Lighted Bell Buoy 14 0.9 miles abeam to starboard at 2111. Your speed made good from 2045 to 2111 is _____.

A. 13.7 knots
B. 14.1 knots
C. 14.5 knots
D. 14.8 knots

15844. Your course made good from 2045 to 2111 is _____.

A. 187°T
B. 190°T
C. 193°T
D. 196°T

15845. If you are going to head directly for Chesapeake Light from your 2111 fix, what is the course to make good?

A. 190°T
B. 193°T
C. 196°T
D. 199°T

15846. At 2200, you alter course to 204°T at 14 knots. You expect a current on this leg of the trip setting 325° at 1.5 knots. Which course should you steer per gyrocompass to make good the true course?

A. 184° pgc
B. 190° pgc
C. 194° pgc
D. 201° pgc

The following questions should be answered using chart 12354TR, Long Island Sound - Eastern Part, and supporting publications. The draft of your vessel is 8.5 feet (2.6 meters). Gyro error is 3°E. "Per standard magnetic compass" is abbreviated "psc." Use a variation of 14°W for the entire plot. The deviation table is:

HDG.	M.DEV.	HDG.	M.DEV.	HDG.	M.DEV.
000°	0°	120°	2°W	240°	3°E
030°	1°W	150°	1°W	270°	3°E
060°	2°W	180°	1°E	300°	2°E
090°	4°W	210°	2°E	330°	1°E

15856. What type of bottom is found at Long Sand Shoal?

A. Rocky
B. Hard
C. Sandy
D. Muddy

15857. You are southeast of Saybrook Breakwater Light passing a horizontally banded buoy. This buoy marks _____.

A. a sunken wreck
B. a tide rips area
C. the junction with the Connecticut R
D. shoal water

15858. At 0005, on 26 January, your position is LAT 41°11.8'N; LONG 72°20.5'W. From this position, you plot a course to a position one mile north of Mattituck Breakwater Light MI. If there are no set and drift, what course should you steer per gyrocompass?

A. 219° pgc
B. 222° pgc
C. 225° pgc
D. 228° pgc

747

15859. You are turning for 9 knots on course 230°T. At 0023, Horton Point Light bears 208° pgc. At 0053, Horton Point Light bears 126° pgc. What is the position of your 0053 running fix?

A. LAT 41°05.7'N, LONG 72°27.6'W
B. LAT 41°05.8'N, LONG 72°28.1'W
C. LAT 41°05.9'N, LONG 72°27.4'W
D. LAT 41°06.0'N, LONG 72°28.2'W

15860. At 0100, your position is LAT 41°05.3 N, LONG 72°29.2 W. You head for the position one mile north of Mattituck Inlet Light and turn to make good 9.0 knots. If the visibility is about 2 miles, at what approximate time will you sight the light?

A. The light is visible at 0100
B. 0109
C. 0120
D. 0128

15861. At 0125, Mattituck Inlet Light bears 203° pgc at 2.1 miles. What is the approximate depth of the water under the keel?

A. 46 fathoms (83.6 meters)
B. 44 fathoms (80.0 meters)
C. 43 feet (13.0 meters)
D. 38 feet (11.5 meters)

15862. At 0125, you change course to make good 280°T. What is the course per standard magnetic compass?

A. 290° psc
B. 292° psc
C. 294° psc
D. 296° psc

15863. If the current is 050° at 0.9 knot, and a northerly wind causes 3° of leeway. What is the course to steer per gyrocompass to make good 280°T if you are turning for 9 knots?

A. 284° pgc
B. 279° pgc
C. 276° pgc
D. 273° pgc

15864. At 0200, you take the following loran readings: 9960-W-14966.0; 9960-X-26410.5; 9960-Y-43933.9. What is the position of your 0200 fix?

A. LAT 41°03.9'N, LONG 72°38.9'W
B. LAT 41°03.8'N, LONG 72°39.1'W
C. LAT 41°03.7'N, LONG 72°38.5'W
D. LAT 41°03.5'N, LONG 72°38.8'W

15865. From your 0200 position, you change course to 272° pgc. How far north of Stratford Shoal Middle Ground Light does this track pass?

A. 2.1 miles
B. 1.6 miles
C. 1.3 miles
D. 1.0 miles

15866. What is your ETA at a point where Stratford Shoal Middle Ground Light bears 180°T if you make good 9.0 knots?

A. 0409
B. 0416
C. 0425
D. 0433

15867. You anticipate a maximum flood current north of Stratford Shoal. You will be set in which general direction?

A. Northerly
B. Easterly
C. Southerly
D. Westerly

15868. Stratford Shoal Middle Ground Light is _____.

A. 13 feet high
B. a fixed white light
C. shown from a white tower
D. equipped with a horn

15869. After you raise Stratford Shoal Middle Ground Light, how will the bearings change if you pass to the north of the light?

A. The bearings will change to the left.
B. The bearings will remain steady.
C. The bearings will change to the right.
D. Magnetic compass bearings will change to the left and gyrocompass bearings will change to the right.

15870. What is the approximate distance from a point three miles south of Stratford Point to Perth Amboy, NJ?

A. 53 miles
B. 62 miles
C. 73 miles
D. 136 miles

The following questions should be answered using chart number 12354TR, Long Island Sound - Eastern Part, and the supporting publications. Your vessel has a draft of 9 feet

(2.7 meters). You are turning for 7.5 knots. Your height of eye is 25 feet (7.6 meters). The variation for the area is 14°W. The deviation table is:

HDG.	M.DEV.	HDG.	M.DEV.	HDG.	M.DEV.
000°	*0.0°*	*120°*	*1.0°W*	*240°*	*2.0°E*
030°	*1°W*	*150°*	*0.0°*	*270°*	*1.5°E*
060°	*3.0°W*	*180°*	*0.0°*	*300°*	*1.0°E*
090°	*2.0°W*	*210°*	*1.0°E*	*330°*	*0.0°*

15906. As you enter the New Haven Outer Channel, you sight the range markers in line directly over the stern. Your heading at the time is 155.5° per gyrocompass. What is the gyro error?

A. 1.0°E
B. 1.0°W
C. 2.0°W
D. 0°

15907. At 0720, you are in the outer channel between buoy 1 and buoy 2 and change course to pass Townshend Ledge Lighted Gong Buoy 10A abeam to port at 200 yards. What is your ETA off the buoy?

A. 0734
B. 0738
C. 0741
D. 0745

15908. At 0740, you plot a loran fix from the following readings: 9960-X-26542.0; 9960-Y-44023.0; 9960-W-15027.0. What is your position?

A. LAT 41°12.6'N, LONG 72°51.3'W
B. LAT 41°12.6'N, LONG 72°51.8'W
C. LAT 41°12.4'N, LONG 72°51.5'W
D. LAT 41°12.3'N, LONG 72°52.0'W

15909. From your 0740 position, you change course to pass 1.1 miles north of Falkner Island Light. What loran reading will ensure that you will remain clear of the 18' shoal located 1 mile NW of Falkner Island Light?

A. 9960 W: not less than 14942
B. 9960 X: not more than 26452
C. 9960 Y: not less than 44013
D. None of the above

15910. At 0802, Branford Reef Light bears 348°T at 0.75 mile, and the north point of Falkner Island bears 088°T at 6.7 miles. What were the set and drift since 0740?

A. Set 040°T, drift 0.3 knot
B. Set 220°T, drift 0.9 knot
C. Set 220°T, drift 0.3 knot
D. You are making good your intended course and speed.

15911. What publication contains information on the navigational hazards in the vicinity of Falkner Island?

A. The navigational regulations in Title 46, Code of Federal Regulations
B. Inland Navigation Rules
C. U.S. Coast Guard Light List
D. U.S. Coast Pilot

15912. If there is no current, what is the course per standard magnetic compass from your 0802 fix to the position 1.1 miles north of Falkner Island Light?

A. 064°
B. 068°
C. 095°
D. 099°

15913. At 0830, you wish to get the latest weather forecasts for the Falkner Island area. On what frequency would you set your FM radio for this information?

A. 2181 kHz
B. 156.65 MHz
C. 156.80 MHz
D. 162.40 MHz

15914. At 0844, the range to the north end of Falkner Island is 2.0 miles and the left tangent bearing is 102°T. What is the approximate charted depth of the water?

A. 14 ft. (4.2 meters)
B. 19 ft. (5.8 meters)
C. 22 ft. (6.7 meters)
D. 29 ft. (8.8 meters)

15915. At 0925, you plot the following loran fix: 9960-W-14931.5; 9960-X-26418.2; 9960-Y-44006.5. If you correct for a current setting 215°T at 0.5 knot, what course will you steer from the 0925 position to arrive at a position 0.5 mile south of Long Sand Shoal West End Horn Buoy W?

A. 089°T
B. 093°T
C. 096°T
D. 102°T

15916. If you correct for the current in question 15 (215°T at 0.5 knot) and maintain an engine speed of 7.5 knots, what is your ETA 0.5 mile south of buoy W?

A. 1016
B. 1021
C. 1026
D. 1030

15917. At what approximate distance would you expect Bartlett Reef Light to break the horizon, if the visibility is 27 nautical miles?

A. 5.9 nm
B. 6.9 nm
C. 12.0 nm
D. 12.8 nm

15918. At 1038, you are 0.4 mile south of Long Sand Shoal Buoy 8A on course 090°T when visibility is reduced to 1 mile in rain and haze. You intend to stay on 090°T until your Loran shows a reading that you can safely follow to the approaches of New London. Which of the following Loran readings will you look for?

A. 9960-W-14720
B. 9960-X-26290
C. 9960-Y-43980
D. 9960-W-14810

15919. At 1200, your position is 2.0 miles southwest of Bartlett Reef Light. Your heading is 075°T. Visibility is less than 0.2 mile in fog and rain. Which of the following signals is most likely to be from another vessel?

A. Whistle from 125° relative
B. Whistle from 075° relative
C. Bell from 350° relative
D. Horn from 330° relative

15920. What chart should you use after you enter New London Harbor?

A. 13211
B. 13213
C. 13214
D. 13272

The following questions are to be answered using chart 13205 TR, Block Island Sound, and supporting publications. Your vessel has just taken departure from New London harbor. Your height of eye is 65 feet and your vessel's draft is 22 feet. Use 15°W variation where required.

15938. At 1910 you obtain the following bearings: Bartlett Reef Light—268°T; Race Rock Light—147°T; Little Gull Island Light—198°T. Which of the following is your position at 1910?

A. LAT 41°17.4'N, LONG 72°05.6'W
B. LAT 41°17.0'N, LONG 72°07.1'W
C. LAT 41°16.6'N, LONG 72°04.6'W
D. LAT 41°16.2'N, LONG 72°06.4'W

15939. From your 1910 position, you set a course of 162°T at a speed of 14 knots. What will serve as a definite warning that you are being set towards Race Rock Light?

A. Decreasing bearings to Race Rock Light
B. Decreasing loran readings on loran rate 9960-W
C. Increasing soundings
D. Decreasing radar ranges to Race Point

15940. At 1934 Little Gull Island Light bears 277°T and Race Rock Light bears 000°T. Which were the set and drift between 1910 and 1934?

A. 321°T, 2.2 knots
B. 321°T, 0.9 knot
C. 331°T, 2.2 knots
D. 331°T, 0.9 knot

15941. From your 1934 position, you change course to pass 2.0 miles due north of Block Island Sound South Entrance Obstruction Lighted BIS Buoy. If you adjust your course only (while maintaining an engine speed of 14 knots) for a set and drift of 230°T at 3.5 knots, what is your ETA and distance off when abeam of Shagwong Reef Lighted Bell Buoy 7SR?

A. 2003, 4.2 miles
B. 2009, 4.2 miles
C. 2003, 3.7 miles
D. 2009, 3.7 miles

15942. At 1959 Watch Hill Point Light bears 030°T, Montauk Point Light bears 146°T, and Little Gull Light bears 283°T. What is the approximate fathometer reading?

A. 51 feet
B. 73 feet
C. 95 feet
D. 111 feet

15943. At 2038 Block Island North Light bears 065°T, Montauk Point Light bears 216°T, and a reading of 25959 is obtained on loran rate 9960-X. Which statement is TRUE?

A. Your speed made good between your 1959 fix and 2038 fix is 11.0 knots.
B. Your course made good between your 1959 fix and 2038 fix is 102°T.
C. At your 2038 fix, your vessel is governed by the Inland Rules of the Road.
D. Block Island Sound South Entrance Obstruction Lighted BIS Buoy is located 3.6 miles off your starboard bow.

15944. From your 2038 position you change course to 104°T and increase engine speed to 18 knots. If you make good this course and speed, at what time will Southwest Ledge Lighted Bell Buoy 2 bear 157°T?

A. 2047
B. 2052
C. 2056
D. 2101

15945. At 2107 Southeast Point Light bears 062°T, and at 2112 this light bears 038°T. What is your distance off Southeast Point Light at 2112 (assume no set and drift)?

A. 2.1 miles
B. 2.5 miles
C. 2.9 miles
D. 3.3 miles

15946. At 2132 you sight Block Island Southest Point Light in line with the Aerobeacon (rotating white and green) bearing 308.5° pgc. The helmsman reports he was heading 106° pgc and 119° psc. What is the deviation on that heading?

A. 4°W
B. 2°W
C. 2°E
D. 4°E

The following questions should be answered using chart 12221TR, Chesapeake Bay Entrance, and the supporting publications. The height of eye is 25 feet (7.6 meters). The gyro error is 3°W. "Per standard magnetic compass" is abbreviated "psc." Use a variation of 10°W for the entire plot. The deviation table is:

HDG.	M.DEV.	HDG.	M.DEV.	HDG.	M.DEV.
000°	0°	120°	2°W	240°	3°E
030°	1°W	150°	1°W	270°	3°E
060°	2°W	180°	1°E	300°	2°E
090°	4°W	210°	2°E	330°	1°E

15956. The National Weather Service provides 24-hour weather broadcasts to vessels transiting the Chesapeake Bay Bridge Tunnel. The broadcasts may be found on _____.

A. 202.35 MHz
B. 181.15 MHz
C. 162.55 MHz
D. 147.45 MHz

15957. At 1752, your position is LAT 37°04.3'N, LONG 76°06.4'W. On an ebb current you should expect to be set to the _____.

A. north-northeast
B. south-southeast
C. south-southwest
D. north-northwest

15958. Your 1752 position is _____.

A. less than 0.2 mile to the west of York Spit Channel
B. less than 0.2 mile to the east of York Spit Channel
C. more than 0.2 mile to the west of York Spit Channel
D. more than 0.2 mile to the east of York Spit Channel

15959. What is the average velocity of the maximum ebb current in the channel west of Middle Ground?

A. 0.8 knot
B. 1.0 knot
C. 1.3 knots
D. 1.6 knots

15960. From your 1752 position, you steer 313° pgc at 9 knots. At 1805, you obtain the following visual bearings: Old Pt. Comfort Light—238° pgc; Chesapeake Bay Tunnel North Light—136° pgc. What are the latitude and longitude of your 1805 position?

A. LAT 37°05.9'N, LONG 76°08.0'W
B. LAT 37°06.0'N, LONG 76°08.4'W
C. LAT 37°05.0'N, LONG 76°08.7'W
D. LAT 37°06.1'N, LONG 76°08.1'W

15961. At 1810, a red buoy bears 010° relative. This buoy marks _____.

A. the side of York Spit Channel
B. the visibility limit of the red sector of Cape Henry Light

C. a submerged obstruction in York Spit Channel
D. the York River Entrance Channel

15962. Based on dead reckoning, at approximately 1817 you would expect to _____.

A. enter a traffic separation zone
B. depart a restricted area
C. cross a submerged pipeline
D. depart a regulated area

15963. At 1845, you obtain a loran fix using the following information: 9960-X-27251.0; 9960-Y-41432.0; 9960-Z-58537.9. Your

latitude is _____.
A. 37°11.4'N
B. 37°11.2'N
C. 37°10.9'N
D. 37°10.7'N

15964. Your 1900 position is LAT 37°12.9'N, LONG 76°13.5'W. You change course to 323° pgc. What is the course per standard magnetic compass?

A. 309° psc
B. 311° psc
C. 329° psc
D. 331° psc

15965. If the visibility is 5 miles, what is the luminous range of New Point Comfort Spit Light 4?

A. 0.5 mile
B. 3.4 miles
C. 4.8 miles
D. 5.0 miles

15966. The yellow buoys on either side of your vessel that lead to Mobjack Bay mark _____.

A. the limits of the dredged channel
B. fishtrap areas
C. underwater cable areas
D. ferry routes

15967. At 1925, you take a fix using the following radar ranges: York Spit Light—3.4 miles away; New Point Comfort Spit Light 2—2.1 miles away; York Spit Swash Channel Light 3—2.7 miles away. Your longitude is _____.

A. 76°16.6'W
B. 76°16.8'W

C. 76°17.0'W
D. 76°17.2'W

5968. What was the speed made good from 1900 to 1925?

A. 8.5 knots
B. 8.7 knots
C. 8.8 knots
D. 9.1 knots

5969. What is the height above water of New Point Comfort Spit Light 2?

A. 6 feet (1.8 meters)
B. 15 feet (4.6 meters)
C. 18 feet (5.5 meters)
D. 24 feet (7.3 meters)

5970. If you have 16.3 miles to reach your destination from your 2000 position and want to be there at 2230, what speed should you make good?

A. 5.7 knots
B. 6.1 knots
C. 6.5 knots
D. 6.9 knots

The following questions are based on chart 12354TR, Long Island Sound - Eastern Part, and the supporting publications. Your vessel has a draft of 12 feet (3.6 meters). Your height of eye is 16 feet (4.8 meters). The gyro error is 2°E. Use 14°W variation where required. The deviation table is:

HDG.	M.DEV.	HDG.	M.DEV.	HDG.	M.DEV.
000°	0°	120°	2°W	240°	3°E
030°	1°W	150°	1°W	270°	3°E
060°	2°W	180°	1°E	300°	2°E
090°	4°W	210°	2°E	330°	1°E

16006. You are on course 082°T, and the engines are turning for 8 knots. At 0352, you take the following bearings: Stratford Point Light—016° pgc; Stratford Shoal (Middle Ground) Light—137° pgc. What is your 0352 position?

A. LAT 41°05.0'N, LONG 73°08.0'W
B. LAT 41°05.2'N, LONG 73°07.8'W
C. LAT 41°05.3'N, LONG 73°07.5'W
D. LAT 41°05.4'N, LONG 73°07.7'W

16007. If the visibility is 11 miles, what is the earliest time you can expect to see New Haven Light?

A. The light is visible at 0352.
B. 0414
C. 0443
D. You will not sight the light.

16008. While on a heading of 082°T, you sight Middle Ground Light in line with Old Field Point Light bearing 206° per standard magnetic compass. From this you can determine the _____.

A. variation
B. deviation table is correct for that heading
C. compass error is 17.5°E
D. deviation is 3.5°E for a bearing of 206° per standard magnetic compass

16009. The maximum ebb current at a location 4.3 miles south of Stratford Point will occur at 0413. The predicted current will be 1.0 knot at 075°. What will be your course made good if you steer 082°T at 8 knots?

A. 081°T
B. 083°T
C. 085°T
D. 087°T

16010. The characteristic of Branford Reef Light is _____.

A. flashing red every 4 seconds
B. flashing red every 3 seconds
C. flashing white every 6 seconds
D. flashing yellow every 4 seconds

16011. At 0415, you take the following bearings: Stratford Point Light—329.5° pgc; Middle Ground Light—223.5° pgc; Old Field Point Light—199.5° pgc. Which statement is TRUE?

A. You are to the right of your intended track line.
B. The current's drift is greater than predicted.
C. The course made good since 0452 is 081°T.
D. Your fathometer reads about 76 fathoms.

16012. If you change course at 0420, what is the course to make good to leave Twenty Eight Foot Shoal Lighted Buoy abeam to port at 1 mile?
A. 079°T
B. 082°T

C. 084°T
D. 086°T

16013. At 0430, you take the following loran readings: 9960-X-26605.5; 9960-Y-43985.0. What is your 0430 position?

A. LAT 41°08.9'N, LONG 73°00.0'W
B. LAT 41°05.0'N, LONG 73°01.1'W
C. LAT 41°05.5'N, LONG 72°59.7'W
D. LAT 41°05.8'N, LONG 73°00.8'W

16014. From your 0430 position, what is the course per standard magnetic compass to a position where Twenty-Eight Foot Shoal lighted buoy TE is abeam to port at 1 mile?

A. 082.5°
B. 086.0°
C. 098.0°
D. 101.5°

16015. By 0430, the wind has increased, and the visibility cleared due to passage of a front. You estimate 3° leeway due to NW'ly winds. What is the course per gyro-compass to pass 1.2 miles due south of Twenty-Eight Foot Shoal Lighted Buoy TE?

A. 080°
B. 083°
C. 086°
D. 090°

16016. At 0430, you change course and speed to make good 090°T at 10 knots. At 0433, you slow due to an engineering casualty and estimate you are making good 5.5 knots. At what time will Branford Reef Light bear 000°T?

A. 0601
B. 0609
C. 0620
D. 0624

16017. What is the approximate distance to New Bedford, MA, from your 0530 DR position, if your 0352 position was 7 miles from Bridgeport, CT?

A. 77 miles
B. 91 miles
C. 104 miles
D. 115 miles

16018. At 0550, engineering repairs are complete and speed is increased to 9.6 knots. At 0630, Falkner Island Light bears

023° pgc and Horton Point Light bears 097° pgc. From your 0630 fix you steer to make good a course of 086°T while turning for 9.6 knots. At 0700, Falkner Island Light bears 336.0° pgc and Horton Point Light bears 105.5° pgc. The radar range to the south tip of Falkner Island is 5.7 miles. Which statement is TRUE?

A. Your course made good from 0630 to 0700 was 082°T.
B. The speed made good from 0630 to 0700 was 10.1 knots.
C. The current from 0630 to 0700 was 279°T at 0.6 knot.
D. You are making good your intended speed.

16019. The south shore of Long Island Sound from Horton Point to Orient Point is _____.

A. low and marshy
B. bluff and rocky
C. marked by sandy beaches and wooded uplands
D. bound by gradual shoaling

16020. If visibility permits, Orient Point Light will break the horizon at a range of about _____.

A. 9.3 miles
B. 10.8 miles
C. 13.9 miles
D. 17.0 miles

The following questions are to be answered using chart 12354 TR, Long Island Sound - Eastern Part, and supporting publications. You are on a coastwise voyage from Bridgeport, Conn., to Boston, Mass. You intend to divert to a position off New Haven, Conn., to evacuate an injured crew member. Your height of eye is 53 feet and your vessel's deep draft is 34 feet. Gyro error is 2°W. Use 14°W variation where required.

16038. At 0820 Old Field Point Light bears 206° per gyrocompass; and Stratford Shoals Middle Ground Light bears 322° per gyrocompass. The radar range to Middle Ground Light is 1.5 miles. Your 0820 fix gives you a position of _____.

A. LAT 41°02.6'N, LONG 73°05.2'W
B. LAT 41°02.5'N, LONG 73°04.9'W
C. LAT 41°02.3'N, LONG 73°05.2'W
D. LAT 41°02.0'N, LONG 73°05.1'W

16039. From your 0820 position you change course to your rendezvous position, one mile due south of buoy NH, speed 14.5 knots. You estimate the current to be 260°T at 0.5 knot. The wind is northwesterly at 20 knots and you estimate 2° leeway. What is your course per gyrocompass (pgc) to the rendezvous position, if you correct your heading for current and leeway?

A. 039°
B. 041°
C. 043°
D. 045°

16040. At 0847 you take a round of bearings as follows: Middle Ground Shoal Light—237° pgc; Stratford Point Light—289° pgc; New Haven Light—019° pgc. What were the set and drift since your 0820 position?

A. Set 180°T, drift 0.6 kt
B. Set 360°T, drift 0.3 kt
C. Set 180°T, drift 0.3 kt
D. Set 360°T, drift 0.6 kt

16041. From your 0847 fix, you change course to arrive at the rendezvous position and, correcting for current, you estimate your speed over the ground at 15 knots. What is your ETA at the rendezvous?

A. 0902
B. 0905
C. 0908
D. 0911

16042. At 1022 when you complete the evacuation, you get underway on course 098°T and order turns for 14.5 knots. You take the following round of bearings at that time: Stratford Point Light—260° per gyrocompass; New Haven Light—326° per gyrocompass; SW Ledge Light—358° per gyrocompass. Determine your ETA and distance off when abeam of Falkner Island Light, if there are no set and drift.

A. 1102, 3.0 miles
B. 1108, 3.3 miles
C. 1114, 3.1 miles
D. 1118, 3.3 miles

16043. As you cross the New Haven Outer Channel range, you observe the range in line bearing 335.5° per gyrocompass. The helmsman reports that he was heading 100° per gyrocompass and that the

standard magnetic compass read 109° at the time of the observation. What are the gyro error and deviation of the standard magnetic compass on this heading?

A. Gyro error 2°E, deviation 3°E
B. Gyro error 0°, deviation 2°W
C. Gyro error 2°W, deviation 9°W
D. Gyro error 2°W, deviation 3°E

16044. At 1038 Branford Reef Light bears 019° pgc, Falkner Island Light bears 075° pgc, and the radar range to Branford Reef Light is 3.0 miles. Which statement is TRUE of your 1038 position?

A. You are required by regulation to change course to avoid steaming through the dumping ground.
B. You are making more speed over the ground, since your 1002 fix, than indicated by your engine RPM.
C. When the loran reads 9960-Y-43964.0, you should follow that loran reading to the approaches to the Race.
D. Your fathometer reads about 25 feet.

16045. The north shore of Long Island, from Horton Point to Orient Point is _____.

A. bluff and rocky
B. low and sparsely wooded
C. marked by long sandy beaches at low water
D. marshy and backed with sand dunes

16046. The visibility is excellent. When Race Rock Light Tower breaks the horizon, how far will you be from the Tower?

A. 8.5 miles
B. 9.6 miles
C. 14.0 miles
D. 17.9 miles

The following questions should be answered using chart 12221TR, Chesapeake Bay Entrance, and the supporting publications. The draft of your vessel is 8.0 feet. The gyro error is 2°W. You are heading down the York River bound for Norfolk, VA. "Per standard magnetic compass" is abbreviated "psc." Use a variation of 10°W for the entire plot. The deviation table is:

HDG.	M.DEV.	HDG.	M.DEV.	HDG.	M.DEV.
000°	0°	120°	2°W	240°	3°E
030°	1°W	150°	1°W	270°	3°E
060°	2°W	180°	1°E	300°	2°E
090°	4°W	210°	2°E	330°	1°E

16056. At 1730, your position is LAT 37°13.9'N, LONG 76°26.4'W. What is your distance off Tue Marshes Light?

A. 2.2 miles
B. 2.6 miles
C. 3.0 miles
D. 3.4 miles

16057. What is the maximum allowable speed of vessels underway up river from Tue Marshes Light?

A. 8 knots
B. 10 knots
C. 12 knots
D. 14 knots

16058. At 1750, your position is LAT 37°14.5'N, LONG 76°22.9'W. What was the speed made good between 1730 and 1750?

A. 7.5 knots
B. 7.8 knots
C. 8.1 knots
D. 8.4 knots

16059. At 1800, Tue Marshes Light bears 270° pgc, and York Spit Swash Channel Light 3 bears 007° pgc. Your position is _____.

A. LAT 37°14.0'N, LONG 76°19.8'W
B. LAT 37°14.2'N, LONG 76°20.3'W
C. LAT 37°14.2'N, LONG 76°20.1'W
D. LAT 37°14.5'N, LONG 76°20.0'W

16060. The short-long dashed, magenta lines parallel to York River Entrance Channel mark _____.

A. fish trap areas
B. naval exercise areas
C. underwater cables
D. recommended track lines

16061. You have just passed York River Entrance Channel Lighted Buoys 13 and 14. The chart shows a light approximately 1.0 mile off your port beam with a light characteristic Fl 6 sec. What is the name of this light?

A. Mobjack Bay Entrance Light
B. York Spit Light
C. New Point Comfort Light
D. York River Entrance Channel Light 1

16062. At 1930, your vessel is between York

River Entrance Channel Lighted Buoys 1YR and 2. From this position, you change course to 142° pgc at an engine speed of 8.0 knots. At 2000, you take the following bearings: Chesapeake Channel Tunnel North Light—131° pgc; Thimble Shoal Light—247° pgc. What were the set and drift between 1930 and 2000?

A. 140°T at 0.2 knot
B. 140°T at 0.4 knot
C. 320°T at 0.2 knot
D. 320°T at 0.4 knot

16063. At 2013, you sight Thimble Shoal Light in line with Old Point Comfort Light bearing 258° pgc. At the time of the bearing, the vessel was headed 142° pgc and 151° psc. Based on this, you _____.

A. know the gyro error is 2°E
B. should adjust the magnetic compass
C. verified that the variation is 10°W
D. have checked the deviation table for a magnetic heading of 150°

16064. At 2015, your vessel is at the Chesapeake Bay Bridge and Tunnel midway between buoys 13 and 14. If the height of tide is −1 foot (−0.3 meter). What is the approximate depth under the keel?

A. 51 feet (15.5 meters)
B. 45 feet (13.6 meters)
C. 40 feet (12.1 meters)
D. 35 feet (10.6 meters)

16065. If you steer 143° pgc at an engine speed of 8.0 knots from your 2015 position, at what time would you reach a point midway between buoys 11 and 12 (ignore set and drift)?

A. 2020
B. 2029
C. 2032
D. 2039

16066. Which statement concerning Thimble Shoal Channel is TRUE?

A. The project width of the main channel is 1000 feet (30.3 meters)
B. The channel is 14.5 miles in length.
C. A tow drawing 30 feet (9.1 meters) is excluded from the main channel.
D. Thimble Shoal Channel is in international waters.

16067. At 2118, you obtain the following

information: Cape Henry Light—151° pgc; Cape Charles Light—033° pgc; Thimble Shoal Light—291° pgc. What is your 2118 position?

A. LAT 36°57.4'N, LONG 76°01.9'W
B. LAT 36°57.5'N, LONG 76°01.4'W
C. LAT 36°57.6'N, LONG 76°01.8'W
D. LAT 36°57.6'N, LONG 76°02.2'W

16068. From your 2118 position, you proceed to Norfolk, VA, a distance of approximately 26.0 miles. To arrive at Norfolk by 0200 the next day, what is the minimum speed to make good from your 2118 position to arrive at this time?

A. 5.0 knots
B. 5.3 knots
C. 5.8 knots
D. 5.5 knots

16069. From your 2118 position, you steer a course of 288°T at an engine speed of 7.0 knots. Visibility is 2 miles. Height of eye is 12 feet (3.7 meters). At what time can you expect to see Old Point Comfort Light?

A. The light is visible at 2118
B. 2139
C. 2201
D. 2232

16070. When exiting Thimble Shoal Channel bound for Norfolk, the track line based on the lights of the Norfolk Entrance Reach Range is _____.

A. 220°T
B. 222°T
C. 225°T
D. 228°T

The following questions are based on chart 12221TR, Chesapeake Bay Entrance, and the supporting publications. Your vessel draws 11 feet (3.3 meters), and your height of eye is 24 feet (7.3 meters). Use variation 10°W where necessary. The gyro error is 2°W. The deviation table is:

HDG.	M.DEV.	HDG.	M.DEV.	HDG.	M.DEV.
000°	1.5°E	120°	2.0°E	240°	0.0°
030°	1.5°E	150°	1.0°W	270°	0.0°
060°	3.0°E	180°	3.0°W	300°	1.0°E
090°	2.5°E	210°	1.0°W	330°	1.0°E

16106. At 0410, you take the following bearings: New Point Comfort Light 2—242°T; Wolf Trap Light—313°T; Horn Harbor Entrance Light HH—262°T. What is your 0410 position?

A. LAT 37°21.0'N, LONG 76°08.1'W
B. LAT 37°21.0'N, LONG 76°08.8'W
C. LAT 37°21.1'N, LONG 76°07.9'W
D. LAT 37°21.2'N, LONG 76°08.2'W

16107. If the visibility is 5 miles and you are in the red sector, at what distance off should you sight Cape Henry Light?

A. 15 miles
B. 13 miles
C. 11 miles
D. 09 miles

16108. From your 0410 fix, what is the course per standard magnetic compass to the entrance to York Spit Channel between buoys 37 and 38?

A. 178°
B. 176°
C. 156°
D. 152°

16109. You are turning for 9 knots, a westerly wind is causing 3° of leeway, and the current is 320°T at 1.2 knots. What true course should you steer to remain in the northern leg of York Spit Channel?

A. 191°T
B. 194°T
C. 197°T
D. 203°T

16110. If you are making 8.3 knots over the ground, what is your ETA at the first turning point in York Spit Channel between buoys 29 and 30?

A. 0444
B. 0456
C. 0508
D. 0522

16111. Which publication contains the specific information about navigating in York Spit Channel?

A. Light List
B. Coast Pilot
C. Chesapeake Bay Harbormaster's Regulations Manual
D. Navigator's Manual—Chesapeake Bay

16112. At 0530, the Coast Guard announces that Chesapeake Channel is

closed indefinitely due to a collision occurring in the channel between Trestle B and C of the Chesapeake Bay Bridge and Tunnel. You exit York Spit Channel, leaving buoy 20 abeam to port at 0.1 mile, and alter course to leave Horseshoe Crossing Lighted Bell Buoy abeam to port at 0.2 mile. What is the course per gyrocompass?

A. 185° pgc
B. 187° pgc
C. 190° pgc
D. 193° pgc

16113. After you enter Thimble Shoal Channel, you will alter course to pass between Trestles A and B. Which channel should you use?

A. Thimble Shoal Main Channel or the South Auxiliary Channel
B. Any of the channels but keep to the right hand side
C. The South Auxiliary Channel
D. Thimble Shoal Main Channel

16114. As you pass through the Chesapeake Bay Bridge and Tunnel, you sight Trestle A in line bearing 198° pgc. What is the gyro error?

A. 2°E
B. 0°E
C. 2°W
D. 4°W

16115. You sighted Trestle A in line at 0707 and are steering 108°T. At 0731, Cape Henry Light bears 136°T; Cape Charles Light bears 032.5°T; and Thimble Shoal Tunnel South Light bears 282°T. What was the speed made good between 0707 and 0731?

A. 8.3 knots
B. 8.8 knots
C. 9.2 knots
D. 9.4 knots

16116. At 0731, approximately how much water is under your keel?

A. 31 feet (9.4 meters)
B. 45 feet (13.6 meters)
C. 48 feet (14.5 meters)
D. 54 feet (16.4 meters)

16117. What is the distance from your 0731 fix to Wilmington, NC (LAT 34°14.0'N, LONG 77°57.0'W)?

A. 339 miles
B. 363 miles
C. 402 miles
D. 486 miles

16118. You will enter waters governed by the International Rules when _____.

A. you cross the territorial sea boundary line
B. abeam of buoy CBJ
C. you cross the boundary of the contiguous zone
D. Cape Charles Light bears 022°T

16119. At 0812, you take the following loran readings: 9960-X-27155.2; 9960-Y-41267.9; 9960-Z-58537.8. What is your 0812 position?

A. LAT 36°53.7'N, LONG 75°56.0'W
B. LAT 36°53.8'N, LONG 75°56.1'W
C. LAT 36°54.5'N, LONG 75°56.2'W
D. LAT 36°54.6'N, LONG 75°55.8'W

16120. At 0812, you are on course 132°T. The standard magnetic compass reads 135°. What should you conclude?

A. The deviation table is correct for that heading.
B. You should adjust the magnetic compass.
C. Your compass may be influenced by a local magnetic disturbance.
D. The deviation is increasing as you go south.

The following questions are to be answered using chart 13205 TR, Block Island Sound, and supporting publications. Your height of eye is 55 feet and your vessel's draft is 22 feet. Your present course is 111°T and your vessel's engines are turning RPMs for 13 knots.

16138. At 1930 Race Rock Light bears 111°T, Little Gull Island Light bears 172°T, and a reading of 26157 is obtained on Loran Rate 9960-X. Which of the following is your position at 1930?

A. LAT 41°15.6'N, LONG 72°09.6'W
B. LAT 41°16.1'N, LONG 72°08.3'W
C. LAT 41°15.3'N, LONG 72°12.9'W
D. LAT 41°15.8'N, LONG 72°07.1'W

16139. From your 1930 position, you set a course of 150°T. Your engine speed is 13 knots. What will be your distance off Valiant Rock Bell Buoy 1A when abeam, if you make good your true course of 150°?

0.8 mile
1.0 mile
1.2 miles
1.4 miles

16140. Available information indicates that there is a set and drift in this area of 290°T at 2 knots. Allowing for this set and drift, what course must you steer to make good a true course of 150°, while maintaining an engine speed of 13 knots, from your 1930 position?

A. 141°T
B. 145°T
C. 149°T
D. 153°T

16141. The speed you can expect to make good over your course while steering to make 150°T is _____.

A. 11.0 knots
B. 11.4 knots
C. 14.0 knots
D. 14.4 knots

16142. At 1949 Little Gull Island Light bears 270°T and is 1.7 miles off. From this position, you change course to 118°T and increase engine speed to 18 knots. If you make good your course and speed, at what time should Shagwong Reef Lighted Bell Buoy 7SR bear 180°T?

A. 2016
B. 2019
C. 2022
D. 2025

16144. From your 2027 position you change course to 106°T, while maintaining an engine speed of 18 knots. Your ETA at a position where Block Island Sound South Entrance Obstruction Lighted Buoy BIS is abeam is _____.

A. 2039
B. 2043
C. 2047
D. 2050

16145. At 2054 Block Island Southeast Point Light bears 054°T, Southwest Ledge Lighted Bell Buoy 2 is 1.6 miles off to port, and a reading of 14595 is obtained on loran rate 9960-W. The set and drift from 2027 to 2054 is _____.

A. 127°T at 3.1 knots
B. 127°T at 1.4 knots
C. 307°T at 3.1 knots
D. 307°T at 1.4 knots

16146. From your 2054 position, you change course to 066°T. Maintaining course and speed of 18 knots, at what time can you expect to first cross the 90-foot curve if you experience no set and drift?

A. 2105
B. 2111
C. 2117
D. 2125

The following questions should be answered using chart 12221TR, Chesapeake Bay Entrance, and supporting publications.The height of eye is 24 feet (7.3 meters). Your draft is 11 feet (3.4 meters). The gyro error is 2°W. You are proceeding down Chesapeake Bay bound for sea and then up the coast to Wilmington, DE. "Per standard magnetic compass" is abbreviated "psc." Use a variation of 10°W for the entire plot. The deviation table is:

HDG.	M.DEV.	HDG.	M.DEV.	HDG.	M.DEV.
000°	1.5°E	120°	2.0°E	240°	0.0°
030°	1.5°E	150°	1.0°W	270°	0.0°
060°	3.0°E	180°	3.0°W	300°	1.0°E
090°	2.5°E	210°	1.0°W	330°	1.0°E

16156. At 0410, you take the following bearings: New Point Comfort Light 2—244° pgc, Wolf Trap Light—315° pgc. What is your 0410 position?

A. LAT 37°21.2'N, LONG 76°08.3'W
B. LAT 37°21.1'N, LONG 76°08.8'W
C. LAT 37°21.1'N, LONG 76°07.9'W
D. LAT 37°21.0'N, LONG 76°08.1'W

16157. If the visibility is 10 miles and you are in the red sector, at what distance off should you sight Cape Henry Light?

A. 15 miles
B. 12 miles
C. 10 miles
D. 08 mile

16158. From your 0410 fix, what is the course per standard magnetic compass to enter York Spit Channel with buoy 29 close abeam to starboard?

A. 172° psc
B. 176° psc

C. 198° psc
D. 202° psc

16159. If you are making 8.3 knots over the ground, what is your ETA at the turning point in York Spit Channel at buoy 29?

A. 0521
B. 0509
C. 0459
D. 0448

16160. You are entering the channel at buoy 29 and turning for 9 knots. An easterly wind is causing 3° of leeway and the current is 320°T at 1.2 knots. What true course should you steer to remain in the middle leg of York Spit Channel?

A. 162°T
B. 165°T
C. 168°T
D. 171°T

16161. Which publication contains specific information on the characteristics of Chesapeake Bay entrance?

A. Sailing Directions
B. Coast Pilot
C. Chesapeake Bay Harbormaster's Manual
D. Navigator's Manual—Chesapeake Bay

16162. The Coast Guard announces that Chesapeake Channel is closed indefinitely due to a collision in the channel between Trestle B and C of the Chesapeake Bay Bridge and Tunnel. You exit York Spit Channel, leaving buoy 22 close abeam to port at 0.1 mile, and alter course to leave Horseshoe Crossing Lighted Bell Buoy HC abeam to port at 0.2 mile. What is the course per gyrocompass?

A. 185° pgc
B. 188° pgc
C. 191° pgc
D. 194° pgc

16164. As you pass through the Chesapeake Bay Bridge and Tunnel, you sight Trestle B in line bearing 018° pgc. What is the gyro error by observation?

A. 2°E
B. 0°
C. 2°W
D. 4°W

16165. You sighted Trestle B in line at 0706 and are steering 108°T. At 0731, Cape Henry Light bears 136°T; Cape Charles Light bears 032.5°T; and Thimble Shoal Tunnel South Light bears 282°T. What was the speed made good between 0706 and 0731?

A. 8.3 knots
B. 8.8 knots
C. 9.2 knots
D. 9.4 knots

16166. At 0731, what is the approximate depth of water?

A. 31 feet (9.4 meters)
B. 41 feet (12.5 meters)
C. 52 feet (15.7 meters)
D. 58 feet (17.6 meters)

16167. What is the coastwise distance from your 0731 fix to Wilmington, DE (LAT 39°43.2'N, LONG 75°31.5'W)?

A. 339 miles
B. 309 miles
C. 245 miles
D. 221 miles

16168. You will enter waters governed by the International Rules when _____.

A. you cross the territorial sea boundary line
B. enter the pilotage area
C. you cross the boundary of the contiguous zone
D. Cape Henry Light bears 202°T

16169. At 0812, you take the following loran readings: 9960-X-27155.2; 9960-Y-41264.5; 9960-Z-58536.2. What is your 0812 position?

A. LAT 36°53.7'N, LONG 75°56.0'W
B. LAT 36°53.8'N, LONG 75°56.1'W
C. LAT 36°54.4'N, LONG 75°55.9'W
D. LAT 36°54.6'N, LONG 75°55.8'W

16170. At 0812, you are on course 132°T. The standard magnetic compass reads 135°. What should you conclude?

A. The deviation table is correct for that heading.
B. Your compass may be influenced by a local magnetic disturbance.
C. You should adjust the magnetic compass.
D. The deviation is increasing as you go south.

The following questions are based on chart 13205TR, Block Island Sound, and the supporting publications. Your vessel draws 8 feet (2.4 meters), and the height of eye is 24 feet (7.3 meters). Use 15°W variation where required. The gyro error is 2°W. The deviation table is:

HDG.	M.DEV.	HDG.	M.DEV.	HDG.	M.DEV.
000°	4.0°E	120°	3.0°W	240°	1.0°W
030°	3.0°E	150°	4.0°W	270°	1.0°E
060°	1.0°E	180°	4.0°W	300°	3.0°E
090°	1.0°W	210°	3.0°W	330°	4.0°E

16206. You are steering 087° pgc and turning for 6.8 knots. At 0600, you take the following loran readings: 9960-W-14784.4; 9960-X-26208.3; 9960-Y-43959.1. What is your 0600 position?

A. LAT 41°11.2'N, LONG 72°14.6'W
B. LAT 41°12.1'N, LONG 72°13.8'W
C. LAT 41°12.3'N, LONG 72°14.7'W
D. LAT 41°12.5'N, LONG 71°14.9'W

16207. If you change course at 0610, what is the course to steer to a point where Little Gull Island Light bears 180°T at 0.7 mile (Point A)?

A. 072° pgc
B. 076° pgc
C. 080° pgc
D. 084° pgc

16208. What is your ETA at point A?

A. 0640
B. 0651
C. 0655
D. 0702

16209. You calculate that the current will be ebbing at the Race at 0700. You should expect to be set in which general direction at the Race?

A. West
B. North
C. Northeast
D. East

16210. As you near Little Gull Island, you use your loran to insure that you do not come within 0.5 mile of the island. Which of the following loran readings will act as a danger line and keep you off Little Gull Island by a minimum of 0.5 mile?

A. Not less than 9960-Y-43953.5
B. Not more than 9960-W-14735.9
C. Not less than 9960-Z-60117.6
D. Not more than 9960-X-26149.0

16211. From point A, you lay out an intended track line to a point where Block Island North Light bears 180°T at 2.9 miles (Point B). What is the length of this leg of the voyage?

A. 20.4 miles
B. 23.7 miles
C. 23.9 miles
D. 24.4 miles

16212. What is the course per standard magnetic compass between points A and B?

A. 094.5°
B. 095.5°
C. 098.5°
D. 099.5°

16213. At 0715 you take the following bearings: Race Rock Light—328° pgc; Little Gull Island Light—249° pgc; Mt. Prospect Antenna—036° pgc. Based on your 0715 fix, which statement is TRUE?

A. You are to the left of your track line.
B. Your fathometer reads about 265 fathoms.
C. You are in a cable area.
D. You are governed by the Inland Rules.

16214. From your 0715 position, you set a course of 085°T. At 0745 you take the following bearings: Race Rock Light—278° pgc; Watch Hill Light—049° pgc. Fisher's Island East Harbor Cupola—010° pgc. What was the current encountered between 0715 and 0745?

A. Set 030°T, drift 0.4 knot
B. Set 216°T, drift 0.3 knot
C. Set 070°T, drift 0.6 knot
D. Set 238°T, drift 1.0 knot

16215. The wind is southerly, and you estimate 3° leeway. Allowing for leeway, what is the course to steer from your 0745 position to pass 1 mile south of Watch Hill Buoy WH?

A. 079° pgc
B. 081° pgc
C. 085° pgc
D. 087° pgc

6216. From your 0745 fix, you change course to pass 1.0 mile south of buoy WH and estimate your speed at 7 knots. If the visibility clears, what is the earliest time you can expect to see Block Island North Light Tower?

A. 0750
B. 0807
C. 0838
D. 0845

6217. Which statement describes the shore between Watch Hill Point and Point Judith?

A. Low, rocky cliffs with heavily wooded hills inland
B. Sandy beaches broken by rocky points
C. Sand dunes and beaches with a mud and sand bottom
D. Wooded, barren hills with isolated prominent buildings

6218. At 0830, Watch Hill Point bears 043°T at 3.5 miles by radar. What was the speed made good since 0745?

A. 5.4 knots
B. 5.8 knots
C. 6.7 knots
D. 7.1 knots

6219. At 0900, you take the following radar ranges: Watch Hill Point—5.4 miles; Block Island Grace Point—8.3 miles. Which statement is TRUE?

A. You are within 3 nautical miles of the coast.
B. The bottom in the area is sand and gravel.
C. The fix is indeterminate.
D. You are governed by the Inland Rules.

6220. At 0930, your position is LAT 41°16.5'N, LONG 71°41.4'W, and you are turning for 7 knots. Allowing 3° leeway for southerly winds and estimating the current is 035° at 0.3 knot, what is the course to steer to point B?

A. 089° pgc
B. 091° pgc
C. 093° pgc
D. 096° pgc

The following questions are to be answered using chart 12221 TR, Chesapeake Bay Entrance, and supporting publications. Your present course is 200°T and your vessel's engines are turning RPMs for 16 knots. Your height of eye is 55 feet and your vessel's draft is 32 feet. Use 10°W variation where required.

16238. At 2045, you obtain the following Loran-C information: 9960-X-27102; 9960-Y-41627; 9960-Z-58743. Your vessel's position is _____.

A. LAT 37°22.8'N, LONG 75°30.8'W
B. LAT 37°22.3'N, LONG 75°31.7'W
C. LAT 37°22.0'N, LONG 75°29.3'W
D. LAT 37°21.8'N, LONG 75°30.7'W

16239. From your 2045 position, you set a course to pass 1.5 miles due east of the charted position of Hog Island Lighted Bell Buoy 12. The known set and drift in the area are 068°T at 3 knots. What is the course to steer, with no change in engine speed, to make good your desired course?

A. 200°T
B. 203°T
C. 206°T
D. 209°T

16240. The speed that you can expect to make good, while steering to make good your desired course, is _____.

A. 13.5 knots
B. 14.3 knots
C. 15.1 knots
D. 15.9 knots

16241. At 2129 Cape Charles Light bears 253°T, Hog Island Lighted Bell Buoy 12 bears 351°T, and Cape Charles Lighted Bell Buoy 14 bears 230°T. Which statement is TRUE?

A. The fathometer reads about 62 feet (18.9 meters).
B. The bottom is hard sand and oysters.
C. You are to seaward of the contiguous zone.
D. You are governed by the International Rules of the Road.

16243. At 2207 Cape Charles Light bears 276°T, Chesapeake Light bears 194°T, and Cape Charles Lighted Bell Buoy 14 bears 312°T and is 2.0 miles off. What were the set and drift of the current acting on your vessel from 2129 to 2207?

A. 258°T at 2.4 knots
B. 258°T at 1.5 knots
C. 078°T at 1.5 knots
D. 078°T at 2.4 knots

16245. At 2259 Cape Henry Light bears 250°T, Chesapeake Light bears 122°T, and North Chesapeake Entrance Lighted Whistle Buoy NCA has a radar range of 1.8 miles. Which statement is TRUE?

A. The course made good is 226°T.
B. You are in the red sector of Cape Henry Light.
C. You are in a submerged submarine transit lane.
D. Chesapeake Light is 7.6 miles off.

16246. From your 2259 fix, you alter course to 250°T. At 2300 Cape Henry Light bears 250°T. At 2326 Cape Henry Light bears 252°T. Which statement is TRUE?

A. You are being set to the right.
B. The bearing change should be expected as you transit the inbound lane.
C. You should alter course to starboard.
D. You should slow to reduce the effect of the current.

The following questions should be answered using chart 12221TR, Chesapeake Bay Entrance, and the supporting publications. On 31 July, you are anchored at LAT 37°22.4'N, LONG 75°39.9'W. You get underway at 0240 enroute to to Yorktown, VA. The draft of your vessel is 9.0 feet (2.75 meters). The gyro error is 2°W. "Per standard magnetic compass" is abbreviated "psc." Use a variation of 10°W for the entire plot. The deviation table is:

HDG.	M.DEV.	HDG.	M.DEV.	HDG.	M.DEV.
000°	1.5°E	120°	1.0°W	240°	1.0°W
030°	2.0°E	150°	1.5°W	270°	0.5°W
060°	1.0°E	180°	2.5°W	300°	0°
090°	0°	210°	1.5°W	330°	0.5°E

16256. What is the course per gyrocompass from the anchorage to point A located 0.5 mile east of Cape Charles Lighted Bell Buoy 14?

A. 180°
B. 184°
C. 198°
D. 199.5°

16257. If your engines turn for 6.5 knots, and you encounter a 0.5 knot southerly current after weighing anchor, what is your ETA at point A?

A. 0511
B. 0501
C. 0450
D. 0440

16258. What is the course to steer per standard magnetic compass from the anchorage to point A, if easterly winds are causing 3° of leeway?

A. 187°
B. 191°
C. 194°
D. 197°

16259. You are on track from the anchorage to point A. At 0250, Great Machipongo Inlet Light 5 (37°21.8'N, 75°43.7'W) bears 279° pgc. At 0320, the light bears 320° pgc. What is the position of your 0320 running fix if you are making good 6.5 knots?

A. LAT 37°18.1'N, LONG 75°39.5'W
B. LAT 37°18.1'N, LONG 75°39.3'W
C. LAT 37°18.1'N, LONG 75°39.7'W
D. LAT 37°18.2'N, LONG 75°39.6'W

16260. If your vessel draws 6.5 feet (2 meters), what is the approximate depth of water under your keel at 0320?

A. 52 feet (15.8 meters)
B. 48 feet (14.5 meters)
C. 44 feet (13.3 meters)
D. 40 feet (12.0 meters)

16261. At 0400, you take a loran fix with the following readings: 9960-X-27120.9; 9960-Y-41524.8; 9960-Z-58681.9. What is your 0400 position?

A. LAT 37°14.2'N, LONG 75°39.2'W
B. LAT 37°14.4'N, LONG 75°39.3'W
C. LAT 37°14.4'N, LONG 75°39.0'W
D. LAT 37°14.6'N, LONG 75°39.2'W

16262. What was the speed made good from 0240 to 0400?

A. 5.2 knots
B. 5.6 knots
C. 6.0 knots
D. 6.4 knots

16263. If you increase speed to 8 knots, and the current is 240° at 0.7 knot, what course should you steer from your 0400 position to arrive at point A?

A. 178°T
B. 180°T
C. 183°T
D. 186°T

16264. Which statement about your 0400 position is true?

A. You are governed by the Inland Rules of the Road.
B. Anchoring, trawling and fishing are prohibited.
C. The ocean floor is composed of shingle.
D. You are within the Territorial Sea and the contiguous zone.

16265. At 0600, you are on course 241° psc at 6.5 knots. Chesapeake Light bears 153° per standard magnetic compass and Cape Henry Light bears 261° per standard magnetic compass. What is the position of your 0600 fix?

A. LAT 36°59.0'N, LONG 75°47.4'W
B. LAT 36°59.1'N, LONG 75°47.8'W
C. LAT 36°59.2'N, LONG 75°47.4'W
D. LAT 36°59.3'N, LONG 75°47.6'W

16266. The abandoned lighthouse at Cape Henry is a (n) _____.

A. octagonal, black and white tower
B. black skelton structure
C. mound of broken rubble
D. grey, pyramidal tower

16267. When Cape Henry Light is abeam, what is the approximate distance to Yorktown, VA?

A. 34 miles
B. 42 miles
C. 55 miles
D. 58 miles

16268. As you pass between trestle B and trestle C of the Chesapeake Bay Bridge Tunnel, you sight along the trestle C when it is in line. The gyro bearing is 048°. What is the gyro error by observation?

A. 4°E
B. 1°E
C. 0°
D. 2°W

16269. On either side of York River Entrance Channel, there are areas bounded by short- long magenta lines and marked by yellow buoys. These areas are _____.

A. fish trap areas
B. designated anchorages
C. spoil areas
D. naval exercise areas

16270. The wind is northerly and will cause 2° leeway. The current is 018° at 0.5 knot. If your engines are turning for 8.0 knots, what should you steer to remain in York River Entrance Channel?

A. 304°T
B. 307°T
C. 309°T
D. 314°T

The following questions are based on chart 12354TR, Long Island Sound - Eastern Part, and the supporting publications. Your vessel has a draft of 10 feet (3.1 meters). Your height of eye is 35 feet (10.6 meters). Use 14°W variation where required. The deviation table is:

HDG.	M.DEV.	HDG.	M.DEV.	HDG.	M.DEV.
000°	0°	120°	2°W	240°	3°E
030°	1°W	150°	1°W	270°	3°E
060°	2°W	180°	1°E	300°	2°E
090°	4°W	210°	2°E	330°	1°E

16306. At 0345, you set a course to depart New London Harbor. Assuming no set and drift, which standard magnetic compass course must you steer to stay in the middle of the channel?

A. 175° psc
B. 187° psc
C. 190° psc
D. 192° psc

16307. Which statement regarding the wreck 0.2 mile south of buoys 1 and 2 at the entrance to New London Harbor is TRUE?

A. The wreck presents a danger to all vessels with drafts in excess of 30 feet (9.1 meters).
B. The wreck is visible above the sounding datum between the months of March and June.
C. The wreck is shown on the chart, but its actual existence is doubtful.
D. The wreck was cleared by wire drag in 1982 and will not appear on future charts.

16308. At 0530, your position is LAT 41°13.6'N, LONG 72°08.5'W. What is the color of New London Light?

. Red
. White
. Green
. Alternating white and green

6309. From your 0530 position, you set a ourse of 271° psc with an engine speed of knots. At 0645, Cornfield Safe-Water Buoy F is abeam to port. What speed have you veraged since 0530?

. 7.5 knots
. 8.6 knots
. 9.0 knots
. 9.5 knots

6310. At 0730, your position is LAT 1°10.5'N, LONG 72°32.2'W. From this posi-on you steer course 286° psc with an en-ine speed of 9.0 knots. What is the pproximate depth of water under your eel?

. 52 feet (15.8 meters)
. 57 feet (17.3 meters)
. 62 feet (18.8 meters)
. 67 feet (20.3 meters)

6311. The broken magenta line which uns parallel to the shore between Roanoke oint and Mattituck Inlet marks a _____.

. pipeline
. fish trap area
. demarcation line
. cable area

6312. Assuming no current, at what time an you expect to be abeam of Townshend edge Lighted Buoy?

. 0859
. 0902
. 0905
. 0910

6313. At 0730, visibility is 5.5 miles. At vhat time will you lose sight of Horton oint Light?

. It is not visible at 0730
. 0751
. 0812
. 0825

6314. At 0820, you take the following oran-C readings: 9960-W-14978.0; 9960-Y-3993.5; 9960-X-26464.1. What are the set nd drift since 0730?

A. Set 052°T, drift 1.1 knots
B. Set 052°T, drift 1.3 knots
C. Set 236°T, drift 1.1 knots
D. Set 236°T, drift 1.3 knots

16315. At 0820, you change course to 301° psc and reduce speed to 7.5 knots. At 0900, you take the following visual bearings: Branford Reef Light—023° psc; New Haven Light—293° psc; Tweed Airport Aerobea-con—332° psc. Your 0900 position is _____.

A. LAT 41°11.9'N, LONG 72°50.6'W
B. LAT 41°11.9'N, LONG 72°49.5'W
C. LAT 41°12.1'N, LONG 72°48.6'W
D. LAT 41°12.5'N, LONG 72°44.3'W

16316. At 0900, the current is flooding in a direction of 350°T at 1.2 knots. If your en-gines are turning RPMs for 9 knots, which course should you steer per standard mag-netic compass to make good a course of 297° true?

A. 302° psc
B. 311° psc
C. 317° psc
D. 319° psc

16317. Which chart would you use for more detailed information on New Haven Harbor?

A. 12370
B. 12371
C. 12372
D. 12373

16318. What true course and speed did you make good between 0730 and 0900?

A. 273°T, 8.7 knots
B. 277°T, 8.4 knots
C. 279°T, 8.0 knots
D. 284°T, 7.5 knots

16319. As you enter the New Haven Outer Channel, you sight the outer range markers in line directly ahead. Your heading at this time is 347° psc. What is your compass de-viation by observation?

A. 0.5°East
B. 3.0°East
C. 3.5°West
D. 4.5°East

16320. Which course should you change to per standard magnetic compass as you pass SW Ledge Light to remain in the channel?

A. 007° psc
B. 014° psc
C. 021° psc
D. 026° psc

The following questions are to be answered using chart 13205 TR, Block Island Sound, and supporting publications. You are turning for 12.4 knots. Your draft is 28 feet. The gyro error is 2°E. Your course is 340°T. Your height of eye is 36 feet. The deviation table is:

HDG.	M.DEV.
315°	1°E
330°	1°W
345°	3°W
360°	5°W

16338. At 2209 you take the following loran readings: 9960-W-14617.0; 9960-X-25834.3; 9960-Y-43716.5. There is a strong WSW'ly wind causing an estimated 3° leeway. What course will you steer by standard magnetic compass from your 2209 position to make good 340°T?

A. 322°
B. 348°
C. 356°
D. 002°

16339. Based on your 2209 fix, which would be a warning that you are being set down on Block Island Sound South Entrance Obstruction Lighted BIS Buoy?

A. Decreasing loran readings on 9960-W
B. Visual bearings of Montauk Point Lt. changing to the left
C. Increasing bearings of Southeast Point Light
D. Decreasing soundings

16340. If you make good your intended course and speed, at what time will you cross the 150-foot curve?

A. 2237
B. 2249
C. 2256
D. 2301

16341. At 2230 you take the following vi-sual bearings: Montauk Point Light, Long Island—317° pgc; Southeast Point Light, Block Island—009° pgc. What is your position?

A. LAT 40°51.2'N, LONG 71°35.9'W
B. LAT 40°51.5'N, LONG 71°36.4'W

C. LAT 40°52.2'N, LONG 71°36.6'W
D. LAT 40°52.0'N, LONG 71°37.4'W

16342. At 2302 you fix your position at LAT 40°57.8'N, LONG 71°39.3'W. What current have you experienced since your 2209 fix?

A. 105°T at 1.0 knot
B. 105°T at 0.9 knot
C. 285°T at 1.0 knot
D. 285°T at 0.9 knot

16343. At 2302 you change course to compensate for an estimated current of 090°T at 1.0 knot. What course per gyrocompass will you steer to leave Endeavor Shoals Lighted Gong Buoy 3 abeam to port at 1 mile?

A. 324° pgc
B. 327° pgc
C. 330° pgc
D. 333° pgc

16344. After changing course to allow for a current of 090°T at 1.0 knot, what time will Endeavor Shoals Lighted Gong Buoy 3 be abeam to port?

A. 2340
B. 2345
C. 2350
D. 2355

16345. Where will you cross the demarcation line between the International and Inland Rules of the Road?

A. Between Montauk Point and Block Island
B. In the Race
C. At the mouth of Bridgeport Harbor
D. Between Plum Gut and Niantic Bay

16346. After passing through the Race, enroute to to Bridgeport, CT, and Race Rock Light is 2 miles astern, you notice an equal interval flashing red light on the starboard side. This light is _____.

A. New London Airport Aerobeacon
B. New London Harbor Light
C. New London Ledge Light
D. Bartlett Reef Light

The following questions should be answered using chart 12221TR, and the supporting publications. On 31 July, you are anchored at LAT 37°22.4' N, LONG 75°39.9' W. You get underway at 0240 enroute to to Yorktown, VA. The draft of your vessel is 9.0 feet (2.75

meters). The gyro error is 2°W. "Per standard magnetic compass" is abbreviated "psc." Use a variation of 10°W for the entire plot. The deviation table is:

HDG.	M.DEV.	HDG.	M.DEV.	HDG.	M.DEV.
000°	1.5°E	120°	1.0°W	240°	1.0°W
030°	2.0°E	150°	1.5°W	270°	0.5°W
060°	1.0°E	180°	2.5°W	300°	0°
090°	0°	210°	1.5°W	330°	0.5°E

16356. What is the course per standard magnetic compass from the anchorage to point A located 0.5 mile east of Cape Charles Lighted Bell Buoy 14?

A. 185°
B. 188°
C. 191°
D. 194°

16357. The coast between Great Machipongo Inlet and Cape Charles is _____.

A. composed of high rocky bluffs and wooded uplands
B. marked by prominent isolated barren hills
C. broken by the mouths of several major rivers
D. low with sandy beaches bordered by marsh and woodland

16358. What is the distance from the anchorage to point A?

A. 13.9 miles
B. 15.1 miles
C. 15.9 miles
D. 17.0 miles

16359. Your engines are turning for 6.5 knots and the estimated current is north at 0.5 knot, what is the ETA at point A?

A. 0511
B. 0501
C. 0450
D. 0440

16360. What is the course to steer per gyrocompass from the anchorage to point A if westerly winds are causing 3° of leeway?

A. 178° pgc
B. 182° pgc
C. 184° pgc
D. 187° pgc

16361. At 0400, you take a loran fix with the following readings: 9960-X-27126.4; 9960-Y-41516.6; 9960-Z-58674.4. What was the course made good since 0240?

A. 182°T
B. 185°T
C. 189°T
D. 192°T

16362. The visibility is about 5 miles. Which statement about Cape Charles Light is TRUE?

A. The light has been visible from the time you departed the anchorage.
B. You should see Cape Charles Light at about 0400.
C. The light will become visible when you enter the inbound leg of the traffic separation scheme.
D. The light will not be visible until you are within 5 miles of the light.

16363. At 0405, you increase speed and at 0500 your position is LAT 37°06.0'N, LONG 75°41.1'W. What is the approximate depth of water?

A. 46 feet (13.9 meters)
B. 54 feet (16.4 meters)
C. 62 feet (18.8 meters)
D. 66 feet (20.0 meters)

16364. If you proceed from your 0500 position to Chesapeake Bay via the inbound traffic lane, what is the distance to Yorktown, VA?

A. 34.0 miles
B. 42.6 miles
C. 51.7 miles
D. 62.1 miles

16365. From your 0500 position, you change course to 221°T and order turns for 9.8 knots. At 0600 Chesapeake Light bears 143° pgc at a radar range of 6.5 miles. Cape Henry Light bears 252° pgc. What is the position of your 0600 fix?

A. LAT 36°59.1'N, LONG 75°48.1'W
B. LAT 36°59.1'N, LONG 75°47.6'W
C. LAT 36°59.2'N, LONG 75°47.8'W
D. LAT 36°58.9'N, LONG 75°48.5'W

16366. From your 0600 fix, you change course to 250°T. At 0605, Cape Henry Light bears 250°T. At 0615, it bears 251°T. At 0625, it bears 252°T. Based on this you know you are _____.

A. being set to the south
B. being set to the north
C. meeting a current from dead ahead
D. running with a current from dead astern

6367. Weather broadcasts for the Norfolk area are broadcast on what frequency?

A. 162.25 MHz
B. 162.30 MHz
C. 162.55 MHz
D. 162.65 MHz

6368. Why should mariners use extreme care when navigating within the precautionary area centered on Chesapeake Bay Entrance Junction Lighted Gong Buoy CBJ?

A. There are numerous underwater obstructions that are a hazard to vessels with drafts exceeding 2 meters (6.5 feet).
B. Fishing vessels of limited maneuverability routinely operate in this area when hunting oysters and crabs.
C. Vessels may approach from different directions from the inbound separation lanes and from Chesapeake and Thimble Shoal Channel.
D. Large naval vessels having the right of way often enter the area when bound to or from the Norfolk Naval Base.

6369. As you pass between Trestle B and Trestle C of the Chesapeake Bay Bridge Tunnel, you sight along Trestle C when it is in line. The gyro bearing is 051°. What is the gyro error by observation?

A. 4°E
B. 2°E
C. 0°
D. 2°W

16370. The wind is westerly and will cause 2° of leeway. The current is 180° at 0.5 knot. If your engines are turning for 8.0 knots, what should you steer to remain in York River Entrance Channel?

A. 304°T
B. 307°T
C. 311°T
D. 314°T

The following questions are based on chart 13205TR, Block Island Sound, and the supporting publications. Your vessel has a draft of 11 feet (3.4 meters). Your height of eye is 32 feet (9.7 meters). Gyro error is 2°W.

Use 15°W variation where required. The deviation table is:

HDG.	M.DEV.	HDG.	M.DEV.	HDG.	M.DEV.
000°	0°	120°	2°W	240°	3°E
030°	1°W	150°	1°W	270°	3°E
060°	2°W	180°	1°E	300°	2°E
090°	4°W	210°	2°E	330°	1°E

16406. At 0227, you take the following radar ranges and bearings: Bartlett Reef Light—359°T at 2.4 miles; Race Rock Light—083°T at 4.1 miles. What is your 0227 position?

A. LAT 41°14.1′N, LONG 72°08.2′W
B. LAT 41°14.2′N, LONG 72°08.4′W
C. LAT 41°14.0′N, LONG 72°08.5′W
D. LAT 41°14.3′N, LONG 72°08.5′W

16407. At 0227, you are on course 087°T at 10 knots. What course per standard magnetic compass should you steer to make good your true course?

A. 099° psc
B. 102° psc
C. 105° psc
D. 109° psc

16408. You estimate that you are making 9.3 knots over the ground. At what time will you enter waters governed by the COLREGS?

A. 0247
B. 0251
C. 0255
D. 0258

16409. At 0337, fog closes in and you anchor under the following radar ranges and bearing: South tip of Watch Hill Point—3.0 miles;

East point of Fishers Island—1.4 miles; Latimer Reef Light—331°T. What is the approximate depth of water at your anchorage?
A. 83 feet (25.2 meters)
B. 100 feet (30.3 meters)
C. 120 feet (36.4 meters)
D. 135 feet (40.9 meters)

16410. By 1015, visibility has increased to 5.0 miles and you can see Fishers Island. Fishers Island has _____.

A. low and sandy beaches with salt ponds and marsh grass

B. sheer cliffs rising from the sea to a high, flat plateau
C. barren, rocky hills with prominent sandy beaches
D. sparsely wooded hills and is fringed with shoals to the south

16411. You get underway at 1030. The wind is out of the SSE and you estimate 3° leeway. What course should you steer per gyrocompass to make good a desired course of 075°T?

A. 074° pgc
B. 076° pgc
C. 078° pgc
D. 080° pgc

16412. Shortly after getting underway, you sight Stonington Outer Breakwater Light in line with Stonington Inner Breakwater Light bearing 000° per gyrocompass. Which statement is TRUE?

A. The gyro error is 2.5°W.
B. The variation is 2°E.
C. The compass error is 16°W.
D. The deviation is 2°W.

16413. At 1104, Watch Hill Point Light is in line with Stonington Outer Breakwater Light, the range to the south tip of Watch Hill Point is 2.6 miles and the range to the beach is 1.9 miles. You are steering to make good 075°T, speed 10.0 knots. At 1110, you change course to head for a position of LAT 41°05.0′N, LONG 71°50.0′W. What is the true course?

A. 185°
B. 187°
C. 190°
D. 193°

16414. At 1110, you increase speed to 12 knots. What is your ETA at the new position?
A. 1157
B. 1208
C. 1215
D. 1219

16415. You can follow what loran reading between your two positions?

A. There is no loran reading to follow.
B. 9960-Y-43958
C. 9960-W-14655
D. 9960-X-25982

16416. At 1345, you depart from a position 1 mile due east of Montauk Point Light and set course for Block Island Southeast Light at 9 knots. At 1430, you take the following loran readings: 9960-W-14600.8; 9960-Y-43866.3; 9960-X-25912.3. What was the current encountered since 1345?

A. Set 015°, drift 0.5 knot
B. Set 195°, drift 0.5 knot
C. Set 015°, drift 0.7 knot
D. Set 195°, drift 0.7 knot

16417. You are encountering heavy weather. What action should you take based on your 1430 fix?

A. Alter course to the right, to pass well clear of Southwest Ledge.
B. Continue on the same course at the same speed.
C. Slow to 8.3 knots to compensate for the current.
D. Continue on the same course but increase speed.

16418. At 2100, you set course of 000°T, speed 10 knots from LAT 41°07.0'N, LONG 71°30.0'W. Visibility is 5.5 n.m. What is the earliest time you can expect to sight Point Judith Light? (Use charted range of 20 miles as nominal range.)

A. The light is visible at 2100.
B. 2114
C. 2123
D. 2131

16419. You estimate the current to be 160°T at 1.2 knots. What should your course and speed be in order to make good 000°T at 10 knots?

A. 358°T at 11.1 knots
B. 358°T at 09.8 knots
C. 002°T at 11.2 knots
D. 002°T at 09.9 knots

16420. If you want to put into Point Judith Harbor of Refuge, what chart should you use?

A. 13205
B. 13209
C. 13217
D. 13219

The following questions are to be answered using chart 12221 TR, Chesapeake Bay Entrance, and supporting publications.

You are on an oceanographic research vessel equipped with standard navigational equipment. The gyro error is 2°W. The maximum draft is 13 feet. Use 10°W variation where required.

HDG.	M.DEV.
060°	1°W
075°	0°
090°	1°E

16438. Chesapeake Channel is temporarily closed to traffic. At 2215 you anchor on the following bearings: Wolf Trap Light—358° pgc; Light HH—301° pgc; New Point Comfort Light 2—263° pgc. What is your 2215 position?

A. LAT 37°18.3'N, LONG 76°10.9'W
B. LAT 37°18.2'N, LONG 76°11.2'W
C. LAT 37°18.1'N, LONG 76°10.8'W
D. LAT 37°18.0'N, LONG 76°11.2'W

16439. While you are at anchor, what will serve as a positive warning that you are drifting toward the wrecks located to the NW and SW of your 2215 position?

A. A decreasing reading on loran pair 9960-X
B. The bearing of Wolf Trap Light changing to the right
C. Increasing soundings
D. The bearing of Wolf Trap Light changing to the left

16440. What course per gyrocompass would you need to steer from the anchorage to York Spit Channel buoy 29?

A. 172° pgc
B. 175° pgc
C. 178° pgc
D. 181° pgc

16441. When you get underway, you will take the most direct route to buoy CBJ, while remaining west of York Spit Channel. You will be turning for 9.7 knots and estimate an average ebb of 0.3 knot during the transit. How long will it take to steam from the anchor position to buoy CBJ?

A. 2h 16m
B. 2h 33m
C. 2h 42m
D. 2h 51m

16442. The area bounded by the buoys C51 to C47A to M6 to M14, west of your anchorage, is _____.

A. a training area for naval small craft
B. restricted to oil and mineral exploration
C. an anchorage for ammunition barges
D. a fish trap area

16443. As you transit the Chesapeake Bay Bridge and Tunnel, you take a gyro bearing of trestle C when it is in line. The gyro bearing was 050°. At that time, the helmsman noted that he was heading 139° pgc and 146° per standard magnetic compass. What is the deviation?

A. 2°E
B. 0°
C. 2°W
D. 4°W

16444. At 1042 you take the following round of bearings: Cape Henry Light—259°T; Chesapeake Light—101°T; Cape Charles Light—006°T. From this position, you set course 070°T at a speed of 9.5 knots. What is the course per standard magnetic compass?

A. 069.5° psc
B. 060.5° psc
C. 079.5° psc
D. 080.5° psc

16445. At 1126 you take the following loran readings: 9960-X-27125.7; 9960-Y-41329.0; 9960-Z-58588.6. What was the current encountered since your 1042 fix?

A. Set 276°, Drift 0.5 knot
B. Set 276°, Drift 0.7 knot
C. Set 096°, Drift 0.5 knot
D. Set 096°, Drift 0.7 knot

The following questions should be answered using chart 12221TR, Chesapeake Bay Entrance, and the supporting publications. On 31 July, you are anchored at LAT 37°22.4' N, LONG 75°39.9' W. You get underway at 0240 enroute to to Yorktown,VA. The draft of your vessel is 9.0 feet (2.75 meters). The gyro error is 2°W. "Per standard magnetic compass" is abbreviated "psc." Use a variation of 10°W for the entire plot. The deviation table is:

HDG.	M.DEV.	HDG.	M.DEV.	HDG.	M.DEV.
000°	1.5°E	120°	1.0°W	240°	1.0°W
030°	2.0°E	150°	1.5°W	270°	0.5°W
060°	1.0°E	180°	2.5°W	300°	0°
090°	0°	210°	1.5°W	330°	0.5°E

16456. What is the course per standard magnetic compass from the anchorage to point A located 0.5 mile east of Cape Charles Lighted Bell Buoy 14?

A. 194° psc
B. 190° psc
C. 187° psc
D. 180° psc

16457. The coast between Great Machipongo Inlet and Cape Charles is _____.

A. broken by the mouths of several major rivers
B. low, with sandy beaches bordered by marsh and woodlands
C. marked by prominent, isolated, barren hills
D. composed of high, rocky bluffs and wooded uplands

16458. If your engines turn for 6.5 knots, and you encounter a 0.5 knot southerly current, what is your ETA at point A?

A. 0400
B. 0450
C. 0501
D. 0511

16459. What is the course to steer per gyrocompass from the anchorage to point A if easterly winds are causing 3° of leeway?

A. 178° pgc
B. 181° pgc
C. 185° pgc
D. 189° pgc

16460. At 0250, Great Machipongo Inlet Light 5 (27°21.8'N; 75°43.7'W) bears 279° pgc. At 0320, the light bears 320° pgc. If you are steering 184°T and making good 9.5 knots, what is the position of your 0320 running fix?

A. LAT 37°18.3'N, LONG 75°39.6'W
B. LAT 37°18.2'N, LONG 75°39.7'W
C. LAT 37°18.1'N, LONG 75°39.2'W
D. LAT 37°18.1'N, LONG 75°39.5'W

16461. At 0400, you take the following loran readings: 9960-X-27126.4; 9960-Y-41516.6; 9960-Z-58674.4. What is your 0400 position?

A. LAT 37°14.2'N, LONG 75°40.7'W
B. LAT 37°14.1'N, LONG 75°41.3'W
C. LAT 37°14.1'N, LONG 75°40.5'W
D. LAT 37°14.0'N, LONG 75°40.7'W

16462. Which statement about your 0400 position is TRUE?

A. You are within the territorial sea and contiguous zone.
B. You are governed by the Inland Rules of the Road.
C. The ocean floor is composed of shale.
D. Anchoring, trawling and fishing are prohibited.

16463. The visibility is about 5 miles. Which statement about Cape Charles Light is TRUE?

A. The light has been visible since you departed the anchorage.
B. You will not see the light until you are within 5 miles of the light.
C. The light will become visible about 0400.
D. The light will not be visible until you enter the inbound leg of the traffic separation scheme.

16464. At 0405, you increase speed. At 0500, your position is LAT 37°06.0'N, LONG 75°41.1'W. What is the approximate depth of the water under the keel?

A. 66 feet (20.0 meters)
B. 62 feet (18.8 meters)
C. 54 feet (16.4 meters)
D. 46 feet (13.9 meters)

16465. At 0600, you are entering the inbound leg of the traffic separation scheme at position LAT 36°59.2'N, LONG 75°47.6'W. Course is 250°T. At 0605, Cape Henry Light bears 249°T. At 0610, it bears 248°T. At 0625, it bears 247°T. Based on this, you know you are _____.

A. meeting a current from dead ahead
B. running with a current from dead ahead
C. being set to the north
D. being set to the south

16466. The abandoned lighthouse at Cape Henry is a (n) _____.

A. grey, pyramidal tower
B. mound of broken rubble
C. octagonal, black and white tower
D. black, skeleton structure

16467. Weather broadcasts for the Norfolk area are broadcast on which frequency?

A. 162.30 MHz
B. 162.35 MHz
C. 162.50 MHz
D. 162.55 MHz

16468. When Cape Henry Light is abeam, what is the approximate distance to Yorktown?

A. 58 miles
B. 55 miles
C. 42 miles
D. 34 miles

16469. As you pass between trestle B and trestle C of the Chesapeake Bay Bridge Tunnel, you sight along the trestle C when it is in line. The trestle bears 057° per standard magnetic compass while the vessel is heading 320°T. From this you know the _____.

A. vessel should be swung to check the deviation table
B. compass error is 12°W
C. deviation table is correct for that bearing
D. deviation is 10°W

16470. The wind is easterly and will cause 2° of leeway. The current is 180° at 0.5 knot. If your engines are turning for 8.0 knots, what should you steer to remain in York River Entrance Channel?

A. 304°T
B. 307°T
C. 311°T
D. 315°T

The following questions are based on chart 13205TR, Block Island Sound, and the supporting publications. Your vessel draws 8 feet (2.4 meters), and the height of eye is 20 feet (6.1 meters). Use 15°W variation where required. The gyro error is 3°E. The deviation table is:

HDG.	M.DEV.	HDG.	M.DEV.	HDG.	M.DEV.
000°	1.5°E	120°	1.0°W	240°	1.5°E
030°	2.5°W	150°	0.5°W	270°	2.0°E
060°	2.5°W	180°	0°	300°	1.0°E
090°	2.0°W	210°	1.0°E	330°	0.5°W

16506. At 0630, you pass Buoy PI close abeam on the starboard side. You are steering 078°T and are headed directly toward Race Rock Light. At 0654, Little Gull Island Light is bearing 207°T and Race Rock Light is bearing 072°T. What is your 0654 position?

A. LAT 41°14.0'N, LONG 72°05.3'W
B. LAT 41°14.2'N, LONG 71°54.6'W
C. LAT 41°14.4'N, LONG 72°06.8'W
D. LAT 41°19.0'N, LONG 72°05.2'W

16507. What is your speed from your 0630 position, with Buoy PI close abeam, to your 0654 position?

A. 8.2 knots
B. 9.3 knots
C. 10.5 knots
D. 11.4 knots

16508. At 0700, your gyro alarm sounds. What course should you steer by the standard magnetic compass in order to maintain your original heading of 078°T?

A. 062° psc
B. 080° psc
C. 090° psc
D. 095° psc

16509. At 0705, with your gyro again functioning properly, you change course to 096°T. At this time Race Rock Light is bearing 000°T at 0.35 mile. You are now governed by which Navigation Rules?

A. Inland Rules
B. Local Pilot Rules
C. International Rules
D. Coastal Fishery Rules

16510. At 0728, Race Rock Light is bearing 282°T at 3.8 miles and the closest point on Fishers Island is at a radar range of 2.0

miles. What speed have you been making since you changed course at 0705?
A. 9.2 knots
B. 9.8 knots
C. 10.6 knots
D. 11.4 knots

16511. At 0728, you change course to 080°T. When steady on course, the standard magnetic compass reads 097°. Which statement is TRUE?

A. The gyro course is 083° pgc.
B. The magnetic heading is 090°.
C. The deviation is 1.0°E.
D. The magnetic compass error is 17°W.

16512. At 0748, you take the following Loran-C readings: 9960-W-14651.0; 9960-X-26034.8; 9960-Y-43943.8. What is the approximate depth of water at this position?

A. 325 feet
B. 175 feet
C. 130 feet
D. 104 feet

16513. At 0748, you change course to 160°T. What loran reading can you follow to remain on this course?

A. 9960-W-14651.0
B. 9960-W-14660.0
C. 9960-Y-43852.0
D. 9960-Y-43943.8

16514. At 0815, Montauk Pt. Light House is bearing 167°T, Shagwong Pt. has a radar range of 4.5 miles, and Cerberus Shoal 9 Buoy is bearing 284°T. If the engine is making turns for 10 knots, what was the set and drift of the current since 0748?

A. Set 065°T, drift 1.1 knots
B. Set 065°T, drift 2.4 knots
C. Set 245°T, drift 1.1 knots
D. Set 245°T, drift 2.4 knots

16515. What action should you take to compensate for the above current?

A. Continue on the same course and speed.
B. Alter your course to the left.
C. Slow to 8.5 knots.
D. Alter your course to the right.

16516. At 0815, visibility is excellent and you can see Montauk Point. Montauk Point is _____.

A. low and rocky with scattered small pine trees
B. a low lying wetland
C. a flat wooded plain
D. a high sandy bluff

16517. At 0815, you change course to 079°T and head for the entrance of Great Salt Pond on Block Island. To compensate for a northerly wind, you estimate a 5° leeway is necessary. What course should you steer per gyrocompass to make good 079°T?

A. 079° pgc
B. 076° pgc
C. 074° pgc
D. 071° pgc

16518. At 0845, Montauk Pt. Light is bearing 205°T at a radar distance of 6.6 miles. What is your speed made good from your 0815 position?

A. 8.4 knots
B. 9.2 knots
C. 10.0 knots
D. 10.5 knots

16519. As you head toward Great Salt Pond, visibility is unlimited. At what time will you lose sight of Montauk Pt. Light?

A. 0905
B. 0928
C. 0950
D. It will remain visible to Great Salt Pond.

16520. Which chart should you use to enter Great Salt Pond?

A. 13214
B. 13205
C. 13217
D. 13207

The following questions are to be answered using chart 12354 TR, Long Island Sound - Eastern Part, and supporting publications. You are turning for 12.5 knots and on a course of 255°T. Your vessel's deep draft is 24 feet. Gyro error is 3°E. Use 14°W variation where required.

HDG.	M.DEV.
240°	2°W
255°	0°
270°	2°E
285°	4°E

16538. At 2216 your position is LAT 41°16.0'N, LONG 72°08.0'W. Which statement is TRUE?

A. You are in the red sector of New London Harbor Light.
B. Your fathometer reads approximately 40 feet.
C. You can follow loran reading 9960-Y-43990 to remain clear of all dangers until west of Stratford Shoal.
D. Little Gull Island Light bears 339°T at 4.3 miles.

16539. If you estimate 3° leeway due to northerly winds, which course will you steer per standard magnetic compass (psc) to make good 255°T?

A. 267° psc
B. 270° psc
C. 272° psc
D. 274° psc

16540. You sight Bartlett Reef Light in range with New London Harbor Light bearing 038° pgc. At the time of the bearing, the helmsman reports he was heading 253° pgc and 269° per standard magnetic compass. What is the deviation for that heading?

A. 1°E
B. 1°W
C. 4°E
D. 4°W

16541. At 2255 you take the following visual bearings: Saybrook Breakwater Light—333° pgc; Little Gull Island Light—094° pgc; Horton Point Light—211° pgc. What is your position?

A. LAT 41°13.6'N, LONG 72°19.2'W
B. LAT 41°13.8'N, LONG 72°19.6'W
C. LAT 41°14.0'N, LONG 72°19.0'W
D. LAT 41°14.2'N, LONG 72°19.7'W

16542. At 2308 your position is LAT 41°12.7'N, LONG 72°22.8'W. You steer a course to make good 255°T from this position. At 2310 you receive a distress call from a vessel anchored 2.1 miles due north of Mattituck Inlet Light. If you change course at 2314, what is the course to steer per gyrocompass to arrive at the distress site if you allow 2° leeway for northerly winds, 3°E gyro error and correct your course for a current of 073°T at 1.3 knots?

A. 208° pgc
B. 212° pgc
C. 216° pgc
D. 220° pgc

16543. Based on the information in the previous question, what is your ETA at the distress scene?

A. 0006
B. 0010
C. 0016
D. 0021

16544. At 2347 you are advised that your assistance is no longer needed. At 2350 you change course to make good 268°T. At 0015 you take the following round of bearings: Kelsey Point Breakwater Light—024° pgc; Horton Point Light—100° pgc; Falkner

Island Light—333° pgc. At 0030 Falkner Island Lt. bears 000°T at 5.9 miles. What is the course and speed made good between 0015 and 0030?

A. CMG 262°T, SMG 10.4 knots
B. CMG 268°T, SMG 10.8 knots
C. CMG 268°T, SMG 10.4 knots
D. CMG 272°T, SMG 10.8 knots

16545. At 0030 you alter course and speed to make good 265°T at 10 knots. What is your ETA at a point where Stratford Shoal Middle Ground Light is abeam?

A. 0218
B. 0223
C. 0228
D. 0233

16546. At 0100 you notice that the wind has become SSW'ly and has freshened. At 0200 you sight Stratford Point Lighted Bell Buoy 18 bearing 268° pgc. At 0215 the buoy bears 269° pgc. Which statement is TRUE?

A. You should alter course to the right to increase the rate of the bearing change.
B. You are making more speed over the ground than you estimated.
C. You should alter course to decrease the distance that you will pass off Middle Ground Shoal.
D. You can hold the present course and safely pass buoy 18.

The following questions should be answered using chart 13205TR, Block Island Sound and Approaches, and supporting publications. You are steering a westerly course and approaching Block Island Sound. The gyro error is 2°W. "Per standard magnetic compass" is abbreviated "psc." Use a variation of 15°W for the entire plot. The deviation table is:

HDG.	M.DEV.	HDG.	M.DEV.	HDG.	M.DEV.
000°	0.0°	120°	1.0°W	240°	2.0°E
030°	1°W	150°	0.0°	270°	1.5°E
060°	3.0°W	180°	0.0°	300°	1.0°E
090°	2.0°W	210°	1.0°E	330°	0.0°

16556. You are underway in the vicinity of Block Island and obtain the following lines of position: Montauk Point Light—267° pgc; Block Island Southeast Light—030° pgc; Radar Bearing to Block Island Southwest Point (tangent)—352° pgc. What is your position at the time of these sightings?

A. LAT 41°05.2'N, LONG 71°36.2'W
B. LAT 41°05.3'N, LONG 71°35.8'W
C. LAT 41°05.4'N, LONG 71°36.0'W
D. LAT 41°05.4'N, LONG 71°35.9'W

16557. Which course would you steer by your standard magnetic compass to make good a course of 275°T?

A. 266° psc
B. 272° psc
C. 289° psc
D. 294° psc

16558. From your position you observe a rotating white and green light to the north. This light is most likely _____.

A. at an airport
B. on a naval mine-countermeasures vessel
C. Block Island North Light
D. on a vessel engauged in public safety activity

16559. At 1800, your position is LAT 41°06.5'N, LONG 71°43.5'W. How should the buoy which bears 030°T from your position at a range of approximately 0.5 mile be painted?

A. Horizontally banded, red over green, with a red buoyancy chamber
B. Horizontally banded, green over red, with a green buoyancy chamber
C. Vertically striped, red and green
D. Solid red with green letters BIS

16560. From your 1800 position, you steer a course of 355° psc at a speed of 10.0 knots. At 1830, your position is LAT 41°11.7'N, LONG 71°45.8'W. What are the set and drift of the current?

A. 005°T, 1.0 knot
B. 005°T, 0.5 knot
C. 180°T, 0.5 knot
D. 208°T, 1.0 knot

16561. From your 1830 fix, you come left to a course of 290°T. Which statement concerning Watch Hill Light is TRUE?

A. The nominal range of its white light is 16 miles.
B. It displays both red and white lights.
C. Its horn blasts every 15 seconds in fog.
D. Its geographic range is 18.5 miles at a 35-foot (10.7 meters) height of eye.

16562. At 1850, you obtain the following bearings and distance: Block Island North Light—085°T; Watch Hill Light—342°T, 5.8 miles. What true speed did you make good between 1830 and 1850?

A. 2.9 knots
B. 5.7 knots
C. 8.0 knots
D. 8.7 knots

16563. From your 1850 fix, you come left to a course of 280°T while maintaining a speed of 10 knots. Which combination of available Loran-C lines would be best for position determination?

A. 9960-Y and 9960-W
B. 9960-X and 9960-Y
C. 9960-W and 9960-X
D. All 3 combinations are equal.

16564. If your height of eye is 45 feet (13.7 meters), what is the approximate geographic range of Block Island North Light?

A. 7.8 nm
B. 8.9 nm
C. 13.0 nm
D. 16.7 nm

16565. You decide to use the 9960-Y and 9960-W rates. At 1915, you obtain the following readings: 9960-Y-43937.5; 9960-W-14651.2. What is your 1915 position?

A. LAT 41°13.6'N, LONG 71°54.0'W
B. LAT 41°13.5'N, LONG 71°53.4'W
C. LAT 41°13.4'N, LONG 71°53.1'W
D. LAT 41°14.4'N, LONG 71°53.7'W

16566. If you were to head into New London Harbor, which chart should you switch to for the best detail?

A. 13209
B. 13212
C. 13213
D. 13214

16567. From your 1915 position, you come left and set a course for Gardiners Point. At 1930, your position is LAT 41°12.7'N, LONG 71°56.8'W. What type of bottom is charted at this position?

A. Blue mud, gritty shells
B. Buried mussels, gritty shells
C. Blue mud, gray sand
D. Bumpy mud with gravel surface

16568. From your 1930 position, you plot a course to pass 0.5 mile due south of Race Rock Light. If your vessel's speed is 8.0 knots, the current's set and drift are 040°T at 1.4 knots, and a south wind produces a 3° leeway, what true course should you steer to make good your desired course?

A. 275°T
B. 280°T
C. 290°T
D. 294°T

16569. The short-long dashed magenta line around Gardiners Island marks _____.

A. a regulated anchorage
B. fish trap areas
C. an area closed to the public
D. underwater cables

16570. NOAA VHF-FM weather broadcasts from Providence, RI, are on _____.

A. 162.25 MHz
B. 162.30 MHz
C. 162.40 MHz
D. 162.55 MHz

The following questions are based on chart 12354TR, Long Island Sound - Eastern Part, and the supporting publications. Your vessel has a draft of 12 feet (3.7 meters). Your height of eye is 24 feet (7.3 meters). Use 14°W variation where required. The deviation table is:

HDG.	M.DEV.	HDG.	M.DEV.	HDG.	M.DEV.
000°	0°	120°	2°W	240°	3°E
030°	1°W	150°	1°W	270°	3°E
060°	2°W	180°	1°E	300°	2°E
090°	4°W	210°	2°E	330°	1°E

16606. Your position is LAT 40°59.0'N, LONG 73°06.2'W. What is the course per standard magnetic compass to New Haven Harbor Lighted Whistle Buoy NH?

A. 035°
B. 046°
C. 049°
D. 052°

16607. You depart from the position in question 16606 at 2114 and make good 12 knots on a course of 040°T. At what time will you sight New Haven Light if the visibility is 11 miles?

A. The light is visible at 2114.
B. 2140

C. 2152
D. 2159

16608. At 2142, you take the following bearings: Stratford Point Light—331°T; Stratford Shoal Middle Ground Light—280°T; Old Field Point Light—223°T. What is your 2142 position?

A. LAT 41°03.0'N, LONG 73°01.7'W
B. LAT 41°03.1'N, LONG 73°02.1'W
C. LAT 41°03.1'N, LONG 73°01.3'W
D. LAT 41°03.3'N, LONG 73°01.9'W

16609. What was the speed made good between 2114 and 2142?

A. 12.3 knots
B. 12.0 knots
C. 11.7 knots
D. 11.4 knots

16610. At 2142, you change course to make good 030°T and increase speed to 14 knots. You rendezvous with another vessel and receive fresh supplies while off New Haven Harbor Lighted Whistle Buoy NH. What is the light characteristic of this buoy?

A. — .
B. — —
C. . —
D. . .

16611. At 0109 you get underway, and at 0112 you take the following Loran-C readings: 9960-W-15026.9; 9960-X-26536.9; 9960-Y-44015.7. What is your 0112 position?

A. LAT 41°11.2'N, LONG 72°51.7'W
B. LAT 41°11.4'N, LONG 72°50.5'W
C. LAT 41°11.4'N, LONG 72°51.3'W
D. LAT 41°11.8'N, LONG 72°51.5'W

16612. At 0112, what is the approximate depth under the keel?

A. 38 feet (11.5 meters)
B. 47 feet (14.2 meters)
C. 51 feet (15.5 meters)
D. 57 feet (17.3 meters)

16613. At 0112, you are on course 124°T and turning for 12.0 knots. What course will you make good if the current is 255°T at 1.2 knots?

A. 132°
B. 129°

C. 120°
D. 118°

6614. Branford reef is _____.

A. completely submerged at all stages of the tide
B. a hard sand shoal
C. surrounded by rocks awash at low water spring tides
D. a small, low, sandy islet surrounded by shoal water

16615. At 0112, the radar range to Branford Reef Light is 2.9 miles. At 0125, the range is 3.6 miles. What is the position of your 0125 running fix if you are steering 124°T at 12 knots?

A. LAT 41°09.7'N, LONG 72°48.1'W
B. LAT 41°09.7'N, LONG 72°48.7'W
C. LAT 41°09.8'N, LONG 72°47.2'W
D. LAT 41°10.2'N, LONG 72°47.7'W

16616. At 0130, your position is LAT 41°09.3'N, LONG 72°46.9'W when you change course to 086°T. If you make good 086°T, what is the closest point of approach to Twenty-Eight Foot Shoal Lighted Buoy?

A. 0.7 mile
B. 0.9 mile
C. 1.1 miles
D. 1.2 miles

16617. At 0200, you take the following bearings: Falkner Island Light—004.5°T; Kelsey Pt. Breakwater Lt.—054.0°T; Horton Point Light—115.0°T. What were the set and drift from 0130?

A. 260° at 0.5 knot
B. 080° at 1.0 knot
C. 260° at 1.0 knot
D. There is no current.

16618. What is the distance from your 0200 position to the point where Twenty-Eight Foot Shoal Lighted Buoy is abeam to starboard?

A. 6.6 miles
B. 6.9 miles
C. 7.1 miles
D. 7.3 miles

16619. The shoreline along Rocky Point should give a good radar return because _____.

A. the lookout tower is marked with radar reflectors
B. of offshore exposed rocks
C. submerged reefs cause prominent breakers
D. the shore is bluff and rocky

16620. You sight Bartlett Reef Light in line with New London Harbor Light bearing 043° pgc. You are heading 088° pgc and 098.5° per standard magnetic compass at the time of the observation. Which statement is TRUE?

A. The true heading at the observation was 090°.
B. The deviation is 1.5°E by observation.
C. The magnetic compass error is 9.5°W.
D. The gyro error is 2°E.

The following questions are to be answered using chart 13205 TR, Block Island Sound, and supporting publications. Your height of eye is 42 feet and your vessel's draft is 34 feet. The gyro error is 2°E. You are keeping daylight savings time (ZT+4). Use 15°W variation where required.

HDG.	M.DEV.	HDG.	M.DEV.	HDG.	M.DEV.
000°	3°W	120°	2°W	240°	3°E
030°	3°W	150°	0°	270°	2°E
060°	4°W	180°	1°E	300°	1°E
090°	3°W	210°	2°E	330°	1°W

16638. At 0400 you take the following loran readings: 9960-X-25841.8; 9960-Y-43736.7. From your 0400 fix, you steer a course to make good 347°T at 12.5 knots. Visibility is good. What is the earliest time you can expect to raise Montauk Point Light? (Nominal range—24 miles, height above water—168 feet.)

A. The light is visible at 0400.
B. 0426
C. 0435
D. 0442

16639. You estimate the current to be 125° at 0.6 knot, and the wind is westerly causing 3° of leeway. What course should you steer per gyrocompass to make good 347°T while turning for 12.5 knots?

A. 340° pgc
B. 343° pgc
C. 346° pgc
D. 349° pgc

16640. At 0445 you take the following lines of position: Montauk Point Light—292° pgc; Block Island Southeast Point Light—024° pgc. What was the current encountered since your 0400 fix?

A. 004°, 0.7 knot
B. 004°, 0.9 knot
C. 184°, 0.7 knot
D. 184°, 0.9 knot

16641. At 0455 you encounter fog and slow to 5 knots. At 0500, you obtain a radar fix from the following information: radar range to Montauk Point is 9.1 miles; tangent bearing to western edge of Block Is. is 015° pgc; distance off the nearest part of Block Is. is 5.9 miles. What is your 0500 position?

A. LAT 41°02.8'N, LONG 71°39.5'W
B. LAT 41°02.9'N, LONG 71°39.8'W
C. LAT 41°03.1'N, LONG 71°39.6'W
D. LAT 41°03.5'N, LONG 71°39.3'W

16642. Based on your 0500 fix, which statement is TRUE?

A. You are seaward of the 120 fathom curve.
B. The course made good between 0445 and 0500 was 345°T.
C. You should alter course to port to clear Southwest Ledge Shoal.
D. A radar contact bearing 020°T at 4.8 miles is buoy 2A.

16643. At 0520 your position is LAT 41°07.2'N, LONG 71°41.6'W. You set course to leave Race Rock Light abeam to starboard at 0.5 mile. What is the course to steer per standard magnetic compass (assume no current)?

A. 301.5°
B. 305.0°
C. 307.5°
D. 309.0°

16644. Visibility becomes variable in patchy fog and you maintain 5 knots speed. At 0610 you sight Montauk Point Light bearing 239° pgc, and at 0630 you sight Watch Hill Point Light bearing 333° pgc. What is the position of your 0630 running fix?

A. LAT 41°08.3'N, LONG 71°45.4'W
B. LAT 41°08.2'N, LONG 71°45.8'W
C. LAT 41°08.1'N, LONG 71°45.1'W
D. LAT 41°08.0'N, LONG 71°45.2'W

16645. At 0630 you increase speed to

12.0 knots. At 0645 Race Rock Light bears 294° pgc. At 0700 Race Rock Light bears 293° pgc. Based on this, you should _____.
A. alter course to port
B. maintain course and speed
C. alter course to starboard
D. maintain course and reduce speed

16646. The Tidal Current Tables indicate the following for the Race:

SLACK WATER	MAXIMUM	CURRENT
0328	0642	3.9 F
0947	1301	3.2 E

What current should you expect when transiting the Race?
A. 3.9 knots, flooding
B. 3.5 knots, flooding
C. 3.3 knots, flooding
D. 3.0 knots, flooding

The following questions are based on chart 13205TR, Block Island Sound, and the supporting publications. Your vessel has a draft of 12 feet (3.7 meters). Your height of eye is 16 feet (4.8 meters). The gyro error is 2°E. Use 15°W variation where required. The deviation table is:

HDG.	M.DEV.	HDG.	M.DEV.	HDG.	M.DEV.
000°	2.0°E	120°	1.0°E	240°	3.0°W
030°	3.0°E	150°	1.0°W	270°	3.5°W
060°	4.0°E	180°	2.0°W	300°	0°
090°	2.0°E	210°	3.5°W	330°	1.5°E

16706. At 0520, you take the following observations: Point Judith Light—032° pgc; Point Judith Harbor of Refuge Main Breakwater Center Light—308° pgc. What is the position of your 0520 fix?

A. LAT 41°20.8'N, Long 71°30.3'W
B. LAT 41°20.8'N, Long 71°29.7'W
C. LAT 41°20.6'N, Long 71°30.0'W
D. LAT 41°20.5'N, Long 71°29.8'W

16707. Point Judith Harbor of Refuge _____.

A. is used mostly by towing vessels
B. has a maximum depth of 14 feet at MHW
C. is easily accessible in heavy southerly seas
D. is entered through the East Gap or the West Gap

16708. At 0520 you are on course 243° pgc at 12 knots. What is the course per standard magnetic compass?

A. 262° psc
B. 258° psc
C. 233° psc
D. 227° psc

16709. The coastline between Point Judith and Watch Hill is _____.

A. steep with rocky bluffs
B. low and marshy
C. sandy and broken by rocky points
D. heavily forested

16710. In clear weather, how far away will you sight Point Judith Light?

A. 9.2 nm
B. 10.6 nm
C. 12.3 nm
D. 14.0 nm

16711. At what time will you cross the 60 foot curve if you make good 12 knots?

A. 0528
B. 0534
C. 0541
D. 0544

16712. The two wavy magenta lines running to Green Hill Point represent _____.

A. recommended approaches to Green Hill Point
B. areas of unreliable loran readings
C. prohibited fishing areas
D. submarine cables

16713. At 0600 your loran reads: 9960-W-14542.5; 9960-X-25909.5; 9960-Y-43950.0. What is your 0600 position?

A. LAT 41°18.1'N, LONG 71°38.3'W
B. LAT 41°18.3'N, LONG 71°38.7'W
C. LAT 41°18.4'N, LONG 72°38.1'W
D. LAT 41°18.5'N, LONG 71°38.9'W

16714. What was the current between 0520 and 0600?

A. 201° at 1.0 knot
B. 201° at 1.5 knots
C. 021° at 1.0 knot
D. 021° at 1.5 knots

16715. From your 0600 position, what is the course per gyrocompass to leave Watch Hill Light abeam to starboard at 2.0 miles if a southerly wind is producing 3° of leeway?

A. 252° pgc
B. 256° pgc
C. 258° pgc
D. 262° pgc

16716. At 0645, Watch Hill Point (left tangent) bears 314.5°T at 2.75 miles. What was the speed made good between 0600 and 0645?

A. 8.1 knots
B. 9.8 knots
C. 10.7 knots
D. 11.4 knots

16717. At 0705, you take the following bearings: Watch Hill Light—030.5° pgc; Latimer Reef Light—329.0° pgc; Race Rock Light—262.0° pgc. What was the true course made good between 0645 and 0705?

A. 252°T
B. 256°T
C. 263°T
D. 266°T

16718. At 0705, you change course to head for The Race. You wish to leave Race Rock Light bearing due north at 0.4 mile. If the current is 100°T at 2.8 knots, and you are turning for 12.0 knots, what course (pgc) should you steer?

A. 250° pgc
B. 255° pgc
C. 263° pgc
D. 267° pgc

16719. You are bound for New London. Where will you cross the demarcation line and be governed by the Inland Rules of the Road?

A. You are already governed by the Inland Rules.
B. In the Race
C. Above the Thames River Bridge
D. You will not be governed by the Inland Rules.

16720. In order to check your compasses, you sight North Dumpling Island Light in line with Latimer Reef Light bearing 074° pgc. The helmsman was steering 303° pgc and 315° per standard magnetic compass at the time. Which of the following is TRUE?

A. The gyro error is still 2°E.
B. The deviation based on the observation is 15°W.

C. The magnetic compass error is 12°W.
D. The true line of the range is 072°.

...ions are to be answered using chart 13205
TR, Block Island Sound, and supporting
...ublications. Your height of eye is 36 feet
and your vessel's draft is 16 feet. The gyro
error is 2°E. There is a light haze. Use 15°W
variation where required.

HDG.	M.DEV.	HDG.	M.DEV.	HDG.	M.DEV.
000°	2.0°E	120°	1.0°E	240°	3.0°W
030°	3.0°E	150°	1.0°W	270°	1.5°W
060°	4.0°E	180°	2.0°W	300°	0°
090°	2.0°E	210°	3.5°W	330°	1.5°E

16738. At 2212 you take the following loran
readings: 9960-W-14715.8; 9960-X-25991.2;
9960-Y-43764.8. What is the course to
steer, per gyrocompass from your 2212 position, to leave Montauk Point Buoy MP
abeam to port at 1 mile if easterly winds
are causing 3° of leeway?

A. 027° pgc
B. 030° pgc
C. 032° pgc
D. 035° pgc

16739. What is the earliest time you should
sight Montauk Point Light (nominal
range—24 miles) if you are turning for 9.2
knots? Visibility is 5 nautical miles.

A. The light is visible at 2212
B. 2221
C. 2243
D. You will not sight the light on this
course.

16740. At 2245 visibility improves and
Montauk Point Light bears 355° pgc. At
2314 Montauk Point Light bears 331° pgc,
and at 2329 the light bears 311° pgc. Based
on your 2329 running fix which statement
is TRUE?

A. You are shoreward of the 90 foot curve.
B. Your fathometer reads about 136 feet.
C. You are being set to the left of the track.
D. You allowed too much leeway for the
easterly winds.

16741. At 2346 Montauk Point Light bears
285° pgc, and the radar range to Montauk
Point is 5.9 miles. You are steering to make
good 034°T. In order to remain westward of
Southwest Ledge you should _____.

A. come left before the loran reads 9960-X-
25900 or less
B. remain on your present course and you
will clear Southwest Ledge
C. keep Block Island North Light bearing
033°T or less
D. alter course to the right when Block Island Aerobeacon bears 055°T

16742. At 2352 you hear a MAYDAY call
from a vessel reporting her position as 1.5
miles due east of Block Island Southeast
Point Light. What is the course to steer, per
gyrocompass to the distress site, if you
change course at midnight and allow 1°
leeway for easterly winds?

A. 049.5° pgc
B. 052.5° pgc
C. 055.5° pgc
D. 059.0° pgc

16743. At 0040 you are south of Lewis Point
when you receive word that the distress is
terminated. You alter course to head for
The Race. At 0052 you take the following
relative bearings because the starboard
gyro repeater is inoperative: Race Rock
Light—002°; Watch Hill Light—034°; Block
Island North Light—122°. Your heading at
each bearing was 285° pgc. What is your
0052 position?

A. LAT 41°08.8'N, LONG 71°41.4'W
B. LAT 41°09.0'N, LONG 71°42.3'W
C. LAT 41°09.0'N, LONG 71°41.1'W
D. LAT 41°09.1'N, LONG 71°41.7'W

16744. You continue to steer 285° pgc from
your 0052 fix. Your speed is 9.2 knots. What
is the course per standard magnetic compass?

A. 273.5°
B. 276.0°
C. 298.0°
D. 302.0°

16745. At 0100 Race Rock Light bears 001°
relative, and at 0110 it bears 000° relative.
Based on this you know you _____.

A. are being set to the right of the track
B. are making good more than 9.2 knots
C. are making good less than 9.2 knots
D. have an unknown gyro error

16746. In order to check your compasses,
you sight Race Rock Light in line with New
London Harbor Light bearing 336° per gy-

rocompass. The helmsman reports the vessel was heading 275.0° pgc and 290.5° per
standard magnetic compass at the time of
the observation. Which statement is TRUE?

A. The gyro error is now 2°E.
B. The deviation table is correct for that
heading.
C. The vessel should be swung to check the
deviation table.
D. The compass error is 0.5°W.

*The following questions are to be answered
using chart 12221 TR, Chesapeake Bay
Entrance, and supporting publications. Your
present course is 202°T and your vessel's engines are turning RPMs for 18 knots. Your
height of eye is 54 feet (16.5 meters) and your
vessel's draft is 28 feet (8.5 meters). Use 10°W
variation where required.*

6838. At 0800 you obtain the following
Loran-C readings: 9960-X-27101; 9960-Y-
41612; 9960-Z-58737. What is your vessel's
position?

A. LAT 37°20.9'N, LONG 75°29.5'W
B. LAT 37°21.0'N, LONG 75°32.0'W
C. LAT 37°19.8'N, LONG 75°30.6'W
D. LAT 37°20.8'N, LONG 75°31.2'W

16839. At 0800 you reduce speed from sea
speed. Speed was reduced by the time you
passed abeam of Cape Charles Lighted Bell
Buoy 12 at 0814. At this time Buoy 12 was
abeam on your starboard side at a distance
of 0.65 mile. Assuming you continue to
make good your course of 202°T, what is
your new speed if you pass abeam of Cape
Charles Lighted Bell Buoy 14 at a distance
of 1.5 miles at 0907?

A. 13.6 knots
B. 12.9 knots
C. 12.3 knots
D. 12.0 knots

16840. Visibility is exceptionally clear. At
approximately what distance did
Chesapeake Light become visible?

A. 19.2 miles
B. 21.0 miles
C. 22.7 miles
D. 24.0 miles

16841. At 0907 you change course to
224°T, and your speed is now 13.0 knots. At
0939 Chesapeake Light is bearing 168°T at
a distance of 7.1 miles, and Cape Henry

Light is bearing 246°T. What were the set and drift since 0907?

A. 326°T at 0.7 knot
B. 326°T at 1.4 knots
C. 146°T at 1.4 knots
D. 146°T at 0.7 knot

16842. From your 0939 position, you wish to change course in order to pass 0.3 mile north of Buoy NCA (LL #375) in the inbound traffic lane. You estimate the current to be 150°T at 2.0 knots. What course should you steer to make good the desired course? Your speed is still 13.0 knots.

A. 232°T
B. 235°T
C. 245°T
D. 249°T

16843. At what time will you enter the inbound traffic lane with Buoy NCA (LL #375) bearing 180°T at 0.3 mile?

A. 1003
B. 0957
C. 0951
D. 0948

16845. After the pilot boards, he tells you the gyro has a 2°E error. If this is true, what should the bearing be along Trestle C of the Chesapeake Bay Bridge–Tunnel as your vessel passes abeam of it?

A. 052° pgc
B. 049° pgc
C. 047° pgc
D. 045° pgc

16846. Your vessel's heading is 330° pgc and 345° psc with a 2°E gyro error. What is the deviation on this heading?

A. 0°
B. 3°W
C. 4°E
D. 7°W

NAVIGATION PROBLEMS— ANSWERS

NAVIGATION PROBLEMS—ANSWERS

NBR	ANS	NBR	ANS	NBR	ANS	NBR	ANS	NBR	ANS	NBR	ANS	NBR	ANS	NBR	ANS
		95	B	160	C	236	C	296	C	368	C	516	D	637	B
33	A	96	A	161	B	237	B	297	C	369	C	517	A	638	A
34	D	97	C	162	D	238	C	298	A	370	D	518	C	640	C
35	B	98	C	163	B	239	A	299	A	425	D	519	D	641	A
36	D	99	B	164	C	240	C	313	A	426	A	521	B	642	B
37	B	100	A	165	A	241	B	314	B	427	A	522	A	643	C
38	A	101	D	166	D	242	B	315	C	428	C	523	D	644	A
39	A	102	A	167	A	243	A	316	C	429	C	524	C	645	B
40	C	103	C	181	D	244	D	317	C	430	B	525	A	646	C
41	C	108	C	182	B	245	C	318	A	431	D	544	D	647	D
42	C	110	D	183	A	246	D	319	D	432	A	545	B	648	C
43	C	111	A	184	B	247	C	320	A	433	C	546	C	649	B
44	B	112	A	185	A	248	D	321	C	434	D	547	B	650	A
45	B	113	B	186	D	249	C	322	B	435	B	548	C	663	D
46	D	114	C	187	C	250	C	323	C	436	B	549	D	664	B
47	C	115	D	188	B	251	A	324	B	437	B	550	B	665	C
48	C	116	C	189	C	252	B	325	B	438	C	551	A	672	A
49	A	117	B	191	C	253	C	326	C	439	C	552	D	673	C
51	B	118	C	192	D	254	B	327	C	440	A	553	D	674	B
53	A	119	C	193	D	255	C	328	D	441	A	554	A	681	D
54	D	120	B	194	C	256	D	329	B	442	D	555	D	682	B
55	A	121	D	196	A	257	D	330	D	443	B	556	A	683	D
56	B	122	B	197	A	259	D	331	B	444	B	557	B	684	B
57	D	123	A	198	B	260	D	332	A	445	C	558	C	685	C
58	D	124	C	199	B	261	D	333	C	446	D	559	B	686	A
59	B	125	A	201	A	262	A	334	D	447	D	560	A	687	A
60	C	126	C	202	B	263	D	335	C	448	C	561	A	688	D
62	B	127	D	203	B	264	C	336	A	449	B	562	C	689	C
63	A	128	B	204	A	265	A	337	D	450	A	563	B	690	B
64	B	129	D	205	C	266	A	338	C	456	B	564	C	691	A
65	D	130	D	206	A	267	C	339	C	486	B	565	B	692	C
66	D	131	C	207	C	268	B	340	D	487	A	566	C	693	C
67	C	132	B	208	B	269	B	341	A	488	A	567	A	694	D
68	C	133	A	209	A	270	B	342	B	489	C	568	B	695	B
69	C	134	D	211	C	271	A	343	A	490	A	569	B	696	D
70	B	135	B	212	C	272	D	344	D	491	B	571	B	697	C
71	D	136	C	213	D	273	D	345	D	492	B	572	B	698	C
72	A	137	C	214	D	274	A	346	B	493	C	573	A	699	D
73	A	138	D	215	D	275	A	347	B	494	D	574	D	700	B
74	D	139	B	216	A	276	C	348	C	495	C	575	B	701	D
75	C	140	B	217	D	277	C	349	A	496	A	576	C	702	C
76	B	141	A	218	C	278	A	350	D	497	D	577	B	703	D
77	B	142	D	219	A	279	D	351	C	498	D	578	C	704	C
78	D	143	C	220	B	280	B	352	C	499	D	579	A	705	A
79	A	144	D	221	A	281	C	353	C	500	A	580	C	706	B
80	C	145	A	222	A	282	A	354	A	501	C	581	A	707	C
81	C	146	C	223	B	283	A	355	D	502	B	593	C	756	B
82	A	147	D	224	B	284	C	356	B	503	A	594	B	1117	C
84	D	149	A	225	C	285	C	357	A	504	D	595	D	1118	A
85	A	150	C	226	D	286	A	358	C	505	B	596	B	1119	D
86	B	151	D	227	A	287	B	359	C	506	D	597	D	1120	B
87	B	152	C	228	D	288	B	360	A	507	C	598	C	1122	C
88	B	153	A	229	C	289	C	361	A	508	B	599	A	1123	D
89	C	154	B	230	A	290	D	362	A	509	B	600	D	1124	B
90	D	155	A	231	C	291	A	363	D	511	C	632	A	1125	A
91	B	156	D	232	D	292	A	364	D	512	A	633	C	1126	A
92	A	157	D	233	D	293	D	365	C	513	C	634	B	1127	B
93	D	158	A	234	A	294	A	366	B	514	A	635	C	1128	D
94	B	159	C	235	C	295	B	367	D	515	A	636	D	1129	C

1130 C	1245 D	1429 D	1544 D	1709 C	1787 C	1846 D	1985 B
1131 B	1246 C	1430 C	1545 D	1710 B	1788 A	1847 C	1986 D
1132 A	1247 B	1431 B	1546 C	1711 C	1789 C	1848 B	1987 B
1133 D	1248 A	1432 B	1547 B	1712 D	1790 B	1849 A	1988 C
1134 B	1249 C	1433 B	1548 D	1716 B	1791 A	1850 D	1989 A
1135 C	1250 D	1434 A	1549 A	1720 C	1792 B	1931 A	1990 C
1136 A	1286 B	1435 D	1550 A	1721 A	1793 D	1932 C	1991 A
1137 D	1287 D	1436 D	1551 A	1722 B	1794 D	1933 C	1992 B
1138 A	1288 C	1437 A	1552 B	1723 D	1795 D	1934 C	1993 A
1139 D	1289 D	1438 C	1553 A	1724 D	1796 C	1935 C	1994 C
1140 C	1290 C	1439 C	1554 A	1725 C	1797 B	1936 D	1995 A
1141 A	1291 B	1440 C	1555 A	1726 A	1798 C	1937 B	1996 D
1142 B	1292 B	1441 B	1556 D	1727 B	1799 A	1938 D	1997 D
1143 B	1293 A	1442 C	1557 C	1728 C	1800 B	1939 C	1998 A
1144 C	1294 B	1443 D	1558 D	1729 B	1801 C	1940 B	1999 D
1145 D	1295 C	1444 D	1559 D	1730 A	1802 D	1941 D	
1146 D	1296 D	1445 C	1560 A	1731 B	1803 C	1942 D	2039 C
1147 C	1297 D	1446 B	1561 B	1732 B	1804 A	1943 C	2040 D
1148 B	1298 A	1447 D	1562 B	1733 C	1805 D	1944 B	2041 A
1149 B	1299 B	1448 C	1563 C	1734 C	1806 B	1945 D	2042 C
1150 A	1300 C	1449 B	1564 D	1735 A	1807 A	1946 D	2043 B
1163 D	1301 C	1506 C	1565 C	1736 D	1808 D	1947 B	2044 D
1164 C	1302 A	1507 A	1566 C	1737 C	1809 C	1948 C	2045 D
1165 D	1303 B	1508 B	1567 A	1738 A	1810 A	1949 C	2046 A
1166 D	1304 D	1509 A	1568 C	1739 D	1811 A	1950 C	2047 C
1167 C	1305 B	1510 C	1569 A	1740 D	1812 B	1951 B	2048 D
1168 A	1306 D	1511 C	1570 D	1741 D	1813 D	1952 B	2049 B
1169 B	1307 A	1512 C	1571 D	1742 A	1814 A	1953 A	2050 A
1170 A	1308 C	1513 B	1622 D	1743 C	1815 A	1954 A	2051 B
1171 A	1309 D	1514 D	1623 B	1744 B	1816 D	1955 A	2052 A
1172 C	1310 A	1515 C	1624 D	1745 D	1817 C	1956 B	2053 A
1173 B	1311 B	1516 A	1625 C	1746 A	1818 C	1957 C	2054 B
1174 D	1312 C	1517 C	1626 C	1747 C	1819 B	1958 C	2055 A
1219 D	1313 B	1518 A	1627 D	1748 D	1820 C	1959 D	2056 B
1220 C	1314 C	1519 D	1628 B	1750 B	1821 A	1960 C	2057 A
1221 A	1315 C	1520 A	1629 D	1751 C	1822 B	1961 A	2058 A
1222 C	1316 A	1521 B	1630 A	1752 B	1823 B	1962 C	2059 A
1223 D	1317 D	1522 C	1631 B	1753 D	1824 B	1963 C	2060 A
1224 B	1318 A	1523 B	1632 C	1754 C	1825 A	1964 B	2061 D
1125 B	1339 B	1524 A	1633 B	1756 D	1826 B	1965 D	2062 D
1226 C	1410 A	1525 D	1634 A	1757 A	1827 A	1966 D	2063 B
1227 C	1411 C	1526 B	1635 C	1759 A	1828 D	1967 C	2064 D
1228 A	1412 C	1527 A	1636 B	1760 B	1829 C	1968 A	2065 A
1229 C	1413 B	1528 D	1637 C	1761 A	1830 A	1969 B	2066 D
1230 A	1414 D	1529 C	1639 C	1762 B	1831 C	1970 B	2067 B
1231 D	1415 C	1530 C	1640 A	1763 C	1832 C	1971 D	2068 D
1232 B	1416 D	1531 D	1642 C	1764 D	1833 C	1972 D	2069 B
1233 D	1417 D	1532 B	1643 D	1765 A	1834 C	1973 C	2070 A
1234 A	1418 D	1533 A	1644 A	1766 D	1835 B	1974 A	2071 B
1235 C	1419 A	1534 B	1646 A	1767 A	1836 C	1975 C	2072 A
1236 D	1420 B	1535 A	1647 B	1768 B	1837 A	1976 D	2073 D
1237 C	1421 A	1536 C	1701 C	1769 D	1838 B	1977 C	2074 C
1238 B	1422 B	1537 D	1702 A	1770 C	1839 D	1978 A	2075 D
1239 D	1423 B	1538 D	1703 D	1771 C	1840 B	1979 C	2076 A
1240 D	1424 C	1539 A	1704 C	1772 D	1841 C	1980 B	2077 D
1241 B	1425 D	1540 B	1705 B	1773 A	1842 D	1981 B	2078 B
1242 A	1426 D	1541 C	1706 B	1774 A	1843 C	1982 B	2079 C
1243 B	1427 B	1542 B	1707 D	1775 B	1844 B	1983 B	2080 A
1244 A	1428 D	1543 C	1708 D	1786 A	1845 D	1984 C	2081 B

2082 C	2205 B	2274 C	2590 C	2707 A	2909 D	3104 D	3301 B
2083 A	2206 B	2296 A	2591 D	2708 C	2910 D	3105 A	3302 D
2084 D	2207 A	2297 C	2592 A	2851 B	2911 B	3106 B	3303 C
2085 A	2208 B	2298 D	2593 B	2852 C	2912 B	3107 C	3304 A
2086 B	2209 D	2299 A	2594 D	2853 A	2913 A	3108 D	3305 B
2087 D	2210 C	2300 B	2595 A	2854 C	3050 D	3109 D	3306 C
2088 C	2211 D	2301 D	2651 B	2855 B	3051 A	3110 C	3307 B
2089 B	2212 A	2302 A	2652 C	2856 D	3052 D	3111 C	3308 C
2090 A	2213 A	2303 C	2653 C	2857 A	3053 A	3112 A	3309 B
2091 D	2214 B	2304 A	2654 A	2858 D	3054 B	3251 C	3310 A
2092 C	2215 D	2305 D	2655 B	2859 B	3055 C	3252 A	3311 A
2093 A	2216 B	2306 C	2656 A	2860 B	3056 A	3253 B	3312 C
2094 C	2217 D	2307 B	2657 C	2861 A	3057 C	3254 B	3313 A
2095 D	2218 B	2308 D	2658 B	2862 B	3058 D	3255 B	3314 D
2096 B	2219 D	2309 D	2659 A	2863 B	3059 B	3256 C	3317 C
2097 D	2220 C	2310 A	2660 C	2864 A	3060 C	3257 C	3318 C
2098 B	2221 A	2311 B	2661 B	2865 C	3061 A	3258 B	3451 B
2099 A	2222 D	2312 B	2662 A	2866 C	3062 C	3259 D	3452 C
2127 D	2223 C	2313 C	2663 D	2867 B	3063 C	3260 D	3453 B
2128 A	2224 C	2314 C	2664 B	2868 A	3064 A	3261 C	3454 C
2129 B	2225 C	2315 C	2665 C	2869 C	3065 C	3262 D	3455 B
2130 B	2226 C	2316 C	2666 A	2870 B	3066 B	3263 B	3456 D
2131 C	2227 C	2317 B	2667 C	2871 D	3067 B	3264 D	3457 C
2132 B	2228 B	2318 A	2668 B	2872 B	3068 B	3265 C	3458 B
2133 D	2229 B	2319 C	2671 B	2873 D	3069 A	3266 C	3459 A
2134 A	2230 B	2320 B	2672 C	2874 D	3070 B	3267 A	3460 C
2135 D	2231 A	2321 C	2673 C	2875 C	3071 C	3268 C	3461 D
2136 C	2232 C	2322 A	2674 A	2877 B	3072 C	3269 B	3462 C
2137 B	2233 B	2381 D	2675 D	2878 C	3073 C	3270 D	3463 C
2138 C	2234 D	2382 A	2676 B	2879 A	3074 B	3271 A	3464 B
2139 A	2235 D	2383 C	2677 A	2880 B	3075 A	3272 A	3465 A
2140 C	2236 D	2384 C	2678 C	2881 A	3076 B	3273 C	3466 B
2141 A	2237 C	2385 D	2680 B	2882 C	3077 A	3274 B	3467 A
2142 D	2248 A	2386 B	2681 B	2883 B	3078 D	3275 C	3468 B
2143 A	2249 C	2387 D	2682 A	2884 C	3079 C	3276 A	3469 A
2144 C	2250 A	2388 A	2683 C	2885 C	3080 D	3277 C	3470 C
2145 D	2251 C	2389 A	2684 C	2886 B	3081 D	3278 B	3471 A
2146 C	2252 D	2390 D	2685 C	2887 B	3082 D	3279 D	3601 D
2147 B	2253 B	2391 A	2686 B	2888 C	3083 A	3280 C	3602 A
2148 C	2254 A	2392 C	2687 D	2889 A	3084 A	3281 C	3603 D
2149 D	2255 D	2393 B	2688 C	2890 B	3085 A	3282 D	3604 C
2150 B	2256 B	2394 A	2689 A	2891 A	3086 B	3283 B	3605 B
2188 C	2257 D	2395 A	2690 B	2892 C	3087 A	3284 D	3606 A
2189 C	2258 B	2396 C	2691 A	2893 D	3088 D	3285 B	3607 D
2190 A	2259 D	2397 D	2692 C	2894 B	3089 B	3286 D	3608 A
2191 C	2260 D	2398 C	2693 B	2895 C	3090 C	3287 B	3609 A
2192 B	2261 C	2399 B	2694 B	2896 D	3091 A	3288 C	3610 A
2193 A	2262 A	2400 A	2695 C	2897 B	3092 B	3289 D	3611 D
2194 B	2263 D	2401 B	2696 B	2898 A	3093 D	3290 B	3612 D
2195 A	2264 D	2424 C	2697 C	2899 B	3094 C	3291 A	3613 B
2196 A	2265 C	2581 D	2698 A	2900 C	3095 A	3292 B	3614 A
2197 C	2266 A	2582 B	2699 A	2901 A	3096 D	3293 A	3615 A
2198 C	2267 D	2583 C	2700 A	2902 C	3097 B	3294 A	3616 A
2199 A	2268 A	2584 B	2701 C	2903 D	3098 C	3295 D	3617 A
2200 D	2269 C	2585 A	2702 B	2904 C	3099 A	3296 A	3618 B
2201 D	2270 B	2586 C	2703 C	2905 D	3100 D	3297 B	3619 D
2202 A	2271 B	2587 C	2704 D	2906 C	3101 C	3298 D	3620 C
2203 C	2272 C	2588 B	2705 D	2907 D	3102 A	3299 C	3621 B
2204 D	2273 B	2589 D	2706 D	2908 C	3103 D	3300 C	3622 C

3623	A	4005	C	10605	B	11400	C	12107	B	12907	A	13707	C	14703	B
3624	C	4006	B	10606	B	11401	C	12108	D	12908	B	13708	A	14704	D
3625	D	4007	A	10607	D	11402	A	12109	A	12909	B	13709	A	15038	B
3626	B	4008	A	10608	C	11403	C	12200	B	13000	C	13801	C	15039	C
3627	D	4009	B	10609	A	11404	C	12201	C	13001	B	13802	D	15040	A
3628	C	4010	C	10610	B	11405	A	12203	D	13002	D	13803	A	15041	A
3629	A	4011	D	10700	B	11406	A	12204	C	13003	B	13804	C	15042	C
3630	B	4012	A	10701	B	11407	C	12205	A	13004	C	13805	D	15043	C
3631	C	4013	D	10702	A	11408	B	12206	B	13005	D	13806	B	15044	A
3632	D	4014	B	10703	C	11409	B	12207	A	13006	C	13807	D	15045	B
3633	C	4015	C	10704	B	11410	C	12208	D	13007	D	13808	B	15046	C
3634	B	4016	D	10705	B	11500	C	12209	A	13008	B	13809	A	15056	A
3635	A	4017	D	10706	C	11501	D	12210	D	13009	A	13810	A	15057	D
3636	C	10100	A	10707	C	11502	C	12300	D	13010	C	13900	C	15058	D
3637	C	10101	B	10708	A	11503	B	12301	C	13100	A	13901	A	15059	C
3638	A	10102	D	10709	D	11504	A	12302	B	13101	C	13902	D	15060	B
3639	A	10103	A	10900	C	11505	C	12303	C	13102	B	13903	B	15061	C
3640	B	10104	D	10901	A	11506	A	12304	A	13104	D	13904	C	15062	D
3641	C	10105	C	10902	D	11507	C	12305	C	13105	D	13905	D	15063	D
3642	C	10106	B	10903	B	11508	B	12306	D	13106	A	13906	A	15064	B
3643	B	10107	D	10904	A	11509	B	12307	B	13107	C	13908	D	15065	C
3644	A	10108	D	10905	C	11700	A	12308	A	13108	D	13909	B	15066	B
3645	C	10109	A	10906	C	11701	D	12309	C	13109	B	14001	B	15067	A
3646	D	10200	C	10907	B	11702	A	12500	A	13210	A	14002	C	15068	B
3647	A	10201	D	10908	A	11703	A	12501	D	13300	A	14003	D	15069	C
3648	B	10202	C	10909	D	11704	B	12502	A	13301	B	14004	C	15070	A
3649	A	10203	C	11001	C	11705	C	12505	A	13302	D	14005	C	15106	B
3650	C	10204	B	11002	D	11706	D	12506	B	13303	C	14100	B	15107	A
3651	A	10205	A	11003	B	11707	B	12507	B	13305	C	14101	D	15108	A
3652	D	10206	D	11004	B	11708	A	12508	D	13306	C	14102	C	15109	B
3653	C	10207	A	11005	D	11709	C	12509	D	13307	B	14103	A	15110	D
3708	A	10208	D	11006	C	11800	A	12600	C	13308	C	14104	B	15111	C
3751	A	10209	B	11007	B	11801	A	12601	B	13309	D	14200	B	15112	B
3752	A	10210	D	11009	D	11802	B	12602	D	13400	D	14201	D	15113	D
3753	C	10300	D	11010	A	11803	C	12603	B	13401	C	14202	B	15114	B
3754	D	10301	C	11011	C	11804	A	12604	C	13402	B	14203	A	15115	D
3755	A	10302	A	11012	B	11805	B	12605	A	13403	B	14204	C	15116	A
3756	D	10303	D	11013	B	11806	D	12606	B	13404	C	14300	A	15117	B
3757	B	10304	B	11014	C	11807	B	12607	C	13405	A	14301	D	15118	C
3758	C	10305	C	11100	C	11808	A	12608	D	13406	C	14302	A	15119	B
3759	D	10306	B	11101	A	11809	C	12609	A	13407	A	14303	B	15120	D
3760	A	10307	A	11102	D	11810	D	12610	B	13409	B	14304	C	15138	C
3761	D	10308	D	11103	D	11900	D	12700	D	13410	C	14401	C	15139	C
3762	B	10309	B	11104	D	11901	B	12701	B	13500	A	14402	D	15140	B
3763	C	10500	C	11105	D	11902	A	12702	A	13501	C	14403	B	15141	D
3764	D	10501	B	11106	B	11903	C	12703	C	13502	D	14404	A	15142	A
3765	C	10502	A	11107	A	11904	A	12704	A	13503	C	14500	D	15143	B
3766	A	10503	C	11108	C	11905	A	12705	A	13504	C	14501	C	15144	C
3767	C	10504	D	11109	A	11906	D	12706	B	13505	B	14502	A	15145	B
3768	D	10505	B	11300	C	11907	B	12707	C	13506	B	14503	B	15146	D
3769	B	10506	B	11301	D	11908	A	12708	D	13507	C	14504	D	15156	C
3770	A	10507	D	11302	A	11909	B	12709	B	13508	A	14600	C	15157	D
3771	A	10508	D	11303	D	12100	A	12900	B	13509	B	14601	B	15158	B
3772	A	10509	B	11304	B	12101	A	12901	A	13700	B	14602	C	15159	B
4000	C	10600	D	11305	C	12102	D	12902	C	13701	C	14603	A	15160	D
4001	A	10601	B	11306	D	12103	C	12903	D	13702	D	14604	D	15161	C
4002	D	10602	D	11307	C	12104	B	12904	C	13703	B	14700	A	15162	A
4003	A	10603	C	11308	A	12105	A	12905	D	13705	C	14701	B	15163	A
4004	B	10604	D	11309	B	12106	C	12906	C	13706	B	14702	C	15164	C

15165 A	15320 A	15468 D	15645 B	15766 C	15911 D	16057 C	16214 C
15166 C	15338 C	15469 B	15646 C	15767 B	15912 C	16058 D	16215 D
15167 B	15339 B	15470 D	15656 D	15768 A	15913 D	16059 C	16216 B
15168 C	15340 C	15506 C	15657 B	15769 D	15914 D	16060 A	16217 B
15169 A	15341 A	15507 D	15658 D	15770 B	15915 A	16061 B	16218 D
15170 C	15342 C	15508 C	15659 A	15799 C	15916 C	16062 B	16219 C
15206 A	15343 D	15509 A	15660 C	15806 D	15917 D	16063 D	16220 D
15207 D	15344 C	15510 B	15661 D	15807 A	15918 C	16064 B	16238 B
15208 C	15345 A	15511 D	15662 D	15808 D	15919 B	16065 B	16239 A
15209 D	15346 B	15512 B	15663 A	15809 D	15920 B	16066 A	16240 B
15210 B	15356 B	15513 D	15664 C	15810 B	15938 C	16067 A	16241 D
15211 C	15357 D	15514 A	15665 B	15811 A	15939 B	16068 D	16243 D
15212 B	15358 C	15515 D	15666 C	15813 B	15940 C	16069 D	16245 D
15213 A	15359 B	15516 D	15667 D	15814 A	15941 D	16070 C	16246 C
15214 B	15360 A	15517 C	15668 B	15815 D	15942 A	16106 A	16256 B
15215 A	15361 D	15518 B	15669 C	15816 C	15943 D	16107 D	16257 C
15216 C	15362 D	15519 A	15670 D	15817 C	15944 B	16108 B	16258 B
15217 B	15363 B	15520 D	15706 C	15818 A	15945 B	16109 B	16259 A
15218 B	15364 A	15538 A	15707 A	15819 A	15946 C	16110 D	16260 D
15219 D	15365 D	15539 C	15708 B	15820 C	15956 C	16111 B	16261 B
15220 C	15366 D	15540 B	15709 D	15821 A	15957 B	16112 D	16262 C
15238 B	15367 B	15541 C	15710 B	15822 B	15958 C	16113 C	16263 C
15239 A	15368 C	15542 D	15712 D	15823 A	15959 C	16114 C	16264 D
15240 D	15369 A	15543 B	15713 C	15824 C	15960 A	16115 B	16265 B
15241 C	15370 C	15544 C	15714 A	15825 C	15961 D	16116 A	16266 D
15242 D	15406 D	15545 D	15715 C	15826 A	15962 D	16117 A	16267 A
15243 B	15407 D	15546 A	15716 A	15827 C	15963 B	16118 D	16268 B
15244 A	15408 B	15606 A	15717 B	15828 C	15964 C	16119 D	16269 A
15245 B	15409 D	15607 B	15718 A	15829 D	15965 B	16120 C	16270 C
15246 C	15410 C	15608 C	15719 A	15830 A	15966 B	16138 D	16306 B
15256 B	15411 B	15609 A	15720 B	15838 B	15967 A	16139 B	16307 C
15257 A	15412 D	15610 D	15721 A	15839 B	15968 D	16140 B	16308 A
15258 A	15413 D	15611 D	15722 B	15840 A	15969 C	16141 B	16309 B
15259 D	15414 A	15612 C	15723 D	15841 D	15970 C	16142 A	16310 A
15260 D	15416 B	15613 A	15724 C	15842 A	16006 B	16144 D	16311 B
15261 B	15418 B	15614 B	15725 C	15843 D	16007 C	16145 A	16312 D
15262 C	15419 A	15615 A	15726 D	15844 C	16008 B	16146 A	16313 B
15263 D	15420 D	15616 D	15727 B	15845 A	16009 A	16156 D	16314 D
15264 B	15438 A	15617 A	15728 A	15846 D	16010 C	16157 A	16315 C
15265 D	15439 A	15618 B	15729 D	15856 B	16011 A	16158 C	16316 A
15266 B	15440 D	15619 D	15738 C	15857 D	16012 C	16159 A	16317 B
15267 A	15441 C	15620 B	15739 B	15858 B	16013 D	16160 B	16318 B
15268 D	15442 B	15621 C	15740 B	15859 D	16014 D	16161 B	16319 A
15269 A	15443 B	15622 A	15741 A	15860 C	16015 A	16162 A	16320 C
15270 C	15444 A	15623 A	15742 B	15861 D	16016 B	16164 B	16338 C
15306 B	15445 D	15624 B	15743 A	15862 B	16017 C	16165 A	16339 A
15307 B	15446 B	15625 B	15744 A	15863 C	16018 D	16166 B	16340 C
15308 A	15456 B	15626 C	15745 D	15864 A	16019 B	16167 D	16341 D
15309 C	15457 D	15627 C	15746 C	15865 A	16020 C	16168 D	16342 A
15310 A	15458 C	15628 A	15756 A	15866 B	16038 B	16169 C	16343 B
15311 C	15459 A	15629 C	15757 B	15867 D	16039 D	16170 B	16344 C
15312 C	15460 A	15630 C	15758 C	15868 D	16040 D	16206 B	16345 B
15313 B	15461 C	15638 C	15759 A	15869 A	16041 C	16207 C	16346 B
15314 A	15462 D	15639 A	15760 D	15870 C	16042 B	16208 B	16356 D
15315 D	15463 C	15640 B	15761 C	15906 C	16043 D	16209 D	16357 D
15316 D	15464 C	15641 A	15762 D	15907 B	16044 D	16210 A	16358 B
15317 A	15465 B	15642 D	15763 B	15908 C	16045 A	16211 D	16359 A
15318 D	15466 C	15643 D	15764 B	15909 C	16046 D	16212 C	16360 D
15319 B	15467 B	15644 A	15765 A	15910 B	16056 B	16213 A	16361 B

16362 B	16518 A	16714 D
16363 B	16519 D	16715 A
16364 C	16520 C	16716 C
16365 C	16538 A	16717 B
16366 A	16539 B	16718 C
16367 C	16540 A	16719 B
16368 C	16541 A	16720 A
16369 D	16542 D	16738 D
16370 C	16543 C	16739 A
16406 A	16544 D	16740 C
16407 C	16545 D	16741 A
16408 B	16546 C	16742 D
16409 B	16556 B	16743 D
16410 D	16557 C	16744 D
16411 D	16558 A	16745 A
16412 A	16559 B	16746 B
16413 C	16560 A	16838 B
16414 C	16561 B	16839 B
16415 D	16562 C	16840 B
16416 B	16563 A	16841 C
16417 A	16564 D	16842 C
16418 B	16565 B	16843 B
16419 A	16566 C	16845 C
16420 D	16567 C	16846 B
16438 A	16568 A	
16439 B	16569 B	
16440 A	16570 C	
16441 B	16606 D	
16442 D	16607 D	
16443 A	16608 A	
16444 C	16609 D	
16445 D	16610 C	
16456 A	16611 C	
16457 B	16612 A	
16458 B	16613 B	
16459 B	16614 A	
16460 D	16615 A	
16461 D	16616 B	
16462 A	16617 C	
16463 C	16618 B	
16464 D	16619 D	
16465 C	16620 B	
16466 A	16638 A	
16467 D	16639 A	
16468 D	16640 B	
16469 A	16641 D	
16470 D	16642 C	
16506 A	16643 C	
16507 C	16644 A	
16508 D	16645 A	
16509 C	16646 A	
16510 B	16706 B	
16511 D	16707 D	
16512 C	16708 A	
16513 A	16709 C	
16514 D	16710 D	
16515 B	16711 A	
16516 D	16712 D	
16517 D	16713 B	

AUXILIARY SAIL ENDORSEMENT

Auxiliary Sailing Vessel

A vessel having both sails and an engine is an auxiliary sailing vessel. Such a vessel is considered a power-driven vessel—whether motoring or motor-sailing—under both Inland and International Rules of the Road.

Terminology

Bobstay—stay running from the end of the bowsprit down and in to the stem of the hull. It balances the upward force of the headstay.

Bow Sprit—spar projecting forward from the bow to support headsails and supported laterally by shrouds, by a headstay from above, and a bobstay from below.

Centerboard—movable vertical board that can be lowered below the hull to minimize sideslip when working to windward.

Chain Plates—metal strength members in the hull to which standing rigging is attached.

Gudgeons—hull fittings on the stern or rudder post to receive the rudder pintles.

Guy—line supporting a spar in a horizontal or inclined position.

Halyard—line used to hoist a sail or gaff (or a yard on a square-rigger).

Heel—(a) bottom of the mast that fits into mast step; (b) leaning of a sailing vessel in response to the pressure of wind on its sails.

Jibe—to change the direction of the vessel relative to the apparent wind by bringing the stern through the wind. (See Tack.)

Marconi—triangular sail.

Mast—heavy vertical spar for sails (or on a merchantman, cargo booms).

Mast Step—supporting structure for the mast heel.

Pintles—rudder fittings which set into gudgeons allowing for lateral rudder swing.

Running Rigging—movable lines used for sail control (sheets, guys, halyards, outhauls and downhauls).

Shrouds—wires running from the hull-mounted chainplates on the beams via spreaders to the mast, supporting it athwartship.

Spars—pole-like structures for supporting sails (mast, yard, boom, gaff).

Spreaders—horizontal braces on the mast which, with the shrouds, prevent bending of the mast.

Standing Rigging—wire (usually) static supports for the mast.

Stays—wires running from forward (forestay) and aft (backstay) to the upper mast supporting it in a fore and aft direction.

Tack—(a) the bottom forward corner of a sail; (b) to change direction of a vessel relative to the apparent wind by bringing the bow through the wind (see Jibe); (c) to denote the side of the vessel the apparent wind comes over (as in port or starboard tack).

Topping Lift—line running from the end of the boom to a block at the head of the mast and down to a cleat; it is set up before dropping sail in order to support the boom.

Sailing Rigs

Cat—a vessel having its mast stepped on the bow, and having no headsails.

Cutter—a vessel with a single mast stepped farther aft than on a sloop, allowing for two headsails (jib and staysail).

Ketch—a two-masted (main and mizzen) vessel, with the latter stepped forward of the rudder post.

Schooner—a fore and aft rigged vessel with two or more masts, and with the aftmost the largest.

Sloop—a single-masted vessel, carrying one headsail.

Yawl—the same rig as the ketch except with the mizzen mast stepped aft of the rudder post.

Definitions

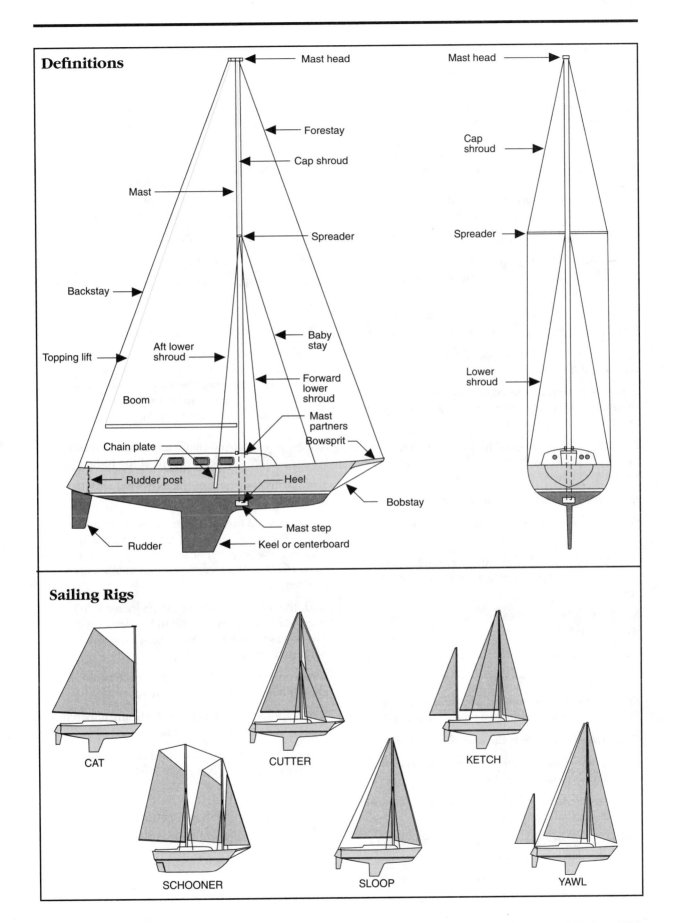

Mast head

Forestay

Cap shroud

Mast

Spreader

Backstay

Baby stay

Topping lift

Aft lower shroud

Forward lower shroud

Boom

Mast partners

Chain plate

Bowsprit

Rudder post

Heel

Bobstay

Mast step

Rudder

Keel or centerboard

Mast head

Cap shroud

Spreader

Lower shroud

Sailing Rigs

CAT

CUTTER

KETCH

SCHOONER

SLOOP

YAWL

SAILS

Terminology

Triangular (Marconi) sails have 3 sides and 3 corners:

Corners	Edges
Clew—after bottom corner	*Foot*—horizontal edge between tack and clew
Head—topmost corner	*Luff*—vertical edge between head and tack
Tack—bottom forward corner	*Leech*—transverse edge between head and clew

Bolt Rope—rope sewn into sail edge for strengthening.

Boom Vang—tackle providing downward tension on the boom, allowing for tensioning the sail when off the wind.

Bumkin—small spar projecting over the stern of a ketch or yawl to support a block for the mizzen sheet.

Clew Outhaul—running rigging controlling clew tension on the foot.

Cringle—grommet formed of rope lining a metal thimble at each sail corner providing for fitting attachments (the halyard to the head cringle, etc.).

Downhaul—line attached to the gooseneck providing tack tension on the luff. A downhaul can also be rigged to the head of a sail to assist in haul-down.

Gaff—small spar at the head of a fore/aft sail.

Gooseneck—a universal fitting attaching the boom to the mast.

Headboard—wood or fiberglass triangular shape into which is stitched the head of the mainsail for strength.

Jib Hanks—fittings sewn into the luff of a sail which snap to the forestay.

Mizzen—sail carried in the mizzen mast.

Peak—upper-after corner of a gaffed sail.

Reef Band—narrow horizontal material sewn into the sail parallel to the foot for attachments of reef points.

Reef Cringle—cringle at the end of a reef band.

Reef Points—small lengths of line attached to the reef band used in reefing the sail.

Roach—curved shape taken by a side of a sail (as in the convex shape of the leech).

Spinnaker—large triangular sail used on points of sail from beam reach to running.

Throat—that part of a gaff closest to the mast.

Traveler—horizontally moving roller assembly supporting the main sheet block allowing for positioning the boom as dictated by point of sail.

Turnbuckles—fittings with a central threaded barrel which receives a bolt at each end, allowing for tensioning stays, shrouds, etc.

Points of Sail

These refer to the direction of the vessel relative to the apparent wind. Starting from the bow and moving aft, the points are (angles approximate):

Close hauled—up to about 45 degrees

Close reach—in between

Beam reach—about 90 degrees

Broad reach—in between

Running—about 160 degrees to dead astern

On any of these points, the vessel can be on either port or starboard tack. When running, although both jib and main could be carried on the same side, the main would blanket the jib, so the sails are put to opposite sides, *wing-and-wing*.

Apparent Wind

It is *apparent wind* that drives the boat—apparent wind being the result of the true wind and that created by the boat speed.

With the wind forward, an increase in boat speed causes the apparent wind to draw forward. An increase in the true wind causes the apparent wind to draw aft. In both cases, the apparent wind increases in strength.

With the wind abaft the beam, an increase in boat speed causes the apparent wind to draw forward. An increase in the true wind causes the apparent wind to draw aft.

When apparent wind is forward of the beam, apparent wind is stronger than true wind.

When apparent wind is abaft the beam, apparent wind is weaker than true wind.

When bringing the wind toward the bow (as in close reach to close haul), the following occur:

- speed decreases
- apparent wind moves forward
- heeling force increases
- sideslip increases.

Sails and Fittings

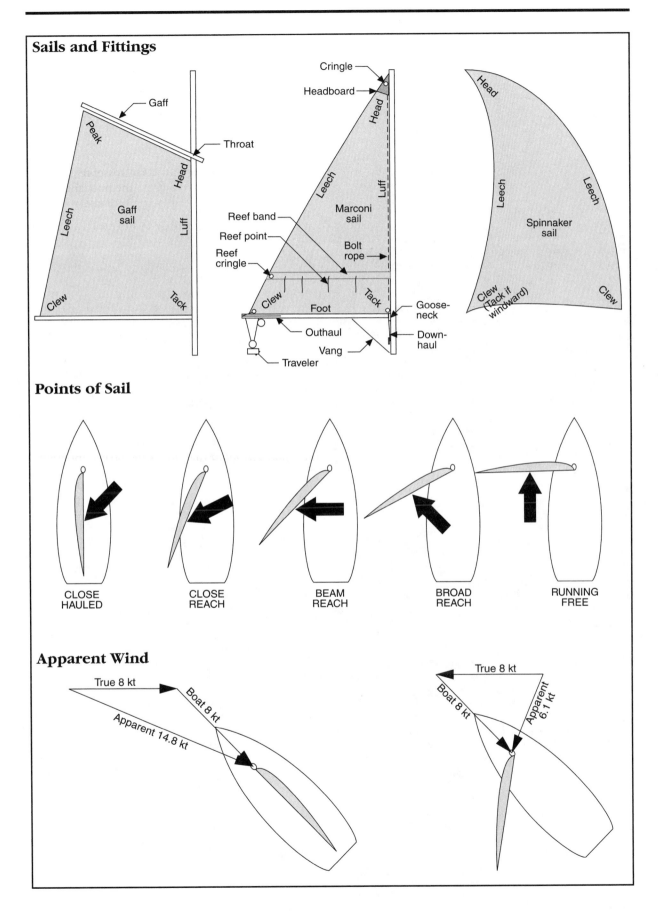

Points of Sail

CLOSE HAULED

CLOSE REACH

BEAM REACH

BROAD REACH

RUNNING FREE

Apparent Wind

True 8 kt

Boat 8 kt

Apparent 14.8 kt

True 8 kt

Boat 8 kt

Apparent 6.1 Kt

AUXILIARY SAIL QUESTIONS

The illustrations cited in the questions are shown on page 812.

NOTE: You may find redundant questions and a few answers which appear to be wrong. All questions and answers are as they appear in the CG database, however.

0631. You are at the helm of a ketch-rigged sailing vessel under sail on the starboard tack, close hauled, with all appropriate sails set and properly trimmed. You are instructed to "bear off quickly." To utilize your sails to assist with the turn, you should _____.

A. slack the mizzen sheet
B. trim the mizzen vang
C. slack the jib sheet
D. trim the main outhaul

1333. If you reef a Marconi mainsail, the sail area _____.

A. moves forward and up
B. moves aft and down
C. becomes larger
D. becomes smaller

1628. You are running before a rough sea and a strong wind. Your sailing vessel is yawing. If the wind should catch the mainsail on the reverse side you will _____.

A. broach
B. tack
C. jibe
D. go in irons

1649. The sails are properly set and trimmed. As a vessel heads up from a beam reach to close hauled the _____.

A. true wind velocity increases
B. heeling moment decreases
C. sideslip decreases
D. jib sheet must be hardened up

1683. You are running before a strong wind in a sloop. The most dangerous thing to do is _____.

A. jibe
B. tack about
C. reef the mainsail
D. strike the jib

1684. You are sailing before the wind in heavy weather. The failure of what will affect the vessel's safety most?

A. The main halyard
B. The jib sheet
C. The helm
D. The outhaul

1691. When anchoring a small sailing vessel in rough weather, the best anchor line would be composed of _____.

A. chain-wire
B. chain-manila
C. chain-nylon
D. all chain

1693. Every different type of sailing rig can be dangerous in certain circumstances. Which situation would most likely be dangerous?

A. A gaff rig is dangerous in a calm wind and sea.
B. A gaff rig is dangerous in a calm wind and large swell.
C. A square rig, such as a ship rig, is dangerous to jibe.
D. A tall, Marconi, sloop rig is dangerous to tack.

1694. When repairing a torn sail at sea, you should _____.

A. use perfectly aligned stitches in old sail-cloth so as to get the strain properly aligned
B. avoid using glued patches on old sailcloth
C. be sure to orient the weave of the patch material, on large patches, in the same orientation as the sail cloth being repaired
D. All of the above

1696. Which statement(s) is(are) TRUE?

A. Polyester sailcloth, such as Dacron, is resistant to rot due to moisture but susceptible to UV degradation and should be kept covered as much as possible.
B. Canvas sailcloth is susceptible to rot due to moisture and should never be covered when wet.
C. Kevlar sailcloth is susceptible to weakening due to repeated folding and therefore should be draped loosely over the boom when stowed.
D. All of the above are true.

1702. You are sailing at 8 knots on a beam reach in an apparent wind of 25 knots. Which statement is TRUE?

A. The true wind is a little abaft your beam, at just under 25 knots.
B. The apparent wind at the top of your mast will be slightly stronger than 25 knots and slightly farther forward than the wind at deck level.

C. If you turn to a close reach, the apparent wind will reduce in strength.
D. None of the above are true.

1703. With regard to aerodynamic lift, which statement is TRUE?

A. If the thrust on a sail becomes excessive when close-hauled, it is likely to capsize the vessel rather than drive it.
B. When a sail is trimmed too tight, turbulence will break out on the windward side of the sail and cause a telltale there to flutter.
C. A properly trimmed sail should have laminar flow on the windward side and turbulent flow on the leeward side.
D. Adjusting the angle of attack on a mainsail is accomplished by adjusting the outhaul or the vang, if fitted.

1704. Which statement is TRUE about sail shape?

A. A high-aspect ratio Marconi mainsail is more efficient for downwind sailing than a gaff-rigged mainsail.
B. You should put more belly in a sail in light airs than in a strong breeze.
C. You can reduce the belly in a boomed mainsail by easing the sheet.
D. You can move the belly up in a mainsail by easing the luff tension.

1706. The major lift-producing part of a sail is the _____.

A. leading edge
B. trailing edge
C. head
D. foil

1707. Your 40-foot auxiliary sailing vessel has just run aground on a bar. She has a relatively long, deep keel and the tide is falling. You have checked the bilges for damage and found none. Which is the most prudent action to take immediately?

A. Sheet the sails in flat to try to heel her over with the wind and sail off.
B. Start the engine and run it hard in forward to try to drive over and off the bar.
C. Strike the sails. Then run a kedge anchor out to one side, hook the main halyard to it, and heave the boat down onto one side.
D. Take soundings visually, by sounding pole, or leadline all around the vessel to locate the deepest water.

805. A sloop is a sailing vessel with
_____.

A. one mast
B. two masts: with the mizzen stepped abaft the rudder post
C. two masts: with the mizzen stepped forward of the rudder post
D. two masts: a foremast and mainmast

807. Which is standing rigging?

A. Halyards
B. Stays
C. Sheets
D. Downhauls

811. What should be your FIRST action if you discover a fire aboard ship?

A. Sound the alarm.
B. Attempt to put out the fire.
C. Confine it by closing doors, ports, vents, etc.
D. Call the Master.

1812. The sails are properly set and trimmed. As a vessel heads up from a beam reach to close hauled the _____.

A. apparent wind moves forward
B. heeling moment decreases
C. sideslip decreases
D. speed increases

1815. The sails are properly set and trimmed. As a vessel heads up from a beam reach to close hauled the _____.

A. speed increases
B. sideslip decreases
C. heeling moment decreases
D. apparent wind moves forward

1824. Most recreational sailing craft have triangular sails and are said to be _____.

A. Gaff rigged
B. Spinnaker rigged
C. Marconi rigged
D. Square rigged

1829. A sailing vessel with the wind coming from 220° relative would be _____.

A. close hauled on the port tack
B. close hauled on the starboard tack
C. running before the wind
D. on a broad reach

1836. A ketch-rigged sailing vessel is sailing to windward with the wind about 50° on the port bow. All the sails are set and drawing properly. Which statement is TRUE?

A. If you slack the mizzen sheet, the center of effort will move aft.
B. If you slack the main sheet, the lift to drag ratio of the mainsail will increase.
C. If you sheet in the mainsail without changing course, the vessel will heel farther and speed up.
D. If you strike the mainsail, the center of effort of the whole rig will move down.

1838. When a sail is reefed, the sail area is _____ .

A. reduced
B. increased
C. widened
D. unchanged

1839. A sailing vessel with the wind coming from 020° relative would be _____.

A. coming about
B. close hauled on the port tack
C. running before the wind
D. on a broad reach on the starboard tack

1846. You are under sail, and the wind is steady. While steady on course, you reef the mainsail and your speed slows. The apparent wind _____.

A. is unchanged
B. increases and draws aft
C. increases and draws forward
D. decreases and draws aft

1856. A sailing vessel with the wind coming from 180° relative would be _____.

A. close hauled on the starboard tack
B. close hauled on the port tack
C. on a broad reach on a port tack
D. running before the wind

1858. A sailing vessel with the wind coming from 180° relative would be _____.

A. close hauled on the port tack
B. close hauled on the starboard tack
C. running before the wind
D. on a broad reach

1859. (Ill. D003SL) The parts of the sail shown are correctly labeled EXCEPT the _____.

A. head
B. leech
C. luff
D. tack

1869. (Ill. D003SL) The three corners of the main sail are called _____.

A. head, fore, and aft
B. luff, leech, and spar
C. headboard, foot, and tail
D. head, tack, and clew

1876. A sailing vessel with the wind coming from 140° relative would be _____.

A. close hauled on the starboard tack
B. close hauled on the port tack
C. on a broad reach
D. running before the wind

1882. A sailing vessel with the wind coming from 260° relative would be _____.

A. on a close reach
B. on a broad reach
C. on a starboard tack
D. running before the wind

1896. (Ill. D001SL) The edge of the sail labeled "A" is called the _____.

A. leech
B. clew
C. luff
D. headboard

1897. Which is a part of a vessel's standing rigging?

A. Sheet
B. Backstay
C. Topping lift
D. Downhaul

1904. A sailing vessel with the wind coming over the port side is said to be on a _____.

A. port jibe
B. starboard jibe
C. port tack
D. starboard tack

1905. What fitting on the mast works in conjunction with the shrouds to control side bend of the mast?

A. Chainplate
B. Hound
C. Crowfoot
D. Spreader

1911. A ketch is a sailing vessel with
_____.

A. one mast
B. two masts: with the mizzen stepped
abaft the rudder post
C. two masts: with the mizzen stepped for-
ward of the rudder post
D. two masts: a foremast and a mainmast

1915. The sails are properly set and
trimmed. As a vessel heads up from a beam
reach to close hauled the _____.

A. apparent wind moves aft
B. heeling moment increases
C. sideslip decreases
D. mainsheet must be eased

1916. What is part of a vessel's standing
rigging?

A. Sheet
B. Backstay
C. Topping lift
D. Downhaul

1919. A sailing vessel with the wind coming from 050° relative would be _____.

A. close hauled on the starboard tack
B. reaching on a starboard tack
C. on a broad reach on a port tack
D. running before the wind

1926. A "reaching" course is one in which
the wind _____.

A. comes directly over the bow
B. comes directly over the stern
C. comes over an area extending from
broad on the bow to the quarter
D. has no effect on the vessel

1932. Which statement about sailing close-
hauled is TRUE?

A. If you ease the sheets, you can sail faster
and closer to the wind.
B. If you ease the sheets, you can sail faster
on the same course.
C. If you steer closer to the wind, you will
slow down.
D. If you sheet your sails closer to the centerline, you must bear away from the wind.

1953. Which fitting is used to connect the
boom to the mast?

A. Clevis pin
B. Gunter-lug
C. Gooseneck
D. Transom

1966. A sailing vessel with the wind
coming from 090° relative would be
_____.

A. close hauled on the starboard tack
B. reaching on the starboard tack
C. on a broad reach on the starboard tack
D. close hauled on the port tack

1969. A sailing vessel with the wind
coming from 290° relative would be
_____.

A. on a close reach on a port tack
B. close hauled on a starboard tack
C. on a broad reach on a port tack
D. on a beam reach on a starboard tack

1972. Which statement about sailing close-
hauled is TRUE?

A. If you ease the sheets and change heading, you can sail faster but not so close to
the wind.
B. If you ease the sheets you will be in
irons.
C. If you sheet your sails closer to the centerline, you can sail closer to the wind and
decrease leeway.
D. If you sheet your sails closer to the centerline, you will luff.

1974. When experiencing heavy winds, you
should reef sails to _____.

A. bring the sails parallel to the wind
B. reduce sail area exposed to the wind
C. allow the sails to catch more wind
D. remove all tension on the main and jib
sheets

1976. A capsized small sail vessel is best
righted when what part of the vessel is
downwind?

A. Stern
B. Bow
C. Centerboard
D. Mast

1977. A stay is _____.

A. standing rigging
B. a downhaul
C. a halyard
D. a jib

1978. How should you try to right a capsized small sailing vessel?

A. Position all personnel at the stern and
rock the vessel upright.
B. Position all personnel around the mast
and lift the vessel upright.
C. Lock the centerboard in the down position, stand on the centerboard, and pull on
a shroud or a halyard.
D. Put the centerboard in the up position
and have all personnel haul in on the line
attached to the mast.

1989. What is the proper method to fix running rigging to a cleat?

A. Half-hitches then a round turn
B. One round turn
C. A series of half-hitches
D. A round turn, figure eights, and a half-
hitch

1992. A deep keel on a sailing vessel increases the _____.

A. resistance to lateral movement
B. length-depth ratio resulting in a faster
hull design
C. height of the center of gravity above the
hull resulting in a more stable vessel
D. mast height to compensate for
increased lateral resistance

2007. The bottom of the mast rests on the
_____.

A. foot plate
B. sole plate
C. hounds
D. mast step

2015. A shroud is _____.

A. a light sail
B. a topmast stay
C. a sheet
D. standing rigging

2021. The sails are properly set and
trimmed. As a vessel heads up from a beam
reach to close hauled the _____.

A. true wind velocity increases
B. heeling moment decreases
C. sideslip increases
D. jib sheet must be eased

2023. If you were to jibe in a strong wind, the part of the rigging most likely to fail would be the _____.

A. forestay
B. backstay
C. jumper stay
D. halyard

2026. Which statement is TRUE concerning the gooseneck?

A. It is a sailing maneuver which brings the vessel's head through the wind.
B. It connects the boom to the mast and allows the boom to swing freely.
C. It is a sailing condition where there is a loss of air flow over the sails.
D. None of the above

2029. A yawl is a sailing vessel with _____.

A. a single mast
B. two masts: with the mizzen stepped abaft the rudder post
C. two masts: with the mizzen stepped forward of the rudder post
D. two masts: foremast and mainmast

2042. Which line would be used to hoist a sail?

A. Forestay
B. Halyard
C. Mainsheet
D. Foreguy

2049. The bottom of the mast rests on a part of the keel called the mast _____.

A. foot
B. heel
C. step
D. sole

2059. What standing rigging supports the mast in the fore-and-aft and athwartships directions?

A. Sheets and guys
B. Guys and vangs
C. Vangs and shrouds
D. Shrouds and stays

2062. You are running before the wind in a fresh breeze. The boom may be prevented from accidentally jibing by using a(n) _____.

A. buntline
B. clewline
C. outhaul
D. preventer

2066. A boom vang _____.

A. holds the boom down and flattens the main sail
B. draws the head of the sail to windward
C. tautens the standing rigging
D. douses the gaff topsail

2069. The metal horseshoe-shaped pieces used to bend a sail onto a stay or boom are called _____.

A. hanks
B. shackles
C. warps
D. gudgeons

2095. Sails may be wing and wing when _____.

A. close hauled
B. tacking
C. wearing
D. sailing with the wind aft

2097. If you reef a Marconi mainsail, the sail area _____.

A. becomes less
B. becomes larger
C. does not change
D. moves aft

2102. The sails are properly set and trimmed. As a vessel heads up from a beam reach to close-hauled the _____.

A. apparent wind remains steady
B. heeling moment decreases
C. sideslip decreases
D. speed decreases

2107. What is NOT running rigging?

A. Downhaul
B. Backstay
C. Halyard
D. Sheet

2111. The hinge fitting used to attach the boom to the mast is the _____.

A. gooseneck
B. step
C. swivel
D. pintle

2155. When sailing with the wind aft, a vessel may carry sails on both sides at the same time. The sails are _____.

A. wing and wing
B. luffed
C. reefed
D. cringled

2165. A schooner is a fore-and-aft rigged vessel with _____.

A. a single mast
B. two masts: with the mizzen stepped abaft the rudder post
C. two masts: with the mizzen stepped forward of the rudder post
D. at least two masts: a foremast and a mainmast

2189. Changing direction by bringing the stern of the vessel through the eye of the wind is known as _____.

A. jibing
B. running before the wind
C. tacking
D. reefing

2198. Which statement is TRUE concerning a sailing vessel with the sails properly trimmed?

A. The more the sails are sheeted in, the greater your speed will be when sailing downwind.
B. As the sails are sheeted in, the vessel will heel less when close hauled.
C. As the sails are sheeted in on a close hauled course, speed will increase as the side forces on the vessel decrease.
D. Sheeting in the sails will allow the vessel to sail closer to the wind but will decrease speed.

2206. Which action will NOT reduce heeling of a vessel when sailing on a tack?

A. Heading up until your sails begin to luff
B. Easing sheets
C. Reefing sails
D. Changing to larger sails

2208. Your 20-ton ketch-rigged sailing vessel is sailing close hauled on the port tack in a moderate breeze with all sails properly trimmed. You wish to bear off quickly to avoid a floating hazard. To utilize your sails to assist with the turn, you should _____.

A. slack the jib sheet
B. slack the mizzen sheet
C. put your rudder hard to port
D. All of the above

2212. In order to maintain speed while changing course from a close reach to a broad reach, the sails should be _____.

A. lowered
B. reefed
C. hauled in
D. eased out

2224. Your vessel is drifting with the wind broad on the port beam. The Marconi sail is set and flapping free. As you sheet in, the maximum drive is attained when the sail _____.

A. is at right angles to the true wind
B. first takes the shape of an airfoil
C. is filled with a slight flap at the leech
D. is 45° from the apparent wind

2226. You are sailing on a close reach when a strong wind suddenly heels the vessel hard over. To reduce the heeling and yet maintain speed, you should _____.

A. ease the mainsheet and bear more away from the wind
B. haul in on the mainsheet and steer more towards the wind
C. haul in on the mainsheet and ease the jib sheet
D. ease all sheets and bear more into the wind

2228. Your sails are properly trimmed while on a reaching course. Changing to a close hauled course will _____.

A. require you to sheet in for best speed
B. result in a reduction of speed
C. cause a greater heeling force to leeward
D. All of the above

2229. To get the best speed when tacking and using a mainsail and jib, the sails should be trimmed such that _____.

A. the jib is on one side of the vessel and the mainsail on the other
B. an air slot is formed between the two sails
C. one sail is as close to a right angle as possible to the other
D. as much of a gap as possible exists between the two sails in order to catch the most wind

2232. Your vessel is sailing on a port tack when a sudden gust of wind heels the vessel sharply to starboard. Which action will reduce the heeling of the vessel?

A. Attempt to sail the vessel closer to the wind
B. Ease the sheets to allow air flow to spill off the sail
C. Shift weight to the port side of the vessel
D. Any of the above

2239. You can slow or stop a sailing vessel by _____.

A. putting the wind off the beam and sheeting in
B. putting the wind off the stern and easing all sheets
C. bringing the vessel's head into the wind and letting the sails luff
D. raising the centerboard when running before the wind

2283. Sails may be wing and wing when _____.

A. tacking
B. on a close reach
C. sailing with the wind aft
D. anchored or drifting

2330. What is the purpose of a centerboard when sailing on a tack?

A. To reduce heeling of the vessel
B. To add weight stability
C. To reduce sideslip of the vessel
D. To prevent the vessel from jibing

2333. You are sailing into a harbor with the intention of picking up your mooring. There is no current. Which statement(s) is(are) TRUE?

A. On a ketch, you will most likely strike the jib before making your final approach.
B. On a yawl, the last sail you will strike after you have picked up the mooring will normally be the mainsail.

C. On a sloop, if your initial approach is to be downwind you could slow your approach by striking the jib and letting your main sheet out as far as it will go.
D. All of the above are correct.

2537. Which statement(s) is(are) TRUE regarding heaving-to?

A. A sloop will heave to with her jib and mainsail aback.
B. A ketch will heave to with her jib and mizzen aback.
C. A yawl will heave to with her jib aback, main sheet eased, and her mizzen sheeted in.
D. All of the above are correct.

2642. When properly set and drawing, a fore-and-aft sail has a cross-section that _____.

A. is a uniform curve
B. is a curve with more curve at the luff
C. is a curve with more curve at the leech
D. approximates a straight line

2851. Kevlar sails, when not in use, may be damaged if _____.

A. left in the sunlight
B. stowed wet
C. folded frequently
D. washed with soap and water

3128. You are Master of a 20-ton ketch. You wish to heave-to on the starboard tack in 35 knots of wind. Which action would be appropriate?

A. Set your storm jib aback to port and secure your rudder hard to starboard.
B. Secure your reefed mizzen aback to starboard and your storm jib aback to port. Secure your rudder hard to port.
C. Sheet your mizzen in flat and secure your rudder amidships.
D. Secure your storm jib aback to starboard and sheet your reefed mizzen in flat. Secure your rudder hard to starboard.

3205. On a sailing vessel, it is best to approach a person in the water by placing them on your _____.

A. leeward side
B. windward side
C. bow
D. transom

3264. If you reef a Marconi mainsail, the sail area _____.

A. stays the same
B. moves aft
C. becomes more
D. becomes less

3293. Your sailing vessel is docked during a storm and is in continuous motion. If a mooring line parts due to vessel motion, it will most likely do so _____.

A. where it is made fast on the vessel
B. midway between the vessel and the dock
C. at the eye
D. at the chock

3484. Your 80-ton schooner is hove to on the starboard tack under storm trysail and fore-staysail in 45 knots of wind. Your heading is averaging about 000° true and the wind is from the northeast. There is a dangerous shoal bearing 270° true, range 5 miles. Which action would be appropriate?

A. You need only stay alert for changes, as your present drift will carry you away from the danger.
B. You should strike all sails and get underway under bare poles, making as much way as possible to the north.
C. You should set a reefed foresail and strike the jib.
D. You should tack or jibe to the port tack and make all possible headway to the south.

4258. Dacron sails, when not in use, may be damaged if _____.

A. left in the sunlight
B. stowed wet
C. washed with soap
D. folded frequently

6042. Canvas sails, when not in use, may be damaged if _____.

A. left in the sunlight
B. stowed wet
C. folded frequently
D. washed with soap and water

AUXILIARY SAIL
ANSWERS

0631	A	2059	D
1333	D	2062	D
1628	C	2066	A
1649	D	2069	A
1683	A	2095	D
1684	C	2097	A
1691	C	2102	D
1693	B	2107	B
1694	C	2111	A
1696	D	2155	A
1702	D	2165	D
1703	A	2189	A
1704	B	2198	D
1706	A	2206	D
1707	C	2208	B
1805	A	2212	D
1807	B	2224	B
1812	A	2226	A
1815	D	2228	D
1824	C	2229	B
1829	D	2232	D
1836	D	2234	B
1838	A	2239	C
1839	A	2283	C
1846	D	2330	C
1856	D	2333	A
1858	C	2537	C
1859	C	2642	B
1869	D	2851	C
1876	C	3128	D
1882	B	3205	B
1896	C	3264	D
1897	B	3293	D
1904	C	3484	D
1905	D	4258	A
1911	C	6042	B
1915	B		
1916	B		
1919	A		
1926	C		
1932	C		
1953	C		
1966	B		
1969	A		
1972	A		
1974	B		
1976	D		
1977	A		
1978	C		
1989	D		
1992	A		
2007	D		
2015	D		
2021	C		
2023	B		
2026	B		
2029	B		
2042	B		
2049	C		

EXAMINATION ILLUSTRATIONS

RULES OF THE ROAD

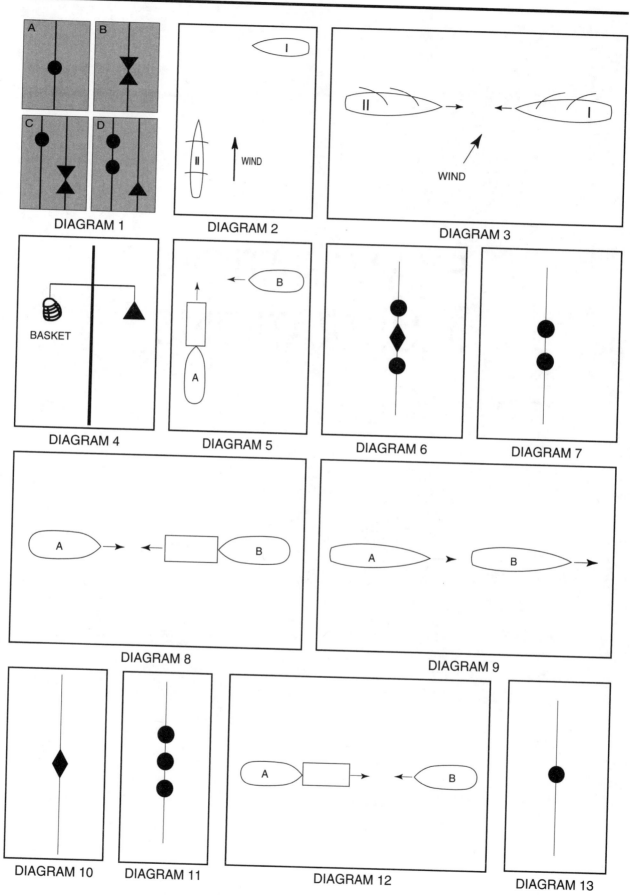

DIAGRAM 1

DIAGRAM 2

DIAGRAM 3

DIAGRAM 4

DIAGRAM 5

DIAGRAM 6

DIAGRAM 7

DIAGRAM 8

DIAGRAM 9

DIAGRAM 10

DIAGRAM 11

DIAGRAM 12

DIAGRAM 13

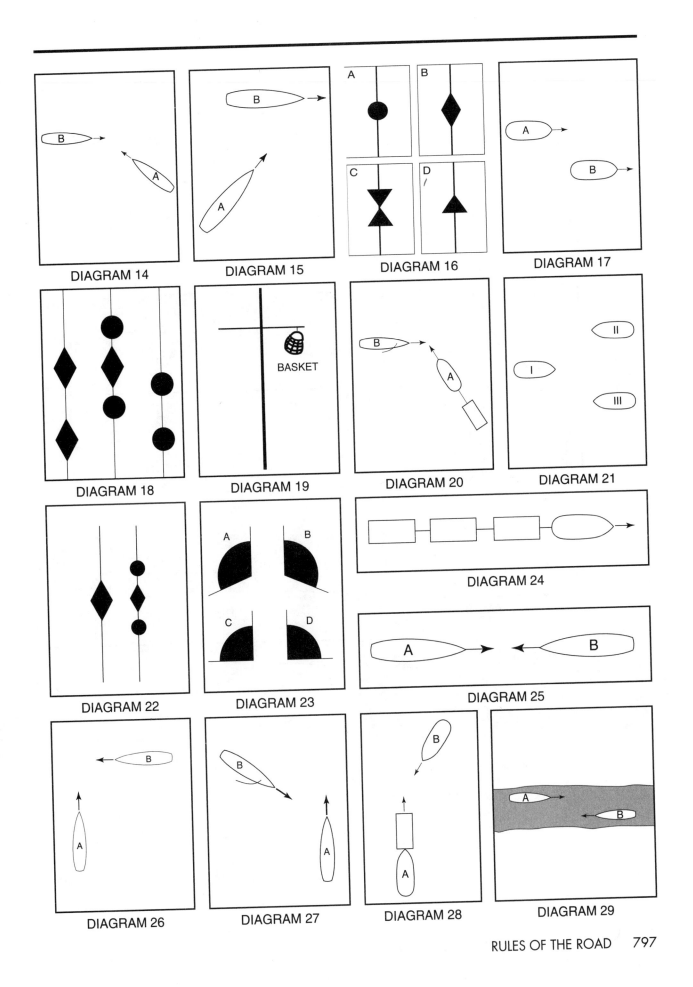

DIAGRAM 14

DIAGRAM 15

DIAGRAM 16

DIAGRAM 17

DIAGRAM 18

DIAGRAM 19

DIAGRAM 20

DIAGRAM 21

DIAGRAM 22

DIAGRAM 23

DIAGRAM 24

DIAGRAM 25

DIAGRAM 26

DIAGRAM 27

DIAGRAM 28

DIAGRAM 29

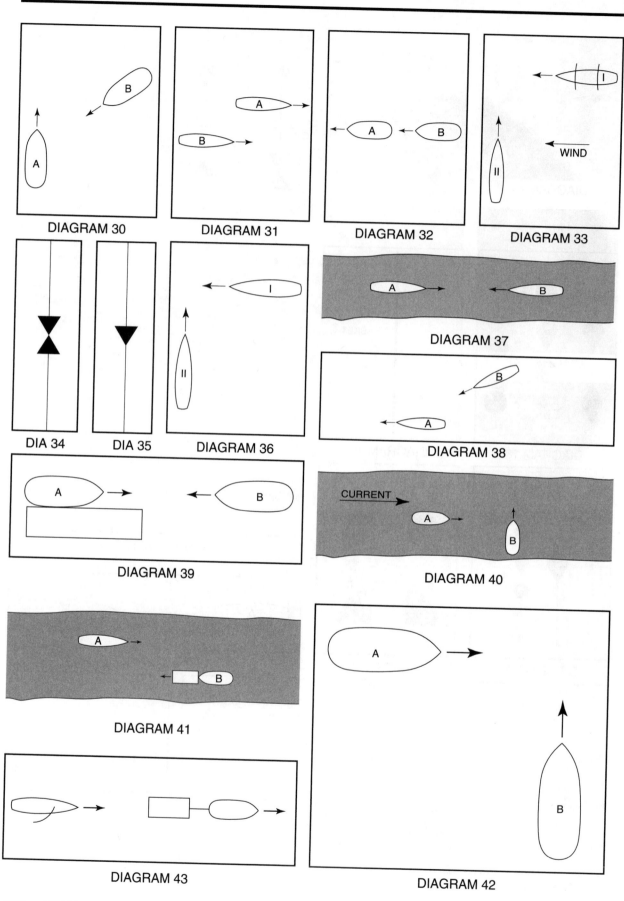

DIAGRAM 30

DIAGRAM 31

DIAGRAM 32

DIAGRAM 33

DIA 34

DIA 35

DIAGRAM 36

DIAGRAM 37

DIAGRAM 38

DIAGRAM 39

DIAGRAM 40

DIAGRAM 41

DIAGRAM 43

DIAGRAM 42

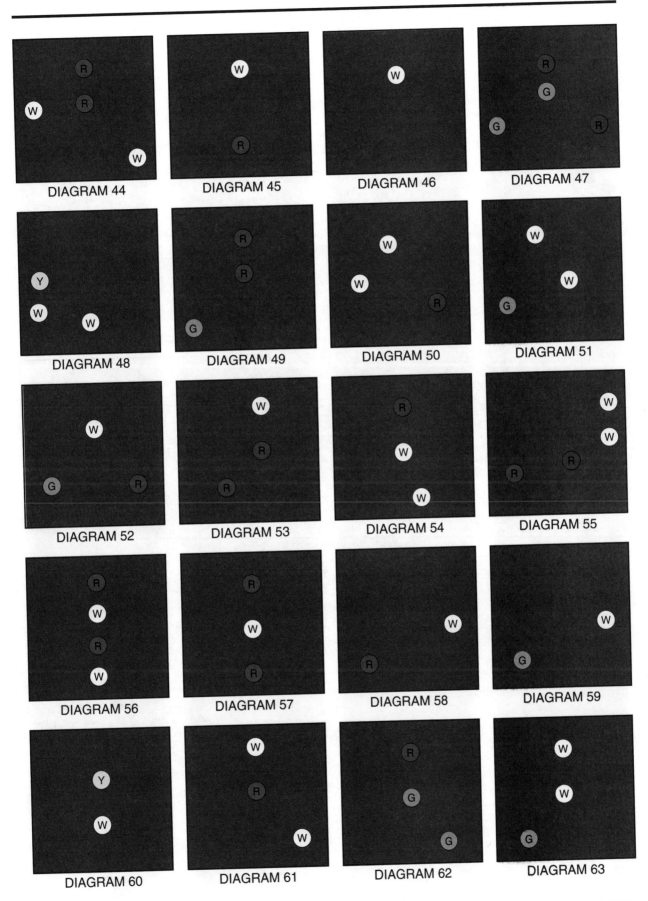

DIAGRAM 44   DIAGRAM 45   DIAGRAM 46   DIAGRAM 47

DIAGRAM 48   DIAGRAM 49   DIAGRAM 50   DIAGRAM 51

DIAGRAM 52   DIAGRAM 53   DIAGRAM 54   DIAGRAM 55

DIAGRAM 56   DIAGRAM 57   DIAGRAM 58   DIAGRAM 59

DIAGRAM 60   DIAGRAM 61   DIAGRAM 62   DIAGRAM 63

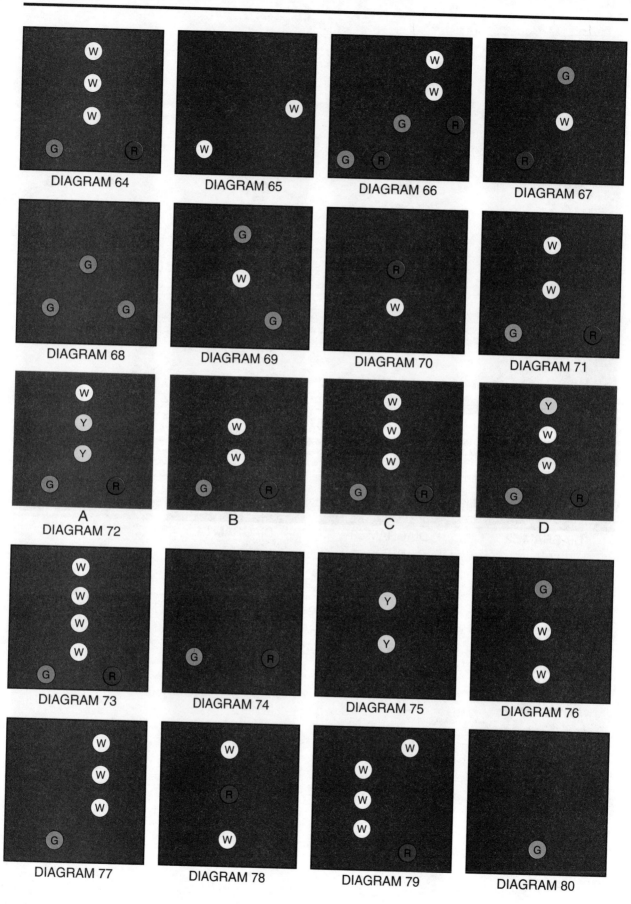

DIAGRAM 64

DIAGRAM 65

DIAGRAM 66

DIAGRAM 67

DIAGRAM 68

DIAGRAM 69

DIAGRAM 70

DIAGRAM 71

A

DIAGRAM 72

B

C

D

DIAGRAM 73

DIAGRAM 74

DIAGRAM 75

DIAGRAM 76

DIAGRAM 77

DIAGRAM 78

DIAGRAM 79

DIAGRAM 80

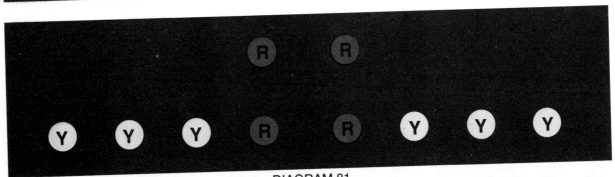

DIAGRAM 81

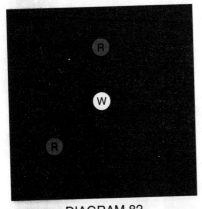

DIAGRAM 82

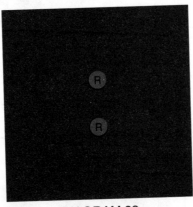

DIAGRAM 83

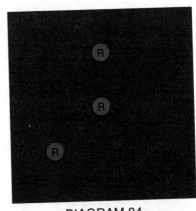

DIAGRAM 84

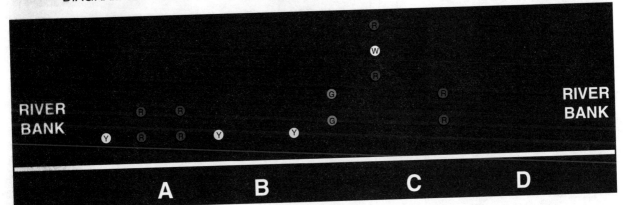

DIAGRAM 85

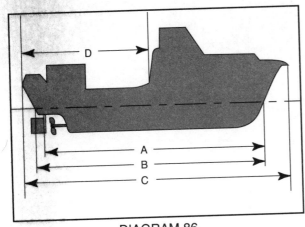

DIAGRAM 86

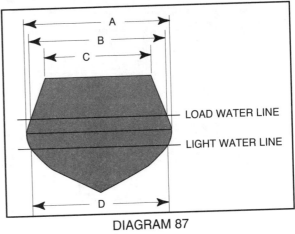

DIAGRAM 87

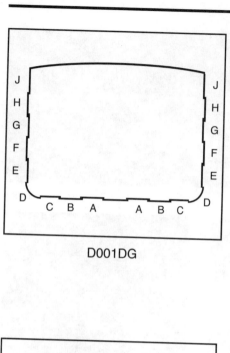

D001DG

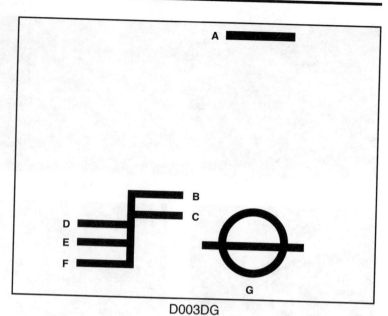

D003DG

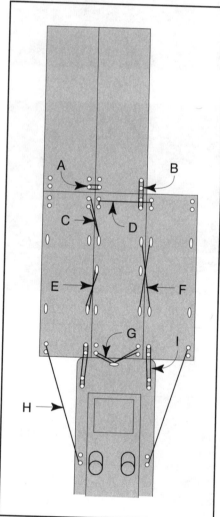

D024DG

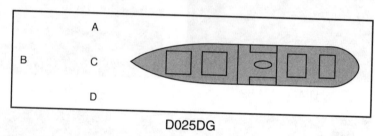

D025DG

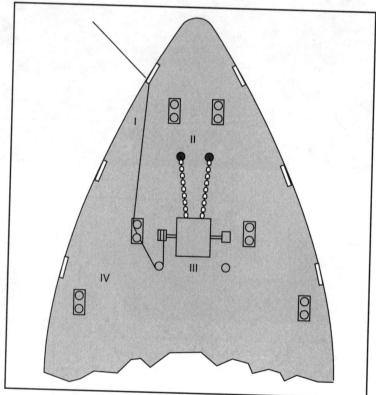

D019DG

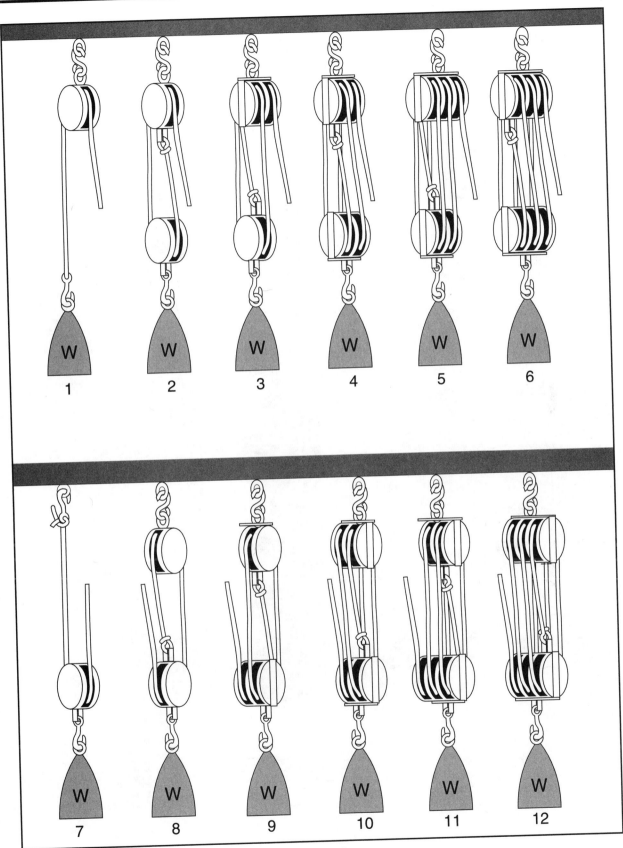

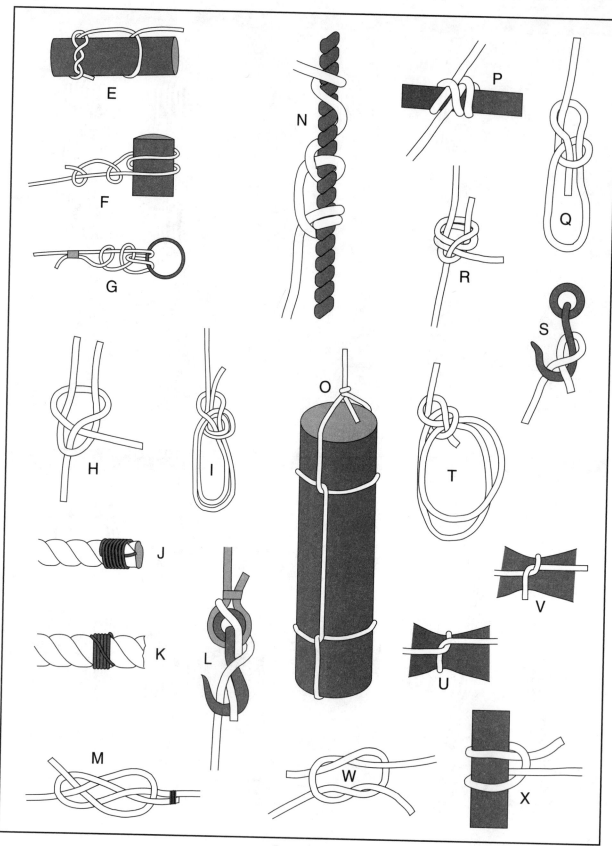

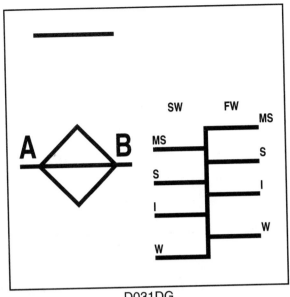

D031DG

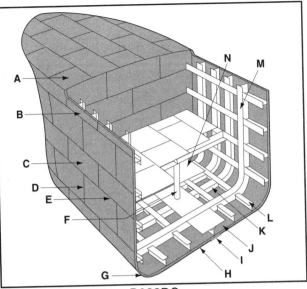

D033DG

HEADING (TRUE)	BEARING (TRUE)	RANGE (YARDS)	REMARKS
228°			Initial heading on initial course.
228°	232°	2260	
228°	234°	1700	Right full rudder ordered
230°	236°	1490	
252°	235°	1275	
275°	231°	1000	
316°	214°	850	
352°	198°	975	
022°	194°	1210	
053°	197°	1430	
087°	202°	1600	
115°	209°	1690	
151°	217°	1700	
183°	225°	1600	
218°	232°	1350	
228°	235°	1125	Rudder amidships Steady on 228° T

D034DG

HEADING (TRUE)	BEARING (TRUE)	RANGE (YARDS)	REMARKS
333°			Initial heading on initial course.
333°	315°	2125	
333°	310°	1650	LEFT full rudder ordered
327°	307°	1475	
310°	303°	1250	
278°	302°	1050	
268°	305°	900	
236°	318°	750	
196°	337°	800	
157°	344°	1100	
113°	340°	1350	
079°	332°	1525	
050°	324°	1575	
022°	318°	1550	
343°	308°	1400	
333°	302°	1175	Rudder amidships Steady on 333° T

D035DG

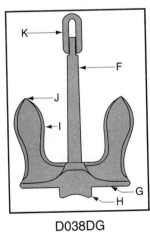

D038DG

D044DG

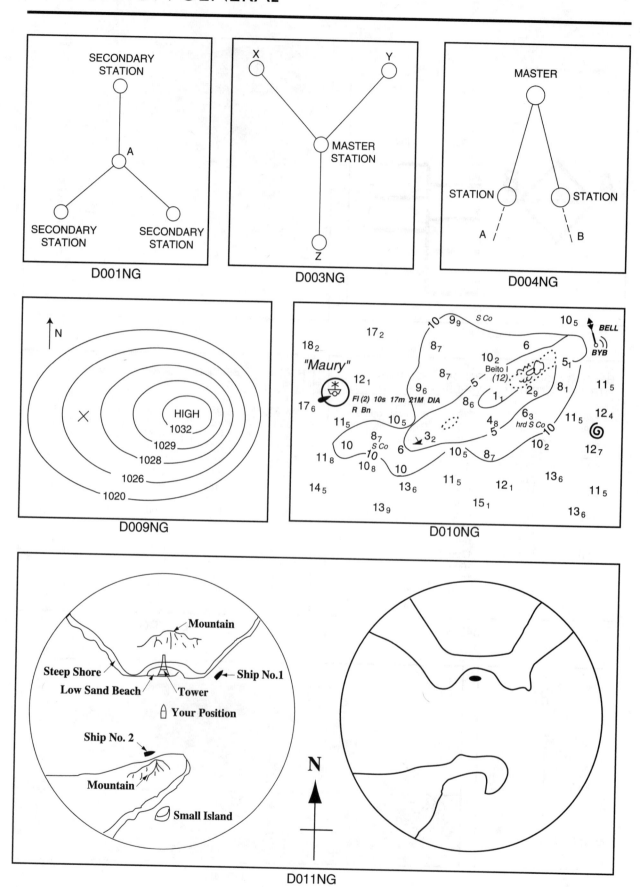

D001NG

D003NG

D004NG

D009NG

D010NG

D011NG

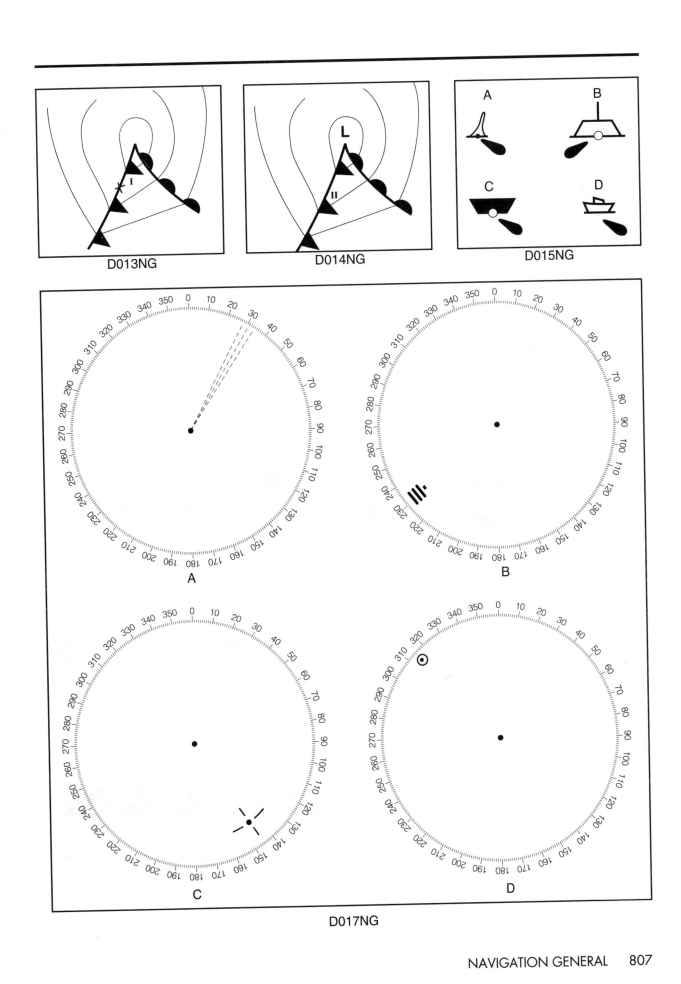

D013NG

D014NG

D015NG

A

B

C

D

D017NG

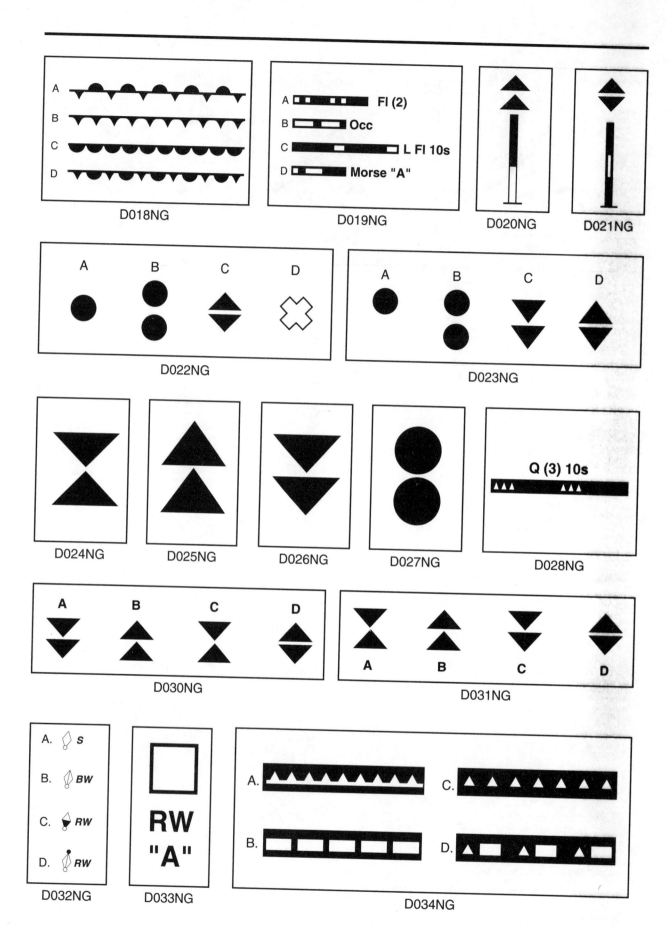

D018NG

D019NG
- A   Fl (2)
- B   Occ
- C   L Fl 10s
- D   Morse "A"

D020NG

D021NG

D022NG
A   B   C   D

D023NG
A   B   C   D

D024NG

D025NG

D026NG

D027NG

D028NG
Q (3) 10s

D030NG
A   B   C   D

D031NG
A   B   C   D

D032NG
- A.   S
- B.   BW
- C.   RW
- D.   RW

D033NG
RW "A"

D034NG
- A.
- B.
- C.
- D.

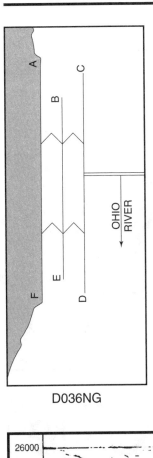

D036NG

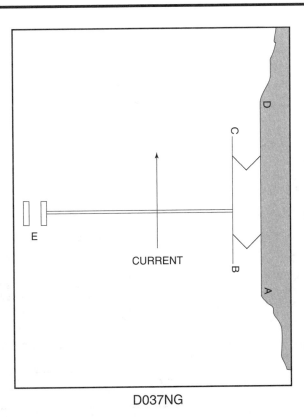

D037NG

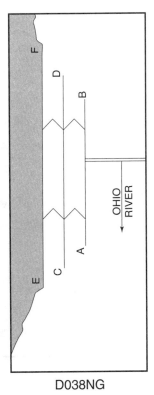

D038NG

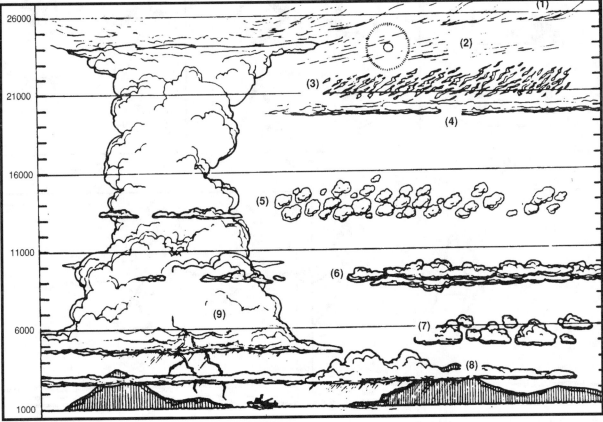

D039NG

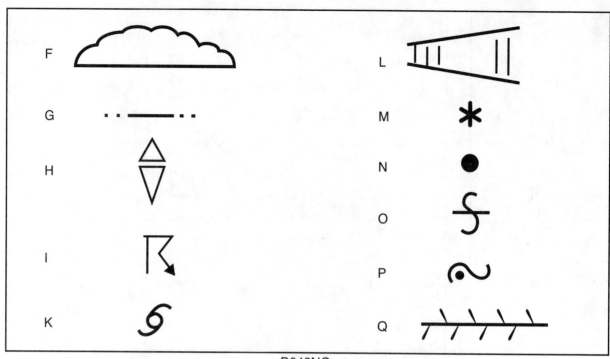

D042NG

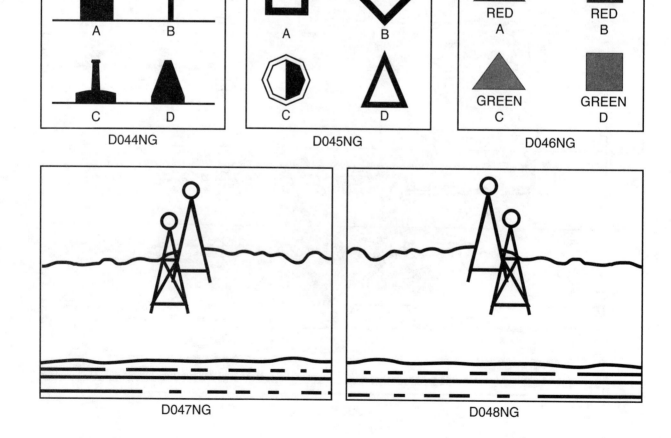

D044NG

D045NG

D046NG

D047NG

D048NG

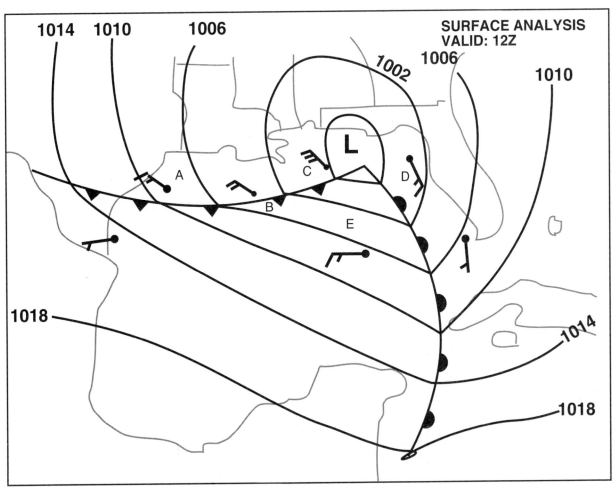

D049NG

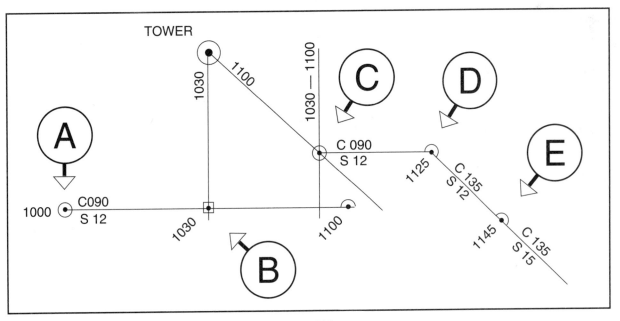

D051NG

SAFETY

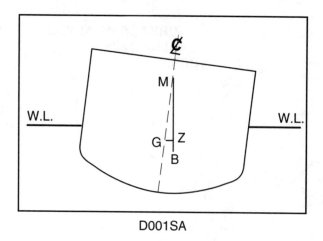

D001SA

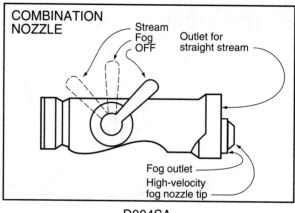

D004SA

AUXILIARY SAIL

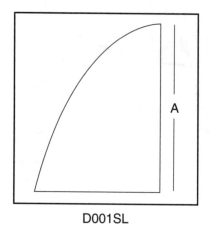

D001SL

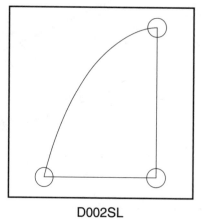

D002SL

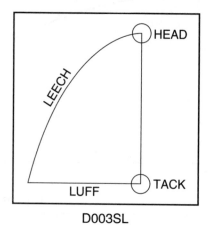

D003SL

APPENDIX: COLREGS

PART A—GENERAL

RULE 1
Application

(a) These Rules shall apply to all vessels upon the high seas and in all waters connected therewith navigable by seagoing vessels.

These Rules apply to all vessels upon the inland waters of the United States, and to vessels of the United States on the Canadian waters of the Great Lakes to the extent that there is no conflict with Canadian law.

(b) Nothing in these Rules shall interfere with the operation of special rules made by an appropriate authority for roadsteads, harbors, rivers, lakes or inland waterways connected with the high seas and navigable by seagoing vessels. Such special rules shall conform as closely as possible to these Rules.

(c) Nothing in these Rules shall interfere with the operation of any special rules made by the government of any State with respect to additional station or signal lights, shapes or whistle signals for ships of war and vessels proceeding under convoy, or with respect to additional station or signal lights or shapes for fishing vessels engaged in fishing as a fleet. These additional station or signal lights, shapes or whistle signals shall, so far as possible, be such that they cannot be mistaken for any light, shape or signal authorized elsewhere under these Rules.

(d) Traffic separation schemes may be adopted by the Organization for the purpose of these Rules.

(e) Whenever the Government concerned shall have determined that a vessel of special construction or purpose cannot comply fully with the provisions of any of these rules with respect to the number, position, range or arc of visibility of lights or shapes, as well as to the disposition and characteristics of sound-signaling appliances, without interfering with the special function of the vessel, such vessel shall comply with such other provisions in regard to the number, position, range or arc of visibility of lights or shapes, as well as to the disposition and characteristics of sound-signaling appliances, as her Government shall have determined to be the closest possible compliance with these Rules in respect to that vessel.

RULE 2
Responsibility

(a) Nothing in these Rules shall exonerate any vessel, or the owner, master or crew thereof, from the consequences of any neglect to comply with these Rules or of the neglect of any precaution which may be required by the ordinary practice of seamen, or by the special circumstances of the case.

(b) In construing and complying with these Rules due regard shall be had to all dangers of navigation and collision and to any special circumstances, including the limitations of the vessels involved, which may make a departure from these Rules necessary to avoid immediate danger.

RULE 3
General Definitions

For the purpose of these Rules, except where the context otherwise requires:

(a) The word "vessel" includes every description of water craft, including nondisplacement craft, WIG craft and seaplanes, used or capable of being used as a means of transportation on water.

(b) The term "power-driven vessel" means any vessel propelled by machinery.

(c) The term "sailing vessel" means any vessel under sail provided that propelling machinery, if fitted, is not being used.

(d) The term "vessel engaged in fishing" means any vessel fishing with nets, lines, trawls or other fishing apparatus which restrict maneuverability, but does not include a vessel fishing with trolling lines or other fishing apparatus which do not restrict maneuverability.

(e) The word "seaplane" includes any aircraft designed to maneuver on the water.

(f) The term "vessel not under command" means a vessel which through some exceptional circumstance is unable to maneuver as required by these Rules and is therefore unable to keep out of the way of another vessel.

(g) The term "vessel restricted in her ability to maneuver" means a vessel which from the nature of her work is restricted in her ability to maneuver as required by these Rules and is therefore unable to keep out of the way of another vessel.

The term "vessels restricted in their ability to maneuver" shall include but not be limited to:

(i) a vessel engaged in laying, servicing or picking up a navigation mark, submarine cable or pipeline;

(ii) a vessel engaged in dredging, surveying or underwater operations;

(iii) a vessel engaged in replenishment or transferring persons, provisions or cargo while underway;

(iv) a vessel engaged in the launching or recovery of aircraft;

(v) a vessel engaged in mineclearance operations;

(vi) a vessel engaged in a towing operation such as severely restricts the towing vessel and her tow in their ability to deviate from their course.

(h) The term "vessel constrained by her draft" means a power-driven vessel which because of her draft in relation to the available depth of water is severely restricted in her ability to deviate from the course she is following.

NOTE: There is no mention of a "vessel constrained by her draft" anywhere in the Inland Rules.

(i) The word "underway" means that a vessel is not at anchor, or made fast to the shore, or aground.

(j) The words "length" and "breadth" of a vessel means her length overall and greatest breadth.

(k) Vessels shall be deemed to be in sight of one another only when one can be observed visually from the other.

(l) The term "restricted visibility" means any condition in which visibility is restricted by fog, mist, falling snow, heavy rainstorms, sandstorms or any other similar causes.

PART B
STEERING AND SAILING RULES

Section I—Conduct of Vessels in Any Condition of Visibility

RULE 4
Application

Rules in this Section apply to any condition of visibility.

RULE 5
Look-Out

Every vessel shall at all times maintain a proper look-out by sight and hearing as well as by all available means appropriate in the prevailing circumstances and conditions so as to make a full appraisal of the situation and of the risk of collision.

RULE 6
Safe Speed

Every vessel shall at all times proceed at a safe speed so that she can take proper and effective action to avoid collision and be stopped within a distance appropriate to the prevailing circumstances and conditions.

In determining a safe speed the following factors shall be among those taken into account:

(a) By all vessels:

(i) the state of visibility;

(ii) the traffic density including concentrations of fishing vessels or any other vessels;

(iii) the maneuverability of the vessel with special reference to stopping distance and turning ability in the prevailing conditions;

(iv) at night the presence of background light such as from shore lights or from back scatter of her own lights;

(v) the state of wind, sea and current, and the proximity of navigational hazards;

(vi) the draft in relation to the available depth of water.

(b) Additionally, by vessels with operational radar:

(i) the characteristics, efficiency and limitations of the radar equipment;

(ii) any constraints imposed by the radar range scale in use;

(iii) the effect on radar detection of the sea state, weather and other sources of interference;

(iv) the possibility that small vessels, ice and other floating objects may not be detected by radar at an adequate range;

(v) the number, location and movement of vessels detected by radar;

(vi) the more exact assessment of the visibility that may be possible when radar is used to determine the range of vessels or other objects in the vicinity.

RULE 7
Risk of Collision

(a) Every vessel shall use all available means appropriate to the prevailing circumstances and conditions to determine if risk of collision exists. If there is any doubt such risk shall be deemed to exist.

(b) Proper use shall be made of radar equipment if fitted and operational, including long-range scanning to obtain early warning of risk of collision and radar plotting or equivalent systematic observation of detected objects.

(c) Assumptions shall not be made on the basis of scanty information, especially scanty radar information.

(d) In determining if risk of collision exists the following considerations shall be among those taken into account:

(i) such risk shall be deemed to exist if the compass bearing of an approaching vessel does not appreciably change;

(ii) such risk may sometimes exist even when an appreciable bearing change is evident, particularly when approaching a very large vessel or a tow or when approaching a vessel at close range.

RULE 8
Action to Avoid Collision

(a) Any action taken to avoid collision shall, if the circumstances of the case admit, be positive, made in ample time and with due regard to the observance of good seamanship.

(b) Any alteration of course and/or speed to avoid collision shall, if the circumstances of the case admit, be large enough to be readily apparent to another vessel observing visually or by radar; a succession of small alterations of course and/or speed should be avoided.

(c) If there is sufficient sea room, alteration of course alone may be the most effective action to avoid a close-quarters situation provided that it is made in good time, is substantial and doesn't result in another close-quarters situation.

(d) Action taken to avoid collision with another vessel shall be such as to result in passing at a safe distance. The effectiveness of the action shall be carefully checked until the other vessel is finally past and clear.

(e) If necessary to avoid collision or allow more time to assess the situation, a vessel shall slacken her speed or take all way off by stopping or reversing her means of propulsion.

(f) (i) A WIG craft only when taking off, landing and in flight near the surface, shall keep well clear of other vessels and avoid impeding their navi-gation.

(ii) A WIG craft operating on the water surface shall comply with the Rules of this part as a power-driven vessel.

RULE 9
Narrow Channels

(a) A vessel proceeding along the course of a narrow channel or fairway shall keep as near to the outer limit of the channel or fairway which lies on her starboard side as is safe and practicable.

A vessel proceeding along the course of a narrow channel or fairway shall keep as near to the outer limit of the channel or fairway which lies on her starboard side as is safe and practicable.

Notwithstanding paragraph (a)(i) and Rule 14(a), a power-driven vessel operating in narrow channels or fairways on the Great Lakes, Western Rivers, or waters specified by the Secretary, and proceeding downbound with a following current shall have the right-of-way over an upbound vessel, shall propose the manner and place of passage, and shall initiate the maneuvering signals prescribed by Rule 34(a)(i), as appropriate. The vessel proceeding upbound against the current shall hold as necessary to permit safe passing.

(b) A vessel of less than 20 meters in length or a sailing vessel shall not impede the passage of a vessel which can safely navigate only within a narrow channel or fairway.

(c) A vessel engaged in fishing shall not impede the passage of any other vessel navigating within a narrow channel or fairway.

(d) A vessel shall not cross a narrow channel or fairway if such crossing impedes the passage of a vessel which can safely navigate only within such channel or fairway. The latter vessel may use the sound signal prescribed in Rule 34(d) if in doubt as to the intention of the crossing vessel.

(e)(i) In a narrow channel or fairway when overtaking can take place only if the vessel to be overtaken has to take action to permit safe passing, the vessel intending to overtake shall indicate her intention by sounding the appropriate signal prescribed in Rule 34(c)(i). The vessel to be overtaken shall, if in agreement, sound the appropriate signal prescribed in Rule 34(c)(ii) and take steps to permit safe passing. If in doubt she may sound the signals prescribed in Rule 34(d).

In a narrow channel or fairway when overtaking, the power-driven vessel intending to overtake another power-driven vessel shall indicate her intention by sounding the appropriate signal prescribed in Rule 34(c) and take steps to permit safe passing. The power-driven vessel being overtaken, if in agreement, shall sound the same signal and may, if specifically agreed, to take steps to permit safe passing. If in doubt she shall sound the danger signal prescribed in Rule 34(d).

(ii) This Rule does not relieve the overtaking vessel of her obligation under Rule 13.

(f) A vessel nearing a bend or an area of a narrow channel or fairway where other vessels may be obscured by an intervening obstruction shall navigate with particular alertness and caution and shall sound the appropriate signal prescribed in Rule 34(e).

(g) Any vessel shall, if the circumstances of the case admit, avoid anchoring in a narrow channel.

RULE 10
Traffic Separation Schemes

(a) This Rule applies to traffic separation schemes adopted by the Organization.

(b) A vessel using a traffic separation scheme shall:

(i) proceed in the appropriate traffic lane in the general direction of traffic flow for that lane;

(ii) so far as practicable keep clear of a traffic separation line or separation zone;

(iii) normally join or leave a traffic lane at the termination of the lane, but when joining or leaving from either side shall do so at as small an angle to the general direction of traffic flow as practicable.

(c) A vessel shall so far as practicable avoid crossing traffic lanes, but if obliged to do so shall cross as nearly as practicable at right angles to the general direction of traffic flow.

(d) Inshore traffic zones shall not normally be used by through traffic which can safely use the appropriate traffic lane within the adjacent traffic separation scheme. However, vessels of less than 20 meters in length and sailing vessels may under all circumstances use inshore traffic zones.

(e) A vessel other than a crossing vessel or a vessel joining or leaving a lane shall not normally enter a separation zone or cross a separation line except:

(i) in cases of emergency to avoid immediate danger;

(ii) to engage in fishing within a separation zone.

(f) A vessel navigating in areas near the terminations of traffic separation schemes shall do so with particular caution.

(g) A vessel shall so far as practicable avoid anchoring in a traffic separation scheme or in areas near its terminations.

(h) A vessel not using a traffic separation scheme shall avoid it by as wide a margin as is practicable.

(i) A vessel engaged in fishing shall not impede the passage of any vessel following a traffic lane.

(j) A vessel of less than 20 meters in length or a sailing vessel shall not impede the safe passage of a power-driven vessel following a traffic lane.

(k) A vessel restricted in her ability to maneuver when engaged in an operation for the maintenance of safety of navigation in a traffic separation scheme is exempted from complying with this Rule to the extent necessary to carry out the operation.

(l) A vessel restricted in her ability to maneuver when engaged in an operation for the laying, servicing or picking up of a submarine cable, within a traffic separation scheme, is exempted from complying with this Rule to the extent necessary to carry out the operation.

Section II—Conduct of Vessels in Sight of One Another

RULE 11
Application

Rules in this Section apply to vessels in sight of one another.

RULE 12
Sailing Vessels

(a) When two sailing vessels are approaching one another, so as to involve risk of collision, one of them shall keep out of the way of the other as follows:

(i) when each has the wind on a different side, the vessel which has the wind on the port side shall keep out of the way of the other;

(ii) when both have the wind on the same side, the vessel which is to windward shall keep out of the way of the vessel which is to leeward;

(iii) if a vessel with the wind on the port side sees a vessel to windward and cannot determine with certainty whether the other vessel has the wind on the port or on the starboard side, she shall keep out of the way of the other.

(b) For the purposes of this Rule the windward side shall be deemed to be the side opposite to that on which the mainsail is carried or, in the case of a square-rigged vessel, the side opposite to that on which the largest fore-and-aft sail is carried.

RULE 13
Overtaking

(a) Notwithstanding anything contained in the Rules of Part B, Sections I and II, any vessel overtaking any other shall keep out of the way of the vessel being overtaken.

(b) A vessel shall be deemed to be overtaking when coming up with another vessel from a direction more than 22.5 degrees abaft her beam, that is, in such a position with reference to the vessel she is overtaking, that at night she would be able to see only the sternlight of that vessel but neither of her sidelights.

(c) When a vessel is in any doubt as to whether she is overtaking another, she shall assume that this is the case and act accordingly.

(d) Any subsequent alteration of the bearing between the two vessels shall not make the overtaking vessel a crossing vessel within the meaning of these Rules or relieve her of the duty of keeping clear of the overtaken vessel until she is finally past and clear.

RULE 14
Head-On Situation

(a) When two power-driven vessels are meeting on reciprocal or nearly reciprocal courses so as to involve risk of collision each shall alter her course to starboard so that each shall pass on the port side of the other.

(b) Such a situation shall be deemed to exist when a vessel sees the other ahead or nearly ahead and by night she could see the masthead lights of the other in a line or nearly in a line and/or both sidelights and by day she observes the corresponding aspect of the other vessel.

(c) When a vessel is in any doubt as to whether such a situation exists she shall assume that it does exist and act accordingly.

Notwithstanding paragraph (a) of this Rule, a power-driven vessel operating on the Great Lakes, Western Rivers, or waters specified by the Secretary, and proceeding downbound with a following current shall have the right-of-way over an upbound vessel, shall propose the manner of passage, and shall initiate the maneuvering signals prescribed by Rule 34(a)(i), as appropriate.

RULE 15
Crossing Situation

When two power-driven vessels are crossing so as to involve risk of collision, the vessel which has the other on her own starboard side shall keep out of the way and shall, if the circumstances of the case admit, avoid crossing ahead of the other vessel.

Notwithstanding paragraph (a), on the Great Lakes, Western Rivers, or water specified by the Secretary, a power-driven vessel crossing a river shall keep out of the way of a power-driven vessel ascending or descending the river.

RULE 16
Action by Give-Way Vessel

Every vessel which is directed to keep out of the way of another vessel shall, so far as possible, take early and substantial action to keep well clear.

RULE 17
Action by Stand-On Vessel

(a)(i) Where one of two vessels is to keep out of the way the other shall keep her course and speed.

(ii) The latter vessel may however take action to avoid collision by her maneuver alone, as soon as it becomes apparent to her that the vessel required to keep out of the way is not taking appropriate action in compliance with these Rules.

(b) When, from any cause, the vessel required to keep her course and speed finds herself so close that collision cannot be avoided by the action of the give-way vessel alone, she shall take such action as will best aid to avoid collision.

(c) A power-driven vessel which takes action in a crossing situation in accordance with subparagraph (a)(ii) of this Rule to avoid collision with another power-driven vessel shall, if the circumstances of the case admit, not alter course to port for a vessel on her own port side.

(d) This Rule does not relieve the give-way vessel of her obligation to keep out of the way.

RULE 18
Responsibilities between Vessels

Except where Rules 9, 10 and 13 otherwise require:

(a) A power-driven vessel underway shall keep out of the way of:

(i) a vessel not under command;

(ii) a vessel restricted in her ability to maneuver;

(iii) a vessel engaged in fishing;

(iv) a sailing vessel.

(b) A sailing vessel underway shall keep out of the way of:

(i) a vessel not under command;

(ii) a vessel restricted in her ability to maneuver;

(iii) a vessel engaged in fishing.

(c) A vessel engaged in fishing when underway shall, so far as possible, keep out of the way of:

(i) a vessel not under command;

(ii) a vessel restricted in her ability to maneuver.

(d) (i) Any vessel other than a vessel not under command or a vessel restricted in her ability to maneuver shall, if the circumstances of the case admit, avoid impeding the safe passage of a vessel

PART C—LIGHTS AND SHAPES

constrained by her draft, exhibiting the signals in Rule 28.

(ii) A vessel constrained by her draft shall navigate with particular caution having full regard to her special condition.

NOTE: There is no mention of a "vessel constrained by her draft" anywhere in the Inland Rules.

(e) A seaplane on the water shall, in general, keep well clear of all vessels and avoid impeding their navigation. In circumstances, however, where risk of collision exists, she shall comply with the Rules of this Part.

Section III—Conduct of Vessels in Restricted Visibility

RULE 19
Conduct of Vessels in Restricted Visibility

(a) This Rule applies to vessels not in sight of one another when navigating in or near an area of restricted visibility.

(b) Every vessel shall proceed at a safe speed adapted to the prevailing circumstances and conditions of restricted visibility. A power-driven vessel shall have her engines ready for immediate maneuver.

(c) Every vessel shall have due regard to the prevailing circumstances and conditions of restricted visibility when complying with the Rules of Section I of this Part.

(d) A vessel which detects by radar alone the presence of another vessel shall determine if a close-quarters situation is developing and/or risk of collision exists. If so, she shall take avoiding action in ample time, provided that when such action consists of an alteration of course, so far as possible the following shall be avoided:

(i) an alteration of course to port for a vessel forward of the beam, other than for a vessel being overtaken;

(ii) an alteration of course toward a vessel abeam or abaft the beam.

(e) Except where it has been determined that a risk of collision does not exist, every vessel which hears apparently forward of her beam the fog signal of another vessel, or which cannot avoid a close-quarters situation with another vessel forward of her beam, shall reduce her speed to the minimum at which she can be kept on her course. She shall if necessary take all her way off and in any event navigate with extreme caution until danger of collision is over.

PART C—LIGHTS AND SHAPES

RULE 20
Application

(a) Rules in this Part shall be complied with in all weathers.

(b) The Rules concerning lights shall be complied with from sunset to sunrise, and during such times no other lights shall be exhibited, except such lights as cannot be mistaken for the lights specified in these Rules or do not impair their visibility or distinctive character, or interfere with the keeping of a proper look-out.

(c) The lights prescribed by these Rules shall, if carried, also be exhibited from sunrise to sunset in restricted visibility and may be exhibited in all other circumstances when it is deemed necessary.

(d) The Rules concerning shapes shall be complied with by day.

(e) The lights and shapes specified in these Rules shall comply with the provisions of Annex I to these Regulations.

RULE 21
Definitions

(a) "Masthead light" means a white light placed over the fore and aft centerline of the vessel showing an unbroken light over an arc of the horizon of 225 degrees and so fixed as to show the light from right ahead to 22.5 degrees abaft the beam on either side of the vessel *except that on a vessel of less than 12 meters in length the masthead light shall be placed as nearly as practicable to the fore and aft centerline of the vessel.*

(b) "Sidelights" means a green light on the starboard side and a red light on the port side each showing an unbroken light over an arc of the horizon of 112.5 degrees and so fixed as to show the light from right ahead to 22.5 degrees abaft the beam on its respective side. In a vessel of less than 20 meters in length the sidelights may be combined in one lantern carried on the fore and aft centerline of the vessel *except that on a vessel of less than 12 meters in length the sidelights when combined in one lantern shall be placed as nearly as practicable to the fore and aft centerline of the vessel.*

(c) "Sternlight" means a white light placed as nearly as practicable at the stern showing an unbroken light over an arc of the horizon of 135 degrees and so fixed as to show the light 67.5 degrees from right aft on each side of the vessel.

(d) "Towing light" means a yellow light having the same characteristics as the "sternlight" defined in paragraph (c) of this Rule.

(e) "All-round light" means a light showing an unbroken light over an arc of the horizon of 360 degrees.

(f) "Flashing light" means a light flashing at regular intervals at a frequency of 120 flashes or more per minute.

"Special flashing light" means a yellow light flashing at regular intervals at a frequency of 50 to 70 flashes per minute, placed as far forward and as nearly as practicable on the fore and aft centerline of the tow and showing an unbroken light over an arc of the horizon of not less than 180 degrees nor more than 225 degrees and so fixed as to show the light from right ahead to abeam and no more than 22.5 degrees abaft the beam on either side of the vessel.

RULE 22
Visibility of Lights

The lights prescribed in these Rules shall have an intensity as specified in Section 8 of Annex I to these Regulations so as to be visible at the following minimum ranges:

(a) In vessels of 50 meters or more in length:

—a masthead light, 6 miles;

—a sidelight, 3 miles;

—a sternlight, 3 miles;

—a towing light, 3 miles;

—a white, red, green or yellow all-round light, 3 miles.

—*a special flashing light, 2 miles.*

(b) In vessels of 12 meters or more in length but less than 50 meters in length:

—a masthead light, 5 miles; except that where the length of the vessel is less than 20 meters, 3 miles;

—a sidelight, 2 miles;

—a sternlight, 2 miles;

—a towing light, 2 miles;

—a white, red, green or yellow all-round light, 2 miles.

—*a special flashing light, 2 miles.*

(c) In vessels of less than 12 meters in length:

—a masthead light, 2 miles;

—a sidelight, 1 mile;

—a sternlight, 2 miles;

—a towing light, 2 miles;

—a white, red, green or yellow all-round light, 2 miles.

—*a special flashing light, 2 miles.*

(d) In inconspicuous, partly submerged vessels or objects being towed:

—a white all-round light, 3 miles.

RULE 23
Power-Driven Vessels Underway

(a) A power-driven vessel underway shall exhibit:

(i) a masthead light forward;

(ii) a second masthead light abaft of and higher than the forward one; except that a vessel of less than 50 meters in length shall not be obliged to exhibit such light but may do so;

(iii) sidelights;

(iv) a stern light.

(b) An air-cushion vessel when operating in the non-displacement mode shall, in addition to the lights prescribed in paragraph (a) of this Rule, exhibit an all-round flashing yellow light.

(c) A WIG aircraft only when taking off, landing and in flight near the surface shall, in addition to the lights prescribed in paragraph (a) of this Rule, exhibit a high intensity all-around flashing red light.

(d)(i) A power-driven vessel of less than 12 meters in length may in lieu of the lights prescribed in paragraph (a) of this Rule exhibit an all-round white light and sidelights;

(ii) a power-driven vessel of less than 7 meters in length whose maximum speed does not exceed 7 knots may in lieu of the lights prescribed in paragraph (a) of this Rule exhibit an all-round white light and shall, if practicable, also exhibit sidelights; *(This exception does exist in Inland Rules.)*

(iii) the masthead light or all-round white light on a power-driven vessel of less than 12 meters in length may be displaced from the fore and aft centerline of the vessel if centerline fitting is not practicable, provided that the sidelights are combined in one lantern which shall be carried on the fore and aft centerline of the vessel or located as nearly as practicable in the same fore and aft line as the masthead light or the all-round white light. *(This exception does exist in Inland Rules.)*

A power-driven vessel when operating on the Great Lakes may carry an all-round white light in lieu of the second masthead light and sternlight prescribed in paragraph (a) of this Rule. The light shall be carried in the position of the second masthead light and be visible at the same minimum range.

RULE 24
Towing and Pushing

(a) A power-driven vessel when towing shall exhibit:

(i) instead of the light prescribed in Rule 23(a)(i) or (a)(ii), two masthead lights in a vertical line. When the length of the tow, measuring from the stern of the towing vessel to the after end of the tow exceeds 200 meters, three such lights in a vertical line;

(ii) sidelights;

(iii) a sternlight;

(iv) a towing light in a vertical line above the sternlight;

(v) when the length of the tow exceeds 200 meters, a diamond shape where it can best be seen.

(b) When a pushing vessel and a vessel being pushed ahead are rigidly connected in a composite unit they shall be regarded as a power-driven vessel and exhibit the lights prescribed in Rule 23.

(c) A power-driven vessel when pushing ahead or towing alongside, except in the case of a composite unit, shall exhibit:

(i) instead of the light prescribed in Rule 23(a)(i) or (a)(ii), two masthead lights in a vertical line;

(ii) sidelights;

(iii) a sternlight.

(iii) two towing lights in a vertical line.

(d) A power-driven vessel to which paragraph (a) or (c) of this Rule apply shall also comply with Rule 23(a)(ii).

(e) A vessel or object being towed, other than those mentioned in paragraph (g) of this Rule, shall exhibit:

(i) sidelights;

(ii) a stern light; and

(iii) when the length of the tow exceeds 200 meters, a diamond shape where it can best be seen.

(f) Provided that any number of vessels being towed alongside or pushed in a group shall be lighted as one vessel, *except as provided in paragraph (iii):*

(i) a vessel being pushed ahead, not being part of a composite unit, shall exhibit at the forward end, sidelights *and a special flashing light;*

(ii) a vessel being towed alongside shall exhibit a sternlight and at the forward end, sidelights *and a special flashing light; and*

(iii) when vessels are towed alongside on both sides of the towing vessels a sternlight shall be exhibited on the stern of the outboard vessel on each side of the towing vessel, and a single set of sidelights *as far forward and as far outboard as is practicable, and a single special flashing light.*

(g) An inconspicuous, partly submerged vessel or object, or combination of such vessels or objects being towed, shall exhibit:

(i) if it is less than 25 meters in breadth, one all-round white light at or near the forward end and one at or near the after end except that dracones need not exhibit a light at or near the forward end;

(ii) if it is 25 meters or more in breadth, two additional all-round white lights at or near the extremities of its breadth;

(iii) if it exceeds 100 meters in length, additional all-round white lights between the lights prescribed in subparagraphs (i) and (ii) so that the distance between the lights shall not exceed 100 meters;

(iv) a diamond shape at or near the aftermost extremity of the last vessel or object being towed and if the length of the tow exceeds 200 meters an additional diamond shape where it can best be seen and located as far forward as is practicable.

(iv) a diamond shape at or near the aftermost extremity of the last vessel or object being towed; and

(v) the towing vessel may direct a searchlight in the direction of the tow to indicate its presence to an approaching vessel.

(h) Where from any sufficient cause it is impracticable for a vessel or object being towed to exhibit the lights or shapes prescribed in paragraph (e) or (g) of this Rule, all possible measures shall be taken to light the vessel or object towed or at least to indicate the presence of such vessel or object.

(i) Where from any sufficient cause it is impracticable for a vessel not normally engaged in towing operations to display the lights prescribed in paragraph (a) or (c) of this Rule, such vessel shall not be required to exhibit those lights when engaged in towing another vessel in distress or otherwise in need of assistance. All possible measures shall be taken to indicate the nature of the relationship between the towing vessel and the vessel being towed as authorized by Rule 36, in particular by illuminating the towline.

Notwithstanding paragraph (c), on the Western Rivers (except below the Huey P. Long Bridge on the Mississippi River) and on waters specified by the Secretary, a power-driven vessel when pushing ahead or towing alongside, except as paragraph (b) applies, shall exhibit:

(i) sidelights; and

(ii) two towing lights in a vertical line.

RULE 25
Sailing Vessels Underway and Vessels under Oars

(a) A sailing vessel underway shall exhibit:

(i) sidelights;

(ii) a sternlight.

(b) In a sailing vessel of less than 20 meters in length the lights prescribed in paragraph (a) of this Rule may be combined in one lantern carried at or near the top of the mast where it can best be seen.

(c) A sailing vessel underway may, in addition to the lights prescribed in paragraph (a) of this Rule, exhibit at or near the top of the mast, where they can best be seen, two all-round lights in a vertical line, the upper being red and the lower green, but these lights shall not be exhibited in conjunction with the combined lantern permitted by paragraph (b) of this Rule.

(d)(i) A sailing vessel of less than 7 meters in length shall, if practicable, exhibit the lights prescribed in paragraph (a) or (b) of this Rule, but if she does not, she shall have ready at hand an electric torch or lighted lantern showing a white light which shall be exhibited in sufficient time to prevent collision.

(ii) A vessel under oars may exhibit the lights prescribed in this Rule for sailing vessels, but if she does not, she shall have ready at hand an electric torch or lighted lantern showing a white light which shall be exhibited in sufficient time to prevent collision.

(e) A vessel proceeding under sail when also being propelled by machinery shall exhibit forward where it can best be seen a conical shape, apex downwards. *A vessel of less than 12 meters in length is not required to exhibit this shape, but may do so.*

RULE 26
Fishing Vessels

(a) A vessel engaged in fishing, whether underway or at anchor, shall exhibit only the lights and shapes prescribed in this Rule.

(b) A vessel when engaged in trawling, by which is meant dragging through the water a dredge net or other apparatus used as a fishing appliance, shall exhibit:

(i) two all-round lights in a vertical line, the upper being green and the lower white, or a shape consisting of two cones with their apexes together in a vertical line one above the other;

(ii) a masthead light abaft of and higher than the all-round green light; a vessel of less than 50 me-

ters in length shall not be obliged to exhibit such a light but may do so;

(iii) when making way through the water, in addition to the lights prescribed in this paragraph, sidelights and a sternlight.

(c) A vessel engaged in fishing, other than trawling, shall exhibit:

(i) two all-round lights in a vertical line, the upper being red and the lower white, or a shape consisting of two cones with apexes together in a vertical line one above the other;

(ii) when there is outlying gear extending more than 150 meters horizontally from the vessel, an all-round white light or a cone apex upwards in the direction of the gear;

(iii) when making way through the water, in addition to the lights prescribed in this paragraph, sidelights and a sternlight.

(d) A vessel engaged in fishing in close proximity to other vessels engaged in fishing may exhibit the additional signals described in Annex II to these Regulations.

(e) A vessel when not engaged in fishing shall not exhibit the lights or shapes prescribed in this Rule, but only those prescribed for a vessel of her length.

RULE 27
Vessels Not under Command or Restricted in Their Ability to Maneuver

(a) A vessel not under command shall exhibit:

(i) two all-round red lights in a vertical line where they can best be seen;

(ii) two balls or similar shapes in a vertical line where they can best be seen;

(iii) when making way through the water, in addition to the lights prescribed in this paragraph, sidelights and a sternlight.

(b) A vessel restricted in her ability to maneuver, except a vessel engaged in mineclearance operations, shall exhibit:

(i) three all-round lights in a vertical line where they can best be seen. The highest and lowest of these lights shall be red and the middle light shall be white;

(ii) three shapes in a vertical line where they can best be seen. The highest and lowest of these shapes shall be balls and the middle one a diamond;

(iii) when making way through the water, a masthead light or lights, sidelights and a sternlight, in addition to the lights prescribed in subparagraph (i);

(iv) when at anchor, in addition to the lights or shapes prescribed in subparagraphs (i) and (ii), the light, lights or shape prescribed in Rule 30.

(c) A power-driven vessel engaged in a towing operation such as severely restricts the towing vessel and her tow in their ability to deviate from their course shall, in addition to the lights or shapes prescribed in Rule 24(a), exhibit the lights or shapes prescribed in subparagraphs (b)(i) and (ii) of this Rule.

(d) A vessel engaged in dredging or underwater operations, when restricted in her ability to maneuver, shall exhibit the lights and shapes prescribed in subparagraphs (b)(i), (ii) and (iii) of this Rule and shall in addition, when an obstruction exists, exhibit:

(i) two all-round red lights or two balls in a vertical line to indicate the side on which the obstruction exists;

(ii) two all-round green lights or two diamonds in a vertical line to indicate the side on which another vessel may pass;

(iii) when at anchor, the lights or shapes prescribed in this paragraph instead of the lights or shape prescribed in Rule 30.

(e) Whenever the size of a vessel engaged in diving operations makes it impracticable to exhibit all lights and shapes prescribed in paragraph (d) of this Rule, the following shall be exhibited:

(i) three all-round lights in a vertical line where they can best be seen. The highest and lowest of these lights shall be red and the middle light shall be white;

(ii) a rigid replica of the International Code flag "A" not less than 1 meter in height. Measures shall be taken to ensure its all-round visibility.

(f) A vessel engaged in mineclearance operations shall in addition to the lights prescribed for a power-driven vessel in Rule 23 or to the lights or shape prescribed for a vessel at anchor in Rule 30 as appropriate, exhibit three all-round green lights or three balls. One of these lights or shapes shall be exhibited near the foremast head and one at each end of the fore yard. These lights or shapes indicate that it is dangerous for another vessel to approach within 1000 meters of the mineclearance vessel, *or 500 meters on either side of the minesweeper.*

(g) Vessels of less than 12 meters in length, ex-cept those engaged in diving operations, shall not be required to exhibit the lights and shapes prescribed in this Rule.

(h) The signals prescribed in this Rule are not signals of vessels in distress and requiring assistance. Such signals are contained in Annex IV to these Regulations.

RULE 28
Vessels Constrained by Their Draft

A vessel constrained by her draft may, in addition to the lights prescribed for power-driven vessels in Rule 23, exhibit where they can best be seen three all-round red lights in a vertical line, or a cylinder.

NOTE: There is no mention of a "vessel constrained by draft" anywhere in the Inland Rules.

RULE 29
Pilot Vessels

(a) A vessel engaged on pilotage duty shall exhibit:

(i) at or near the masthead, two all-round lights in a vertical line, the upper being white and the lower red;

(ii) when underway, in addition, sidelights and a sternlight;

(iii) when at anchor, in addition to the lights prescribed in subparagraph (i), the light, lights or shape prescribed in Rule 30 for vessels at anchor.

(b) A pilot vessel when not engaged on pilotage duty shall exhibit the lights or shapes prescribed for a similar vessel of her length.

RULE 30
Anchored Vessels
and Vessels Aground

(a) A vessel at anchor shall exhibit where it can best be seen:

(i) in the fore part, an all-round white light or one ball;

(ii) at or near the stern and at a lower level than the light prescribed in subparagraph (i), an all-round white light.

(b) A vessel of less than 50 meters in length may exhibit an all-round white light where it can best be seen instead of the lights prescribed in paragraph (a) of this Rule.

(c) A vessel at anchor may, and a vessel of 100 meters and more in length shall, also use the available working or equivalent lights to illuminate her decks.

(d) A vessel aground shall exhibit the lights prescribed in paragraph (a) or (b) of this Rule and in addition, where they can best be seen:

(i) two all-round red lights in a vertical line;

(ii) three balls in a vertical line.

(e) A vessel of less than 7 meters in length, when at anchor, not in or near a narrow channel, fairway or anchorage, or where other vessels normally navigate, shall not be required to exhibit the lights or shape prescribed in paragraphs (a) and (b) of this Rule.

(f) A vessel of less than 12 meters in length, when aground, shall not be required to exhibit the lights or shapes prescribed in subparagraphs (d)(i) and (ii) of this Rule.

A vessel of less than 20 meters in length, when at anchor in a special anchorage area designated by the Secretary, shall not be required to exhibit the anchor lights and shapes required by this Rule.

RULE 31
Seaplanes

Where it is impracticable for a seaplane or WIG craft to exhibit lights and shapes of the characteristics or in the positions prescribed in the Rules of this Part she shall exhibit lights and shapes as closely similar in characteristics and position as is possible.

PART D
SOUND AND LIGHT SIGNALS
RULE 32
Definitions

(a) The word "whistle" means any sound signaling appliance capable of producing the prescribed blasts and which complies with the specifications in Annex III to these Regulations.

(b) The term "short blast" means a blast of about one second's duration.

(c) The term "prolonged blast" means a blast of from four to six seconds' duration.

RULE 33
Equipment for Sound Signals

(a) A vessel of 12 meters or more in length shall be provided with a whistle, a vessel of 20 meters or more in length shall be provided with a bell in addition to the whistle, and a vessel of 100 meters or more in length shall, in addition, be provided with a gong, the tone and sound of which cannot be con-

fused with that of the bell. The whistle, bell and gong shall comply with the specifications in Annex III to these Regulations. The bell or gong or both may be replaced by other equipment having the same respective sound characteristics, provided that manual sounding of the prescribed signals shall always be possible.

(b) A vessel of less than 12 meters in length shall not be obliged to carry the sound-signaling appliances prescribed in paragraph (a) of this Rule but if she does not, she shall be provided with some other means of making an efficient sound signal.

RULE 34
Maneuvering and Warning Signals

(a) When vessels are in sight of one another, a power-driven vessel underway, when maneuvering as authorized or required by these Rules, shall indicate that maneuver by the following signals on her whistle:

—one short blast to mean "I am altering my course to starboard";

—two short blasts to mean "I am altering my course to port";

—three short blasts to mean "I am operating astern propulsion."

(b) Any vessel may supplement the whistle signals prescribed in paragraph (a) of this Rule by light signals, repeated as appropriate, whilst the maneuver is being carried out:

(i) these light signals shall have the following significance:

—one flash to mean "I am altering my course to starboard";

—two flashes to mean "I am altering my course to port";

—three flashes to mean "I am operating astern propulsion";

(ii) the duration of each flash shall be about one second, the interval between flashes shall be about one second, and the interval between successive signals shall be not less than ten seconds;

(iii) the light used for this signal shall, if fitted, be an all-round white light, visible at a minimum range of 5 miles, and shall comply with the provisions of Annex I to these Regulations.

(c) When in sight of one another in a narrow channel or fairway:

(i) a vessel intending to overtake another shall in compliance with Rule 9(e)(i) indicate her intention by the following signals on her whistle:

—two prolonged blasts followed by one short blast to mean "I intend to overtake you on your starboard side";

—two prolonged blasts followed by two short blasts to mean "I intend to overtake you on your port side."

(ii) the vessel about to be overtaken when acting in accordance with Rule 9(e)(i) shall indicate her agreement by the following signal on her whistle:

—one prolonged, one short, one prolonged and one short blast, in that order.

(d) When vessels in sight of one another are approaching each other and from any cause either vessel fails to understand the intentions or actions of the other, or is in doubt whether sufficient action is being taken by the other to avoid collision, the vessel in doubt shall immediately indicate such doubt by giving at least five short and rapid blasts on the whistle. Such signal may be supplemented by a light signal of at least five short and rapid flashes.

(e) A vessel nearing a bend or an area of a channel or fairway where other vessels may be obscured by an intervening obstruction shall sound one prolonged blast. Such signal shall be answered with a prolonged blast by any approaching vessel that may be within hearing around the bend or behind the intervening obstruction.

(f) If whistles are fitted on a vessel at a distance apart of more than 100 meters, one whistle only shall be used for giving maneuvering and warning signals.

RULE 34
Maneuvering and Warning Signals

(a) When power-driven vessels are in sight of one another and meeting or crossing at a distance within half a mile of each other, each vessel underway, when maneuvering as authorized or required by these Rules:

(i) shall indicate that maneuver by the following signals on her whistle: one short blast to mean "I intend to leave you on my port side"; two short blasts to mean "I intend to leave you on my starboard side"; and three short blasts to mean "I am operating astern propulsion."

(ii) upon hearing the one or two blast signal of the other shall, if in agreement, sound the same whistle signal and take the steps necessary to effect a safe passing. If, however, from any cause, the vessel doubts the safety of the proposed maneuver, she shall sound the danger signal specified in paragraph (d) of this Rule and each vessel shall take appropriate precautionary action until a safe passing agreement is made.

(b) A vessel may supplement the whistle signals prescribed in paragraph (a) of this Rule by light signals:

(i) These signals shall have the following significance: one flash to mean "I intend to leave you on my port side"; two flashes to mean "I intend to leave you on my starboard side"; three flashes to mean "I am operating astern propulsion";

(ii) The duration of each flash shall be about 1 second; and

(iii) The light used for this signal shall, if fitted, be one all-round white or yellow light, visible at a minimum range of 2 miles, synchronized with the whistle, and shall comply with the provisions of Annex I to these Rules.

(c) When in sight of one another:

(i) a power-driven vessel intending to overtake another power-driven vessel shall indicate her intention by the following signals on her whistle: one short blast to mean "I intend to overtake you on your starboard side"; two short blasts to mean "I intend to overtake you on your port side"; and

(ii) the power-driven vessel about to be overtaken shall, if in agreement, sound a similar sound signal. If in doubt she shall sound the danger signal prescribed in paragraph (d).

(d) When vessels in sight of one another are approaching each other and from any cause either vessel fails to understand the intentions or actions of the other, or is in doubt whether sufficient action is being taken by the other to avoid collision, the vessel in doubt shall immediately indicate such doubt by giving at least five short and rapid blasts on the whistle. This signal may be supplemented by a light signal of at least five short and rapid flashes.

(e) A vessel nearing a bend or an area of a channel or fairway where other vessels may be obscured by an intervening obstruction shall sound one prolonged blast. This signal shall be answered with a prolonged blast by any approaching vessel that may be within hearing around the bend or behind the intervening obstruction.

(f) If whistles are fitted on a vessel at a distance apart of more than 100 meters, one whistle only shall be used for giving maneuvering and warning signals.

(g) When a power-driven vessel is leaving a dock or berth, she shall sound one prolonged blast.

(h) A vessel that reaches agreement with another vessel in a head-on, crossing, or overtak-

ing situation by using the radiotelephone as prescribed by the Bridge-to-Bridge Radiotelephone Act (85 Stat. 165; 33 U.S.C. 1207 et seq.), is not obliged to sound the whistle signals prescribed by this Rule, but may do so. If agreement is not reached, then whistle signals shall be exchanged in a timely manner and shall prevail.

RULE 35
Sound Signals in Restricted Visibility

In or near an area of restricted visibility, whether by day or night, the signals prescribed in this Rule shall be used as follows:

(a) A power-driven vessel making way through the water shall sound at intervals of not more than 2 minutes one prolonged blast.

(b) A power-driven vessel underway but stopped and making no way through the water shall sound at intervals of not more than 2 minutes two prolonged blasts in succession with an interval of about 2 seconds between them.

(c) A vessel not under command, a vessel restricted in her ability to maneuver (a vessel constrained by her draft—*not in Inland*), a sailing vessel, a vessel engaged in fishing, *whether underway or at anchor,* and a vessel engaged in towing or pushing another vessel shall, instead of the signals prescribed in paragraphs (a) or (b) of this Rule, sound at intervals of not more than 2 minutes three blasts in succession, namely one prolonged followed by two short blasts.

(d) A vessel engaged in fishing, when at anchor, and a vessel restricted in her ability to maneuver when carrying out her work at anchor, shall instead of the signals prescribed in paragraph (g) of this Rule sound the signal prescribed in paragraph (c) of this Rule.

(e)*(d)* A vessel towed or if more than one vessel is towed the last vessel of the tow, if manned, shall at intervals of not more than 2 minutes sound four blasts in succession, namely one prolonged followed by three short blasts. When practicable, this signal shall be made immediately after the signal made by the towing vessel.

(f)*(e)* When a pushing vessel and a vessel being pushed ahead are rigidly connected in a composite unit they shall be regarded as a power-driven vessel and shall give the signals prescribed in paragraphs (a) or (b) of this Rule.

(g)*(f)* A vessel at anchor shall at intervals of not more than one minute ring the bell rapidly for about 5 seconds. In a vessel of 100 meters or more in length the bell shall be sounded in the forepart of the vessel and immediately after the ringing of the bell the gong shall be sounded rapidly for about 5 seconds in the after part of the vessel. A vessel at anchor may in addition sound three blasts in succession, namely one short, one prolonged and one short blast, to give warning of her position and of the possibility of collision to an approaching vessel.

(h)*(g)* A vessel aground shall give the bell signal and if required the gong signal prescribed in paragraph (g)*(f)* of this Rule and shall, in addition, give three separate and distinct strokes on the bell immediately before and after the rapid ringing of the bell. A vessel aground may in addition sound an appropriate whistle signal.

(i) A vessel of 12 meters or more but less than 20 meters in length shall not be obliged to give the bell signals prescribed in paragraphs (g) and (h) of this Rule. However, if she does not, she shall make some other efficient sound signals at intervals of not more than two minutes.

(j)*(h)* A vessel of less than 12 meters in length shall not be obliged to give the above-mentioned signals but, if she does not, shall make some other efficient sound signal at intervals of not more than 2 minutes.

(k)*(i)* A pilot vessel when engaged on pilotage duty may in addition to the signals prescribed in paragraphs (a), (b) or (g) of this Rule sound an identity signal consisting of four short blasts.

(k) The following vessels shall not be required to sound signals as prescribed in paragraph (f) of this Rule when anchored in a special anchorage area designated by the Secretary:

(i) a vessel of less than 20 meters in length;

(ii) a barge, canal boat, scow, or other nondescript craft.

RULE 36
Signals to Attract Attention

If necessary to attract the attention of another vessel, any vessel may make light or sound signals that cannot be mistaken for any signal authorized elsewhere in these Rules, or may direct the beam of her searchlight in the direction of the danger, in such a way as not to embarrass any vessel. Any light to attract the attention of another vessel shall be such that it cannot be mistaken for any aid to navigation. For the purpose of this Rule the use of high intensity intermittent or revolving lights, such as strobe lights, shall be avoided.

NOTE: There is no restriction on the use of strobe lights in the Inland Rules.

RULE 37
Distress Signals

When a vessel is in distress and requires assistance she shall use or exhibit the signals described in Annex IV to these Regulations.

The distress signals for inland waters are the same as those for international waters with the following additional signal described: A high intensity white light flashing at regular intervals from 50 to 70 times per minute.

PART E
EXEMPTIONS
RULE 38
Exemptions

Any vessel (or class of vessels) provided that she complies with the requirements of the International Regulations for Preventing Collisions at Sea, 1960, the keel of which is laid or which is at a corresponding stage of construction before the entry into force of these Regulations may be exempted from compliance therewith as follows:

Any vessel or class of vessels, the keel of which is laid or which is at a corresponding stage of construction before the date of enactment of this Act, provided that she complies with the requirements of—

(a) The Act of June 7, 1897 (30 Stat. 96), as amended (33 U.S.C. 154–232) for vessels navigating the waters subject to that statute;

(b) Section 4233 of the Revised Statutes (33 U.S.C. 301-356) for vessels navigating the waters subject to that statute;

(c) The Act of February 8, 1895 (28 Stat. 645), as amended (33 U.S.C. 241-295) for vessels navigating the waters subject to that statute; or

(d) Sections 3, 4, and 5 of the Act of April 25, 1940 (54 Stat. 163), as amended (46 U.S.C. 526 b, c, and d) for motorboats navigating the waters subject to that statute; shall be exempted from compliance with the technical Annexes to these Rules as follows:

(a) The installation of lights with ranges prescribed in Rule 22, until four years after the date of entry into force of these Regulations, *except that vessels of less than 20 meters in length are permanently exempt.*

(b) The installation of lights with color specifications as prescribed in Section 7 of Annex I to these Regulations, until four years after the date of entry into force of these Regulations, *except that vessels of less than 20 meters in length are permanently exempt.*

(c) The repositioning of lights as a result of conversion from Imperial to metric units and rounding off measurement figures, permanent exemption.

(d)(i) The repositioning of masthead lights on vessels of less than 150 meters in length, resulting from the prescriptions of Section 3(a) of Annex I to these Regulations, permanent exemption.

(ii) The repositioning of masthead lights on vessels of 150 meters or more in length, resulting from the prescriptions of Section 3(a) of Annex I to these Regulations, until 9 years after the date of entry into force of these Regulations.

(e) The repositioning of masthead lights resulting from the prescriptions of Section 2(b) of Annex I to these Regulations, until 9 years after the date of entry into force of these Regulations.

(f) The repositioning of sidelights resulting from the prescriptions of Sections 2(9) and 3(b) of Annex I to these Regulations, until 9 years after the date of entry into force of these Regulations.

(g) The requirements for sound signal appliances prescribed in Annex III to these Regulations, until 9 years after the date of entry into force of these Regulations.

The requirements for sound signal appliances prescribed in Annex III to these Rules, until 9 years after the effective date of these Rules.

(h) The repositioning of all-round lights resulting from the prescription of Section 9(b) of Annex I to these Regulations, permanent exemption.

(vi) Power-driven vessels of 12 meters or more but less than 20 meters in length are permanently exempt from the provisions of Rule 23(a)(i) and 23(a)(iv) provided that, in place of these lights, the vessel exhibits a white light aft visible all round the horizon; and

(vii) The requirements for sound signal appliances prescribed in Annex III to these Rules, until 9 years after the effective date of these Rules.

ANNEX I

ANNEX I—Positioning and Technical Details of Lights and Shapes

1. Definition: The term "height above the hull" means height above the uppermost continuous deck. This height shall be measured from the position vertically beneath the location of the light.

High-speed craft means a craft capable of maximum speed in meters per second (m/s) equal to or exceeding: 3.7 s 0.1667; where s = displacement corresponding to the design waterline (meters³).

The term "practical cut-off" means, for vessels 20 meters or more in length, 12.5 percent of the minimum luminous intensity (Table 84.15(b)) corresponding to the greatest range of visibility for which the requirements of Annex I are met.

The term "Rule" or "Rules" means the Inland Navigation Rules contained in Sec. 2 of the Inland Navigational Rules Act of 1980 (Pub. L. 96-591, 94 Stat. 3415, 33 U.S.C. 2001, December 24, 1980) as amended.

2. Vertical positioning and spacing of lights

(a) On a power-driven vessel of 20 meters or more the masthead lights shall be placed as follows:

(i) the forward masthead light, or if only one masthead light is carried, then that light, at a height above the hull of not less than 6 meters, and, if the breadth of the vessel exceeds 6 meters, then at a height above the hull not less than such breadth, so however that the light need not be placed at a greater height above the hull than 12 meters;

The forward masthead light, or if only one masthead light is carried, then that light, at a height above the hull of not less than 5 meters, and, if the breadth of the vessel exceeds 5 meters, then at a height above the hull not less than such breadth, so however that the light need not be placed at a greater height above the hull than 8 meters;

(ii) when two masthead lights are carried the after one shall be at least 4.5 meters vertically higher than the forward one.

When two masthead lights are carried the after one shall be at least 2 meters vertically higher than the forward one.

(b) The vertical separation of masthead lights of power-driven vessels shall be such that in all normal conditions of trim the after light will be seen over and separate from the forward light at a distance of 1000 meters from the stem when viewed from sea level.

(c) The masthead light of a power-driven vessel of 12 meters but less than 20 meters in length shall be placed at a height above the gunwale of not less than 2.5 meters.

(d) A power-driven vessel of less than 12 meters in length may carry the uppermost light at a height of less than 2.5 meters above the gunwale. When however a masthead light is carried in addition to sidelights and a sternlight, then such masthead light shall be carried at least 1 meter higher than the sidelights.

The masthead light, or the all-round light described in Rule 23(c), of a power-driven vessel of less than 12 meters in length shall be carried at least one meter higher than the sidelights.

(e) One of the two or three masthead lights prescribed for a power-driven vessel when engaged in towing or pushing another vessel shall be placed in the same position as either the forward masthead light or the after masthead light; provided that, if carried on the aftermast, the lowest after masthead light shall be at least 4.5 meters vertically higher than the forward masthead light.

One of the two or three masthead lights prescribed for a power-driven vessel when engaged in towing or pushing another vessel shall be placed in the same position as either the forward masthead light or the after masthead light, provided that the lowest after masthead light shall be at least 2 meters vertically higher than the highest forward masthead light.

(f)(i) The masthead light or lights prescribed in Rule 23(a) shall be so placed as to be above and clear of all other lights and obstructions except as described in subparagraph (ii).

(ii) When it is impracticable to carry the all-round lights prescribed by Rule 27(b)(i) or Rule 28 below the masthead lights, they may be carried above the after masthead light(s) or vertically in between the forward masthead light(s) and after masthead light(s), provided that in the latter case the requirement of Section 3(c) of this Annex shall be complied with.

(g) The sidelights of a power-driven vessel shall be placed at a height above the hull not greater than three quarters of that of the forward masthead light. They shall not be so low as to be interfered with by deck lights.

The sidelights of a power-driven vessel shall be placed at least one meter lower than the forward masthead light. They shall not be so low as to be interfered with by deck lights.

(h) The sidelights, if in a combined lantern and carried on a power-driven vessel of less than 20 meters in length, shall be placed not less than 1 meter below the masthead light. *[(b) Reserved]*

(b) (i) When the Rules prescribe two or three lights to be carried in a vertical line, they shall be spaced as follows:

(i) on a vessel of 20 meters in length or more such lights shall be spaced not less than 2 meters apart, and the lowest of these lights shall, except where a towing light is required, be placed at a height of not less than 4 meters above the hull;

On a vessel of 20 meters in length or more such lights shall be spaced not less than 1 meter apart, and the lowest of these lights shall, except where a towing light is required, be placed at a height of not less than 4 meters above the hull;

(ii) on a vessel of less than 20 meters in length such lights shall be spaced not less than 1 meter apart and the lowest of these lights shall, except where a towing light is required, be placed at a height of not less than 2 meters above the hull;

(iii) when three lights are carried they shall be equally spaced.

(j) The lower of the two all-round lights prescribed for a vessel when engaged in fishing shall be at a height above the sidelights not less than twice the distance between the two vertical lights.

(k) The forward anchor light prescribed in Rule 30(a)(i), when two are carried, shall not be less than 4.5 meters above the after one. On a vessel of 50 meters or more in length this forward anchor light shall be placed at a height of not less than 6 meters above the hull.

3. Horizontal positioning and spacing of lights

(a) When two masthead lights are prescribed for a power-driven vessel, the horizontal distance between them shall not be less than one half of the length of the vessel but need not be more than 100 meters. The forward light shall be placed not more than one quarter of the length of the vessel from the stem.

Except as specified in paragraph (b) of this section, when two masthead lights are prescribed for a power-driven vessel, the horizontal distance between them shall not be less than one quarter of the length of the vessel but need not be more than 50 meters. The forward light shall be placed not more than one half of the length of the vessel from the stem.

(b) On a power-driven vessel of 20 meters or more in length the sidelights shall not be placed in front of the forward masthead lights. They shall be placed at or near the side of the vessel.

(c) When the lights prescribed in Rule 27(b)(i) or Rule 28 are placed vertically between the forward masthead light(s) and the after masthead light(s) these all-round lights shall be placed at a horizontal distance of not less than 2 meters from the fore and aft centerline of the vessel in the athwartship direction.

(d) When only one masthead light is prescribed for a power-driven vessel, this light shall be exhibited forward of amidships; except that a vessel of less than 20 meters in length need not exhibit this light forward of amidships but shall exhibit it as far forward as is practicable.

(e) On power-driven vessels 50 meters but less than 60 meters in length operated on the Western Rivers, the horizontal distance between masthead lights shall not be less than 10 meters.

4. Details of location of direction-indicating lights for fishing vessels, dredges and vessels engaged in underwater operations

(a) The light indicating the direction of the outlying gear from a vessel engaged in fishing as prescribed in Rule 26(c)(ii) shall be placed at a horizontal distance of not less than 2 meters and not more than 6 meters away from the two all-round red and white lights. This light shall be placed not higher than the all-round white light prescribed in Rule 26(c)(i) and not lower than the sidelights.

(b) The lights and shapes on a vessel engaged in dredging or underwater operations to indicate the obstructed side and/or the side on which it is safe to pass, as prescribed in Rule 27(d)(i) and (ii), shall be placed at the maximum practical horizontal distance, but in no case less than 2 meters, from the lights or shapes prescribed in Rule 27(b)(i) and (ii). In no case shall the upper of these lights or shapes be at a greater height than the lower of the three.

5. Screens for sidelights

The sidelights of vessels of 20 meters or more in length shall be fitted with inboard screens painted matt black, and meeting the requirements of Section 9 of this Annex. On vessels of less than 20 meters in length the sidelights, if necessary to meet the requirements of Section 9 of this Annex, shall be fitted with inboard matt black screens. With a combined lantern, using a single vertical filament and a very narrow division between the green and red sections, external screens need not be fitted.

On power-driven vessels less than 12 meters in length constructed after July 31, 1983, the masthead light, or the all-round light described in Rule 23(c) shall be screened to prevent direct illumination of the vessel forward of the operator's position.

6. Shapes

(a) Shapes shall be black and of the following sizes:

(i) a ball shall have a diameter of not less than 0.6 meter;

(ii) a cone shall have a base diameter of not less than 0.6 meter and a height equal to its diameter;

(iii) a cylinder shall have a diameter of at least 0.6 meter and a height of twice its diameter; *(There is no cylinder in Inland Rules.)*

(iv) a diamond shape shall consist of two cones as defined in (ii) above having a common base.

(b) The vertical distance between shapes shall be at least 1.5 meters.

(c) In a vessel of less than 20 meters in length shapes of lesser dimensions but commensurate with the size of the vessel may be used and the distance apart may be correspondingly reduced.

7. Color specification of lights

The chromaticity of all navigation lights shall conform to the following standards, which lie within the boundaries of the area of the diagram specified for each color by the International Commission on Illumination (CIE).

The boundaries of the area for each color are given by indicating the corner coordinates, which are as follows:

(i) White:

x	0.525	0.525	0.452	0.310	0.310	0.443
y	0.382	0.440	0.440	0.348	0.283	0.382

(ii) Green:

x	0.028	0.009	0.300	0.203
y	0.385	0.723	0.511	0.356

(iii) Red:

x	0.680	0.660	0.735	0.721
y	0.320	0.320	0.265	0.259

(iv) Yellow:

x	0.612	0.618	0.575	0.575
y	0.382	0.382	0.425	0.406

8. Intensity of lights

(a) The minimum luminous intensity of lights shall be calculated by using the formula:

$$I = 3.43 \times 10^6 \times T \times D^2 \times K^{-D}$$

where   I is luminous intensity in candelas under service conditions

T is threshold factor 2×10^{-7} lux,

D is range of visibility (luminous range) of the light in nautical miles,

K is atmospheric transmissivity. For prescribed lights the value of K shall be 0.8, corresponding to a meteorological visibility of approximately 13 nautical miles.

(b) A selection of figures derived from the formula is given in the following table:

Range of visibility (luminous range) of light in nm, D	Luminous intensity of light in candelas for K = 0.8
1	0.9
2	4.3
3	12
4	27
5	52
6	94

Note: The maximum luminous intensity of navigation lights should be limited to avoid undue glare. This shall not be achieved by a variable control of the luminous intensity.

9. Horizontal sectors

(a)(i) In the forward direction, sidelights as fitted on the vessel shall show the minimum required intensities. The intensities shall decrease to reach practical cut-off between 1 degree and 3 degrees outside the prescribed sectors.

(ii) For sternlights and masthead lights and at 22.5 degrees abaft the beam for sidelights, the minimum required intensities shall be maintained over the arc of the horizon up to 5 degrees within the limits of the sectors prescribed in Rule 21. From 5 degrees within the prescribed sectors the intensity may decrease by 50 percent up to the pre-scribed limits; it shall decrease steadily to reach practical cut-off at not more than 5 degrees outside the prescribed sectors.

(b) All-round lights shall be so located as not to be obscured by masts, topmasts or structures within angular sectors of more than 6 degrees, except anchor lights prescribed in Rule 30, which need not be placed at an impracticable height above the hull, *and the all-round white light described in Rule 23(d), which may not be obscured at all.*

(c) If it is impracticable to comply with paragraph (b) of this section by exhibiting only one

all-round light, two all-round lights shall be used suitably positioned or screened to appear, as far as practicable, as one light at a minimum distance of one nautical mile. NOTE to paragraph (c): Two unscreened all-round lights that are 1.28 meters apart or less will appear as one light to the naked eye at a distance of one nautical mile.

10. Vertical sectors

(a) The vertical sectors of electric lights as fitted, with the exception of lights on sailing vessels, *and on unmanned barges,* shall ensure that:

(i) at least the required minimum intensity is maintained at all angles from 5 degrees above to 5 degrees below the horizontal;

(ii) at least 60 percent of the required minimum intensity is maintained from 7.5 degrees above to 7.5 degrees below the horizontal.

(b) In the case of sailing vessels the vertical sectors of electric lights as fitted shall ensure that:

(i) at least the required minimum intensity is maintained at all angles from 5 degrees above to 5 degrees below the horizontal;

(ii) at least 50 percent of the required minimum intensity is maintained from 25 degrees above to 25 degrees below the horizontal.

In the case of unmanned barges the minimum required intensity of electric lights as fitted shall be maintained on the horizontal.

c) In the case of lights other than electric these specifications shall be met as closely as possible.

11. Intensity of non-electric lights

Non-electric lights shall so far as practicable comply with the minimum intensities, as specified in the Table given in Section 8 of this Annex.

12. Maneuvering light

Notwithstanding the provisions of paragraph 2(f) of this Annex the maneuvering light described in Rule 34(b) shall be placed in the same fore and aft vertical plane as the masthead light or lights and, where practicable, at a minimum height of 2 meters (*0.5 meter*) vertically above the forward masthead light, provided that it shall be carried not less than 2 meters (*0.5 meter*) vertically above or below the after masthead light. On a vessel where only one masthead light is carried the maneuvering light, if fitted, shall be carried where it can best be seen, not less than 2 meters (*0.5 meter*) vertically apart from the masthead light.

84.24 High Speed Craft

The masthead light of high speed craft with a length to breadth ratio of less than 3.0 may be placed at a height related to the breadth lower than that precribed in Sec. 84.03(a)(1), provided that the base angle of the isosceles triangle formed by the sidelights and masthead light when seen in end elevation is not less than 27 degrees as determined by the formula in paragraph (b) of this section.

(b) The minimum height of masthead light above sidelights is to be determined by the following formula: Tan 27°=x/y; where Y is the horizontal distance between the sidelights and X is the height of the forward masthead light.

14. Approval

The construction of lights and shapes and the installation of lights on board the vessel shall be to the satisfaction of the appropriate authority of the State whose flag the vessel is entitled to fly.

ANNEX II—Additional Signals for Fishing Vessels Fishing in Close Proximity

1. General

The lights mentioned herein shall, if exhibited in pursuance of Rule 26(d), be placed where they can best be seen. They shall be at least 0.9 meter apart but at a lower level than lights prescribed in Rule 26(b)(i) and (c)(i). The lights shall be visible all around the horizon at a distance of at least 1 mile but at a lesser distance than the lights prescribed by these Rules for fishing vessels.

2. Signals for trawlers

(a) Vessels when engaged in trawling, whether using demersal or pelagic gear, may exhibit:

(i) when shooting their nets: two white lights in a vertical line;

(ii) when hauling their nets: one white light over one red light in a vertical line;

(iii) when the net has come fast upon an obstruction: two red lights in a vertical line.

(b) Each vessel engaged in pair trawling may exhibit:

(i) by night, a searchlight directed forward and in the direction of the other vessel of the pair;

(ii) when shooting or hauling their nets or when their nets have come fast upon an obstruction, the lights prescribed in 2(a) above.

(c) A vessel of less than 20 meters in length engaged in trawling, whether using demersal or pelagic gear, or engaged in pair trawling, may exhibit the lights prescribed in paragraphs (a) or (b) of this section, as appropriate.

3. Signals for purse seiners

Vessels engaged in fishing with purse seine gear may exhibit two yellow lights in a vertical line. These lights shall flash alternately every second and with equal light and occultation duration. These lights may be exhibited only when the vessel is hampered by its fishing gear.

ANNEX III—Technical Details of Sound Signal Appliances

1. Whistles

(a) Frequencies and range of audibility.

The fundamental frequency of the signal shall lie within the range 70–700 Hz *(70–525 Hz)*. The range of audibility of the signal from a whistle shall be determined by those frequencies, which may include the fundamental and/or one or more higher frequencies, which lie within the range 180–700 Hz (±1 percent) and which provide the sound pressure levels specified in paragraph 1(c) below.

(b) Limits of fundamental frequencies.

To ensure a wide variety of whistle characteristics, the fundamental frequency of a whistle shall be between:

(i) 70–200 Hz, for a vessel 200 meters or more in length;

(ii) 130–350 Hz, for a vessel 75 meters but less than 200 meters in length;

(iii) 250–700 Hz *(250–525 Hz)*, for a vessel less than 75 meters in length.

(c) Sound signal intensity and range of audibility.

A whistle fitted in a vessel shall provide, in the direction of maximum intensity of the whistle and at a distance of 1 meter from it, a sound pressure level in at least one $^1/_3$-octave band within the range of frequencies 180–700 Hz (±1 percent) of not less than the appropriate figure given in the following table.

The range of audibility in the following table is for information and is approximately the range at which a whistle may be heard on its forward axis with 90

Length of vessel in meters	$^1/_3$-octave band level at 1 m in dB referred to 2×10^{-5} nm^2	Audibility range in nm
200 or more	143	2
75 but less than 200	138	1.5
20 but less than 75	130	1
less than 20	120	0.5

percent probability in conditions of still air on board a vessel having average background noise level at the listening posts (taken to be 68 dB in the octave band centered on 250 Hz and 63 dB in the octave band centered on 500 Hz).

In practice the range at which a whistle may be heard is extremely variable and depends critically on weather conditions; the values given can be regarded as typical but under conditions of strong wind or high ambient noise level at the listening post the range may be much reduced.

(d) Directional properties.

The sound pressure level of a directional whistle shall be not more than 4 dB below the prescribed sound pressure level on that axis at any direction in the horizontal plane within ±45 degrees of the axis. The sound pressure level at any other direction in the horizontal plane shall be not more than 10 dB below the prescribed sound pressure level on the axis, so that the range in any direction will be at least half the range on the forward axis. The sound pressure level shall be measured in that $^1/_3$-octave band which determines the audibility range.

(e) Positioning of whistles.

When a directional whistle is to be used as the only whistle on a vessel, it shall be installed with its maximum intensity directed straight ahead.

A whistle shall be placed as high as practicable on a vessel, in order to reduce interception of the emitted sound by obstructions and also to minimize hearing damage risk to personnel. The sound pressure level of the vessel's own signal at listening posts shall not exceed 110 dB (A) and so far as practicable should not exceed 100 dB (A).

(f) Fitting of more than one whistle.

If whistles are fitted at a distance apart of no more than 100 meters, it shall be so arranged that they are not sounded simultaneously.

(g) Combined whistle systems.

If due to the presence of obstructions the sound field of a single whistle or of one of the whistles referred to in paragraph 1(f) above is likely to have a zone of greatly reduced signal level, it is recommended that a combined whistle system be fitted so as to overcome this reduction. For the purposes of the Rules a combined whistle system is to be regarded as a single whistle. The whistles of a combined system shall be located at a distance apart of not more than 100 meters and arranged to be sounded simultaneously. The frequency of any one whistle shall differ from those of the others by at least 10 Hz.

Towing vessel whistles. A power-driven vessel normally engaged in pushing ahead or towing alongside may, at all times, use a whistle whose characteristic falls within the limits prescribed for the longest customary composite length of the vessel and its tow.

2. Bell or gong

(a) Intensity of signal.

A bell or gong, or other device having similar sound characteristics shall produce a sound pressure level of not less than 110 dB at a distance of 1 meter from it.

(b) Construction.

Bells and gongs shall be made of corrosion-resistant material and be designed to give a clear tone. The diameter of the mouth of the bell shall be no less than 300 mm for vessels of 20 meters or more in length, and shall be no less than 200 mm for vessels of 12 meters or more but of less than 20 meters. Where practicable, a power-driven bell striker is recommended to ensure constant force but manual operation shall be possible. The mass of the striker shall be not less than 3 percent of the mass of the bell.

3. Approval.

The construction of sound signal appliances, their performance and their installation on board the vessel shall be to the satisfaction of the appropriate authority of the State whose flag the vessel is entitled to fly.

ANNEX IV—Distress Signals

1. Need of assistance.
The following signals, used or exhibited together or separately, indicate distress and need of assistance:

(a) a gun or other explosive signal fired at intervals of about a minute;

(b) a continuous sounding with any fog-signaling apparatus;

(c) rockets or shells, throwing red stars fired one at a time at short intervals;

(d) a signal made by radiotelegraphy or by any other signaling method consisting of the group · · · — — — · · · (SOS) in the Morse Code;

(e) a signal sent by radiotelephony consisting of the spoken word "Mayday";

(f) the International Code Signal of distress indicated by N.C.;

(g) a signal consisting of a square flag having above or below it a ball or anything resembling a ball;

(h) flames on the vessel (as from a burning tar barrel, oil barrel, etc.);

(i) a rocket parachute flare or a hand flare showing a red light;

(j) a smoke signal giving off orange-colored smoke;

(k) slowly and repeatedly raising and lowering arms outstretched to each side;

(l) the radiotelegraph alarm signal;

(m) the radiotelephone alarm signal;

(n) signals transmitted by emergency position-indicating radio beacons.

(o) A high intensity white light flashing at regular intervals from 50 to 70 times per minute.

2. The use or exhibition of any of the foregoing signals except for the purpose of indicating distress and need of assistance and the use of other signals which may be confused with any of the above signals is prohibited.

3. Attention is drawn to the relevant sections of the International Code of Signals, the Merchant Ship Search and Rescue Manual and the following signals: (a) a piece of orange-colored canvas with either a black square and circle or other appropriate symbol (for identification from the air); (b) a dye marker.

ANNEX V—Pilot Rules

Purpose and applicability.

This part applies to all vessels operating on United States Inland waters and to United States vessels operating on the Canadian waters of the Great Lakes to the extent there is no conflict with Canadian law.

Definitions.
The terms used in this part have the same meaning as defined in the Inland Navigational Rules Act of 1980.

Copy of Rules.

After January 1, 1983, the operator of each self-propelled vessel 12 meters or more in length shall carry on board and maintain for ready reference a copy of the Inland Navigation Rules.

Temporary exemption from light and shape requirements when operating under bridges.

A vessel's navigation lights and shapes may be lowered if necessary to pass under a bridge.

Law enforcement vessels.

(a) Law enforcement vessels may display a flashing blue light when engaged in direct law enforcement activities. This light shall be located so that it does not interfere with the visibility of the vessel's navigation lights.

(b) The blue light described in this section may be displayed by law enforcement vessels of the United States and the States and their political subdivisions.

Lights on barges at bank or dock.

(a) The following barges shall display at night and, if practicable, in periods of restricted visibility the lights described in paragraph (b) of this section—

(1) Every barge projecting into a buoyed or restricted channel.

(2) Every barge so moored that it reduces the available navigable width of any channel to less than 80 meters.

(3) Barges moored in groups more than two barges wide or to a maximum width of over 25 meters.

(4) Every barge not moored parallel to the bank or dock.

(b) Barges described in paragraph (a) of this section shall carry two unobstructed all-round white lights of an intensity to be visible for at least one nautical mile and meeting the technical requirements as prescribed in § 84.15 of this chapter.

(c) A barge or a group of barges at anchor or made fast to one or more mooring bouys or other similar device, in lieu of the provisions of Inland Navigation Rule 30, may carry unobstructed all-round white lights of an intensity to be visible for at least one nautical mile that meet the requirements of § 84.15 of this chapter and shall be arranged as follows:

(1) Any barge that projects from a group formation, shall be lighted on its outboard corners.

(2) On a single barge moored in water where other vessels normally navigate on both sides of the barge, lights shall be placed to mark the corner extremities of the barge.

(3) On barges moored in group formation, moored in water where other vessels normally navigate on both sides of the group, lights shall be placed to mark the corner extremities of the group.

(d) The following are exempt from the requirements of this section:

(1) A barge or group of barges moored in a slip or slough used primarily for mooring purposes.

(2) A barge or group of barges moored behind a pierhead.

(3) A barge less than 20 meters in length when moored in a special anchorage area designated in accordance with § 109.10 of this chapter.

Lights on dredge pipelines.

Dredge pipelines that are floating or supported on trestles shall display the following lights at night and in periods of restricted visibility.

(a) One row of yellow lights. The lights must be—

(1) Flashing 50 to 70 times per minute,

(2) Visible all around the horizon,

(3) Visible for at least 2 miles on a clear dark night,

(4) Not less than 1 and not more than 3.5 meters above the water,

(5) Approximately equally spaced, and

(6) Not more than 10 meters apart where the pipeline crosses a navigable channel. Where the pipeline does not cross a navigable channel the lights must be sufficient in number to clearly show the pipeline's length and course.

(b) Two red lights at each end of the pipeline, including the ends in a channel where the pipeline is separated to allow vessels to pass (whether open or closed). The lights must be—

(1) Visible all around the horizon, and

(2) Visible for at least 2 miles on a clear dark night, and

(3) One meter apart in a vertical line with the lower light at the same height above the water as the flashing yellow light.

INDEX

Numbers in **bold** refer to pages with illustrations. The question and answer sections are not indexed.